Praise for the Reformation Commentary on Scripture

"Protestant reformers were fundamentally exegetes as much as theologians, yet (except for figures like Luther and Calvin) their commentaries and sermons have been neglected because these writings are not available in modern editions or languages. That makes this new series of Reformation Commentary on Scripture most welcome as a way to provide access to some of the wealth of biblical exposition of the sixteenth and seventeenth centuries. The editor's introduction explains the nature of the sources and the selection process; the intended audience of modern pastors and students of the Bible has led to a focus on theological and practical comments. Although it will be of use to students of the Reformation, this series is far from being an esoteric study of largely forgotten voices; this collection of reforming comments, comprehending every verse and provided with topical headings, will serve contemporary pastors and preachers very well."

Elsie Anne McKee, *Archibald Alexander Professor of Reformation Studies and the History of Worship, Princeton Theological Seminary*

"This series provides an excellent introduction to the history of biblical exegesis in the Reformation period. The introductions are accurate, clear and informative, and the passages intelligently chosen to give the reader a good idea of methods deployed and issues at stake. It puts precritical exegesis in its context and so presents it in its correct light. Highly recommended as reference book, course book and general reading for students and all interested lay and clerical readers."

Irena Backus, *Professeure Ordinaire, Institut d'histoire de la Réformation, Université de Genève*

"The Reformation Commentary on Scripture is a major publishing event—for those with historical interest in the founding convictions of Protestantism, but even more for those who care about understanding the Bible. As with IVP Academic's earlier Ancient Christian Commentary on Scripture, this effort brings flesh and blood to 'the communion of saints' by letting believers of our day look over the shoulders of giants from the past. By connecting the past with the present, and by doing so with the Bible at the center, the editors of this series perform a great service for the church. The series deserves the widest possible support."

Mark A. Noll, *Francis A. McAnaney Professor of History, University of Notre Dame*

"For those who preach and teach Scripture in the church, the Reformation Commentary on Scripture is a significant publishing event. Pastors and other church leaders will find delightful surprises, challenging enigmas and edifying insights in this series, as many Reformational voices are newly translated into English. The lively conversation in these pages can ignite today's pastoral imagination for fresh and faithful expositions of Scripture."

J. Todd Billings, *Gordon H. Girod Research Professor of Reformed Theology, Western Theological Seminary*

"The reformers discerned rightly what the church desperately needed in the sixteenth century—the bold proclamation of the Word based on careful study of the sacred Scriptures. We need not only to hear that same call again for our own day but also to learn from the Reformation how to do it. This commentary series is a godsend!"

Richard J. Mouw, *President Emeritus, Fuller Theological Seminary*

"Like the Ancient Christian Commentary on Scripture, the Reformation Commentary on Scripture does a masterful job of offering excellent selections from well-known and not-so-well-known exegetes. The editor's introductory survey is, by itself, worth the price of the book. It is easy to forget that there were more hands, hearts and minds involved in the Reformation than Luther and Calvin. Furthermore, encounters even with these figures are often limited to familiar quotes on familiar topics. However, the Reformation Commentary helps us to recognize the breadth and depth of exegetical interests and skill that fueled and continue to fuel faithful meditation on God's Word. I heartily recommend this series as a tremendous resource not only for ministry but for personal edification."

Michael S. Horton, *J. G. Machen Professor of Systematic Theology and Apologetics,*
Westminster Seminary, California

"The Reformation was ignited by a fresh reading of Scripture. In this series of commentaries, we contemporary interpreters are allowed to feel some of the excitement, surprise and wonder of our spiritual forebears. Luther, Calvin and their fellow revolutionaries were masterful interpreters of the Word. Now, in this remarkable series, some of our very best Reformation scholars open up the riches of the Reformation's reading of the Scripture."

William H. Willimon, *Professor of the Practice of Christian Ministry, Duke Divinity School*

"The Reformation Scripture principle set the entirety of Christian life and thought under the governance of the divine Word, and pressed the church to renew its exegetical labors. This series promises to place before the contemporary church the fruit of those labors, and so to exemplify life under the Word."

John Webster, *Professor of Divinity, University of St. Andrews*[†]

"Since Gerhard Ebeling's pioneering work on Luther's exegesis seventy years ago, the history of biblical interpretation has occupied many Reformation scholars and become a vital part of study of the period. The Reformation Commentary on Scripture provides fresh materials for students of Reformation-era biblical interpretation and for twenty-first-century preachers to mine the rich stores of insights from leading reformers of the sixteenth century into both the text of Scripture itself and its application in sixteenth-century contexts. This series will strengthen our understanding of the period of the Reformation and enable us to apply its insights to our own days and its challenges to the church."

Robert Kolb, *Professor Emeritus, Concordia Theological Seminary*

"The multivolume Ancient Christian Commentary on Scripture is a valuable resource for those who wish to know how the Fathers interpreted a passage of Scripture but who lack the time or the opportunity to search through the many individual works. This new Reformation Commentary on Scripture will do the same for the reformers and is to be warmly welcomed. It will provide much easier access to the exegetical treasures of the Reformation and will hopefully encourage readers to go back to some of the original works themselves."

Anthony N. S. Lane, *Professor of Historical Theology and Director of Research, London School of Theology*

"This volume of the RCS project is an invaluable source for pastors and the historically/biblically interested that provides unparalleled access not only to commentaries of the leading Protestant reformers but also to a host of nowadays unknown commentaters on Galatians and Ephesians. The RCS is sure to enhance and enliven contemporary exegesis. With its wide scope, the collection will enrich our understanding of the variety of Reformation thought and biblical exegesis."

Sigrun Haude, *Associate Professor of Reformation and Early Modern European History,*
University of Cincinnati

"This grand project sets before scholars, pastors, teachers, students and growing Christians an experience that can only be likened to stumbling into a group Bible study only to discover that your fellow participants include some of the most significant Christians of the Reformation and post-Reformation (for that matter, of any) era. Here the Word of God is explained in a variety of accents: German, Swiss, French, Dutch, English, Scottish and more. Each one vibrates with a thrilling sense of the living nature of God's Word and its power to transform individuals, churches and even whole communities. Here is a series to anticipate, enjoy and treasure."

Sinclair Ferguson, *Senior Minister, First Presbyterian Church, Columbia, South Carolina*

"I strongly endorse the Reformation Commentary on Scripture. Introducing how the Bible was interpreted during the age of the Reformation, these volumes will not only renew contemporary preaching, but they will also help us understand more fully how reading and meditating on Scripture can, in fact, change our lives!"

Lois Malcolm, *Associate Professor of Systematic Theology, Luther Seminary*

"Discerning the true significance of movements in theology requires acquaintance with their biblical exegesis. This is supremely so with the Reformation, which was essentially a biblical revival. The Reformation Commentary on Scripture will fill a yawning gap, just as the Ancient Christian Commentary did before it, and the first volume gets the series off to a fine start, whetting the appetite for more. Most heartily do I welcome and commend this long overdue project."

J. I. Packer, *Retired Board of Governors Professor of Theology, Regent College*

"There is no telling the benefits to emerge from the publication of this magnificent Reformation Commentary on Scripture series! Now exegetical and theological treasures from Reformation era commentators will be at our fingertips, providing new insights from old sources to give light for the present and future. This series is a gift to scholars and to the church; a wonderful resource to enhance our study of the written Word of God for generations to come!"

Donald K. McKim, *Executive Editor of Theology and Reference, Westminster John Knox Press*

"Why was this not done before? The publication of the Reformation Commentary on Scripture should be greeted with enthusiasm by every believing Christian—but especially by those who will preach and teach the Word of God. This commentary series brings the very best of the Reformation heritage to the task of exegesis and exposition, and each volume in this series represents a veritable feast that takes us back to the sixteenth century to enrich the preaching and teaching of God's Word in our own time."

R. Albert Mohler Jr., *President, The Southern Baptist Theological Seminary*

"Today more than ever, the Christian past is the church's future. InterVarsity Press has already brought the voice of the ancients to our ears. Now, in the Reformation Commentary on Scripture, we hear a timely word from the first Protestants as well."

Bryan Litfin, *Professor of Theology, Moody Bible Institute*

"I am delighted to see the Reformation Commentary on Scripture. The editors of this series have done us all a service by gleaning from these rich fields of biblical reflection. May God use this new life for these old words to give him glory and to build his church."

Mark Dever, *Senior Pastor, Capitol Hill Baptist Church, and President of 9Marks.org Ministries*

"Monumental and magisterial, the Reformation Commentary on Scripture, edited by Timothy George, is a remarkably bold and visionary undertaking. Bringing together a wealth of resources, these volumes will provide historians, theologians, biblical scholars, pastors and students with a fresh look at the exegetical insights of those who shaped and influenced the sixteenth-century Reformation. With this marvelous publication, InterVarsity Press has reached yet another plateau of excellence. We pray that this superb series will be used of God to strengthen both church and academy."

David S. Dockery, *President, Trinity International University*

"Detached from her roots, the church cannot reach the world as God intends. While every generation must steward the scriptural insights God grants it, only arrogance or ignorance causes leaders to ignore the contributions of those faithful leaders before us. The Reformation Commentary on Scripture roots our thought in great insights of faithful leaders of the Reformation to further biblical preaching and teaching in this generation."

Bryan Chapell, *Chancellor and Professor of Practical Theology, Covenant Theological Seminary*

"After reading several volumes of the Reformation Commentary on Scripture, I exclaimed, 'Hey, this is just what the doctor ordered—I mean Doctor Martinus Lutherus!' The church of today bearing his name needs a strong dose of the medicine this doctor prescribed for the ailing church of the sixteenth century. The reforming fire of Christ-centered preaching that Luther ignited is the only hope to reclaim the impact of the gospel to keep the Reformation going, not for its own sake but to further the renewal of the worldwide church of Christ today. This series of commentaries will equip preachers to step into their pulpits with confidence in the same living Word that inspired the witness of Luther and Calvin and many other lesser-known Reformers."

Carl E. Braaten, *Cofounder of the Center for Catholic and Evangelical Theology*

"As a pastor, how does one cultivate a knowledge of the history of interpretation? That's where IVP's Reformation Commentary on Scripture and its forerunner, the Ancient Christian Commentary on Scripture, come in. They do an excellent job in helping pastors become more aware of the history of exegesis for the benefit of their congregations. Every pastor should have access to a set of each."

Carl R. Trueman, *Paul Woolley Chair of Church History, Westminster Theological Seminary*

REFORMATION COMMENTARY ON SCRIPTURE

NEW TESTAMENT
VII

ROMANS 1–8

EDITED BY
GWENFAIR WALTERS ADAMS

GENERAL EDITOR
TIMOTHY GEORGE

ASSOCIATE GENERAL EDITOR
SCOTT M. MANETSCH

IVP Academic

An imprint of InterVarsity Press
Downers Grove, Illinois

InterVarsity Press
P.O. Box 1400, Downers Grove, IL 60515-1426
ivpress.com
email@ivpress.com

InterVarsity Press® is the book-publishing division of InterVarsity Christian Fellowship/USA®, a movement of students and faculty active on campus at hundreds of universities, colleges and schools of nursing in the United States of America, and a member movement of the International Fellowship of Evangelical Students. For information about local and regional activities, visit intervarsity.org.

This publication contains The Holy Bible, English Standard Version®, copyright © 2001 by Crossway, a publishing ministry of Good News Publishers. The ESV® text appearing in this publication is reproduced and published by cooperation between Good News Publishers and InterVarsity Press and by permission of Good News Publishers. Unauthorized reproduction of this publication is prohibited.

The Holy Bible, English Standard Version (ESV) is adapted from the Revised Standard Version of the Bible, copyright Division of Christian Education of the National Council of the Churches of Christ in the U.S.A. All rights reserved.

English Standard Version®, ESV® and ESV® logo are trademarks of Good News Publishers located in Wheaton, Illinois. Used by permission.

Excerpts from Luther's Works, *vol. 25, are copyright © 1972 by Concordia Publishing House, www.cph.org. Used by permission. All rights reserved.*
Excerpts from Luther's Works, *vol. 75, are copyright © 2013 by Concordia Publishing House, www.cph.org. Used by permission. All rights reserved.*
Excerpts from Luther's Works, *vol. 77, are copyright © 2014 by Concordia Publishing House, www.cph.org. Used by permission. All rights reserved.*
Excerpts from Luther's Works, *vol. 78, are copyright © 2015 by Concordia Publishing House, www.cph.org. Used by permission. All rights reserved.*
Excerpts from Philipp Melanchthon, Commentary on Romans, *translated by Fred Kramer, are copyright © 1992 by Concordia Publishing House, www.cph.org. Used by permission. All rights reserved.*
Excerpts from Philipp Melanchthon, Commonplaces: Loci Communes, 1521, *translated by Christian Preus, are copyright © 2014 by Concordia Publishing House, www.cph.org. Used by permission. All rights reserved.*

Every effort has been made to trace and contact copyright holders for materials quoted in this book. The publisher will be pleased to rectify any omissions in future printings if notified by copyright holders.

Design: Cindy Kiple
Images: wooden cross: iStockphoto
    The Protestant Church in Lyon: The Protestant Church in Lyon, called "The Paradise" at Bibliotheque Publique et Universitaire, Geneva, Switzerland. Erich Lessing/Art Resource, NY.

ISBN 978-0-8308-2970-5 (print)
ISBN 978-0-8308-7299-2 (digital)

Printed in the United States of America ∞

Library of Congress Cataloging-in-Publication Data

Names: Adams, Gwenfair Walters, editor.
Title: Romans 1-8 / edited by Gwenfair Walters Adams ; general editor, Timothy George ; associate general editor, Scott M. Manetsch.
Description: Downers Grove : InterVarsity Press, 2019. | Series: Reformation commentary on Scripture. Old Testament ; 7 | Includes bibliographical references and index.
Identifiers: LCCN 2018059526 (print) | LCCN 2019006391 (ebook) | ISBN 9780830872992 (eBook) | ISBN 9780830829705 (hardcover : alk. paper)
Subjects: LCSH: Bible. Romans, I-VIII--Commentaries..
Classification: LCC BS2665.53 (ebook) | LCC BS2665.53 .R66239 2016 (print) | DDC 227/.107--dc23
LC record available at https://lccn.loc.gov/2018059526

P	26	25	24	23	22	21	20	19	18	17	16	15	14	13	12	11	10	9	8	7	6	5	4	3	2	1
Y	41	40	39	38	37	36	35	34	33	32	31	30	29	28	27	26	25	24	23	22	21	20	19			

For

Mair L. Walters, M.D.

D. Kevin Adams

Donna D. Langford

Reformation Commentary on Scripture
Project Staff

Project Editor
David W. McNutt

---

*Senior Production Manager
and Managing Editor*
Benjamin M. McCoy

Associate Managing Editor
Elissa Schauer

Copyeditor
Jeffrey A. Reimer

Assistant Project Editor
André A. Gazal

Editorial and Research Assistants
David J. Hooper
Ashley Davila

Assistants to the General Editors
Le-Ann Little
Jason Odom

Design
Cindy Kiple

Design Assistant
Beth McGill

Content Production
Maureen G. Tobey
Daniel van Loon
Jeanna L. Wiggins

Proofreader
Travis Ables

InterVarsity Press

Publisher
Jeff Crosby

Associate Publisher, Director of Editorial
Cindy Bunch

Editorial Director, IVP Academic
Jon Boyd

CONTENTS

ACKNOWLEDGMENTS

My late father, Gwyn Walters, a preaching professor and Calvin scholar, inculcated in me an enduring love of the Word and of the Reformation from an early age, and it has been my joy to spend these past seven years steeped in Romans 1-8 and in the writings of Calvin and the many other sixteenth- and seventeenth-century men and women who explored this theologically rich epistle. Being immersed in the text and in the commentaries, treatises, sermons, letters, and poetry has profoundly deepened my appreciation for the power and beauty of the gospel of Jesus Christ.

I would like to thank Timothy George and Scott M. Manetsch, General Editor and Associate General Editor of the Reformation Commentary on Scripture series, for their kind invitation to participate in this valuable enterprise; and the project editors, Michael Gibson, Brannon Ellis, and David McNutt, and their teams at InterVarsity Press, who have been wonderful to work with.

When I first started on the project, it soon became apparent that with the significant amount of material published on Romans during the Reformation—most of it having never been translated into English—this endeavor would require more hands than just mine. Paul Watkins became my right-hand man for the Latin translations, and I am profoundly grateful to him as well as to Aaron Gies, Steve Mapa, and Ian Drummond. Their careful work graces much of the originally Latin material in this volume. I am also thankful to a number of other Gordon-Conwell alumni and teaching assistants for their able assistance along the journey: Sarah Wilsey, Simone Baird, Hope Crelin, Sam Alberty, Liz Marvel, Adrienne Willhoft, Jason Mackey, and Nina Walters.

I am grateful to the Trustees and Administration of Gordon-Conwell Theological Seminary and to my Faculty colleagues for the sabbatical that made it possible for me to work exclusively on the project for a year. I also wish to thank Janet Grant, my literary agent at Books and Such Literary Management, and my brother, Meirwyn Walters, for their kind assistance.

My dear husband, Kevin, has been a strong encourager through the years in which Romans-in-the-Reformation has absorbed my attention. I am exceedingly grateful to him for his support.

In his preface to Romans, Martin Luther wrote, "It is impossible to read or to meditate on this letter too much or too well. The more one deals with it, the more precious it becomes and the better it tastes."[1] That has proved true for me, and my hope is that it will be so for readers of this volume.

Soli Deo Gloria.

---

[1] Luther, "Preface to the Letter"*.

ABBREVIATIONS

CNTC	*Calvin's New Testament Commentaries.* 12 vols. Edited by David W. Torrance and Thomas F. Torrance. Grand Rapids: Eerdmans, 1959–1972.
CO	*Ioannis Calvini Opera Quae Supersunt Omnia.* 59 vols. Corpus Reformatorum 29-88. Edited by G. Baum, E. Cunitz, and E. Reuss. Brunswick and Berlin, 1863–1900.
CRR	*Classics of the Radical Reformation.* 12 vols. Waterloo, ON, and Scottsdale, PA: Herald Press, 1973–.
CTS	Calvin Translation Society
CWE	*Collected Works of Erasmus.* 86 vols. planned. Toronto: University of Toronto Press, 1969–.
DLCPT	The Digital Library of Classic Protestant Texts
EEBO	Early English Books Online
EEBO-TCP	Early English Books Online-Text Creation Partnership
LCC	Library of Christian Classics
LW	*Luther's Works.* American edition. 82 vols. planned. St. Louis: Concordia; Philadelphia: Fortress, 1955–1986; 2009–.
OER	Oxford Encyclopedia of the Reformation. 4 vols. Edited by Hans J. Hillebrand. Oxford: Oxford University Press, 1996.
RCS	*The Reformation Commentary on Scripture.* 27 vols. projected. Downers Grove, IL: InterVarsity Press, 2010–.
WA	*D. Martin Luthers Werke: Kritische Gesamtausgabe.* 66 vols. Weimar: Hermann Böhlaus Nachfolger, 1883–1987.
WA, Tr	*D. Martin Luthers Werke: Kritische Gesamtausgabe: Tischreden.* 6 vols. Weimar: Hermann Böhlaus Nachfolger, 1912–21.

BIBLE TRANSLATIONS

CEB	Common English Bible
ESV	English Standard Version
KJV	King James Version
LXX	Septuagint
NASB	New American Standard Bible
NIV	New International Version
NKJV	New King James Version
NRSV	New Revised Standard Version
VG	Vulgate

A GUIDE TO USING THIS COMMENTARY

Several features have been incorporated into the design of this commentary. The following comments are intended to assist readers in making full use of this volume.

Pericopes of Scripture

The scriptural text has been divided into pericopes, or passages, usually several verses in length. Each of these pericopes is given a heading, which appears at the beginning of the pericope. For example, the first section in this commentary is Romans 1:1-7, "Greeting to the Christians in Rome." This heading is followed by the Scripture passage quoted in the English Standard Version (ESV). The Scripture passage is provided for the convenience of readers, but it is also in keeping with Reformation-era commentaries, which often followed the patristic and medieval commentary tradition, in which the citations of the reformers were arranged according to the text of Scripture.

Overviews

Following each pericope of text is an overview of the Reformation authors' comments on that pericope. The format of this overview varies among the volumes of this series, depending on the requirements of the specific book(s) of Scripture. The function of the overview is to identify succinctly the key exegetical, theological, and pastoral concerns of the Reformation writers arising from the pericope, providing the reader with an orientation to Reformation-era approaches and emphases. It tracks a reasonably cohesive thread of argument among reformers' comments, even though they are derived from diverse sources and generations. Thus, the summaries do not proceed chronologically or by verse sequence. Rather, they seek to rehearse the overall course of the reformers' comments on that pericope.

We do not assume that the commentators themselves anticipated or expressed a formally received cohesive argument but rather that the various arguments tend to flow in a plausible, recognizable pattern. Modern readers can thus glimpse aspects of continuity in the flow of diverse exegetical traditions representing various generations and geographical locations.

Topical Headings

An abundance of varied Reformation-era comment is available for each pericope. For this reason we have broken the pericopes into two levels. First is the verse with its topical heading. The reformers' comments are then focused on aspects of each verse, with topical headings summarizing the essence of the individual comment by evoking a key phrase, metaphor, or idea. This feature provides a bridge by which modern readers can enter into the heart of the Reformation-era comment.

Identifying the Reformation Authors, Texts, and Events

Following the topical heading of each section of comment, the name of the Reformation commentator is given. An English translation (where needed) of the reformer's comment is then provided. This is immediately followed by the title of the original work rendered in English.

Readers who wish to pursue a deeper investigation of the reformers' works cited in this commentary will find full bibliographic detail for each Reformation title provided in the bibliography at the back of the volume. Information on English translations (where available) and standard original-language editions and critical editions of the works cited is found in the bibliography. The Biographical Sketches section provides brief overviews of the life and work of each commentator, and each confession or collaborative work, appearing in the present volume (as well as in any previous volumes). Finally, a Timeline of the Reformation offers broader context for people, places, and events relevant to the commentators and their works.

Footnotes and Back Matter

To aid the reader in exploring the background and texts in further detail, this commentary utilizes footnotes. The use and content of footnotes may vary among the volumes in this series. Where footnotes appear, a footnote number directs the reader to a note at the bottom of the page, where one will find annotations (clarifications or biblical cross references), information on English translations (where available) or standard original-language editions of the work cited.

Where original-language texts have remained untranslated into English, we provide new translations. Where there is any serious ambiguity or textual problem in the selection, we have tried to reflect the best available textual tradition. Wherever current English translations are already well rendered, they are utilized, but where necessary they are stylistically updated. A single asterisk (*) indicates that a previous English translation has been updated to modern English or amended for easier reading. We have standardized spellings and made grammatical variables uniform so that our English references will not reflect the linguistic oddities of the older English translations. For ease of reading we have in some cases removed superfluous conjunctions.

GENERAL INTRODUCTION

The Reformation Commentary on Scripture (RCS) is a twenty-eight-volume series of exegetical comment covering the entire Bible and gathered from the writings of sixteenth-century preachers, scholars and reformers. The RCS is intended as a sequel to the highly acclaimed Ancient Christian Commentary on Scripture (ACCS), and as such its overall concept, method, format, and audience are similar to the earlier series. Both series are committed to the renewal of the church through careful study and meditative reflection on the Old and New Testaments, the charter documents of Christianity, read in the context of the worshiping, believing community of faith across the centuries. However, the patristic and Reformation eras are separated by nearly a millennium, and the challenges of reading Scripture with the reformers require special attention to their context, resources and assumptions. The purpose of this general introduction is to present an overview of the context and process of biblical interpretation in the age of the Reformation.

Goals

The Reformation Commentary on Scripture seeks to introduce its readers to the depth and richness of exegetical ferment that defined the Reformation era. The RCS has four goals: the enrichment of contemporary biblical interpretation through exposure to Reformation-era biblical exegesis; the renewal of contemporary preaching through exposure to the biblical insights of the Reformation writers; a deeper understanding of the Reformation itself and the breadth of perspectives represented within it; and a recovery of the profound integration of the life of faith and the life of the mind that should characterize Christian scholarship. Each of these goals requires a brief comment.

Renewing contemporary biblical interpretation. During the past half-century, biblical hermeneutics has become a major growth industry in the academic world. One of the consequences of the historical-critical hegemony of biblical studies has been the privileging of contemporary philosophies and ideologies at the expense of a commitment to the Christian church as the primary reading community within which and for which biblical exegesis is done. Reading Scripture with the church fathers and the reformers is a corrective to all such imperialism of the present. One of the greatest skills required for a fruitful interpretation of the Bible is the ability to listen. We rightly emphasize the importance of listening to the voices of contextual theologies today, but in doing so we often marginalize or ignore another crucial context—the community of believing Christians through the centuries. The serious study of Scripture requires more than the latest

Bible translation in one hand and the latest commentary (or niche study Bible) in the other. John L. Thompson has called on Christians today to practice the art of "reading the Bible with the dead."[1] The RCS presents carefully selected comments from the extant commentaries of the Reformation as an encouragement to more in-depth study of this important epoch in the history of biblical interpretation.

Strengthening contemporary preaching. The Protestant reformers identified the public preaching of the Word of God as an indispensible means of grace and a sure sign of the true church. Through the words of the preacher, the living voice of the gospel (*viva vox evangelii*) is heard. Luther famously said that the church is not a "pen house" but a "mouth house."[2] The Reformation in Switzerland began when Huldrych Zwingli entered the pulpit of the Grossmünster in Zurich on January 1, 1519, and began to preach a series of expositional sermons chapter by chapter from the Gospel of Matthew. In the following years he extended this homiletical approach to other books of the Old and New Testaments. Calvin followed a similar pattern in Geneva. Many of the commentaries represented in this series were either originally presented as sermons or were written to support the regular preaching ministry of local church pastors. Luther said that the preacher should be a *bonus textualis*—a good one with a text—well-versed in the Scriptures. Preachers in the Reformation traditions preached not only about the Bible but also from it, and this required more than a passing acquaintance with its contents. Those who have been charged with the office of preaching in the church today can find wisdom and insight—and fresh perspectives—in the sermons of the Reformation and the biblical commentaries read and studied by preachers of the sixteenth century.

Deepening understanding of the Reformation. Some scholars of the sixteenth century prefer to speak of the period they study in the plural, the European Reformations, to indicate that many diverse impulses for reform were at work in this turbulent age of transition from medieval to modern times.[3] While this point is well taken, the RCS follows the time-honored tradition of using *Reformation* in the singular form to indicate not only a major moment in the history of Christianity in the West but also, as Hans J. Hillerbrand has put it, "an essential cohesiveness in the heterogeneous pursuits of religious reform in the sixteenth century."[4] At the same time, in developing guidelines to assist the volume editors in making judicious selections from the vast amount of commentary material available in this period, we have stressed the multifaceted character of the Reformation across many confessions, theological orientations, and political settings.

Advancing Christian scholarship. By assembling and disseminating numerous voices from such a signal period as the Reformation, the RCS aims to make a significant contribution to the ever-growing stream of Christian scholarship. The post-Enlightenment split between the study of the Bible as an academic discipline and the reading of the Bible as spiritual nurture was foreign

---

[1] John L. Thompson, *Reading the Bible with the Dead* (Grand Rapids: Eerdmans, 2007).

[2] WA 10,2:48.

[3] See Carter Lindberg, *The European Reformations*, 2nd ed. (Malden, MA: Wiley-Blackwell, 2010).

[4] Hans J. Hillerbrand, *The Division of Christendom* (Louisville, KY: Westminster John Knox, 2007), x. Hillerbrand has also edited the standard reference work in Reformation studies, *OER*. See also Diarmaid MacCulloch, *The Reformation* (New York: Viking, 2003), and Patrick Collinson, *The Reformation: A History* (New York: Random House, 2004).

to the reformers. For them the study of the Bible was transformative at the most basic level of the human person: *coram deo*.

The reformers all repudiated the idea that the Bible could be studied and understood with dispassionate objectivity, as a cold artifact from antiquity. Luther's famous Reformation breakthrough triggered by his laborious study of the Psalms and Paul's letter to the Romans is well known, but the experience of Cambridge scholar Thomas Bilney was perhaps more typical. When Erasmus's critical edition of the Greek New Testament was published in 1516, it was accompanied by a new translation in elegant Latin. Attracted by the classical beauty of Erasmus's Latin, Bilney came across this statement in 1 Timothy 1:15: "Christ Jesus came into the world to save sinners." In the Greek this sentence is described as *pistos ho logos*, which the Vulgate had rendered *fidelis sermo*, "a faithful saying." Erasmus chose a different word for the Greek *pistos—certus*, "sure, certain." When Bilney grasped the meaning of this word applied to the announcement of salvation in Christ, he tells us that "immediately, I felt a marvellous comfort and quietness, insomuch as 'my bruised bones leaped for joy.'"[5]

Luther described the way the Bible was meant to function in the minds and hearts of believers when he reproached himself and others for studying the nativity narrative with such cool unconcern:

> I hate myself because when I see Christ laid in the manger or in the lap of his mother and hear the angels sing, my heart does not leap into flame. With what good reason should we all despise ourselves that we remain so cold when this word is spoken to us, over which everyone should dance and leap and burn for joy! We act as though it were a frigid historical fact that does not smite our hearts, as if someone were merely relating that the sultan has a crown of gold.[6]

It was a core conviction of the Reformation that the careful study and meditative listening to the Scriptures, what the monks called *lectio divina*, could yield transformative results for *all* of life. The value of such a rich commentary, therefore, lies not only in the impressive volume of Reformation-era voices that are presented throughout the course of the series but in the many particular fields for which their respective lives and ministries are relevant. The Reformation is consequential for historical studies, both church as well as secular history. Biblical and theological studies, to say nothing of pastoral and spiritual studies, also stand to benefit and progress immensely from renewed engagement today, as mediated through the RCS, with the reformers of yesteryear.

Perspectives

In setting forth the perspectives and parameters of the RCS, the following considerations have proved helpful.

Chronology. When did the Reformation begin, and how long did it last? In some traditional accounts, the answer was clear: the Reformation began with the posting of Luther's Ninety-five

---

[5]John Foxe, *The Acts and Monuments of John Foxe: A New and Complete Edition*, 8 vols., ed. Stephen Reed Cattley (London: R. B. Seeley & W. Burnside, 1837), 4:635; quoting Ps 51:8; cited in A. G. Dickens, *The English Reformation*, 2nd ed. (University Park, PA: The Pennsylvannia State University Press, 1991), 102.

[6]WA 49:176-77, quoted in Roland Bainton, "The Bible in the Reformation," in *CHB*, 3:23.

Theses at Wittenberg in 1517 and ended with the death of Calvin in Geneva in 1564. Apart from reducing the Reformation to a largely German event with a side trip to Switzerland, this perspective fails to do justice to the important events that led up to Luther's break with Rome and its many reverberations throughout Europe and beyond. In choosing commentary selections for the RCS, we have adopted the concept of the long sixteenth century, say, from the late 1400s to the mid-seventeenth century. Thus we have included commentary selections from early or pre-Reformation writers such as John Colet and Jacques Lefèvre d'Étaples to seventeenth-century figures such as Henry Ainsworth and Johann Gerhard.

Confession. The RCS concentrates primarily, though not exclusively, on the exegetical writings of the Protestant reformers. While the ACCS provided a compendium of key consensual exegetes of the early Christian centuries, the Catholic/Protestant confessional divide in the sixteenth century tested the very idea of consensus, especially with reference to ecclesiology and soteriology. While many able and worthy exegetes faithful to the Roman Catholic Church were active during this period, this project has chosen to include primarily those figures that represent perspectives within the Protestant Reformation. For this reason we have not included comments on the apocryphal or deuterocanonical writings.

We recognize that "Protestant" and "Catholic" as contradistinctive labels are anachronistic terms for the early decades of the sixteenth century before the hardening of confessional identities surrounding the Council of Trent (1545–1563). Protestant figures such as Philipp Melanchthon, Johannes Oecolampadius and John Calvin were all products of the revival of sacred letters known as biblical humanism. They shared an approach to biblical interpretation that owed much to Desiderius Erasmus and other scholars who remained loyal to the Church of Rome. Careful comparative studies of Protestant and Catholic exegesis in the sixteenth century have shown surprising areas of agreement when the focus was the study of a particular biblical text rather than the standard confessional debates.

At the same time, exegetical differences among the various Protestant groups could become strident and church-dividing. The most famous example of this is the interpretive impasse between Luther and Zwingli over the meaning of "This is my body" (Mt 26:26) in the words of institution. Their disagreement at the Colloquy of Marburg in 1529 had important christological and pastoral implications, as well as social and political consequences. Luther refused fellowship with Zwingli and his party at the end of the colloquy; in no small measure this bitter division led to the separate trajectories pursued by Lutheran and Reformed Protestantism to this day. In Elizabethan England, Puritans and Anglicans agreed that "Holy Scripture containeth all things necessary to salvation: so that whatsoever is not read therein, nor may be proved thereby, is not to be required of any man" (article 6 of the Thirty-Nine Articles of Religion), yet on the basis of their differing interpretations of the Bible they fought bitterly over the structures of the church, the clothing of the clergy and the ways of worship. On the matter of infant baptism, Catholics and Protestants alike agreed on its propriety, though there were various theories as to how a practice not mentioned in the Bible could be justified biblically. The Anabaptists were outliers on this subject. They rejected infant baptism altogether. They appealed to the example of the baptism of Jesus and to his final words as recorded in the Gospel of Matthew (Mt 28:19-20): "Go therefore, and make disciples of all nations, baptizing them in the name of the Father, and of the Son, and of the Holy Spirit, teaching them to observe all that I have commanded you." New Testament Christians, they argued, are to follow not only the commands of Jesus in the Great Commission, but also the exact order in which they were given: evangelize, baptize, catechize.

These and many other differences of interpretation among the various Protestant groups are reflected in their many sermons, commentaries and public disputations. In the RCS, the volume editors' introduction to each volume is intended to help the reader understand the nature and significance of doctrinal conversations and disputes that resulted in particular, and frequently clashing, interpretations. Footnotes throughout the text will be provided to explain obscure references, unusual expressions and other matters that require special comment. Volume editors have chosen comments on the Bible across a wide range of sixteenth-century confessions and schools of interpretation: biblical humanists, Lutheran, Reformed, Anglican, Puritan, and Anabaptist. We have not pursued passages from post-Tridentine Catholic authors or from radical spiritualists and antitrinitarian writers, though sufficient material is available from these sources to justify another series.

Format. The design of the RCS is intended to offer reader-friendly access to these classic texts. The availability of digital resources has given access to a huge residual database of sixteenth-century exegetical comment hitherto available only in major research universities and rare book collections. The RCS has benefited greatly from online databases such as Alexander Street Press's Digital Library of Classical Protestant Texts (DLCPT) and Early English Books Online as well as freely accessible databases like the Post-Reformation Digital Library (prdl.org). Through the help of RCS editorial advisor Herman Selderhuis, we have also had access to the special Reformation collections of the Johannes a Lasco Bibliothek in Emden, Germany. In addition, modern critical editions and translations of Reformation sources have been published over the past generation. Original translations of Reformation sources are given unless an acceptable translation already exists.

Each volume in the RCS will include an introduction by the volume editor placing that portion of the canon within the historical context of the Protestant Reformation and presenting a summary of the theological themes, interpretive issues and reception of the particular book(s). The commentary itself consists of particular pericopes identified by a pericope heading; the biblical text in the English Standard Version (ESV), with significant textual variants registered in the footnotes; an overview of the pericope in which principal exegetical and theological concerns of the Reformation writers are succinctly noted; and excerpts from the Reformation writers identified by name according to the conventions of the *Oxford Encyclopedia of the Reformation*. Each volume will also include a bibliography of sources cited, as well as an appendix of authors and source works.

The Reformation era was a time of verbal as well as physical violence, and this fact has presented a challenge for this project. Without unduly sanitizing the texts, where they contain anti-Semitic, sexist or inordinately polemical rhetoric, we have not felt obliged to parade such comments either. We have noted the abridgement of texts with ellipses and an explanatory footnote.

While this procedure would not be valid in the critical edition of such a text, we have deemed it appropriate in a series whose primary purpose is pastoral and devotional. When translating *homo* or similar terms that refer to the human race as a whole or to individual persons without reference to gender, we have used alternative English expressions to the word *man* (or derivative constructions that formerly were used generically to signify humanity at large), whenever such substitutions can be made without producing an awkward or artificial construction.

As is true in the ACCS, we have made a special effort where possible to include the voices of women, though we acknowledge the difficulty of doing so for the early modern period when for a variety of social and cultural reasons few theological and biblical works were published by women. However, recent scholarship has focused on a number of female leaders whose literary remains show us how they understood and interpreted the Bible. Women who made significant contributions to the Reformation include Marguerite d'Angoulême, sister of King Francis I, who supported French reformist evangelicals including Calvin and who published a religious poem influenced by Luther's theology, *The Mirror of the Sinful Soul*; Argula von Grumbach, a Bavarian noblewoman who defended the teachings of Luther and Melanchthon before the theologians of the University of Ingolstadt; Katharina Schütz Zell, the wife of a former priest, Matthias Zell, and a remarkable reformer in her own right—she conducted funerals, compiled hymnbooks, defended the downtrodden, and published a defense of clerical marriage as well as composing works of consolation on divine comfort and pleas for the toleration of Anabaptists and Catholics alike; and Anne Askew, a Protestant martyr put to death in 1546 after demonstrating remarkable biblical prowess in her examinations by church officials. Other echoes of faithful women in the age of the Reformation are found in their letters, translations, poems, hymns, court depositions, and martyr records.

Lay culture, learned culture. In recent decades, much attention has been given to what is called "reforming from below," that is, the expressions of religious beliefs and churchly life that characterized the popular culture of the majority of the population in the era of the Reformation. Social historians have taught us to examine the diverse pieties of townspeople and city folk, of rural religion and village life, the emergence of lay theologies, and the experiences of women in the religious tumults of Reformation Europe.[7] Formal commentaries by their nature are artifacts of learned culture. Almost all of them were written in Latin, the lingua franca of learned discourse well past the age of the Reformation. Biblical commentaries were certainly not the primary means by which the Protestant Reformation spread so rapidly across wide sectors of sixteenth-century society. Small pamphlets and broadsheets, later called *Flugschriften* ("flying writings"), with their graphic woodcuts and cartoon-like depictions of Reformation personalities and events, became the means of choice for mass communication in the early age of printing. Sermons and works of devotion were also printed with appealing visual aids. Luther's early writings were often accompanied by drawings and sketches from Lucas Cranach and other artists. This was done "above all for the sake of children and simple folk," as Luther

---

[7]See Peter Matheson, ed., *Reformation Christianity* (Minneapolis: Fortress, 2007).

put it, "who are more easily moved by pictures and images to recall divine history than through mere words or doctrines."[8]

We should be cautious, however, in drawing too sharp a distinction between learned and lay culture in this period. The phenomenon of preaching was a kind of verbal bridge between scholars at their desks and the thousands of illiterate or semiliterate listeners whose views were shaped by the results of Reformation exegesis. According to contemporary witness, more than one thousand people were crowding into Geneva to hear Calvin expound the Scriptures every day.[9] An example of how learned theological works by Reformation scholars were received across divisions of class and social status comes from Lazare Drilhon, an apothecary of Toulon. He was accused of heresy in May 1545 when a cache of prohibited books was found hidden in his garden shed. In addition to devotional works, the French New Testament and a copy of Calvin's Genevan liturgy, there was found a series of biblical commentaries, translated from the Latin into French: Martin Bucer's on Matthew, François Lambert's on the Apocalypse and one by Oecolampadius on 1 John.[10] Biblical exegesis in the sixteenth century was not limited to the kind of full-length commentaries found in Drilhon's shed. Citations from the Bible and expositions of its meaning permeate the extant literature of sermons, letters, court depositions, doctrinal treatises, records of public disputations and even last wills and testaments. While most of the selections in the RCS will be drawn from formal commentary literature, other sources of biblical reflection will also be considered.

Historical Context

The medieval legacy. On October 18, 1512, the degree *Doctor in Biblia* was conferred on Martin Luther, and he began his career as a professor in the University of Wittenberg. As is well known, Luther was also a monk who had taken solemn vows in the Augustinian Order of Hermits at Erfurt. These two settings—the university and the monastery—both deeply rooted in the Middle Ages, form the background not only for Luther's personal vocation as a reformer but also for the history of the biblical commentary in the age of the Reformation. Since the time of the Venerable Bede (d. 735), sometimes called "the last of the Fathers," serious study of the Bible had taken place primarily in the context of cloistered monasteries. The Rule of St. Benedict brought together *lectio* and *meditatio*, the knowledge of letters and the life of prayer. The liturgy was the medium through which the daily reading of the Bible, especially the Psalms, and the sayings of the church fathers came together in the spiritual formation of the monks.[11] Essential to this understanding was a belief in the unity of the people of God throughout time as well as space, and an awareness that life in this world was a preparation for the beatific vision in the next.

---

[8]Martin Luther, "Personal Prayer Book," LW 43:42-43* (WA 10,2:458); quoted in R. W. Scribner, *For the Sake of Simple Folk: Popular Propaganda for the German Reformation* (Cambridge: Cambridge University Press, 1981), xi.

[9]Letter of De Beaulieu to Guillaume Farel (1561) in *Theodor Beza nach handschriftlichen und anderen gleichzeitigen Quellen*, ed. J. W. Baum (Leipzig: Weidmann, 1851), 2:92.

[10]Francis Higman, "A Heretic's Library: The Drilhon Inventory" (1545), in Francis Higman, *Lire et Découvire: la circulation des idées au temps de la Réforme* (Geneva: Droz, 1998), 65-85.

[11]See the classic study by Jean Leclercq, *The Love of Learning and the Desire for God* (New York: Fordham University Press, 1961).

The source of theology was the study of the sacred page (*sacra pagina*); its object was the accumulation of knowledge not for its own sake but for the obtaining of eternal life. For these monks, the Bible had God for its author, salvation for its end and unadulterated truth for its matter, though they would not have expressed it in such an Aristotelian way. The medieval method of interpreting the Bible owed much to Augustine's *On Christian Doctrine*. In addition to setting forth a series of rules (drawn from an earlier work by Tyconius), Augustine stressed the importance of distinguishing the literal and spiritual or allegorical senses of Scripture. While the literal sense was not disparaged, the allegorical was valued because it enabled the believer to obtain spiritual benefit from the obscure places in the Bible, especially in the Old Testament. For Augustine, as for the monks who followed him, the goal of scriptural exegesis was freighted with eschatological meaning; its purpose was to induce faith, hope, and love and so to advance in one's pilgrimage toward that city with foundations (see Heb 11:10).

Building on the work of Augustine and other church fathers going back to Origen, medieval exegetes came to understand Scripture as possessed of four possible meanings, the famous *quadriga*. The literal meaning was retained, of course, but the spiritual meaning was now subdivided into three senses: the allegorical, the moral, and the anagogical. Medieval exegetes often referred to the four meanings of Scripture in a popular rhyme:

> The letter shows us what God and our fathers did;
> The allegory shows us where our faith is hid;
> The moral meaning gives us rules of daily life;
> The anagogy shows us where we end our strife.[12]

In this schema, the three spiritual meanings of the text correspond to the three theological virtues: faith (allegory), hope (anagogy), and love (the moral meaning). It should be noted that this way of approaching the Bible assumed a high doctrine of scriptural inspiration: the multiple meanings inherent in the text had been placed there by the Holy Spirit for the benefit of the people of God. The biblical justification for this method went back to the apostle Paul, who had used the words *allegory* and *type* when applying Old Testament events to believers in Christ (Gal 4:21-31; 1 Cor 10:1-11). The problem with this approach was knowing how to relate each of the four senses to one another and how to prevent Scripture from becoming a nose of wax turned this way and that by various interpreters. As G. R. Evans explains, "Any interpretation which could be put upon the text and was in keeping with the faith and edifying, had the warrant of God himself, for no human reader had the ingenuity to find more than God had put there."[13]

With the rise of the universities in the eleventh century, theology and the study of Scripture moved from the cloister into the classroom. Scripture and the Fathers were still important, but they came to function more as footnotes to the theological questions debated in the schools and brought together in an impressive systematic way in works such as Peter Lombard's *Books of Sentences* (the standard theology textbook of the Middle Ages) and the great scholastic *summae* of the thirteenth

---

[12]Robert M. Grant, *A Short History of the Interpretation of the Bible* (New York: Macmillan, 1963), 119. A translation of the well-known Latin quatrain: *Littera gesta docet/Quid credas allegoria/Moralis quid agas/Quo tendas anagogia.*

[13]G. R. Evans, *The Language and Logic of the Bible: The Road to Reformation* (Cambridge: Cambridge University Press, 1985), 42.

century. Indispensible to the study of the Bible in the later Middle Ages was the *Glossa ordinaria*, a collection of exegetical opinions by the church fathers and other commentators. Heiko Oberman summarized the transition from devotion to dialectic this way: "When, due to the scientific revolution of the twelfth century, Scripture became the *object* of study rather than the *subject* through which God speaks to the student, the difference between the two modes of speaking was investigated in terms of the texts themselves rather than in their relation to the recipients."[14] It was possible, of course, to be both a scholastic theologian and a master of the spiritual life. Meister Eckhart, for example, wrote commentaries on the Old Testament in Latin and works of mystical theology in German, reflecting what had come to be seen as a division of labor between the two.

An increasing focus on the text of Scripture led to a revival of interest in its literal sense. The two key figures in this development were Thomas Aquinas (d. 1274) and Nicholas of Lyra (d. 1340). Thomas is best remembered for his *Summa Theologiae*, but he was also a prolific commentator on the Bible. Thomas did not abandon the multiple senses of Scripture but declared that all the senses were founded on one—the literal—and this sense eclipsed allegory as the basis of sacred doctrine. Nicholas of Lyra was a Franciscan scholar who made use of the Hebrew text of the Old Testament and quoted liberally from works of Jewish scholars, especially the learned French rabbi Salomon Rashi (d. 1105). After Aquinas, Lyra was the strongest defender of the literal, historical meaning of Scripture as the primary basis of theological disputation. His *Postilla*, as his notes were called—the abbreviated form of *post illa verba textus*, meaning "after these words from Scripture"—were widely circulated in the late Middle Ages and became the first biblical commentary to be printed in the fifteenth century. More than any other commentator from the period of high scholasticism, Lyra and his work were greatly valued by the early reformers. According to an old Latin pun, *Nisi Lyra lyrasset, Lutherus non saltasset*, "If Lyra had not played his lyre, Luther would not have danced."[15] While Luther was never an uncritical disciple of any teacher, he did praise Lyra as a good Hebraist and quoted him more than one hundred times in his lectures on Genesis, where he declared, "I prefer him to almost all other interpreters of Scripture."[16]

Sacred philology. The sixteenth century has been called a golden age of biblical interpretation, and it is a fact that the age of the Reformation witnessed an explosion of commentary writing unparalleled in the history of the Christian church. Kenneth Hagen has cataloged forty-five commentaries on Hebrews between 1516 (Erasmus) and 1598 (Beza).[17] During the sixteenth century, more than seventy new commentaries on Romans were published, five of them by Melanchthon alone, and nearly one hundred commentaries on the Bible's prayer book, the Psalms.[18] There were two developments in the fifteenth century that presaged this development and without which it

---

[14]Heiko Oberman, *Forerunners of the Reformation* (Philadelphia: Fortress, 1966), 284.

[15]Nicholas of Lyra, *The Postilla of Nicolas of Lyra on the Song of Songs*, trans. and ed. James George Kiecker (Milwaukee: Marquette University Press, 1998), 19.

[16]LW 2:164 (WA 42:377).

[17]Kenneth Hagen, *Hebrews Commenting from Erasmus to Bèze, 1516–1598* (Tübingen: Mohr, 1981).

[18]R. Gerald Hobbs, "Biblical Commentaries," *OER* 1:167-71. See in general David C. Steinmetz, ed., *The Bible in the Sixteenth Century* (Durham: Duke University Press, 1990).

could not have taken place: the invention of printing and the rediscovery of a vast store of ancient learning hitherto unknown or unavailable to scholars in the West.

It is now commonplace to say that what the computer has become in our generation, the printing press was to the world of Erasmus, Luther, and other leaders of the Reformation. Johannes Gutenberg, a goldsmith by trade, developed a metal alloy suitable for type and a machine that would allow printed characters to be cast with relative ease, placed in even lines of composition and then manipulated again and again, making possible the mass production of an unbelievable number of texts. In 1455, the Gutenberg Bible, the masterpiece of the typographical revolution, was published at Mainz in double columns in gothic type. Forty-seven copies of the beautiful Gutenberg Bible are still extant, each consisting of more than one thousand colorfully illuminated and impeccably printed pages. What began at Gutenberg's print shop in Mainz on the Rhine River soon spread, like McDonald's or Starbucks in our day, into every nook and cranny of the known world. Printing presses sprang up in Rome (1464), Venice (1469), Paris (1470), the Netherlands (1471), Switzerland (1472), Spain (1474), England (1476), Sweden (1483), and Constantinople (1490). By 1500, these and other presses across Europe had published some twenty-seven thousand titles, most of them in Latin. Erasmus once compared himself with an obscure preacher whose sermons were heard by only a few people in one or two churches while his books were read in every country in the world. Erasmus was not known for his humility, but in this case he was simply telling the truth.[19]

The Italian humanist Lorenzo Valla (d. 1457) died in the early dawn of the age of printing, but his critical and philological studies would be taken up by others who believed that genuine reform in church and society could come about only by returning to the wellsprings of ancient learning and wisdom—*ad fontes*, "back to the sources!" Valla is best remembered for undermining a major claim made by defenders of the papacy when he proved by philological research that the so-called Donation of Constantine, which had bolstered papal assertions of temporal sovereignty, was a forgery. But it was Valla's *Collatio Novi Testamenti* of 1444 that would have such a great effect on the renewal of biblical studies in the next century. Erasmus discovered the manuscript of this work while rummaging through an old library in Belgium and published it at Paris in 1505. In the preface to his edition of Valla, Erasmus gave the rationale that would guide his own labors in textual criticism. Just as Jerome had translated the Latin Vulgate from older versions and copies of the Scriptures in his day, so now Jerome's own text must be subjected to careful scrutiny and correction. Erasmus would be *Hieronymus redivivus*, a new Jerome come back to life to advance the cause of sacred philology. The restoration of the Scriptures and the writings of the church fathers would usher in what Erasmus believed would be a golden age of peace and learning. In 1516, the Basel publisher Froben brought out Erasmus's *Novum Instrumentum*, the first published edition of the Greek New Testament. Erasmus's Greek New Testament would go through five editions in his lifetime, each one with new emendations to the text and a growing section of annotations that expanded to include not only technical notes about the text but also theological comment. The influence of Erasmus's Greek New

---

[19]E. Harris Harbison, *The Christian Scholar in the Age of the Reformation* (New York: Charles Scribner's Sons, 1956), 80.

Testament was enormous. It formed the basis for Robert Estienne's *Novum Testamentum Graece* of 1550, which in turn was used to establish the Greek *Textus Receptus* for a number of late Reformation translations including the King James Version of 1611.

For all his expertise in Greek, Erasmus was a poor student of Hebrew and only published commentaries on several of the psalms. However, the renaissance of Hebrew letters was part of the wider program of biblical humanism as reflected in the establishment of trilingual colleges devoted to the study of Hebrew, Greek and Latin (the three languages written on the *titulus* of Jesus' cross [Jn 19:20]) at Alcalá in Spain, Wittenberg in Germany, Louvain in Belgium, and Paris in France. While it is true that some medieval commentators, especially Nicholas of Lyra, had been informed by the study of Hebrew and rabbinics in their biblical work, it was the publication of Johannes Reuchlin's *De rudimentis hebraicis* (1506), a combined grammar and dictionary, that led to the recovery of *veritas Hebraica*, as Jerome had referred to the true voice of the Hebrew Scriptures. The pursuit of Hebrew studies was carried forward in the Reformation by two great scholars, Konrad Pellikan and Sebastian Münster. Pellikan was a former Franciscan friar who embraced the Protestant cause and played a major role in the Zurich reformation. He had published a Hebrew grammar even prior to Reuchlin and produced a commentary on nearly the entire Bible that appeared in seven volumes between 1532 and 1539. Münster was Pellikan's student and taught Hebrew at the University of Heidelberg before taking up a similar position in Basel. Like his mentor, Münster was a great collector of Hebraica and published a series of excellent grammars, dictionaries and rabbinic texts. Münster did for the Hebrew Old Testament what Erasmus had done for the Greek New Testament. His *Hebraica Biblia* offered a fresh Latin translation of the Old Testament with annotations from medieval rabbinic exegesis.

Luther first learned Hebrew with Reuchlin's grammar in hand but took advantage of other published resources, such as the four-volume Hebrew Bible published at Venice by Daniel Bomberg in 1516 to 1517. He also gathered his own circle of Hebrew experts, his *sanhedrin* he called it, who helped him with his German translation of the Old Testament. We do not know where William Tyndale learned Hebrew, though perhaps it was in Worms, where there was a thriving rabbinical school during his stay there. In any event, he had sufficiently mastered the language to bring out a freshly translated Pentateuch that was published at Antwerp in 1530. By the time the English separatist scholar Henry Ainsworth published his prolix commentaries on the Pentateuch in 1616, the knowledge of Hebrew, as well as Greek, was taken for granted by every serious scholar of the Bible. In the preface to his commentary on Genesis, Ainsworth explained that "the literal sense of Moses's Hebrew (which is the tongue wherein he wrote the law), is the ground of all interpretation, and that language hath figures and properties of speech, different from ours: These therefore in the first place are to be opened that the natural meaning of the Scripture, being known, the mysteries of godliness therein implied, may be better discerned."[20]

The restoration of the biblical text in the original languages made possible the revival of scriptural exposition reflected in the floodtide of sermon literature and commentary work. Of even

---

[20]Henry Ainsworth, *Annotations upon the First Book of Moses Called Genesis* (Amsterdam, 1616), preface (unpaginated).

more far-reaching import was the steady stream of vernacular Bibles in the sixteenth century. In the introduction to his 1516 edition of the New Testament, Erasmus had expressed his desire that the Scriptures be translated into all languages so that "the lowliest women" could read the Gospels and the Pauline epistles and "the farmer sing some portion of them at the plow, the weaver hum some parts of them to the movement of his shuttle, the traveler lighten the weariness of the journey with stories of this kind."[21] Like Erasmus, Tyndale wanted the Bible to be available in the language of the common people. He once said to a learned divine that if God spared his life he would cause the boy who drives the plow to know more of the Scriptures than he did![22] The project of allowing the Bible to speak in the language of the mother in the house, the children in the street and the cheesemonger in the marketplace was met with stiff opposition by certain Catholic polemicists such as Johann Eck, Luther's antagonist at the Leipzig Debate of 1519. In his *Enchiridion* (1525), Eck derided the "inky theologians" whose translations paraded the Bible before "the untutored crowd" and subjected it to the judgment of "laymen and crazy old women."[23] In fact, some fourteen German Bibles had already been published prior to Luther's September Testament of 1522, which he translated from Erasmus's Greek New Testament in less than three months' time while sequestered in the Wartburg. Luther's German New Testament became the first bestseller in the world, appearing in forty-three distinct editions between 1522 and 1525 with upward of one hundred thousand copies issued in these three years. It is estimated that 5 percent of the German population may have been literate at this time, but this rate increased as the century wore on due in no small part to the unmitigated success of vernacular Bibles.[24]

Luther's German Bible (inclusive of the Old Testament from 1534) was the most successful venture of its kind, but it was not alone in the field. Hans Denck and Ludwig Hätzer, leaders in the early Anabaptist movement, translated the prophetic books of the Old Testament from Hebrew into German in 1527. This work influenced the Swiss-German Bible of 1531 published by Leo Jud and other pastors in Zurich. Tyndale's influence on the English language rivaled that of Luther on German. At a time when English was regarded as "that obscure and remote dialect of German spoken in an off-shore island," Tyndale, with his remarkable linguistic ability (he was fluent in eight languages), "made a language for England," as his modern editor David Daniell has put it.[25] Tyndale was imprisoned and executed near Brussels in 1536, but the influence of his biblical work among the common people of England was already being felt. There is no reason to doubt the authenticity of John Foxe's recollection of how Tyndale's New Testament was received in England during the 1520s and 1530s:

---

[21]John C. Olin, *Christian Humanism and the Reformation* (New York: Fordham University Press, 1987), 101.

[22]This famous statement of Tyndale was quoted by John Foxe in his *Acts and Monuments of Matters Happening in the Church* (London, 1563). See Henry Wansbrough, "Tyndale," in *The Bible in the Renaissance*, ed. Richard Griffith (Aldershot, UK: Ashgate, 2001), 124.

[23]John Eck, *Enchiridion of Commonplaces*, trans. Ford Lewis Battles (Grand Rapids: Baker, 1979), 47-49.

[24]The effect of printing on the spread of the Reformation has been much debated. See the classic study by Elizabeth L. Eisenstein, *The Printing Press as an Agent of Change* (Cambridge: Cambridge University Press, 1979). More recent studies include Mark U. Edwards Jr., *Printing, Propaganda and Martin Luther* (Minneapolis: Fortress, 1994), and Andrew Pettegree and Matthew Hall, "The Reformation and the Book: A Reconsideration," *Historical Journal* 47 (2004): 1-24.

[25]David Daniell, *William Tyndale: A Biography* (New Haven: Yale University Press, 1994), 3.

The fervent zeal of those Christian days seemed much superior to these our days and times; as manifestly may appear by their sitting up all night in reading and hearing; also by their expenses and charges in buying of books in English, of whom some gave five marks, some more, some less, for a book: some gave a load of hay for a few chapters of St. James, or of St. Paul in English.[26]

Calvin helped to revise and contributed three prefaces to the French Bible translated by his cousin Pierre Robert Olivétan and originally published at Neuchâtel in 1535. Clément Marot and Beza provided a fresh translation of the Psalms with each psalm rendered in poetic form and accompanied by monophonic musical settings for congregational singing. The Bay Psalter, the first book printed in America, was an English adaptation of this work. Geneva also provided the provenance of the most influential Italian Bible published by Giovanni Diodati in 1607. The flowering of biblical humanism in vernacular Bibles resulted in new translations in all of the major language groups of Europe: Spanish (1569), Portuguese (1681), Dutch (New Testament, 1523; Old Testament, 1527), Danish (1550), Czech (1579–1593/94), Hungarian (New Testament, 1541; complete Bible, 1590), Polish (1563), Swedish (1541), and even Arabic (1591).[27]

Patterns of Reformation

Once the text of the Bible had been placed in the hands of the people, in cheap and easily available editions, what further need was there of published expositions such as commentaries? Given the Protestant doctrine of the priesthood of all believers, was there any longer a need for learned clergy and their bookish religion? Some radical reformers thought not. Sebastian Franck searched for the true church of the Spirit "scattered among the heathen and the weeds" but could not find it in any of the institutional structures of his time. *Veritas non potest scribi, aut exprimi*, he said, "truth can neither be spoken nor written."[28] Kaspar von Schwenckfeld so emphasized religious inwardness that he suspended external observance of the Lord's Supper and downplayed the readable, audible Scriptures in favor of the Word within. This trajectory would lead to the rise of the Quakers in the next century, but it was pursued neither by the mainline reformers nor by most of the Anabaptists. Article 7 of the Augsburg Confession (1530) declared the one holy Christian church to be "the assembly of all believers among whom the Gospel is purely preached and the holy sacraments are administered according to the Gospel."[29]

Historians of the nineteenth century referred to the material and formal principles of the Reformation. In this construal, the matter at stake was the meaning of the Christian gospel: the liberating insight that helpless sinners are graciously justified by the gift of faith alone, apart from any works or merits of their own, entirely on the basis of Christ's atoning work on the cross. For Luther especially, justification by faith alone became the criterion by which all other doctrines and

---

[26]Foxe, *Acts and Monuments*, 4:218.

[27]On vernacular translations of the Bible, see *CHB* 3:94-140 and Jaroslav Pelikan, *The Reformation of the Bible/The Bible of the Reformation* (New Haven: Yale University Press, 1996), 41-62.

[28]Sebastian Franck, *280 Paradoxes or Wondrous Sayings*, trans. E. J. Furcha (Lewiston, NY: Edwin Mellen Press, 1986), 10, 212.

[29]BoC 42 (BSLK 61).

practices of the church were to be judged. The cross proves everything, he said at the Heidelberg disputation in 1518. The distinction between law and gospel thus became the primary hermeneutical key that unlocked the true meaning of Scripture.

The formal principle of the Reformation, *sola Scriptura*, was closely bound up with proper distinctions between Scripture and tradition. "Scripture alone," said Luther, "is the true lord and master of all writings and doctrine on earth. If that is not granted, what is Scripture good for? The more we reject it, the more we become satisfied with human books and human teachers."[30] On the basis of this principle, the reformers challenged the structures and institutions of the medieval Catholic Church. Even a simple layperson, they asserted, armed with Scripture should be believed above a pope or a council without it. But, however boldly asserted, the doctrine of the primacy of Scripture did not absolve the reformers from dealing with a host of hermeneutical issues that became matters of contention both between Rome and the Reformation and within each of these two communities: the extent of the biblical canon, the validity of critical study of the Bible, the perspicuity of Scripture and its relation to preaching, and the retention of devotional and liturgical practices such as holy days, incense, the burning of candles, the sprinkling of holy water, church art, and musical instruments. Zwingli, the Puritans, and the radicals dismissed such things as a rubbish heap of ceremonials that amounted to nothing but tomfoolery, while Lutherans and Anglicans retained most of them as consonant with Scripture and valuable aids to worship.

It is important to note that while the mainline reformers differed among themselves on many matters, overwhelmingly they saw themselves as part of the ongoing Catholic tradition, indeed as the legitimate bearers of it. This was seen in numerous ways including their sense of continuity with the church of the preceding centuries; their embrace of the ecumenical orthodoxy of the early church; and their desire to read the Bible in dialogue with the exegetical tradition of the church.

In their biblical commentaries, the reformers of the sixteenth century revealed a close familiarity with the preceding exegetical tradition, and they used it respectfully as well as critically in their own expositions of the sacred text. For them, *sola Scriptura* was not *nuda Scriptura*. Rather, the Scriptures were seen as the book given to the church, gathered and guided by the Holy Spirit. In his restatement of the Vincentian canon, Calvin defined the church as "a society of all the saints, a society which, spread over the whole world, and existing in all ages, and bound together by the one doctrine and the one spirit of Christ, cultivates and observes unity of faith and brotherly concord. With this church we deny that we have any disagreement. Nay, rather, as we revere her as our mother, so we desire to remain in her bosom." Defined thus, the church has a real, albeit relative and circumscribed, authority since, as Calvin admits, "We cannot fly without wings."[31] While the reformers could not agree with the Council of Trent (though some recent Catholic theologians have challenged this interpretation) that Scripture and tradition were two separate and equal sources of divine revelation,

---

[30]LW 32:11-12* (WA 7:317).

[31]John C. Olin, ed., *John Calvin and Jacopo Sadoleto: A Reformation Debate* (New York: Harper Torchbooks, 1966), 61-62, 77.

they did believe in the coinherence of Scripture and tradition. This conviction shaped the way they read and interpreted the Bible.[32]

Schools of Exegesis

The reformers were passionate about biblical exegesis, but they showed little concern for hermeneutics as a separate field of inquiry. Niels Hemmingsen, a Lutheran theologian in Denmark, did write a treatise, *De methodis* (1555), in which he offered a philosophical and theological framework for the interpretation of Scripture. This was followed by the *Clavis Scripturae Sacrae* (1567) of Matthias Flacius Illyricus, which contains some fifty rules for studying the Bible drawn from Scripture itself.[33] However, hermeneutics as we know it came of age only in the Enlightenment and should not be backloaded into the Reformation. It is also true that the word *commentary* did not mean in the sixteenth century what it means for us today. Erasmus provided both annotations and paraphrases on the New Testament, the former a series of critical notes on the text but also containing points of doctrinal substance, the latter a theological overview and brief exposition. Most of Calvin's commentaries began as sermons or lectures presented in the course of his pastoral ministry. In the dedication to his 1519 study of Galatians, Luther declared that his work was "not so much a commentary as a testimony of my faith in Christ."[34] The exegetical work of the reformers was embodied in a wide variety of forms and genres, and the RCS has worked with this broader concept in setting the guidelines for this compendium.

The Protestant reformers shared in common a number of key interpretive principles such as the priority of the grammatical-historical sense of Scripture and the christological centeredness of the entire Bible, but they also developed a number of distinct approaches and schools of exegesis.[35] For the purposes of the RCS, we note the following key figures and families of interpretation in this period.

Biblical humanism. The key figure is Erasmus, whose importance is hard to exaggerate for Catholic and Protestant exegetes alike. His annotated Greek New Testament and fresh Latin translation challenged the hegemony of the Vulgate tradition and was doubtless a factor in the decision of the Council of Trent to establish the Vulgate edition as authentic and normative. Erasmus believed that the wide distribution of the Scriptures would contribute to personal spiritual renewal and the reform of society. In 1547, the English translation of Erasmus's *Paraphrases* was ordered to be placed in every parish church in England. John Colet first encouraged Erasmus

---

[32]See Timothy George, "An Evangelical Reflection on Scripture and Tradition," *Pro Ecclesia* 9 (2000): 184-207.

[33]See Kenneth G. Hagen, "'*De Exegetica Methodo*': Niels Hemmingsen's *De Methodis* (1555)," in *The Bible in the Sixteenth Century*, ed. David C. Steinmetz (Durham: Duke University Press, 1990), 181-96.

[34]LW 27:1-9 (WA 2:449). See Kenneth Hagen, "What Did the Term *Commentarius* Mean to Sixteenth-Century Theologians?" in *Théorie e pratique de l'exégèse*, eds. Irena Backus and Francis M. Higman (Geneva: Droz, 1990), 13-38.

[35]I follow here the sketch of Irena Backus, "Biblical Hermeneutics and Exegesis," *OER* 1:152-58. In this work, Backus confines herself to Continental developments, whereas we have noted the exegetical contribution of the English Reformation as well. For more comprehensive listings of sixteenth-century commentators, see Gerald Bray, *Biblical Interpretation* (Downers Grove, IL: InterVarsity Press, 1996), 165-212; and Richard A. Muller, "Biblical Interpretation in the Sixteenth and Seventeenth Centuries," *DMBI* 22-44.

to learn Greek, though he never took up the language himself. Colet's lectures on Paul's epistles at Oxford are reflected in his commentaries on Romans and 1 Corinthians.

Jacques Lefèvre d'Étaples has been called the "French Erasmus" because of his great learning and support for early reform movements in his native land. He published a major edition of the Psalter, as well as commentaries on the Pauline Epistles (1512), the Gospels (1522), and the General Epistles (1527). Guillaume Farel, the early reformer of Geneva, was a disciple of Lefèvre, and the young Calvin also came within his sphere of influence.

Among pre-Tridentine Catholic reformers, special attention should be given to Thomas de Vio, better known as Cajetan. He is best remembered for confronting Martin Luther on behalf of the pope in 1518, but his biblical commentaries (on nearly every book of the Bible) are virtually free of polemic. Like Erasmus, he dared to criticize the Vulgate on linguistic grounds. His commentary on Romans supported the doctrine of justification by grace applied by faith based on the "alien righteousness" of God in Christ. Jared Wicks sums up Cajetan's significance in this way: "Cajetan's combination of passion for pristine biblical meaning with his fully developed theological horizon of understanding indicates, in an intriguing manner, something of the breadth of possibilities open to Roman Catholics before a more restrictive settlement came to exercise its hold on many Catholic interpreters in the wake of the Council of Trent."[36] Girolamo Seripando, like Cajetan, was a cardinal in the Catholic Church, though he belonged to the Augustinian rather than the Dominican order. He was an outstanding classical scholar and published commentaries on Romans and Galatians. Also important is Jacopo Sadoleto, another cardinal, best known for his 1539 letter to the people of Geneva beseeching them to return to the Church of Rome, to which Calvin replied with a manifesto of his own. Sadoleto published a commentary on Romans in 1535. Bucer once commended Sadoleto's teaching on justification as approximating that of the reformers, while others saw him tilting away from the Augustinian tradition toward Pelagianism.[37]

Luther and the Wittenberg School. It was in the name of the Word of God, and specifically as a doctor of Scripture, that Luther challenged the church of his day and inaugurated the Reformation. Though Luther renounced his monastic vows, he never lost that sense of intimacy with *sacra pagina* he first acquired as a young monk. Luther provided three rules for reading the Bible: prayer, meditation, and struggle *(tentatio)*. His exegetical output was enormous. In the American edition of Luther's works, thirty out of the fifty-five volumes are devoted to his biblical studies, and additional translations are planned. Many of his commentaries originated as sermons or lecture notes presented to his students at the university and to his parishioners at Wittenberg's parish church of St. Mary. Luther referred to Galatians as his bride: "The Epistle to the Galatians is my dear epistle. I have betrothed myself to it. It is my Käthe von Bora."[38] He considered his 1535 commentary on Galatians his greatest exegetical work, although his massive commentary on Genesis

---

[36]Jared Wicks, "Tommaso de Vio Cajetan (1469-1534)," *DMBI* 283-87, here 286.

[37]See the discussion by Bernard Roussel, "Martin Bucer et Jacques Sadolet: la concorde possible," *Bulletin de la Société de l'histoire de protestantisme français* (1976): 525-50, and T. H. L. Parker, *Commentaries on the Epistle to the Romans, 1532–1542* (Edinburgh: T&T Clark, 1986), 25-34.

[38]WATR 1:69 no. 146; cf. LW 54:20 no. 146. I have followed Rörer's variant on Dietrich's notes.

(eight volumes in LW), which he worked on for ten years (1535–1545), must be considered his crowning work. Luther's principles of biblical interpretation are found in his *Open Letter on Translating* and in the prefaces he wrote to all the books of the Bible.

Philipp Melanchthon was brought to Wittenberg to teach Greek in 1518 and proved to be an able associate to Luther in the reform of the church. A set of his lecture notes on Romans was published without his knowledge in 1522. This was revised and expanded many times until his large commentary of 1556. Melanchthon also commented on other New Testament books including Matthew, John, Galatians, and the Petrine epistles, as well as Proverbs, Daniel, and Ecclesiastes. Though he was well trained in the humanist disciplines, Melanchthon devoted little attention to critical and textual matters in his commentaries. Rather, he followed the primary argument of the biblical writer and gathered from this exposition a series of doctrinal topics for special consideration. This method lay behind Melanchthon's *Loci communes* (1521), the first Protestant theology textbook to be published. Another Wittenberger was Johannes Bugenhagen of Pomerania, a prolific commentator on both the Old and New Testaments. His commentary on the Psalms (1524), translated into German by Bucer, applied Luther's teaching on justification to the Psalter. He also wrote a commentary on Job and annotations on many of the books in the Bible. The Lutheran exegetical tradition was shaped by many other scholar-reformers including Andreas Osiander, Johannes Brenz, Caspar Cruciger, Erasmus Sarcerius, Georg Maior, Jacob Andreae, Nikolaus Selnecker, and Johann Gerhard.

The Strasbourg-Basel tradition. Bucer, the son of a shoemaker in Alsace, became the leader of the Reformation in Strasbourg. A former Dominican, he was early on influenced by Erasmus and continued to share his passion for Christian unity. Bucer was the most ecumenical of the Protestant reformers seeking rapprochement with Catholics on justification and an armistice between Luther and Zwingli in their strife over the Lord's Supper. Bucer also had a decisive influence on Calvin, though the latter characterized his biblical commentaries as longwinded and repetitious.[39] In his exegetical work, Bucer made ample use of patristic and medieval sources, though he criticized the abuse and overuse of allegory as "the most blatant insult to the Holy Spirit."[40] He declared that the purpose of his commentaries was "to help inexperienced brethren [perhaps like the apothecary Drilhon, who owned a French translation of Bucer's *Commentary on Matthew*] to understand each of the words and actions of Christ, and in their proper order as far as possible, and to retain an explanation of them in their natural meaning, so that they will not distort God's Word through age-old aberrations or by inept interpretation, but rather with a faithful comprehension of everything as written by the Spirit of God, they may expound to all the churches in their firm upbuilding in faith and love."[41] In addition to writing commentaries on all four Gospels, Bucer published commentaries on Judges, the Psalms, Zephaniah, Romans, and Ephesians. In the early years of the Reformation, there was a great deal of back and forth between Strasbourg and Basel, and both

---

[39]CNTC 8:3 (CO 10:404).

[40]*DMBI* 249; P. Scherding and F. Wendel, eds., "Un Traité d'exégèse pratique de Bucer," *Revue d'histoire et de philosophie religieuses* 26 (1946): 32-75, here 56.

[41]Martin Bucer, *Enarrationes perpetuae in sacra quatuor evangelia*, 2nd ed. (Strasbourg: Georg Ulrich Andlanus, 1530), 10r; quoted in D. F. Wright, "Martin Bucer," *DMBI* 290.

were centers of a lively publishing trade. Wolfgang Capito, Bucer's associate at Strasbourg, was a notable Hebraist and composed commentaries on Hosea (1529) and Habakkuk (1527).

At Basel, the great Sebastian Münster defended the use of Jewish sources in the Christian study of the Old Testament and published, in addition to his famous Hebrew grammar, an annotated version of the Gospel of Matthew translated from Greek into Hebrew. Oecolampadius, Basel's chief reformer, had been a proofreader in Froben's publishing house and worked with Erasmus on his Greek New Testament and his critical edition of Jerome. From 1523 he was both a preacher and professor of Holy Scripture at Basel. He defended Zwingli's eucharistic theology at the Colloquy of Marburg and published commentaries on 1 John (1524), Romans (1525), and Haggai–Malachi (1525). Oecolampadius was succeeded by Simon Grynaeus, a classical scholar who taught Greek and supported Bucer's efforts to bring Lutherans and Zwinglians together. More in line with Erasmus was Sebastian Castellio, who came to Basel after his expulsion from Geneva in 1545. He is best remembered for questioning the canonicity of the Song of Songs and for his annotations and French translation of the Bible.

The Zurich group. Biblical exegesis in Zurich was centered on the distinctive institution of the *Prophezei*, which began on June 19, 1525. On five days a week, at seven o'clock in the morning, all of the ministers and theological students in Zurich gathered into the choir of the Grossmünster to engage in a period of intense exegesis and interpretation of Scripture. After Zwingli had opened the meeting with prayer, the text of the day was read in Latin, Greek, and Hebrew, followed by appropriate textual or exegetical comments. One of the ministers then delivered a sermon on the passage in German that was heard by many of Zurich's citizens who stopped by the cathedral on their way to work. This institute for advanced biblical studies had an enormous influence as a model for Reformed academies and seminaries throughout Europe. It was also the seedbed for sermon series in Zurich's churches and the extensive exegetical publications of Zwingli, Leo Jud, Konrad Pellikan, Heinrich Bullinger, Oswald Myconius, and Rudolf Gwalther. Zwingli had memorized in Greek all of the Pauline epistles, and this bore fruit in his powerful expository preaching and biblical exegesis. He took seriously the role of grammar, rhetoric, and historical research in explaining the biblical text. For example, he disagreed with Bucer on the value of the Septuagint, regarding it as a trustworthy witness to a proto-Hebrew version earlier than the Masoretic text.

Zwingli's work was carried forward by his successor Bullinger, one of the most formidable scholars and networkers among the reformers. He composed commentaries on Daniel (1565), the Gospels (1542–1546), the Epistles (1537), Acts (1533), and Revelation (1557). He collaborated with Calvin to produce the *Consensus Tigurinus* (1549), a Reformed accord on the nature of the Lord's Supper, and produced a series of fifty sermons on Christian doctrine, known as *Decades*, which became required reading in Elizabethan England. As the *Antistes* ("overseer") of the Zurich church for forty-four years, Bullinger faced opposition from nascent Anabaptism on the one hand and resurgent Catholicism on the other. The need for a well-trained clergy and scholarly resources, including Scripture commentaries, arose from the fact that the Bible was "difficult or obscure to the unlearned, unskillful, unexercised, and malicious or corrupted wills." While forswearing papal claims to infallibility, Bullinger and other leaders of the magisterial Reformation saw the need for a kind of Protestant magisterium as a check against the tendency to read the Bible in "such sense as everyone shall be persuaded in himself to be most convenient."[42]

Two other commentators can be treated in connection with the Zurich group, though each of them had a wide-ranging ministry across the Reformation fronts. A former Benedictine monk, Wolfgang Musculus, embraced the Reformation in the 1520s and served briefly as the secretary to Bucer in Strasbourg. He shared Bucer's desire for Protestant unity and served for seventeen years (1531–1548) as a pastor and reformer in Augsburg. After a brief time in Zurich, where he came under the influence of Bullinger, Musculus was called to Bern, where he taught the Scriptures and published commentaries on the Psalms, the Decalogue, Genesis, Romans, Isaiah, 1 and 2 Corinthians, Galatians and Ephesians, Philippians, Colossians, 1 and 2 Thessalonians, and 1 Timothy. Drawing on his exegetical writings, Musculus also produced a compendium of Protestant theology that was translated into English in 1563 as *Commonplaces of Christian Religion*.

Peter Martyr Vermigli was a Florentine-born scholar and Augustinian friar who embraced the Reformation and fled to Switzerland in 1542. Over the next twenty years, he would gain an international reputation as a prolific scholar and leading theologian within the Reformed community. He lectured on the Old Testament at Strasbourg, was made regius professor at Oxford, corresponded with the Italian refugee church in Geneva and spent the last years of his life as professor of Hebrew at Zurich. Vermigli published commentaries on 1 Corinthians, Romans, and Judges during his lifetime. His biblical lectures on Genesis, Lamentations, 1 and 2 Samuel, and 1 and 2 Kings were published posthumously. The most influential of his writings was the *Loci communes* (*Commonplaces*), a theological compendium drawn from his exegetical writings.

The Genevan reformers. What Zwingli and Bullinger were to Zurich, Calvin and Beza were to Geneva. Calvin has been called "the father of modern biblical scholarship," and his exegetical work is without parallel in the Reformation. Because of the success of his *Institutes of the Christian Religion* Calvin has sometimes been thought of as a man of one book, but he always intended the *Institutes*, which went through eight editions in Latin and five in French during his lifetime, to serve as a guide to the study of the Bible, to show the reader "what he ought especially to seek in Scripture and to what end he ought to relate its contents." Jacob Arminius, who modified several principles of Calvin's theology, recommended his commentaries next to the Bible, for, as he said, Calvin "is incomparable in the interpretation of Scripture."[43] Drawing on his superb knowledge of Greek and Hebrew and his thorough training in humanist rhetoric, Calvin produced commentaries on all of the New Testament books except 2 and 3 John and Revelation. Calvin's Old Testament commentaries originated as sermon and lecture series and include Genesis, Psalms, Hosea, Isaiah, minor prophets, Daniel, Jeremiah and Lamentations, a harmony of the last four books of Moses,

---

[42]Euan Cameron, *The European Reformation* (Oxford: Oxford University Press, 1991), 120.

[43]Letter to Sebastian Egbert (May 3, 1607), in *Praestantium ac eruditorum virorum epistolae ecclesiasticae et theologicae varii argumenti*, ed. Christiaan Hartsoeker (Amsterdam: Henricus Dendrinus, 1660), 236-37. Quoted in A. M. Hunter, *The Teaching of Calvin* (London: James Clarke, 1950), 20.

Ezekiel 1–20, and Joshua. Calvin sought for brevity and clarity in all of his exegetical work. He emphasized the illumination of the Holy Spirit as essential to a proper understanding of the text. Calvin underscored the continuity between the two Testaments (one covenant in two dispensations) and sought to apply the plain or natural sense of the text to the church of his day. In the preface to his own influential commentary on Romans, Karl Barth described how Calvin worked to recover the mind of Paul and make the apostle's message relevant to his day:

> How energetically Calvin goes to work, first scientifically establishing the text ("what stands there?"), then following along the footsteps of its thought; that is to say, he conducts a discussion with it until the wall between the first and the sixteenth centuries becomes transparent, and until there in the first century Paul speaks and here the man of the sixteenth century hears, until indeed the conversation between document and reader becomes concentrated upon the substance (which must be the same now as then).[44]

Beza was elected moderator of Geneva's Company of Pastors after Calvin's death in 1564 and guided the Genevan Reformation over the next four decades. His annotated Latin translation of the Greek New Testament (1556) and his further revisions of the Greek text established his reputation as the leading textual critic of the sixteenth century after Erasmus. Beza completed the translation of Marot's metrical Psalter, which became a centerpiece of Huguenot piety and Reformed church life. Though known for his polemical writings on grace, free will, and predestination, Beza's work is marked by a strong pastoral orientation and concern for a Scripture-based spirituality.

Robert Estienne (Stephanus) was a printer-scholar who had served the royal household in Paris. After his conversion to Protestantism, in 1550 he moved to Geneva, where he published a series of notable editions and translations of the Bible. He also produced sermons and commentaries on Job, Ecclesiastes, the Song of Songs, Romans and Hebrews, as well as dictionaries, concordances, and a thesaurus of biblical terms. He also published the first editions of the Bible with chapters divided into verses, an innovation that quickly became universally accepted.

The British Reformation. Commentary writing in England and Scotland lagged behind the continental Reformation for several reasons. In 1500, there were only three publishing houses in England compared with more than two hundred on the Continent. A 1408 statute against publishing or reading the Bible in English, stemming from the days of Lollardy, stifled the free flow of ideas, as was seen in the fate of Tyndale. Moreover, the nature of the English Reformation from Henry through Elizabeth provided little stability for the flourishing of biblical scholarship. In the sixteenth century, many "hot-gospel" Protestants in England were edified by the English translations of commentaries and theological writings by the Continental reformers. The influence of Calvin and Beza was felt especially in the Geneva Bible with its "Protestant glosses" of theological notes and references.

During the later Elizabethan and Stuart church, however, the indigenous English commentary came into its own. Both Anglicans and Puritans contributed to this outpouring of biblical studies.

---

[44]Karl Barth, *Die Römerbrief* (Zurich: TVZ, 1940), 11, translated by T. H. L. Parker as the epigraph to *Calvin's New Testament Commentaries*, 2nd ed. (Louisville, KY: Westminster John Knox, 1993).

The sermons of Lancelot Andrewes and John Donne are replete with exegetical insights based on a close study of the Greek and Hebrew texts. Among the Reformed authors in England, none was more influential than William Perkins, the greatest of the early Puritan theologians, who published commentaries on Galatians, Jude, Revelation, and the Sermon on the Mount (Mt 5–7). John Cotton, one of his students, wrote commentaries on the Song of Songs, Ecclesiastes, and Revelation before departing for New England in 1633. The separatist pastor Henry Ainsworth was an outstanding scholar of Hebrew and wrote major commentaries on the Pentateuch, the Psalms, and the Song of Songs. In Scotland, Robert Rollock, the first principal of Edinburgh University (1585), wrote numerous commentaries including those on the Psalms, Ephesians, Daniel, Romans, 1 and 2 Thessalonians, John, Colossians, and Hebrews. Joseph Mede and Thomas Brightman were leading authorities on Revelation and contributed to the apocalyptic thought of the seventeenth century. Mention should also be made of Archbishop James Ussher, whose *Annals of the Old Testament* was published in 1650. Ussher developed a keen interest in biblical chronology and calculated that the creation of the world had taken place on October 26, 4004 B.C. As late as 1945, the Scofield Reference Bible still retained this date next to Genesis 1:1, but later editions omitted it because of the lack of evidence on which to fix such dates.[45]

Anabaptism. Irena Backus has noted that there was no school of "dissident" exegesis during the Reformation, and the reasons are not hard to find. The radical Reformation was an ill-defined movement that existed on the margins of official church life in the sixteenth century. The denial of infant baptism and the refusal to swear an oath marked radicals as a seditious element in society, and they were persecuted by Protestants and Catholics alike. However, in the RCS we have made an attempt to include some voices of the radical Reformation, especially among the Anabaptists. While the Anabaptists published few commentaries in the sixteenth century, they were avid readers and quoters of the Bible. Numerous exegetical gems can be found in their letters, treatises, martyr acts (especially *The Martyrs' Mirror*), hymns, and histories. They placed a strong emphasis on the memorizing of Scripture and quoted liberally from vernacular translations of the Bible. George H. Williams has noted that "many an Anabaptist theological tract was really a beautiful mosaic of Scripture texts."[46] In general, most Anabaptists accepted the apocryphal books as canonical, contrasted outer word and inner spirit with relative degrees of strictness and saw the New Testament as normative for church life and social ethics (witness their pacifism, nonswearing, emphasis on believers' baptism and congregational discipline).

We have noted the Old Testament translation of Ludwig Hätzer, who became an antitrinitarian, and Hans Denck that they published at Worms in 1527. Denck also wrote a notable commentary on Micah. Conrad Grebel belonged to a Greek reading circle in Zurich and came to his Anabaptist convictions while poring over the text of Erasmus's New Testament. The only Anabaptist leader with university credentials was Balthasar Hubmaier, who was made a doctor of theology (Ingolstadt, 1512) in the same year as Luther. His reflections on the Bible are found in his numerous

---

[45]*The New Scofield Reference Bible* (New York: Oxford University Press, 1967), vi.
[46]George H. Williams, *The Radical Reformation*, 3rd ed. (Kirksville, MO: Sixteenth Century Journal Publishers, 1992), 1247.

writings, which include the first catechism of the Reformation (1526), a two-part treatise on the freedom of the will and a major work (*On the Sword*) setting forth positive attitudes toward the role of government and the Christian's place in society. Melchior Hoffman was an apocalyptic seer who wrote commentaries on Romans, Revelation, and Daniel 12. He predicted that Christ would return in 1533. More temperate was Pilgram Marpeck, a mining engineer who embraced Anabaptism and traveled widely throughout Switzerland and south Germany, from Strasbourg to Augsburg. His "Admonition of 1542" is the longest published defense of Anabaptist views on baptism and the Lord's Supper. He also wrote many letters that functioned as theological tracts for the congregations he had founded dealing with topics such as the fruits of repentance, the lowliness of Christ, and the unity of the church. Menno Simons, a former Catholic priest, became the most outstanding leader of the Dutch Anabaptist movement. His masterpiece was the *Foundation of Christian Doctrine* published in 1540. His other writings include *Meditation on the Twenty-fifth Psalm* (1537); *A Personal Exegesis of Psalm Twenty-five* modeled on the style of Augustine's *Confessions*; *Confession of the Triune God* (1550), directed against Adam Pastor, a former disciple of Menno who came to doubt the divinity of Christ; *Meditations and Prayers for Mealtime* (1557); and the *Cross of the Saints* (1554), an exhortation to faithfulness in the face of persecution. Like many other Anabaptists, Menno emphasized the centrality of discipleship (*Nachfolge*) as a deliberate repudiation of the old life and a radical commitment to follow Jesus as Lord.

Reading Scripture with the Reformers

In 1947, Gerhard Ebeling set forth his thesis that the history of the Christian church is the history of the interpretation of Scripture. Since that time, the place of the Bible in the story of the church has been investigated from many angles. A better understanding of the history of exegesis has been aided by new critical editions and scholarly discussions of the primary sources. The *Cambridge History of the Bible*, published in three volumes (1963–1970), remains a standard reference work in the field. The ACCS built on, and itself contributed to, the recovery of patristic biblical wisdom of both East and West. Beryl Smalley's *The Study of the Bible in the Middle Ages* (1940) and Henri de Lubac's *Medieval Exegesis: The Four Senses of Scripture* (1959) are essential reading for understanding the monastic and scholastic settings of commentary work between Augustine and Luther. The Reformation took place during what has been called "le grand siècle de la Bible."[47] Aided by the tools of Renaissance humanism and the dynamic impetus of Reformation theology (including permutations and reactions against it), the sixteenth century produced an unprecedented number of commentaries on every book in the Bible. Drawing from this vast storehouse of exegetical treasures, the RCS allows us to read Scripture along with the reformers. In doing so, it serves as a practical homiletic and devotional guide to some of the greatest masters of biblical interpretation in the history of the church.

The RCS gladly acknowledges its affinity with and dependence on recent scholarly investigations of Reformation-era exegesis. Between 1976 and 1990, three international colloquia on the

---

[47]J-R. Aarmogathe, ed., *Bible de tous les temps*, 8 vols.; vol. 6, *Le grand siècle de la Bible* (Paris: Beauchesne, 1989).

history of biblical exegesis in the sixteenth century took place in Geneva and in Durham, North Carolina.[48] Among those participating in these three gatherings were a number of scholars who have produced groundbreaking works in the study of biblical interpretation in the Reformation. These include Elsie McKee, Irena Backus, Kenneth Hagen, Scott H. Hendrix, Richard A. Muller, Guy Bedouelle, Gerald Hobbs, John B. Payne, Bernard Roussel, Pierre Fraenkel, and David C. Steinmetz (1936–2015). Among other scholars whose works are indispensible for the study of this field are Heinrich Bornkamm, Jaroslav Pelikan, Heiko A. Oberman, James S. Preus, T. H. L. Parker, David F. Wright, Tony Lane, John L. Thompson, Frank A. James, and Timothy J. Wengert.[49] Among these scholars no one has had a greater influence on the study of Reformation exegesis than David C. Steinmetz. A student of Oberman, he emphasized the importance of understanding the Reformation in medieval perspective. In addition to important studies on Luther and Staupitz, he pioneered the method of comparative exegesis showing both continuity and discontinuity between major Reformation figures and the preceding exegetical traditions (see his *Luther in Context* and *Calvin in Context*). From his base at Duke University, he spawned what might be called a Steinmetz school, a cadre of students and scholars whose work on the Bible in the Reformation era continues to shape the field. Steinmetz served on the RCS Board of Editorial Advisors, and a number of our volume editors pursued doctoral studies under his supervision.

In 1980, Steinmetz published "The Superiority of Pre-critical Exegesis," a seminal essay that not only placed Reformation exegesis in the context of the preceding fifteen centuries of the church's study of the Bible but also challenged certain assumptions underlying the hegemony of historical-critical exegesis of the post-Enlightenment academy.[50] Steinmetz helps us to approach the reformers and other precritical interpreters of the Bible on their own terms as faithful witnesses to the church's apostolic tradition. For them, a specific book or pericope had to be understood within the scope of the consensus of the canon. Thus the reformers, no less than the Fathers and the schoolmen, interpreted the hymn of the Johannine prologue about the preexistent Christ in consonance with the creation narrative of Genesis 1. In the same way, Psalm 22, Isaiah 53, and Daniel 7 are seen as part of an overarching storyline that finds ultimate fulfillment in Jesus Christ. Reading the Bible with the resources of the new learning, the reformers challenged the exegetical conclusions of their medieval predecessors at many points. However, unlike Alexander Campbell in the nineteenth century, their aim was not to "open the New Testament as if mortal man had never seen it before."[51]

---

[48]Olivier Fatio and Pierre Fraenkel, eds., *Histoire de l'exégèse au XVIe siècle: texts du colloque international tenu à Genève en 1976* (Geneva: Droz, 1978); David C. Steinmetz, ed., *The Bible in the Sixteenth Century* [Second International Colloquy on the History of Biblical Exegesis in the Sixteenth Century] (Durham: Duke University Press, 1990); Irena Backus and Francis M. Higman, eds., *Théorie et pratique de l'exégèse. Actes du troisième colloque international sur l'histoire de l'exégèse biblique au XVIe siècle, Genève, 31 aôut–2 septembre 1988* (Geneva: Droz, 1990); see also Guy Bedouelle and Bernard Roussel, eds., *Bible de tous les temps*, 8 vols.; vol. 5, *Le temps des Réformes et la Bible* (Paris: Beauchesne, 1989).

[49]For bibliographical references and evaluation of these and other contributors to the scholarly study of Reformation-era exegesis, see Richard A. Muller, "Biblical Interpretation in the Era of the Reformation: The View From the Middle Ages," in *Biblical Interpretation in the Era of the Reformation: Essays Presented to David C. Steinmetz in Honor of His Sixtieth Birthday*, ed. Richard A. Muller and John L. Thompson (Grand Rapids: Eerdmans, 1996), 3-22.

[50]David C. Steinmetz, "The Superiority of Pre-Critical Exegesis," *Theology Today* 37 (1980): 27-38.

[51]Alexander Campbell, *Memoirs of Alexander Campbell*, ed. Robert Richardson (Cincinnati: Standard Publishing Company, 1872), 97.

Rather, they wanted to do their biblical work as part of an interpretive conversation within the family of the people of God. In the reformers' emphatic turn to the literal sense, which prompted their many blasts against the unrestrained use of allegory, their work was an extension of a similar impulse made by Thomas Aquinas and Nicholas of Lyra.

This is not to discount the radically new insights gained by the reformers in their dynamic engagement with the text of Scripture; nor should we dismiss in a reactionary way the light shed on the meaning of the Bible by the scholarly accomplishments of the past two centuries. However, it is to acknowledge that the church's exegetical tradition is an indispensible aid for the proper interpretation of Scripture. And this means, as Richard Muller has said, that "while it is often appropriate to recognize that traditionary readings of the text are erroneous on the grounds offered by the historical-critical method, we ought also to recognize that the conclusions offered by historical-critical exegesis may themselves be quite erroneous on the grounds provided by the exegesis of the patristic, medieval, and reformation periods."[52] The RCS wishes to commend the exegetical work of the Reformation era as a program of retrieval for the sake of renewal—spiritual réssourcement for believers committed to the life of faith today.

George Herbert was an English pastor and poet who reaped the benefits of the renewal of biblical studies in the age of the Reformation. He referred to the Scriptures as a book of infinite sweetness, "a mass of strange delights," a book with secrets to make the life of anyone good. In describing the various means pastors require to be fully furnished in the work of their calling, Herbert provided a rationale for the history of exegesis and for the Reformation Commentary on Scripture:

> The fourth means are commenters and Fathers, who have handled the places controverted, which the parson by no means refuseth. As he doth not so study others as to neglect the grace of God in himself and what the Holy Spirit teacheth him, so doth he assure himself that God in all ages hath had his servants to whom he hath revealed his Truth, as well as to him; and that as one country doth not bear all things that there may be a commerce, so neither hath God opened or will open all to one, that there may be a traffic in knowledge between the servants of God for the planting both of love and humility. Wherefore he hath one comment[ary] at least upon every book of Scripture, and ploughing with this, and his own meditations, he enters into the secrets of God treasured in the holy Scripture.[53]

Timothy George
General Editor

---

[52]Richard A. Muller and John L. Thompson, "The Significance of Precritical Exegesis: Retrospect and Prospect," in *Biblical Interpretation in the Era of the Reformation: Essays Presented to David C. Steinmetz in Honor of His Sixtieth Birthday*, ed. Richard A. Muller and John L. Thompson (Grand Rapids: Eerdmans, 1996), 342.

[53]George Herbert, *The Complete English Poems* (London: Penguin, 1991), 205.

INTRODUCTION TO ROMANS 1–8

Paul's letter to the Romans opened the gates of paradise for Martin Luther. He wrote of it, "This epistle is really the chief part of the New Testament, and is truly the purest gospel."[1] He believed that Christians should not only memorize it but also meditate on it daily as the "daily bread of the soul."[2] Other reformers expressed a similar preference for Romans. Philipp Melanchthon wrote that Romans is "didactic, teaching what the gospel is and, indeed, the source of justification, and it is truly like a *methodus* [way of teaching] of the entire Scripture."[3] For John Calvin, it was the key that gave access to all the deepest treasures of the Scriptures. Cyriacus Spangenberg stated, "In sum, this epistle is a light. It shines before the dull and the ignorant to teach them, to enlighten them and to give them correct understanding."[4] And for Juan de Valdés, it was Romans that illuminated the essential content of Scripture, which is the illustration of God's glory:

> Paul proceeds throughout to treat and touch on many things very worthy of consideration, very lofty, and most divine: so much so, that there is much reason for what is said, that this epistle being understood, it is easy to understand all that is essential in Holy Scripture; and I call essential that which pertains to our justification, vivification, resurrection and glorification, because this is the principal design of Holy Scripture: by this to illustrate the glory of God, and of the Son of God, Jesus Christ our Lord.[5]

During the sixteenth century, as far as we can tell, there were more commentaries written on Romans than on any other book of the Bible; from 1500 to 1650 there are at least seventy.[6] In many ways, the Reformation hinges on Romans. And the key theological paradigm shift of the Reformation occurs in one man's wrestling with a verse in its opening chapter.

---

[1]LW 35:365*.

[2]Martin Luther, *Preface to the Letter of St. Paul to the Romans*, trans. Andrew Thornton, OSB (Manchester, NH: Saint Anselm College Humanities Program, 1983), www.ccel.org*.

[3]Timothy Wengert, "Philip Melanchthon's 1522 Annotations on Romans and the Lutheran Origins of Rhetorical Criticism," in *Biblical Interpretation in the Reformation*, ed. Richard A. Muller and John L. Thompson (Grand Rapids: Eerdmans, 1996), 128, cites it from Melanchthon's 1521 notes on his Greek text.

[4]Quoted in RCS 8:liii.

[5]Juan de Valdés, *Commentary on St. Paul's Epistle Commentary Upon St. Paul's Epistle to the Romans*, trans. John T. Betts (London: Trübner, 1883), xxxii*.

[6]For a chronological list of Romans commentaries, see Eckhard Schnabel, *Der Brief des Paulus an die Römer*, vol. 1, *Kapitel 1–5*, Historisch-Theologische Auslegung (Witten: SCM R-Brockhaus, 2015), 591-95.

The Medieval Background

Romans was one of the places in Scripture where the reformers responded most clearly and directly to the medieval world in which they were raised. Theirs was a world marked by a devout piety exemplified by the cathedrals scattered across Europe. Each medieval cathedral soared above its city. The tallest, Lincoln Cathedral, reputedly—perhaps apocryphally—reached 525 feet, about 100 times the height of a human being.[7] Multicolored light poured in through its stained-glass walls. The cathedral provided the medieval person with a concretized experience of theology. It captured something of the transcendence of God, serving as a physically embodied metaphor of the majesty and magnificence of the Creator, Redeemer, and Judge. The cathedral (or parish church, in the case of towns) was the center point for medieval life, piety, and theology.

Medieval theology was complex, varying over time and between theologians, so it is impossible to capture all the nuances in a short overview. However, one can try to delineate its broad contours in the late medieval period into which the reformers were born, for there was a common core that held together the piety of the time.

This piety emphasized the idea that humanity was sinful and needed to participate in paying the penalty for that sin. It was commonly believed, and affirmed by sermon illustrations, that each person had a good angel and a bad angel following them around at all times, keeping track respectively of all their good and bad deeds, and that these written records would be weighed in the two pans of the judgment scales on Doomsday. The sacrament of penance was meant to provide a way to undo the bad deeds. If one confessed one's sins to the priest, then one could receive the priest's absolution and be assigned a penance. The absolution got rid of the guilt, but the penalty remained to be paid, and thus the performance of penance was necessary. Most people did not confess all their sins or complete all their penance, and thus most would go to purgatory, where the remaining sins would be purged. Many medieval depictions of purgatory, whether in art or sermons or visionary accounts, were rather terrifying, portraying details of torture by demons and monsters, flames, burning oil, beds of nails, and so on. Only the saints would avoid this and go straight to heaven. Average medieval persons did not have a sense of security about their eternal destiny. Many believed that priests and monks and nuns had a more certain path to heaven, but even then, one could not be sure.[8]

Throughout the Middle Ages, the ransom theory of the atonement[9] eventually gave way to Anselm's satisfaction theory. In reflection of the feudal, hierarchical society in which honor was due to those above one—for example, from knights to their lords—Anselm taught that Adam and Eve had dishonored God with their disobedience, and that satisfaction needed to be made.

---

[7]This spire, because of its massive weight and height, collapsed in 1549.

[8]See Jacques Le Goff, *The Birth of Purgatory*, trans. Arthur Goldhammer (Chicago: University of Chicago Press, 1984), 209-34, 289-333.

[9]Advocated by such early Christian thinkers as Origen (184–253) and Gregory the Great (540–604), the ransom theory of the atonement maintained that the death of Christ constituted a ransom paid to Satan in order to nullify the latter's claims on humanity. However, Christ deceived Satan in this bargain by rising from the dead, thereby proving that Satan was unable to retain any hold on him.

Christ, as the only one who was both God and man, made that satisfaction on the cross. And this satisfaction could be applied, initially, to individuals who believed in him. After this first application, further satisfactions would be made if the individual also made acceptable acts of satisfaction. Building on this, late medieval theology taught that the individual received justification in the sacrament of baptism, but that it had to be renewed by the sacrament of penance. The work that Christ had done on the cross was applied to believers through their fulfillment of certain conditions, such as participation in the sacraments, belief in the articles of faith, and the performance of good works.

At the same time that there was a strong emphasis on the weight of human responsibility in appropriating Christ's satisfaction, there was also a focus on the costly suffering of Christ that made that satisfaction possible. Peter Abelard had proposed an alternative atonement theory to Anselm's, and it had been initially rejected, but Thomas Aquinas later combined it in some ways with Anselm's theory. Abelard's treatment undergirded a strong emphasis on the suffering of Christ, which was enhanced by Franciscan piety and a focus in art on the physical pain of the crucifixion. Abelard taught that the love Christ exemplified on the cross should enkindle love in the hearts of those who meditated on it. And St. Francis's stigmata and visions of the crucified Christ helped fuel a highly affective spirituality. Parishioners were exhorted to spend significant time and emotion in contemplation of the images of the Suffering Servant (Is 53), to weep along with the Blessed Virgin Mary and John the Evangelist at the foot of the cross. The crucifixion was one of the most frequently portrayed subjects in medieval art, appearing in stained-glass windows, wooden crucifixes, painted altarpieces, devotional triptychs, illuminated manuscripts, rosary beads, and so on. Its sorrow sat at the center of the medieval world.[10] Thus, during the Middle Ages, there were various approaches to explaining the details of the atonement.

The Material Principle of the Reformation

This medieval world prepared the reformers to understand Romans in a profound way, but the reformers' fresh interpretation of Romans would also dramatically change the theology they had inherited. The reformers were born into a culture that inculcated in them a strong sense of the holiness of God and the sinfulness of humanity. They were keenly aware of the deep suffering of Christ on their behalf. For many of them, this created a mixture of fear, guilt, and uncertainty. It was an encounter within Martin Luther—between this intense emotion and a verse in Romans 1—that triggered the key material principle (i.e., central doctrine) of the Reformation: *sola fide*, salvation is by faith alone.[11]

Luther was an Augustinian monk at the time. He had tried living medieval theology and piety to its extremes, going on pilgrimage, practicing vigorous asceticism, confessing his sins with

---

[10]For studies on the history of the cross, see Robin M. Jensen, *The Cross: History, Art, and Controversy* (Cambridge, MA: Harvard University Press, 2017), and Richard Viladesau, *The Beauty of the Cross: The Passion of Christ in Theology and the Arts from the Catacombs to the Eve of the Renaissance* (Oxford: Oxford University Press, 2005).

[11]Historians speak of the key formal principle (i.e., authoritative source of the teaching) of the Reformation being *sola Scriptura*, and *sola fide* being the primary material principle (i.e., theological content). See Timothy George, *Theology of the Reformers*, rev. ed. (Nashville: B&H Academic, 2013), 328.

scrupulous rigor while desperately attempting to muster up perfect contrition but finding himself hating God, the angry Judge that terrified him. He was struggling with *Anfechtungen*-induced depression.[12] In concerned response, his confessor, Johann von Staupitz, had sent him from his monastery to the University of Wittenberg to study the Scriptures and earn a doctorate in biblical studies. After completing that doctorate and lecturing on the Psalms, Luther turned to Romans (1515–1516). His lecture notes are extant, as well as manuscripts of his students' notes, remaining unpublished until they were discovered in the early twentieth century. These notes show that although his thought revealed signs of a theology in flux, it was still very early in his development, coming before even his posting of the Ninety-Five Theses. Luther was still using the glosses and scholia approach of the scholastics.[13] And for Romans 1–8, he used Jacques Lefèvre d'Étaples's Latin and Lorenzo Valla's Greek edition rather than Erasmus's since the latter had not been published before Luther's studies took him to Romans 9.[14] His lectures on Romans, therefore, do not reflect his mature thinking on either content or methodology. Yet, although Luther would never write a full commentary on Romans, we do have glimpses into his more mature thought on the letter. And in these reflections, we discover the pivotal theological "moment" that changed everything for him and that helped trigger the Reformation. Luther's preface to the 1545 edition of his Latin writings recounts that story—often referred to as the Tower Experience since he refers to it as having taken place in the tower at his monastery—in which he discovers the doctrine of justification by faith alone. We don't know exactly when that moment occurred or whether it was, instead, a season rather than a specific point in time; scholars suggest dates between 1512 and 1519. In any case, Luther had been reflecting on Romans 1:17.[15] The phrase *iustitia Dei*, the "righteousness of God," had long discouraged him because of his belief that it set a standard that he was required to meet, yet never could. But now suddenly, with a change in his interpretation of its genitive, it became, instead of a righteousness demanded *by* God from him, a righteousness that came *from* God *to* him. That meant the righteousness came as a gift. The implications of this change were dramatic, bringing in the doctrines of *sola fide, sola gratia* (by grace alone), *and solus Christus* (by Christ alone). For Luther and the Protestant reformers to come, it would be Christ's righteousness imputed to the believer through *faith*—rather than faith plus the works of the believer—that was the means by which salvation came, for the "righteous shall live by faith" (Rom 1:17).

Luther would go on to translate Romans into German during the eleven weeks in which he turned Erasmus's Greek New Testament into a lay-accessible text. This was in 1521–1522, while he was hiding out in Wartburg Castle after his courageous "Here I stand" stance at the Diet of Worms. Given that the entire New Testament took him fewer than three months, proportionately speaking, Luther may have translated Romans in less than four days! Perhaps the most controversial piece of his translation (1522 version) was Romans 3:28, to which he added the word

---

[12]*Anfechtungen* was a key term for Luther. It is difficult to capture in one English word, but refers to a combination of torments, temptations, and trials.

[13]For helpful discussion of the various literary genres of commentaries, annotations, postils, etc., see RCS 9a:xlix-lii.

[14]Brian Cummings, *The Literary Culture of the Reformation: Grammar and Grace* (Oxford: Oxford University Press, 2002), 77-78.

[15]See the excerpt below at Rom 1:17.

"alone" to "through faith." This expressed, of course, his belief in *sola fide*, which would become one of the five *solas* of the Reformation. His 1522 preface to Romans, albeit brief, reveals his maturing thought, expressed in his definitions of key terms and his summaries of the main themes of each of the chapters in the letter. In it Luther defines faith:

> Faith is a work of God in us, which changes us and brings us to birth anew from God (cf. John 1). It kills the old Adam, makes us completely different people in heart, mind, senses, and all our powers, and brings the Holy Spirit with it. What a living, creative, active powerful thing is faith! It is impossible that faith ever stop doing good. . . . Faith is a living, unshakeable confidence in God's grace; it is so certain, that someone would die a thousand times for it. This kind of trust in and knowledge of God's grace makes a person joyful, confident, and happy with regard to God and all creatures. This is what the Holy Spirit does by faith.[16]

The Commentators' Encounters with Romans

Luther's experience in Romans set the Reformation trajectory. Almost every major reformer would lecture, preach a series, or write a commentary on the letter. This volume includes more than 140 different commentators and preachers from the period 1500–1650, incorporating Lutheran, Reformed, Anabaptist, and Anglican/Puritan writers, as well as late medieval and pre-Tridentine Catholic writers whose theology bore similarity to or sympathy with the reformers. There are professors, preachers and pastors, royals and aristocrats, poets, hymn writers, and an artist. Their documents range from hymns to poems, from surreptitiously published lecture notes to massive commentaries, from verbatim court-trial accounts to an eleven-year-old princess's translation of a queen's book and a sixteen-year-old's conversation in the tower as she awaited beheading. The largest category is that of commentaries. Many of these developed from preaching, others from lecturing; all arose from the need to spiritually feed parishioners or train pastors. They incorporated everything from biblical exegesis and theological exposition to worshipful proclamation and practical application. The vast majority of the excerpts in the volume have not been published since the sixteenth or seventeenth centuries, and most of them have never been translated into English until now.

Luther and the Lutheran reformers. Luther had an extremely bright student at Wittenberg, Philipp Melanchthon (1497–1560). In 1519, Melanchthon took over from Luther the teaching of Romans at Wittenberg. His early lecture notes, which he termed *Lucubratiuncula* (nightwork), were published in 1520 without his consent or knowledge.[17] Melanchthon's exegesis of Romans had been influenced by the humanist approach of Rudolf Agricola and the Aristotelian approach of looking for themes and topics in the text. Instead of producing a verse-by-verse exposition, he searched for and described the various topics (*loci*) that he found there: sin, law, gospel, grace, justification and faith, Old and New Testaments, signs (baptism, repentance and

---

[16]Luther, *Preface to the Letter**.
[17]Philipp Melanchthon, *Loci Communes 1521*, trans. Christian Preus (St. Louis: Concordia, 2014), 9.

private confession, Lord's supper), love, and magistrates. A revised version of this was published in 1521 as the *Loci Communes*, bringing Melanchthon to prominence while Luther was hidden away in the Wartburg Castle.[18] Luther thought so highly of this book that in *Bondage of the Will* (1525) he remarked that it was worthy of being in the biblical canon.[19] Melanchthon revised the *Loci* significantly, both stylistically and theologically, throughout many subsequent editions. It became what some refer to as the first systematic theology of the Reformation and was the work that eventually replaced Peter Lombard's *Sentences* as the theological textbook for about fifty years in Lutheran seminaries.

Meanwhile, in 1522, Luther had taken another set of Melanchthon's Romans lectures, together with those on Corinthians, and published them as *Annotations*.[20] And in 1532, Melanchthon started publishing his own commentaries on Romans. Melanchthon made Romans part of the core of "Wittenberg's theological curriculum" and lectured on it nine times, six of which were turned into published works.[21] He was the reformer who published the largest number of different versions of work on Romans.

From the beginning, Melanchthon approached interpretation from a humanist rather than a scholastic perspective. He had been lecturing on rhetoric and on Romans at the same time in 1520, and he thus adopted rhetorical analysis as his approach to his exegesis, perhaps being the first exegete to look at Romans thoroughly through this lens.[22] He regarded Romans as a model letter and was so fascinated by its shape that in 1529/1530, he wrote *Dispositio orationis in Epistolam Pauli ad Romans* (The shape of the oration in Paul's epistle to the Romans).[23] He saw Romans as Paul's defense of the gospel, presented in the classic *causa* format.[24] Each work has a *scopus* or *status*, that is, a principal argument, and for Romans that was "that we are justified by faith."[25]

Several other faculty members at Wittenberg also taught or wrote commentaries on Romans. These included Justus Jonas, who translated Melanchthon's 1535 edition of the *Loci Communes* into German, but unlike Luther's and Melanchthon's students' notes, his own teachings on Romans do not appear to have ever been published. Other Wittenberg professors, however, would publish works on Romans: Johann Agricola, who published on Romans in 1530; Georg Mylius (1548–1607), professor of theology, published in 1590; Johannes Bugenhagen (1485–1558) published a commentary on Romans in 1527. Bugenhagen was known as a popularizer of Luther's

---

[18]Ibid., 1.

[19]Martin Luther, *The Bondage of the Will*, trans. J. I. Packer and O. R. Johnston (1957; repr., Grand Rapids: Baker Academic, 2012), 63. Cf. LW 33:16.

[20]Philipp Melanchthon, *Commentary on Romans*, trans. Fred Kramer (St. Louis: Concordia, 1992), 8.

[21]Timothy Wengert, "Biblical Interpretation in the Works of Philip Melanchthon" in *A History of Biblical Interpretation*, vol. 2, *The Medieval Through Reformation Periods*, ed. Alan J. Hauser and Duane F. Watson (Grand Rapids: Eerdmans, 2009), 329, citing E. Bizer, ed., *Texte aus der Anfangszeit Melanchthons* (Neukirchen-Vluyn: Neukirchener, 1966), 9-30, 39-85.

[22]Wengert, "Biblical Interpretation," 321-22; see also Wengert, "Philip Melanchthon's 1522 Annotations," 118-40. John Schneider, "The Hermeneutics of Commentary: Origins of Melanchthon's Integration of Dialectic into Rhetoric," in *Philip Melanchthon (1497–1560) and the Commentary*, ed. Timothy Wengert and M. Patrick Graham (Sheffield: Sheffield Academic, 1997), 20-47.

[23]Wengert, "Biblical Interpretation," 322.

[24]See T. H. L. Parker, *Commentaries on Romans, 1532–1542* (Edinburgh: T&T Clark, 1986), 5.

[25]Wengert, "Philip Melanchthon's 1522 Annotations," 129.

ideas, and his commentary on Romans reflects this easy-to-read style. Also at Wittenberg as a professor of theology was Georg Major, who wrote commentaries on all of Paul's letters, which were published in 1569.

Many other Romans commentators studied and/or taught at Wittenberg. Niels Hemmingsen (1513–1600) wrote a commentary on Romans (published in 1562). Caspar Cruciger (1504–1548) wrote a commentary on Romans that was published posthumously in 1567. Tilemann Hesshus's (1527–1588) Romans commentary was published in 1571. Johann Wigand's (c. 1523–1587) work on Romans was published in 1580, and Georg Mylius's (1548–1607) disputations in 1590. David Runge (1564–1604), a professor of theology at Wittenberg, began publishing disputations on Romans in Wittenberg in 1595. And in 1611, Friedrich Balduin (1575–1627) first published his commentary on Romans.

The University of Tübingen was another hub for Lutheran Romans commentaries on Romans. Lucas Osiander (1534–1604), son of the controversial reformer Andreas Osiander (1498–1552), published explications of Romans in 1583; Dietrich Schnepff (1525–1586) published disputations on Romans in 1585; and Matthias Hafenreffer (1561–1619) wrote disputations on justification based on Romans (1606).

Elsewhere, Andreas Knopken, a student of Johannes Bugenhagen's, published a commentary on Romans in 1524.[26] The theologian Johannes Brenz's commentary was written in light of his being present at many of the key events of the Reformation, having entered the Protestant movement early on, and being the last of the first generation of reformers to die. His commentary on Romans was first published in 1564. It is is warm, pastoral, creative, and filled with illustrations that make abstract concepts accessible.

Other Lutheran writers, again all mostly professors, but not in Wittenberg, included the following, in chronological order according to the date of publication of their Romans writings: Johannes Lonicer (1499–1569) produced an exegesis of Romans (1537); Antonius Corvinus (1501–1553) published his "postilla" on Letters and Gospels in 1540; Alexander Alesius (1500–1565) was a Scottish theologian who first published his commentary on Romans in 1533; Erasmus Sarcerius (1501–1559), a Gnesio-Lutheran theologian, published his commentary in 1541; Viktorin Strigel (1524–1569), a Philippist, published his notes on the Letters in 1565; Christoph Corner (1518–1594) published a commentary in 1583; Aegidius Hunnius (1550–1603), a Gnesio-Lutheran theologian, published his exposition on Romans in 1592; Johann Gerhard (1582–1637), a highly regarded theologian of his time, published his Romans works in 1635 and 1645; and in his mid-thirties, Michael Cobabus (1610–1686) published five volumes of disputations on Romans (1644–1645).

The Reformed commentators. Meanwhile, in the Reformed wing in Zurich, a commentary by Huldrych Zwingli (1484–1531) was published in 1539, eight years after he died in battle. He did not place as much emphasis on Romans 1:17 as Luther had, but he also held to justification by faith alone. Heinrich Bullinger (1504–1575) succeeded Zwingli as pastor of the Grossmünster in

---

[26]Peter G. Bietenholz and Thomas B. Deutscher, eds., *Contemporaries of Erasmus: A Biographical Register of the Renaissance and Reformation*, 3 vols. in 1 (Toronto: University of Toronto Press, 2003), 2:267.

Zurich. At age twenty-one, he lectured on Romans at Kappel. The notes for that lecture survive. At twenty-nine (1533), he published his Romans commentary. Calvin would refer to it as being both scholarly and accessible. Rudolf Gwalther (1519–1586), who succeeded Bullinger at Grossmünster, began to publish a series of sermons on Romans in 1566 that would go through dozens of editions.

Meanwhile, in Strasbourg, Martin Bucer (1491–1551) published his commentary in 1536. Bucer's commentary was extraordinarily detailed, spanning almost four hundred double-columned pages for Romans 1–8. He treated each pericope using many different approaches, exploring Paul's intent and the church fathers' comments (*expositio*), theological content (*interpretatio*), harmonizations of biblical passages that seem to contradict verses in Romans (*conciliatio*), and various issues (*quaestiones*). Bucer wrote his commentary a year after Cardinal Sadoleto published one of his own. Directly after his comments on Romans 8, he tucked in a response to the cardinal in which he waxed eloquent about *sola fide*, arguing against Sadoleto's claim that the reformers were advocating a "dead faith."[27] Bucer's commentary on Romans is regarded as his most mature theological work.[28]

In 1540, John Calvin (1509–1564) published his first commentary on Scripture: it was on Romans. It is likely that it emerged from lectures he gave in Geneva from 1536 to 1538, during his early years in the city. He continued to work on it during his exile in Strasbourg after being thrown out of Geneva.[29] Calvin had read, appreciated, and praised at least three other Protestant commentaries on Romans. He thought that Melanchthon's was more illuminating than commentaries before him; Bullinger's handled doctrine well, combining simplicity with erudition; and Bucer's was extraordinarily diligent and greater than most. He, however, considered Melanchthon's commentary to be too sparse, treating many things with clarity but letting many others go; and Bucer's was too long for busy people to read and too difficult for the simple to understand.[30] Because he had already published two Latin editions of his *Institutes of the Christian Religion*—the second three times larger than the first—Calvin believed that readers did not need as much detail in his commentaries, so he kept his relatively short, especially when compared to Bucer's. In this, his first scriptural commentary, Calvin set out to carry through on a discussion he had with Simon Grynaeus about hermeneutics, in which they had agreed that what was crucial in exegesis was *perspicua brevitas* (lucid brevity) and that it should aim to discover the *mentem scriptoris* (author's intent).[31] He would revise the 1540 version in subsequent editions, both in Latin and French, and merge it into volumes with other letters, and then into a commentary on the entire New Testament. Meanwhile, Calvin's *Institutes of the Christian Religion*—published in numerous,

---

[27]Martin Bucer, *Metaphrases et Enarrationes Perpetuae Epistolarum D. Pauli Apostoli* . . . (Wendelinus Rihelius, 1536), 370-73. Cf. Brian Lugioyo, *Martin Bucer's Doctrine of Justification: Reformation Theology and Early Modern Irenicism*, Oxford Studies in Historical Theology (Oxford: Oxford University Press, 2010), 195.

[28]Lugioyo, *Martin Bucer's Doctrine*, 41.

[29]T. H. L. Parker, *Calvin's New Testament Commentaries* (1971; repr., Edinburgh: T&T Clark, 1993), 15.

[30]John Calvin, *The Epistles of Paul the Apostle to the Romans and to the Thessalonians*, trans. Ross Mackenzie, Calvin's New Testament Commentaries 8 (Grand Rapids: Eerdmans, 1960), 2.

[31]Ibid., 1.

ever-expanding editions—in its final, 1559 version included more references to Romans than to any other New Testament book. The only Old Testament book that was referenced more was the Psalms, and that by only twenty or so additional entries.

Theodore Beza (1519–1605) published the first edition of his annotations on the New Testament in 1556, which would have an impact on the Geneva Bible (English, 1560).[32] In 1565, another of Beza's many revisions of his Greek New Testament was published, again including his detailed annotations. There would be ever-expanding editions in the 1580s and 1590s. Beza was a strong Latinist, and his expertise in language flavored his annotations,[33] as did his views on double predestination. In addition, in his first years of leading Geneva, Beza lectured on Romans at the Academy, and the notes taken by two of his students survive.[34]

Numerous other reformed commentators wrote about Romans as well. Johannes Oecolampadius (1482–1531) published his Romans commentary in 1525, with short paragraphs on various phrases from the letter. Konrad Pellikan (1478–1556) published a volume on all the apostles' letters in 1539. In so doing, he almost became the first person in the Reformation to complete a commentary on the entire Bible, but fell short by neglecting Revelation. Bernard Ochino (1487–1564) published a commentary on Romans in 1545, Andreas Hyperius (1511–1564) published one in 1548, and Wolfgang Musculus (1497–1563) in 1555. Peter Martyr Vermigli (1499–1562) published his Romans commentary in 1560. His commentary is lively and fresh, filled with metaphors and illustrations from everyday life. Antonio Del Corro's (1527–1591) *Theological Dialogue* (1574) focused on Romans and grew out of lectures given in London a few years before he became a professor at Oxford University. Kaspar Olevianus (1536–1587) published his notes on Romans in 1579. The Romans commentary of Benedict Aretius (d. 1574), professor of theology at Bern, was also published posthumously, in 1579. Daniel Toussain (1541–1602), professor of New Testament at Heidelberg, wrote a synopsis of the doctrine of justification based on Romans 1, published in 1588. The analysis of Romans by Johannes Piscator (1546–1625) was first published in 1589. David Pareus's (1548–1622) Romans commentary was published initially in 1608 and numerous times after, going verse by verse, even phrase by phrase, through the letter. In 1642, Parliament ordered that the annotations on the Bible by Geneva professor of theology Giovanni Diodati (1576–1649) be printed in England, in English. Louis de Dieu (1590–1642) published his observations on Romans in 1646, focusing on linguistic issues. Charles Ferme (c. 1566–1617), the principal of Fraserburgh University, Scotland, did not publish his writings during his life. Published posthumously in 1651, his "Logical Analysis" of Romans is his only extant work. And Johannes Cocceius's (1603–1669) commentary was published in 1668, while he was professor of theology at Leiden.

Anabaptists and others. Romans was perhaps not as central to the Anabaptists as to the magisterial reformers. It played a role, but not a prominent one, in the origins of the movement. Zwingli

---

[32]Shawn Wright, *Theodore Beza: The Man and the Myth* (Tain, Scotland: Christian Focus, 2015), 25.

[33]Ibid., 19.

[34]Theodore Beza, *Cours Sur Les Épîtres aux Romains et aux Hébreux: 1564–1566 d'après les notes de Marcus Widler. Thèses disputées à l'Académie de Genève: 1564–1567*, ed. Pierre Fraenkel and Luc Perrotet, Travaux d'Humanisme et Renaissance (Geneva: Librarie Droz, 1988), 34.

had encouraged laypeople to read the Scriptures and discuss them in groups. One such group formed in 1523 under the leadership of Andreas Castelberger, a book peddler. When an investigation was done of the group two years later, it so happened that they were reading the letter to the Romans. It was their Bible study group and others throughout Zurich that began to develop the views that became foundational for Anabaptism.

The Anabaptists did not publish commentaries on Romans, for they tended to distrust human commentary on the Scriptures in general. Their works often functioned as pastiches of Scripture verses, with very little prose analysis. Interpretation was implied in the clustering of particular texts to illustrate theological points. Thus it is difficult to find many Anabaptist comments on texts in Romans. In addition, they tended to emphasize the Gospels over the Pauline letters.

The four radical reformers that have the most number of excerpts in this volume are the Dutch theologians Dirk Philips and Menno Simons, the German theologian Balthasar Hubmaier, and the Austrian theologian and key second-generation leader Pilgram Marpeck, who sought to bring unity among Anabaptists. Additional radical reformers included in this volume are the Dutch pastor David Joris; Austrian elder Leupold Scharnschlager; German theologian Peter Riedemann; German radical leaders Hans Hut and Andreas Karlstadt; German preachers Thomas Müntzer and Jörg Haug; Austrian martyrs Hans Schaffler, Leonhard Frick, Leonhard Schiemer, and imprisoned hymnwriter Ursula Hellrigel; Swiss martyrs Felix Mantz and Hans Hotz; and Hutterian Brethren preacher Paul Glock (Jung Paul).

The Anabaptists agreed, in large part, with the magisterial reformers on the issue of justification by faith alone and the reduction in number of sacraments from seven to two (although some did not consider them sacraments per se). The issues that distinguish the radical reformers from the magisterial in their interpretation of Romans are their prohibition of oath-making (see excerpts below at Rom 1:9, 27), their eschewal of infant baptism (see, for examples, excerpts below at Rom 2:29; 3:1; 4:11; 5:18; 6:3), and their self-identification as those who place a greater emphasis on living righteously. As Peter Riedemann stated, "Faith is a power that works righteousness" and enables believers to follow God's will.[35] As victims of often severe persecution, the early Anabaptists' most frequently referenced chapter in Romans was Romans 8, and their favorite verse within that, Romans 8:17, which brings together themes of being like Christ and suffering with him.[36]

Pre-Tridentine Catholic commentators. Before Trent, a number of Catholics wrote commentaries on Romans that showed some sympathy to Reformation principles. Prior to the Reformation, the humanist John Colet (1467–1519) lectured on Romans at Oxford around 1497, interpreting Paul in light of Plato. His preaching was popular with Lollards and even brought him trouble from the authorities. Scholars suggest that Colet influenced Erasmus through his Romans lectures in 1499.[37] Jacques Lefèvre d'Étaples (c. 1455–1536), the French humanist theologian,

---

[35]Peter Riedemann, *Love Is Like Fire: The Confession of an Anabaptist Prisoner*, ed. Emmy Barth Maendel (1993; repr., Walden, NY: Plough, 2016), 19. See excerpt at Rom 1:16-17.

[36]R. Emmet McLaughlin, "Paul in Early Anabaptism," in *A Companion to Paul in the Reformation*, ed. R. Ward Holder, Brill's Companions to the Christian Tradition (Leiden: Brill, 2009), 217, 220.

[37]Colet's influence on Erasmus has been challenged by some scholars. See John B. Gleason, *John Colet* (Berkeley: University of California Press, 1989).

predated and foreshadowed Luther by first interpreting the Psalms (1509) and then Romans (as part of his 1512 commentary on Paul's letters). There were hints of the coming Reformation in his commentary, and many believe his work influenced Luther.[38] Lefèvre never entirely identified with the Reformation movement, but his views on justification would come under censure by Noël Beda, member of the Faculty of the Sorbonne. His commentary on Romans is rhetorically beautiful, many of the passages evoking the style of Augustine. The Dutch humanist scholar Erasmus of Rotterdam (1466–1536) worked on the book of Romans over the course of years. His critical edition (first ed., 1516) of the Greek version of Romans informed many of the reformers' works on the letter. In 1517, Romans was the first book he worked on in his *Paraphrases*. Henry VIII's wife Katherine Parr had the *Paraphrases* translated into English, and they became quite popular.[39] Erasmus sought to understand Paul's theology in light of humanist principles and by privileging the early church fathers over the medieval scholastic theologians. He changed his views as he interacted with Luther through debate and with Melanchthon through extensive correspondence, adapting his *Annotations* in 1527 and 1535 and his *Paraphrases* in 1532. As time passed, his views on faith tilted more toward Luther's.[40] Several phrases in Romans 3:28 in his 1532 *Paraphrases*—including his appending of "through faith" to "righteousness"—seem to indicate an emerging belief that Paul regarded the law of faith as replacing the law of Moses.[41] And, although he did not write a Romans commentary, Johann von Staupitz (d. 1524), Luther's confessor and the vicar general of the Reformed Congregation of the Hermits of Augustine, of which Luther was a member, introduced Luther to a number of ideas from Romans that related to grace and laid the foundations for his discovery of *sola fide*.[42]

During the Reformation, other Catholic ecclesiastical and monastic leaders wrote Romans commentaries that overlapped with Reformation ideals. Cardinal Cajetan (1469–1534) sought to bring reform to, and remained within, the Catholic Church even though his writings show agreement with some of the reformers' views. He integrated scholasticism and humanism with his interest in both Aquinas and Erasmus.[43] His commentary on Romans shows his interest in correcting the errors of the Vulgate and emphasizes the literal sense over the allegorical. He remarked that the Gospel of John and the letter to the Romans were the two books that required the greatest attention in revising the Vulgate; his Romans commentary took him two and a half months to complete in 1528 and was published in 1532.[44] Cardinal Jacopo Sadoleto (1477–1547)—who would in 1539 write his famous letter to Geneva seeking to bring the city back into the Catholic fold while Calvin was in exile from them, and to which Calvin would respond—published a commentary on Romans in 1535 that would get him in trouble with the Catholic Church.

---

[38]See, e.g., his excerpt in Rom 3:21 below.

[39]Timothy George, *Reading Scripture with the Reformers* (Downers Grove, IL: IVP Academic, 2011), 92, 94.

[40]Greta Grace Kroeker, *Erasmus in the Footsteps of Paul: A Pauline Theologian* (Toronto: University of Toronto Press, 2011), 3, 134-37.

[41]See Erasmus's excerpt in Rom 3:28 below.

[42]See his excerpt at Rom 8:30.

[43]Michael O'Connor, "Cajetan on Paul" in Holder, *Companion to Paul*, 340.

[44]Ibid., 338.

This was ironic, for he had written the commentary as an anti-Protestant work, but his section on Romans 8:29-31[45] was judged as not having enough clarity about human merit. A second edition would add more detail. Johann (Ferus) Wild (1495–1554) was a Franciscan commentator, many of whose commentaries, including Romans (1558), were placed on the Index because of ideas that were redolent of Lutheranism; he was known for being highly anticlerical, for grounding his preaching in the Scriptures, and for advocating the reform of the Catholic Church.

Juan de Valdés (c. 1500/1510–1541), a Spanish theologian, led the "Valdesian circle" in Naples (1535–1541), a Catholic reforming group that included figures such as Peter Martyr Vermigli, Bernard Ochino, and Signora Donna Giulia de Gonzaga (1513–1566). Valdés favored evangelical theology but didn't want to cause disunity in the church, so, unlike Vermigli and Ochino, he did not come fully over to the Reformation. He taught in favor of justification by faith, speaking of the *beneficio di Cristo* (the benefits that came to the believer from Christ's death). In the context of the circle, he worked on a commentary on Romans. He included in it a Spanish translation of Romans based on the Greek and dedicated the commentary to Giulia, a beautiful countess in the convent at Naples. In another work (*Alfabeta Cristiano*), also dedicated to the countess, Valdés included a verbatim account of a dialogue with her, in which he at one point discusses law and gospel in Romans 8.[46] After Valdés's death, Giulia paid for his works to be printed. Ochino wrote his *Expositio epistolae divi Pauli ad Romanos* in 1545 in Geneva. One can imagine him discussing the letter with Calvin, who had published his own commentary only a few years earlier.[47]

Closely related to the Valdesian circle was the Viterbo circle, which included figures who, although they did not write commentaries, left writings that show their defense of the theology of Romans. Vittoria Colonna (1492–1547) was a famous lyric poet and a friend to the artist Michelangelo di Lodovico Buonarroti Simoni (commonly known as Michelangelo). She was influenced by Valdés and Ochino and wrote poetry that incorporated Reformation themes, particularly on the importance of faith.[48] For a season from the late 1530s through the 1540s, she and Michelangelo wrote sonnets for each other, a number of them expressing their views on faith and salvation. Michelangelo was also a proponent of justification by faith alone.[49] Another member of the circle, Pietro Carnesecchi, was tried for heresy and condemned to death for his views on justification by faith and its many implications. He was also condemned for his association with Valdés and Flaminio, with Lutheran and Calvinist ideas, and with the book *The Benefit of Christ's Death* (see below). Excerpts from the trial that relate to theological concepts in Romans are included below.[50]

The *Beneficio di Cristo* (translated in the mid-sixteenth century into English as *The Benefit of Christ's Death*) was very popular, reflecting themes from Romans and Calvin's *Institutes*. It is estimated that as many as forty thousand copies were in print before it was banned by the Catholic

---

[45]See excerpt in Rom 8:29 below.
[46]See an excerpt at Rom 5:20.
[47]See Ochino excerpt at Rom 1:28.
[48]See her poems at Rom 8:26.
[49]See Michelangelo's poem at Rom 1:17, 5:9, 7:17, 24; 8:26.
[50]See excerpts from the trial at Rom 5:1.

Church. Although its author's name was not on the document, scholars argue that it was written by a Benedictine monk named Benedetto de Mantova and adapted by Marcantonio Flaminio, incorporating Valdés's teachings and Calvin's *Institutes*.[51] It is possible that Vittoria Colonna had been friends with Flaminio and had shown an unpublished manuscript version of it to Michelangelo in the early 1540s.[52] The second edition was published in 1543. It was later placed on the *Index Librorum Prohibitorum* (first operating in 1559), the copies of it were destroyed, and it was believed to no longer be extant—until, that is, in the nineteenth century, when an English translation of it was discovered, and then another English translation manuscript that seems to have been read and commented on by Edward VI.

The Valdesian and Viterbo circles were part of a larger movement called the *spirituali* (those who worked for reform within the Catholic Church). Several cardinals were members of the *spirituali*, including Gasparo Contarini (1483–1542), who wrote *scholia* on the Pauline letters.

Anglicans and Puritans. There are far fewer Romans commentaries from England, Scotland, and Wales than on the Continent, but one can find Romans being dealt with in Bible translations, homilies, sermons, and other sources. One of the earliest English reformers, William Tyndale (1494–1536), would base his 1536 translation of the New Testament on Erasmus's Greek rather than Luther's German, but when it came to writing his *Prologue to Romans*, he would incorporate mostly a translation and adaptation of Luther's preface to the letter in his German translation of the New Testament.[53] Archbishop Thomas Cranmer (1489–1556), arguably the most influential English reformer, did not write a commentary on Romans. His most direct teachings on Romans are in his homily on salvation, which was part of the *First Book of Homilies*, published by 1547 under the reign of the young king Edward VI, for use in the churches. There are also his corrections of Henry VIII's corrections of *Institutions of the Christian Man*, which reveal his emerging Reformation views on justification.[54] During Elizabeth I's reign, one of the secretaries of state was Laurence Tomson (1539–1608), a Reformed theologian who had taught Hebrew in Geneva while in exile during Mary's reign. He translated the New Testament into English from Theodore Beza's edition for the Geneva Bible, and contributed annotations that include numerous comments on Romans.

Most of what survives from England are sermons. Well-known Puritan preachers William Perkins (1558–1602), Richard Rogers (c. 1550–1618), John Owen (1616–1683), Richard Sibbes (1577–1635), and Richard Baxter (1615–1691) did not preach extensively on Romans. But Sibbes and Owen each have at least one extant sermon on the book. Sibbes's sermon on Romans 8:2 is a robustly theological meditation published posthumously as "Spiritual Jubilee" in 1538. After traveling with Oliver Cromwell to Ireland as his chaplain, John Owen preached his sermon on Romans 4:20, "The Steadfastness of the Promises, and the Sinfulness of Staggering" to the Commons of

---

[51]Dermot Fenlon, *Heresy and Obedience in Tridentine Italy: Cardinal Pole and the Counter Reformation* (Cambridge: Cambridge University Press, 1972), 73-74, 77-78.

[52]Vittoria Colonna, *Sonnets for Michelangelo: A Bilingual Edition*, ed. Abigail Brundin (Chicago: University of Chicago Press, 2005), 17; Abigail Brundin, *Vittoria Colonna and the Spiritual Poetics of the Italian Reformation* (New York: Routledge, 2008), 79n49.

[53]For part of Tyndale's preface that is original to him, see excerpt in Romans introduction below.

[54]See excerpt at Rom 3:24.

England in the Parliamentary Assembly, pleading for the spiritual needs of Ireland, exhorting the leaders to trust boldly in the promises of God as Abraham had. And Perkins and Rogers both refer to the golden chain of Romans 8:30, the former doing so in a treatise called *Golden Chaine*, named for the concept and teaching on all the stages of the chain. Baxter, influenced by Perkins and Sibbes, was a pastor at Kidderminster. He was the first to refuse to sign the Act of Uniformity, was ejected, and defended the other seventeen hundred or so who were ejected as well. He didn't write a commentary on Romans but has a relevant treatise, *Aphorismes of Justification* (1649 ed.).

Many other Anglicans and/or Puritans also preached, commented, or wrote hymns on Romans in the seventeenth century. Although a number of Latin Romans commentaries from the Continent had been previously translated into English, the first Romans commentary written originally in English was by Andrew Willet (1562–1621), a former professor turned Anglican vicar. It is a *Hexapla*, a sixfold commentary, published in 1611. It beat out Thomas Wilson's English commentary by three years. William Ames delivered a series of lectures published after his death, titled *The Substance of Christian Religion*. Five of them were explications of verses from Romans. Renowned metaphysical poets John Donne (1572–1631) and George Herbert (1593–1633) explored sundry themes in Romans through their verse. Anthony Maxey (d. 1618) preached a sermon on Romans 8:30 called "The Golden Chaine of Mans Saluation" before King James I around 1606. Puritan Edward Elton (c. 1569–1624) wrote a highly detailed sermon series (1618) on Romans 7. The Reformed Anglican Anthony Cade (c. 1564–1641) wrote *Paul's Agony* (1618), a sermon on the inner turmoil faced by Paul in Romans 7:24. Puritan Thomas Goodwin (1600–1680) preached a sermon on Romans 8:34 in 1642. George Wither (1588–1667), increasingly a Puritan, in 1623 published one of the earliest hymnbooks in England, *Hymns and Songs of the Church*. He wrote a long defense of the hymns when the Stationers Company refused to print them since he wasn't sticking only to psalms and canticles (hymns other than psalms, and pieces directly from the Scriptures). Several of the hymns incorporate texts from Romans 1–8. John Preston's (1587–1628) four sermons titled "On Faith" in his *The Breast-Plate of Faith and Love* (1634) focus on Romans 1:17. He concludes the series with a focus on God's glory, and then admits, "I cannot stand to press it further. So much for this time, and for this text."[55] He had just written 138 pages on one verse! And English Puritan divine John Downame (c. 1571–1652), along with other unnamed editors, compiled the *English Annotations*, a digest of continental commentaries, first published in 1645.

Several Welsh Puritans wrote or preached on Romans in the mid-seventeenth century. Vavasor Powell (1617–1670) had already been imprisoned under Archbishop William Laud in the early 1640s for his Puritan views. When the Puritans took over later in the decade, the new government passed an act for the propagation of the gospel in Wales, and invited Powell to preach before Parliament, which he did in 1649. Later that year, he preached before the mayor of London and other officials. The sermon, "God the Father Glorified," which dealt with salvation, engages with Romans at several points. In 1655, during Oliver Cromwell's term as Lord Protector, another Welsh Puritan

---

[55] John Preston, *Breast-Plate of Faith and Love* (London: George Purflow, 1651), 138*.

clergyman, Walter Cradock (c. 1606–1659), published a series of sermons on Romans 8:4-5 titled *Gospel Holiness*. A third Welsh reformer was Gabriel Powel (1576–1611), a Welsh Anglican who was highly anti-Catholic in his writings and who composed a detailed analysis of Romans 1.

In Scotland, the Puritan William Guild (1586–1657) wrote a treatise (1649) against Catholicism arguing that Paul's letter to the Romans, together with the writings of the early church, constitute the true "Old Roman Catholicism," which is "apostolic" in contrast with the new Catholicism of the medieval and Tridentine church, which is "apostatical." Point by point, he opposed contemporary Catholic teaching with Paul's teachings and excerpts from patristic authors such as Augustine, Jerome, and Gregory. The Reformed David Dickson (1583?–1663), professor of theology at Edinburgh, published his exposition of Paul's letters (1659) in the decade after the Puritan Revolution. It set out with great clarity the ideas of Reformed commentators before him. Scottish Presbyterian Samuel Rutherford (1600–1661), known particularly for his letters, utilizes Romans texts in a number of them.

Meanwhile, with the Puritans in the New World, during the antinomian controversy, John Cotton (1585–1652) held a conference with the elders of Boston, for which a copy of the proceedings were acquired and published in London in 1646 by Francis Cornwell, a minister. It referenced Romans at several points, including on whether someone can gather evidence for their justification from their sanctification; and the problems with liturgical prayers. Cotton also refers frequently to Romans in a 1641 collection of sermons. Finally, the preface of *The Book of the General Laws and Libertyes Concerning the Inhabitants of Massachusetts* (1648) incorporated verses from Romans.

Women. As far as we know, no woman wrote a full commentary on Romans during the period covered in this volume. However, it is possible to find the traces of the reading and interpretation of Romans in the writings of women, including their hymns, ballads, prayers, and letters. In addition to the women already mentioned, we find the following:

Marguerite d'Angoulême (1492–1549) was the sister of Francis I, king of France. She was highly supportive of the circle of Meaux and wrote a number of works herself. Her *Miroir de l'âme pécheresse* explores themes from Romans 7, and her *Discord étant en l'homme par la contrariété de l'esprit et de la chair* is a commentary on Romans 7–8. Elizabeth I, at age eleven, translated the *Miroir* into English. Marguerite was a courageous political supporter of many of the French reformers.[56]

In a letter to Marguerite d'Angoulême in April 1539, Marie Dentière (c. 1495–1561) defended Calvin after he was expelled from Geneva. She spoke positively about Calvin while also encouraging Marguerite and other women to study the Scriptures for themselves. The letter would be published in Geneva as a theological treatise.[57]

Katharina Schütz Zell (1497/1498–1562), in 1524, at age twenty-six wrote a letter of encouragement to the women of Kentzingen who were remaining with their children in the city to face

---

[56]Marguerite also wrote a fictional work, the *Heptameron*, in which a group of men and women stranded together by a flood that had destroyed the only bridge between them and freedom whiled away the time in which the bridge was being rebuilt by sharing one hundred stories in ten days, beginning each of the first five days by reading from Romans.

[57]See Rom 4:16 below for an excerpt from the letter.

persecution as their husbands had been exiled by authorities for their Reformation beliefs. In it, she draws on numerous Scriptures, including Romans 8:5-8. Also, in a long prayer based on the Miserere Psalm, she alludes to Romans numerous times.

An Italian woman, Olympia Fulvia Morata (1526–1555), in one of her surviving letters (dated 1554), quotes Romans 8:29, drawing on Paul's words to explain how the suffering she endured during the capture of her city of Schweinfurt served a redemptive purpose. In her poem titled "Poem to Johannes of Lanzhut," Argula von Grumbach (c. 1490–c. 1554) wrote in defense of women being used by the Holy Spirit to read and interpret Scripture. In it, she references numerous scriptural passages, including Romans 8. Women also wrote hymns that incorporated Romans themes. Caspar Cruciger's wife, Elisabeth (c. 1500–1535), wrote a hymn, "Herr Christ, der einig Gotts Sohn," in her early twenties, dealing with the Romans 6:6 theme of old self and new self.[58] It remains in Lutheran hymnbooks to this day. Ursula Hellrigel (born c. 1521), an Anabaptist, is credited with writing a hymn that is printed in the *Ausbund*, a Swiss Brethren hymnal.[59] And Catharina Regina von Greiffenberg (1633–1694), an Austrian poet and Protestant, wrote meditations that touched on Romans.[60]

In the final years of Henry VIII's reign, Anne Askew (1521–1546), while she was in prison at Newgate, wrote and sang a ballad that focuses on faith as her shield and points to her belief in Abraham's faith being counted as righteousness and giving her boldness.[61] Elizabeth I, Henry VIII's daughter who would become the popular and long-reigning Virgin Queen of England, at age eleven (see above) translated Marguerite d'Angoulême's *Miroir* into English.[62] Then, at age twelve, she translated chapter one from Calvin's *Institutes*. Her "Prayer to God for the Auspicious Administration of the Kingdom and the Safety of the People" incorporates the concept of dying and being reborn with Christ.[63] Finally, in the reign of Charles II, Lady Anne Clifford (1590–1676), the Countess Dowager of Dorset, Pembroke, and Montgomery, when dying in 1676, turned to Romans 8, which had long been a focus of her meditation. Bishop Rainbow, preaching her funeral sermon, told the story of her final hours and how the chapter comforted her in her dying moments and shaped her last words.[64]

The Theology of Romans 1–8

For the interpreters in this volume, Romans 1–8 was a prism through which all the colors of the rainbow of doctrine were refracted. Their commentary on this half of the letter touches on virtually every area of medieval theology, and most of the major theological shifts of the Reformation appear in their writings on these eight chapters.

---

[58]See the hymn at Rom 6:6 below.
[59]See the hymn in her excerpt at Rom 8:30. It is sometimes attributed to Annelein of Freiburg, an Anabaptist martyred in 1529.
[60]See excerpts at Rom 8:30.
[61]See the excerpt at Rom 4:9.
[62]See the excerpts at Rom 5:6-8; 7:19.
[63]See the excerpt at Rom 6:4.
[64]See the excerpt at Rom 8:39.

Human sin and God's holiness. The first key area is the doctrine of sin, a major theme in Romans, which uses the term far more than any other New Testament book. Early on, Luther found in the letter reason to counter medieval thought on original sin. He stated:

> The chief purpose of this letter is to break down, to pluck up, and to destroy all wisdom and righteousness of the flesh. This includes all the works which in the eyes of people or even in our own eyes may be great works. No matter whether these works are done with a sincere heart and mind, this letter is to affirm and state and magnify sin, no matter how much someone insists that it does not exist, or that it was believed not to exist.[65]

Nominalist theologians had taught a toned-down version of original sin as merely the privation of righteousness and Adam's original standing with God, and the impairment of the human will; it required baptism, penance, and the Eucharist to provide healing through sacramental grace.[66] In discussing Romans 1:21-32 and Romans 5:12-14, Luther and the other reformers paint a more serious picture of sin and its effects. Brenz (Rom 5:12) speaks of Adam losing the Holy Spirit and righteousness and becoming an unbeliever who despised God and his neighbor to the point of becoming the "scum of all evil" and inheriting "bodily death and continuous damnation." Bucer describes persons as being "stripped of the bright image of God" and of being so "ruined by this" that they will "not be able to do anything but live for Satan, unto their eternal damnation."[67]

Romans 1:18-32 engendered discussion about the nature, role, and limits of natural knowledge. The commentators had a variety of views on what was included in the natural knowledge. For Melanchthon, the knowledge of the Gentiles was one of law, not of gospel. Gentiles sense that God is a God of justice. But they cannot, apart from revelation, know that he wishes to remit their sins through his Son. Their knowledge is limited, however, to God's actions; they do not have knowledge of his essence. Bucer speaks of the *notio Dei*, the "idea of God" implanted by God himself in the human soul. It assures all that God exists, "that he possesses power over all things, and is the Highest Good."[68] Brenz, on the other hand, argues that original sin has obscured humans' ability to be sure that there is a God. Only the Scriptures could "scatter this obscurity and darkness."[69] At the same time, however, the beauty and order of the natural world points to a Mind, and certain of God's characteristics are reflected in the world he created.[70] Lucas Osiander warns readers not to blame the gardener for the bad tree; it is humans, not God, who have, by their idolatry, obscured what they once knew about God.[71]

The theme of God's holiness permeates the commentaries on Romans. It is in contrast to this righteousness (*iustitia Dei*) that human unrighteousness stands out so starkly. The strong

---

[65]LW 25:135*.

[66]Timothy George, "Martin Luther," in *Reading Romans Through the Centuries: From the Early Church to Karl Barth*, ed. Jeffrey P. Greenman and Timothy Larsen (Grand Rapids: Brazos, 2005), 114.

[67]See the excerpt in Romans 5:12.

[68]Bucer at Rom 1:19.

[69]Brenz at Rom 1:19.

[70]Brenz at Rom 1:20.

[71]Osiander at Rom 1:24.

language of the commentators toward sin, reflecting Paul's, sets up the reader for the surprise that *sola fide* then brings. No one can rise above their own sin. No one can merit God's favor. No one deserves salvation. Only God himself can save. It is Christ alone who can restore. But why would he do that for sinners? And why would he do that as a gift? The juxtaposition of our sinfulness and God's gracious, free gift of his Son, shocked the reformers. And the intensity of the resulting emotion reverberates throughout their writings. They cannot get over the joy of *sola fide*.

Iustitia Dei *and justification by faith alone.* At the same time that Romans opened the door for reformers to discuss virtually every doctrine, every verse seemed to offer the opportunity to focus on this one doctrine in particular: justification by faith alone. Reading the commentators, one gets the sense that on this issue, all roads lead not *to* Rome but *away* from it. For all of the reformers, and most of our commentators, justification is by faith alone. *Sola fide*. It was the material principle of the Reformation. As narrated above, Luther's major turning point came when he discovered this doctrine through Romans 1:17. And Melanchthon states that the entire letter of Romans "consists in one locus: the source of justification."[72]

In medieval thought, the doctrine of justification was closely related to the Anselmian satisfaction theory of the atonement (mentioned above). Justification meant being made righteous. In scholastic theology, there were four elements (not necessarily stages) in the *processus justificationis* (process of justification).[73] The first element is an infusion of grace. The second is a movement of the free will, which is also a movement of love—that is, of faith formed by love.[74] This *fides caritate formata* is a justifying faith, and it involves a movement toward God. The third is contrition; this involves a movement away from sin. The fourth is the remission of sins. All four together constitute justification.[75] *Facere quod in se est* (do what lies within you) came, for the nominalists, to replace the second and third elements of the *processus justificationis*.[76] The phrase had first been used in the thirteenth century but became popular in the later Middle Ages. It indicated that God would not withhold his grace from those who did their best. Stephen Gardiner, a key Catholic bishop under Henry VIII, for example, said, "He is worthy of love and favor who will seek for it and do his duty to attain it."[77] Doing one's best involves two elements, the love of God and the hatred of sin. The former requires loving God "above all else" (*propter Deum*, "for his own sake").

The reformers spoke strongly against this. For example, Vermigli labels as presumptuous those who claim that "a praiseworthy intention and good end are enough."[78] Justification comes by faith,

---

[72]Cited in Wengert, "Philip Melanchthon's 1522 Annotations," 128.

[73]Charles P. Carlson Jr., *Justification in Earlier Medieval Theology* (The Hague: Martinus Nijhoff, 1975), 126.

[74]Carlson, *Justification in Earlier Medieval Theology*, 119-20.

[75]Alister E. McGrath, *Iustitia Dei: A History of the Christian Doctrine of Justification*, 3rd ed. (Cambridge: Cambridge University Press, 2005), 64-65.

[76]Carlson, *Justification in Earlier Medieval Theology*, 126.

[77]Stephen Gardiner, *A Declaration of such true articles as George Ioye hath gone about to confute as false* (London: Johannes Herford for Robert Toye, 1546), fol. 12v*; modernized from excerpt in Ashley Null, "Thomas Cranmer's Reading of Paul's Letters," in *Reformation Readings of Paul: Explorations in History and Exegesis*, ed. Michael Allen and Jonathan A. Linebaugh (Downers Grove, IL: IVP Academic, 2015), 218.

[78]See his excerpts in Rom 3:8; 5:5.

not by one's intentions or the mustering up of love, or the doing of one's best. And faith comes as a gift from God, not as a response on God's part to some initial thought or action on the part of the human. For the vast majority of the commentators, God is the initiator of salvation.

Scholastic theologians had debated the role of grace in salvation. Categories such as *gratia gratis data* (gratuitously given grace) and *gratia gratum faciens* (sanctifying, habitual, indwelling grace) differentiate between grace that comes externally from God as a form of ongoing aid, and grace that is infused by God into the human heart. This latter form could be lost by mortal sins and needs to be restored by engaging in the sacrament of penance. Operative (*operans*) grace refers to God's actions on the human being that do not require a response, whereas cooperative (*cooperans*) grace enables human beings' cooperation with God's actions. Some theologians also differentiated between *praeveniens* (prevenient) and *subsequens* (subsequent) grace, as the grace that prepared a soul and the grace that enabled the soul to continue. The commentators argued against—or at least modified—these categories. The Anglican (and Calvinist) rector Andrew Willet[79] summarizes their arguments: The first distinction, by referring to only one of the terms as "gratuitously given," seems to imply that there are forms of grace that are not freely given, which is an error since grace, by definition, is freely given. It also errs in attributing salvation to the grace that is infused in us as a habit rather than the grace that is grounded in Christ. The second distinction, that between "working" grace and "working together" grace, can work only if the former, rather than the latter, is what saves a person. The latter is what enables one to live the Christian life, but it does not save one's soul. Third, the distinction between prevenient and subsequent grace is mistaken if it implies that how people use the former will determine whether the latter will be given to them. It is the same grace that goes before and that follows along, and the former doesn't earn one the latter.

Some scholastic theologians had attempted to make a connection between grace, the stages of justification, and the discussion of merit. The doing of one's best prepared one to receive grace and *meritum de congruo*. *Meritum de congruo* is the merit that God gives to those who have done good works of their own free will (although many theologians agreed that there must be grace present to enable even these works). These initial works are not significant enough to earn one salvation, but they put one in a position to receive grace that will enable one to do works that are worthy of merit, the *meritum de condigno*. God has put himself under obligation to himself to grant merit for this second category of works. Reformers objected to this. There are no works that humans can do, with or without grace, that can earn enough merit to put God in our debt. Only Christ's work on the cross can earn the merit that is worthy.

The clear line through the Reformation writings on Romans is that believers appropriate Christ's work on the cross through faith alone. Not through works, earning of merit, penance, indulgences, prayers, the giving of alms, pilgrimages, veneration of saints, priests' absolutions, the monastic life, or through engagement in the sacraments.

---

[79]See Andrew Willet excerpt at Rom 5:21.

The sacraments. In medieval theology, the primary method through which the acts of satisfaction and the gaining of merit and the infusing of grace occurred was the sacramental system. There were seven sacraments. According to this system, the individual soul is born already tainted by original sin, and the sacramental system makes it possible to deal with that sin, so an infant is baptized soon after birth. This remits the original sin, but of course, all persons continue to sin, and so many of the other sacraments are essential as well. It was believed that salvific grace is mediated through the sacraments. The two key sacraments are penance and the Eucharist—the latter often referred to as the Mass—and the medieval person was expected to participate in both annually.

In this understanding there is a strong relationship between the doctrine of justification and the sacrament of penance. The third element of the *processus justificationis* is contrition, a key factor in penance. The scholastic debate on attrition (defined variously as repenting out of fear of punishment, or repenting only with human will rather than with grace) and contrition (repenting out of a love of God; or, repentance perfected by God's grace) had not been formally resolved as to whether the latter was essential to the effectiveness of the sacrament. There was pressure to perform the sacrament properly, out of a pure motive of love for God. So anyone with a hint of scrupulosity could have a painful time of it.

Luther had fallen into this camp. His scrupulosity combined with medieval theology had led to profound depression. He believed that for the sacrament of penance to work, he had to come to it with utter contrition, but he could not do that, for he hated God, and pure contrition required a love of God. He would later write to his confessor, Staupitz, that "formerly almost no word in the whole Scripture was more bitter to me than *poenitentia* (although I zealously made a pretense before God and tried to express a feigned and constrained love for him)."[80] Luther wrestled with this in his *Lectures on Romans*. His rediscovery of the doctrine of justification by faith alone, in his encounter with Romans 1:17, changed things dramatically in relation to penance. Luther would soon reject *facere quod in se est* and eliminate penance as a sacrament.

Along with Luther, the majority of the commentators would reduce the sacraments from the medieval seven to two: baptism and the Lord's Supper (variously referred to as Eucharist, communion, Lord's Table, breaking bread, etc.). The Eucharist was not much of a focus in Reformation commentaries on Romans 1–8, but baptism shows up in their comments on several passages. Both Paul's mentions of circumcision (Rom 2:25–3:1; 4:9-12) and his statement that we are baptized with Christ into his death (Rom 6:1-4) raised the issue of baptism. Many of the magisterial reformers saw baptism as the new circumcision and thus supported infant baptism.[81] Most followed Augustine's view of a sacrament as a visible sign of an invisible reality. Some saw the sacraments as seals of the covenant.[82] On the other hand, the Anabaptists took the opportunity to argue for the necessity of adult baptism. They saw Romans 6:4 as evidence that faith must

---

[80]LW 48:65*.
[81]See, e.g., Zwingli excerpt at Rom 4:11.
[82]See Kaspar Olevianus at Rom 2:25.

precede baptism and that therefore infant baptism is not warranted,[83] and also that baptism should initiate a life of holiness and transformation. The magisterial reformers argued against what they perceived as the Anabaptists' rebaptisms.

Imputation of Christ's righteousness. Rather than believing in a sacramental outworking of a satisfaction theory of atonement, many of the Reformers held a forensic (legal) view of justification. For Calvin, for example, to justify meant to acquit from charges of guilt.[84] Melanchthon explained that "to justify is to pronounce or to consider as just," giving the example of Scipio before the tribunes. Building on Romans 4, he stated that "when we say we are justified by faith it is the same thing as saying that we are accounted just by God on account of Christ when we believe."[85]

For most who held to the forensic view, this meant the imputation of Christ's righteousness. Beza, for example, stated that there were only two ways to have the righteousness that will allow us to be "approved by God": "We are righteous before God either through faith, the alien righteousness of Christ being imputed to us, *or* by our own righteousness, that is, by observing the divine law."[86] But of course, no one fully observed the law, so the only way, in the end, to have right standing with God was through the imputation of Christ's righteousness.

Andreas Osiander objected to this approach and instead taught an infused, essential righteousness, that the believer is justified not by God's pardon but by being made righteous by the indwelling of Christ. The Spanish theologian Antonio del Corro agreed with him. Both faced conflict from Calvin and others who advocated the imputation of Christ's righteousness. Calvin dealt with Osiander in the *Institutes*, referring to Romans 4:6-7.[87] Where Osiander taught that it was incumbent on us to be righteous and that it would be inappropriate for God to justify those who were still sinful, Calvin argued that if it is about our actual righteousness, then God cannot be pleased, because our righteousness is always partial. Imputation of Christ's righteousness is therefore essential to our salvation. Toussain also spoke out against Osiander, as seen in the commentary on Romans 5:1.

One of the key differences between the reformers and the medieval theologians on justification was in their differentiation of it from sanctification. Whereas the medieval theologians held that justification, like sanctification, is a lifelong process of transformation, most of the reformers believed that justification is God's external pronouncement of righteousness, one that occurs at the point of conversion, whereas sanctification is the lifelong process of inner transformation. Although there was some variety in the way the commentators explored the definitions of and relationship between justification and sanctification, for most, the good works that accompany sanctification are evidence of salvation but do not earn merit toward one's salvation.

Law and gospel. Another key theme in Romans is the pairing of law and gospel. This was a particularly important theme for Melanchthon, who differentiated sharply between the two, emphasizing their differences and seeing them as two key works of God in human beings. The job of the former was

---

[83]See Felix Manz excerpt at Rom 6:4.
[84]John Calvin, *Institutes of the Christian Religion* 3.11.11.
[85]Melanchthon, *Commentary on Romans*, 25-26*. See excerpt at Rom 4:7.
[86]See Rom 1:18 below.
[87]See Calvin excerpt at Rom 4:6 below.

to invoke fear. The latter's purpose was to justify and bring to life those who had been driven to it by the fear. The former revealed sin and condemned it. The latter promised grace and delivered it through Christ.[88] The pairing of law and gospel came to serve as a hermeneutical principle for Melanchthon. He viewed all of Scripture through the dual lens, finding law in certain parts, gospel in others.[89]

Reflecting on Romans 3:20, Melanchthon identifies two uses of the moral law. The first is the political, involving an "external justice" that is meant to coerce unbelievers to behave, but it does not relate to the remission of sins.[90] This use is present in Romans 2:12 and Romans 3:19. The second use of moral law is the one present in the law-and-gospel pairing, accusing the conscience so as to drive it to the gospel. Later, in the second edition of his *Loci Communes* (1535), he would add a third use, that of providing the standards for believers' sanctification.

Calvin took a different approach toward the law-and-gospel pairing, viewing them as differing in clarity of manifestation rather than primarily being in opposition to each other. The term *law*, according to Calvin, was used frequently by Paul to be "that rule of holy living in which God exacts what is his due."[91] He did not see the gospel as offering a new method of salvation. Rather, it was the "substance" that was foreshadowed in the law. The patriarchs had spoken of it in advance, though without the clarity it takes on in the New Testament. The gospel thus confirms and fulfills the law. Calvin believed that the law served three purposes. The first is to reveal the reality of the individual's sin. Second, the law restrains sin and its effects in society. Third, the law functions as an instrument that teaches the Christian how to live in a manner that glorifies and honors God.

Good works and the transformed life. Given their emphasis on justification by faith alone, the reformers were vulnerable to the accusation of teaching that works did not matter at all. Many of the commentators responded to this directly, making it clear that although works do not save a person, they are nevertheless important. The gospel should transform one's life. For example, Vermigli, commenting on Romans 3:8, argues that "God does remit sins freely. But he does not, therefore, grant his people the freedom to sin." And thus he gives us the Holy Spirit and brings renewal to our lives. Justifying faith needs to be "accompanied continually by good works."[92]

Melanchthon, in seeking compromise in the Leipzig Interim, initially agreed to a statement that good works were essential to salvation. He meant it in the sense that they were necessary signs of the justification that did not itself include works, but he later regretted signing on to it since it could so easily be mistaken for claiming that good works earn merit. Georg Major, intending it to guard against antinomianism, picked up the idea, claiming in 1551 that "good works are essential to salvation." This resulted in the Majoristic Controversy, with Gnesio-Lutherans (ardent followers of Luther) becoming increasingly polarized from the Philippists (staunch followers of Melanchthon).

One of the ongoing tasks for the commentators on Romans was to harmonize Paul and James, since James's statement that faith without works is dead seemed at first to contradict Paul's saying

---

[88]For similar sentiments, see Luther excerpt in Rom 2:15.
[89]Melanchthon, *Loci Communes*, 91.
[90]See below at Rom 3:20.
[91]See Calvin excerpt in Rom 1:16 below.
[92]See Vermigli excerpt in Rom 3:8 below.

in Romans 3:28 that we are saved by faith, not works. A few reformers resorted to claiming that James was not canonical. But most found other ways of solving the seeming contradiction. One popular way was that Paul was speaking of the Christian being justified before God, whereas James was referring to someone being justified before other people.[93]

Most of the reformers held, in keeping with Augustine, that in Romans 7 Paul is speaking as a redeemed person.[94] This interpretation is very much in keeping with Luther's view of *simul iustus et peccator*, that the believer is simultaneously justified and still a sinner. The flesh and the spirit fight against each other, and sometimes the flesh wins, but the regenerate part is the stronger.[95] Anne Bradstreet turned Flesh and Spirit into characters and portrayed their battle in poetry.[96] There were only a few who disagreed that the Romans 7 Paul was regenerate. These included Jacobus Arminius and Faustus Sozzini (Socinus), who argued that Paul was referring to himself as he used to be under, before, or apart from the law rather than as a regenerate believer. When Arminius preached a series of sermons in 1592 on Romans 7, he was accused of Pelagianism for implying that someone could feel such concern about their sin before having the Holy Spirit in them.[97]

The golden chain. Richard Muller traces the roots of the theological term *ordo salutis* (order of salvation) back to the reformers' use of the phrase *armilla aurea* (golden chain) to refer to the series of stages of salvation listed in Romans 8:30. The phrase *ordo salutis* itself would not be used as a technical term until the early eighteenth century, but one can see the beginnings of the concept in the reformers' comments on this verse.[98] In the excerpts included in this volume, Calvin refers to this list as a "climax" (a rhetorical term for concepts listed in ascending order). Anthony Maxey (1606) and William Perkins each wrote treatises on the golden chain. The chain is composed of predestination, calling, justification, and glorification. All of the stages come from God and by his grace, and the four are linked together so that if the believer has one, he or she will have all of them. For many reformers, this implied that predestination thus necessarily included perseverance, and this could lead to a sense of eternal security and thus peace and joy.

The use of the early church fathers. In explicating the biblical text, the reformers made extensive use of a few of the early church fathers. David Steinmetz notes that, other than John Chrysostom's, there were very few full commentaries on Romans from the patristic era extant during the Reformation. One commentary was believed at the time to have been Ambrose's but is currently thought to have been by an anonymous person who is now referred to as Ambrosiaster. Another commentary, believed by the reformers to be by Jerome, was in fact by Pelagius. Origen's had been

---

[93]Balduin excerpt at Rom 3:20.

[94]See David C. Steinmetz, "Calvin and the Divided Self of Romans 7," in *Augustine, the Harvest, and Theology: Essays Dedicated to Heiko Augustinus Oberman in Honor of his Sixtieth Birthday*, ed. Kenneth Hagen (Leiden: Brill, 1990), 300-313.

[95]See Rollock excerpt in Rom 7:14.

[96]See Bradstreet excerpt in Rom 7:14.

[97]His treatise the *True and Genuine Sense of Romans 7* was published in 1612 after his death, by his nine children. Sozzini also published a treatise on Rom 7 around the same time. See their excerpts in Rom 7:14.

[98]See Richard Muller, *Calvin and the Reformed Tradition: On the Work of Christ and the Order of Salvation* (Grand Rapids: Baker Academic, 2012), 161-63.

translated into Latin by Rufinus. And a ninth-century collection of comments on Romans by Augustine had been compiled by Florus of Lyon; Augustine had not completed his commentary on Romans.[99] The reformers made generous use of these ancient commentaries, engaging them as conversation partners, and even sparring with them from time to time. Although they treated the fathers with respect, they did not grant them the same high level of authority the medieval commentators had.

Translation Matters

In keeping with the guidelines for the Reformation Commentary on Scripture, the occasional vitriolic rhetoric, characteristic of the time, has been cut out or toned down. Gender language in relation to humans has often been substituted with "person," "self," "us," "one," or "humanity," or adding "women" or "sisters" to "men" and "brothers." Terms such as "papist" or "papistical" have been replaced with "Roman Catholic" or "Catholic"; "sophists" with "scholastic theologians." Long sentences have been broken up. As often as possible, figures of speech have been kept in order to preserve flavor. Nineteenth-century translations have been modernized. Where syllogisms or enthymemes are emphasized, I have added (P1) for the major premise, (P2) for the minor premise, and (C) for the conclusion, in order to make the structure clearer. Overall, I have striven for dynamic equivalence rather than literal rendering, aiming for readability while still maintaining the accuracy of the theological wording.

The number and length of excerpts per historical figure does not necessarily relate to their prominence. Zwingli, for example, wrote a commentary, but his entries were very short. Cranmer didn't write a commentary on Romans at all, so it is difficult to find much by him on Romans. On the other hand, a few lesser-known figures such as Erasmus Sarcerius wrote highly detailed commentaries, so they are fairly frequently represented in the volume. At the same time, however, there are highly influential figures such as Bucer, Brenz, and Bugenhagen who have had very little translated from their Romans commentaries until now. They are therefore included in significant quantities in this volume.

Reading the Reformers on Romans 1–8

Reading the letter to the Romans with the reformers is a fascinating adventure, for in many ways they were going through the very transition that Paul discusses in Romans 1–8, which gave the letter an added sense of urgency and relevance to them. Luther expressed the deep emotion of that transition. He wrote, "I did not learn my theology all at once, but I had to search deeper for it, where my . . . *Anfechtungen* took me. . . . Not understanding, reading, or speculation, but living, nay, rather dying and being damned make a theologian."[100] *Anfechtung* is a combination of trial, tribulation, suffering, even depression. One could argue that *Anfechtungen* not only made Luther a theologian but also made the Reformation happen. In this it served a function parallel to what

---

[99]David C. Steinmetz, *The Bible in the Sixteenth Century* (Durham, NC: Duke University Press, 1990), 102 (the list is from him).
[100]WA, Tr 1:146; WA 5:163, in George, *Theology of the Reformers*, 61.

Paul pointed to with the law: it killed. Therefore, it led to the gospel. Luther's agony over his sin and the impossibility of being able to fully and adequately address it perhaps finds its parallel in the Old Testament law, whose role, according to Paul (Rom 7:7), was to bring acute awareness of sin. Here is where the medieval sacrament of penance had served an analogous function of highlighting sin on a daily basis. Thus, when Luther discovered—or rediscovered—the doctrine of justification by faith alone, it was as if he were personally moving from law to gospel, from Romans 1:18–3:20 to Romans 3:21–5:21. The resulting joy in his writing, and that of other reformers in his wake, is palpable. They exhort readers to make that same transition, from law (whether natural or Mosaic) to gospel, from death to life, from sorrow and fear to exultation.

Reading through the volume as a whole is also a bit like listening to a symphony.[101] The orchestra is large, comprising over 140 musicians. Some—such as Luther, Calvin, Melanchthon, Bucer, Vermigli, and Bugenhagen—like oboes and violins, carry the melody throughout. Others—John Bunyan and Samuel Rutherford, for example—like triangles, come in only once or twice. At first the music may feel unfamiliar and foreign. There are strange—occasionally off-putting—passages, bracing moments, and complex, highly intricate harmonies. But as one perseveres, one starts to hear the themes, and variations on themes, repeating motifs of *sola fide* and gratitude, of law and impossibility, of grace, of sin and sacrifice, and love. It begins in the dark tones of the early chapters, and builds slowly but surely from the law, to David and Abraham and Adam, to the second Adam, Christ, and in crescendo to a climax in Romans 8, where nothing, absolutely nothing, can separate us from God's love. When you listen to the symphony from beginning to end, beauty breaks through repeatedly.

At the heart of the symphony is what English Puritan John Preston refers to as "the great glorious mystery of the gospel."[102] In every pericope, verse after verse, writers keep bringing us back to the paired motifs of our sinful state and Christ's saving work. At the same time, the arc of the symphony as a whole tells the story of Romans 1–8, which is itself shaped by the gospel. The first movement evokes the darkness of sin, with long lists and detailed descriptions of transgressions put forward by the apostle and the psalmist(s) and elaborated by the commentators. No one is immune. All have sinned. All are responsible, whether by natural knowledge or by the law that God sends through Moses to invoke fear and force one to face one's distance from the holy God. Father Abraham appears, modeling the faith that will be the sole approach to God. He points toward the One to come, whose righteousness will be key. Then comes the startling arrival of the foreshadowed One, the holy God, in Christ, who stands in our place in bearing the consequences of Adam's sin and ours by becoming the second Adam, who atones for our sins. His righteousness is credited to us who believe. It is by faith alone, by grace alone, by Christ alone. Although we seek to grow in his likeness, by the power of the Holy Spirit, we continue to struggle with sin. But we need not be anxious, for the symphony rises to its climax. Now the lists are of what

---

[101]See an adaptation of this in Gwenfair Walters Adams, "Shock and Awe: The Reformers and the Stunning Joy of Romans 1–8," *Journal of the Evangelical Theological Society* 61, no. 2 (2018): 231-44.
[102]See John Preston excerpt at Rom 1:17.

Christ has conquered, of what we do not need to fear. For no matter what comes, we will be safe in Christ, both in facing the judgment of God and in whatever life brings, for nothing will be able to separate us from the love of our Savior. And thus in the climactic notes of the performance, an Anabaptist woman asks God to keep her "pure in joy" in the midst of imprisonment and potential martyrdom; the author of the *Institutes* speaks of the "fountain of love" that "flows to us from Christ"; an Anglican aristocrat finds peace and joy in her dying days through the comfort of Romans 8, which in turn gives form to her final words; and an Austrian pastor rejoices in the "something lovely and wonderful" that God reveals to us even in the midst of our suffering.

And then in the final notes of the final movement, the man who published more lectures and commentaries on Romans than anyone else in the 150-year period, brings it to resolution, boiling it all down to one simple declaration: "At the end of the consolation Paul repeats this proper and chief voice of the gospel—that God loves us. . . . In all terrors look on this comfort, *that God certainly loves you*."[103]

The reformers responded with stunned joy to the idea that "while we were still sinners, Christ died for us" (Rom 5:8). Martin Bucer exemplifies this and provides an appropriate exhortation to us with which to close the introduction to this volume. Commenting on Romans 5:6-8, he notes Paul's repeated juxtaposition of our sinfulness with Christ's suffering. Bucer—overcome by the love thus demonstrated by God and the extraordinary news that he offers salvation to us freely, through faith—asks us, his readers:

> If we carefully consider that although we were being completely carried away contrary to his one, holy, and perfect will, and although we were offending him in the gravest possible manner, he nevertheless, embraced us with such love that he willed that his Son should die in order to redeem us, and the Son himself submitted to this death with ardent longing—what could stand in the way that would prevent you from entirely handing yourself over and devoting yourself completely to this God and Savior of yours who loves you in such an incomparable way? How could you doubt that you will receive from him anything whatever that could be to your advantage? What thing could be burdensome for you to do or to suffer when you know that you're accepted by him? What else, finally, could there be that could so inflame us with true and lasting love toward our neighbors, and even toward our enemies? Such love could never take up residence in your soul as long as you were nothing but an ungodly person, a sinner, and an enemy to God—who is not only the Highest Good but also All Good. Nevertheless, he in his infinite love for you restored you to himself in fellowship of eternal life. With this thought carefully pondered by faith and always repeated within the heart, who would not let go of all other things that are not God and devote themselves to him alone so much that they would freely wish to think upon, seek after and live for nothing other than God?[104]

Soli Deo gloria.

---

[103]See Lady Anne Clifford, John Calvin, Hans Has von Halstatt, and Melanchthon (from which the quotation above is drawn) excerpts at Rom 8:30 below (emphasis added). Melanchthon, *Commentary on Romans*, 183*.
[104]Bucer, *Metaphrases et Enarrationes*, 250; citing Rom 5:6, 8, 10.

COMMENTARY ON ROMANS 1–8

OVERVIEW: In their prefatory comments, the Reformation-era interpreters extol the importance of the letter to the Romans, noting its centrality to all of Christian doctrine. They celebrate the letter in verse, summarize its contents and argument, and observe that it especially focuses on one central doctrine: justification by faith alone. Key concepts such as the law, gospel, and grace are introduced, as is the author of the letter, the apostle Paul. The reformers dedicate their commentaries to individuals and situate their work in relation to previously written commentaries. Finally, they address the reader, requesting prayer and suggesting how to approach the text spiritually.

THE MOST IMPORTANT PIECE IN THE NEW TESTAMENT. MARTIN LUTHER: This letter is truly the most important piece in the New Testament. It is purest gospel. It is well worth a Christian's while not only to memorize it word for word but also to occupy himself with it daily, as though it were the daily bread of the soul. It is impossible to read or to meditate on this letter too much or too well. The more one deals with it, the more precious it becomes and the better it tastes. Therefore I want to carry out my service and, with this preface, provide an introduction to the letter, insofar as God gives me the ability, so that everyone can gain the fullest possible understanding of it. Up to now it has been darkened by glosses† . . . and by many a useless comment, but it is in itself a bright light, almost bright enough to illumine the entire Scripture. . . .

We find in this letter, then, the richest possible teaching about what a Christian should know: the meaning of law, gospel, sin, punishment, grace, faith, justice, Christ, God, good works, love, hope, and the cross. We learn how we are to act toward everyone, toward the virtuous and sinful, toward the strong and the weak, friend and foe, and toward ourselves. Paul bases everything firmly on Scripture and proves his points with examples from his own experience and from the prophets, so that nothing more could be desired. Therefore it seems that St. Paul, in writing this letter, wanted to compose a summary of the whole of Christian and evangelical teaching that would also be an introduction to the whole Old Testament. Without doubt, whoever takes this letter to heart possesses the light and power of the Old Testament. Therefore each and every Christian should make this letter the habitual and constant object of their study. God grant us his grace to do so. Amen. PREFACE TO THE LETTER OF ST. PAUL TO THE ROMANS (1545).[1]

ALL CHRISTIAN DOCTRINE REVOLVES AROUND THIS BOOK. JOHANN WILD: Among the Pauline letters the one that he wrote to the Romans has been assigned the first place. That's not because he wrote it first, for at least two others, that to the Corinthians and that to the Thessalonians, had already preceded it. But this letter is deservedly given the first place, not only because it was written to the Romans among whom the most important affairs and the empire itself was then located, but also because it presents a particular

---

[1]Luther, *Preface to the Letter**. †Glosses are brief, interpretive notations.

text of Christian doctrine containing, as it were, a method of teaching of the whole of Scripture. Those who are even moderately literate are aware how profitable it may be to possess a way of teaching in accordance with the whole of doctrine. The whole of Christian teaching revolves around this book. The explanation of how we are justified before God, or what Christian righteousness really is, is the head and chief point of the whole of Christian doctrine. Hence Paul undertakes to clarify and illustrate this point in this letter. EXEGESIS OF ROMANS (1558).[2]

PURITY OF DOCTRINE, FOUND IN ROMANS, PROTECTS THE ROSE. NIELS HEMMINGSEN: The church of God in this world is not improperly compared to a rose born among thorns. For as thorns encircling a rose press against it and puncture it, they thereby only render it more fragrant. Similarly, the church, when hard-pressed on all sides, breathes out her fragrance all the more widely. By this exhaling, she emits her fragrance more effectively, and as a result, she also grows larger by new additions. This is what the history of the church sets in front of those who read it, and that to which the experience of all the saints bears witness.

The thorns surrounding this rose that crowd it and puncture it are the thistles and tares of heresy, of tyranny, hypocrisy, shameful acts, and various scandals in doctrine and morals, and—to say no more—spurious, woody, and dry stalks that cause no small harm to the true and genuine rose. Satan, that *aspondos* [implacable] enemy of Christ, scatters and sows these thorns so that he might squeeze and suffocate the rose that Christ planted with his own hand, clearly wishing to reduce her to nonexistence. Or, if he is unable to do that, he aims to at least prevent her from spreading her flowers and branches more widely. . . .

What is truly necessary for preserving the church is purity of doctrine. This has been found to be one and the same thing in all the church

histories that have been written, and holy discipline in morals serves as its handmaid. For this purity of doctrine is that life-giving spring out of which the Lord's rose blooms, so that she will not be suffocated or wither away even among the many thorns of tyranny, hypocrisy, sophistry, and scandals. This purity of doctrine is not to be sought after from any other source than from that saving fountain, that is, the writings of the prophets and apostles, among which the letters of Paul hold no mean rank, and especially that which he wrote to the Romans.

For this letter in a particular way demonstrates and explains the chief points of true doctrine. For this reason I believe it should be read and known with singular diligence by all pious persons. But so that it might be more properly understood by simpler persons and by novices with less experience in sacred theology, I have resolved to publish a commentary of sorts on this book, hoping that good and pious men and women will not disapprove of my intention. But even though I am aware that the judgment of certain persons opposes us, still I did not wish to defraud the many good men and women who await my small work on account of a few who think ill of it. COMMENTARY ON ROMANS (1562).[3]

INTRODUCTION TO PAUL. JOHANNES BRENZ: In order to explain this letter that the apostle Paul wrote to the Romans, before anything else I will first say a few things about Paul, the author of this letter, and then I will set forth in a few words the essence of this letter, so that we will know what we should expect to find in it.

Now as to what pertains to Paul, Christ himself, the only-begotten Son of God, gave a testimony concerning him. For when he was divinely converted from the synagogue of the Jews to the church of the sons of God, and from being a persecutor became instead an apostle of Christ, he was called by a heavenly voice a *skeuos tēs eklogēs*, or a "chosen instrument," "to bear my name before Gentiles and

---

[2]Wild, *Exegesis in Epistolam*, 4r-4v.

[3]Hemmingsen, *Commentarius in Epistolam*, A2r-A2v; B2v-B3r.

kings, and before the children of Israel." Even though at first he had cruelly persecuted the church and the gospel of Christ, his teaching has thereby more authority insofar as it was all the more amazing that he came to a knowledge of Christ. For he did not abandon the Pharisaism that he once professed by any kind of fickleness of mind, but he converted to Christianity only when moved by a miracle from heaven. And he learned his gospel not from men and women here on earth, but from Christ himself in heaven, now sitting and reigning at the right hand of God. For he was caught up to Paradise, and also to the third heaven, and apart from the many secrets that he heard and that cannot be revealed on this earth with human words, he received also the very gospel from Christ himself, which he would later publish through the whole world. Nor was this another gospel than the one that Christ had earlier taught in this world and that the other apostles had learned. Therefore, the greatest confirmation of the truth of his doctrine is that Paul had come to know the very same thing in heaven that the rest of the apostles had received on earth. "Paul an apostle," he says, "not from men and women, nor by men and women, but by Jesus Christ and God the Father who raised him from the dead"; and "the gospel that is preached by me is not according to men and women. For neither did I receive it from men and women, nor did I learn it, but through a revelation of Jesus Christ." So that Paul would not be lacking in any authority to preach the gospel, Christ did not send him in secret and without public commendation, but adorned and marked him with such a great gift of working miracles that he not only raised the dead with his presence, but even the handkerchiefs and aprons taken from his body (according to Luke) laid on the sick pulled them back from sickness and caused evil spirits to depart. These were his letters of commendation, which are commonly called "letters of credit," by which the heavenly Father wished to commend to the world the authority of Paul and the truthfulness of his gospel. One could rightly say many other things about Paul, but since a man's speech shows the true shape of his soul, I would rather that by

this commemoration of mine we come to know who Paul is from his own words, which he has given us in written letters. COMMENTARY ON ROMANS (1564).[4]

THE BACKGROUND TO ROMANS. HULDRYCH ZWINGLI: The apostle gives thanks to Christ for prospering the Romans, and rejoices greatly on account of their faith, which was reported throughout the whole world. Then he attempts to settle a disagreement and controversy that existed among them. For it so happened that there were Roman believers from both the Jews and the Gentiles, and each was haughty in thinking too highly of themselves. Each side was setting themselves above the other and esteeming themselves as more loved by God and pleasing to him than the other. The Gentiles (who opposed the Jews as being profane and unworthy of Christ) think that they have an excuse before God for their unbelief, since they possessed neither the law, nor the prophets, nor a covenant by which they could know and worship God. They therefore thought of themselves as being excused in the sight of God and the world, or at least as being far better than the Jews. For the Jews had the law and the prophets and the divine oracles, including prophecies of the coming Christ, and nevertheless they crucified Christ the Savior, and therefore were made unworthy of Christ. The Jews, on the other hand, were so envious of the gospel going to the Gentiles that they would not allow it to be preached to them in any way, claiming that the promise of a Savior was given to them alone, not to the Gentiles. Paul explodes this quarrel, placing himself as an intermediary between the Jews and Gentiles, and shows that both are sinners, and that through Christ those of both origins are now one and same people, one holy church. He then proves by the strongest witnesses drawn from the Old Testament that both were going to be saved through Christ, and that not because of any works but only by the grace of God through Christ. In the end he adds a moral section concerning the true worship of God

---

[4]Brenz, *In Epistolam*, 5-6; citing Acts 9:15; Gal 1:1, 11-12; Acts 19:12.

and works, and how they should act in external matters. ANNOTATIONS ON ROMANS (1539).[5]

THE TIMING OF THE LETTER IN PAUL'S LIFE.
GEORG MAJOR: In the twenty-second year of Paul's conversion, the fifty-fifth year after Christ's birth, and the thirteenth year of Claudius's reign—after the Ephesian tumult had been sedated—Paul traveled to Macedonia, visiting the cities and churches where he had taught before. In the city of Philippi, having written the second letter to the Corinthians, which he sent through Titus and Luke, whom he sent ahead to collect alms in Corinth and Achaia and coming soon after them, he remained in Greece and particularly in Corinth for three months. At that time the letter to the Romans, written in Corinth, was sent through Phoebe a minister of the church at Cenchreae. Now Paul had spent his time continually proclaiming the gospel to all from Jerusalem to Illyricum, as he reports in Romans 15, where he says, "Now I must travel to Jerusalem to minister to the saints." For it seems that to Macedonia and Achaia . . . he sent ahead Titus and Luke from Corinth to collect alms in order to share fellowship with the poor saints who were in Jerusalem. LIFE OF PAUL.[6]

PREPARATION FOR PREACHING THE GOSPEL.
CHARLES FERME AND ANDREW MELVILLE: The apostle, being about to proceed to Rome, sends this letter on before him, in which it appears to be his aim and design to prepare the minds of the Romans by it—as by a sort of *Isagoge*[†]—for hearing and eagerly embracing the gospel when he himself should come and preach it. He seems, therefore, purposely to select for discussion in this letter the position "that the gospel is the power of God unto salvation," that is, that the gospel is the sole truth according to which God is rightly worshiped, and that brings righteousness, peace, and eternal life to men and women. Having discussed this, he, by way of an appendix or

inference, exhorts us to a life worthy of the gospel, which is the second part of the preparation. LOGICAL ANALYSIS OF THE EPISTLE OF PAUL TO THE ROMANS (1651).[7]

THE SCOPE OF THE EPISTLE. THOMAS WILSON:
Timotheus:[†] What is the scope of this letter?

Silas: To teach the way of obtaining true righteousness, which is not by works but by a lively faith in Christ Jesus.

Timotheus: Are there any more matters handled in this letter?

Silas: Yes, sundry and most weighty, as namely: about original corruption; sanctification; spiritual combat; the use of the law; of the remnants of sin; the benefits of afflictions; the constancy of believers; election; reprobation; rejection; provocation of the Jews; moral, ecclesiastical, and political duties; Christian liberty; and familiar matters.

Timotheus: What reasons may move us to love and study this letter?

Silas: (1) The worthiness and variety of the matter. (2) The method and order of writing, which is very exact. (3) The dignity of the instrument or pen-man, who was an apostle that had seen visions and revelations. (4) The majesty and wisdom of the Author, who is the God of wisdom and majesty. . . .

Timotheus: Why was this letter set before the rest of Paul's letter?

Silas: It was not because it was written before all the others, nor because of the great dignity of the Roman nation—being then lords of almost the whole earth—nor for the excellency of the Roman church—which consisted of Gentiles and was inferior to the church of the Jews, who were the olive tree, others being wild olives—nor yet for the length of this letter, as some have imagined, but for the exceeding worth and use of the matter handled in it. For besides the main article of justification by faith, defined, debated, and determined, there are other

---

[5]Zwingli, *In Evangelicam Historiam*, 497.
[6]Major, *Vita S. Pauli Apostoli*, C7v-C8r; citing Rom 16:1-2; 15:25. Cf. RCS NT 6:274-75.

[7]Ferme and Melville, *Logical Analysis*, 1*. [†]Isagogue: an introduction, opening a case. Ferme may be referring specifically to Porphyry's *Isagogue*, an introduction to Aristotle's *Categories* and a well-known medieval university textbook.

questions and points of Christian faith of great moment and profit: the fall of humanity, the force of original corruption, the restoration of men and women by Christ; of the sweet and manifold fruits of justifying faith, also of sanctification; of the cross and comfort to those that bear it; of predestination; of the vocation of Gentiles; of the breaking off and grafting in again of the Jews; of good works; of magistracy, of charity, of the use of things indifferent,[†] of the diversity of gifts, and functions of the church. So this letter was, out of good respect, set before the rest as the key to open the way to understand the others, and as a catechism or introduction to our most holy religion. Also, the most exact and accurate method of this letter deserved that it have a preface; so, after the proem, Paul defines justification, declaring what it is. . . . Also, he expresses the various causes of it: (1) Efficient: God's grace (2) Material: Christ Jesus dead and raised to life. (3) The Formal: our belief of the gospel (4) The Final or remote end: the praise of God's righteousness; the nearest end, our salvation.[§] A COMMENTARY UPON THE MOST DIVINE EPISTLE OF ST. PAUL TO THE ROMANS (1614).[8]

Summaries of the Content of Romans 1–8

CONDENSED FORM OF ERASMUS'S ARGUMENT.

ANDREAS KNOPKEN: Erasmus weaves together a rather complex argument, but it can be more concisely stated this way: that Paul teaches that both Jews and Gentiles who have come together within Christianity by virtue of faith in Christ are transgressors of the divine law. Neither did the written law profit the Jews, nor the law divinely inscribed on the minds of men and women— which they call the "law of nature"—profit the Gentiles, but both are guilty before God, as many scriptural testimonies prove. To both, he then

offers Christ, through justifying faith, who is the *end*, or the fulfillment, "of the law for righteousness to all who believe." He both forgives sins and imparts the justifying Spirit, who transforms our affections so that we are made into a new creation and so that we might be righteous not only in the eyes of men and women by our works, which is what the law demands of us, but also inwardly in our mind and affections, which are known only to God. Only the Spirit of Christ can make this happen, who transforms whomever he moves upon into new men and women, just as Samuel said to Saul. Then he goes on to teach, last, that however it might be the case that we are righteous in the eyes of God only by faith in Christ, that works do not confer righteousness, and that by them "no flesh will be justified before God." Yet because we are still burdened by impure flesh and justification is required until the day that "this mortal shall put on immortality," we must keep the flesh in subjection to our mind by virtuous efforts.

And so that we might not think that the preaching of the grace of God means we no longer have to do good works—and so change that liberty into which Christ set us free into an occasion for the flesh so that we make it into a cloak for wickedness—he then launches into the moral section of the letter, along various topics. Just before the end he admonishes them to show tolerance toward the weak and superstitious until they also mature in Christ "into a perfect man or woman."

This letter was written from Corinth, a city of Achaia, and carried by Phoebe, a Roman woman from Cenchreae who was sent by the apostle. It is in this letter especially, along with that written to the Galatians, that Paul pays special attention to and exalts the role of faith, against the Pharisaic "workers," showing that trust in Christ alone justifies for obtaining salvation or glory. But the works belonging to those who are thus justified are the fruits of a good tree, and such works without faith are sins, however much they might be marvelous and magnificent in the eyes of men and women: "for whatever is not of faith is sin," and

---

[8]Wilson, *Commentarie*, 3-4*. [†]Wilson uses a fictional dialogue format. [‡]Referring to the *adiaphora*, theological and spiritual matters that are debatable rather than essential to the faith. [§]Aristotle's four causes.

"without faith no person can please God." OF THE EPISTLE TO THE ROMANS.[9]

SUMMARY OF CHAPTERS 1–4. JOHN OWEN: In the first chapters of this letter, the apostle, from Scripture and the constant practice of all sorts of men and women of all ages, Jews and Gentiles, wise and barbarians, proves all the world, and every individual in it, to "have sinned and come short of the glory of God." And not only so, but that it was utterly impossible that by their own strength, or by virtue of any assistance communicated or privileges enjoyed, they would ever be able to attain to a righteousness of their own that might be acceptable to God.

So, he concludes that discourse with these two positive assertions:

First, that for what is past, "every mouth must be stopped, and all the world become guilty before God."

Second, for the future, though they should labor to amend their ways, and improve their assistances and privileges to a better advantage than formerly, "yet by the deeds of the law no flesh will be justified in the sight of God."

Now, since it is the main drift of the apostle in this letter, and in his whole employment, to manifest that God has not shut up all of humanity hopeless and remediless under this condition, he immediately discovers and opens the rich supply that God, in free grace, has made and provided for the deliverance of his own from this calamitous estate. That is, by the righteousness of faith in Christ, which he unfolds, asserts, proves, and vindicates from objections, to the end of the third chapter.

This is a matter of great weight, comprising in itself the sum of the gospel with which Paul was entrusted. It involves the honor and exaltation of Christ, which above all he desired; the great design of God to be glorious in his saints; and, in a word, is the chief subject of the message committed to him from Christ. This gospel is that those who neither have, nor by any means can attain, a

righteousness of their own by the best of their own working, may yet have that which is complete and *irrefusable* in Christ, by believing. Paul, therefore, strongly confirms this in the fourth chapter, by testimony and example from the Scripture, with the ancient saints. He thus also declares that though the manifestation of this mystery was not more fully opened by Christ from the bosom of the Father, yet, ever since sin entered the world, this has been the only way for anyone to appear in the presence of God.

To make his demonstrations even more evident, he singles out one person as an example: someone who was eminently known and confessed by all to have been the friend of God, to have been righteous and justified before him, and thereby to have held sweet communion with him all his days. To wit, Abraham. . . .

Now, concerning him, the apostle proves abundantly, in the beginning of the fourth chapter, that the justification that he found, and the righteousness he attained, was purely that—and no other—which he described before; to wit, a righteousness in the forgiveness of sins through faith in the blood of Christ. Yes, and that all the privileges and exaltations of this Abraham, which made him so signal and eminent among the saints of God as to be called "the father of the faithful," were merely from this, that this righteousness of grace was freely discovered and fully established to him. An enjoyment was granted to him in a peculiar manner by faith whereby the Lord Christ—with the whole spring of the righteousness previously mentioned—was enwrapped. This the apostle pursues, with sundry and various inferences and conclusions, to the end of verse 17, chapter 14.

Having laid this down, in the next place Paul gives us a description of the faith by which Abraham became the inheritor of those excellent things. . . . So that, just as his justification was proposed as an example of God's dealing with us by his grace, so his faith might be laid down as a pattern for us in receiving that grace. SERMON ON ROMANS 4:20.[10]

---

[9]Knopken, *In Epistolam ad Romanos* (1524), A4r-A4v; citing Rom 10:4; 1 Sam 10:6; Rom 3:20; 1 Cor 15:54; Eph 4:13; Rom 14:23; Heb 11:6.

[10]Owen, *Works*, 8:211-12*; citing Rom 3:19-20.

The Argument of Romans 1–8. Giovanni Diodati: Now, although the New Testament letters were written for particular occasions, yet divine providence directed the apostles to include in them the necessary exposition of all the chief topics of Christian doctrine, and St. Paul, who spoke more than anyone else, also wrote more; and he more expansively and deeply unfolded all the mysteries of salvation, the duties of serving God, and the rules of lawful government and discipline in the church. He also mixed in excellent revelations of things to come, which God had manifested to him. Among all the letters of this great "vessel of election," the one to the Romans holds the first degree in all categories, for in it, Paul lays open each part of Christ's benefit in most exquisite order, as well as the duties of grateful response and service to which all believers are bound. The Romans to whom he writes were believers among the Gentiles that were assembled in Rome, where the gospel had been carried even before the apostles came there. And as the apostleship of the Gentiles had fallen to Paul's lot, so he performed this great duty toward it—after he had for a long time caused it to shine with the incomparable gifts of God's grace—to instruct and edify it with this divine letter, which may very well be called the great sea of Christian doctrine. And in it, after he had in the beginning set down his vocation and desire to contribute to the advancement of the faith of those who believed in Rome, he shows that the gospel received by faith is the only and most powerful means to obtain true righteousness before God, and by the means of it, life—seeing that all men and women, because of sin, are subject to God's wrath and curse. The Gentiles are condemned by the law of nature imprinted in their hearts, and the Jews much more by Moses' law, which yields no man or woman any prerogative to righteousness, but instead makes their coming judgment worse, since having the knowledge of the law, they do not live in correspondence with it by obeying it entirely. And therefore Paul concludes that all men and women, to avoid being condemned, must seek outside themselves the

righteousness that they lack, looking to Christ in whom this treasure is laid up, for the remission of sins, and full justification of sinners. And that as God presents this righteousness out of his mere grace, and to all nations, so the only means to receive it is by lively faith. It is without any necessity or use of circumcision or other ceremonies of the law. And men and women's own works do not in any way contribute power to it. And Paul demonstrates it by the example of Abraham, the father of all believers, and the general pattern of faith. Then he goes on to declare the effects of faith, and of God's fatherly love in Christ, which are peace and quiet of conscience toward God, security, joy, and spiritual rejoicing in tribulations, and assured hope of everlasting glory. And he concludes this part by showing the foundation and ground of all this communication of Christ to his believers, which is God's order, who has established Christ to be the head and stock of his church. He did this so that from him might derive into her the virtue of his righteousness to justification, everlasting life and happiness—just as Adam was the natural head of all men and women, enclosing and enfolding them all in his sin, and consequently into his death and condemnation. Then Paul comes to the subsequent, and inseparable benefit of sanctification, which is brought forth in believers by the Holy Spirit, so that they may resemble Jesus Christ their head, by virtue of which the believer does not fight any more against the law of God. And again, the law is not an instigation for the believer to sin, to incense and harden him, but rather, a loving and friendly guide and rule of holiness. The believer willingly and peaceably frames and co-orders his will and actions to the law, though still with much weakness and repugnancy at the remainders of flesh within. God leaves those remainders in those that are his for a continual exercise and spur to their sides, to cause them to sigh after their perfect deliverance and freedom in the heavenly life to come. And therefore Paul comforts them by telling them that those firstfruits of the Holy Spirit—his motions and strivings—are to them a sure earnest of God's love, of their conjunction with Christ, and of their adoption, justification, and future inheritance and glory, which they at the present taste, but only in faith and hope, but which is nevertheless infallible, being grounded on God's everlasting decree. And therefore there also grows in them a firm confidence against all the assaults of the devil and the world, both internal or external. PIOUS AND LEARNED ANNOTATIONS.[11]

ROMANS 1–8 IN VERSE. RUDOLF GWALTHER:

Chapter 1
I often wished to come and see my Roman
    brothers,
But mighty God obstructed my prayer.
Then [Paul] teaches from where all vicious evils
    come;
They come from disregarding the holy will of God.

Chapter 2
All those born in the human race have sinned
And all deserve God's anger.
And lest the Jewish peoples think they are exempt,
Paul teaches what it will mean to be truly a Jew.

Chapter 3
Glorious Israel, howevermuch the fame of the
    nation rises,
Nevertheless, incurred penalties for sins.
And indeed, they do not benefit from the sacred
    writings of the law;
The abounding grace of God alone helps sinful
    people.

Chapter 4
The prophet Abraham believed in the truthful-
    ness of God
This faith gave pleasure to God, not being
    doubted.
Thus all who believe are declared children of
    Abraham.
Faith alone is able to reconcile [us] to the Lord.

Chapter 5
He describes the beginning of the holy gift of
    faith,

Revealing how great the grace of the Lord will
    be
He tells of the fount whence the error of sin
    arose,
And that Fount from whence the grace of faith
    now flows.

Chapter 6
To sin the doors must now be closed, he says.
It's faith's duty then to live in holy deeds.
Being recently made pure from the filth of sin,
Now with a holy mind go on to strive after God.

Chapter 7
He teaches with heavenly [wisdom] the
    function of the law,
And how it lays its heavy yoke upon us.
It shows us hidden sin that escapes our notice.
But for us who are in Christ, our nurturing
    faith has set us free.

Chapter 8
No condemnation is able to afflict the faithful.
Truly, God becomes our Father when the Spirit
    makes it so.
And [Paul] writes that the summit of the
    Father's love is so great
That neither cross nor violent death is able to
    steal it.

SUMMARY OF THE BIBLE IN POETRY (1543).[12]

Key Concepts

THE ESSENTIAL CHARACTER OF THE LETTER. JOHANNES BUGENHAGEN: The first thing to be observed in this letter is that herein Paul charges that all men and women are sinners and very plainly shows that they are all sons and daughters of wrath and of eternal damnation. After he achieves this, he declares how we may be justified, that is, through Christ by faith alone. This is the essential character of this letter, and everything else that he discusses throughout this whole letter is

---

[11]Diodati, *Pious and Learned Annotations*, Cc3v*.

[12]Gwalther, *Argumenta Omnium*, 118r-118v. Adapted from original translation and versification by Paul Watkins.

referred back to this. Therefore, let those who seek true righteousness from some other source be ashamed. But all men and women do this. There is nobody who does not know that the Jews seek after righteousness in their ceremonies, by which they confess themselves to be, in fact, unrighteous. The Gentiles likewise seek the same thing by the worship of idols, thus accusing themselves of their own unrighteousness. But if they seek righteousness by means of their works, what else are such miserable people doing than trying to wash away excrement with excrement? For an evil tree cannot possibly bear good fruit, nor can Israel attain to righteousness by pursuing the righteousness of the law. INTERPRETATION OF ROMANS (1527).[13]

THE WHOLE CAUSE OF WRITING THE LETTER. WILLIAM TYNDALE: The sum and whole cause of the writing of this letter is to prove that we are justified by faith alone. If you deny this proposition, not only will this letter and all that Paul writes, but also the whole of Scripture, be so locked up that you shall never understand it to your soul's health. And to bring us to the understanding and feeling that faith alone justifies, Paul proves that the whole nature of humanity is so poisoned, so corrupt, and so dead concerning godly living or godly thinking that it is impossible for anyone to keep the law in the sight of God. That is to say, it is impossible to love the law—and out of love and willingness, to do it as naturally as a person eats or drinks—unless we have been quickened again and healed through faith. And by "justifying" understand no other thing than to be reconciled to God, to be restored to his favor, and to have your sins forgiven. And when I say God justifies us, understand thereby that God, for Christ's sake, merits, and deserving alone, receives us unto his mercy, favor, and grace, and forgives us our sins. And when I say Christ justifies us, understand thereby that Christ alone has redeemed us, bought, and delivered us out of the wrath of God and damnation, and has

with his works alone purchased us the mercy, the favor, and grace of God, and the forgiveness of our sins. And when I say that faith justifies, understand thereby that faith and trust in the truth of God and in the mercy promised us for Christ's sake—and for his deserving and works alone—that quiets the conscience and certifies her that our sins are forgiven and that we are in the favor of God.

Furthermore, set before your eyes Christ's works and your own works. Christ's works alone justify you and make satisfaction for your sin; your own works do not. That is to say, only Christ's works can quiet your conscience and make sure that your sins are forgiven; your own works cannot. For the promise of mercy is made to you for Christ's work's sake, and not for your own work's sake.

Therefore, seeing that God has not promised that your own works will save you, therefore faith in your own works can never quiet your conscience nor certify you before God that your sins are forgiven when God comes to judge and to take a reckoning. Beyond all this, my own works can never satisfy the law or pay what I owe it. For I owe the law to love it with all my heart, soul, power, and might, which I will never be able to pay while I am enclosed with flesh. No, I cannot begin to love the law until I first am sure, by faith, that God loves me and forgives me.

Finally, it ought to offend no one that we say, "Faith alone justifies." For if it is true that Christ alone redeemed us, that Christ alone bore our sins, made satisfaction for us, and purchased for us the favor of God, then it must be true that only trust in Christ's deserving and in the promises of God the Father—made to us for Christ's sake—can quiet the conscience and certify that our sins are forgiven. And when they say, "People must repent, forsake sin, and purpose to sin no more, as much as they can, and love the law of God. Therefore, faith alone does not justify," I answer, "That and all similar arguments are nothing, such as: I must repent and be sorry; the gospel must be preached to me, and I must believe it, or else I cannot be a partaker of mercy, which Christ has deserved for

---

[13]Bugenhagen, *In Epistolam Pauli ad Romanos*, IV-2r; citing Rom 9:31.

me. Therefore Christ alone does not justify me; or Christ alone has not made satisfaction for my sins." Just as this is a naughty argument, so is the other.

Now, reader, go and act according to the order of Paul's writing. First, behold yourself diligently in the law of God, and there observe your just damnation. Second, turn your eyes to Christ, and see there the exceeding mercy of your most kind and loving Father. Third, remember that Christ did not make this atonement so that you would anger God again. Nor did he die for your sins so that you would return, as a swine, to your old puddle again; but rather so that you would be a new creature and live a new life according to the will of God, and not to the flesh. And be diligent, so that you do not lose this favor and mercy again through your own negligence and ingratitude. Farewell. PROLOGUE UPON THE EPISTLE OF ST. PAUL TO THE ROMANS (1526).[14]

WHAT IS THE MORAL LAW? CASPAR CRUCIGER: The moral law is the eternal and unchanging wisdom in the divine mind and the rule in God's will that he has made evident in creation inasmuch as glimmers of his wisdom have been instilled in creatures that possess reason, and which, therefore, gives knowledge about the nature of God, in his very own voice. It sanctifies us so that as rational creatures, we might agree with his mind and righteousness. And it condemns with horrible wrath those natures that are disagreeable, that is, who do not render full obedience. Those who stupidly imagine that these decrees are outside of God and changeable like Solon's tablets[†] or that of a Roman council[‡] posted on the city walls where they could later be removed, think of the law in a poor and paltry way. Men and women are greatly ensnared by this childish conception. And a blind sense of security, without feeling any great discomfort, is strengthened in men's and women's minds by such antinomian dreams. It behooves us instead to believe that God, the just judge, will destroy with horrible wrath those natures disagreeable to

his, as the conscience experiences this judgment with genuine discomfort when it begins to understand this saying: "the law brings about wrath," and also "by the law, sin becomes more abundantly chargeable," and in 1 Corinthians 15: "the sting of death is sin, and the strength of sin is the law." COMMENTARY ON ROMANS (1567).[15]

WHAT IS THE GOSPEL? CASPAR CRUCIGER: The "gospel" is the preaching of repentance and the promise. Because reason does not naturally comprehend it, it must be divinely revealed, having been disclosed from the eternal Father's bosom through the Son as mediator, in which on whose account God (1) affirms that he remits sins, (2) regards men and women as righteous, and also (3) sanctifies them, the Holy Spirit being through that very Son placed in their hearts, and (4) gives them eternal life. And that he gives all these good things freely through faith, that is, to those believing the gospel, its peculiar promise being this: that these goods are given on account of the Son of God, not because of our worthiness. Here we must carefully consider a distinction between promises. There are promises in the law, as in Leviticus 18 and Ezekiel 20: "whoever shall do them shall live by them"; but the promises of the law are conditional; that is, they stipulate the condition of full obedience, requiring that the whole self be conformed to God. Accordingly, men and women *would* live by them if life (that is, God himself) were in them rather than sin being in them. But the promise of the gospel is offered freely; that is, it is granted on account of the Son of God, not because of our worthiness or any of our works.

Therefore, so that the distinction between the law and the gospel might be more evident, two terms must be kept in view: "on account of Christ" and "freely [*gratis*]." This is how we understand in

---

[14]Tyndale, *Doctrinal Treatises*, 508-10*.

[15]Cruciger, *In Epistolam Pauli*, 6-7; citing Rom 4:15, 5:20, 1 Cor 15:56. [†]Solon was the sixth-century-BC Athenian who posted the laws on wooden tablets, but with only a one-hundred-year term of enactment, after which they would cease to be valid. [‡]Lit. *decemvir* (ten men), a fifth-century-BC council of ten magistrates who wrote up laws for Rome.

the [Apostles'] Creed that article "I believe in the remission of sins": it is given to me freely on account of the Son of God as mediator. For the conscience does not suffer pangs in disputing whether God remits sin or whether he is merciful, but whether he *freely* remits the sins of the unworthy and also whether he remits them to *you*. This preaching of the gospel is to be believed, which so often repeats the exclusive particle "freely." It is also a universal promise, according to Matthew 11: "Come to me all you who labor and are heavy laden, and I will give you rest." And yet it is still necessary that the gospel be heard and accepted by faith, and indeed when we are strengthened by the preaching and contemplation of the gospel the Son of God works effectively within us at the same time, kindling faith and rejoicing the heart by the Holy Spirit which is given to us, according to Romans 1, "The gospel is the power of God unto salvation for all who believe," and Galatians 3, "that we might receive the promise of the Spirit through faith." COMMENTARY ON ROMANS (1567).[16]

WHAT IS GRACE? CASPAR CRUCIGER: It is to be lamented that the word "grace" (*gratia*) is so greatly obscured by the interpretations of the monks, the greater part of whom understand grace to be a new quality that is divinely infused. . . . For when speaking of this subject when we say that "sins are remitted for man and woman by grace," the term "grace" does not properly mean infused qualities but is understood in a relative sense to refer to God's promised mercy or freely given acceptance of us on account of the Son of God. For it is necessary when encountering the word "grace" to understand that both the terms "freely given" (*gratis*) and "mediator" are implied in it. And yet it is also true that when the remission of sins is received, the Holy Spirit is also always given, through whom the self is made into a temple of God when its heart is made alive and raised up out of the terrors of hell.

Let this then serve as a definition: Grace is the (1) freely granted remission of sins, and (2) reconciliation or acceptance of us bestowed *freely* by God's mercy on account of the Son of God. Although it is certain that it is always accompanied by the gift of the Holy Spirit, by whom the Father and the Son breathing on us sanctify our hearts and join us to themselves that we might become God's temple as is stated in 1 John 3, "by his Spirit which he gave to us" and in Galatians 4, "God sent the Spirit of his Son into our hearts, crying out 'Abba, Father.'" Now, the remission of sins is a liberation from real terrors and pains, a liberation in which the Son of God himself makes us alive and comforts us by his Holy Spirit, whom we truly receive when the preaching of the gospel is heard and laid hold of by faith. As a result of this comforting, our hearts experience a rejoicing and become acquainted with God's mercy and presence, and a true invocation is kindled within us, like what is said in that sweetest discourse in Zechariah 12: "I will pour out upon the house of David the spirit of grace and of prayer." That is, the Holy Spirit bears witness both in the ministration of the gospel and within our hearts that we are "in grace"—that is, that we are accepted freely by God on account of the Mediator. The Spirit is also he who in the ministration of the gospel shows us how to genuinely call on God, and also moves our hearts so that they grow in trust toward God through the Mediator. In this way a new beginning and eternal life are kindled within us. COMMENTARY ON ROMANS (1567).[17]

ON PREVIOUS COMMENTATORS. JOHN CALVIN: Of the ancients who have, by their piety, learning, holiness, and also by their age, gained so much authority that we ought to despise nothing of what they have adduced, I will say nothing; and with regard to those who live at this day, it is of no benefit to mention them all by name: Of those who have spent most labor in this work, I will express my opinion.

---

[16]Cruciger, *In Epistolam Pauli*, 10-11; citing Lev 18:5; Ezek 20:11; Mt 11:28; Rom 1:16; Gal 3:14.

[17]Cruciger, *In Epistolam Pauli*, 12-13; citing Zech 12:10; 1 Jn 3:24; Gal 4:6.

Philipp Melanchthon, who, by his singular learning and industry, and by that readiness in all kinds of knowledge in which he excels, has introduced more light than those who had preceded him. But as it seems to have been his object to examine only those things that are mainly worthy of attention, he dwelt at large on these, and designedly passed by many things that common minds find to be difficult. Then follows Bullinger, who has justly attained no small praise; for with learning he has connected plainness, for which he has been highly commended. In the last place comes Bucer, who, by publishing his works, has given as it were the finishing stroke. For in addition to his recondite learning and enlarged knowledge of things, and to the clearness of his mind, and much reading and many other excellencies, in which he is hardly surpassed by any at this day, equaled by few and excelled by still fewer—he possesses, as you know—this praise as his own— that no one in our age has been with so much labor engaged in the work of expounding Scripture. EPISTLE TO GRYNAEUS.[18]

A PRAYER, AN APPEAL, AND AN EXHORTATION. DAVID RUNGE: We pray that the Son of God, that Fount of all wisdom and knowledge, by whose Spirit this letter was dictated and written, would mercifully see fit to bestow on us the firstfruits of his celestial heavens so that we might happily carry out to its end this holy endeavor of ours. We appeal to benevolent and honest readers that they might help our effort with their dedicated and pious prayers. We exhort studious youths to diligently read the apostle's text and thus equipped, also tie in the analyses of others. In this way we trust that our labor in the Lord will by no means be in vain. DISPUTATION ON ROMANS (1595).[19]

DEDICATION OF COMMENTARY. ANDREW WILLET: To the most Christian, right noble, most excellent, and mighty prince, James, by the grace of God, king of Great Britain, France, and Ireland, Defender of the True Christian Faith, and so on, and Gracious Sovereign.

As I have this far (by God's special grace assisting me) travailed in some books of the Old Testament, so now I have attempted to do the like in the New: "For as one cannot sail in the sea without fear who has not first tried the rivers," so the deep sea of mysteries in the new law cannot well be sounded, unless we have first coasted by the old. . . .

And thus having made an entrance into the apostolic writings, I have made the choice of St. Paul's letters, and among them of this to the Romans, which is as a key to the rest. . . . There are few old heretical positions or new [Roman Catholic] errors, which if they are propounded plainly, may not be confuted by this letter. . . .

We bless God, who has raised up Your Majesty as a notable instrument both of discovering and dissuading papal errors. . . . God has made Your Highness the pilot and steersman to guide this little ship of the English Church, so that it does not dash on the rocks of false religion. The ministers of God are the oarsmen: those who are lusty and strong to work should be set to their tackling.[†] . . . Thus, while both the sturdy mariners get to their business and the weak sailors are heartened to play their parts, with your sacred authority guiding the helm we may at length bring the ship, by God's grace, safely to the shore, fearing nothing while we follow our loadstar, Christ Jesus. And as Ambrose says, "Observe that star that brought the wise men unto Christ,"[‡] who in his good time, we trust, will conduct our ship, with our Sovereign Pilot, the noble officers, the painstaking mariners, and the patient passengers, into the haven of everlasting life. Amen.

Your Majesty's most humble subject, Andrew Willet. SIX-FOLD COMMENTARY ON THE EPISTLE TO THE ROMANS (1620).[20]

---

[18]CTS 38:xxiv-xxv (CO 10:403-4).
[19]Runge, *Disputatio Prima*, A2v.

[20]Willet, *Hexapla*, 3r-v*. [†]I.e., handling the ship's equipment. [‡]Possibly paraphrased from Ambrose, *Exposition on Luke* 2.46-48 (CSEL 32/4:67-68).

NOTE TO THE READER. CASPAR CRUCIGER:

> Reader, if you wish to draw Paul's doctrine from
>   the bubbling spring,
>   This book shows you the path to the
>   fountain.
> The Father sent the eternal Word,
>   Willing that his utterances might not reach
>   us with uncertain sound,
> Therefore, I wish to present heavenly things—as
>   they are properly called;
>   Nor would I want mud sprinkled in these
>   springs.
> But darkness has stolen away the minds of men
>   and women,
>   So that in their fallen state they stray from
>   the right path toward some other way.
> But the censure of the godly still calls the
>   straying back,
>   And the pious mind shows love by issuing
>   these warnings.
> Thus I ask to be instructed by the judgments of
>   the readers,
>   As long as a kind appraisal is joined to them.
> May we always be one Church in Christ;
>   May one faith and one love join our hearts
>   together.
> God wishes us to be united and one with
>   himself,
>   And rage harms us both when it tears us
>   apart.
> You, O Redeemer Christ, have joined us
>   together, as your own, to be a single entity.
> So join us by the eternal covenant to yourself.

COMMENTARY ON ROMANS (1567).[21]

HOW TO READ THE LETTER. JOHN TRAPP: The whole letter is the confession of our churches, as Melanchthon calls it, who therefore taught it ten times in his ordinary lectures, the letter being such that no one will ever be able to think, speak, or write sufficiently of its words and excellency. Mr. Perkins advises that in reading the Scripture one first begin with the Gospel of John and this letter to the Romans, their being the keys of the New Testament. And, for the letter to the Romans, Cardinal Pole advises to begin at the twelfth chapter and read to the end and practice the precepts of repentance and mortification. And then to set on the former part of the letter, where justification and predestination are handled. COMMENTARY ON ROMANS (1656).[22]

PRAY FOR THE HOLY SPIRIT TO BE YOUR GUIDE. JUAN DE VALDÉS: You will find in St. Paul some things that you will not find in yourself, and you will find others that you will not understand, and others that will appear strange to you. I suggest that you let all those things pass, so that you will not greatly fatigue yourself in attempting to understand them, since your purpose in reading St. Paul is not to understand all that St. Paul says, but to form your mind with what God will give you to understand, to feel, and to relish in St. Paul. I also counsel you, when you begin to read a letter, to read the argument that you find prefixed to it, because it throws great light on the whole letter. But all these counsels are nothing, and there is one that is worth much more than them all. It is this: that you always, when taking St. Paul into your hands, commend yourself to God, praying to him to send his Holy Spirit to be your guide in this reading, and that you seek to have him, through the mediation of the only-begotten Son of God, Jesus Christ our Lord, to whom be glory for ever. Amen. PREFATORY LETTER TO GIULIA GONZAGA IN COMMENTARY ON ROMANS (1556).[23]

---

[21]Cruciger, *In Epistolam Pauli*, a viii v.

[22]Trapp, *A Commentary or Exposition upon the Epistle of St. Paul*, 618*. Citing Puritan William Perkins, *Prophetica Sive de Sacra et Unica Ratione Concionandi, Tractatus* (Hanau, Germany: Guilielmuin Antonium, 1602), 22; *The Art of Prophecying*, 26; and Reginald Pole, Cardinal Archbishop of Canterbury.

[23]Valdés, *Commentary upon St. Paul's Epistle*, xxix*.

1:1-7 GREETING TO THE CHRISTIANS IN ROME

Paul, a servant of Christ Jesus, called to be an apostle, set apart for the gospel of God, ²which he promised beforehand through his prophets in the holy Scriptures, ³concerning his Son, who was descended from David^a according to the flesh ⁴and was declared to be the Son of God in power according to the Spirit of holiness by his resurrection from the dead, Jesus Christ our Lord, ⁵through whom we have received grace and apostleship to bring about the obedience of faith for the sake of his name among all the nations, ⁶including you who are called to belong to Jesus Christ,

⁷To all those in Rome who are loved by God and called to be saints:

Grace to you and peace from God our Father and the Lord Jesus Christ.

a Or who came from the offspring of David

OVERVIEW: The commentators note that Paul introduces himself in a way that intends to glorify God while also establishing his authority so that his readers will be able to trust his writing. He does this by mentioning his various titles and roles. First, he is a servant of Christ, and this servanthood should be a model for all those in episcopal leadership and should entail their serving the church in fear and love. All other Christians are called to be servants of Christ as well. Second, Paul is an apostle, and as such, his apostleship is a higher calling than a bishop's, thus giving him leadership over the other leaders of the church and undergirding the reformers' belief that the Scriptures have more authority than the bishops of the Catholic Church.

Paul, like the other apostles, is called to deliver the gospel, but as they are called to the Jews, he is called to the Gentiles. He is not creating a new gospel, but rather it is what the promise of the Old Testament prophets pointed to but has become buried under incorrect interpretations of the Pharisees. In a parallel way, the reformers explain that they are not proclaiming a new gospel, but rather one that has been buried under erroneous teachings. This gospel is bound up in Christ, and thus, if we move away from Christ, we move away from the gospel. In light of Paul's affirmation of the two natures of Christ, as both the Son of David

and the Son of God, the interpreters reflect on the necessity of the incarnation to salvation and how the human and divine natures relate.

Faith plays a key role in the gospel and the Reformation, and the reformers here start to explore the connection between obedience and faith, which will be an important theme throughout the first eight chapters. Faith should lead to obedience, but the obedience of faith differs from the obedience of law. It involves a shift from the wisdom of the flesh to the simplicity of faith, from the servitude of the law to the servitude of Christ.

Although Paul's salutation is to the Romans, it applies to all Christians, and it implies that all Christians should be allowed to read the Scriptures, a key desire of the reformers. It is the Christian's "peculiar glory" to be loved by God. God, in his beneficence, gives them both grace and peace. All Christians are called to be saints, being called to be holy, but first having sanctity bestowed on them through the forgiveness of their sins.

PAUL'S CALL TO PREACH THE GOSPEL. DESIDERIUS ERASMUS: I am Paul, who used to be Saul. I have come from creating turbulence to making peace. Freed from subjection to the law, I am now the servant of Jesus Christ. I am not, however, like a false soldier who has deserted his captain, or like a truant who has forgone his old profession.

Rather, I have been called forth to proclaim this message. I am much more content to be set apart now than at the time I was part of the "set apart" Pharisaical sect, who with ungodly zeal and light (i.e., not heavy) persuasion wandered out of the right way. Now—as one never before deserving to be referred to as "of unfeigned devotion"—I am one set apart and chosen by Christ himself to labor and travail in a much more weighty matter, namely, to preach, I say, the joyful tidings of God, which is no newfound fantasy. But rather, it was preached many years before, in his prophecies, which remain still in books of no small credence, ones about the holy and most undoubted truth of his Son. This truth relates to his frail manhood, born in time, of the seed of David. He was declared, by the Holy Spirit, to be the everlasting Son of the everlasting God. Various other professions appeared as well, most especially that he overcame death, rose again from the dead, and has now become to all who in him are born again, the Prince and Chief Author of resurrection. I mean Jesus Christ our Lord, by whom we have obtained not only such favor as the keeping of the law could not help us to, but also strength to be his messengers. As Christ's gospel has been spread abroad among the Jews by other apostles, so may it be set forth among all heathens by me. And may it not trouble them with the burden of the law, but make them yield and submit themselves obediently to the doctrine of Christ's faith, steadfastly clinging to it, rather than to the vain wisdom of philosophers. In relation to your nation, you Romans are also included in those heathens. But you are all called—by adoption and fathering—to the right title of inheritance and the surname "of Jesus Christ." Incidentally, I also make this point to warn you, lest either sects or other countries cause you to square up against others who, through a favorable and gentle fathering, are now made one man's children. PARAPHRASE OF ROMANS (1549).[1]

1:1 *Paul, a Servant of Christ*

PAUL'S THREE-PART TITLE. JOHANNES OECOLAMPADIUS: "Paul." Many have said many things about this name Paul, especially Chrysostom in his sermon on Paul's conversion. In brief, it seems to us that Saul had been called by his ethnic name, since he was from the tribe and people of Benjamin among whom Saul was the first to reign. But he was also called Paul, since he was born a citizen of Rome. The name Paul was more pleasing to the Romans, among whom there were certain eminent Pauls. For he was said to have been born in the village of Gyscal in the region of Tarsus of Cilicia.

"Servant." Paul is among those servants whom the man sent out—when the king was going to put on a wedding for his son—to invite many guests. His friends are called apostles with respect to their service, and servants with respect to the knowledge of the mysteries. But to be called a servant means more than to be called an attendant [minister]. For a servant is more subject. . . . Also, learn firmly from this passage that ecclesiastical rule is nothing other than service, as in Luke 22: "Whoever is greater among you, let him be a servant."

"Of Jesus Christ." He is contrasting Jesus with kings and emperors, to whom the rest of mortal men and women were subject. It is more praiseworthy to serve Christ than the emperor. Additionally, he sets Christ against Moses, since he proclaimed the gospel rather than the burden of the law.

Paul introduces himself well, as striving for nothing else than the glory of his Lord. ANNOTATIONS ON ROMANS.[2]

PAUL, A SERVANT OF CHRIST. THEODORE BEZA: The name "servant" might seem too unflattering and unfitting for such a great authority as Paul. But this title is more honorable than all the titles of bishops and kings and is most fitting for Paul's purpose. For it is the same as if he had said that he who was a master over them was

---

[1] Erasmus, *The Seconde Tome*, Air-v*.

[2] Oecolampadius, *Epistolam B. Pauli* (1525), b1r; citing Lk 22:26.

himself a servant to his own master. Therefore they ought to listen attentively to the things that the master of the family commands: "By God's commandment, I bring a word from him who is both your and my Lord." On the other hand, the term "servant" is not taken here to refer to the condition of men and women as they are regarded by law. It is, therefore, not necessary to discourse here on the duty of a servant toward his master . . . for "servant" here refers to nothing other than the labors of someone who is employed by the Lord in announcing the gospel. And, however much the name "servant" might be appropriate for all who possess the name of Christ, it is nevertheless in this case particularly applied to ministers. LECTURES ON THE EPISTLES.[3]

WHAT IT MEANS TO BE A SERVANT OF CHRIST. PETER MARTYR VERMIGLI: In the introduction, Paul gives three titles by which he graces his own name. The first is "a servant of Jesus Christ," which is common to all the faithful. For it is the property of a servant to not be in possession of his own rights, but rather to be about the business of his master. For this reason, if we are the servants of Christ, it is necessary that whatever we live, breathe and think, we direct it all to Christ. Also, false apostles appear to be censured by these words, for they seek after their own interests so that they may fill their bellies and advance their own designs. They do not claim men and women for Christ, but rather for Moses or for themselves. When it says that we are the servants of Christ, the metaphor should be carefully pondered so that it may be applied commonly to us all, by which it can be said of us all that we ought to be as subject to God as servants are to their masters. But we are so very far from rendering this kind of servitude, for servants care for their own affairs during only a small portion of the day, but for all the rest of the time they carry out the affairs of their master. But we do far otherwise. How little space or few hours of our life we give to pursuing divine things; rather,

whatever time we have, we turn ourselves to human and earthly matters. A servant possesses nothing of his own or that belongs to him; but we desire to privately possess many things that we will expend neither for God nor for Christ. When at times servants are killed or beaten, they seek refuge with pleading and supplicating voices; but when we are in adversities, we fight back against God, we murmur, and we blaspheme. Servants receive only food and clothing and are content with them; we place neither measure nor limit to wealth and luxury. Servants, upon hearing threats, tremble from head to toe; but we are not moved at all by the threats of prophets, apostles, or of learned churchmen. Servants do not mix the words of their master with those of their enemies, nor do they exhibit any civility or signs of friendship with them; but we perpetually join ourselves to the devil, the flesh, and the world. For which reason we are very far from that servitude that we owe to God, although we ought to obey and serve him far more than our servants ought to obey us. For God, beyond the fact that he feeds and nourishes us, also brought us forth and granted that we might exist. Whatever servants do for us is done entirely for our well-being, whereas it is no benefit to them. So also we, when we serve God, render none of our labors either for our own utility or benefit. Since even if we live righteously, he is made no better or more blessed than he was before. Also, we give our servants either nothing or only a little; but God sent forth his only Son for us, and at the same time, with him granted us all things. We promise our servants rather meager wages, while God has promised us that same happiness which Christ himself enjoys. COMMENTARY ON ROMANS.[4]

TWICE SEPARATED. THE ENGLISH ANNOTATIONS: Paul was separated from his mother's womb by God's appointment; however, he was actually set apart by the command of the Holy Ghost to preach the gospel among the Gentiles. In the word "separate," he seems to allude to the name

---

[3]Beza, *Cours sur les Épîtres*, 21.

[4]Vermigli, *In Epistolam S. Pauli Apostoli*, 2-3.

of "Pharisee," which signifies a person who is separate, of which sect he was before his conversion. And by this he implies that he is still a separated person, but to a better purpose, namely, to the preaching of the gospel of Christ. ANNOTATIONS ON ROMANS 1:1.[5]

PASTORS SHOULD SERVE WITH LOVE AND FEAR. MARTIN LUTHER: Every pastor in the church, following the example of the apostle . . . considering himself always the lowliest of all servants, should administer his office with a mixture of fear and love. He should do only those things that are good and profitable for his charges, so that, knowing that the whole office exists for the benefit of his charges, he should rather resign from the office if his experience should show that the welfare and the good of his charges does not follow or that it is being hindered by him personally. LECTURES ON ROMANS.[6]

APOSTOLIC VERSUS EPISCOPAL APPOINTMENTS. PHILIPP MELANCHTHON: It is for a necessary reason that he makes mention of his office, that the church might know that the teaching of Paul is to be believed just as much as if it had boomed forth by the voice of God from heaven. Therefore, as Moses prefaced his comments: "The Lord God has spoken all these words," and so on, that the people might know that he was putting forward not human teaching, but that which had been undeniably and expressly handed over to him by God, so also Paul starts out by asserting that he is an apostle, not chosen by any human judgment, but by the voice of Christ, and that he carries a gospel divinely handed to him, and that the position that he puts forward concerning the law, the promises, sin, grace, and faith was not a human invention but was divinely revealed and entrusted to him that he might pass it on to the churches. Therefore, he does not pointlessly insist on mere titles—either here or in other places—as

often as he repeats the mention of his office. These things are, therefore, to be remembered, so that we should read Paul as we read Ambrose or Augustine, not only as erudite interpreters of the prophetic Scriptures, but as firmly setting forth heavenly teaching to which it is necessary to assent.

Further, in this passage the apostolic calling is to be carefully distinguished from the episcopal calling. An apostle is called directly by Christ to teach the gospel, and he possesses a firm testimony that his teaching is divine. And it is certain that he possesses the Holy Spirit, does not err in doctrine, and is able to teach everywhere in all the churches. Whereas a bishop is called by human beings to teach the gospel in a certain region, can err, and may not necessarily possess the Holy Spirit.

Many things can be judged from these descriptions. For as the prophets among the people of Israel far surpassed the priests in excellence and did many heroic things the law did not permit the priests to do, so they hold that the calling of an apostle is far superior to that of bishops. They abrogate the law, call the Gentiles into community with the people of God, and narrate obscure points concerning the Messiah, such as that he is the Son of God, and that he would not take possession of a political kingdom. They also expressly impart the remission of sins, which the Levitical priests had never done. They explain in detail the doctrine of the justification by faith, which few among the people of the law had previously heard, whereas bishops are obliged to receive the things written by the apostles and not innovate some new or different kind of teaching. Therefore, Paul makes mention of his calling when he says, "a servant of Jesus Christ, called to be an apostle" so that he may admonish all to heed the authority of his teaching, COMMENTARY ON ROMANS (1540).[7]

A SUPERIOR APOSTOLIC CALLING. CASPAR CRUCIGER: I previously stated that the apostolic calling was superior to the common, intermediate calling that bishops have. A prophet in the Old

---

[5]Downame, ed., *Annotations*, AAA1r*; citing Gal 1:15; Acts 13:2.
[6]LW 25:140*.

[7]Melanchthon, *Commentarii in Epistolam Pauli*, 22v-23r.

Testament was a person called directly by God to shed light on the promise of a Messiah, as well as to give counsel on certain civil matters, having testimony from God that they would not go astray in their teaching. An apostle is a person called directly by the Son of God to teach the gospel that he entrusted to them, not for any administration of civil affairs, having testimony that their teaching would be divine and that it would not err in doctrine, and also having the authority to teach this wherever they pleased. A bishop is a person called by the church to teach the gospel, which he must preserve incorrupt as it was received from the apostles. But bishops err when they permit corruptions (which can and does happen), and they only have authority to teach in their own assigned place. These things are, therefore, to be kept in mind that their ravings might be censured when they pretend that the authority of bishops is equal to that of the apostles, and dream that Paul, who seems to wander about like the meandering Iris,[†] was far inferior to a bishop who has canonical authority in one place, as they say. COMMENTARY ON ROMANS (1567).[8]

SERVING IN THE GOSPEL OF CHRIST. JUAN DE VALDÉS: Here I understand that in calling himself "the servant of Christ," Paul does not deprive himself of the dignity of a child of God, it being a fact that he was a child of God by regeneration. For he had received the grace of the gospel, he was a member of Christ, he had the spirit of Christ, and he was the servant of Christ through the apostolate, because in preaching the gospel he served Christ, illustrating Christ's name and his righteousness. The name of "servant of Christ" properly attaches itself to those who serve in the gospel of Christ, discharging the duty of apostles.

And I understand that those who proclaim to men and women the righteousness of God expected in Christ serve in the gospel. They affirm that through it God has already pardoned all men

and women solely upon their believing in the gospel, and upon their accepting this righteousness as their own, and upon their submitting themselves to it.

Where it is to be understood that because this is the best news that ever might, or ever could be brought to humanity, it is called the gospel, which means good tidings, something worthy of reward (*albricias*, paid to the one who first brings good news). At times St. Paul calls it the "gospel of God," because he sent it; at other times, the "gospel of Christ," because Christ was the bearer of it, and confirmed it by his death. And on some occasions, "my gospel," because he published it among the Gentiles. COMMENTARY ON ROMANS (1556).[9]

A MOST PROFITABLE PREFACE. LAURENCE TOMSON (OR PIERRE L'OISELEUR): The first part of the letter through verse 16 contains a highly profitable preface. Paul moves the Romans to pay diligent care to him, showing that he does not come in his own name, but as God's messenger to the Gentiles. He entreats them with the weightiest matter, which was promised long ago by God, proclaimed through many fit witnesses, and now at last, is performed in deed. THE GENEVA BIBLE (1595).[10]

1:2 *The Gospel's Ancient Pedigree*

DO NOT CONFUSE THE PROMISE AND THE GOSPEL. JOHN CALVIN: "Which he had promised before," and so on. Since many withdraw from a doctrine that is suspected of novelty, he establishes the gospel faith from antiquity. It is as if he had said that Christ had not descended unexpectedly to Earth, nor had he brought some new and previously unheard-of teaching. But rather, Christ along with his gospel was promised from the beginning of the world and had always been expected. Now, since the testimony of antiquity is frequently fictitious, he adds certain classical witnesses who were exempt from any suspicion,

---

[8]Cruciger, *In Epistolam Pauli*, 28. [†]In Greek mythology, the goddess of the rainbow, who wanders all over the earth.

[9]Valdés, *Commentary upon St. Paul's Epistle*, 1-2*. [10]Tomson, *The Bible*, 61v*.

namely, the prophets of God. Third, he adds that their testimony was solemnly sealed when they were recorded in the Scriptures. One can gather what the gospel is from this passage: the gospel teaches that which had not been promulgated by the prophets, but had only been promised. Therefore if the prophets were only promising the gospel, it follows that the gospel was at length openly exhibited when the Lord took on flesh. Therefore those who confuse the promises with the gospel are deceived, since properly speaking, the gospel is the solemn proclamation of the revealed Christ, in whom the promises themselves are exhibited. COMMENTARY ON ROMANS (1556).[11]

PAUL'S MESSAGE IS NOT NEW. PHILIPP MELANCHTHON: He inserts this so that he might quietly meet an objection. Since a new kind of teaching was being proclaimed, without doubt the Pharisees declaimed against it. Since the church of God in some form had always existed since the beginning of the world, she necessarily had to always be in possession of that doctrine necessary for salvation. Therefore the Pharisees were grumbling over whether they also held to this teaching of the apostles. If they did not hold to it, the Pharisees clamored that it was a new and invented doctrine. Paul responds that there is one and the same gospel concerning the Messiah which was promised to the fathers and shown to the prophets and which had now been openly set forth: "We do not set forward a teaching unknown to the fathers and the prophets, but one buried under human opinions about the righteousness of the law, and about a political reign of the Messiah. You condemn this kind of teaching as new and invented because you do not understand the liberation that the fathers and prophets were expecting. You pretend that we are righteous by the law, that the Messiah was to come so that he might take up a worldly empire, that he might give you provinces to be ruled so that you might be affluent in wealth and pleasures. This is the liberation of which you

drunkards dream. But the fathers and prophets were waiting for the Messiah who would abolish sin and death by divine power, and who would destroy the kingdom of the devil. They looked forward to the promised Seed that would crush the head of the serpent."

In the same way the papal church now opposes us. They vociferously charge that we are bringing a kind of doctrine that is unknown to the church. We cry in reply and testify that our doctrine was supported in the church of the fathers, of the prophets, and of the apostles, and among the faithful in succession. We call forward the witness of [these] churches, namely, of the prophets, apostles, and the other saints. No doctrine ought to be received that has always been unknown to the churches of Christ. But the position of the true churches has been obscured for many centuries now. For popes, priests, and monarchs have scattered false and Pharisaic opinions in the church concerning the righteousness of works; they have thought up human forms of worship; they have gathered pagan superstitions, the invocation of the dead—a manifest *idolomania*—and have profaned the Lord's Supper with horrid impiety.

These things were thought up partly by superstition, partly by inquiry, and partly for the support of tyranny. This assembly of impious popes and kings is not the church of Christ, for which reason they unjustly arrogate this most noble title for themselves and oppose their invented authority—not the authority of the true churches—against us. Therefore, in this passage Paul warns his readers that they not receive dogmas without the testimonies of divine Scripture. He also warns that we must inquire into the opinions of the true churches and distinguish the true church from the false. COMMENTARY ON ROMANS (1540).[12]

THE GOSPEL IS THE ESSENTIAL POINT OF THE PROPHETS' TEACHINGS. JOHANNES BRENZ: Next, Paul explains in this introduction of what kind his doctrines are, whether he is setting forth

---

[11]Calvin, *In Omnes Pauli*, 2.   [12]Melanchthon, *Commentarii in Epistolam Pauli*, 22v-23r.

some new and never-before-heard-of teaching. In this section, not only does he teach the true and genuine interpretation of the prophetic Scriptures, but he also defines and expounds the true person of our Lord Jesus Christ. For Paul's doctrine, even if it appeared to be new, was nevertheless—if rightly assayed—not new, but had already been promised beforehand to the patriarchs and preached by the prophets. "Set apart," he says, "to the gospel." Not to the Ten Commandments, as Moses was, but to the gospel of God, not of men and women. Nor is there anything in the gospel that was so unknown or unheard of, but that God had promised it beforehand through his prophets and in the holy Scriptures. Therefore the gospel—in which it is preached that we might obtain the remission of sins before God, not on account of the merits of our human righteousness, but only on account of the merit of Christ, by faith—is not a new heresy, as the sycophants abusively label it, but is the ancient doctrine of the prophets and the sacred Scriptures. Here you have, not the interpretation of only a few passages, but the chief argument from the whole of the prophetic Scriptures. But if you should ask what the essential point of the prophetic Scriptures might be, no more fitting or truer answer could be given than that it has to do with Christ and his gospel, nor does it have any other goal than Christ. "Set apart," he says, "to the gospel of God, which he had before promised by his prophets, in the holy Scriptures concerning his Son," and so on. Peter says something similar: "Receiving back," he writes, "the end of your faith, the salvation of souls, concerning which salvation the prophets inquired into and searched carefully, who foretold the grace that was to come to you, searching out when or in what kind of time the Spirit of Christ who was in them was indicating." COMMENTARY ON ROMANS.[13]

IMPORTANCE OF THE PREACHED GOSPEL.

MARTIN LUTHER: Thus Scripture teaches that Christ comes, though he was previously in all the fathers; but he did not come to everyone through public preaching until after his resurrection from the dead. Scripture speaks most of this coming, for the sake of which he also came bodily in the human nature. His incarnation would have been useful to no one if the gospel had not come from it, through which he came into all the world and made known why he became man, so that the promised blessing would be distributed to all who believed on Christ through the gospel. Paul certainly says that the gospel was promised by God, as if he would say that God paid more attention to the gospel and the public coming through the Word than to the bodily birth or his coming in human form. For him, it had to do with the gospel and our faith, and for that reason he had his Son become man, so that the gospel would be preached by him, and thus his salvation would come to all the world through the public [preaching of the] Word. CHURCH POSTIL (1540 / 1544).[14]

PAUL EMPHASIZES THE DIGNITY OF THE GOSPEL. HEINRICH BULLINGER: Now he renders his hearers receptive and attentive by means of the subject itself that was to be discussed. So that they will not despise the preaching of the gospel as something recent and novel, he emphasizes its antiquity and authority from the oracles of the prophets. More than that, he adds dignity to it. For it is the preaching of Christ Jesus as true God and man. Here in the beginning of his letter he sets forth in passing—as if looking through a lattice— all the things to be considered that he would at length discuss more amply one by one. From this we learn the same thing that the apostle Peter said in the first chapter of his second letter that the gospel was made firm by the prophetic Scriptures, or rather was sought after by them. For while Paul was defending himself before Agrippa, the Jews (he said) had tried to kill their captive, but having survived until this day he was witnessing to both small and great, speaking nothing other than those things that Moses and the prophets had foretold

---

[13]Brenz, *In Epistolam* (1564), 12-13; citing 1 Pet 1:9-11.

[14]LW 75:17*.

were to come, such as that the Christ would suffer, and so on. These were the very things that those writing of gospel realities affirmed in all their writings. Nor does he refer to any writings whatever, but to the holy Scriptures, that is, to those inspired by the Holy Spirit who spoke by the prophets to the one, holy, and apostolic church. Last, we learn that the scope of the gospel is Jesus Christ, the salvation of the world. COMMENTARY ON PAUL'S EPISTLES (1582).[15]

PREORDAINED NATURE OF THE GOSPEL PRECLUDES OUR RIGHTEOUSNESS. MARTIN LUTHER: "Which he promised beforehand." He says this so that we should not think that this gift has been received on account of our merits or that it is the result of human wisdom. This is the greatest power and the proof of the gospel, that it has the witness of the old law and prophets that it would be so in the future. For the gospel proclaims only what prophecy has said it would proclaim, so that we may say that it has been ordained by God's previous decision to be so before it should happen, and thus God alone should receive the glory for this doctrine and not our own merits and endeavors, obviously because this gospel was ordained before we existed. LECTURES ON ROMANS.[16]

1:3 Christ Is Human

THE GOSPEL BOUND UP IN CHRIST. JOHN CALVIN: This is a principal passage in which we are taught that the whole gospel is bound up in Christ, so that if anybody moves a single foot away from Christ they withdraw themselves from the gospel. Since he is the natural and express image of the Father, it is no wonder that he is revealed only to those of us who direct our whole faith to him. This verse is, therefore, a kind of definition of the gospel by which Paul designates what is principally contained in it. COMMENTARY ON ROMANS (1556).[17]

THE SON OF GOD AND THE SON OF DAVID. MARTIN LUTHER: "Concerning his Son." This is the gospel, which deals not merely with the Son of God in general but with him who has become incarnate and is of the seed of David. In effect he says: "He has emptied himself and has become weak. He who was before all and created everything new has a beginning himself and has been made." But the gospel speaks not only of the humiliation of the Son of God, by which he emptied himself, but also of his glory and the power which after his humiliation he received from God in his humanity. In other words, just as the Son of God became the Son of David by humbling and emptying himself in the weakness of the flesh, so on the other hand the Son of David, though weak according to the flesh, has now in turn been established and designated the Son of God in all power and glory. And as according to his divine form he emptied himself to the point of the nothingness of the flesh by being born into the world, so in the form of a servant he has brought himself to completion to the point of fullness of divine essence by ascending into heaven. LECTURES ON ROMANS.[18]

CHRIST TOOK ON HUMAN FLESH. PETER MARTYR VERMIGLI: "Who was made from the seed of David." This touches on the incarnation of the Son of God. He is said to be "made" with respect to his person, although such a thing does not properly apply to him except only with respect to his humanity. But it says "from the Seed of David" because that illustrious promise was made to David, so that the Son of David came to be popularly called the Messiah, just as we read in the Gospels that the scribes and Pharisees were witnesses to whom Christ objected, asking how it was that David calls him his Lord. Here in this passage are condemned those impious heretics who wish to say that Christ did not possess a body from the nature and essence of the Virgin, but one brought down with him from heaven.[†] They

---

[15]Bullinger, *Commentarii in Omnes Pauli*, 1-2; citing 2 Pet 1:16-21; Acts 26:23.
[16]LW 25:144-45*.
[17]Calvin, *In Omnes Pauli*, 2.

[18]LW 25:146-47*; citing Phil 2:7.

fashion for themselves the argument that our flesh is subject to condemnation and to a curse. Therefore, it is not exactly true, they say, that the Son of God took it on himself. This argument can be easily blown to pieces: for curse and condemnation are accidents, so God could easily take them away while preserving intact the nature and substance of humanity.[†] For which reason he was not less able to bestow on Christ a holy and pure body from the Virgin than he was able to bring forth the noble and perfectly pure body of Adam from filthy mud. And since we read that the Son of God so emptied himself that he took on human flesh, this should be no small stimulus to us, so that there might be nothing that he embraced that would be so difficult that we would not be willing to embrace it for Christ's sake. It is asked by many, "Why did the Son of God wish to take on himself human flesh?" And although it is possible to offer many reasons, I would refer to that which Ambrose answered from this passage, namely, that the punishment should be exacted on the flesh that had sinned, just as men and women who are evildoers, according to custom suffer their punishment in the place where they committed their notorious crimes. COMMENTARY ON ROMANS (1560).[19]

HOW THE HUMAN AND DIVINE NATURES RELATE. FRIEDRICH BALDUIN: When the Son of God is said to be "made from the seed of David according to the flesh," it is asked whether the distinguishing particle "according" takes away the majesty communicated to the flesh of Christ; so that, just as the Son of God is said to be born from David according to the flesh, so in like manner should it be said that the Son of Man is omnipotent or omnipresent according to deity? I answer . . . the position of our churches is not that the communication of attributes is an impressing or mixing of attributes between the natures. For we believe and confess that the things proper to one nature never become

proper to the other nature, neither by mixing, nor by inhering, nor by any other way whatsoever, since it is fitting to maintain the differences of the natures and the distinction of properties. However, because it is also necessary to preserve the unity of the person, therefore we say that to one and the same person who consists of two natures, all the attributes are communicated or attributed, whether they are essentially fitting to the divine or to the human nature. However, so that there may not be a confusion of natures, it is added, by the example of Scripture, according to which nature it is predicated of the person, since the attributes of both natures cannot essentially coincide at the same time. COMMENTARY ON ROMANS.[20]

FROM SEED, FROM EVERLASTING. LAURENCE TOMSON (OR PIERRE L'OISELEUR): By declaring the sum of the doctrine of the gospel, he sets up the Romans to consider well the matter about which he entreats them. So then he shows that Christ (who is the very substance and sum of the gospel) is the only Son of God the Father, who as touching his humanity is made of the seed of David, but touching his divine and spiritual nature whereby he sanctified himself, is begotten of the Father from everlasting, as appears manifestly by his mighty resurrection. THE GENEVA BIBLE (1595).[21]

1:4 Christ Is Divine

"SHOWN TO BE" RATHER THAN "PREDESTINED." GASPARO CONTARINI: "Jesus Christ our Lord, who was predestined the Son of God in power according to the Spirit of holiness, by the resurrection from the dead." This is a difficult passage. First of all, recent theologians offer many explanations for how Christ could be "predestined the Son of God."[†] But the Greek text is better than the Latin and removes the difficulty, so that we read instead "designated," that is, "shown to be." All of what follows refers to this showing: namely, that he was

---

[19]Vermigli, *In Epistolam S. Pauli*, 11. [†]Vermigli is likely referring to those, such as Melchior Hoffman and Menno Simons, who advocated the doctrine of the celestial flesh of Christ. [‡]Refers to the Aristotelian/scholastic distinction between substance and accidents.

[20]Balduin, *Catechesis Apostolica*, 56.
[21]Tomson, *The Bible*, 61v*.

shown to be the Son of God on account of the power by which he raised himself from the dead through the Holy Spirit. In Acts 13, Paul implies this meaning when he says that the verse from the Psalm, "You are my Son; today I have begotten you" refers to the day in which Christ was raised from the dead. COMMENTARY ON ROMANS (1571).[22]

THE GOSPEL. MARTIN LUTHER: Let us summarize: The gospel deals with his Son, who was born of the seed of David but now has been manifested as the Son of God with power over all things through the Holy Spirit, given from the resurrection of the dead, even Jesus Christ, our Lord. See, there you have it: The gospel is the message concerning Christ, the Son of God, who was first humbled and then glorified. LECTURES ON ROMANS.[23]

CONTRARIES TO CONTRARIES. DESIDERIUS ERASMUS: By a wonderful plan, Paul has opposed contraries to contraries. For first he set in contrast "Paul" with Saul; he set "a servant of Jesus Christ" in contrast with the servitude of the Mosaic law; an "apostle called" with those who were taking the office on themselves; "set apart for the gospel" with the Pharisaism that he professed before. Thus far he has commended himself and the office he filled. The words that follow relate to the commendation of Christ, who was promised not by just anyone, but by God himself; and promised not through just anyone but through his own prophets, that is, men who were true and inspired by God; and not with just any instruments, but in the holy Scriptures. Then with words wonderful in their suggestive power, he describes the double nature of Christ in the same *hypostasis*: concerning the man, he says he "was made," so that you may understand that something that was not came into existence; concerning the divinity he says "he

was shown." To the former clause he adds "according to the flesh," whose companions are weakness and impurity—hence: "The spirit is willing, but the flesh is weak." And the desires of the flesh are called affections that incite us to sins. Accordingly, he set in contrast to the flesh the power of God and the spirit of sanctification, that is, power in contrast to weakness, holiness to uncleanness. [Christ] assumed, therefore, our flesh; and he demonstrated his power, above all by the fact that through his own power he rose from the dead, and the life that by his own will he had laid down at his death he received back again in his own good time. Further, because morality belongs to the flesh, to this, too, [Paul] opposed the resurrection of the dead, which is immortality. ANNOTATIONS ON THE EPISTLE TO THE ROMANS (1516, 1519, 1522, 1527, 1535).[24]

ARGUMENTS FOR THE DIVINITY OF CHRIST. HEINRICH BULLINGER: He therefore adds to the gospel three proofs of the deity of Christ. First is the power of his miracles. Of these we read in the Gospel according to John: "If," said the Lord, "you do not believe my words, at least believe my works." Second, the Holy Spirit, which according to Hebrew usage he calls the "Spirit who sanctifies," concerning which there are many testimonies in the same Gospel of John (chapters 1, 15, and 16). To this also pertains that which John said in his letter, "And it is the Spirit who testifies." But the third proof of the deity of Christ is the resurrection. For Thomas, having understood these things, acclaims Christ as "my Lord and my God." COMMENTARY ON PAUL'S EPISTLES (1582).[25]

COMBINING THREE ARGUMENTS FOR CHRIST'S DIVINITY. JOHN CALVIN: However, three separate types of proofs for the deity of Christ are made here: understanding by the power of miracles, then by the testimony of the Spirit, and last by the resurrection from the dead. I prefer

---

[22]Contarini, *Opera*, 435; citing Acts 13:33; Ps 2:7. †Nicholas of Lyra, for example, assumes the Vulgate use of the term *predestination* and, therefore, attempts to explain that it is the humanity rather than the divinity of Christ that is predestined to be the Son of God. Lyra, *Postilla litteralis*, 159v-160r.
[23]LW 25:148*.

[24]CWE 56:16*.
[25]Bullinger, *Commentarii in Omnes Pauli*, 2; citing Jn 10:38.

to connect these together and to refer these three to a single point in this way: that Christ was declared to be the Son of God (openly and truly shown by the heavenly power of the Spirit) when he arose from the dead; but that that power is grasped in hearts only when it is sealed by the same Spirit. The statement of the apostle supports this interpretation well, when he says that Christ had been declared by power, in that the power that is proper to God alone had flashed within him, and had proved without doubt that he was God. Truly this power shone forth in his resurrection, just as elsewhere the same Paul, where he had confessed that he had appeared in the weakness of mortal flesh, praises the power of the Spirit in the resurrection. But that glory does not become known to us until it is sealed in our hearts by the same Spirit. COMMENTARY ON ROMANS (1540, 1550, 1556).[26]

DECLARATIONS OF CHRIST'S SONSHIP IN POWER. JACQUES LEFÈVRE D'ÉTAPLES: Next, he says that Christ had come from David according to the flesh. It is this that prophecy had declared: "From the fruit of your womb I will place One on your throne." And also Matthew in the beginning of his Gospel: "The book of the generations of Jesus Christ, the Son of David." But he is also defined and declared to be the Son of God in power—who will deny that? For who was it that performed powers and signs and wonders? By such things even the demons confessed that he was the Son of God, for Mark says they fell down before him, and they cried out saying, "You are the Son of God." He was declared the Son of God "by the Holy Spirit" when he visibly descended on him and the Father's voice sounded with, "Here is my beloved Son in whom I greatly delight." He was also declared to be the Son of God by his resurrection from the dead. For who ever raised himself from the dead by his own power, except for the Son of God who said, "Destroy this temple and in three days I will raise it up"? And again, "I lay

down my soul, that I might take it up again. Nobody will take it from me, but I lay it down myself. For I have the power of laying it down, and I have the power of taking it up again." See, therefore, how he was defined and declared to be the Son of God by his display of power, by the Spirit of holiness, which is the Holy Spirit, and by the resurrection from the dead. COMMENTARY ON ROMANS (1517).[27]

GREATER THAN A MERELY HUMAN LEADER. PHILIPP MELANCHTHON: But this stands contrary to all the opinions of the Jews, who were certainly expecting the Messiah to be merely a man, although one who was distinguished by heroic victories and who would bestow on them wealth rather than a new nature and eternal life. But Paul says that this Messiah has power, and that he gives us the Spirit who sanctifies, by whom a new law is established within believers, and righteousness and eternal life, and by whom the devil is defeated. He said that this is the true redemption that the fathers both understood and experienced in the training of their faith when struggling against the devil, death, and manifold dangers. This is far greater than that redemption that you Jews are expecting, who think that the Messiah will hand out provinces like Alexander distributed his kingdom to his military colleagues. Paul here reprehends those errors, although by only a short description. Now when he uses this name, "Christ," we are brought to lively contemplation of all those ancient promises of the prophets, so that we might see that they truly line up with this proclamation of the gospel, and so that by the contemplation of the benefits of Christ, we might ignite faith within us and also call on him. For unless faith is exercised by calling on him, the power and the presence of Christ cannot be experienced. COMMENTARY ON ROMANS.[28]

---

[26]Calvin, *Commentarius in Epistolam Pauli*, 14.

[27]Lefèvre, *Epistole divi Pauli*, 1:3-4; citing Mk 5:7; Mt 3:17; Jn 2:19; 10:18.

[28]Melanchthon, *Commentarii in epistolam Pauli* (1540), av v; citing Mt 1:1; 8:29; 3:17; Jn 10:17-18.

THE HUMAN NATURE OF CHRIST. PETER RIEDEMANN: As the time of compassion drew near when God wanted to fulfill his promise and have mercy on the lost human race, he sent his Word, who was in and with God in the beginning. By means of his messenger Gabriel he sent the Word to a virgin whom he had previously chosen. As soon as she believed, she was sealed with the Holy Spirit. Then she was told, "Power from on high will overshadow you, and the Holy Spirit will come down from above into you. Therefore, the Holy One who is to be born of you, shall be called the Son of God."

The Holy Spirit worked together with her faith so that the Word she believed took human nature from her and became a living fruit. In this way what God had undertaken to do was fulfilled, and it was revealed how, and through what means, God wanted to send his Christ into the world.

Sin was brought into the world by Adam and was passed on to all his descendants. They had been commanded by God to multiply by mingling the seed of man and woman. Hence, it was necessary that he who was to do away with this sin should have a different origin from the human one. We were conceived in the weakness of the flesh, but Christ was conceived in the power of God.

Through the union of the Holy Spirit with Mary's faith, the Word was conceived and became human. He did not bring his human nature with him from heaven but received it from Mary. Therefore, Paul distinguishes the two natures of Christ in this way: "He was a descendant of David according to the flesh, and was powerfully declared to be the Son of God according to the Spirit, the one who sanctifies, from the time he was raised from the dead." ARTICLE ON "CONCEIVED OF THE HOLY SPIRIT" IN THE HUTTERITE CONFESSION.[29]

SON OF GOD, SON OF MAN. JOHN CALVIN: But if his filiation (if I may so express it) had a beginning at the time when he was manifested in the flesh, it follows that he was also a Son, in respect to human nature. Servetus, and others who are similarly frenzied, hold that Christ, who appeared in the flesh, is the Son of God, in that if it were not for his incarnation he could not have possessed this name. Let them now answer me whether he is a Son according to, and in respect to, both natures. They will foolishly claim that he is not. But Paul's doctrine is very different. We acknowledge, indeed, that Christ in his human nature is called a Son, not like believers who are so merely by gratuitous adoption, but as the true, natural, and therefore only Son, this being the mark that distinguishes him from all others. God honors with the name of sons and daughters those of us who are regenerated to a new life; he bestows the name of "true and only-begotten Son" on Christ alone. But how is he an only Son in so great a multitude of brothers, except that he possesses by nature what we acquire by gift? This honor we extend to his whole character of Mediator, so that he who was born of a Virgin, and on the cross offered himself in sacrifice to the Father, is truly and properly the Son of God. But when Paul says that he "was separated unto the gospel of God (which he had promised before by his prophets in the holy Scriptures), concerning his Son Jesus Christ our Lord, which was made of the seed of David according to the flesh; and declared to be the Son of God with power," Paul teaches us about Christ's Godhead. When distinctly calling him the Son of David according to the flesh, why would he also say that he was "declared to be the Son of God" if he did not mean to intimate that this depended on something other than his incarnation? INSTITUTES OF THE CHRISTIAN RELIGION 1.14.6 (1559).[30]

CHRIST IS BOTH GOD AND MAN. DAVID RUNGE: Paul here, writing briefly but clearly, describes Christ the Savior, as far as his person and office. Respecting his person, he declares him to be true God and true man. God: (1) Because he is the Son of God. (2) Because his divine majesty is

---

[29]CRR 9:68*.

[30]Calvin, *Institutes*, 1:420-421*.

revealed by indisputable testimonies, by the power or strength of issuing miracles, by the outpouring of the Spirit he brought about (who, in the Hebrew phrasing, is called the Spirit of holiness both from his essential holiness and for the work of our holiness); and finally from the resurrection from the dead, whereby having set aside his life, he recovered it by particular power. That Christ is human is asserted by three arguments. (1) Because he was made. (2) From the seed of David. (3) Because he had flesh—which phrase is common to the Scriptures—he was taken for an entire man. The office of Christ touches so far as the titles noted: for he is Jesus, who will save his people from sin. He is Christ, who was anointed with the fullness of the Holy Spirit without measure. And he is our King and Priest. He is our Lord, not only by reason of creation, but also because he purchased us by his blood, and acquired for himself a flock, the church. DISPUTATION ON ROMANS (1595).[31]

SIMULTANEOUSLY OUR BROTHER AND THE EVERLASTING GOD. JOHN CALVIN: St. Paul says in Romans 1, "Jesus Christ our Lord was made of the seed of David." He likewise adds, "He was declared to be the Son of God."

It is not enough for us to behold him with our natural eyes, for then we rise no higher than his humanity. But when we see that by miracles and mighty works, he shows himself to be the Son of God, it is a seal and proof that in abasing himself he did not discard his heavenly majesty. Therefore, we may come to him as our brother and at the same time worship him as the everlasting God, by whom we were made, and by whom we are preserved. SERMON ON 1 TIMOTHY 3:16.[32]

1:5 Bringing the Obedience of Faith

WE MUST LISTEN DIFFERENTLY TO APOSTLES THAN TO OTHER MINISTERS. TILEMANN HESSHUS: Other ministers of the church—such as bishops, pastors, and teachers—are not of the same authority as the apostles. They are called by men, by magistrates, or through the church. They are attached to a certain place. They did not receive the Holy Spirit in visible form. They are not equipped with miracles; nor do they have any evidence that they would not err. But they are bound to the writings of the prophets and apostles. . . . If they have departed from their teachings, it is not necessary to trust them. So Paul wisely advises us we should not listen closely to matters of the Spirit without investigation. We wisely distinguish the rest of ministry from the apostolic function in order that we might accurately judge the evidence of the testimonies of the apostolic function. And to assent to the voice of God with reverence and without hesitation. COMMENTARY ON PAUL'S EPISTLES (1605).[33]

OBEDIENCE OF FAITH. DESIDERIUS ERASMUS: By "obedience of faith" he means, as Chrysostom explains, that [faith] is not obtained by a painstaking process of logical reasoning, but by simple obedience and quiet compliance. And this applies to both peoples: to the Jews who sought for signs, and to the Gentiles who demanded philosophical arguments; and perhaps today it applies to the convoluted labyrinths of the questions of the scholastics concerning those matters of which it is pious to be ignorant. ANNOTATIONS ON THE EPISTLE TO THE ROMANS (1516, 1519, 1522, 1527, 1535).[34]

OBEDIENCE OF FAITH AND THE KINGDOM OF CHRIST. MARTIN LUTHER: He shows from the testimony of these same prophets what the kingdom of this Christ is to be, namely, that it would not be an external, worldly power and dominion like that of other lords, kings, and emperors over land and people, goods, and temporal life. Rather, it would be a spiritual, eternal kingdom in the hearts of people, and a power and

---

[31]Runge, *Disputatio Prima*, B2v; citing Jn 10:17; Jn 1:14; Mt 1:21; Ps 4:5; Jn 3:34; Acts 10:38.
[32]Calvin, *Selection of Most Celebrated Sermons*, 32*.
[33]Hesshus, *Commentarius in Omnes*, 12.
[34]CWE 56:27*.

dominion over and against sin, eternal death, and the might of hell in order to redeem us from them. It would bring and give us these things through this office for preaching of the gospel, which we receive through faith. This is the obedience that everyone should give to this Lord and, by doing so, subject themselves to him and so partake of his grace and benefits, which St. Paul also calls "the obedience of faith." SUMMER POSTIL (1544).[35]

THE OBEDIENCE OF FAITH. MARTIN BUCER: This obedience can be understood twofold, as both faith itself and as that obedience by which men and women strive in all things by faith in the Lord Christ and are obedient to his Word. For who can be persuaded and truly believe that Christ seeks nothing but our salvation and certainly gives it to those who follow him, and yet not wholly assent to him in every single thing and render themselves compliant to him? It is to this effect that the apostle is seen to have spoken to the Corinthians about obedience: "I wrote to you for this purpose, that I might know how you have proved yourselves, and whether you are obedient in all things." Again, "Taking captive every thought to obedience to Christ, and being ready to punish all disobedience, when your obedience is complete." And also to the Philippians, "Therefore, my beloved, as you have always obeyed, do so not only in my presence but now much more in my absence." In these passages the apostle seems to be speaking of that obedience by which those believing in the Lord assent in all things, insofar as they come from him, because by faith they firmly acknowledge him as Lord. But when he writes to the Romans, "But not all have obeyed the gospel, for Isaiah said, 'Who has believed our report?'" and in the second letter to the Thessalonians, "He will take vengeance on those who did not know God and who have not obeyed the gospel." In these passages it seems that "to obey" is taken to mean "to believe." For just as those who obey simply embrace commandments, so also those who possess faith simply embrace what is said,

which things they also lay hold of without examination and to which they render assent, so that obedience might be wholly implanted into the one believing. But in whichever way you understand this obedience, one can hardly render any such thing until by faith one is firmly brought to birth by the command of the Lord to render such obedience with all one's heart, for nobody is able to render themselves a hearer of the Lord's command in all things unless they have truly believed on him. COMMENTARY ON ROMANS (1562).[36]

THE SIMPLICITY OF FAITH. MARTIN BUCER: St. Chrysostom observed . . . that the role of the apostles is simply to pass on the proclamation of those things which they had received from the Lord, but that to persuade a soul is the work of God. Further, to be of faith is simply to embrace the things proclaimed by the Word of God without inquiry and over-curious investigation. St. Ambrose thinks that the power of miracles is referred to here, by which that is made believable which otherwise was unbelievable to the world. But by no means can even miracles persuade the soul of the truth without the power of the Spirit. Augustine understood this obedience precisely as faith in Christ, and so also did Origen. Erasmus further observes that obedience of the faith is referred to by the apostle in contrast to obedience of the law, by which he also calls the reader away from the vain wisdom of the philosophers who sought to support the faith with reasons and could not bear to simply believe the Word of God. This certainly very strongly agrees with Paul's custom, since he everywhere exhorts his readers to turn from the servitude of the law to the servitude of Christ, and from the wisdom of the flesh to the simplicity of faith. And whenever he was inflamed in whatever he said or wrote, he was aiming against all those things that are contrary to the simplicity of faith. COMMENTARY ON ROMANS (1562).[37]

---

[35]LW 77:42-43*.

[36]Bucer, *Metaphrasis et Enarratio*, 18 (this is a reprint of the 1536 edition); citing 2 Cor 2:9; 10:5; Phil 2:12; Rom 10:16; 2 Thess 1:8.
[37]Bucer, *Metaphrasis et Enarratio*, 18-19 (this is a reprint of the 1536 edition).

THE GOSPEL IS OBEYED BY FAITH. JOHN CALVIN: That is, we received the commandment to carry forth the gospel to all peoples that they might obey it by faith. In accordance with the goal of his calling, Paul admonishes the Romans of their duties to one another. It is as if he had said, "It is my responsibility to carry out the duty committed to me, which is to proclaim the Word, but your part is to give ear to the Word with all obedience, unless you wish to render void the calling which the Lord placed on me." From this we conclude that they who irreverently and contemptuously despise the preaching of the gospel are stubbornly resisting the rule of God and overturning his entire order, the goal of which is to summon us to submission to God. Here also the nature of faith is observed, which is, therefore, signified by the word "obedience," since the Lord calls us through the gospel, and we who are called answer by faith. The same is true of the converse: unbelief is the source of all stubbornness against God. I chose to translate *eis hypakoēn* as "in obedience of faith" rather than "unto obedience," since the latter cannot be said except improperly and figuratively, even though it is read this way once in Acts. For faith is properly that by which the gospel is obeyed. COMMENTARY ON ROMANS (1556).[38]

1:6 Called to Christ

THE CALLED OF JESUS CHRIST. JOHN CALVIN: He assigns the principal reason: namely, that the Lord had raised up among them an example by which he declared himself to be calling them to the communication of the gospel. From this it follows that if they willed to stand fast in their calling, that the ministry of Paul was not to be repudiated by them, who had in a similar way been set apart by the Lord's choosing. Likewise, I understand this phrase "the called of Jesus Christ" as a declaration, as if he had inserted the words "without doubt." For it undoubtedly means that they were sharers in Christ by calling. For those who are heirs of future eternal life are also chosen by the heavenly Father to be sons and daughters in Christ, and elect in him, just as their care and their faith are entrusted to pastors. COMMENTARY ON ROMANS (1556).[39]

THE NATURE OF THE CALL. PETER MARTYR VERMIGLI: Paul says that they are "the called of Christ," since they would not have come to him if they had not been called. Nor does the participle "calling" imply a temporary state. Thus Paul was predicting that they would have constancy and steadfastness in the purpose they had undertaken, for they had not received a temporary calling, but a firm and constant one. Whenever he employs the noun "calling"—as he does very frequently—he amply indicates the nature of our conversion when we embrace Christ. It is certainly voluntary, by no means coerced nor violent. Rather, we are persuaded when we are efficaciously called by the Word of God within. COMMENTARY ON ROMANS (1560).[40]

PREACHING THE NAME OF CHRIST. MARTIN BUCER: In the same place he treats them as worthy of communion with Christ, in that he calls them the "called of Jesus Christ," called, that is, by the firm decree of God, into which communion the Lord of his own accord summoned them by his benevolence, and which communion he had so decreed would be theirs that they were destined to bear at length the new and holy name, *klētoi*, "the called of Jesus Christ." For those who were among them whom the Father gave to his Son ought rightly to receive and listen with the highest respect to the one who had been especially commissioned by the same Lord and Savior as theirs in this very thing, that he should proclaim the gospel to them as well.

For this duty was not anything other than to preach the name of Christ, that is, to celebrate Christ with their praises, to commend him as our one and only Savior, King and Author of life, which these names "Jesus" and "Christ" signified. For a name in the Scriptures is understood to

---

[38]Calvin, *In Omnes Pauli*, 3.

[39]Calvin, *In Omnes Pauli*, 3.
[40]Vermigli, *In Epistolam S. Pauli*, 14-15.

stand for one's praise and honor. The Lord said to David through Nathan, "I have made your name great, like the name of the great ones who are in the earth. Has there until now ever been another name more highly regarded, shining and illustrious than I have given to you?" For this reason those famous giants of old were called 'nshy hshm, "men of name." The Lord spoke to Ananias concerning Paul himself: "This one is my instrument, that he might carry my Name, that is, my praise, my splendor. He will preach those things by which I am known, and extol my praise before nations, kings and the sons of Israel." So we pray that the name of our heavenly Father might be hallowed, that is, that it would be granted to us that we might rightly know him, and that we might so regard him as One to be worshiped and adored with the highest devotion so that every good thing that God—the Father, the heavenly Father, the Lord—agrees with should be ours as well. COMMENTARY ON ROMANS (1562).[41]

1:7 Salutation to All Christians

Not Only for the Romans. JOHANNES BRENZ: This letter was initially written to the Romans. But what shall we say? That it pertains to the Romans alone? By no means. We could wish that the Roman church would have continued always to be acquainted with the doctrine of this letter and to have kept their eyes on it, but it is instead to be deplored that this doctrine opposes nobody more than it does Rome. This is not the place, however, for speaking of such a matter at the present time. Therefore, although this letter is by name written only to the Romans, its doctrine pertains to the universal church of Christ. "For I am not ashamed," says Paul, "of the gospel, for it is the power of God unto salvation for all who believe, not only for the Roman, but first to the Jew and then also to the Greek." COMMENTARY ON ROMANS (1588).[42]

Rome Is Not the Mother Church. JOHN CALVIN: Here, by the way, we see how fond the Catholics are of tying God to Rome, under the claim, as they say, that it is the apostolic see. Let us put the case that it were so, although we do not know why, for all that they allege of St. Peter is but tales and stark lies. It is very certain that St. Paul was held prisoner at Rome, and it may be gathered that he was even put to death there. Behold, all the holiness of Rome is this: that the gospel was persecuted there, and that the devilish dungeon has been defiled with the blood of the martyrs, as it were to provoke God's wrath, and to confederate itself to fight against the truth, and as much as possible to abolish the name and memory of our Lord Jesus Christ. See, that's all the worthiness of Rome. But now compare them to the references to the city of Jerusalem in the holy Scripture, and you will not find even one syllable in common. The Scriptures do not say that God will reign or have any dwelling in the city of Rome, nor that it should be named the mother church, nor have any other dignity or preeminence at all. Indeed, St. Paul says that the faith of the Romans (and at that time they were then only a handful of people) was at the time known everywhere, even to their great renown. For you must not think that those that bore the sword there were the Christians. Rather, the Christians were a few folk gathered together covertly. St. Paul praises and commends them. But it does not mean that the church was over the whole town of Rome. SERMONS ON GALATIANS (1574).[43]

An Argument for Listening to Paul's Teaching. DAVID DICKSON: Argument 7. In the inscription of the letter, there remains the description and salutation of those to whom he writes: . . . You are the beloved of God, effectually called, and in part sanctified, and heirs of grace and peace; so that I may justly in the name of God, apply to you the blessing of the gospel, and wish you grace (i.e., all good things that by way of sanctification flow from the special favor of God). Peace (i.e., all those

---

[41]Bucer, *Metaphrasis et Enarratio*, 19-20 (this is a reprint of the 1536 edition); citing 2 Sam 7:9.
[42]Brenz, *In Epistolam*, 487; citing Rom 1:16.
[43]Calvin, *Sermons on Galatians* [sic], 218v*.

things that help bring about your happiness, either in this present life, or that which is to come) from God, through Christ the Mediator, to be communicated to you. Therefore, you ought to listen to my doctrine with a fully willing mind. EXPOSITION OF PAUL'S EPISTLES.[44]

ALL CHRISTIANS MAY READ THE SCRIPTURES. WILLIAM GUILD: That people should not be barred from reading the Scriptures. . . . The apostle directs his letter "to all that are in Rome," he says, "beloved of God, called to be saints."

From which it follows: If the apostle directs his letter—as a part of divine Scripture—to all Christians in common that were at Rome, then all Christians were permitted to read the letter. And, consequently, it implies that no Christian should be prevented from reading holy Scripture. THE OLD ROMAN CATHOLIC (1649).[45]

THE CHRISTIAN'S PECULIAR GLORY. JUAN DE VALDÈS: This is St. Paul's ordinary salutation, the desire that grace and peace from God, and from Christ, may come to them, whom God loves, and who are saints. Whence I understand that "it is the Christian's peculiar glory to be beloved of God." COMMENTARY ON ROMANS (1556).[46]

CALLED TO BE SAINTS. PETER MARTYR VERMIGLI: He added, "called to be saints," by which expression he reminds them of their former state. If they are called to sanctity, since no movement can take place without both an origin and a destination, they would therefore have been able to conclude that they had been called to holiness out of a state of filth and impurity. Nor must you tell me, "Not all who were from Rome should have been called saints, since there were many in that city who were barely absolved from their sins, but not yet perfect," since these two states are not opposed to each other. Since Paul first cast his eyes on the better kind, by their name and reputation

he honored with them the entire church as well. For the particular honors enjoyed by individual members redounds to the other members. Then the apostle observed the end to which they had been called, namely, that they might be made saints. He saw them as having been called into the communion of the saints, whence also they received the title of saints. Augustine in book six of *Against Julian* admonishes us not to suppose that the word *sanctity* means perfection. He cites that passage of Paul from 1 Corinthians, where he says, "The temple of God is holy, which temple you are," although it is not hidden to anybody how much the Corinthians struggled with the greatest number of vices. And if we would thoroughly investigate the semantic force of this word, "saints," as the very same one Augustine teaches in his book *Of Faith and the Creed*, we would find that it is taken from the verb "to make sacred" or "render inviolable." For that is called "sacred" which is constant and firm and esteemed as something to be kept inviolate. But truly there is nothing that impedes us more than sin does, so that we endure less lastingly. For it is said, "The wages of sin is death." Therefore it happens that the highest possible sanctity is conferred by the forgiveness and remission of sins. That which Paul says in 1 Corinthians is not at all disagreeable to this way of reckoning when he says, after having gone over a whole catalog of shocking sins, "But now you have been washed, you have been sanctified." Forgiveness of sins is obtained through the Holy Spirit. If we say that someone is sacred on account of the Spirit's preparatory work, those who have believed in Christ could genuinely be called saints when they are prepared by the Spirit and the grace of Christ for glory and the highest purity in the life to come. COMMENTARY ON ROMANS (1560).[47]

GRACE AND PEACE. PHILIPP MELANCHTHON: First he wishes them "grace," which is reconciliation and the gift of the Holy Spirit. Then "peace," which

---

[44]Dickson, *Exposition of All Paul's Epistles*, 2*.
[45]Guild, *Old Roman Catholik*, 31*.
[46]Valdés, *Commentary upon St. Paul's Epistle*, 5*.

[47]Vermigli, *In Epistolam S. Pauli*, 16; citing 1 Cor 3:17; Rom 6:23; 1 Cor 6:11.

is all the other good things that are beneficial for anyone. For the word *peace* according to Hebrew custom generally signifies favorable and flourishing conditions. In the church many gifts must be exercised, as must purity of doctrine, the growth of virtue, concord, constancy, nourishment, and hospitality. All these things are included in the word *peace*. Then he conjoins God the Father and the Lord Jesus Christ, first that he might remind us that both grace and the other gifts are given by God on account of the Son as mediator, and second that we might know how we might with certainty obtain these things—namely, if we ask for them on the basis of the Son. Third, this conjunction means that Christ is of the very nature of God, equal in power with the Father, reigning and helping us by his divine power as is promised in the psalm, "Help, O Lord, all who stumble, and raise up all who are bowed down." COMMENTARY ON ROMANS (1540).[48]

OUR PEACE COMES FROM GOD'S GRACE. JOHN CALVIN: Nothing should be desired more principally than that God would be propitious toward us, which is here designated as "grace." Second, that prosperity and success in all things might flow from him, which is here signified by the word *peace*. For however everything might appear to be favorable to us, if God is hostile, then even blessing itself will be turned into a curse. Therefore, there is only one foundation of our happiness, God's benevolence, by which it happens that we enjoy true and secure prosperity, and our salvation is advanced even by the things that are against us. Then, since peace is asked for from the Lord, we understand that whatever good thing comes on us is the fruit of divine beneficence. Nor is it to be passed over that these goods are at the same time asked for from the Lord Jesus. This is an honor

deservedly rendered to him who is not only the Administrator and Dispenser of the Father's kindness toward us, but who also works in common with him. But the apostle wished to note properly that all benefits come to us from God through him. There are those who prefer to understand by the word *peace* tranquility of conscience, which interpretation I do not deny is sometimes appropriate, but since it is certain that the apostle wished to treat of the highest of goods, that earlier interpretation that was suggested by Bucer is far more fitting. Therefore, wanting to desire for the saints the highest happiness, he turns to its source, as he did before, namely, to the grace of God, which not only brings us eternal blessedness, but is also the cause of all good things in this life. COMMENTARY ON ROMANS (1556).[49]

ARIANS INTERPRETED THIS PASSAGE WRONGLY. JOHANNES OECOLAMPADIUS: The Arians plundered this present passage for themselves, as if to say that the Son was less than the Father, since here the Father is called "God," but the Son is only called "Lord." But truly, their throats are cut by their own sword—for if the Son gives the same things, namely, grace and peace, and does the same things that the Father does, he must likewise be God along with the Father. For the working of God and that of a creature are not one and the same. For if some creature were to be placed within the dignity of the divine essence, then God would be pulled down to the level of his creatures. But it is said of Christ that "he is Lord," that we might not be ashamed of his cross. But because he himself ministered to us as a servant, he is worthy that we should serve him in return and that we should acknowledge him as Lord even over the whole human race. ANNOTATIONS ON ROMANS (1525).[50]

---

[48]Melanchthon, *Commentarii in Epistolam Pauli*, a vii r-v; citing Ps 145:14.

[49]Calvin, *In Omnes Pauli*, 3-4.
[50]Oecolampadius, *In Epistolam B. Pauli*, 4r.

1:8-15 PAUL'S DESIRE TO VISIT
THE CHURCH AT ROME

⁸First, I thank my God through Jesus Christ for all of you, because your faith is proclaimed in all the world. ⁹For God is my witness, whom I serve with my spirit in the gospel of his Son, that without ceasing I mention you ¹⁰always in my prayers, asking that somehow by God's will I may now at last succeed in coming to you. ¹¹For I long to see you, that I may impart to you some spiritual gift to strengthen you— ¹²that is, that we may be mutually encouraged by each other's faith, both yours and mine. ¹³I do not want you to be unaware, brothers,ᵃ that I have often intended to come to you (but thus far have been prevented), in order that I may reap some harvest among you as well as among the rest of the Gentiles. ¹⁴I am under obligation both to Greeks and to barbarians,ᵇ both to the wise and to the foolish. ¹⁵So I am eager to preach the gospel to you also who are in Rome.

a Or *brothers and sisters*. In New Testament usage, depending on the context, the plural Greek word *adelphoi* (translated "brothers") may refer either to brothers or to brothers and sisters   b That is, non-Greeks

OVERVIEW: The interpreters see Paul's gratitude as a model to be followed in appreciating both God and fellow believers, and they exhort readers to follow his example of demonstrating love through prayer and action.

Along the way, the commentators take the opportunity to explore several contemporary issues. One differentiates Paul's use of the term *catholic* from the claims of the Roman Catholic Church to be the universal church. Another discusses the permissibility of swearing oaths, in contrast to the Anabaptists, who were against them. The interpreters begin to look at the role of God's providence, a theme that will weave its way through the first eight chapters of the letter. God sometimes overturns our plans in order to humble us, and we need to seek the Shepherd's guidance in making our plans.

The reformers also begin to explore another theme they will touch on throughout these chapters, that of spirit and the Holy Spirit. When Paul refers to serving God in his "spirit," they examine whether the passage differentiates between spiritual and ceremonial worship, spirit and law, or spirit and body; or whether it refers to Paul's wholehearted service to God, or to worship as teaching and learning the gospel. God gives us gifts in order that we may both impart and strengthen faith, and these gifts are given to us by the Holy Spirit, their author, through the preaching of the gospel.

Erasmus argues that "wise and foolish" should be translated "educated and uneducated," but Calvin disagrees. Some may have thought Paul arrogant to claim to teach the wise, but he was an apostle bringing "heavenly teaching," and the gospel trumps the human wisdom of law and philosophy. Paul is impelled to proclaim this gospel, one in which the Lord Jesus is "for us," and he is prepared and willing to overcome any danger in order to gain souls for Christ.

1:8 *Gratitude to God for Their Faith*

PAUL ESTABLISHES GOODWILL USING AN EXORDIUM. PHILIPP MELANCHTHON: Learned men and women know that such a lingering over expressing our goodwill in the introduction is customary. Nor is it difficult to assign the parts of the *exordium*† to common rhetorical guidelines. It consists of these parts: "I congratulate you for your knowledge of the gospel, and I wish that that knowledge might increase among you." Then the proposition of the *exordium* follows: "I desire to teach you in person," to which he immediately adds a difficulty, "but until now the churches in these regions have detained me so that I have not been able to continue on to you." Third follows the reason for this proposition, why he wished to teach them in person. Because, he says, I must aid study of the gospel among all learned and unlearned persons. All such things belong to passages aimed at garnering goodwill. COMMENTARY ON ROMANS (1540).[1]

WHY WE SHOULD REJOICE IN THE WELL-DOING OF OTHERS. THOMAS WILSON: Timotheus: What does Paul mean that he gives thanks to God?

Silas: That he was glad and praised God with joy for their conversion to the gospel, and that their fame had grown, not so much because of their conquests over many nations as because of their zeal and fervency for the Christian religion. From this we learn that it is the duty of every faithful man or woman to rejoice for the well-doing of others when they thrive and prosper in godliness. The reasons of this duty are as follows: First, because we are members of one another and therefore ought to suffer together and rejoice together. Second, the well-doing and spiritual prosperity of other Christians redounds to us who have an interest in all their gifts, as related to the use and profit of them, though not for the propriety of them. For every saint is the possessor of his or her own graces, yet in the fruition and benefits there is a communion, according to that which we profess in our creed concerning the "communion of saints," in which we have a just and great matter for rejoicing and thanksgiving. Third, to rejoice at the welfare and the well-doing of the brethren is a testimony that we have Christ, his Spirit, which is a spirit of charity, chasing envy out of the heart, and instead planting brotherly love in it. This

doctrine serves to reprove the envious and malicious that regard and rejoice either little or not at all. A COMMENTARY UPON THE MOST DIVINE EPISTLE OF ST. PAUL TO THE ROMANS (1614).[2]

THREE PURPOSES OF PAUL'S THANKSGIVING. WILLIAM DAY: Here the apostle begins the letter itself, for that which went before was just the salutation that was prefixed before the letter. And note here that the apostle—in almost all his letters (the more to insinuate himself)—begins with the commendation of those to whom he writes, which commendation he ushers in with thanks to God for them. And these thanks he uses first to commend the graces (for which he does commend them to whom he writes) as being such as proceed from God. Second, to show them that—and to whom—they should return thanks for what they have. Third, to manifest his love toward them, for whereas such gifts and graces may procure envy in some, yet such is his love to them that they do not procure envy in him, but rather, thanksgiving to God in their behalf. PARAPHRASE AND COMMENTARY ON ROMANS.[3]

THE HOLINESS OF REJOICING IN OTHERS' GOOD. GEORGE HERBERT: The Country Parson preaches constantly; the pulpit is his joy and his throne . . . the character of his sermon is holiness. He is not witty, or learned, or eloquent, but holy. . . . [This holiness is shown] by his frequent wishes for the people's good and his finding joy therein, even though he himself might, like St. Paul, be sacrificed while in the service of their faith. For there is no greater sign of holiness than in the procuring and rejoicing in another's good. And in this St. Paul excelled in all his letters. How he put the Romans in all his prayers! And never ceased to give thanks for the Ephesians. And for the Corinthians. And for the Philippians, he made requests with joy. THE COUNTRY PARSON.[4]

---

[1]Melanchthon, *Commentarii in epistolam Pauli*, Ai9. †An *exordium* is the beginning part of an oration and typically introduces the audience to the purpose and theme(s) of the speech.

[2]Wilson, *Commentarie*, 31*; citing 1 Cor 12:26; Gal 5:22; 1 Cor 14:4; Eph 1:4. †Wilson uses a fictional dialogue format.
[3]Day, *Paraphrase*, 11*.
[4]Herbert, *Works*, 223-25*; citing Eph 1:16; 1 Cor 1:4; Phil 1:4.

CHRIST OFFERS UP OUR THANKS AS THE ETERNAL PRIEST. ANDREAS KNOPKEN: This is his *narratio,*[†] in which he first gives thanks to God, but does so through Christ, thereby teaching that nothing is pleasing to the Father if Christ the eternal Priest does not offer it to him. He gives thanks for the faith of the Romans just as he did for the Ephesians, for faith is the sole means by which we can appropriate the grace of God and of Christ himself. From this we learn that faith is the gift of God, as he says to the Philippians: "It has been given to you by God, not only that you believe in Christ, but also that you suffer on his account." OF THE EPISTLE TO THE ROMANS (1524).[5]

INCULCATING AN ATTITUDE OF GRATITUDE. JOHN CALVIN: First, it is worth consideration that Paul praises their faith in such a way that he still considers it as something received from God. From this we learn that faith is a gift from God. For if the giving of thanks is the acknowledgment of benefits received, then faith is confessed to come from God by the one who gives God thanks for it. But when we see the apostle always commencing his praise of others with a word of thanksgiving, we should know that we are thereby admonished that all our good things are benefits received from God. For this reason it is fitting to make it our custom to employ similar forms when speaking, by which we might more fervently stir ourselves up to always acknowledging God to be the bountiful giver of all good things. We ought therefore to elevate our thinking about other blessings in one and the same way. Now, if it is fitting to observe this practice in very small blessings, how much more fitting is it when it comes to faith? COMMENTARY ON ROMANS (1540, 1667).[6]

WHAT DOES IT MEAN TO BE "CATHOLIC"? FRIEDRICH BALDUIN: Q: The apostle declares concerning the Roman church, that her faith is proclaimed throughout the world. Therefore, should not the Roman church of today rightly call itself "catholic" [i.e., universal] since her faith is catholic?

A: I answer: . . . The "catholic church" is spoken of in two ways: (1) by reason of place, (2) by reason of faith and doctrine. By reason of place, because it is Christian, that is, not shut up in any one place, as the Jewish church was, but is spread over the whole circle of the earth, embracing all places, peoples, and nations. And in this proper sense the Roman church cannot be called "catholic," because she is only a piece of the church, made up neither of all places, nor peoples nor nations. And if the title "catholic church" were fitting only for the Roman, it would follow that before the foundation of the Roman church there was no catholic church in the world. For the Roman only began to be a church when the gospel was preached in Rome. At which time there were already so many other kinds of churches, the Jerusalemite, Antiochene, Samaritan, Egyptian, and Greek churches, all of which were founded before the Roman. But by reason of faith and doctrine, the church is called "catholic" because it is the guardian of the catholic faith and doctrine, that is, the orthodox, prophetic, and apostolic doctrine, which was also openly confessed: and in this respect the ancient Roman church was said to be catholic, but not alone—because many parts of the church held to the same faith and therefore are not to be excluded from this *elogio* (inscription). And accordingly those churches are parts of the catholic church, not the catholic church itself. COMMENTARY ON ROMANS (1620).[7]

1:9 Paul Prays Frequently for the Roman Christians

THE NATURE OF OATHS. JOHN CALVIN: Since he recognized that for the establishing of their faith by his preaching it was expedient that the Romans be

---

[5]Knopken, *In Epistolam ad Romanos*, B2r; citing Eph 1:15-16, Phil 1:29. [†]Rhetorical term for the second part of a speech, in which what has happened is narrated.
[6]Calvin, *Commentarii in Omnes Epistolas*, 3.

[7]Balduin, *Catechesis Apostolica*, 61-62.

persuaded well of his sincerity, he employs an oath, a necessary remedy that is the price for a matter to be all the more firm and beyond doubt whenever an affirmation could vacillate in uncertainty. For if an oath is nothing other than invoking God as witness for the confirmation of our words, it would be most foolish for anyone to blame the apostle for having sworn an oath. Nor did he transgress Christ's prohibition against swearing. It follows therefore that Christ's counsel did not abolish oath-swearing altogether (as the superstitious Anabaptists dream), but rather calls us back to a true keeping of the law. But the law, permitting oaths, condemns only perjury and swearing in vain. Therefore if we want to swear rightly, we will imitate the sobriety and piety in oath-taking that we find in the apostles. But when you perceive this formula, know for certain that God is called as a witness in such a way that he is also summoned as an avenger if we prove false, which Paul elsewhere expresses with these words, "God is my witness against my soul." COMMENTARY ON ROMANS (1540, 1667).[8]

THE CONTRAST OF SPIRIT AND THE EXTERNAL. HEINRICH BULLINGER: "Whom I serve in my spirit." Here also in passing he weaves in the excellent truth that God is not to be worshiped bodily, but in spirit. For he sets spirit contrary to all external things. For "God is Spirit," as Christ also taught in John 4. But when he adds "in the gospel of his Son," he expresses the same thing as if he had said, "according to the doctrine and authority of the gospel of the Son of God." For the gospel shatters all typal shadows[†] with its brightness, and places the worship of God wholly in the realm of spirit. For this reason the Lord departed the earth in his flesh, and sent the power of the Holy Spirit in his place. COMMENTARY ON ROMANS (1533).[9]

WHOLEHEARTEDLY SURRENDERED. THEODORE BEZA: "With my spirit," *en tō pneumati mou.* That is, fully willing and wholeheartedly surrendered to him. For although the antithesis between ceremonial and spiritual worship may be tacitly implied, nevertheless I do not think that Paul is referring to this, but rather is saying this so as to cause their trust in him to be confirmed. He has called God as his witness, whose majesty and glory he could not demonstrate in a better way or with greater certainty by anything else he might have done than he did by the diligence that he employed in announcing the gospel that was entrusted to him. MAJOR ANNOTATIONS (1594).[10]

PERSISTENCE IN PRAYER. JOHN CALVIN: "How continually." By his very persistence in praying, he expresses a greater vehemence of love for the Romans than he has until now. . . . He is, therefore, speaking particularly of those prayers for which the saints deliberately gather their thoughts, just as we see that the Lord himself sought solitude for the purpose of such prayers. At the same time, he implies how frequently, or better, how continuously he was at this task, when he said that he devoted himself unceasingly to it. COMMENTARY ON ROMANS (1540, 1667).[11]

1:10 Paul Demonstrates His Love for the Roman Christians

LOVE SHOULD BE DEMONSTRATED. MARTIN BUCER: To possess true charity is not only to choose to treat as equals, share in all things, spend time together, and converse with those whom you love, but to do so aiming at the glory of God. For that is true love that sincerely embraces all men and women in the Lord. For this reason, an empty pretense of words—that those who are not moved by the glory of God brag about to the people who they want to believe they care about—is not true love. "Our love is in spirit," they say. "It cares

---

[8]Calvin, *Commentarii in Omnes Epistolas*, 4; citing 2 Cor 1:23.
[9]Bullinger, *In Sanctissimam Pauli ad Romanos*, 3; citing Jn 4:23-24.
[†]Old Testament types (symbols, images, figures) that point toward New Testament fulfillments.

[10]Beza, *Annotationes Majores*, 10-11.
[11]Calvin, *Commentarii in Omnes Epistolas*, 4.

nothing for carnal addresses and custom and letters and all the other courtesies of this life. They are mere words." Did the apostle Paul love people in the flesh or did he love them in spirit? It was undoubtedly in spirit. And yet, who else at any time ever more fully rendered those courtesies that belong to true and natural love, though without sin? Over what lands and through what seas and through what hazards to his life did he cross, with so much willingness and eagerness, so that he might see his brethren face-to-face and refresh them? So that where he was not permitted to do so, he had the habit of sending letters in his stead (though he was not content with this alone), even those letters that he regarded as among his most important. How much did he strive to be better informed of the affairs of his brothers, even in those matters pertaining to the flesh? How much did he have his hands full trying to ensure that he did not fail them even on the point of some external comfort? For the Spirit of Christ does not take away nature, but restores it. So also in this matter, the Spirit is far more solid and more efficacious than all the powers of nature, so that that love that springs forth from this Spirit is more powerful and suffers longer and pervades everything and really grips the heart. He only removes those things that are improper for true love, but the rest he stretches and perfects. The law of love says, "You shall love your neighbor as yourself." Therefore let anybody ask himself whether he wishes that the benevolence of others toward him should be restricted to the thoughts of the heart alone? Would he not also rejoice in the greetings and company of friends, the interchange of letters, and other things that belong to courtesy? "Our friendship," they say, "is not constituted by seeing each other in the flesh, or by the courtesy of letters, so neither will it be lost by the intermission of such things." However, neither is a tree constituted by its fruits, and yet who would judge that tree to be tolerated, or who would rightly think it to be a fruit tree as long as it remains unproductive? It is true that love is long lasting, even if nothing of this kind of courtesies is received from those whom it

loves—as long as the opportunity for showing such courtesies is not at their disposal. Otherwise the courtesies will certainly not be omitted. But an enclosed fire does not spread to everything—if somehow it should break out—quite as much as solid love searches for every possible occasion for courtesy. Therefore, so that we do not deceive both ourselves and others, men and women are to be loved with the heart, not with the tongue alone, so that we love them with true charity and not by some empty dream of the mind. Commentary on Romans (1562).[12]

Impelled by Affection, Not Curiosity. Lucas Osiander: "Always in my prayers to God," entreating him that he might preserve and also strengthen you in true faith, and at the same time "praying, if by some means I might at last find some opportune way to come to you in the will of God." I implore God that at some time, by his benign will, he would permit me a happy departure to come to you. Moreover, I am not enticed to journey to distant lands out of curiosity. Rather, I am compelled to it by the affection of Christian love. Brief and Perspicuous Explication of Paul's Epistles (1583).[13]

1:11 Paul's Desire to Visit and Strengthen Them

God's Gifts Are for Imparting and Strengthening Faith. Martin Bucer: Here we ought to ponder how much the Lord desires to bring about the salvation of our brothers and sisters through our ministry. God's spiritual gifts are given not only to impart faith but also to strengthen it, and Paul deservedly regards himself as a minister and instrument of Christ for both. That the Lord may connect those of us who are heirs of eternal salvation more firmly to each other and unite us as one, he

---

[12]Bucer, *Metaphrasis et Enarratio*, 42 (this is a reprint of the 1536 edition).
[13]Osiander, *Epistolae S. Pauli*, 8.

commands us to minister in this way to each other. Undoubtedly, therefore, if there were a greater earnestness among us for discipling and admonishing our brothers and sisters, by no means would the Lord disdain to more fervently and ardently give increase to our gifts. In this way, with spiritual gifts being shared mutually among us, we would immediately find ourselves more richly bestowed with them. And in that very day, becoming more confirmed, our faith would enlarge itself, and would spread out into the whole life of God and into a full measure of holiness.... It causes Paul no shame to admit here that his own faith can be strengthened by the faith of the Romans. For, as we've said, it very much agrees with the custom and character of Paul to write this truthfully, even to write about how he desired from the Romans an aid of this kind to his faith. COMMENTARY ON ROMANS.[14]

PREACHING CONFERS SPIRITUAL GIFTS.

JOHANNES BRENZ: Next, Paul once again points to the purpose for the external preaching of the gospel. He says: "that I might impart to you a spiritual gift," and "that I might be strengthened in faith together with you." It was not his habit to confer any spiritual gift on anyone, nor to strengthen either his own faith or that of another, by means of tapestries woven by artisans[†] or by making the sign of the cross with his hands, as the popes are accustomed to blessing their adorers, but rather by the ministry of preaching the gospel. Therefore, the preaching of the gospel is the instrument by which spiritual gifts are conferred on us, and by which we receive both consolation in times of difficulty and the strengthening of our faith. Consequently, these things that we ought to be familiar with are set forth so that we may know by what instrument a remedy should be sought in the midst of afflictions, errors, turmoil of soul, and in times of desperation. For there is no affliction so great or severe, nor any turmoil of soul so vehement, nor any error so perplexing for which the

Word of the Lord is not the medicine and remover of difficulties.

The spiritual gifts that are conferred on us through the gospel by the Holy Spirit as their author are precisely these: faith, strengthening in faith, hope in adverse circumstances, comfort, constancy, patience, charity toward one's neighbor, generosity, temperance, chastity, and the other virtues of this kind. COMMENTARY ON ROMANS (1588).[15]

WHY PAUL WANTS TO VISIT.

JOHN MAYER: Touching which, so that they might be more confirmed, he gave them to understand that he had often determined to come to them but, so far, had been prevented. That is, the Lord, whom he besought for a voyage to them, had detained him from coming by employing him in other parts, where there was first need for his labors. And this prevention is also intimated in Romans 15:20.

"That I might have some fruit, and so on." That is, that by my coming I might benefit you in respect to grace, as I have done with the other Gentiles. For in regard to the apostle's office being to gather fruit to God by converting and establishing souls, he referred to the fruit that would be had through his coming, so much did he find joy in doing this good wherever he went.

Again, to confirm further to them his goodwill to do this, he sets himself forth as a debtor to all sorts, which name he took upon himself in respect to his apostolic calling, which was to preach to all. So he became a debtor by God's binding him to preach to the people of all nations. The particulars [about whom this includes] are reckoned by the phrase "the Greeks and barbarians," wise and unwise. By the Greeks he means those that had more humane learning and civility; by the barbarians, people who were more rude and illiterate; to declare which, he varied the phrase, calling the Greeks wise, and the barbarians unwise. COMMENTARY ON ROMANS.[16]

---

[14]Bucer, *Metaphrasis et Enarratio*, 42.

[15]Brenz, *In Epistolam*, 490-91. [†]May refer to the pallium, a vestment granted by the pope to an archbishop.
[16]Mayer, *A Commentarie upon all the Epistles*, 7*.

EXAMPLE TO PASTORS AND LISTENERS.
TILEMANN HESSHUS: In this well-wishing, Paul teaches us what manner of affection should exist in a godly pastor as well as a diligent disciple and what it should aim at. For when Paul says that he prays to the Lord that an opportunity would be given him for instructing and strengthening the Romans in the faith, he is admonishing all pastors that they ought to expend such great effort in the pursuit of advancing the health of the church that they should put her before all the comforts of this life, and that they should not hesitate to undertake for her whatever hardships and troubles and dangers and labors might come. For because the Son of God did not hesitate to give up his own life for the sake of our salvation, it is entirely fitting for us not to flee from labors or dangers when we are serving the divine glory and the salvation of the church.

In turn, the hearer should have a genuine and ardent effort to learn. They should also acknowledge the special gift of God that works in prophets, apostles, and teachers. Let them hold pious teachers in reverent regard; let them fervently ask God that the ministry of the gospel will be illumined, that carelessness in its teaching will not increase its hardships and dangers, that ministers will earnestly seek the undoubted truth, and that they will not flee from the hardships and sufferings that accompany the profession of the gospel. COMMENTARY ON PAUL'S EPISTLES (1606).[17]

1:12 Mutual Encouragement

MUTUAL STRENGTHENING. PHILIPP MELANCHTHON: [This next point] deals with mutual strengthening in faith. Paul desires to teach and strengthen them, and also to stir up the same from them toward each other. Christ spoke to Peter of this mutual strengthening when he said: "But when you have returned to me, strengthen your brethren." It is beneficial in matters of doctrine for the faithful to pay heed to the testimony of the godly and the experienced. COMMENTARY ON ROMANS (1540).[18]

STRENGTHENING IN THE TRUE FAITH. HEINRICH BULLINGER: For I desire to see you, most certainly not so that I might gain some free advantage from you, like extorting money or robbing from you, but rather that I might confer some spiritual gift. So that you will rightly understand me: I long to strengthen you in the true faith. Even this is sometimes misunderstood, as if in the name of "faith" I desire to lord it over you, whereas I desire from you only a mutual comfort and joy of soul, so that together with you, you might hear me speaking of my faith and I in return might hear you speaking of your faith. For truly, mutual conference and exhortation greatly strengthen the human heart. COMMENTARY ON ROMANS (1533).[19]

PAUL'S HUMILITY. JOHN CALVIN: See with how much moderation the pious soul abases itself, since it does not refuse to seek strengthening even from unskilled novices! Nor is Paul speaking insincerely, since there is nobody so weak in the church of Christ that they cannot offer us something for our advancement. But we are impeded by our own ill-will and arrogance, which keep us from gathering nearly as much fruit as we should. It is our pride—that drunkenness with self-glory—that makes people despise and take leave of others, thinking themselves to be quite self-capable. COMMENTARY ON ROMANS (1540, 1667).[20]

ENCOURAGE WITH THE WORD THAT CONSOLES. KATHARINA SCHÜTZ ZELL: He does not want us to fear human beings, as he also says in Matthew 10 and Luke 12. Equally little does he want us to trust in human beings and their help, and he cries in the prophet Isaiah in chapter 31, "Woe to those who trust in the great number and

---

[17]Hesshus, *Commentarius in Omnes*, 15.

[18]Melanchthon, *Commentarii in Epistolam Pauli*, 219-20; citing Lk 22:32.
[19]Bullinger, *In Sanctissimam Pauli ad Romanos*, 3.
[20]Calvin, *Commentarii in Omnes Epistolas*, 5.

strength of human beings and not in the Holy One of Israel and who do not seek God." And he tells how he intends to send evil on them and not allow his word to be overcome and will rise up against the wicked and their help. We have consolations enough in all the Scripture, which we should have always before the eyes of our hearts. If, however, we are weak in our flesh, we should always encourage each other with the Word of God, by which we will be consoled through our faith that we share among ourselves, as Paul says to the Romans in chapter 1. APOLOGIA FOR MASTER MATTHEW ZELL.[21]

1:13 Hindered in Coming

OBSTRUCTION IS THE WORK OF GOD. JUAN DE VALDÉS: St. Paul, in saying that his pious inclination to go and visit the Romans had been prohibited or obstructed by God in order that the fruit might be greater when he went, teaches godly persons that when they are obstructed in any desires which may appear holy and pious to them, they may rest assured that that obstruction is the work of God, who purposes by that obstruction something greater, more pious, and more holy.

Human wisdom is incapable of this, while the Holy Spirit is capable of it. COMMENTARY ON ROMANS (1556).[22]

WHY PAUL HAS BEEN DELAYED. NIELS HEMMINGSEN: This approval is also an answer in advance of an objection. For when he gives his reasons why he had not come, he makes clearer the whole affair as to why he had fallen short of his original purpose. He thus overturns the objection of those who were anxiously waiting for his coming. Also, it was due to a redirection of task: "For I," he says, "intended to come to you, but I was hindered." But this hindrance appears to have been the difficult struggle that Paul had against false apostles whose mouths needed to be shut, lest the

seed of the heavenly Word which he had cast in various places should be choked by . . . thorns. COMMENTARY ON ROMANS (1562).[23]

GOD KEEPS US HUMBLE AND DEPENDENT. JOHN CALVIN: He says this because he had to this point testified that he persistently made request of the Lord that he might permit him to visit them sometime; as this could have appeared an empty request unless he actually seized opportunities that presented themselves to visit, he now strengthens their confidence in him. For he says that it was not for lack of effort that he hadn't yet come, but lack of ability, since he had frequently been impeded in carrying out his desired plan. We learn from this that the Lord frequently overturns the plans of the saints, by which he might humble us and by such humility train us to look instead to his providence, that we might depend on it. However, the holy ones who deliberate nothing without the Lord's will are not strictly speaking driven off course. For it is an impious audacity to omit God when making future arrangements, as if the future was in our power! James sharply castigates this audacity. COMMENTARY ON ROMANS (1540, 1667).[24]

FOLLOWING THE SHEPHERD'S LEADING. MARTIN BUCER: With regard to the saints, the best of them seek counsel, and those who inquire after the Lord's will with holy modesty and solicitude will make greater progress. Let us keep in mind that just like sheep, that Shepherd under whose hand we will then gladly abide will not fail us in any respect; we will not be lacking in any good thing; he will grant us to lie down in green pastures and gently lead us to flowing waters; he will conduct us along the paths of righteousness for his name's sake. We should confess, to the glory of the Lord, that which the seer elsewhere mused: "I am truly stupid and know nothing, and am as a dumb animal before you. Therefore I remain always in your presence; you have held me by my

---

[21]Zell, *Church Mother*, 80*; citing Mt 10:26, 28; Lk 12:4; Is 31:1-2; Mt 26:41.
[22]Valdés, *Commentary upon St. Paul's Epistle*, 8*.
[23]Hemmingsen, *Commentarius in Epistolam*, 35-36.
[24]Calvin, *Commentarii in Omnes Epistolas*, 5; citing Jas 4:13.

right hand; you direct and lead me by your counsel, and thus glory pursues me and will overtake me." COMMENTARY ON ROMANS (1562).[25]

PROPAGATION OF THE GOSPEL AS FRUIT. NIELS HEMMINGSEN: He adds the motive for his coming: "So that," he says, "I might have some fruit among you." Without doubt, this fruit was the propagation of the gospel, and the strengthening of the Romans in true doctrine.... Sincere ministers of God should imitate this example of Paul, by which the church might daily increase through ministerial visits, and doctrinal purity might be preserved. COMMENTARY ON ROMANS (1562).[26]

ANOTHER ARGUMENT FOR LISTENING TO PAUL'S TEACHING. DAVID DICKSON: Although I have been hitherto hindered from coming to you, yet after many impediments, I resumed my purpose of coming to you again, that, by the preaching of the gospel, I might not only confirm you in the faith and obedience of the gospel, but might be a means of converting some among you to the faith, even as among the other Gentiles I have gained some to God. Therefore, you ought to hearken to my teaching on the doctrine [of justification by faith]. EXPOSITION OF PAUL'S EPISTLES.[27]

1:14 A Gospel for the Wise and the Foolish

THE GREEKS AND BARBARIANS. DESIDERIUS ERASMUS: "To Greeks and to Barbarians." In the Greek the conjunction "and" is doubled: *Hellēsin te kai Barbarois*, that is, "to both Greeks and also to the Barbarians." And again with *sophois te kai anoētois*: "to both the wise and also to the foolish." The repetition of the conjunction is not without reason, as it signifies that Paul is a debtor to all equally, without any favoritism toward a particular

people. What's more, he presses against the Jews who wished to restrict the preaching of the gospel to themselves alone. As for the rest, here *sophois* does not mean "the wise" as much as it does "the learned," and *anoētois* is better understood as "uneducated" and "uninstructed." For the Greeks claimed wisdom or learning for themselves. Last, the "Greeks," which you will sometimes find used to represent Gentiles of any kind, he sets against the barbarians whom he calls *anoētois*, or unlearned in philosophy and uninstructed. ANNOTATIONS ON ROMANS (1527).[28]

A GOSPEL FOR ALL. JOHN CALVIN: What he meant by "Greeks" and "barbarians" he explains when he calls them by the epithets "wise" and "foolish." Although Erasmus is not wrong to alter these to "learned" and "uneducated," I prefer to retain the words of Paul himself. It has been argued that out of courtesy Paul did not claim for himself the right to be arrogant on account of his believing himself capable of teaching something to the Romans, who were a people thought in every way to surpass preeminently the whole world in learning, prudence, and expertise. For it would appear that the Lord put him under obligation to the wise as well. Here two things should be considered: (1) That he was directed to bring the gospel to the wise by a heavenly mandate, by which the Lord might subject to himself all the wisdom of this world, and make all acumen and every kind of knowledge and all loftiness of the arts give way to the simplicity of his doctrine. (2) And what is more, how the Romans are reduced to the same class with the unlearned and thus softened so that they might receive as fellow disciples under the same master, Christ, those whom previously they would not have regarded as worthy of being students. Therefore, the unlearned are by no means to be kept away from this school, nor should we run away from them out of foolish fears. COMMENTARY ON ROMANS (1540, 1667).[29]

---

[25]Bucer, *Metaphrasis et Enarratio*, 43 (this is a reprint of the 1536 edition); citing Ps 23:1-6; 73:22-23.
[26]Hemmingsen, *Commentarius in Epistolam*, 36.
[27]Dickson, *Exposition of All Paul's Epistles* (1659), 3*.

[28]Erasmus, *In Novum Testamentum*, 328.
[29]Calvin, *Commentarii in Omnes Epistolas*, 5.

TEACHING THE "WISE." PHILIPP MELANCH-THON: He touches on the apostolic office. "I am," he says, "a debtor to both the wise and the foolish." This certainly appears to be a boastful thing to say. The apostle dares to claim that he is capable of teaching even the wise! What kind of arrogance this must have looked like to the leading men—the Romans—for the Jewish wanderer to offer himself as a teacher even of the wise! Since for the most part they excel in temperament and teaching, they admire themselves too much, especially when they persuade themselves they are holy and they demand that divine honors be paid to them. Some of this I've seen myself. People like these look down on Paul from on high and deride this statement in which he claims to be a teacher of the wise. But we must remember that he is an apostle who brings not human but heavenly teaching, like Elijah, Elisha, and Isaiah, who were the teachers and governors of kings and high priests. Thus, let us pay attention to Paul as well, and may the wise not be ashamed to learn from God, since we experience all the time how human wisdom basely digresses and goes far astray, as all wise men and women have complained. For God said, "I will destroy the wisdom of the wise," which every period of history has clearly demonstrated, and everyday life bears witness. COMMENTARY ON ROMANS (1540).[30]

THE GOSPEL BESTS LAW AND PHILOSOPHY. PETER MARTYR VERMIGLI: If the gospel is so widely accessible that nobody is excluded from it, it is evident that it greatly surpasses philosophy in excellence, for not everyone is suited for philosophy. It even surpasses the law of Moses, which was revered by one nation only, whereas the gospel sounds forth everywhere. Chrysostom[†] concluded from this passage that neither the syllogisms of the philosophers nor the preparatory study of human sciences should be admitted when it comes to the gospel. And certainly we regard old women and peasants and the aged as just as much suited for the gospel as nobles, the wealthy and philosophers. And, in a word, there is no one so illustrious and brilliant, nor on the other hand anyone so common and unlearned who cannot be saved by the gospel. Also on this text Chrysostom calls forward an example, in asserting the dignity of the gospel, of how Plato, the most highly celebrated and honored of philosophers, had gone to Sicily three times to minister healing to the afflicted and to be a guide to the tyrant so that he might enact fair and just laws.[†] He was not at all successful in these things. For Dionysius became even worse in those days so that he was in the end stripped of his rule. And that kingdom was left no better off for Plato's efforts, even though for this cause Plato had put his own head in danger, and had been captured by pirates and reduced to slavery. By this example it is manifestly apparent how weak philosophy is for improving human affairs. COMMENTARY ON ROMANS (1560).[31]

GOSPEL PREACHING. NIELS HEMMINGSEN: By juxtaposing contrasting terms, Paul points to the distinguishing characteristics of persons in the various nations, some of whom are wise, and others unlearned. First, let us conclude from this that the preaching of the gospel is universal. By it all persons, without distinction, are called to a free salvation. For public preaching, said Chrysostom, is placed before all people. It does not recognize differences in rank, ethnic prominence, or anything else of this kind. Second, the gospel is a different kind of teaching from philosophy. Indeed, it is unknown to the philosophers of the world. Third, a singular readiness of heart for preaching the gospel is required of ministers of the gospel. COMMENTARY ON ROMANS (1562).[32]

---

[30]Melanchthon, *Commentarii in Epistolam Pauli*, 220.

[31]Vermigli, *In Epistolam S. Pauli Apostoli*, 39-40. [†]Citing Chrysostom, *Homilies on The Epistle to the Romans* (Homily 2). [†]See Diogenes Laertius, *Lives of Eminent Philosophers* 3.18 (*Life of Plato*).

[32]Hemmingsen, *Commentarius in Epistolam*, 36-37.

1:15 *Called to Proclaim the Gospel*

PROCLAIMER OF GOOD NEWS. MARTIN BUCER: "To proclaim the gospel." Paul speaks eagerly, especially because he is impelled—brought forth by Christ—to proclaim salvation. The apostle truly is a *basar* (proclaimer of good news) and *euangelizein* (evangelist), for which reason he delivers the preaching of Christ from the Scriptures. And those who share Christ warn, rebuke, and exhort. But they do it all from this: that the Lord Jesus receives us as his friends, as those whom he restores to grace with the Father. Therefore, Paul will be announcing the gospel to them: that the Lord Jesus is for us, and he is deemed worthy to excel. He is the first and most prominent one. COMMENTARY ON ROMANS (1562).[33]

EQUIPPED FOR THE DANGEROUS JOURNEY. PETER MARTYR VERMIGLI: Factors that often cause people to lose heart and not grab ahold of a task are: not knowing the outcome, the dangers to be faced, the hardships that will be confronted, and anything for which we are not sufficiently equipped with abilities and resources for carrying out the work. But against ignorance of the outcome, Paul counters the certainty of the promise that he had come to understand would be the means of converting the nations to Christ. Against the dangers that remained before him, he counters the profitability of the enterprise, since by it he would gain for Christ an infinite number of men and women. Merchants demonstrate how powerful this motive is for shaking off sluggishness and sloth. Given the opportunity for a profit, they do not hesitate even in the face of danger from storms, difficulties of travel, and the risk of being attacked by robbers. The love and charity that ignited and enflamed Paul's heart lightened the hardships that he was yet to encounter. He was not concerned about the means of his abilities and strengths, for he trusted that they would be equal to the work. Paul was wholly depending on Christ to equip him with spiritual gifts and gifts of the Holy Spirit, as much as the place and time would require. COMMENTARY ON ROMANS (1560).[34]

---

[33]Bucer, *Metaphrasis et Enarratio*, 47 (this is a reprint of the 1536 edition).

[34]Vermigli, *In Epistolam S. Pauli*, 40-41.

1:16-17 THE GOSPEL AND THE RIGHTEOUSNESS OF GOD

¹⁶*For I am not ashamed of the gospel, for it is the power of God for salvation to everyone who believes, to the Jew first and also to the Greek.* ¹⁷*For in it the righteousness of God is revealed from faith for faith,*[a] *as it is written, "The righteous shall live by faith."*[b]

a Or *beginning and ending in faith* b Or *The one who by faith is righteous shall live*

OVERVIEW: In these verses, Paul deals with the issue of shame in relation to the gospel. He is not ashamed of the gospel even though it is a stumbling block and appears foolish to many, for it is the power of God. The reformers remind their readers that Paul's readers, like them, were under attack, and that the gospel is not a myth, but rather the revelation of the mind of God, and that they need to be bold rather than fearful in proclaiming it.

The gospel is a joyful message for all. But although the gospel invites all, it doesn't work efficaciously with all. The result is either destruction or eternal life, so it is important that one believe, for the gospel offers life to "all who *believe*." This illustrates the importance of faith in salvation, the major theme for the reformers throughout these eight chapters.

In Romans 1:17 we find the key turning point for the Reformation. This is the verse that triggered the paradigm shift in Martin Luther's theology as he came to believe that the "righteousness of God" referred to here is God's rather than ours, and that it is imputed to us rather than demanded from us. Following Luther's lead, most of the reformers teach that "justification" is more accurately translated as "reckoning righteous" rather than "making righteous," and they explore the way that God's righteousness and the justification of the believer relate to each other.

Many of the reformers immediately warn that justification by "faith alone" does not imply that works don't matter in the Christian life. At the same time, they make it clear that although those who are saved are called to holiness, works are not part of *earning* one's salvation.

1:16 *Not Ashamed of the Powerful Gospel*

NEITHER AFRAID NOR ASHAMED. DESIDERIUS ERASMUS: I am, therefore, a debtor not only to the Greeks but to the barbarian nations, not only to the learned and eloquent but also to the unrefined and unlearned, whoever they are who do not renounce or disdain the gospel. So that, as much as is in me, I am joyfully ready to preach the gospel, even to those of you in Rome. The majesty of the Roman Empire doesn't make me afraid. Nor am I ashamed of preaching the gospel. To the wicked and unfaithful, the gospel seems vain and a matter to be laughed at. But to those who believe, the gospel is the mighty power of God, effective for salvation and the perfect quieting of men's and women's consciences. These are things that neither Jewish traditions nor your philosophy nor your dominion are able to bring about. Although this mighty power of the gospel is equally available to all humans, yet, in God's pleasure, for honor's sake, it was first offered to the Jews and then straight away, the preachers of the gospel spread it abroad to the Greeks and all other nations of the world, to the end that all people should know their own unrighteousness and seek to be made righteous by God, whether they be English or French. For far from salvation are those who neither know their own disease or where to seek for its remedy. PARAPHRASE OF ROMANS.[1]

---

[1]Erasmus, *Seconde Tome*, A2r*.

1535 English Translation. Miles Coverdale: For I am not ashamed of the gospel of Christ. For it is the power of God, which saves all that believe thereon, the Jew first, also the Greek. For in it the righteousness that is of value before God, is opened, which comes out of faith in to faith. As it is written, "The just shall live by his faith." The Bible, that is the Holy Scripture of the Old and New Testaments (1535).[2]

Unashamed of the "Foolishness" of the Gospel. Huldrych Zwingli: "For I am not ashamed." As if Paul were saying that the gospel—which is what he was now calling the gospel story, the objective content itself, the story of Christ—proclaims how Christ is the Son of God, and was seized by the Jews and crucified. When this is preached before the nations it is foolishness, and it is a stumbling block to many, especially the Jews. For example, if someone were to proclaim the virtues of some person and in the end after an extended oration and commendation concerning him were to say that the same person perished on a torture wheel or a cross, many would be offended by this, and many would drive the speaker away with hissing. Accordingly the nations, before whom if Christ were proclaimed the Savior of the whole world, when it was then added that he had been nailed to a cross between two robbers, would say that if he had been the Savior of the world he would never have been crucified, or if he was God, he would never have permitted himself to be crucified—not being mindful that this had been decreed by God before the ages. And so it happens that many are ashamed of the gospel. Let them learn here that those sent by God to preach the gospel must be resolute, lest they be frightened away from their duty out of shame. Notes on Romans (1539).[3]

Why Many Are Ashamed of the Gospel. Georg Mylius: In the third part of the chapter,

since the apostle rejoices in this apothegmatic saying:[†] "I am not ashamed of the gospel," he teaches not only *ho deon* of all the faithful commonly, but also shows *ho ginomenon*, indicating that there are many who are ashamed of the gospel. For the Jews are ashamed; the Gentiles are ashamed; the philosophers are ashamed; the wise of this world are ashamed; even hypocrites are ashamed. For the gospel proposes in part what should be believed: that of which, when asked by any person, one is able to give an account. Indeed, all human reason struggles with the gospel, partly because it takes away the glory of righteousness even from some of the best people in the world, and partly because it commands that, after having spurned all worldly things, we follow Christ through any adversities whatever. Disputation from Romans 1 (1590).[4]

Why Paul Is Not Ashamed of the Gospel. Juan de Valdés: It is as though the apostle had said, "For this is why I am not ashamed of the gospel: because I understand it to be the efficient instrument by which God exhibits himself powerful, saving all who believe, both Jews and Gentiles." He means to say that God exhibits his power by a preached gospel, for that is how he draws those whom he wills unto obedience to the faith, and those who are drawn, he justifies and saves. And in doing that, he operates with the same effect on Gentiles as on Jews.

And I understand him to say "to the Jew first" in conformity with the declaration, "Salvation is of the Jews," for Christ was principally promised to them, and he was born of and among them. Commentary on Romans (1556).[5]

Standing for the Gospel amid Attack. Philipp Melanchthon: The Pharisees were seeing the ceremonies of the law and their traditions being abolished. So they murmured and

---

[2]Coverdale, *Biblia*, 1999v*.

[3]Zwingli, *In Evangelicam Historiam*, 408; citing 1 Cor 1:18.

[4]Mylius, *Disputatio Ex Capite Primo*, A3v. [†]An apothegm is a concise, witty saying.

[5]Valdés, *Commentary upon St. Paul's Epistle*, 10*; citing Jn 4:22.

complained that God was being offered insult, that works that propitiated God were being prohibited, and that a license for sinning was being permitted. It further appeared to them that, with the law abolished, their society was being altered, the distinction between priest and people was being blurred, and the particular glory of their society . . . was being taken away. Such a change brought enormous anguish to the wise. The devil stoked these flames of hate and enflamed rulers to cruelty and to putting the apostles to death. So also in the present day are we mocked with the utmost arrogance by Epicureans, since we believe that the gospel is not a fabrication, and because we believe that it must be seriously submitted to. Kings and rulers howl that the tranquility of their citizens is being disturbed by differences in doctrine. Popes do not want idolatry to be rebuked, lest their own authority should be shaken. Monks, who are fascinated by a little superstition, are anxious for profit and contend that good works are being prohibited. From all these causes arises a savage hatred of the gospel. But against this enormous sentiment we assert that the profession of the gospel is not to be reproached. We are not ashamed of this doctrine. For it is not an empty myth, nor a foreign superstition, but it is the mind of God, divinely revealed, by which he wills to impart eternal salvation to all. COMMENTARY ON ROMANS (1541).[6]

COMPELLED TO LISTEN, NOT BELIEVE. URBA-NUS RHEGIUS: It is true that one cannot force faith into the heart of the godless with sword, stocks, nor rope, nor drive it out. Otherwise not so many Jews would allow themselves to be killed and in former times there would not have been so many martyrs. God the Father must himself draw the sinner in his heart to Christ, give faith and the Holy Spirit through the gospel, otherwise we would eternally remain without faith. But it is God's order in the conversion of the sinner that he uses the preaching of the gospel, which is a power

of God to salvation of all who believe it. To his Word he connects his holy seals, the sacraments, so that the faith that makes us pious and also the Holy Spirit comes into our hearts through the hearing of the gospel, as the Acts of the Apostles prove. Therefore, although one can force no one to believe this or that, for we cannot illumate another person's heart, and not even our own, that being alone the work of God through the Word, yet one can and ought to compel the erring one and the unbeliever to hear the Word of faith. It is the responsibility of the government as a duty of its office to induce subjects to hear the Word of God. For the worldly government has been ordained for us by God for our protection, shelter, and for the furthering of all that is good as much as father and mother, for which it is called fathers with the Father. Now if it is the father's duty to teach his child and to require the child to attend to God's Word and all godliness, if there is need, then the government must also do so and as much as is in them, to require and compel them to this best of all, namely, to hear God's Word and to believe. They do not give faith, nor do they force anyone to believe, but they do force you to hear the Word of salvation, and it is hoped that God would give his grace and faith so that the listener would be converted and believe in Christ. Who now says that the government has no power to force those who believe wrongly to the right faith in this way denies God's Word, which clearly says that the government is God's servant for good. Thus you must either deny that it is good to encourage a person to believe, or else you admit that it is good, as you truly must confess. JUSTIFICATION FOR THE PROSECUTION OF ANABAPTISTS.[7]

PREACH WITHOUT WORRYING IF YOU WILL LOOK FOOLISH. BALTHASAR HUBMAIER: But Satan can well stand to have us build something up today and break it down again after a short time, for thereby many persons are seriously weakened, confused, and scandalized, so that they

---

[6]Melanchthon, *Operum Philippi Melanchtonis*, 219.

[7]CRR 10:216-17*; citing Jn 6; Rom 10; Gal 3; Eph 2; Phil 1; Rom 13.

no longer know at all what they are supposed to believe or practice.

Yes indeed, says our carnal wisdom, which in such matters above all does not want to look like a fool: "We must have forbearance with the weak. Right now it is not fitting to preach that. In a while it will be fitting. Now I preach what, if I had preached it a year ago, I would long ago have been chased out. But now I am still with my sheep." O you of little faith, you are speaking as if it was through your own counsel that the people have stood by the Word of God, and that God would not have been able to sustain it. Here you rob the divine Word of its power and of the efficacy that is ascribed to it everywhere in Scripture. A FORM OF WATER BAPTISM.[8]

LIKE A BEGGAR RESCUING A KING. MARTIN BUCER: With these words he transitions from his introduction to the principal question concerning which he wrote this letter: that we are assuredly justified by faith alone in the Lord Jesus. Who would be ashamed of a thing like this that has such power to save, whether they are a person of great eminence who is receiving the gospel from whomever it is, or whether they are a person of no importance at all who is ministering it to the greatest of persons? For there is a subtle irony in the assertion that he is not ashamed. For while this certainly shows that Paul justly recognizes himself as occupying a lowly position—so that he should deservedly be ashamed to arrogate to himself the role of a teacher and advisor among those who were eminent for their great wisdom, fame, and power—it also means that the matter which he was bringing to them was of such great importance that it should cause shame to nobody, however common they might be, to convey it to the most eminent of people. A beggar is deservedly ashamed to touch or pull at a king's person; but if he discovers that the king has fallen into a pit and there are no others present who can pull him out,

in that case, a beggar can save the life of the king by touching and pulling. He is not afraid of handling the body of the king in any way whatever, as long as he can rescue him from the danger to his life. The apostle was therefore correct when he said this. COMMENTARY ON ROMANS (1562).[9]

THE DIGNITY OF PREACHING. GABRIEL POWEL: The dignity of the ecclesiastical ministry is great, seeing that no man ought to "be ashamed" of it. Whatever the world thinks of it, yet in the sight of God it is so glorious that the Son of God himself, being on earth, doubted not to undertake the office of preaching. They, therefore, that are ashamed, condemn, or think basely of this function are insolent and reproachful against the Son of God himself. A LOGICAL RESOLUTION OF ROMANS I (1602).[10]

THE GOSPEL IS A JOYFUL MESSAGE. PETER RIEDEMANN: The gospel is a joyful message from God and Christ, proclaimed, put into practice, and accepted through the Holy Spirit. It is a word of liberty that sets people free and makes them devout and blessed. As Paul says, "The gospel is the power of God, providing salvation to all who believe it." And again Paul says, "It is the true grace of God on which you have taken your stand and by which you will find salvation, if you hold fast to it as you have received it."

The Word shows us that God has restored his promised grace through Christ, making us heirs of his grace and sharers in its fellowship. It raises up the conscience that has been beaten down by the law and accomplishes what the law demands but cannot achieve. It makes people children of God, and at one with him. They become a new creation with a godly character. HUTTERITE CONFESSION OF FAITH (1565).[11]

---

[8]CRR 5:390*; citing Is 40:8, 55:11; Gen 1:1-31; Jer 6:1-30; 23:29; Heb 4:12.

[9]Bucer, *Metaphrasis et Enarratio*, 44 (this is a reprint of the 1536 edition).
[10]Powel, *Prodromus*, 118-19*.
[11]CRR 9:100-101*; citing Is 61:1-2; Lk 4:16-19; Rom 8:1-2; Rom 1:16; 1 Cor 1:18; 1 Cor 15:-1-2.

SALVATION FOR THOSE WHO BELIEVE. JOHN CALVIN: Because the gospel does not operate efficaciously in everyone, but only where the Spirit as the inner teacher casts light upon hearts, he, therefore, qualifies this with "to all who believe." The gospel is truly offered to all unto salvation; but its power does not appear in every place. But that it is the odor of death to the ungodly does not so much arise from its own nature as it does from their malice. By showing the one way of salvation, he cuts off every other source of confidence. But when they steal themselves away from this one and only salvation the gospel becomes to them a manifestation of their destruction. Therefore, since the gospel invites all to salvation without distinction, it is properly called the doctrine of salvation. For in it Christ is offered, whose proper office is to save those who have been lost. But those who refuse to be saved by him will experience judgment. Last, throughout the Scriptures the word *salvation* is simply opposed to *destruction*. Therefore when the word *salvation* is named, it must be understood in light of the plight it addresses. Since the gospel liberates from destruction and the curse of eternal death, the salvation it offers is eternal life. COMMENTARY ON ROMANS (1540, 1667).[12]

THE GREAT GLORIOUS MYSTERY OF THE GOSPEL. JOHN PRESTON: The point to be gathered out of these words is this: *That righteousness by which alone we can be saved, now in the time of the gospel is revealed and offered to all that will take it.*

When you hear this, it may be that at reading it, you may not have as much of an understanding of the thing as you should. But it is not a matter of light moment, but an exceedingly great thing, to see the righteousness of God revealed. It is the great, glorious mystery of the gospel, which the angels desire to pry into, which made Paul in his ministry so glorious, which swallowed up his thoughts, that he could not tell how to express. That now in this last age, Christ has revealed through us the

unsearchable riches of his grace, that is, riches that I do not know how to express. Therefore, he prays that "God would open their eyes, so that they might comprehend with all the saints, the height and length and breadth of that redemption that Christ has worked for them." It is beyond full comprehension, yet he prays that they may comprehend it in as much measure as is possible, though there is a height, and breadth, and depth in it that cannot be measured. And this is what is revealed to the souls of men and women: the escaping of hell and death; the free access to the throne of grace that no one had before; the liberty to be made the sons and daughters of God and heirs of heaven, yes, kings and priests to God; and the making good of all God's promises, and the entailing of them to our posterity and making them "Yes and Amen." All this, I say, is now revealed, which was not before. SERMON "ON FAITH" (1634).[13]

LAW AND GOSPEL DIFFER IN CLARITY OF MANIFESTATION. JOHN CALVIN: From this also we see the error of those who, in comparing the law with the gospel, represent it merely as a comparison between the merit of works and the gratuitous imputation of righteousness. The contrast thus made is by no means to be rejected, because, by the term law, Paul frequently understands that rule of holy living in which God exacts what is his due, giving no hope of life unless we obey it in every respect; and, on the other hand, denouncing by curse for the slightest failure. Paul does this when showing that we are freely accepted by God and accounted righteous by being pardoned, because that obedience of the law to which the award is promised is nowhere to be found. Thus he appropriately represents the righteousness of the law and the gospel as opposed to each other. But the gospel has not succeeded the whole law in such a sense as to introduce a different method of salvation. Rather, it confirms the law and proves that everything that it promised is fulfilled. What

---

[12]Calvin, *Commentarii in Omnes Epistolas*, 6.

[13]Preston, *Breast-Plate of Faith and Love*, 3-4*.

was shadow, it has made substance. When Christ says that the law and the prophets were in effect until John, he does not consign the fathers to the curse, which, as the slaves of the law, they could not escape. Rather, he intimates that they were only imbued with the rudiments and remained far beneath the height of the gospel doctrine. Accordingly Paul, after calling the gospel "the power of God unto salvation to every one that believes," shortly after adds that it was "witnessed by the law and the prophets." And in the end of the same letter, though he describes "the preaching of Jesus Christ" as "the revelation of the mystery which was kept secret since the world began," he modifies the expression by adding, that it is "now made manifest" "by the Scriptures of the prophets." Hence we infer that when the whole law is spoken of, the gospel differs from it only in respect of its clarity of manifestation. Still, on account of the inestimable riches of grace set before us in Christ, there is good reason for saying that by his advent the kingdom of heaven was erected on the earth. INSTITUTES OF THE CHRISTIAN RELIGION 2.9.4 (1559).[14]

1:17 The Righteous Shall Live By Faith

LUTHER'S TURNING POINT. MARTIN LUTHER: Meanwhile in that same year, 1519, I had begun interpreting the Psalms once again. I felt confident that I was now more experienced, since I had dealt in university courses with St. Paul's letters to the Romans, to the Galatians, and the letter to the Hebrews. I had conceived a burning desire to understand what Paul meant in his letter to the Romans, but thus far there had stood in my way, not the cold blood around my heart, but that one word that is in chapter 1: "The justice of God is revealed in it." I hated that word, "justice of God," which, by the use and custom of all my teachers, I had been taught to understand philosophically as referring to formal or active justice, as they call it, namely, that justice by which God is just and by which he punishes sinners and the unjust. But I,

blameless monk that I was, felt that before God I was a sinner with an extremely troubled conscience. I couldn't be sure that God was appeased by my satisfaction. I did not love, no, rather I hated the just God who punishes sinners. In silence, if I did not blaspheme, then certainly I grumbled vehemently and got angry at God. I said, "Isn't it enough that we miserable sinners, lost for all eternity because of original sin, are oppressed by every kind of calamity through the Ten Commandments? Why does God heap sorrow on sorrow through the gospel and through the gospel threaten us with his justice and his wrath?" This was how I was raging with wild and disturbed conscience. I constantly badgered St. Paul about that spot in Romans 1 and anxiously wanted to know what he meant. I meditated night and day on those words until at last, by the mercy of God, I paid attention to their context: "The justice of God is revealed in it, as it is written: 'The just person lives by faith.'" I began to understand that in this verse the justice of God is that by which the just person lives by a gift of God, that is, by faith. I began to understand that this verse means that the justice of God is revealed through the gospel, but it is a passive justice, namely, that by which the merciful God justifies us by faith, as it is written: "The just person lives by faith." All at once I felt that I had been born again and entered into paradise itself through open gates. Immediately I saw the whole of Scripture in a different light. I ran through the Scriptures from memory and found that other terms had analogous meanings, for example, the work of God, that is, what God works in us; the power of God, by which he makes us powerful; the wisdom of God, by which he makes us wise; the strength of God, the salvation of God, the glory of God. I exalted this sweetest word of mine, "the justice of God," with as much love as before I had hated it with hate. This phrase of Paul was for me the very gate of paradise. Afterward I read Augustine's *On the Spirit and the Letter*, in which I found what I had not dared hope for. I discovered that he too interpreted "the justice of God" in a similar way,

---

[14]Calvin, *Institutes*, 1:366-67*; citing Rom 3:21; 16:25-26; Mt 12:28.

namely, as that with which God clothes us when he justifies us. Although Augustine had said it imperfectly and did not explain in detail how God imputes justice to us, still it pleased me that he taught the justice of God by which we are justified. PREFACE TO THE COMPLETE EDITION OF LUTHER'S LATIN WORKS (1545).[15]

PREACHING THE RIGHTEOUSNESS OF GOD.

MARTIN BUCER: "In it is revealed the righteousness of God." We are first taught that the gospel is only rightly preached when nothing else is preached but the righteousness of God, his perfect goodness and mercy, by which he freely remits sins and bestows the Spirit of righteousness. We then learn that this blessing is received when, by faith, we embrace this righteousness of God toward us, in no way doubting that God now counts us among those whom, snatched from among all the wicked, he will save eternally. In this manner, the righteousness of God is revealed and exhibited to us, which will in due time shine brightly, since he enkindles in us the pursuit of true righteousness. Therefore, nothing is to be more quickly, eagerly, and promptly preached, impressed, and pounded in than that God is righteous: that is, that he is perfectly just and the justifier of the ungodly. For unless this is believed, nothing of genuine love for or pursuit of God can ever be obtained—no divine threats, no fear of judgment will be able to stir up repentance unto salvation. There is no other thing that takes away the neglect of God and damning carnal security, and that stirs up a lively eagerness to correct one's life. COMMENTARY ON ROMANS (1562).[16]

RIGHTEOUSNESS AS THE POWER OF GOD.

HEINRICH BULLINGER: He shapes what follows to explain this (i.e., the power to become children of God), for through it the righteousness of God is revealed, because even if there is a slightly more evi-

dent cause why he should not be ashamed of the gospel—as for example that he is taught by it what true wisdom and righteousness are—nevertheless it is no less an explanation. For that which he called the power of God earlier, he now more openly names the righteousness of God. As if, indeed, preaching speaks about that power of God, not only regarding the terrible majesty of God—omnipotent and ineffable—but even more was established with regard to the righteousness of God, that is, with regard to the way in which a person might be rendered righteous before God. COMMENTARY ON ROMANS (1582).[17]

THE GOSPEL BRINGS LIFE.

THE ENGLISH ANNOTATIONS: Either the just shall live by his faith, or he that is just by faith shall live, which well agrees with the Hebrew and likewise with the main point of the apostle. Here he proves that one obtains life and salvation by the gospel. Forasmuch as the gospel offers to us the only cause of life, namely, the true righteousness, which is Christ's righteousness imputed to human beings by grace and embraced by them through a lively faith, whereunto the allegation out of Habakkuk is pertinent; for the prophet, attributing to faith the obtaining and possessing of spiritual life, consequently attributes to the same the means of getting that righteousness which is the only cause of life. ANNOTATIONS ON ROMANS 1:17.[18]

TO BE RECKONED RIGHTEOUS, NOT MADE RIGHTEOUS.

JOHANNES BRENZ: So we have said that this letter consists of three parts: one about faith, the other about hope, and the third about love. In the first part, therefore, he explains faith, and dwells in its explication up to the fifth chapter. The proposition of this part is: "The just will live by his faith." The arguments that follow this through to the fifth chapter refer back to this. Paul does not simply put forward his own words, but he uses the saying of the prophet for his proposition. Indeed,

---

[15]Luther, *Preface to the Complete Edition*.

[16]Bucer, *Metaphrasis et Enarratio*, 53 (this is a reprint of the 1536 edition).

[17]Bullinger, *Commentarii in Omnes Pauli*, 4.

[18]Downame, ed., *Annotations*, AAA1v*; citing Hab 2:4; Gal 3:26.

these words, "The just lives by his faith," are written in Habakkuk 2. And it is a notable and memorable saying that so delights Paul that he even repeats it in the letter to the Galatians, chapter 3.

... The common person calls someone "just" who is adorned with a certain external honesty. The Philosopher calls someone "just" who is faithful to promises and who does not defraud anyone in business negotiations. The law of Moses calls someone "just" who abides in all things that are written in the law and does them. However, in this saying, "The just shall live by his faith," the title "just" is received in a very different way. For it does not mean this: one who has no defilement, no unrighteousness in their own flesh. "For there is no one righteous on the earth, there is no one who does good, not even one." Rather, it means this: for whom God absolves unrighteousness and does not impute sins to him, on account of Christ his own Son, by faith.

"To be justified" usually means "to be made actually righteous." However, in Paul's discussion, it does not mean "to be made actually righteous," but means (according to the Hebrew phrasing) to be absolved from unrighteousness, to receive forgiveness of unrighteousness, to be reckoned righteous, and to be taken back into grace, on account of Christ, through faith. Thus, and in another place, Paul uses this word with the same meaning, in Acts 13: "Through this is announced to you the remission of sins, from all things from which you were not able to be justified"—that is, absolved and freed—"through the law of Moses." And it follows: Through this, everyone who believes is justified, that is, is absolved from unrighteousness, and is pronounced righteous, or is accepted by God. And so when it is said, "The just one lives by his faith," or "a person is justified by faith," it has this meaning: the person is absolved before God from unrighteousness, by reason of this: because he believes in Christ the Son of God. And so, the soul, by which the person lives in the presence of God, is reckoned justified by faith in Christ. For to be reckoned righteous before God is life, righteousness, and the salvation of a person. You now know how

Paul is using "just" and "justified" in this discussion. COMMENTARY ON ROMANS (1588).[19]

What Is the Righteousness of God?

ANDREW WILLET: "The justice or righteousness of God is revealed." What justice is the apostle speaking of?

There is a justice of God, in which he is righteous and just in himself, as with Psalm 11:7: "The righteous Lord loves righteousness." But the apostle is not speaking of this. The essential justice of God is not communicated to us by faith. There is a distributive justice in God, by which he renders to men and women according to their works. This is Origen's understanding of the justice of God. But this is not the justice whereby a man or woman is justified to salvation, for if the Lord would mark what is done amiss, no man or woman would be able to abide it. The justice of God signifies his verity and truth in keeping his promises; so Gorrhan takes it here. It is true that God graciously performs whatever is performed in Christ, yet his mercy must go before in promising. Theodoret understands the perfect justice of Christ to be that by which he satisfied the wrath of God for our sins and accomplished our redemption. And this perfect justice of Christ is revealed in the gospel. But the apostle speaks evidently of such justice whereby a man or woman is justified before God, which is not that perfect justice inherent in Christ, but the applying of it to us by faith. Therefore Chrysostom's exposition is the best, who in *Homilia* 3 takes it for that justice which is communicated and infused to us by that justice of Christ. And so Augustine understands that justice, not by which God is just in himself, *sed qua hominem induit, cum eum iustificat*, but by which he judges men and women when he justifies them.[†] Of this the apostle speaks in Romans 3:28: "We conclude that a man is justified by faith, without the works of the law." But this justice is not a habit infused into the mind, whereby a man or woman is

---

[19]Brenz, *In Epistolam*, 493-94; citing Hab 2:4; Gal 3:11; Rom 3:10, 12; Acts 13:38.

prepared to exercise good works, as Pererius says, that this justice comprehends two things, *remissionem peccatorum*, the remission of sins, *et animi rectitudinem*, and the uprightness of the mind, by which it is now acceptable to God, and is exercised in good works. For the apostle says of this justice of God that it is "made manifest without the law, by the faith of Jesus." But this infused habit, which is charity and the exercising of good works, is not revealed without the law, for the law requires and commands charity. This justice then consists only in the remission of sins, and in imputing to us the righteousness of Christ by faith. "Blessed is the man to whom the Lord imputes not sin" (Pareus). It is called the justice of God, both because it is given us from God, not procured by our own works, and because we are made righteous by it, not before men and women, but in the sight of God (Tolet). And this justice is sometimes called the righteousness of God because he is the author of it; sometimes of Christ—he is our righteousness—because we are justified by his obedience; sometimes of faith, because it is the instrument by which Christ's righteousness is applied to us (Grynaeus). A Six-fold COMMENTARY ON THE EPISTLE TO THE ROMANS (1620).[20]

THE RIGHTEOUSNESS OF THE MERIT OF CHRIST. JOHANN WIGAND: "Righteousness." As it pertains to the gospel, let this discussion clearly explain what it contains and what it grants. Paul here refers to the righteousness of God—not the essential righteousness of God, nor the active righteousness of the law, but the righteousness of the merit of Christ, or the fulfillment of the law rendered by Christ, which is imputed to all believers in him, freely, out of his mercy. Now it is called the "righteousness of God" because men and women did not render it as they ought to have, but rather the Son of God becoming man and "obedient unto the death of the cross" brought it into being, and because God in his mercy imputes and

grants it to believers, and because God regards it, accepts it, and reckons it for righteousness. The sure foundation of this understanding is the voice of Christ himself, "I have come to fulfill the law," and of Paul, "Christ is the end of the law for justification to all who believe," and "That I might be found in him, not having my own righteousness that is of the law, but that which is of faith, of Christ, which is the righteousness of God through faith." This is the clear meaning of this phrase, "the righteousness of God" in the writings of Paul. Luther rendered it with great clarity: *Die Gerechtigheit die för im gilt* (the righteousness that avails for him). Augustine also regards the "righteousness of God" in this light, namely, that it is not that by which he himself is righteous, but that by which he justifies the ungodly. Thus Luther was accustomed to call this "passive righteousness," that is, which we do not produce ourselves, but which is imputed and given freely to us based on the merit of Christ. Those who fail to understand this phrase of the apostle in this manner sail blindly in the night and make shipwreck among the rocks. ANNOTATIONS ON ROMANS (1580).[21]

FAITH AS SMALL AS A PEARL. THOMAS TAYLOR: In regard to the hidden virtue and secret excellence of them: The body and quantity of a pearl is small, but the virtue and power of it are great. So the gospel seems small and contemptible, but it is the power of God to salvation. And faith in the gospel draws virtue from Christ to open blind eyes; to cure all spiritual diseases; to raise from death in sin; to drive away devils and break the force of temptation. All the pearls between heaven and earth do not have such power. Only faith, as small as a grain of mustard seed, draws virtue from Christ. And grace, even if ever so little (if sound), it has the power to open blind eyes and to carry the saints along to their salvation. THE PEARL OF THE GOSPEL.[22]

[20]Willet, *Hexapla*, 54-55; citing Ps 11:7; 130:3; Rom 3:28, 21; 4:5; Phil 3:9; 1 Cor 1:30; Phil 3:9. †Augustine, *On the Spirit and the Letter* 9.

[21]Wigand, *In Epistolam S. Pauli*, 15r-v; citing Phil 2:8; Mt 5:17; Rom 10:4; Phil 3:9.
[22]Taylor, *Pearl of the Gospel*, 9-10*.

Faith Before and After Christ. Martin Luther: Just as they [the patriarchs] previously believed the promise of God, so we believe in the same promise, which has now been fulfilled; the one faith is just like the other, except that it follows the other, just as the promise and the fulfillment follow each other. They both depend on the Seed of Abraham (that is, on Christ)—one before, the other after his coming. Whoever would now believe, as the Jews do, that Christ has not yet come, as if the promise were still unfulfilled, would be condemned because he calls God a liar and asserts that he has not fulfilled his promise, which he has fulfilled. Then salvation would still be far away from us, and we would have to wait for it.

These two kinds of faith may be what St. Paul had in mind when he said, "In the gospel the righteousness of God is revealed from faith to faith." "From faith to faith" is nothing other than saying there is one kind of faith, the faith of the fathers and our faith, one which believes in the coming Christ, and the other, in the Christ who has appeared; yet the gospel leads from the one faith to the other. It is now necessary to believe not only the promise but also its fulfillment, which Abraham and the ancients did not yet have to believe, though they had the same Christ as we do. There is one faith, one spirit, one Christ, one communion of all saints, except that they were before Christ and we are after him.

Thus we (that is, the fathers and us) have believed with the same common faith in the one Christ, and still do believe in him, but in different ways. Just as we, because of this common faith in Christ, say, "We have believed," even though we were not alive at that time but "the fathers believed," so in turn they say, "They will hear, see, and believe Christ," even though they are not alive at our time, but we do that. David says, "I look at your heavens, the work of your hands," even though he did not witness it. There are many similar passages in which one person applies another person's [actions] to themselves because of the common faith; in that way they have Christ in the middle and are one body. Church Postil (1540 /1544).[23]

"From Faith to Faith" Is About Growth. John Calvin: In the place of what he had earlier said, "to all who believe," he now says, "from faith." For righteousness is conveyed through the gospel and is laid hold of by faith. Then he adds, "to faith," for however much our faith progresses and we advance in this knowledge, the righteousness of God will correspondingly grow within us and, in a certain way, his possession will be sanctified. When we first get a taste of the gospel, we certainly do observe God's countenance toward us to be cheerful and relaxed, but only at a distance. The more our schooling in godliness increases, as our approach to him draws closer we observe the grace of God more clearly and intimately. As for the idea that some have who think that in this verse there is an implied comparison between the Old and New Testaments, that's more clever than it is sound. For Paul is not comparing us here with the fathers who lived under the law, but rather is referring to the everyday progress made by individual believers. Commentary on Romans (1540, 1667).[24]

The Meaning of Faith. Heinrich Bullinger: For this cause the apostle subjoins, "from faith to faith," from which phrase many expositors hand down many and various meanings. For there are some who explain it as, "from unformed faith to formed faith." Others indeed explain it as "from faith to faith," that is, "in whatever place there had been faithful ones." Others, "from faith, namely, the obscure faith of the fathers to gospel faith." Moreover, there are those who refer to the increase of faith. What if we call the phrase in question a pleonasm† of speech? So that the sense would be: "and this righteousness is nothing but solid and true faith," or, "and this righteousness of God is not shared with you except through sound faith." In a similar form, also, we read that John said, "And from his fullness we have all received grace on grace," that is, the most unconditional grace and gift. . . . Or certainly faith will be a metastasis‡ of speech, so that faith is in the first place the faith of the Christian

---

[23]LW 75:16*; citing Eph 4:4-6; Ps 8:3.

[24]Calvin, *Commentarii in Omnes Epistolas*, 6.

mind. Afterward, in the second place, the truth and constancy of God. For *ĕmet* means "truth" and "faith" in Hebrew, just as in Latin, faith is very often used to designate steadfastness. And Paul says, *pistos ho Theos*, and *pistos ho logos*, which the interpreter translated partly "God is faithful," and partly "true" or "a true saying." And with this meaning, the sense of Paul will be, "The righteousness by which we are made truly righteous before God arises from the faith that is supported and propped up by faith, that is, by the firm and most certain promises of God." COMMENTARY ON ROMANS (1582).[25]

LIKE A SEAL'S IMPRESS ON WAX. CHARLES FERME AND ANDREW MELVILLE: The apostle speaks about his ministry of the gospel, of which the apostles are its ministers, as not having his face veiled as Moses did, but uncovered—there is not here that gleaming brightness that vanishes away, but the boundless glory of God brilliantly shining in the face of Christ; not on stony tablets on which are inscribed letters whose twilight was approaching, but on soft tablets of the heart such as are made of flesh, on which the law of Yahweh is inscribed; depicting that which needed to be seen not by the ministry of the law, but by the preaching of the gospel, for it is by the sight of the gospel's glory that the hearers are transformed and by which they are conformed to the glorious Christ, that image being copied from the glory that is in Christ's face and transferred to a glory that is being impressed on the hearers, and that not by the power of ministers but by the spiritual power of the Lord, who is the Spirit. This glory is therefore twofold, one being the cause of the other: that which belongs to Christ is reflected in the preaching of the gospel and is the cause of the glory in its hearers, just like the writing on a seal impresses its image on wax and is therefore the cause of the copied image that is impressed in the wax. COMMENTARY ON ROMANS (1601).[26]

---

[25]Bullinger, *Commentarii in Omnes Pauli*, 4-5; citing Jn 1:16. †A pleonasm is the use of redundant words either out of error or for emphasis. ‡A metastasis quickly shifts from one idea to another.
[26]Ferme and Melville, *Logical Analysis*, 400.

FROM FIRST TO LAST. GEORGE HERBERT:

> Lord, how couldst thou so much appease
> Thy wrath for sin, as when man's sight was dim,
> And could see little, to regard his ease,
> And bring by Faith all things to him?
>
> Hungry I was, and had no meat:
> I did conceit a most delicious feast;
> I had it straight, and did as truly eat,
> As ever did a welcome guest.
>
> There is a rare outlandish root,
> Which when I could not get, I thought it here:
> That apprehension cured so well my foot,
> That I can walk to heaven well near.
>
> I owed thousands and much more:
> I did believe that I did nothing owe,
> And lived accordingly; my creditor
> Believes so too, and lets me go.
>
> Faith makes me anything, or all
> That I believe is in the sacred story:
> And when sin places me in Adam's fall,
> Faith sets me higher in his glory
>
> If I go lower in the book,
> What can be lower than the common manger?
> Faith puts me there with him, who sweetly took
> Our flesh and frailty, death and danger
>
> If bliss had lien in art or strength,
> None but the wise and strong had gained it:
> Where now by Faith all arms are of a length;
> One size doth all conditions fit.
>
> A peasant may believe as much
> As a great Clerk, and reach the highest stature.
> Thus dost thou make proud knowledge bend
>   and crouch,
> While grace fills up uneven nature
>
> When creatures had no real light
> Inherent in them, thou didst make the sun,
> Impute a luster, and allow them bright:
> And in this show, what Christ hath done.
>
> That which before was darkened clean
> With bushy groves, pricking the looker's eye,

Vanished away, when Faith did change the scene:
And then appeared a glorious sky.

What though my body run to dust?
Faith cleaves unto it, counting every grain,
With an exact and most particular trust,
Reserving all for flesh again.

FAITH.[27]

CHRIST DWELLS ONLY IN SINNERS. MARTIN
LUTHER: Now I would like to know whether your
soul, tired of her own righteousness, would learn
to breathe and confide in the righteousness of
Christ. For nowadays the presumption besets
many, especially those who with all their powers
try to be righteous and good. They do not know
the righteousness of God, which is most bounti-
fully and freely given us in Christ, and so they seek
to do good in and by themselves until such a time
as they feel confident that they can stand before
God adorned with their own virtues and merits,
but this cannot possibly be done. You yourself
were of this opinion, or rather error, and so was I,
and even now I fight against this error and have
not yet conquered it.

Therefore, my dear brother, learn Christ and
him crucified, learn to pray to him, despairing of
yourself, saying: "You, Lord Jesus, are my righteousness, but I am your sin; you have taken on yourself
what you were not, and have given to me what I
was not." Beware of ever aspiring to such purity
that you do not want to seem to yourself, or to be,
a sinner. For Christ dwells only in sinners.

It was for this that he came down from heaven,
where he dwelled in the righteous, that he might
also dwell in sinners. Think about his love and you
will see how beautifully it will comfort and sustain
you. For if it is only by our own efforts and
strivings that we can achieve a quiet conscience,
what did he die for? You will therefore find peace
only in him, in faith despairing in yourself and
your own works; and thus you will learn that as he
took you up and made your sins his own, he made

his righteousness yours. LETTER TO GEORGE
SPENLEIN (APRIL 8, 1516).[28]

THE MODE OF JUSTIFICATION. HEINRICH
BULLINGER: Righteousness in this passage doesn't
refer to God's busy court, that is, for that which
deals with punishments for crimes—or for that
perfection by which God is righteous in his own
nature, even if all these things are also taught by the
gospel. Truly, he speaks here particularly about the
mode of justification: what, I mean, the gospel gives
as the method for being justified. Again, Christ
Jesus has been made our wisdom, sanctification,
redemption, and righteousness by God. Therefore,
the gospel preaches Jesus Christ, the righteousness
of God, who becomes our righteousness if we truly
believe in him. COMMENTARY ON ROMANS (1582).[29]

REFORMED VIEW ON JUSTIFICATION. GABRIEL
POWEL: The doctrine of the Reformed churches
concerning justification is this: Men and women,
being unjust and children of wrath by nature, are
accounted as just and pronounced to be so by God,
inasmuch as he forgives them of their sins and
imputes the righteousness of Christ to them for
the merits and satisfaction of Christ performed for
them, and apprehended by them by faith. At which
time they are justified by faith alone because they
are counted righteous and by consequence
pronounced just, for Christ's satisfaction only. This
is imputed to them by faith only, because they do
not apprehend and apply it to themselves except by
faith. And so, men and women are justified partly
by the grace and free love of God, whereby he
ordained Christ to be a Satisfier and Mediator for
the elect, and partly by the justice of God, whereby
accepting Christ's satisfaction for the elect, he
imputes the same to them and immediately
receives them into favor and adopts them for sons
and daughters and heirs of eternal life. A LOGICAL
RESOLUTION OF ROMANS I (1602).[30]

---

[27]Herbert, *The Temple*, 42-44*.

[28]LCC 15:lvii-lviii*.
[29]Bullinger, *Commentarii in Omnes Pauli*, 4.
[30]Powel, *Prodromus*, 135-36*.

WHAT IS FAITH? PIETER RIEDEMANN: Faith is a certain assurance of what we hope for, a clear revelation and a conviction of things that are not seen, a conquest of the world, the devil, and the flesh. It is a sure guide to God, an assurance of the hope and purification of the heart; through it one becomes completely pure, holy, and godly. But faith is also a justification, because through faith in Christ we become devout and just before God—as a gift. Faith is a power that can do everything—nothing is impossible for it. As Christ testifies, "If you have faith like a mustard seed, say to this mountain, 'Get up from here and cast yourself into the sea,' and it will obey." Or, "Be it done for you as you have believed." Faith is also an assurance of the conscience that it stands firm and trusts God's promise. Thus it is a confirmation of the supplication, for God does not disdain the prayer of the believer, but must grant the request since it comes from faith. John says, "We are certain that we have received what we have asked him for."

As Paul teaches, faith is a power that works righteousness and easily carries out all God's will. People who say they cannot carry out God's will show that they are not believers but unbelievers, for all things are possible to those who believe. It is easy for them to walk in the footsteps of Christ, who has said, "My yoke is easy and my burden light." LOVE IS LIKE FIRE (1529–1532).[31]

FAITH IS RIGHTEOUSNESS. HEINRICH BULLINGER: Here is the essential position of this letter: that true faith is righteousness, which fact, in case it should seem very difficult to someone, he confirms with a prophetic saying drawn from Habakkuk 2: "The righteous one shall live by faith." Wherefore, it is no wonder he testifies that faith will be life for the faithful. For just as a body without a soul is more truly a cadaver than a body, so a righteous person without faith is more truly a hypocrite than a just person. In sum, here is the whole gospel, and the single goal of this letter:

Faith is righteousness. COMMENTARY ON ROMANS (1582).[32]

FAITH IS NOT A HUMAN ILLUSION. MARTIN LUTHER: Faith is not that human illusion and dream that some people think it is. When they hear and talk a lot about faith and yet see that no moral improvement and no good works result from it, they fall into error and say, "Faith is not enough. You must do works if you want to be virtuous and get to heaven." The result is that, when they hear the gospel, they stumble and make for themselves with their own powers a concept in their hearts, which says, "I believe." This concept they hold to be true faith. But since it is a human fabrication and thought and not an experience of the heart, it accomplishes nothing, and there follows no improvement.

Faith is a work of God in us, which changes us and brings us to birth anew from God (see John 1). It kills the old Adam, makes us completely different people in heart, mind, senses, and all our powers, and brings the Holy Spirit with it. What a living, creative, active powerful thing is faith! It is impossible for faith to ever stop doing good. Faith doesn't ask whether good works are to be done, but, before it is asked, it has done them. It is always active. Those who don't do such works are without faith; they grope and search about themselves for faith and good works but don't know what faith or good works are. Even so, they chatter on with a great many words about faith and good works.

Faith is a living, unshakeable confidence in God's grace; it is so certain, that someone would die a thousand times for it. This kind of trust in and knowledge of God's grace makes a person joyful, confident, and happy with regard to God and all creatures. This is what the Holy Spirit does by faith. Through faith, a person will do good to everyone without coercion, willingly and happily; he will serve everyone, suffer everything for the love and praise of God, who has shown him such grace. It is as impossible to separate works from faith as burning and shining from fire. Therefore be on

---

[31]Riedemann, *Love Is Like Fire*, 19-20*; citing Heb 11:1; Mt 17:20; Mt 8:13; 1 Jn 5:14.

[32]Bullinger, *Commentarii in Omnes Pauli*, 5; citing Heb 2:4.

guard against your own false ideas and against the chatterers who think they are clever enough to make judgments about faith and good works but who are in reality the biggest fools. Ask God to work faith in you; otherwise you will remain eternally without faith, no matter what you try to do or fabricate. PREFACE TO THE LETTER OF ST. PAUL TO THE ROMANS (1545).[33]

THE DIFFERENCE BETWEEN OPINION, KNOWLEDGE, AND FAITH. HEINRICH BULLINGER: The wisdom of the Christians is this very thing, which is not taught by the books of the philosophers, but by the oracles of the Holy Spirit, I say, in the gospel of Jesus Christ. Nevertheless, here at the beginning, we should observe what Johannes Oecolampadius warned should be observed, that if you are speaking exactly, the righteousness of our faith is not to be attributed to our own work. For it would be to abuse faith if, as I say, I seem to trust God by my own faith, as if there were something worthy in me that God should reward. But rather, righteousness is attributed to faith, because faith attributes the whole to divine compassion. The same man warns that there are many differences between opinion, knowledge, and faith. He warns that opinion, by which things are not firmly assented to, but one feels now this, now that, is doubtful. Indeed, knowledge is certainly more sure, as for example that by which one consents to reliable arguments, and because of them it cannot be contradicted, but it contains nothing in itself for salvation. From this cause, he warns that there are some who call faith historical. But faith itself is alive, certain, effective, as for example that by which one leans on the Word of God. It arises from God and is founded in God, the substance of eternal things. COMMENTARY ON ROMANS (1582).[34]

FAITH THAT SUSTAINS IN SUFFERING. JOHANN GERHARD: "The just will live by faith." This phrase

is taken from Habakkuk 2:4, where in the context of their calamity under the Chaldeans it was proclaimed to the Israelite people that the welfare of the godly or of believers was going to be different from that of the ungodly or of unbelievers. The latter, because of their distrust toward God and empty confidence in human protections would become like water bubbles that quickly vanish, whereas the former because of the faith by which they know that God is kindly disposed toward them will live; that is, they will enjoy true and life-giving consolation.

The apostle applies this phrase, which is a general one, to the doctrine of the gospel, which is the doctrine of faith. For the faith that can sustain us in tribulation requires as a precondition a free remission of sins and reconciliation with God to occur before it can be apprehended by faith.

The occasion for and application of a saying can be specific, while the saying itself may be a general one. The prophet explained how it is possible for them to sustain themselves in any temptations and calamities whatsoever, and that they could be calmly composed even in the midst of waves—namely, by true faith in the Messiah alone, for since by faith they know themselves to be justified and placed in a state of grace before God, they endure—or rather mock—all adversities with strong courage. Consequently in the specific case of the evils that would be brought on the Israelites by the Chaldeans, he admonishes them that they should sustain themselves by faith. Rightly therefore does the apostle apply what the prophet had said in general, to the specific case of the principal role of faith, showing that just as in bodily torments, even more so in the face of spiritual torments and the impending trial of eternal death, that the self feels in its senses what it fully deserves due to its sins. Nobody can live—that is, be sustained, survive, and enjoy life-giving consolation—except he or she be justified by faith in the Messiah. ANNOTATIONS ON ROMANS I (1645).[35]

---

[33]Luther, *Preface to the Letter**.
[34]Bullinger, *Commentarii in Omnes Pauli*, 5.
[35]Gerhard, *Annotationes ad Priora*, 39-40; citing Hab 2:4.

RECKONED RIGHTEOUS BY FAITH. JOHANNES BRENZ: Let us now see about the word "faith." First of all, when it is said, "The person is justified 'by faith,'" the word "faith" is not set in opposition to God the Father, nor Christ the Son, nor the Holy Spirit, nor the preaching of the gospel, nor the sacraments. And for instance, God the Father justifies (that is, he absolves from unrighteousness) by his own authority, Christ by his own merit, the Holy Spirit by his own power, the preaching of the gospel by its own ministry, the sacraments by their own instrument. By which means, when it is said, "We are justified by faith," the word "faith" is not set in opposition to these things that we have now enumerated, but only is set in opposition to works of the law (which are good works), and to their merits, so that this sentence might be: In the gathering of the faith and of good works, we are not justified, we are not absolved from sins, we are not reckoned righteous before God on account of good works, or their merits, but only on account of Christ, if we believe in him. COMMENTARY ON ROMANS (1588).[36]

YOU NEED ONLY TO TAKE IT. JOHN PRESTON: How is this righteousness of Christ made ours? Or What is to be done by him to whom it belongs?

To this I answer: Although no precedent qualification is required, yet you must take it. You must not reflect on yourself and consider, "Am I worthy of it?" Rather, you must take it, like a plaster, which will not heal unless it is applied; or as meat, which if it is not eaten, does not nourish. As the husband woos his spouse, and says thus, "I require nothing at your hands, no condition at all; I do not examine whether you are wealthy or not; whether you are beautiful or not; whether you are out of debt, or well-conditioned. It does not matter what you are. I require you simply to take me for your husband." Christ comes to us in this way. We must not say, "Am I worthy to be a spouse for Christ? Am I fit to receive great mercies?" You are meant only to take him. When we exclude all

conditions, we exclude the frame and habit of mind that we think is required to make us worthy to take him. It is as if a physician came and offered you a medicine by which you might be healed and says, "I require nothing at your hands, only to drink it, for otherwise it will do you no good." So God offers the righteousness of Christ, which is that which heals the souls of men and women. God looks for nothing in your hands; it matters not what your person is; only, you must take it. So you will find him expressing it in Isaiah, where he compares this to the offer of wine and milk: "Come buy wine and milk without money. Let him who is thirsty come, and he that has no money." It is as if he had said, "It is freely offered; you need only to take it." SERMON "ON FAITH" (1634).[37]

FAITH AND GOOD WORKS. JOHANNES BRENZ: A person is justified by faith, not on account of the completeness and worth of the faith in the person, but only on account of Christ, who by faith (however weak) is received. . . . In no way, however, should it be thought that since we are justified before God only by faith, therefore, good works should not be done. But rather let us know that wherever there is true faith in Christ, there it cannot be grasped unless one eagerly desires to excel in all sorts of good works. . . . Just as a kindled light not only brings heat with it, but also casts in front of it splendor on every side. And also as the good root of the tree and the innermost part not only preserve the inner goodness of the tree, but also bring forth good fruits from without. Thus faith in Christ not only brings with it righteousness before God but also produces righteousness, which is the exercise of good works before people. By which means, when a person is said to be justified through faith, the reigns for the desire of the flesh are not relaxed, with the result that they might do whatever they want, but rather it is demanded that the flesh be mortified and placed under the spirit, and moreover that the person walk in every kind of good works. But Paul will

---

[36]Brenz, *In Epistolam*, 494-95.

[37]Preston, *Breast-Plate of Faith and Love*, 15-16*; citing Is 55:1.

discuss this matter later in many words. Finally, even if the righteousness of good works follows by necessity out of faith, nevertheless, when we say that a person is justified through faith, it should not be understood that a person should be justified by faith on account of those good works that follow. COMMENTARY ON ROMANS (1588).[38]

LIVING BY THE POWER OF THE NEW LIFE. MENNO SIMONS: Paul calls baptism "the washing of regeneration." O Lord, how lamentably your Holy Word is abused. Is it not greatly to be lamented, that people are attempting—notwithstanding these plain passages—to maintain their idolatrous invention of infant baptism and set forth that infants are regenerated by it, as if regeneration were simply a pressing into the water? Oh no, regeneration is not such a work of hypocrisy but is an inward change that converts a person by the power of God through faith from evil to good, from carnality to spirituality, from unrighteousness to righteousness, out of Adam into Christ, which can in no way take place with infants. The regenerated live by the power of the new life; they crucify the flesh with its evil lusts; they put off the old Adam with his deeds; they avoid every appearance of evil; they are taught, governed, and influenced by the Holy Spirit. CONCERNING BAPTISM.[39]

THE MEANINGS OF *FIDES* AND *PISTIS*. DESIDERIUS ERASMUS: The sacred text frequently employs these expressions. For "faith" is frequently used in the sense of "trust in God" so that it does not differ much from "hope." Occasionally it is used in the sense of "a believing" or "a persuasion" by which we assent to those things that have been handed down to us concerning God, by which "faith" even the demons believe. Sometimes the word "faith" embraces all of these senses: (1) assent in both the historical facts as well as the promises, (2) inward formation of trust in his omnipotent

goodness, (3) but not without hope, which is an eager expectation of the fulfillment of his promises. What is more, until now, only human faith has been spoken of. There is a "faith" of God that is also spoken of, by which he keeps his promises, for which reason God is said to be trustworthy or faithful [*fidelis*], that is, *pistos*, since he does not deceive anyone. But a man or woman who believes in the One promising is also said to be faithful [*fidelis*]. Although this is outside of customary Latin usage, the sacred text nevertheless frequently speaks in this way. For in Latin a steward is said to be *fidelis*, but one is said to be *infidelis*—not in Latin but in the Scriptures—who disbelieves (or better, in Greek: *apistos* . . .). Sometimes the "faith of God" refers to that faith by which we trust in him more than we do in humanity, where "faith" is said to be his not only because it has him for its object but because it is given by him. Sometimes it is both, such as in the "just will live by faith"—both the faith *of God* who does not deceive with his promises and the faith *of the man or woman* who trusts in God. It also refers to both senses here when it says "from faith to faith." For just as God at determined points in time began to reveal what he was like and to fulfill the things he had promised, so also the knowledge of God and trust in him grew among men and women in stages. Few of the prophets believed the things that they had prophesied, before the Lord displayed them in front of their eyes. It is otherwise with us, whose faith is confirmed by the things we have already seen as well as by the things predicted of the second coming that we will yet see. ANNOTATIONS ON THE NEW TESTAMENT (1527).[40]

DISCUSSING FAITH. LADY JANE GREY: Feckenham—what thing is required in a Christian?

Jane—To believe in God the Father, in God the Son, and in God the Holy Ghost.

Feckenham—Is there nothing else required in a Christian but to believe in God?

---

[38]Brenz, *In Epistolam*, 496.
[39]Simons, *Complete Works*, 26-27*; citing Rom 1:7.
[40]Erasmus, *In Novum Testamentum*, 329.

Jane—Yes, truly, we must believe in him, we must love him, with all our heart, with all our soul, and all our mind, and our neighbor as ourselves.

Feckenham—Why, then *faith* does not justify or save us.

Jane—Yes, truly, faith only—as St. Paul says—justifies.

Feckenham—Why, St. Paul says, if I have all faith, without love, it is nothing.

Jane—True it is, for how can I love him I do not trust, or how can I trust in him whom I do not love? Faith and love both go together, and love is comprehended in faith.

Feckenham—How shall we love our neighbor?

Jane—To love our neighbor is to feed the hungry, clothe the naked, with such other deeds of mercy, and to do to him as we would do to ourselves.

Feckenham—Why then, it is necessary to salvation to do good works also, and it is not sufficient only to believe.

Jane—I deny that, and I affirm that faith alone saves. And yet, it is appropriate for all Christians—in token that they follow their master Christ—to do good works. Yet we may not say that they profit to salvation. For when we have done all, yet we are unprofitable servants, and only the faith we have in Christ's blood will save us. A COMMUNICATION BETWEEN FECKENHAM AND LADY JANE DUDLEY.[41]

TEARS SPRING IN MY HEART. MICHELANGELO:

No earthly object is more base and vile
Than I, without you, miserable am.
My spirit now, midst errors multiform,
Weak, wearied, and infirm, pardon implores.
O Lord most high! Extend to me that chain
Which with itself links every gift divine:
Chiefest, to faith, I bid my soul aspire,

Flying from sense, whose paths conduct to death.
The rarer be this gift of gifts, the more
May it to me abound; and still the more,
Since the world yields not true content and peace.
By faith alone the fount of bitter tears
Can spring within my heart, made penitent:
No other key unlocks the gate of heaven.

SONNET 54.[42]

BENEFITS OF FAITH. KONRAD PELLIKAN: The just always live by their faith. This is what the apostle concludes from the prophecy of Habakkuk, who when he had complained before God of the prosperity enjoyed by the wicked and of the hardships endured by the godly was commanded by God to write upon tablets: "Behold, as for the one who is stubborn and unbelieving, his soul will not be upright within him, but the just will live by his faith." That is, the one who does not subject himself to God but is haughty in his spirit, such a one will never live with an upright, secure, and tranquil heart. But the just person will live by his faith, in which he rests on the promises of God and by hope lays hold of future happiness, and by the present certitude of the Spirit that belongs to the sons and daughters of God will enjoy to the full both tranquility and rejoicing in the Lord's goodness. "For it does not yet appear what we will be, for that which we eagerly await is not yet seen. For we know in part." Therefore, it is by faith, by which hope rests on the promise of future happiness, a happiness that we discern as it were by our own eyes through faith, and by faith hold fast to. By this faith we stand firm, we live, and by it we are both saved and made blessed. It has always been by this that they have lived and been comforted, whenever it was that they were deemed righteous and approved by God. And this is the thesis of the entire disputation undertaken by the apostle: that the righteousness of God is revealed in the gospel, and that we are justified by faith—which is the

---

[41]Grey, *Here in This Book* (1554), A7v- A8r*. This is part of a conversation in which John Feckenham, Queen Mary's chaplain, attempted (unsuccessfully) to convert Lady Jane to Catholicism in the days leading up to her execution.

[42]Michelangelo, *Life of Michael Angelo*, 163*.

same thing. For when the gospel declares the righteousness of God—that goodness of God by which he remits our sins and bestows on us the Spirit of righteousness—it demands nothing other than true faith in order to benefit from it and be begotten of God and end up as sharers in eternal life. COMMENTARY ON ALL THE APOSTOLIC EPISTLES (1539).[43]

---

[43]Pellikan, *In Omnes Apostolicas Epistolas*, 14; citing Hab 2:4; 1 Jn 3:2.

1:18-32 GOD'S RESPONSE TO HUMANITY'S SIN

¹⁸For the wrath of God is revealed from heaven against all ungodliness and unrighteousness of men, who by their unrighteousness suppress the truth. ¹⁹For what can be known about God is plain to them, because God has shown it to them. ²⁰For his invisible attributes, namely, his eternal power and divine nature, have been clearly perceived, ever since the creation of the world,^a in the things that have been made. So they are without excuse. ²¹For although they knew God, they did not honor him as God or give thanks to him, but they became futile in their thinking, and their foolish hearts were darkened. ²²Claiming to be wise, they became fools, ²³and exchanged the glory of the immortal God for images resembling mortal man and birds and animals and creeping things.

²⁴Therefore God gave them up in the lusts of their hearts to impurity, to the dishonoring of their bodies among themselves, ²⁵because they exchanged the truth about God for a lie and worshiped and served the creature rather than the Creator, who is blessed forever! Amen.

²⁶For this reason God gave them up to dishonorable passions. For their women exchanged natural relations for those that are contrary to nature; ²⁷and the men likewise gave up natural relations with women and were consumed with passion for one another, men committing shameless acts with men and receiving in themselves the due penalty for their error.

²⁸And since they did not see fit to acknowledge God, God gave them up to a debased mind to do what ought not to be done. ²⁹They were filled with all manner of unrighteousness, evil, covetousness, malice. They are full of envy, murder, strife, deceit, maliciousness. They are gossips, ³⁰slanderers, haters of God, insolent, haughty, boastful, inventors of evil, disobedient to parents, ³¹foolish, faithless, heartless, ruthless. ³²Though they know God's righteous decree that those who practice such things deserve to die, they not only do them but give approval to those who practice them.

a Or *clearly perceived from the creation of the world*

OVERVIEW: Following Paul's argument, the reformers move from their emphasis on our need to be justified (i.e., "reckoned righteous") to demonstrate *why* we need to be justified, by illuminating the stark contrast between the high standard of God's righteousness and our unrighteousness.

First, they explain that there are two kinds of law that make humans responsible before God. The Jews had the law that came to them engraved on tablets of stone. The Greeks (Gentiles) did not have that Mosaic law, but they have the law of nature within them as the *notio Dei* (the notion that has been engraved on all minds or souls that there is a God). The reformers explore the concepts of natural law and reason and what the responsibilities and limits of each are, and they warn their readers not to suppress the truth of God or they will find their hearts darkened.

Second, the reformers explore the various facets of humanity's initial sins that triggered God's "handing over" of them to deeper sin. The resulting sins of lust were both the effect of, and the wages of, idolatry and, importantly, do not entail that God is the author of evil. For the reformers, idolatry seems to be an existential concern more than the issue of "unnatural relations," for they apply the concept of idolatry to the veneration of images and the elaborations of the Lord's Supper by the Roman Catholic Church of their day and judge them to be dishonoring to God, believing they strip him of his majesty. Nonetheless, the reformers see sexual sins as a portion of the many sins of the body, and they define each of the terms in the even broader and longer list of sins provided by Paul. This extensive list leaves no one innocent or capable of living the sinless life that is essential for perfect obedience to the law, demonstrating the breadth and ugliness of sin, and thereby pointing to our unrighteousness and the necessity of salvation through Christ, through faith.

1:18 God's Wrath Against the Unrighteous

God's Wrath Points to Our Unrighteousness. THEODORE BEZA: "For the wrath of God is made manifest" (*apokalyptetai*). It seems to me that Paul is alluding to the words of the prophet in Psalm 50:6. The Vulgate reads "is revealed" (*revelatur*), and Erasmus renders it "is disclosed" (*patefit*) as if this wrath were disclosed by the gospel also. For, Erasmus says, it cannot be doubted that there is nothing that charges the world with sin as much as the light of the gospel does. . . . [But] in most respects to charge with sin pertains rather to the ministry of the law than it does to that of the gospel. But then what is Paul doing here? Has Paul here assumed the very thing that is asked by the posed question, namely, whether the gospel is the power of God unto salvation? That is, whether it is by the gospel that God asserts his power in saving men and women? Paul said that he was going to prove that faith—which is mutually related to the preaching of the gospel—conveys to us that righteousness by which we will be approved to God, and that it therefore also shows us the way that leads to salvation. It is now redundant that he should prove this, that we obtain this righteousness by no other instrument than faith. But this is proved by this immediate argument: we are righteous before God either through faith, the alien righteousness of Christ being imputed to us, *or* by our own righteousness, that is, by observing the divine law. But in fact the whole life of men and women cries out that God has poured out his wrath from heaven on men and women. Therefore, persons in themselves are not righteous. For God is not indignant toward the righteous, but the unrighteous. Shall I go on to state from where this wrath of God arises? It results from the fact that men and women, once given any slack, are carried away to every wicked deed—which would become clearly apparent if someone were to subject his life to obeying a prescribed law, whether it be natural law or the law of Moses. This is the main thread of Paul's disputation up until the third chapter, verse 20, where this either/or syllogism is brought to a conclusion. MAJOR ANNOTATIONS (1594).[1]

People Do Not Glorify God. ALEXANDER ALESIUS: With severe words, Paul threatens all people with eternal punishments on account of their ungodliness and unrighteousness, unless they repent and flee for refuge to the Son of God. For he says that the wrath of God is revealed from heaven, from which place the Holy Spirit descending on the apostles with a spirit of burning warns of the wrath of God through them by their preaching of repentance. The invisible things of God, when they are reflected on, prove that people comprehend his eternal power, and deity, and the things that belong to deity: goodness, wisdom, justice, a love of piety, and wrath kindled against impiety and the unrighteousness of those who suppress the truth in unrighteousness. They can also perceive this wrath revealed from heaven in such a clear fashion that the nations are handed over to a reprobate mind and to shameful passions and even a manifest perversity and insanity. This happens because although God has been known from the creation of the world, they did not glorify him with true piety or veneration in their heart or by obedience to the law. And even now they do not glorify him with true faith according to the evangelical doctrine, nor do they give him thanks for the generous gift of redemption by the Son of God. But by common natural knowledge and contempt for the truth revealed in the gospel, they contend that true piety is in the veneration of images, and that they are righteous on account of their own virtues, and they even condemn the doctrine of righteousness before God by faith and

---

[1]Beza, *Annotationes Majores*, 15-16; citing Ps 50:6.

trust in the mercies of Christ, and they assail it with all manner of cruelty. Disputations on Romans (1553).[2]

Disgraceful Lives as a Sign of God's Wrath.

Wolfgang Musculus: We see in this passage how the disgraceful mode of life of unbelieving people is itself the unmistakable judgment of an angry God. Sometimes, the wrath of God is not recognized because a person appears to be virtuous, as if covered by snow. When, however, someone is being hurled forward into a life of crime, this is a clear sign of the wrath of God. Indeed, God is angry at the failure of humans to respect him, and his wrath is being revealed against all their impiety and injustice. . . .

What shall we say of our time? For what kind of scandal does not clearly reign in the midst of the Christian sphere? If the wrath of God expresses disapproval of an impious mode of life, what can we anticipate? What great destruction will he unfold? Commentary on Romans (1555).[3]

Two Species of Unrighteousness.

Friedrich Balduin: He shows that unrighteousness by means of its effects, for it provokes "the wrath of God from heaven"; that is, it deserves the most just heavenly punishments, inflicted by God's intentional governance, not happening by chance (for the "wrath of God" in this passage refers to God's indignation and most just vengeance by which he will punish crimes previously committed), which punishments, he writes, "have been revealed." That is, they have been aptly declared by many examples of people who miserably perished in their sins. Now he lays down two species of this unrighteousness: (1) ungodliness, and (2) wrongdoing, or impiety and injury. The former includes profanity or sins against the first table of the law;[†] the latter, sins against the second table, or violence done to oneself and to one's neighbor. Commentary on Romans (1620).[4]

Why the Unrighteous Suppress the Truth.

Thomas Hooker: Question one: What is the power of the truth, or what does it do that leads wicked persons to oppose it?

Answer: It appears in four particulars: First, it is a word of information that is the first work to discover all things to us in their proper colors. The text Proverbs 6:23 tells us the commandment is a lamp, and the law is a light, and the reproofs of instruction are the way of life as a lamp in the night, so that the way may be discovered. So it is with the power of the word of truth, and he that has a mind to attend carefully may be able to judge and see right from wrong. Men and women cannot go astray as long as they are directed by the light of truth. As the sun shows all the motes and blemishes in the house, so the truth is like the sun in discovering and showing every mote and blemish in us and discovering every secret and corrupt corner. All things that are reproved are made manifest by the light, for whatever makes things manifest is light. You cannot inquire to do anything without it advising you.

Second, since it is about information, it is also about quickening, a word of power that not only tells the way but enables us to walk in it; it promotes virtue and the ability to walk on cheerfully.

Truth works not only like the sun to show us the way but like a stream to carry us in the way that God would have us walk. There is not a light in the shining sun (Christ) that is not a warning to make our benumbed joints nimble. In 1 Timothy 6:3, Paul calls it the wholesome word of truth that he says nourished Timothy. Psalm 119: "I will never forget your commandments because thereby you have quickened me."

In the third place it is a cord; if you are dull, it will pluck you on. And, in the fourth place, it is a word of conviction with power to overthrow all the gainsaying of a man or woman; it meets with every cavil, it stops all the base tricks and devices of our sinful minds. In Luke 21:10, Christ says to the disciples—if they should be brought before magistrates—"Take no care what you shall say," and in verse 15, "For I will give you a mouth and

---

[2]Alesius, *Omnes Disputationes*, E2v.
[3]Musculus, *In Epistolam Apostoli Pauli*, 29-30.
[4]Balduin, *Catechesis Apostolica*, 79-80. [†]I.e., the first four of the Ten Commandments.

wisdom, which all your adversaries will not be able to gainsay, nor resist." THE WRATH OF GOD AGAINST SINNERS (1639).[5]

WE CANNOT FULFILL THE LAW. MARTIN LUTHER: Christ always begins his preaching of the gospel with this point. He first reveals and teaches what reason cannot have or know from the law, namely, that all people, no matter how they are and live by nature, are damned and under sin. Right at the beginning of his letter to the Romans, St. Paul also demonstrates and concludes this. Thus this decree and conclusion is stated first, namely, that, in their natural state and with all their abilities, people cannot fulfill God's law, even though they presume to keep it. Keeping the law does not mean doing the works externally according to human powers. Consequently, the law cannot help people to righteousness before God nor deliver them from sin and eternal wrath. SUMMER POSTIL (MAY 27, 1526).[6]

1:19 God Has Revealed Himself to All

THE TWO KINDS OF LAW THAT MAKE HUMANS RESPONSIBLE. JOHANNES BRENZ: The whole human race is distinguished into two orders: Greeks, which we customarily call "the nations," and Jews. But Paul clearly teaches that they both are altogether without excuse for their ungodliness, even those to whom no law had been given like the Jews had. For even though they had not received a law written in tablets of stone, a law had been divinely engraved within them. They call this *prolēpsin* and "the law of nature." So even if they did not possess the law written in the Scriptures, they nevertheless possessed the law of nature. COMMENTARY ON ROMANS (1588).[7]

THE INEXPUNGABLE *NOTIO DEI* IMPLANTED BY GOD. MARTIN BUCER: "For God revealed it to them." This is the proof of what he had just said, that an idea of God is manifested to them. For

since God himself revealed himself to humanity, the things that are lawful for men and women to know about him cannot be hidden from them. Thus it is most certain that this idea of God—that he possesses power over all things, and is the Highest Good—is impressed on and engraved in the minds of all, so that nobody willing to admit that he believes it to be the truth can deny that this idea was put within him by God. For those ideas that are not formed within us by the Author of nature himself are usually, in the common experience of all men and women, found to be uncertain and to not last very long. But that God exists is innate to us all and, as it were, engraved in the soul. Not only has this idea not grown old with the passage of time and the ages of humankind, but it has been confirmed and increased in strength to such a point that no matter how many people may strive by the most diligent efforts, they will nevertheless be unable to expunge this idea of God from the soul. COMMENTARY ON ROMANS (1562).[8]

IF WE HAVE REASON, WHY DO WE NEED THE SCRIPTURES? JOHANNES BRENZ: You will say: if human reason can, by itself, pursue so much knowledge of divine things by the light of nature, what need do we have of the Scriptures? Or what is the usefulness of preaching the gospel of Jesus Christ our only Savior? I answer: we should know that although human reason does possess by its own nature a certain awareness of divine things, on account of that sin commonly called "original sin," people, in their natures, are deprived of the Holy Spirit. Therefore, this natural awareness is obscured, and sometimes is so drowned out that people hold opinions that are a long way away from what right reason would teach. For this reason there have been those who have not only doubted, but even firmly denied, that there is a God. We, therefore, have need of the Scriptures, which scatter this obscurity and darkness. COMMENTARY ON ROMANS (1588).[9]

---

[5]Hooker, *Three Godly Sermons*, 12-15*; citing Eph 5:14; Lk 24:2.
[6]LW 78:34*; citing Rom 1:18-3:20.
[7]Brenz, *In Epistolam*, 498.

[8]Bucer, *Metaphrasis et Enarratio*, 57 (this is a reprint of the 1536 edition).
[9]Brenz, *In Epistolam*, 500.

1:20 *Creation Reveals God*

THE GOODNESS OF CREATION POINTS TO GOD'S GOODNESS. HEINRICH BULLINGER: By these words, all things are understood to carry this revelation, as long, of course, as the works of God are weighed with careful judgment. For God in and of himself is the omnipotent, highest, true, eternal, good, wise, and righteous subsistence of all things. The great mass of the world is the most unassailable proof that all other things also subsist in God. For it was formed by his power and wisdom, was guided by his righteousness and truth, and is most beautiful and most useful as a result of his goodness. Clearly it could not have been these things unless its Maker were eternal, omnipotent, and truly the greatest. COMMENTARY ON ROMANS (1533).[10]

UNIVERSE'S ORDER REVEALS THE MIND OF GOD. JOHANNES BRENZ: Let us see, therefore, in what way God has made himself known to the Gentiles, or rather to us as well, by means of this visible and tangible world. In the first place, although the truth that there is a God is not seen with external eyes, it is nevertheless established by a certain use of their reasoning faculty reflecting on this visible world. The human intellect was capable of discovering this truth. For the Gentiles saw from the nature of things that the alternation of seasons and movements in the heavens were entirely predictable. They perceived that everything, as much in the heavens as on earth, is administered and governed by an astonishing, orderly arrangement. But that such things should be governed with such an immensely long lasting regularity cannot happen by chance or without design. For which reason, by the judgment even of human reason by itself, it is necessary to confess that there exists some Mind that governs such a universal mass and conserves it in such a remarkably orderly way. We call this Mind, *to agathon* (the Good), or God. For if someone should

carefully consider man himself who is called a *mikrokosmon*, which means a "little world," he will necessarily have to confess that there is a God. For a person's mind, which is his supreme faculty, does not have its existence from itself, but from something else. But a cause is far superior to its effect. Therefore, that Mind which is the cause of the human mind is necessarily superior to it. And this most supreme Mind is called God. For in not only their writings but also in their sacred rites, the Gentiles bear testimony that they have discovered by these arguments and other reasoning of this kind that there is a God. And this is what Paul said: that his eternal power and deity has been understood from the creation of the world. In other words, from this world it can be known—by natural reasoning—that there is a God and that he is eternal. Therefore, whereas the essence of God as it is in itself is not seen, nor is his essential power, wisdom, goodness, or severity seen, nevertheless they are set before human reason as things to be perceived from reflection on this world. For where it is understood from the governance of the world that there is a God, by the same intellect we also comprehend that God is infinitely powerful and wise. For who could govern and conserve with such perpetuity and order such a great mass unless they were endowed with the highest power and wisdom? For he sets forth his visible goodness when he gives profitable temporal things and we discover from the nature of the thing itself that all things have been fashioned for human utility. That God personally watches over and cares for all things is not in itself visible, but is made visible in the things he has created. "For he who created the eye, does he not see? He who created the ear, does he not hear?" He who created within parents a care for their children, will he not care for his own creatures? Therefore, in eyes, ears, and the care of parents is revealed to us the watchful care that God exercises for all, his hearing of their groans, and his yearning for their salvation. COMMENTARY ON ROMANS.[11]

---

[10]Bullinger, *In Sanctissimam Pauli ad Romanos*, fol. 18r.

[11]Brenz, *In Epistolam* (1564), 499-500; citing Ps 94:9.

GOD REVEALS THE INVISIBLE THROUGH THE VISIBLE. MARTIN BUCER: "For his invisible things." That God has revealed himself to men and women and that he has made manifest that which can be known about him, Paul proves by those things that, when they arise among men and women, could not exist unless they were infused by God himself. For those things that are known about God are invisible things that are deduced from things that are visible, the deduction of which is so far beyond the grasp of men and women that it can by no means be confessed without a peculiar and certain revelation of God. He also at the same time explains the manner in which he effects this awareness within us. This is clear from the fact that we have no awareness of God apart from his own self-revelation. "The eternal power and deity of God." This means that he holds all things in his hand and controls them according to a most perfect order (this is what is meant by the term "eternal power"), while showing himself to be the Highest Good and the Father of those who seek him (this is what is implied by the term "divinity"). I assert that these invisible things of God are such that cannot be observed by the senses and are, therefore, not perceived by the mind. But they are comprehended—clearly and firmly known—by God himself revealing the *noumena* (things deduced by the mind's reasoning). COMMENTARY ON ROMANS (1562).[12]

CHRIST TAUGHT BY POINTING TO CREATION. HANS HUT: If someone wants to comprehend and confess God's power and divinity, God's invisible essence, through the works (or creatures) of all creation since the beginning of the world, then he must note and consider that Christ always communicated the kingdom of heaven and the power of God to the common person through the use of parables, pointing to a creature or to different handicrafts or different human occupations. He never sent the poor and simple to books

(as our scholars do now). Rather, he taught and witnessed the gospel to them through their work—to peasants by their fields, seeds, thistles, thorns, and rocks. A BEGINNING OF A TRUE CHRISTIAN LIFE.[13]

PHILOSOPHERS AND THE INVISIBLE THINGS. JUAN DE VALDÉS: Paul means to say that by this fabric of the world, which is the work of his hands, God manifested to humanity those things that are invisible in him, including his eternal power and his Godhead. Among the invisible things of God I understand St. Paul to mean his goodness, his truth, and his justice. And those who have read the works of the philosophers well know that where discussing God—although, due to pride, they have not conjectured rightly—they still to a certain extent have succeeded in hitting on these things through their use of reason, and through the understanding that God has given them. COMMENTARY ON ROMANS (1556).[14]

WHY THOSE WITHOUT THE GOSPEL ARE NOT EXCUSED. JOHANNES BRENZ: Although the Gentiles, or nations, in their natural state had no awareness of the gospel of Christ and lacked the Holy Spirit, they ought not nor can be accordingly excused from their sin. For what reason? Here Paul explains what he meant when he had said a bit earlier, that the Gentiles "suppress the truth in unrighteousness." For the "truth" is that there is a God, that God is eternal, powerful, wise, good, and the Governor of all things. The Gentiles recognized this truth. But it is "unrighteousness" that God be likened to mortal men and women, beasts, reptiles, gold, silver, stones, wood, and other things of this kind. It is also unrighteousness and a lie that God needs human service and is cared for by human hands. To "suppress the truth in unrighteousness," therefore, is to clearly know that God is—that he is eternal, powerful, and the Governor of all things—but nevertheless to not honor him as

---

[12]Bucer, *Metaphrasis et Enarratio*, 72 (this is a reprint of the 1536 edition).

[13]CRR 12:123-4*; citing Mt 13:3-8; Mk 4:26-34; Lk 8:5-8; Jn 12:24.
[14]Valdés, *Commentary upon St. Paul's Epistle*, 13*.

God, and as eternal, powerful, and the Governor of all things. Or, in other words, to not believe in him, to not put one's trust in him, to not call on him in times of need, but instead to change his glory into an image fashioned in the likeness of a creature, and to drag down his heavenly majesty to the lowliness of bodily and earthly things. COMMENTARY ON ROMANS (1588).[15]

1:21 *The Darkening of Foolish Hearts*

DESCRIBING DECEPTION. DESIDERIUS ERASMUS: *Evanescere* (to vanish) refers to something that first appeared to the eyes as a false image, then later vanishes like vapor. Paul refers to those who have been deceived by their own reasoning. That is, things happened far otherwise than they had anticipated. What follows next testifies to that: "Asserting themselves to be wise, they were made foolish." In fact, "to be deceived" is this: When you have hoped for the highest wisdom, but encounter the summit of stupidity; when you have dreamed of the brightest light, only to be plunged in deepest darkness; when at one time you proposed for yourself a glory rare among humans, only to collapse into shameful lusts, from which even brutish animals instinctively shrink back. ANNOTATIONS ON THE NEW TESTAMENT (1527).[16]

BEWARE OF YOUR HEART DARKENING. RUDOLF GWALTHER: "And their foolish heart was darkened." For they covered themselves in dark clouds when, not being zealous for the things that God had manifested about himself, they followed the principles of their own flesh, concerning the nature of which many things will be said in what follows. Let us remember that this is what is clearly stated by Paul concerning the Gentiles. . . . But in the same manner this can even be said of Christians, and of some it can be said with great reproach, who having abandoned the Word of God have set up a worship of God fashioned out of

their own mind and pretend that there are new gods and so cover themselves in darkness by which the light revealed in the gospel of truth is obscured. Therefore, let us be on our guard against the reasoning of our flesh, nor let us give admittance to commonly held human superstitions; but rather let us be zealous for the Word of God alone, which Jesus Christ proclaimed, who is the catholic Teacher of eternal truth and the light of the world. Those "who follow" him "will not walk in darkness." To him is due blessing, honor, glory, and power for eternity. Amen. SERMONS ON ROMANS (1590).[17]

ONLY THOSE WHO WANT TO ERR ARE HARDENED. BALTHASAR HUBMAIER: To that God answers, not I: "Therefore, Israel, because you wanted to err, be blinded and be hardened, because you wanted to follow your dreams and human laws, not hearing me, but doing that which was good in your eyes, and because you despised my commandments, therefore, this happened to you as also to the Romans, for thus I punish sins with sins." Christ also says: "Jerusalem, Jerusalem, how often did I want to gather you like a hen gathers its chicks under its wings, but you did not want to." Therefore, your house will be waste. For God does not want to make anyone err or be hardened, except the one who himself wants to err wantonly and be hardened. Thus the doctor abandons the sick one who does not obey him nor take his medicine. FREEDOM OF THE WILL.[18]

THE LIMITS OF HUMAN REASON. JOHANN WIGAND: "Knowing." That is, insofar as they are able by the light of nature and reason, for he is speaking of the nations. It needs to be noted how far into truth the nations are able to advance by such lights as these: they are able to know that there is a God, that his essence is without bounds, that he existed before the world was, that he is wise, just, all-powerful, good, and the avenger of crimes. They also know that God is to be

---

[15]Brenz, *In Epistolam*, 501.
[16]Erasmus, *In Novum Testamentum*, 331.
[17]Gwalther, *In d. Pauli Apostoli*, 13v; citing Jn 8:12.
[18]CRR 5:487*; citing Mt 23:37.

worshiped and called on, that he sees all things, governs all things, and sustains all things. Thus far human reason can arrive at the truth, but it is not able on its own or by rational arguments to determine anything about the true and proper essence of God or his purpose of grace toward sinners. That is, it cannot ascertain that God is one essence but in three persons, or that out of merciful compassion on account of Christ's blood he is willing to receive and save those sinners who believe. In such matters a thick darkness reigns and continues its hold in the hearts of all men and women after the fall, except for in the church of God. ANNOTATIONS ON ROMANS (1580).[19]

IDOLATROUS WORSHIP VERSUS THE LORD'S SUPPER. PETER MARTYR VERMIGLI: On the one hand, creation had taught them that the one God whom they had acknowledged was to be worshiped with the greatest zeal and purity. But on the other hand, it also incited the passions and allurements of the pleasures that ought to be cast out in that true and lawful worship of God. But clever men and women thought up ways that both could be joined together at the same time: for they introduced a worship of God that was composed of gold and silver, choice sacrificial victims, extravagant banquets, games, shows, and other things of this kind, that might minister to the pleasures of their flesh. As a result, the same activities served both God and their own sensual amusements.

Nor any less than this are some in our own day doing the things that Paul is now railing against, things that correspond to the idolatries of those times. For Christ instituted the Lord's Supper so that in it the Lord's death might be commemorated and communicants might receive the fruit of that death, that they might be joined to Christ, that they might be always united to one another in greater friendship, that they might mortify depraved passions, and that they might be again and again renewed with new life by the divine food. This is the worship that God requires in this

sacrament from his people. But not content with this, people—either because it was difficult to do, or because they always wished to add their own inventions to divine things—dreamed up external ornaments, vestments, gold, silver, precious stones, candles, little bells, and innumerable ceremonies by which they tried to commend this sacrament. But these serve their own interests also. They desired that men and women stand on the sidelines as merely spectators and hearers of the Mass, while they mutter their . . . prayers and imagine they have thereby performed the divine mysteries. By human judgments of this kind the true and lawful use of the sacrament instituted by Christ is nearly abolished. This is what human inventions lead to. In this way the foolish heart is rendered fatuous, so that it prefers lightsome and frivolous things before the necessary and weighty. COMMENTARY ON ROMANS (1560).[20]

1:22-23 Exchanging God's Glory for Idols

HOW THE GENTILES BECAME FOOLISH. HEINRICH BULLINGER: Here Paul explains most clearly how it is that they suppressed the truth in unrighteousness, and also how they did not glorify God, but became foolish. It was because they believed themselves to be wise, since they considered themselves to have discovered that the ideas derived particularly from idolatry—which the foolish minds of philosophers were appropriating for themselves through their powers of reasoning—are what is true and righteous. As a result, they became utterly foolish and exhibited this folly as a sign of what was in their soul. For they altered the incorruptible glory of God and, as much as they could, adulterated his ineffable majesty. As if by a miserable human image, or by the likeness of living things that are less than human, they could picture or represent that Beginning of all things, and the Highest Good and Being of the universe itself! Certainly nothing more foolish could possibly be

---

[19]Wigand, *In Epistolam S. Pauli*, 18v.   [20]Vermigli, *In Epistolam S. Pauli*, 71-72.

imagined. This is how the greatest apostle of Christ convicted the Gentiles of ungodliness. The wrath of God deservedly falls on such great impiety. COMMENTARY ON ROMANS (1533).[21]

EXCHANGING GOD'S GLORY FOR AN ONION AND A MOUSE. JOHANN WILD: "And change the glory." That is, though knowing God they did not render him honor by expecting and asking him for all things, but placed their confidence in creatures; not only in living ones but in stones and wood: "Saying to stones: 'you are my father' and to wood, 'you have brought me forth.'" Notice here first of all the progress of sin, how much impiety grows unless it is immediately uprooted by repentance. Learn also how much we should abhor idols, for something of the divine glory is diminished by them and "truth is exchanged for a lie." Now, he mentions four kinds of idols: (1) the "likeness of men and women," as were the idols of Venus, Minerva, Jupiter, and so on; (2) "of flying things," for the Egyptians worshiped the hawk and the ibis; (3) "of four-footed things," for some worshiped cattle, sheep, rabbits, and others; (4) "of creeping things" such as serpents and dragons. Men and women were so blinded that they could even worship pitiful living things like the mouse. For it is found in the histories that such things as the onion, insects, the oven, fever, and sickness were dignified with the names of deities. Further, take note here that outward idolatry has its root in impiety within the heart. For since men and women are self-sufficient in nothing, they have need of help from another, and since they will not wait on the true God or ask him, it necessarily follows that they will invent for themselves another, or rather many other gods, from whom they might have recourse to for help. For because men and women are lacking in many things, they did not believe that one God was sufficient to meet all needs, so they fabricated many gods. EXEGESIS OF ROMANS.[22]

IDOLATERS DIDN'T THINK THE IDOLS THEMSELVES WERE GODS. NIELS HEMMINGSEN: He is describing the vanity and foolishness of the powers of human reasoning when it comes to God and the worship paid to him, which is that crude and monstrous idolatry into which the whole earth has fallen. Nor was there other occasion for the invention of idols and images than that mistaken opinion in which men and women thought themselves to be serving the true God by prostrating themselves before idols or images. Nor should it be thought that the makers of images were so crude as to think that wood and stones were gods, but rather they said that they were stirred up to worship the true God by means of such helps, and this is why those wishing to pray prostrated themselves before them—which rite of worshiping God the Holy Spirit condemns here. A prudent and pious disciple of Christ will easily be able to learn from this passage how we should regard those heathenish and diabolical abominations that today are observed to the disgracing of the gospel of Christ, so much so that on their account ministers of the gospel are being persecuted. COMMENTARY ON ROMANS (1562).[23]

FOLLOW MOSES AND PAUL BY SHUNNING IMAGES. ANDREAS BODENSTEIN VON KARLSTADT: You will have to admit that Paul is a fulsome preacher of the gospel and the new law. He reached the depth of Moses' meaning and brought it to light. He proclaimed Christian promise in an abundantly comforting fashion. You must then also say that when Paul prohibits images, I will also shun them. Now hear this. Paul says, "They exchanged the glory of the immortal God for an image not only of a dead human being, but also of birds, four-legged, and crawling animals." Can you perceive how evil and harmful Paul considers images to be? He says that those who honor images rob God of his glory and equate him with creatures. In this way they diminish and blaspheme God. Moses also says repeatedly that God cannot

[21]Bullinger, *In Sanctissimam Pauli ad Romanos*, C3v.
[22]Wild, *Exegesis in Epistolam* (1558), 60r-61r; citing Jer 2:27.

[23]Hemmingsen, *Commentarius in Epistolam*, 52-53.

tolerate our images and likenesses. Thus Moses and Paul agree. And I have shown from the letters of Paul that no one who honors images comes to God. On the Removal of Images.[24]

Placing Anything Above God or His Word Is Idolatry. Dirk Philips: But some, who worship the molten calf and want to have a visible God, forsake Moses who tarries on the mountain. That is, they turn away from the living God, and from the Lord Jesus Christ who ascended to heaven and delays his return as they imagine. Therefore they fall on a strange worship and choose for themselves idols that are visible. Thus they play and leap around the golden calf. For whoever loves or honors any creature above the Creator, or instead of God, or whoever regards any human doctrine as equal to or above God's Word, or whoever sets his righteousness or seeks his salvation in any false worship which God himself has not instituted with one express word, without doubt worships the golden calf and is reckoned before the Lord as a servant of idols. However gloriously he may embellish or adorn his idolatry with the appearance of holiness, calling it true worship, it is, nevertheless, before God nothing other than idolatry. For God alone will be God and Lord and be confessed as such. He will also not be served according to our opinions but according to his Word alone. Concerning Spiritual Restitution.[25]

Parallels to the Golden Calf and to Veneration of Images. Huldrych Zwingli: "They changed the glory." He explains how it is that they desired to serve this divine power and energy, since it was clearly apparent to them. Sometimes they fashioned the greatest winged god, and at other times a serpent, and they served such things in place of God. Sometimes they even fashioned images of some human, such as Mars, Saturn, or Venus. It was their custom to set up both pleasant and unpleasant gods over the nations—one to turn them away from evils, another to furnish them with good things that should be followed. Accordingly, we have both Jove and Vejovis[†] and so on. (It might also here be noted in passing that the nations did not serve the idols themselves, but the god whom the idol stood for and in whose image the idols were fashioned, a god whom they believed was in the heavens.) Therefore, Paul lays a charge against the nations, that they knew of God but did not rightly serve the One they knew. He thereby takes away from them all excuse, charging them to be no less sinners than the Jews who had served a calf or rather, served God through a calf. And we, when we were under the reign of the pope, were in no way inferior to the Gentiles in this sin. For what didn't we serve? Annotations on Romans (1539).[26]

1:24 God Gave Them Over to Lust

Handed Over to Sinful Desires. Martin Bucer: "On account of which God handed them over." It was with utmost wrath that God resolved to hand over, give over, and deliver up to the desires of their hearts those whom he had fashioned in his own image that by his Spirit they might do all that is virtuous, holy, and divine. Today, these desires, where the Spirit of Christ is absent, are altogether beastly; or rather, because men and women are capable of reason, they are much more deviant and monstrous than beasts, who, unlike beasts, cannot at all restrain themselves even within natural boundaries. For what monsters are there that throw themselves like this into sexual behaviors that do not serve the production of offspring, to say nothing of being contrary to nature? Who so insanely take pleasure in food and drink that results in their own destruction? How many escape such madness by their desires for receiving honors and influence, by which motives irrational creatures are unmoved? All things are greater when

---

[24]CRR 8:120*.
[25]CRR 6:330-31*; citing Ex 32:1; 1 Cor 10:7; Acts 1:9-11; Deut 5:7; 12:2-4; Is 28:9; Mt 15:2.

[26]Zwingli, *In Evangelicam Historiam*, 409. [†]The anti-Jove.

it comes to humankind, for which reason the sins committed by them are more monstrous and more impetuous where perversity takes possession of them. Without doubt, since the fall of our first parents this claims possession of every faculty that humanity has. Therefore, there is no clearer or more certain proof of divine wrath than that a person has been handed over to his or her lusts. COMMENTARY ON ROMANS (1562).[27]

DON'T BLAME THE GARDENER FOR THE BAD TREE. LUCAS OSIANDER: As we said a bit earlier, there is no graver sin than idolatry. "On account of which" God also punishes this sin in the gravest manner, permitting the Gentiles to fall into detestable crimes, the very mention of which is abhorrent to the virtuous soul. "God handed them over" (says Paul) "to the desire of their hearts." He removed from them the whole of his governance (as it relates to their manner of life) and permitted them to freely follow their ungodly desires so that they act on whatever things their corrupt flesh might suggest to them. God is not the author of sin. For just as a bad tree that a gardener does not reckon worthy of being cared for any further (since it is bad) in time will without doubt become worse, but the blame for its badness cannot be charged to the gardener, just so, when God deserts depraved people so that in time they fall headlong into a worse depravity, one must not assign any blame at all to God. It was in this way that God handed the Gentiles over, Paul says, that they might fall straightway "into uncleanness"—that is, "that they might dishonor their own bodies among themselves." Or more correctly, "mutually," so that they reproachfully contaminate their bodies by detestable carnal passions toward each other—we will speak in more detail about this kind of sin a bit later. It is by the just judgment of God that they have fallen into such infamous and shameful deeds, "since they changed the truth of God into a lie." For that which they

knew concerning God, they corrupted, obscured, and perverted, and what's more, they contaminated it with unlawful, foolish, and utterly empty idolatrous worship. EXPLICATION OF PAUL'S EPISTLES (1583).[28]

ADMITTING GOD'S SOVEREIGNTY OVER ALL THINGS. MARTIN BUCER: Let us grant this, that in everything God inclines the hearts of each according to their own judgment. A man can do absolutely nothing to make himself good. And he, therefore, can never fail to follow his evil desires, being sentenced by God. We deny God if we do not acknowledge he brings about all things. Therefore, when people before God's judgment seat of reckoning attribute ability to themselves, they flee the smoke and throw themselves headlong into the fire. . . . Who knows the reason why God made wolves to devour sheep rather than sheep to devour wolves? Or why he created fleas, lice, and countless others? And how extraordinary it is that God directs not only human beings but also the rest of the world in such a way that most would not want it to change. COMMENTARY ON ROMANS (1562).[29]

CONSEQUENCES FOR IGNORING GOD'S CALL. BALTHASAR HUBMAIER: Leonhart: How does God draw or call a person?

Hans: In two forms, outwardly and inwardly. The outward drawing occurs through the public proclamation of his holy gospel, that Christ has commanded to preach to all creatures in the whole world, which is now proclaimed everywhere. The inward drawing is this, that God also illuminates the person's soul inwardly, so that it understands the incontrovertible truth, convinced by the Spirit and the preached Word in such a way that one must in one's own conscience confess that this is the case and it cannot be otherwise.

Leonhart: Explain this by an example.

---

[27]Bucer, *Metaphrasis et Enarratio*, 70 (this is a reprint of the 1536 edition).

[28]Osiander, *Epistolae S. Pauli*, 15.

[29]Bucer, *Metaphrasis et Enarratio*, 72-73 (this is a reprint of the 1536 edition).

Hans: Gladly. Just as one hears outwardly with his ears and inwardly understands: All that enters into the mouth does not make one unclean. He knows too that Christ said this. In his conscience he is now convinced that this must be true, and he cannot oppose it at all with clear Scripture. That is the outward and inward drawing of God, which everyone can safely believe and trust. But if he does not do this, God will abandon him and with just judgment give him over to a perverted mind, blind, harden, and strike him with a deceiving mind like Babylon, the Jews, and the Romans. A CHRISTIAN CATECHISM.[30]

LUSTS MORE TYRANNICAL THAN LIONS AND TIGERS. ANDREW WILLET: The Lord at one time gave the idolatrous Samaritans over to lions, but he gives over these idolatrous Gentiles to their own hearts' lusts and vile affections, which more tyrannized over them than lions and tigers, for when the body is given up to wild beasts and deprived of life nothing happens against the condition of our mortal nature, but when the mind is ruled by lust and so the affection prevails against reason, this is monstrous and unnatural. A SIX-FOLD COMMENTARY UPON THE EPISTLE OF ROMANS (1611).[31]

FLESH OR SPIRIT MUST BE AFIRE. MARTIN LUTHER: Rule: When young persons have no spark of reverence for God in their hearts but go their way without a thought about God, I can hardly believe that they are chaste. For as they must live either by the flesh or by the spirit, either their flesh or their spirit must be afire. There is no better victory over the burning of the flesh than to have the heart flee and turn away from it in devout prayer. Where the flame of the spirit is burning, the flesh soon cools off and becomes cold, and vice versa. LECTURES ON ROMANS (1516).[32]

1:25 Unholy Exchanges

HUMANS EXCHANGED UNTRUTH FOR TRUTH. KONRAD PELLIKAN: By way of repetition, he explains again why God, in wrath, has handed over so many who are wise according to the flesh and destitute of true faith in God to such a sick mind that they turn out more wretched and filthy than beasts. "For the truth of God"—is that there is One who creates, reigns over, and most perfectly orders all things, that he appears and shows himself through his works, and that he invites us to a true worship of him. But by their carved images, men and women have set before themselves and venerated a lie, contrary to the dictate of right reason and the interior witness of a good conscience, the voice of which nobody fails to hear frequently, but those who live according to the flesh pay it no attention. So also do those who venerate and value their false and foolish divine images and human gestures as containing more truth than—and who choose to adhere to their theologians more closely than—the Word of the Lord and the sacred Scriptures. So also do those whose sluggishness of body and sensual desires do not very willingly obey that faculty of judging of what is proper that was implanted in the human heart, but instead necessarily push them to become increasingly worse, unless the faith of true religion and the fear of God should persuade them otherwise. [Although], therefore, the heavens, the stars, the earth, animals, and even men and women themselves are living examples of the wisdom, goodness, and power of God, so that by these things the Maker can clearly be learned of and known, men and women nevertheless prefer to fashion and set before themselves the productions of their arts, from which things they most foolishly presumed to learn about and search out a God who is infinitely dissimilar to such things. They also choose to believe and obey their own thoughts rather than the Word of God and the will of the Creator who so severely prohibits and abominates all such things as these. COMMENTARY ON ALL THE APOSTOLIC EPISTLES (1539).[33]

---

[30]CRR 5:362-63*; citing Mk 16:15; Mt 15:17; Jer 51:7; Mt 13:15-17.
[31]Willet, *Hexapla*, 98; citing 2 Kings 17:25.
[32]LW 25:167*.

[33]Pellikan, *In Omnes Apostolicas Epistolas*, 20-21.

STRIPPING THE CREATOR OF HIS MAJESTY.
LOUIS DE DIEU: Even if they wished to purify themselves from idolatry, that they should worship not only creatures but also the Creator, they are still *anapologētoi* (without excuse) because they worship the creatures above the Creator, and where the Creator is held to be lower than creatures, he is stripped of all his majesty. OBSERVATIONS ON ROMANS (1646).[34]

GOD KNOWS AND TESTS YOUR HEART. ANDREAS BODENSTEIN VON KARLSTADT: Thus God helps the godless and wicked, even though they seek help with creatures contrary to divine counsel and will. He tolerates when you say, Blessed Mary in Grünthal in Franconia restored my sight, or, the blessed blood in the marches made me walk straight again, or, St. Anne at Denten preserved me from poison and death, even though the saints do not hear or know of our pleas and vows. However, out of great goodness, God helps by being silent for a time, even though you rob God of his honor by ascribing it to a creature.

God does this because he knows your heart better than you do; he sees that you have forsaken him and that you have made for yourself new gods of the saints; yes, what is even greater, God sees how you run after the images of saints. For this reason God leaves you to the desires and lust of your heart and allows you to run to your eternal loss, as is written in Romans 1.

It is not without reason that God overlooks your faults and allows that you thus go astray. For you first left God and carried his glory in and to a creature. This is for one. For the other, it is written that God imposes times when deceiving gods such as lying prophets and preachers will arise, and he does not prevent false prophets, such as popes, bishops, and monks, from preaching to us. Why does God do this? Because he tests us by this to see whether we desire to cling to and stay with him. So that it may become apparent to everyone whether we love God with all our heart and whether we follow him alone. This is what Paul says also that there must be quarrels and divisions so that true believers might become known. REGARDING VOWS (1522).[35]

PAUL BREAKS OUT IN PRAISE. KONRAD PELLIKAN: This is so evil, so unworthy of God, that in describing such things the apostle is most deeply disturbed in his thoughts and is compelled by the Holy Spirit to cry out and be amazed at the vileness of such human evil and foolishness and exclaim in a contrary and most holy sense, "Who is to be praised forever and ever, Amen." It is as if he were saying, "What savage impiety! What an abominable insult to God—to him who alone is God, who alone is to be praised, who fashioned all things, who is the only Good One and Potentate—these wretched people neglect this God; by their lies they strive against honoring him. It is by means of this sacrilege of theirs that they presume to understand matters with greater prudence, to be taking thought of their fellow human as to what the best way of making progress in righteousness might be, which sacrilege both the Word of God and God himself condemns by his finger, and frequently cries out that those idols, which they contend persuade people and promote the things that stir up piety toward him, are to be altogether abominated. And yet, they even erase the second commandment of the first table of the law about not worshiping idols, as being superfluous, and by passing over it they effectively cancel it out as something written unadvisedly into the Ten Commandments by the finger of God.

As for the addition "Amen," it confirms that all praise and worship is owed to the one and only true God, and that faithful and true worshipers must guard against the worship of any other. COMMENTARY ON ALL THE APOSTOLIC EPISTLES (1539).[36]

---

[34]De Dieu, *Animadversiones in D. Pauli*, 14.

[35]CRR 8:60*; citing Deut 13:3; 1 Cor 11:19.
[36]Pellikan, *In Omnes Apostolicas Epistolas*, 21.

1:26-27 Handed Over to Sin Because of Sin

MISUSE OF OUR BODY DISHONORS US.
JOHANNES BRENZ: Let us learn from this passage that our bodies and their members are dishonored not only in the manner that is mentioned here, but also by any unlawful, inordinate abuse whatever. For example: the tongue was created so that it might glorify God, speak the truth, and say those things that promote the edification of our neighbor. Therefore, people who abuse the name of God in profanity, or who lie, or who rip apart their neighbors with insults, or who are stumbling blocks to the weak on account of their impious or foul words—such people dishonor their tongues. Ears were created that they might hear the Word of God and the things that promote piety and character. For which reason, if we should turn our ears away from hearing the Word of God and toward hearing trifles, speech that tears down the reputation of another person, and other things of this kind, we dishonor our ears. In brief: our whole body was created so that it might offer itself in obedience to the Word of God. For which reason, if it passes over to the service of Satan in obedience to sins, the whole body is dishonored. Therefore, nobody, no matter how powerful an enemy they might be, can dishonor us as much as we ourselves do by the abuse of our own bodies. COMMENTARY ON ROMANS (1588).[37]

THE SIN IS BOTH THE EFFECT OF AND THE WAGES OF IDOLATRY. AEGIDIUS HUNNIUS: "For they even changed the natural use of their women." This is an exposition of those things that he had earlier begun to mention concerning the Gentiles' manner of life, which they horribly defiled in both sexes by the most evil sins, especially by lusts contrary to nature. This abominable uncleanness, he says, was not only the effect of idolatry but also its just punishment and wages; so that in this way,

sins were being punished by sins. For, considered in themselves, these shameful acts are sins, in which respect they have Satan for their author. But they are also punishments, with respect to the preceding idolatry. Certainly God does not cause these sins in themselves, but by his just judgment he permits the Gentiles to tumble down into them with Satan pushing them. EXPOSITION ON ROMANS (1592).[38]

THE PROGRESSION OF DISOBEDIENCE TO GOD'S WORD. PILGRAM MARPECK: The beginning of the disobedience to God's Word consists of arrogance, presumption, pride, self-importance, boasting, and stubbornness about one's own self-will and vainglory. From these follow murders, those who shed the blood of the innocent, mockers, blasphemers, persecutors of the truth; those who disobey parents, murderers of father and mother, liars, deceivers, and seducers; those who are envious, hateful, and hold grudges, and those who always resist the good, who tend to all wickedness; the blasphemers, those who, because of their malice, are deniers of the truth; playing, eating, drinking, whoring, backbiting, and slandering the neighbor; idolaters, servants of idols, magicians, and venerators of images. All these are delivered over to a perverted mind. They change the way of nature and, against nature, enflame themselves and others with passion, man for man, woman for woman, and for dumb animals; they are seducers of children, brawlers, quarrelers, falsely zealous rioters, rebels, creators of false sects, on whom the sudden judgment of God will fall before long. Usury, avarice, which is the root of all idolatry, wrath, bad temper, villainy, slanderous talk, disgraceful words, swearers of oaths, and perjurers, all of these are the fruit of wickedness, and there can never be any hope that such fruit could become good. JUDGMENT AND DECISION (C. 1541).[39]

---

[37]Brenz, *In Epistolam*, 505-6.

[38]Hunnius, collating *Epistolae Divi Pauli*, 85 and *Thesaurus*, 21.
[39]CRR 2:345-46*.

1:28 A Debased Mind

Given Over to a Perverse Mind. Bernardino Ochino: "And because they did not see fit." Nor did they show themselves, by the doing of upright deeds, "to retain God in their knowledge," for not acknowledging God in Christ, they did not know God sufficiently, nor did they retain an experience, discovery, inward perception, or a clear and full view of his goodness, even though they possessed a certain kind of awareness of God from the nature of things. But this awareness was so crippled that, being dominated by the lusts that were in them, they were influenced more by the deceitful appearance of the empty shadows of this life and by images than they were by that true and substantive goodness of God. "Them." Since they did not regard God as of great worth, nor One to be treated with honor—what they ought to have been animated by—"God released them to a perverse mind." That is, he so took vengeance on them that he handed them over to an evil, unreasonable, insane, blind, and perverse mind, "to do abominable deeds," so that because they did not know God in an appropriate way, "they were filled with all manner of unrighteousness." Exposition on Romans.[40]

A Mind Void of Judgment. The English Annotations: Into a perverse and contrary mind, whereby it comes to pass that the light of conscience being once put out, and having almost no more remorse of sin, men and women run headlong into all kinds of mischief. The word in the original, *adokimon*, may be taken either actively or passively. Actively, for a mind which disapproves of all good courses, or does not prove or try good or bad nor put difference between that which is vile and that which is honorable; or passively, for a mind disallowed of God, and so in this sense is a metaphor taken from goldsmiths trying metals and choosing that which is good and precious and rejecting and reprobating that which is vile. Annotations on Romans 1:28.[41]

Paul's List of Sins Leaves No One Innocent. Lucas Osiander: But lest the Gentiles should object to Paul that they had not been contaminated by all the evil deeds mentioned earlier, and that, therefore, not everyone can be charged as guilty of sins and crimes, Paul here adds such a list of vices that nobody among the Gentiles could wholly exempt himself from, but rather would be forced to confess himself to be guilty of at least one or another vice of this kind. He does this so that all might be convinced that humanity can not be justified in any way other than the free clemency of God, through faith. Then Paul goes on, saying: "And since they did not see fit to retain God in their knowledge." For in a manner fitting with how they did not watch jealously over these duties, particularly those that he was just teaching about—that they should rightly acknowledge God, learn how to lawfully worship him, and then conduct it with care—they also became most dissolute in their common life together. "God handed them over by his just judgment to a reprobate mind," that they might straightway become even more perverse, "to do those things which are not fitting," things that are plainly unworthy of good, virtuous, and just men and women. Explication of Paul's Epistle (1583).[42]

1:29-31 A Catalog of Sins

Every Kind of Sin. Peter Martyr Vermigli: "Filled with every kind of unrighteousness." A catalog of sins is here reviewed, as God's avengers and agents of punishment, as it were. That they are said to be "filled" with these sins is wonderfully emphasized. Nor does it say merely "with unrighteousness," but the adjective "all manner of" is added by way of *epitasin* (a stretching or an increase), since even godly men and women can occasionally slip a little and experience within themselves the beginnings of these vices. But the people in this passage are said to be not only "filled" but even to have their entire nature stuffed full of such evils. "Injustice," by which we

---

[40]Ochino, *Expositio Epistolae Divi Pauli*, 18.
[41]Downame, ed., *Annotations*, AAA1v*.
[42]Osiander, *Epistolae S. Pauli*, 17.

cause injury to our neighbor, is placed first. Then "fornication" is added without explicit mention of adultery, for, as Ambrose says, a graver sin is condemned by the condemnation of a lighter one. For if fornication is a sin, so much more is adultery. And if he had passed over fornication and mentioned only adultery, perhaps they might think that fornication is not a sin. This is what they say that the laws of the Romans did, which, passing over fornication, punished only adultery. *Ponēria* (wickedness)—this means laboring with the intention of doing evil to another. The word *pleonechia* (greediness) is derived from *pleon et echein* (carrying more), and those are called *pleonektai* (those who have) who busy themselves at every opportunity to possess more than others do, and to take for themselves more than is fitting even if it harms their neighbor and comes at a high cost, whether this pursuit is for wealth, or for sensual pleasures, or for public honors. *Kakia* (maliciousness)—if understood broadly this means "vice," the opposite of *tē aretē* (virtue). Wherever there is slothfulness, there *to ekakoun* (to speak negligently) means to fall short of virtue. *Kakia* is also that vice by which we grow weary of steadfastly doing good. It also can mean "affliction" by which we do harm to neighbors. *Mestous phthonou, phonou, eridos* (full of ill will, murder, and strife)—he once again shows that they are not only in some ways stained by evils, but that they overflow with evil. He rightly conjoins "jealousy" and "murder": the first homicide, by Cain, arose out of jealousy. Then, following the committing of murders come contentions once again. *Dolou* (deceit)—this means "fraud"; for those whom they do not possess the power to kill or oppress, they overthrow with deceit and cunning. *Kakoētheias* (evil disposition)—here we find reproached all harsh, morose, and ill-tempered manners. These people are among those whom almost nobody can stay around. *Psithyristas* (whisperers)—whisperers are those who secretly spread abroad the things they hear or see, and lie in wait against the closest of friendships and, to the best of one's ability, to break them up and dissolve them. COMMENTARY ON ROMANS (1560).[43]

---

[43]Vermigli, *In Epistolam S. Pauli*, 101-2.

AVARICE DEFINED. JOHANNES BRENZ: "Avarice." What, then, is avarice? Men and women are accustomed to invert the names of things. They call diligence in conserving personal property "attentiveness." And similarly, they call the pursuit of gathering wealth, in whatever way it can be done, whether justly or unjustly, "prudence" and "honest business." But these things must be judged for what they are. "Avarice" is not the desire to legitimately obtain and possess honest food and clothing, appropriate to the manner and condition of one's occupation, but rather it is to not be content with one's possessions, either those things that you already possess by the gift of God or those that you can lawfully obtain, and to crave for more than necessity requires and that is lawful, even if it causes harm to others. For that which some monarchs take for their creed, namely, "I must have even more!" is a natural instinct in nearly all men and women, so that they crave more than they can honestly acquire. This is what "avarice" means. For the desire of legitimately obtaining and possessing the things that are necessary for an honest life is a natural sense engrafted and created in men and women by God. This is why even Christ commanded us to pray, "Give us this day our daily bread." And in the twenty-eighth chapter of Genesis, Jacob says: "if the Lord will give me bread to eat, and clothing to wear," and so on. And the thirtieth chapter of Proverbs says: "give me neither poverty nor riches. Grant me only my necessary food." And Paul when he wrote in the fourth chapter of Ephesians: "He who formerly stole must not steal any longer, but rather must labor by working with his hands." These passages do not teach avarice, but rather teach a duty that is worthy of an honest man or woman. Therefore, avarice is not the natural impulse of honestly acquiring and possessing the necessary food appropriate for one's condition of life, but it is to pay more attention to wealth than to the righteousness of God, to obtain wealth at the cost of others and by cheating, and to trust more in wealth than in the promise of God. For this reason Paul elsewhere calls avarice "idolatry,"

and he calls avaricious people "idolaters." COM-
MENTARY ON ROMANS (1588).[44]

FORNICATION DEFINED. NIELS HEMMINGSEN:
"Fornication." In the enumeration of the kinds of
unrighteousness, he puts in first place that kind
in which man commits an injustice against his
own self, not rendering due honor to his own
body, but foully contaminating it and exposing it
to every kind of uncleanness. He is using the
term "fornication" as a synecdoche for all unlawful sexual acts. For how gravely serious this vice
is, see 1 Corinthians 6. COMMENTARY ON
ROMANS (1562).[45]

FIVE TERMS DEFINED. JOHANN WILD: "Full of
envy." Envy is jealousy of the happiness of others.
To be envious means wishing good on themselves
alone; neither is it enough for them to be afflicted
with their own misery, unless they also torment
themselves by their own choice because of the
happiness of others.

"Murder." Murder comes about not only from
the act of killing itself, but in words and thoughts,
wherefore Christ plainly says (and John as well),
"he who hates his brother" is a murderer.

"Contention." Contention is where some
position is defended not by reason, but by stubbornness. Or it is where the truth is not sought,
but animosity is encouraged. They were filled with
contention because even knowing that they are
wrong, they nonetheless refused to yield, but rather
continued defending their error and sin.

"Deceit." Those who cannot overcome by
contention build with deceit. Who can sufficiently
estimate how many deceits ungodly men and
women have rolling around in their minds? Like a
sharp knife (which wounds before it is felt), you
have worked deceit. They sin all the more because
they cannot avoid doing harm to others.

"Maliciousness." This seems to indicate a craving
to offend. Herein you can see how much humanity
has fallen off from its likeness to God, whose
character is to show mercy to all. But humanity is
full of a craving to cause offense. EXEGESIS ON
ROMANS (1558).[46]

WHISPERERS AND DETRACTORS. MARTIN
LUTHER: "Whisperer" and "detractor" differ in that
the detractor undermines the good reputation of
another person, but the whisperer sows discord
among those who live in harmony by secretly
informing one person of one thing and another
person of another thing. Every whisperer is
double-tongued, but not every detractor is.
LECTURES ON ROMANS.[47]

THOSE WHO INVENT EVIL. HEINRICH BULL-
INGER: Next to be recounted are the inventors of
evils, who, not being content with those evils with
which men and women have customarily polluted
themselves, in addition contrive certain new evils;
or rather, you can find monsters of a certain character who measure out rewards to those who invent
new forms of either torture or novel sensual
pleasures. It is read that Phalaris[†] rewarded the
former, Sardanapalus[†] the latter. What shall I say
of those ministers of haughtiness, arrogance,
extravagance, and ostentatious displays who invent
new styles of vestments? What of those merchants
who trade in the shrewdest imaginable inventions
of evil deceits, shams, and frauds? What shall I say
of certain lawyers before whom there is no
jurisprudence but that involving the gravest
injustice? For they entangle what is plain, obscure
what is clear, and distort what is simple so that a
judicial proceeding might be even further prolonged and thereby be more costly. I need say
nothing of princes and the means of acquiring
wealth invented by certain nobles. For the whole
world knows how shrewd they are in inventing and
collecting new tributes and taxes. This is the very

[44]Brenz, *In Epistolam*, 509; citing Mt 6:11; Gen 28:20; Prov 30:8;
Eph 4:28; Col 3:5; Eph 5:5.
[45]Hemmingsen, *Commentarius in Epistolam*, 57; citing 1 Cor
6:13-20.

[46]Wild, *Exegesis in Epistolam*, 69r-70r; citing Mt 5:22; 1 Jn 3:15.
[47]LW 25:170*.

thing that Erasmus, in *A Thousand Proverbs*,§ accused the rich of doing: demanding tribute even from the dead. But those who refuse to comply with the authors of these laws or those who represent them are condemned by not only divine law, but by human law as well. Commentary on Romans (1533).[48]

Paul's List Continues. Peter Martyr Vermigli: *Katalalous* (backbiters)—or, "disparagers." These differ from whisperers only inasmuch as they speak against people openly, whereas whisperers spread their poison secretly. *Theos tigeis* (God-haters)—These have a hatred for God and do not wish to ever hear, think, or speak about him. Julius Pollux said in his *Onomasticon*† that this word is an epithet for the impious, and he also said that it is a horrible word. For there are those who say to God, "Depart from us! We do not want a knowledge of your ways." *Ybristas* (insolent persons)—These are those revilers who by their reproach heap verbal abuse and wrongful injuries on their neighbors. *Hyperēphanous* (arrogant)—these are those who wish everywhere to be famous, proud and haughty. *Alazonas* (boasters)—the boastful; refers to those like Thraso,‡ boastful military commanders who attribute to themselves feats that have never been seen, written, or pictured. *Epheuretas kakōn* (inventors of evil)—these are so wicked that you can propose nothing good, solid, or firm to them without their discovering something of evil in it. Or, they are those who, not being content with the forms and variety of vices that already exist, think up new kinds of wicked deeds. *Goneusin apeitheis* (disobedient to their parents)—he understands by "parents" not only progenitors but also magistrates, teachers, and pastors.

Asynetous (without understanding). These are those who do nothing with good judgment or right reason but manage all their affairs in foolishness and insanity. *Asynthetous* (covenant breakers). These do not keep their promises, agreements, or covenants. They are treacherous and covenant breakers. *Astorgous* (without natural affection). These are those who aren't in any way moved with affection toward those who by some necessary relationship are closely connected to them. They are moved with affection toward neither parents, nor fellow freemen, nor their brothers or sisters, nor their own country, nor friends, nay, toward almost nobody. *Aspondous*—you could call these the irreconcilable, the implacable, who would start a war as soon as they become irate. *Aneleēmonas* (unmerciful)—in the last place, Paul places those who are so cruel that nothing touches them with a feeling of mercy.

Chrysostom, however, so lays out these last four vices such that by *asynthetous* (covenant breakers) he understands those who will not be reconciled with even those who are closely related to them by nature. A horse will join itself to another horse, and a cow to another cow, but these people will join themselves to no one. He takes the *astorgous* (without natural affection) as those who are unmoved by necessary relationships, and the *aspondous* (those that can never be appeased) as those who regard no covenant or society as unbreakable. *Aneleēmonas* (unmerciful), he says, are those who show mercy to nobody. These four vices are so diligently recounted because by them or by certain signs of them ungodliness can be discovered. They are, therefore, also for our benefit, partly so that we might behold the destruction of those who live without Christ and his gospel, and partly that we might have before our eyes who the enemy is, against whom we are to fight. Commentary on Paul's Epistles (1560).[49]

---

[48]Bullinger, *In Sanctissimam Pauli ad Romanos*, 32v-33r. †Phalaris was a cruel tyrant in Sicily (c. 570–554 BC) rumored to have engaged in cannibalism and to have roasted people alive inside a large brass bull. ‡Sardanapalus was described by Ctesias of Cnidus as the last king of Assyria (7th century BC), renowned for his decadence. §Erasmus, *Adagio* 1.9.12 critiques the excessive taxes of the sixteenth century, including priests charging the poor for burial on sacred ground.

[49]Vermigli, *In Epistolam S. Pauli*, 102-3; and *Learned and Fruitfull Commentaries*, 34r-34v. †Julius Pollux was a second-century Roman scholar who compiled the *Onomasticon*, a thesaurus of synonyms and phrases. ‡Thraso, a boastful captain, was a character in Terence's *Eunuchus*.

1:32 *Those Who Approve of Evil*

Definition of the Law of Nature. Tile-mann Hesshus: Here a definition of the law of nature can be sought: the law of nature is the natural knowledge divinely implanted into the human mind, which remains even after the fall, in conformity to the standard of God's own right-eousness. This knowledge bears witness that there is a God and that he is both just and an avenger of wicked deeds; it shows us the difference between good and evil, and it regulates our manner of life. The whole sum of the law of nature is contained in the Ten Commandments: for God wished by that repetition of his law, both to establish the judg-ment of the human mind concerning God and to illuminate and stir up the sparks that remain in the ashes within humanity, whose light was almost entirely extinguished, and at the same time to disclose evidence against his spiritual sin, and the unclean nature of humanity. Commentary on Romans (1605).[50]

Approving or Grieving Others' Crimes. Johannes Brenz: A clergyman, if he does not explain the magnitude and gravity of evil deeds with as much diligence as the law of God demands, in effect consents with these deeds and is guilty of the very crimes that his listeners perpetrate. A magistrate, if he does not guard honest laws with very much care, nor warn against public crimes as much as his vocation requires of him, becomes guilty of every crime that his subjects commit. The paternal head of a family, if he winks at the sins of his family and passes over them, or even if he should be displeased with it but does not do his duty so that it is punished in a manner fitting his calling, he is rightly said to consent to it. They are masters of workers and do not care about the honesty of their servants or disciples, but only that the household completes its tasks. They are, therefore, in the eyes of God, said to consent to the crimes of their family. Common people are not as bothered by others' sins as by their own inconve-niences. Such people do not plead with God, nor burn in their souls while invoking God's name that such horrific kinds of crimes might be removed from their midst. In God's eyes this undoubtedly amounts to consent to those crimes and an approval of such sins.

Now, for a collection of examples of the opposite: Moses was so distraught at the sins of his people that he wished to be erased from the Book of Life rather than that his people should perish; Jeremiah interceded for the sins of his fellow citizens without ceasing; and Paul said, "Who is weak, and I am not weak? Who is caused to stumble, and I do not burn?" For even if, in times past, all of these men had their own weaknesses, they are nevertheless examples by which it can in some way be understood what kind of feelings the godly should have toward the sins of others. Because this was lacking in the Gentiles, even the most noble among them consented in God's eyes to the wicked deeds of others and approved them. It is, therefore, a manifest and true axiom that the doer and the consenter are worthy of the same punishment. For this reason the noble Gentiles, as much as the criminal ones, are guilty of ungodli-ness and of the crimes committed by those who are still celebrated among them. Commentary on Romans (1588).[51]

To Hold the Bag Is as Bad as to Fill It. John Trapp: They patronize, applaud, and approve. This is set last, as worst of all. It compre-hends all kinds of consent. To hold the bag is as bad as to fill it. The law of God requires not only our observation but our preservation, to cause others to keep it, as well as ourselves. And to rebuke, at least by the expression of our counte-nance (as God does in Psalm 80:16), those that violate it. There is little difference . . . whether you commit sin or consent to it. Commentary on Romans (1656).[52]

---

[50]Hesshus, *Commentarius in Omnes*, 23.

[51]Brenz, *In Epistolam*, 511; citing 2 Cor 11:29.
[52]Trapp, *A Commentary or Exposition upon the Epistle of St. Paul*, 621*; citing Ps 80:16.

Those Who Tolerate Wrong Even Though They Know Better. Rudolf Gwalther: Let us, therefore, see what it is that Paul most strenuously accuses the Gentiles of: namely, that though they possessed the law of nature inscribed in their hearts, not only did they sin against it, but they also gave their support to wicked deeds and in this way became authors of the sins of many others. How commonplace is this—oh, what agony!—in this, our own age? For, if we should begin with faith and religion, there are many who acknowledge that there is one God who alone governs all things, who alone can help in every danger, and, therefore, ought alone to be invoked in prayer. They further acknowledge that there is only one Mediator between God and us: Jesus Christ, who having become a sacrificial victim on our behalf, expiated our sins and led us with him back into grace. So how is it that we see so many who, though they know these things, nevertheless turn to creatures, invoke the saints, trust in the merits of their own works, heap up superstitious worship by which the merit of Christ is for the most part emptied of meaning? Not content with this alone, they offer their full support to the inventors of superstitions: if some should have a more correct opinion, they drive them away from the confession of the truth by force of arms. This is a sin of the most savage character, all the more grave because it brings with it both insult to God and the destruction of many souls, and because it is generally committed by those who ought to be guarding among themselves and spreading true doctrine and the worship of the true God. Similar things can be said of others whose manners and custom of life people are watching. . . . They know that all these things are unrighteous and iniquitous, but when they ought to be correcting them in themselves, they instead persuade many others to do the same things, and even take pleasure in the iniquity of others. They are examples of a perverse mind, who unless they are corrected in the course of time will at length become incurable. Therefore, we must be zealous to amend ourselves in these matters, and because it has never been granted to anybody to achieve perfection as long as we live in this flesh, let us with an unwavering faith lay hold of the righteousness of God that through the gospel he offers us in his Son, Jesus Christ, to whom is due blessing, honor, glory, and power forever and ever, Amen. Sermons on Romans (1590).[53]

---

[53]Gwalther, *In d. Pauli Apostoli*, 19-20.

2:1-11 UNRIGHTEOUS AND RIGHTEOUS JUDGMENT

Therefore you have no excuse, O man, every one of you who judges. For in passing judgment on another you condemn yourself, because you, the judge, practice the very same things. ²We know that the judgment of God rightly falls on those who practice such things. ³Do you suppose, O man—you who judge those who practice such things and yet do them yourself—that you will escape the judgment of God? ⁴Or do you presume on the riches of his kindness and forbearance and patience, not knowing that God's kindness is meant to lead you to repentance? ⁵But because of your hard and impenitent heart you are storing up wrath for yourself on the day of wrath when God's righteous judgment will be revealed.

⁶He will render to each one according to his works: ⁷to those who by patience in well-doing seek for glory and honor and immortality, he will give eternal life; ⁸but for those who are self-seeking^a and do not obey the truth, but obey unrighteousness, there will be wrath and fury. ⁹There will be tribulation and distress for every human being who does evil, the Jew first and also the Greek, ¹⁰but glory and honor and peace for everyone who does good, the Jew first and also the Greek. ¹¹For God shows no partiality.

a Or *contentious*

OVERVIEW: The commentators echo Paul by warning that those who think that they are innocent or that they can merit salvation need to take care. God does not judge like the world judges, on the basis only of outward appearances. For God judges according to truth, which means that he looks at the heart. Thus he does not judge simply external actions but also the motivations, desires, and thoughts. And none of us is pure. Many people judge others while ignoring their own sin, but Paul exhorts us to pay attention to our own culpability. Moreover, one must not interpret God's long-suffering as approval; if God is slow in punishing, it is not that he does not see our sin, but rather that he is patient and does not desire any to perish. The delay in punishment is an invitation to repentance. But those who reject that invitation are storing up wrath for themselves.

Responding to medieval theology, the reformers argue for different approaches to the phrase "[God] will render to each one according to his works" (Rom 2:6). Medieval interpreters had purported that Romans 2:10 was evidence supporting the role of good works in salvation. The verse must be interpreted in light of the gospel, not the law; for our works do not earn us salvation. The reformers argue that the good works referred to here arise from grace, and so are divinely given gifts. God will repay us not *because* of our works, but *according* to works, for the works that are done in belief are the fruit of faith and thus considered godly works, whereas the works done in a state of unbelief are regarded as ungodly works. God will reward us in accordance with our godly works, not on the basis of their merit but rather on the basis of his promise of grace, and we should not seek to earn merit by them.

At the same time, there are numerous incentives for Christians to do good works even though they are not what earn salvation. The more we receive from God, the more that is expected from us. In addition, we should not be surprised if when we seek to do good works it is attacked, for what is of God will be crucified, since we follow a crucified Christ. For those who refuse God's good invitation and continue in unrighteousness, there will be no hope in their tribulations, for they have refused to place their hope in God. Unless they repent and produce fruits worthy of repentance, they will perish eternally. The good news is that, unlike corrupt judges, God does not show partiality on the basis of wealth or social status or ethnicity (Jew or Gentile). The commentators emphasize that no matter what our standing is in the world, if we call on the name of Christ and believe in him, we will be saved.

2:1 Those Who Judge Others When Guilty Themselves

UNIVERSAL SIN. ROBERT ROLLOCK: In the above chapter, the universality of sin was demonstrated. In this chapter, the universality of humans sinning is demonstrated. For it is axiomatic of all humans that they are impious and unjust. Moreover, it is understood that there are two sections, the first more general, pertaining to all, whether Jews or Gentiles (to verse 17), and then, more specifically, considering the Jews by name (to the end of the chapter). COMMENTARY ON ROMANS.[1]

THOSE WHO THINK THEY ARE INNOCENT. JOHANNES BRENZ: That which Paul began to say at the end of the previous chapter he now fully works out at the start of the present chapter. For the more noble among the Gentiles, since they are endowed with a token of virtue and lead a life that is blameless in the eyes of the world, cannot patiently endure being reduced to the level of criminal men or women, and because they cannot be accused of any kind of crime before a human tribunal, they therefore judge themselves to be innocent even before the tribunal of God. And like the Pharisee who, according to Luke, disdained the tax collector before him and remained a great distance away from him on account of having judged him as lacking righteousness, the more noble Gentiles likewise have no thought whatever that they belong in the list of sinful men and women. But Paul teaches that they have no excuse and cannot stand before the judgment of God any more than those guilty of crimes can.

Why so? Because even if they may not sin in outward deed, they nevertheless sin by their consent, as was explained a little earlier. Furthermore, this consent is composed not only of the heart's conscious approval, but also of ungodliness hidden in the recesses of the heart. For "from the heart," Christ said, "go forth evil thoughts, murder, adultery," and so on. There is, therefore, within the heart an insubordination toward God, out of which flow all other sins. But where there is insubordination toward God, how will you promise yourself impunity in the day of God's judgment? For the judgment of God is not according to outward appearance but according to truth. "I do not judge (the Lord said to Samuel) according to what man can see. Men and women see those things which are visible; but the Lord looks into the heart." For which reason, since the noble Gentile has a heart no less insubordinate to God and full of ungodliness than a criminal person's, there is no injustice whatever when they are convicted before God of the same sins. This is an accurate dictum: the judgment of God is according to truth against those who act in these ways; even human reason itself acknowledges that it is fitting that things should be judged in this way. Give me an apple that is a shiny red on the outside but rotten on the inside—would you pronounce it to be good? Give me a nut that is intact on the outside but consumed by worms on the inside— would you say that it is good? Give me a man who speaks flattering words but who has hatred in his heart—would you affirm that he is a friend and of goodwill toward you? But, you ask, if God judges according to the truth concerning men and women, who then can be saved? Who can say, "My heart is pure"? I answer, "No one can." "Who then will be preserved in the day of God's judgment?" I answer, "No one will." If then the sentence required by the law of God is pronounced against us, to whom should we turn? Away from judgment and toward mercy! Away from the law and toward the gospel! Away from Moses and toward Christ! For if you look only to the severity of the law or of the divine judgment, all men and women are liable for

[1]Rollock, *In Epistolam S. Pauli*, 22.

damnation. "No one living is justified," he said, "in the sight of God." If, however, you should become converted to Christ the Son of God and believe that your sins have been expiated by his death and that the wrath of God has been placated toward you, the Judge's sentence concerning you will be pronounced not according to the severity of the law but according to the promise of the gospel. COMMENTARY ON ROMANS (1588).[2]

TURN FROM JUDGMENT TO MERCY. WOLFGANG MUSCULUS: This line of argumentation by Paul, in which he proves that both Jews and Gentiles are guilty of sin and inexcusable, has the form of a syllogism of this type:

(P1) Whoever condemns himself is inexcusable.

(P2) But you who judge another condemn yourself.

Ergo: You who judge another are inexcusable.

The minor premise (P2) needs a proof of its own. He therefore adds: "for you who judge are also doing the same thing." But this is conceded by their own consciences, the testimony of which is insuperable, nor is there any need for further witnesses. The major premise (P1) needs no further proof, for nobody denies that those who condemn themselves by their own judgment cannot be excused in any way. COMMENTARY ON ROMANS (1555).[3]

HYPOCRISY IN JUDGMENT. THE ENGLISH ANNOTATIONS: Here the apostle taxes those among the Gentiles who were lawgivers and judges, or who led a more strict or austere life than the rest, as some of the philosophers did, whereby they seemed to judge and condemn the practice of others, while they were inwardly full of hatred, envy, arrogance, and so on, and committed the same sins in secret, when they thought they could hide them from the eye of man. All these men's seeming wisdom and justice serves but to condemn them, and therefore though they thought them-

selves exempted from the ordinary sort of people, yet they are in the same, or a worse condition with them. And if they will be saved, they must have recourse to the only righteousness of the gospel, seeing that their own is nothing but a mask or false show. ANNOTATIONS ON ROMANS 2:1.[4]

2:2 God's Judgment Is Just

GOD KNOWS OUR HEARTS. HULDRYCH ZWINGLI: "For we know that the judgment of God." Someone was saying, "*I do not act in the way that that Gentile or that Jew does!*" The apostle answers with an *anthypophora*,[†] saying: "A person can easily excuse himself in the sight of men and women, advertising himself as a just and innocent person." For the self judges by external things and can easily be deceived. But nobody deceives God; nobody can conceal oneself from him. Because he looks on the heart and examines the inner parts, therefore his judgment is accurate. This is what we read in Luke 16: "You are those who justify yourself before men and women, but God knows your heart." Nearly all of us act in this way by nature—but that we might be inwardly pure is something we must zealously strive for. Let us, therefore, recover our senses that we might be approved in the eyes of God. NOTES ON ROMANS (1539).[5]

THE CONTRAST OF THE WORLD'S AND GOD'S JUDGMENTS. ERASMUS SARCERIUS: "For we know" from the Word that only God does not judge according to external things, but according to the heart. It is the opinion of the philosophers and of the world that God does not judge the affections. But it is the opinion of the Word that God judges the affections even of the ungodly.

"That the judgment of God" is that judgment that God reserves exclusively for himself, which goes beyond the powers of human reason and of men and women whose judgment is not the

---

[2]Brenz, *In Epistolam*, 511-12.
[3]Musculus, *In Epistolam Apostoli Pauli*, 41; citing 1 Sam 16:7; Ps 143:2.
[4]Downame, ed., *Annotations*, AAA2r*.
[5]Zwingli, *In Evangelicam Historiam*, 410; citing Lk 16:15. [†]An *anthypophora* is a rhetorical device in which one raises a question and immediately answers it.

same as his since theirs reaches only as far as external things.

A comparison between the judgment of God and that of men and women can be established here. The judgment of the world is according to external things alone. That is, it is according to openly committed deeds and to the circumstances involved. The true judgment of God is not according to external things alone, but also according to the heart, without any respect of circumstances.

Since it is good to know the reason for needing before God a freely given righteousness, learn here that God judges not only according to external things but also according to the heart, and that, therefore, righteousness before God is obtained not only by external uprightness but also by purity of mind. Further, since it is good to know why our works lack righteousness, learn here that the world judges them according to external factors only, and does not give any consideration to the unclean inner thoughts of the mind. NOTES ON ROMANS (1541).[6]

GOD JUDGES ACCORDING TO TRUTH. CHRISTOPH CORNER: Here is an exposition and filling out of the argument drawn from the fact that God righteously judges with grave reproach both internal and external sins. Major premise: God rightly and justly judges and condemns those who commit such sins. Minor premise: you who are judging others are yourself doing the same kinds of things. Therefore, God rightly condemns you such that you can in no way escape his judgment, condemnation, and divine punishment. But God is praised because he will judge *kat' alētheian* (according to truth), not only according to the outer surface of our actions but also according to men's and women's minds and the fountains of our actions. For he omnipotently and omnisciently searches out the hearts and inner parts of men and women, and therefore prohibits and punishes not only external sins but also internal sins that are of the heart, desires and thoughts. And he requires both cleanness and purity of mind, and innocence

of soul. The judgment of God, which is according to truth, is therefore one thing, and the judgment of men and women, which often errs and only observes and considers external sins, is quite another. Therefore, those who either conceal their sins from God or falsely hope that they will escape his judgment are deceived. COMMENTARY ON ROMANS (1583).[7]

THE JUDGMENT OF GOD. JUAN DE VALDÉS: By "the judgment of God" the holy Scriptures mean God's rigorous examination, whereupon he chastises ungodliness, together with all its practices. And these judgments of God are seen in his works in which he chastised the unbelief of the Jewish nation by the maltreatment which they experienced at the hands of their enemies, and in the instance of David's vainglory, which God chastised by pestilence. Though, indeed, these were parental chastisements intended to induce amendment. They were not meant to confound, unlike the "hardness of heart" by which God chastised Pharaoh; or the "reprobate mind" with which he chastised the heathen. And therefore every godly and Christian person should be alert to see and consider the works in which God shows and manifests his judgments that are intended to correct, as well as those which are intended to confound, although the ones in the latter category never befall the godly and the truly Christian. COMMENTARY ON ROMANS (1556).[8]

2:3-4 Presuming on the Patience of God

THOSE WHO JUDGE OTHERS FOR SINS THEY ALSO COMMIT. PETER MARTYR VERMIGLI: As he said, we condemn ourselves by the very thing we judge others for. By the same punishment we sentence others to, we harm ourselves. And since we cannot escape our own judgment, how will we escape the judgment of God, which is according to truth? For it will not then happen as we see it

---

[6]Sarcerius, *In Apostolam ad Romanos*, F5r.

[7]Corner, *In Epistolam ad Romanos*, 27v.
[8]Valdés, *Commentary upon St. Paul's Epistle*, 20-21*.

happening in this age that for the same kind of crime one person is condemned while another escapes. We will be judged exactly according to our deeds. In the present, men and women spare themselves and are severe toward others. But this will never happen with the judgment of God. It therefore follows that we should show the same severity toward ourselves that we apply to others who are to be judged. It is evident from this how poorly the adversaries of religion behave; how they everywhere cry out against the marriage of priests, which seems to them something impure, but meanwhile they pass lightly over themselves even though they are completely covered with every kind of lust. They cry that vows are not being fulfilled, but they don't give the least thought to what they themselves vowed to God in their baptism. They complain that fasts, which men have commanded, are being laid aside, and yet they do absolutely nothing about their own luxuries and carnal delights. They lament that the sacraments are being neglected unworthily by us, while they have so wretchedly sold, mutilated, and deformed the sacraments with their lies about transubstantiation.

The gist of Paul's teaching is that when we blame others we should examine ourselves also, since it is most certain that the judgment of God will be according to truth. Therefore, we must make every effort within our power so that our life and manners are approved by such a judgment. COMMENTARY ON ROMANS (1560).[9]

DON'T MISTAKE GOD'S LONG-SUFFERING FOR APPROVAL OF YOUR SIN. HEINRICH BULLINGER: It is as if they were saying, "If he does not leave evil unpunished, but we are evil men and women, why are you being so dishonest with us? Certainly such a long time passing without our being punished is a powerful argument that we are not the kind of people you say we are, Paul." This is like a benign creditor whose debtor denies that he owes him anything since he has not demanded the payment of the debt for a very long time. He will answer: "Is

this how you thank me for my goodness and delay, by now denying me what is owed because I, having compassion on you, have for so long put off demanding it back?" Indeed, Paul vehemently sets his oration ablaze with an interrogation, as if he were saying, "With what impudence, may I ask, do you dare to invoke the long-suffering of the most blessed God as a defense of your ungodly behavior? As if he favors your misdeeds because until now he has employed such abundant goodness toward you! He is not delaying your punishment because he is pleased with your manner of life, but rather because by his long-suffering he wishes to call you to your senses. For in the same way that God does not desire iniquity, he also "does not desire the death of a sinner, but rather that he should be converted and live." COMMENTARY ON ROMANS (1582).[10]

AN INVERSION OF CAUSES. NIELS HEMMINGSEN: There is here an inversion of causes, as if he had said: "You think, O hypocrites, that your innocence is the cause for which God will not exact his judgment against you—but you are wrong. For the goodness of God that invites you to repentance delays your judgment only so that you might have time for repentance. It is principally to be observed from this passage that the delaying of punishment is an invitation to repentance that has for its true cause the goodness of God toward men and women." COMMENTARY ON ROMANS (1562).[11]

DON'T PRESUME ON GOD'S PATIENCE. MARTIN BUCER: As we said before, this creates a dilemma. You know that God will punish sins, but despite this, as long as God is putting off exacting punishment from you on account of his leniency, you continue in every respect to live sinfully. Therefore, either you must think that you will escape God's judgment, or you despise the goodness of God. The former is impossible, while the latter renders you liable to even more serious

---

[9]Vermigli, *In Epistolam S. Pauli*, 109.

[10]Bullinger, *Commentarii in Omnes Epistolas*, 15; citing Ezek 18:23. [11]Hemmingsen, *Commentarius in Epistolam*, 66-67.

punishments. They were able to reason along these lines: "Since God treats us so indulgently and blesses us so abundantly, why should we have such a great fear of his judging us? Why should we not trust that we will escape it? For the things that he confers on us are not evidence of a wrathful Being or of One about to exact punishment." The apostle therefore answers, "On account of this very thing—that while God shows you so much leniency and directs you to himself by such profuse goodness, you, hardened in your ungodliness, will not allow yourselves to be moved by these things to repentance for your perversities— there hangs over you a more severe judgment, and the wrath of God will make up for this slowness of punishment with an intolerable severity. Therefore, while you continue to despise the goodness and leniency of God that is, as it were, urging you to come to your senses out of your sins, you are doing nothing else than depositing something more everyday to the cumulative weight of your punishment, which will be unleashed on you all at once when the determined time for this judgment arrives." Therefore we have this proposition: the more amply you enjoy the benefits of God while living in an ungodly way, and the less you feel sorry for evil, the more severe will be the punishments for your ungodliness that will be meted out to you. But, in case you may be entertaining doubts, let it be far from any of you to conclude that when that time comes you will escape the judgment of God. COMMENTARY ON ROMANS (1562).[12]

GOD LEADS US BY THE HAND TO MERCY. JOHN CALVIN: "Not knowing that the goodness." The Lord in his leniency toward us declares that he is the one to whom we ought to turn, if we wish to fare well. He also strengthens our confidence that we will receive mercy. But if we do not use the good things that God gives to this end, we abuse them. Although not everything is always to be received in the same way. For when the Lord treats his servants with indulgence and attends them with earthly blessings, he demonstrates his benevolence by tokens of this kind, and at the same time disposes us to seek in him our highest of all goods. And when his indulgence falls on transgressors of the law, he is wanting to mitigate their stubborn disobedience by means of his goodness. And yet he does not thereby testify that he is at peace with them, but rather by this he calls them to repentance. Now if someone were to object that the Lord is singing to the deaf as long as he does not move the inner heart, it must be answered that nothing here can be blamed except for our own depravity. As for the rest, I prefer the verb "leads" rather than "invites," for the former word means more. Nor, on the other hand, do I understand this in the sense of "compel," but rather to "lead by the hand." COMMENTARY ON ROMANS (1540, 1667).[13]

2:5 Impenitent Hearts Store Up Wrath

WHY IMPENITENCE STORES WRATH. FRIEDRICH BALDUIN: Q: How is it that humans by impenitence store up wrath for themselves, when neither repentance nor conversion is within our power, but is the work of God, according to Jeremiah 31: "Turn me, Lord, and I will turn"?

A: I answer: Conversion—insofar as it denotes the restitution of the original integrity of humankind, by which he is made a child of grace out of a child of wrath—wholly and thoroughly is the work of God alone. Humans have a purely passive role, and they can neither apply nor dispose themselves to the grace of God, nor do anything else at all toward their own conversions. And this is what that saying of Christ means in John 6, "No one comes to me unless the Father draws him." But God does not forcibly drag anybody, either by a certain hidden movement or inspiration. Rather, he offers the Word to the unconverted person. That person is then rationally able—and is naturally accustomed—to resist the Word, and to impede their conversion for a time, just as the

---

[12]Bucer, *Metaphrasis et Enarratio*, 92 (this is a reprint of the 1536 edition).

[13]Calvin, *Commentarii in Omnes Epistolas*, 11.

Pharisees were doing when they were spurning the council of God against themselves. Therefore, when a person is able to have and hear the Word—when God, with a loud voice is standing at the door and knocking and they not only don't let him in but cast him out with great indignation—then the wrath of God is more and more heaped up. For which reason also Christ said that the coming punishment for Capernaum and Chorazin and Bethsaida would be much heavier in the last day than for other cities in which there was not as much abundance of the Word or as much of the splendor of Christ's miracles. COMMENTARY ON ROMANS (1620).[14]

THE DAY OF THE REVELATION OF GOD'S RIGHTEOUS JUDGMENT. WOLFGANG MUSCULUS: He adds, "and of the revelation of the righteous judgment of God." He notably does not simply say, "and of the righteous judgment of God," but "of the revelation of the righteous judgment of God," thereby attributing to that day that revelation by which what each person has merited will be disclosed. Meanwhile, when the ungodly are doing well and the godly are afflicted, when the hypocrites flourish and the godly are weighed down, then the righteous judgment of God that will be revealed in the end—in which he will repay to each one according to his works, something we will see in the future judgment—is hidden in some degree for now. Therefore, he rightly calls that day the day of the revelation of the righteous judgment of God. Until then, each person will sleep on their own account and on that day rise again on their own account to stand before the tribunal to receive their final and perpetual sentence. COMMENTARY ON ROMANS (1555).[15]

TRUE CONVERSION. FRIEDRICH BALDUIN: True conversion is understood as repentance, when the old self is being renewed day by day, where the converted person is able to contend against the flesh and cooperate with the Holy Spirit to do good and flee evil, by truly instigating, impelling, and igniting. For truly converted people cooperate, not by their own power, but by the gift of God who illuminates them. On the other hand, when persons do not do good, do not allow the operation and impulse of the Holy Spirit, neglect one admonition after another, and indulge the flesh and its lusts, they only offend more gravely against the goodness of God and hasten a harsher judgment against themselves. By their stubbornness and crimes of eager sin, they place obstacles to the Holy Spirit's inward work and put to flight the precious guest dwelling within. COMMENTARY ON ROMANS (1620).[16]

2:6 Rewarded According to Works

THE PHRASE NEEDS TO BE INTERPRETED WITH THE GOSPEL. PHILIPP MELANCHTHON: The entire divine Scripture sets forth the law in some places, in others the gospel, so some of its statements are statements of the law, and some of its statements are statements of the gospel. Nevertheless, the gospel is the light and interpretation of the law. This is a phrase of the law: "He will reward everyone according to his works." The meaning is: "He will give rewards to the righteous, and the unjust he will punish." Neither is there any doubt that the explanation of who the righteous are and what works please God must be added from the gospel. For the pronouncements of the law without the gospel produce despair. Never can a conscience in the midst of true terrors declare that it has works worthy of the forgiveness of sins or eternal life. Thus when Christ says: "if you wish to enter into life, keep the commandments," it is necessary to mitigate what is said by adding the interpretation from the gospel. For no one satisfies the law. COMMENTARY ON ROMANS (1540).[17]

---

[14]Balduin, *Catechesis Apostolica*, 125-26; citing Jer 31:18; Jn 6:44; Lk 7:30; Mt.11:21.
[15]Musculus, *In Epistolam Apostoli Pauli*, 44.

[16]Balduin, *Catechesis Apostolica*,126.
[17]Melanchthon, *Commentary on Romans*, 88*; citing Mt. 19:17.

ACCORDING TO WORKS. FRIEDRICH BALDUIN: God does indeed repay "according to works," not "on account of works." This does not refer to the meritorious cause, but rather to the attributes, character, and testimony of those who are to come before God's judgment. For since the action of that future judgment is visible, it is appropriate that that which ought to bear witness to the person being justified should pass before all eyes; of which kind are the works of men and women that bear witness either of their faith or their faithlessness, for which cause also they are brought forth by the Savior as witnesses of either those who are to be saved, or those who are to be condemned. COMMENTARY ON ROMANS (1620).[18]

RENDERING TO THE UNGODLY VERSUS THE GODLY. JUAN DE VALDÉS: On this day, says he, "God will render to every man according to his works," meaning that he will chastise the ungodliness of the wicked and their ungodly works, and that he will crown the godliness of the saints and their godly works. In the ungodly he will find nothing to crown, however much they may have labored to do the thing that is right. For as Christ says, the evil tree brings forth corrupt fruit; and thus they will be treated according to their ungodliness. While in the godly, he will on that day find nothing to condemn or to chastise, however heedless they may have been in the doing of that which is right, for he will contemplate them, not by that which they are in themselves, but by that which they are in Christ, they having accepted the gospel, and having made the righteousness of Christ their own, which acceptance will be crowned in them, together with the works that will have proceeded from this good root. For, as Christ says, the good tree brings forth good fruit. COMMENTARY ON ROMANS (1556).[19]

FAITH PERFORMS GOOD WORKS. HULDRYCH ZWINGLI: "He will repay to each one according to

his works." Works are performed either in faith or in unbelief. For works are either good or evil with respect to one's fidelity or infidelity. "Whatever does not come from faith is sin." "Every tree that does not bear fruit." Therefore, wages will be repaid for works, not simply and on account of the works themselves, but with respect to faith and unbelief. God grants to humans his grace and Spirit, and faith (which itself is the gift of God) performs good works. Unbelief produces evil fruits. God will not repay us for works that come from our own powers, for as far as they are from us they are evil. In this letter, Paul is addressing those of the Gentiles and Jews who were Christians and who were either trusting in their works or attributing righteousness to them. NOTES ON ROMANS (1539).[20]

2:7-8 Eternal Life or Condemnation?

IS IT WRONG TO WORK TOWARD ETERNAL REWARDS? FRIEDRICH BALDUIN: Q: Honor and glory and eternal life are promised to those persevering in good works. Is it, therefore, permissible to do good with an eye to eternal rewards?

A: I answer: The Council of Trent 16[†] indiscriminately condemns those who answer this question in the negative. For so run the words of the canon: "If anyone should say that justified persons sin when they do good with an eye to eternal rewards, let them be anathema!" And thus also write our own Bellarmine and Pererius. But it is expedient that we distinguish between a meritorious reward and a free promise. For it is this that we constantly deny from Scripture, that humans ought to do good in order that they should be owed eternal life for their works, as merit that is condign or truly meritorious in and of itself as the [Catholics] contend. For this is contrary in many ways to Scripture, which testifies that we are God's debtors even in our most perfect works. Since where there is debt, merit can have no place, much less is God obliged to us out of debt to repay

---

[18]Balduin, *Catechesis Apostolica*, 118-119; citing Mt 25:14-26.
[19]Valdés, *Commentary upon St. Paul's Epistle*, 23*.

[20]Zwingli, *In Evangelicam Historiam*, 410; citing Rom 14:23; Mt 7:12.

us with rewards for our good works. These are the sayings of Scripture: "When you will have done all things, say 'we are useless servants, for we have done what we were obliged to do,'" and "You are not your own, for you were bought with a price," and "We are debtors, but not to living according to the flesh." It also teaches that our works, on account of the corruption of our nature—even the highest, most carefully rendered to the law—are greatly imperfect. Therefore, if they are adorned with rewards, it is surely not out of a debt of justice but rather out of merciful divine grace. For it says of the law, that "whoever does not continue in all things which are written in it, let him be accursed." But the gospel promises blessing even upon imperfect works, as long as they have their origin in faith. It expressly denies any worthiness of eternal glory to our works and sufferings. It teaches that those works are not ours, but are God's who is working through us. Therefore, God does not adorn our merits with rewards, but he rewards his own gifts. Therefore, we say that it is sin in this situation, for the reasons already indicated, if someone were to do good with an eye on rewards due to us as condign merit, that is, if that person should desire to merit something by their works, and in some way legally demand a reward from God as if it were meritoriously owed. For grace and merit are opposites. However, we do not deny that people should be moved to doing good by the hope of rewards promised by grace. It is to this that all those passages pertain that in a long catalog Bellarmine and Pererius heap praise on the cited verses. For we know that the promises of this and the future life require piety, but the promises depend on the grace of God alone, not on any of our merits. Whenever this reward is freely promised, however, it is not given to the lazy but to those who labor. It rightly happens that the pursuit of good works is excited within us either by an eye toward them or a memory of them. From this it is understood that even the beginnings of our obedience are pleasing to God, so that he is pleased to adorn them in this life with spiritual and corporal goods, and in the other life with eternal glory on the basis of sheer grace by Christ. COMMENTARY ON ROMANS (1620).[21]

WORRY IF YOUR GOOD WORKS ARE NOT ATTACKED. MARTIN LUTHER: "By patience in well-doing." So necessary is patience that no work can be good when patience is lacking, for the world is so perverted and the devil so wicked that he cannot pass a good work by without challenging it, but it is through this challenge that God in his wonderful good judgment tests the good work that pleases him. Let us therefore keep the following canonical and practical rule: As long as we are doing good and do not experience as a result of it opposition, hatred, trouble, or harm, so long we have reason to worry that our work has not pleased God as yet, for trial and patience have not been applied as yet, and God has not yet approved it, because he has not yet tested it. For he does not approve what he has not tested before. But if our work is immediately attacked, then let us be of good cheer and firmly trust that it is well-pleasing to God, that is, believe that it is of God himself, for what is of God must be crucified in the world. So long as it does not lead to the cross (that is, to shameful suffering), it is not recognized as a work that comes from God, inasmuch as the only-begotten Son was not protected against this experience but rather was appointed the example of it. "Blessed are those who are persecuted for righteousness' sake." "Rejoice and be glad, for your reward is great in heaven." LECTURES ON ROMANS (1516).[22]

THOSE WHO ARE CONTENTIOUS AGAINST THE TRUTH. MARTIN BUCER: "But to those who are 'of the contention.'" That is, those who are given to contention. Paul customarily speaks in this manner: to be "of the law," "of the circumcision," "of faith" to refer to that which rests in the law, is given

---

[21]Balduin, *Catechesis Apostolica*, 130-31; citing Lk 17:10; 1 Cor 6:19-20; Rom 8:12; Deut 27:26; 1 Tim 4; Rev 3:3; Rom 8:4; 2 Cor 3:1-18. †Citing Council of Trent, session 6, canon 31, chapter 16; Bellarmine, *On Justification* 5.8; Pererius, *Epistle to the Romans*, chap. 2, disputation 3, number 32, p. 268.
[22]LW 25:177*; citing Mt 5:10, 12.

to the circumcision and that depends on faith. So by "those of the contention" he understands those who are always straining themselves in contentions. These are the ones who do not yield to the truth; who cannot endure being persuaded by things that are true; that yield and hand themselves over instead to lies—not to any lie whatever—but to those by which they can persuade themselves to be left alone in their iniquity. Although reason was demanding the opposite, they obeyed a lie. So that he might show this evil to be more atrocious he did not say "who obey a lie," but rather "who obey iniquity," showing what a destructive lie it was that they had given themselves to after having repudiated saving truth. Quite appropriately, then, he said, "to those who are of the contention." For to "be of the contention" is properly understood to have a negative meaning, indicating someone contradicting the truth without good reason. But this is what anyone who does not consent to the truth in holy doctrine does. For that truth is so evident, its light is so great, that it forces itself to be seen even by those who are unwilling, so that when they contradict it, they always do so with their conscience objecting, and for reasons which not even they are convinced of. COMMENTARY ON ROMANS (1562).[23]

THE CONTENTIOUS WILL BE CONDEMNED. HEINRICH BULLINGER: Those who will be deemed to have been contentious will be condemned. The contentious are those who are puffed up by pride. They are rude with an obstinacy arising from a depraved soul that will not move the width of a straw from their opinions. They always have something at hand to say, object to, twist out of context, and fight against with insults. This is what Paul was also referring to when he said, "who do not obey the truth, but obey unrighteousness." It is people like this, I say, that are the contentious. They do not acknowledge their own sins, and therefore they do not confess their sins before

God—for which reason "their sin remains." Therefore, the apostle wished to put an end to these contentions in which the Gentiles were forever seeking to excuse themselves. It is as if he were saying, "What need is there of words? You are all sinners. Why are you contending? There is already more than enough sin—it will not serve you to add a contentious obstinacy to a great heap of sins that is already more than enough." COMMENTARY ON ROMANS (1582).[24]

OBEYING UNRIGHTEOUSNESS. ALEXANDER ALESIUS: This threatens with eternal punishment the ungodly who contend that the gospel teaching concerning the righteousness of humanity before God by faith is false. Paul names these with a Hebrew idiom, "those who are of the contention," that is, the contentious—and he adds as reasons for their just condemnation that they do not obey the truth. (This truth is also called "the gospel," for Christ said, "Your word is truth.") They do not repent, and they hand themselves over to shameful behavior. He calls this "obeying unrighteousness" as he will also later in chapter 6: "in the way you exhibited your members that they might serve unrighteousness." DISPUTATION ON ROMANS (1553).[25]

2:9-10 Anguish for the Ungodly, Rewards for Those Who Do Good

THE UNGODLY PERSON'S ANGUISH IN TRIBULATION. MARTIN LUTHER: "Tribulation and distress." This is to be the explanation of the expression "wrath and indignation." I take these words as belonging together and meaning the same thing. This does not refer to any kind of tribulation but to a tribulation that is connected with anguish, that is, one from which there is no way out nor hope of a way out, where comfort is lacking in tribulation. To be sure, the faithful are also suffering tribulation, but they are consoled in it. . . . Hope and trust in God have given us this comfort.

---

[23]Bucer, *Metaphrasis et Enarratio*, 96 (this is a reprint of the 1536 edition).

[24]Bullinger, *Commentarii in Omnes Epistolas*, 16; citing Jn 9:41.
[25]Alesius, *Omnes Disputationes*, G5iv v; citing Jn 17:20; Rom 6:19.

But the ungodly are tortured by anguish in tribulation through despair. They do not have hope and reliance on anything, because they do not place their hope in God that they might be freed some day. Just as joy is a certain freedom of the heart, even in tribulation, so distress represents a certain narrowing and constriction in tribulation. LECTURES ON ROMANS (1516).[26]

ALL WILL BE JUDGED. NIELS HEMMINGSEN: Paul magnifies by repetition the idea of distributive justice, as if he were saying, "I declare that the things I'm saying about the repaying of good and evil works apply to all people, in such a way that I want to affirm that absolutely nobody is given an exception to being subjected to this most righteous judgment of God." These things apply so universally that we should gravely ponder that judicial fairness that the perfectly just Judge will observe in the future judgment, from which nobody can escape. Second, unless we prefer to eternally perish with the enemies of Christ, we should repent of sins and produce fruits worthy of repentance, according to which the just Judge will pass sentence. Here let us once again call to mind that principle that eternal life is the gift of God through Jesus Christ our Lord. Further, let this rule be held fast: that God gives rewards not on account of the worthiness of the works by way of a debt, but on account of his fatherly promise by way of grace, for there cannot be any other proportionality between good works and eternal life. This is why those who twist this saying of Paul against the doctrine of a free justification and salvation are in error. Those also are in error who boast that they have faith without true revivification, which is a change from one's prior way of life and a resolution to live a new life by way of mortification and vivification. COMMENTARY ON ROMANS.[27]

RESTORATION TO THE IMAGE OF GOD. MARTIN BUCER: It is here reasonably obvious that in these words the reward for righteousness being expressed is that highest dignity, excellence, and beauty, which will shine on the saints perfected by Christ when it then will appear in them fully, which Psalm 8 sings about, "You have surrounded him with glory and honor"; that is, "You have heaped on him glory and honor from all sides; you have made him lord over all the works of your hands; you have placed all things under his feet." For even if the letter to the Hebrews applies this passage particularly to the Lord Jesus, it nevertheless is fittingly applied at the same time to all who are restored by Christ. Further, this dignity and excellency of humans principally rests on the fact that the image of God is restored by them in a whole and complete righteousness, so much so that they are already regarded as holy and righteous by God himself and by his angels. They are, in other words, the blessed, whom God declares to be inherently precious and choice in his sight. And all understand the noun "peace" to mean "happiness." COMMENTARY ON ROMANS (1562).[28]

FINDING PEACE. KATHARINA SCHÜTZ ZELL: So it was for me also and for many afflicted hearts who were then in great distress along with me: many honorable old women and virgins who sought out my company and were glad to be my companions. We were in such anxiety and worry about the grace of God, but we could never find any peace in all our many works, practices, and sacraments of that [Roman] church. Then God had mercy on us and many people. He awakened and sent out by tongue and writings the dear and now blessed Dr. Martin Luther, who described the Lord Jesus Christ for me and others in such a lovely way that I thought I had been drawn up out of the depths of the earth, yes, out of grim bitter hell, into the sweet lovely kingdom of heaven. A LETTER TO THE WHOLE CITIZENSHIP.[29]

---

[26]LW 25:179*; citing Ps 4:2; 2 Cor 1:4.
[27]Hemmingsen, *Commentarius in Epistolam* (1562), 71.
[28]Bucer, *Metaphrasis et Enarratio*, 98 (this is a reprint of the 1536 edition); citing Ps 8:5-6.
[29]Zell, *Church Mother*, 226*.

Our Good Works Come from Grace.

Heinrich Bullinger: In these antitheses he sets contrary terms in opposition: "but glory and honor," and so on, where the words "glory and honor" are used for everything that is glorious, delightful, heavenly, and eternal. There is nothing better, sweeter, or more noble than tranquility of conscience or of soul. And this is the reward of righteousness. This passage would demand that I now discuss more extensively the topic of rewards and the merit for works, if St. Augustine had not already so fully discharged this task among the fathers, and many eminent men with as much learning as piety have taken up the same thing. Therefore I will say but a few words. Just as nobody, unless they are the most impious of persons, would go so far as to deny that evil comes from us, and that by that evil we earn damnation from the just judgment of God, so also nobody has denied that the reward is given on account of our virtue. But in to the passage it should be added that these rewards are for virtues that are not of own powers, and are owed only with respect to divine goodness and grace. For every virtue we have comes not from us, but rather is from God. Therefore, since the reward is owed to virtue, it is only with respect to God's grace, not to us. Even when the Lord grants us grace so that we believe, faith is not then passive but is working actively. Therefore, whatever is done is done by the virtue of faith, so that it always returns in a circle back to the source. Commentary on Romans (1582).[30]

Incentives to Do Good. Andreas Hyperius:

The more gifts we receive from God, the more we are obligated to doing good, and the more severely all that we have done (according to God's standard of judgment) will be demanded of us, according to Christ's word in Luke 12, "To whom much is given, much will be required." Second, there is laid up in these words a doctrine, namely, that God reserves for himself a certain care for all things, but especially for his elect whom he always loves and helps above all others—namely, those who are prepared as vessels of mercy for the display of God's glory and power.

"But glory and honor." This is a universal appeal interposed, with great effect, in order to inflame souls to doing good in the most useful ways. The antitheses here should be noticed: peace especially is opposed to affliction and anxiety. For this refers chiefly to peace of conscience. Commentary on Romans (1583).[31]

On Good Works. Juan de Valdés: The wicked

seek glory, honor, immortality, and eternal life, but not by belief in the truth which the gospel preaches. They, by belief in the falsehood which human prudence preaches, will not attain what they seek; but the godly will attain it, who, by the gift of God, believe in the gospel, stopping their ears to the persuasions of human wisdom. The gospel declares that people attain all this by accepting as their own the justice of God executed on Christ. And human wisdom declares that people attain all this by living virtuously, and by making satisfaction with good works for having failed to live virtuously; as though people were able of themselves to satisfy God, without Christ, in relation to their wickedness and wicked works; and as though people were capable of producing good works acceptable to the divine majesty without Christ. Commentary on Romans (1556).[32]

2:11 God Is an Impartial Judge

God Treats All Sinners Equally. David

Pareus: "For there is no respecting of persons": Here we begin the third section of the chapter, which discusses a pretext of the Gentiles, which they could oppose to the judgment of God. Notice the connection. The apostle terrifies the impenitent by the threat of divine wrath from the *dikaiokrisia* (righteous judgment) of God. He demonstrated

---

[30]Bullinger, *Commentarii in Omnes Epistolas*, 16.

[31]Hyperius, *Commentarii D. Andrea Hyperii*, 44; citing Lk 12:48; Rom 9:23.

[32]Valdés, *Commentary upon St. Paul's Epistle*, 24*.

this from the rule of distributive justice, according to which God is about to judge, that is, about to render rewards to the good, oppression and wrath to the wicked, without respect to nation or occupation, whether those working evil are Jews or Greeks. The apostle does not belabor the matter at the beginning about the rewards of the good, for that was acceptable on its face, since all desire that the good have rewards that are worthy of them. Therefore, he omits that in the present. Afterward, the matter of the penalties to be inflicted on those doing evil might seem foreign to equity. For equal judgments must not be attributed to unequal parties, and the Jews and the Gentiles would certainly seem to be unequal when they sin. For the former have the law; the latter do not. Therefore, they do not seem equally liable to damnation. The apostle, anticipating that some will scoff at this—because he said that they were both alike to be punished—confirms it from the office of judge, which is to judge *aneu pathōn kai prosōpolempsias* (without passion and favoritism). Because of this, he says, notwithstanding distinction of the latter and former, God will punish both sinners equally, whether they have the law or not. Because each one sins, they are deserving of death whether they sin without the law or according to the law, otherwise God would be a *prosōpoleptis*, a respecter of persons. But with God there is no *prosōpolempsia* (favoritism). Vice is severely condemned by the law of God and altogether foreign to the office of a just judge. Therefore, although the Jews and Gentiles differ in that the former have and the latter do not have the law, they are nevertheless equals in the cause of punishment, that is, in sin. This is the connection. For there is *prosōpolempsia* (favoritism) in judgment when unequals are actually treated equally by the judge in the cause of a lawsuit. That is, one of two equal defendants is condemned, the other absolved, because of an external circumstance that does not pertain to the lawsuit, presumably because one is rich and the other is not; one gave a bribe, the other did not; one influences by authority or favor, the other does not; or because of external circumstances of this kind a

defendant is absolved contrary to the laws, and an innocent party is condemned, which plague on judgments is condemned by the law of God: "You shall not show partiality to the poor, neither shall you show favoritism to the great in judgment; you shall judge your neighbor in justice." How, therefore, could God be a respecter of persons, who so severely condemned this plague on judgments? Therefore, let no one deceive himself with vain persuasion, as if the sinner is not to be condemned by the judgment of God because he is powerful, rich, strong, educated, and so on. What the apostle discusses here concerning the judgment of God against both the Jews and the Greeks—that it is fixed and established for all—is indeed of interest for human salvation and divine glory. Therefore, no one will absolve themselves of all sin. And no one will accuse God of injustice if all persons who sin are condemned. COMMENTARY ON ROMANS (1608).[33]

THE GOOD NEWS THAT GOD IS NO RESPECTER OF PERSONS. JOHANNES BRENZ: "For there is no respect of persons with God," whether one might be a Jew or a Gentile, whether a prince or a subject, whether a rich person or a pauper. If persons have acted wickedly they will be condemned, but if rightly, they will be spared. Now, to respect persons in judgment means to pass judgment not according to the arguments presented or the evidence of the case, but according to the kind of persons involved. For example, if a charge is laid before a judge against someone who is influential or a rich person or a friend of the judge and who has a poor defense, the judge is said to respect persons when, in his act of passing judgment, he dismisses the accusation on account of the defendant's influential status or friendship with him. Or, if a pauper or an outsider brings a charge before him against a friend of the judge or some influential person, the judge is said to respect persons when he decides the case against the

---

[33]Pareus, *In Divinam ad Romanos*, 191-92; citing Lev 19:15; Deut 19:15, Prov 6:35; 18:5.

pauper—not being even willing to consider his case despite it being a solid one—simply because he is an unimportant person and his opponent is either a friend of the judge or someone distinguished for his wealth. When this sin occurs among judges, it is not simply a sin such as theft or murder, but it is also an injurious crime against the divine majesty. For to judge is the work of God, but God entrusts the execution of this work to lawful judges. For which reason, if a judge should pervert his judgment, he injures not only people, but even the very majesty of God itself. But because God is not a respecter of persons in his judgment, not only are public judges admonished in their duties, but also a right understanding of this is useful for us privately as well. For just as God is not a respecter of persons in his judgment against sin, so also he is not a respecter of persons in his gospel with respect to faith. For which reason, when we are overwhelmed with great misery and calamity, knowing that God does not look at us through the lens of our misery and calamity, trust is then stirred up within us when we contemplate that God is not a respecter of persons but that among all nations whoever should place his faith in his gospel and call on him will obtain salvation. "For all," he said, "who believe in him will not perish but have everlasting life"; and, "All who will call upon the name of the Lord will be saved." Commentary on Romans (1588).[34]

God's Twofold Acceptance. John Calvin: If any object and say, "Then there is no such thing as the gratuitous election of God," it may be answered that there is a twofold acceptation of mortals before God. The first when he chooses and calls us from nothing, through gratuitous goodness, as there is nothing in our nature that can be approved by him. The second when, after having regenerated us, he confers on us his gifts, and shows favor to the image of his Son, which he recognizes in us. Commentary on Romans 2:11.[35]

---

[34]Brenz, *In Epistolam*, 517-18; citing Jn 3:16; Joel 2:32; Acts 2:21; Rom 10:13.
[35]CTS 38:94* (CO 49:36).

2:12-16 THE LAW AND JUDGMENT

¹²*For all who have sinned without the law will also perish without the law, and all who have sinned under the law will be judged by the law. ¹³For it is not the hearers of the law who are righteous before God, but the doers of the law who will be justified. ¹⁴For when Gentiles, who do not have the law, by nature do what the law requires, they are a law to themselves, even though they do not have the law. ¹⁵They show that the work of the law is written on their hearts, while their conscience also bears witness, and their conflicting thoughts accuse or even excuse them ¹⁶on that day when, according to my gospel, God judges the secrets of men by Christ Jesus.*

OVERVIEW: In this section, our Reformation-era commentators reflect on Paul's contention that all people need the gospel. Jews will be judged by the law of Moses, and Gentiles will be judged by the law of nature, but in all cases, they will be condemned, for no one keeps either law perfectly. Only those who actually *do* the law—rather than simply hear it—will be saved, but no one can fully do the law. So, all are in need of God's mercy and grace. More particularly, the reformers seek to harmonize Romans 2:13 with Romans 3:20. They argue against medieval theologians who claimed that Paul's statement that it is "the doers of the law who will be justified" means that it is possible to be saved by works. No one has kept the law perfectly, so no one will be justified according to their works. They develop these reflections by appealing to two kinds of justification: the legally owed, which requires perfect obedience to the law and is therefore impossible; and the freely imputed, which is available through the gospel, through God's grace, through faith alone, and for which the righteous, meritorious deeds on which it depends are not ours but Christ's. This justification comes in phases: the first appoints us to eternal life, the second gives us a glimpse of eternal life in the here and now, and the third will come to fruition in heaven.

2:12 Both Jews and Gentiles Will Be Judged

ALL WILL BE JUDGED. PETER MARTYR VERMIGLI: "And whoever has sinned according to the law will be judged by the law." This teaches the same thing, that God does not respect persons, nor will he show injustice to anyone in his judgment. He treats Jews and Gentiles the same: whenever persons from either group conduct themselves wickedly, they will perish. And, as it pertains to the form of judgment, the Jews who are to be condemned will be judged by the law of Moses that they will have accusing and condemning them; whereas the reprobate Gentiles will be neither accused nor condemned by that law, but rather by the light of nature and by their own thoughts. In this passage, it is proper to understand "by the law" as referring to the Mosaic law. For it is the only perfect law, and it was on account of it that contention had arisen. Otherwise, there has never been a nation, or scarcely any, that has not been governed by some sort of institutions or laws. There are two objections implied here. The first is that it was seen by the Jews to be a wonderful thing that they had been adorned with the benefit of a law that came from God, even if it did nothing to help their case. To those making this objection, Paul answers that this only makes their case more serious, since it is not those who hear the law but those who do it that will be justified before God. The other objection is that it seemed to the Gentiles to be overly harsh that they should perish simply because they lacked the law of God. To which Paul says, "You were not entirely lacking the law." He uses two reasons to prove that they possessed a law: first, that by nature they had done those things that are of the law, and second that they possessed thoughts within themselves that alternately accused and defended themselves. As for the Jews, he treats them more severely since they acted so unreasonably in judging themselves to be justified simply because they had received the law. He is just now beginning to gradually engage them in dispute, which he will do more openly a bit later. COMMENTARY ON ROMANS (1560).[1]

GOD'S IMPARTIALITY PROVED. NIELS HEMMINGSEN: That with God there is no respect of persons he proves from the event of the coming judgment in which God will repay destruction and damnation to all sinners according to their deeds. That is, God will punish all sinners without making distinctions, whether they are Gentiles who do not possess the written law, or whether they are Jews. COMMENTARY ON ROMANS (1562).[2]

2:13 The Hearers Versus Doers of the Law

THE DOERS, NOT THE HEARERS, OF THE LAW WILL BE SAVED. CARDINAL CAJETAN: "For it is not the hearers of the law who are righteous before God." The logic[†] here can be understood in two ways. One is according to the literal words, along the lines of the last mentioned reason, namely, that "whoever has sinned in the law will be judged by the law." This same reasoning is again rehearsed, that it is not enough to hear the law but one must also keep it. According to this logic, the doctrine that follows concerning the righteousness of the Gentiles has slipped in unnoticed. The other way of making sense out of the text appeals to what is said implicitly. For when it is said, "whoever has sinned without the law will perish without the law," it has the same meaning as its inverse, that "whoever has done good works without the law will be justified without the merit of the law." Likewise, when it says "and whoever has sinned in the law will be judged by

the law," its inverse also has the same meaning: "whoever has done good works in the law will be justified by the merits of the law." Each statement implies an understanding of its inverse. Thus, when he immediately afterward adds "it is not the hearers of the law," what is meant is "it is not by reason of the merits of good deeds," which is what Paul is principally aiming at. A few people, however, point to the other way that the text was introduced, for it renders the same sense throughout: that the hearing of the law has no weight before God, but only its doing, since before God what has weight is not the personal prerogatives of those who hear the law, but rather that the law be done. This is, therefore, the reason first for the judgment of those who have sinned in the law, and then for the common judgment of all according to our deeds.

"But the doers of the law will be justified." This would raise a huge question against the teaching of the same apostle if the main substance of the discussion is not held in view, since a little later he himself will expressly condemn those who were saying that men and women are justified by the works of the law, but these words here sound like they are contradicting that. But the question goes away if we examine what is understood by divine judgment being delivered to each one "according to their works." What is understood by this is not absolute merits, but merits of works. It is well known that, speaking of the merits of works, it is most truly said that "the doer of the law is justified by God." It is understood, accordingly, how much it is from the reason of works. Nor does this exclude the merits of faith, which exceed the merits of works. It is not the "founders of the law" (i.e., the Jews) but the ones doing deeds that are of the law who are called "doers of the law," whether or not they have the written law. OF THE EPISTLES OF PAUL (1550).[3]

SIMPLY HEARING DOES NOT SAVE. HULDRYCH ZWINGLI: He is giving a reason for the

---

[1]Vermigli, *In Epistolam S. Pauli*, 127-28.
[2]Hemmingsen, *Commentarius in Epistolam*, 72-73.

[3]Cajetan, *Epistolae Pauli*, 12v [collated with (1639)], 11. [†]Lit. *ratio contextus*, an explanation of how points fit together.

things he just said. For someone to be deemed righteous it is not enough to have heard the law, but also to have kept the law and to establish their righteousness with deeds. Therefore, since nobody has ever fulfilled the law of the Jews by his or her deeds, nobody will be deemed righteous or be saved. And therefore, not only did they receive no profit from the law, on account of which they flattered themselves, but it resulted in them all becoming liable to judgment. Now, just as the hearing of the law does not excuse the Jews, since they did not obey it in their actions as they should have, but rather subjects them to greater condemnation, so also the hearing of the law of Christ will not excuse us Christians unless we bring forth fruits of repentance that are worthy of the gospel. But if someone should object, "What do these things written for the Romans have to do with us?" I answer, the same vices that were in the Romans are in us also. Therefore, we should expect the same punishment. The same medicine is always applied to the same sicknesses. NOTES ON ROMANS.[4]

NO ONE IS A DOER OF THE LAW. ALEXANDER ALESIUS: That which some people here clamor about and wish to prove from this sentence—"for not the hearers of the law, but the doers will be justified"—that works justify, is not only out of place but also unlearned. For Paul has just proved that all Gentiles are under the wrath of God on account of their transgression of the law of nature, and he will soon show in his accusation against the Jews that they are even worse than the Gentiles and are even more unpleasing to God. Therefore, even if we accept the hypothesis that the doers of the law are justified, this sentence is a blanket accusation against both Jews and Gentiles. For, throughout this entire accusation Paul is refuting the minor premise, that there are those who do the law, the conclusion is that "we have proved that all are under sin," "that the whole world might be made accountable to God," "so that no flesh will

glory in his sight" on account of their works of the law. DISPUTATIONS ON ROMANS (1553).[5]

NOBODY IS JUSTIFIED AS A LEGALLY OWED DEBT. NIELS HEMMINGSEN: The [Catholics] twist this Pauline text, and use it as their defense to attempt to overturn the free justification that the gospel proclaims. Rather what the apostle says about this condition, that "the man or woman who does these things will by live by them," is confirmed by the conclusion of his whole argument, which he states by these words in the third chapter: "Therefore, no flesh will be justified in the sight of God by the works of the law." Further, a distinction must be maintained between two kinds of justification, which Paul teaches in the fourth chapter of this letter. For there is one kind of legally owed justification, such as that which is rendered as a debt owed to obedience to the law, and there is another kind of justification that is given by grace, such as that which is imputed to the believer by grace. Now the kind of justification that Paul is speaking about in this passage, one that is legally owed as a debt, no mortal can possess. The gospel, however, sets forth a free justification, which will be dealt with at the end of the third chapter and in the fourth and fifth chapters. Therefore let us think logically according to Paul's mind as expressed in the text before us:

(P1) Only doers of the law are justified before God as a legally owed debt.

(P2) But there are no doers of the law.

(C) Therefore, nobody can be justified as a legally owed debt.

COMMENTARY ON ROMANS (1562).[6]

TWO GROUNDS FOR JUSTIFICATION. WOLF-GANG MUSCULUS: There are two grounds for justification before God. One is according to debt, the other by imputation. I invent nothing here; the

---

[4]Zwingli, *In Evangelicam Historiam* (1539), 411; citing Lk 3:8.

[5]Alesius, *Omnes Disputationes*, H2r; citing Rom 3:9, 19; 1 Cor 1:29.
[6]Hemmingsen, *Commentarius in Epistolam*, 73-74; citing Lev 18:5; Rom 3:20.

apostle himself sets forth both of them, as we will see later in chapter 4. Debt-based justification pertains to those who do works. Imputation-based justification pertains to those "who do not work but who believe on him who justifies the ungodly." One belongs to the law, the other to the gospel. Show me someone who fully satisfies the law of God by his good works so that he cannot be condemned for any transgression, and such a person will certainly be regarded as righteous before God and will receive as a debt owed to him the wages of his righteousness. For "to him who works," the apostle says, "wages are not reckoned according to grace but according to debt." But who will you show me who does good and does not sin? "There is none," he says, "who does good and does not sin, no, not even one." And David says, "Do not enter into judgment, for no living person will be justified in your sight." David also calls those "'blessed' whose iniquities are forgiven and whose sins are covered." The apostle says the same thing here in Romans. His statement that "it is not the hearers of the law who will be justified before God, but the doers of the law" pertains to those who seek righteousness by works of the law, which he calls "their own righteousness" in chapter 10, making a distinction between it and that "righteousness of God which is by faith in Christ Jesus." It is as if he were saying, "But if you are seeking that righteousness before God that is of the works of the law, know most certainly that such righteousness comes not by hearing the law, but by performing and fulfilling it with one's works. According to the law, God will not be able to justify him who only hears the law but does not do the things the law commands. Rather, he will justify him who in his deeds adheres to the law in its entirety. But as for you, since you are hearers of the law but do not keep the law's commands, what insanity is this, that you promise yourselves righteousness and salvation on the basis of works of the law, when you will be condemned even more by the sentence of a law which you have not obeyed? Therefore, leaving behind your own righteousness—which by works you vainly seek

from a law you have not kept—lay hold on the imputation of righteousness, which is through faith in Christ." This is what the apostle has in mind in this passage. It, therefore, becomes quite clear how we are to understand what he says later, that nobody is justified by works of the law. He does not mean that if there should be someone who were to keep the whole law that there would be no future wages of righteousness awarded him before God. Far from it! For this would not be fitting for a just judge. But, rather, you should understand that there is no mortal who keeps the law, that is, who fully satisfies the righteousness of a law that clearly requires a heavenly and spiritual soul. It is, therefore, evident why he says that nobody is justified by works of the law, which in themselves are certainly good and holy. They should be set aside, and, instead, we should seek after that righteousness which—according to faith in Christ—is freely imputed to those who believe. COMMENTARY ON ROMANS (1555).[7]

HARMONIZING ROMANS 2:13 AND ROMANS 3:20. MARTIN BUCER: God saves us solely on the basis of his clemency and by regarding the merits of Christ that are given to us and become ours when we believe in Christ. For those righteous deeds on account of which God justifies us—that is, awards us with eternal life—are none other than the works of Christ within us, when they are given by him out of the sheer gracious benevolence of God, so that the goodness of God might always be the first, proper, and entire cause of our salvation, and so that we might accept the fact that we are justified solely by faith, which is the means by which this grace embraces us, and not by works. By these statements it is being asked what is the first and proper cause of our justification, and they further deny that there even exists such righteous works that nobody can possess unless he is already justified and possesses a share of eternal life. On this point St. Augustine makes this sound

---

[7]Musculus, *In Epistolam Apostoli Pauli*, 53-54; citing Rom 4:5; Rom 4:4; 3:12; Ps 143:2; 32:1; Rom 10:3; Phil 3:9; Rom 3:20.

statement, "Works do not justify"; "Good works follow one who is justified, they do not precede one who is yet to be justified."[†] Commentary on Romans (1536).[8]

Good Works Come from Election, Faith, and the Holy Spirit. Martin Bucer: Since God desires that we cooperate with him in our salvation by our good works, or rather that we might "complete it" (*katergazesthai*) (Phil 2), he had so determined to repay us according to our deeds that even our justification—that is, when he awards us with eternal life—would be according to works. But that was then. Now, when this life of God by the grace of God and the merits of Christ has already been awarded to us before the foundation of the world by means of our election (Eph 1 and 3), it is again awarded through faith. That is, after believing in Christ, we are in some sense made sharers in him by that happy beginning of faith that is wrought in us by the Spirit of the sons and daughters of God, who is also the guarantee of this inheritance. Good works are the fruit of this faith and of the Spirit. Commentary on Romans (1536).[9]

Analogies That Reconcile These Texts. Wolfgang Musculus: There is, therefore, no discrepancy between these two sentences of the apostle [Rom 2:13 and Rom 3:20]. It is true that works justify. On the other hand, it is also true that works do not justify, but rather faith does. Works do justify, but clearly they do not justify sinners, since they have no works. Works do not justify, but faith does, since "there is nobody who does good and does not sin," or to whom wages are owed by way of debt because of their own righteousness. But righteousness will be imputed to believers by the grace that is in Christ. See if you can understand how the following statements can both be true: (1) Nectar, the drink of the gods as the poets

had it in their fables, intoxicates, and ambrosia, the food of the gods, satiates. According to them, Jupiter was sated with ambrosia and lived drinking the nectar. Now, place this next to its opposite: (2) Nobody is sated with ambrosia and nobody is inebriated with nectar, but mortals are sated and inebriated with bread and wine. Couldn't both statements be true? They can, if you understand that ambrosia does not satiate humans nor does nectar inebriate them, not because they do not have the ability to do this in themselves if one were to partake of it, but because mortals cannot partake of them.

Beer inebriates. That is true, *if* you drink it. Nobody is inebriated by beer, but [only] by wine. This is also true, if you are thinking of those who do not have any beer and so drink wine instead. Now compare the beer to one's own righteousness, and the wine to the righteousness of God by which hearts are made glad. Now apply the situation of those who neither have any beer nor any grain from which it can be made, that is, of people for whom beer is entirely foreign, and who therefore drink and are intoxicated by wine instead.

Or again, it is true that bread strengthens the heart of man or woman as it says in Psalm 104. But it is, on the other hand, also true that the heart of man or woman is strengthened not by bread, but by manna. How can both be true? They can, if you consider those who were wandering about for forty years in the wilderness, who had neither bread nor grain from which bread could be made, but who were nevertheless fed with heavenly food.

In this same way it is clearly true that those who by their deeds adhere to the law are justified before God. And, on the other hand, it is likewise true that nobody is justified before God by the works of the law, but only by faith. Surely this is not due to a defect of the law itself, but rather a defect in our flesh. The grace of Christ resolves this such that we, who cannot be saved by our good works or lay hold of the wages of righteousness according to debt by satisfying the law of God, are saved by grace according to an imputed

---

[8]Bucer, *Metaphrases et Enarrationes*, 129. [†]Augustine, *Concerning Faith and Works* 14.
[9]Bucer, *Metaphrases et Enarrationes*, 129-30; citing Phil 2:12; Eph 1:5; 3:11.

righteousness, the gift of Christ, which is promised to those who believe on him. COMMENTARY ON ROMANS (1555).[10]

THREEFOLD JUSTIFICATION. MARTIN BUCER: Our justification is therefore threefold. That is, God awards us with eternal life in three ways. The first kind of justification is that in which he appoints us to eternal life, and that is strictly according to his goodness alone and a regard for the merits of Christ. Scholastic theologians add, "with respect to the merits that God foresees will exist in his people." But, I ask, how can he foresee merits that nobody at all can possess unless he himself were to give them, and which he decreed that he himself would give only after he had already decreed to give them salvation? The second kind of justification is that by which he in some manner gives us a glimpse of eternal life even now and grants that it might be enjoyed by means of his Spirit given to us, "by whom we cry, 'Abba, Father.'" This justification has additional reference to our faith, but that itself is something that God also gives us out of his gracious goodness and that he effects in us by his Spirit. The third kind of justification is when he at last furnishes us fully with eternal life in its very essence, or even when we enjoy the good things he gives us in this life, no longer only in faith and hope. Our deeds work together toward this kind of justification, but even then those very deeds are also the gifts and works of the freely bestowed goodness of God. COMMENTARY ON ROMANS (1536).[11]

INVITATION TO GOOD WORKS. MARTIN BUCER: Now, we must show how the fact that God holds out to us the full enjoyment of eternal life as following and being awarded according to works in no way contradicts our grasping this same hope by faith in the gospel through trust in the goodness of God and the merits of Christ

alone, which very things themselves—I mean faith and hope—God effects in us solely on account of his goodness and according to the merit of Christ. Therefore, neither of these texts, either by themselves or together, are in any way opposed to our belief that the first and entire self-sufficient cause of all these things is the goodness of God alone and the merit of Christ, so that there is nothing in these passages of Scripture that disagrees with what they themselves everywhere proclaim. It can also be easily seen that when the Scriptures touch on what especially concerns us they commend to us good works, and invite us to the practice of them in such a way that it does not at all contradict itself when it merely makes mention of and expounds the fact that good works are profitable for our happiness. For it is by God's will that good works result in wages being repaid for them in abundance, that he judges us according to them, and that on their account he declares us heirs of eternal life—or rather, he offers eternal life more fully—that is, on account of works he justifies us in a final and consummate sense. How then could Scripture not express, proclaim, and inculcate this in the very places where it undertakes to stir up and inflame in us the pursuit of good works? For this reason, all of Scripture, in other passages, abundantly preaches that these good works do pertain to us, but also uniformly says that when the wages of eternal life are repaid for them, that they are in absolutely no way equal to such a great reward, and that they are never finally of such a quality that we can trust in them, but rather that the clemency of God and the satisfaction that Christ rendered is altogether alone to be rested on. Nor do the Scriptures preach on works except to those who already properly grasp the truth about God's voluntary goodness, Christ's merit, the nature of faith, and the insufficiency of our works. COMMENTARY ON ROMANS (1536).[12]

---

[10]Musculus, *In Epistolam Apostoli Pauli*, 54; citing Rom 3:20, 12; Ps 104:15.
[11]Bucer, *Metaphrases et Enarrationes*, 130; citing Rom 8:15.

[12]Bucer, *Metaphrases et Enarrationes*, 130.

2:14 The Gentiles Observe the Law by Nature

BOTH JEWS AND GENTILES NEED GOD'S MERCY. MARTIN LUTHER: Both are under sin, no matter how much good they may have done, the Jews according to the inner person because they have observed merely the letter of the law, the Gentiles in a twofold way, because they have fulfilled the law only in part and not with their whole heart. I accept this interpretation because the whole tenor of this chapter (as Paul himself says below in Rom 3:9: "For we have charged that both Jews and Greeks are all under sin") is nothing else than a proof that all people, and therefore both of these, are sinners and in need of the mercy of God. LECTURES ON ROMANS.[13]

THE GENTILES AND THE LAW. PETER MARTYR VERMIGLI: Now he deals with the Gentiles, who ought not complain if they perish even if they did not possess the law of Moses. He shows that they were not entirely without the law, since by nature they had observed the things that were of the law. But when he says, "by nature" this does not wholly exclude the help of God. For it is always true that what men and women understand from God also comes from the Holy Spirit. Here, "nature" means the power of understanding that was implanted in our minds, just as the faculty of seeing was implanted by God in our bodily eyes. In this verse, Paul doesn't tell us by what powers the Gentiles are enabled to render this obedience. That will be declared later, how the power of living uprightly is given to the regenerate by the Spirit and the grace of Christ. For now, he is only speaking of certain external, virtuous, and upright actions that, since they pertain to civil justice, can be naturally observed by men and women. Nor does he say that the Gentiles have fully obeyed the law such that they have kept it in its entirety, or that they would be justified on this account. He only means that they have observed some of its precepts. He

concludes from this that by natural acumen they have been able to discern between what is virtuous and what is not, what is just and what is unjust. Or rather, if we should look into the habits of Cato, Atticus, Socrates, and Aristides, we will see justice, and how by their civil propriety they acted better than very many Christians do, not to mention the Jews. COMMENTARY ON ROMANS (1560).[14]

THE NATURAL LAW IS FROM GOD. HEINRICH BULLINGER: Since this idea has been engraved in all minds, I would not doubt that it should be identified as the law of nature. I would even say that inasmuch as it either arises from our corrupt nature or passes through it, not much is accomplished by it, for unless God touches our heart nobody would do unto others what he wishes to be done to himself. That which seems to have been implanted in us by God as part of our nature is therefore called the "law of nature." And what, I pray, is nature other than God's constant operative and disposing work in us? It teaches us that the Deity is to be worshiped, that effort is to be given to the virtues, that nobody is to be harmed, that good is to be done to all, and other things similar to these, which things are certainly from God and not from our own nature. For in the first chapter we read, "for God has revealed it to them." But in this verse we read plainly that the work of the law is written in the hearts of the Gentiles. Who wrote it on the hearts of men and women, if not the one God? Therefore, if something is righteous in the law of nature, it most certainly comes from God. For that reason, just as God revealed himself to the Gentiles through visible things, so he also inserted a certain command into their hearts, not a corruption or an inclination to sin, but a certain light by the rays of which they could discern what is true, just, and equitable. COMMENTARY ON ROMANS (1533).[15]

---

[13]LW 25:186*; citing Rom 3:9.

[14]Vermigli, *In Epistolam S. Pauli*, 129.
[15]Bullinger, *In Sanctissimam Pauli*, 40r-40v; citing Rom 1:19.

IT APPLIES TO GENTILES EVEN THOUGH WITHOUT THE WRITTEN LAW. ERASMUS SARCERIUS: Here is yet another explanatory clause that anticipates an objection. For the Gentiles could have objected: "How is it that we are sinners, since we do not possess the written law?" Paul answers that while it is true that the Gentiles do not have the written law, they nevertheless do possess the law of nature, and since they did not live up to this law, they have become sinners equally with the Jews.

Or, it may be that the explanatory clause makes sense as an anticipation of a slightly different objection: the Gentiles could have objected, "The preceding verse concerning doers of the law does not apply to us, but only to the Jews who possess the written law." The apostle responds to this objection and teaches that the preceding verse concerning doers of the law does apply even to the Gentiles, who are those who possess the law of nature and are able to keep it by an outward obedience. NOTES ON ROMANS (1541).[16]

CONSCIENCES LIKE THEATERS, EXECUTIONERS, AND WORMS. ANDREAS HYPERIUS: Paul is saying that all people naturally feel themselves to be moved by occasional stirrings of conscience, especially when, fearing that most severe judgment that will one day be executed by God, they accuse or condemn themselves on account of their evil deeds, or, alternatively, they excuse and feel good about themselves on account of their good deeds. It therefore becomes quite obvious that they have an awareness of the divine law, and it is on this basis alone that the judgment of their good and evil deeds is being prepared. Paul's first argument is especially applicable to good people who are esteemed to have diligently performed the work of the law. But the latter argument pertains just as much to bad people as it does to good, such that in the most fitting manner all people are together without exception shown to possess a knowledge of the law. This evidence is clearer than a more detailed

proof would require. For we have just read, a little bit earlier, how some of the Gentiles had boasted of their performing external works of the kind commanded by the law of God, and even dared to judge and condemn others whom everyone could plainly see were stained by outward crimes. But everywhere among the philosophers and poets one can find testimonies concerning the stirrings of conscience and of thoughts accusing people inwardly with a powerful struggle, something which all men and women—but especially the evil—continually feel within themselves. And it is from this common experience of all people that such popular sayings as these come: "Conscience is as good as a thousand witnesses," "A good conscience is the largest theater," "An evil conscience is the cruelest executioner," and "a worm that never ceases to gnaw." COMMENTARY ON ROMANS (1583).[17]

MASSACHUSETTS COVENANT EVEN BETTER THAN THE LAW OF NATURE. MASSACHUSETTS GOVERNMENT: As soon as God had set up a political government among his people Israel, he gave them a body of laws for use in judgment in both civil and criminal cases. These were brief and fundamental principles, yet so full and comprehensive that clear deductions could be drawn from them to all specific cases in future times. For a commonwealth without laws is like a ship without rigging and steerage. Nor is it sufficient to have principles or fundamentals; one needs to draw out their implications for various times and conditions for the people's use. And it is unsafe and injurious to the body of the people to require them to learn their duties and liberties from general rules. Nor is it enough merely to have laws: they must also be just laws. Therefore, among other privileges that the Lord gave to his special people, he calls them to especially consider these: that God was nearer to them, and that their laws were more righteous than other nations'. God was said to be among them or near to them because of the ordinances he had himself established. And their laws were righteous

---

[16]Sarcerius, *In Apostolam ad Romanos*, G7v.

[17]Hyperius, *Commentarii D. Andrea Hyperii*, 46.

because he himself was their Lawgiver. Yet two things are implied in the comparison: first, that other nations had something of God's presence among them. Second, that there was also some equity in their laws, for it pleased the Father (upon the covenant of redemption with his Son) to restore enough of his image to lost men and women in order to predispose all nations to worship God, and to advance righteousness, which appears in the teaching of the apostle in Romans 1:21 ("They knew God") and in Romans 2:14 ("They did by nature the things contained in the law of God.") But when the nations corrupted his ordinances (both of religion and justice), God withdrew his presence from them, proportionately giving them up to abominable lusts. If they had walked according to that light and law of nature, they might have been preserved from such moral evils and might have enjoyed a common blessing in all their natural and civil ordinances. Now, if it could have been so with the nations who were strangers to the covenant of grace, consider what advantage they have who have interest in that covenant, and who may enjoy the special presence of God in the purity and native simplicity of all his ordinances, by which he is so near to his own people. LAWS AND LIBERTIES OF THE INHABITANTS OF MASSACHUSETTS (1647).[18]

THE BLIND WOULD GLADLY SEE. BALTHASAR HUBMAIER: Just so is it with our soul after the transgression of Adam. As soon as he ate from the tree of the knowledge of good and evil, from that hour on he lost the taste of the knowledge of good and evil so that he can neither know nor judge what is right, good, or evil before God, what righteousness is sufficient before God, or what works are pleasing to God; all this even though he would gladly do right according to the spirit. This desire is still present today in all people, in Jews and heathen, as Paul writes to the Romans. Indeed, if one is blind, he would gladly see. FREEDOM OF THE WILL, I.[19]

CORNELIUS AND THE NATURAL LAW. PILGRAM MARPECK: As there is in all men and women, there was a struggle in Cornelius between the light, the Word, and the natural law. God permitted this struggle to burn freely in him, without resistance, and perform its preaching office. This conflict revealed to him a God to whom he owed praise and thanks, and it placed him in the fear of God that he might begin to pray and to do good. But without the Holy Spirit, he did not know what he was praying. Likewise the eunuch, along with other pagans who unknowingly served God, was driven by something within him to Jerusalem, but he did not exactly know what he was doing. Such persons are still found today. Cornelius could not receive the Holy Spirit without outward preaching and faith in Christ. When Cornelius had received the Holy Spirit, he, from that moment on, had a clear knowledge of what he had to do. He was no longer permitted to pray in ignorance and to remain passive, as he had been before. His former prayer had occurred apart from the Spirit and truth and therefore it had not been pleasing to God. For he was not yet a Christian nor a child of God; he had not the spirit of sonship, but only the spirit of servitude. He could not pray the Lord's Prayer; he was not freed from the fear of death nor was he freed from the curse of the natural law, which, although he was a pagan, was written in his heart. A CLEAR AND USEFUL INSTRUCTION.[20]

WE WANT TO DO RIGHT, BUT WE CAN'T. BALTHASAR HUBMAIER: A Comparison: Wounded or feverish people cannot or will not eat or drink anything wholesome. Only cold water and harmful food appeal to them. That is because their sound natures and healthy constitutions have been deranged by illness, for they have lost the right, sound taste of knowledge. Each has a bitter tongue. They judge to be good what is harmful to them and deem as evil what is good to them. So it is with our soul since the defection of Adam. As soon as he

---

[18]*The Book of the General Lauues and Libertyes*; citing Rom 1:21.
[19]CRR 5:436*.

[20]CRR 2:102*; citing Deut 30:19; Mt 6:24; Acts 8:26, 27; 17:23; Rom 10:7; Gal 3:2; Rom 8:26; Heb 2:15.

had eaten of the tree of the knowledge of good and evil, from that very hour he lost the taste to recognize good and evil and thus could no longer know or judge what is good or evil in the sight of God, what deeds of piety are pleasing to God, or what works God will bless, although according to his spirit, he would have liked to do it right. That wish exists today in all people, in Jews and pagans, as Paul writes to the Romans. If people are blind, they would like to see. If they are lame, they would like to be able to walk. If they have fallen among murderers and have been left for dead, they would like to be healed. But as to the right way and means of arriving at this health of the soul, all are confused, except for those who are instructed by the Word of God. ON FREE WILL.[21]

BECOMING LAW TO ONE'S OWN SELF IS IDOLATROUS. PILGRAM MARPECK: God himself is the wisest order in and through his Word, that is, Jesus Christ his only begotten from eternity. Whoever manipulates the omnipotence of God outside of this order is a deceiver and seducer. Again, whoever establishes, commands, or prohibits any order outside of the divine order and omnipotence denies God's power and glory. Thus all the heathen have, by their own violence, become their own law and order. Thereby, they also condemn themselves, according to divine decision, without law, for they are a law to themselves in imitation of God. This imitation, as their poets say, they have stolen from God. As Paul says, "Men are God's imitators." Such condemnation and imitation happens as a result of their own order and law, which is outside God's order and law. The consequence is that God's wisdom and order is made into foolishness, and is despised. He who establishes, commands, or prohibits that which has not been established, commanded, or prohibited by the Word of God makes God and his Word into foolishness, as if God did not know or understand, and thus he makes himself into God. Whoever acts against any statute sins against the Lord of

that statute. That is to say, God's honor is stolen, for he alone is sinned against and his place usurped. JUDGMENT AND DECISION.[22]

2:15 *The Gentiles' Consciences*

HOW THE LAW AND THE GOSPEL EACH PREACH. MARTIN LUTHER: The knowledge of the law has naturally been written and implanted in all human hearts, as St. Paul says. The law teaches us what we are to do and accuses our disobedience. It does this in many ways, not only with the frightful signs and feelings of punishment and God's wrath but also from all kinds of gifts and works of God, which a person sees and hears and which point out to him his sin and God's wrath, because he misuses them in contempt and disobedience toward God. He himself must conclude from this that those who are unthankful to God for his gifts and benefits are worthy of his wrath and damnation.

Thus all God's benefits are nothing but a living preaching of repentance (when they touch a heart), which leads people to the knowledge of their sins and thus throws them into fright. St. Paul once again in Romans 2 says to the impenitent, hardened hypocrites: "Do you despise the riches of divine goodness, patience, and long-suffering? Do you not know that God's goodness leads you to repentance?"

Therefore, there is nothing in what our antinomians make out of this example, when they say that people should preach and urge repentance not through the law but through the gospel (or, as they call it, *per violationem Filii* [through the profanation of the Son]). They reverse the two points, the *revelatio gratiae* [revelation of grace] and the *revelatio irae* [revelation of wrath], as if we should first preach and give consolation about grace, and only then frighten with wrath. These are only the blind and foolish assertions of people who do not understand either wrath or grace, repentance or comfort of conscience.

---

[21]LCC 25:121-22* (CRR 5:436).

[22]CRR 2:341-42*.

Everything that preaches about our sins and God's wrath is the law's preaching, no matter how or when it happens. On the other hand, the gospel is the preaching that shows and gives nothing but grace and forgiveness in Christ. It is true and correct that the apostles and preachers of the gospel (as Christ also himself did) confirmed the preaching of the law, and began with this among those who still did not know their sins and were not frightened of God's wrath, as Christ says, "The Holy Spirit will rebuke the world because of sin." What is a more serious, frightful pointing out and preaching of God's wrath at sin than the suffering and dying of Christ, his Son?

However, as long as all of this preaches God's wrath and frightens people, it is not yet the gospel's or Christ's own preaching, but Moses' and the law's [preaching] to the impenitent. The gospel and Christ were not instituted or given to frighten or condemn, but to comfort and raise up those who are frightened and fearful. From this it follows that if the suffering of Christ genuinely strikes a man's heart, he certainly must himself see and feel in this the unbearable wrath of God against sin and be frightened of it, so that the world becomes too narrow for him. St. Bernard testifies that this happened to him when he genuinely looked at the suffering of Christ; he says, "I thought I was safe and did not know about the verdict and wrath that had come upon me, until I saw that God's only Son had to step in for me." SUMMER POSTIL (JULY 12, 1528).[23]

THE DEFINITION OF CONSCIENCE. JOHN CALVIN: To solve this difficulty, the first thing of importance is to understand what is meant by *conscience*. The definition must be sought in the etymology of the word. For as people, when they apprehend the knowledge of things by the mind and intellect, are said to know, and hence arises the term knowledge or *science*, so when they have a sense of the divine justice added as a witness that allows them not to conceal their sins but drags

them forward as culprits to the bar of God, that sense is called *conscience*. For it stands, as it were, between God and man, not suffering man to suppress what he knows in himself; but following him on even to conviction. It is this that Paul means when he says, "Their conscience also bearing witness, and their thoughts the meanwhile accusing, or else excusing one another." Simple knowledge may exist in a person, shut up, as it were; therefore this sense, which summons us before the bar of God, is set over us as a kind of sentinel to observe and spy out all our secrets, that nothing may remain buried in darkness. Hence the ancient proverb, "Conscience is a thousand witnesses." For the same reason, Peter also employs the expression, "the answer of a good conscience," for tranquility of mind. When persuaded of the grace of Christ, we boldly present ourselves before God. And the author of the letter to the Hebrews says that we have "no more conscience of sins," that we are held as freed or acquitted, so that sin no longer accuses us. INSTITUTES OF THE CHRISTIAN RELIGION 3.19.15 (1559).[24]

CONSCIENCES LIKE FURIES. JOHANNES BRENZ: The Gentiles not only possessed a knowledge of what things are just and unjust, noble and shameful, they also had a conscience of things done rightly or wrongly. For someone who has been bringing hope to some suffering person among the Gentiles, their conscience will have been bearing them witness that they have been acting rightly and piously. But for someone who has been killing others or at least harassing them out of jealousy, this very same conscience, which has the weight of a thousand witnesses, will have been accusing them and objecting to it, whispering in the ear of their minds that what they have been doing is most wicked. It is like the Furies that tormented Orestes and Nero, both of whom had killed their mothers. Therefore, both conscience's approval of good deeds and its accusations and Furies unleashed against evil deeds are manifest proofs that the Gentiles did

---

[23]LW 78:215-16*; citing Jn 16:8.

[24]Calvin, *Institutes*, 2:141*; citing 1 Pet 3:21; Heb 10:2.

in fact have the work of the law written on their hearts, that is, that they possessed a knowledge of what things are noble and what are shameful, divinely inscribed on their natural powers of reason. COMMENTARY ON ROMANS (1564).[25]

SEEDS RATHER THAN FULL KNOWLEDGE. JOHN CALVIN: We cannot conclude from this passage that there is in people a full knowledge of the law, but that there are only some seeds of what is right planted in their nature, evidenced by such acts as these: All the Gentiles alike instituted religious rites; they made laws to punish adultery, and theft, and murder; they commended good faith in bargains and contracts. They have thus indeed proved, that God ought to be worshiped; that adultery, and theft, and murder are evils; that honesty is commendable. It is not to our purpose to inquire what sort of God they imagined him to be, or how many gods they devised. It is enough to know that they thought there is a God, and that honor and worship are due to him. It matters not whether they are permitted the coveting of another man's wife, or of his possessions, or of anything that was his—whether they connived at wrath and hatred; inasmuch as it was right for them to covet what they knew to be evil when done. COMMENTARY ON ROMANS 2:15.[26]

OUR HEARTS ACCUSE US, BUT CHRIST DEFENDS US. MARTIN LUTHER: From where shall we take thoughts to defend us? Only from Christ, and only in him will we find them. For if the heart of a believer in Christ accuses him and reprimands him and witnesses against him that he has done evil, he will immediately turn away from evil and will take his refuge in Christ and say, "Christ has done enough for me. He is just. He is my defense. He has died for me. He has made his righteousness my righteousness, and my sin his sin. If he has made my sin to be his sin, then I do not have it, and I am free. If he has made his

righteousness my righteousness, then I am righteous now with the same righteousness as he. My sin cannot devour him, but it is engulfed in the unfathomable depths of his righteousness for he himself is God, who is blessed forever." Thus we can say, "God is greater than our heart." The Defender is greater than the accuser, immeasurably greater. It is God who is my defender. It is my heart that accuses me. LECTURES ON ROMANS (1516).[27]

2:16 God Will Judge the Secrets of Humans

THE GOSPEL INCLUDES JUDGMENT. JOHN CALVIN: It is indeed no matter of surprise that the gospel is in part called the messenger and the announcer of future judgment, for if the fulfilment and completion of what it promises is deferred to the full revelation of the heavenly kingdom, it must necessarily be connected with the last judgment. And further, Christ cannot be preached without being a resurrection to some and a destruction to others, and both these things have a reference to the day of judgment. The words "through Jesus Christ" I apply to the day of judgment, though they are regarded otherwise by some. The meaning is that the Lord will execute judgment by Christ, for he is appointed by the Father to be the judge of the living and of the dead, which the apostles always mention among the main articles of the gospel. Thus the sentence will be full and complete, which would otherwise be defective. COMMENTARY OF ROMANS 2:16.[28]

SINS WILL BE REVEALED UNLESS REPENTED OF. JOHANNES BRENZ: He . . . adds to this verse the phrase "according to my gospel." For he had been preaching not only that Christ had expiated our sins but also that by Christ God was to judge the living and the dead. Let us therefore learn the fear of God. For first, we possess both natural

---

[25]Brenz, *In Epistolam*, 60-61.
[26]CTS 38:98* (CO 49:38).
[27]LW 25:188*; citing Rom 8:33, 34, 31; 1 Jn 3:20.
[28]CTS 38:100* (CO 49:39).

reason, as the Gentiles did, and the Ten Commandments, as the Jews did, and also the revelation of the gospel, which was hidden from the Gentiles and shown in some manner to the Jews. For this reason, if we should sin and not repent of it we will be more gravely condemned the more we have been furnished with more excellent gifts. Then, when Paul says, "the secrets of men that will be disclosed on the day of judgment," this should rightly deter us from sinning. For if we tremble with terror when we think about a sin that we have conceived being revealed before a small assembly of mere men and women, how much more ought we to be terrified of the thought of any sin whatever, since nothing can be perpetrated in a hidden enough way that it will not be revealed and judged before the eyes of the whole world. Sins must therefore be fled from, or if we perchance should sin, it must be repented of in Christ, in whom alone sins are not only hidden but also so wiped away that there remains no lingering memory of it. COMMENTARY ON ROMANS (1564).[29]

THE PERSECUTED ONE WILL BE THE JUDGE.
KASPAR OLEVIANUS: "By Jesus Christ, according

to whose gospel." In other words, the One whom idolaters today are persecuting will himself judge them. They persecute him who holds life, death, and eternal judgment in his hands. But someone might object: "But I thought such and such!" He will answer, "I know and felt in my body what you thought of me." Let the merchants of souls hear and read what is written, "They will say to the mountains and the rocks, 'Fall on us; hide us from the face of him who sits on the throne and from the wrath of the Lamb!'" And similarly, "But outside will be the dogs, sorcerers, fornicators, murderers, idolaters, and all those who love and practice lies." The Lord will in that day reveal the idolatry of the heart. NOTES ON ROMANS (1579).[30]

THE GOSPEL AS STANDARD FOR THE FINAL JUDGMENT. FRIEDRICH BALDUIN: The gospel of Paul concerning Jesus Christ will be the standard for the final judgment: since in the gospel is revealed the voice and decisive sentence of the Judge: "Whoever believes in the Son is not judged: whoever does not believe, is judged already." COMMENTARY ON ROMANS (1620).[31]

---

[29]Brenz, *In Epistolam*, 61.

[30]Olevianus, *In Epistolam D. Pauli*, 103; citing Rev 18: 3, 9, 13; Rev 6:10, 11, 16.
[31]Balduin, *Catechesis Apostolica*, 147; citing Jn 3:18.

2:17-29 THE LAW AND CIRCUMCISION

[17]But if you call yourself a Jew and rely on the law and boast in God [18]and know his will and approve what is excellent, because you are instructed from the law; [19]and if you are sure that you yourself are a guide to the blind, a light to those who are in darkness, [20]an instructor of the foolish, a teacher of children, having in the law the embodiment of knowledge and truth— [21]you then who teach others, do you not teach yourself? While you preach against stealing, do you steal? [22]You who say that one must not commit adultery, do you commit adultery? You who abhor idols, do you rob temples? [23]You who boast in the law dishonor God by breaking the law. [24]For, as it is written, "The name of God is blasphemed among the Gentiles because of you."

[25]For circumcision indeed is of value if you obey the law, but if you break the law, your circumcision becomes uncircumcision. [26]So, if a man who is uncircumcised keeps the precepts of the law, will not his uncircumcision be regarded[a] as circumcision? [27]Then he who is physically[b] uncircumcised but keeps the law will condemn you who have the written code[c] and circumcision but break the law. [28]For no one is a Jew who is merely one outwardly, nor is circumcision outward and physical. [29]But a Jew is one inwardly, and circumcision is a matter of the heart, by the Spirit, not by the letter. His praise is not from man but from God.

a Or counted   b Or is by nature   c Or the letter

OVERVIEW: Paul teaches that reliance on the law and on circumcision for one's salvation is futile, and he draws attention to the hypocrisy of those who boast that they have the law but then do not live up to its standards. Our Reformation-era commentators elaborate on Paul's metaphors—and create additional ones—that illustrate this hypocrisy of teaching one thing while doing another. They define the four sins of theft, adultery, idolatry, and blasphemy, which one interpreter suggests may be in ascending order.

Continuing with the theme of our utter inability to reach God's high standards, the reformers teach that circumcision is only effective if it is fully lived up to, that is, by following the law completely. But it is impossible to keep it fully. So there is a need for a new circumcision, one that can be kept by faith. For many of the reformers—although it is not mentioned directly in the text—this points to the sacraments (or ordinances). In contrast to the medieval Catholic belief in seven sacraments, the Protestant reformers taught only two: baptism and the Lord's Supper. Their comments on the role of faith and law in relation to the sacraments must be read in distinction from the Catholic theologians' teaching that salvific grace was mediated through the sacraments *ex opere operato* (literally "out of the work worked"); that is, that if rightly performed, a sacrament would convey grace. For the reformers, although the sacraments needed to be received by faith, salvation itself came via faith alone, not via the sacraments. Various commentators apply the contrast between external and internal circumcision to the church, to baptism and the Lord's Supper, and to the individual believer's life. Although they hold a variety of views on the sacraments, they agree that the stance of the recipient is key, that merely external sacraments are insufficient. Circumcision of the heart is what matters, but we cannot have this deeper circumcision of our hearts without grace from above, so we must seek after Christ, repent, and receive grace in order to be saved. The dead letter (*gramma*)—variously interpreted as the law, reason, or virtue—is contrasted with the Holy Spirit's vital, life-giving work that brings joy and light to the believer.

2:17 Those Who Rely on the Law

THREE GIFTS CONFERRED ON THE JEWS.
PETER MARTYR VERMIGLI: He calls to mind the gifts conferred on the Jews from the beginning, and reduces them to approximately three categories. The first is the nobility of the title that was added to them from being the family and holy seed of the patriarchs. The second is that they knew the will of God through the law established with their ancestors. The third is that they had been commissioned to teach other nations. These were magnificent things, but they were of no profit to them since the Jews had deteriorated since the time of the patriarchs in matters pertaining to morality and justice, and since they had by their sins lived contrary to the law they had received, and also since they had neglected to teach even themselves, let alone teach other peoples. But with these words, Paul most powerfully reminds them of the things they had freely received. For they were not conferred on them due to any merit of their own. COMMENTARY ON ROMANS (1560).[1]

FAITH DISTINGUISHES THE GODLY. NIELS HEMMINGSEN: "If you are called a Jew." In other words, since you are proud of belonging to the special people of God and being members of his household, which I do not deny to be a noble thing, only show yourself to be worthy of such a family. Observe that it is not the title, but faith that distinguishes the godly from the ungodly. COMMENTARY ON ROMANS (1562).[2]

LEARNING FEAR AND COMFORTING THE TERRIFIED. PHILIPP MELANCHTHON: "If the law were sufficient for justification, all who have received the law and are observing the outward acts of worship would be righteous." But these are not righteous, so the law is not sufficient for justification. It must be diligently considered what Paul's purpose was when he wrote this. He accuses the Jews in order that they may understand that there is need for a different benefit for justification. This is a serious rebuke of the arrogance in hypocrites, who are puffed up with confidence in their own righteousness. Such passages must be noted both in order that we may learn fear and that terrified minds may receive comfort. For such passages do much for both sides because they both curb carnal security and again raise up fear-filled minds according to the saying, "Let him that boasts, boast of the Lord." COMMENTARY ON ROMANS (1540).[3]

SCRIPTURE IS NOT A CANTERBURY TALE.
THOMAS CRANMER: The church of God, most dearly beloved brothers and sisters, ought not to be reputed and taken as a place where people go only to stare and listen, either for their solace or as a pastime. But whatever is declared there from the Word of God, that we should receive devoutly and earnestly print on our minds, so that we will both believe it as most certain truth, and diligently endeavor to express the same in the way we live. If we receive and repute the gospel to be true and godly, why don't we live according to the same? If we count it as fables and trifles, why do we take it on ourselves to give such credit and authority to it? To what purpose is such dissimulation and hypocrisy? If we take it for a Canterbury tale, why do we not refuse it? Why do we not laugh it out of place and whistle at it? Why do we approve it with words and receive and allow it with our consciences, give credit to it, repute, and take it as a thing most true, wholesome, and godly, and then in our living clearly reject it? Brothers and sisters, God will not be mocked. For this cause God so severely and grievously punished the Jews above all other nations. And since our cause is the same, the same anger and displeasure of God is now provoked and kindled against us. SERMON CONCERNING THE TIME OF REBELLION (1549).[4]

---

[1]Vermigli, *In Epistolam S. Pauli*, 133.
[2]Hemmingsen, *Commentarius in Epistolam*, 78.
[3]Melanchthon, *Commentary on Romans*, 90*; citing 2 Cor 10:17.
[4]Cranmer, *Miscellaneous*, 198*. This may have been partially written by Peter Martyr Vermigli. Probably refers to Kett's Rebellion in Norfolk in 1549.

2:18 *If Knowledgeable of the Law*

THE DECALOGUE BRINGS SIGHT TO HUMANITY'S BLINDNESS. JOHANNES BRENZ: For the Ten Commandments, according to their own true and correct opinion, which the Holy Spirit exposited in the writings of the prophets and apostles, was a "guide to the blind and a light for those who were walking in darkness." For we have by nature a knowledge of what is right and wrong, as has been shown above, but this knowledge has so long been obscured by the power of original sin, false doctrine, perverse upbringing, and the bad example of crowds, that you would not be far from the truth if you said that humans labor under a monstrous blindness and are like a blind person groping around at midday, so that they do not know what direction they are turning or what way they should walk to true life. But the Ten Commandments call men and women back from that blindness to their original power of sight. COMMENTARY ON ROMANS (1588).[5]

THEY OVERESTIMATED THEIR KNOWLEDGE. RUDOLF GWALTHER: Even if they were speaking truthfully, they still were not free of the vice of exaggeration, since they were not that much wiser than the Gentiles. For even if they did possess, by the law, a conception of true knowledge, the very people whom it was meant to illuminate more than any others cast it off from their souls. Similar to these were the scholastic theologians and those showing off their empty knowledge or learning, who possess the fullest libraries, who at great cost purchase dictations of lectures by famous teachers, and who carry about in their hands books decorated as sumptuously as they are finely crafted. . . . The Jews, I say, were such as these, whom Malachi censured in ancient times. And how unlearned the common person among them was is evident in the case of Nicodemus, who although he was a most celebrated teacher was nevertheless ignorant of the basic principles of human salvation. Therefore,

Paul rightly sets out to place before their eyes those gifts that God had seen fit to bestow on them, so that they might come to acknowledge their vice by such weighty words as if in a kind of mirror. SERMONS ON ROMANS (1590).[6]

2:19 *If a Guide to the Blind*

THE METAPHORS APPLY ALSO TO THE LAW AND GOSPEL. CHRISTOPH CORNER: These are excellent compliments and are spoken to "the person" of the Jews. However, these are metaphorical commendations and also amount to a praise of the law and the gospel, of which they are brief, commendatory descriptions. For the law or Ten Commandments is a guide for the blind, a teacher of the ignorant, a rule of truth. The gospel is likewise rightly called a guide for the blind, for by it alone is the truth known; it is also the "true light shining in the darkness," that is, the true knowledge that brings people to God; and it is the rule of divine truth and true doctrine and the means of truly worshiping and pleasing God. COMMENTARY ON ROMANS (1583).[7]

IF YOU CLAIM TO BE A GUIDE TO THE BLIND. HEINRICH BULLINGER: It is as if he were saying, with these magnificent words, "You are indeed versed in the law, know the will of God, prove the things that are excellent, are a guide for the blind, a light, a teacher, and a corrector of the foolish, and you also possess the rule for how to live. In short, you lack nothing that pertains to a full knowledge of the truth. But is there something else? This one thing you lack, without which all the rest are powerless, or rather, without which no knowledge whatever will profit you: a change of habits and the practicing of a way of life consistent with the things you know." COMMENTARY ON ROMANS (1533).[8]

---

[5]Brenz, *In Epistolam*, 522.

[6]Gwalther, *In d. Pauli Apostoli*. 28r.
[7]Corner, *In Epistolam ad Romanos*, 35-36; citing Jn 1:5, 9.
[8]Bullinger, *In Sanctissimam Pauli*, 43r.

PAUL REVEALS THE PHARISEES' DANGEROUS ERROR. TILEMANN HESSHUS: The Pharisees and others were misusing these very praises to prop up their own pride. For they wished to be thought righteous before God on account of their profession of doctrine, knowledge of the divine law, and external practices of various kinds. Therefore, in order for Paul to take this dangerous error away from them, he shows that these titles—that someone should be called a Jew, possess the law, be an instructor of the foolish, a teacher of the ignorant, and a guide for the blind—contribute nothing to one's obtaining justification before God. This is because the law, he says, requires not only that it be known and professed, but much more so that it be entirely obeyed in absolutely every one of its points. Since the Jews are far from having done this, they accuse themselves by the very law that they are trying to teach to others. For the very thing that they complain about in the external behavior of other sinners and Epicureans, they themselves commit in the depraved desires and erring impulses of their hearts. COMMENTARY ON PAUL'S EPISTLES (1605).[9]

2:20 If a Teacher of the Law

ONLY AN IMAGE OF KNOWLEDGE AND GODLINESS. JOHANNES LONICER: He very purposely said a "form" of knowledge and godliness, thereby indicating that they do not possess a true knowledge or a true godliness, but only a kind of feigned image, which appearance of the truth they did in fact display, but that there was nothing of the truth itself. It is therefore rightly said that in the law it is necessary to possess a true image of it in one's conscience and works. But you, he says, are hugely proud of the fact that you are such an image of the law; but the truth is that this is not at all true of you, inasmuch as you are not a doer of the law. EXEGESIS OF ROMANS (1537).[10]

THE KNOWLEDGE MUST BE TRULY BELIEVED AND LIVED. MARTIN BUCER: Here he says plainly what he had just said by way of metaphor. For to instruct the foolish and teach the ignorant is nothing different than to offer oneself as a guide for the blind and a light in the darkness. The Jews assumed these for themselves, since they trusted in the law of God in which all of these assertions can be found. But these apply only to a person who gives himself to the law with unshakable faith and meditates on it day and night. "The testimony of the Lord," said the psalmist, "is sure, making wise the foolish," but only when it is truly believed. As for them, since they had not yet lived according to the law, they neither truly grasped it and were therefore themselves blind, groping around in darkness; those who had not yet encountered true learning or wisdom did "not yet know as they ought to know." Since, however, they were fully versed in the letter of the law, when they were having their grandiose discussions about words in the law of the Lord it certainly appeared that those outward elements set down in ceremonial precepts were being piously observed. But they were displaying an empty form of knowledge and of the truth of the One who is in the law, that is, he whom the law sets forth when it is rightly understood. But the one who truly possesses that knowledge and that truth is the one who so comprehends what things are true and just, that he inclines toward them with his whole heart and does not waver at all toward the opposite. "By this we know that we know God, if we keep his commandments. And he who says 'I know him' but does not keep his commandments is a liar, and the truth is not in him." COMMENTARY ON ROMANS (1536).[11]

2:21 Teachers Who Do Not Learn

A PARSON MUST PREACH FIRST TO HIMSELF. GEORGE HERBERT: And consequently the Parson

---

[9]Hesshus, *Commentarius in Omnes*, 28.
[10]Lonicer, *Exegesis Romanos*, 15.

[11]Bucer, *Metaphrases et Enarrationes*, 134-35; citing Ps 19:7; 1 Cor 8:2; 1 Jn 2:3-4.

found that the essence of repentance—that it may be alike in all God's children—consists in a true detestation of the soul, abhorring and renouncing sin, and turning to God in truth of heart and newness of life, which acts of repentance are and must be found in all God's servants. Weeping cannot be essential to it, for some are of a softer temperament than others. Not that weeping is not useful, when someone can weep. It makes it so that the body may join in the grief, as it did in the sin. But, unlike the other acts of repentance, it is not necessary. So those who perform the other acts of repentance repent just as truly, even when they cannot weep, as those that weep a flood of tears. When, after receiving this instruction and comfort for himself, the Parson tells it to others, it becomes a sermon. The same happens with other Christian virtues such as faith, love, and the cases of conscience belonging to them. Thus—as St. Paul implies that he should, in Romans 2—he first preaches to himself, and then to others. A PRIEST TO THE TEMPLE.[12]

SHEPHERDS WHO STRANGLE THEIR SHEEP. DIRK PHILIPS: Oh, that many (who accept their teaching position and yet are so selfish, haughty, unrighteous, idolatrous, and lead such godless lives) would earnestly observe and consider well what great complaints are in all Scripture about the false prophets and shepherds, with the implication that the corruption of the people has most of its origin from them. For it behooves the shepherds to feed the sheep, just as Christ commanded Peter and Peter commanded the elders. But how is this to take place when the shepherds trample the precious pasture of the divine Word with their feet and then give the sheep to eat the same which they have trampled with their feet? It behooves the shepherds also to dip the water of divine teaching out of the fountain of salvation and give the sheep to drink; but how lamentable is it when the shepherds become Philistines and stop up the spring of living water by throwing in earth.

Yes, when they are wolves who do not save the flock [but] feed themselves and scatter and strangle the sheep? THE SENDING OF PREACHERS.[13]

LIKE A PAINTER WHO NEVER PAINTS. PETER MARTYR VERMIGLI: "You who teach another, do you not teach yourself?" They could not endure to be taught by others, which is clear from what they said to the man who was born blind: "You were wholly born in sin, and are you teaching us?" They ought at least to have taught themselves. But since they didn't, and concerned themselves only with seeing that their works were adhered to by others, they were therefore like the fig tree that had leaves without any fruit and that withered at the curse of Christ. That which he had said earlier to the Gentiles, "You who judge another and yet do the same things which you condemn," he now applies to the Jews, since they were teaching others and yet transgressing themselves. Certainly, when it comes to matters of this world, we are not of that disposition, for you will see nobody distributing alms without first providing goods for himself or herself. Why does it happen then, that we teach our doctrine to others while we do not embrace it ourselves? Chrysostom compares this kind of man with a painter who has a painting before his eyes that he perpetually contemplates, but yet does not himself paint anything at all that he sees in it. Paul had just said that "it is not the hearers of the law but the doers who will be justified." In our day this would accuse those preachers who hardly practice at all the things they teach. It must, therefore, be concluded that it is not enough to preach or to hear sound doctrine: it must also be put into practice. COMMENTARY ON ROMANS (1560).[14]

INTERNAL SINS MATTER. CHRISTOPH CORNER: There is also an amplification of their transgression of the law as a consequence of the following aggravating factors: by their many sins and

---

[12]Herbert, *Works*, 1:235-36*.

[13]CRR 6:212*; citing Jn 21:17; 1 Pet 5:2; Ezek 34:18-19; Acts 20:29-30.
[14]Vermigli, *In Epistolam S. Pauli*, 136; citing Jn 9:34; Rom 2:1, 13.

impieties they were causing injury to and cursing the name and honor of God, as is written in Isaiah 52 and Ezekiel 36. But you might say, "Not all the Jews were guilty of such crimes as these." There were in fact many "godly" persons among them, at least some who were not contaminated by outward idols and sins, but one must carefully weigh Paul's meaning here, who with this name, "Jew," condemns all who were guilty of either external or internal sins. For there were many hypocrites who felt themselves secure, but who had no repentance, no fear of God, and no true faith. But where there is hypocrisy, there many sins and evils flourish alongside it: security, pride, trust in and admiration of oneself, impatience, and in the end, a lack of hope. Therefore, Paul refers as much to internal impulses and desires of a depraved soul and heart as he does to external acts like theft and adultery. COMMENTARY ON ROMANS (1583).[15]

WE COMPARE OURSELVES TOO POSITIVELY TO OTHERS. HULDRYCH ZWINGLI: It is according to the law that one ought not to steal—that is, that one must not cheat another, or defraud them in any business dealings, nor must anyone harm another in any way whatever. But you, when you act contrary to the law, the law profits you nothing, but is instead a liability. So it is in our day also. We all wish to be righteous in comparison with other people, since we do not do what some others do, or because we are free of certain vices and crimes, and we therefore judge others but do not judge ourselves. We interrogate others' lives but do not weigh our own in the balance. A thief cannot be said to be righteous because he is not a murderer of his parents. NOTES ON ROMANS (1539).[16]

FOUR SINS IN ORDER OF INCREASING GRAVITY. CHRISTOPH CORNER: He now proves that the Jews are also sinners and that their privileges are of no help to them. He makes a mockery of those privileges by turning them upside down and laying a serious charge against the Jews, declaring that they are guilty of the same crimes that they reprehend and condemn in others. He does this by way of division (*diamerismō*). First he speaks in a general way: "You who teach others, do you not teach yourselves what things should be done and what avoided?" There is a rebuke (*epitimēsis*) in these words. He then condemns, in order of increasing gravity, four sins that they were guilty of: theft, adultery, idolatry, and blasphemy. For the Jews were in the habit of stealing and committing adultery; they were sacrilegious and by their profaning of the divine name, their blasphemy and their many scandals they stained the name of God with disrepute, as much as by their making a sham of the law as by their corrupt lives. In other words, they dishonored God (*theōn atimazein*). This is why he added the words, "the name of God is blasphemed because of you." COMMENTARY ON ROMANS (1583).[17]

STEALING DEFINED. RUDOLF GWALTHER: People steal when they claim for themselves in an unjust way something that belongs to another, or keep back something from their masters without their consent. There are, in fact, many kinds of theft that Moses enumerates in the law. Under this label ought also to be referred such things as plundering, the confiscation of inheritances which happens under the pretense of law, and deceit and trickery of all kinds that unscrupulous merchants and money-changers employ, such as adulterating their wares, cheating in their measures and weights or in their counting of money, and other things of this kind. The practices of those who lend money at interest also amount to theft, by which those who have once fallen into their hands are reduced to extreme poverty. Those who defraud contractors or workers of the wages due their labor are also thieves. HOMILY 12 ON ROMANS 2:17-24 (1590).[18]

---

[15]Corner, *In Epistolam Ad Romanos*, 36v; citing Is 52:1-15; Ezek 36:20, 22.
[16]Zwingli, *In Evangelicam Historiam*, 412.
[17]Corner, *In Epistolam Ad Romanos*, 36r.
[18]Gwalther, *In d. Pauli Apostoli*, 28v.

CONSISTENCY OF WORD AND DEED. MENNO SIMONS: It is not sufficient for sincere Christians merely to speak the truth; they must also demonstrate in power and in deed that which they speak, confirming themselves to it. Or they shall hear with the Pharisees, "You say, and do not"; and also as Paul, in writing to the Romans, says of the Jews, "You that preach that a person should not steal, do you steal? You who say a person should not commit adultery, do you commit adultery? You that abhor idols, do you commit sacrilege? You that make your boast of the law, do you break the law, thus dishonoring God?"

In short, Christians teach and act; profess and practice; believe and obey; direct and advance. Their hearts, words, and deeds are in unison; if not they are hypocrites, and not Christians; as, alas! THE CROSS OF CHRIST.[19]

2:22 Adulterers Who Condemn Adultery

VIOLATING BOTH TABLES OF THE LAW. NIELS HEMMINGSEN: Does this argument turn back against the Jews the very thing they commonly took great pride in?

(P1) If those who possess the law and teach it to others should themselves fail to keep it, they are unrighteous and hold the law out before them in vain.

(P2) The Jews possess the law and teach it to others, but they do not keep it themselves.

(C) Therefore, the Jews are unrighteous and hold the law out before them in vain.

Only the minor premise (P2) is stated, and that by means of a question, in order to make his rebuke sharper and to better pierce their hypocrisy. Paul supports the minor premise with a double proof. First, he accuses them of violating the second table of the law by theft and adultery. Second, they violate the first table of the law by sacrilege and blasphemy, by which the honor and glory of God

are aggrieved. When he accuses the Jews of being guilty of theft, adultery, sacrilege, and blasphemy, he does not refer so much to external deeds as he does to the internal impurity of the heart, since external deeds proceed as the outflow of an impure heart. COMMENTARY ON ROMANS (1562).[20]

ADULTERY DEFINED. RUDOLF GWALTHER: Adultery is another type of sin. Now, it is understood that in the law not only is the pollution of another's marriage bed prohibited, but also all unlawful sexual activity. For in the exposition of the law there are precepts concerning rape, incest, and similar things. And, of course, Christ, refocusing its meaning more sharply, calls the desiring the wife of another the crime of adultery: "Whoever sees a woman so as to desire her has already committed adultery with her in his heart." Therefore, since Paul was writing to Jews who had already been converted to Christ, he was able to rightly say this and at the same time accuse them all of adultery, since hardly anyone can be found who can say that he is free from all lust. A general teaching ought to be sought from this, that those who are free of more serious crimes and who are irreproachable in the judgment of this world are not for this reason righteous before God. For, since God claims for himself the whole person—the more principle part of whom is the soul—those who withhold their souls from God and alienate themselves from him by depraved desires can never be said to have rendered due obedience to the law. This being observed, it is most fitting that Paul numbers adultery among those crimes that render us liable to the wrath of God and to condemnation. And it is also fitting because it foully pollutes the body, which ought to be the temple of the Holy Spirit, and snatches away the soul so that, on account of one's modesty being completely extinguished, one falls headlong into lustful desires. He therefore lays down serious punishments for

---

[19]Simons, *Complete Works*, 208*.

[20]Hemmingsen, *Commentarius in Epistolam*, 80-81.

adulterers, which punishments we have shown elsewhere to have been accepted among all nations by unanimous consent. What is more, there are awful examples found everywhere in the histories, in which God gave warning to those whom he had allowed to commit rape and adultery with apparent impunity. For this reason, the fact that things so severely prohibited by the divine law are being treated almost like a game or a joke is no small proof of the extreme corruption of our present time. Homily 12 on Romans 2:17-24 (1590).[21]

2:23-24 Falsely Glorying in God's Law

FALSE BOASTING. Martin Bucer: To "glory" is to boast of those things that we consider to be especially good. Accordingly, the Jews gloried in the law when they carried about before them the high regard they had for the law. But they declared how insincere they were in this when they lived in every way contrary to the written law. Therefore, as much as they appeared to honor God when they gloried in his law, insofar as they bore witness that it was exceedingly good and saving for them, they made it equally evident by their deeds that they really regarded the law of God as nothing, since they most brazenly trampled it underfoot their entire life. In so doing they brought a more serious reproach on God, since deeds are more authentic and a more reliable witness of one's soul than words are. For it is precisely due to the fact that they were so vainly glorying in the law of God that they were bringing reproach on God, whom they were clearly mocking by glorying in the words of his law while deeply despising it in their heart. For to greatly boast of God and of divine things contrary to your heart's true thoughts of him, what else do you call this but to hold God in ridicule and insult him to his face? Especially when he is everywhere present and everything we do we do right before him? Commentary on Romans (1536).[22]

WE WERE CREATED TO GLORIFY GOD. Peter Martyr Vermigli: To act this way is truly to resist the very purpose for which we were formed, since we were created to glorify the name of God. Paul asserts that we were created in order to live to the praise of his glory and grace. Christ also said, "So let your light shine before men and women that they might see your good works and glorify your Father who is in heaven." They mock God who boast of him and yet by their works are constantly resisting his will. Commentary on Romans (1560).[23]

BEWARE OF PRETENDING DEVOTION TO THE GOSPEL. Andreas Hyperius: That daily petition "hallowed be thy name" refers to the same thing. There are those who act contrary to this so that on account of their reprobate life they present to adversaries a religion and evangelical doctrine as something to be despised, and even the name of God himself as something to be blasphemed. Such people should know that they not only cause harm to weak men and women, but also do the gravest injury to God himself, and that they will therefore by no means escape the hands of God. Indeed it would have been better if these men and women had never been born than to have lived as authors of stumbling blocks and blasphemies against God. Let those beware who go around appearing as those who are greatly devoted to the gospel and with empty words make every effort to promote this view of themselves among the common people, but who all the while are in their habits the furthest thing from gospel charity, temperance, and modesty. Such people are less fit for the business of the gospel than those who openly profess themselves to be God's sworn enemies. Commentary on Romans (1583).[24]

2:25 Circumcision Without Works Profits Nothing

CIRCUMCISION AND WORKS. Cardinal Cajetan: "Circumcision in work has profit." There

---

[21]Gwalther, In d. Pauli Apostoli, 28v-29; citing Mt 5:28.
[22]Bucer, Metaphrases et Enarrationes, 135.

[23]Vermigli, In Epistolam S. Pauli, 138; citing Eph 1:12, 14; Mt 5:16.
[24]Hyperius, Commentarii D. Andrea Hyperii, 49-50.

are two main principles for the Jews. The first is the law of Moses, and the other is the circumcision given to Abraham. Therefore, after he has proved to this point that works are weighed before the divine tribunal in such a way that the divine judgment considers not the law itself but the works done in conformity with law as much in the case of the Jews as in that of Gentiles, he now shows the same thing by declaring that both Jews and Gentiles have a similar status with regard to circumcision. Just as he had proved, by referring both to the written law, that there is no respecting of persons but only of works before the divine tribunal, so likewise by referring both to circumcision, he proves the same point. Just as he pushed back against the Jews by making them equal to Gentiles with respect to their merits of the works of the law, so he again pushes back against them by equating them with Gentiles even with respect to the "work" of circumcision. This serves his overarching purpose to show that the righteousness of circumcision does not exist unless there is a righteousness by virtue of works as well. He does this by using the same argument, namely, that Gentiles are able to attain to the righteousness of circumcision by their works and that circumcision without works profits nothing. ON THE EPISTLES OF PAUL (1550).[25]

CIRCUMCISION PROFITS IF YOU KEEP THE LAW. CARDINAL CAJETAN: Notice here that the sense of these words is understood as a manner of speaking, and therefore these words of Paul, "circumcision indeed profits," are to be kept in balance as merely a manner of speaking. But certainly this manner of speaking makes a stark distinction: on the one side circumcised Jews, and on the other Gentiles in their uncircumcision with respect to the light of nature, for it is clearly explained that "he will judge that which is by nature uncircumcision." From this it is clearly understood that the present discussion concerns circumcision and uncircumcision in an absolute

sense, and does not refer to that state in which Christians that had been converted from Jews and Gentiles then stood. Consequently, the apostle spoke truly when he says in an absolute sense, "circumcision indeed profits"—without doubt he means unto eternal life—"if you observe the law by your deeds." For circumcision was a sign of just such a calling, for which reason he also writes to the Galatians, "I testify to any who is circumcised that he is a debtor to the whole law." Just as we said that the calling to the pontificate or to a religious life is profitable if it is attested by good works, so likewise the apostle says that the circumcision that was commanded to Abraham would profit too, if you keep the law. COMMENTARY ON THE EPISTLES OF PAUL (1550).[26]

ACCEPTING THE SIGN IMPLIES AGREEMENT TO THE COVENANT AND ITS CONDITIONS. KASPAR OLEVIANUS: It must be understood that there are two parts of a covenant: promise and counter-promise. Now the covenant is called a "sign," which is, of course, a "testimony" or a visible sign. Hence, just as in his audible word or covenant he does not make a promise without attaching a condition to it, so neither does he promise any differently when giving a visible word or "sign." And by receiving the covenant by means of a sign, we thereby bind ourselves to the conditions of the covenant.

Now the Jews did not keep the law, neither in a legal sense by works, nor by faith. Paul, therefore, concludes that not only are they not justified by the "work" of circumcision, but that circumcision is not even the sign of the covenant of God itself—for sacraments in their external use are not sacraments—and that contrary to its testimony, insofar as they are covenant-breakers, circumcision actually counts against them. How then did circumcision profit Abraham? Because by faith he truly kept the law.

You ask: "What profit then is circumcision?" I answer: it was not for the purpose of justification by the law, unless the entire law were to be kept,

---

[25]Cajetan, *Epistolae Pauli*, 15r.

[26]Cajetan, *Epistolae Pauli*, 15r-15v; citing Gal 5:3.

which can be done by no one, but rather its purpose was the sealing of the righteousness of faith. "Circumcision is of profit," he says, "if you keep the law." Just as, when God audibly spoke the law which the Jews heard and to which circumcision bound them, he did not promise life except under the condition that they obey the law (which is done by faith), just so in the visible word signifying the same thing he gives the promise under the same condition. And by accepting the sign of the covenant they were binding themselves to that condition. Notes on Romans (1579).[27]

Circumcision's Benefit to Law-Keepers.
Kaspar Olevianus: Objection: surely nobody keeps the law. Why then did Paul say, "Circumcision is profitable if you keep the law?" I answer, because circumcision bound the people that were constituted under the law to observe the whole law by their own strength, which as creatures was right for them to do. Then it is certain that insofar as it was a sign of the pact or covenant of law, Paul rightly said that it would do them no good unless they kept the whole law. And since outside of Christ the law has dominion, whereas these people apart from Christ were trusting in circumcision, Paul rightly sends them back to the law-covenant, to which covenant circumcision was still binding them even now in the age of fuller liberty. Thus reads Galatians 5:3, "I bear witness to every man who is circumcised that he is a debtor to keep the whole law." Also, "those who are under the law are under a curse." But this effect of circumcision, that it would bring someone into the law-covenant, was not its main purpose. Its proper end was to bring Abraham and his seed to faith in the promised Seed, as well as to seal to them their freely given righteousness by faith and renewal of the heart. For that is the true circumcision that happens by faith in the spirit and the mind of a man or woman, as he will explain later, not that which occurs only outwardly in the flesh and by the letter. The latter

binds a person to that very letter or law-covenant, meaning the letters inscribed on tablets of stone, but not written on the heart, a covenant that neither they nor their fathers were able to keep. The praise for such circumcision as this comes only from men and women, since it binds a person to the law, which demands obedience by virtue of one's own human powers, which if someone could manage such obedience they would indeed deserve praise. But the praise for the other kind of circumcision comes from God, for it is the free gift of God, consisting not only of the writing of the law on the heart, but also a freely given righteousness, as he explains in the last verses of this chapter. In summary, Paul deprives the Jews of their legal obedience to the covenant unto which circumcision binds them, as well as any advantage of circumcision itself since that depends upon the keeping of the law, and he leads them away toward the law of faith as he explains in chapter 3. This is the freely given righteousness that is by faith, to which is added the inscription of the law of God on the heart, or that renewal that takes place by the Holy Spirit. Notes on Romans (1579).[28]

How Can the Law Be Kept? Johannes Brenz: To this Paul answers, "Circumcision indeed benefits you, if you keep the law. Because if you are a transgressor of the law." Here is the beginning. Before we proceed to the interpretation, it must be inquired how the law of God can be observed. It is no longer asked how we might attain true and eternal salvation. The answer to that is indeed certain, namely, that we should observe the law. "If you want," says Christ, "to enter into life, keep the commandments." But the question is *how* the law or the commandments of God can be kept. Here, there are numerous varying opinions.

Some indeed think that the whole law is able to be kept by people, and that people are able to love God with their whole heart, and this with their inherent strength. But this contends with the

---

[27]Olevianus, *In Epistolam D. Pauli*, 109-10; citing Col 2:11-14; Phil 3:3.

[28]Olevianus, *In Epistolam D. Pauli*, 113-14; citing Gal 5:3; 3:10; Jer 31:33; Acts 15:10-11.

whole of Scripture, and even with experience itself, just as is demonstrated abundantly elsewhere. Others think that the law is satisfied by external works of the law. But the law does not demand external works only. Rather, it demands perfect holiness and absolute righteousness, as much internal as external. Others think that although they do not fulfill the law, nevertheless, if they sin, they will be able to expiate their sins by the merits of their own rites and good works, so that they may be reckoned fulfillers of the law on account of this satisfaction. But no sacred rites, no works are pleasing to God, unless the worker is reconciled to God. As one of the Gentiles has said, "The impious one should not dare to placate the wrath of the gods with gifts."[†] And with Isaiah, God himself says: "What, to me, is the multitude of your sacrifices?" And then, "Incense is an abomination to me." And again: "When you hold out your hands, I will turn my eyes from you, and when you make many prayers, I will not listen, for your hands are full of blood." Therefore, it is not possible that sinners, while in sin—and for this reason God's enemies—are able to expiate their sins by their own works, in the presence of God.

Therefore, what will we say? By what way, at last, are we able to keep the law of God, so that we may attain salvation? About this way Paul will preach later, saying Israel did not fulfill the law of righteousness, because they did so not by faith, but by works. With these few words he teaches that the law is able to be kept by them, since they have embraced Christ by faith. This, however, is accustomed to happen in this way. In the first place, one must believe in Christ, because he himself will expiate our sins, and will reconcile us to God the Father. Christ is given to us by this faith, together with all his good things. Moreover, among these good things is contained both the fulfillment of the law, and the Holy Spirit. For he himself has fulfilled the law perfectly, and accepted the gifts of the Holy Spirit, so that he may dispense them to those who believe. "He who did not spare his own Son," says Paul, "but handed him over for us all, how will he not, in the same way, give to us all

things?" Therefore, the fulfilling of the law, which has happened through Christ, becomes ours by faith, so that we may even be reckoned, on account of Christ, as fulfillers of the law. Then, after we are reckoned as fulfillers of the law by faith, we are gifted with the Holy Spirit, who leads us away from works of the flesh toward works of righteousness. And even though, while we are still in this flesh, those works are not perfect, nevertheless our obedience pleases God. COMMENTARY ON ROMANS (1564).[29]

THE COVENANT HAS A CONDITION. KASPAR OLEVIANUS: The Jews were drawing this conclusion: "We are not under damnation, nor will we be condemned by God, since we are God's friends and covenant partners. And why are we covenant members? Because of the 'sign of the covenant between me and you.'" Paul answers: "That's true. Circumcision is the seal of the covenant, but of the *whole* covenant, not only half of it. Therefore, you have no grounds to put forward in your defense one part of the covenant only, wherein God had given a promise and confirmed it with a sign; no, you must also include the other part, in which he had given the promise *with a condition*, namely, that you fulfill what you promised him in return: that you would surely 'walk before his face and be blameless.'"

I wish that this were understood—for not even the sign of the covenant can be said to bear fruit if we're ignorant of the covenant—and that we would recognize the mistake the Jews had made and that Christians are making even today. The covenant formula and the institution of the sign that are found in Genesis 17 need to be carefully looked at. "I will be God to you and to your descendants" was said under the condition of the counterpromise: "Walk before me and be perfect," which means, "Be faithful to me and keep my commandments."

Someone might ask: "Why did God wish to bind himself with a covenant?" I answer: it would certainly have been sufficient for him to have

---

[29]Brenz, *In Epistolam*, 64-65; citing Jn 14:15; Is 1:11, 15; Rom 8:32.
[†]Cicero, *On the Laws* 2.

simply promised. But because he is good and aids our weakness, he went so far as to put himself under obligation with an oath and a covenant. NOTES ON ROMANS (1579).[30]

ONE IS MADE A JEW BY SPIRIT AND HEART.

HULDRYCH ZWINGLI: Here is an *anthypophora*.[†] For the Jew might have asked, "If it is the same thing to be circumcised and uncircumcised, for what reason, therefore, did God give to us the law and circumcision, if we differ in no way from the Gentiles?" To this Paul now answers, saying, "To be Jewish and circumcised would be something certainly great, if you kept the law. However, you do not serve the law, for this is impossible for you. Therefore, you have nothing, because you cast aside circumcision if you do not serve that on account of which that circumcision was given. For the one who is circumcised is made a debtor to and observer of the whole law. Moreover, he receives the law by circumcision, which is that by which the Jews regarded themselves as Jews, and by which they used to exalt themselves above others, saying that external circumcision displays something else, namely, the heart's circumcision and purification. Likewise, one is not made a Jew by birth, but by spirit and heart. Truly, the Gentile can have this no less than the Jew. You understand the same with regard to Christians being baptized." Paul makes Jews and Gentiles equal, showing each to be sinners, with nothing by which the Jews excel or are better than the Gentiles. NOTES ON ROMANS (1539).[31]

THE PROPER USE OF SACRAMENTS. KASPAR

OLEVIANUS: Doctrinal conclusions: "What are the sacraments, and what is their proper use?" Against those who improperly define certain things to be sacraments: sacraments are the visible signs of the covenant that take their name[†] from the covenant itself, since they are testimonies of our whole covenant with God. They testify as much of the

will of God toward us—that he wishes to be our God and the God of our offspring under the condition that we walk uprightly before him—as of our faith and obedience toward God. Therefore, the proper use of the sacraments of initiation, as much circumcision as baptism, is that they bind us to repentance and faith, and in return seal to the penitent and believing the free promise of *koinōnias* (communion) with Christ. Consequently, if someone were to scorn the repentance and faith to which he is thereby bound, neither circumcision nor baptism would be of any profit to such a person. For they do not promise anything at all, nor seal anything at all, to the impenitent and unbelieving. NOTES ON ROMANS (1579).[32]

SACRAMENTS EFFECTIVE IF YOU BELIEVE IN

CHRIST. NIELS HEMMINGSEN: Let us seek here a general doctrine concerning our sacraments, in which those who do not keep their law boast of in vain. Baptism indeed has profit, and the sacred Supper also has profit, if you keep the law of baptism, or the law of the Supper, that is, if you believe in Christ, if you are genuinely penitent, and if you render obedience to God on the basis of faith. COMMENTARY ON ROMANS (1562).[33]

RIGHTLY USING ORDINANCES. DIRK PHILIPS:

In the same way circumcision was given to Abraham from God as a sign of his covenant, but afterward through misunderstanding became a Jewish superstition or was not rightly used nor viewed by the pompousness of many, for they sought righteousness thereby, as the prophets complain over it in many places, and the letter to the Romans testifies to it. For circumcision has still remained according to its original institution and was used orderly according to the purpose of God in their children. For that is clearly to be noted that John the Baptist, yes, the child Jesus himself was circumcised on the eighth day

---

[30]Olevianus, *In Epistolam D. Pauli*, 108-9; citing Gen 17:11, 1.
[31]Zwingli, *In Evangelicam Historiam*, 412. [†]Rhetorical term for answering one's own question.
[32]Olevianus, *In Epistolam D. Pauli*, 108-9. [†]The Latin *sacramentum* was rooted in the ancient soldier's oath of allegiance, hence a "sacrament" meant an oath binding one to a covenant.
[33]Hemmingsen, *Commentarius Romanos*, 83.

according to the will of his heavenly Father and according to his ordinance.

Therefore, no one may reject or let fall into disuse any ordinance of God on account of misuse. But one is to deal rightly therewith according to the Lord's command and first formulation, for if circumcision (which was certainly figurative) had remained in its proper use by the God-fearing (as related above) until Christ fulfilled the law, took away the figures and shadows and in their place established the true being, how much more then must the ordinances of the Lord (which are certainly genuine) have their continuance and remain in existence. For no one will come after Jesus Christ with the right to be able to change one tittle in his teaching, in his work and commands. For Jesus Christ (the apostle says) is today and yesterday, and also eternally. Do not let yourself be misled by various and strange teachings.

Out of such reasons baptism and the Lord's Supper were restored to the former divine institution through God's grace, and it is fitting for all repentants and believers to receive it thus, just as John and Christ himself accepted circumcision. ANSWER TO SEBASTIAN FRANCK.[34]

CIRCUMCISION AND THE SACRAMENTS. PETER MARTYR VERMIGLI: It should nevertheless be known that it is proper to conclude from the apostle's words that if the faith and piety of those who receive the sacraments is added to them, then the external things have a certain usefulness. For since they are instituted by God, they must be admitted to be good things, unless it happens that they are made harmful by our own vice. But they are good and useful things to the righteous, those in whom justification by faith has already taken place. But the sacraments, if I might speak of them as a whole, are visible signs that signify—and by which the Holy Spirit exhibits—grace and union with Christ to those who receive them as believers, and which seal to them the promises of salvation. And if we might say something about circumcision,

it was a sign—if I might put it more clearly—of the sealing of the promise and of the covenant with God that is entered into through Christ. It was branded on the organ of generation that Christ might be signified who would be born of human seed by which he became man. Also by that sign they would be perpetually reminded of the covenant entered into with God, and by it they openly confessed their obedience to the law. Hence it says in Galatians that anyone who had been circumcised was "a debtor to keep the whole law." It also played the role of a token by which that people might be distinguished from the other nations. That's why they were not circumcised while they made their way through the desert, for there were no other nations present from whom they needed to be distinguished by such a sign. This is what the commentaries attributed to Jerome. However much this may have been the case, a different reason can more plausibly be assigned. This sacrament signifies the mortification of the flesh and of lusts, indicating that all superfluous things are to be avoided; things are superfluous if they displease God.

For the ancients, this rite stood in the place of baptism, and was regarded as the sacrament of regeneration. From this it is clear that our infants should be baptized, since they have not received something inferior to what the children of the Hebrews received, but rather something that is superior in many respects. For, I would remind you, our baptism is not restricted to the eighth day as the circumcision of the Jews was of old, since we have been set free by Christ from the circumstances of time and place. And sacred rites are, as it were, external professions of piety. It was not only the Jews that had them, but also any who lived piously in their original state of nature. Therefore, the outward symbols of the rites, according to the change of times, were eventually changed, whereas their essential meanings remain the same. Further, it can be concluded from these words of Paul that circumcision is profitable if keeping the law is added. For it is useful to follow regeneration, to have a sign of the covenant and a perpetual

---

[34]CRR 6:456*; citing Gen 17:2, 9-14; Lk 2:27.

reminder of the mortification of the flesh, and to have a seal of the divine promises and of the heavenly gift given to us. COMMENTARY ON ROMANS (1560).[35]

CIRCUMCISION, BAPTISM, AND COVENANT. JUAN DE VALDÉS: I understand the benefit of circumcision to have consisted in the circumcised person defining himself thereby, reminded of the pact and covenant that God had established with Abraham when he promised him the inheritance of the world; and of that which God had established with all the Jewish nation when he promised them temporal happiness through observance of the law. For circumcision was given as a sign in connection with both these promises.

In like manner I understand the benefit of baptism to consist in the baptized person's remembrance that they are, by baptism, reminded of the covenant which God established with men and women through the mediation of Jesus Christ, when he promised them justification and eternal life through faith, by believing in the covenant; for baptism is the sign of the acceptance of the covenant, since none are baptized save those who believe. Now those who receive baptism without possessing the faith with which the covenant is accepted, and being without the Christian habits that are annexed to faith, are like those who received circumcision without having faith in the promise made to Abraham, and who lived disregarding the law, concerning whom St. Paul here states that their circumcision was useless. COMMENTARY ON ROMANS (1556).[36]

2:26-27 Circumcision and Keeping the Law

UNCIRCUMCISION TO CIRCUMCISION. THEODORE BEZA: In this earlier passage, "foreskin" [praeputium] is used for "uncircumcised" [praeputiatus], that is, for uncircumcision itself, using

metonymy.[†] . . . However, in the following passage, it is used not for uncircumcision itself, but for its condition and situation, that is, for "Gentilism." Thus, I will say that as in the short verse above, when he said that circumcision changed into uncircumcision, Paul meant that Judaism is changed into Gentilism. For certainly, he did not use either word to refer simply to "skin." MAJOR ANNOTATIONS (1594).[37]

BAPTISM IS NECESSARY. JOHANNES BRENZ: Surely we will not infer in a similar way, that if those who have not been baptized should observe the law, then they would be regarded the same as if they were baptized? Certainly this follows unavoidably from the words of Paul. But meanwhile, it ought to be observed that in Mosaic polity, before the coming of Christ in the flesh, circumcision was included among the commands of the divine decrees, and therefore, in its time, had to be observed. Nor was anyone in the family of Abraham who used to observe the law able to keep the law unless they had been circumcised, if in any way it was possible. In the same way, baptism is understood as part of the list of divine decrees in Christianity. And so, however many observe the law, as far as they are able to, they must be baptized. Baptism is necessary, except when some catechumen may be dragged off to death by a tyrant, on account of a confession of Christ before he is able to be baptized. So then his confession is reckoned instead of baptism. COMMENTARY ON ROMANS (1588).[38]

GOD SETS ON OUR SCORE CHRIST'S RIGHTEOUSNESS. GEORGE WALKER: Now all laid together, the meaning of the apostle in these words is this: that if an uncircumcised man keeps all the commandments and performs the righteousness of the law, his state of "Gentilism" comprehending in it the righteousness of the law shall be counted and

---

[35] Vermigli, *In Epistolam S. Pauli* 141-43; citing Gal 5:3.
[36] Valdés, *Commentary upon St. Paul's Epistle*, 30*.
[37] Beza, *Annotationes Majores*, 29. [†] Rhetorical device that substitutes an associated item for the original term.
[38] Brenz, *In Epistolam*, 524.

accepted for the state of a holy and righteous man circumcised in heart. And he, though uncircumcised in flesh and a Gentile in his outward estate, will be counted by God as a true Israelite without guile, truly circumcised with inward spiritual circumcision of the heart in the spirit, whose praise is not of humans but of God. This sense and meaning of the words and of this phrase is so clear and manifest and so perfectly agreeable to all true reason, that people cannot deny it, unless they set themselves to rebel against the light. And this phrase being one that this apostle uses again where he mentions counting and imputing faith and belief as righteousness to Abraham and to every true believer, provides light for discovering the true sense and meaning of the words, the phrase being exactly the same. As a result of which, if we will follow the apostle himself and tread after him in the same steps (since he is the surest guide and best expounder of his own words and meaning), we must by "Abraham's believing," by a metalepsis[†] or double trope—along with our learned ministers—understand Abraham to be standing in the state of a true believer. He is united by one spirit to God or Christ and has the communion of Christ's satisfaction and righteousness, which were in force from the beginning to save and justify, and to make God the reward of the believer. And by "faith imputed or counted for righteousness," we must not understand faith in a proper [narrow/literal] sense, but by a double trope, for the state and condition of a true, faithful person, and for that which faith comprehends and includes in it, even the perfect righteousness and full satisfaction of Christ, God and human. By "righteousness" we must understand the state of a justified person, or evangelical righteousness communicated to the justified person and made his for justification. And by "counting and imputing" we must understand the accepting, approving, esteeming, and judging of Abraham, and every true believer as soon as he appears faithful, to be in a justified state, with God's setting on his score, and counting, and imputing to his being faithful, the righteousness of Christ apprehended by faith. This faith is indeed

and in truth made his by spiritual union and communion with Christ.

Here then is the true paraphrase of the apostle's words showing the true sense and meaning of them: Abraham, upon a true inward spiritual sense of his union and communion with Christ, believed and was surely persuaded that God was his reward, and this his belief and faith comprehending Christ for righteousness, and containing in it after a sort the righteousness of Christ, God counted it to him for righteousness. That is, he set it on his score, and reckoned it to him for justification, and judged, esteemed, and accepted him as a truly righteous man, as indeed he was. And so, whoever does not rest on his own works for justification nor seek to be justified by them, but by faith seeks that righteousness that makes him righteous by the communion of it, when in himself by nature he is ungodly, his faith comprehending in it Christ and his righteousness, is counted for righteousness, because it settles him in the state of a righteous person; and God's setting on his score Christ's satisfaction and righteousness accepts him for a justified person. A DEFENSE OF THE TRUE SENSE AND MEANING OF THE WORDS OF THE HOLY APOSTLE (1641).[39]

2:28-29 *True Circumcision*

CIRCUMCISED IN FLESH ALONE IS UNCIRCUMCISED. GEORGE WITHER: Song 48—For the Feast of Circumcision

1.

This day your flesh, oh Christ, did bleed,
Marked by the circumcision knife;
Because the law, for man's misdeed,
Required that earnest of your life:
Those drops divined that shower of blood,
Which in your agony began:

---

[39]Walker, *Defense of the True Sense*, 14-15*; citing Rom 4:3. Arguing against Socinus and Arminius and the Arminian John Goodwin. [†]Metalepsis is a figure of speech in which another figure of speech is alluded to. It adds layers of symbolism and poetic expression.

And that great shower foreshowed the flood,
Which from your side the next day ran.

2.

Then, through that milder sacrament,
Succeeding this, your grace inspire;
Yes, let your pain make us repent,
And circumcised hearts desire.
For he that either is baptized,
Or circumcised in flesh alone,
Is but as an uncircumcised,
Or as an unbaptized one.

3.

The year anew we now begin,
And outward gifts received have we;
Renew us also, Lord, within,
And make us new year's gifts for thee:
Yes, let us, with the passed year,
Our old affections cast away;
That we new creatures may appear,
And to redeem the time essay.

HYMNS AND SONGS OF THE CHURCH (1625)[40]

TRUE SIGNS OF THE COVENANT. DIRK
PHILIPS: In the same manner, God gave Noah
the rainbow and Abraham circumcision, as signs
of his covenant, and both of these signs image
Jesus Christ for us, who is a sign of our peace in
heaven, at his Father's right hand, and his
circumcision is the true circumcision that occurs
without hands, with the stone knife of the divine
Word on the foreskin of the heart, through the
laying aside of the sinful flesh, that is, all wicked
lusts, desires, and works that come out of the
flesh. Therefore, Paul says that he is not a Jew
who is a Jew externally. Also that is no circumcision which occurs externally in the flesh, but
that one is a Jew who is hidden internally, and
that is circumcision, the circumcision of the
heart that happens in the spirit and does not
happen in the letter, whose praise is not out of
people but out of God.

In the same manner, almighty God has
instituted, given, and left to us baptism and the
Lord's Supper so that we thereby and through
them would be admonished of the divine covenant
and our debt which we once again owe to God.
THREE ADMONITIONS.[41]

**THE MERELY APPARENT VERSUS THE TRUE
CHURCH.** DAVID PAREUS: Therefore, those who
are merely publicly bathed are not true Christians;
rather it is those who with their baptism render
faith and obedience toward God. Nor is that a
true church which appears to be such only
outwardly to the eyes of men and women, but
rather that which is inwardly bathed by the blood
and the Spirit of Christ and appears such in the
eyes of God. "For the Lord knows those" among
the mixed, gathered church *who are his*, and those
who are not. This text is the foundation for the
distinction between the visible and the invisible
church, which has been handed down by our
theologians and which the Sophists[†] keep criticizing. For the distinction between merely apparent
and true members of the church is rightly applied
to the merely apparent and the true church.
COMMENTARY ON ROMANS (1608).[42]

THE IMPORTANCE OF THE INTERNAL. JO-
HANNES BRENZ: It is not the one who is publicly
a Christian who is a true Christian, but the one
who is a Christian in the secret place. Each person
individually should make certain of their own
faith and, without any doubting, believe that they
are accepted by God because of Jesus Christ, and
judge their neighbor with that charity that "hopes
all things and believes all things," as Paul says, and
not rashly condemn anybody. But it must be
known that true and perfect piety is perfected not
by works, ceremonies, virtues, nor even by
miracles, for all these are public and are (as Paul
puts it) *gramma*, that is, "letters." Someone might

---

[40]Wither, *Hymns and Songs*, 184-85*.

[41]CRR 6:419*; citing Gen 9:12-13; 17:9-14; Eph 2:13-14; Col 2:11.
[42]Pareus, *In Divinam ad Romanos*, 216; citing 2 Tim 2:19. [†]The
medieval scholastic theologians.

ask: "But isn't it especially needful to leave all things and follow after Christ, as Peter and the other apostles did?" Ah, but it can happen that this can be done with a soul that is greedy, or ambitious, or addicted to some other carnal desire, and done in order to seek from Christ not true and spiritual goods, but only bodily goods. COMMENTARY ON ROMANS (1564).[43]

OUTWARD AND INWARD CIRCUMCISION.
DAVID PAREUS: Where ceremonies are received by the outward senses, grace is received by the inward spirit. The apostle said that one kind of circumcision is done in the flesh, but another in the spirit—not that there are two circumcisions but because when the sacrament is rightly administered, both of these things are as a whole signified by the name of the outward act.

Further, a ceremony accompanied by grace is beneficial because it produces the effect of the sacrament by signifying the benefits of the gospel and by strengthening believers. Apart from grace, however, nothing is beneficial—the ceremony becomes useless. As it is said, "Circumcision profits if you keep the law, but if you do not, it becomes uncircumcision." Hence two conclusions logically follow: (1) the grace of a sacrament is not tied to the outward sign, and (2) unbelievers receive the sacraments without the inward reality[†] of the sacrament. COMMENTARY ON ROMANS (1608).[44]

GRAMMA AS THE BARE LAW. THEODORE BEZA: Paul is in the habit of opposing the words "letter" and "spirit" to signify something particular. For first of all, because the law that is called Moses' was not only engraved on tablets by the finger of God himself—as the Scripture says—and holds the Decalogue, but also because, by the command of God himself, it was handed down by Moses as written monuments. That is the best reason why

that law would be called *gramma*[†] by *antonomasia*,[‡] because you would have more rightly translated it "written document" than "letter." Nevertheless, we preferred that it be interpreted as "letter." But Paul saw something greater. For since the law is not only ceremonial but also moral—what they call the Decalogue—it is used to lead to Christ, who for us in every way has become righteousness. Of this use of the law, however, the Jews were partly ignorant and partly rejecting. From here it happened that Paul spoke of the law in two ways: first, according to the hypothesis of the Jews, who used to apply to themselves the law separate from Christ; and second, according to its proper use and the will of the Lawgiver. Thus Paul contrived words suitable to the distinction between the two ways. And so it is customary to call the bare law separated from Christ the *gramma*, as if it were some dead writing, which profits nothing for salvation for the sin of our flesh. Because, namely, as long as it is able to reveal a vice lying hidden in our heart, it is not likewise possible to truly consecrate it. Moreover, because that law, considered outside the Spirit of Christ, stirs up sin in us so that it becomes greater and gives us to death. MAJOR ANNOTATIONS (1594).[45]

ON "LETTER" AND "SPIRIT." CASPAR CRUCIGER: Origen distinguished them in this way: the "letter" refers to ceremonies, whereas the "spirit" refers to allegorical interpretations, nor is it to be understood as a reference to the Holy Spirit or the lively motions of the Holy Spirit. We, however, know that for Paul "the letter" includes all actions, both moral and ceremonial, all noble thoughts and intentions or determinations conceived of apart from the Holy Spirit, that is to say, outside of the gospel, apart from the true fear of God and apart from true faith kindled by the Holy Spirit. For those deliberations of reason apart from the Holy Spirit that are here called "the letter" are like a mere

---

[43]Brenz, *In Epistola*, 66-67; citing 1 Cor 13:7.

[44]Pareus, *In Divinam ad Romanos*, 217-18. [†]*Re sacramenti. Re* refers to the grace or heavenly reality that a sacrament signifies and makes present, as opposed to *sacramenti*, which refers to the outward form or ceremony.

[45]Beza, *Annotationes Majores*, 30. [†]Greek for something written or drawn. [‡]Rhetorical device that substitutes a proper name for a general concept, or a title or epithet for a proper name.

painting by the hand of reason; they are not the life and motions of the divine within the will and heart. They are most certainly not God moving the heart so that it comes alive and is fired up with spiritual motions within it. Similarly, the kind of virtue that Alexander the Great displayed when he left Darius's daughters untouched† is far too small—like a painting smeared by reason—and able to govern only one's outer movements. That kind of virtue is certainly not the life of the heart and living motion that looks toward God. Whereas "the spirit" signifies the Holy Spirit, or that burning motion, light, life, and joy that spring from the Holy Spirit as it is said in John 3, "that which is born of the Spirit is spirit," and in 2 Corinthians 3, "we with unveiled face beholding the glory of the Lord are transformed into that same image as by the Spirit of the Lord." That is, when in true terrors and a realization of God's wrath we acknowledge the Son and are raised up by faith, our hearts are made alive by the Son and the Holy Spirit so that, being irradiated by a new light they firmly believe in God and feel a new joy in God and new motions within. He said that when we behold the glory or the brightness or the light of Christ, by his promise of bestowing reconciliation, we are transformed by that same light, that is, by him illuminating and consoling us in the light or brightness, that is, in radiant knowledge and life and joy like that which is in himself, and this happens, he says, through the Holy Spirit.

These things are understood and believed for genuine consolation when in conversion we are raised up by the preaching of the gospel, whereupon we learn the difference between the "letter" and the "Spirit." Saul heard such consolations in vain, for to him they were only letters, that is, pictures and momentary thoughts. But when David was pulled back from the pains of hell by this consolation, the Lord took away his sin and he was made alive by the power of the Son of God, and in the contemplation of this consolation he received the Holy Spirit so that he experienced new light and joy in God. Thus the words of Psalm 51 are understood: "Create in me a clean heart, O

God, and renew a right spirit in my inward parts." The "clean heart" is one purified by faith, which receives remission of sins and reconciliation, and "a right spirit" is a firm one that does not doubt God's promise. In the verse "Do not cast me away from your presence, and do not take away your Holy Spirit from me," the "Holy Spirit" is the One sanctifying or producing new motions within that please God, such as the fear of God, trust, hope, love, and other motions that are congruent with the Holy Spirit. "Restore to me the joy of your salvation and strengthen me with a willing spirit," that is, "being strengthened by your Holy Spirit may I not fail in difficulty, so that I retain my faith, calling and inheritance of eternal life and am not shattered in my soul, suffering the cruelty of devils and people." COMMENTARY ON ROMANS (1567).[46]

OUTWARD AND INWARD BAPTISM. DAVID PAREUS: There are two things that happen in baptism: an outward washing with water, which is the "sacrament," and inner washing with the blood and Spirit of Christ, which is the "grace of the sacrament." There is, therefore, a baptism of water and a baptism of the Spirit—not that there are two baptisms, but these two aspects of one and the same baptism both receive the name of "baptism" in the church's language. When rightly administered, when believers are baptized both of these things occur together, and all such who are baptized are engrafted into Christ, as it is said, "whoever will believe and be baptized will be saved," and "for as many of you as have been baptized into Christ have put on Christ." In the event that they are denied the ceremony, still the faithful are washed by the Spirit. But no regeneration or salvation is conferred on unbelievers through baptism, for it is said that "whoever will not believe will be condemned." Baptism of water is received outwardly by the body; baptism of the Spirit is received inwardly by faith. Further, baptism of

---

[46]Cruciger, *In Epistolam Pauli*, 23-25; citing Jn 3:6; 2 Cor 3:18; Ps 51:10, 11, 12. †After Alexander defeated Darius III in battle, he made sure that Darius's two unmarried daughters were protected and treated respectfully. See Plutarch's *Life of Alexander*.

water brings much benefit if it is accompanied by baptism of the Spirit. For "as many as are baptized into Christ, put on Christ." But without the Spirit the ceremony is useless, for even Simon the magician was said to have been baptized: "You have no part in this matter, for your heart is not upright." Two conclusions logically follow: (1) the grace of regeneration is not tied to the ceremony, and therefore not all who are dipped in water are regenerated, nor are all those not dipped in water deprived of the regeneration of the Spirit; (2) unbelievers and hypocrites washed outwardly in baptism are not regenerated inwardly. COMMENTARY ON ROMANS (1608).[47]

BAPTISM OF THE HEART IS TRUE BAPTISM.
NIELS HEMMINGSEN: The one who is merely outwardly a Christian is not a Christian. Nor is that baptism that is merely outward a baptism. But the one is a Christian who is inwardly a Christian. And baptism of the heart, by which consciences are cleansed from all dead works, is true baptism. This in no way takes away from the worth of the sacraments, nor of the Old or New Testament, as will be explained more copiously in the fourth chapter. COMMENTARY ON ROMANS (1562).[48]

OUTWARD AND INWARD EATING OF THE HOLY SUPPER. DAVID PAREUS: There are two things that happen in the Holy Supper: (1) an outward partaking of bread and wine, and (2) an inward communion with the body and blood of Christ. There is a twofold eating, one of the outward symbols, the other of the inward realities—not that there are two sacraments, but rather two aspects of but one sacrament. Both are partaken of together by believers, who alone eat and drink worthily. In the event that they are denied the Supper, the faithful are not deprived of communion with Christ, but this principle applies: "Believe, and you have already eaten."[†] But apart

from its right reception (that is, without faith and repentance) the sacrament is partaken of without the inner reality, although they do receive the guilt of having profaned the body and blood of Christ, as it is said, "Whoever eats of this bread unworthily is guilty of the Lord's body." The partaking of bread and wine occurs in the mouth; the enjoyment of the body and blood, however, happens by faith. When combined together it becomes very profitable, for "whoever eats and drinks the flesh and blood of the Son of God has eternal life." But no benefit is received by a merely outward reception without its inward reality. Two conclusions follow from this: (1) that outward and inward eating do not so cling together that all who eat outwardly also eat inwardly, otherwise all who are deprived of communion in the sacrament would be deprived of communion with Christ; (2) unbelievers receive symbols in their reception of the Eucharist, but do not feed on the body and blood of Christ nor do they receive any of the benefits of the gospel, as Cyprian said, "Did they not die as a result of their receiving it?" The following argument in favor of unbelievers is therefore frivolous:

(P1) In the Supper the body and blood of Christ is received.

(P2) Unbelievers receive the Supper.

(C) Therefore, they also receive the body of Christ.

The major premise (P1), however, assumes a *right* reception of the Supper, which requires faith. Otherwise it is false, such as when the Supper is partaken of by unbelievers or by hypocrites. To them their "supper" is not the Supper but only a ceremony that earns them judgment, just as circumcision for the impenitent was not circumcision but uncircumcision. Therefore, contrary to this we must reason:

(P1) Apart from the Supper the body of Christ is not eaten in the mouth.

(P2) The "supper" is not the Supper for unbelievers.

---

[47]Pareus, *In Divinam ad Romanos*, 218; citing Gal 3:27; Mk 16:16; Gal 3:27; Acts 8:21.

[48]Hemmingsen, *Commentarius in Epistolam* 86; citing Heb 9:14; see Hemmingsen on the sacraments, in Rom 4:11 below.

(C) Therefore, unbelievers do not eat the body of Christ in the mouth, and much less do they do so by faith.

COMMENTARY ON ROMANS (1608).[49]

CIRCUMCISION OF THE HEART. ALEXANDER ALESIUS: Paul answers and proposes a single sacrament for all. Circumcision is advantageous, if you observe the law, if you accept not only a sacred rite in the flesh, but the thing signified by means of the ceremony. That is the circumcision of the heart, the forgiveness of sins, and the gift of the Holy Spirit. He renews the heart and uncovers the eyes of the mind in order that not only the letter of the law and its outward instruction is considered. But it is understood that a perfect and spiritual obedience of the heart is also required, for which work the Spirit of Christ is given. He is received by faith, which Christ alone has perfectly brought about, for he satisfied the law on behalf of those who believe. DISPUTATIONS ON ROMANS (1553).[50]

HEART CIRCUMCISION REQUIRES HELP FROM ABOVE. MARTIN LUTHER: Somebody may object and say that this circumcision of the heart is brought about only by grace, for our nature, as I said above, inclines toward evil, is impotent to do good, abhors rather than loves the law, which drives toward the good and prohibits from the evil, and so by itself it has no desire for the law but only displeasure. And thus our nature, unless helped from above, remains captive to evil lusts opposed to the law and is full of evil desires, no matter how much it may produce works when it is prompted externally by fear of punishment or drawn by the love of secular things. . . . The whole task of the apostle and of his Lord is to humiliate the proud and to bring them to a realization of this condition,

to teach them that they need grace, to destroy their own righteousness so that in humility they will seek Christ and confess that they are sinners and thus receive grace and be saved. LECTURES ON ROMANS (1516).[51]

CIRCUMCISION OF THE HEART COMES ONLY THROUGH FAITH. PILGRAM MARPECK: Now, however, in the revealed kingdom of our Lord Jesus, there is no longer any "you must." Rather, those who will, let them come and be baptized in the name of Jesus Christ, and find remission and forgiveness of sin; he who is outwardly circumcised is no Jew, and never shall be one. And such circumcision shall no longer be valid. The only true circumcision shall be that of the heart. This circumcision can only occur when man recognizes it himself through his faith in Christ. Only through such faith can the hearts become circumcised. As Paul says, you are circumcised without hands; through the laying aside of the body of sin, you are buried with him through baptism.

Here it is clear to whom Paul is referring. He refers not to the circumcision of young children, which was practiced among the ancients. Rather, he refers to the true circumcision of the heart, performed without hands. If infant baptism, then, constitutes a parallel to the circumcision performed with hands, which Paul rejects here, one would baptize, but without the Spirit, only the flesh of children. How, then, can such a baptism be done according to Paul's word? He draws a parallel between baptism and the circumcision without hands. Baptism without circumcision takes place through a recognized, unconcealed confession of faith in Christ. Baptism is based on the faith, and not on external circumcision performed on the unknowing flesh; children cannot lay aside the body of sin nor can they be questioned as to whether their heart is circumcised through the faith in Christ. THE ADMONITION OF 1542.[52]

---

[49]Pareus, *In Divinam ad Romanos*, 218-220; citing 1 Cor 11:27; Jn 6:54. †See Augustine, *Tractates on the Gospel of John* 25.12, and, for example, Sarum Rite of extreme unction.
[50]Alesius, *Omnes Disputationes*, H5vii; citing Rom 8:32; 2 Cor 2:5-6; 2 Cor 3:1-18.

[51]LW 25:191*.
[52]CRR 2:238-39*.

SPIRITUAL CHILDREN OF ABRAHAM. DIRK PHILIPS: The third reason is that only the boys were circumcised in Israel, but the girls without circumcision and external signs, nevertheless, were God's children in his covenant as well as the boys. From this it is clearly to be understood that circumcision is nowhere a figure of baptism and has no similarity with it, otherwise boys alone would have to be baptized. But now baptism is given to girls as well as boys without distinction of persons. What similarity then has the practice of circumcision with the practice of Christian baptism? That boys only were circumcised in Israel is, according to our understanding, a figure of the spiritual children of Abraham, the Israel of God, those who are circumcised in the heart, have a strong nature, character, and the power of faith. THE BAPTISM OF OUR LORD JESUS CHRIST.[53]

WHOSE PRAISE IS NOT OF MAN OR WOMAN. WOLFGANG MUSCULUS: "Whose praise is not from men or women." This is not expounded in the same way. Ambrose understood him to say "whose circumcision not by men but by God is praised," adducing that Abraham did not please God by his circumcision in the flesh but rather by the circumcision of his mind by faith. But Augustine, whose reading I prefer, understands him to say "whose praise, that is, whose worthiness or that which is praiseworthy in it in that it merits praise, is not from men but from God"; that is, he does not have this from men or women but from God, whose Spirit, without the help of man or woman, brings about this circumcision in the heart. According to this reading, the apostle is not here speaking of who it is that would praise circumcision of the heart so that he might deny that it is praised by men and women, for that does not serve his present purpose. Rather, he is declaring that the praise for our inner circumcision comes from God alone, that is, that it is the work of God alone without any human works being adjoined to it, so that in this way he might elevate the Gentile who is circumcised in his heart above him who glories in the circumcision of his flesh, and in order to reject that praise and glory which the Jewish circumcisers were always seeking for themselves among the Gentiles, among whom also they were trying to introduce the circumcision of the flesh. See the last chapter of Galatians: "Not even they keep the law" who wish you to be circumcised, "but they desire you to be circumcised that they might glory in your flesh." COMMENTARY ON ROMANS (1555).[54]

---

[53]CRR 6:105; citing Eph 4:2-3; Gal 6:15; Col 2:11.

[54]Musculus, *In Epistolam Apostoli Pauli*, 61; citing Gal 6:13.

3:1-8 OUR UNRIGHTEOUSNESS REVEALS GOD'S RIGHTEOUSNESS

Then what advantage has the Jew? Or what is the value of circumcision? ²*Much in every way. To begin with, the Jews were entrusted with the oracles of God.* ³*What if some were unfaithful? Does their faithlessness nullify the faithfulness of God?* ⁴*By no means! Let God be true though every one were a liar, as it is written,*

"That you may be justified in your words,
and prevail when you are judged."

⁵*But if our unrighteousness serves to show the righteousness of God, what shall we say? That God is unrighteous to inflict wrath on us? (I speak in a human way.)* ⁶*By no means! For then how could God judge the world?* ⁷*But if through my lie God's truth abounds to his glory, why am I still being condemned as a sinner?* ⁸*And why not do evil that good may come?—as some people slanderously charge us with saying. Their condemnation is just.*

Overview: Paul asks whether there are advantages to being a Jew or to circumcision. Yes, he says, for the revelation of God was given to the Jews, as well as circumcision, which confirmed their covenant with him. The reformers argue that both circumcision and baptism have value, even though salvation does not come through them but through Christ. In the medieval sacramental system, baptism, as one of seven sacraments, had been seen as essential to salvation. In shifting to faith in Christ, rather than the sacraments, as the instrumental cause of justification, the reformers do not intend to negate the importance of baptism to the Christian life. Although they agree with each other on its value, as they discuss baptism, the differences between the magisterial and Radical reformers are displayed. The former argue for infant baptism. The latter allude to the persecution they have endured for their views against it.

In keeping with their emphasis on God's righteousness (*iustitia Dei*), the interpreters state that God is faithful and true even when we are faithless liars; therefore we should trust in God's righteousness rather than our own. His promises stand on his character, not our own worthiness.

The commentators explain that Paul is responding to accusations from others who claim that he is saying that God does not have a right to punish sinners, since their lying makes his truthfulness shine more brightly and their faithlessness casts his faithfulness into flattering relief, and all of it gives him the opportunity to display his great mercy. These accusations are absurd; the ends do not justify the means.

The commentators accuse some of their Catholic contemporaries of defending evils under the pretext of doing good. They point out three such examples from medieval church life. First, in many places, the priests allowed the laity to receive Communion only in one kind (the host rather than the chalice) in order to prevent them spilling the wine—given the medieval Catholic belief in transubstantiation and the real presence, the possibility of Christ's blood being spilled on the floor, without hope of being reclaimed, brought fears of sacrilege. The reformers, not believing in transubstantiation, advocated that the laity should receive both the bread and the wine. Second, medieval confessors required the people to pray in Latin since they had forbidden the Scriptures to them, saying all that was needed was a praiseworthy intention on the part of the laity. With rare exceptions, the medieval Scriptures were in Latin (the Latin Vulgate, in particular), and most laity could not read them. The reformers, on the other hand, believed that the Scriptures and worship practices should be made accessible to the laity in their own language. Third, the Catholic authorities accused the reformers of encouraging lax lives by preaching justification by faith alone. The reformers were concerned that the medieval church's emphasis on purgatory, the seven deadly sins, the seven works of mercy, the sacrament of penance, and annual confession were what were driving people to change their behavior. In response, the reformers argue that *sola fide* should not lead to loose living. They preach that justification is possible only when faith is accompanied by continual good works. They exhort believers not only not to do evil in order to display God's mercy and forgiveness, but to do good, since God has prescribed obedience to him as a way that we can glorify him.

3:1 *The Value of Circumcision*

God Honors the Jews First. Jacques Lefèvre d'Étaples: You speak the truth. But if the true circumcision is "that which is of the heart and in the Spirit" and not that which is of the flesh and "in the letter," then what advantage do the Jewish people have over other nations? And "what is the usefulness of circumcision" according to the flesh above that of uncircumcision? Paul raises this question and then answers it when he says, "What advantage has the Jew? Or what is the usefulness of circumcision? Much in every way. First and foremost in that it was to them that the oracles of God were entrusted." Most certainly God did a great thing to the Jewish people when he handed over to them his oracles and his ritual of worship and the ceremonies and precepts of life, as the prophet testifies saying, "He has not done anything like this with all the other nations, nor to them has he revealed his judgments." Most assuredly so, for he gave them circumcision, the sign of faith and belief, but to the rest of the nations he had not as of then given any sign of faith. And later, the sacred gospel shed the light of God's Word on the Jews first and only then to the Gentiles, when it gave baptism to all as a sign of faith. Accordingly, God has always honored the Jews above all others. Commentary on Romans.[1]

The Jews Do and Do Not Excel Gentiles. Heinrich Bullinger: Paul answers certain objections with somewhat of a digression. He immediately returns to the regular path and proves that all men and women are sinners. He seems to have opened himself up to these objections by treating the Gentiles as nearly equal to Jews. The Jews would then be able to say, "If it is of no value to be Jewish men, and if there is no glory in circumcision, and if moreover we are constituted sinners by the law, for what purpose were we obliged to be circumcised and by means of circumcision separated from other nations, if we do not thereby excel them even in the slightest way?" The apostle answers, "We do excel them, and we do not excel them. For if we look at the native inclination of the soul of either group, we are all sinners (on which he will say more later). But if we pay attention to certain externals and to the divine service, the Jews have excelled the Gentiles for a very long time." For the prophet said in the 147th Psalm: "He declared his word to Jacob, his statutes and his judgments to Israel. He did not do this for any other nation, and they did not know his judgments" (concerning which see Romans 9). For to them belonged the establishment of the law, the divine worship, and the promises. And by the term *logia* (oracles), he means the promises in general. Commentary on Romans (1533).[2]

Overcoming Objections. Johannes Piscator: First we have an objection, which is also twofold, arising from the last part of the previous chapter. This objection can be formulated with the following syllogisms, in this manner:

(P1) If the Jews did not excel the Gentiles on account of their circumcision, they excelled them in nothing.

---

[1]Lefèvre, *Epistole divi Pauli*, 58v; citing Rom 2:29; Ps 147:20.
[2]Bullinger, *In Sanctissimam Pauli*, 46r-46v; citing Ps 147:19-20; Rom 9:1-33.

(P2) But they excelled them in some way.

(C) Therefore, they excelled them on account of their circumcision.

The second objection is this:

(P1) If circumcision does not render the Jews more acceptable to God than the Gentiles, circumcision is of no usefulness at all.

(P2) But circumcision does have some usefulness.

(C) Therefore, circumcision renders Jews more acceptable to God than the Gentiles.

The apostle responds to the first objection by proving the contrary proposition and thus implicitly denying the proposition made by the objection. He proves that the Jews excel the Gentiles even if they do not excel them by means of their circumcision, since the tables of the covenant were entrusted to them by God, which were most certainly useful for confirming them in their faith. Against the second objection concerning the usefulness of circumcision, he does not give an answer right here, but will deal with this question later in verse 11 of the next chapter. From that explanation it will be evident that the proposition set forth in the second syllogism is false, since even if circumcision did not itself commend the Jews to God over and above the Gentiles, nevertheless it was useful to them for confirming them in the faith as a sign of the covenant. LOGICAL ANALYSIS OF ROMANS (1589).[3]

PRAISING WHAT HE CAN. MARTIN BUCER: "In what way does the Jew excel?" Let us learn from this that mild patience with which we are to take away from people the things they falsely put their trust in, and that moderation with which we are to lead them to an acknowledgment of their sins. It is in this way that false trust in good things is to be cast off; it is in this way that people are to be convicted of their depravity, when you clearly carry before you how much you value whatever in them

is good, and that you will not condemn them in any matter unless it cannot be defended in any sense. The Jews were trusting in ceremonies, a thing that by God's institution is assuredly most salutary for those who make use of them in faith. Their life, however, was riddled with vice, despite the fact that they were endowed by God with holy things more than all the other nations. Therefore, since there was one particular thing that needed to be corrected because it was a sin, as a master of this art—even though he wished to violently throw down their vain hope in these sacred ceremonies that were not at all agreeable to them inwardly—Paul nevertheless loudly praised them because they were exceedingly great in and of themselves on account of their being a gift from God. It is in this way that he was resolved to reproach their vices, so that if there was anything that in any way could be considered worthy of praise he would most gladly render it. For anyone who would undertake to profitably admonish men and women and reprove them in a way that reaches their soul, it is first necessary that he not omit anything by which he might show himself to be as eager as possible to be equitable and sincere, as well as being the greatest possible lover of men and women. COMMENTARY ON ROMANS (1536).[4]

CIRCUMCISION AND BAPTISM IMPORTANT, BUT NOT SALVIFIC. DIRK PHILIPS: We are neither weakened, nor made to err [by the fact] that some (who, after the nature of spiders, turn good into evil, yes, honey into poison) mock us and ask what baptism benefits us, and why we suffer persecution since we ourselves confess that salvation is not bound to the external sign. Likewise, they say also that faith and love can break or alter all external ordinances and institutions of the Lord, such as baptism, the Lord's Supper, and whatever more there is. They argue that just as Moses discontinued circumcision in the wilderness, so Christians may also discontinue these practices and deal with them according to their own discretion.

---

[3]Piscator, *Analysis Logica*, 15.

[4]Bucer, *Metaphrases et Enarrationes*, 164-65; citing Rom 4:11.

Although we do not take such sharp-witted objections and questions seriously and have already answered them sufficiently, we will nevertheless give a further response as follows: First, that just as in the Old Testament salvation rested primarily in the grace of God and not in circumcision, nevertheless, circumcision as an ordinance of God was profitable to those who observed the law, so now in the New Testament, salvation rests primarily on the mercy and grace of God, the heavenly Father, and in the merits of Jesus Christ. However, baptism is nevertheless (as an ordinance of the Lord Jesus Christ) profitable and beneficial to all who believe the gospel and are obedient to it. THE BAPTISM OF OUR LORD JESUS CHRIST.[5]

3:2 *The Oracles of God*

DISSEMINATING THE TREASURE OF THE ORACLES. PETER MARTYR VERMIGLI: Now as for the words he wrote in the previous verse, the apostle did not intend by the word "first" to commence a series, as if he wished to list the many other benefits of God shown to the Jews, but gives only something of an introduction to such a list. Or by "first" he perhaps means that the oracles of God are the highest and chiefest of those things that were granted to them. Indeed, the oracles of God were as it were an immensely rich treasure that had for a long time been hidden away among the Hebrews and not shared with the Gentiles until the times of the apostles. For the apostles had the task of disseminating that treasure among the Gentiles. It is true that Ptolemy II Philadelphus wished to translate the laws of the Hebrews into the Greek language by the seventy translators,[†] but he was not acknowledging thereby that the oracles then being translated pertained also to the Gentiles. The apostles alone began to disclose to the whole world that the promises concerning Christ and eternal salvation belonged to the Gentiles also. COMMENTARY ON ROMANS.[6]

CIRCUMCISION'S GREATEST VALUE. MARTIN LUTHER: Its greatest value is that "the oracles of God were believed"; that is, circumcision was useful to this end, that in it the promises of God were believed and thus their fulfillment was awaited, and in this the Jews had an advantage over the Gentiles, to whom God promised nothing but in pure mercy in the fullness of time he deigned to make them equal with the Jews. However, to the Jews he was not only merciful but also truthful, for he demonstrated that mercy which he had promised. Thus these two concepts are frequently joined together in Scripture: mercy and truthfulness. LECTURES ON ROMANS.[7]

THE CHIEF PURPOSE OF THE JEWISH STATE. PHILIPP MELANCHTHON: Therefore this passage is already teaching about the chief purpose of the Jewish state. The unlearned imagine that these laws were given in order that the people might be justified through them, but Paul takes away the glory of justification from the law, and shows that the purpose was political. For it was necessary that there should be a certain people in which the promises about Christ should be revealed by sure and clear testimonies of God. Therefore God separated this people from the Gentiles, and bore witness with many evident miracles that they had the Word of God. The cultus and the entire setup of the state were external things ordained chiefly for this political purpose, that they should distinguish this people from the other nations. Meanwhile miracles, laws given out, and other things were testimonies that God had given his Word to this people. The acts of worship themselves had been ordained by God in order to remind people that the Word of God and indeed the promise of Christ was among this people. And the just had exercises of faith, likewise they admonished others, and so on. Therefore this passage of Paul usefully teaches

---

[5]CRR 6:107*; citing Rom 3:24; 5:1; 8:1; 11:22.
[6]Vermigli, *In Epistolam S. Pauli*, 150-51. [†]Referring to the

Septuagint, a Greek translation of the Hebrew Scriptures made in the third century BC.
[7]LW 25:195*.

that acts of worship did not merit forgiveness of sins, that they did not justify. COMMENTARY ON ROMANS (1540).[8]

3:3 God's Faithfulness in Spite of Our Unfaithfulness

GOD IS FAITHFUL EVEN WHEN WE ARE NOT. JACQUES LEFÈVRE D'ÉTAPLES: But you will say, "The Word, and the light of the Word, and the sign of faith was entrusted to the Jews, but they did not all believe." What of it? The good counsel and precepts of a physician are not less true or less good nor is the physician less faithful if not everyone receives what they prescribe and therefore not everyone is healed. Paul, therefore, adds, "For what if there were some who did not believe? Their unbelief does not nullify the faithfulness of God, does it? By no means! But as it is written, 'Let God be true, but everyone a liar, so that you will be justified by your words, and will prevail when you are judged.'" For if God is faithful, he is therefore true and therefore righteous, so that our unfaithfulness only shows him to be faithful, our lies show him to be true, and our unrighteousness shows him to be righteous. Will he, being faithful, not punish the unfaithful? Or will he, being true, not punish liars? Or will he, being righteous, not punish the unrighteous? COMMENTARY ON ROMANS.[9]

SACRAMENTS ARE REAL EVEN WHEN NOT BELIEVED. JOHANNES BRENZ: "If we deny him, he also will deny us"; that is, we will not profit from his benefits. "If we do not believe, he still remains faithful; he is not able to deny himself," so that we may be turned from unbelief to faith. Let us understand, therefore, this saying of Paul. People's unbelief does not make faith in God useless. Rather they are able to make the greatest use of it, especially those who have either denied Christ and his gospel in persecution, or who have repeatedly fallen back into sins and think that no more hope

of pardon is left to them. For even if people have forsaken the Word of God and have either rejected Christ, or in some other way have perpetrated dreadful sins, the Word of God nevertheless remains truthful and firm, so that they may come to their senses and return through faith and seek after the benefits that are promised to those who believe. For all those who, recovering their senses, call on the name of the Lord—whether previously unbelieving, or having fallen back into sin—will be saved. The truth of the sacraments of Christ may also be judged by this saying. For Christ instituted two sacraments in the church: baptism and the Lord's Supper. And about baptism, indeed, he says, "He who believes and is baptized will be saved." However, regarding the bread of his own supper he says that this is his body handed over for sins, and about the wine, that it is his blood, poured out for sins. These sayings are as certain as they are true, and are thus most well founded. For even though many receive these sacraments without faith, they are nevertheless still divine. Baptism is the bath of regeneration and salvation, even if Simon Magus was not regenerated, nor pursued salvation. The bread of the Lord's Supper is the true body of Christ, and the wine his blood, even if many do not believe nor enjoy their offered benefits, which are taken up in the sacraments. For the truth of the sacraments does not depend on the faith or assertion of people, but on the truth and certainty of the Word of God. "The meaning of the sacrament," says Augustine, "does not depend on the belief of the one who receives it." COMMENTARY ON ROMANS (1533).[10]

ARGUMENT FOR INFANT BAPTISM. ERASMUS SARCERIUS: Here also arises the question of whether our unworthiness and unbelief overturns the grace or promises of God? From Paul's statements we must answer no. It is appropriate to take this as an unassailable argument against the Anabaptists, who argue in this way:

---

[8]Melanchthon, *Commentary on Romans*, 92*.
[9]Lefèvre, *Epistole divi Pauli*, 58v.
[10]Brenz, *In Epistolam*, 528-29; citing 2 Tim 2:12-13; Mk 16:16.

(P2) Small children are unworthy.

(C) Therefore small children should not be baptized.

And:

(P2) Small children do not possess faith that comes by hearing the Word.

(C) Therefore, small children ought not be baptized.

The same arguments can be drawn from the objection addressed in this verse:

(P2) The Jews did not believe the promise.

(C) Therefore the promise of God was rendered void and made of no effect.

In Mark 10, the disciples are in agreement with the Anabaptists in their arguments against small children:

(P2) Children are ignorant of and not capable of [understanding] Christ's teaching.

(C) Therefore, children are to be kept away and should not be brought to Christ.

Against the disciples, Christ himself answers: "Permit the children to come to me, for theirs is the kingdom of God." In other words, the grace of God is universally offered to all people and to all ages, to the learned and the unlearned. The promise of God's grace remains true even if they are ignorant children, and even if they are not yet able to possess faith by the hearing of the Word. By this answer that Christ gave, the Anabaptists can be overthrown with a single blow. For if the promise of grace is universally offered to all ages, baptism is as well, since baptism is the sign of promised grace. Therefore, both Paul's answer to the objection in our verse and Christ's answer to the disciples in Mark 10 result in the same conclusion against the Anabaptists. NOTES ON ROMANS (1541).[11]

3:4 God Is True

GOD IS TRUTH ITSELF. PETER MARTYR VERMIGLI: "What then, if some were unbelieving, does their unbelief render void the faithfulness of God? By no means!" These things are said by way of *anthypophora*,[†] as if there were Gentiles who would wish to obscure this honor belonging to Jews on the grounds that they did not believe the words of God that were entrusted to them. But the opposite conclusion is subjoined, to wit, that their vice cannot possibly have overturned the truthfulness of God. For since he is truth itself, who promised—and who was also the content of that promise—that he would be their God and that they would be his people, their sins were not able to prevent what he had promised from happening. For, among that people there have always been some good people who both believed the promises of God and lived incorrupt lives. Therefore to them, albeit not to all, that which was promised was fulfilled. Let it be far from us to think that depravity of life could detract anything from the truthfulness of God's oracles, but rather that by depravity, God's truthfulness has been demonstrated and has gleamed forth more brightly. COMMENTARY ON ROMANS (1560).[12]

EVERYONE IS A LIAR. PHILIPP MELANCHTHON: He adds an antithesis in order that it may become clearer that God is truthful because he keeps his promises to the unworthy, on account of his truthfulness and goodness. Every man is a liar; he does not judge rightly about God, does not truly fear God; he does not truly believe God; does not think that God is angry at sin or that he takes pity on those who repent. He doubts, neglects, and mistrusts God. Remnants of these sins and of this darkness remain also in the saints. Therefore he says: "Every man is a liar." Therefore the promises do not depend on our worthiness, but on the fact that God is truthful. COMMENTARY ON ROMANS (1540).[13]

---

[11]Sarcerius, *In Apostolam ad Romanos*, J8v; citing Mk 10:14.

[12]Vermigli, *In Epistolam S. Pauli*, 150-51. [†]Rhetorical device in which one raises a question and immediately answers it.
[13]Melanchthon, *Commentary on Romans*, 93*.

GOD IS TRUTHFUL; I AM A SINNER. JOHANNES BUGENHAGEN: It all boils down to this: as God is true, it is necessary that I be a sinner. All of Scripture cries out that we are sinners, and that through Christ alone we are justified. Therefore, it is necessary that sin proceed, and the righteousness of God be declared. How then will God take away my sin, if I have had no sin? As Isaiah says, "If the Lord will have washed away the sin. . . ." INTERPRETATION OF ROMANS (1531).[14]

TRUST GOD'S GOODNESS RATHER THAN YOUR MERITS. PETER MARTYR VERMIGLI: The Holy Spirit was always in the church, and he inspired other good people so that they might cry out against the ones who establish their own decrees against the Word of God. In sum, the apostle wants to demonstrate that the divine promises are not connected to our merits but rather to the goodness of God. As it is thus proved by the words of David, when he says, "Against you only have I sinned." When we pray to God, we bring nothing except sins to him. Therefore, let us direct our prayers in such a way that he may hear us, and therefore he may be vindicated in accordance with his own words. The hypocrites want to be heard according to their own merits and good works because they don't recognize their own sins. Those who rightly understand these things take great comfort from them, because they may trust that they themselves will be heard on account of the very goodness of God. COMMENTARY ON ROMANS (1560).[15]

PASSIVE AND ACTIVE JUSTIFICATION. MARTIN LUTHER: That "God is justified in his words" means that he is made just and true in his words or that his words are made just and true. And this takes place in believing them, accepting them, and holding them as true and just. . . . Through the fact that "God is justified" we are justified. And this passive justification of God by which he is justified by us is our active justification by God. For he

regards that faith that justifies his words as righteousness, as it says in 4:5 and 1:17, "The just shall live by faith." And on the contrary, the passive justification of God, by which he is judged by unbelievers is their own condemnation. For he rejects as unrighteousness and damnation that unbelief by which they judge and condemn his words. LECTURES ON ROMANS (1516).[16]

DAVID'S FALL AND GOD'S FORGIVENESS. ANDREW MELVILLE: "That you might be justified." . . . According to these words, the treachery and unrighteousness of David in the matter of Bathsheba and the murder of Uriah did not only not cause the truthfulness and justice of God to collapse, but actually made it all the more illustrious. For whereas David, violating the trust many had invested in him, involved himself in the gravest of crimes, yet God on the basis of the covenant of grace in Christ, and David's repentance, both granted the forgiveness of all his sins and abundantly reconfirmed all his promises toward him. For in judicial condemnations and in the carrying out of sentences of condemnation he does not show himself less faithful than just, even if it was God's purpose to display his truthfulness and justice when he permitted David to fall, and even if David when he acknowledged and confessed his crime intended that God would receive glory as a result of his disgrace. COMMENTARY ON ROMANS (1601).[17]

ETERNAL AND TRUSTWORTHY TRUTH. DIRK PHILIPS: The knowledge of the Holy Spirit's divinity teaches us that we should believe his teaching and witness, because he is God who alone is real and cannot fail. Therefore everything that the Holy Spirit has declared and spoken through the prophets and apostles, yes, through Jesus Christ himself, that is the eternal and trustworthy truth, and the testimony of God. THE TRUE KNOWLEDGE OF GOD.[18]

---

[14]Bugenhagen, *In D. Pauli ad Romanos*, 26r; citing Is 4:4.
[15]Vermigli, *In Epistolam S. Pauli*, 156-57; citing Ps 51:4.
[16]LW 25:210-11*; citing Ps 51:4; Rom 4:5; 1:17.
[17]Melville, *Commentarius in Divinam Pauli*, 430.
[18]CRR 6:259*; citing Ps 116:11; Rom 3:4; 2 Pet 1:21.

3:5-6 Our Unrighteousness and God's Righteousness

OUR SIN AND GOD'S RIGHTEOUSNESS.
JACQUES LEFÈVRE D'ÉTAPLES: It has already been said that "wrath" means retribution and vengeance. And as to why this is said to be spoken "in the manner of humans," I suggest that you interpret this like we would say "speaking according to human judgment," for it is absurd to say that God is unjust who inflicts retribution and a scourge on the unrighteous. Is it not rather precisely because he punishes the unrighteous that he is recognized as being just? And if he were not just, how would he judge the world? For what does it mean "to judge" but to assign to each his due, which is the role of justice and of the just judge. And Paul is certainly extraordinary— as has been stated—at proving and establishing the faithfulness of God through our unfaithfulness, the truth of God through our lie, and the righteousness of God through our unrighteousness. He acknowledges God as faithful on the basis of our unfaithfulness. That he is true on the basis of our lie, and that he is righteous on the basis of our injustice, even as God punishes this unfaithfulness, lie, and unrighteousness. For when he punishes unfaithfulness, he punishes it as One who is faithful; when he punishes the lie, he does so as One who is true; and when he punishes unrighteousness, it is as the Righteous One. For don't we see fire scatter and exterminate things that are cold, wet, and dark? It exterminates and scatters the cold because it is hot, and wetness because it is dry, and darkness because it is bright. On the other hand, fire does not exterminate hot things, nor dry things, nor bright things, but rather embraces them, nourishes them, and gives them health. In this way, God punishes and exterminates the unfaithful and the liars and the unrighteous, but he embraces and nourishes and saves the faithful, the true, and the righteous. God is, therefore, faithful and true and just. And to the degree that infidelity, the lie, and unrighteousness abounds, to that degree God punishes more severely, and thus more fully displays his faithfulness, truth, and righteousness unto his glory and the consternation of those who have transgressed so egregiously. This was the case as long as of their own accord they continued stubborn in their unbelief and their lie and their unrighteousness. But when they stop persisting in these things and, begging for mercy, are converted to God, they come to enjoy his grace and goodness. "Where transgression abounded, there grace superabounded." For the goodness and grace of God manifest themselves more notably and abundantly when he receives evildoers and ingrates. Or rather, when he receives many evildoers and many ingrates when they confess and detest their evildoing equally with their ingratitude. COMMENTARY ON ROMANS.[19]

THE RIGHTEOUSNESS BY WHICH HE MAKES US RIGHTEOUS. MARTIN LUTHER: He is not speaking here of the righteousness by which he is righteous himself, but of that by which he who is righteous makes us righteous, and he himself alone is righteous with respect to us; for our unrighteousness, if it truly has become ours (that is, by being acknowledged and confessed), does commend his righteousness, for it humbles us, makes us bow before our God and seek his righteousness; and when we have received it, we glorify, praise, and love God who imparted it to us. On the other hand, when our righteousness disparages the righteousness of God, and even destroys and denies it and argues that it is lying and false, as when, for example, we resist the words of God and regard his righteousness as unnecessary and believe in the sufficiency of our own, then we have to say, "Against you, you only have I sinned . . . so that you are justified," that is, "that you alone may be extolled with praise and glory as our righteous Justifier"; "in your sentence," that is, "as you have promised and testified." LECTURES ON ROMANS.[20]

---

[19]Lefèvre, *Epistole divi Pauli*, 58v-59r; citing Rom 5:20.
[20]LW 25:201*; citing Ps 51:4.

GETTING SICK IN ORDER TO REVEAL A DOC-TOR'S SKILL. PETER MARTYR VERMIGLI: Some people loosen the reigns of their sin under the pretense of desiring to give God victory and justify him. They are like patients who have been sick with a harsh disease and then are restored by a doctor, revealing the doctor's clear skill. They then desire to fall back into the same type of disease in order to make the doctor better known. Or it is as if the poor and beggars wanted to be without or to beg so that they might show forth more and more the liberality of the wealthy. It is not necessary for something to be reprehensible and disgraceful in order to lead to the glory of God. The virtues that are united with true praise promote the glory of God by themselves. COMMENTARY ON ROMANS (1560).[21]

THE MORE LOST THE SINNER, THE MORE GLORIOUS THE MERCY. MARTIN BUCER: Paul, that he might show how much we are to look to Christ alone for all things, and how that he offers himself as Savior to all men and women no matter how lost they are, everywhere was freely bearing witness that Christ had come so that "where sin abounded, grace might abound" also. God, so that he might show himself to be "just and the justifier of the ungodly," willed to send his Christ at that time when every vice would be at the brink of a precipice, and every crime reigning as much among the Jews as among Gentiles. Paul was preaching with great earnestness, even at such a time as that, that there is no perversity so bothersome to God that those who believe in Christ cannot be forgiven them, neither the law nor any of its works being of any use for this purpose, but only faith in Christ. And since the Jews wished to believe that the Gentiles were alienated from the kingdom of God, inasmuch as they were cast down into every kind of ungodliness and all manner of shameful acts and crimes, Paul would customarily respond that the more lost they were, the more glorious God's mercy toward them in Christ appears, and that therefore it was fitting that sin should abound,

so that grace might shine even more abundantly. In a word, just as righteousness is not furnished to anybody except by faith in Christ, so Paul was having to attribute everything to faith. Since they trusted vainly in the works of the law and, wishing to establish their own righteousness, would not suffer themselves to submit to God's righteousness, Paul was diligently repeating his teaching that Christ came to save sinners, and that sinners are closer to the kingdom of God than those who are righteous in their own eyes. That is also what our Lord and Savior was everywhere pressing on the Pharisees, affirming that prostitutes and tax collectors would enter the kingdom of God before the "righteous" did.

For these reasons, the enemies of the truth constructed this false charge against Paul: that it followed from what he was teaching both that God "is unjust when he punishes sin" and also that those who are inclined to evil would take the opportunity to sin more freely. Or rather, they were charging him and those who were professing the same doctrine with expressly teaching that "evil should be done that good might come of it." Therefore, as was fitting, the apostle wished to dispel this false charge and defamation of the truth, and the present passage was a very suitable occasion for doing so. COMMENTARY ON ROMANS (1536).[22]

PROVING GOD'S TRUTHFULNESS. HEINRICH BULLINGER: Because indeed many might take these Scripture passages and wrongly interpret and twist these good words, Paul immediately refutes, with a brief digression. And in the beginning, he will speak not his own opinion, but that of his adversaries. Likewise, he added, "I speak in a human manner." That is, "What I'm saying is truly not my own opinion but that of the impious."

For they have taunted, "We have heard that our lying makes it known openly that God alone is truthful. Likewise, we have heard a prophet saying, 'Against you have I sinned, so that you may be

---

[21]Vermigli, *In Epistolam S. Pauli*, 158.

[22]Bucer, *Metaphrases et Enarrationes*, 166; citing Rom 5:20; 3:26, 5, 8.

justified in your words and overcome when you are judged.' Therefore, it necessarily follows that our unrighteousness is not able to offend God. It increases the display of God's glory. Indeed, if we were not sinners and liars, it would not shine out to such a degree that God alone is righteous and true; nor would he be able to exercise his mercy as much. Second, it follows that God, if he should proceed to become angry on account of being sinned against—that is, if he should inflict vengeance (anger indeed is understood for vengeance)—he is unrighteous, and obviously, one who would condemn good deeds."

However, it was not with this intention that Paul had brought up the prophetic testimonies, but only for the proving of God's truthfulness. And the other is that they are . . . simple and good words. COMMENTARY ON ROMANS (1533).[23]

THE WORDS OF HUMANS, NOT OF THE HOLY SPIRIT. RUDOLF GWALTHER: First, so that no one will think that this question sprang from the Holy Spirit, Paul inserts in parenthesis: "I'm speaking as a human." That is, this question does not have the Holy Spirit as its author, but is an invention of human reasoning. And so, for people of sound judgment, who are accustomed to true piety, there is no need for a laborious refutation. But by saying this he slays, in one word, human wisdom and the whole cunning of human natural ability. . . . While people follow their reason, they do not perceive the things which are of the Spirit of God. And it has been noted in Isaiah 55, when God himself announces: "My thoughts are not your thoughts, nor my ways your ways," says the Lord. "But as the heavens are higher than the earth, so are my ways higher than your ways, and my thoughts than your thoughts."

This one thing, if correctly observed, will suffice to refute the errors of many who are eager to force against us the intercession of the saints, the sacrifice of the Mass, the righteousness of our works, and an innumerable quantity of other things.

Why then do they assert this, that there is a need for mediators with Christ as with the princes of this world? Likewise, that the merit of Christ does not benefit us unless it should be applied to us, and that this comes about most properly through the Mass, which both has the clear traces of old sacrifices, and presents again the entire history of the death itself for display, or in addition to the benefit of some work. Is it required that Christ be obligated to us in order to impart his own righteousness to us? After they first forwarded these reasons, they soon enumerated them, which in the papacy in the name of good works are offered up for sale: fasts, purchased prayers, holy days, pilgrimages, couches, rosaries, brotherhoods of monks, candles, incense, ecclesiastical song, the sounds of the resounding organs, and other such things of this kind.

But we say that they say all these things "as a human," nor is there any similarity between those things and that reason of our salvation which is handed down in the Scriptures. And so they are false and erroneous and should not be agreed to by the pious. Then they throw before us the Fathers, the councils, the canons, and the decrees. Because truly they are not able to deny that these are also of human origin, in vain do they argue with them, and so much so that they betray themselves with their own evidence, as long as they oppose human authority to divine. SERMONS ON ROMANS (1590).[24]

GOD IS NOT UNRIGHTEOUS. JOHANNES BRENZ: Undoubtedly, Paul wrote to the Romans that the truth of God makes clear the falsehood of humanity, and that the righteousness of God reveals and proves the unrighteousness of humans. He was often, too, publicly preaching this with other words. Hence, tricksters took the opportunity to misrepresent and circulate rumors that Paul was preaching that God is unrighteous when he punishes sinners, since God makes clearer the glory of his own name by our sin. And that evil is to be done in order that

---

[23]Bullinger, *In Sanctissimam Pauli*, 47r-47v; citing Ps 51:4.

[24]Gwalther, *In d. Pauli Apostoli*, 34v; citing Is 58:8-9.

good may come. Therefore, Paul takes up these false accusations to refute them, but he spends only a little time on them in order to continue on with his teaching.

There are two false accusations. First, that he teaches that God is unrighteous. Second, that he teaches that evil is to be done in order that good may come. The former one he answers by refusing to acknowledge it as true: "I have not taught that God is unrighteous, nor is God unrighteous when he punishes the unrighteous or sinners. For I teach that God is judge of the whole world. Therefore, how could I teach that God is unrighteous? For even if many judges among humans are unrighteous, yet God, on that account, is judge of the world, in order that he may justly punish the unjust judges. Abraham said to the Lord, 'Far be it from you that you should do this thing, that you should kill the just with the wicked, and the just should be treated the same as the wicked. This is not you, who judges all the earth.'" And it appears to be true that what Paul was looking back to here were Abraham's words. COMMENTARY ON ROMANS (1588).[25]

GOD IS JUST IN CONDEMNING UNBELIEF. GEORG MAJOR: The third objection is that if our unbelief and unrighteousness commend the justice and mercy of God—while although we might not believe in the promise itself, nevertheless it itself remains certain and immovable—and all who embrace the faith are shown mercy, then God unjustly punishes the unbelieving. This objection is absurd and full of pretense and wholly wicked. Therefore, Paul concludes it is unworthy for him to answer. And yet he answers with a concise word. He says of those who abuse both the goodness and mercy of God so rudely, wickedly, criminally, and impiously to their own destruction, that their damnation is just. And God is just, who punishes such people. EXPOSITION OF THE EPISTLES OF PAUL (1569).[26]

3:7 What If Our Lying Reveals God's Truthfulness?

LIKE A DOCTOR WITH A PATIENT IN DENIAL. MARTIN LUTHER: This is like the case of the doctor (as Persius tells us[†]) who wishes to heal his patient, but finds that he is a man who denies that he is sick, calling the doctor a fool and an even sicker person than himself for presuming to cure a healthy man. And because of the man's resistance the doctor cannot get around to recommending his skill and his medicine. For he could do so only if the sick man would admit his illness and permit him to cure him by saying, "I certainly am sick in order that you may be praised, that is, be a man of health and be spoken of as such, that is, when you have healed me."

Thus these ungodly and arrogant men, although they are sick before God, seem most healthy to themselves. Therefore they not only reject God as their physician, but they even regard him as a fool and a liar and even sicker than themselves for presuming to heal such wonderfully healthy men and treating them as if they were sick. LECTURES ON ROMANS (1516).[27]

PAUL INTENDS TO GLORIFY GOD. JACQUES LEFÈVRE D'ÉTAPLES: Of course, because Paul offers this divinely inspired opinion in saying that our unrighteousness commends the righteousness of God, and that the truth of God abounds by our lie to his glory, many who failed to understand this were saying that Paul was blaspheming and were heaping abuse on him as a blasphemer. They were accusing him of being a sinner by their words, as if he had been saying, "Let us do evil that good may come," that is, that the goodness of God might be commended through us, for if we do evil, the goodness of God will be demonstrated and displayed in us, whether we enjoy his kindness or the Avenger punishes us. But Paul did not say that this happens to our own commendation, but only that of God's glory. The person who is good cannot

[25]Brenz, *In Epistolam*, 531; citing Gen 18:25.
[26]Major, *Enarrationes Epistolarum S. Pauli*, 43.
[27]LW 25:202-3*. †Persius, *Satires* 3.88-106.

do evil, regardless of whether God wipes it away in his goodness or punishes it as Avenger. And so to believe and speak in this way is not to be a sinner, nor to blaspheme, but rather to attribute glory to God for his eminence in all goodness, faithfulness, truthfulness, and righteousness. . . . In all of his sayings, Paul always honored God, aiming to make the supereminent goodness of God to be clear to all. COMMENTARY ON ROMANS.[28]

LIKE A CRAFTSMAN COMMENDED IN THREE WAYS. MARTIN LUTHER: In the same way a good craftsman is commended in three ways. First, when he criticizes the inexperienced and reproves them when they make mistakes. Second, when in comparison with them he appears better trained than they. Third when he transmits the perfection of his skill to others who did not yet possess it. And this is the true commendation. For to reprove others or to appear as a craftsman, this is not being a praiseworthy artist, but to cause others to become artists, this is being a truly good artist. In the same way, God is truly praiseworthy for being righteous in us. . . . But just as that craftsman cannot pass on his skill to those who do not have confidence in him and those who are well satisfied with their own skill, and just as he cannot draw praise and commendation from them for his art and mastery unless they first recognize their own lack of skill and believe him when he asserts that they are unskillful—but their pride will not let them believe him—so the ungodly do not believe that they are ungodly and thus do not acknowledge the fact. Hence they do not allow God to be justified in them, or to be declared truthful, and thus glorified or commended. LECTURES ON ROMANS (1516).[29]

3:8 Should We Do Evil So That Good May Come?

MISTAKEN CAUSATION. NIELS HEMMINGSEN: Paul's opponents gather two absurd conclusions

out of the last response. First, if truth, that is, the unchanging promises of God are given glory by my lying, that is, by my sin, I should not be accused, punished, or damned on account of sin. For nothing that makes clear the glory of God would be rightly condemned. Second, if the truth of God is made clear by sinning greatly, the greater the glory of God will be praised. For if out of evil good comes, to do evil is useful for those who would render great good. However, Paul destroys these conclusions by *exuthenismus*,[†] and he emphasizes that those who hold them are to be condemned justly. In dialectic, you would rightly call it committing a fallacy of mistaking a noncause for a cause. For by no means is sin a cause[‡] that brings light to the glory of God. Nor is evil the cause of good, except by chance. COMMENTARY ON ROMANS (1562).[30]

DOING EVIL UNDER PRETEXT OF A GOOD END. PETER MARTYR VERMIGLI: Certainly, in our time as well, it has been lamented that there are people who defend many evils under the pretext of their having a good end. They have dared to mutilate the sacrament of the Eucharist, for they believed that the cup would spill if given to laypeople. Likewise, they want the people to pray in an unknown language,[†] which has been forbidden by the Word of God, and they say that a praiseworthy intention and good end are enough. And thus they presume upon the infinite, not weighing out what the Holy Spirit makes known in this passage. And they throw the same things against us that were objected to in Paul. For when we preach justification, free and apart from works, they say that we open up the entrance to a lax life and condemn good works, when, in fact, we in no way teach those things. Indeed, God does remit sins freely. But he does not, therefore, grant his people the freedom to sin. Rather, together with justification,

[28]Lefèvre, *Epistole divi Pauli*, 59r.
[29]LW 25:205-7*.

[30]Hemmingsen, *Commentarius in Epistolam*, 93-94. [†]*Exuthenismus* is a rhetorical figure in which a person or thing is spoken of with contempt. [‡]The common Latin form is *non causa pro causa*. Also called "mistaken causation/cause" or "false cause." It involves mistaking correlation for causality.

the Holy Spirit is given, and renewal of life. From which a great devotion to good works arises. But if we wanted to spur banter of this kind against them, perhaps they would be embarrassed that they give much more occasion for lax lives. For they teach that if people confess their sins and receive ecclesiastical absolution, even though they have no good and holy motives, yet they will receive justification. . . . But that is an exceedingly easy thing, and it opens the way for sins, as does their purgatory. But by no means do we promise justification, unless there is a genuine and firm faith that is accompanied continually by good works. COMMENTARY ON ROMANS (1560).[31]

THE ENDS DO NOT MAKE THE MEANS GOOD.
JOHANNES BRENZ: But to the next false accusation he answers with indeed the simplest—but also the most severe—rebuttal, "Those who say such things are justly damned." For this false accusation is most obvious, not deserving any additional refutation, as it should be clear to whomever is not exceedingly severe by nature. For when Paul says that from the falsehood of humanity shines forth the truth of God, or that the injustice of persons commends the justice of God, he does not think that injustice or falsehood is pleasing to God, or that by bringing about justice injustice becomes by its nature good, or that injustice must be done to make justice clear. . . .

Someone says, "A great and dangerous sickness commends the diligence of a doctor." What? Does he believe that sickness is a pleasant thing to bring about in order to make the doctor diligent, or that sickness deserves to be undertaken in order to prove the diligence of the doctor? Not in the least! Rather, it signifies that the diligence of the doctor shines forth from the cure of the dangerous sickness. Another says, "An undeveloped student commends a learned instructor." This does not mean that the instructor is delighted in an undeveloped student, or that the student ought to remain undeveloped in order that the teacher

might become skilled. What is this perverse understanding? Rather, the meaning is that to the degree a student has been undeveloped, the more the learning of the instructor is made clear, if the student himself becomes learned.

So God is not pleased by our falsehood or injustice, neither does our falsehood bring about the truth of God. But to the degree we are unjust, to that greater degree the justice of God is made clear, either when he is compared with our injustice, or when God freely forgives us our injustice on account of Christ. From which Paul, after chapter 5, says, "Where sin is abundant, there grace is more greatly abundant." In that place Paul will handle this thing at length. That idea carries over to this context as well, for we should apply it to our experience. For before the judgment seat of God, the multitude and greatness of our sin will be cast before us. They say, "What? Is anyone able to be one's own hope of salvation when one has committed so many and such great sins?" But it is necessary to answer with these sayings of Paul. "Let God be truthful, but every person false." And, "Our injustice commends the justice of God." And, "The truth of God excels to the glory of God through my falsehood." And, "Where sin overflows, there grace is more greatly abundant."

For when he says, "Do not hope for salvation in the case of so many sins, and call on Christ, the Son of God," what else is it, I ask, than if he were to say to an invalid, "Your sickness is great and dangerous. Therefore, take precautions; you should call the doctor to come to you and should make use of his care. Indeed for that reason you ought to call the doctor and make use of his work because you are sick." So by no means on that account should Christ be rejected because you are a sinner, but because you are a sinner, on that account it is necessary that your hope be in Christ. Formerly, Peter cried out to Christ in the boat, "Depart from me, Lord, because I am a sinful man." However, we should say, "Come to me, Lord, because I am a sinner."

There is that saying of Paul, "Do not do evil in order that good may come," a noble thought worth repeating. For there are those who think it is all

---

[31]Vermigli, *In Epistolam S. Pauli*, 161, conflated with *Learned and Fruitfull Commentaries*, 54*. †That is, Latin.

right to do evil in order that good may come. It is good for you to feed and nourish your family. Therefore, is it permissible to resort to deception in order to feed your family, in order that good may come? Not in the least! It is good to give alms. Therefore, should you seize another's means so that you can give alms, in order that good may come? God forbid! Good authority protects. Therefore, is it all right for Saul to murder innocent David in order that authority may protect? The damnation of these, Paul says, is just. For the one who brings forth iniquity cannot be good, accepted by God, nor blessed. Therefore, whoever produces iniquity is cursed and detested. COMMENTARY ON ROMANS (1588).[32]

GODLINESS GLORIFIES GOD. JOHN CALVIN: The pretense is this: "If God is by our iniquity glorified, and if nothing can be done by people in this life more befitting than to promote the glory of God, then let us sin to advance his glory!" Now the answer to this is evident: "That evil cannot of itself produce anything but evil, and that God's glory is illustrated through our sin is not the work of people but of God, who as a wonderful worker knows how to overcome our wickedness and to convert it to another end, so as to turn it contrary to what we intend, to the promotion of his own glory." God has prescribed to us the way by which he would have himself to be glorified by us, even by true piety, which consists in obedience to his Word. He who leaps over this boundary strives not to honor God but to dishonor him. That it turns out otherwise is to be ascribed to the providence of God, and not to human wickedness, through which it does not come, that the majesty of God is not injured, nay, wholly overthrown. COMMENTARY ON ROMANS 3:8.[33]

---

[32]Brenz, *In Epistolam*, 531-32; citing Rom 5:20; 3:4-7; Lk 5:8.

[33]CTS 38:122* (CO 49:51).

3:9-20 THE LAW REVEALS OUR UNRIGHTEOUSNESS

⁹*What then? Are we Jews*ᵃ *any better off?*ᵇ *No, not at all. For we have already charged that all, both Jews and Greeks, are under sin,* ¹⁰*as it is written:*

"None is righteous, no, not one;
ᵃ¹*no one understands;*
no one seeks for God.
¹²*All have turned aside; together they have become worthless;*
no one does good,
not even one."
¹³*"Their throat is an open grave;*
they use their tongues to deceive."
"The venom of asps is under their lips."

¹⁴*"Their mouth is full of curses and bitterness."*
¹⁵*"Their feet are swift to shed blood;*
¹⁶*in their paths are ruin and misery,*
¹⁷*and the way of peace they have not known."*
¹⁸*"There is no fear of God before their eyes."*

¹⁹*Now we know that whatever the law says it speaks to those who are under the law, so that every mouth may be stopped, and the whole world may be held accountable to God.* ²⁰*For by works of the law no human being*ᶜ *will be justified in his sight, since through the law comes knowledge of sin.*

a Greek *Are we*   b Or *at any disadvantage?*   c Greek *flesh*

OVERVIEW: The reformers see Paul as modeling how the gospel should be proclaimed. He starts by showing that the law convicts us by uncovering our sins, for without our first becoming aware of our unrighteousness, we would not realize our need to flee to Christ for *his* righteousness. And in our fallen nature, apart from grace, we do not have the free will requisite for doing good works perfectly. Paul draws on biblical metaphors from the Old Testament to describe the kinds of ways in which people sin.

Here the commentators start to harmonize Paul and James on works, a task that will continue in later passages. Catholic opponents of *sola fide* often turned to James to argue that his emphasis on works spoke against faith alone saving. In response, one reformer suggests that when Paul writes that no person is justified by works, he is referring to justification before God, whereas when James writes that Abraham is justified by works, he is speaking of justification before people.

The reformers explore whether the law referred to here includes the ceremonial law, some claiming that Paul expands his argument to include the whole law in order to prevent people from arguing that justification can be based on moral works. Some see parallels in the Israelites sinning by going further than God's prescribed law to seek humanly created ceremonies, to medieval Catholic practices —such as the Mass or the invocation of saints—that went beyond what Christ had handed down. In either case, the law does not justify, nor does it get rid of sin. Rather, the law brings *knowledge* of sin.

3:9 Do the Jews Surpass the Gentiles?

DO WE SURPASS THEM? THEODORE BEZA: "What then? Do we surpass them?" The old codices translate it this way, and there is no doubt that this is the true translation of this passage. Previously, Paul had, up to a point, assuaged the displeasure of the Jews by placing them before the Gentiles. Now, fearing that the Jews might become arrogant, he declares that such "surpassing" ought not to be considered as something inherent to the Jews, but rather, as coming from the bounty of God. For both the Jews and Gentiles are equal in this, since they are two sides of the same thing and within themselves are guilty of sins and worthy of God's wrath. Thus, in Christ, they may be made equal. Nor has the apostle said, "you surpass," but rather, "*we* surpass." In order to take away every reason for offense, he speaks of Jewish matters as a Jew himself, placing himself in the same position as them. MAJOR ANNOTATIONS (1594).[1]

THE GOSPEL FIRST UNCOVERS OUR NEED.

JOHANNES BUGENHAGEN: So far, therefore, Paul has treated the proposition. Now he will demonstrate and confirm it with most reliable Scriptures, so that we will not be able to slip away in any way. In addition, you will learn from this the correct order for preaching the gospel. First, people's sins should be uncovered through the law, so that they begin to be displeased with themselves, and despair of their own skin. Then comfort must be brought, namely, that Christ is our justifier. He takes away our sins because he satisfies the Father. No one uses medicines unless he first recognizes the disease. In this way, how do you understand that God is merciful unless you see that you are a child of wrath and damnation? The gospel reveals the heart's thoughts. That is, it reveals how great the iniquity in us is, so that we might flee to Christ at last. It urges us on, just as a mother is accustomed to urge on her own child. Thus when Christ was preaching, he would first say: "Repent, discern your sins, and the kingdom of God will come to you." For this reason, Paul wisely speaks of our condemnation before he describes righteousness through Christ. INTERPRETATION OF ROMANS (1531).[2]

JEWS AND GENTILES EQUALLY LIABLE TO JUDGMENT.

LOUIS DE DIEU: The apostle had stated in verse 1 that the Jews were advantaged above the Gentiles, and circumcision over uncircumcision. But he then immediately added in verse 2 that this profits only believers who embrace by faith the faithfulness of God, that is, the promise

of his grace that was announced by the covenant and sealed by circumcision. But unbelievers were those who wished to be justified by works, though this did not nullify the truthfulness of the divine promise or God's excellency, but rather had the result that their lives were spent with no other usefulness than that being discovered as liars and unrighteous men and women they might all the more demonstrate God's truthfulness and glory. Nor can this be seized on as an excuse, as if this would make them immune from blame. Supposing that such an excuse should be acceptable in the eyes of humanity and in the depraved judgment of the human mind, it would follow that God will not be the judge of the world, nor could any be condemned as a sinner, and it would be permissible "to do evil so that good might come." But if the situation is understood with sound reasoning and as God sees it, then it is equally true that unbelievers commend the truthfulness of God by their unbelief, and that God is nonetheless the just judge of the world, that he will judge all as sinners, and those who claim to have a license to sin will be justly condemned. From this it is rightly concluded that in and of themselves the Jews are better than the Gentiles in nothing, nor are they less guilty of sin or liable to judgment. OBSERVATIONS ON ROMANS (1646).[3]

3:10 No One Is Righteous

NO ONE IS COMPLETELY PURE.

JOHN BUNYAN: But let us take Paul's definition of a person: "There is none righteous. . . ." I would rather give you this definition from Paul than any of my own, because it is the soundest description of the soul, one the Holy Spirit himself could draw. Here there is no purity in human nature. Nor is the soul's complexion such that it can keep itself from mixing with that which is contrary to itself. And note that this is the state of all people, as they stand before God. Therefore, even if all the humans in the world were together—even in their most pure natural state

---

[1]Beza, *Annotationes Majores*, 35-36.
[2]Bugenhagen, *In D. Pauli ad Romanos*, 28v; citing Mt 4:17.
[3]De Dieu, *Animadversiones in D. Pauli*, 35-36; citing Rom 3:8.

and with all the purity of humanity that they can make—they would still be unprofitable, and so must come short of doing good, "that every mouth might be stopped, and all the world become guilty before God." A Defense of the Doctrine of Justification (1672).[4]

Human Nature and Grace. Niels Hemmingsen: The form of the proposition repeated from the aforementioned Scripture is an argument from the contrary:

(P2) There are none who are righteous.

(C) Therefore all are sinners.

The antecedent is proved by the remote causes of righteousness, which are right judgment, will, and effort or the ability of acting on it. For these three things are required for there to be righteous actions. For when he says, "there are none who understand," the standard of justice is taken away, which is right judgment. When he adds, "there are none who seek God," the will is denied. When he then adds that "all have turned aside (namely, from the right path of justice) and have become unprofitable; there is none that does good (namely, according to the prescript of the law), not even one," then the ability or faculty of acting is taken away.

But Paul is here speaking about men and women as they are by nature, not by grace. Then he speaks not about the righteousness of faith but rather that of works. For David, when he said these things, without any doubt was already righteous by faith even if he was not righteous by works. In this passage an unassailable argument is therefore observed against the defenders of free will as it relates to spiritual righteousness. For however much may remain in humanity's power apart from grace, there is nothing at all of free will pertaining to saving actions that is left within us. For this reason, we are reminded of our corruption, so that by acknowledging our natural infirmity we will flee to the Word by whom our judgment was formed. And let us ask the Holy Spirit so that he may both bend our wills and supply to us the power of acting out those things that are pleasing to him. Commentary on Romans (1562).[5]

God Curbs Human Nature. John Calvin: Here again, we are met with a question very much the same as that which was previously solved. In every age there have been some who, under the guidance of nature, were all their lives devoted to virtue. It is of no consequence that many blots may be detected in their conduct; by the mere study of their virtue, they evidenced that there was some purity in their nature. The value that virtues of this kind have in the sight of God will be considered more fully when we treat of the merit of works. Meanwhile, however, it will be proper to consider it in this place also, insofar as necessary for the exposition of the subject in hand. Such examples, then, seem to warn us against supposing that human nature is utterly vicious, since, under its guidance, some have not only excelled in illustrious deeds but have conducted themselves most honorably through the whole course of their lives. But we ought to consider that, notwithstanding the corruption of our nature, there is some room for divine grace; such grace as, without purifying the corruption itself, may at least lay it under internal restraint. For, if the Lord let loose every mind to wallow in its lusts, doubtless there is no one who would not show that his nature is capable of all the crimes with which Paul charges it (Rom 3 compared with Ps 14:3). What? Can you exempt yourself from the number of those whose feet are swift to shed blood; whose hands are foul with rapine and murder; whose throats are like open sepulchers; whose tongues are deceitful; whose lips are venomous; whose actions are useless, unjust, rotten, deadly; whose soul is without God; whose inward parts are full of evil; whose eyes are on the watch for deception; whose minds are prepared for insult; whose every part, in short, is framed for

---

[4]Bunyan, *A Defence of the Doctrine of Iustification*, 4*; written from prison against "Mr. Fowler's Pretended Design of Christianity."

[5]Hemmingsen, *Commentarius in Epistolam*, 95-96.

endless sinful deeds? If every soul is capable of such abominations (and the apostle declares this boldly), it is surely easy to see what the result would be if the Lord were to permit human passion to follow its bent. No ravenous beast would rush so furiously, no stream, however rapid and violent, would so impetuously burst its banks. In the elect, God cures the diseases in the mode which will be explained shortly; in others, he only lays them under such restraint as may prevent them from breaking forth to a degree incompatible with the preservation of the established order of things. Hence, however much people may disguise their impurity, some are restrained only by shame, others by a fear of the laws, from breaking out into many kinds of evil. Some aspire to an honest life, deeming it most conducive to their interest, while others are raised above the vulgar lot so that by the dignity of their station they may keep inferiors to their duty. Thus God, by his providence, curbs the perverseness of nature, preventing it from breaking forth into action, yet without rendering it inwardly pure. INSTITUTES OF THE CHRISTIAN RELIGION 2.3.2 (1559).[6]

3:11-12 No One Seeks After God or Does Good

DAMNING IGNORANCE OF GOD. DAVID PAREUS: "There is no one that understands." . . . He damns blindness and ignorance of God, which is the mother of all profanity, cutting off the fear of God. Therefore the knowledge of God is here and there used in place of the fear of God. To the question of David, whether God, looking down from heaven, sees anyone who understands and seeks God, the apostle asserts the negative from the following denial. For even if the Jews had and knew the law, they nevertheless did not understand it, nor were they led to seek God. ("Seek God," which is said several times in Hosea.) COMMENTARY ON ROMANS (1562).[7]

SCIENCES AND ARTS EMPTY WITHOUT KNOWLEDGE OF GOD. JOHN CALVIN: The first effect is that "there is none that understands," and then this ignorance is immediately proved, for they "seek not God." Empty are those in whom there is not the knowledge of God, whatever other learning they may possess. The sciences and the arts, which in themselves are good, are empty things when they are without this groundwork. COMMENTARY ON ROMANS 3:11.[8]

ALL HAVE TURNED AWAY FROM GOD. KONRAD PELLIKAN: All people, not only the Gentiles, but many sinful Jews and Israelites, had turned away from the path of the law of righteousness and common sense, living entirely apart from that law that God the Creator had enjoined on them, abandoning that path of humanity and natural instinct, not moved to expend effort to help one's neighbor, and all seeking not the Lord's will, but their own. Even among the Jews, they obliterated their public duty to humanity a long time ago, and have become useless like rotten fruit that is of no use to anybody. For they have fallen away from all charity and concern to do good works to anyone near them, so that not even one can be found who is completely innocent of these charges, and they do not give thanks to God through Christ as Mediator, from whom alone comes anyone's righteousness or goodness. And although all these sinful people have been in possession of the law given to them by God, the law of God does not bestow righteousness on its disciples, nor do the works of the law make one a sharer in righteousness. COMMENTARY ON ALL THE APOSTOLIC EPISTLES (1539).[9]

NOT EVEN ONE. WOLFGANG MUSCULUS: Here certain people—such as Augustine—exclusively read in Psalm 14, "only one," understanding by "one," Christ, who alone is removed from the corruption of humankind and is clean of every depravity; who

---

[6]Calvin, *Institutes*, 1:251-52*.

[7]Pareus, *In Divinam ad Romanos*, 269-70; citing Ps 14:2; 53:2; Hos 3:5; 5:15.

[8]CTS 38:126* (CO 49:53).

[9]Pellikan, *In Omnes Apostolicas Epistolas*, 40.

alone understands God and seeks him; and is helpful and does that which is good.

Although this is true in itself, it is not what is in that passage. For the Hebrew does not have "only one," but "not even one." And the apostle in this passage does not write this to prove that Christ is free from corruption.

Some, siding with the Jews, weaken the apostle's argument by synecdoche, understanding by *all*, "many," which word is of course sometimes found. as in, "There went out to him *all* Jerusalem." That is, a *great* number from Jerusalem.

Or that David desires to speak only about the people of his own time, because they are by no means loyal. However, although David demonstrates the ill will of his own age, nevertheless he introduces the testimony of Scripture, from Genesis 6, from which he demonstrates that the whole nature of mortals is corrupt. And this is from God's testimony, who has looked down from heaven. So those statements must be most strongly noted: "There is not one who does good; they have all turned away." Also: "They have become unprofitable; there is not even one."

Some have objected that many in the Scriptures are praised using the term "righteous," such as Noah, Job, Abraham, and others. We answer: They are called righteous when compared to wicked persons. But obviously, they are not without sin.

If you say: But there are those who are not characterized by such great wickedness, and yet here, how strongly the apostle attributes it to all. I answer: By *nature*, things are a certain way, but by the *grace of God* they become better. Paul, however, places in front of our eyes the corruption of human nature, in and of itself, outside the energy of divine grace, so that he may prepare the way of grace. COMMENTARY ON ROMANS (1555).[10]

3:13-14 *The Mouth Used to Sin*

OPEN GRAVES AND ASPS' POISON. KONRAD PELLIKAN: These two prior metaphors have been

chosen from Psalm 5, and they each mean the same thing: that those impious ones—about whom it is here inquired—devour people with their lies and deceits, just like the grave. Moreover, they utterly consume them. In this, however, because he says, "the open grave," he means that they are ready and equipped to destroy their neighbors with deceit. Regarding the poison under their lips, Psalm 140:3 has the same metaphor, which is almost as powerful as the preceding metaphor. However it means the harmful and destructive deceit with which the impious suddenly destroy the innocent.

The next sentence is quoted from Psalm 10. It pertains, as also do the foregoing sentences, to the description of destructive and pestilential speech by which the impious defraud and destroy the pious. The whole law of God is fulfilled in love and service to neighbor. In the same way, the greatest perversity is to provoke others to injury, to defraud by trickery, and to cheat or injure brothers. Paul exaggerates beautifully, in elegant, explanatory metaphors the injuries and greatest losses. COMMENTARY ON ALL THE APOSTOLIC EPISTLES (1539).[11]

FALSE TEACHING AS AN OPEN GRAVE. ERASMUS SARCERIUS: The previously mentioned sins are particularly internal to the mind; they are sins from our corrupted nature, and they ought to be assigned to wicked thinking, opinions, tendencies, and pursuits of the mind. Now the sins that follow are these: the corruption of the mind and irreverent fruit. For an evil tree can bear nothing but evil fruit. As Christ said, "From a wicked heart proceeds every type of sin." But the sins that follow are those that are partly against the second commandment, partly against the third. For the sins are: the misuse of the name of God, and false teaching by which false teachers damage and torment the consciences of men and women. And indeed, we ourselves have all been distressed by false teaching from birth. For there is no one who

---

[10]Musculus, *In Epistolam Apostoli Pauli*, 72; citing Ps 14:3; Mk 1:5.

[11]Pellikan, *In Omnes Apostolicas Epistolas*, 40; citing Ps 5:9; 140:3; 10:7. Parts of this excerpt are from Bucer's commentary. See, for example, Bucer at 3:14 below.

has not had, from birth, a throat lying open in the likeness of a grave, a crafty tongue, and the poison of asps being under his lips. That is, one who does not more greatly desire false doctrine than true, who does not more greatly follow his own dreams than the pure Word, and who does not confess with more pleasure his own cogitations and speculations than the pure Word. "Their throat is an open grave." The paraphrase is that all men and women from birth follow and profess false teaching. The next paraphrase in this place is that all false teaching is a false teaching that damages the conscience into ruination. Disaster and ruin are signified by the expression, "the grave," because it announces false doctrine. For as the grave is a place and deep hole for a dead person (so to speak), so false doctrine leads men and women to the extremity of ruin and casts them down into perniciously deep holes. Likewise, as a person thrown into a grave is devoured by worms, so men and women are devoured by false doctrine. NOTES ON ROMANS (1541).[12]

TONGUES WERE GIVEN TO PRAISE, NOT TO POISON. AEGIDIUS HUNNIUS: He eloquently quotes "their throat is an open grave." For in the same way that graves, no matter how splendidly they may be decorated, if opened, immediately exhale deadly and harmful odors from the bodies of the dead, so it happens that nothing else comes forth from the heart of the ungodly, that is, through their throat as if it were an open doorway, except that which because of its extraordinary foulness is utterly displeasing to God.

He described their tongues in the same fashion. Although they were given for declaring God's praise and for setting forth what is profitable to our neighbor, he says that it is by their tongues that men and women commit themselves to deceit, fraud, malevolent shams, and abusive language of all kinds against other people, and that behind their lips is a most hideous and most harmful poison equal to that of asps, inasmuch as they

open their lips with a most destructive effect on others. Hence he does not merely say that the mouth of the ungodly utters blasphemies against God and hateful bitterness toward one's neighbor, but rather that it does these things to the fullest possible extent.

He says also that their "feet are swift to shed human blood, and in all their ways," that is, in every part of their life and manner of conduct (which is what is meant by "ways") there is nothing but "misery and destruction" in that they try to subject their neighbor to the utmost misery and calamity. And, because they walk at full speed in such ungodly ways as these, conversely they are utterly "ignorant of the way of peace" toward their neighbor.

Last, he brings all this to an abrupt close with: "there is no fear of God before their eyes." EXPOSITION ON ROMANS (1592).[13]

ALL PEOPLE ARE EQUALLY SINNERS. HULDRYCH ZWINGLI: So far, he demonstrates, with testimonies, that our actions are unprofitable. Now, following, these testimonies demonstrate that our mind and even our will are impure. . . . Even if people do not sin by an external action such as homicide or adultery, there is no good in them. Rather, they are like open graves that exhale nothing but harmful and putrid stench. In addition, Paul begins from the tongue and proceeds through all the limbs, showing that there is nothing good in us, but only a swamp[†] of all evils. Nothing but impurity comes out of the throat. The tongue is used for deceit, emitting the poison of asps, which is most harmful and incurable. The feet hurry to the shedding of blood. There is grief and ruin in all their ways. There is no peace or gentleness among them. Thus Paul demonstrates that all people are equally sinners. ANNOTATIONS ON ROMANS (1539).[14]

---

[12]Sarcerius, *In Apostolam ad Romanos*, L2v; citing Mt 15:19.

[13]Hunnius, *Epistolae Divi Pauli*, 132-33.
[14]Zwingli, *In Apostolam ad Romanos*, 414. [†]"A Lerna of evils" was a common phrase (cf. Erasmus, *Adages* 4.1.1). *Lerna* is the term for the body of water, sometimes referred to as a swamp, in which Heracles killed the Hydra. It was considered by some to be the mouth of hell.

FULL OF CURSES AND BITTERNESS. MARTIN BUCER: "Whose mouth is full of curses and bitterness." . . . It pertains to and expresses to the highest level the harmful and destructive speech of the ungodly who may attack and destroy the pious. The whole law is fulfilled in the love of—and good works toward—one's neighbor. Accordingly, Scripture describes the greatest perversity and sinfulness as injuries against one's neighbor. When these injuries are greatest, they come about by deceit, and Scripture describes them with these metaphors, magnifying and exaggerating them. They perfectly express the remarkable injury that is in this kind of offense, which is like an open grave or asps' venom. "The mouth full of bitterness and deceit" signifies the particular zeal and power of destroying one's neighbor with lies. COMMENTARY ON ROMANS (1536).[15]

BRINGING FORTH WICKEDNESS. JOHN CALVIN: Then he says that "their mouth is full of cursing and bitterness," a vice of opposite character to the former. The meaning is that they are in every way full of wickedness, for if they speak fair, they deceive and blend poison with their flatteries, but if they draw forth what they have in their hearts, bitterness and cursing stream out. COMMENTARY ON ROMANS 3:14.[16]

3:15-18 Paths of Ruin and Misery

DESTRUCTIVE PATHS. KONRAD PELLIKAN: "Swift feet run to shed blood." This passage is in Isaiah 59, where the prophet amply and deeply complains about piety and innocence being overturned in the people of Israel, where the same things are considered that follow here, although in other words. In Isaiah, what follows is, "Their thoughts are corrupt thoughts, desolation and destruction are in their paths, and they do not know the way of peace. Nor is justice in their footpath; their ways are perverse. The one who steps along them does not know peace."

The apostle passes over certain things, but one can understand those things on one's own from the ones that he has enumerated. The impious pretend to be hurt by good persons, while inside they are prepared and eager to utterly finish them off. But from Psalm 36:1 is at last added, "There is no fear of God before their eyes." And this is the beginning of the whole error of human life. Indeed, the one who does not return to God is led as utterly captive to Satan. From all these things it is clear that the Israelites, wholly guilty of their weighty sins, have had a righteousness from the law given to and known by them, which is not able to return righteousness by itself. And thus, righteousness from the law is waited for in vain. Therefore, another author of righteousness must be sought. He is the Savior who, being reconciled, may have mercy on those who are lost in sin. COMMENTARY ON ALL THE APOSTOLIC EPISTLES (1539).[17]

AGAINST CIVIC AND ECCLESIASTICAL VIOLENCE. DAVID PAREUS: "And the way of peace they have not known." He condemns civic and ecclesiastical violence—from the same passage of the prophet in verse 8—because, by sedition and obstinacy, they disturb every rank of men and women in the church and the state. Nor are they able to bear the laws and decrees that are composed for the peace and safety of them and others. COMMENTARY ON ROMANS (1608).[18]

THE TWOFOLD WAY. JOHANNES BUGENHAGEN: You see, there is a twofold way of the ungodly and the godly. Compare this with the preceding verses, and you will realize what his or her grief and calamity are. In the way of the wicked, they and others lose miserably. The way of peace is that in which we acknowledge the only God, the Father, by whose mercy our consciences are pacified. INTERPRETATION OF ROMANS (1531).[19]

---

[15]Bucer, *Metaphrases et Enarrationes*, 173-74; citing Ps 10:7.
[16]CTS 38:127* (CO 49:54).

[17]Pellikan, *In Omnes Apostolicas Epistolas*, 41; citing Is 59:7; Ps 36:1.
[18]Pareus, *In Divinam ad Romanos*, 271; citing Is 59:8.
[19]Bugenhagen, *In D. Pauli ad Romanos*, 30v.

THE SOURCE AND SEAT OF SIN. FRIEDRICH BALDUIN: For this is truly the source of all those criminal acts that he had a little while before recited: that they had removed God from before their eyes. For he who does not fear God, how will he ever respect people? But it must be known that the apostle in this list of sins does not speak only of actual sins, but also of original sin, from which it is evident that he speaks generally of all, not excluding even infants. And he speaks of original sin, from which we are liberated by the grace of God, and last because those actual sins presuppose original sin as their cause. And it clearly follows that the apostle places the seat of original sin not only in one part of man or woman, but in the whole self, in the intellect as well as the will, to all the faculties of the soul and all members of the body. COMMENTARY ON ROMANS (1620).[20]

WE DO NOT HAVE THE FEAR OF GOD. MARTIN LUTHER: But they nevertheless imagine that they have as much fear of God as possible. For what virtue will proud men or women not arrogate to themselves? Just as they consider themselves righteous in their search for God, so also they believe they have the fear of God and all the things which the apostle here denies to them, and all the things that he ascribes to them, these they presumptuously believe are as far away from them as possible. Therefore, unless one believes with faith in these words of the Holy Spirit to this psalm, that they are true and that no one is righteous before God, they will never think this about themselves so long as they seem righteous in their own eyes. Hence, it will always be necessary to realize that these things are true about us and that it can be said of each of us that we are unjust people, without fear of God, so that being thus humbled and confessing ourselves to be ungodly and foolish before God, we may deserve to be justified by him. LECTURES ON ROMANS.[21]

3:19 *That All Mouths Will Be Silenced*

ENTHYMEMES ON OUR ALL BECOMING SINNERS. ERASMUS SARCERIUS: It did not come about blindly that all people would become sinners. Rather, so that God alone would have the glory, the occasion of boasting was removed from us. So that at last, we might have occasion to flee to free grace.

An enthymeme:[†] God alone ought to have all glory; therefore we have all become sinners.

Likewise, to God alone is owed all glory. Therefore we all have become sinners, for which reason the occasion of boasting has been removed from us.

Likewise, if we were not all sinners, and we were able to be justified by our works, no one would have fled to the mercy of God. On the contrary, no one would have had occasion to flee to him. Therefore we all have been made sinners, so that for us there might be occasion for the mercy of God. Similar passages are found in Ephesians 2:8 and Galatians 3:22.

The arrangement of the enthymeme is thus clearer: So that every mouth is silenced, therefore, from the works of the law, no flesh is justified. Therefore, we are all sinners. "So that every mouth is silenced." Namely, so that the mouth may not boast in its own works of righteousness. Moreover, this shows, on the other hand, how great the cause for our boasting would be if we were justified by our works, and if we were not all (equally) sinners. NOTES ON ROMANS (1541).[22]

AN *ANTHYPOPHORA* ON THE LAW. HULDRYCH ZWINGLI: Paul answers the Jews through an *anthypophora*,[†] for they could say: "What is this to us?" Paul says, "The law has been given especially to you." Moreover, he understands that even the prophets are under the law. It is as if Paul is saying, "These things first of all apply to you, although the Gentiles have not been excepted. For all are sinners,

---

[20]Balduin, *Catechesis Apostolica*, 197-98.
[21]LW 25:233*; citing Ps 12:3.

[22]Sarcerius, *In Apostolam ad Romanos*, L6r*; citing Eph 2:8; Gal 3:22. [†]An enthymeme is a syllogism in which one of the premises is implied rather than stated.

so that the mouth of everyone may be silenced. Therefore, I have brought forth these things so clearly that I have silenced all of your mouths. And, therefore, no one may say, 'I am not a sinner,' but rather, all people will recognize themselves to be sinners—unprofitable and infirm. And so that with all their faith, they will cast themselves onto God. And so that they will recognize themselves as lacking divine grace, and thus they will not boast at all about themselves." ANNOTATIONS ON ROMANS (1539).[23]

No One Fulfills the Law Perfectly.

JOHANNES BRENZ: Although there are those who follow the law and who do the works of the law most diligently, nevertheless they are not justified by works. That is, they are not acquitted from unrighteousness before God. Certainly the law requires the perfect work of righteousness. For what is more excellent than to love God from one's entire heart and one's neighbor as oneself? And if people would do these works perfectly, they would certainly be justified by works of the law. But there is not one person who fulfills these works perfectly. And that is on account of original sin, which has remained even in those who are born again because of Christ. Original sin still clings to their flesh by its action, so that they do what they do not desire. Therefore, there is no one who is justified by works of the law. COMMENTARY ON ROMANS (1564).[24]

The Law of God Leads to Lament for Sins.

DIRK PHILIPS: Therefore, now the sin of Adam and Eve may neither judge nor condemn anyone, since Christ Jesus, through his death and blood, has taken it away, (as we with God's help will further clarify). But just as sin had its origin in disobedience and began with the knowledge of good and evil in Adam and Eve, in like measure it also occurs with children. For, though they all come from a sinful Adam, yet original sin (as

people call it) is not imputed to them by God to damnation, for the sake of Jesus Christ. For they are in part like Adam and Eve were before the fall, namely this, that they being simply both good and bad, understand neither good nor evil. But as soon as they come to a knowledge of good and evil and step from simple ignorance into conscious wickedness, and they sin against the Lord through their own disobedience and transgression of the divine Word and command, then it is the proper and appointed time that they first be taught, yes, with the law of God be heartily admonished to penitence so that they amend themselves, lament their sins before God, confess, and bear remorse over them. Thereafter, they must again be comforted with the gospel. THE BAPTISM OF OUR LORD JESUS CHRIST.[25]

3:20 The Law Brings Knowledge Rather Than Justification

Grace Alone Justifies.

MARTIN LUTHER: Other people work in such a way that they think they are fulfilling the law and thus are righteous, even though they neither desire grace nor realize and hate the fact that they are sinners; because they have worked according to the outward form of the law, they do not dispose themselves to seek righteousness but rather boast as if through these works it were already in their possession, being totally unaware in their thinking that they are observing the law either with no will or with a will which is unwilling and hostile, or at least out of love and desire for earthly things, but not out of a love for God. And thus they stand still, content and without plans for works worth seeking in behalf of grace, by which they might have also willingness in the law. The fact is that neither the works which precede nor those which follow justify. How much less the works of the law! The works that precede do not justify because they prepare for righteousness; those that follow do not

---

[23]Zwingli, *In Epistolam Romanos*, 414. †An *anthypophora* is a rhetorical device in which one raises a question and immediately answers it.
[24]Brenz, *In Epistolam*, 78-79.

[25]CRR 6:77*; citing Rom 5:1, 12; Mt 28:19; Mk 1:4; Acts 2:38; Eph 2:7.

justify because they demand a justification that has already been accomplished. For we are not made righteous by doing righteous works, but rather we do righteous works by being righteous. Therefore grace alone justifies. LECTURES ON ROMANS (1516).[26]

RECONCILING PAUL AND JAMES. FRIEDRICH BALDUIN: Q: How is it that our Paul could write that nobody is justified by the works of the law, when the apostle James expressly writes the contrary, that Abraham was justified by works? . . .

A: From these things, therefore, insofar as they are said concerning justification and works, the reconciliation of these two apostolic passages, of Paul and James, is easy. When Paul writes "no flesh is justified by works" he speaks of justification before God, to which he expressly adds the qualification. In this matter it is not works but faith that applies, which is that sole instrument by which we apprehend the righteousness of Christ imputed to us. But when James writes, "you see that Abraham was justified by works" he is speaking of justification before men and women, or rather of the declaration, by its effects, of the righteousness of faith. COMMENTARY ON ROMANS (1620).[27]

TWO WAYS THE PURITAN DIVINES RECONCILE PAUL AND JAMES. WILLIAM PEMBLE:

1. The first is by distinguishing the word *justification*, which may be taken either:

a. For the absolution of a sinner in God's judgment.

b. For the declaration of a person's righteousness before people.

This distinction is certain and has its ground in Scripture, which uses the word *justify* in both ways: for the quitting of us in God's sight, and for the manifestation of our innocence before other people against accusation or suspicion of faultiness. They apply this distinction for the reconciling of the two

apostles. Thus St. Paul speaks of justification *in foro Dei*. St. James speaks of justification *in foro hominis*. A person is justified by faith without works, says St. Paul. That is, in God's sight, a person obtains remission of sins and is reputed righteous only for his faith in Christ, not for his works' sake. A man or a woman is justified by works, and not by faith alone, says St. James. That is, in people's sight, we are declared to be just by our good works, not by our faith alone, which with other inward and invisible graces are made visible to others only in the good works that they see us perform. That this application is not unfit for reconciling this difference, may be shown by the following parts:

a. For St. Paul, it's agreed on all sides that he speaks of a person's justification in God's sight.

b. For St. James, we are to show that with just probability he may be understood to be speaking of the declaration of our justification and righteousness before others. . . .

2. The second way then of reconciling these places is by distinguishing of the word (i.e., faith), which is taken in a doubled sense.

a. First, for that faith that is true and living (i.e., faith that works through love) and is fruitful in all manner of obedience.

b. Second, for that faith that is false and dead, being only a bare acknowledgment of the truth of all articles of religion accompanied with an outward formality of profession, but yet destitute of sincere obedience.

This distinction of this word *faith* is certain by the Scriptures, as has already been shown in the handling of that grace. Our men now apply it thus. St. Paul when he affirms that we are justified by faith alone, speaks of that faith which is true and living, working by charity. St. James, when he denies a person is justified by faith alone, is disputing against that faith which is false and dead, without power to bring forth any good works. Thus the apostles speak no contradictions, where Paul

[26]LW 25:241-42*.
[27]Balduin, *Commentario Romanos*, 205, 208; citing Jas 2:21.

teaches we are justified by a true faith, and St. James affirms that we are not justified by a false faith.

Again, St. Paul says we are not justified by works. St. James says we are justified by works. And there is no contradiction at all here either. For St. James understands by works, a working faith in opposition to the idle and dead faith before-spoken of (by a metonymy of the effect). From this it is plain that these two propositions, "We are not justified by works," which is Paul's, and "We are justified by a working faith," which is James, sweetly consort together. Paul severs works from our justification, but not from our faith. James joined works to our faith, but not to our justification. TREATISE OF JUSTIFICATION BY FAITH (1625).[28]

To Make or to Declare Righteous?

FRIEDRICH BALDUIN: To "justify" in Scripture is not to "make righteous" or to infuse new qualities of righteousness, but to constitute, pronounce, and declare as righteous, in the same way that God was said earlier to be justified by his words. The publicans had justified God, not because he had become righteous from being unrighteous, but because he was acknowledged and declared to be righteous. In the same way he is also said to be sanctified and magnified. But that declaration either happens before God or before others. Before God, men and women are justified when they are absolved from sins on account of the righteousness of Christ freely imputed to them. And this justification Paul attributes to faith. One is justified before men and women when one is acknowledged as being righteous and as being received in grace by God. And this latter kind of justification happens a posteriori, for it is attributed even to works, which bear witness of the faith of the justified person as an effect bears witness of its cause. St. Paul speaks of the first kind of justification, whereas St. James speaks of the latter, as is clear from James 2:18. Both kinds have a forensic meaning. For this is the unifying thread in justification terminology. COMMENTARY ON ROMANS (1620).[29]

Neither Ceremonial Nor Moral Law
Justifies. PETER MARTYR VERMIGLI: It is necessary that we know of what works of the law the apostle is dealing with here. And here we affirm that he speaks universally of all works, so that those things that are mentioned here ought not to be exclusively applied to ceremonies, since it is the whole law that is referred to. However, we admit that the controversy sprang from the reason of ceremonies, for false apostles went about imposing them as necessary for those who believed in Christ, as though Christ could not bring salvation to believers without them. . . . Yet, although the contention sprang by reason of ceremonies, yet by the guidance of the Holy Spirit it nevertheless happens that Paul redirects the question away from this narrower issue (species) and considers the larger question (genus) of the law as a whole. For if the whole thing were overthrown then it would follow that the smaller parts within that whole would likewise be done away with. For if the law as a whole does not justify, certainly neither will their ceremonies justify, for they are but a narrower aspect and part of the law. (The reason ceremonies are in view is that the schism among them began over questions of ritual.) . . .

We can see this in his letter to the Galatians: "We who are by nature Jews, and not sinners of the Gentiles—since we know that humans are not justified by works of the law without faith in Jesus Christ—we also have believed in Christ Jesus that we might be justified by faith in Christ and not by the works of the law, for by the works of the law no flesh will be justified." And it is beyond all controversy that Paul did not rebuke Peter on any matter other than ceremonies. Also in the same book in chapter 3 he says: "Did you receive the Spirit by the works of the law, or by the preaching of the faith? Are you so foolish, as having begun in the Spirit you now seek to be perfected in the flesh?" In that text, since he described the "works of the law" as being done "in the flesh," it is clear that he was talking about Mosaic ceremonies. But, even if the controversy had begun on this question, it nevertheless most helpfully happened that Paul

---

[28]Pemble, *Vindiciae Fidei*, 190-91*; citing Gal 5:6.
[29]Balduin, *Catechesis Apostolica*, 206; citing Rom 3:4; Jas 2:18.

redirected it to the larger question of the law as a whole. For it would come to pass that once ceremonies had been disavowed, in the course of time many would try to attribute justification to *moral* works instead. But this is sufficiently and quite clearly refuted by Paul's logic as it is worked out here.

And it should be noted that the argument works both ways. For just as it is proper to infer that since no works of the law justify, therefore neither do the ceremonies, so likewise we can conclude in reverse, that if the ceremonies do not justify, therefore neither does any other part of the law, since the ceremonies were the chief part of the law. They were the duties first and most chiefly commanded: "I am," says the Lord, "your God. Therefore, it is fitting that I should be worshiped by you both in spirit and in external confession consisting not only in words but also in rituals established by me." Nor were those ceremonies less obligatory for the patriarchs of old than baptism and the Eucharist are for us today. Therefore, just as the Jews were gravely sinning when, not being satisfied with the worship that was prescribed by God himself but in search of new ceremonies and rituals invented by men and women (which is to wish to add to the divine wisdom, for according to Deuteronomy 4 their peculiar wisdom as a people was the worship instituted among them by God), so likewise our people most gravely sin when, going beyond baptism and the Eucharist and the things that we hold were handed down to us by Christ, they establish other things that people have invented as necessary for the worship of God and for salvation, such as the mass, the invocation of saints, and other things of this kind. Commentary on Romans (1560).[30]

Sacred Rites Must Be Done in Faith.
Martin Bucer: "Therefore by the works of the law." This sentence must be inculcated to every person in the most diligent way. For consider how

these words sharply condemn both the Jews and superstitious Christians alike who might seek to be justified before God by means of ceremonies, but who in fact depend on nothing other than themselves. For they put effort into nothing else when they wish to commend themselves to God. But faith, by which we are justified through Christ alone, surrenders us to Christ. Nor does it leave us to walk around in darkness, that is, to abide in any perversity. There are people who continue in perversity—which they cannot fail to realize makes them obnoxious to God and casts reproach upon the blood of Christ—and yet all the while render him works by way of sacred ceremonies. In their ceremonies, they are either mocking God by their hypocrisy, or they are sincere and by this means are seeking to avert God's wrath toward them. But if they were putting their faith in Christ's death, as they are eager to tell us they do through their sacred ceremonies as much as in all their sacred actions, when performing them they would not be able to avoid being deeply convicted and ardently stirred up by true repentance for wrongs committed, to apply themselves to the pursuit of righteousness. If our heart is not in it when we either listen to or handle the Word of God, and we perform sacred rites, taking part in holy supplications and other religious actions, let us have no doubt that we are then casting unspeakable reproach on God and on our Lord Jesus Christ, for we are either mocking him with ungodly hypocrisy, or preferring our own works to him. This evil is of such a kind that ever since the appearance of humankind there has been no period of history in which it has failed to corrupt the greater part of humanity. Fear of God disturbs people, and hence is born a certain shame of being impious, and so it happens that when they see holy people applying themselves devotedly to sacred ceremonies and by them entreating divine favor, they imitate them, but do so only with an outward performance of the ceremonies, not with inward faith. As long as they are not improving and becoming more holy in their lives as a result, for which purpose the ceremonies were established, it can only be that they are doing

---

[30]Vermigli, *In Epistolam S. Pauli*, 169-70; citing Gal 2:15-16; Gal 3:2-3; Deut 4:6-8.

what they do either because they are ashamed of looking like atheists, or because they are placing the protection of their salvation in ceremonies. COMMENTARY ON ROMANS (1536).[31]

BAPTISM, INFANTS, AND THE CONVERTED. THOMAS CRANMER: For the fuller understanding of this, it is our part and duty to always remember the great mercy of God, how that (all the world being wrapped in sin by breaking of the law) God sent his only Son our Savior Christ into this world to fulfill the law for us; and to make a sacrifice and satisfaction by the shedding of his most precious blood, or (as it may be called) to make amends to his Father for our sins, to assuage his wrath and indignation conceived against us for the same. To the point that infants, being baptized and dying in their infancy, are by this sacrifice washed from their sins, brought to God's favor, and made his children, and inheritors of his kingdom of heaven. And those who actually do sin after their baptism, when they convert and genuinely turn again to God, they are likewise washed by this sacrifice from their sins, in such a way that no spot of any sin will be imputed to their damnation. This is that justification or righteousness that St. Paul speaks of, when he says, "No one is justified by the works of the law," but freely by faith in Jesus Christ. And again he says, "We believe in Christ Jesus, that we are justified freely by the faith of Christ, and not by the works of the law, because no one will be justified by the works of the law." HOMILY ON SALVATION (1547 AND 1560).[32]

THE LAW EXPOSES RATHER THAN DISPOSES OF SIN. GEORG MAJOR: The reason why the Jews are not justified by the works of the law is that sin is not taken away by the law, but only exposed and recognized, and thus sin becomes more exceedingly sinful. For the law is a judgment by which God reveals his great wrath against sin, from which arises the pains of death and hell. On the proper

use and effect of the law that he will teach below in chapter 7, he here touches only in passing. EXPOSITION OF THE EPISTLES OF PAUL (1529).[33]

BY THE LAW, WE HAVE KNOWLEDGE OF SIN. DAVID PAREUS: By the law, we have knowledge of sin, and, therefore, of not being righteous. . . . First, he had spoken of nature in Romans 2:15. Have the Gentiles convicted themselves inwardly in their thoughts, by alternating accusations and excuses? Indeed, what is a bad conscience if not the practice (*praxis*) of the law of nature, leading us to an inward knowledge of sin and the wrath of God, from where follows fear and trembling for our sins? For truly, on account of the depravity and carelessness of the flesh, the very law is obliterated, the conscience is held in check, and reason is blinded so that one does not recognize one's sins, or regards them as light matters. For that reason, the written law has come to us, which reveals any small and hidden sins, carnal desire and sensuality, and all disordered affections and emotions. Therefore, how does one gain the strongest possible knowledge of sin (just as below in chapter 7)? By comparing our nature and actions with the standard of the law. Because righteousness is in agreement with it, and because sin differs from it. On the other hand, human nature outside of Christ has been compared to the plumb line of the law. It is recognized as no less corrupted and twisted than a bow is compared to a ruler. The same discord is found in actions, feelings, thoughts, words, the things we say, and deeds, both inward and outward. Thus through the law is all *epignosis* (true knowledge) of sin. First, the original discord, which is the depravity of nature from our parents' fall, which has spread out to all with eternal guilt. Second, a defect in the light in our minds and of uprightness in our wills and hearts, that was present from the first creation of our debt. Third, of all our inclinations, appetites, and emotions that are against God's law. Fourth, of sinful actions in our thoughts and all the things we say and do that are offensive

---

[31]Bucer, *Metaphrases et Enarrationes*, 199.
[32]Cranmer, *Miscellaneous Writings*, 128*; citing Rom 3:22, 24; Gal 2:16.

[33]Major, *Enarrationes Epistolarum S. Pauli*, 108.

to the divine law, or are deficient from it. And finally, of the great number of things we have not done, when the law instructed us to do those things that we omitted or to omit those things that we do. Commentary on Romans.[34]

The Uses of the Law. Philipp Melanchthon: Paul's concern is that one could object: If we are not righteous by the law, for what purpose was the law given? Paul responds (however, more briefly) because this same concern is repeated below. And this response is seen by the world as something wholly new and absurd, that sin is only revealed by the law, not taken away. For lawgivers make laws for kingdoms not only to show sins, but to take them away. The hearer must be reminded that here Paul is not at all preaching about civil righteousness and external morals. He is treating a different matter: how we may be accounted righteous before God; how we may receive remission of sins; and what the law contributes there. Therefore the uses of the law must be distinguished. Moreover we are here talking not only about the law of Moses but about the moral law inscribed in all men and women.

Now there are two uses. One is the political, namely, to coerce carnal persons from the outside. For God also requires this external justice, although we are not righteous before God on account of it and it does not merit remission of sins. He is not speaking about this use in this statement. Elsewhere he does speak about this use: The law is laid down for the unjust.

The other use is not political, but concerns the judgment of God and the conscience, namely, to accuse and to terrify the conscience, as he says elsewhere . . . that is, the law reveals sin and terrifies hearts. It is of such knowledge that he is speaking here. Commentary on Romans (1540).[35]

Transition from Contrition to Repentance. Georg Major: To this point in the letter, Paul has handed down to us [only] the first part of the doctrine of repentance, namely, that of contrition, which is the acknowledgment of sin and a sense of God's wrath against sin, in which he shows that the whole world is guilty and liable to God's judgment. It is therefore asked, "If all righteousness of all men and women and all works and merits are excluded from justification before God, and the whole world remains under condemnation, how then are we justified before God, and by what means does redemption from sin, God's wrath, and death actually happen?" Paul answers, "It happens by faith embracing the righteousness of God as not reckoning sins to us on account of the promised Mediator." Then, in the words that follow, he begins to address the second part of repentance, namely, faith. Exposition of the Epistles of Paul (1529).[36]

---

[34]Pareus, *In Divinam ad Romanos*, 276-77; citing Rom 2:15.

[35]Melanchthon, *Commentary on Romans*, 97-98*; citing Rom 2:12; 1 Cor 15:56.
[36]Major, *Enarrationes Epistolarum S. Pauli*, 108.

3:21-26 THE RIGHTEOUSNESS OF GOD REVEALED

21But now the righteousness of God has been manifested apart from the law, although the Law and the Prophets bear witness to it— 22the righteousness of God through faith in Jesus Christ for all who believe. For there is no distinction: 23for all have sinned and fall short of the glory of God, 24and are justified by his grace as a gift, through the redemption that is in Christ Jesus, 25whom God put forward as a propitiation by his blood, to be received by faith. This was to show God's righteousness, because in his divine forbearance he had passed over former sins. 26It was to show his righteousness at the present time, so that he might be just and the justifier of the one who has faith in Jesus.

OVERVIEW: This passage is highly significant for the Reformation. Luther wrote in the margin of his Bible at Romans 3:23-26, "This is the chief point, and the very central place of the letter, and of the whole Bible."[1] Calvin said of Romans 3:24-26, "There is, perhaps, no passage in the whole Scripture that illustrates in a more striking manner the efficacy of his righteousness."[2] And Melanchthon said of it, "This whole period [i.e., Rom 3:24-26] contains the very head and front of Paul's discussion."[3] For the reformers in general, the doctrine of *sola fide* finds much ballast in these verses.

In the writings of the reformers, the righteousness of God that Paul refers to here is the righteousness by which he justifies, and that is Christ himself, faith in whom alone is the means by which God makes us righteous. This is apart from the law, apart from works. The reformers argue that Paul is not merely implying the discontinuation of the ceremonial law but also indicating that all works of the law, without exception, are not efficacious. This puts them in opposition to the medieval Catholic Church, which taught that certain works could be meritorious.

The reformers explore the relationship between law and gospel in detail. We obtain the righteousness of God by faith in Christ who died for us. This faith is not bare belief, but rather firm belief combined with trust, and it is a gift from God. All people need this faith, for all are sinners and have lost the glory of God that was intended for them as those created in the image of God.

The commentators study the process by which we are justified. Some use the Aristotelian categories of the four causes (efficient, formal/instrumental, material, final) to analyze this. Others point to the fact that Paul's reference here to Christ's passive obedience (i.e., his submission to the cross) does not imply that Christ's active obedience (to the law) is not also essential to our salvation. Both the passion and holiness of Christ are necessary as meritorious causes of our justification. To justify means to acquit one from charges of guilt, and this is what God does for us in Christ. The reference to Christ as our propitiation may be an allusion to the mercy seat, and it is Christ the Propitiator to whom we must look for mercy. Justification by faith and the work of redemption reveal God's righteous character and glory.

3:21 Righteousness Apart from the Law

ALL WORKS ARE EXCLUDED, WITHOUT EXCEPTION. JOHN CALVIN: It is not certain for what distinct reason he calls it the righteousness of God, which we obtain by faith, whether it is because it can stand alone before God, or because the Lord in his mercy confers it on us. As both

---

[1]Quoted in James Morison, *A Critical Exposition of the Third Chapter of St. Paul's Epistle to the Romans* (London: Hamilton, Adams, 1866), 269.
[2]CTS 38:141 (CO 49:61).
[3]Quoted in Morison, *A Critical Exposition*, 270.

interpretations are suitable, we contend for neither. This righteousness, then, which God communicates to people, and accepts alone, and owns as righteousness, has been revealed, he says, "without the law," that is, without the aid of the law. The law is to be understood as meaning works, for it is not proper to refer this to its teaching, which he immediately adduces as bearing witness to the gratuitous righteousness of faith. Some confine it to ceremonies, but this view I shall presently show to be unsound and frigid. We ought then to know that the merits of works are excluded. We also see that he does not blend works with the mercy of God, but having taken away and wholly removed all confidence in works, he sets up mercy alone.

It is not unknown to me that Augustine gives a different explanation, for he thinks that the righteousness of God is the grace of regeneration. This grace he allows to be free, because God renews us, when unworthy, by his Spirit, and from this he excludes the works of the law, that is, those works by which people of themselves endeavor, without renovation, to render God indebted to them. I also well know that some new speculators proudly adduce this sentiment, as though it were at this day revealed to them. But that the apostle includes all works without exception, even those that the Lord produces in his own people, is evident from the context.

For no doubt Abraham was regenerated and led by the Spirit of God at the time when he denied that he was justified by works. Hence he excluded from humanity's justification not only works morally good, as they commonly call them, but also all those that even the faithful can perform. Again, since this is a definition of righteousness of faith, "Blessed are those whose iniquities are forgiven," there is no question to be made about this or that kind of work, but the merit of works being abolished, the remission of sins alone is set down as the cause of righteousness. COMMENTARY ON ROMANS 3:21.[4]

THE RIGHTEOUSNESS OF GOD. ANDREAS KNOPKEN: The righteousness that God confers—and by which he justifies—is Christ himself, faith in whom alone is the basis on which God makes righteous those of the ungodly who become believers, apart from any works or assisting merits. "For being ignorant of the righteousness of God and wanting to establish their own," and in other passages: "Christ has become for us wisdom from God and redemption and sanctification and righteousness," which is the righteousness that is manifested by the preaching of the gospel, witnessed to of old by the law, such as "do not say in your heart." Likewise in the Prophets, such as "I will pardon your iniquities," and "I will spare them as a man spares his son who obeys him." Also in the Psalms, "Blessed is the man to whom the Lord does not impute sin," and "none who hope in him will be condemned."

This is therefore his meaning: The "righteousness of God" is faith in Christ. That is, because we believe the promise in which Christ is promised as the salvation of the world, we are therefore justified, but not by the law, since although it shows us our sin, it is incapable of rehabilitating the sinful nature. Hence our own powers and efforts amount to nothing. OF THE EPISTLE TO THE ROMANS (1524).[5]

THE RIGHTEOUSNESS OF FAITH. JACQUES LEFÈVRE D'ÉTAPLES: This "righteousness of God" was witnessed to by the law. For the "righteousness of God" is the righteousness of faith, a witness to which we find in Genesis: "Abraham believed God, and it was reckoned to him for righteousness." There is also a witness to it in the prophets, as for example, in Isaiah according to the Septuagint: "Behold, I place in Zion a most costly stone, a cornerstone, proved, elect, and precious, and whoever believes in him will not be put to shame." And with respect to this righteousness and justification by faith, neither being a Jew nor a

---

[4]CTS 38:134-35* (CO 49:57-58).

[5]Knopken, *In Epistolam ad Romanos*, C7v; citing Rom 10:3; Ps 32:2; 34:22; 1 Cor 1:30; Rom 10:6; Deut 30:12-14; Mal 3:17.

Gentile, neither a Greek nor a barbarian, has any bearing. And this is solely from God's mercy, "who desires that all people should be saved and come to a knowledge of the truth." Further, people should attribute glory to God alone, for of themselves and by their works they cannot be saved, for by them they more often merit damnation rather than salvation, which Paul explains in this way: "for all have sinned and lack the glory of God." COMMENTARY ON ROMANS (C. 1512).[6]

THE HOLY SPIRIT REVEALS UNRIGHTEOUS-NESS. HEINRICH BULLINGER: Until now, Paul has been speaking about sin. Now he turns to the subject of righteousness. This is in accord with what Christ said, that the time was coming when the Holy Spirit would convict the world concerning sin, since they have not believed in God, and concerning righteousness, since the Son has gone to the Father. For to this point Paul has sufficiently proved that unfaithfulness and wicked deeds are the fruit of unbelief, showing that there is nothing firm, just, true or righteous within humans, and that they are, as a result, children of wrath and condemned by the righteous judgment of God. Let us regard this same verdict as applying to us as well, if we worship idols, do violence to the law of nature, or contrive the most shameful deeds contrary to our consciences, to say nothing yet of hypocrisy. But when we, who are marked with the name of "Christian" ought to have been sincerely cultivating righteousness, we carried all our works out sluggishly, to say nothing of the times when we have wholly neglected them. True Christians are not those who have merely acquired the name, but those who by faith and purity of life exert themselves in sanctification. Literal baptism profits nobody if the heart also is not purged of evil. But to have heard the gospel of God is to have heaped up greater judgment against oneself if one's life does not correspond with one's doctrine. "The servant who knows the will of the master but does not do it will be beaten with many stripes." It is

true that we men and women are but flesh and blood inclined to evil, so that we are not able to render such pure obedience as the law of God demands. Therefore, there is not within us power sufficient to be justified before God. We are able to be regarded as just in the sight of men and women, but God looks on the heart. All things are corrupt and likened to a stinking grave. How, therefore, can we be justified? Certainly not of ourselves, nor by the law, nor by works. For what else is a human being than a creature of base lusts and a "Lerna of evils"?[†] So that if, in such corrupt flesh, you were to try to perform any kind of righteousness whatever, you would be doing nothing more prudent than if you try to collect gems from the sewers or from shells on the beach. Therefore, with every empty hope of righteousness now taken away, Paul shows what true righteousness is and applies a gospel bandage to wounded consciences. COMMENTARY ON ROMANS (1533).[7]

RIGHTEOUSNESS BEFORE PEOPLE VERSUS RIGHTEOUSNESS BEFORE GOD. ERASMUS SARCERIUS: Paul clearly distinguishes between one's righteousness before other humans and righteousness in the eyes of God. The former is afforded by the works of the law, but the same is not true of the latter, which is granted apart from the law, as Paul said.

You must make the distinction that the gospel does not abolish the civil or political righteousness that exists in the eyes of the world, but rather, it demands even more of it. This is what even Christ said, in Matthew 5, where he required of his disciples an even greater righteousness: "Unless your righteousness abounds more than that of the scribes and Pharisees, you will not enter the kingdom of heaven."

He calls the "righteousness of God" a freely bestowed imputation and acceptance, as when

---

[6]Lefèvre, Contenta, 74v; citing Rom 4:3; Is 28:16; 1 Tim 2:4.

[7]Bullinger, In Sanctissimam Pauli, 52v-53r; citing Jn 16:8; Lk 12:4-7. [†]"A Lerna of evils" was a common phrase (cf. Erasmus, Adages 4.1.1). Lerna is the term for the body of water, sometimes referred to as a swamp, in which Heracles killed the Hydra. It was considered by some to be the mouth of hell.

from a judge's compassion a person charged with crime is exonerated and pronounced righteous when that judge freely pardons sins out of sheer mercy. Notes on Romans (1541).[8]

Three Distinctions of Law from Gospel.

Tilemann Hesshus: It must first be observed in this passage what the distinction is between the law and the gospel, which must always be kept clear in the church, and apart from which the discourses of the prophets and the apostles cannot possibly be understood. Paul very clearly states that "the righteousness of God is revealed apart from the law." It must, therefore, follow that a different kind of doctrine is put forth by the apostle, differing from the law, in which a new and wonderful righteousness of God is manifested, differing from the righteousness of the law: namely, the promise of the gospel. Now there are three distinctions according to which the law and the gospel differ from one another.

First, the knowledge of the law was placed within our first parents in creation, for God formed man and woman according to his image in righteousness and holiness. And even though this light within humans has been horribly obscured by sin and scrambled by darkness, so much so that humans now by the light of nature neither regard God himself nor know his will in all things, nor most importantly of all can they understand the works of the first table of the law, nevertheless there remains within them something like a very tiny spark of this light and teaching of the law so that they by their rational judgment naturally understand the difference between noble and wicked conduct. This is why Paul says that "the work of the law is written in their hearts, bearing witness with their own conscience."

But the promise of the gospel is a mystery hidden from the beginning of the ages, revealed by our Lord Jesus Christ. Before that revelation the doctrine of the gospel was unknown to all creatures. Neither Adam nor the angels saw into God's

council of the redemption of the human race before the promise was revealed that the Seed would crush the head of the serpent. For this knowledge was not revealed in creation itself, which is why John says, "Nobody has seen God at any time; the Son who is in the bosom of the Father, he has declared him to us."

Second, they differ in terms of their promises. The law promised God's favor and delight, all pleasant things of this life, and eternal life, but only to those who rendered whole and perfect obedience to the law, as it is said, "If you wish to enter into life, keep the commandments." But if one's obedience is not whole, but is contaminated by sin, then the law not only promises nothing good to such a sinner but it also threatens and calls down a curse and eternal damnation on him, as it is said, "Cursed is everyone who does not continue in all the things that are written in this book of the law." All promises of the law are so conditional that they rigorously demand our perfect obedience and offer life to us *ex debito* (on the basis of what is therefore owed to us).

But the promise of the gospel is not conditional; it does not demand our works, but is given freely; it demonstrates the immense mercy of God toward the unworthy and polluted; it shows us the Mediator Jesus Christ who fulfilled the law in our place, whose obedience acquired life and salvation for us and who also offers and grants the remission of sins and eternal life freely to all who believe in the Son of God as Mediator, as it is been testified to them. To this end does all the testimony of the prophets tend, as they hold out the promise that all who believe in his name will receive the remission of their sins.

Third, they differ as to their effects. For the law divinely discloses to us God's judgment and accuses our uncleanness and declares on us the punishment of eternal death. It does not bring joy to the heart, but horrible terrors, trembling, and desperation, for it places eternal damnation before our eyes, from which we are unable to flee by any of our powers. Paul spoke of this effect of the law: "By the law is the knowledge of sin"; "The law works

---

[8]Sarcerius, *In Apostolam ad Romanos*, M; citing Mt 5:20.

wrath"; "I would not have known that covetousness was sin if the law had not said, 'You shall not covet.'" Also, the law is "the ministration of death."

But the gospel has a much different effect. For it freely offers and grants remission of sins to the unworthy; liberation from the wrath of God, from death, from the tyranny of Satan, and from hell; and it transfers us into the kingdom of light and life. It stirs up neither terrors nor flight, but rather fills the heart with wonderful rejoicing, kindles a new light, brings peace of conscience, raises us up and comforts us, and gives us new life and health. Hence Christ said, "Whoever will drink of the water which I will give to him will never thirst for eternity, but the water which I will give him will spring up within him as a saving fountain of water unto eternal life." And also: "The gospel is the power of God unto salvation for all who believe." Again, "Truly I say to you, if anyone keeps my word, he will never see death." By this distinction between the law and the gospel being observed, not only is this passage of Paul illuminated with a great light, but also all the other discourses of the prophets and the apostles are more easily and accurately understood. EXPOSITION ON ROMANS (1571).[9]

THESE ARE NOT NEW TEACHINGS. JOHANNES BUGENHAGEN: He received the testimony. Paul said these things of necessity in order to again commend the Scripture to us in opposition to the new prophets who presently disregard the Scripture and are bold to say, "What have I to do with the Old Testament? The Spirit is the useful one who teaches me all things." This is certainly right. But at the same time, these miserable people do not see that the things themselves that the Holy Spirit teaches are confirmed and had already been said in Moses and the Prophets, for that which we teach at present is not a new doctrine. Or is Christ someone other than the one who had been promised to Adam, and afterward to Abraham and

the fathers? For this reason Paul said, "Having been revealed"; that is, he is not a new creation, but in truth he always was, although he escaped our notice. INTERPRETATION OF ROMANS (1531).[10]

3:22 Righteousness Through Faith in Christ

THE ORDER OF DISCUSSING JUSTIFICATION. JOHN CALVIN: Paul shows in few words what this justification is, even that which is found in Christ and is apprehended in faith. At the same time, by introducing again the name of God, he seems to make God the founder and not only the approver of the righteousness of which he speaks, as though he had said that it flows from him alone, or that its origin is from heaven, but that it is made manifest to us in Christ.

When, therefore, we discuss this subject, we ought to proceed in this way: First, the question respecting our justification is to be referred, not to human judgment, but to the judgment of God, before whom nothing is counted righteousness but perfect and absolute obedience to the law, which appears clear from its promises and threatenings. If no one is found who has attained such a perfect measure, it follows that all are in themselves destitute of righteousness. Second, it is necessary that Christ should come to our aid, who being alone just can render us just by transferring to us his own righteousness. You now see how the righteousness of faith is the righteousness of Christ. When therefore we are justified, the efficient cause is the mercy of God, the meritorious is Christ, the instrumental is the word in connection with faith. Hence faith is said to justify, because it is the instrument by which we receive Christ, in whom righteousness is conveyed to us. Having been made partakers of Christ, we ourselves are not only just, but our works are counted just before God, and for this reason, because whatever imperfections there may be in them are obliterated by the blood of Christ, the promises that are conditional are also

---

[9]Hesshus, *Explicatio Epistolae Pauli*, 88v-90v; citing Rom 2:15; Gen 3:15; Jn 1:18; Mt 19:17; Deut 27:26; Acts 10:43; Rom 3:20; 4:15; 7:7; 2 Cor 3:7; Jn 4:14; Rom 1:16; Jn 8:51.

[10]Bugenhagen, *In D. Pauli ad Romanos*, 32v.

by the same grace fulfilled to us, for God rewards our works as perfect, inasmuch as their defects are covered by free pardon. Commentary on Romans 3:22.[11]

Why There Is No Need for Doubt. Matthias Hafenreffer: It follows that we ought not to doubt about our justification and our salvation. The reason is that because the godly place the foundation of their trust not in their own worthiness, or merits, or disposition, but in God's mercy and in the superabounding merit of Christ, and are persuaded that "he who has begun a good work will continue it until the day of Christ." Disputation on Justification from Romans (1606).[12]

It Is "Righteous" Because It Fulfills a Promise. Johannes Oecolampadius: "The righteousness of God." You should be wondering why it is called the "righteousness" of God when it is the most lavish mercy. The reason is that this mercy rests on the promises. It is righteous to fulfill a promise, and since God promised salvation through the Son, rather than through our own works, it is rightly called his "righteousness." Further, it is righteousness for him to receive one seeking refuge in him, but it would be unrighteousness and iniquity to not receive him. Lectures on Romans (1525).[13]

How Do We Obtain the Righteousness of God? Johannes Brenz: It must be considered how the righteousness of God is communicated, or how we obtain it, so that God may justify us or forgive our unrighteousness to us and even receive us into his grace. Surely we don't obtain this by circumcision? Indeed, circumcision had its own use in its own times, but we do not obtain the righteousness of God by its merit. Surely it is by the merits of other moral works or of human virtues? No, indeed, not by these. Indeed, otherwise grace would not be grace. Therefore, since we

are saved by grace, it is not possible for us to obtain the righteousness of God by the merits of works. What, therefore, is that thing by which we obtain righteousness? "By faith in Jesus Christ," Paul says. For faith alone in Christ is that instrument by which Christ is received, through the gospel. "For faith comes from hearing, and hearing by the Word of God." Truly, where Christ is, there God is well-disposed. God forgives sin on account of Christ. And if we are believers, he adopts us as his sons and daughters and as heirs of his heavenly blessings. And moreover, good works follow faith. We, however, are not justified—that is, not absolved from our own unrighteousness—either on account of works that precede, nor on account of works that follow faith. Rather, we are justified only on account of Christ, who is embraced by faith. For this reason we must care for faith most of all, so that we might learn about Christ through the gospel, and embrace him through faith. Commentary on Romans (1564).[14]

Faith Is Not Bare Belief. Wolfgang Musculus: The phrase "who believe" is not to be understood as referring to bare faith such as sometimes exists without trust, for it is only trust that lays hold of God's righteousness and mercy. For even the demons believe and tremble, and in Mark 3, Matthew 8, and Luke 4 we see them confessing Christ, and that this Jesus is the Son of God, but even so none of them is justified or saved by such a faith. Commentary on Romans (1555).[15]

All That Is Left to Do Is Trust. John Colet: St. Paul teaches that this one thing remains by which men and women can be justified: namely, for them to trust in God and acknowledge the dispensation and grace of God, which in due time was offered to all humankind through his Son Jesus Christ. For it is by his death and dissolution that men and women's redemption from the power

---

[11]CTS 38:138-39* (CO 49:59-60).
[12]Hafenreffer, *Disputatio de Iustificatione*, 21; citing Phil 1:6.
[13]Oecolampadius, *In Epistolam Pauli*, 34-35.

[14]Brenz, *In Epistolam*, 82-83; citing Rom 10:17.
[15]Musculus, *In Epistolam Apostoli Pauli*, 77; citing Mk 3:11; Mt 8:29; Lk 4:34.

of the devil comes, as well as reconciliation with God. Whoever owns and believes and observes this mystery of salvation, no matter his ethnicity, St. Paul pronounces that he will be saved; and he must also *firmly* believe this in order to have salvation. Accordingly, making Jews equal with Gentiles, and showing both peoples to be on the same level in guilt and wickedness, the apostle draws all together to one faith in Christ Jesus, implying that it was to this that the law of the Jews pointed. EXPOSITION ON ROMANS (1497).[16]

FAITH IS A GIFT FROM GOD. JUAN DE VALDÉS: He means that God communicates his righteousness generally to all who believe in Christ, without making difference between the one and the other. Only let them believe. The communication of his righteousness consists in his making them righteous as he is righteous; not because they work, but because they truly believe that they are accepted by God as righteous, without works, by faith alone. Here I understand that although it appears a thing facile and light, that men and women are brought to believe that God will accept them as righteous, without their works, it is so difficult, so grave, and so hard to the human mind that unless it is by the special gift of God, they will never be brought to it. Because human wisdom is wholly opposed to this faith, it cannot understand it, nor would it desire to entertain it in any way. And therefore St. Paul and St. John rightly say that faith is the gift of God. COMMENTARY ON ROMANS (1556).[17]

OUR FAITH MUST BE IN CHRIST. DAVID PAREUS: "Even," I say, "the righteousness of God is through faith." In the fourth place, he adds a brief description of gospel righteousness, which he will illustrate in verses 24, 25, 26, from principal causes[†]—*efficient*, which is God, and *instrumental*, which is faith—yet not from the subject or *material* in which all believers are. The "righteousness of God," again, names not that righteousness

by which God is righteous, but that by which he justifies us sinners. It is not by the impress of righteousness as a *habitus*, but by the imputation of righteousness through faith, as will become plain in what follows. He will emphasize the same God as the author of this righteousness, so that he may teach that nothing of it is from us or in us.

"Through faith in Jesus Christ": He is not yet describing this righteousness from its *form*, but from its *instrumental* cause, through which it is received, and by which it is clearly enough distinguished from righteousness from works. This is "faith in Jesus Christ," not actively, which Christ himself has, but passively, by which Christ himself is had or possessed. For it is not faith about whatever you please, but faith in Jesus Christ that justifies, on which statement the prophet cited above says: "The righteous by his faith shall live." This faith is a firm assent to the surely known doctrine of Christ with trust in the gracious remission of sins and salvation for Christ's sake. Briefly, it is the trusting avowal of Christ. Earlier, I noted six or seven meanings of faith from the Scriptures, of which the fifth will obviously pertain to this from chapter 4, where faith is a certain persuasion, trust, and fixed confidence in the redemption of the Lord Jesus. Hence, to the Hebrews, Paul names the faith of the fathers as the certainty of those things which were or are in hope as if they already existed in fact. . . . Therefore, faith is not only general assent to unknown doctrine, but certain knowledge, assent, and trust in the gospel promise of the grace and blessings of Christ to each and every believer. And that it pertains in the same manner to me also.

This faith does not *effectively* cause righteousness, as if it made us righteous habitually, or disposed or shaped to habitual righteousness; nor *materially*, as if it were that thing by which we are counted righteous, but *objectively*, so far as it is directed to Christ, who is our righteousness; and *instrumentally*, so far as it apprehends the gift of the righteousness of Christ freely imputed to those rightly believing, so that hereafter it may be more

---

[16]Colet, *Exposition of St. Paul's Epistle*, 7*.
[17]Valdés, *Commentary upon St. Paul's Epistle*, 43*.

clearly taught. Therefore, he indicates the organ of our justification by the phrase "through faith." And this faith is opposed to reason, knowledge, ceremonies, law, works, virtues, and dispositions, through which application is not made to righteousness. COMMENTARY ON ROMANS (1608).[18]

FAITH IN CHRIST, WHO DIED FOR US. MARTIN BUCER: "The righteousness of God by faith in Jesus Christ." Our cause is ever supported by these verses from the chief apostle and Christ's chosen instrument. No other apostle ever inculcated in us the doctrine that righteousness comes to all people solely by faith in Jesus Christ, who died for us. Let us fix our minds on this very thing with greater depth and carefully weigh the matter with a worthy examination. For nobody has ever considered this question fully enough. This is truly a treasure of life and a fountain of eternal salvation. For who can ponder that God, out of his ineffable love toward us for our sakes handed over his only-begotten Son to his enemies to die so that through him we might live forever, and believe this, and yet not believe himself to already be safe and blessed and yield himself entirely to God's breast? From this we also truly learn and firmly acknowledge how lost we are in and of ourselves, that from absolutely nothing that comes from us or from any other creature can it come to pass that God would become pleased with us, so that to restore us it was necessary that the Word of God become incarnate and the Only-Begotten of God die a most horrible death. This thought preserves true modesty within us, causes us to endure in adversities, and kindles in us the endeavor to correct evil lusts and to earnestly give ourselves to the task of sanctification and righteousness. Paul wished to "know nothing beyond the Lord Jesus and him crucified," because he had found that in the cross of our Lord is contained the true philosophy and all saving knowledge. COMMENTARY ON ROMANS (1536).[19]

THE EXTRA WORDS ILLUSTRATE THE LIBERALITY OF GOD'S GRACE. WOLFGANG MUSCULUS: "To all and on all who believe." Some people think there is a pleonasm[†] here. To our mind, there is nothing redundant, however it might appear to be an abundance of words. Ambrose[‡] appears to understand the first "all" to pertain to the Jews and the second to the Gentiles. That is certainly true. The apostle here embraces every race of mortals, which the arguments that follow will make clear also. It seems to me that he wished to commend that immense goodness of God out of which he profusely infuses and communicates his grace through Jesus Christ to everyone who should believe. For even the combining of the prepositions *eis* and *epi* suggest something to this effect. For he wishes to speak at full volume of the grace of God that has been offered to mortals, or rather that has been poured out liberally and copiously on them. And certainly he is not without good reason for doing so, for the Jews did not wish to acknowledge this very thing. COMMENTARY ON ROMANS (1555).[20]

BELIEVERS IN CHRIST AS A SPIRITUAL SEED. DIRK PHILIPS: One may count not only the Jews and Israelites for the congregation of God, but all who truly confessed, feared, and honored God, have lived according to his will out of the law of nature, inscribed by God in their hearts. All those out of the heathen who become believers in Jesus Christ, who are in the foreskin of their flesh [thus uncircumcised], and in their heathendom are reckoned as a spiritual seed of Abraham and the promise. And thus it follows from this that they have been God's and Christ's. THE CONGREGATION OF GOD.[21]

THERE IS NO DISTINCTION. FRIEDRICH BALDUIN: There is no distinction in the matter of justification between the righteousness of God through faith in Jesus Christ to all and on all who

---

[18]Pareus, *In Divinam ad Romanos*, 283-84; citing Rom 4:23-25. [†]Referring to Aristotle's four causes: efficient, instrumental, material, and formal.
[19]Bucer, *Metaphrases et Enarrationes*, 199-200; citing 1 Cor 2:2.

[20]Musculus, *In Epistolam Apostoli Pauli*, 77. [†]A pleonasm is the use of redundant words either out of error or for emphasis. [‡]Or Ambrosiaster.
[21]CRR 6:356*; citing Gal 3:16.

believe. To what end therefore do the Catholics distinguish between first justification and second justification? Or between the inchoate and the perfect? Or between works of the unregenerate and those of the regenerate? Or between works preceding faith and those following it? For only in the former do they consider justification as being by faith, whereas in the latter they consider justification as by works, which futile attempts our apostle always opposes with this Achilles' heel: "There is no distinction." COMMENTARY ON ROMANS (1620).[22]

3:23 Lacking the Glory of God

ALL LACK THE GLORY OF GOD. HEINRICH BULLINGER: Both the explanation and the succinct laying out of reasons, or proof, are rather brief. He said that nobody is excluded from this righteousness and salvation. He now proves this: "for there is no distinction." He also says that this righteousness is not due to our merits, but to grace, nor is anyone justified other than by faith. He provides the reason: "there is no distinction, for *all* have sinned," therefore all must be saved by grace. He thus repeats and condenses with amazing brevity the argument given earlier, by which he convicts all men and women of sin, and then adds something even more serious still: that they are destitute of the glory of God. This "glory of God" is the integrity, holiness, and perfection that God was to possess in humanity as the royalty above all creatures, formed in the image and glory of God. But all are destitute of, or lack, this glory. COMMENTARY ON ROMANS (1533).[23]

NEEDING THE GLORY OF GOD'S GRACE. WOLFGANG MUSCULUS: When some read "and stand in need of the glory of God," they understand "the glory of God" to mean a freely bestowed forgiveness and remission of sins and the imputation of righteousness, which all people universally are in need of since they are destitute of any "glory"

of their own righteousness. It seems that Jerome understood it in this way when he said: "They have need of the glory of God since they have not their own."[†] Several examples of this in Latin can be seen in Erasmus, who, commenting on the phrase "they have need of the glory of God," says that "God is glorified when out of his goodness he preserves the human race." This is why the gospel, that is, the preaching of the grace of Christ, is called "the gospel of the glory of God" by the apostle in 1 Timothy 1. Also in Ephesians 1, not merely once or twice, but four or rather five times, if I am not mistaken, where he speaks of the mystery of redemption he makes mention of the glory and praise of God. "To the praise," he says, "of the glory of his grace, which he bestowed freely upon us in his beloved Son." This is also how it was understood by Primasius of Utica,[‡] whose work was recently discovered. For he interpreted it in this way: "They are in need of the glory of the Redeemer." This latter opinion seems to me to be the most likely, and more fitting to the apostle's teaching. I rather incline to this interpretation since it results in the greatest commendation of the grace of the gospel.

It seems that the verb itself sufficiently indicates that "glory" should be more understood as the glory of God's grace, which all mortals have need of if they are to be saved, than of that "glory" that we lost by Adam's transgression. For if the apostle were speaking of the glory that was lost by Adam, he would not have used a present tense verb, but rather one in the past tense. For it would better suit that sense if he had said, "and they were deprived of the glory of God" after the words "for all have sinned." But because he says "they *are* destitute," I judge it more fitting that it be understood to refer to the glory of God's grace, and I read it in agreement with the Fathers: "they are in need of the glory of God." COMMENTARY ON ROMANS (1555).[24]

---

[24]Musculus, *In Epistolam Apostoli Pauli*, 78-79; citing 1 Tim 1:11; Eph 1:6. [†]Jerome, *Commentary on Romans* (PL 30:661). [‡]Primasius of Utica was the bishop of Hadrumetum in the sixth century. A manuscript attributed to him had recently been discovered in Musculus's time. It may, however, have been a spurious work.

---

[22]Balduin, *Catechesis Apostolica*, 258.
[23]Bullinger, *In Sanctissimam Pauli*, 54r-54v.

The Antithesis of Our Sin and God's Righteousness. Erasmus Sarcerius: This is another explanation for why there is no distinction of persons and why the righteousness of God is available to all, drawn from a minor premise by way of antithesis:

(P2) All have sinned.

(C) Therefore, all have need of God's righteousness, so therefore, the righteousness of God is available to all.

You can see here that the need for a freely bestowed righteousness arises from our weakness in obeying the law. You can also see that the law was not able to serve this purpose, insofar as "it was weak through the flesh." Notes on Romans (1541).[25]

Made Righteous Without Our Contribution. Pilgram Marpeck: Now, however, the righteousness that is acceptable to God has appeared without any help from the law, which is witnessed to by the Law and the Prophets. Paul speaks of righteousness before God, given to all and on all who believe, which comes from faith in Jesus Christ. For here there is no difference; they are all sinners and lack the praise which God desires from them. They are made righteous without any contribution on their part; understand clearly that they were made righteous through the redemption that took place through Christ whom God has set as a mercy seat through faith in his blood; Christ demonstrates the righteousness which God demands in that he forgives sin. Before Christ, no sin was forgiven; he himself, Christ, forgives sins which occurred before, under the patience of God. This sin he carried in order that the righteousness which God requires be demonstrated only in these times and in order that he alone might be just and justify him who has faith in Jesus. Pilgram Marpeck's Confession of 1532.[26]

3:24 Justified by Grace Through Christ's Redemption

If from Grace, Then Not from Works. Thomas Cranmer: The penitent must conceive certain hope and faith that God will forgive him his sins, and repute him justified, and of the number of his elect children, not [Henry VIII's correction: only] for the worthiness of any merit or work done by the penitent, but only [Henry VIII's correction: chiefly] for the merits of the blood and passion of our Savior Jesus Christ.

[Cranmer's annotation on Henry VIII's corrections:] "Only, chiefly." These two words may not be put in this place in any wise: for they signify that our election and justification come partly from our merits, though chiefly they come from the goodness of God. But certain it is that our election comes only and wholly from the benefit and grace of God, for the merits of Christ's passion, and no part from our merits and good works, as St. Paul disputes and proves at length in the letters to the Romans and Galatians, and a variety of other places, saying "If from works, then not from grace; if from grace, then not from works." Cranmer's Annotations on Henry VIII's Corrections of the Institution of the Christian Man.[27]

Preparation for Justification. Friedrich Balduin: Q: Whether by this statement of Paul, "justified freely by the grace of God," it is ignorantly and perversely inferred that people need not prepare themselves for justification?

R: I answer: Concerning the preparation for justification, the Catholics teach differently than do our orthodox churches. When we speak of preparation, we understand only the means and order that, according to the teaching of Scripture, God employs when he wills to lead men and women to justification. It is necessary that a true and sincere contrition precedes justification—and the terrors of a conscience recognizing the anger of God, sorrows on account of sins, a resolution of

[25]Sarcerius, *In Apostolam ad Romanos*, M3r-M4v; citing Rom 8:3-8.
[26]CRR 2:135-36*; citing 1 Pet 3:20.

[27]Cranmer, *Miscellaneous Writings*, 95-97*.

amending one's life—all of these do not proceed from the freedom of our own powers. Rather, they are the movements of the Spirit standing, as it were, outside of us and knocking on our hearts from without. By these kinds of things, by the hearing of the Word, he works as if outside of us until being let in he renews our hearts and begins to graciously indwell within. It was in this sense that the blessed Luther wrote on the third chapter of Galatians that the law in its proper office is a minister and preparer for grace, since it is advantageous to this end, that grace could have entrance into us. But these movements precede the justification of men and women not as in any way cooperating by any worthiness unto justification, nor as some kind of physical alteration that prepares the subject and renders it capable of receiving a new form of the righteousness to be infused. Rather, they precede justification as a removal of the obstacles prohibiting it, or are to be likened to the necessary removal of impurity before the healing of a wound. COMMENTARY ON ROMANS (1620).[28]

GOD'S GRACE AND GOD'S RIGHTEOUSNESS WORK TOGETHER. CARDINAL CAJETAN: The word translated as "justified" is a passive present participle, which is lacking in the Latin language. For this reason, some translators render it "they are justified." And Paul says that "all have sinned and fall short of glory before God," but they are justified. That is, from being sinners they are made to be righteous. "Freely," meaning not on the basis of works, but without cost. And in case you should ask whose free gift this is, he explains that it is "by his grace," namely, God's. Here it is clearly explained that the justifying righteousness of God is had not on the basis of works, but on the basis of God's grace. "Through the redemption that is in Christ Jesus": Paul declares that the grounds for the righteousness of God is rooted in the intervening redemption of men and women that was accomplished by Jesus Christ.

Pay attention to the fact that in this business of people being made righteous from being sinners, the grace of God and the righteousness of God work together in tandem. Grace alone does not do all the work, which it would do if God were to forgive sin without payment for it being made. But this is something God has never done, nor ever does. Instead, in grace he introduces his own righteousness, which the apostle so often refers to as "the righteousness of God." In a moment he'll explain that this righteousness consists in redemption, that is, in the payment of the price, which Jesus accomplished in order to set us free from captivity or enslavement to sin.

But what if, contrary to this, it is insisted that these two things—that we are justified freely by God's grace and that we are justified by the redemption that is in Jesus Christ—are contrary to one another? This is a problem, since if justification is by redemption, then it is not free. But if it is by grace, it is not put forth in redemption by the righteousness of God. Then the answer to this is that the sacred Scriptures do not say that we are justified by grace alone, but by grace and righteousness together at the same time. And both of these are of God—both the grace of God and the righteousness of God. It is not the righteousness of humanity. For this reason the apostle frequently repeats the phrase "the righteousness of God." God's grace does not exclude the righteousness of God, but only the righteousness of man and woman. The redemption that was accomplished by Christ is the righteousness of God, not our righteousness, since Jesus Christ is true God. It is also significant that he does not say "which was accomplished by Christ Jesus" but rather "which is in Christ Jesus," so that we should understand this redemption not as something he accomplished with things or with money, but rather with his own flesh and blood and soul. OF THE EPISTLES OF PAUL.[29]

---

[28]Balduin, *Catechesis Apostolica*, 237-38; citing Gal 3:21-27.

[29]Cajetan, *In Omnes d. Pauli*, 18.

JUSTIFICATION BY GRACE. JOHANNES BRENZ: Although Paul had formerly made mention of the righteousness of God by which persons are freed from their unrighteousness through faith in Jesus Christ, yet because he repeats again that all are sinners and have forsaken the glory of God, therefore he repeats it again even now. Because before, he had begun by regarding the righteousness of God through faith, and had explained it with the most meaningful words in order to teach clearly that it pertains not only to Christ but to all people, truly indeed insofar as people are justified, that is, that they are freed from their unrighteousness freely and without any merit of their own works. But in this verse, Paul makes use of words that should not just be numbered but should be carefully weighed and valued more than gold and topaz. For they contain the highest head of our religion and the way of truth and eternal salvation. "All," he says, "have sinned and have lost the glory of God." Therefore how are they justified? How are they freed from their unrighteousness? How do they obtain the forgiveness of sins? How is it that they are able to have glory in the presence of God? This is surely not through the merit of good works or our strength? Indeed this is a philosophic, pharisaic, scholastic, monastic, and hypocritical teaching that whoever is a sinner and desires to be reconciled with God ought to pay attention to good works and that it is by one's strength that one earns the favor of God and pardon of one's sins. The moral philosopher teaches, "Exercise moral virtues that you should become pleasing to God." The Pharisee teaches sacrifice and long prayers. The monks and hypocrites think their fasting and other works are an atonement for sins and appease the wrath of God. Paul, however, brings from Paradise and indeed from the third heaven a far different teaching. For he says, "They are justified freely." "Freely," he says. This word, "freely," is worth all gold and precious stones. The greatness of neither the Babylonian nor Roman empires was able to suitably purchase for us this one word. For first this word plainly explains to us the will of God toward us, and it reveals to us the entrance of the heavenly kingdom. For unless we are justified, that is, we are freely acquitted from unrighteousness, no man or woman is able to enter into the heavenly kingdom and to be made a partaker of its benefits. For all have sinned and have lost the glory of God. But now, since men and women are justified freely without any merit of their own works, the entrance to heaven is opened, so that now it is lawful for them to enter without any delay, if they believe in Christ. Next, this one word overturns the good of all of human works, or their strength. Indeed, this does not overturn them so that they should not be done, for they are always beneficial, are always in accordance with God's calling, and it is necessary to walk in obedience to God's commands, but it overturns and discredits them in regard to their place in justification. They confer nothing toward obtaining forgiveness of unrighteousness in God's presence, nor are they able to appease the wrath of God and to merit his grace. What more is needed? This singular saying, "Freely," remedies the most serious temptation by which we are incited to be uncertain about the grace of God toward us. COMMENTARY ON ROMANS (1564).[30]

WE WERE BOUGHT BACK. WOLFGANG MUSCULUS: "Through the redemption that is in Christ Jesus." Because he mentions the grace of God by which all are freely justified, he now explains in more detail what he had said in a single word so that we might not only know that we are justified by the grace of God, but also recognize a little more clearly the work that grace accomplished and how justification was achieved. Therefore, in a somewhat rhetorical style he diligently describes the circumstances of our justification:

1. It is God who justifies (on which, see below).

2. He justifies freely by his grace.

3. How? By the redemption that is in Christ.

4. How does he redeem? By his blood.

5. To whom does this grace reach? To believers.

6. Why in this way? To display his righteousness.

---

[30]Brenz, *In Epistolam*, 85-86.

Now observe that in the word "redemption" he implies a certain unseen captivity. For we were "sold under sin." He is employing a metaphor of those who have been captured by their enemies in war, and who are then ransomed and liberated by their friends giving money.

Both Chrysostom and Jerome remark that he did not say "by purchase" but "by redemption,"[†] so that he is implying not simply that we are purchased by Christ in the way things are purchased that were not previously in the rightful possession of the buyer, but rather that we were redeemed like things that were at one time in the possession of the buyer but that were somehow taken away. For we once belonged to God by right of creation, but Satan has stolen us away and brought us into captivity through sin. It is therefore rightly said that we have been "redeemed" by Christ and restored to the Father.

Both Chrysostom and Jerome had good reason for making this remark, so that we might take care that we do not fall back again into the old captivity from which we were redeemed. Those who return again to the enemy after they have been redeemed from captivity by their lord clearly deserve to perish. COMMENTARY ON ROMANS (1555).[31]

TRUE RIGHTEOUSNESS. ERASMUS SARCERIUS: This verse goes with the preceding sentence by way of an enthymeme:[†]

(P2) All have sinned and fall short of the glory of God.

(C) Therefore all are justified freely by grace.

This is a most beautiful enthymeme, in which one can discern the reason why the righteousness of God is needed: since our merits are deficient, grace comes to us in order to fill up the measure of what we lack. Also, "to sin" and "to be justified," as well as "to fall short of the glory of God" and "grace" are

here set in opposition to one another in a most beautiful fashion. In the conclusion of this enthymeme we find a kind of definition of true righteousness drawn from its multiple causes:

Its definition: True righteousness is that by which, by the grace of God, through the redemption that is in Christ Jesus, whom God set forth as a propitiation, through faith, we are justified freely in his blood.

Its causes: (1) Both the grace of God and (2) faith that lays hold of that grace unto righteousness. (3) Christ on whose account a righteousness is available, (4) the redemption that Christ worked, and (5) Christ's merit. The formal cause is the blood of Christ, which by shedding he merited true righteousness for us.

Its "parts": This righteousness is one, nor can it be separated into parts and called "freely bestowed righteousness" while there is another kind of righteousness that is not free but given in accordance with the merits of works.

Its effects: Remission of sins, reconciliation with God, and so on. But a clearer and more concise definition of true righteousness follows in chapter 4.

There are many excellent passages that concur with this definition. First, as to what the causes of true righteousness are; second, to whom righteousness is given; third, how or in what way righteousness is laid hold of; fourth, what moved God to freely bestow this righteousness. NOTES ON ROMANS (1541).[32]

THE EFFICACY OF CHRIST'S RIGHTEOUSNESS. JOHN CALVIN: A participle is here put for the verb according to the usage of the Greek language. The meaning is this, that since there remains nothing for people as to themselves but to perish, being smitten by the just judgment of God, they are being justified freely through his mercy, for Christ comes to the aid of this misery and

---

[31]Musculus, *In Epistolam Apostoli Pauli*, 80-81; citing Rom 7:14. [†]In both Greek and Latin, the words "purchase" and "redemption" are cognates, the latter having a prefix added that makes it, literally, "to buy *back*."

[32]Sarcerius, *In Apostolam ad Romanos*, M3v-M4r. [†]An enthymeme is a syllogism in which one of the premises is implied rather than stated.

communicates himself to believers, so that they find in him alone all those things they are wanting. There is, perhaps, no passage in the whole Scripture that illustrates in a more striking manner the efficacy of his righteousness, for it shows that God's mercy is the efficient cause, that Christ with his blood is the meritorious cause, that the formal or instrumental cause is faith in the word, and that, moreover, the final cause is the glory of the divine justice and goodness.

With regard to the efficient cause, Paul says that we are "justified freely," and further, by his grace. He thus repeats the word to show that the whole is from God, and nothing from us. It might have been enough to oppose grace to merits, but lest we should imagine a half kind of grace, he affirms more strongly what he means by a repetition, and claims for God's mercy alone the whole glory of our righteousness, which the sophists divide into parts and mutilate, that they may not be constrained to confess their own poverty. COMMENTARY ON ROMANS 3:24.[33]

SALVATION RESTS ON MERITS OF CHRIST.

DIRK PHILIPS: In summary, just as circumcision is practiced on the fleshly children of Israel, so also baptism shall be practiced on the spiritual Israelites, on the newborn children of God, that is, on believing Christians. Again, just as circumcision is commanded by God and appointed for the eighth day, so also baptism is instituted by Christ and ordained and commanded upon faith. Again, just as the salvation of children rested primarily in the grace of God and not in the fleshly circumcision in the Old Testament, in the same measure now in the New Testament, the salvation of children rests in the mercy, love, and goodness of the heavenly Father and in the merits of Jesus Christ, not in external baptism. THE BAPTISM OF OUR LORD JESUS CHRIST.[34]

CHRIST THE MERCY SEAT AND MATERIAL CAUSE.

JOHN CALVIN: "Through the redemption." This is the material cause. Christ, by his obedience, satisfied the Father's justice, and by undertaking our cause he liberated us from the tyranny of death, by which we were held captive, as on account of the sacrifice that he offered is our guilt removed. Here again is fully confuted the gloss of those who make righteousness a quality, for if we are counted righteous before God, because we are redeemed by a price, we certainly derive from another what is not in us. And Paul immediately explains more clearly what this redemption is, and what is its object, which is to reconcile us to God, for he calls Christ a propitiation (or, if we prefer an allusion to an ancient type,) a mercy seat. But what he means is that we are not otherwise just than through Christ propitiating the Father for us. COMMENTARY ON ROMANS 3:24.[35]

JUSTIFIED BEFORE GOD, CONSCIENCE, AND OTHERS.

VAVASOR POWELL: God did reckon and account it as a righteous act. Objection: But the Scripture is clear that men and women are justified by faith, and by believing.

Answer: So the Scripture is clear, that men and women are justified by (1) works and by (2) words. But you are to understand in what sense men and women are justified by these. Mark therefore: By (3) Christ his death, sufferings, and resurrection, men and women are really, and virtually justified. By faith, men and women are personally and apprehensively justified, and by works and words, men and women are declaratively justified. In the first sense, men and women are justified before *God*, in the second sense they are justified in their own consciences, and in the third sense they are justified before other men and women. GOD THE FATHER GLORIFIED (1650).[36]

---

[33]CTS 38:140-41* (CO 49:61).
[34]CRR 6:105*; citing Gen 17:12; Mk 16:16; Acts 8:35-38; Rom 5:1; 11:6.

[35]CTS 38:141* (CO 49:61-62).
[36]Powell, *God the Father Glorified*, 44-45*; citing Jas 2:18, 24-25; Mt 12:37; Lk 18:14; Gal 2:1; 1 Cor 6:11.

CHARACTERISTICS OF TRUE REPENTANCE.

DIRK PHILIPS: True repentance always has these following points or characteristics (which one calls properties), and which cannot be separated from it, namely: a proper sadness and sorrowful state about the preceding sin; after that a true confession of the sin before God; praying and sighing before the throne of grace with a genuine faith for the forgiveness of sin and with a firm trust in God's bottomless mercy. But above all there must be a good and firm resolve to sin no more and to refrain from the sin. That is then true repentance that is valid before God, that one refrains from sin, yes, that is the true worship which pleases the Lord. And that one ceases from unrighteousness, that is a true atonement for sin. ABOUT THE MAR-RIAGE OF CHRISTIANS.[37]

THE CAUSES OF JUSTIFICATION.

THE ENGLISH ANNOTATIONS: The apostle describes all the causes and the properties of justification revealed to us in the gospel. The first and supreme cause is the undeserved grace and favor of God. The moving or meritorious cause is redemption and reconciliation purchased by Christ. The instrumental cause whereby the same is imputed is faith in the blood of Christ. The final cause is the glory of God in the declaration of his righteousness and faithfulness. Its property is that all human boasting is excluded by it. ANNOTATIONS ON ROMANS 3:24.[38]

3:25 Christ Our Propitiation

IT IS GOD WHO JUSTIFIES US. WILLIAM AMES:

Doctrine 1: It is God that justifies us. He is said to justify us, not in that he infuses righteousness into us, or that he makes us fit to do things that are just, which is the error of the Catholics who place justification first in the infusion of the habits of faith, hope, and charity, and next in the good works that come from those habits, with which they mix a certain sort of remission of sins. Rather,

therefore, he is said to justify us because by his judicial sentence he absolves us from the guilt of all sin, and accepts or accounts us as fully just and righteous for eternal life, by the righteousness of Christ, which he gives us. It appears from here that this term "justification" is used in Scripture for the opposite of charging with crimes, or for the opposite of condemnation. And this justification is done by God, as it were, by these degrees: (1) In his eternal counsel and decree, because from eternity he intended to justify us. (2) In Christ, our head, rising again from the dead, we were both virtually justified, and in some sort actually justified. As in Adam sinning, all his posterity were virtually condemned to death by the law, and in some sort actually, because they were in some sort actual sinners. (3) He justifies us fuller actually and formally in our selves, and not only in our heads; when by his Spirit and our faith, itself the work of his Spirit, he applies Christ to us, to our justification. (4) And further yet, he justifies us actually and formally to our sense and feeling, when by our own reflective knowledge and examination of our estate, he allows us to perceive that this application of Christ has been made, and thus to have peace and joy in him. THE SUB-STANCE OF CHRISTIAN RELIGION.[39]

THE FATHER PREDESTINED HIS SON TO

REDEEM US. MARTIN BUCER: He had already said that we are justified by the redemption that is in Christ Jesus, that is, the redemption that was accomplished by Jesus Christ. Therefore, he judged that it ought to be explained in what way the Lord Jesus accomplished this redemption. He first proclaims that God from the very beginning had decreed this within himself. For even if the death of Christ is the cause of redemption, it is only so because the Father decreed it to be so, who for this purpose both sent his Son and delivered him up to death. That he might express this he said, "whom God set forth," that is, as St. Chrysostom under-stood it, long before he came in the flesh and

---

[37]CRR 6:565*; citing Mt 3:1-2; Ps 32:1-2; Heb 5:7-8; Sir 35:1-12.
[38]Downame, ed., *Annotations*, AAA3r*.

[39]Ames, *Substance of Christian Religion*, 155-56*; citing Rom 8:33.

redeemed us by his death, the Father decreed and predestined him to this end. COMMENTARY ON ROMANS (1536).[40]

WHY THE FATHER SENT THE SON. HULDRYCH ZWINGLI: "As a Reconciler." In the Greek, this is *hilastērion*, "propitiation." He is perhaps alluding to the lid over the ark of the covenant. In Christ, God shows and renders himself propitious to us. We are then truly reconciled with God when we firmly set our hope on the grace and mercy of God on account of the death and blood of Jesus Christ. For "the blood of Christ cleanses our sins"; "this One is the Lamb of God who takes away the sins of the world"; "there is one Mediator, Jesus Christ," and so on.

"That he might display his righteousness." In other words, this is the reason why he gave his Son as a Mediator for our sins: that he might display his righteousness, that is, that he might show himself to be faithful and just by fulfilling what had been promised.

"On account of the remission of sins." He gave his Son for the remission of the sins which had been committed and perpetrated before his Son had been born.

"To demonstrate his righteousness." It was not only for the remission of sins of old that he had long put up with, but also to demonstrate his righteousness in the present time, in that he who justifies all those who believe in Jesus Christ his Son are themselves just in doing so. Therefore he did not send his Son merely to wipe away and atone for sins previously committed, but also for present and future sins as well. NOTES ON ROMANS (1539).[41]

CHRIST IS OUR PEACE. JACQUES LEFÈVRE D'ÉTAPLES: What does it mean that "whom God set forth as a propitiation through faith," except that God placed before himself an appeasement and peace between himself and sinners? "For he is our peace," so that he shows his "righteousness," the righteousness that is by faith and by grace, to those of us who have faith in the redemption that is through his blood, by forgiving us our sins that we committed prior to faith. For if even those of us who have faith were to transgress into serious error, our sins would not be forgiven if it were not for that propitiation set before God on our behalf, and that blood of redemption interceding for us on the altar of the wood, in his great sacrifice. All these things are granted to us freely, for he "has trodden the winepress alone"; and as Isaiah says, "He took away our grief, and carried away our sorrows . . . the Lord has placed on him the iniquity of us all . . . the chastisement for our peace was on him, and by his bruises we have been healed." And who is [still] a sinner if he turns himself to the contemplation of such great goodness of God and to calling on him from the heart? Who would not find mercy through such a Mediator as this? And when the apostle says "justifying him who is of faith in Jesus," he shows that this righteousness and justification is from God and not from human beings. Hence no persons should boast in themselves or in their works as if they could be saved by them, but should boast only in God, and in Christ's bruises, and in his blood. Paul, therefore, adds in dialogical form, "Where then is boasting? It is excluded. By what law? That of works? No, but by the law of faith." COMMENTARY ON ROMANS.[42]

CHRIST CARRIES ALL SINS. MARTIN LUTHER: The devil, therefore, that master of a thousand tricks, lays traps for us with marvelous cleverness. He leads some astray by getting them involved in open sins. Others, who think themselves righteous, he brings to a stop, makes them lukewarm, and prompts them to give up the desire for righteousness, as Rev 3:14 speaks of the angel of Laodicea. A third group he seduces into superstitions and ascetic sects, so that, for example, in their greater degree of holiness and in their imagined possession of righteousness, they do not at all grow cold but

---

[40]Bucer, *Metaphrases et Enarrationes*, 111.

[41]Zwingli, *In Evangelicam Historiam*, 415; citing 1 Jn 1:7; Jn 1:29; 1 Tim 2:5.

[42]Lefèvre, *Epistole divi Pauli*, 59v; citing Eph 2:14; Is 63:3; 53:4, 6, 5.

feverishly engage in works, setting themselves apart from the others, whom they despise in their pride and disdain. A fourth class of people he urges on with ridiculous labor to the point where they try to be completely pure and holy, without any taint of sin. And as long as they realize that they are sinning and that evil may overwhelm them, he so frightens them with the judgment and wears out their consciences that they all but despair. He senses the weakness of each individual and attacks him in this area. And because these four classes of people are so fervent for righteousness, it is not easy to persuade them to the contrary. Thus he begins by helping them to achieve their goal, so that they become overanxious to rid themselves of every evil desire. And when they cannot accomplish this, he causes them to become sad, dejected, wavering, hopeless, and unsettled in their consciences. Then it only remains for us to stay in our sins and to cry in hope of the mercy of God that he would deliver us from them. Just as the patient who is too anxious to recover can surely have a serious relapse, we must also be healed gradually and for a while put up with certain weaknesses. For it is sufficient that our sin displeases us, even though we do not get entirely rid of it. For Christ carries all sins, if only they are displeasing to us, and thus they are no longer ours but his, and his righteousness in turn is ours. LECTURES ON ROMANS (1516).[43]

CHRIST CONTINUES AS MEDIATOR. PHILIPP MELANCHTHON: Our adversaries also confess that Christ is the mediator and propitiator. But this very thing they afterward change and corrupt. For they say nothing about the application, nor do they teach that one should make use of Christ as the Mediator. And first, they say nothing at all about this faith, that is, about trust in the Mediator. They do not teach that Christ, the Mediator, should be used; rather, they command the conscience to doubt. This doubting clearly militates against the faith which Paul here

demands. Second, they imagine that Christ is a propitiator only so far as the chance for merit is concerned, as when the head of a family, angry with a servant, is placated by some friend. There the friend procures access to the master for the servant. Thereafter he has no business there, but the servant pleases because of his own service. They give to Christ only this, that he merited this beginning and chance for us to merit.

Thus they themselves say that Christ merited a first grace. Afterward they bury him and imagine that he is idle, and that people merit remission of sins and are righteous because of their own fulfillment of the law. On the contrary, we rightly understand that Christ always remains the mediator and must be applied to in faith; that is, it must be stated that we are pleasing to God not on account of our worthiness or fulfillment of the law, but on account of Christ. We ought not oppose our virtues to the judgment of God, but Christ, the sacrificial victim and propitiator. Paul speaks expressly of the application below when he says "Through whom we have access by faith to this grace," as though he said, "We approach God if we use Christ, the mediator, if by faith we flee to this propitiator and think that we are forgiven because of him." COMMENTARY ON ROMANS (1540).[44]

CHRIST'S HOLINESS AND PASSION BOTH MATTER. FRIEDRICH BALDUIN: Q: Our apostle writes that God had put forward his Son as a propitiation in his blood, and thus only mentioned the passive obedience of Christ. Therefore, is it the case that the active obedience of Christ by which he fulfilled the law does not pertain to the meritorious cause of our justification?

A: . . . One half of something being posited, it is not necessary to exclude the other. This is the case in this passage: both active and passive obedience pertain to the meritorious cause and satisfaction of our justification; but the former satisfies the obedience due to the law, whereas the latter satisfies the penalties earned by our disobedience.

---

[43]LW 25:254*; citing Rev 3:14.

[44]Melanchthon, *Commentary on Romans*, 101*.

Both had to be rendered in our place. Therefore one cannot exclude the other. Also, however often Scripture mentions the death and passion of Christ, it always presupposes his active obedience to the law, without which his passion would not have sufficed for reconciling the human race. For not only did sins have to be expiated, but so also did submitting to the law in our place. . . . Partly because the passion and death of Christ was the apex and final end of the obedience of Christ rendered for us, as the apostle Paul testifies in Philippians 2:8; partly because our justification is described as the remission of sins in Psalm 32:2 and Romans 4:3. But the remission of sins does not happen without the spilling of blood. Therefore, where there is true remission of sins, there is both holiness and righteousness imputed to us. For when sin departs, righteousness takes its place. Therefore both the holiness and passion of Christ are necessary as the meritorious cause of our justification. COMMENTARY ON ROMANS (1620).[45]

CHRIST THE MERCY SEAT. DIRK PHILIPS: Thus the ark, that is, the box of the covenant, was made of two substances, as an example that the congregation is also of two different substances. That is, it is from the earth through the birth from Adam, and it is from heaven through the other birth out of God; it is weak and fallible from itself, and it is wonderful and beautiful through the grace of Jesus Christ.

But it is not thus with the mercy seat. That one is of one substance, of pure gold, and is Jesus Christ, the head of his congregation, the genuine mercy seat presented to us from the Father on account of belief in his blood, as the apostle said, through whom God spoke to us. THREE ADMONITIONS.[46]

THE GREATEST PROOF THAT GOD IS KIND. HEINRICH BULLINGER: This is what in French they call a "ransom." For God willed that redemption accomplished by his Son would be perpetual.

It therefore follows that the One whom God set forth as a "propitiation," alluding to the *propitiatorium* [i.e., place of atonement or mercy seat] belonging to the Mosaic tabernacle and understanding it to represent the Son of God, was to be also in future ages the only salvation for all who believe. For which reason we take certain note of the second chapter of the first canonical letter of John.

But he set him forth in such a way that we might "believe in his blood," that is, so that we might trust him on account of his death, which is the greatest proof on earth that God is kind toward humanity, inasmuch as "he spared not even his own Son, but delivered him up for us all," so that "we might be saved from wrath" by his shed blood, by the blood of a pure and spotless Lamb. COMMENTARY ON ROMANS (1533).[47]

THE MERCY SEAT AS A FIGURE OF CHRIST. DIRK PHILIPS: The mercy seat, which was made of the very finest gold, also stood on the ark, and is a figure of Christ Jesus, who is given to us by God the Father as a mercy seat and placed by God as head of the congregation, just as the mercy seat stood on top of the ark. THE TABERNACLE OF MOSES.[48]

BAPTISM AS SIGN OF SPRINKLING OF CHRIST'S BLOOD. DIRK PHILIPS: This is indeed the proper significance of these figures, at least if one wants to let the Scripture be unbroken. For in this manner, the Spirit comes to agreement with the letter and the true being with the figure. On the other hand, if one wants to interpret this literally and on an external symbol [alone], then one must also understand the other in the same way. But now if one must understand Egypt, Pharaoh, the iron furnace, the house of servitude, the bread of heaven, the drink and the rock, only spiritually, how does this agree with the truth that one should understand the baptism of the children of Israel under Moses, the clouds, and the sea in a

---

[45]Balduin, *Catechesis Apostolica*, 248-50; citing Phil 2:8; Ps 32:2; Rom 4:3; Heb 9:7.
[46]CRR 6:415*; citing Jn 3:5; 1 Cor 15:43; Eph 5:6; Song 2:1; Heb 5:3.
[47]Bullinger, *In Sanctissimam Pauli*, 55r; citing Acts 4:12; Heb 10:1-18; 1 Jn 2:2; Rom 8:32; 5:9; Ex 12:5; 1 Pet 1:19; Jn 1:29.
[48]CRR 6:272*; citing Ex 25:17; Heb 5:1-6; Eph 1:22; 4:15; Col 1:18.

literal sense only? In addition, we are not delivered primarily through external baptism, but through the precious blood of Jesus Christ, to whose sprinkling we have come by faith and have thus been baptized into Jesus Christ and his death, of which external baptism is a sign and witness. THE BAPTISM OF OUR LORD JESUS CHRIST.[49]

RECEIVED BY FAITH. CATHERINE PARR: For this is the life everlasting, O Lord, that I must believe you to be the true God, and him whom you sent, Jesus Christ. By this faith I am assured, and by this assurance I feel the remission of my sins. This is what makes me bold. This is what comforts me. This is what quenches all despair.

I know, O my Lord, your eyes look on my faith. St. Paul says, "We are justified by faith in Christ, and not by the deeds of the law; for if righteousness comes by the law, then Christ died in vain." St. Paul doesn't mean here a dead, human, and historical faith, gotten by human industry; but a supernatural and lively faith, which works by love, as he expresses clearly. Dignifying faith does not derogate good works, for all good works spring out of this faith. Yet we may not impute our justification before God to the worthiness of faith or works. Rather, we must ascribe and give the worthiness of it wholly to the merits of Christ's passion, and refer and attribute the knowledge and receiving of it only to faith. Faith's very true and only property is to take, apprehend, and hold fast the promises of God's mercy that makes us righteous. And to cause me continually to hope for the same mercy, and in love to work in all the ways allowed in the Scripture, that I may be thankful for the same. THE LAMENTATION OF A SINNER.[50]

BELIEVING IN THE CRUCIFIED ONE. DIRK PHILIPS: Herewith Christ explained his words that he had spoken about eating his flesh and drinking his blood, namely, that they are not to be understood carnally but spiritually, and that his flesh which he has given us to eat is actually the true living bread of heaven. Whoever now receives this bread of Christ Jesus and eats it, that is whoever receives and keeps the words of Christ, and believes firmly in Jesus Christ the crucified one, that he has given his flesh for us and shed his blood for the forgiveness of our sins, eats spiritually of the flesh of Christ and drinks spiritually of his blood. And through the power of the spiritual food of the flesh and blood of Christ as the true bread of heaven, [that person] is nourished and strengthened to eternal life. CONCERNING THE TRUE KNOWLEDGE OF JESUS CHRIST.[51]

THE INSTRUMENTAL CAUSE OF JUSTIFICATION. FRIEDRICH BALDUIN: The instrumental cause of our justification is nothing other than faith, which the apostle constantly insists on when treating this subject. For Christ without faith is useless to us, for which reason he is called our propitiation "through faith in his blood," that is, by that faith which apprehends the passion and death of Christ and with it the whole of his merit. For we do not understand by "faith" here only that bare knowledge or assent to the articles of faith, which kind of faith can occur even in demons. Rather, we understand a certain trust, the proper and adequate object of which is the merit of the Son of God, on account of which we are received in grace before God. For it happens that when faith apprehends Christ's merit, it causes it to belong to oneself. This faithful apprehension is that hand of the beggar which of itself does nothing toward gathering gifts—it merits nothing, does nothing to dispose people toward conferring a gift, but simply receives a gift freely from another and on account of the merit of another, namely, of Christ, that is conferred on us. It is for this reason that we are said to be justified not "on account of," but "through" faith in Christ. And because it is the instrumental cause with respect to our righteousness before God, it is here called the righteousness of faith. Quite differently do the Catholics argue concerning faith,

---

[49]CRR 6:97-98*; citing 1 Pet 1:2; Rom 6:3-4.
[50]*Writings of Edward VI*, 38-39*; citing Gal 2:21.

[51]CRR 6:171*; citing Gal 1:4; Eph 2:13; Col 1:20.

who while they are not wholly able to eliminate faith from this matter nevertheless assert that it justifies not in an instrumental fashion, but by way of disposition or entreaty, as Bellarmine says in book one *On Justification*, chapter three. That is, they attribute all the power and efficacy of justifying to virtues inherent within us. Therefore they write that we are justified "on account of" faith, which Pererius is always repeating. COMMENTARY ON ROMANS (1620).[52]

TO JUSTIFY IS TO ACQUIT FROM CHARGES OF GUILT. JOHN CALVIN: We simply interpret justification as the acceptance with which God receives us into his favor as if we were righteous; and we say that this justification consists in the forgiveness of sins and the imputation of the righteousness of Christ.

There are many clear passages of Scripture that confirm this. First, it cannot be denied that this is the proper and most usual signification of the term. But since it is too tedious to collect all the passages and compare them with each other, let it suffice to have called the reader's attention to the fact; he will easily convince himself of its truth. I will only mention a few passages that expressly handle the justification of which we speak. First, when Luke relates that all the people that heard Christ "justified God," and when Christ declares, that "Wisdom is justified of all her children," Luke does not mean that they conferred righteousness, which always dwells in perfection with God, even if the whole world attempts to wrest it from him. Nor does Christ mean that the doctrine of salvation is made just; this it is in its own nature. Rather, both modes of expression are equivalent to attributing due praise to God and his doctrine. On the other hand, when Christ upbraids the Pharisees for justifying themselves, he does not mean that they acquired righteousness by acting properly, but that they ambitiously courted a reputation for right-eousness of which they were destitute. Those acquainted with Hebrew understand the meaning

better; for in that language the name of wicked is given not only to those who are conscious of wickedness, but to those who receive a sentence of condemnation. Thus, when Bathsheba says, "I and my son Solomon shall be counted offenders," she does not acknowledge a crime, but complains that she and her son will be exposed to the disgrace of being numbered among reprobates and criminals. It is, indeed, plain from the context that the term even in Latin must be thus understood—that is, relatively—and does not denote any quality. In regard to the use of the term with reference to the present subject, when Paul speaks of the Scripture, "foreseeing that God would justify the heathen through faith," what other meaning can you give it but that God imputes righteousness by faith? Again, when he says "that he (God) might be just, and the justifier of him who believeth in Jesus," what can the meaning be, if not that God, in consideration of their faith, frees them from the condemnation which their wickedness deserves? This appears still more plainly at the conclusion, when he exclaims, "Who shall lay anything to the charge of God's elect? It is God that justifies. Who is he that condemns? It is Christ that died, yea rather, that is risen again, who is even at the right hand of God, who also makes intercession for us." For it is just as if he had said, "Who shall accuse those whom God has acquitted? Who shall condemn those for whom Christ pleads?" To justify, therefore, is nothing else than to acquit from the charge of guilt, as if innocence were proved. Hence, when God justifies us through the intercession of Christ, he does not acquit us on a proof of our own innocence, but by an imputation of righteousness, so that though not righteous in ourselves, we are deemed righteous in Christ. Thus it is said in Paul's discourse, in Acts, "This man is preaching to you the forgiveness of sins; and by him all that believe are justified from all things from which you could not be justified by the law of Moses." You see that after remission of sins, justification is set down by way of explanation; you see plainly that it is used for acquittal; you see how it cannot be obtained by the works of the law; you see that it is

---

[52]Balduin, *Catechesis Apostolica*, 221-22.

entirely through the interposition of Christ; you see that it is obtained by faith; you see, finally, that ratification intervenes, since it is said that we are justified from our sins by Christ. Thus when the publican is said to have gone down to his house "justified," it cannot be held that he obtained this justification by any merit of works. All that is said is that after he obtained the pardon of sins, he was regarded in the sight of God as righteous. He was justified, therefore, not by any approval of works, but by gratuitous acquittal on the part of God. Hence Ambrose elegantly terms confession of sins "legal justification." INSTITUTES OF THE CHRISTIAN RELIGION 3.11.2-3 (1559).[53]

LIKE OPENING EYES TO THE SUN. JOHANNES BRENZ: For if propitiation and redemption were brought about by Christ, insomuch as it pertains to himself, he is sufficient for all men and women, without distinction, and having been proposed to all men and women without distinction he ought to be received by all. Yet not all people acknowledge and receive him, and therefore they do not all delight in him. Indeed, just as the kindness of the state's mercy is displayed to all the poor who receive alms from a city—if they approach the almshouse and receive help with their own hands—just so, while we are all poor and in want of true righteousness, the kindness of Christ's mercy is offered to us, but therefore needs to be received by everyone's own hands. Therefore, whose are the hands by which the mercy of Christ's righteousness is received? They are not fleshly hands, but hands of the heart, namely, faith. Therefore we receive the kindness of Christ when we embrace Christ by faith. For just as the sun certainly shines on everyone, but if any will desire to delight in its light, it is necessary that they have their eyes open to let in the light, just so Christ has been displayed to all and is clear to all, but if any will desire to obtain salvation, it is necessary that he or she has the eyes of the mind open, that is, to

believe in Christ. For there is not another organ by which Christ is accepted besides faith. COMMENTARY ON ROMANS (1564).[54]

DISPLAYING GOD'S RIGHTEOUSNESS AND GLORY. MARTIN BUCER: That the goal of our redemption and the remission of our sins is to display God's righteousness and glory in us should rightly stir us up to the constant pursuit of righteousness. The highest expression of his goodness is that this display of God's righteousness would occur in his giving it to us, by causing us to participate in his own true righteousness. Therefore, this and other similar passages ever aid us . . . in which all might see how propitious God is ever ready to be, and how generous he is to those who are his sons by faith. And most of all in this, that it is to such people as us that he grants to be sharers in his divinity, that is, of a complete righteousness. COMMENTARY ON ROMANS (1536).[55]

A DEFINITION OF RIGHTEOUSNESS. JOHN CALVIN: This is a definition of that righteousness which he has declared was revealed when Christ was given, and which, as he has taught us in the first chapter, is made known in the gospel. He affirms that it consists of two parts. The first is that God is just, not indeed as one among many, but as one who contains within himself all fullness of righteousness. Complete and full praise, such as is his due, is not otherwise given to him, but when he alone obtains the name and honor of being just, while the whole human race is condemned for injustice. Then the other part refers to the communication of righteousness, for God by no means keeps his riches laid up in himself, but pours them forth upon people. Then the righteousness of God shines in us, whenever he justifies us by faith in Christ, for Christ was given for us for righteousness in vain unless there was the enjoyment of him by faith. It hence follows that all were unjust and lost

[53]Calvin, *Institutes*, 2:38-39*; citing Lk 7:29, 35; 16:15, 1 Kings 1:21; Gal 3:8; Rom 8:33-34; Acts 13:38-39; Lk 18:14.

[54]Brenz, *In Epistolam*, 88.
[55]Bucer, *Metaphrases et Enarrationes*, 200; citing Rom 9 conflated with 2 Tim 2:20-21.

in themselves until a remedy from heaven was offered to them. COMMENTARY ON ROMANS 3:26.[56]

FOR FORMER SINS. WOLFGANG MUSCULUS: "By the remission of sins previously committed." The righteousness of God, that is, the goodness of God, is displayed in the remission of sins. But we must not snatch at the phrase "sins previously committed" as if Christ's redemption availed only for those sins that were committed before Christ's passion, as certain impious persons who wish to protect their theological agenda would have us understand. They teach that it is necessary for us to make satisfaction for our own sins, since by his blood Christ only acquired remission for the sins of old, that is, those that were committed before his advent, along with original sin, as well as those sins committed before our baptism. But for all other sins, they assert, each one must make satisfaction to God.

But that by the blood of Christ there is remission not only of sins committed in the old covenant but also of those committed under the new covenant in which we presently live, is very clear from 1 John 2 where we read: "My little children, I write this to you that you might not sin, but if anyone does sin, we have an advocate with the Father: Jesus Christ the Righteous One. And he is the propitiation for our sins, and not for ours only, but also for the whole world." Behold, it is not only for us, he said, but for the whole world! Is the "whole world" restricted only to the time of the old covenant? To whom is he writing, if not to Christians who have already been baptized? He says that Christ is their advocate before God and a propitiation, even if they should sin after baptism. COMMENTARY ON ROMANS (1555).[57]

3:26 Why God Waited

FAITH LOOKS ON THE PROPITIATOR. GEORG MAJOR: For it is God who justifies, but the reason why we are justified is his freely bestowed mercy

and the obedience and intercession of his Son the Propitiator, *not* our work or merit. Because faith looks on this Propitiator alone and rests solely on him, we are therefore, on account of the Mediator, justified by faith alone as the instrument by which we lay hold of the Mediator and apply his mediation to ourselves. EXPOSITION OF THE EPISTLES OF PAUL (1569).[58]

ABSOLVING THE SAINTS OF THE OLD TESTAMENT. HEINRICH BULLINGER: The style of his address or speech and his conciseness leaves the meaning somewhat obscure. It is, therefore, permissible to render the sentence more freely with a paraphrase, in this way: "God set before us his Son as a propitiation for our sins so that he might show us his righteousness, that is, that he might prove himself to be faithful and trustworthy" (for "righteousness" is here used for the "truthfulness of God," as it often is in the Psalms). This righteousness I speak of is that on account of which, or perhaps by which, it happened that he passed over sins that were committed or perpetrated before his Son was born. For he did not put up with it because he either was ignorant of sin or approved of it, but because he intended, at a determined time, to offer a sacrifice with his Son as the sole sacrificial victim. Hence it is clear that the death of Christ absolved even the saints of the Old Testament, which is what both Peter in his first letter, as well as the article of faith, "he descended to hell," sufficiently prove. For he believed that the death of Christ had profited the dead as well, speaking as he was of the power of the death of Christ, or of his person. He also tells us that "hell" is not only the place of punishment and of the damned, but also is a word referring to the dead in general, whom we also refer to as "those below" in the same way we speak of the living as "those above." COMMENTARY ON ROMANS (1533).[59]

---

[56]CTS 38:146* (CO 49:64).
[57]Musculus, *In Epistolam Apostoli Pauli*, 81, 82-83; citing 1 Jn 2:1-2.
[58]Major, *Enarrationes Epistolarum S. Pauli*, 109.
[59]Bullinger, *In Sanctissimam Pauli ad Romanos*, 57r; citing 1 Pet 3:19 and the Apostles' Creed. Latin wordplay on *inferus*, which means both "those below" and "hell."

**WAITING UNTIL THE ILLNESS/SIN IN-
CREASES.** WOLFGANG MUSCULUS: Subjoining
and declaring a kind of reason for such long and
drawn-out tolerance until now, he says that God
tolerated the sins of the prior testament, and sent
his Son in these last days, who would finally
redeem the human race, so that by this his
justice—evidently that by which he himself is just,
true, and good, and the justifier of him who is of
the faith in Jesus Christ, that is, he who is of the
number of those believing in Christ—might be
rendered clearer and more manifest. For this
righteousness of God through faith in Christ—
this redemption through the blood of Christ—
would not even have existed for the best and
brightest if the corrupted human race had been
quickly brought to a close at the beginning. For
this reason it was drawn out into the last days, so
that "where sin abounded, grace might also be
abounding." Just as the goodness and virtue of a
medicine are not made manifest if they are
quickly used on the sick person at the beginning
of a disease when, not yet having been brought to
the desperation of the height of the disease, he
would be returned to health; whereas if, at the last
hopeless end, the sick person who had been
despaired of and mourned and in whom all
remaining medicines could do nothing, were still
moved to the health, he would have been conspicuously cured.

Therefore, since it was to be done in order to
show the divine righteousness, if the advent of
Christ and redemption through his blood were to
come about not hastily, but when the human race
was at its worst, it was certainly necessary that, by
that long-suffering tolerance, he show consideration for the sins of the human race, until the
redemption that he himself had planned from
eternity and predestined to be manifested in the
last days should arrive. COMMENTARY ON
ROMANS (1555).[60]

**JUSTIFICATION BY FAITH REVEALS GOD'S
RIGHTEOUSNESS.** DAVID DICKSON: Argument 8.
God has set forth Christ as a reconcilement and
propitiatory sacrifice, by which the wrath of God is
appeased toward all that lay hold on him by faith.
Therefore, it is not possible for a person to be
justified except by faith in Christ's offering up this
atonement in his blood, unless God should alter
the means of appeasing himself.

"To show forth." Argument 9. God, in the
present time of the gospel, set forth Christ as the
means of appeasing his anger, to those who
embrace the gospel by faith. That by this way of
justifying, his past righteousness might also be
revealed, through his forbearance and forgiveness
of sins in the past, which from the beginning of the
world he has forborne and forgiven. That is, God
did not pardon sins on his own but on account of
the propitiatory sacrifice of Christ that was to
come, and that without any violation of his justice.
Therefore, this ground of our justification is no less
to be asserted than the glory of God's justice is to
be manifested. The matter is clear: If justification
by faith in the blood of Christ shows that God
never pardons sins except for by the satisfaction
made to his justice by the blood of Christ, certainly
anyone who would determine any other ground for
our justification than by faith conceals the righteousness of God.

"That he might be just." This confirms the
argument that God has set forth Christ that he
might be a propitiation through faith in his blood.
It was not only that he might declare himself just
in sending the promised Messiah, for whose sake
freely and also justly he would pardon sin, but that
he might show himself the author and donor of
true righteousness to us (that were without any
righteousness of our own) by believing in Jesus
Christ. Therefore this ground of our justification
by faith is no less to be maintained than the glory
of God's justice, faithfulness, and goodness are to
be declared in his justifying of believers. EXPOSI-
TION ON PAUL'S EPISTLES.[61]

---

[60]Musculus, *In Epistolam Apostoli Pauli*, 83; citing Rom 5:20.

[61]Dickson, *Exposition*, 8*.

THE WORK OF REDEMPTION DISPLAYS GOD'S RIGHTEOUSNESS. DAVID PAREUS: First, God is called "righteous" because of his universal uprightness and holiness from which every blemish and iniquity is foreign. This righteousness is especially on display in the whole work of redemption, since every amazing divine virtue all at once gleams most brightly in this: his immense wisdom, power, justice, goodness, mercy, generosity, and grace. COMMENTARY ON ROMANS (1608).[62]

---

[62]Pareus, *In Divinam ad Romanos*, 297.

3:27-31 JUSTIFICATION AND THE LAW OF FAITH

²⁷Then what becomes of our boasting? It is excluded. By what kind of law? By a law of works? No, but by the law of faith. ²⁸For we hold that one is justified by faith apart from works of the law. ²⁹Or is God the God of Jews only? Is he not the God of Gentiles also?

Yes, of Gentiles also, ³⁰since God is one—who will justify the circumcised by faith and the uncircumcised through faith. ³¹Do we then overthrow the law by this faith? By no means! On the contrary, we uphold the law.

Overview: One of the recurring issues for the reformers is the need to reconcile passages that point to the role of faith with ones that point to works. In this passage, the commentators seek to harmonize Romans 3:27 with Romans 3:20. How does Paul's saying that the law of works does not exclude boasting fit with his statement that the law is what brings awareness of sin? The law of works without faith may allow us to pretend that we are righteous. The doctrine of faith is what eliminates the possibility of our glorying in works. It takes away our masks so that we must acknowledge that we are sinners who need God's grace. It does this by working together with the law to convict us of sin so that we cannot boast about our righteousness.

Romans 3:28 finds Luther famously inserting the word *alone* in his translation of the New Testament into German to complete the phrase "by faith alone." *Sola fide* was, of course, a key theme for the Reformation. In response to it, the Council of Trent would anathematize anyone who believed that faith alone justified. Although not all reformers will add the word *alone* to the biblical verse, they will all support the doctrine that salvation comes by faith alone. Justification is something that God does; it is not our doing, and God does not do it in response to our works.

The Protestant commentators argue against Catholics who agree with them that justification is initially by faith alone but who differ from them by claiming that once one is a believer then one needs to add works to justification. Again, the interpreters seek to reconcile Paul and James, this time

adding the possibility that the two are using the terms *justify, faith,* and *works* in different ways. And they suggest several ways in which the gospel establishes rather than abolishes the law.

3:27 Our Boasting Is Excluded

Faith in Christ Is Greater Than Abraham's Faith. Jacques Lefèvre d'Étaples: The *circumcision* (circumcised), or the Jews, "are justified by the faith" of Abraham, and the *uncircumcision* (uncircumcised), or the Gentiles, are justified *through faith* in Christ. But just as much as Christ is greater than Abraham, so also is faith in Christ greater than justification by Abraham's faith, for it justifies not only the uncircumcised but the circumcised also. The justification that is in Christ is universal, whereas that of Abraham is particular to the Jews. Christ's is the true justification; Abraham's is a foreshadowing. Christ's is perfect; Abraham's is imperfect and receives its power of justification from his perfect justification. For faith in Christ justifies even the circumcised. Therefore that justification by the faith of Abraham was not perfect, whereas circumcision adds nothing at all to the justification that is in Christ, for it is perfect. But he who would believe that the justification of the circumcised that is by the faith of Abraham is necessary to obtain justification in Christ, clearly believes that the justification in Christ is imperfect and unworthy, which is sinful and impious to think. Commentary on Romans.[1]

---

[1]Lefèvre, *Epistole divi Pauli,* 59v.

God Eliminates Glorying in Anyone but Him. Friedrich Balduin: The "law" here he understands generally as "doctrine," wherein he wishes to teach that it is not the merit of our works that reconciles to God but the blood of his Son that apprehends by faith, that we might not have reason to glory, for God does not will to give his glory to another. Therefore, he shuts out all glorying of men and women, not by the doctrine of works but by the doctrine of faith. In other words, not only is it that some of the works of the law do not justify, namely, ceremonial works, or even those moral works done by the unregenerate as the Catholics explain, but all glorying in works whatsoever, of whatever kind they may be, is shut out by this evangelical doctrine concerning faith. For where faith is, there works can have no place in the matter of our justification, although outside of this matter they are distantly conjoined as a cause and its effects. Therefore it must be diligently noted that this passage of the apostle casts wholly to the ground that frivolous Catholic distinction between works of the regenerate and the nonregenerate, as if the latter have nothing for which they might boast in, but the former are able to boast. Commentary on Romans (1620).[2]

Taking Away Masks. Huldrych Zwingli: "It is excluded." Namely, all boasting of either Gentiles or Jews so that nothing remains to anyone but sin. It is as if he were saying, "I have taken away from you, I think, your mask, so that there is nothing left for you but to acknowledge that you are sinners in need of the glory and grace of God." Annotations on Romans (1539).[3]

Boasting Is Excluded from the Jews. Martin Bucer: "Where then is boasting? It is excluded." This boasting, which the Jews arrogated to themselves, arose from the fact that they had accepted from God both the law and his sacred worship, and that they were regarded as the people of God while all the rest of the nations everywhere lived in the world without God. This boasting is now taken away from the Jews and excluded in that the apostle has shown that the Jews themselves, however great the gifts of God may be that they had received, are no better than the Gentiles—or rather, that they are actually worse, because by faith alone in Christ the Gentiles have attained to righteousness and salvation. With these arguments he was clearly pressing the point that the Jews possessed absolutely nothing by which they excelled the Gentiles or on account of which they could boast more than others. Commentary on Romans (1536).[4]

Reconciling 3:27 with 3:20. Martin Bucer: How do we reconcile "boasting is not excluded by the law of works" with "by the law there is an awareness of sin"?

Because the law convicts us of sin, it takes away any boasting in our righteousness. If there is already recognition of sin by means of the law, there is also an awareness out of which one is compelled to condemn oneself. Certainly the law excludes all things that a man or woman could boast in. But this appears to disagree with what Paul here clearly says when he denies that boasting is excluded by the law of works. But, [you might say,] the law of works is the law. Accordingly, if it does not take away this boasting it is true that boasting is not taken away by the law. And if the law does not take away boasting, then neither does it show sin, and therefore, in general there is no knowledge of sin by the law.

It must here be observed that the apostle has placed in opposition to one another these two laws: of works and of faith. It is important, therefore, to understand that faith is here separated out from the law of works, and if faith is absent, then the law of works can not be viewed rightly, nor can what it summons us to and what it requires ever be rightly perceived. When men and women are eager to take from it and implement what it demands with

[2]Balduin, *Catechesis Apostolica*, 224-25.
[3]Zwingli, *In Evangelicam Historiam*, 415.
[4]Bucer, *Metaphrases et Enarrationes*, 200.

external works, it is then being understood only superficially. Thus they wish to acknowledge nothing commanded in the law beyond that which, in reality, they seem to be rendering for their own benefit! They receive commandments from the law so that they might please themselves and have something in which they can boast. In this verse the apostle has spoken of the law in this way, because the matter at hand had to do with those who were making much of the law that they had embraced only in external works, without faith, or even without a proper understanding of the law. The law of works was not taking away boasting from these people, but rather was giving them a further occasion for boasting.

Further, when faith arrives, with its aid, the true understanding of the law makes itself clear. Accordingly, what God demands of us in each of his precepts is acknowledged, so that committing ourselves to him in all of them, we give ourselves in service to the needs of our neighbors with the highest love, looking for nothing but his glory and the salvation of our neighbors. From this it immediately becomes apparent how helpless and lost we are in ourselves, how many are our sins and how much they merit damnation. Then at last is sin truly known by the law, but this is for our salvation. In the same manner that faith shows us the force of the law as it ought to be seen, so likewise hope shows us the power of forgiveness and salvation. It's from this that true repentance from sins arises in the soul, but also, at the same time, with the most ardent exertion being shown by those receiving righteousness. This can be seen in the case of Zacchaeus and of the sinful woman who washed the Lord's feet with her tears, and in similar examples of true repentance. COMMENTARY ON ROMANS (1536).[5]

THE END OF JUSTIFICATION IS THE GLORY OF GOD ALONE. LAURENCE TOMSON (OR PIERRE L'OISELEUR): An argument to prove this conclu-

sion: that we are justified by faith without works, taken from the end of justification. The end of justification is the glory of God alone. Therefore, we are justified by faith without works. For if we were justified either only by our own works or partly by faith and partly by works, the glory of this justification would not be given wholly to God. THE GENEVA BIBLE (1595).[6]

3:28 *Justified by Faith, Apart from Works*

DEFENSE OF LUTHER'S INSERTION OF "ALONE." FRIEDRICH BALDUIN: Q: Whether the blessed Luther committed a grievous crime in his German translation, when to these words: "We reckon that man is justified by faith, without works" he inserted the particle "alone," which is found neither in any Greek nor in any Latin manuscript?

A: I answer: this is the perpetual cuckoo with which the Catholics wish to make us sick, as if some irremissible sin had been committed by our Luther. But it is so far from us that we should be ashamed of this translation, or that we should acknowledge in it some grievous crime, or rather should state that that translation which could not have been better or more perfectly fitting to the apostolic language should be strongly opposed. For Luther himself clearly wrote in his *Apology* concerning his translation in volume five, folio 140ff., in which he manfully and boldly responds to the reproaches and clamors of the Romanists, the climax of whose apology is this: "First," he says, "it was spoken in Germanic idiom, not in Latin nor in Greek." But it is a property of the Germanic idiom that when a word is twofold, by which one affirms and the other denies, that the particle *allein* (alone) added to the affirmation so that the negation of the other part might be all the stronger, which is a fact known by all who know how to speak German. For any language whatever has its idioms that cannot be rightly judged except by those who are experts in that language. "Next," he

---

[5]Bucer, *Metaphrases et Enarrationes*, 204; citing Rom 3:20; Lk 19:1-10; 7:36-50.

[6]Tomson, *The Bible*, 62v*.

said, "The words of Paul required this and not any other sense, for he opposes faith to works as two immediately opposite things. Therefore, when Paul removes works from justification, faith *alone* is necessarily what remains behind, so that it is the same thing to say 'justified by faith without works' and 'justified by faith *alone*.'" . . .

Why, therefore, is our Luther charged with a vice when he adds the exclusive particle "only," if in a similar passage the apostle says that man or woman is not justified by works apart from faith. And it should be added that in the Syriac version of Romans 4:5 it also inserts the exclusive particle *balchud*, to him who does not work but *only* (*balchud*) believes, . . . which also is not found in the Greek text. COMMENTARY ON ROMANS (1620).[7]

AMBROSIASTER ON "FAITH ALONE." WOLF-GANG MUSCULUS: St. Ambrose, commenting on the word "freely" understood that we are justified "by faith alone," which is the gift of God. Ambrose comments: "We are justified," he says, "freely, since we are justified by faith alone, the gift of God, apart from anything we do or render to him in return." So says Ambrose. What will the adversaries of God's grace say to this? Was not Ambrose ortho-dox? Did he not write this in an orthodox manner? Who ever at any time reproved him on this point? And when he says "apart from anything we do," what does this mean other than that we do not merit justification by any preceding works? And by "or render to him in return," what can this mean if not that once we have received justification we do not afterward repay God for it by any work? So here is a holy man who did not think it would be enough to explain the text by "we are justified by faith," unless he said that "we are justified by faith *alone*," and who even added the words "apart from anything we do or render to him in return." If he had wished to oppose the grace of Christ in company with our present-day Sophists,[†] he would have said after their fashion "apart from rendering

any legal [i.e., Mosaic] obedience." And *they* are the ones who cry "heresy!" if we teach that we are justified by faith alone, and who are always objecting to us with "the Fathers!" and the "ortho-dox faith!" COMMENTARY ON ROMANS (1555).[8]

THE MEANING OF "BY FAITH ALONE." THOMAS CRANMER: First, you shall understand, that in our justification by Christ it is not the same thing: God's office to us, and our office to God. Justifica-tion is not our office, but God's. For we cannot justify ourselves by our own works, neither in part, nor in the whole; for that would be the greatest human arrogance and presumption that antichrist could erect against God, to affirm that we might by our own works take away and purge our own sins, and so justify ourselves. But justification is the office of God alone, and is not something that we render to him, but something we receive from him. We do not give it to him, but rather we take it from him, by his free mercy, and only by the merits of his most dearly beloved Son, our only Redeemer, Savior, and Justifier, Jesus Christ. So that the true understanding of this doctrine, that we are justified freely by faith without works, or that we are justified by faith in Christ alone, is not, that this our own act to believe in Christ, or this our faith in Christ, which is within us, justifies us, and merits our justification to us (for that would be to count ourselves to be justified by some act or virtue that is within ourselves). But the true understanding and meaning of it is that although we hear God's Word and believe it; although we have faith, hope, charity, repentance, dread, and fear of God within us, and do many good works in response; yet we must renounce the merit of all our said virtues of faith, hope, charity, and all our other virtues and good deeds, which we either have done, shall do, or can do, as things that are far too weak and insuf-ficient and imperfect to deserve remission of our sins, and our justification. And therefore we must trust only in God's mercy, and in that sacrifice that

---

[7]Balduin, *Catechesis Apostolica*, 250-51, 253; citing Rom 4:5.

[8]Musculus, *In Epistolam Apostoli Pauli*, 80. [†]Referring to Catholic theologians.

our High Priest and Savior Christ Jesus, the Son of God, once offered for us on the cross, to obtain thereby God's grace and remission, as well for our original sin in baptism, as for all actual sin committed by us after our baptism, if we truly repent, and genuinely convert to him again. So that, as St John Baptist, although he was such a virtuous and godly man, yet in this matter of forgiving of sin he directed the people away from him and pointed them to Christ, saying to them, "Behold, yonder is the Lamb of God, who takes away the sins of the world." Even so, as great and as godly a virtue as the lively faith is, yet it directs us away from itself, and remits or points us to Christ, to have by him alone, remission of our sins, or justification. So that our faith in Christ (as it were) says to us this: It is not I that take away your sins, but it is Christ alone; and to him alone I send you for that purpose, renouncing by that all your good virtues, words, thoughts, and works, and putting your trust in Christ alone. HOMILY ON SALVATION (1547 AND 1560). [9]

BY FAITH ALONE, NOT JUST IN THE BEGINNING. WOLFGANG MUSCULUS: From this passage arises a contention over whether or not faith *alone* justifies. We, along with some of the Fathers, have concluded that a man or woman is justified by faith alone. Our adversaries, by whom neither the grace of Christ nor the mind of the apostle has been sufficiently paid attention to, not only deny this but also impugn us with the charge of corrupting and committing forgery with the apostle's sentence.[†] These gentlemen fail to see that this charge attacks the Fathers more than it does us. [Johann] Eck even says that it is a heresy if someone should teach that faith alone without any works justifies.

Certain people who would put an end to this controversy teach that it is true that a person is justified by faith alone apart from works, but only in the beginning of faith in Christ, so that Paul should be understood as building an argument that neither the works of the Jews profit those who

are coming to faith in Christ, nor do the sins of the Gentiles, however many they might be, hinder them from coming to faith, but that as soon as they have begun to believe in Christ, they are regarded as righteous before God. But that *after* justification he does not hold this to be the case, that is, that faith alone no longer justifies those who are already justified, but that good works are necessary for salvation, by which they merit the goods of eternal life. And they are proud of this opinion of theirs as if it had never been heard before but was for the first time ever revealed to them. They took this from the commentaries of Jerome, who holds this opinion about the passage we are now considering: "But the apostle says of the man who is coming to Christ that *when he first believes* he is saved by faith alone."

What shall we say to this? It is good that they admit that a person believing in Christ for the first time is justified by faith alone. But when they teach that works are necessary for justification for someone who is already a believer and already justified, they in effect place a limit on the first justification by attributing only the *beginnings* of justification to faith. This is just as absurd as if you said that while it may be that the soul alone entering into the body immediately brings a person to life, this is no longer the case afterward. What could be more absurd than this? The apostle says in Romans 1 that faith is the life of the righteous; he did not say that it is only the *beginning* of life. What does he believe the life of the just to be? He holds that it is love for God and neighbor. It is hope. It is endurance in suffering. It is the fear of God. It is meekness of soul, and all manner of good works. If the righteous live by faith, it is therefore by faith that a righteous person believes, loves, hopes, fears, worships God, is meek, and does good works, for which reason justification by faith continues throughout the entire life of the righteous. The soul's impartation of life continues in the body all the way until life's last breath, so that you rightly say that it is the soul alone that brings life to the body, not only in the beginning, but also throughout one's entire life. Although the

---

[9]Cranmer, *Miscellaneous Writings*, 131-32*.

body may have its works, the possession of life itself, which belongs to the soul, is not attributed to these works. Likewise, you rightly say that faith alone justifies not only in the beginning but also throughout a just person's entire life. Though one may be very productive in good works, justification itself cannot be attributed to them—that is, performing good works cannot render someone righteous, for he would not do these good works unless he were already righteous by faith. The situation would be the same if we had considered the other half of justification, which is not the imputation of righteousness but the cleansing of the impure heart, concerning which the apostle Peter in Acts 15 says, "cleansing their hearts by faith."

Also, when they speak of the imputation of righteousness that is by faith, it is again not true what they say, that imputed righteousness avails only in the beginning. For it is necessary through-out the entire life of justified saints, who are never lacking in sin and whose works are like a men-strual cloth, as Christ said: "When you have done all these things, say 'we are unprofitable servants.'" And to believers and people already justified, John wrote: "If anyone sins, we have an advocate with the Father, Jesus Christ the Righteous One, and he is the propitiation for our sins." He does not say, "And he *was* the propitiation for our sins, but now in order to obtain righteousness, your good works are necessary." How is this reconciliation appropriated by sinners, if not by faith in Christ, even after that first justification? COMMENTARY ON ROMANS (1555).[10]

APART FROM THE LAW. JOHANNES BRENZ: All men and women, whether Greek or Jew, are sinners, just as was shown above. Christ—placed before us by God in the atonement—is grasped only by faith. Thus, it clearly follows, it is declared, it is pronounced, it is concluded, that one is justified, that is, one is absolved from one's

unrighteousness and is accepted by God, in grace, only by faith, apart from the works of the law. Now, when Paul says, "apart from the law," he does not mean that good works should not be done—he spoke of that above, and will explain it copiously below—but rather, he is referring here to the *merit* of works. Indeed, the law of God makes no work of man or woman righteous. . . . And the "works of the law" refers not only to the ceremonial, but to all of the works of the divine law. Indeed, just as the Jews do not merit remission of their unrigh-teousness by the works of circumcision, Sabbath, or sacrifices, so also they do not receive merit for their works of mercy, beneficent works to the poor, honoring their parents, maintaining chastity in marriage, or telling the truth in their testimonies. Thus, although these and other kinds of works are good, are taught by the law of God, and are meant to be done, nevertheless they are imperfect and damaged by sin, not meriting absolution from unrighteousness before God. So Paul says that knowledge of sins comes through the law. COM-MENTARY ON ROMANS (1564).[11]

EXAMPLES OF THOSE JUSTIFIED APART FROM WORKS. JACQUES LEFÈVRE D'ÉTAPLES: You ask, since Paul says "we judge that a person is justified by faith apart from the works of the law," who has ever been justified apart from the works of the law, whether written or of nature? If I were to answer that this has happened to countless people, I would probably not be lying. It is certainly true of those of the Gentiles and even open sinners who have fled for refuge to the grace of baptism, having only faith in Christ and the confession of his holy name; these emerged from the holy laver immediately justified. And if they had died right after they emerged from baptism, who doubts that they would have attained to the life of the blessed, without any works? We believe the same thing con-cerning baptized infants. And who does not know that the thief was justified by faith alone? When with a firm faith he believed that Christ was the

---

[10]Musculus, *In Epistolam Apostoli Pauli*, 85-86; citing Rom 1:17; Acts 15:9; Lk 17:10; 1 Jn 2:1-2. †Cf. Balduin's discussion above of Luther's adding the German word *allein* (alone) to "justification by faith."

[11]Brenz, *In Epistolam*, 92-93; citing Rom 3:20.

King and said, "Lord, remember me when you come into your kingdom," he immediately heard, "Truly I say to you, today you will be with me in Paradise." COMMENTARY ON ROMANS.[12]

RECEIVING THE TRUE PROMISED LAND. DIRK PHILIPS: So one might then think or ask: If the children do not believe, why are they saved and pleasing to God? We answer, out of grace, through Jesus Christ, who by his death has taken away the sins of the whole world, so that adults in their penitent faith but children in [their] simplicity are pleasing to God so long as they remain therein. The Lord himself testified to this in Deuteronomy thus: "Moreover, your little ones, who you said would become a prey, and your sons, who this day have no understanding of good or evil, shall enter the promised land, and to them I will give it and they shall occupy it." See then that what the adult Israelites could not receive on account of their unbelief and disobedience, the children, who understood neither good nor evil, received from God's grace. Thus now the children of the true Israelites, the Christian believers, receive and inherit the true promised land, that is, the kingdom of heaven out of grace through Jesus Christ in order that the promise of God (from the seed of Abraham, the children of the heavenly Sarah, who are included under the promise), remains fixed on the basis of grace and the election of God in the merit of Jesus Christ, not on the basis of any works or merit of human beings. THE BAPTISM OF OUR LORD JESUS CHRIST.[13]

RESTORED BY ANOTHER WAY. GEORG MAJOR: Therefore, it is asked, "Since all the world is made guilty before God, is under sin, death, and the curse, how and in what way are we freed from this so great and horrible evil? Can it be that liberation should be granted through works of the law or through one's own merit?" But Paul denies that sin

can truly be taken away through the law, or that one can know sin other than through the law. In Corinthians he says, "The power of sin is the law and its ministry death."

However, he reveals that sin, the wrath of God, and the curse are taken away, and that justice and life are restored by another way. This is truly by faith, embracing the Propitiator, our Lord Jesus Christ, with the shedding of his own blood for us. It is by grace and apart from the merit of our own works, and only by the free mercy of God. This he calls the righteousness of God revealed apart from the law and confirmed by the testimony of the law and the prophets.

Therefore, the righteousness of God—that is, the righteousness by which we are justified in the presence of God, having been given the forgiveness of sins, and let into eternal life—is to believe in the Son of God having been crucified and resurrected for us. And through him we freely receive the reconciled Father, on account of the Son, the propitiator and intercessor. God the Father imputes this faith to us as righteousness, on account of Christ the Son.

But while all—the Jews as much as the Gentiles—sinned and are guilty, so these make plain the righteousness of God through faith in Jesus Christ, not only in certain chosen ones, but in all and on all who believe, whether they are Jews, or Greeks, with no consideration of the merit of their work. EXPOSITION OF THE EPISTLES OF PAUL (1569).[14]

EXCLUDING WORKS SHEDS LIGHT ON JUSTIFICATION BY FAITH. JOHN CALVIN: Paul now draws the main proposition as one that is incontrovertible, and adds an explanation. Justification by faith is indeed made very clear, while works are expressly excluded. Hence, in nothing do our adversaries labor more in the present day than in attempts to blend faith with the merits of works. They indeed allow that people are justified by faith, but not by faith alone. Yea, they place the efficacy of justification in love, though in words they ascribe it to faith. But

---

[12]Lefèvre, *Epistole divi Pauli*, 59v; citing Lk 23:42-43.
[13]CRR 6:91*; citing Rom 5:18; Jn 1:29; 3:17; Deut 1:39; Gal 3:29; Eph 2:7.

[14]Major, *Enarrationes Epistolarum S. Pauli*, 43-44; citing 1 Cor 15:56.

Paul affirms in this passage that justification is so gratuitous that he makes it quite evident that it can by no means be associated with the merit of works. I have already explained why he names the works of the law, and I have also proved that is it quite absurd to confine them to ceremonies. Inaccurate also is the gloss that works are to be taken for those that are outward, and done without the Spirit of Christ. On the contrary, the word "law" that is added means the same as though he called them meritorious, for what is referred to is the reward promised in the law. COMMENTARY ON ROMANS 3:28.[15]

JUSTIFIED APART FROM THE LAW. GEORG MAJOR: Another asks, "Why should God justify freely and only by faith?" Paul answers, "For the reason that the boasting of one's own meritorious works should be excluded by faith, that just as 1 Corinthians 1 says, "Whoever boasts should boast in the Lord."

But here someone may object again, "What do you say, Paul? Can it be that you suppose a man or woman is able to be justified apart from the works of the law? Are not circumcision and the law instituted and handed down by God?" Therefore, Paul says they are handed down by God, but not toward justification. Another proposes this objection: "Can it be that he is the God of the Jews only? And not of the Gentiles?" Paul answers that God is surely the God of the Gentiles also, namely, according to the promise given to Abraham: "In your seed all the nations of the earth will be blessed." For if justification is from the law and circumcision, God would be God of the Jews only, but because he is God also of the Gentiles who do not have circumcision and the law (for the blessing of the seed of Abraham indeed reaches to the Gentiles), therefore, he is not justified because of circumcision and the works of the law. Circumcision is only the seal of righteousness, not righteousness itself, and the law is only the pedagogue for Christ, who was made for us wisdom from God, righteousness, sanctification, and redemption.

But from this another question arises, "When you teach, Paul, that man is justified by faith apart from works of the law, do you consider the law to be abolished?" He answers, "I do not make the law invalid by teaching that man is justified through faith in Jesus Christ. On the contrary, by means of this doctrine we establish the law, since Christ is the end and completion of the law, and without Christ it is not possible to fulfill the law. For whoever would desire to fulfill the law, it is necessary that he first believe that on account of Christ his sins are remitted and that God receives him to eternal life by grace apart from his own merits. Then, though the corruption and depravity of nature still survive, nevertheless he should believe that on account of Christ those remains of uncleanness are not imputed to him. Following next, it is necessary, having been born again, to obey the law of God by faith and the Holy Spirit, and though those who are obedient to the law of God are those who have hardly begun and are imperfect in this life, nevertheless he should establish this newness of life pleasing to God through Jesus Christ."

Therefore, those teaching that a person, apart from works of the law, is justified by faith, do not make the law void. Rather, they establish the law while they show that Christ is the end of the law. And they teach how the law is made and is able to be fulfilled. It is by truly receiving by faith the forgiveness of sins and reconciliation and by being established in and believing the law. This law is the perfect obedience of Christ to the law, and it is imputed to us, as if we had fulfilled the entire law, seeing that only a beginning of obedience toward the law of God is in this life. The consummation of it will follow in another life, where the righteous will shine as the sun and as the stars into everlasting immortality. Meanwhile, in this life we are righteous and perfect in Christ Jesus. Therefore, the teaching of faith does not destroy the law and good works, but it makes clear how the law is to be kept and good works ought to be done. EXPOSITION OF THE EPISTLES OF PAUL (1569).[16]

---

[15]CTS 38:148-49* (CO 49:65-66).

[16]Major, *Enarrationes Epistolarum S. Pauli*, 44; citing 1 Cor 1:31.

RECONCILING PAUL AND JAMES. JOHN CALVIN: What James says, that people are not justified by faith alone but also by works, does not at all militate against the preceding view. The reconciling of these two views depends chiefly on the drift of the argument pursued by James. For the question with him is not how people attain righteousness before God, but how they prove to others that they are justified. His object was to confute hypocrites, who vainly boasted that they had faith. Gross then is the sophistry not to admit that the word *justify* is taken in a different sense by James from that in which it is used by Paul, for they handle different subjects. The word *faith* is also no doubt capable of various meanings. These two things must be taken into account before a correct judgment can be formed on the point. We may learn from the context that James meant no more than that people are not made or proved to be just by a feigned or dead faith, and that he must prove his righteousness by his works. See this subject in my *Institutes.* COMMENTARY ON ROMANS 3:28.[17]

3:29-30 The God of Both Jews and Gentiles

WE ARE NOT JUSTIFIED BY THE LAW. THEODORE BEZA: "The God of the Jews," *Ioudaiēn ho Theos.* According to the peculiar mode of speaking found in the Scriptures, God is said to be the God of those whom he embraces with his benevolence, such as in Psalm 33:12. Even though the nations as a class were alienated from God's covenant (as it is written in Eph 2:12), still an access to him was open to proselytes to Judaism, and there are many testimonies of the prophets in which it is testified that God has not cast off the nations forever. But Paul has something else in mind, for he hangs this argument on the preceding conclusion, in this way:

(P1) We are justified only in such a way that all the glory for our justification is attributed solely to the grace of God.

(P2) But a justification by our works does not attribute all the glory of our justification to the grace of God.

(C) Therefore we are justified by justification by faith, not by the law.

MAJOR ANNOTATIONS (1594).[18]

FAITH FROM FOREFATHERS AND FAITH FROM THE GOSPEL. KONRAD PELLIKAN: To be the God of all other nations is to rule over all by his providence, to keep them in his protection, to heap many benefits on them, and last to grant them eternal life. God promises this to all those to whom he promises to be their God. Hence the Lord Jesus concludes that there will be a resurrection of the dead on the grounds that God had testified that he is the God of Abraham, Isaac, and Jacob. "He is not," he said, "the God of the dead, but of the living," who have lived in such manner that they will one day arise to eternal life.

Therefore, the Lord is the God of the Jews: "I," he said, "will be your God." But he also formed all the nations in his image, from whom he chooses his elect, to whom he presents himself as Savior God and author of eternal life. And the Lord had already begun to openly declare this reality by the time that Paul wrote this. For a long while since the dispersion of the Jews, he had been bestowing the eminent and illustrious gift of his Spirit on the Gentiles, not any less than to the Jews who were converting to Christ. But then he adds, "Since God is One, who will account the circumcision righteous?" that is, the circumcised Jews, *by faith,* namely, that faith that they had received as handed down from their ancestors, "and the uncircumcised Gentiles through faith," that faith that came to them through the gospel. Here the faith of the Jews and that of the Gentiles are set side by side, and one faith is preached as obtaining for both of them the same justification and Spirit-given life, for the Jews as well as the Gentiles. But there is discernible here a certain distinction, in that for the

---

[17]CTS 38:149* (CO 49:66).

[18]Beza, *Annotationes Majores,* 44; citing Ps 33:12; Eph 2:12.

Jews it is by that faith that they received from their forefathers, while for the Gentiles it is that faith in the gospel of Christ that was preached by the apostles and by the Jews who had converted to Christ. COMMENTARY ON ALL THE APOSTOLIC EPISTLES (1539).[19]

3:31 *Faith Upholds the Law*

CHRIST WRITES THE LAW ON OUR HEARTS. ANDREAS KNOPKEN: He has several times said that Christ imparts his Spirit to believers, who changes and transforms our human affections (for the law makes demands on them as well) so that we are powerfully drawn to keep the very law that was not able to accomplish that by force. Thus, by grace, Christ writes the law on our inner parts and our hearts. Then, if we do sin in some way, on account of our faith it is not imputed to us, as the psalm says, "Blessed is the man who," and so on. And likewise, "Christ is the fulfillment of the law unto righteousness to everyone who believes." In a similar sense we should understand that verse where he "came not to abolish the law but to fulfill it." OF THE EPISTLE TO THE ROMANS (1524).[20]

THE SPIRIT ENABLES US TO LOVE. JOHANNES BUGENHAGEN: Here is an *occupatio*.[†] "Do you, Paul, cast aside the law of God?" He answers, "I do not cast it aside, on the contrary I establish it, and I teach how it must be fulfilled." Indeed, it is fulfilled not by works, but by faith. The law says, "Love God!" However, no one is able to do this according to nature. Therefore, it is taught that the law is unprofitable if faith is not preached, from which we will learn to recognize our inability. Through faith God grants his own Spirit, which is poured out in our hearts. He supplies us with strength, so that we may do the law unaided. Without the Spirit of faith, no one loves enough, for which reason the law is preached and driven home in vain. If our own leaders had seen this, they would not have estab-

lished such a butchery of good works or the pious and religious ways of living in the monasteries. INTERPRETATION OF ROMANS (1531).[21]

THREE WAYS THE LAW IS ESTABLISHED. GEORG MAJOR: Another objection: If Christ is the end of the law, whom the whole law has been signifying, then the types and shadows of the law have yielded to Christ, who has been presented, just as Christ says, "The law and prophets up to John the Baptist." Therefore, through the doctrine of faith, the ceremonial and forensic law have truly been abolished. Why, therefore, does Paul deny that the law is abolished by faith and, instead, affirms that this very law is established? I answer: Paul speaks about the moral law, which is an eternal and unmoved standard for righteousness in God. It is communicated to angels and people. It demands conformity with God. And it accuses and curses all who do not conform to it. The gospel does not abolish the law. Rather, it establishes it. And it does this in three ways. First, it shows the true and spiritual use of the law, through which sin is not removed, but is shown and increased, so that sin is increased and shown at a higher degree to be sin. Then by imputation, since by faith we receive the remission of sins, reconciliation, the imputation of righteousness, and the obedience of Christ toward the law. Christ satisfied the law for us, and his satisfaction is imputed to us as if it were ours. In the third place, since the Son of God has brought a new light to men and women by the pouring out of the Holy Spirit on believers, he begins our obedience toward the law of God. It must then be completed, since God will be all in all when our whole nature will have been restored according to the image of God and we fully conform to him. Thus by the doctrine of faith, the law is established, not abolished. EXPOSITION OF THE EPISTLES OF PAUL (1569).[22]

---

[19]Pellikan, *In Omnes Apostolicas Epistolas*, 46; citing Mt 22:32; Ex 6:7.
[20]Knopken, *In Epistolam ad Romanos*, C8v; citing Ps 32:2; Rom 10:4, Mt 5:17.

[21]Bugenhagen, *In D. Pauli ad Romanos*, 37v. [†]Rhetorical figure that is a subcategory of *preterition*, which emphasizes something by omitting it.
[22]Major, *Enarrationes Epistolarum S. Pauli*, 110; citing Lk 16:16 or Mt 11:13.

THE LAW IS ESTABLISHED RATHER THAN WEAKENED BY FAITH. HEINRICH BULLINGER: Erasmus elegantly and concisely (as everywhere else) explains this response: "We are so far from abolishing the law or weakening its force that we even strengthen it and establish it firmly, since we proclaim the very thing that the law promised was to come, and we announce him who is the consummate goal to whom the law was pointing." For we read elsewhere that "Christ is the perfection of the law for justification to all who believe." Since faith is diligently devoted to him, truly the law is more established by faith than it is weakened by it. COMMENTARY ON ROMANS (1533).[23]

---

[23]Bullinger, *In Sanctissimam Pauli*, 60v; citing Rom 10:4.

4:1-5 ABRAHAM'S FAITH CREDITED AS RIGHTEOUSNESS

*What then shall we say was gained by Abraham, our forefather according to the flesh? ²For if Abraham was justified by works, he has something to boast about, but not before God. ³For what does the Scripture say? "Abraham believed God, and it was counted to him as righteousness." ⁴Now to the one who works, his wages are not counted as a gift but as his due. ⁵And to the one who does not work but believes in*ᵃ *him who justifies the ungodly, his faith is counted as righteousness,*

a Or *but trusts*; compare verse 24

OVERVIEW: This section of Paul's letter inspires many of the Reformation-era commentators to compile lists. They regard the chapter as a set of seven or eight arguments for justification apart from the law or by faith alone. Or they gather items such as twelve circumstances of Abraham's justification, or nine corollaries from Paul's words, or ten trials that Abraham endured.

The reformers approach again the issue of the seeming disagreement between Paul and James on the relationship between works and faith. Seeking to reconcile Romans 4:1 with James 2:21, many of these interpreters argue that the works that James refers to are ones that follow rather than precede justification. Some posit that they are addressing their letters to different categories of people: James to those who believe that works no longer have any role; Paul to those, like the Pharisees, who believed that their works would justify them. Others suggest that Paul is here addressing justification in relation to our standing before God, but that James is speaking of justification as it is evidenced before other people. A few, particularly Lutherans, dismiss James as an authority.

What all the reformers share, however, is a rejection of the prevailing medieval view that a person is justified by the cooperation of faith and works. They all see Abraham as modeling justification by faith alone. Abraham is an example for us of one who was declared righteous, not because of his good works, but because he

believed God. Wages are granted to those who have earned them, but we cannot earn wages from God, for we are sinful, and our works are inadequate. It is only through grace, through mercy, on account of God's benevolence toward us, that righteousness is imputed to us. And that righteousness comes only through Christ's work and through our faith in him.

Abraham was not justified by his righteousness but by his faith. Faith places the glory in God, whereas our works place the glory in us. The commentators study numerous aspects of faith and advance various definitions. Paul sets up contrasting pairs, and the interpreters explore them in detail: the one who works versus the one who believes, to work versus not to work, debt versus grace, debt versus imputation, wages versus righteousness, and so on. Throughout their discussions, the reformers make it clear that Jesus Christ and *his* works are central, and that it is only in him that we are justified.

4:1 *Studying Abraham*

ABRAHAM AS AN EXAMPLE. MARTIN BUCER: "What shall we say, then?" He has already concluded that "a man or woman is justified by faith, not by any works of the law." From this solidly established principle, it follows that where faith is present, there will be justification (the highest act of divine favor); where faith is absent, whatever works of the law may be present, there the utmost wickedness reigns (the most certain proof of divine wrath). Who, therefore, does not see that faith is that by which we receive God's mercy in freely absolving us, that is, in justifying us? But his style of teaching demands accurate and clear examples wherein the conclusion reached by rational argument can be visually seen as a thing placed before our very eyes. Therefore, the apostle chose to make use of an example—and with good reason, since it is in the understanding of this doctrine he is now discussing that eternal salvation and happiness is to be found, and since his instruction derives from the foremost master of teaching, the Holy Spirit. But even though the chief force of many examples evidently concerns this subject (for as none of the saints were justified except by faith alone, so each one of them that the Scriptures sets forth contains within itself clear evidence of the doctrine here under discussion), he nevertheless selects Abraham, that first father of the saints, since it was on his authority that Paul's adversaries were especially wishing to be seen as relying. He also puts forward this example in his peculiar style of interrogation, for the sake of expressing himself vividly and with confidence. . . .

"What therefore," Paul says, "are we saying that Abraham found?" He is saying, in effect, "We have proved that a man or woman is 'justified by faith apart from the works of the law'; but if perhaps you require an example of this, I do not want to adduce just any common example—let us consider our father Abraham himself. What shall we say that he 'found,' to what thing did he attain, by virtue of which he was at length justified? He is the father of us all. Even if we trace our genealogy according to the flesh from a source common to both me and the Jews, I do not despise this nobility, but I regard myself and anyone else who obtains justification like Abraham did as blessed." COMMENTARY ON ROMANS (1536).[1]

---

[1]Bucer, *Metaphrases et Enarrationes*, 211-12; citing Rom 3:28.

EIGHT ARGUMENTS FOR JUSTIFICATION APART FROM THE LAW. GEORG MAJOR: Having put forward the proposition, "We reckon that a man or woman is justified by faith apart from the works of the law," in the fourth chapter Paul gives his proofs for it.

The first proof is taken from the example of Abraham in this way:

(P1) Since Abraham is the father of all those who would be saved, both of Jews and Gentiles, it must be that both Jews and Gentiles are justified and saved in the same way that Abraham was justified.

(P2) Abraham was justified by faith and not by works.

(C) Therefore, all the children of Abraham, both Jews and Gentiles, are justified by faith and not by works.

The major premise (P1) is clear from Genesis chapter 17: "I have made you a father of many nations." He proves the minor premise (P2) in this way: even though Abraham was a light to his generation and adorned with the highest virtues, he still could not boast of these virtues before God, but in God's sight he is obliged to say: "Lord, do not enter into judgment with your servant, for in your sight no living creature will be justified." Neither does the Scripture attribute the praise of righteousness to Abraham's good works, but to his faith, as Genesis 15 says: "Abraham believed God, and it was reckoned to him as righteousness." Now to whatever thing the Scriptures attribute the praise of righteousness, by that thing we are righteous. But it attributes righteousness to Abraham's faith and not to his works. Therefore, Abraham and all his children are righteous by faith and not by the merits of works.

The second argument by which he shows that righteousness is not by works but by faith and God's freely bestowed mercy and imputation, is taken from an analogy with wage-earners.

(P1) To the wage-earner who labors, their wages are counted as a debt owed and not as grace.

(P2) To the believer, even one who does not labor and is unworthy (such as the thief converted on the cross), their faith is reckoned as righteousness on the basis of sheer grace apart from works.

(C) Therefore, good works do not justify.

Also, since justification is remission of sins and the freely bestowed imputation of righteousness apart from works, it cannot be based on an owed debt or on the merit of good works, but only on the freely bestowed grace and mercy of God on account of Christ the promised Mediator. The testimony of Psalm 32 proves this definition of justification: "Blessed are those whose iniquities are forgiven," where the prophet teaches that the blessedness and justification of men and women is for their sins to be remitted, covered and not imputed.

The third argument is taken from the circumstances of the times.

(P2) Abraham was pronounced righteous on account of his faith while yet uncircumcised.

(C) Therefore, circumcision and the works of the law do not justify, but faith alone does.

Fourth argument:

(P1) The sign and the thing signified are different.

(P2) Circumcision was required of Abraham only to be a sign of the righteousness of faith.

(C) Therefore circumcision cannot be righteousness itself.

Fifth argument:

The inheritance was promised to Abraham through the righteousness of faith, apart from the law. For the law was first given many years after Abraham had already been long before pronounced righteous by faith. Therefore, righteousness is not by the law or by works, nor is the inheritance of eternal life given except *freely* by faith, that it might not be merit but a free gift, and given to us on account of our Lord Jesus Christ and by his merit and obedience.

Sixth argument:

The inheritance is universally promised to all, as much to them that are under the law as to those who do not possess the law, as it is written in Genesis 22: "In your seed all the peoples of the earth will be blessed." Therefore, it is not only those to whom the law pertains who are righteous and heirs of eternal life, but rather all are blessed who by faith lay hold of the Seed of Abraham, our Lord Jesus Christ, whether they be Jews or Gentiles in their uncircumcision.

Also,

(P1) Every promise is received by faith.

(P2) The inheritance was promised, and indeed *freely* without condition or works of the law.

(C) Therefore, the promised inheritance is received by faith, nor is it necessary to be deserving of it by the works of the law.

Also,

(P1) If righteousness and the inheritance are established on the basis of the merit of works, then they are promised in vain.

(P2) But God did not promise them in vain.

(C) Therefore, the inheritance is not established on the basis of works, but rather those who believe are children and heirs of God apart from the merits of works, by faith alone. John 1 says: "He gave to them the power to become sons of God."

The seventh argument is taken from the contrary effects of justification and of the law:

(P1) The justified "have peace and joy with God, through our Lord Jesus Christ."

(P2) But "the law brings about wrath." That is, it produces terrors of conscience, and it accuses and condemns everyone who does not render it a complete obedience, internally and externally.

(C) Therefore, justification cannot be on the basis of the law and its works, since the vivification and renovation that come with it result in eternal life and joy.

Eighth argument:

(P1) A conditional promise is never certain as long as its condition is pending and not yet fulfilled.

(P2) The promise of grace is not conditional, but entirely freely given. In fact it is free so that it might be firm and certain.

(C) Therefore, those who receive that promise by faith are justified freely without any condition of works or merits, whether they are of the law or not, as long as they are of the faith of Abraham, who is the father of all of us who believe in Christ, both Jews and Gentiles.

The proof of the minor premise is: if the promise of remission of sins depended on the condition of fulfilling the law, it would always be uncertain. Or rather, it would be completely in vain because nobody fulfills the law, as Christ said in John 7: "Did not Moses give you the law, and yet none of you keep the law" in your deeds? "Therefore the inheritance is given on the basis of faith, that it might be according to grace, so that the promise might be sure to all the seed." With these words, Paul concludes his set of proofs.

To this conclusion he adds an amplification in which he wondrously commends Abraham's faith for us to imitate. He sets forth the illustrious example of this father of us all, and at the same time illustrates the nature of faith. He teaches us that it does not turn upon visible things subjected to reason, but that it lays hold of the promise and rests upon it and hopes when there is no hope. And having simply rested on the divine promise, it struggles against unbelief and despair, and conquers them even over nature's objections. And this faith of Abraham was reckoned to him as righteousness. But this was written that we might know that righteousness is likewise reckoned to us who believe in Christ who died and was raised for our sakes, for whom it was necessary to be delivered up in order to wipe away our sins, and to be raised

because of our justification, since this could not have happened through the law and our merits.

Thus he concludes his proof with a most beautiful concluding summary, in which the whole doctrine of justification is brought in: Here is that Lord, on whose account sins are not imputed to believers, and on whose account we are righteous, and sons and daughters and heirs of God. EXPOSITION OF THE EPISTLES OF PAUL (1569).[2]

IF ABRAHAM WAS JUSTIFIED BY WORKS.
MARTIN BUCER: He first brings out an opinion that he opposes by reducing it to absurdity: "if Abraham was justified by works" (but he was not so justified before God), then he has "found" something, then "he has something to boast about" (but not before God). But if he was not justified before God, if he has found nothing, if he has attained to nothing that he can boast about before God, what is more absurd than to say that he was justified by works? For the whole judgment of God concerning us is that he who has not shown himself approved has already perished. Further, that Abraham (if we should say that he was justified by works) possessed nothing that he could boast about before God, nothing that was of any particular value before God, he proves by the oracle in which God testified that Abraham was justified by faith. For that statement reads: "He believed God, and it was imputed to him as righteousness." On account of what "thing" could we say that Abraham was counted as righteous, other than that thing here given as the reason why God pronounced him righteous? That "thing" is *faith*. Therefore, he was justified by faith and not by works. Consequently, however many there are who are elect unto eternal life and therefore children of Abraham, it is necessary that they be justified not by works, but by faith, if indeed they want to be justified before God and have a reason to boast before him. COMMENTARY ON ROMANS (1536).[3]

---

[2]Major, *Enarrationes Epistolarum S. Pauli*, 44-46; citing Rom 3:28; Gen 17:5; Ps 143:2; Gen 15:6; Ps 32:1; Gen 22:18; Jn 1:12; Rom 5:1; Rom 4:15; Jn 7:19; Rom 4:16.
[3]Bucer, *Metaphrases et Enarrationes*, 212.

SEVEN ARGUMENTS FOR FAITH ALONE.
JOHANNES BUGENHAGEN: The reader should here diligently pay attention to what has preceded, lest by neglecting to observe Paul's order of argument he fail to grasp what follows. The passage here is one of confirmation, for he here strengthens the proposition that faith in Christ alone justifies with convincing arguments, which we will consider in turn.

"What therefore?" The Jews and legal experts, upon hearing that we are justified by faith alone, object: "Are good works really worth nothing? Abraham our father performed good works—do you think that God didn't have any regard for them?" Paul here answers with seven arguments, which can be further divided into even more, in which you will see more clearly by means of analogy what is proper to faith and what to works, and what is circumstantial to them.

1. "For if Abraham." The first argument is that Abraham was justified by faith, not by works, and therefore we also are justified by faith and not by works, for the reason that nobody is justified in any other way—is equally applicable in either case. It was necessary to prove this to the Jews who were crossing swords with him over the law.

2. "Even as David also." This is the second argument, that righteousness is attained by imputation. "The blessing of the one." This is that by which a man or woman is made righteous and blessed. "To whom God." He calls blessed the person whom God justifies, not the one who does good works. He accepts us as righteous, even though according to our nature we are unrighteous. It is just like when I forgive someone a debt that is not getting paid off, he is then free from debt, not because he paid it off, but because I *reckon* it as being paid off. Otherwise, if I had not reckoned it so, he would have remained a debtor. Thus we are righteous, not because of ourselves, but because of God. You, therefore, hear only of grace in this matter.

3. "For we say." By "we," he means in concert with the Scriptures; it is not "I" alone who say this. This is his third argument: Abraham was justified before he was circumcised; therefore, we also are justified before any of our works.

Circumcision is the first work of the law, without which all the others could not fittingly be done. This is akin to what baptism is for us. Moreover, it is only the sign of the righteousness that is by faith, not the righteousness itself. Look at what is said concerning this in Genesis, where not a few years had passed between the story of Abraham's faith and his circumcision. For before he had received Isaac from Sarah or even Ishmael from Hagar, the Scriptures had already said of him that "Abraham believed, and it was reckoned to him." Therefore, since circumcision is the first work of the law, and Abraham was justified before he was circumcised, what is it to which we should adhere? From this passage you can detect the error of the letter of James, in which book you find an impious line of reasoning, not to mention the absurdities it arrives at. It cites Scripture against Scripture, which the Holy Spirit cannot do. It, therefore, cannot be numbered with the rest of the books of Scripture that proclaim righteousness by faith. The letter to the Hebrews handles these Old Testament examples in a far worthier manner.

4. "For not through the law." He uses this argument multiple times in Galatians: Abraham was justified on the basis of the promise, not on the basis of the law, since it is written that as soon as Abraham had heard God's promise "he believed." That truthful promise concerned his inheritance, which he obtained only by the righteousness of faith. It was, therefore, not by the law but by faith that he was made the heir of the world. That the promise might be fulfilled in the greatest possible way, he did not then immediately inherit the land of Canaan. But in Christ, who is the promised Seed himself, he became the possessor and Lord of that land, or rather of the whole world. Concerning which, see Isaiah 40, Paul's letter to Timothy, and the Psalms: "You have placed all things under his feet." From this testimony it is to be observed that all things are subjected to Christ and to his people, that is, to believers. But nothing belongs to the wicked—they occupy the earth by oppression, by which they themselves are ruined and by which they abuse every creature. They are thieves and

robbers, since while in this land of the promise they make use of it with no good conscience. To even hear of what they do ought to horrify us. . . .

5. "For if they who are of the law are heirs." This argument depends on the previous ones. If righteousness is on the basis of God's promise, who wills that we should sincerely receive what he promised, that righteousness is not from us is also indicated by the name employed for it: it is called *God's* righteousness, not *ours*. It comes *to* us, not because he would find any righteousness in us, but because he provides us with his own, that is, *God's* righteousness. "For all have sinned." He promised it because we did not then possess it. He did not promise in vain, which he would have done if he had promised us that which we already previously possessed. We are impoverished and empty-handed—we possess nothing of righteousness. But we *will* possess it, because he promised it, if we will believe the One making the promise.

6. "For the law brings about wrath." He again proves that it cannot happen that we are justified by the law. In fact, it is far from being able to reconcile us with God in any way whatever. Even if we should fully carry out its requirements, it would continue to terrify our consciences and stir up within us an anger and indignation against God, and under such horror and terror we would find ourselves wishing that the law did not exist, or rather that God were not God. Is this to honor God and keep the law? So that we might perceive our own condemnation, the law brings about the thing about which our nature cannot fail to become enraged and murmur in a most insolent manner against God. It thus happens, so that through the law, sin might become more serious, that it stirs us up against God, which is what is declared in Romans 7. They who do not see this in their own hearts must be the greatest and most arrogant of hypocrites. Therefore, the law aggravates our conscience more than it liberates or justifies.

7. "Therefore it is of faith." A conscience angered with God does not glorify God after it sees itself cast away from him by revealed sin. "For in hell,

who will confess you?" And thus sin becomes greater, and transgression becomes manifest. If, therefore, righteousness were by works, people would not be able to pacify their own consciences. But since God grants righteousness at no cost, we cannot be in doubt about our righteousness, and it is from this that our conscience is set at rest. This argument is powerful—let nobody despise it. INTERPRETATION OF ROMANS (1531).[4]

ABRAHAM JUSTIFIED BY FAITH AND NOT BY WORKS. MARTIN BUCER: Further, since the divine oracle says nothing more than that the fact that he believed was reckoned to Abraham as righteousness, it could appear that he has not yet fully proved that Abraham was justified by faith *alone*, apart from works, or rather by faith and *not* by works. Even if it is fully evident from this oracle that Abraham was justified by faith (for to whom God imputes righteousness, such a one is without question then justified before him, that is, judged as being righteous), it nevertheless seems possible to doubt whether the further point that Abraham was *not* justified by works can be concluded from the oracle.

Now it is true that the letter that St. James wrote, when he made reference to this testimony concerning Abraham's faith and granted that he had indeed been justified by faith, nevertheless affirms that he was at the same time *justified by works*, and that "his faith was made perfect by his works." He then concludes from this that "a man is justified by works and not by faith alone." And yet, in the same way that the apostle Paul affirms that Abraham was justified by faith, he also denies that he was justified by works. Paul wishes us to understand this denial just as much as the affirmation that he adduced from this testimony, which is something that anybody carefully considering it would easily acknowledge as necessarily following from what Paul says about faith. For to Paul, faith is that by which we embrace the freely given

---

[4]Bugenhagen, *In D. Pauli ad Romanos*, 38r-39v, 41r-42v; citing Gen 15:6; Rom 4:13; Is 40:10-11; 2 Tim 2:8; Ps 8:6; Rom 3:23; Ps 6:5.

promise of God with full confidence. Thus to be justified by faith has the same force to the apostle as being justified by grace on the basis of the unobliged goodness of God, by which God offers us salvation without being incited to doing so by our works. While it's to those who have faith that he holds out this offer of his, he is the One who inspired that very faith in them. That he understands that being justified by grace and being justified by works are incompatible with one another is made manifestly clear, from which this conclusion rightly follows: Abraham was justified by faith, and therefore not by works. For this is the same as saying that he was justified by grace, and therefore not of works. Paul's general line of argument goes this way:

(P1) There is no doubt that all the elect are justified in the same way in which Abraham was justified, since he is the father of all the saints, and particularly of the Jews.

(P2) But he was justified by faith, and not by works.

(C) Therefore whoever is elect unto life is justified by faith and not by works.

Further, it is clear that Abraham was justified by faith and not by works from the fact that the Scriptures testify that he was justified by faith. Now if he was justified by faith, since this is the same as being justified by God's freely granted acceptance of him, then he could not have been justified by works. For he could not be justified, that is, be approved by God, both on the basis of God's freely given benevolence and at the same time on the basis of his own works. Just as it cannot be true that someone could be justified at the same time by a freely given worthiness and one that isn't freely given. That passage in James is speaking of a secondary justification that works obtain, not of the primary and essential justification of which Paul speaks . . .

Here it is also to be observed that just as the apostle understands by "faith" the acceptance of the freely offered promise, so he understands by "works"

those things by which you merit something. This is why he subsequently adds that "to the one who works, wages are reckoned not according to grace, but according to debt." From this there is nobody who cannot clearly see that the apostle here is speaking of those works by which wages are earned, and on the basis of debt. In this passage, therefore, the "one who works" is the one meriting something by those works. Whereas "he who does not work" is he who does the same things as a believer and merits nothing by those works. Seeing that to be "justified by grace" and to be "justified by faith," by which of course that grace is laid hold of, are in fact the same thing to Paul, just as it is the same thing to him that "one works," that one is "justified by works," and that one is "justified by the merit of the works and thus by debt," it is therefore plain for all to see that the Scripture that affirms that Abraham was justified by faith affirms at the same time that he was justified freely, and denies it that it was on the basis of works.

What is clearer is that in passing, Paul indicates what the nature of faith is, for nobody will savingly believe in God if he does not before anything else believe that he promises the remission of sins, that is, the justification of the ungodly. But "to believe" in this passage is to embrace as true, on the authority of the One speaking, something which you cannot know to be true or not on the basis of any other consideration. To a person to whom the authority of God stands behind his believing something, what would he be more ready to believe about God than that he promises to be his God, that is, that he will receive remission of sins and salvation? If such a person should not believe God because he believes, from his innate awareness of the divine nature, that he cannot escape God's judgment, then he will hate God and shrink back from everything that belongs to God, and absolutely no real faith at all will find lodging within him. Certainly such a person is being led by his own authority, for there is nothing else that would induce such an opinion. Since he sets the believer against the "one who works," that is, the one who freely accepts the proffered mercy against the one who desires to merit it by his works, he therefore most rightly expresses what is the first point in true faith, that one "believe in God who justifies the ungodly." COMMENTARY ON ROMANS (1536).[5]

TEN TRIALS ABRAHAM ENDURED. PETER MARTYR VERMIGLI: These things, then, which are spoken of here, should not be brought up for the purpose of making life easier and giving license to sin, but rather for being called back toward the goal. Paul does just this, showing that the reason for our justification is not situated in good works. He bequeaths other honors and dignities for them from there; nor, indeed, should one think that Paul, by his teaching, be thought of as desiring to think little of the most noble virtues of such a man as Abraham. For as the Jews remember, Abraham was very often tested, and nonetheless always overcame. God summoned him outside his land and his own kin, so that he wandered in the land of Cana. But there he was not able to live, on account of the famine, so from there he was compelled to go down into Egypt, where he experienced a third trial when Pharaoh snatched away his wife. He endured a fourth trial when Lot compelled him to leave in order to avoid tensions. A fifth in a war he had to wage against many kings and a victorious army, when he himself had only a few on his side. A sixth, when he himself, now an old man, was ordered to receive circumcision. A seventh, when King Abimelech, in Gerar, again stole away his wife. An eighth, when Hagar, who had conceived by him, was compelled to flee by Sarah, who was greatly afflicting her. A ninth, when he was compelled to send away his son Ishmael, born to him in his old age, along with his mother. A tenth, when God required of him that he sacrifice his only-begotten son Isaac. Abraham endured these and other similar, most illustrious accomplishments. And in no way does Paul cast them aside. But he simply shows that these things were not so great that they could be set opposite the wrath and judgment of God. Or that on account of these things, God

would be favorably inclined to him. COMMENTARY ON ROMANS (1560).[6]

CONTRAST OF GLORIFYING SELF AND GOD. JACQUES LEFÈVRE D'ÉTAPLES: Paul does not wish that any persons trust in their works as if they could be justified by them, or as if the one who works is justified on account of his works as if works themselves are what justify. It is not so. But the glory of justification is to be given not to works, but to God, who justifies. They look to themselves, but Paul wants them to look to God. They glorify themselves, but Paul wants them to glorify God. They boast and are puffed up about themselves, but Paul wants them to glory in God and humble themselves on their own account. They are impious, whereas Paul wants them to be pious. They are carnal, whereas Paul wants them to be spiritual. Human knowledge drags them down since they are relying on their fleshly understanding, but divine knowledge raises Paul up as he, in a certain sense, abandons his own understanding and relies on the Spirit. Paul refers all things and all praise to God, whereas they assign it to men and women. COMMENTARY ON ROMANS.[7]

RECONCILING ROMANS 4:1 WITH JAMES 2:21. JACQUES LEFÈVRE D'ÉTAPLES: Paul then adds, "What then will we say that Abraham our father found according to the flesh? For if Abraham was justified by works, he has cause to glory, though not before God." For this praise would then belong not to God, but to Abraham, who had worked and whose own works would have justified him. But when we say that God justified Abraham by faith, the glory of this justification belongs to God and not to Abraham. But perhaps you will say, "But the apostle James said that Abraham was justified by works." He did indeed: "Was not Abraham our father justified by works when he offered Isaac his son on the altar?" Paul neither denies nor opposes anything that was

---

[5]Bucer, *Metaphrases et Enarrationes*, 212-13; citing Jas 2:21-22, 24.

[6]Vermigli, *In Epistolam S. Pauli*, 217.
[7]Lèfvre, *Epistole divi Pauli*, 60v.

uttered by the Spirit,[†] for what Paul denies is the idea that Abraham was justified by works, which is what those who trust in the works of the law believe, as if righteousness were by works and the works themselves justify. Rather he says that Abraham was justified by God on the basis of his faith, which is the same that James expressed under inspiration when he said, "Every good gift and every perfect gift is from above, descending from the Father of lights with whom there is no change nor shadow of turning"; that is, there is no sign or indication of mutability or changeableness in him. Now who would deny that justification is a perfect gift? He does, therefore, not mean to say that anybody is justified by works, as those who trust in works want to understand him, as if works justify. But rather James conjoins works to faith as faith's auxiliary, a help that must be obtained and preserved. For he says, "Do you see how that faith works together with works, and faith is consummated by works?" And that faith that is not preceded, accompanied, or followed by works he calls "dead," just as we call a man or woman dead who is not accompanied by movement, sensation, or breath. But if we see someone moving or having sensation, we know that he or she is alive, and if we perceive some wind of breath, any breathing in and out, we have a sign that there is still life. COMMENTARY ON ROMANS.[8]

THE ROYAL LAW AND WORKS OF FAITH.

JACQUES LEFÈVRE D'ÉTAPLES: The works of faith, being the same as the works of the "royal law," which is what James calls that commandment that encompasses the Ten Commandments, are tokens of faith and of the life of faith, which is followed by justification—that is like the illumination of a healthy eye directed toward the sun—and they also preserve justification.

However, anyone who says that the turning of the eyes toward the solar rays is itself illumination is mistaken, but far more wrong is the one who believes that works, which are eye salves or repeated washings of the eyes, are themselves illumination. The latter are in fact further away from illumination than the former is. It is by the gracious gift and benefit of the sun that eyes are illuminated, not by either the turning of the eyes, nor by one's works. The latter symbolically represents the works of the law, and the former represents faith. But the ray from above that is cast by the sun is justification. Hence, the works of the law cleanse, while faith turns the soul toward God, and justification illuminates. Works are a dark purgation, faith is an attachment to God, and justification is the cleanness that illuminates and brightens every part.

There were in those days two parties. The first was of those who were trusting in works such that, according to their opinion, they sufficed to attain justification. The second party was of those trusting in faith but taking no care to do good works. The apostle James counters the latter, whereas Paul was countering the former. But you, if you are made wise by the Spirit, must trust neither in faith nor in works, but only in God. Based on Paul, attribute to faith the chief role in obtaining salvation from God; and based on James, add works to that faith, for they are a token of life and of a fruit-bearing faith. But a lack of works is a token of an idle and dead faith, and contrary works are like the horrible stink given off by a cadaver only recently deceased. The one who understands the matter in this way will understand it spiritually, and both apostles will agree with one another, though, of course, they were already in agreement even before being "reconciled." For this discord clearly belongs to us and to the flesh, not to the Spirit. For the flesh and the letter cause plenty of discord to be seen. But concord manifestly belongs to the Spirit. COMMENTARY ON ROMANS.[9]

---

[8]Lefèvre, *Epistole divi Pauli*, 60v; citing Jas 2:21; 1:17; 2:22, 20.
[†]*Spiritiloquus*. It is possible that Lefèvre coined the word especially for this occasion. Or perhaps he found it in Paolo Cortesi, *In Sententias* (Froben, 1513), 222v.

---

[9]Lefèvre, *Epistole divi Pauli*, 61r; citing Jas 2:8.

4:2 No Cause to Boast of Works Before God

THE GOSPEL IS ABOUT SPIRITUAL AND ETERNAL LIFE. PHILIPP MELANCHTHON: Paul here as nowhere else refutes and rejects the righteousness of the law in a wonderful manner. One must prudently see where this discussion is headed. He is asking about righteousness before God—whether our righteousness can be set in opposition to the terrors of sin, of the wrath and judgment of God; whether we receive forgiveness of sins on account of our own worthiness; whether our own worthiness can set us free from sin and death; whether in a real struggle our conscience ought to rest on our own worthiness, or indeed on the mercy promised because of Christ. To this debate must be referred these belittlements of the righteousness of the law, not to carnally secure consciences or to external or civil life. For the gospel preaches about spiritual and eternal life. It preaches about true repentance and liberates from sin and death. Outward life has need of discipline and law. But the argument here is not about this external life. COMMENTARY ON ROMANS (1540).[10]

PAUL AND JAMES SPEAK OF DIFFERENT GROUPS. FRIEDRICH BALDUIN: Each apostle, Paul and James, is speaking of a different class of men and women. Paul is dealing with Pharisees who were insisting on the righteousness of their works in the court of justification, while James was dealing with hypocrites and Epicureans who believed in righteousness by faith, but who held that there was no further purpose for good works outside the court of justification and, therefore, were assuming for themselves a permission to sin. Therefore, Paul is arguing against his adversaries concerning good works understood as *efficient causes* of justification and, therefore, excluded them from justification since it is faith, not works, that lays hold of the righteousness of Christ. But James is arguing against his adversaries concerning good

works understood as *effects*, and therefore he presses their necessity on the justified person as marks of true faith. This is also what St. Augustine said about these questions, that Paul is speaking of works that *precede* faith, among which are the works of the law, by which nobody is justified; but that James speaks of works that *follow* faith, which works are said to justify insofar as they declare and put to practice the righteousness one has already received. Therefore let it be sure and undoubted that while each apostle speaks of Abraham as already justified, Paul refers to how he obtained justification, while James refers to how his justification was declared or born witness to. COMMENTARY ON ROMANS (1620).[11]

THE LAW AND GOSPEL ARE DIFFERENT. JOHN CALVIN: The law, Paul says, is different from faith. Why? Because to obtain justification by it, works are required; and from this it follows that to obtain justification by the gospel, works are not required. From this statement, it appears that those who are justified by faith are justified independent of—indeed, in the absence of—the merit of works, because faith receives that righteousness that the gospel bestows. But the gospel differs from the law in this, that it does not confine justification to works, but places it entirely in the mercy of God. In like manner, Paul contends, in the letter to the Romans, that Abraham had no ground of glorying, because faith was imputed to him for righteousness; and he adds in confirmation, that the proper place for justification by faith is where there are no works to which reward is due. "To him that works, the reward is not reckoned of grace, but of debt." What is given to faith is gratuitous, this being the force of the meaning of the words that he employs there. Shortly after, he adds, "Therefore it is of faith, that it might be by grace"; and from this infers that the inheritance is gratuitous because it is procured by faith. How is it so if not because faith, without the aid of works, leans entirely on

---

[10]Melanchthon, *Commentary on Romans*, 106*. [11]Balduin, *Catechesis Apostolica*, 289-90.

the mercy of God? And in the same sense, doubtless, he teaches elsewhere that the righteousness of God without the law was manifested, being witnessed by the law and the prophets. For he excludes the law, declaring that God's righteousness is not aided by works, that we do not obtain it by working, but are destitute when we draw near to receive it. INSTITUTES OF THE CHRISTIAN RELIGION 3.11.18 (1559).[12]

HOLY ABRAHAM NOT JUSTIFIED BY HIS RIGHTEOUSNESS.

JOHANNES BRENZ: This argument clearly describes that we are accepted by God not on account of any merit of our strength, but only on account of Christ, if we believe in him. And it is very much centered on the example of Abraham, for Abraham was the chief of the patriarchs, from whom also began the circumcision about which the Jews loudly boast. Whereby, if it is shown that Abraham was not justified or acquitted of unrighteousness on account of the merit of his righteousness, but only through faith on account of Christ, it is clear that neither are other men and women justified on account of their merit, that is, overcome the sentence of the divine judgment of death and condemnation. Further, Abraham was a most pious man and was gifted with eminent virtue. Therefore, if Abraham is not justified by the purity of his virtue, how is it possible that any other people would be justified by their virtue, especially since theirs is inferior merit? We should, therefore, consider the example of Abraham carefully, and we should hold it, as it were, a most strong argument for the righteousness of faith against the merits of our works. COMMENTARY ON ROMANS (1564).[13]

FAITH REMOVES AND PROVIDES GROUNDS FOR BOASTING.

MARTIN BUCER: "For if Abraham was justified by works." This is the proof of his assertion that Abraham was not justified by works, which he demonstrates by reducing it to the absurd, in this way: "If he was justified by works, he has something to glory in"; that is, he has cause to boast, and that *before God* since all judgment belongs to him. But it is impossible that one might have cause to boast before God on account of one's works. Therefore, the cause for which he would have obtained this boast, that he was justified by works, is also assuredly impossible. He proves this impossibility from the fact that the Scriptures testify that his faith was "reckoned to Abraham as righteousness." Which, as I've already said, is the same as righteousness and salvation being divinely bestowed upon him freely apart from any merit.

A harmonization of these assertions:

The law of faith takes away boasting—*and*—
The one who believes has a boast before God.

A few verses earlier, the apostle had made it proper to faith to take away boasting, which of course the law of works would not take away. But when he writes here that Abraham did not have a boast before God on account of his works, this means that he *did* have a boast before God *by faith*. Consequently, faith both removes *and* provides grounds for boasting, which two assertions appear to be contradictory. But in fact, one kind of boasting is of one's own righteousness, while another kind of boasting is of *God's* righteousness. One kind is about *our* good works, the other about *God's* worthiness. Faith clearly takes away the first, while it establishes the second. "Glorying" is the expression and boast of a soul trusting and exulting in some distinguished thing as belonging to them. The men and women who now truly believe in God through Christ recognize that they were saved by the mercy of God alone, and that all that belonged to them was so incapable of not being cursed by God, that in order to atone for them it was necessary that the Son of God die. Hence it cannot happen that they boast in any thing else but in the grace and goodness of God toward them and in the cross of our Lord Jesus Christ. This is why in Ephesians the apostle wrote concerning our salvation, "It is the gift of God, not of works, lest anyone should boast."

---

[12]Calvin, *Institutes*, 2:54-55*; citing Rom 4:16; 3:21.
[13]Brenz, *In Epistolam*, 98.

But when faith is persuaded that apart from any obligation on God's part eternal happiness has been bestowed on it, it then has cause to boast, but only in the Lord, and especially so as the Lord has been so propitious and so benevolent toward him. COMMENTARY ON ROMANS (1536).[14]

ALL WORKS ARE EXCLUDED FROM BOASTING. ANDREW WILLET: "If Abraham was justified by works." The Catholics are of the opinion that the apostle is here excluding only such works as were done only by the strength of nature without faith in the Mediator: So Stapleton, *Antid.* p. 46, who urges this reason among others to confirm his opinion: The apostle excludes only works that do not expect an eternal reward with God, but the works done in faith do expect an eternal reward; therefore he does not exclude such works.[†]

Contra. 1. But the contrary is evident that the apostle shuts out all works whatsoever from the matter of justification: (1) He speaks of the works of Abraham, now a faithful man not an unbeliever. (2) He mentions works in general without any distinction, denying justification unto them, and ascribing it unto faith. (3) Everything that is rewarded *ex debito*, of due debt, is excluded from justification, but to every work is the wages due out of debt, as verse 4. "To him that works, the wages is counted by debt." Therefore, every work is excluded.

2. Concerning his reason: if he means the reward which is due of debt and not given by favor, then even the works of faithful men and women cannot expect such a reward. If he means a reward given by favor, then both the works that are so rewarded, as well as those that will not be, are excluded.

3. And as the works of faith are excluded together with works done before and without faith; so also not only does the apostle speaking of works mean the reward only, but even the works of the moral law also; for the apostle names works in general and he directly afterward speaks of the moral law, verse 15. "The law causes wrath, and where no law is, there is no transgression," which though it is true of every law in general, yet this generally is seen in the moral law. A SIX-FOLD COMMENTARY ON THE EPISTLE TO THE ROMANS (1611).[15]

4:3 Abraham's Belief Counted as Righteousness

THE FOUNDATION OF TRUE RELIGION. JOHANNES BRENZ: Abraham is not righteous before God by the merits of his works but only because of grace, on account of Christ in whom he believed. Or more concisely, "Whoever believes in him who justifies the wicked, his faith is imputed for righteousness." But Abraham believed God. Therefore this believing was imputed to him for righteousness. This is the first of particular places in Holy Scripture by which the foundation of the doctrine of true religion is established and developed. Therefore, it is to be observed most carefully. For in Genesis, God established a meeting with Abraham, who was lamenting of childlessness, and he promised him an heir, saying, "This one will not be your heir, but the one who comes out from your belly, that one will be your heir." And leading him outside, he said, "Look up toward heaven and number the stars if you are able. So will be your seed." To these the Scriptures add, saying "Abraham believed God and it was imputed to him for righteousness." That is, after Abraham put faith in the divine promise, God laid hold of him by so great favor and grace, that he did not impute unrighteousness to him any longer, but absolved him of all unrighteousness, nor did he pronounce otherwise concerning him than if he were most righteous. COMMENTARY ON ROMANS (1564).[16]

TWELVE CIRCUMSTANCES OF ABRAHAM'S JUSTIFICATION. NIELS HEMMINGSEN: Having briefly noted these points, let us return to the example of Abraham, from whom nearly everything that follows in this chapter has been

---

[14]Bucer, *Metaphrases et Enarrationes*, 217; citing 3:27; Eph 2:9.

[15]Willet, *Hexapla*, 196*. [†]Thomas Stapleton, *Antidota Apostolica in Epistolam Pauli ad Romanos* (Antwerp, 1595).
[16]Brenz, *In Epistolam*, 101.

constructed. Paul, like a master craftsman, considers and examines two things in the example that he put forward: the deed considered in itself, and the circumstances surrounding both it and Abraham personally. From this, if I might summarize, we are taught three things. First, what is the true reckoning of justification. Next, what is the true character of faith. Last, what the personal life of believers should be like. But, though everything else is contained under these three heads, still we will examine apart from this the deed and Abraham's personal circumstances, so that we may have not only a pattern of life in our holy father Abraham, but also that a careful observation of it might assist us in the handling of other such examples and their adaptation to a particular purpose.

Therefore, Abraham's deed in itself teaches, as has already been said, that true righteousness, by which we are made acceptable to God, is by the faith with which we believe the free promise. For others must be justified in the same way that Abraham was justified. I mean that a separate method of justification is not possible since God is equal in his dealings with all. The personal circumstances of the one justified, Abraham, instructs us in a number of very important matters, the most prominent of which I will now go over.

First is Abraham's profession of life before his justification, which testifies that Abraham was received into favor not by his own merit or by his own preparatory works, but by the grace of God alone. Paul thereby takes away every ground of boasting. For what, I ask, is able to be merited by idolatry? Who is able to have "congruous merits" by which God is moved to bestow his grace? This circumstance therefore confounds the doctrine of preparatory works and congruous merits.

The second circumstance concerns when it was that Abraham was justified by faith. This teaches that circumcision is not necessarily required for justification. For Abraham was justified *before* he was circumcised, which would not at all be true if circumcision was either the cause of, or the merit for, or part of, or the fulfillment of, justification.

The third circumstance is also about timing, showing thereby that the righteousness that is by faith pertains to all indiscriminately. For Abraham was justified by faith *before* men and women were distinguished by external marks. It was without any doubt from this circumstance that the prophets constructed their sermons concerning the calling of the Gentiles.

The fourth circumstance is similarly about timing, which teaches that the Mosaic rites are not required for justification. For as Abraham is justified without them, so also those who will be justified after his example do not require them for righteousness, neither as a cause nor a complement.

The fifth circumstance is also about timing, which teaches that we obtain free justification apart from the moral law and the works that are commanded in the Decalogue. For since we are justified according to the pattern of Abraham, who was justified many years—that is 430—before the moral law was entrusted by God to the people of Israel, it cannot happen that that righteousness should be from the moral law. But if anyone should object that the moral law is perpetual, and therefore that Abraham was not without it, the answer is simple: no reward is owed to works except as God covenants to give it. For the works of men and women should not be esteemed as meritorious because of some intrinsic worth they possess, but only because of God's willing acceptance and by reason of the covenant he interposed. Therefore, this reckoning stands unmoved: Abraham was justified by faith in the promise before the covenant of works was published, namely, that "the man or woman who does these things will live by them." Hence Abraham was justified by faith, not by obedience to the moral law.

The sixth circumstance is that of Abraham's faith, which is not a casual belief or hollow persuasion, but a certain full assurance [*plerophoria*], which yields to no rational arguments. On the contrary, it rises up against all reason, steadfastly leaning on the unchangeableness of God's promise.

The seventh circumstance concerns the things that accompanied Abraham's faith, which teach that Abraham's faith was not devoid of good works, but that it had adjoined to it obedience to God. For even though it was by faith alone that he laid hold of the freely given benefit of justification, yet faith will not be despoiled of its own natural properties, as we see in Abraham, who also attributed the glory of truthfulness to God, and he obeyed him, being prepared to sacrifice his only son. Let the godly man and woman learn from this that nothing ought to be more dear to them than obedience to God and eagerness to do good works. This is why when Paul says that Christ rescued us from the present evil age, he adds the reason why: that we should be zealous for good works. Thus we ought to imitate Abraham's obedience. Only, let us glory in our father Abraham for the right reason.

The eighth circumstance is Abraham's economic activity. For though Abraham, had been divinely called, he did not cast aside the care of his family, but rather he showed himself to be industrious not only within the household, but also in the market. This teaches that economic administration, a righteous mode of acquiring wealth, contractual agreements, and lawful warfare do not make us less pleasing to God, as long as we follow in the footsteps of our father Abraham and conduct ourselves in the same manner in those situations.

The ninth circumstance is the wealth of Abraham, which refutes the impious doctrine of the monks who place Christian perfection in beggary. For when Abraham was announced to have been perfect by the testimony of God, although he did not at all have mediocre means, it follows that Christian perfection does not require abdicating possessions. On the contrary, this example of Abraham clearly teaches where true and Christian perfection is placed. For when he obeys the voice of God, being prepared to sacrifice his only-begotten son, he teaches well enough that the only Christian perfection is when someone who believes in God esteems all other matters less than obedience to him, just as Abraham did.

The tenth circumstance is the persecution of Abraham, which teaches that the church has been placed under the cross in order that she might cultivate faith and prayer.

The eleventh circumstance is Abraham's unconquerable faith in the presence of various kinds of stumbling blocks. For he was not broken by suffering by the multitude of his enemies and the scarcity of the godly. But he sustained himself in the midst of hardships by a confidence in a glorious liberation.

The twelfth circumstance is his common lot with the godly: although he was declared a friend of God, yet he was still subject to the common lot of men and women, namely, to death. And yet he was not afraid to face death, but he sustained himself in the midst of death by a contemplation of heavenly glory, and entrusted his holy soul to God in the hope of immortality.

It pleased Paul to set forth these personal circumstances attending Abraham, in order that it might be clear to us why Abraham is called the "father of those who believe," since these facts exhibit for us the faith and the obedience of this holy patriarch of Christians. COMMENTARY ON ROMANS (1562).[17]

FAITH RESTS ON THE MERCY AND GOODNESS OF GOD. MARTIN BUCER: "But what does the Scripture say?" This question that he adds to the discussion is intended to give us confidence in the truth. The passage here cited is Genesis 15. In that passage we read that the Lord spoke these words to Abraham: "Do not fear! I am your shield and your exceedingly great reward." It was when Abraham had complained that his household slave would be his heir, as no son had been given to him, and the Lord answered that that slave would not be his heir, but rather one who would be born to him, and then that having led him outside he commanded him to look up at the heavens and number the stars if he could, and to set them in order, and said "Thus shall your descendants be." It was then that the Scripture adds, "And he believed Jehovah and righteousness was imputed to him."

---

[17]Hemmingsen, *Commentarius in Epistolam*, 133-37; citing Lev 18:5.

It is apparent that the one thing being proclaimed here was this faith of Abraham which he had toward the promise, "The one who will be your heir will proceed from your body," and "Thus shall your descendants be." Paul confidently exposits the nature of faith from this passage. But in his application, he draws a general conclusion about faith "in God who justifies the ungodly" from this particular example of Abraham. It seems then that he infers the whole from a part, which is not a valid construction in logic. However, we have already said in our exposition that nobody applies their faith to the words of God except those who first of all believe what he promised, that he will be their God, that is, their Savior. For what benefits would someone really expect to receive from God if he doubts whether he is propitious toward him? Therefore whenever someone has truly believed in God, it can be confidently inferred from this that he believes that God wills him good or shows him favor. This faith which the apostle is now preaching about is that which forms us anew and satisfies God. Philip Melanchthon piously and perceptively writes that the object of faith is always the mercy of God. Sometimes this is set forth in spiritual matters and sometimes in bodily matters. Hence, in any situation in which we truly embrace his mercy, having faith in God's promises, our faith always rests on the freely bestowed benevolence of God. Faith is always of the same nature, whatever specific act of faith it may be; it is still faith which rests in the mercy of God. Therefore, it is rightly inferred that if Abraham truly believed God in this matter, it is because he possessed faith. And if he possessed faith, since all faith in God looks to him to be merciful, it follows that he believed God to be his God, his highest good and only Savior. Abraham therefore possesses faith in every respect. COMMENTARY ON ROMANS (1536).[18]

FAITH IS TRUST IN THE GOOD GOD. WOLFGANG MUSCULUS: "What then?" This is a proof

taken from the authority of sacred Scripture by which he strengthens both parts of the previous argument: the affirmative part, which, though he did not state it explicitly, can nevertheless be understood from the opposite negative. The affirmative part is that Abraham was justified before God by faith, and the negative is that Abraham was *not* justified by works, otherwise he would not have had a boast before God. But since it is now certain that he *did* have a boast before God, it cannot be doubted that he came to possess it by faith and not by works. This he clearly proves using the Scripture passage he adduced.

The passage appealed to is that of Genesis 15. . . .

There are two things in this passage that must be carefully considered and explained. The first is what Paul said, that "Abraham believed God," and the second is, "and it was reckoned to him as righteousness."

"He believed God." It could appear that this testimony is not well fitted to support the case that the apostle is trying to make with it so as to prove his doctrine of righteousness by faith in Christ, since in it there is only mention of Abraham's faith by which he believed the promise concerning the multiplication of his descendants—an earthly and corporeal matter that is not a very fitting example of faith in Christ. And so along these lines there are some who think that Paul is twisting this passage to make it refer to faith in Christ, and that he misuses it in order to render faith in Christ more praiseworthy by the use of fictitious praises and by this means hopes to entice the Jews to come to Christ.

In this matter it is necessary to understand what faith is, the definition of which has been skillfully annotated by several writers: that faith is trust in promised mercy, such that the proper object of faith is the promised mercy of God, that God will be truthful, propitious, and benevolent. This is the unmovable object of faith in each and every kind of promise that is hoped for and laid hold of by faith, whether it be spiritual or corporeal in nature. However the things promised by God may vary, the object of faith remains always the

---

[18]Bucer, *Metaphrases et Enarrationes*, 214; citing Gen 15:1, 5, 4; Rom 4:6.

same: that God will be benevolent, propitious, truthful, and one's Savior—or in a word, that he will be one's God.

Thus the faith of Abraham was in this passage specifically engaged with the promise of his offspring and posterity; Jacob's faith in Genesis 28 concerned the hope of returning and of provision; David's was about victory over his enemies. And yet Abraham could not have expected by faith the multiplication of his descendants, nor Jacob his return and nourishment, nor David a victory, unless by faith they had first resolved to believe that God was propitious toward them and truthful in his promises. And this trust could not have been warranted without God's promise. In this passage, Abraham already possessed this general promise, not just this one particular promise. For it was promised, "Do not fear, Abraham, I am your shield," which is the principal promise unto which all particular promises, not to speak of this specific one, are to be referred. Therefore, this faith of Abraham was nothing other than faith in the mercy and goodness of God, to which faith in Christ is also referred. For faith is always of the same nature, whatever the particular and specific promise may be that is believed. Consequently, the apostle adduces this passage quite appropriately in order to establish his case. There is nothing awry with it at all if we would only observe in this way what faith really is and what its perpetual and principal object is.

"And it was reckoned to him as righteousness." I said above that the apostle does not merely prove that Abraham was justified by faith, but also that he was justified without works. It is at this point the verb "to reckon" must be carefully examined. This verse seems to look differently to those who immediately say: "We concede that Abraham was justified by faith, but where is that exclusive adverb, 'without works' or 'by faith alone,' or 'freely'? For although he may have been justified by faith, this in no way prevents works from being con-joined to faith so that it could equally have been said that Abraham was justified on account of works." But the verb "to reckon" wars against this

objection in the strongest way. COMMENTARY ON ROMANS (1555).[19]

THE EXAMPLE OF PHINEHAS. PETER MARTYR VERMIGLI: Nor should we pay any attention to those who interpret this sentence in such a way that they understand the "faith" of which Paul speaks here as necessarily having this sense: that God reckoned as righteousness that *action* of Abraham by which he believed, as if he were willing to regard that action in the place of righteous deeds. But that Paul may be discussing a good work is not the point of the text at hand. Rather, what is being demonstrated is the reason why we are justified. So that the main point here might become clear, I assert that "to be reckoned as righteousness" has to be taken in a twofold sense. Sometimes it means that some act is regarded as being validated and approved, or, if I might put it concisely, as being accepted as a righteous act. We grant that in this sense that celebrated deed of Phinehas and the good works of holy men and women are reckoned by God as righteousness. But sometimes it means, in a different sense, that thing by which we ourselves are regarded as enrolled in the list of the righteous. And Paul exclusively attributes this to faith, as if he were saying, "Abraham believed that he was pleasing to God and that when standing before him he would be regarded as a righteous man and would ultimately be blessed, and according to how he believed, so he received." This took place according to his faith. He, therefore, received by faith that which was being offered to him by God, as is understood from the beginning of the fifteenth chapter. For God had said to him, "I am your shield and your reward is exceedingly great." But that which is said of Phinehas and of the works of the saints pertains to the duties that come as a consequence on those who have already been justified. COMMENTARY ON ROMANS (1560).[20]

[19]Musculus, *Commentarii Romanos*, 89-90; citing Gen 15:1-6; Gen 28:1-22; 15:1.
[20]Vermigli, *In Epistolam S. Pauli*, 223; citing Gen 15:1.

Against ex Opere Operato. Erasmus Sarcerius: To "believe" is here to be certain, with a firm confidence, that one obtains remission of sins, or "righteousness," by means of grace or imputation.

To "impute" or reckon is to freely remit and forgive sins. What's more, expressed in the phrase "being imputed" are the causal grounds of righteousness, which are grace and mercy. Likewise, our merits and virtues are excluded by the word *imputed* as the causal grounds of righteousness.

Hereby is removed that cavil of the Sophists[†] who say that faith does indeed justify, but as a work *ex opere operato*,[‡] for, they say, faith is also a work. It must therefore be known that faith does not justify *ex opere operato*, on account of it being a work, but because righteousness is imputed to the believer, which is why Paul adds: "and it was reckoned to him as righteousness." That is, righteousness was imputed and bestowed on believing Abraham.

Consequently, whenever justification by faith is being discussed, it must be established that we are justified *imputatively* by faith, that is, *freely*. For imputation as the causal grounds of righteousness is opposed to any thought of wage, debt, or *ex opere operato*. Notes on Romans (1541).[21]

Good Works Follow Rather Than Precede Justification. Peter Martyr Vermigli: Since many promises are made to works, and in this passage God calls himself a "reward,"[†] and since eternal life is more than once in the sacred text called "wages" as if it is repaid for works, why can't we obtain righteousness in the same way, by works, since it is no lesser thing to glorify than to justify? Well, two things need to be considered here. The first is that it is possible for good works to precede glorification, but not justification. After we are justified we are capable of doing the things that are pleasing to God, but before we are justified we are capable of doing nothing that is truly good and that pleases God. Second, we do not concede that eternal life is gained by works, as if it were merited by them. But when it is called "wages," this is in view of the fact that it is bestowed *after* one's work is done. In a similar fashion, it is customary that the wages we earn by certain civil actions are not given until the work is complete. Only in this temporal sense can eternal life have a kind of similitude to wages.

But it is far different from wages in terms of the reasoning and nature that is proper to it, and that for three reasons. First, because what are rendered and what are received are not of equal value, but this is what is required to have just grounds for merit. Second, because the works that we offer are never really ours. For God bestows them on us, and is the one "who works in us both to will and to work." For this reason, if there were something of merit, it would not be to our credit but to God as the Author of good works. Last, when wages or merit is taken in the strict sense, it is needful that the work rendered by us not be already owed as a debt to him to whom it is rendered. But we, even if we were not going to attain to happiness thereby, are nevertheless obliged to do everything we do to the glory of God. Hence, eternal life cannot be called "wages" except by way of a certain similitude. Commentary on Romans (1560).[22]

A Returning Rebel Treated as Loyal. Juan de Valdés: St. Paul, in seeking to prove that Abraham had found nothing according to the flesh, not having been justified by his works, quotes words from holy Scriptures, which testify that Abraham attained justification, not by works, but by faith, God imputing to him his righteousness for faith. It is like a rebel who has fled from

---

[21]Sarcerius, *In Apostolam ad Romanos*, N6v-N6r. [†]The medieval scholastic theologians. [‡]The Latin phrase *ex opere operato*, "by the work performed," affirmed the medieval Catholic view that the correct and priestly performance of the sacrament conveyed grace to the recipient unless the recipient placed an obstacle to grace. By comparison, *ex opere operantis*, "by the work of the worker," affirmed that the moral condition of the priest or the proper attitude of the recipient in the celebration of the sacrament would determine its efficacy.

[22]Vermigli, *In Epistolam S. Pauli*, 223-24; citing Phil 2:13. [†]Includes the sense of "wages."

the kingdom of which he is a subject, but who should return to it, believing and confiding in his king's word, that his faith and confidence is taken and counted to him as satisfaction and loyalty, and that on this account the king holds and esteems him as if he had always been faithful and loyal. St. Paul takes occasion from this remission of punishment to go on through the whole chapter, to show it to be a fact that man's justification and faithfulness proceed not from merits, but because God does not impute to his condemnation the sins he commits, while God does impute to his justification the faith that he has. COMMENTARY ON ROMANS (1556).[23]

PAUL IS NOT SPEAKING FIGURATIVELY. PETER MARTYR VERMIGLI: Many people wish to receive these sentences of Paul figuratively, as if it were a synecdoche. Faith, they say, is said to justify, since it occupies the preeminent role in justifying, and in this way, they will not agree that works are excluded from the power of justifying. They do indeed concede to us that we ought to commend faith, but they say we ought to commend it in such a way that we should say that faith justifies *in union with* other good works, which they would have us understand to be included by Paul in the word *faith* by way of synecdoche. They think that it is in this way that very many passages in the sacred Scriptures can be harmonized. For in the twentieth [sic] chapter of Genesis, God clearly promises many things to Abraham on account of his deed: "Because," he said, "you have done this thing . . . your descendants will be multiplied, . . . they will possess the gates of their enemies, and by your descendants all nations will be blessed," and also other passages to the same effect. And even James seems to unfold this synecdoche when he asserted that Abraham was justified by works.

To those people who say this we answer that the words of Paul do not in any way allow for a figurative sense in this way, whose words are so

clear that they cannot be twisted or erased. For he did not merely say that we are justified by faith, but he also explicitly excluded works. For he says, "apart from works," and what is even more clearly and more easily understood, he added the word *freely* and other things which openly militate against a figurative use of speech. And it reasonably ought to be seen that men and women, in their very selves, are first made righteous and pleasing to God, and *then* good works follow as a result. Those things found in the twentieth [sic] chapter of Genesis do not at all contradict this position, since it cannot be demonstrated from that passage that Abraham was regarded as righteous before God *on account of* that work. He had already obtained this standing before then; he had received the promises concerning his posterity, that God wished to confer upon them many excellent things. . . .

Nor was James trying to say that Abraham was justified by works in the same way that Paul is speaking of justification here. James was speaking of that "justification" by which it can be recognized by men and women and according to which we are *declared* to have been justified. For we are not able to recognize in other people the *spiritual* justification that we are considering now, except by the things that are done by them outwardly. In sum, whenever passages of Scripture attribute righteousness to works, they are speaking of that righteousness that *follows* justification. COMMENTARY ON ROMANS (1560).[24]

4:4 *Wages Are Owed, Not Given*

JUSTIFICATION IS NOT OWED AS A DEBT. JACQUES LEFÈVRE D'ÉTAPLES: "But to him who works, wages are not reckoned according to grace but according to debt." . . . If someone were to be justified by works in this way, then justification would be owed as a debt and would not be the gift and grace of God. For debt is one thing, grace quite another, for grace is a gift bestowed apart from any

---

[23]Valdés, *Commentary upon St. Paul's Epistle*, 50-51*; citing Gen 15:6.

[24]Vermigli, *In Epistolam S. Pauli*, 224-25; citing Gen 22:16-18; Jas 2:21; Rom 3:28; 4:6 (also Rom 3:24).

debt whatever. But he who says that justification is owed as a debt takes away all grace from God and makes men and women ungrateful toward God and therefore unworthy of justification. For if you dig in a garden and then receive your wages or money for your day's work, what grace is it that you're repaid with? What is repaid is what was owed. Your employer has shown you no grace—you deserved it; he has given you only what you have earned. COMMENTARY ON ROMANS.[25]

ABRAHAM DID NOT MERIT RIGHTEOUSNESS BY HIS WORKS. THEODORE BEZA: There are two opposing views on this argument: the first is between the reward of grace and the reward that is owed for work. From this the scholastic theologians built up the idea of "merit" out of the term "reward."

The second is between payment that is gratuitous and payment that is owed. From this, Paul's syllogism is: (P1) For those who earn righteousness by their works, the reward of righteousness is not imputed freely but as a payment owed. (P2) Yet it does not say that Abraham was being paid the reward of righteousness as something that was owed, but rather, it was imputed freely due to his believing. (C) Therefore, Abraham did not merit righteousness by his works. MAJOR ANNOTATIONS (1594).[26]

TRUE AND FALSE CAUSES OF RIGHTEOUSNESS. ERASMUS SARCERIUS: A comparison of true and false causes of righteousness follows, using an antithesis. The true causes of righteousness are: grace, mercy, imputation, and faith that embraces grace, mercy, and imputation. The causes of righteousness that the hypocrites establish according to their own thoughts are false: works, merits, payments, debt, religious rites, particular virtues, good thoughts, and the rest. This comparison looks toward the amplification or illustration of freely given righteousness in Abraham. The apostle said that Abraham was justified—was imputed—by faith. Now he opposes true causes of

righteousness with false causes. And the sense of this opposition is quite simple. If by the example of Abraham we are justified by an imputed faith, then we are not justified through works and merits. Likewise, if the true causes of righteousness are grace, mercy, imputation, and faith, then works, merits, and debt are false causes. NOTES OF ROMANS (1541).[27]

IMPUTATION IS GIVEN FREELY. WOLFGANG MUSCULUS: With this double sentence he applies the cited passage of Scripture to his argument and shows that Abraham's justification, since it was by way of imputation, could not be attributed to works, but that it must necessarily be attributed to faith alone. Why? Because praise given to works of righteousness is owed on the basis of merit as wages, and not on the basis of grace. What's more, to "impute" does not mean to hand over that which ought to be given due to some debt, but rather to give and assign freely what could be rightfully denied. Therefore, this imputed righteousness cannot be attributed to Abraham's works, since imputation is not a rendering of what is owed but a thing given freely.

The phrases "the one who works" and "the one who does not work but who believes" should prudently be read not as if the apostle were speaking of an idle and dead faith, that is, a merely historical one that we have in common even with demons, nor that Abraham's good works are being stripped away and he is being credited only with faith, since he was conspicuous for many and greatly heroic virtues that the Scriptures likewise commend him for. Rather, let us understand that the only point being made is that he was not justified before God on account of the works that he admirably possessed, but by faith alone. Therefore, when he says "to him who works," understand that this refers to someone who merits righteousness by his works—to such a person righteousness most certainly cannot be imputed by grace, but is owed as wages. And "but he who does not work"

[25]Lefèvre, *Epistole divi Pauli*, 60v-61r.
[26]Beza, *Annotationes Majores*, 47.
[27]Sarcerius, *In Apostolam ad Romanos*, N7v.

refers to someone who does not merit righteousness by his works. "But believes on him who justifies the ungodly" means that he has a sincere confidence in God whose goodness is so great that he would even "justify the ungodly," that is, regard him as righteous if he should have faith in him. In the person of Abraham, Paul is here clearly teaching and explaining that the character of the righteous and of believers is of such a kind that even if they perform innumerable good deeds, they would nevertheless acknowledge that they are unworthy, and on the basis of those deeds, if they should come to be judged by their merits, the "righteous" would be regarded instead as ungodly. They, therefore, place all their faith in the goodness and mercy of God, by the immensity of which it comes to pass that the ungodly are justified before God by grace. You can also clearly see in this passage that the object of faith is not our own merits but the mercy of God who justifies the ungodly. COMMENTARY ON ROMANS (1555).[28]

What Is Imputation? ANDREW WILLET: Question 8. What imputation is, and what to be imputed. 1. This word is distinguished according to that which is imputed, as sometimes that which is evil is said to be imputed, and sometimes that which is good.

An evil thing is imputed two ways, either rightfully, as when a sin is worthily imputed to the person who committed it, as Quintilian put this case[†] whether the murder should be imputed to the one who began the strife; or it is imputed wrongfully, as adultery was imputed to Susanna, the charge being without cause.

2. A good thing is imputed in three ways. (1) *Iure*, by right, as the reward is imputed to the work by debt, as the apostle uses the word here in verse 4. But then this word *imputed* is taken for *to give*, and it is improperly called an imputing. (2) *Iniuria*, by wrong, as when innocence is imputed to a malefactor, which is forbidden. "To justify the wicked." (3) *Gratia*, by grace and favor, a thing is

imputed, but not against right, *propter alienum meritum*, for another's merit, and so we are said to be justified by faith in Christ. *Pareus*: like as when a creditor of grace and favor accepts a debt to be paid, and accounts it discharged, when yet the indebted party is able to pay it. In this sense the word is taken in Numbers 18:27. "Your offering will be reckoned to you as the corn of the barn"; it shall be so counted, or be instead of it, though it be not it. . . .

2. This word *to be imputed*, likewise is taken either *Physice*, in a physical sense, as when a plant is said to be imputed, that is set in or grafted into the stock, or *relate*, by way of relation, when a thing is imputed by way of acceptation and favor, as when the victory achieved by the soldiers is for honor's sake ascribed to the captain though absent, or when the captain to whom the spoil belongs gives it to the soldiers that did not fight for it. And thus is the righteousness of Christ—which we did not work ourselves—imputed to us by faith.

3. And thus for faith to be imputed for righteousness, or to be justified by faith, of faith, or through faith, are taken by St. Paul for one and the same thing. A SIX-FOLD COMMENTARY UPON THE EPISTLE TO THE ROMANS (1611).[29]

Nine Corollaries. NIELS HEMMINGSEN: The conclusion proves the examined proposition, that truly, righteousness is from faith. The consequence from this is highly evident, where the apostle displays righteousness to be either from faith or works. Therefore, since it is not from works, it follows that it is from faith. This is the strength of Paul's argument. In truth, we may gather many corollaries [*hypotheses*] from the words of the apostle. The strongest of these is treated here first. It is that the righteousness with which a man or woman is justified before God is an imputed righteousness received by faith.

The second is that *to impute* is to confer something freely, not to allot from something that

---

[28]Musculus, *In Epistolam Apostoli Pauli*, 90.

[29]Willet, *Hexapla*, 199; citing Prov 17:15; Num 18:27. [†]Lib. 5.c.10 *utrum cades ei imputanda fit*.

is owed. Indeed to impute is from grace and to allot is from debt; they are diametrically opposed.

The third is with respect to the particular reward that is owed for merit. This is a payment of a debt. Although the term *wages* is used to refer to compensation in general, this sort of compensation has two forms: one is a salary due for a debt owed, the other the receiving of compensation *not* owed. When it is said that a salary is given to a laborer, it signifies an offsetting of what is owed, and it applies to both good and bad work. But in another place it is said that your abundant reward is in heaven. That signifies an undue compensation that has been conveyed by grace on account of the promise.

The fourth is that grace and debt are placed in opposition by Paul, so that it is impossible to say they are the same, for they have absolutely contradictory conditions.

The fifth is how the twofold righteousness is of works and of faith: thus that one of them is something owed, and that the other one is applied freely. But this distinction is not intended to imply that someone should then pursue that kind of righteousness that comes from being owed. Rather it makes the distinction—as I have suggested above—in order that the righteousness of faith should be understood to differ from the righteousness of the law. For each of these is a specific form of righteousness.

The sixth is that the sinful are justified by the remission of sins that make them righteous by the imputation of an alien righteousness, namely, Christ's. Don't the Scriptures proclaim, "The one who condemns a just man, and the one who justifies the wicked, either one is an abomination before God"? In what way, therefore, is this appropriate for God? Is he not doing what he abominates in another? By no means. Paul signifies one thing by the word *justification*, and the prophets another. On the one hand, *to justify* among the prophets is a judicial decree to acquit the guilty so that the punishment owed is not paid, and nothing else. However, with Paul *to justify* is not only to acquit the guilty so that they do not pay the penalty derived from their guilt, but it also signifies to make one righteous from

unrighteousness by the imputation of the righteousness of Christ.

The seventh is this phrase: "the one who justifies the wicked." It indicates both what the condition of the man or woman was before the imputation of righteousness—that is, truly sinful—and that there is no congruous merit that precedes justification. But as impiety proceeds from man or woman alone, so the Father's benevolence in the Son comes from God alone.

The eighth overturns the doctrine of those who proclaim that works are necessary for salvation. Salvation, since it cannot be separated from justification, does not have another cause or merit besides justification itself. This also has to be admitted, that works are necessarily required for those justified, but as during the midst of a journey, not as a cause or merit.

The ninth: Since in the present circumstances the ones not working and the ones working are opposed, it must be understood that as the ones working are designated in this place, they earn justification by their own works. So the ones not working are designated as the ones who do not earn justification by their own works, but it is the ones who settle by faith on the grace of God's goodness who are made righteous. This is displayed as a beautiful example in the third chapter of Philippians by Paul himself, who concerning himself wrote in this way, "I consider everything as loss on account of the preeminence of the knowledge of Christ Jesus my Lord, on account of whom I have suffered the loss of all things, and all things I consider as refuse in order that I may gain Christ and be found in him, not having my own righteousness which is from the law, but one which is through faith in Jesus Christ." Here the apostle does not rob himself of good works, but rather he casts aside confidence in works and places it instead in the righteousness of God, which is received and seized by faith in Jesus Christ. COMMENTARY ON ROMANS (1562).[30]

---

[30]Hemmingsen, *Commentarius in Epistolam*, 139-41; citing Mt 5:12; Prov 17:15; Phil 3:8-9.

RECONCILING ROMANS 4:4, ROMANS 6:23, AND THE PARABLE OF THE WORKERS. FRIEDRICH BALDUIN: Q: How is it that wages are not of grace when they are given to one who works (as the apostle writes in verse 4) when elsewhere we read that the wages of eternal life are given by grace, while at the same time being given only to those who work, according to the parable of the workers in Matthew 20?

R: I answer: When Paul writes that wages given to one who works are not of grace but of debt, he refers to meritorious works where there is a just worthiness and proportion to the wages earned. In that case nothing is *given* to the person working. Rather, he receives the price of his labor that is justly owed him. According to this, the worker is worthy of his wages. But when it is said that eternal life is *given* to those who work, then works are not to be understood as meritorious, for there is no proportion or comparison between even the most perfect works with the infinite and eternal weight of eternal glory. They are, instead, "declaratory works," if I may speak in this way, which are only the display and marks of a person who truly believes and is a candidate for eternal life. COMMENTARY ON ROMANS (1620).[31]

THREE PAIRS OF OPPOSITES. MARTIN BUCER: The apostle sets down three sets of opposites: the one who works versus the one who believes, grace versus debt, and wages versus righteousness. When we say "the one who works," what is meant is "the one who works for pay." "The one who believes" means "the one who by believing accepts the things that the mercy of God freely offers." On one side are aligned together "to work," "wages," and "debt," while on the other side belong "to believe," "grace," and "freely given righteousness." Later on in chapter 11 the apostle expresses in the clearest manner possible that the following concepts are diametrically opposed to each other: the procuring of the gifts of God by one's works, and the laying hold of them by grace. "If by grace,"

he says, "it is no longer of works, else grace would no longer be grace." But if it is of works, then it would no longer be of grace. Otherwise work would no longer be work—at least as defined as that by which somebody can merit something— for that's how Paul understands the term "works." COMMENTARY ON ROMANS (1536).[32]

FAITH AND GRACE VERSUS MERIT AND DEBT. HEINRICH BULLINGER: Taking opportunity from the selected passage of Moses that he had just quoted, he now explains the text more clearly and at the same time also puts together a certain incontrovertible argument in favor of his point. Having with a wonderful art appropriated the term *imputation*, he here makes his case by way of allusion and opposites, concluding the entire affair with a double proposition.

"To work" and "to not work" are opposites, as are "wages" versus "grace," and "debt" versus "imputation." These pairs cannot exist together at the same time, for if righteousness is conferred by grace,[†] it can by no means be the wages for a work. And again: when God *imputes* righteousness, he most certainly does not owe it. For we do not "impute" things we already owe. Therefore, righteousness is by faith (that is, by grace), not by merit (that is, by works). Paul did not intend this passage to say that faith is without works, but was only employing a similitude. For he alluded to those who perform manual labor and receive wages equal to their labors, or that are "owed" to them. This is also what Christ referred to in the Gospel according to Matthew, where the master of the house paid wages to the laborers, for it was a reward for their virtue,[†] but he paid it by grace and on the basis of their agreement, not as being owed according to the value of their labor (because salvation is a free gift, not one that is merited). This is why he adds, "I do you no wrong—did you not agree with me to work for a denarius? Take what is yours and go—I wish to give to the last the same as to you. Or is it not

---

[31]Balduin, *Catechesis Apostolica*, 292; citing Rom 6:23; Mt 20:1-16.

[32]Bucer, *Metaphrases et Enarrationes*, 217; citing Rom 11:6.

permitted for me to do what I wish with what is mine?" Therefore, Paul said "the one who works," not "the believer in whom faith is made effective through love," because of the allusion to the laborers who depend on their works and wish by them to merit something.

Now we will see what the meaning is. All agree to this much, that righteousness was imputed to Abraham our father, the unique type from whom believers take their pattern. But now let us examine what the word *impute* could mean. It is immediately explained by the double proposition that is set forth, "for if the one who works," which takes the form of a dilemma. From this text we reason in this fashion:

(P1) To whomever something is imputed, it is clearly imputed to him on the basis of grace and not owed on the basis of debt (this is proved by Paul's aforementioned double proposition)

(P2) Faith was imputed to Abraham as righteousness (which is proved by the Scripture already cited).

(C) (It necessarily follows:) Therefore Abraham was justified on the basis of faith or grace, not on the basis of merit or debt.

I ask those who defend merit to give an answer to this—and also those who distinguish between the works of the law and the works of grace in such a manner as not to yield all the glory to God through Christ, but rather so as to twist the words and look for a knot in a bulrush. That most holy man of God, Abraham, was not justified by his holy works. According to the witness of the apostle to the Hebrews, he did not do these works apart from faith. For at the call of God he emigrated from his homeland, left behind all that was pleasing to his flesh, personally believed God, exposed his head to dangers, patiently struggled, lived in constancy, delivered Lot by the force of arms along with others who were oppressed in life and in critical straights, received angels with hospitality, and offered his own son as a sacrifice. He did not fail to do anything that was required of him, and yet for all this he was not justified by his

truly good works. Nor did he believe in any of his works. COMMENTARY ON ROMANS (1533).[33]

WE CAN HAVE CONFIDENCE OF SALVATION.

WOLFGANG MUSCULUS: These things do not please the scholastic theologians, in that they think that a firm confidence of salvation is not granted to our consciences. But I think they look for this as much as those who wish to see the doctrine of grace advanced. For both sides seek after a doctrine whereby in our consciences there might be a firm and certain confidence and persuasion of salvation. But the scholastics rely more on reason and on the normal course of human life than they do the authority of sacred Scriptures, and therefore think that they establish a more certain hope of salvation if it is looked for as something owed rather than on the basis of grace. For they think that any hope that does not arise from merits is in vain, and so they seek after and establish merit and debt in order to fabricate a certain hope of salvation after the fashion of that famous saying: "Hope that is founded on merit is a just hope."[†] But our theologians, although they have the same hope, being admonished by the Scriptures have seen that a persuasion of one's salvation could not be certain and unshakable in any conscience if it were to depend upon our works or the merits of our works, which plainly are worthless if they should be examined by the Lord's judgment. For we never satisfy the law of God. They therefore also instruct us that we must heed the holy Scriptures, in which we are taught that the divine promises are to be trusted in—promises that do not depend on our merits but rather on the divine truthfulness, though they are laid hold of by faith. As a result, the salvation that is expected from God's mercy is made certain by virtue of God's promise. For "God is true, but every man is a liar." COMMENTARY ON ROMANS (1555).[34]

---

[33]Bullinger, *In Sanctissimam Pauli*, 62r-63r; citing Mt 20:13-15. [†]Lit. "freely." [‡]Presumably referring to their willingness to work.
[34]Musculus, *In Epistolam Apostoli Pauli*, 91; citing Rom 3:4. [†]Ovid, *Heroides* 2.62.

WAKING UP THROUGH THE SIGHING OF THE HEART. JACQUES LEFÈVRE D'ÉTAPLES: Let us not say that we are justified by works in this way. Those who say this are trusting in themselves, attributing deservingness to themselves. That which is grace they think is owed to them. They are ungrateful and puffed up, boasting in their works. Rather, let us say that any and everybody is justified by faith, such that we understand that justification is the gift and grace of God, not something owed. For when an ungodly man or woman is justified by God, who does not see that his or her justification is a gift and a grace from God? Which works do the ungodly do for which justification is owed to them? But was it not said, "I said, 'I will confess against myself my transgressions,' and you forgave the ungodliness of my sin," believing that it was God who could justify the ungodly and that justification was a grace, not wages owed to works? Clearly so. And Paul appeals to another testimony from this same Psalm 32 to the same effect. And truly whether someone performs works or does not perform works, if he sighs [in repentance] because of his offense committed against God, then as a result of a conversion to God by means of faith, his justification will come from the grace of God alone. Those who say this do not trust in themselves but rather in God. They do not attribute deservingness to themselves, nor treat justification as wages owed, but as it really is, grace. They are not ungrateful, but with affections perpetually inflamed they give thanks to God who justifies, for such an ineffable gift that could be merited by nobody. They do not boast, nor swell up with pride, but with all their mind and devotion humble themselves with prostration, knowing that they owe an infinite amount of thanksgiving. It was so that we might learn this piety and possess this humility, that we might not trust in ourselves but in the generosity of God that the apostle divinely instructed us when he said that we are not justified "by works but according to the purpose of God's grace." For he wished that the grace of justification might be imparted to us by God, but in a way that we

should turn to him, not trusting in ourselves but only in his goodness and in the gift of his purposed grace and his goodwill. For he said through Isaiah, "Seek the Lord while he may be found; call on him while he is near. Let the ungodly forsake their way, and the unrighteous their thoughts, and let them turn to the Lord and he will have mercy on them, and to our God, for he will abundantly pardon."

If God has enabled some to do good works, let them not trust in themselves but in God. Let them not think that they are justified by those works. But when they have done everything let them say, as is true, "We are unprofitable servants, for we have done what was our duty to do." What does it mean that "we are unprofitable servants," if not "undeserving"? What he has done for us belongs to the goodness of God, to the grace of the Lord, and to his mercy. It is not because of our merits, not something owed by the Lord, but the gift of his super-exuberant goodness, and only a gift. And so forever blessed is that supereminent goodness that cannot be grasped by our thoughts, that he cannot possibly owe any of it but only give it. For how could he who is all-good and all-generous owe anything? And to whom could he owe anything? For whatever one has, he has from him. . . . But if justification were owed to the works of the law, it could be obtained by only the very fewest people. But the one who understands that justification is the grace of God, who does not justify on the basis of merit but who forgives the sins of those hearts turned toward him (for he alone sees everyone's heart), sees that he can offer justification to a great many. But those who judge on the basis of works save few and condemn many, making themselves a rash judge. For judgment does not belong to them, but to God who alone is the One who justifies and who alone "has the power to cast into hell." But the one who pays heed to the grace of God keeps silent and judges nobody, for it would be foolish to wish to confine the infinite grace of God to human judgment, or rather to the narrowness of human temerity. Therefore, justification is common as much to those who do works as to those who do not, or even those who perpetrate things contrary to the works of the law. It can be given most widely and to the greatest number, as much to the circumcised as to the uncircumcised, as much to the good as to the bad who wake up out of their sinfulness through sighing of heart. COMMENTARY ON ROMANS.[35]

THOSE WHO FLEE PARDONED BY A PRINCE. JUAN DE VALDÉS: If anyone says to me, "I deserve because I believe," I will reply to them that God does not give them justification by way of recompensing their faith, but that they enjoy the general justification because they believe. It is as if a prince were generally to pardon all those who had fled from his dominions in order that they might return to their homes, and some, believing the prince's pardon, returned to their homes. They could not say, "The prince has pardoned us by way of recompensing our faith," but "The prince has graciously and liberally pardoned us, and we enjoy the pardon because we have believed." And I shall further answer him that faith is the gift of God, and thus this sentence will remain true: that all who attain justification attain it by grace and not by debt, nor by personal desert. COMMENTARY ON ROMANS (1556).[36]

4:5 Faith Counted as Righteousness

STRUGGLING TO ESCAPE UNGODLINESS. FRIEDRICH BALDUIN: Q: How can God be said to justify the ungodly when we read in Proverbs 17:15 and Isaiah 5:25 that whoever does this same thing is an abomination to the Lord?

R: I answer: we must make a distinction between the ungodly person who remains in their ungodliness and one who is struggling to escape it. The Lord justifies the latter in the court of his judgment, while the former will not stand in the judgment of God. But an ungodly person struggles to escape their ungodliness when they acknowl-

edge their ungodliness and detest it and then lay hold in their heart by faith in the One who became our righteousness. . . . Also, we must make a distinction between different ways of justifying the ungodly. When an ungodly person is justified or absolved in a court of judgment without in any way paying for their crimes, then that justification or absolution is an abomination to God, and in this respect God denies that he justifies the ungodly. But when there is a payment for those crimes, whether by the ungodly person or by another in their place, then that justice, which has already been satisfied, requires absolution. Indeed, such a payment as this for the sins of the ungodly was most sufficiently rendered by Christ who, "although he knew not sin, God made him to be sin for us that we might be made the righteousness of God in him." COMMENTARY ON ROMANS (1620).[37]

IMPUTED RATHER THAN REPUTED. CARDINAL CAJETAN: "But to him who does not work." He does not say "who works against it" but only denies that there is merit in works. In other words, their faith justifies them even if they have not worked, even though there are no merits of works accompanying their faith. "But believes on him who justifies the ungodly by forgiving sins." "Reputed," in place of "imputed." Translators interchange the words, sometimes rendering it "imputed" and sometimes "reputed," although Paul uses the same word each time. It more accurately means "to be imputed" than it does "to be reputed," for it means "to be ascribed" or "attributed."

"Is his faith unto righteousness?" Precisely because it is faith that is imputed unto righteousness, it means that righteousness is not conferred because it is owed or on the basis of merit, the opposite of which is said in the case of the one who works. From the fact that the Scriptures say that "his faith was imputed for righteousness," Paul draws a distinction between the one who believes and the one who works; the believer does not merit

---

[35]Lèfevre, *Epistole divi Pauli*, 61r; citing Ps 32:5; 2 Tim 1:9; Is 55:6-7; Lk 17:10; 12:5.
[36]Valdés, *Commentary upon St. Paul's Epistle*, 51-52*.

[37]Balduin, *Catechesis Apostolica*, 292-93; citing Ps 1:5 Ex 34:7; 2 Cor 5:21.

righteousness nor is it owed to the believer. But those who work, as long as they continue working, receive the wages of their own justification, though, as has been stated often, it is not a justification such as remits sin. OF THE EPISTLES OF PAUL (1639).[38]

THE GOODNESS THAT WE ALLOW TO ENTER Us. MARTIN BUCER: "Faith is imputed as righteousness." Let us never fail to carefully weigh this. We are forever to be considering along these lines our absolute uselessness toward all that is good as well as the infinite goodness of God toward us—the goodness of God toward us that in the last analysis occupies the place of our highest virtue, that goodness that we allow to bless us and confer salvation on us, that goodness that we allow to enter us so that it might forgive us our sins and makes us heirs of eternal life. But to indeed have faith in the One who promises these things, what is greater than to allow him to be our God, that is, to act as our Savior and Benefactor? How priceless will this be to us when we realize that neither we ourselves nor anything else is able to offer us any hope, and that God alone is our every good? But we are not able to do even this by our own power—it is also necessary that the Lord breathe this very thing on us. We therefore most clearly discern our uselessness in this matter, who are altogether able to do nothing but to sin, so much so that our entire salvation consists in this: that we believe in God who offers us remission of sins. COMMENTARY ON ROMANS (1536).[39]

NO HALF REMISSION. JOHN CALVIN: Dissipated also, in like manner, by the words of the prophet are the puerile fancies of the schoolmen respecting half remission. Their childish fiction is that though the fault is remitted, the punishment is still retained by God. But the prophet not only declares that our sins are covered, that is, removed from the presence of God, but also adds that they are not imputed. How can it be consistent that God should punish

those sins that he does not impute? This most glorious declaration, then, remains safe to us, "that they are justified by faith who are cleared before God by a gratuitous remission of their sins." We may also hence learn the unceasing perpetuity of gratuitous righteousness through life. For when David, being wearied with the continual anguish of his own conscience, gave utterance to this declaration, he no doubt spoke according to his own experience, and he had now served God for many years. He then had found by experience, after having made great advances, that all are miserable when summoned before God's tribunal, and he made this avowal, that there is no other way of obtaining blessedness except the Lord receives us into favor by not imputing our sins. Thus fully refuted also is the romance of those who dream that the righteousness of faith is but initial, and that the faithful afterward retain by works possession of that righteousness which they had first attained by no merits. COMMENTARY ON ROMANS 4:6.[40]

THE INVISIBLE CHURCH IS MANIFEST AS ABRAHAM WAS. DIRK PHILIPS: The congregation of God is not only invisible, as some permit themselves to think and imagine an invisible Christian people, but also visible. . . . And this is the reason the apostles wrote all their letters to the Christians, to their brothers and companions of faith and not to the world. This would not have taken place if they had not known the Christians and had not known the difference between Christians and the world.

Yes, the Christian congregation is also in part manifest to the world, just as Abraham was manifest to the world through his faith, righteousness, and glorious deeds according to God's Word, and left to us as an example in Scripture to teach and admonish that we should follow in his footsteps with sincere trust and fruitfulness of works that God commands us. THE SENDING OF PREACHERS.[41]

---

[38]Cajetan, *In Omnes d. Pauli*, 20.
[39]Bucer, *Metaphrases et Enarrationes*, 219.
[40]CTS 38:160-61* (CO 49:72).
[41]CRR 6:221*; citing Gen 15:6; Gal 3:6; Jas 2:23.

4:6-12 BLESSEDNESS OF THE RIGHTEOUS BY FAITH

⁶*just as David also speaks of the blessing of the one to whom God counts righteousness apart from works:*

⁷*"Blessed are those whose lawless deeds are forgiven,*
and whose sins are covered;
⁸*blessed is the man against whom the Lord will not count his sin."*

⁹*Is this blessing then only for the circumcised, or also for the uncircumcised? For we say that faith was counted to Abraham as righteousness.* ¹⁰*How then was it counted to him? Was it before or after he had been circumcised? It was not after, but before he was circumcised.* ¹¹*He received the sign of circumcision as a seal of the righteousness that he had by faith while he was still uncircumcised. The purpose was to make him the father of all who believe without being circumcised, so that righteousness would be counted to them as well,* ¹²*and to make him the father of the circumcised who are not merely circumcised but who also walk in the footsteps of the faith that our father Abraham had before he was circumcised.*

OVERVIEW: Continuing with the theme of justification, Paul extends his argument by drawing on Psalm 32. The commentators see this as Paul's offering several definitions of justification or as adding another Old Testament figure to show that Abraham is not the only one who was justified by faith. They continue the discussion from the preceding pericope on the relationship between the views on faith and works taught by Paul and James.

They argue against the medieval Catholic theologians who claim that faith justifies only in the beginning (*initium fidei*) of one's progress toward salvation, when someone is first starting to believe. This justification comes to the circumcised and uncircumcised, to those who have done works and those who have not, for it is neither circumcision nor good works that saves a person. On the other hand, although good works have no effect *before* one's justification, they are of value afterward in glorifying God, even though they do not earn us salvation.

The commentators argue against the medieval Catholic emphasis on the role of the sacraments in salvation. Abraham was not justified by works but rather by grace. The interpreters see the timing of the promise to Abraham, of his belief, and of his circumcision as important, since Abraham received the circumcision *after* receiving and believing the initial promise. So his faith was reckoned to him as righteousness *before* he received the ceremony. The implication is that his justification did not come to him through his circumcision and further, therefore, that our justification is not due to the sacraments. The sacraments thus confirm rather than confer justification.

The reformers take the opportunity here to discuss sacraments in general, and baptism in particular. Most of them follow Augustine's teaching that a sacrament is a visible sign of invisible grace. Zwingli, who tended more toward seeing the sacraments as primarily symbolic, refers to baptism as a testimony. Various Reformed writers speak of them as seals of the promises of God, as brands that mark our high value to God, or as instruments of God's grace. In line with the Lutheran emphasis on the necessity of a promise of forgiveness being attached to a sacrament, one Lutheran writer outlines four essential components of sacraments: God's command and institution, an external sign, a promise of grace, and a belief in the promise. The Anabaptists encourage enthusiasm toward baptism and perseverance in suffering persecution, two things that in their case were often connected since both magisterial reformers and Catholics objected to their being against infant baptism and regarded their adult baptisms as rebaptisms and thus heretical. Although the reformers express a variety of approaches to the sacraments, one thing they agree on is that the sacraments do not function in the *ex opere operato* (by the work worked) fashion taught by the medieval church.

4:6 *David on the Blessing*

Four Definitions of Justification from Psalm 32. Christoph Corner: Here the "blessing" or "justification" (*makarismos*) of a person is defined. And there are four definitions from the authority or testimony of David in Psalm 32. First, justification is a free imputation of righteousness, by which we are received by God into grace. It is when God imputes to believers righteousness without works, that is, he pronounces persons righteous, and accepts them, and decrees to them freely the righteousness of his Son entirely on account of his merit. Second, justification is the free remission of sins (*aphesis tōn anomiōn*), on account of the deeds of the Mediator. For David says, "whose sins are forgiven" (*hōn aphethēsan hai anomiai*). Or as the Hebrews say, "Blessed is the one who is released from sin, whose sin God releases as a heavy burden," and as John says, he "takes up" or "takes away" (*airei*). The third definition is: "The righteous one, whose sins are covered," is the person who is justified, whose sins are covered by the shelter of the Mediator, who is Christ, through whom and on account of whom God "covers" or "hides away" and does not want his sins to be brought forth into his sight. He also covers and bears our infirmity (*epikalyptei*), so that there may be "no more condemnation for those who are incorporated into Christ." The fourth definition (*horismos*) is: Blessed is *hōu ou mē logisētai kyrios hamartian,* "the one to whom the Lord has not imputed sin"... whose sin has been introduced, destroyed, and no more is found on the tablets of

their accounts, nor from there will be recalled for punishment. Commentary on Romans (1583).[1]

David as Proof That Abraham Is Not Alone. Johannes Brenz: When he brought up the example of Abraham from Genesis, someone could have rejected it, saying, "I certainly confess that Abraham was considered righteous insofar as he believed, but surely no other person will be justified or achieve the forgiveness of unrighteousness in that way. Perhaps what is truly said about Abraham is falsely said about other people." Paul answers this objection, and he brings in the testimony of Psalm 32, where he demonstrates that what is said in Genesis specifically concerning Abraham is true for all people. He says, "Just as David also explains the blessing of man or woman," that is, whoever are pronounced blessed, these are pronounced righteous. For blessing is not apart from righteousness. But David, filled by the Holy Spirit, pronounces not only to one person, but to all men and women, "Blessed are those whose sins are forgiven and to whom sins are not imputed but are covered." Therefore, the example of Abraham pertains to all men and women, to the extent that as Abraham is righteous and was blessed according to it because righteousness and blessing was imputed to him, so also others are righteous and blessed, not because they earned righteousness or blessing by their works, but because God forgives their sins freely, and he imputes righteousness to them by a great and free mercy. That is, if indeed they have believed—just as Abraham did—in the promise to Abraham in Christ. One can see this in the saying from the psalm that is cited in this passage. For he clearly recites the reason why men and women before the tribunal of God are freed from condemnation and achieve true and eternal salvation. When it is asked for what reason David now delights in heavenly blessedness, what is the answer? Surely not because he did many good works? In fact he did horrible and detestable sins as well. Surely he did not atone for these sins by the merits of his good works? Nothing could be

---

[1]Corner, *In Epistolam Ad Romanos*, 62r-62v.

219

less! Certainly he did good things and he had a cause to boast, but not before God. Therefore, he has obtained the heavenly blessedness, not on account of his own righteousness, but because his unrighteousness has been forgiven and his sins covered, and the Lord did not reckon his sin, on account of Christ his Son, in whom he believed. Commentary on Romans (1564).[2]

David and Imputed Righteousness.
Wolfgang Musculus: Even though the example of Abraham was sufficient to establish his point, he nevertheless adduces also the testimony of David in order to heap up an abundance of testimony, so that the Jews might see that this idea of imputed righteousness by God's grace apart from works was not recently invented by himself, but that it was known and disclosed by David before him, and that in very clear words. "Just as David also," he says. He selects this testimony from Psalm 32, in which the following points are to be noted:

First, the remission of sins is to be our righteousness. This is clear from the fact that the apostle applies this text, which is about the remission of sins, to prove his case in which he is dealing with the justification of man and woman by faith apart from works. Otherwise, how would this testimony serve the apostle's purpose? Just as David also, he says, describes the blessedness of the man or woman to whom God imputes righteousness apart from works, by which words he shows that the same thing is declared by David's testimony as he himself had undertaken to declare. He did not simply say, "David describes the blessedness of the man or woman," but rather "Just as David also," and then shortly after, "Blessed is the man or woman to whom the Lord does not impute sin." To the apostle, this is the same as if he had said, "Blessed is the man or woman to whom the Lord imputes righteousness apart from works." Therefore the righteousness of God is that which is freely imputed; it is for sin to be *not* imputed. What does it mean "to be righteous" if not that one is set free

from sin? For nobody is pure and free from sin unless it is by the free imputation of righteousness and the remission of sins.

Next we see in this text that in the apostle's mind, this freely imputed "righteousness" is the same thing as the "blessedness" of the prophet David, when he says: "Blessed is the man" and "Blessed are those whose iniquities are forgiven," which is the same thing as if he had said, "The righteous are those whose iniquities are forgiven" and "That man or woman is righteous to whom the Lord does not impute sin." Consequently, blessedness is that very righteousness freely imputed apart from works.

Third, it is also to be observed of this blessedness, which is freely imputed righteousness, that it must necessarily be by faith, since the apostle is arguing concerning a righteousness that is imputed on account of faith. Therefore, "He who believes is righteous and blessed, due to the remission of sins, apart from the merits of works."

Let those who say that faith justifies only in the beginning when we first begin to believe give an answer to this. How do these observations square with their opinion by which they weaken the force of the apostle's words? If the righteousness of God is by faith apart from works, imputed freely by means of the remission of sins, can we really say that that righteousness is imputed by faith only in the beginning of our believing? If so, then the free remission of sins, after baptism, would not be attained by faith alone but would be attributable to works, contrary to the clear text of 1 John 2, which I have already cited earlier.

Next, who will be able to claim, and prove it, that in this text David is speaking only of the beginning of faith[†]—that is, of those only who just now have begun to believe, so that the cause of this blessedness is no longer to be found in those who, already previously justified, have fallen into sin afterward and are seeking pardon by faith in the goodness of God?

Third, if we would carefully ponder the passage cited from Genesis that ascribes righteousness to Abraham's faith apart from works and to it alone, who would not see that this righteousness is not

[2]Brenz, *In Epistolam*, 103-4; citing Ps 32.

imputed, in that text, to a man who was first beginning to believe? We read in Genesis 12 that he had already long before believed God and, by faith, had abandoned his homeland for the calling of God, as Hebrews 11 tells us. COMMENTARY ON ROMANS (1555).[3]

AGAINST OSIANDER ON JUSTIFICATION. JOHN CALVIN: But more poison lurks in the second branch, when Osiander says that we are righteous with God.[†] I think I have already sufficiently proved that although that dogma is not so pestiferous, yet because it is frigid and jejune, and falls by its own vanity, all sound and pious readers must dislike it. But it is impossible to tolerate the impiety that, under the pretense of a twofold righteousness, undermines our assurance of salvation and, hurrying us into the clouds, tries to prevent us from embracing the gift of expiation in faith, and the invoking of God with quiet minds. Osiander derides us for teaching that "to be justified" is a forensic term, because it is incumbent on us to be righteous in reality. Also, there is nothing to which he is more opposed than the idea of our being justified by a free imputation. Say, then, if God does not justify us by acquitting and pardoning, what does Paul mean when he says, "God was in Christ reconciling the world to himself, not imputing their trespasses unto them"? "He made him to be sin for us who knew no sin; that we might be made the righteousness of God in him." Here I learn, first, that those who are reconciled to God are regarded as righteous. Then the method is stated: God justifies by pardoning; and therefore, in another place, justification is opposed to accusation. This antithesis clearly demonstrates that the mode of expression is derived from forensic use. And indeed, no person moderately conversant in the Hebrew tongue (provided he is also of sedate brain) is ignorant that this phrase thus took its rise, and thereafter derived

its tendency and force. Now, then, when Paul says that David "describes the blessedness of the person to whom God imputes righteousness without works, saying, 'Blessed are those whose iniquities are forgiven,'" let Osiander say whether this is a complete or only a partial definition. He certainly does not adduce the psalmist as a witness that pardon of sins is a part of righteousness, or concurs with something else in justifying, but he includes the whole of righteousness in gratuitous forgiveness, declaring those to be blessed "whose iniquities are forgiven, and whose sins are covered," and "to whom the Lord will not impute sin." He assesses and judges his happiness from this, that in this way he is righteous not in reality, but by imputation.

Osiander objects that it would be insulting to God, and contrary to his nature, to justify those who still remain wicked. But it ought to be remembered, as I already observed, that the gift of justification is not separated from regeneration, though the two things are distinct. But as it is too well known by experience that the remains of sin always exist in the righteous, it is necessary that justification should be something very different from reformation to newness of life. God begins the latter in his elect, and carries it on during the whole course of life, gradually and sometimes slowly, so that if placed at his judgment seat they would always deserve sentence of death. He justifies not partially, but freely, so that they can appear in the heavens as if clothed with the purity of Christ. No portion of righteousness could pacify the conscience. It must be decided that we are pleasing to God, as being without exception righteous in his sight. From this it follows that the doctrine of justification is perverted and completely overthrown whenever doubt is instilled into the mind, confidence in salvation is shaken, and free and intrepid prayer is impeded; indeed, whenever rest and tranquility with spiritual joy are not established. INSTITUTES OF THE CHRISTIAN RELIGION 3.11.11 (1559).[4]

---

[3]Musculus, *In Epistolam Apostoli Pauli*, 91-92; citing Ps 32; 1 Jn 2; Gen 12; Heb 11. [†]*Initium fidei* is a theological term that explores the first movement toward faith. It raises the issue of the roles of the Holy Spirit and of the believer in the process.

[4]Calvin, *Institutes*, 2:47-48*; citing 2 Cor 5:19-21; Rom 8:33; Ps 32:1. [†]Andreas Osiander taught that Christ's indwelling the believer (rather than the imputation of justification by grace) is what made the believer righteous in God's sight.

Difficulties Reconciling with James.
Wolfgang Musculus: On this account I openly
admit that I fail to see how the letter of James can
be brought into agreement with Paul, not only
because it disparages righteousness by faith alone
with clear words (which perhaps could be excused
by making a distinction between historical faith
and justifying, or living and efficacious, faith), but
also because that passage of Scripture is misused in
order to confirm belief in works righteousness,
whereas here in Romans no mention is made of
any works, and the apostle here draws the conclusion that righteousness is imputed by faith apart
from works, and even expressly says "apart from
works." I therefore prefer, along with some writers
of antiquity, to doubt the authorship of the letter
of James, rather than to allow his authority to
obscure the pure, firm, and sound doctrine of the
apostle Paul, especially since Jerome himself says
that it was asserted by some of old that it was not
from the apostle James, but from some other
unknown person, and had gained authority with
the passage of time. It is to be wondered at why
James was not held in authority among the
ancients when the letters of Paul *were* held in
authority. It gained its authority only afterward
with the advance of time, as the lie began little by
little to stamp out the truth according to the
prophet Paul that was increasingly growing weaker.

It is nevertheless true what James says, that the
faith that lacks deeds is useless and dead. But you
must take into account its context and capacity. For
in general, in the winter a tree could not be said to
be barren and bad even though it bears no fruit;
nor can a man who is sleeping be called blind, or
deaf, or mute, even though while he sleeps he
neither sees nor hears nor speaks.

It is also true that faith is made perfect by
works—that is, it is pronounced as being or is
acknowledged to be—authentic and living. But
this is still not the same as a man or woman
being justified by works. For it is one thing for
faith to be justified and another for a man or
woman to be justified. In the sight of men
and women, faith is justified by works. In the sight

of men and women, a man or woman is also
justified by works. But it is in a quite different way
before God. In God's eyes, not only is faith that is
without works not really dead but living, even if it
lacks the opportunity to exert itself. The same is
true even of bodies that are without respiration
and apparently dead. For why would God need to
see the fruit of works in order to know there is
faith? Is he ignorant that there is faith in the heart
unless it announces itself by its fruit? But as it is,
since he regards only faith and looks for it alone, it
is surely ill-advised for works to be allowed into
the matter of justification by an appeal to James.

"But James speaks of authentic and living faith,"
you say. That's true. But Paul speaks of the same
thing, and yet he expressly excludes works in this
matter. But, as I have said, even if everything else
James says could be excused, in my judgment this
one thing cannot be excused: that he said that
Abraham was justified on account of his having
offered up his son, while there is no mention
whatever of justification in Genesis 22. What's
more, James says that Genesis 15:6 is fulfilled by
works righteousness, whereas Paul, to the contrary,
invokes that same passage *against* works righteousness. However, I do not judge anybody, nor do I
wish to be obstinate in asserting anything, but am
merely offering my opinion. Let a wiser person be
the judge. Commentary on Romans (1555).[5]

**David's Blessedness Is Paul's Righteous-
ness.** Erasmus Sarcerius: The third argument
drawn from the authority of Scripture is that
righteousness is attained freely, or by means of
imputation through faith, and that we are justified
freely by faith after the pattern of Abraham.

Enthymeme:[†]

(P2) The Scriptures say that righteousness is that
which is attained by imputation.

(C) Therefore it is true that righteousness is
attained by imputation.

---

[5]Musculus, *In Epistolam Apostoli Pauli*, 92-93; citing Jas 2:24, 21;
Gen 22:1-24; Jas 2:23; Gen 15:6.

Taking an opportunity from the word "to impute," he argues from the etymology of the word that we are justified freely. It is not rashly nor without great deliberation that the apostle argues that the cause of righteousness is this very imputation, since he undoubtedly foresaw in the Spirit that there would be those who would attack the true cause of righteousness. That which Paul calls "righteousness" David calls "blessedness." For if true righteousness consists in blessedness, then whoever is righteous is also blessed. Blessedness and righteousness are therefore closely akin.

The cited Davidic text contains a definition of true righteousness that is not inconsistent with the definition drawn from the text of Genesis cited above. For in this Davidic text, righteousness is the remission of sins by means of imputation. Imputation as the cause of righteousness is opposed to the merits of works and all such things. From this text, the righteous person to whom God imputes righteousness apart from works is blessed. Righteousness is blessedness when God imputes it apart from works.

But you may object: isn't faith here excluded? To which I answer: it is enough to have set forth imputation as the cause or object that faith lays hold of unto righteousness. By no means can righteousness be attained apart from faith, since indeed he said earlier, "even the righteousness of God by faith in Jesus Christ to all and on all who believe in him," and in John: "to those who would believe in his name." NOTES ON ROMANS (1541).[6]

JUSTIFICATION IS THE BEGINNING OF HAPPINESS. PETER MARTYR VERMIGLI: David also, just like Abraham, was gifted with many good works, and yet he did not think that he could be justified on their account, but that it could be only on account of having his sins remitted. Also from this scriptural testimony it is clear that justification and blessedness are the same thing, or Paul's conclusion could not be soundly arrived at. Justification, if one considers it rightly, is surely nothing other than the beginning of happiness. David testifies of this blessedness, or justification, that it is located not only in the fact that sins are *not imputed*, but also, to express the truly great thing, in the fact that sins *are remitted*. A person who is assured that justification is the remission of sins is someone who can easily understand that it is not good works that are brought to God—by the working and merit of which he might justify us—but rather we bring only sins for him to forgive. COMMENTARY ON ROMANS (1560).[7]

4:7-8 Blessed Are the Forgiven

BOTH SINNER AND SAINT. MARTIN LUTHER: It is similar to the case of a sick man who believes the doctor who promises him a sure recovery and in the meantime obeys the doctor's order in the hope of the promised recovery and abstains from those things which have been forbidden him, so that he may in no way hinder the promised return to health or increase his sickness until the doctor can fulfill his promise to him. Now is this sick man well? The fact is that he is both sick and well at the same time. He is sick in fact, but he is well because of the sure promise of the doctor, whom he trusts and who has reckoned him as already cured, because he is sure that he will cure him; for he has already begun to cure him and no longer reckons to him a sickness unto death. In the same way Christ, our Samaritan, has brought his half-dead man into the inn to be cared for, and he has begun to heal him, having promised him the most complete cure unto eternal life, and he does not impute his sins, that is, his wicked desires, unto death, but in the meantime in the hope of the promised recovery he prohibits him from doing or omitting things by which his cure might be impeded and his sin, that is, his concupiscence,[†] might be increased. Now, is he perfectly righteous? No, for he is at the same time both a sinner and a

---

[6]Sarcerius, *In Apostolam ad Romanos*, Oiv; citing Rom 3:22; Jn 1:12.
[†]An enthymeme is a syllogism in which one of the premises is implied rather than stated.

[7]Vermigli, *In Epistolam S. Pauli*, 227.

righteous man; a sinner in fact, but a righteous man by the sure imputation and promise of God that he will continue to deliver him from sin until he has completely cured him. And thus he is entirely healthy in hope, but in fact he is still a sinner; but he has the beginning of righteousness, so that he continues more and more always to seek it, yet he realizes that he is always unrighteous. LECTURES ON ROMANS.[8]

FORENSIC JUSTIFICATION. PHILIPP MELANCH-THON: According to the Hebrew usage of the term, *to justify* is to pronounce or to consider as just, as is said in Hebrew: "The Roman people justified Scipio when he was accused by the tribunes," that is, absolved him or pronounce him just. Thus we know for certain that in these disputations of Paul justification signifies the remission of sins and acceptance to eternal life, as the fourth chapter of Romans testifies in a sufficiently clear manner, where it defines justification as the forgiveness of sins. Therefore when we say we are justified by faith it is the same thing as saying that we are accounted just by God on account of Christ when we believe. And the word *iustitia* does not signify the righteousness of the law, or universal obedi-ence, or our qualities, when it is said, "By faith there is given us *iustitia*." It signifies the imputa-tion of *iustitia*, or acceptance. And *iustus* is in this way understood relationally as acceptance to eternal life.

. . . When a terrified conscience asks how we may be justified, it does not ask what virtues we possess, but how we can receive forgiveness and reconciliation with God. It is worried about the will of God toward us; it does not contemplate its own virtues, and does not oppose them to the judgment of God. Therefore those who interpret justification as infusion of virtues do not notice that the question here is about the forgiveness of sins, and about peace of conscience in the sight of God, or about reconciliation. We are asking how we may be justified, namely, when we may have

remission of sins, and why it can be said that God is favorable toward us. Therefore it is necessary to understand justification as forgiveness of sins and divine acceptance, or imputation of righteousness. COMMENTARY ON ROMANS (1540).[9]

SCRIPTURE USES "RIGHTEOUSNESS" DIFFER-ENTLY FROM PHILOSOPHERS. MARTIN LUTHER: Scripture uses the terms *righteousness* and *unrighteousness* very differently from the philosophers and lawyers. This is obvious, because they consider these things as a quality of the soul. But the "righteousness" of Scripture depends on the imputation of God more than on the essence of a thing itself. For those do not have righteousness who only have a quality, indeed, they are altogether sinners and unrighteous; but those alone have righteousness whom God mercifully regards as righteous because of their confession of their own unrighteousness and because of their prayer for the righteousness of God and whom God wills to be considered righteous before him. Therefore we are all born of iniquity, that is, in unrighteousness, and we die in it, and we are righteous only by the imputation of a merciful God through faith in his Word. LECTURES ON ROMANS.[10]

CHRIST'S INNOCENT DEATH BRINGS ETER-NAL RECONCILIATION. DIRK PHILIPS: One must now know that all Christians have sin and must confess themselves sinners, so that they humble themselves under the mighty hand of God and pray to the Lord for his grace; and thus the Scripture remains true and unbroken, which accuses and disciplines all persons as sinners. But sin is not reckoned to the account of the Christian, but is already forgiven him through the innocent death of Jesus Christ, and covered with his eternal love whereby he has offered himself for us as an eternal reconciliation for our sins, and has taken our burden upon himself, paid our debt with his

---

[8]LW 25:260*. [†]Sinful desires.

[9]Melanchthon, *Commentary on Romans*, 25-26*.
[10]LW 25:274-275*.

bitter suffering, and given us out of grace all that he has. Thus he is one with us and we with him; through which we are well pleasing to God, yes, are reckoned as God's saints. THE TABERNACLE OF MOSES (1556).[11]

JUSTIFICATION IS NOT ONLY AT THE BEGINNING. KASPAR OLEVIANUS: It must be understood that when we begin to believe, we are justified freely by faith. But—unlike what the Sophists[†] say—it does not happen just once in the beginning and then later righteousness is obtained by our merits. Rather, we are justified by continual progression, in no other way than freely by faith. For faith is from grace and by the power of the Holy Spirit. It involves receiving something from God, namely, the promised righteousness. It is not about giving something to God. This is proved from the context. For David is not speaking about those who have only begun to believe, and that they are justified freely *once*. Rather, he is speaking about himself. And since he had already believed for a long time, he was not establishing another happiness other than the free remission of sins. Therefore, Catholics fight openly with sacred Scripture when they say to those who believe that in the beginning their sins are forgiven freely once, but that if anyone sins afterward, their sins must be absolved and expiated by works. And this is against this clear passage from David, who after having believed for a long time, fell into sin. And in no other way did he discover the blessed peace than in the free remission. It is also against the clear text in 1 John 2: "Little children, I write these things to you so that you may not sin, but if, however, we should sin, we have an advocate, Jesus Christ the righteous one." He writes about sins, which are forgiven after faith has been received. NOTES ON ROMANS (1579).[12]

4:9 *How Circumcision Relates to Justification*

ABRAHAM WAS JUSTIFIED BEFORE HE WAS CIRCUMCISED. JOHANNES PISCATOR: He composes a question about the particular subject of imputed righteousness. That is, will righteousness be imputed by faith to all people, not only to the uncircumcised, namely, the Jews, but also in truth to the uncircumcised, namely, the rest of the nations? This question seems to be enjoined by *prolepsis*[†]—on account of the example of Abraham that had preceded—to the Jews who had understood it in this way: that the reason for righteousness, which the Scripture proclaims about Abraham, pertained only to the circumcised, that is, the Jews. And consequently, that they alone had arisen from Abraham according to the flesh. Therefore, the apostle demonstrates in the example of Abraham—from the circumstance of time—that that imputed righteousness of faith was common to both the uncircumcised and the circumcised. For righteousness was imputed to Abraham—who was not yet circumcised—on account of his faith.

We may compose a syllogism according to this mode:

(P1) If righteousness were imputed only to circumcised believers, it would not have been imputed to Abraham, who was a believer but not yet circumcised.

(P2) And moreover, righteousness was imputed to Abraham, who believed, but was not yet circumcised.

(C) Therefore, righteousness is not imputed only to circumcised believers, and consequently, it is also imputed to the uncircumcised.

The meaning of the conclusion proceeds from this verse. It is in the form of a question, illustrated by exposition of the contrary objection. An *assumptio* follows verse 10, the rhetoric embellished by *dialogismus* and *communicatio*.[†] Moreover, one must know the meaning and confirmation of the

---

[11]CRR 6:285*; citing Rom 4:7.
[12]Olevianus, *In Epistolam D. Pauli*, 162-163; citing 1 Jn 2:1. [†]The medieval scholastic theologians.

assumptio, that the testimony of righteousness had been given to Abraham before Ishmael's birth, namely, as in the passages in Genesis 15 and 16. For the testimony of righteousness was given to Abraham, as in Genesis 15:6. At that very time he was yet without children. Just as in that same place in verse 2, however, Ishmael later was finally born in Abraham's eighty-sixth year, as told in the last verse of Genesis 16. Circumcision truly had at last been instituted in Abraham's ninety-ninth year, as is understood in chapter 17, from the combination of the first and tenth verse. From all these things it is perceived that the testimony of the righteousness of faith had been given to Abraham more than thirteen years before circumcision was instituted. This is also clear from the compilation of verses 24 and 25 from the same chapter 17, where it is told that Abraham was circumcised in his ninety-ninth year. Ishmael, however, was in his thirteenth year. On the same day, indeed, he was circumcised, as verse 23 says. Since, therefore, Abraham obtained that testimony of righteousness before Ishmael was born, it is necessary that he obtained that testimony more than thirteen years before his circumcision.

The apostle extends the other assumption of the syllogism set forth in the *prolepsis* of verse 11, when he expounds the use of circumcision. Objection: If Abraham had been justified before he was circumcised, why then was he circumcised? The apostle asserts two reasons: first, so that the righteousness of Abraham himself would be sealed, and second, so that he himself might become the father of all believers, certainly of the circumcised, then of the uncircumcised. This latter reason at the same time pertains to confirming the opinion set forth by the apostle about those to whom justification by faith pertains. Logical Analysis of Romans (1589).[13]

---

[13]Piscator, *Analysis Logica*, 70-72; citing Gen 15:6; 16:16; 17:1, 10, 24, 25, 23. †Answering potential objections. †*Assumptio*: to introduce a point for consideration; *dialogismo*: to speak as someone else; and *communicatio*: to explicitly include one's audience in one's discourse.

Made Bold by the Fathers' Faith.

Anne Askew:

> Like as the armed knight
> Appointed to the field,
> With this world will I fight,
> And faith shall be my shield.
>
> Faith is that weapon strong
> Which will not fail at need;
> My foes therefore among
> Therewith will I proceed.
>
> As it is had in strength
> And force of Christ his way,
> It will prevail at length
> Though all the devils say, Nay.
>
> Faith in the fathers old
> Obtained righteousness,
> Which makes me very bold
> To fear no world's distress.
>
> I now rejoice in heart,
> And hope bids me do so,
> That Christ will take my part,
> And ease me of my woe.
>
> You say'st Lord, Whoso knock
> To them thou wilt attend;
> Undo therefore the lock,
> And your strong power send.
>
> More enemies now I have,
> Than hairs upon my head,
> Let them not me deprave,
> But fight thou in my stead.
>
> On you my care I cast,
> For all their cruel spite,
> I set not by their haste
> For thou art my delight
>
> I am not she that list
> My anchor to let fall,
> For every drizzling mist;
> My ship's substantial.
>
> Not oft use I to write,
> In prose, nor yet in rhyme,

Yet will I show one sight,
That I saw in my time.

I saw a royal throne
Where justice should have sit,
But in her stead was one
Of moody, cruel wit.

Absorbed was righteousness
As of the raging flood;
Satan in fierce excess
Sucked up the guiltless blood.

Then thought I, Jesus, Lord,
When you shalt judge us all,
Hard is it to record
On these men what will fall.

Yet Lord, I you desire,
For that they do to me,
Let them not taste the hire
Of their iniquity.

BALLAD WRITTEN IN NEWGATE PRISON.[14]

SEALS OF JUSTIFICATION BY FAITH. JACQUES LEFÈVRE D'ÉTAPLES: The Jews were very much going astray in believing that without circumcision and works of the law it is not possible for whoever believes to be justified. Paul refutes this, and he sheds light on it. For not even Abraham was circumcised from works of the law, but believing God, he was justified. For when Abraham had as of yet no offspring, the Lord led him outside and spoke to him. "Look to the heavens and number the stars if you are able," he said to him. "Such will your seed be." Abraham believed God, and it was considered as righteousness for him. Afterward, Hagar bore a son while Abraham was eighty-six years old and still uncircumcised, for Abraham was ninety-nine years old when he was circumcised. These things are known from the Genesis account. Therefore, justification by grace is as common to the circumcised as to the uncircumcised. Nor is

the salvation of men and women by the grace and the gift of God a small thing—as the Jews believe—narrowly confined. And the circumcision that the Hebrews believe justifies, does not justify. Rather, it is the sign of justification by faith. And so are the works that follow on faith; they are a sign of a living faith, as our breathing and breath are signs of life. For justification is the mode of the life of faith, which, if it is present, faith is alive and whoever would live that life must have the sign of living works. And our washing with the material of water in baptism does not justify, but is a sign of our justification by faith in Christ. For they are sensible symbols. They are signs of spiritual things and of divine infusion. The signs are the things being perceived: the faith is what is real. This mode of ablution (i.e., baptism) is a sign of being justified by faith in Christ. Just as for Abraham, circumcision was the material sign that he was justified by faith. And so speaks Paul concerning circumcision. COMMENTARY ON ROMANS.[15]

THE PROMISE OF HOLY OFFSPRING. MARTIN BUCER: When he begins, he proves two things at the same time, both that faith justifies, and that works do not justify. It is true that he expressly asserts that *circumcision* does not justify. But having proved this, anybody will easily see that no work of the law justifies, for if circumcision doesn't, neither will any other. He follows the example of Abraham and therein observes the time at which, having believed, he obtained the praise of righteousness, and at the same time received the honor of being constituted the father—that is, the religious leader and progenitor—of all believers, no less of uncircumcision than of circumcision. Even though according to the flesh he is the father of all the circumcised, he is nevertheless, in respect of that paternity that is here specially granted on the basis of his faith, properly the father only of those who by faith follow in his footsteps. And it was at a time when he was not yet circumcised that he received these things from God. It was, therefore,

---

[14]*Writings of Edward VI*, 4:33-35*; Askew composed the ballad while a prisoner at Newgate Prison, awaiting being burned at the stake at Smithfield, England, as a heretic.

[15]Lefèvre, *Epistole divi Pauli*, 61r.

as an uncircumcised man that his faith brought both things to pass: that he was regarded as righteous before God, and that he was appointed as the head of the holy people. So in the same way faith renders any others whomsoever as righteous before God and truly engrafts them into the holy race. Lest someone should object that circumcision would then have been conferred in vain, he anticipates this objection and declares why it is that Abraham was circumcised: it was in order that by this symbol the righteousness that he had obtained by faith might be sealed and confirmed. For it was through him that righteousness was to spread to his offspring, and through them to the whole earth, by the power of the one and true Seed of Abraham, our Lord Jesus Christ.

He arranges his proof in the following manner:

(P1) When Abraham was pronounced by God as righteous and the people of God was instituted with him, something that did not yet exist could not have contributed anything to either of these.

(P2) Circumcision did not yet exist at that time.

(C) Therefore, etc.

Further:

(P1) That which in Abraham is praised in the Scriptures as the cause of his justification and the origin of the holy people will—undoubtedly to anybody who considers it—stand out as the cause of both righteousness and holy kinship.

(P2) But it is faith that is praised.

(C) Etc.

Nor is it any accident that, whenever it proclaims the faith of Abraham, the Scriptures place this promise: "So shall your seed be" (to which is further added the promise that he would be the father of many nations) before any praise of the righteousness that it memorializes him as having obtained by faith. By no means was a purely carnal posterity of great value to either God or to that holy man. It would be good to lament that the ungodly had ever been born, as the Lord himself said of Judas. None of the saints would have wished for themselves to have ungodly children, but that is just what all the unregenerate are. In this passage, therefore, God made a promise of a *holy* offspring, and did so on account of Abraham's faith. Therefore it is by faith that the promise is established. COMMENTARY ON ROMANS (1536).[16]

BAPTISM REPLACES CIRCUMCISION. THE ENGLISH ANNOTATIONS: Previously, circumcision was called a sign with respect to the outward ceremony. Now St. Paul shows the force and substance of that sign, that is, to what end it is used, which is not only to signify, but also to seal the righteousness of faith, whereby we come to possess Christ himself. For the Holy Spirit works that inwardly and indeed, it is that which the sacrament, being joined with the word, outwardly represents.

God was pleased to dispose of the sign at the time with Abraham, to show that the Gentiles as well as the Jews are to be reputed true children of Abraham, and comprised in the covenant that he made with him and his posterity. So they followed his faith, whether they were circumcised, as during the time of the ceremonial law they were to be according to God's order, or not circumcised, that is, after God had instituted another sacrament instead of that, to wit, baptism. ANNOTATIONS ON ROMANS 4:9.[17]

ARGUMENT FROM THE CIRCUMSTANCE OF TIME. ERASMUS SARCERIUS: "Did not impute sin": that is, he freely remitted it. "Does this blessedness then rest only on the circumcision, or also on the uncircumcision?" With this question, Paul confirms from the example of Abraham's circumcision that the cause of righteousness is imputation itself, for in his case God imputed righteousness before circumcision.

There is in this question yet a fourth argument, in which Paul proves that righteousness is attained

---

[16]Bucer, *Metaphrases et Enarrationes*, 219; citing Gen 15:5; 17:4.
[17]Downame, ed., *Annotations*, AAA3v*.

freely, that Abraham himself had been justified by imputation, and that we also are justified by means of imputation after the example of Abraham.

The argument is derived from the circumstance of time. Abraham was justified before circumcision. Therefore Abraham was not justified by circumcision. Also, Abraham was justified before circumcision. Therefore, we are justified apart from the works of the law.

Similar in every respect is the passage found in Galatians 3 that says: "Now this I say, that the law which came into being after four hundred thirty years could not have nullified the covenant that was ratified earlier, such that the promise should be annulled." This could be the enthymeme[†] governing that verse: Righteousness was attained before the law was given. Therefore the law is not the cause of righteousness.

The question concerns the causes of justification, argued from the circumstance of time. These causes cannot be the works of the law or merits, since Abraham received righteousness before the law was given. This question asks, therefore, whether righteousness is attained by the law or apart from the law.

Certain people argue that works are the sine qua non cause of justification. But just such a cause is here precluded by the example of Abraham, for Abraham received righteousness before the law was given. NOTES ON ROMANS (1541).[18]

4:10 Abraham Justified Before Circumcised

JUSTIFICATION FOR THE CIRCUMCISED AND UNCIRCUMCISED. JOHANNES BRENZ: Paul . . . returns to the example of Abraham in order to show from the circumstance of the occasion that the imputation of righteousness and blessing does not happen on account of the merit of circumcision, but only by free mercy through faith. He says,

"Then did this blessing come only to the circumcision, that is, to the Jews who were circumcised, or also to the uncircumcised, that is, to the uncircumcised Gentiles? Indeed, you of the Pharisees contend that the blessing concerning which David addresses in the psalm pertains to the Jews only—on account of circumcision and the merits of other works of the law—and not also to the Gentiles who are not circumcised and do not have other works of the law. I will surely demonstrate by the example of Abraham, from the circumstance of the occasion itself, that that blessing—which comes from the forgiveness of iniquities and by not imputing sins—pertains as much to the uncircumcised as to the circumcised. For we consider the time in which it was spoken concerning Abraham that his faith was imputed to him as righteousness. Therefore look for yourself. It is written concerning Abraham in the fifteenth chapter of Genesis that because he believed God, it was imputed to him as righteousness. He, however, at the time was not yet circumcised, for circumcision was not yet instituted. Rather, it was instituted thirteen years afterward, as can be deduced from the sixteenth chapter in Genesis, and afterward in the twenty-second chapter. Therefore, just as Abraham's faith was imputed as righteousness, without circumcision, so it cannot be denied that imputation pertains also to the uncircumcised." This argument is recited in such a way in chapter 3 of the Galatian letter. The Scripture, foreseeing that God would justify the Gentiles by faith, previously (evidently before Abraham was circumcised) delivered the gospel to Abraham: "In you all the nations will be blessed." Therefore, those who are of faith are blessed together with faithful Abraham. COMMENTARY ON ROMANS (1564).[19]

DID ABRAHAM DO GOOD WORKS FROM THE LAW OF NATURE? JOHANNES BRENZ: Again, it can be objected: Although Abraham was not justified or absolved from unrighteousness on account of circumcision, nevertheless he was

---

[18]Sarcerius, In Apostolam ad Romanos, O2r-O2v; citing Gal 3:17.
  [†]An enthymeme is a syllogism in which one of the premises is implied rather than stated.

[19]Brenz, In Epistolam, 104-5; citing Gen 15:1-21; 16:1-16; 22:18.

justified on account of other good works that are instructed in the divine law. Concerning this objection, Paul answers in Galatians 3, and that similarly, from the circumstance of the occasion, just as also in this place concerning circumcision. Saying, "I say that the law, which began four hundred thirty years afterward, could not make the covenant invalid and take away the promise that would be ratified by Christ." That is, the blessing was not so much about the multiplication of posterity as about the forgiveness of sins and eternal salvation, which were promised to Abraham—on account of Christ—430 years before the time the law was given that instructed good works. Therefore, how did he obtain the blessing? On account of good works of the law? Again you will say, "But Abraham did good works from the law of nature"? But above, it was explained that all men and women are sinners, whether under the law of nature or under the written law. And it is not obscure that if Abraham or any other man is not justified or is not absolved from unrighteousness on account of circumcision, certainly he will not be justified on account of any other good works of the law, whether that law is engraved by divine operation in men and women, or written on a tablet of stone. For the institution of circumcision was after Abraham's circumcision; it is a particular and most sacred rite in the Israelite church. For it is the door to the heavenly inheritance. And it has the most serious threat, saying, "The life of the uncircumcised male will be blotted out from his people because he has made my covenant void." And the Lord was willing to kill Moses because he did not circumcise his son. Wherefore, if the merit of circumcision did not justify or absolve from unrighteousness either Abraham or other men, it is clear that there is no other work—whether preceding or following merit—able to justify the doer of works. Abraham obeyed God's calling, and he left his home on account of the Word of God. A great work, but it did not justify Abraham. That is, it did not absolve him from unrighteousness. Abraham forgave the injustice committed against him by his relative Lot, and he submitted to him.

An eminent work, but it did not justify Abraham. Why so? Because all men and women are sinners in the sight of God. And, "If the Lord should observe iniquity, O Lord, who could stand?" Further, when it says that all men and women are sinners, it does not mean that men and women sometimes sin and sometimes do right. This is a political, not an ecclesiastical opinion. But it must be understood that all men and women always by their nature are and remain sinners in the presence of God, from the beginning of conception all the way until the final moment of their life. For though one is justified or absolved from unrighteousness through faith on account of Christ, so that one's faith is regarded as righteousness, nevertheless flesh is not changed into spirit. Indeed it always fights with the spirit, in order that whatever the men and women who are born again do not desire, they do. And it may be to such a degree that they may give in and perpetrate dreadful crimes, such as David, Peter, and others did. Or one may take a stand, yet it will not be perfect enough to satisfy the law of God by one's works. COMMENTARY ON ROMANS (1564).[20]

JUSTIFICATION NOT TIED TO THE SACRAMENTS. DAVID PAREUS: "When, therefore?" In order to untangle the knot of how the imputation of righteousness relates to the uncircumcised, Paul teaches from the circumstance of time, using the device of asking and responding . . . as if to say, consider the story, whether righteousness was said to be imputed to Abraham before or after circumcision. Certainly not after, but before—fourteen years, in fact. For he received the promise by faith—by which he was called justified—in the year of the confirmation of the covenant. This year was the tenth after his entry into Canaan, and Abraham was eighty-five years old. It was the same year in which he took Hagar the maid as a wife, from whom in the following year, at the age of eighty-six, he fathered Ishmael. He received

---

[20]Brenz, *In Epistolam*, 105-6; citing Gal 3:1-29; Gen 17:14; Gen 13:1-18; Ps 130:3.

circumcision at age ninety-nine, Ishmael having been born thirteen years before.

Hence it is obviously a true statement that justice was imputed to Abraham not in circumcision, but in uncircumcision. From there it follows *in hypothesis* that Abraham had been justified while uncircumcised, not through circumcision; *in thesis* that circumcision does not convey justification; and *in general*, that sacraments were not instituted to confer justice "from the action of the worker" or "by being enacted," as the scholastic theologians say, but that the righteousness of faith is often had before the sacraments. And therefore, it is not tied to the sacraments, since it often comes about without them. *In sum*, this is what is from the mind of the apostle: the imputed justice of faith does not pertain only to Jews, but also to Gentiles; yet nevertheless not to whomever you please, but to those who follow in the footsteps of the faith of Abraham, as Paul will teach in verse 12. COMMENTARY ON ROMANS (1608).[21]

OBEDIENCE, FAITH, AND SPIRITUAL BAPTISM. MENNO SIMONS: Behold, beloved brothers and sisters. Baptism saves us in this manner, as Peter teaches: not as the outward literal baptism, but the inward, spiritual baptism, which as obedient children of God, has led us, through the power of faith, to the outward literal baptism. For the outward, literal baptism is nothing more than obedience to the divine Word, and thus it is a seal or proof of the righteousness from where the true, fruitful faith comes, in the same way that the literal circumcision was to the believing and obedient Abraham. CHRISTIAN BAPTISM.[22]

4:11 Circumcision as a Seal of Righteousness

BAPTISM IS THE CIRCUMCISION OF CHRIST.
HULDRYCH ZWINGLI: Now I want to tell with which places in Scripture I support my view that

infants must be baptized. For in such argumentation of ideas one must be able to come up with a sure reference in which our view is very clearly contained. Therefore, hear the passage in Romans 4: Circumcision was the sign of a faith that was already there. But it was always performed eight days after birth on infants who would only many years later come to faith. Baptism then took the place of circumcision. It follows then that baptism, like circumcision, should be performed also on those who will not come to faith until later. Of course, secondary circumstances of place, person, time, and method must be taken into consideration. All of this is clear and plain, except the middle clause, that baptism is the Christian's circumcision. But this assertion is also as clearly stated when Paul in Colossians 2 says, "In whom also you are circumcised with the circumcision made without hands, by putting off the body of the sins of the flesh by the circumcision of Christ, buried with him in baptism." In regard to the meaning of this passage, it is very clear what Paul meant to say here, that the one who becomes a Christian is a new creation. But I want to come back to what I was going to say. What, I ask, could have been said more clearly than this, that the circumcision of Christ has been performed on us when we are buried with him in baptism? Consequently, the circumcision of Christ is also administered to infants on the authority of God's word, not the pope's, just like earlier the circumcision of Abraham. LETTER TO THE STRASBOURG BRETHREN.[23]

GOD SEALS WITH HIS SIGNET RING.
HEINRICH BULLINGER: I am inclined to think that this is both an *anthypophora* and an *antistrephon* all in one.[†] It is an *anthypophora* because the Jews were objecting: "If he was absolutely righteous before circumcision, what was the point of circumcision?" And by way of *antistrephon*, Paul in this verse now answers in such a way as to twist their objection about circumcision back around against them, making it to serve his own purposes. Abraham, he

---

[21]Pareus, *In Divinam ad Romanos*, 395-96; citing Gal 3:17.
[22]Simons, *Complete Works*, 202*.

[23]CRR 4:306*; citing Col 2:11; 2 Cor 5:17; Rom 6:4.

says, believed while he was not yet circumcised and was justified on that account. Circumcision came later, not in order to justify, but to be "a seal of the righteousness of faith," that is, as a witness to and sacrament of the reality that righteousness is by faith. For not only did he say "he received the sign of circumcision," but he further added the concept of a seal: "in order to be a seal (*sphragida*), I say, of the righteousness of faith (*tēs dikaiosynēs tēs pisteōs*)." The word *sphragida* is used for a mark impressed into something, and even the seal of a signet ring. It is our custom, in order to strengthen faith, to sign something that we wish to make certain and beyond doubt. But with a seal we both guarantee our trust and bind ourselves to a written agreement. Paul, therefore, thinks that by circumcision, God wished to sign, as with a seal, the fact that justification is by faith and by no other thing, and, what is more, he wanted those who received circumcision to bind themselves as with an oath [*sacramenta*] that they would not attempt to seek after righteousness in anything other than God through faith. This is the force of the rhetorical stress of the words, since he did not say merely that it was a "seal of righteousness," but added further, "a seal of the righteousness of faith," that is, that faith is righteousness. It is in this way, I assert, that he has with great effectiveness twisted back against the Jews the very thing that they themselves were objecting with in order to defend works righteousness. The verses that follow simply shed further light upon and strengthen this point. COMMENTARY ON PAUL'S EPISTLES (1582).[24]

SIGN AND SEAL. DESIDERIUS ERASMUS: *Signaculum*, "seal." Paul uses two words, *sēmeion* and *sphragis* (the one used second is *sphragis*), that is, *signum* [sign, *sēmeion*] and *nota impressa* [impressed mark, *sphragis*]. For to ensure reliability we are accustomed to "seal" [*obsignare*] what we wish to be established. And in the same way we

"seal" what we desire to put away and store up for a time, to be brought forth in its proper place. Otherwise, it could appear that Paul had said the same thing twice, when he had just now said *signum* [mark, or sign] then spoke again of *signaculum* [mark, or seal]. The first of these is, in Greek, *sēmeion*, "a sign" by which something else is designated. For even at that time the carnal circumcision bore the figure of the Christian circumcision, which does not remove the foreskin from the glans but cuts away all harmful desires from the heart. It was also a "seal," because for a time it concealed the mystery that was to be opened up later, namely, [the mystery] of righteousness, which is conferred through faith. But it is possible for something to be a "sign" that is not a "seal," as a statue is a "sign," but the symbol on a ring, marked on a promissory note, is a *sphragis* [seal]. These two terms, however, are in apposition to each other. For the same thing is said to be a *sēmeion* [sign], insofar as it points to the righteousness from faith that was in Abraham before circumcision, and also a *sphragis* [seal], insofar as by the example of Abraham righteousness from faith without circumcision was promised to all who believe. This has been carefully noted by Origen. ANNOTATIONS ON THE EPISTLE TO THE ROMANS (1516, 1519, 1522, 1527, 1535).[25]

LIKE A SEAL ON A LETTER OF RECOMMENDATION. MICHAEL COBABUS AND JOHANN QUISTORP: Abraham was circumcised. It is particular to—and has reference only to—the Jews to follow the example of Abraham. For if circumcision by itself were the cause of the blessedness or righteousness that was imputed to Abraham, it would then follow that (1) the effect would precede its cause, for righteousness was imputed to Abraham not in a state of circumcision, but in uncircumcision before he was circumcised, so how would righteousness have been imputed in his condition of uncircumcision? It happened not in his circumcision but in his uncircumcision.

---

[24]Bullinger, *Commentarii in Omnes*, 64v-65r. †An *anthypophora* is a rhetorical device in which one raises a question and immediately answers it; an *antistrephon* uses an argument from one's opponent.

[25]CWE 56:112*.

(2) It would also follow that the antecedent would come after the consequent, for circumcision in Abraham was like a seal with which a letter of recommendation is guaranteed, and he received the sign of circumcision as a token of the righteousness of faith which was already there in uncircumcision. Therefore just as the seal is not affixed before the letter of recommendation is written, but rather follows it, so also circumcision in Abraham followed the righteousness of faith and confirmed it. In this way the apostle (in this passage) shows that justification in Abraham's case in no way depended on his circumcision, so that he might also show that all other works confer no justification on man or woman, since they do not precede being justified but rather follow after one is already justified. DISPUTATIONS ON ROMANS (1644).[26]

SACRAMENTS SEAL GOD'S GRACE ON OUR HEARTS. JOHN CALVIN: We have indeed here a remarkable passage with regard to the general benefits of sacraments. According to the testimony of Paul, they are seals by which the promises of God are in a manner imprinted on our hearts, and the certainty of grace confirmed. And though by themselves they profit nothing, yet God has designed them to be the instruments of his grace, and he effects by the secret grace of his Spirit that they should not be without benefit to the elect. And though they are dead and unprofitable symbols to the reprobate, they yet ever retain their import and character, for though our unbelief may deprive them of their effect, yet it cannot weaken or extinguish the truth of God. Hence it remains a fixed principle that sacred symbols are testimonies by which God seals his grace on our hearts. COMMENTARY ON ROMANS 4:11.[27]

FOUR COMPONENTS OF A SACRAMENT. NIELS HEMMINGSEN: Again, because in this place he advises us concerning the use of the sacraments, I desire, albeit most briefly, to develop a general

account of the sacraments. In the first place, it is worth observing the covenant—which God made with his church and by which he reigned and governed her—at the time when the promise of the seed was first given. For the observation itself, and whatever the parts of the work may be, and in what way they were mutually consistent, will be made abundantly clear.

From the time of the beginning of the world, God had always preserved this custom with respect to either his promises, or later, to his decrees or solemn repetitions: he added external signs as visible declarations of his promises. These signs indicate those sacred things that are called *sacramentum* in Latin and are called *mysterion* by the Greeks, by which visible things contain the hidden and spiritual things. And moreover, Augustine rightly said concerning this subject, "The sacrament is a visible word." For what the Lord offers with his Word, he seals with a sacrament as a visible testimony. And both of these, whether Word or Sacrament, require faith, because both are declarations of some promise.

From these things it is easily understood that concerning the nature of each sacrament, we need to seek four things, in order. First, God's command and institution. Then the external sign—and that is not simple, but symbolic. Then the promise of grace. Finally, the belief of the promise. These four Paul has connected when he says, "And the sign of circumcision he received as a seal of the righteousness which is by faith." When it is said, "Abraham received," a divine command and institution are noted, according to Genesis 17. When "circumcision" is named, an external sign is displayed. When the seal is joined with justification, it is shown that the external sign of the promised grace of justification is a sure seal. In the last place, when faith is added, the promised righteousness is shown to be received by faith. In this way, these four should come together in the account of any sacrament: the divine command or institution, the analogous or symbolic sign, the Word of promise, and belief of the promise. Nor does the brief saying of

---

[26]Cobabus and Quistorp, *Disputatione*, 13.
[27]CTS 38:164-65* (CO 49:64).

Augustine on John 15 lack any of the four: "The Word comes together with the element and becomes a sacrament." He understands the Word of God to be establishing and promising, which Word requires faith and obedience. The element is an outward thing meeting up with an internal sense. Thus, by these things which have been seen and spoken, we build up a general definition of a sacrament in this way: a sacrament is a visible sign commanded and instituted by God, by which God gives evidence of his grace and seals people so that his people in turn profess faith in God, and they declare it by use of the sacrament. For this reason it is also apparent to any that the principal end of the sacraments is evidently to seal the grace promised, which is received and held by faith. But what was said above, that it is an external sign that clothes the analogical or symbolic, must be carefully heeded. But it is called analogical or symbolic on account of its purpose. For a sign ought to be like a visible word, that is, as something that teaches by displaying to the senses a certain likeness. And, therefore, it is properly called a symbol, that is, a sign, because it teaches by a comparison—which the visible thing holds toward the thing that is promised and offered in the sacrament. So Augustine said, "If the sacraments do not contain a comparison to that thing signified, they are not sacraments."[†] Circumcision as an external symbol teaches in this way: as the foreskin of the reproductive member is cut off in circumcision, so figuratively, the old nature is being cut off in regeneration. In baptism there is an analogical or symbolic reckoning between the water and the blood of Christ in their effects. For as water washes away bodily uncleanness, so the sprinkling of the Lord's blood signifies the virtue by which men and women are cleansed from their sins. In the Supper there is a clear analogy between bread and the body, and between wine and the blood. For just as bread nourishes and wine refreshes our bodies, so by the body and blood of the Lord in the Supper—but only should faith be present—are we spiritually fed. These are general statements about the sacraments. More may be sought from other writings. COMMENTARY ON ROMANS (1562).[28]

A SACRAMENT OF THE COVENANT OF GRACE. WILLIAM AMES: Here the apostle deals with the justification of Abraham, ascribing it to him in such a way that he sets down a pattern of justification to life that applies to both uncircumcised Gentiles and to the Jews themselves. For this end the apostle observes—and proposes to be observed—that faith was reputed to Abraham as righteousness, while he was yet uncircumcised or in the foreskin. Against this proposition—because it might be objected that then circumcision was of no use to Abraham—the apostle . . . answers that there was another purpose and use of that sacrament. For he was not circumcised in order to be justified by circumcision. Rather, circumcision, as by a seal and sign, confirmed the righteousness that had already been imputed to him. We have then in these words a description of a sacrament of the covenant of grace. THE SUBSTANCE OF CHRISTIAN RELIGION.[29]

THE BENEFITS OF EXTERNAL SIGNS. JOHANNES BUGENHAGEN: What was the advantage of Abraham's circumcision if he was not justified because of it? You have here a notable passage about external signs, the sort that nearly all Jewish ceremonies were, and that our present sacraments are. These do not justify by means of themselves, just as not even the outward hearing of the Word by itself justifies, but they are sure signs of an inward righteousness. So Abraham received the external sign of the cutting of his skin as a sign of the righteousness that he had within his heart. The true righteousness of Abraham himself was signified by the sign, but through itself it was not righteous. Also, the people of God were recognized through that sign. It is true that signs of this kind are often able to deceive, especially when used by

---

[28]Hemmingsen, *Commentarius in Epistolam*, 146-49; citing Gen 17; Jn 15. [†]Augustine, *Epistula* 98.9.
[29]Ames, *Substance of Christian Religion*, 166-67*.

hypocrites. But then they may only be called signs, not signs of God. And signs are not really true unless they are inwardly what they signify outwardly. So we see the sacraments of God accomplish the same as the external Word, for they speak to us as the Word of God, testifying of God's good purpose toward us. Wherefore, I do not say that without the Word of God they are nothing. Faith accepting the Word of God justifies, and faith accepting the sacraments justifies. For we are justified by faith, "but faith comes by hearing, and hearing through the Word of God." Therefore, the sacraments are signs and seals of the covenant between us sinners and the benevolent God, for we receive them from his hand.

But second, through such we indicate to others that we are considered the faithful. A sign and covenant between God and me . . . does not deceive me. But a sign only in the presence of men and women often deceives and is hypocrisy. Thus, when sins bother our conscience, we receive the sacrament of the Eucharist in order that we might reassure our conscience concerning the forgiveness of sins, which is only because of faith in Christ. In the end, good works flow from such a faith, by which also I reassure myself concerning my faith. For I would not do these things unless the Holy Spirit impelled me to do them. INTERPRETATION OF ROMANS (1531).[30]

SACRAMENTS MARK OUR HIGH VALUE TO GOD. PETER MARTYR VERMIGLI: The reason that letters are signed, and the documents of princes are protected with seals, is that no one may be in doubt about their authority or fidelity. In this way, God handed over the sacraments to us as signatures of his promises. Therefore, circumcision signified two things, both that base desires were to be severed from the mind, and that the children of Israel were to be separate from other nations. Then it was a small sign of the divine will and promise that was offered to Abraham—of justice, of the remission of sins through Christ, of making a

covenant with God, and of many goods of this kind. This, I say, was the promise signed for by the symbol of circumcision. And two other advantages not to be despised are added to these significations of sacraments. For things are claimed by their masters with signs in this way, since with horses, bulls, and other items of this kind, brands [*characteres*] and burned-on signs indicate to whom they belong. In this case, such external signs indicate for what price and value the things labeled may be had, as is obvious in the case of gold coins, and also in horses. Some signs indicate a horse of noble stock, others of common. Furthermore, the sacraments that God commended to us indicate how much God values us. For the images of the reminders of circumcision and the other sacraments are signs of the will and promises of God. For since, because we were sick, we could not easily believe in the promises of God, it was necessary that his works be signified to our wills not only with words, but signed for with things which we can perceive. For this reason, Augustine very wisely says that sacraments are visible words. COMMENTARY ON ROMANS (1560).[31]

SIGNS CONFIRM RATHER THAN CONFER. WILLIAM GUILD: That sacraments do not confer grace on the receivers *ex opere operato*. . . . Whereby we see from this verse that this is the nature of sacraments: to wit, that they are signs for representation, and seals for confirming or ratifying. Seals serve to confirm, but they do not confer on anyone the thing that they confirm. In the same way, sacraments *ex opere operato*, or by the mere receiving, do not confer grace or salvation on anyone. Only God does, who is the giver of all grace and glory. THE OLD ROMAN CATHOLIC (1649).[32]

THE VARIETY OF SIGNS. PETER MARTYR VERMIGLI: Now that enough has been said about the term, we will add the definition of a sacrament,

---

[30]Bugenhagen, *In D. Pauli ad Romanos*, 39v-40r; citing Rom 10:17.

[31]Vermigli, *In Epistolam S. Pauli*, 234.
[32]Guild, *The Old Roman Catholik*, 66*.

and this is the most well received one: a sacrament is a visible form or visible sign of an invisible grace. Indeed, it is said to be a sign because beyond the form that it carries to our senses, it introduces something else into our knowledge. A sign is also divided—as Augustine writes and the Master of the Sentences [Peter Lombard] affirms—into the natural and the given. Smoke is the natural sign of fire, and clouds, of rain. There are many different kinds of signs, such as letters, messages, stories, gestures, and many other things of this kind. These different kinds of signs can also refer to many, various senses. They can signify the past, present, or future. The preserved tables of the law, manna, and the rod of Aaron signified the past, for God wished for these and certain monuments of past events to remain. Others designate future things, such as the arc in the clouds given in the time of Noah, the fleece of Gideon, the shadow of the sun that went backward in the time of Hezekiah. Many signified present things, such as the priestly vestments of the Levites, or in the ornaments of magistrates, or in the miracles of Christ. For all these things signified the power of God in the present. Our sacraments are visible signs, not by their own nature, but rather because they are given to us by the will of God, and they pertain to many senses. For the words that are pronounced in the sacraments are perceived by the ears; the notes and external symbols are sensed either by sight, by touch, by smell, or by taste. They demonstrate things from the past, present, and future. Thus the death of Christ is represented in them, which has already happened; and the promise and gift of God that, to the mind and to faith, surround us as if present; and purity of life, mortification, and the offices of charity, which are necessarily to be fulfilled by us in the future. From these things it is proved: we may hold signs of this kind to be sacraments. But it could seem to be enough that one accept the definition from Paul, that we say that sacraments are *sphragidas*, that is, seals of the righteousness of faith. For they seal the promises of God, by which, when applied by faith, we are justified. For if you were to ask what it may

be that God promises to us, if I may respond in one word, it is that God will be our God—that, when it shall have come to pass, he preserves us, he blesses us, and renders us happy. COMMENTARY ON ROMANS (1560).[33]

BAPTISM IS A TESTIMONY. HULDRYCH ZWINGLI: "And he received the sign of circumcision." Indeed, the patriarch received circumcision, but not so that he might be justified, but simply as a token and a seal of that righteousness that had already been granted to him by the grace of God, when he was still a Gentile, or uncircumcised. According to this testimony, he is the father—that is, the model—of all who believed while uncircumcised, that is, of faithful Gentiles, who, while uncircumcised in the flesh, nevertheless have trusted in the mercy of God that they might be righteous. And then, also, he is the father of the circumcised, that is, of the Jews, or of those who believed because of circumcision. This is in order that God might reveal through Abraham, or in Abraham, that all nations would share in salvation, if only they would believe. Observe that Paul calls this circumcision a sign that—in Abraham—precedes faith. He is not of this opinion because his faith—which came before—was sealed by the external circumcision. Nor because no one who is circumcised ought to accept this sign unless he first believes, as the Anabaptists contend. Rather, it is because it was a sign to him while uncircumcised that the mercy and grace of God would come, and it was just as a token or a public testimony. Thus the sign of baptism should not be undertaken so that faith may be established or that sin may be atoned for through it. Rather, it should be undertaken as a testimony that the one baptized has been washed of his or her sins through the blood of Christ and that righteousness and the forgiveness of sins has been granted by grace alone, not from work or merit. NOTES ON ROMANS (1539).[34]

---

[33]Vermigli, *In Epistolam S. Pauli*, 238-39.
[34]Zwingli, *In Evangelicam Historiam*, 416-17.

INFANT BAPTISM PARALLELS CIRCUMCISION.
FRIEDRICH BALDUIN: Q: The circumcision of
Abraham is called a seal, *sphragis* of the righteousness he had already received. Therefore, isn't
baptism also only a seal or a sign of righteousness
rather than the instrument of conferring the grace
of righteousness?

R: I answer: we must here distinguish between
the circumcision of Abraham and that of others
who received that sacrament in infancy. Righteousness was not conferred at that time on Abraham,
but having already been conferred it was signified by
this sacrament—his circumcision was therefore a
sign pointing to the righteousness he had first
received some forty years earlier. And yet it was the
instrument of conferring grace with respect to an
increase of faith and other gifts that follow that
received righteousness. On infants, however, on
whom righteousness has not yet been conferred,
righteousness was at that time conferred by means
of circumcision as the normal instrument [*organon*]
of grace and, at the same time, was a sign of the
righteousness received. Therefore, it is not the
circumcision of Abraham but the circumcision of
infants that this assumes, which is to be compared
with baptism, by which today both the grace of God
is conferred and also that which has already been
received is sealed. APOSTOLIC CATECHISM (1620).[35]

**CHRISTIANS SHOULD ACCEPT BAPTISM WITH
ZEAL.** DIRK PHILIPS: Thus also the believing
Abraham (whom all believers must follow and in
whose footsteps of faith they must walk) through
his faith did not reject external circumcision (even
though it was only a sign and a small thing in
itself), but received and accepted it as a seal of his
faith. In like manner, Christians should also,
because of their faith, not reject baptism, but
accept and receive it with wholehearted zeal and
earnestness, since they have not only Abraham but
Jesus Christ himself as an example. THE BAPTISM
OF OUR LORD JESUS CHRIST.[36]

**LIKE ABRAHAM, WE DO NOT RECEIVE THE
PROMISE BY WORKS.** JACQUES LEFÈVRE
D'ÉTAPLES: I believe that this bears a clear mean-
ing; however, there is another reason, because
justification comes from the promise made to
Abraham. But when the promise was made to
Abraham, he was believing God, as is found in
Genesis; it was not according to works. For
Abraham was seventy-five years old when the Lord
said to him, "Depart from your country and place
of birth and from your father's household, and go
into the land which I will show you. . . ." And so
Abraham went out just as the Lord commanded
him. Is not Abraham's departure from his land and
place of birth and from his father's house a sign of
his faith effecting works? Certainly they are
evidence of faith. But even concerning the earthly
promise, according to the same account of the law
in Genesis, Abraham believed God, and it was
considered for him as righteousness. And God said
to him, "I am the Lord who brought you out from
Ur of the Chaldeans that I might give to you that
land in order that you might take possession of it."
Look at the manner in which the promise was
made to Abraham. It was not by works of the law,
but only from believing God. To be sure, if the
seed of Abraham is said to be those who receive
the inheritance of the Earth because of works, faith
is made unnecessary and the promise destroyed.
For neither faith nor the promise would be
bringing anything about. For in that case, whether
faith existed or not, or the promise existed or not,
the inheritance would be received, because it would
be owed to the works. Therefore, to say that the
seed of Abraham receives the earthly inheritance
according to works of the law is equal to making
justification and faith invalid and to destroying the
promise that the sacred pronouncements commended. COMMENTARY ON ROMANS.[37]

BECOMING LIKE FATHER ABRAHAM. LEUPOLD
SCHARNSCHLAGER: For what kind of test, what
kind of faith and hope would it be, in which our

---

[35]Balduin, *Catechesis Apostolica*, 296-97.
[36]CRR 6:108*; citing Gen 17:10.

[37]Lefèvre, *Epistole divi Pauli*, 61r-61v; citing Gen 12:1-2.

future comfort, location, or place did not remain hidden, invisible, or unknown, but were physically or visibly present? The Lord and Peter only pronounce as blessed those who believe yet have not seen. And Paul says it is not hope if one sees it, so that we become like the faithful Abraham who is a father and shaper of all the faithful, who went out "to the place that he should receive as his inheritance, though not knowing where he would end up." Let us rejoice in such testing and tribulations, because they will produce only goodness and patience. Consider that they come upon us only for our good; that is why he sends you such tribulations. Admonition and Comfort in All Manner of Sorrow.[38]

4:12 The Father of Those Who Walk in the Faith

Circumcision of the Flesh and of the Heart. Dirk Philips: The figure of Abraham must be understood according to the true being of the Spirit in a twofold manner. In the first place, God the heavenly Father is signified to us through Abraham; Isaac is a figure of Jesus Christ and of all Christians; Sarah, of the New Testament; circumcision of the flesh, of the circumcision of the hearts, which is the circumcision of Christ that takes place in the Spirit. This is the meaning and interpretation of circumcision everywhere in Scripture as we have also explained above. The Baptism of Our Lord Jesus Christ.[39]

Old and New Testament Agree on Sacraments. Friedrich Balduin: Q: Since circumcision is called a "sign and seal of the righteousness of faith," is it not rightly inferred that the sacraments of the Old and New Testaments differed as respects their efficacy in bestowing grace, such that the latter actually conferred grace while the former did not, but merely

signified the grace that would be conferred after the passion of Christ?

R: I answer, this is what many Catholics . . . conclude from this passage. In the Council of Florence that was called by Pope Eugene in the year 1439, it was dogmatically affirmed that the sacraments of the old law did not effect grace, but only prefigured that grace that would be given through the passion of Christ, but that the sacraments of our new law both contain grace and confer it on those worthily receiving them. Pererius wavers on this question, which he argues on both sides, but in the end he finally inclines to say that by circumcision grace was also given, but less so than is given in baptism. . . . But let us hold the scriptural fundamentals, by which it is proved that the two Testaments do not differ from each other as to the efficacy of bestowing grace, and that circumcision was in the same manner as baptism the ordinary instrument God willed should be used by which to obtain the gifts of his grace that were being offered, exhibited, and signified. Apostolic Catechism (1620).[40]

Spiritual Children of Sarah. Dirk Philips: This is also clearly to be understood from the fact that Ishmael according to the flesh was a son of Abraham and also circumcised as was Isaac. Nevertheless, God made his covenant with Isaac, not with Ishmael. Thus not Ishmael, but only Isaac, had an inheritance in the house of Abraham. [Isaac] was born from free Sarah through the promise, signifying that God, the heavenly Father, has chosen the spiritual children of Sarah, that is, of the New Testament, out of grace. These are the children of his promise, and are counted as that seed, and their salvation lies in the boundless grace and mercy of God, in the innocent death of our Lord and Savior, Jesus Christ. The Baptism of Our Lord Jesus Christ.[41]

---

[38]CRR 12:522*; citing Jn 20:29; 1 Pet 1:8; Rom 8:24; Heb 11:8; Jas 1:3; Rom 5:3.
[39]CRR 6:102*; citing Phil 3:3; Col 2:11.
[40]Balduin, *Catechesis Apostolica*, 300-301.
[41]CRR 6:105*; citing Gen 16:15; 17:10-11; Rom 9:7; Gen 21:2; Gal 4:23; Rom 9:7; Gal 3:29; Eph 1:7; Col 1:14.

The Nature of True and Saving Faith.
William Guild: From this verse and Romans 4:20-21, it follows that the nature of a true and saving faith—to which we are exhorted, following the example of the godly before us—is not an uncertain conjecture, or probable opinion only, but a full persuasion, without staggering or doubting (which the apostle calls unbelief and contrary to faith). And this full persuasion of the performance of God's promises to a penitent believer, is so far from sinful presumption . . . that, on the contrary, the apostle declares that God is thereby glorified, and acknowledged to be true to his promises. And on the other side, doubting that God will perform his promises to us is rather presumptuous, for we make God a liar. The Old Roman Catholic (1649).[42]

---

[42]Guild, *The Old Roman Catholik*, 57-58*; citing Rom 4:20-21.

4:13-25 BELIEF CREDITED AS RIGHTEOUSNESS

¹³*For the promise to Abraham and his offspring that he would be heir of the world did not come through the law but through the righteousness of faith.* ¹⁴*For if it is the adherents of the law who are to be the heirs, faith is null and the promise is void.* ¹⁵*For the law brings wrath, but where there is no law there is no transgression.*

¹⁶*That is why it depends on faith, in order that the promise may rest on grace and be guaranteed to all his offspring—not only to the adherent of the law but also to the one who shares the faith of Abraham, who is the father of us all,* ¹⁷*as it is written, "I have made you the father of many nations"—in the presence of the God in whom he believed, who gives life to the dead and calls into existence the things that do not exist.* ¹⁸*In hope he believed against hope, that he should become the father of many nations, as he had been told, "So shall your offspring be."* ¹⁹*He did not weaken in faith when he considered his own body, which was as good as dead (since he was about a hundred years old), or when he considered the barrenness*ᵃ *of Sarah's womb.* ²⁰*No unbelief made him waver concerning the promise of God, but he grew strong in his faith as he gave glory to God,* ²¹*fully convinced that God was able to do what he had promised.* ²²*That is why his faith was "counted to him as righteousness."* ²³*But the words "it was counted to him" were not written for his sake alone,* ²⁴*but for ours also. It will be counted to us who believe in him who raised from the dead Jesus our Lord,* ²⁵*who was delivered up for our trespasses and raised for our justification.*

a Greek *deadness*

OVERVIEW: The main focus of this pericope is the nature of faith. The reformers continue to emphasize justification by faith alone, contrasting it to fulfillment of the law. The timing of the law being given 430 years *later than* the promise to Abraham (as mentioned in Gal 3:17) and Abraham's being credited with righteousness demonstrate, they argue, that the gift of righteousness and the inheritance of eternal life are not dependent on the law. The law, however, is helpful to us, for in bringing wrath, it points to the sin in us and alerts us to our need for a Savior. If salvation were by works, God's promise to Abraham would have been empty, and salvation would have applied only to the Jews, since the Gentiles did not receive the law. We can have assurance of salvation since it does not depend on our perfectly following the law, doing good works, being of a particular ethnicity, and so on. It is by faith alone. Here the reformers continue to argue against medieval Catholic faith, as well as the Council of Trent, which stated that one is justified by faith and works rather than by faith alone.

The commentators together create a paean to faith. Faith and hope are closely linked. Faith believes God's Word, and hope waits for the promise to be fulfilled. Hope mounts on wings toward the wonders of God that await, and faith is strengthened by focusing on the faithful God. The reformers, many of whom faced persecution themselves, contend that believers must continue to have faith, even when in the midst of tribulations and when under spiritual attack, and sometimes even contrary to reason. Once we know what God has said, we need to believe it and trust him. Our faith brings God glory, as did Abraham's, for he believed God's promise to him even though he had no model of God having miraculously brought forth a child from barrenness. In turn, faith makes us strong. Faith is not mere knowledge of the law or of history; faith is a firm certainty, a trust in the promises of God. And the God who Abraham believed in is the same God whose promises we too can trust.

The interpreters then give center stage to the gospel. Believing in the one who raised Christ from the dead is the heart of the gospel. It encapsulates and implies the larger story of Christ's perfect, obedient life, his suffering on the cross, and his resurrection. And the highest point of God's love was his handing over his Son so that we might be delivered from our sins.

4:13 The Promise Came Through Faith, Not Law

WE ARE HEIRS OF THE WORLD. JOHN CALVIN: The apostle in Hebrews 1:2 calls Christ the heir of all the good things of God, for the adoption that we obtain through his favor restores to us the possession of the inheritance we lost in Adam. And as under the type of the land of Canaan, not only the hope of a heavenly life was exhibited to Abraham, but also the full and complete blessing of God, the apostle rightly teaches us that the dominion of the world was promised to him. The godly have some taste of this in the present life, for however much they may at times be oppressed with want, yet as they partake with a peaceable conscience of those things that God has created for their use, and as they enjoy through his mercy and goodwill his earthly benefits not otherwise than as pledges and earnests of eternal life, their poverty does in no degree prevent them from acknowledging heaven, and the earth, and the sea, as their own possessions.

Though the ungodly swallow up the riches of the world, they can yet call nothing their own, but rather they snatch them as it were by stealth, for they possess them under the curse of God. It is indeed a great comfort to the godly in their poverty that though they fare slenderly, they steal nothing of what belongs to another, but receive their lawful allowance from the hand of their celestial Father, until they enter on the full possession of their inheritance, when all creatures shall be made subservient to their glory. Both heaven and earth shall be renewed for this end, that according to their measure they may contribute to render

glorious the kingdom of God. COMMENTARY ON ROMANS 4:13.[1]

THE LAW AND FAITH DESERVE OPPOSITE THINGS. MARTIN LUTHER: Again he proves that righteousness does not come from the law but from faith, according to the fruit and merit of both. For the law and faith deserve opposite things. That is, the law merits wrath and the loss of the promise, but faith deserves grace and the fulfillment of the promise; as if to say, if you do not believe the Scripture and its example, at least believe your own experience. For through the law you have deserved wrath and desolation, but through faith, grace and the possession of the whole world, as is clear in the case of the apostles, who reign with Christ in all the world. Thus also the promise was not given to Abraham through the law but through faith, and the same will be the case with you who are his seed. LECTURE ON ROMANS (1516).[2]

THE LAW CREATES GUILTY PARTIES, NOT HEIRS. PETER MARTYR VERMIGLI: It was proved above that Abraham did not possess righteousness because of circumcision, since he had gained it before he was circumcised. Now he proves the same thing by something greater. He says that the promise was made to Abraham "not through the law," therefore neither through circumcision. Since the law is obviously broader than circumcision, the argument from it is plain. For it does not contain circumcision alone, but also innumerable excellent precepts. And it can be confirmed in two ways that the promise was not conditional on being through the law. First, as is held in Galatians, the law was later than the promise by 430 years. It could not, therefore, be the condition of the promise made at a point when it did not yet exist. "A man's covenant," says Paul, "no one voids, or adds anything to whatever." But here Paul omits the argument drawn from time: partly because it was used by Paul before, when he said that circumcision was

---

[1]CTS 38:169* (CO 49:77).
[2]LW 25:278-79*.

given after Abraham had already been justified; and also partly because he wishes to use a different argument, which is more plain.

The law, he says, if it were added to the promise, would make it useless and abolish faith. For the law, entering our sinful minds, sets nothing before us except the wrath of God. The law cannot produce the promise or the inheritance of happiness. And Paul proves that the wrath of God comes by the law, since when there was no law, there was no transgression either. Ambrose says, "The law brought about wrath, so that it might create guilty parties." They become culprits, or are condemned, or are made less than fit to receive the promises. For the son who is disinherited for transgressions does not receive the inheritance. So we also, being cursed by the law, are sentenced to Gehenna, rather than made fit by the law to inherit the ensuing promises. COMMENTARY ON ROMANS (1560).[3]

ARGUMENT FROM TIME. GEORG MAJOR: The promised inheritance is Abraham's *apart* from the law. For the law was first proclaimed after many years, *after* Abraham had been declared righteous by faith much earlier. Therefore, neither righteousness nor the inheritance of eternal life is given as a result of the law, but freely, by faith so that it might not be merited, but a free gift, on account of the Lord Jesus Christ. EXPOSITION OF THE EPISTLES OF PAUL (1569).[4]

4:14-15 *The Law Brings Wrath*

ARGUMENTS FOR RECEIVING THE PROMISES BY FAITH, NOT THE LAW. HEINRICH BULLINGER: The heirs are those who are participants in the heirship of Christ and in that one and only salvific Soul. But those of the law are those who wish to be justified by the law and who trust in their works. The following are the arguments employed to support the summary above. For Paul proves with various arguments that Abraham was not justified by the law but by faith. Anybody can infer as much from the word "inheritance." (P1) That which comes by inheritance comes freely (for children do not purchase their inheritance from their parents). (P2) Righteousness comes by inheritance. (C) Therefore, righteousness also comes freely.

It's along these lines that the following two responses to reductions to absurdity pertain. First, if righteousness were owed to those of the law, surely "faith would be made void." For the law rests on merit, whereas faith rests on grace. Indeed, it is certain that faith could not at any time confide in works and find repose in them, since it never happens that the soul of man or woman can trust with certainty that it has sufficiently kept the law enough. As a result there eventually arises a hesitation and desperation in which faith is made void. Second, "the promise would be dissolved" and to no avail. For when faith collapses, at the same time the promise is emptied. For in vain is something promised if we either already possess it or are able to provide it for ourselves. So reads Galatians 3: "If the inheritance is by the law, it is no longer of promise. But God gave it to Abraham by way of promise," therefore it is not by the law.

The next arguments are drawn from contraries. The following are derived from contrary functions as well as from the force of the law: righteousness makes us peaceful, but the law terrifies and therefore does not justify, for that which justifies creates peace. He then adds a statement that provides the reason why: "for where there is no law, there is no transgression." By this is proved the statement that "the law works wrath," concerning which see chapter 7.

From all these arguments we learn that the promises of God are to be received by faith. We also learn what the force of the law is, and that all those who defend works and merits empty faith of meaning and dissolve the promises of God. COMMENTARY ON ROMANS (1582).[5]

---

[3]Vermigli, *In Epistolam S. Pauli*, 267-68; collated with *Learned and Fruitfull Commentaries*, 87v; citing Gal 3:17.
[4]Major, *Enarrationes Epistolarum S. Pauli*, 111.

[5]Bullinger, *Commentarii in Omnes*, 33; and *In Sanctissimam Pauli* (1533), 68r; citing Gal 3:18.

Resting Securely in the Goodness of God. John Calvin: The apostle teaches us that faith perishes unless the soul rests on the goodness of God. Faith then is not a naked knowledge of either God or his truth, nor is it a simple persuasion that God is, that his word is the truth, but a sure knowledge of God's mercy, which is received from the gospel and brings peace of conscience with regard to God and rest to the mind. The sum of the matter then is this, that if salvation depends on keeping the law, the soul can entertain no confidence respecting it, yea that all the promises offered to us by God will become void. We must thus become wretched and lost, if we are sent back to works to find the cause or certainty of our salvation. Commentary on Romans 4:14.[6]

Effects of the Law. Erasmus Sarcerius: "For the law works wrath." The *aetiologia*[†] from the effect of the law is that the law is not the cause of the promise or of righteousness. This is the seventh argument for free righteousness through faith, and it is taken from the effect of the law.

A syllogism:

(P1) Whatever works wrath does not justify, nor is it the cause of righteousness.

(P2) The law works wrath.

(C) Therefore, the law does not justify, nor is it the cause of righteousness.

Another syllogism:

(P1) Whatever stirs consciences is not the cause of righteousness. Nor does it justify.

(P2) The law stirs consciences.

(P3) Therefore, the law is not the cause of righteousness, nor does it justify.

But, I ask, how might the law work wrath? I answer: thus does it work wrath. . . . The law seeks pure affections and at the same time a spirit that is harmonious with our outward actions. [But] when we see that we are not able to satisfy the law, we begin to get angry not only with the law, but even with the Author of the law; intranquility of the conscience afterward follows wrath, as does doubt, desperation, and deceit. The law works wrath. The difficulty of the law is in its outcomes. It is an occasion for wrath, indignation, intranquility, and desperation.

Above, Paul demonstrated from another effect of the law, that the law does not justify, nor is it the cause for justification. Indeed he said, "The awareness of sin comes through the law."

Syllogism:

Whatever makes sin known, does not remove it. The law makes sin known. Therefore, the law does not remove sin.

Notes on Romans (1541).[7]

How the Law Works Wrath. Martin Bucer: "The law works wrath." It would be appropriate for us to consider at this point the reason why God wished to restore us to himself. By its very nature, the law shows us what is right and wrong. But we are born with such an innate disposition that not only do we run after the knowledge of evil and repudiate the knowledge of good, but it also happens that the more the law calls us away from evil and drives us toward good, that much more do we shrink back from good and insanely lose ourselves in evil. Hence it happens that every admonition of the law increases sin within us, stirs up God's wrath against us and entirely consumes and exhausts us, whereas the Spirit of Christ arouses in us the hope of pardon and kindles in us the true study of the law. But although this may be the case, the law nevertheless does have a saving function, and "blessed is he who . . . meditates on it day and night." God has determined to save sinners, not the righteous, and for this reason sent his Son into the world. It is,

---

[7]Sarcerius, *In Apostolam ad Romanos*, P2r. [†]Term of rhetoric for providing a cause or reason.

[6]CTS 38:170-71* (CO 49:78).

therefore, necessary that we recognize and feel appropriately about our sins, and the law serves this function. To be sure, all of God's teaching does this—even that which sets forth the promises of grace and announces the gospel. For it everywhere calls us to deny ourselves and depend entirely on the grace of God. There is nothing that we are less able to do than this. For we wish to be gods, to know for ourselves both good and evil, to provide for ourselves and to govern ourselves. It is therefore necessary that we always be reminded how lost we are by nature, and how we endlessly provoke the wrath of God against us. Despite knowing what his goodwill is, we endlessly strive in the opposite direction. When we thoroughly sense that this is so, and when we are altogether condemned and consigned to hell in our very own judgment, then with our whole heart let us flee to the mercy of God for refuge and adore the one good God and Christ our only Savior. Perhaps in this way we are intended to obtain a more perfect communion in which we will have humbled ourselves more completely.

Therefore, the "law works wrath," since by showing what is right it convicts us of our sins more heavily, but for this purpose: that by causing us to despair of ourselves it might drive us more forcefully toward Christ. It increases sin, but only so that in so doing it might more firmly teach us how much we ought to long for Christ the physician. It constitutes us transgressors, but only so that we might repair to him who inscribes his law upon our hearts once pardon of our transgressions has been obtained. It is therefore desirable that it should increase sin, render us liable to divine wrath and condemn us, for it was for this very purpose that God instituted the law. It does no harm to us in so doing; it only reveals the evil that is innate within us and urges us to seek the remedy.

It is, therefore, no valid argument against the laws of human beings that it is harmful for many to be made since the more laws there are, the more transgressions there must be as a result. If laws are unjust, they are not really laws and for that very

reason are to be rejected. But if they *are* just, then they are nothing other than explications of divine law. We have, deep within, a knowledge of this most salutary law, in such fashion that whenever our nature rears its head against it, even more transgressions are committed. The otherwise inescapable evil that lies hidden in our nature is thus brought forward so that it might be removed once we have demonstrated an awareness of it by our confession of it to Christ. Commentary on Romans (1536).[8]

The Law Points to Sin and Condemnation. Dirk Philips: The law is that commanded Word of God given through Moses on Mount Sinai, with such terrible voice, with such a storm, thunder, and lightning, that the children of Israel could not bear it, but they said to Moses, speak with the Lord, and do not let the Lord speak with us, so that we do not die. Yes, Moses himself was afraid and terrified, which indicated the severity of the law. For it points us to sin and condemnation, since it requires of all people perfect righteousness of the internal person, the entire nature created holy and of high understanding, full of the true knowledge of God, and in addition, a holy, pure heart that is zealous in the love of God. The Congregation of God.[9]

4:16-17 *The Father of All and the God Who Gives Life*

Only Faith Calms the Soul. Heinrich Bullinger: This is the conclusion or inference of this disputation: that Jews and Gentiles are both justified freely. In this context he was using the concept of inheritance to represent salvation or righteousness, with this intended meaning: *therefore* righteousness is conferred *through faith*. Now lest anything ambiguous still remain he further adds, *hina kata charin* (that it might be

---

[8]Bucer, *Metaphrases et Enarrationes*, 228; citing Ps 1:1-2.
[9]CRR 6:358*; citing Ex 19:16-20:1; Heb 12:18-21; Deut 6:4, Mt 22:37.

according to grace). In other words, "that it might be a gift freely given," for this is the idea present in the morphology of the word "grace." There is also another reason why he wished to assert that righteousness is given freely: so that the promise might be certain, which otherwise would be emptied if we merited righteousness by works. And add to that the fact that, if this were the case, righteousness could not possibly be conferred on Gentiles. For if it were owed to circumcision and the law, the Gentiles who lack these things would be shut out. But if they were excluded from the blessing, how would the promise of God be fulfilled that "in your seed all nations will be blessed"? Therefore, in order to make the promise certain to his seed universally, since it is comprised as much of Gentiles as it is of Jews, God wished to justify the world by faith and not by works.

And so you see that excellent reasons have been affixed to this conclusion. Others have referred this verse to the idea that only faith in God calms the soul, whereas works do not. For our conscience knows that all our works have something of vice in them, so it is always doubtful whether the works that we do are sufficient. Hence in human affairs the one and only Rock and ground of certainty is God himself—there is nothing certain within creatures. But God is grasped by faith alone, so it follows that the promise was to have its certainty by means of faith alone. So much for the conclusion, in which with remarkable skill all this has been enfolded into so few words: namely, that we are justified freely by faith, not by our works, or by circumcision, or by privileges of ethnicity, but that all who believe are children of God and of Abraham. COMMENTARY ON ROMANS (1582).[10]

IMITATE ABRAHAM'S FAITH. JOHN COLET: For what else was the meaning of Abraham's circumcision and cutting off the foreskin than a cutting off from the mind of all distrust, that the faith of a man or woman may appear naked and undis-

guised before God? This faith existed in Abraham, to his great praise and justification, before the rite of circumcision was adopted as a sign of the mind's being circumcised and believing in God without any distrust. And so great was it in Abraham, that if only God had promised anything, even though it seemed impossible to men and women, he trusted in it without doubting and looked for its coming to pass. For which cause he was both accounted righteous before God and marked out to be the heir of the world along with his seed, that is, his faithful seed and offspring. And the promise of this inheritance to the faithful may picture to us Abraham's great faith, and the expression, so to speak, of his mind. That we may judge of his posterity according to their imitation of his faith. For theirs assuredly is the inheritance and the world—even God himself, who is the true world.

He of his grace imparts himself to those who believe and trust in him, who have also been taken and drawn away by him from unbelief, that they may trust in him alone and believe that by no other means whatever can they be justified than by the divine grace. For the law, in which the Jews hoped, points out sin, defines boundaries, threatens transgressors; but it does not take away the fault nor draw men and women out of their straits, nor graciously cherish and sustain them, which very things divine grace does, with both strength and sweetness, so that men and women may be able to trust in God alone. And this grace touched and drew and justified Abraham and gave him a promise that others would be justified equally and in a similar manner. Such were to be counted as his sons and daughters; partly by virtue of the above-mentioned likeness to Abraham, and partly and chiefly because the parent and second ancestor of the faith, Jesus Christ, would draw his descent in the flesh from Abraham. He was the Son, and the promised seed. It was to Abraham's issue that the divine promises given to him had regard. EXPOSITION ON ROMANS (1497).[11]

---

[10]Bullinger, *Commentarii in Omnes*, 33-34; citing Gen 22:18; Jn 1:12.

[11]Colet, *Exposition of St. Paul's Epistle*, 10*.

Meditate on Strong Abraham. Katharina Schütz Zell: I beg you, loyal believing women, also to do this: take on you the manly, Abraham-like courage while you too are in distress and while you are abused with all kinds of insult and suffering. When you may meet with imprisonment in towers, chains, drowning, banishment, and such like things; when your husbands and you your-selves may be killed, meditate then on strong Abraham, father of us all; struggle after him as a good child should follow his father in a faith like the father's. Do you not think that Abraham also suffered when God told him to kill his only son?! When He told Abraham to do it himself!—to kill the son in whom also the blessing of human beings was promised. Yes, indeed, he was very grieved, for he was also flesh and blood like all of us; but he knew (as the Scripture says) that God could bring his son back to life. Letter to the Suffering Women of Kentzingen (1524).[12]

Faith Justifies the Thief and the Perse-cutor. Marie Dentière: There is still a general reason behind all of this, which is enough to close the mouths of all blasphemers against the truth. He makes known to his creatures his justice and mercy, to some by his condemnation, as to the Pharaoh, showing his great power through Moses; but the Pharaoh rebelled against God's commandments, even though he saw the great signs and miracles that Moses performed in his presence by God's power, because his heart was hardened. To others he shows his power for their consolation and salvation, without their having deserved it; his goodness and mercy alone give them the grace to recognize it and to have full, perfect faith in his son Jesus, who died for our sins and was resurrected for our justification. That faith alone justifies us, without the works of the law, making us pleasing to God by means of Jesus Christ. It also justifies the thief hanging on the cross, Paul persecuting the Christians on the road to Damascus, and Jacob in the womb of his mother, loved by God but hated by his brother Esau,

without any of them having done either good or evil. The justice and mercy of God is manifest in them. Epistle to Marguerite De Navarre.[13]

A Double Similarity. Martin Bucer: "According to God." Paul uses the term *katenanti*, and Chrysostom writes that it means the same as *homoiōs*, that is, similarly, or according to a similitude. Indeed he places this similarity in two points: just as God is not the Father of only some, but of all, so also is Abraham; and just as God is Father, not according to natural bloodline, but according to a kinship of faith, so it is the case with Abraham. Some read this as meaning "before" God. For *katenanti*, even *enantion*, that is, "in the presence of." Certainly "in the presence of God" Abraham has been made father of all of us. According to the flesh, and therefore in the eyes of men and women, he is the father of no one but the Jews. However, the first interpretation seems to agree better with what the apostle says next, according to which one can detect in Abraham a certain "similarity" with God. Further, it seems that he places this "similarity" with Abraham in the fact that God restores the dead to life, and by his word brings into existence those things that are not, and as if they were: "Thus Abraham, supported by hope against hope, embraced the promise, that although the body, his own as much as his wife's, was already half dead, nevertheless he would become the father not only of Isaac, who was born from him at that time, but of all nations, which were not yet in existence." For it seems that this whole thing is an explanation of that which he said first: "who is the father of us all," in this sense—the father, I say, of us all, which is like unto God, for just as God restores the dead to life and by his Word confers existence on those things which are not, so Abraham, by his own faith, called himself and his wife back to life as though from the dead, and the power of begetting which had already been lost due to age now being recovered, he obtained sons and daughters, who not only had no sacred kinship

---

[12]Zell, *Church Mother*, 51*; citing Gen 22:1-2; Heb 11:17-19.

[13]Dentière, *Epistle to Marguerite De Navarre*, 82-83*.

with him, but who didn't even yet exist, for whoever until the end of the world is taken into the lot of the sons of God, these he accepts as sons. That faith worked effectively in him, causing him to hope against hope. It is to this that he owes that he was made the father of many nations, so much so that his sons would surpass the number of grains of sand and the stars, according to that divine assertion, believing which, it is announced that he has been justified: "So shall your seed be." COMMENTARY ON ROMANS (1536).[14]

4:18 Hope Against Hope

THE DIFFERENCE BETWEEN ORDINARY AND CHRISTIAN HOPE. MARTIN LUTHER: In the first place, "hope" signifies a thing that is naturally hoped for, but this hope was not of this kind. In the second place, however, it also signifies something which is supernaturally hoped for. In both instances "hope" must be taken in the sense of a thing to be hoped for and not in the sense of the power of hoping. And this beautifully suggests the difference between the hope of people generally and the hope of Christians. For the hope of people in general is not contrary to hope but according to hope, that is, what can reasonably be expected to happen. For people do not hope where only that which is contrary to their hopes appears, but rather when that appears which is very similar to their hopes or that which has a definite potentiality to occur. Hence this faith is more a negative than a positive thing; that is, they presume that when certain things have begun, then that which was hoped for will come to pass. And then, finally, they hope that there will be no impediment to prevent what they have hoped for. Thus in regard to what is positively hoped for, this hope wants to be certain and to know, but in regard to the negative it is compelled to remain uncertain. By contrast, the hope of Christians is certain about the negative aspects. For it knows that the thing hoped for must come to pass and will not be hindered, as long as it

is hoped for. For no one can hinder God. LECTURES ON ROMANS (1516).[15]

FAITH MUST ASCEND ON HEAVENLY WINGS. JOHN CALVIN: If thus we read, the sense is that when there was no probable reason, yea, when all things were against him, he yet continued to believe. And doubtless there is nothing more injurious to faith than to fasten our minds to our eyes, that we may from what we see seek a reason for hope. We may also read "above hope," and perhaps more suitably, as though he said that by his faith he far surpassed all that he could conceive, for unless faith flies upward on celestial wings, so as to look down on all the perceptions of the flesh as on things far below, it will stick fast in the mud of the world. COMMENTARY ON ROMANS 4:18.[16]

HOPE AWAITS THE PROMISE. WOLFGANG MUSCULUS: Although the apostle will make himself clear, it is nevertheless worthwhile to explain these phrases. "To believe" is, per se, to have faith in the words of God. For the faith of Christians is not a foolish opinion conceived in the mind apart from the Word of God. Paul explains it in two ways. In the first way, some deed is proclaimed, such as when it was preached to us that Christ was crucified for our salvation. Thereupon, by faith we have already taken hold of the benefit that has been presented. In the second way, something is promised. We believe that this is not only going to come about, but also we hope—that is, we await with longing; we are rightly said to believe "in hope." For where hope is joined to faith, faith believes the Word of God, and hope awaits the promise. Thus, when Abraham had the word of promise regarding the multiplication of his seed, he first believed, so to speak, in God, who is unable to lie. Then, because he was brought by desire into that which was promised, hope was added to faith, and so the phrase, "Who in hope believed." COMMENTARY ON ROMANS (1555).[17]

---

[14]Bucer, *Metaphrases et Enarrationes*, 226; citing Gen 15.
[15]LW 25:283*.
[16]CTS 38:176* (CO 49:81).
[17]Musculus, *Commentarii Romanos*, 102.

HOPE LEADS TO THE LORD, WHO WORKS WONDERS. THOMAS MÜNTZER: People cannot know this teaching or know whether Christ is mendacious or truthful, unless their wills are conformed to the crucified one, unless they too have first endured the swells and surges of the waters, which for most of the time are cascading over the heads of the elect from all sides. After a struggle, however, they are rescued again, having cried out hoarsely and learned to hope against hope and to seek his will alone on the day of visitation that comes after prolonged waiting. Then their feet will be set on the rock and the Lord who works wonders will appear from afar; at long last authentic testimonies of God will be rendered. LETTER TO MARTIN LUTHER, JULY 9, 1523.[18]

THE KIND OF FAITH BEFITTING RIGHTEOUS-NESS. ERASMUS SARCERIUS: "Who against hope believed in hope." To this point we have heard the arguments by which the apostle has proved that righteousness is freely given through faith. Now let us next hear what kind of faith one must have and what the means of obtaining righteousness is. And because he said that the promise, or this righteousness, ought to be sure, he will now teach that the faith that is the means of obtaining the promise, or this righteousness, ought likewise to be certain.

An enthymeme,[†] arguing backwards from the effect to the cause:

(P2) The promise, or this righteousness, ought to be certain.

(C) Therefore faith by which we obtain the promise, or this righteousness [ought also to be certain].

There occasion, therefore, arises in the verses that follow to show from the certainty of faith that existed in Abraham, that faith in the One who justifies cannot coexist with doubt, but ought to be certain. The following verses also contain a definition of faith, which though it can be put in

various ways all amount to the same thing, which is outlined here:

1. Faith is first of all that trust that "against hope believed in hope."

2. Faith is also to not grow weak, not considering either this or that thing, nor these nor those circumstances, but trusting in the bare promise.

3. Faith is also to "not waver in unbelief" toward the promise, but to "be strengthened by faith and give glory to God" and to "be fully assured that what God promised he is able also to perform."

This is similar to the definition that is found in Hebrews 11: "faith is the *elenchos* of things hoped for," that is, an absolutely certain knowledge without any doubting. It is also a *hypostasis*, that is, the expectation or realization of the promises of God, and that which obtains the promises.

You also have here a clear statement of the nature of faith, which is to entrust oneself to the mere Word of God without any respect to the circumstances; it is to not enter into reasoning, with either reason itself or "flesh and blood"; it is to not weigh this or that, and to not waver in doubt, even if both reason and the common sense of nature argue otherwise.

This is also why Christ said to Peter in Matthew 16 when by faith he confessed Christ to be the Son of the living God: "Flesh and blood did not reveal this to you," as if to say, "Flesh and blood, being offended by my common and humble person, would not have believed that my common and humble person is the Son of the living God." So also if Abraham had entered into counsel with reason, flesh and blood, then he would have "considered his flesh to be dead (he being nearly a hundred years old) and Sarah's womb as dead," and would not have believed in the simple promise.

The subsequent verses also deal particularly with the object of faith, that which faith lays hold of unto righteousness, and that is: the promise.

It is, therefore, of the nature of faith to believe in the bare promise, even if reason, flesh, and blood, and all circumstances argue otherwise, as the facts

---

[18]Müntzer, *Works*, 57*; citing Ps 93:3; 69:3; Ps 40:2.

were arguing against the promise of a son being born to Abraham. NOTES ON ROMANS.[19]

4:19 Abraham Believed in Spite of Circumstances

FIRM FAITH OVERCOMES REASON'S OBJECTIONS. NIELS HEMMINGSEN: This is the second part of the description of faith. Just as Abraham shut off all objections from his reason and his flesh when the promise of offspring was made to him, so true faith shuts off every sense of the flesh when it perceives the promises of God. Indeed, first, reason told Abraham that it was impossible for him as a worn out old man to became a father. Then reason objected because of the barrenness of Sarah, on two counts. She was by nature barren, and she was too old to conceive or to carry in her womb. Abraham did not submit to rational arguments, but on the contrary, all the more became unconquerable. He stood fast persistently by faith in the promise. And moreover, what he says here in no way impairs this but makes it stronger. For it is by the familiar litote[†] for the Hebrews, who by contradicting what they deny, they strongly assert. Therefore, by this statement he demonstrates what is said above: "Against hope, in hope, he believed." And this passage teaches that faith must not be mere acquaintance and assent, but rather, firm faith that submits to no arguments of reason. COMMENTARY ON ROMANS (1562).[20]

OBSTACLES ABRAHAM'S FAITH OVERCAME. JOHANNES LONICER: There were many considerations that could have rendered his faith sluggish and without effect, but his noble soul did not grow faint in the face of any of these things. First there was the fact that he had no example to which he could look by which his mind could find a support—the promise of producing offspring was first given to him contrary to hope. Second, the fact of his old age being already far advanced and effectively dead could have made his soul to collapse and did nothing to encourage his faith. Third, there was the fact that his wife Sarah as a mother was equally as good as half dead, and barren and sterile in her old age and utterly incapable of either conceiving or of giving birth to children. EXEGESIS OF ROMANS (1537).[21]

FAITH IS A FIRM PERSUASION OF THE DIVINE PROMISE. MARTIN BUCER: In this section Paul provides an exposition of Abraham's example, along with an application to us as well as a description of our own faith. In his exposition he places the nature of faith before our eyes, and in so doing teaches us how those who by faith follow in Abraham's footsteps can be recognized. Faith is a firm persuasion concerning the divine promise, depending solely on that which God promised. Hence the apostle, wishing to declare how full and firm the faith of Abraham had been, shows the impossibility, on both the part of Abraham himself as well as that of Sarah his wife, of having a child at that very time when they had faith in God who was promising a child. For Abraham was one hundred years old, and Sarah ninety, and thus both of their bodies were utterly dead in terms of being able to bear a child. For when we see the reasons for something in the nature of things themselves, and in these see a natural facility for producing the things that God promised, we frequently do not believe in God so much as we do in our own cleverness and reasoning. Rightly, therefore, does the apostle proclaim Abraham's faith precisely in this, that in his case not only did no natural cause or faculty stand out, but it appeared in every respect to be an impossibility. In this it became apparent that he was clinging solely to God's promise with a pure and full persuasion.

---

[19]Sarcerius, In Apostolam ad Romanos (1541), P4r-P5r; citing Heb 11:1; Mt 16:17. [†]An enthymeme is a syllogism in which one of the premises is implied rather than stated.

[20]Hemmingsen, Commentarius in Epistolam, 162. [†]A litote is an understatement in which an affirmative is expressed by the negative of the contrary (as in "not a bad singer" or "not unhappy").

[21]Lonicer, Veteris Cuiuspiam Theologi, 31.

This is what the apostle wanted to express when he wrote that Abraham did not consider the deadness of his own body or that of his wife, that he did not doubt concerning the promise of God that he was strengthened in faith, that he gave glory to God, and that he received a firm persuasion that God was able to perform what he had promised, for the promise itself was showing him God's will. It is certain that since everything in him, considered apart from God, was cutting off any hope of having children, it was therefore necessary that with his whole heart he look to the promise of God alone, supported by an utterly unwavering faith. Paul therefore declared that when Abraham had faith in the promise concerning a son and a holy offspring, he was entrusting himself to God purely and without wavering. And thus it is in this passage more than any other that the Scriptures testify that this faith was imputed to him as righteousness. Indeed, our highest and only righteousness is to have faith in God who offers us his own worthiness, that is, our justification. COMMENTARY ON ROMANS (1536).[22]

FOCUSING ON THE FAITHFUL GOD. JUAN DE VALDÉS: Pious Christians, emulating Abraham's faith, when they hear that the gospel promises them justification, resurrection, and eternal life through Christ, do not set themselves to examine either their virtues or their vices, because either of them would lead them to doubt. Rather, they occupy themselves with the consideration that God who promises it to them is mighty to fulfill it, and that God is true in fulfilling to men and women what he promises them. COMMENTARY ON ROMANS (1556).[23]

4:20 Abraham's Faith Gave God Glory

GOD FULFILLS HIS PROMISES. JOHANNES BUGENHAGEN: To believe every word of God is to give glory to God, even when it may be contrary to every natural sense. For "nothing is impossible with God," as the angel says to Mary in Luke. Therefore, God expects this glory, and nothing else, from us. This is why we should not despair in any trials or straights, nor in any spiritual temptations, nor in sins. Let it be that even when everything appears grave and terrible, that we give glory to God, who is truthful, for he has promised forgiveness of sins. Do not—I ask you, O man or woman—believe your sins to be greater than the divine promises, or in some other way accuse God of a lie and despair like Judas, so that you become a fornicator, a murderer, and so on. When your sin is revealed to you, watch out that you do not, in desperation, sin worse. God has not imputed your sin to you. Just believe that he is truthful. Meanwhile, Satan does not want you to believe. He proposes that sins are much greater than the promises of God. Here you must stand strong and come together against this enemy. See to it that you grind his stronghold to dust. It will then come about, if against all hope, in spite of your senses, you should believe in God, he will rescue you from your own hellish season, and he will not permit you to be taken under the waves, which are greater than you. Thus in every outward requirement, even if you should experience infertility,[†] he would take care of you. God is omnipotent. Whatever he promises through his own Word, he supplies, as long as we have cried out from the heart, "Forgive us our sins." INTERPRETATION OF ROMANS (1531).[24]

BELIEVING GOD'S PROMISE. MARTIN BUCER: "But he did not waver concerning the promise of God." Let us here take note that "faith" means to lay hold of the words of God in the simplest manner possible without any questioning and without passing judgment on it. This is the highest honor, and equally so the one most owed, that we are obliged to render to God. God knows all things, loves us more than we do ourselves, and can do all things. It is, therefore, enough for us if he should

[22]Bucer, *Metaphrases et Enarrationes*, 229.
[23]Valdés, *Commentary upon St. Paul's Epistle*, 58-59*.

[24]Bugenhagen, *In D. Pauli ad Romanos*, 44v-45r; Lk 1:37. †Lit. "scarcity of the womb."

say something; it is enough that it is promised. Whatever kind of promise it may be, however difficult it may be for you, remember it is God who spoke and brought all things into existence.

We ought, however, to investigate just as religiously *what* God has said. If it is not certain that he said something, there is nothing else for faith to hang on to. In this case the whole mind and all our powers must be strained toward that to which he summons us. But even in this endeavor Satan employs his devices and with even the very least of the things that God has said he displaces God's sayings with his own lies. There are an endless number of things that have to be expressed not only by a limited number of words but by only the barest few. There are as a result many ambiguous things in the Scriptures. It is everywhere necessary to interpret one thing in light of another. Satan's abuse is such that he often persuades us that something diametrically opposed to God's Word is the very Word of God itself, fetched as it is, though in a depraved manner, from the sacred text. For this reason God must be always diligently entreated to guard a simplicity within us and to strengthen the soul that seriously seeks his will. Thus all things will be clear, and he will straightway illuminate the mind so that it inclines toward his intended meaning. Where this is established, there can be no further hesitation, no further inquiry; there is nothing to do but to repeat, "God said so. God has spoken. Let all things be silenced, fall down, and submit." This is the true glory that we owe to God. He knows all things, can do all things, and does all things, and he does them for better reasons than any power of creatures could do or even attempt doing. COMMENTARY ON ROMANS (1536).[25]

BOARDING THE BOAT TAKES FAITH. JOHN OWEN: When someone comes close to committing to the promise, indeed, to making a life on it, he is very ready to question and inquire whether it is possible that its word will ever be made good to him. He that sees a little boat swimming at sea observes no great difficulty in it, looks on it without any solicitousness of mind at all, beholds how it tosses up and down without any fears of its sinking. But now, let this person commit his own life to sea in that boat—what inquiries will he make! What a search into the vessel! Is it possible, he says, that this little thing could safeguard my life in the ocean? It is so with us, in our view of God's promises. While we consider them at large, as they lie in the Word, alas! They are all true—all yea and amen—shall all be accomplished. But when we go to venture our souls on a promise, in an ocean of wrath and temptations, then we think every blast will overturn it; it will not bear us above all these waves. Is it possible we could swim safely on the plank of a pinnace[†] in the middle of the ocean? STEADFASTNESS OF THE PROMISES (c. 1649).[26]

FOUR CONDITIONS AND REQUIREMENTS OF FAITH. HEINRICH BULLINGER: It is wonderful to find agreement in opposites, and even more wonderful to treat of the advantages of things. For we learn here what the true conditions and requirements of faith are:

First, faith does not hesitate, pass judgment on, or contend, but cleaves to the One making a promise with a firm and simple heart. Earlier he had said, "he did not consider," and here he says, "he did not hesitate." . . . There is a most beautiful description of a hesitating soul found in Virgil, who speaks of Aeneas wavering in perplexity under weighty concerns:

> He divides his mind swiftly now in one
>   direction, now in another;
> He seizes upon different lines of thought; he
>   turns over absolutely every idea.
> He is like quivering light from water in a bronze
>   basin.
> When reflected by the sun or by the glowing
>   image of the moon,
> It flickers about all over the place, then bends
>   upward and strikes the paneled ceiling.[†]

---

[25]Bucer, *Metaphrases et Enarrationes*, 132-33.

[26]Owen, *Works*, 8:225*. [†]A ship's small boat.

Something similar is said by James in chapter 1: "The man who doubts is like the sea . . . let him not suppose that he will receive anything."

Second, because faith is steadfast, it continually expands and grows incrementally a bit stronger every day. This strength of faith corresponds to that which we heard above, "not being weakened in faith."

Third, what is proper to faith is that which gives glory to God; believes him to be true, living, and omnipotent; and calls on, adores, and serves him and nobody else, which is the singular glory of God.

Fourth, faith is a sure thing and not to be doubted of. COMMENTARY ON ROMANS (1533).[27]

WHY ONE MIGHT DISTRUST A PROMISE. JOHN OWEN: Now, the fact that Abraham did not have any reason to waver from the promise will be clear if we consider what reasons could have arisen. All the stability of a promise depends on the qualifications of the promise-maker in relation to the ends and purposes of the promise. If someone makes me a promise to do such and such thing for me, and I question whether it will ever be so, it must be from a doubt about one of these things in relation to the one who made the promise: (1) their truthfulness, (2) their ability to make good their word, especially if the thing itself is difficult, (3) their sincerity of intent in relation to what they say to me, (4) their constancy of memory to take the opportunity to do the intended thing, (5) their stability to be still of the same mind over time.

Now, if the person whose promises we speak of does not lack any of these, then there is certainly no ground for our wavering. It is only from our own unbelief. STEADFASTNESS OF THE PROMISES (c. 1649).[28]

OUR BEST GIFT TO GOD. PETER MARTYR VERMIGLI: "Giving glory to God." Here is set forth the goal to which faith looks, namely, that the glory of God would be manifest and would increase, which is set forth so that we might entertain worthy thoughts of God. Abraham is said to have been nearly one hundred years old, as the story in Genesis 27 has him being ninety-nine years of age when this promise was made to him. Nor did he have for himself a similar example by looking to which he could be strengthened in his faith, for he was the very first that we read of in the Scriptures to whom the power of having children was restored. Nor is it any wonder that the glory of God is promoted by a work of faith, since therein by his grace we deny the better of our efforts. For this faith is the mindset and faculty of reason by which we either assent or dissent to things proposed to us. Hence it is evident that there is nothing more excellent that we can offer to God. COMMENTARY ON ROMANS (1560).[29]

4:21 *Certain of God's Promise*

CERTAINTY IN GOD'S WORD. WOLFGANG MUSCULUS: Faith makes the soul strong. "He was made strong," he says, "by faith." And, "did not waver toward God's promise." And again, the promise was received with "a firm persuasion." These things show us the character of faith, which makes the believing soul to be solid, firm, sure, and strong in arduous and doubtful situations and in things that are impossible according to human judgment. Faith is therefore the furthest thing from some kind of rash and uncertain opinion; it is rather a firm and indubitable certainty. This is also how it is defined in Hebrews 11: "Faith is the *hypostasis* (that is, the firm substance) of things hoped for, the *elenchos* (that is, the proof, discovery, and evidence) of things not seen." And as Chrysostom comments, this certainty that faith furnishes is far more solid than that which rational judgments can provide. For whatever the judgment of reason concludes, it can be called into doubt by other reasons and rendered null. But faith fortifies itself contrary to all reasons, as if moved by its own certainty of the truth and of God's power, which is

[27]Bullinger, *In Sanctissimam Pauli*, 70v-71r; citing Jas 1:6-7. †Virgil, *Aeneid* 8.20-25.
[28]Owen, *Works*, 8:221*.

[29]Vermigli, *In Epistolam S. Pauli*, 287; citing Gen 27.

far more firm and solid than the whole course of nature. Indeed, the Creator is so reliable in what he says that Christ says, "Heaven and earth will pass away, but my words will not pass away." Those who trust in changeable things and in their rational judgment are not capable of being certain of the things in which they hope. But those who believe the Word of God are made absolutely sure of all things and are freed from all wavering of the mind by the very certainty and truthfulness of the Word of God. COMMENTARY ON ROMANS (1555).[30]

EXALTING THE POWER OF GOD. JOHN CALVIN: As all people acknowledge God's power, Paul seems to say nothing very extraordinary of the faith of Abraham, but experience proves that nothing is more uncommon, or more difficult, than to ascribe to God's power the honor it deserves. There is indeed no obstacle, however small and insignificant, by which the flesh imagines the hand of God restrained from working. Hence it is that in the slightest trials, the promises of God slide away from us. When there is no contest, it is true, no one, as I have said, denies that God can do all things, but as soon as anything comes in the way to impede the course of God's promise, we cast down God's power from its eminence. Hence, that it may obtain from us its right and honor, when a contest comes, we ought to determine thus, that it is no less sufficient to overcome the obstacles of the world than the strong rays of the sun are to dissipate the mists. We are indeed wont ever to excuse ourselves, that we derogate nothing from God's power, whenever we hesitate respecting his promises, and we commonly say, "The thought that God promises more in his Word than he can perform (which would be a falsehood and blasphemy against him), is by no means the cause of our hesitation, but that it is the defect which we feel in ourselves." But we do not sufficiently exalt the power of God unless we think it to be greater than our weakness. Faith then ought not to regard

our weakness, our misery, and defects, but to fix wholly its attention on the power of God alone, for if it depends on our righteousness or worthiness, it can never ascend to the consideration of God's power. And it is a proof of the unbelief, of which he had before spoken, when we mete the Lord's power with our own measure. For faith does not think that God can do all things while it leaves him sitting still, but when, on the contrary, it regards his power in continual exercise, and applies it, especially to the accomplishment of his Word, for the hand of God is ever ready to execute whatever he has declared by his mouth. COMMENTARY ON ROMANS 4:21.[31]

A SHIP IN FULL SAIL BREAKING THROUGH THE STORMS. JOHN OWEN: He was "fully persuaded." . . . This is the third thing that is observed in the manner of his believing. He fully, quietly, resolvedly cast himself on this, that "he who had promised was able to perform it." As a ship at sea (for so the word imports), looking about, and seeing storms and winds arising, sets up all her sails, and with all speed makes to the harbor. Abraham, seeing the storms of doubts and temptations likely to rise against the promise made to him, with full sail breaks through all, to lie down quietly in God's all-sufficiency. THE STEADFASTNESS OF THE PROMISES (1649).[32]

4:22 Faith Counted as Righteousness

DEFINITIONS OF FAITH. NIELS HEMMINGSEN: Paul has explained of what sort Abraham's faith was. Now he adds what that faith profited him, and he reports that righteousness was imputed to Abraham. That is, that Abraham laid hold of the righteousness of Christ by faith, which having it been imputed to him, he was made righteous and acceptable to God. So far, the apostle has put forward—through the illustrious example of Abraham—the true character of faith. Now in this

---

[30]Musculus, *In Epistolam Apostoli Pauli*, 105-6; citing Heb 11:1; Mt 24:35; Mk 13:21; Lk 21:33.

[31]CTS 38:180-81* (CO 84-85).
[32]Owen, *Works*, 8:214*.

passage, putting together a complete definition of faith, we may build it in this way: Faith is the awareness of and constant trust in the divine promises, excluding the senses of the flesh, and fighting the sophistry of reason with the Word of divine promise, as well as submitting every hesitation to the Word of divine promise. Faith's constancy conquers every unbelief, which truly assigns glory to God. The fullest faith awaits the promises of God.

This is the reason for justifying faith, which can be briefly summarized: Faith is the knowledge, assent, desire, and certain trust in the promises of salvation on account of Christ. Here I add the memorable saying of Bernard concerning faith; he says, "Faith surpasses the limits of reason, the skill of natural humanity, and the boundaries of experience." COMMENTARY ON ROMANS (1562).[33]

IT WAS IMPUTED. MARTIN BUCER: It does indeed seem to most expositors that the force of Paul's argumentation lies mainly in the words "it was imputed," to which expression the apostle had earlier subjoined the testimony of Psalm 32, "to whom he does not impute sin." But if one should examine each word more closely, I judge that he would fully acknowledge that the apostle is by no means building his argument on the basis of the word "to impute" but rather on the basis of what Scripture says that God imputed, namely, since in this chapter we read that to the one who believes, "*God* imputes righteousness" (and, what is also in Psalm 32) "apart from works," that is, graciously. I have no doubt that the proof that the apostle is seeking to establish in this passage is affirming the same thing that we deduced earlier. The Scriptures testify that God imputed Abraham's righteousness to him as righteousness. That is, the Scriptures assert that because he had conformed his faith to God's promise, he possessed something so pleasing to God and regarded as such an extraordinary obedience of righteousness, that it does not speak with such high regard of any of his other esteemed

deeds. Abraham never did anything so praiseworthy that it was worth as much to God as his faith was. But this was a faith in God's gracious promise. Therefore Abraham attained to being acceptable to God first and foremost because grace was given to him to embrace his voluntary and gracious promise. Thus, by laying hold by faith of the benevolent promise of God—and not at all by any of his works—he was justified. It is necessary that others also be justified in this way. What's more, he was justified before God immediately, as soon as he had first believed him, even if the Scriptures declared his justification only later when it set forth his more distinguished example of faith.

When Psalm [32] declares that they are blessed whose iniquities God forgives, and whose sins God covers and does not impute, it clearly teaches the very same thing: that righteousness is imputed to nobody on account of their works or merits, but only by the gracious remission of sins. When he was about to invoke this passage the apostle did not say merely, "David pronounces blessing on the man to whom God imputes righteousness," but "to whom he imputes righteousness *apart from works*." Now, the word *logizesthai*, "to impute," in the apostle's mind is common to both gracious imputation and owed imputation, so immediately after invoking the utterance concerning Abraham's imputed righteousness he adds, "to the one who works (i.e., so as to merit something) wages are imputed according to debt." Even God imputes to his people their good works unto wages, as in the oracle we cited earlier concerning Phinehas. But above all, what he imputes to them and regards as righteousness is when they set their faith in him when he promises remission of sins and gracious beneficence in every area of life. Accordingly, it is overwhelmingly proved that we obtain salvation and righteousness before God not by any of our works, but only by the gracious goodness of God. This is clearly what the apostle is especially arguing in this disputation. COMMENTARY ON ROMANS (1536).[34]

---

[33]Hemmingsen, *Commentarius in Epistolam*, 164-65.

[34]Bucer, *Metaphrases et Enarrationes*, 230-31; citing Rom 4:8; Ps 32:2; Rom 4:6; 4:4.

BEATING BACK THE TWADDLE. PHILIPP MELANCHTHON: I have spoken here to explain the nature of faith, because its object is described first. The proper object of faith is the Word, which fights with the outward appearance, as Abraham is promised the Seed and posterity whom God wants to bless. Meanwhile, his wife is sterile and he himself was exhausted . . .

I have spoken of the object; now I shall speak about the formal side of faith. And this subject shows clearly that what Paul calls faith is trust which assents to the promise of the gospel and fights against doubt. Faith does not mean knowledge of the law, or merely a knowledge of history. It signifies assent to the promise, not doubt that God will carry out his promise.

This subject must also be observed in order that it may be opposed to those who deny that faith is confidence that fights against doubt. Four descriptions are placed here expressly. Mistrust did not harbor doubt concerning the promise; it was certain. Likewise, it gave glory to God. Thus Paul above puts together faith and the promise, and shows that they are interconnected like correlatives. It is certain that with Paul faith signifies trust which assents to the promise of the gospel, and which accepts the promised forgiveness of sins and reconciliation. There is no doubt that Paul is speaking about a faith which accomplishes something in the midst of terrors of conscience and comforts consciences, as he says below: "Having been justified by faith, we have peace." Furthermore, this comfort is not brought about by knowledge of the law, or by the knowledge of only history, but by trust in the promise that fights against doubt.

All things are full of darkness and fog in the Christian doctrine where this proper meaning of the word *faith* has been lost. These passages in Paul should be carefully observed in order that one may be able to judge and establish for certain what faith really signifies, and to beat back the twaddle of those who deny that faith is confidence which fights against doubt, but imagine that it is only a knowledge of history. COMMENTARY ON ROMANS (1540).[35]

FAITH IS INSTRUMENTAL, BUT NOT MERITORIOUS. ANDREW WILLET: Faith does not justify by the merit or act, but only instrumentally, as it applies and apprehends the righteousness of Christ . . . Abraham was not justified because he in believing gave glory to God. That indeed was an act and fruit of his faith, but it was by his faith only that he was justified. As the apostle says afterward in verse 24, "It shall be likewise imputed to us for righteousness, which believe." The apostle says, "To him that does not work but believes, faith is counted for righteousness." Therefore it will follow that where faith is counted or imputed for righteousness, there is no work. Faith then justifies not as a work by the act of believing, for then faith would not justify without works, which is the scope of all the apostle's discourse "that by faith righteousness is imputed without works." Faith then does not justify actively, as if a work, but passively, as it apprehends the righteousness of Christ. If faith is the gift of God, as Bellarmine confesses, then it cannot merit, for he that merits must merit of his own. Where there is grace and favor, as in the free bestowing of gifts, there is no merit. A SIX-FOLD COMMENTARY ON THE EPISTLE TO THE ROMANS.[36]

IMPUTATION AND THE PEPPERCORN RENT. RICHARD BAXTER: In this sense also it is so far from being an error to affirm that faith itself is our righteousness, that it is a truth necessary for every Christian to know. That is, faith is our evangelical righteousness (in the sense beforehand explained), just as Christ is our legal righteousness.

Answer. It is plainly this: men and women become unrighteous by breaking the law of righteousness that was given to them; Christ fully satisfies for this transgression and buys the

---

[35]Melanchthon, *Commentary on Romans*, 117-18*; citing Rom 5:1.
[36]Willet, *Hexapla*, 230*; citing Rom 4:6, 4.

prisoners back into his own hands, and makes a new covenant with them so that whoever will accept him and believe in him who has thus made satisfaction, it will be as effective for their justification as if they had fulfilled the law of works themselves. A tenant forfeits his lease to his landlord by not paying his rent; he runs deep in debt to him and is unable to pay him any more rent for the future, whereupon he is put out of his house and cast into prison until he pays the debt. His landlord's son pays it for him, takes him out of prison, and puts him in his house again as his tenant, having purchased the house and all for himself. He makes him a new lease in this tenor, that paying just a peppercorn yearly to him, he shall be acquitted both from his debt and from all other rent for the future that was to be paid according to his old lease. Yet he does not cancel the old lease, but instead keeps it in his hands to put in a suit against the tenant if he should be so foolish as to deny the payment of the peppercorn. In this case, the payment of the grain of pepper is imputed to the tenant as if he had paid the rent of the old lease. Yet this imputation does not extol the peppercorn, nor vilify the benefit of his benefactor who redeemed him. Nor can it be said that the purchase only served to advance the value and efficacy of the grain of pepper. But thus, a personal rent must be paid for as an attestation of his homage; he was never deemed to be independent of his own landlord and maker. He cannot pay the old rent; his new landlord's clemency is such that he has resolved that this grain shall serve the turn.

Do I need to apply this in the present case, or can't every one apply it? In a similar way, our evangelical righteousness or faith is imputed to us for a real righteousness, as perfect obedience. Two things are taken into account with this debt of righteousness: the value, and the personal performance or interest. The value of Christ's satisfaction is imputed to us instead of the value of a perfect obedience of our own performing; and the value of our faith is not so imputed. But because there must be some personal performance of homage, therefore the personal performance of faith shall be

imputed to us for a sufficient personal payment, as if we had paid the full rent, because Christ, in whom we believe, has paid it, and he will take this for satisfactory homage. So faith is imputed in relation to personal performance, rather than to value. APHORISMS OF JUSTIFICATION.[37]

4:23 Not Just for Abraham's Sake

GOD IS THE SAME TODAY. HULDRYCH ZWINGLI: "Not for his sake alone." Lest someone might think that this was written solely for Abraham's benefit, Paul shows that it pertains to all believers, who are the children of Abraham. God is always the same, nor does he ever act contrary to his nature. Therefore, if we have placed our hope in him, as Abraham did, he will be to us what he was to Abraham of old: if he was then forgiving and merciful, he still is today. If he was then just, he is still just today. NOTES ON ROMANS (1539).[38]

WRITTEN FOR OUR SAKE AS WELL. MARTIN BUCER: Paul applies the example of Abraham to us when he says that this "was not written for his sake alone" (for Scripture does recount this as an event to be celebrated for his sake also), "but for our sakes also." For "all things ... were written for our instruction." He then goes on to instruct us that what can be learned from this passage was also written for our sakes, that if we will believe in God's promise that he offers to us just as Abraham believed in the promise that was made to him, then our faith "would be imputed to us" for righteousness "also."

Last, he tells us that the promise that was made to us through the gospel is that God has "delivered up to death" his own Son, the Lord Jesus, "on account of our sins" that needed atoning, and then recalled him back "from the dead ... on account of our righteousness,"[†] that is, the righteousness that is to be conveyed to us. Accordingly, "to believe in him who raised the Lord Jesus from the dead" is to

---

[37]Baxter, Aphorismes, 82-84*.
[38]Zwingli, In Evangelicam Historiam, 418.

hold with a firm persuasion the truth that God raised his Son from the dead for this purpose, that just as he made satisfaction for our sins by his death, so also by now reigning in life immortal, he gives us his own righteousness, thus making us conformed to his own image. This is what it means to have faith in the gospel. COMMENTARY ON ROMANS (1536).[39]

THE RULE OF JUSTIFICATION IS FAITH IN GOD.

LAURENCE TOMSON (OR PIERRE L'OISELEUR): The rule of justification is always one, both in Abraham, and in all the faithful. That is to say, faith in God, who after Christ our mediator made full satisfaction for our sins, raised him from the dead, that we also being justified might be saved in him. THE GENEVA BIBLE (1595).[40]

4:24 For Those Who Believe in the One Who Raised Jesus

IF CHRIST HAD REMAINED IN DEATH. ERASMUS SARCERIUS: He adds of Christ the Mediator that it is of necessity because Christ, by his resurrection and his victory, merited and brought back a free righteousness for us, and also because Christ has been cast down, he is the person that having faith in obtains free righteousness. Therefore, because we have been justified freely through grace, Christ himself produces in us his victory against the devil, sin, death, and so on. For if Christ had remained in death, and we had remained in sin, we would never have been made partakers of the free righteousness. NOTES ON ROMANS (1541).[41]

THE BENEFITS OF CHRIST'S WORK. NIELS

HEMMINGSEN: Here Paul makes the transfer from hypothesis to thesis, adapting the pattern of Abraham to believers. The apostle develops these adaptations from the object of faith, and at the same time as that, he explains the means of our righteousness, but briefly, for he will pursue this broadly in the fifth chapter. Here he observes the catholic teaching concerning the benefits of Christ that come from his death. That is to say, Christ expiated our sin by his complete obedience on the cross, for he is the sacrifice—*lytron* and *sōphron* (ransom and salvation)—who freed and redeemed men and women from the law of sin and gave eternal salvation. Truly, he obtained our righteousness by his resurrection. For unless the Lord had been raised, his sacrifice would not have been satisfactory for redeeming us from the law of sin. For at that time he was not the conqueror of death, but he was overcome by death. In this place we observe a synecdoche, common in the Scriptures, by which the part frequently is ascribed to the whole. Here it is the attribution of the resurrection of Christ as our justification. In the fifth chapter the synecdoche Paul uses is "the blood of Christ," referring to Christ's sacrifice. From this, we teach that the benefits of salvation come not only by the obedience of Christ as a whole but also by the bestowal of its individual parts. So then it is rightly said: Christ was born, circumcised, presented at the temple, suffered, and raised from the dead on account of our sins. And on the other hand, it is possible that the same effects are to be assigned to the various actions of Christ, so that Christ redeemed us by his birth. Thus also concerning the others. Therefore our entire salvation hangs not from our, but from Christ's merits, of which we are truly partakers when we put on Christ by faith. For then he becomes to us both a shelter by which he covers our sin, and a righteousness by which we are pleasing to God, being loved in the beloved. COMMENTARY ON ROMANS (1562).[42]

THE PRINCE OF LIFE AND RIGHTEOUSNESS.

MARTIN BUCER: To "believe him who raised the Lord Jesus" is nothing else than to have faith in the gospel in which it is proclaimed to us that God the Father raised up to heavenly and blessed life the

---

[39]Bucer, *Metaphrases et Enarrationes*, 229; citing Rom 15:4.
 †Contrary to both the Greek and the Vulgate versions, Bucer uses "righteousness" rather than "justification" here.
[40]Tomson, *The Bible*, 63r*.
[41]Sarcerius, *In Apostolam ad Romanos*, Q1r.

[42]Hemmingsen, *Commentarius in Epistolam*, 165-66.

Lord Jesus, the Prince of life and of righteousness, out of a death whereby he had atoned for our sins. Due to the sin of our first parents, we are all born by nature so prone to every evil and opposed to the righteous will of God, that it is necessary for us to perish. But it pleased God that the eternal Word, his only-begotten Son, should put on our flesh, and in this new Man by his death should wash away this perversity and perdition that belonged to us and to open for us the way back to life and to God. It was therefore necessary in the course of time for this Man to be born and by his death to offer the price by which, both afterward and previously, not only the remission of sins but also a full communion with the divine life is made sure to all the elect. So that it might be manifest to the whole earth that our Lord conquered our death by his own, and by his resurrection laid up heavenly life for those who believe in him, he willed that the gospel of this redemption of ours be "preached to every creature" and that his "Spirit be poured out on all flesh," and further that this very thing be declared: that "he died because of our sins and rose again because of our righteousness" and that it might instruct us that, now reigning "at the right hand of the Father," Christ "saves us from all wrath." The "Spirit of the Father who raised Jesus from the dead" is also the One who "sets us free from sin" and "the wages of sin, death" and from all things contrary to us. The apostle will deal explicitly with each of these matters in the following two chapters and in chapter 8, where there will be occasion for learning things that pertain further to this subject. COMMENTARY ON ROMANS (1536).[43]

4:25 Jesus Died and Rose for Our Justification

LETTING GO OF A MONK'S COWL. MARTIN LUTHER: For if I had accepted as true and certain what St. Paul says in Romans 4:25 that Christ died for our sins and was raised again for our justifica-tion in order that we might become his brothers and sisters, then I would thereby have learned that my own works and my monk's hood could not obtain this for me. Otherwise what need would there have been for Christ to go and take my sins and the wrath of God on himself in his cross and death, and by his resurrection to place me into the inheritance of the forgiveness of sins, of eternal salvation and glory?

But now, inasmuch as they cling to their monkery, and seek God's grace by their own merits, desiring thereby to get rid of and atone for their sins, they bear witness against themselves that they do not believe what they say with their lips. I believe in Jesus Christ who died for me and rose again; but they believe, on the contrary, in the cowl and cord of the barefooted monks, in St. Ann, St. Anthony, and in the devil (pardon me), in his rump. Because it is impossible for one who knows Christ in this brotherhood to be engaged in such follies as are taught and observed not only without faith and contrary to it, but also contrary to the command-ments, and which are real diabolical sins, the sins of all sins. SERMONS.[44]

OUR JUSTIFICATION DUE ENTIRELY TO CHRIST'S MERITS. FRIEDRICH BALDUIN: Q: When our Paul distinctly writes that Christ was handed over for our sins and raised on account of our justification in verse 25, does this not support the Catholics who think that our justification does not consist solely in the remission of sins but that its principal part is the renovation of life, the great exemplar of which is seen in the resurrec-tion of Christ?

R: I answer . . . when Paul treats the resurrec-tion as a kind of justification, this is by the customary synecdoche found in Scripture in which it attributes our justification partly to the obedience of Christ, as in Romans 5, and partly to his death and passion, as in Romans 4, and partly to his resurrection, as in this passage and also in Philippians 3, but in each case it is always

---

[43]Bucer, *Metaphrases et Enarrationes*, 232; citing Mk 16:15; Acts 2:17; Rom 8:34; 5:9; 8:11; 6:22-23.

[44]Luther, *Sermons*, 2:263*.

understood to owe itself entirely to his merits. APOSTOLIC CATECHISM (1620).[45]

CHRIST, THE PUBLIC PERSON. RICHARD SIBBES: All this was for our good. What Christ did was not for himself, but for us. And in his birth, and life, and death, and resurrection, we must consider him as a public person,[†] and so go along with all that he did as a public person. Whatsoever may be terrible to us, we must look on it first in Christ. If we look on the corruption and defilement in our nature, look on the pure nature of Christ. His nature was sanctified in his birth, and he is a public person: therefore this is for me; and though I am defiled in my own nature, and carry the remainders of corruption about me, yet the Spirit of life in Christ sanctified his nature, and there is more sanctity in him than there can be sin in me. When we look on our sins, let us not so much look on them in our consciences, as in our surety, Christ. When we look on death, look not upon it in ourselves, in its own visage, but as it is in Christ, undergone and conquered: for the power of the Spirit of life in Christ overcame death, in himself first, and for us, and will overcome in us in time. When the wrath of God is on our consciences, do not look on it as it is in ourselves, but as undergone by Christ, and as Christ, by the Spirit of life now in him, is raised up, not from death alone, but from all terrors. "My God, my God, why have you forsaken me?" See Christ, by the Spirit of life, quickened from all, not just from natural death, but from all the enemies you need to fear. From the law: it is nailed to his cross; he now triumphs over it. And from sin: he was a sacrifice for it. And from the wrath of God: he has satisfied it, or else he would not have come out of his grave. So whatever is terrifying, look on it in Christ first, and see a full discharge from all that might frighten your conscience or trouble your peace in any way. See him in his death, dying for every one that will believe. Consider him in his resurrection as a public person, not rising for himself alone, but for

all of us. Therefore in 1 Peter 1:8, there is an excellent verse, "Blessed be God, the Father of our Lord Jesus Christ, who has begotten us again to a lively hope by the resurrection of Jesus Christ, to an inheritance immortal, undefiled." And then go along with him to his ascension, and see ourselves "sitting with him in heavenly places," as St. Paul says in Ephesians 2:6. O, this is a sweet meditation on Christ! To see ourselves in him, in all the passages of his birth, and life, and death, and resurrection, and ascension to glory in heaven. For all that he did was as a public person, as the second Adam. But now, before the Spirit of life in Christ comes to free me, I and Christ must be one. There must be a union between me and Christ. I must be a member of Christ mystical. For as Christ brought to life his own body, every joint when it was dead, because it was his body, so he brings to life his mystical body, every member of it. But I must be a member first; I must not be severed from Christ. Christ by his death obtained all good, and by his resurrection he declared it; but it must be applied to me. Now this Spirit of life that is in Christ, which brought him back to life and raised him up, and all for my good, must apply this to me. SERMON ON THE SPIRITUAL JUBILEE.[46]

PARALLELS OF BAPTISM TO CHRIST'S RESURRECTION. DIRK PHILIPS: With these words the apostle gives us to understand what Christian baptism means to the believer, namely, the dying of the flesh or putting to death the old Adam, the burial of sins, the putting off of the sinful body, and a resurrection to a new life. For this reason and with this instruction, since Christ has died, was buried on behalf of our sins, and was raised from the dead for our justification, we through faith are first incorporated into him and then become partakers of his death, his righteousness, his holiness, yes, of all that is his. To this his fellowship we have been called by God out of grace and become established in and through

---

[45]Balduin, *Catechesis Apostolica*, 321-23; citing Rom 5; Phil 3.

[46]Sibbes, *Complete Works*, 5:240*. [†]As one representing a community.

baptism. Therefore, we must also for his sake die to sin, bury it, and live in righteousness in the Spirit so that we may be his true members. THE BAPTISM OF OUR LORD JESUS CHRIST.[47]

EMBRACING THE MEDIATOR. PHILIPP MELANCHTHON: Finally, it is not enough just to speak about faith or trust in the promise. It is necessary to embrace the Mediator. Paul says that it is imputed to those who believe in him who raised from the dead Jesus, who was delivered for our offenses and raised again for our justification. Here again you have an argument that faith does not signify knowledge of the law or only of history, but signifies trust which lays hold of the imputation made on account of Christ, the Mediator, who suffered and now reigns. COMMENTARY ON ROMANS (1540).[48]

ABRAHAM'S FAITH AS MODEL FOR OUR OWN. HEINRICH BULLINGER: The Holy Spirit in the Scriptures did not wish merely to demonstrate how Abraham alone was justified, but rather how every race of mortal men and women can be justified. For Abraham is the father and model of all believers. What do those who contend with Paul in speaking of their works, who are under the law and not under grace, have to say to this? For we hear that both the old way of being justified and that of our own is one and the same way. Therefore, even if Abraham was faithful and already under grace, it was still by none of his merits but only by faith that he was justified. Therefore, it must be that all Christians are justified by nothing else but faith or by grace.

We further hear that the object of Abraham's faith was "God who gives life to the dead." The same thing is held out to us, that we might "believe in him who raised up his Son Jesus from the dead." Abraham's faith increased as various proofs of God's goodness came to him day after day. So also our own faith grows as often as we thoughtfully

ponder the fact that it was for us that he delivered up his Son, to whom he imparted "all the fullness." He was delivered up to death that he might expiate our sins by the offering of his own body, and he arose from the dead so that he might prove that by this means death had been abolished, life restored, and that true righteousness had been brought forth in the earth.

Finally, the Spirit wants us to understand that we also are to walk in newness of life. Our own faith ought to be of a similar kind, and then beyond a shadow of a doubt it will, by grace, be imputed as righteousness to us also. COMMENTARY ON ROMANS (1533).[49]

THE CAUSE AND THE END FOR THE BIRTH, RESURRECTION, AND SUFFERING. ERASMUS SARCERIUS: He adds these benefits of Christ in order that he might acquire Christ, the cause of free righteousness, and that he might teach the manner in which and through whom the free righteousness has come to us. A simple understanding of these is that Christ earned the free righteousness for us by his suffering and resurrection, and is himself its cause.

The discussion: Christ was delivered over for our transgressions and he was raised for our righteousness. We are, therefore, justified freely. You have this impulse or reason for the birth, the suffering, and the resurrection of Christ: our sins. Isaiah 43:24: "But yet you have made me to serve with regard to your sin, you have wearied me with regard to your iniquity." So also Isaiah 53:5: "But he was wounded on account of our iniquities. Why was he bruised? On account of our sins." Therefore, our sins are the cause of the birth, the suffering, and the resurrection of Christ. And he was resurrected for our justification. Consider this ultimate end of the birth, suffering, and resurrection of Christ: the cause of our justification: Isaiah 43: "I myself am he, I blot out your sins on my own account, and your sins I will not remember any

---

[47]CRR 6:75*; citing Col 2:11-12.
[48]Melanchthon, *Commentary on Romans*, 120*.

[49]Bullinger, *In Sanctissimam Pauli*, 72r; citing Rom 4:17, 24; Col 1:19; 1 Cor 1, 15.

longer." Isaiah 53: "By his stripes we are healed." NOTES ON ROMANS (1541).[50]

THE RESURRECTION AS THE OBJECT OF FAITH. JOHANN GERHARD: Question: Why is the resurrection of Christ, in particular, constituted as the proper object of justifying faith?

It should briefly be said that this is not done in an exclusive sense that pushes other things out, as if justification pertained only to this one doctrine, but rather (1) in a complex sense, for the resurrection of Christ presupposes and includes within it his passion and death and the other things that pertain to the satisfaction for our sins accomplished for us by Christ, and is such a summary of the whole gospel that by naming this one thing all the others are at once included in it. It is also said (2) by way of synecdoche, for this is the manner and custom of the Scriptures that it attributes remission of sins as well as justification sometimes to one deed or work of Christ and sometimes to another, in an indiscriminate way, employing synecdoche as is its custom. By this variety in manner of speech both the sufficiency of our redemption and the goodness of the Redeemer are hinted at. It is third said (3) in a declarative sense, for by God raising his Son, our surety from the dead, he made a manifest public display and demonstrated that through his death he had been fully satisfied. Last, it was said (4) in a step by step fashion, for the heavenly Father by raising him from the dead exercised his power in Christ, so that this might be transferred to his argument and applied to the example of Abraham who is then praised for having glorified God, convinced of his power. CONSIDERATION OF ROMANS 4:25 (1635).[51]

THE RESURRECTION AS SURETY OF OUR JUSTIFICATION. RICHARD SIBBES: The Holy Spirit supported Christ in his death . . . but especially in his resurrection. . . . Especially then, the Spirit of life that had sanctified Christ, and

quickened him, and enriched his nature, and supported him, and done all, that Spirit of life quickened the dead body of Christ. "And he was mightily declared to be the Son of God by the Spirit of sanctification, by his resurrection from the dead." The Spirit of life raised him from the dead, and put an end to all that misery that he had undergone before for our sakes. For until his resurrection, there was, as it were, some conflict with some enemies of Christ, either with Satan, or the world, or with death itself. He lay under death three days. Until Christ's body was raised, our enemies were not overcome. God's wrath was not fully satisfied. At least, it was not declared to be satisfied. For he being our surety, until he came out of the grave, we could not know that our sins were satisfied for. But now, when the Spirit of life in Christ comes and quickens that body of his in the grave, and so justifies us, as it is in Romans 4:25, "He died for our sins, and rose again for our justification." That is, by the Spirit of life in Christ quickening his dead body, he declared that we are fully discharged from our sins because he was fully discharged from our sins; being our surety, he showed by his resurrection that he was fully discharged from all that he took on him. When a man comes out of prison, that is a surety; his very coming out of prison shows that he has a full discharge of all the debt he undertook to pay. So the Spirit of life, raising Christ's body the third day, manifestly declared that the debt he took on him was fully discharged. And so as he died for sin, to satisfy God's justice for them, so he rose again for our justification, to show that he had a full discharge for all. SERMON ON THE SPIRITUAL JUBILEE.[52]

THE HIGHEST POINT OF GOD'S LOVE. PETER MARTYR VERMIGLI: The forgiveness of sins corresponds quite well to the death of Christ, since it was due to sin that we were indebted to die. Just as Christ died, as far as it pertains to perishable life, so ought we to die to sin when we are justified.

---

[50]Sarcerius, *In Apostolam ad Romanos*, Q1r-Q1v; citing Is 43:24; 53:5.
[51]Gerhard, *Summae Evangelii Aphorism*, C1v-C2r; citing Eph 1:20.

[52]Sibbes, *Complete Works* 5:239*.

Likewise, because justification appears to be pronounced in the context of our beginning a new life, it therefore corresponds to Christ's resurrection, since he was then seen to have begun a heavenly and happy life. Paul employed a similar form of words elsewhere in this letter when he said, "With the heart one believes unto righteousness, but with the mouth one makes confession unto salvation." For faith in the heart both brings about righteousness as well as confers salvation. But since both salvation and renewal are most effectively declared by an act, he therefore wrote that it results from confession. But I will neither argue nor can I easily say which of these expositions is more correct.

A most sweet consolation is elicited from what has been said. For by it we know not only of the weight of sin, but we also perceive that the highest point of God's love for us was shown when he delivered up his only-begotten Son to death that we might be delivered from our sins. Also, when Christ is said to have "risen from the dead on account of our justification" we can easily see that by this we are called to a new life, unto which, however, we could not aspire unless we had first been chosen by him. COMMENTARY ON Romans (1560).[53]

---

[53]Vermigli, *In Epistolam S. Pauli*, 298; citing Rom 10:10.

5:1-11 RECONCILIATION THROUGH FAITH IN CHRIST

Therefore, since we have been justified by faith, we[a] *have peace with God through our Lord Jesus Christ.* [2]*Through him we have also obtained access by faith*[b] *into this grace in which we stand, and we*[c] *rejoice*[d] *in hope of the glory of God.* [3]*Not only that, but we rejoice in our sufferings, knowing that suffering produces endurance,* [4]*and endurance produces character, and character produces hope,* [5]*and hope does not put us to shame, because God's love has been poured into our hearts through the Holy Spirit who has been given to us.*

[6]*For while we were still weak, at the right time Christ died for the ungodly.* [7]*For one will scarcely die for a righteous person—though perhaps for a good person one would dare even to die—* [8]*but God shows his love for us in that while we were still sinners, Christ died for us.* [9]*Since, therefore, we have now been justified by his blood, much more shall we be saved by him from the wrath of God.* [10]*For if while we were enemies we were reconciled to God by the death of his Son, much more, now that we are reconciled, shall we be saved by his life.* [11]*More than that, we also rejoice in God through our Lord Jesus Christ, through whom we have now received reconciliation.*

a Some manuscripts *let us*   b Some manuscripts omit *by faith*   c Or *let us*; also verse 3   d Or *boast*; also verses 3, 11

OVERVIEW: Having argued for justification by faith alone, these early modern commentators now turn to explore Paul's explication of the benefits of being justified by God. First, we have peace with God. Because of what Christ has done, our consciences can be at rest, no longer striving to earn God's favor through our works. Second, we have hope, which comes as a result of faith. Where faith receives forgiveness in this life, hope anticipates the glory that awaits us. Third, we can glory in our tribulations, for they work in parallel fashion to physical exercises, strengthening us spiritually. Suffering—especially with faith's help—develops patience in us. And faith and hope fight against the doubt and despair that can come in affliction, for they bring certainty that one is in the grace of God.

Where faith and hope thrive, love follows as their consummation, and this love comes from the Holy Spirit. The reformers argue that the phrase here, "the love of God"—contrary to some medieval theologians (including early Luther)—refers to God's love for us rather than ours for him, empha-

sizing his role rather than ours, in salvation. Christ's death on the cross, especially in light of it being for sinners, demonstrates God's immense love for us. The reformers meditate on the importance of the blood of Christ being shed, particularly in light of the sacrifice of the Passover lamb. Knowing how much Christ loves us and what he endured for us, how can we not be willing to endure everything for him? In him, the hope of happiness awaits.

5:1 *We Have Peace Through Justification*

BENEFITS OF JUSTIFICATION. NIELS HEMMINGSEN: Being absolutely confident of this justification by faith, in the beginning of this chapter the apostle fittingly enumerates these benefits that were connected with justification, as they are peace with God through Christ, access to God, hope of the glory of God, comfort at the foot of the cross, and glorying in God. Of all these, he introduces the principal cause, that is, the love of God toward men and women. He amplifies that love by a sign and comparison. In the third place then, in order that he might teach us what the righteousness of God is—by which anyone who believes is justified—he shows that what proceeds from Adam is sin, death, and condemnation, and so what proceeds from Christ is righteousness, life, and salvation. Commentary on Romans (1562).[1]

First Proof That We Are Justified by Faith: Inner Sense of God's Love.

Martin Bucer: The premise that we are justified by faith in Christ—that is, being convinced of the remission of our sins and having a title to eternal life, by faith in Christ, we have not the slightest doubt concerning the great and perpetual favor that God has for us, so that we boast with overflowing hearts that we are enrolled in the number of the blessed and that God is ours in every respect, even when those things happen outside of us that seem to testify openly of God's wrath and indignation—this premise, I say, the apostle proves in four parts.

First, it is proved from the inner sense of the saints and by spiritual experience. For they do indeed feel and experience, by the Spirit conferred upon them, the great and genuine fatherly love of God toward them. Such great love cannot be contemplated without seeing that whosoever should be persuaded of this love ought to be absolutely certain of their justification and adoption as sons and daughters of God, and to such a degree that they cannot fail to boast with all their heart in this God who is now theirs, and do so even in the midst of any and all circumstances no matter how adverse they might appear. This is the proof found in the first part. Commentary on Romans (1536).[2]

Second Proof: The Death of Christ.

Martin Bucer: The second proof of his premise is drawn from the death of the Lord Jesus Christ and reasons in the following manner. Faith in

Christ is firmly convinced that he was delivered up by the Father that he might meet death on our behalf, even while we were still ungodly and his enemies, a task he fulfilled voluntarily and readily. Now, neither could the Father have commanded this nor could the Son have eagerly submitted to it unless the greatest possible love for us had induced them to these things. Accordingly, faith toward Christ, when the gospel is believed, causes us to be fully convinced that we are so loved by both the Father and the Son that, now that our sins are forgiven, there is no evil that will not be turned away, nor anything good that will not be provided for us. This faith makes for the fullest boasting in God even in adverse circumstances, in addition to conveying a most perfect justification. These are the ideas present in the second part. Commentary on Romans (1536).[3]

Third Proof: The Life of Christ.

Martin Bucer: The third argument by which he proves the same premise is drawn from a comparison between the death and life of Christ, in the following sense. Faith in Christ does not doubt that by the death of Christ we are reconciled to God and rendered exempt from all punishment that was laid up for us while we were God's enemies. It is therefore much more certain, now that we have been brought back to God in grace by the blood of Christ, that by means of the life of Christ, in which life our Head, Champion and Restorer reigns with the aim of bringing our salvation to completion, we will be set free from every evil and crowned with every kind of good. It is therefore as a result of this faith that we boast in God as being ours, even in the midst of what appear to be the greatest difficulties and calamities. Commentary on Romans (1536).[4]

Fourth Proof: Comparison of Adam and Christ.

Martin Bucer: The fourth argument is drawn from a comparison between Adam and

---

[1]Hemmingsen, *Commentarius in Epistolam*, 167.
[2]Bucer, *Metaphrases et Enarrationes*, 235.
[3]Bucer, *Metaphrases et Enarrationes*, 235.
[4]Bucer, *Metaphrases et Enarrationes*, 235.

Christ. Faith in Christ knows full well that in Christ there is provided for us a salvation much greater than the calamity brought upon us by Adam's sin. Faith, therefore, so believes itself to have received from Christ both justification and a participation in divine righteousness that it is able to boast in its God in every situation, even when the flesh is beset by troubles. The apostle deals with this in parts 3, 4 and 5. He here dwells on this subject and so presses the point fully that it is fitting that the merits of Christ are far more efficacious in restoring us than the Fall of Adam was in casting us down, so that he restores far more than was lost by the sin our first parents committed. COMMENTARY ON ROMANS (1536).[5]

THE PRINCIPAL HINGE OF FAITH. JOHN
CALVIN: The principal hinge on which faith turns is this: We must not suppose that any promises of mercy that the Lord offers are true only outside of us, and not at all in us; rather, we should make them ours by inwardly embracing them. Only in this way is that confidence engendered that he elsewhere terms peace; though perhaps instead he means to make peace follow from it. This is the security that quiets and calms the conscience in the view of the judgment of God, and without which it is necessarily vexed and almost torn with tumultuous dread, except when it happens to slumber for a moment, forgetful both of God and of itself. And truly it is but for a moment. It never long enjoys that miserable obliviousness, for the memory of the divine judgment, ever and again recurring, stings it to the quick. In one word, he alone is a true believer who, firmly persuaded that God is reconciled to him and is a kind Father to him, hopes everything from his kindness. He, trusting to the promises of the divine favor, with undoubting confidence anticipates salvation; as the apostle shows in these words, "We are made partakers of Christ, if we hold the beginning of our confidence steadfast until the end." He thus holds that no one hopes well in the Lord except for those who confidently glory in

being the heirs of the heavenly kingdom. No one, I say, is a believer but he who, trusting to the security of his salvation, confidently triumphs over the devil and death, as we are taught by the noble exclamation of Paul, "I am persuaded, that neither death, nor life, nor angels, nor principalities, nor powers, nor things present, nor things to come, nor height, nor depth, nor any other creature, shall be able to separate us from the love of God, which is in Christ Jesus our Lord." In a similar manner, the same apostle does not consider that the eyes of our understanding are enlightened unless we know what is the hope of the eternal inheritance to which we are called. Thus he uniformly intimates throughout his writings, that the goodness of God is not properly comprehended when security does not follow as its fruit. INSTITUTES OF THE CHRISTIAN RELIGION 3.2.16 (1559).[6]

THREE STAGES OF OUR SALVATION. MARTIN
BUCER: "We have peace with God." Let us carefully consider that the apostle attributes to Christ our Lord the beginning, middle and end of our salvation, and also whatever follows its consummation, and he presses the point that this salvation is received by faith alone. The *end* of our restoration is peace with God; the *beginning* is when we receive access into this grace by faith, that is, when we trust in Christ when he calls us and follow where he leads. The *middle* is when we are strengthened in this faith so that we might continue firm in the hope and expectation that, as we have been divinely destined, we will at last without any doubt attain to a *consortium divinitatis*, full participation in deity, that is, in the glory of God. In these three stages our salvation is perfected. Further, a confident and effusive boasting in these truths accompanies our salvation, to such a degree that it remains prominent even in adversity, which, no matter how dire they may be, we can have no doubt whatever that they exist for our good. All these things have been acquired for us, and are now bestowed, preserved and perfected by Christ. We hold out to him

---

[5]Bucer, *Metaphrases et Enarrationes*, 235-36.

[6]Calvin, *Institutes*, 1:483-84*; citing Rom 8:38; Eph 1:18.

nothing but faith, that is, we embrace these things by believing on Christ, and it is also he who effects, preserves and perfects this faith. For "it is by him," says Paul, "that we have by faith obtained access into this grace in which we stand." You must therefore clearly understand that your having come to this grace and having continued in it is Christ's doing. So much so, that *nothing* belongs to us in this matter; everything belongs to our Lord Jesus Christ. But if he were to grant us to fully understand and always ponder this matter, we would realize that we are assuredly able to think nothing, say nothing, and do nothing apart from the one Lord Jesus Christ, by whom alone it is we are able to strive after anything at all. O Lord Jesus, cause these truths at last to live within us! COMMENTARY ON ROMANS (1536).[7]

SCRIPTURE REQUIRES A TWOFOLD RIGHTEOUSNESS.

DANIEL TOUSSAIN: Now as to what pertains to Osiander,[†] our theologians have always responded with remarkable agreement that by his teaching, Osiander overturns (1) first, all our consolation and faith if he takes away from us the essential righteousness of God; (2) and second, the full obedience of Christ, since he would have rendered it in vain unless, as the apostle teaches, that obedience being opposed to the disobedience of Adam and imputed to us justifies us. The answer to all of these in general is that the Scriptures require of us a twofold righteousness, but in different modes and respects: (1) the righteousness of God that Christ alone supplies, gives, and imputes to believers, which renders consciences at peace, as the apostle teaches in the clearest possible terms in Romans 5, and (2) the righteousness of *works*, or of that new obedience which is a consequence and a fruit of the former kind and inseparable from it. The first righteousness belongs to Another, but in such a way that it becomes ours, just as Christ himself is ours, not only because he was rendered for our benefit, but also by way of the communion that we have with him. Christians should not give heed to that principle of the philosophers in this particular point of doctrine, who would have it that nothing can be regarded as this or that unless it first becomes it, as for instance a person could not be said to be learned or white unless teaching or whiteness inhered within him. These are the mysteries of salvation that only faith is able to understand. Our theologians also have answered that our righteousness of works cannot be the cause of our justification before God or any aspect thereof, because it is imperfect, because it follows justification, and because however much is attributed to the righteousness of works, that much is taken away from the merit of Christ and his most perfect obedience. SYNOPSIS OF THE DOCTRINE OF JUSTIFICATION FROM ROMANS 1 (1588).[8]

HIS SACRIFICE HAS SANCTIFIED US.

DIRK PHILIPS: He is entirely heavenly, entirely from God, entirely holy, who also through the only sacrifice of his unblemished flesh and precious blood has sanctified and made perfect all those who believe in his name. For it happened thus that the one who would pay all the guilt of the trespasser Adam with his innocence[†]—would make as nothing all our unrighteousness with his righteousness, destroying death with his life, as that only innocent Lamb of God, taking away the sins of the world, and completing the wonderful work of our redemption—that one had to be a divine person, yes, true God and human in one person. For with his divinity he could thus help us, and according to his humanity could he thus as the only high priest of God anointed and instituted according to the order of Melchizedek, offer himself for us through the Holy Spirit, and set on fire that precious incense on the altar of the cross with the fire of his immeasurable love to us, a sweet smell to the Father and as a reconciliation with God and as a forgiveness of our sins. THREE ADMONITIONS.[9]

---

[7]Bucer, *Metaphrases et Enarrationes*, 244.

[8]Toussain, *Synopsis Doctrinae Apostoli Pauli*, thesis 35. [†]Osiander had published two works (*De Lege et Evangelio* and *De Justificatio*) in 1550 which argued that justification was located in Christ's divinity indwelling in the believer.
[9]CRR 6:416*; citing Jn 3:13; 6:32; Heb 10:14; Jn 1:29; 1 Jn 2:1; Heb 5:1; 9:11; 10:11; Eph 5:2. [†]Lit. "unguilt."

CHEERFUL ADMISSION THROUGH FAITH IN CHRIST. MARTIN LUTHER: It is the greatest joy the human heart can feel when it again sees and recognizes Christ who had previously been in death and with him all comfort and joy were gone. But now it can cheerfully take comfort and know that in him it has a dear and friendly Savior and, through him, pure grace and comfort with God against all the fear of sin and death and against the power of the world and of hell. This is the same thing St. Paul says, "Since we have been justified by faith, we have peace with God through our Lord Jesus Christ, through whom we also have a cheerful admission or access in faith." SUMMER POSTIL (APRIL 19, 1523).[10]

THE JOYFUL MESSAGE OF THE GRACE OF GOD. DIRK PHILIPS: This New Testament (a word of the saving grace, witness of divine love, a comfort of the conscience, and eternal salvation of souls) Jesus Christ, as the true and only mediator of the New Testament, has received from God his Father. He has proclaimed the same to his chosen apostles and all God-fearing persons and with his Holy Spirit written it in their hearts. And, therefore, this is basically called a testament, even as is the testament of the outer and inner will of a dying person, who allows his will to be written in order that he might give his friends to know his will and desire, and gives his decision how after his death the right heirs should divide his estate. Thus Jesus Christ has also done. Before his death he called the apostles, his dear friends, to himself, revealed his Word to them, and gave them to know his will, and commanded them after his death to preach his gospel, that is, the joyful message of the grace of God, the merits of Christ, namely, that he with his suffering and shedding of blood has made sin and eternal damnation into nothing and has overcome death and the devil, and over against this has earned salvation and eternal life for us, to all creatures, and has given as a possession to all who believe all his goods, that is, all his glory, righteous-ness, and salvation with which he has endowed us and made us partakers of eternal life. THE SUPPER OF OUR LORD JESUS CHRIST.[11]

THE SWEET FRUITS OF JUSTIFICATION. DANIEL TOUSSAIN: These are the beautiful and sweet fruits and truly divine effects of our freely granted justification: that the consciences of believers are at peace toward God, that they have access to him and to his blessings, that they glory in the midst of their afflictions and hope for a good end, having as a foundation of their hope that they cannot be smitten even by the very gates of hell, and they love him in return, and they love their neighbor because of him, whose love they feel most abundantly poured into their hearts by the Holy Spirit, and so they are conforming themselves daily in obedience to his will. SYNOPSIS OF THE DOCTRINE OF JUSTIFICATION FROM ROMANS 1 (1588).[12]

THE FRUITS OF FAITH. JOHANNES BUGENHA-GEN: And so you see here that the most noble fruits of faith are described, which cannot be corrupted nor die. First, that you are certain about the glory of God, from which you have peace. Second, in adverse conditions, no matter how terrible they are, nothing will be able to separate you from hope. Nor will behaviors nor sin strike you down. That is to say, you will be the strongest rock. Third, lest you, feeling unworthy, doubt anything regarding grace, know that grace is given to the unworthy, not to the worthy and holy, because Christ loved us though we were unrigh-teous. Fourth, our conscience is sure, saying that the grace that comes through Christ is greater than the sin that was propagated from Adam to us. Therefore, if our condemnation on account of Adam is so great, you should know that the grace of God through Christ is greater. And so this is the summary, full of consolation, Adam's and Christ's. See the rest in Paul's words. INTERPRETATION OF ROMANS (1531).[13]

---

[10]LW 77:129*.

[11]CRR 6:125-26*; citing Heb 12:24; Col 2:13; Mt 28:19; Mk 16:15.
[12]Toussain, *Synopsis Doctrinae Apostoli Pauli*, B2v.
[13]Bugenhagen, *In D. Pauli ad Romanos*, 47r-47v.

A TRIAL FOR THE HERESY OF JUSTIFICATION BY FAITH. PIETRO CARNESECCHI: Having been conducted to Rome, and your cause having been carefully investigated in the Holy Office, after various apologies and many inconsistencies and evasions on your part, in which you showed yourself to be rigid and intractable, by shrinking from a free confession of your heterodox sentiments opposed to the holy Catholic faith, as well as by your palliation of your faults and misconceptions; and while you frequently waited to be convicted by your own writings, notwithstanding the countless warnings that were given to you; we have finally ascertained, by the testimony that exists against you, and by letters and documents written by your own hand, and also by your own voluntary confession, that the things recited are true, and that they occurred in the manner stated; and that from 1540 and in succeeding years, you have held and believed the following propositions, which are, respectively, heretical, erroneous, rash, and scandalous:

1. Justification by faith alone, without the participation of our works therein; according to the doctrine of the heresiarch Luther, on the letter to the Galatians.

2. The certainty of grace and of salvation, according to the same Luther.

3. That our works were not essential to salvation, which is to be obtained through faith; but that the justified man or woman would inevitably perform them whenever they should have time and opportunity.

4. And consequently that the said good works could not merit everlasting life, but should indeed be rewarded with a higher degree of glory after the general resurrection.

. . . 13. You have held that the Satisfaction which consists of penitential works, imposed by Priests upon those who are contrite, was not necessary (upon the presumption that it took the place of the merit of Christ, as sufficient to atone for the sins of the whole world) but that such works were good for the purposes of mortifying the flesh, and giving life to the spirit.

. . . 19. That the most holy sacrifice of the Mass was not truly propitiatory, except so far as it excites in us the remembrance of the passion of Christ, and consequently that faith by which the forgiveness of sins is obtained.

. . . 33. From the year 1543 until 1545, and from 1557 till 1559, you have held that, Christ being the only Mediator between God and humanity, it was unnecessary to pray to the saints; and for some time you have not done so.

34. And, last, you have believed all the errors and heresies comprised in the said book *Of the Benefit of Christ*, as well as the false doctrine and principles taught by the said Juan Valdés your master.

. . . Admitting, however, in respect to the tenets of justification through faith, the perpetuity of grace, and those which are inconsistent with the belief that good works are indispensable and meritorious, that you had absolutely adopted views in which you concurred with Valdés, up to the time of the final resolution and ratifying ordinance of the Council of Trent.

. . . And so it appears that you have agreed not only with Valdés, but also with Luther, respecting the doctrine of justification, and therefore as to those principles that are subordinate to it, and as to others which you have mentioned.

. . . Having invoked the most holy name of our Lord Jesus Christ, and of the glorious Virgin Mary . . . we issue in this writ, pronounce, adjudge, determine, and declare, that you, Pietro Carnesecchi, from 1540 and the years that followed, have been a heretic, who confided in heretics, and who was their abettor and entertainer, severally . . .

. . . And we condemn you to the forfeiture of all your property, personal and real.

. . . And we, in like manner pronounce and ordain that you ought to be degraded, as we direct that you be actually degraded, from the orders to which you have attained. And as a person so depressed, henceforward, as well as from the previous time, we expel you, as an unprofitable branch, from our ecclesiastical court, and from the safeguard of our holy church. And we surrender and deliver you up to the secular court.

... So we cardinals, inquisitors general, whose names are written beneath, decree. VERBATIM ACCOUNT OF THE TRIAL OF PIETRO CARNESECCHI.[14]

GLORYING IN PEACE AND IN SUFFERING.

JACQUES LEFÈVRE D'ÉTAPLES: Our sins are wiped away through the death of Christ, that is, they are dismissed and forgiven by Christ dying on our behalf and they continue to be dismissed and forgiven in Christ as often as we go amiss and then through genuine faith run back to him, with penance [or repentance] acting as our guide. And it is through his resurrection that after the remission of our sins justification is granted to us in him, that is, to him in our place. This is followed by peace and reconciliation to God so that we receive an eternal inheritance with Christ that we possess now in this age by means of hope, but in the next age by enjoyment of everlasting blessings. For the remission of all sins is "in Christ," the justification of all is "in Christ," and the reconciliation of all is "in Christ." And so Paul goes on to say, "being justified therefore by faith, we have peace with God through our Lord Jesus Christ, through whom we have access through faith and this grace in which we stand and in which we rejoice in hope of the glory of God." A wonderful thing indeed is this grace! The justification in us is received from Christ. In Christ himself this grace is total and universal, whereas in us and in any one particular justified person it is that in which we are to remain standing, and the expectation of the glory of God in the immortality of life is an occasion for great glorying and exulting in spirit. But Paul and the other apostles did not glory only in that certain hope of God's glory, but also in their tribulations, as it was written, "And they went out rejoicing from the presence of the council since they were regarded worthy of suffering reproach on account of the name of Jesus." For they recognized that tribulations were producing in them patience, bearing with them with a calm and cheerful spirit for Christ's sake. And their patience was causing them to be proved, as genuine gold is proved which does not give in to the violence of the fire but rather persists and is rendered more beautiful and, if I may say so, more joyful. And their being proved was causing to grow in them a much greater hope. For hope does not produce any effect of confusion, whereas a lack of hope squanders, confuses, and removes life and conveys death. Hence hope saves; it protects us from confusion, and it takes away death and conveys life. Add to this that by this means they were conformed to Christ and imitators of Christ, who suffered tribulation, showed the greatest patience, and was proved, while hoping more than all others. He suffered tribulation: "Man tramples on me; all day long an attacker oppresses me." He displayed the greatest patience: "Lord, You are my patience, my hope from my youth." He was proved: "You have tested my heart and visited me at night; you have examined me by fire, and iniquity was not found in me." And likewise he was hoping: "I will hope continually and will add to all your praises." COMMENTARY ON ROMANS (1517).[15]

THE PEACE OF CONSCIENCE. HULDRYCH

ZWINGLI: Paul contends against those who have been attributing righteousness to works. And after he has made the point that faith is apprehended by faith alone, now in this chapter, he repeats it—as though in an epilogue—that peace and tranquility of conscience stand by faith, not by works. For however splendid those works might be, nevertheless no one is ever able to have faith in them without danger. The one who truly has faith in God through Christ, he now has a conscience at peace. Christ is the one through whom we are led into this grace, for by him we have access to God. NOTES ON ROMANS (1539).[16]

---

[14]Carnesecchi, *Report of the Trial*, 31-33, 35, 37-38, 43, 46-47, 49, 50-53*. Carnesecchi, having been a member of the circle of Juan de Valdés, was put on trial by the Roman Inquisition for his Reformation views. He was condemned to death and beheaded.

[15]Lefèvre, *Epistole divi Pauli*, 63; citing Acts 5:41; Ps 56:1; 71:5; 17:3; 71:14.
[16]Zwingli, *In Evangelicam Historiam*, 418.

Peace Through Christ. Balthasar Hubmaier: And by that they also heard how Christ
had suffered for them, that he paid for them and
gave satisfaction for them on the cross. That again
gives joy to people, enlivens sinners, and brings
them on the right path, so that they place their
faith, hope, and love in God and trust him for all
good, through Jesus Christ, our Lord. Precisely for
that reason, and that is the ultimate one, Christ
sent out his disciples as God his Father had sent
him: that as he, Christ himself, said on earth to the
believers, "Take heart, rise, go forth, your sins are
forgiven you." Likewise his disciples should now
represent him henceforth during the time of his
bodily absence and guarantee to all believers a sure
and certain remission of their sin through him,
Jesus Christ. Through this the believers came to
rest and peace in their consciences, because they
knew that through the suffering of Christ they had
acquired a graceful and merciful God in heaven, to
whom they were permitted to cry: "Father, Father . . .
our Father who is in heaven." On the Christian
Baptism of Believers.[17]

Peace with God and One Another. Dirk
Philips: We must believe the teaching of Jesus
Christ entirely, earnestly keep his commandments,
and in addition neither introduce nor accept
anything new, so that true peace may be and
remain among us. For to that we are called, and
therefore Christ has reconciled us with his
precious blood to God the Father, so that we
should have peace with God and with each other
in truth and righteousness. Again, therefore, we are
baptized through one Spirit, into one body. Yes,
therefore Christ is our head, and his Holy Spirit is
our life so that we should all alike hold firmly to
Christ, become conformed to him, and proceed in
the one Holy Spirit, speak through him alone, and
be driven of him to all true peace, to all perfect love
and unity. The Tabernacle of Moses.[18]

Only Faith Brings Peace. Johannes Bugenhagen: He says from the beginning of the chapter,
throughout the whole chapter: Being justified by
faith, we have peace. To this point, Paul's letter has
seemed difficult, and many have even feared it, but
if its order is observed, there will be no difficulty in
it. Above, Paul taught that righteousness is by faith,
and he now follows with this, that by this faith, our
consciences have peace with God, and there is
nothing else in this chapter. . . .

Don't we all seek righteousness by works and
by other things, so that in this way we might have
peace with God? At one time, we all marched
along this road, living in our righteous deeds,
confessing and fasting, not on account of anything
except that our sins might be taken away and our
consciences pacified.

But the same thing happens to us that happened to the Israelites, as you see in chapter 9:
"striving after righteousness, they did not attain it."
Even we used to think that righteousness would
come from our works, but we were deceived.

No matter what you make up about the
righteousness of works, you will not achieve the
peace of conscience. You are able to be deceived for
a time, likewise you are able to imagine holiness
and peace, but with the consciousness of sin
returning, where is your invented peace and
holiness? Clearly, the same disturbance and
disquietude of conscience that you previously
perceived returned. You said and dreamed that you
had peace, but then you saw that there is no peace,
because there is no peace for the impious. Such are
all who claim righteousness by works, and not by
faith in Christ.

And so the outstanding commendation of the
righteousness of faith in this passage is, as Paul says,
"Test and seek, and you will find peace whenever
you believe that Christ has made satisfaction for
your sins." You have experience herself as a teacher
in your heart, which convinces you that righteousness is by faith. And even while resisting, your
mind and flesh are being compelled to confess and
to say, "You have the thing itself. Why do you need

---

[17]CRR 5:115-16*; citing Rom 8:15; Mt 6:9.
[18]CRR 6:265-66*; citing Eph 2:13; 1 Cor 12:13; Eph 4:16; Rom 8:29.

more witnesses here?" Our spirit gives testimony to the Spirit of God, because the righteousness by which the conscience finds peace may not be any other than faith's when we perceive and believe in the forgiveness of sins through Christ. Now the conscience exults in the sight of God and sings— with great freedom from care—the triumphant song, namely this: "Christ is my righteousness, my strength. He has erased sin's handwriting, conquered Satan, chief of the devils, and now there is nothing I need fear. All my enemies and adversaries are like stubble that is immediately consumed by fire and is like dust that the wind scatters." No one is able to grasp these words, so great are their joys. They are as great as the proclamation of this peace in the conscience, which sees and senses the forgiveness of sins. Let someone try to prove it is not possible to have this peace and happiness of conscience from any of those other things from which the flesh hopes for salvation—or that surely, certainly, it was never possible to be certain regarding God's paternal will toward oneself. INTERPRETATION OF ROMANS (1531).[19]

OUR RECONCILIATION DEPENDS ON CHRIST.

JOHN CALVIN: Our reconciliation with God depends only on Christ, for he only is the beloved Son, and we are all by nature the children of wrath. But this favor is communicated to us by the gospel, for the gospel is the ministry of reconciliation, by the means of which we are in a manner brought into the kingdom of God. Rightly then does Paul set before our eyes in Christ a sure pledge of God's favor, that he might more easily draw us away from every confidence in works. And as he teaches us by the word "access," that salvation begins with Christ, he excludes those preparations by which foolish people imagine that they can anticipate God's mercy, as though he said, "Christ comes to you, nor helps you, on account of your merits." He afterward immediately adds that it is through the continuance of the same favor that our salvation becomes certain and sure, by which he intimates

that perseverance is not founded in our power and diligence, but on Christ. COMMENTARY ON ROMANS 5:2.[20]

5:2 Access by Faith to Grace, Hope, and Glory

WANTING BOTH THE SUN AND THE LIGHT.

MARTIN LUTHER: In our day the hypocrites and legalists swell up with horrifying pride and think that they are now saved and sufficiently righteous because they believe in Christ, but they are unwilling to be considered unrighteous or regarded as fools. And what is this except the rejection of Christ's protection and a desire to approach God only from faith but not through Christ? Indeed, then there is not faith at all, but only the appearance. So at sunset the rays of the sun and the light of the sun go down together. But he who is wise does not set such high value on the light that he no longer needs the sun, rather he wants to have both the sun and the light at the same time. Therefore those who approach God through faith and not at the same time through Christ actually depart from him. LECTURES ON ROMANS (1516).[21]

HOPE AND FAITH.

ALEXANDER ALESIUS: Hope is, therefore, the effect of justification by faith. And the object of hope is the glory of the sons of God being revealed. The object of faith is the remission of sins. And these two virtues[†] of faith and hope differ by their acts and objects. Aristotle said that habits are distinguished by their acts, and acts by their objects. The act of hope is to anticipate the glory of the sons and daughters of God, whereas the act of faith is to receive the forgiveness of sins in the present life. DISPUTATIONS ON ROMANS (1553).[22]

A BEGGAR'S INHERITANCE.

JOHANNES BRENZ: The true inheritance of righteousness pertains to us and yet we do not feel changed in the flesh, which is still sinful. The inheritance of perpetual life and

---

[19]Bugenhagen, In D. Pauli ad Romanos, 46r-47r; citing Rom 9:31.

[20]CTS 38:188-89* (CO 49:89).
[21]LW 25:287*.
[22]Alesius, Omnes Disputationes, N2v. †A virtue is a good habitus.

happiness pertains to us, and yet in the present it does not appear without death and ruin. Therefore we boast through faith because we possess these benefits of God, even if by human reckoning nothing appears less important. Let us imagine a poor man living among us to whom a reliable witness, letters, and a seal promises the crown of an empire across the sea. Also, safe navigation is promised to him even if many and various dangers in the crossing of the sea are undertaken. But while he undertakes the voyage, he must at the same time retain the garment of a beggar, until he reaches the country across the sea. How do you think this beggar will be affected? How can he not be affected as if he already is dressed in purple, even if up to this point he is wearing the beggar's cloak and is driven here and there on the waves of the sea? But the glory of God was promised much more certainly to us than any earthly crown can be promised. Hence although we must walk for some time in this world dressed as beggars, nevertheless faith is proved when we boast in the good things of the glory and majesty of God no differently than if we were perceptibly inheriting them today. COMMENTARY ON ROMANS (1564).[23]

EAT THE FOOD OF FAITH. WOLFGANG MUSCULUS: It should be observed how the apostle places together in this passage the two things necessary for our salvation: Christ as Mediator and Lord, and faith in Christ. He teaches us that all these good things are obtained through Christ, but in such a way that it does not happen apart from faith. He, therefore, inserts the word "faith" twice: "being justified," he says, "by faith we have peace" . . . and, "it is by faith that we are led into this grace." We learn from this that neither faith apart from Christ, nor Christ apart from faith, profits us even the slightest, but that these two necessary things must be conjoined together if we are to obtain salvation. For these two require each other in such a way that neither does us any good without the other. In like fashion (if I may illustrate this with an analogy),

two things are necessary for the feeding and nourishment of the stomach: food, and the eating or intake of food. If you do not eat the food, its wholesomeness will do you no good; it will not take away hunger and satisfy the stomach unless it is eaten. On the contrary, even if you should eat something, unless it is food that you're eating, you will eat in vain. If you should eat poison, you will eat for yourself death rather than life; if you eat useless rubbish, you merely weigh your stomach down rather than feed it, and so you'll end up afflicting it rather than nourishing it. These two things are necessary for nourishment: that you have food, and then that you eat it—not simply that you eat anything you please, but that you eat food. Christ and faith have a similar relation to each other: the true bread is Christ, the sole Mediator and Savior who alone can justify us, set us at peace, feed us and save us, through whom everything necessary for salvation is to be sought by us; then there is faith in Christ, which is nothing other than the eating of this food. I said faith *in Christ*, not any kind of faith you please. For both the Jews and Gentiles have their own kind of faith, but they are not saved by it. They also eat, but because it is useless trash—or rather, poison—that they eat instead of food, they are thereby dissipated rather than satiated. COMMENTARY ON ROMANS (1555).[24]

JESUS, NOT BAPTISM, IS THE TRUE SIGN OF GRACE. DIRK PHILIPS: This grace and this covenant of God with all believing Christians is bound to no external symbol, but to Jesus Christ alone, who is the only and true sign of grace, and faith alone grasps this through the Holy Spirit, who assures our spirit that we are God's children. Therefore, some lack understanding who hold not Christ Jesus but primarily baptism for the true sign of grace, and therefore ascribe to baptism what belongs primarily to Christ himself. THE BAPTISM OF OUR LORD JESUS CHRIST.[25]

---

[23]Brenz, *In Epistolam*, 124.

[24]Musculus, *In Epistolam Apostoli Pauli*, 112-13.
[25]CRR 6:102-3*; citing Heb 5:3; 11:1; Rom 8:16.

5:3 Rejoicing in Suffering

WHY WE CAN GLORY IN OUR SUFFERING.
PETER MARTYR VERMIGLI: These sufferings are
the tools by which the power and goodness of God
are exercised in us for consolation and for edification at one and the same time. They are occasions
for the most glorious goods. "The strength of God
is perfected in our weakness." Daily lapses are
corrected by these as if by a kind of paternal
chastisement. Haughtiness and pride are suppressed, the flesh and licentiousness are beaten
back, our old self decays, but the inner self is
renewed. Laziness and dullness are driven out, the
confession of faith is expressed; the weakness of
our powers is laid bare, and we are spurred on to
pray more fervently and implore the divine favor,
and for days to come we better understand the
wickedness of our nature. By such afflictions we are
made like Christ: "For it was opportune that
Christ should suffer, and so obtain his kingdom,
that we also might follow in his steps. For the
kingdom of God suffers violence, and narrow is the
way that leads to life." But just as he was exalted
after the obedience of the cross, and "given the
name which is above every name," so we also, "if we
have suffered with him, shall reign with him" as
well. It is sweet for the lover, then, to suffer for that
which he loves. Thus we are accustomed to
endurance, so that, as if we were made like steel, we
tire out our persecutors rather than being broken
by them. For they are like exercises are to the
human body, which rather strengthen health and
condition the powers than prostrate or debilitate
them, for which reason, the righteous glory in
sufferings with some justification. COMMENTARY
ON ROMANS (1560).[26]

AFFLICTIONS ARE A GLORIOUS THING.
VIKTORIN STRIGEL: We rejoice and have established that afflictions are a glorious thing, not only
because they will have a glorious end in eternal life,
but also because the presence of God is discerned

in the cross, and the splendor of the church
properly shines—that is, the true knowledge, the
calling on and celebration of God. Tertullian in his
Apology wrote: "It is our battle that we are called
before the tribunals so that under threat of capital
punishment in that place, we might contend for the
truth. However, victory is to obtain that for which
you have struggled. This victory includes both the
glory of pleasing God, and the spoils of eternal life."
And a little later he says about the martyr, "This is
the garment of our victory, this our clothing
embroidered with palm branches.[†] In such a
chariot do we celebrate our triumph." NOTES ON
THE EPISTLES OF PAUL (1565).[27]

SINGING WHILE GLORYING IN TRIBULATION.
NATHANIEL HOLMES: How do we follow the
example of Christ when receiving communion if
after the administration of it we do not sing a
hymn or psalm? When are we Christian-like merry,
if not when receiving mercies from the hand of
God? And how are we merry according to the
prescript of Scriptures, if we do not sing? Often,
saints "glory in tribulation," so that Paul and Silas
sing psalms in the prison, even in the stocks. What
kind of Christians then are we that will not sing at
all? That season no duties with singing? The
churches in the primitive times, in the ten persecutions, sugared and sweetened their meetings and
duties with singing of psalms before they parted, as
we heard before. The truth is, devout singing of
psalms is a savory sauce to relish every condition
and ordinance that is an iterated ordinance. For
baptism, after one administration, is never to be
repeated. But churches sing before sermons, to
enliven their hearts to prayer. They sing after
Communion, to raise them up in praise. Yes, I may
say, this spiritual sauce is meat itself. In singing we
pray, we praise, we confess, we petition, we exhort,
we meditate, we believe, we joy, we mourn. GOSPEL
MUSIC (1644).[28]

---

[26]Vermigli, *In Epistolam S. Pauli*, 305; citing Phil 2:9; 2 Tim 2:12.

[27]Strigel, *Hypomnemata Epistolas*, 33; citing Tertullian, *Apology*, 50.
[†]Roman victors often wore brightly colored tunics embroidered with palms to denote their triumph.
[28]Holmes, *Gospel Musick*, 8; citing James 5.

LIKE GOOD MEDICINE COMPOUNDED FROM POISONOUS INGREDIENTS. PETER MARTYR VERMIGLI: "Knowing that your affliction produces patience." A common way of speaking in sacred Scripture should be noted here, by which that which belongs to a "thing" is attributed to an instrument or a "sign," which is often done with the sacraments. (We have not once alluded to the saying of Augustine, with which our enemies especially disagree.)† Here Paul attributes to afflictions that which is obviously the work of God and the Holy Spirit to bring about. When things by their nature are evil and hateful, they do not attract patience but instead, cast it off. We see this happen among the wicked, who, when they are very seriously afflicted, erupt in blasphemies and often even in despair. So, as a doctor compounds potent health-giving medicines from poisonous and noxious ingredients, so God the greatest and most perfect, in his wisdom, produces the most glorious virtues—such as patience—from afflictions, no matter how evil the events themselves may be. COMMENTARY ON ROMANS (1560).[29]

PATIENCE COMES THROUGH FAITH. JOHANNES BRENZ: "Suffering brings forth patience." What is this? It appears to be the first in many absurdities. For suffering brings forth more impatience than patience. We should understand, therefore, that when it says that suffering brings forth patience it must be understood and inserted at this place what was said above, through *faith*. Where there is not faith, there is impatience in suffering. But where faith is, there suffering produces true patience. For it is learned through faith that suffering does not occur blindly, but by the will of God. COMMENTARY ON ROMANS (1564).[30]

SUFFERING A "NECESSARY" CAUSE OF PATIENCE. WOLFGANG MUSCULUS: But it will be asked, How does the apostle say that endurance is produced from suffering since that brings forth impatience instead? Here it is necessary to observe the twofold derivation with regard to these things. One is what the dialecticians call a "sufficient cause," a certain "cause through which." Put this way, the effect follows unavoidably. For example, since the sun rises, therefore there is light. According to this type of cause, the thinking of the apostle would not be true. For it does not necessarily follow that where suffering is, soon there is patience, trial, and hope. Rather, with those who are afflicted, we see mostly impatience, dejection, despair, and an aversion to that suffering. It is far from being the case that patience, trial, and hope are brought about by suffering.

The other cause is what they call a "necessary" cause, without which something is not. It is as if you would say iron is the cause of the sword, stones, and wood and the remaining materials the cause of the house. For the sword cannot exist except by reason of the iron, nor the house except from the necessary materials. According to this method, what the apostle says is true: "Patience is brought forth from suffering." Neither is it possible for patience to exist without suffering. In fact, no one should say patience is the calm of that person to whom no suffering has befallen. And so, seeing that the great virtue of patience—which brings forth trial, from which is the solidity of hope—cannot be without suffering, the apostle says the virtue that comes from suffering is patience. And the pious also boast in tribulation since without it these good things cannot exist.

Therefore, the truth of this thinking must be observed to be useful, even when another cause is added—namely, faith in Christ, love for Christ, the hope of a future glory, knowledge of the divine works, and chiefly the power of the Spirit (the Spirit concerning whom he will speak next). For just as it is granted that children are not born without a woman, yet a woman is not a sufficient cause for giving birth, unless the following factors are added: the union with a man, age, fertility, and so on, therefore this holds. Even if patience cannot exist without suffering, nevertheless, suffering is

---

[29]Vermigli, *In Epistolam S. Pauli*, 305. †Augustine, *On the Catechising of the Uninstructed* 26.50.
[30]Brenz, *In Epistolam*, 124-25.

not a sufficient cause for patience unless those things I have spoken of are added. COMMENTARY ON ROMANS (1555).[31]

THE IMPORTANCE OF KNOWING. MARTIN BUCER: The apostle is here treating of things that are true of all Christians, for in this passage he is discussing that justification—as well as explaining its nature—that is possessed by all the saints. It is to all the saints that "the peace of God" comes; it is to all the saints that "an access into this grace" is opened up, so that "they eagerly wait for the glory of God," and do not doubt that "all things work together for their good" on the grounds that God loves them, and also because of the witness of the Holy Spirit, whom, "if anyone does not have, he does not belong to Christ."

Therefore, it also applies to all Christians when he says, "We know that suffering produces perseverance." There are no Christians of whom this is not true. What's more, what we "know" we have certainty of, and to "know" in this case is to rest on the Word of God and is, therefore, by faith which comes by the persuasion of the Holy Spirit. There is, therefore, greater certainty in this knowledge of faith than in any other kind of knowledge. Therefore, if Christians eagerly await the inheritance of the sons and daughters of God, it would be truly destructive for them not to know whether or not they are in the grace of God. COMMENTARY ON ROMANS (1536).[32]

5:4 Endurance Produces Character Produces Hope

ENTRUSTING OURSELVES TO GOD IN AFFLIC-TION. MARTIN BUCER: "Endurance produces a proven character." This ascending sequence, which furnishes all believers in Christ with what is needed for a confident and unimpeded journey, starts with bitter affliction and ends with a genuine

boasting in the goodness of God. We should accordingly impress upon our souls the confidence that as often as the Lord sees us undergoing these things he will always be there to aid our soul and exercise his ministry in our midst.

There are certain *axiōmata* or singularly noteworthy dogmas of our faith drawn from these verses that are profitable to recall to mind repeatedly and carefully ponder. Or to put it differently, since we are perpetually experiencing adverse circumstances and our cross must always be taken up and carried, this sentence in front of us should never be dismissed from our mind. "By your endurance you will possess your souls." It is fitting to always keep that text in mind along with what comes first: this step-by-step sequence and ascension from trying afflictions to a hope that does not put to shame. We entrust ourselves to the love of God because he gave up his Son to death for us while we were still his enemies, and because he bestowed his Spirit on us so that those of us who believe in this Son of his will come to possess eternal life. If we rightly call this to mind, we will be persuaded that even in the smallest matter absolutely nothing can come between us and God except what is singularly suited to our salvation. COMMENTARY ON ROMANS (1536).[33]

FAITH, HOPE, AND PATIENCE. PHILIPP MEL-ANCHTHON: This means that in this exercise, faith and hope are aroused and strengthened. For although faith and hope are related impulses and are not separated from each other, there is some difference. Faith is confidence by which we at present accept forgiveness of sins and declare that we have a gracious God. We are comforted at present by this mercy; its object also is God, apprehended in the Word by which the remission is bestowed. But hope is the expectation of future deliverance. It speaks not only about present mercy, but also about a future event.

These impulses, he says, increase in that exercise, and patience does not consider itself as merit on

[31]Musculus, *In Epistolam Apostoli Pauli*, 117-18.
[32]Bucer, *Metaphrases et Enarrationes*, 244-45; citing Rom 5:1; 5:2; 8:28; 8:16; 8:9; 5:3.
[33]Bucer, *Metaphrases et Enarrationes*, 245; citing Lk 21:19.

which hope depends, but considers itself an occasion for its exercise. For faith and hope are there when in affliction they fight against doubt and despair. Neither does patience come before hope, but Paul wants there to be hope in that struggle. That struggle is patience, obeying God and expecting liberation. And faith and hope depend on the gratuitous promise, otherwise they would become uncertain. COMMENTARY ON ROMANS (1540).[34]

EXPERIENCE GIVES BIRTH TO HOPE. PILGRAM MARPECK: Faith is the brother of love. For where there is no faith, love can have no brother. And where there is no hope, love has no sister. For love and faith cannot exist without hope. Experience is the mother of hope, for experience gives birth to hope, and hope will not disappoint. Everything comes from one Father who is God, and faith, love, and hope will also be born with him who is born of God, to live with him in this world. Beyond this time faith and hope cease, but love remains eternally in the knowledge of God and of his Christ, for she remains in God and God in her. CONCERNING LOVE.[35]

HOPE HAS THE HIGHEST PLACE. JOHANNES BUGENHAGEN: Why does Paul here place hope in the highest place when he previously called it the cause of all of these things that you see in the text? I answer that it is necessary that hope—which preserves faith—exist, lest temptations overwhelm us. Concerning this, he says here that testing brings forth hope. The apostle desires them to become stronger and more certain in trials. Everyone puts it to the test themselves when they once again conquer the adversary in the arena, having greater and more resolute courage in the face of many dangers. In such a way, godly souls who have been tested and afflicted more than once, endure in adversity so that they do not abandon their Christ, who is their only hope. INTERPRETATION OF ROMANS (1531).[36]

5:5 Hope and the Love of God

FOOLISH HOPE, WISE HOPE. JOHN TRAPP: As among humankind, many lie languishing at Hope's hospital, as he did at the pool of Bethesda, and return as they did from the Brooks of Tema. Or, as people go to a lottery with heads full of hopes but return with hearts full of blanks. The Dutch have a proverb to this purpose: *Sperare et expectare, multos reddit stultos* (To hope and to expect makes many foolish). And we say, he that hopes for dead men's shoes may have to go barefoot. Bad people's hopes may hope headless; they may perish in the height of their expectancies. Not so those that hope in God. They shall yet praise him who is the help of their countenance, and their God. COMMENTARY ON ROMANS (1656).[37]

FAITH, HOPE, AND LOVE. JACQUES LEFÈVRE D'ÉTAPLES: The order that Paul places between these three virtues, faith, hope and love, is noteworthy. Faith is first, then hope, and third love. From faith comes hope, but the love of God always follows behind faith and hope. For if you do not believe, you do not have faith, and therefore do not hope. If you do not hope, you do not love. But if you both believe and hope, then you love constantly. And the "love of God" is the perfection and consummation of the other two, faith and hope, which, according to the apostles and St. Paul, is poured out abundantly by the Holy Spirit. He says that hope does not disappoint, and he then follows with the reason why: "because the love of God is poured out in our hearts by the Holy Spirit who has been given to us." If hope were without love, it would be in vain and would disappoint when it comes upon death instead of life. Therefore, let us imitate the glorious apostles, having a firm faith, which is accompanied by hope of the glory of God that is to be ours, in which let us rejoice in our minds. And let us rejoice not only in the hope of glory, but also by calmly enduring tribulations,

---

[34]Melanchthon, *Commentary on Romans*, 127*.
[35]CRR 2:517-18*.
[36]Bugenhagen, *In D. Pauli ad Romanos*, 49r.

[37]Trapp, *A Commentary or Exposition upon the Epistle of St. Paul*, 629*; citing Jn 5; Job 6:18-20; Ps 43.

recognizing our being proved by our patience, and growing in hope, to which we ask that charity be added by the gift of the Holy Spirit. And how could we not have hope? How could we not have the love of God? "For when we were weak and powerless to return to health, at the right time Christ died for us, the ungodly. Scarcely would any of you be willing to die for a righteous person; though perhaps someone might for a good person," or perhaps in order to achieve some good end they might dare to commit themselves in some critical moment facing death. But we were not righteous; rather we were unrighteous and ungodly. Nor was Christ seeking his own good or some profit for himself in dying for us, but only our good. For he who already had from the Father the status of being greater than all, sought nothing of his own advantage. For he said, "The Father has given to me: he is greater than all." And by this he showed us his great and ineffable love toward us for the purpose of increasing hope and love in us. COMMENTARY ON ROMANS (1517).[38]

CERTAINTY AND HOPE. JOHN CALVIN: But why employ a more obscure testimony? Paul uniformly declares that the conscience can have no peace or quiet joy until it is held for certain that we are justified by faith. And he at the same time declares from what this certainty is derived. That is, when "the love of God is shed abroad in our hearts by the Holy Ghost"; it is as if he had said that our souls cannot have peace until we are fully assured that we are pleasing to God. Thus he elsewhere exclaims in the person of believers in general, "Who shall separate us from the love of Christ?" Until we have reached that haven, the slightest breeze will make us tremble, but so long as the Lord is our Shepherd, we shall walk without fear in the valley of the shadow of death. Thus those who pretend that justification by faith consists in being regenerated and made just by living spiritually, have never tasted the sweetness of grace in trusting that God will be propitious. Hence also,

they know no more of praying aright than do . . . any heathen people. For, as Paul declares, faith is not true, unless it suggests and dictates the delightful name of Father. Indeed, unless it opens our mouths and enables us to cry freely, "Abba, Father." This he expresses more clearly in another passage: "In whom we have boldness and access with confidence by the faith of him." This, certainly, is not obtained by the gift of regeneration, which, as it is always defective in the present state, contains within it many grounds of doubt. Whereby, we must have recourse to this remedy; we must hold that the only hope that believers have of the heavenly inheritance is, that being engrafted into the body of Christ, they are justified freely. For, in regard to justification, faith is merely passive, bringing nothing of our own to procure the favor of God, but receiving from Christ everything that we want. INSTITUTES OF THE CHRISTIAN RELIGION 3.13.5 (1559).[39]

EXULTING IN THE GLORY OF GOD. JACQUES LEFÈVRE D'ÉTAPLES: If hope had been without love, it would have been empty and brought disorder, so that by it one would have found not life, but death. Therefore, let us imitate the glorious apostles, having the firm faith that hope follows to arrive at the glory of God in which we exult in our minds. And we do not exult in the hope of glory alone, but calmly bearing tribulations, acknowledging our testing by suffering and increasing hope, we also pray for love to be adjoined to it by the gift of the Holy Spirit. If we do not yet hope, we do not yet have the love of God. Yet, "when we were weak" and sick—at that time, "Christ died for us, the ungodly"—so that we might return to health. Hardly anyone would wish to die for a righteous person, even though they, for another good—for the sake of any good you like—might dare to commit themselves to the crisis of death. But neither were we righteous, but unrighteous and ungodly. He asks, "Was Christ not seeking our true good when dying for us? For he sought no

---

[38]Lèfevre, *Epistole divi Pauli*, 62v; citing Jn 10:29.

[39]Calvin, *Institutes*, 2:72*; citing Rom 8:35; Ps 23; Eph 3:12.

advantage for himself, who held from his Father that which was greater than all." "That which," he said, "the Father has given me is greater than all." And in that great and ineffable work he showed us his love to increase hope and charity in us, that "while we were still sinners" and certainly at that time, "he died for us." What then? Shall we (whom he redeemed, justified, reconciled to the Father), not much more be saved through him, being snatched from eternal damnation? Must we not much more hope and burn with love and exult in God through Christ our Lord who loves and loved us and brought together such plans for our benefit? If death reconciled the sons of God to God when enemies, will his immortal life not much more save those already reconciled and made friends? These are arguments from the lesser to the greater, and this is how Paul reasons. COMMENTARY ON ROMANS (1517).[40]

THE SCHOLASTICS AND THEIR UNCERTAINTY OF HOPE.

PETER MARTYR VERMIGLI: The scholastics taught something far different. For the Master of Sentences [Peter Lombard] in his third book defined "hope" in this way: "Hope is the certain expectation of that future blessedness that is coming to us from the grace of God and by our merits that precede it." That this definition, especially in its last phrase, is completely absurd, is clearly seen in the case of those who are newly converted to Christ out of the most serious and abominable vices. For such people most certainly cannot have any good merits, since they were formerly destitute of the love (*caritas*) from which the scholastics asserted that all our merits proceed. At the same time, it is even more certain that those who have been converted to Christ cannot possibly lack hope. Augustine in his exposition of the psalm "Out of the Depths" (*De Profundis*) exhorts those who had fallen away and those who had turned back to the evil depths that they should not cast away all hope, pointing them to the example of the thief on the cross and of many others. We will,

therefore, investigate from what merits hope is granted to men and women in this fashion. The scholastics customarily answer that "merits do not always precede hope, but they do always precede the thing hoped for." And they explain this opinion of theirs on this subject in such a way that they conclude that merits precede hope, either real merit itself or at least the intention thereof. For men and women who are newly converted, when they take hold of the hope of salvation, usually intend in their soul and their thoughts to do good works, by which these scholastics would have us believe they merit the ultimate reward. But how much present hope can these good works produce, that the soul intends but hasn't yet actually done? An effect that already exists cannot be from a cause that hasn't yet happened. To the contrary, it is far more properly stated that a good will arises from both faith and hope, than that either hope or faith proceed from a good will as their cause.

But it is a sport to see how it is that these scholastics change their colors, when on the one hand they say that "hope is the certain expectation" and yet on the other hand want us to regard it as a most infallible dogma that nobody can be certain about his salvation unless it is revealed to him by God himself in some extraordinary fashion. This they think they have themselves, and they confess that it is difficult to see what this certainty of hope could be. Because of this, these miserable men are in turmoil, and nervously sweat and contrive many explanations. They first assert that all certainty of hope flows from the certainty of faith (and this at least they say rightly), so we therefore hope with certainty because it is by faith that the most certain promise of God is embraced. But they proceed further and say that it is by *faith* that we believe in a general and absolute sense that all the elect and those predestined will be saved, but we *hope* when we trust that we are among the number of the elect. They speak as if hope possesses a special knowledge within the larger scope of faith, so that whatever can be understood by faith in a general sense is applied to us personally by hope. They then assert that this certainty of hope is only

---

[40]Lèfevre, *Epistole divi Pauli*, 62v; citing Jn 10:29.

hypothetical, for it holds only if we are among the elect and if we persevere to the end—and so they wish to compose this kind of certainty out of only probable conjectures. And finally they conclude that there is less certainty of hope than there is of faith. COMMENTARY ON ROMANS (1560).[41]

HOPE PERSONALIZES THE GOODNESS OF GOD. PETER MARTYR VERMIGLI: We, on the other hand, derive a certainty out of both faith and hope: however much we have with regard to faith, that much we have also toward hope. Nor does faith reserve for itself some measure of certainty that does not also pass over to hope. They assert a pure fiction when they say that it is by hope that we apply those things to ourselves that we believe in a general and absolute sense by faith. For we do not believe merely that God is good, or Father, or the source of human happiness, but rather each and every pious person is assured by faith in his own mind that God is good *to him*, that he is *his* Father, the source of *his* happiness and present and future existence. This is what the certainty of hope does, and this is why Paul writes that it cannot be disappointed. Whereas faith regards God as truthful, hope regards him as faithful and eagerly poised to grant his promises, knowing that God is not less faithful in making good on his promises than he is true in making them. Hence it is demonstrated that hope has as much certainty as faith has. Nor does it help their case when they finally prate that hope has a certainty as it pertains to the object hoped for, but not as it pertains to the subject who hopes. For although, they say, hope has regard to God's clemency, goodness, grace, and power, it is certain of nothing except that each one of these attributes of God will remain intact. Thus they place a solid certainty on hope only in this sense. But if you consider the subject, that is, the soul and will of the one who is hoping, since our will is bendable and both wavers and changes, it can never be certain of or secure about its salvation. To tell the truth, these people seem to me to be just

like those who, when they are defending a city under siege, diligently close and bar all the other doors, yet all the while leave one open, for which reason they realize that they were taking their task too lightly when their enemies come in and plunder everything. In this way, these men expend great pains lest any uncertainty should be seen arising from God's goodness, power, and mercy, or from the merits of Christ. At the same time, however, they assert that our will is so liable to change that it neither can nor should promise itself perseverance even on the basis of God's Word. They therefore entirely do away with all certainty, leaving no room for Paul's assertion that "hope does not disappoint," nor does that "certainty" which they attempt to establish actually do us any real good.

If, however, we would consult the sacred text, we understand not only that God is generally good, and generally powerful, but that he is good and propitious to us personally. He will, therefore, undertake to strengthen our will so that it will never fall away from him. For as we cited a little above, "He will not allow us to be tempted beyond that which we are able to endure, but will along with the temptation make a way of escape." And in the first chapter of 1 Corinthians: "He will confirm you unto the end, that you might be blameless in the Day of our Lord Jesus Christ. God is faithful, by whom you have been called." And there are many other testimonies of this kind in the sacred text that promise us both perseverance and the strengthening of our will through Christ. For this reason, we say that this certainty of hope is a firm clinging to the promises offered to us and received in faith, which we are not to wander from because of the final end to follow. COMMENTARY ON ROMANS (1560).[42]

THE "LOVE OF GOD" REFERS TO HIS LOVE FOR US. JOHANNES BRENZ: It is clear that a few of the ecclesiastical writers explain the love of God in this verse as the love with which we love

---

[41]Vermigli, *In Epistolam S. Pauli*, 311-12; citing Ps 130.

[42]Vermigli, *In Epistolam S. Pauli*, 312-13; citing 1 Cor 10:13; 1 Cor 1:8-9.

God and which the Holy Spirit stirs up in us. And, indeed, in its own place, this is rightly said. For we are entirely obligated to love God—according to his command—from the whole heart and the whole soul. Even though in this world we are not able to fulfill this command perfectly by natural strength, nevertheless by the gift of the Holy Spirit it is possible, or at least we can begin to love God partially in this life. And we testify to what sort of obedience our obligation is. Wherefore, when it is said that the Holy Spirit works that we may love God, it is a true thought, in its place. But it is utterly alien from this place in Paul. For in this verse, he does not refer to that love of God by which we love God, but rather to that by which God loves us. For Paul soon explains his own words: "God commends his own love toward us. . . ."

Seeing that the faith by which we freely obtain the forgiveness of sins is on account of Christ, Paul disputes that if it depended on any merit of his own love with which he loves God he should look forward to the pardon of sins and the heavenly salvation. Therefore, when Paul says, "The love of God is poured forth into our hearts through the Holy Spirit," he does not mean by the term "love of God" our love toward God, but God's love toward us. Commentary on Romans (1564).[43]

Possible Meanings of the "Love of God."

Heinrich Bullinger: To all these things, the efficient cause, the Holy Spirit, is added, who abundantly pours forth the love of God into our hearts. Indeed, this love easily overcomes the most savage and insurmountable things, because nothing is too difficult for the one who loves. Or this may be the sense: For that reason, those who believe cannot be brought to ruin, because through the inspiration of the Holy Spirit they learn how great is that love of God toward the human race by which he delivered himself over for us. Commentary on Romans (1533).[44]

Loving into the Midst of the Shadows.

Martin Luther: It is called "God's love" because by it we love God alone, where nothing is visible, nothing experiential, either inwardly or outwardly, in which we can trust or which is to be loved or feared; but it is carried away beyond all things into the invisible God, who cannot be experienced, who cannot be comprehended, that is, into the midst of the shadows, not knowing what it loves, only knowing what it does not love; turning away from everything which it has known and experienced, and desiring only that which it has not yet known, saying: "I am sick with love"; that is, I do not want what I have and I do not have what I want. But this gift is far removed from those who still are looking at their own righteousnesses and love them, and are sad and despairing when they cannot be seen, and trust in them when they are seen, and feel secure in them and thus do not "rejoice in sufferings," are not tested, and thus have no hope. Lectures on Romans (1516).[45]

We Are Not Justified by the Inherent Habit of Love.

Andrew Willet: Whereas the apostle says, "The love of God is shed abroad in our hearts." Pererius—understanding the apostle to speak here of that love and charity that is infused as a habit into the mind, by which we love God—sets down here certain positions concerning this inherent charity. (1) He affirms that this charity is that justice by which we are formally made just and righteous before God (Disputation 2.10). (2) This charity by which we are justified he affirms to be a gift far exceeding all other gifts. (3) This charity is not indeed distinguished from grace making us acceptable to God. (4) Against the opinion of Cajetan, Scotus, and Gabriel,[†] he holds that in those who are justified, there is a habit of charity that is permanent and remains when the act ceases by which they are formally made just before God; otherwise they would not be held to be just before God in their sleep or when they cease to work (Disputation 3.17-18).

---

[43]Brenz, *In Epistolam*, 129 & 131.
[44]Bullinger, *In Sanctissimam Pauli*, 73v-74r.

[45]LW 25:294*; citing Song 2:5.

Contra: Although all these questions are not pertinent here because the apostle doesn't deal here with the charity or love that is in a man or woman toward God but of God's love toward us, . . . yet it will not be amiss to briefly counterpoise these erroneous assertions with the contrary true and sound positions:

1. We do not deny that there is an inherent righteousness and infused charity in the faithful, but it is not such as by which we are formally made righteous and justified before God, both because all our righteousness is as a stained cloth, it is imperfect and weak, and therefore not able to justify us. And because the Scripture testifies that it is the righteousness of Christ that is applied by faith by which we are justified before God, as the apostle calls it, "The righteousness of God, through the faith of Christ."

2. Charity is not simply the greatest of all other gifts and so absolutely preferred before faith, but only wherein they are compared together, namely, in respect to the continuance, because faith and hope shall cease, when we enjoy those things that are believed and hoped for, but love will remain still. So Chrysostom expounds the apostle. Thus Hugo says well that charity is said to be the greatest because it does not fall away, but otherwise faith is the greater, as it is a knowledge and engenders all other virtues.

3. The Thomists are herein contrary to the Jesuits who affirm that *gratia gratum faciens*, grace that makes us acceptable to God, is in respect of charity as the soul is to the powers and faculties that proceed from it. And so indeed the grace that makes us acceptable to God is the love and favor of God in Christ, that is, as the sufficient cause of that other love and charity that is infused into us and worked in us by the Holy Spirit. And that our love of God makes us not first acceptable to him, the apostle evidently testifies, "Herein is love, not that we loved him, but that he loved us." We were first accepted and beloved of God before we could love him again.

4. We grant that faith, hope, and charity are habits of the mind infused by the Spirit and permanent in the soul. For as the wicked do attain to evil habits of vice and sin, so the faithful have the habit of virtue. But this is the difference: that an evil habit is *acquisitus*, got by evil custom, but the good habits of the intellectual virtues of faith, love, and hope are infused and worked in us by the Spirit.

But we deny that by any such inherent habit we are made formally just. They are not causes of our justification, but rather the fruits and effects. We have the habit of faith because the Spirit of God works in us belief. And we love God because he loved us first and gave us his Spirit, which works his love in us. . . . So then the faithful, even in their sleep, are justified, not by any inherent habit, but because they are accepted of God in Christ, as the apostle says, "Christ died for us, that whether we wake or sleep, we should live together with him." A Six-fold Commentary on the Epistle to the Romans (1611).[46]

Let Love Ignite Our Hearts. Leupold Scharnschlager: Christ himself bears the burden he has called us to take up and carry after him, through his Holy Spirit and the love of God poured out in our hearts. That is the true power that makes the burden of Christ light. Thus I ask of you that this love shape us, encircle us, and take us captive. May this love give us its strong wine to drink, that we may forget ourselves. Let love inscribe herself in our hearts through her self-revelation and the inflowing confirmation of her faithfulness, friendship, and goodness. Let her ignite our hearts toward her with fiery brilliance and become such a lovely aromatic bag of myrrh that we will never relinquish it in eternity. An Epistle of Comfort Concerning the Love of God.[47]

---

[46]Willet, *Hexapla*, 267-68; citing Is 64; Rom 3:22; Phil 3:9; 1 Cor 13:13; 1 Jn 4:10; 1 Thess 5:10. †Gabriel Biel (1410–1495) was a German scholastic, nominalist theologian. His views on justification and soteriology are frequently described as "semi-Pelagian."
[47]CRR 12:527*; citing Mt 11:29f.

LOVE COMES THROUGH THE HOLY SPIRIT.
DIRK PHILIPS: And this is now the principal
teaching and the highest command of our Lord
Jesus Christ, that we shall have love one for another
just as he has loved us. And this love is not only in
words, but lies in power and truth and must be
shown in deeds. For since God is love, as John says,
so it is powerful and according to Solomon's word,
stronger than death and firmer than hell, for love is
fiery and a flame of the Lord, that waters also
cannot extinguish love, nor streams drown it. And
if someone wanted to give all his goods for love, he
cannot buy it with them, for it is a gift of the Lord
and a special power of God. It comes into the heart
of believers through the Holy Spirit, and apart
from love nothing counts that a person does; as
little as anything counts that is outside of God.
THE FRISIAN FLEMISH DIVISION.[48]

5:6-8 *Christ Died for Us Sinners*

ACCORDING TO THE TIME. ANDREW WILLET:
How Christ is said to have died according to the
time. Some refer these words to the former clause
and read thus, "When we were yet weak according
to the time," that is, we were weak in the time of
the law, when grace had not yet appeared. So
Chrysostom, Theodore, and Erasmus think this is
added as a mitigation of their infirmity. But it is
against the apostle's use to qualify the corruption
and evil of human nature. And he speaks to the
Gentiles that did not have the law, as well as to
the Jews.

Most apply it to the latter clause, that Christ
died in his time. And there are diverse opinions.
Some understand it of the short time that Christ's
death continued . . . namely, only three days. But
that time being assigned to Christ's resurrection, it
is not fitly expounded of his death. Sedulius
interpreted it thus: . . . because he died in the last
time or age of the world. According to the time,
that is, he died temporally in the flesh, which is

mortal, for eternity knows no time. . . . Jerome . . .
refers it to the opportunity of time: Christ died in
a fit time, when the world stood most in need of
his redemption. But the best exposition is that
Christ died in the fullness of time, as the apostle
says, the time decreed and appointed of his father.
SIX-FOLD COMMENTARY ON THE EPISTLE TO THE
ROMANS (1611).[49]

**WE ARE WANDERING SHEEP DRAWN BY HIS
LOVE.** JOHANNES BUGENHAGEN: An argument
based on timing. We exist within time, while God
exists outside of time. We are, therefore, the saints
and the blessed according to predestination, since
he loved us in Christ "before the foundation of the
world." But when we are in the flesh, we exist
within time, and consequently in our ungodliness
we do not acknowledge God or his grace. We are
wandering sheep and will not be snatched away
from that error unless that drawing by love lays
hold of us—that love with which he loved us from
eternity past. Here you can once again see how
impious it is for us to pretend to have merits, for if
salvation depended on our works, our righteousness would last only for a moment, just like our
works do. Therefore only grace can assure us of
God's good will toward us when he pours this
peace into us, something works can never accomplish. Or why would the apostle have said that we
are all "weak," if not because we can do nothing
good, not even cooperate with grace? INTERPRETA-
TION OF ROMANS (1531).[50]

THE ALPHA AND OMEGA OF OUR SALVATION.
AEGIDIUS HUNNIUS: As Paul writes, Christ died
for us while we were yet his enemies. From this we
learn that God, by his grace and mercy, preceded us.
And so then, there is no congruous merit, of which
the scholastics talked foolishly. They taught that
we could anticipate the grace of God by congruous
merit. Truly, however, the enemies of God are able
to merit nothing, whether *ex congruo* or *ex*

---

[48]CRR 6:479-80*; citing Jn 15:12; 1 Jn 3:18; 1 Jn 4:7; Song 8:6f.;
1 Cor 1; Rom 5:5; 1 Cor 13:1-2.
[49]Willet, *Hexapla*, 242*; citing Gal 4:4.
[50]Bugenhagen, *In D. Pauli ad Romanos*, 50r-v; citing Eph 1:4.

condigno,† except for damnation. Therefore the mercy and grace of God in perfecting our salvation both precedes and follows us, and is for all our salvation, the alpha and omega, the beginning and the end. EXPOSITION ON ROMANS (1592).[51]

CHRIST'S ARDENT LONGING INSPIRES OUR LASTING LOVE. MARTIN BUCER: Let us take note of something that the apostle was trying to express, which he here repeats for the third time: this antithesis of our ungodliness with the death of Christ. He first said, "died for the ungodly," then a bit later, "died for . . . sinners," and last, "we were reconciled by" his "death while were still his enemies." Surely in this collation a most holy doctrine is proposed to us, and there is no limit to how much it would increase piety among us all if this were always religiously kept in mind. For when we contemplate that before Christ had reconciled us to the Father, we were capable of being nothing but sinners, ungodly and the enemies of God, what can we give ourselves credit for? What reason could there be for not wholly detesting our own nature, being as lost as it is, and hence utterly denying ourselves? If we were to do this, the root of every sin would at once be cut out. On the other hand, if we carefully consider that although we were being completely carried away contrary to his one, holy, and perfect will, and although we were offending him in the gravest possible manner, he nevertheless embraced us with such love that he willed that his Son should die in order to redeem us, and the Son himself submitted to this death with ardent longing—what could stand in the way that would prevent you from entirely handing yourself over and devoting yourself completely to this God and Savior of yours who loves you in such an incomparable way? How could you doubt that you will receive from him anything whatever that could be to your advantage? What thing could be burdensome for you to do or to suffer when you know that you're accepted by him? What else,

finally, could there be that could so inflame us with true and lasting love toward our neighbors, and even toward our enemies? Such love could never take up residence in your soul as long as you were nothing but an ungodly person, a sinner, and an enemy to God—who is not only the Highest Good but also All Good. Nevertheless, he in his infinite love for you restored you to himself in fellowship of eternal life. With this thought carefully pondered by faith and always repeated within the heart, who would not let go of all other things that are not God and devote themselves to him alone so much that they would freely wish to think on, seek after, and live for nothing other than God? COMMENTARY ON ROMANS (1536).[52]

HERE GOD REVEALS HIS ANATOMY. JOHN TRAPP: Herein God lays naked to us the tenderest innards of his fatherly compassions, as in an anatomy. A young student in history, Polybius says, should have the whole history of the world under his view and should reduce it all into one body. God, by giving his Son for us, showed us all his love at once, as it were embodied. All other spiritual blessings meet in this, as the lines in the center, as the streams in the fountain. If the centurion were held worthy of respect because he loved our nation, they said, and built us a synagogue, what shall we say of Almighty God, who so loved our souls that he gave his only-begotten Son. COMMENTARY ON ROMANS (1656).[53]

I SEE NOTHING ELSE BUT LOVE. MARGUERITE DE NAVARRE: Alas, good Jesus! You saw my blindness and that in my need I would have no human aid. Then you opened the way to my salvation. O what goodness and sweetness! Is there any father to the daughter or else brother to the sister that would ever do as he has done? For he came into hell to aid my soul, where against his will she was willing to perish because she did not love

---

[51]Hunnius, *Epistolae Divi Pauli*, 199-200; †see the introduction for a discussion of *congruo* and *condigno* merit.

[52]Bucer, *Metaphrases et Enarrationes*, 250; citing Rom 5:6; 5:8; 5:10.
[53]Trapp, *A Commentary or Exposition upon the Epistle of St. Paul*, 629*; citing Luke 7:5.

you, alas! You have loved her. O Charity, fervent and inflamed, you are not slack in loving, you who love everybody, yes, and also your enemies, not only forgiving them their offenses, but also giving yourself (for their salvation, liberty, and deliverance) to the death, cross, travail, pain, and suffering. When I consider the occasion of your love toward me, I can see nothing else but the love that incites you to give me what I cannot deserve. THE MIRROR OF THE SINFUL SOUL (1544).[54]

WHY GOD CHOSE THE CROSS AS THE METHOD OF SALVATION. PETER MARTYR VERMIGLI: He wished to come, and to undergo the most bitter death on the cross. It was fitting that something good be offered to God in order to redeem us, which was able either equally or even more to appease him than all the sins of the world had displeased him. That is what Christ offered for us. For if you ask why the death of Christ was so acceptable to God, no other reason can be found than his immense love and goodwill. For God certainly could have been contented by any other thing, but rather, he willed this. Not so that he could feed on the affliction and supplications of Christ with his eyes or mind, for this would have been savage of the Father, nor because he foresaw the great love and humility in the Son—although these were also at their greatest in Christ, and valued greatly by the Father. Rather, I judge that it was for this single purpose: that his love could be declared to us most perfectly by his works, and an example could be given to human beings for living in the most holy way. For if you ask whether it were necessary for the Son of God to die thus, I respond that no necessity of action can be established here, for there is no coercion in God. And neither do we establish a necessity here by the goal of the supposition, for human salvation could have been provided by many other plans and ways in a fashion he wished. But it was necessary for Christ

to die from the supposition of the divine providence and counsel: for God had decreed it beforehand, and he did this in the most powerful way in order to declare his boundless love. COMMENTARY ON ROMANS (1560).[55]

WILLING TO DIE? THE ENGLISH ANNOTATIONS: Some will have these words to be read with an interrogative point, and render them thus: "Scarce will one die for a righteous man, for even for a good man will any man easily undertake to die?" But if the words are to be read without an interrogative point, then the apostle's meaning is that though it may be that some are found courageous and kind enough that they would undertake such a task as dying for another, especially for a very good person, yet it is a very rare thing that seldom happens. ANNOTATIONS ON ROMANS 5:7.[56]

DOCTRINE, CONSOLATION, AND CONFUTATION. NIELS HEMMINGSEN: Here is an adaptation of the text into a collection of its propositions, the main force of which is:

(P1) If someone should endure to die for those who are righteous and good, he would certainly be declaring his deepest love toward them.

(P2) But now Christ the Son of God died for us who are not righteous, but unrighteous, for us who are not good, but wicked, and therefore did not do so expecting some benefit or anything useful he might receive from us.

(C) Therefore God's love, that moved him to deliver up his only-begotten Son for our sakes must necessarily be immense and ineffable.

This homily of Paul's on God's love toward us should be carefully observed, for it contains within it both the most useful doctrine, the most abundant consolation, and the soundest confutation of the law-enforcers. Its doctrine is that the death of Christ was accomplished by grace for expiating the

---

[54]De Navarre, *The Mirror of the Sinful Soul*, 71-72*; citing Acts 4; 1 Jn 4. Translated into English by Elizabeth I when she was eleven years old.

[55]Vermigli, *In Epistolam S. Pauli*, 329-30.
[56]Downame, ed., *Annotations*, AAA4r*.

impiety of men and women, and that it alone has earned our salvation.

A consolation is here provided in the face of God's great wrath, in that the Son of God loved men and women so much that he diverted his Father's wrath toward himself so that men and women, who are made in God's image, might not eternally perish. Its confutation is of the errors of the Pharisees of every age, who think that men and women are delivered from sin and death by means other than by the sacrifice of the Son of God alone. COMMENTARY ON ROMANS (1562).[57]

NOT THE WORLD'S WISDOM, RIGHTEOUSNESS, OR LOVE. DIRK PHILIPS: That is not the world's wisdom, nor of the angels in heaven, but it is God's wisdom hidden in secrecy, which was preached by the apostles, not with words of human cleverness, but with such words as the Holy Spirit had taught them. That is also a severe, exalted, and valiant, yes, eternal righteousness of God, that he has punished so severely and made his own beloved Son to pay for our sins (which could be paid or taken away through no other means). And that is also no human love and mercy, but it is God's eternal love, God's bottomless grace and mercy that Jesus Christ has died for us while we were sinners, godless, and God's enemies. THE CONGREGATION OF GOD.[58]

INCOMPREHENSIBLE, AMAZING LOVE. RICHARD BAXTER: Such incomprehensible, amazing love of God the Father and of Christ is manifested in this new covenant, that the glorifying of it does seem to be the main end in this design. O sweet and blessed end! Shouldn't then the searching into it be our main study? And the contemplating of it—the admiring of it—be our main employment? No wonder, therefore, that God did not prevent the fall of humanity, even though he foresaw it, when he could make it an occasion preparative to such happy ends. APHORISMS OF JUSTIFICATION.[59]

---

[57]Hemmingsen, *Commentarius in Epistolam*, 182-83.
[58]CRR 6:362*; citing 1 Cor. 2:6f.; Is 53:8; 1 Pet 2:24; Gal 1:4; Rom 5:8.
[59]Baxter, *Aphorismes*, 50*; citing Rom 5:8, Tit 3:4, 1 Jn 4:9; Eph 3:18-19; Jn 15:13.

5:9 Saved by Christ's Blood

THE INSTRUMENTAL RATHER THAN INHERENT WORTH OF FAITH. WOLFGANG MUSCULUS: "Having been justified by his blood we will be saved." We see this justification of ours that he had earlier attributed to faith here being attributed to the blood, that is, the death, of Christ. Consequently, he does not assign justification to faith as if faith possessed some inherent worth that merits our being justified, but rather as that which by believing instrumentally "lays hold of" what was acquired by the blood of Christ. The merit for our justification is not in our faith, but in the blood of Christ. But, because justification is not apprehended by any other thing but by faith alone, it is therefore correctly attributed to faith as well. COMMENTARY ON ROMANS (1555).[60]

CHRIST, THE GIFT-GIVER. GEORG MAJOR: The phrase "being reconciled" explains the term "being justified," letting us know in regard to the word "righteousness" that a repayment is implied, namely, a reconciliation or an acceptance that is made by means of the Mediator between God and humanity. . . . Through Christ, grace and gift are given, as we lay hold of reconciliation by faith, and are brought back to life through the Son. Just as he says: "I give them eternal life." Likewise, "He who has the Son, has life." EXPOSITION OF THE EPISTLES OF PAUL (1569).[61]

THE NECESSITY OF A BLOODY DEATH. WOLFGANG MUSCULUS: Why doesn't it say that we are justified by Christ having breathed out his spirit on the cross? The satisfaction of divine justice is not located in the breathing out of his spirit because it does not involve the bloody and violent death that is denoted by "the shedding of blood." For satisfaction, it was necessary that that Lamb be slain and offered as One slain by a bloody death. A merely common death occurred in breathing out his spirit,

---

[60]Musculus, *In Epistolam Apostoli Pauli*, 117.
[61]Major, *Enarrationes Epistolarum S. Pauli*, 114; citing Jn 10:28; 1 Jn 5:12.

but it is not so with the shedding of his blood—this is rightly understood as signifying that Christ died for our sins in order to satisfy divine justice. A bloody death is required of those who are punished for evil deeds, not simply that they breathe out their spirit. This is what the slaughter of bulls and the blood of the Passover lamb was all about. COMMENTARY ON ROMANS (1555).[62]

SAVED BY BLOOD FROM WRATH. MICHELANGELO:

From a vexatious, heavy load, set free,
Eternal Lord, and from the world unloosed,
Wearied to you I turn, like a frail bark
Escaped from fierce storms, into a placid sea.
The thorns, the nails, the one and the other hand,
Together with your aspect, meek, benign,
And mangled, pledge the grace to mourning souls,
Of deep repentance, and Salvation's hope.
View not my sins in the condemning light,
Of justice strict; avert your awful ear,
Nor stretch forth on me your avenging arm.
May your blood wash my guilt and sins away;
As age creeps on may it abound the more,
With timely aid, and full forgiveness.

SONNET 49.[63]

THE LAMB SLAIN BEFORE THE FOUNDATION OF THE WORLD. WOLFGANG MUSCULUS: Now, so that no persons will say to themselves: "If we are justified by the blood of Christ alone, in such a way that we lay hold of that justification by means of faith—that is, if faith does not justify in and of itself, but merely lays hold of what was obtained by the blood of Christ, then since it is said to justify us in the same way that Abraham was justified by faith, although the blood of Christ was not at that time yet available, how are we not to conclude that it was shed needlessly?" It should here be understood that this blood of Christ was shed in the last days with respect to this world, in which world there exist ages and turning points in time; but that

in God's sight, before whom there is no passage of time, it had already been shed from the beginning of the world. That's why it is said "the Lamb who was slain from the foundation of the world." The effects of the blood of Christ extend not only to subsequent ages but to preceding ones as well. For inasmuch as Christ was appointed by the Father as the sole Mediator of all men and women, as much of those of the old covenant as those of the new, so also by his blood was redemption accomplished for all men and women, of all the ages. Now as for the fact that in Hebrew this blood of Christ is called the "blood of the new covenant," this was said to distinguish between the blood of the old covenant that was poured out repeatedly in a symbolic, figurative way through the slaughtering of the Passover lamb and of bulls. This is not to be taken as meaning that the blood of Christ pertains only to the new covenant with respect to its effects and the work of redemption. COMMENTARY ON ROMANS (1555).[64]

SEPARATION AND RESTORATION. JOHN CALVIN: Let us now consider the truth of what was said in the definition—that is, that justification by faith is reconciliation with God, and that this consists solely in the remission of sins. We must always return to the axiom that the wrath of God lies on all people as long as they continue to be sinners. This is elegantly expressed by Isaiah in these words: "Behold, the Lord's hand is not shortened, that it cannot save; neither his ear heavy, that it cannot hear. But your iniquities have separated between you and your God, and your sins have hid his face from you, that he will not hear." We are here told that sin is a separation between God and humans; that his countenance is turned away from the sinner; and that it cannot be otherwise, since to have any engagement with sin is repugnant to his righteousness. Hence the apostle shows that we are at enmity with God until we are restored to favor by Christ. When the Lord, therefore, admits us to union, he is said to justify

---

[62]Musculus, *In Epistolam Apostoli Pauli*, 117; citing Heb 9:22.
[63]Michelangelo, *Life of Michael Angelo*, 169-170*.
[64]Musculus, *In Epistolam Apostoli Pauli*, 117-18; citing Rev. 13:8.

us, because he can neither receive us into favor, nor unite us to himself, without changing our condition from that of sinners into that of righteous persons. We add that this is done by remission of sins. For if those whom the Lord has reconciled to himself are assessed by their works, they will still prove to be, in reality, sinners, while they ought to be pure and free from sin. It is evident, therefore, that the only way in which those whom God embraces are made righteous, is by having their pollutions wiped away by the remission of sins, so that this justification may be termed in one word: the remission of sins. INSTITUTES OF THE CHRISTIAN RELIGION 3.11.21 (1559).[65]

5:10 Reconciled by Christ's Death and Life

CHRIST, THE PERFECT SAVIOR. WILLIAM GUILD: From this verse we reason in this way: God's love is no less to us, now that we are reconciled to him by the death of his Son, than when we were enemies and unreconciled. Rather, it is greater. When we were enemies, he reconciled us to himself by the death of his Son, perfectly saving us, both from the guilt of sin here and from all satisfaction-making punishment for the same here or hereafter, as the apostle testifies in Hebrews.

Therefore, now that we are reconciled, how much more shall he perfectly save us, both from the guilt of sin here and from all satisfaction-making punishment whatsoever that it deserves here or hereafter. Otherwise, Christ could not be to us a perfect Savior. But we, in part—by our satisfactory sufferings here, and in purgatory—would be saviors to ourselves. THE OLD ROMAN CATHOLIC (1649).[66]

DYING FOR ENEMIES SHOWS GREATER LOVE. JOHANNES BRENZ: There are among men and women those who certainly do not deserve death

on account of crimes, but who, rather, sustain death on behalf of a good thing, that is, for a beloved thing, for one's country, for spouses, for friends, or even for a soldier's pay. And these have a spirit of courage, preferring to undergo death than to abandon either homeland or friends to dangers. These have most distinguished strength, and they are commended by public eulogies and celebrated with great praise in the chronicles and histories. Curtius, a Roman, drove himself headlong into the chasm of the Roman forum in order to protect the safety of his country. The two Philaeni brothers having suffered with regard to the dispute about the borders between the Carthaginians and the Cyrenes, buried themselves alive with earth in order that the borders of their countries might be extended. Here also Zaleucus Locrensis can be recalled, who suffered to be deprived of one of his own eyes instead of his son. The slave of Panopionis having exchanged clothes with his master, and also having exchanged a ring, secretly sent him out the back door and he kept back in his own bedroom so that he would be killed instead of him.[†] These and many other examples of this type are on record. But these met death either for their country, or for children, or for friends, or for their beloved master. But God the Father gave his son for enemies, and in that condition up till that point they were enemies. And Christ, the Son of God, died for the wicked, including for his persecutors, who also crucified him, and who long before had cruelly killed their ambassadors the prophets. It is, therefore, most obvious that the love of God toward us is in the death of his Son is the most evidenced and attested of all things. COMMENTARY ON ROMANS (1564).[67]

GREATER THAN A PARENT OR A PRINCE. MARTIN BUCER: As a result of this reconciliation that he once again speaks of, we should set our

[67]Brenz, In Epistolam, 132. [†]Marcus Curtis was a mythical hero. The Philaeni brothers appear in Sallust, History of the Jugurthine War 79; Zaleucus's story and that of the slave of Panopionis are told in Valerius Maximus, Memorable Doings and Sayings (Factorum et Dictorum Memorabilium) 6.5 ext. 3 and 6.8.6.

[65]Calvin, Institutes, 2:57*; citing Is 59:1-2; Rom 5:8-10.
[66]Guild, The Old Roman Catholik, 63; citing Heb 7:25; 10:14.

minds on the truth that it is now fitting that our own wills be yielded entirely over to the will of God, just as much as they formerly used to fight against it. And that, consequently, we should now walk in that benevolence of God by which he was able to restore us—though not without the death of the Son of God—and to take such care to apply ourselves to please him with so much effort in every situation that our very way of life gives a public witness that all our happiness is to be found in this grace of God alone.

We see how the hearts of children can be reconciled to their parents after some grave offense against them, or how those who rely on princes can be received back into their good graces after they have fallen away from their favor, and finally how such princes respond when their benevolence is extolled by those who return to them in grace. The benevolence of God is incomparably more to be implored than all such human benevolence. This must be applied to with the greatest earnestness so that we do not incite against us God's indignation, from which we boast that we have been delivered by the blood of Christ. That would be, as the letter to the Hebrews puts it, to "trample the Son of God underfoot and profane the blood of the covenant." COMMENTARY ON ROMANS (1536).[68]

5:11 Rejoicing with God

GOD IS OURS. JOHANNES BUGENHAGEN: Not only do we boast in the hope of the glory of God and of the cross, by which God accepts us, but there is also a third glorying by which we boast: it is that God is ours. We do not only boast because such a king, God, gives and is going to give many good things to enrich us. Rather, *this* is the greatest of all things: because he belongs to us, and he desires us to say it. All of God's people are his, and he desires to be ours, and this happens through Christ Jesus the Mediator. But these things surpass all sense. Consequently, Paul means to strengthen

and establish the peace of our feeble consciences. When we think of sins, we are pulled into doubt, which is most destructive in opposing peace. Therefore, Paul declares that grace is greater than sin, and that salvation does not depend on what we feel and think, but rather on the favor of God through Christ, in whom alone we obtain that peace. Paul is thorough in this, since he has placed right before our eyes the power of both grace and of sin, by which we recognize that there is nothing that can take us away from God. INTERPRETATION OF ROMANS (1531).[69]

RECONCILED REBELS REJOICE IN THEIR KING. JUAN DE VALDÉS: Here I understand that only those who inwardly feel the effects of justification attained by reconciliation with God feel joy in having God for their God and share in the enjoyment of this glorying. Those who do not feel these effects not only do not feel joy in God, but they do not glory in God. In fact, were it possible, they would wish that there were no God, because of the intrinsic enmity they have toward him, for there rises between God and humans that which rises between a king's vassals and their king. I mean that just as when there has been a general rebellion in a kingdom and some of the rebels have effected a reconciliation with the king while others remain in a state of rebellion, the reconciled ones feel joy and rejoice in having the king for their king, while the unreconciled wish there were no king. . . .

Now, the reconciled are the justified, and the justified are those who experience in their souls the effects of justification that St. Paul has here discussed, who are glorying in hope, rejoicing in tribulations, and rejoicing in God. COMMENTARY ON ROMANS (1556).[70]

WE GLORY IN TRIBULATIONS BECAUSE WE FEEL OURSELVES BELOVED OF GOD. PETER MARTYR VERMIGLI: This is to glory in God, not in

---

[68]Bucer, *Metaphrases et Enarrationes*, 251; citing Heb 10:29.

[69]Bugenhagen, *In D. Pauli ad Romanos*, 51r-v.
[70]Valdés, *Commentary upon St. Paul's Epistle*, 67*.

our works; hence what Paul has said above, that the elect glory in tribulations, depends on this fact. For we do not glory in afflictions themselves per se, but that in them we feel ourselves beloved of God. Our glory is that afterward we will obtain God himself, both lover and father, and because of this happiness nothing better could happen to us. COMMENTARY ON ROMANS (1560).[71]

---

[71]Vermigli, *In Epistolam S. Pauli,* 334.

5:12-21 FROM DEATH IN ADAM
TO LIFE IN CHRIST

[12]*Therefore, just as sin came into the world through one man, and death through sin, and so death spread to all men[a] because all sinned—* [13]*for sin indeed was in the world before the law was given, but sin is not counted where there is no law.* [14]*Yet death reigned from Adam to Moses, even over those whose sinning was not like the transgression of Adam, who was a type of the one who was to come.*

[15]*But the free gift is not like the trespass. For if many died through one man's trespass, much more have the grace of God and the free gift by the grace of that one man Jesus Christ abounded for many.* [16]*And the free gift is not like the result of that one man's sin. For the judgment following one trespass brought condemnation, but the free gift following many trespasses brought justification.* [17]*For if, because of one man's trespass, death reigned through that one man, much more will those who receive the abundance of grace and the free gift of righteousness reign in life through the one man Jesus Christ.*

[18]*Therefore, as one trespass[b] led to condemnation for all men, so one act of righteousness[c] leads to justification and life for all men.* [19]*For as by the one man's disobedience the many were made sinners, so by the one man's obedience the many will be made righteous.* [20]*Now the law came in to increase the trespass, but where sin increased, grace abounded all the more,* [21]*so that, as sin reigned in death, grace also might reign through righteousness leading to eternal life through Jesus Christ our Lord.*

a The Greek word *anthropoi* refers here to both men and women; also twice in verse 18   b Or *the trespass of one*   c Or *the act of righteousness of one*

OVERVIEW: In their commentary, the reformers expand on two contrasting pairs that Paul sets up in this passage: Adam versus Christ, and law versus grace.

Our interpreters, echoing Paul, develop the contrast between Adam and Christ in an elaborate series of paired contrasts. Through one man, sin came into the world, and it brought with it a tremendously destructive force. But there is a greater, more powerful force for good, and where sin brought death, this force brings life. Where sin brought eternal damnation, this one brings eternal life. There is violence in sin, but this force is gentle yet powerful in its impact. The life-giving force is grace, and it comes to us through the one whose obedience countered the disobedience of Adam. Sin estranged us from God, but grace restores us to God. Adam infected us with one sin (original sin), but Christ frees us from all sins. Adam gave us sin; Christ gives us righteousness. Adam gave us suffering; Christ gives us peace. Adam gave us death; Christ gives us life. Adam gave us hell; Christ gives us heaven. Adam's sin may, at first glance, appear small and insignificant, but it is not. It involved scorning and blatantly disobeying the word of the God who created all things. Christ's obedience may, at first glance, appear small and insignificant, but it is not. He lived a perfect life of obedience and went all the way to the bitter death of the cross, which he could have stopped at any moment. With each of the pairs, Christ's side overwhelms Adam's side in both scope and power.

With the other contrast, that of law and grace, the commentators first discuss whether sin and death existed before the law. For those who might argue that sin didn't come into the world until the law of Moses, the interpreters point to natural law and the reigning of death from the time of Adam. Most of the reformers follow in Augustine's and others' footsteps in believing that this passage teaches original sin. And they explore the concept of grace, responding to scholastic categories such as *gratia gratis data* (gratuitously given grace) and *gratia gratum faciens* (sanctifying grace); *operans* (operative) and *cooperans* (cooperative); *praeveniens* (prevenient) and *subsequens* (subsequent).[1] They proclaim that grace is greater than sin, and forgiveness is more powerful than guilt. Ultimately, the gospel is more powerful than the law, and Christ is more powerful than death. Where sin reigned, grace will reign. Christ is the king of both righteousness and grace, and we must pursue both.

5:12 Death Came into the World Through One Person

ADDRESSING RIGHTEOUSNESS DIRECTLY. NIELS HEMMINGSEN: Several times now the apostle has said that it is by Christ that we are reconciled to God, which assertion he here again repeats, in order to furnish himself with a means of declaring that aspect of justification that his argument is dealing with, which is the imputation of Christ's righteousness. To this point he has been explaining something of justification in general, something further of its chief aspect, the expiation of sin or absolution from sin, to which the "remission of sins" refers to, and also something of the acceptance unto eternal life of those who have been reconciled. For these reasons, justification comes to us freely on account of Christ. But now because both the remission of sins and acceptance of our persons rests on Christ as its foundation and Author, whose righteousness is imputed to believers so that they appear righteous in God's sight, he therefore proceeds to a discussion of that righteousness itself. For it can deservedly be inquired what this "righteousness of God" is that he has already spoken of several times, and since it is defined as belonging properly to Christ, it can also be inquired how the righteousness of One can suffice for many and be imputed to them. He, therefore, proceeds from this point until the end of this chapter to show this righteousness that needs to be explained as well as its method of imputation,

and he does so in the most beautiful style by a comparison of causes and effects. Sin and righteousness correspond to one another, as do Christ and Adam, death and life, the law and grace, from which comparison not only is it clearly concluded what the sole means of our justification is, but also many prominent passages of Scripture are brought forward that are useful in declaring the mystery of our salvation and restoration to God. Therefore, this section especially should be known and paid attention to, not only because it contains the chief head of heavenly doctrine, but also because it powerfully refutes the error of Osiander, and that of other both older and more recent writers, who have strayed from the true source of our justification. COMMENTARY ON ROMANS (1562).[2]

THIS PASSAGE DOES NOT POINT TO ORIGINAL SIN. DESIDERIUS ERASMUS: I do not say this to call into question whether there was some original sin, but to point out that those lie who say that I alone record this interpretation, and that it is a fabrication peculiar to Pelagius and me. I condemn the opinion of Pelagius, and I am aware of the consensus of the ancients on this matter; [but] the dispute is concerned only with the sense of this passage, whether properly it refers to original sin. . . . There remains the uproar over this, that I supposedly aid the Pelagians by disarming the church, since the most powerful weapon of all, as they say, has been wrenched away. First of all, I have shown that there are other passages that are more effective weapons. Second, how do I support the Pelagians when I openly denounce their view? "But" [you say] "I show that both readings are valid." Even if I keep silent, the evidence cries out that the passage is more easily understood to refer to the sin of individuals. One passage of Scripture was enough against Pelagius, and the church would be safe if it lost even this weapon. "But the whole church interprets the passage in this way!" Do

---

[1]For discussion of these terms, see the volume introduction.

[2]Hemmingsen, *Commentarius in Epistolam*, 186-87. Andreas Osiander taught that Christ's indwelling the believer (rather than the imputation of justification by grace) is what made the believer righteous in God's sight.

three or four doctors constitute the whole church? The whole church teaches that all the descendants of Adam are born subject to punishment because of the sin of Adam; but nowhere does the universal church teach that this passage can be understood only of original sin. And yet this was the only point I made in my annotation. ANNOTATIONS ON THE EPISTLE TO THE ROMANS (1516, 1519, 1522, 1527, 1535).[3]

ORIGINAL SIN, THE VERY TINDER OF SIN.

MARTIN LUTHER: Therefore, as the ancient holy fathers so correctly said, this original sin is the very tinder of sin, the law of the flesh, the law of the members, the weakness of our nature, the tyrant, the original sickness. For it is like a sick man whose mortal illness is not only the loss of health of one of his members, but it is, in addition to the lack of health in all his members, the weakness of all of his senses and powers, culminating even in his disdain for those things which are healthful and in his desire for those things which make him sick. LECTURES ON ROMANS.[4]

JUDGMENT FROM ONE SIN LED TO CONDEMNATION FOR ALL.

BALTHASAR HUBMAIER: In particular St. Paul also wholeheartedly laments everywhere in his letters. Namely, how through one person, that is, through Adam, sin has come into the world and death through sin and thus death has come to all people and the judgment from one sin unto condemnation has come over all people. He also confesses openly that there is nothing good in him, that is, in his flesh. Therefore he calls out very loudly: "Miserable person that I am, who will relieve me from the body of this death?" We have all died once in Adam and have all become children of wrath by nature. FREEDOM OF THE WILL, II.[5]

THE CONSEQUENCES OF ADAM'S SIN.

JOHANNES BRENZ: We see what Adam did, that we might know from this what came to pass

through Adam to us, his descendants. For Adam, when he was created by God in the beginning, was different from the way human beings are now, unjust, wretched, and mortal. Rather, he was created in the likeness and image of God, that is, created holy, righteous, knowing God, blessed, and not subject to death. For this is the likeness and image of God. And if he had not sinned, all of his posterity would have been born from him holy, righteous, knowing God, blessed, and not subject to death. The entire earth would have been our Paradise. Men, by no labor or sweat—on the contrary, with great enjoyment—would have cultivated the land. Women would have given birth to children without pain. In short, all of humanity's way of life would have been holy, blissful, and blessed. And on the occasion he and everyone would have arrived at the end of this earthly and creaturely life, he would have been transferred, and that suddenly, in the stroke of an eye, without pain, but with the greatest delight into spiritual and heavenly life. For man and woman were not created to remain forever on the earth and in this animal life, but in their own ordained times to be translated to heavenly blessedness. But what happened? Adam did not remain in this happiness, but when he ate from the tree of wisdom, from the forbidden fruit, he sinned against God. Therefore, by this first sin, he lost the Holy Spirit, after whose loss the spirit of Satan advanced. Next he lost righteousness, after which loss, the unrighteous one advanced with his entire army. Therefore, Adam became an unbeliever, one who did not fear or love God, but rather, despised him. Indeed, he did not know God. He became a despiser of his neighbor, zealous for evil things, hateful, greedy, and lustful—in short, the scum of all evil. For although he retained some knowledge of God and some integrity—just as chapter 1 has said above—nevertheless it was not, on the whole, secure. He was easily shaken by temptations, and in addition, he denied that God existed. And he considered all piety and integrity with hatred. Afterward, he became liable to all kinds of bodily and spiritual sufferings, famine, cold, sweat, sickness, weakness,

---

[3] CWE 56:144, 148*.
[4] LW 25:300*.
[5] CRR 5:456*; citing Rom 7:24; 1 Cor 15:22; Eph 2:3.

fear, sadness, despair—in short, to all types of moods. Finally, he became liable to bodily death and continuous damnation. COMMENTARY ON ROMANS (1564).[6]

THE DEPTH OF GOD'S HATRED FOR SIN REVEALED. DIRK PHILIPS: Thereby the righteousness of God is now fully revealed in that he has . . . humbled his only-begotten Son on account of the sins of his people. For how very much God hates sin is revealed out of this—that he because of the disobedience and transgression of one man (through whom then we have all become sinners), did not allow himself to be reconciled (for his righteousness endures forever) before he allowed his beloved only-begotten Son to be so miserably handled by the godless and the heathen. His pure and holy body he also allowed to be wounded, and allowed his head to be crowned with a crown of thorns, and finally, he allowed him to suffer the bitter and most shameful death for us on the cross. CONCERNING THE TRUE KNOWLEDGE OF JESUS CHRIST.[7]

SIN CAUSES DEATH. MARTIN BUCER: "And through sin, death." Let us here observe that the apostle makes sin the proper cause of death, so that we should not doubt that whatever sin we commit carries with it death to us and to our children. Nor can that common distinction between venial and mortal sins stand scrutiny, a distinction invented by the schools,[†] who say that the latter are of their very nature irremissible while the former can be forgiven. What is there that, if you do not refer it to the glory of God "with all your heart, all your soul, and all your strength," will not cause you to merit eternal death, since, even if you don't do it with premeditation or in open contempt for God, in doing it you still turn yourself away from God who is the highest good? But I have written on this subject elsewhere.

We who have been engrafted into Christ know that through this One, we will obtain forgiveness of *all* sins, anything at all that has not been done rightly, however tiny a sin we may think it is that we've committed. Let us not doubt that we merit eternal death not only for ourselves, but also for all of our children. Or rather, by our sinning we push them precipitously toward such a death. Thinking of this will cause us to conduct ourselves more seriously and carefully and to exert a greater effort in placing a bridle on our death-carrying lusts. COMMENTARY ON ROMANS (1536).[8]

DESCENDANTS OF ADAM PARTAKE OF HIS SINFUL NATURE. DIRK PHILIPS: We also confess that we of ourselves are poor sinners, born according to the sinful flesh of Adam who was bitten and poisoned by the serpent, and all those who are descended from him, these have become partakers of his sinful nature. Against this poison of the serpent and sinful nature of the flesh, our merciful heavenly Father has given a true saving sign, namely, his only-begotten and beloved Son, Jesus Christ, who has been raised up from the earth and exalted so that whoever looks on him with true faith does not die but lives eternally. And just as no herb or plaster could heal the Israelites when they were bitten by the serpent, nor may also heal them, but the Lord's Word which heals all things and which they also have believed has healed and made them well; so also Jesus Christ alone heals and makes us well, and there is no other means to salvation. Yes, to us there is no other name given under heaven whereby we must be saved. THE NEW BIRTH AND THE NEW CREATURE.[9]

CHRIST SPEAKS TO SIN. VAVASOR POWELL: The first enemy that Jesus Christ conquered—I beg you to note it—was humanity's own sin; sin is the cause of death, and men and women would never have died had not humanity sinned. Sin interposed and intervened between God and humans, and so shut the door of God's mercy and grace, that men

---

[6]Brenz, *In Epistolam*, 135-36.
[7]CRR 6:163*; citing Mt 27; Jn 19.

[8]Bucer, *Metaphrases et Enarrationes*, 258; citing Lk 10:27.
[†]Scholastic theologians.
[9]CRR 6:308-309*; citing Jn 3:14-15; 12:32; Wis 16:12; Acts 4:12.

and women could not come in. But Jesus Christ comes and takes hold of this enemy of humanity, sin, and says, "Well, you and I must have a single bout concerning these men and women's redemption and salvation. You would hinder them from being saved; I would have them saved. You would shut the door of my Father's grace and glory from these men and women, and I would have it open. Now I will try whether you are stronger to keep them from glory or I to bring them to glory."

At this, sin comes with all its number, calls in all its forces—yes, all the sins that have been committed, or shall be committed, from Adam's time to the day of the resurrection. All these sins—I mean the sins of those that shall be saved—they came in together and in heaps on the Lord Jesus Christ. In addition, my beloved, God the Father, when he saw that his Son would undertake for humanity, to save humanity, he gathered all the sins that were committed or to be committed by any of the previously mentioned against him, and he laid them on the shoulders of his Son. And he—if I may speak with reverence—said thus to his Son, "Well, my Son, seeing you have so much delight in the sons and daughters of men, seeing you will have them saved and not damned, seeing you will undergo what is due for their sins since you will be surety for them, I must reckon with you. If you will undergo the sorrow, shame and misery that is due to their sins—I had rather take your word, and have you to satisfy me—yet look you to it, for you must bear all the sins of those that you are willing to save, and satisfy for them, for I intend not to deal any more with such sinners, but I will place it all on your score and account."

Now Jesus Christ might answer his Father this way, "O Father, such is my love, such is my delight, and such is my pity toward my sons and daughters, that I had rather undergo ten thousand times so many sins, yes, ten thousand thousand times so many sufferings for sin, than that these poor souls should be damned." GOD THE FATHER GLORIFIED (1650).[10]

CHRIST AND THE IMPUTATION OF RIGHTEOUSNESS. NIELS HEMMINGSEN: By "one man" is understood the first man, namely, Adam, who was like a lump of kneaded dough from whom all other human beings originated. Through this one, Paul says, sin entered into the world. He means original sin. Moreover, there are two things regarding original sin that must be considered: guilt, of course, and corruption. These two things, although they cannot be separated, nevertheless ought to be carefully distinguished. For Adam, by having let sin in, became the first one liable to the wrath of God. Then, because he was guilty, he was placed under the penalty of sin, that is, the corruption not only of the mind but of the body also. And this is what Paul says, "And through sin came death." Thus likewise he transmitted not only guilt but also corruption to those who would be born after him. Therefore, in this passage concerning the propagation of guilt, the apostle urges the opposite, the imputation of the righteousness of Christ. For when, by means of his death, Christ washes away guilt, at the same time the faithful are clothed with an imputed righteousness. COMMENTARY ON ROMANS (1562).[11]

THE WORD THAT GAVE ADAM FLESH BECAME FLESH. MENNO SIMONS: The commandment was not given to the heavenly Christ, but to the earthly Adam and his seed, through Christ, that is, through the Word. Adam, transgressing, was condemned to death through the Word Christ. As the righteousness of God is unchangeable and eternal, as you yourselves say, therefore disobedient Adam must die according to the immutable righteousness of God. As Adam was earthly and of earth, and was cursed by the word on account of his disobedience and had to die, therefore nothing could be expected nor taken from earth but earth, from curse nothing but curse, and from death nothing but death, as Paul plainly shows. Adam, being disobedient to the Word that created him, in not giving heed to it, and eating what it had

---

[10] V. Powell, *God the Father Glorified*, 18-19*.

[11] Hemmingsen, *Commentarius in Epistolam*, 189.

forbidden, had to die involuntarily the death, with his seed, which the Word had promised him. Because it was for righteousness' sake that Adam and his descendants had to die, he having sinned and not having the ability to requite it; therefore, it is solely by grace, mercy and love that he is allowed to live. But how? Through the righteousness of Adam's flesh? Not at all; but the Word that had made Adam a living being, which gave him the commandment and promised him death if he should commit iniquity, as was said above. This same Word (as death had to be the consequence, according to righteousness, as truth had spoken) that God again promised to Adam, was to become flesh; that, as he was deceived by the liar, and therefore, according to the justice of God, had to die, he might again be delivered by the promised truth, and thus by grace and mercy alone, inherit life eternal. Adam believed it and was consoled, and as a sign of the truth of the promised favor and love, God made for Adam and for his consort coats of skins, and clothed them. CONFESSION OF THE INCARNATION OF JESUS CHRIST.[12]

CHRIST'S POWER GREATER THAN ADAM'S. JOHANNES BRENZ: We should wake up, in order to become acquainted with the power of Christ from the antithesis Paul considers in this passage. For if Adam was so powerful that sin, suffering, death, and hell poured from him into his posterity from the start, much more powerful is Christ, the only-begotten Son of God, from whom righteousness, blessing, life, and happiness are poured from himself into all of his posterity (those who believe in him and who are born again through faith in him). COMMENTARY ON ROMANS (1564).[13]

REMADE THROUGH CHRIST. DAVID JORIS: I maintain that the true restitution is the first, which has thus occurred in Christ. Put briefly, everything we have lost in the first Adam, by disobedience through the devil, is restored by and

through the obedience of Jesus Christ. Also, that those who now believe in the name of Jesus, that he is Christ, and call on him as their head and prove to be obedient, in these people all things will be restored and renewed, changed from flesh into spirit, from death into life, from the earthly into the heavenly beings, until they have become once again the likeness and true image of God through Christ Jesus by grace. They will be just as God made Adam in the beginning as an image of God: immortal, pure, without spot or sin, simple and innocent, just like God. We must again put on these clean, unspotted, white garments of simplicity and innocence, else we cannot enter into Eden, that is, into the life and kingdom of God. Pay attention. OF THE WONDERFUL WORKING OF GOD.[14]

THE IMPACT ON PARENTING. MARTIN BUCER: By thinking along these lines we will be more firmly persuaded that we, in and of ourselves, are nothing except lost and consigned to death. We will thus more fully entrust ourselves to our Restorer, our Lord Jesus Christ, who alone restored that which Adam lost. What's more, he not only restored it, but he heaps on us goods far more bountiful than those Adam squandered. If we pondered this more attentively and often, we would never fix our eyes on ourselves or on our family, but rather would supplicate Christ, lifting up our minds most fervently to our Savior that we might be deemed worthy of exchanging that innate oldness and lostness of our nature, by the newness of his life, for an everlasting and happy constancy. And with all our hearts, we would reshape everything that is ours to this end.

And how much this would beautifully temper that excessive love and indulgence we have toward children! We would never again look on them without groaning at the sight of them so stripped of the bright image of God by our own guilt and by the guilt of their first parents. They have been so ruined by this that if Christ does not restore them, they will

---

[12]Simons, *Complete Works*, 338*; citing Gen 3:21.
[13]Brenz, *In Epistolam*, 136.

[14]CRR 7:122-23*.

not be able to do anything but live for Satan, unto their eternal destruction. If we pondered this truth, our efforts in consecrating them most devotedly to Christ and in educating them with all our powers would be stirred up and inflamed.

But the consideration of this innate lostness should not, however, move us so that we merely lament of it, and as the Thracians of old are reputed to have done,[†] to bewail our birth into so many miseries. Rather, let it move us to offer and yield ourselves and our children to Christ all the more eagerly, for it is in him that those who have been lost in Adam and by us are brought back to life. COMMENTARY ON ROMANS (1536).[15]

SIN AND DEATH ARE AN ADAMANTINE CHAIN.

RICHARD SIBBES: Now, note the joining of both these together. We are under sin and death by nature. Where a man is under sin he is under death; for as the apostle says in Romans 5:12, "Sin entered into the world, and by sin death." Neither was God's creature, neither sin nor death. But sin entered into the world by Satan, and death by sin. "Oh, you will not die," says Satan. From the beginning, he was always a liar. So now he says to men and women, you will not die; you may do this and do well enough. But he is a liar and a murderer. When he solicits us to sin, he is a murderer. Let us take heed of solicitations to sin, from our own nature or from Satan. Note how God has linked sin and death, "The wages of sin is death." When we are tempted to sin, we think, I shall have this honor, or profit, or contentment, or preferment, and advancement in the world. Yes, but what you get by sin is not as great as you expect, when you get it, if you get it at all. But afterward comes death, the beginnings of eternal death. And terrors of conscience universally follow, if a man is himself, if he is not stupefied. The more confident a person is and enjoys the liberty of their judgment to judge things, the more they see the misery that is due

after sin, with a fearful expectation of worse things to come. Sin and death are an adamantine chain and link that none can sever. Who shall separate that which God in his justice has put together? If sin goes before, death will follow. If the conception goes before, the birth will follow after; if the smoke goes before, the fire will follow. There is not a more constant order in nature than this in God's appointment: first sin, and then death and damnation after. SERMON ON THE SPIRITUAL JUBILEE.[16]

JESUS IS STRONGER THAN ADAM.

BENEDETTO DA MANTOVA AND MARCANTONIO FLAMINIO: It is not to be believed that the sin of Adam, which we have by inheritance from him, should be of more force than the righteousness of Christ, that which we also inherit by faith. It seems that we have great cause to complain, that (without any reason why) we are conceived and born in sin, and in the sinfulness of our parents, by means of whom death reigns over all people. But now all our sorrow is taken away, in that by similar means—without any occasion given by us—righteousness and everlasting life have come by Jesus Christ, and by him death has been slain; about which St. Paul makes a very godly discourse, which I purpose to set down here. . . . By these words of St. Paul, we manifestly perceive the thing to be true that we have said above; that is, that the law was given to make sin known; which sin we also know is not of greater force than Christ's righteousness, by which we are justified before God. For, even as Jesus is stronger than Adam was, so is his righteousness mightier than the sin of Adam. And, if the sin of Adam was sufficient enough to make all of us sinners and children of wrath, without any misdeeds of our own, much more will Christ's righteousness be of greater force to make us all righteous and the children of grace, without any of our own good works, which cannot be good, unless, before we do them, we ourselves are made good. THE BENEFIT OF CHRIST'S DEATH.[17]

---

[15]Bucer, *Metaphrases et Enarrationes*, 257-58. [†]Herodotus describes the custom of the Trausi (related to the Thracians) mourning at a child's birth and rejoicing at a person's funeral, because of the trials of life. See *The History of Herodotus 5*.

[16]Sibbes, *Collected Works*, 5:235*; citing Rom 6:23.
[17]Benedetto and Flaminio, *Benefit of Christ's Death*, 17-19*; citing Romans 5:12-21.

5:13-14 *Sin and Death Before the Law*

WAS THERE SIN BEFORE MOSES? JOHANNES BRENZ: Someone will say, "Indeed, I acknowledge that sin was already in the world from the time of the law of Moses, for through the law is the knowledge of sin." And, "I would not have known concupiscence if the law did not say, 'You should not lust.' But I do not see how sin entered into the world through Adam. For the law, which was given afterward at Mount Sinai, did not yet exist in Adam's time or his posterity's before Moses published it. But where there is no law, there is no transgression or sin. Therefore, it seems preferable to say that sin entered into the world through Moses rather than through Adam." To this it must be answered that indeed it is true that sin is not imputed when no law exists, but nonetheless, it must be understood that sin was already in the world from the time of Adam continuously to the law, and this is proved by two arguments. The one is that although the law written on stone tablets did not exist from Adam until Moses, nevertheless, it was engraved on the human heart, which they call the natural law. The other is that death reigned from Adam all the way until Moses and it proceeded to reign thereafter. COMMENTARY ON ROMANS (1564).[18]

SIN AND DEATH EXISTED BEFORE THE LAW. PETER MARTYR VERMIGLI: These are still in and of themselves sins, even if they are not imputed on account of Christ, just as the apostle says in this passage, that before the law there were many sins committed, but that they were not counted against men and women. However, there is a distinction to be drawn here: in the former case the imputation of sins is removed by God's mercy, but in the latter case it was due to the man or woman's ignorance. And although it is said, "until the law," even the era of the law was hardly constituted immune from sin, for the law does not possess the power of uprooting it. . . . Paul's manner of speaking is akin to how pagan writers say, "The war was waged by the

Greeks against Troy until the tenth year." They do not intend by this to exclude the tenth year itself. So also when Paul says, "Sin was in the world until the law," he does not exclude the time that falls under the law itself.

Also, this marvelously proclaims the grace of Christ, since it alone was able to overcome and cast down sin, as it possessed such a great power for ruin and had been roaming about so widely and for such a long time that it could not be restrained even by the law. When Paul says, "death reigned," he employs a *prosopopoeia*,[†] so we ought not to suspect that there is any kind of beneficial dominion implied by the word "reign." Death does, however, hold power, and for this reason Paul calls it a "reign" so as to indicate that it holds uncontested sway to which everything yields and a most surpassing power that reduces everything to compliance. The same way of speaking will be used again in this very letter when he says, "Do not let sin reign in your mortal body," as if he were saying, "Even though you are not able to prohibit sin from dwelling in you, do not permit it to have a reign or ultimate power over you such that all your efforts and designs yield to it and obey it."

Further, he added "death reigned from Adam until Moses," in order to show that sin had already been in the world. For death inseparably accompanies sin, and sin and death mutually occasion each other. Hence, those who argue that infants are without sin—and that they are said to die and to be subject to the condition of mortality because of Adam's sin alone, even though they themselves are innocent and pure from all vice—are deceived. If this were true, then the apostle would have proved nothing in this passage. For he would have been able to answer quite easily that although men and women were dying before the law, sin did not exist at that time. [But this is not what he says.] Therefore, let us say along with Paul that death and sin are so conjoined to each other that they cannot be pulled apart. COMMENTARY ON ROMANS (1560).[19]

---

[18]Brenz, *In Epistolam*, 136.

[19]Vermigli, *In Epistolam S. Pauli Apostoli*, 354-55; citing Rom 6:12.
[†]The personification of an abstract thing or a nonhuman entity.

A Definition of Original Sin. Niels Hemmingsen: From this description of the apostle we may conclude with a definition of original sin, in this manner: Original sin is when a sinner, who is born guilty on account of the sin of Adam, and the corruption of human nature propagated from Adam, is liable to death and damnation, if forgiveness does not take place. Commentary on Romans (1562).[20]

Experiencing Original Sin in Both Flesh and Mind. Juan de Valdés: There have been some calling themselves Christians who have wholly denied original sin; and there have been others who have denied its existence in the mind, confessing its existence in the flesh. And there have been others who, confessing its existence in the flesh and in the mind, have said that it is a thing that is more easily made a subject of conversation and of belief than of comprehension or of experience. And among these, some understand St. Paul's words in one way, and some in another. I understand them in the way in which I have expounded them, understanding original sin to be in the flesh and in the mind, for I feel the effect of sin in the flesh and in the mind. I feel it in the flesh, finding it to be passible, more wretched and meaner than that of other animals, and finding it to be mortal and corruptible. And I feel it in my mind, finding it to be disposed to evil, and in my inability to bring it to confide in God and to hope for the fulfillment of what he promises or to love God and obey him as he commands. And since I know for certain that God created men and women in his image and likeness, I hold it to be certain too that he created them perfect in the flesh, neither passible, nor mortal, and that God created them perfect in mind, well disposed, ready to trust in God and to love God. I learn this from Scripture. And I feel this inwardly, and to such a degree that I might have ventured to confess it even without Scripture. Commentary on Romans (1556).[21]

Original Sin Existed Before the Law. David Pareus: "Yet death reigned." In this verse he establishes with two reasons the assertion that original sin had been imputed even before the law: it is "prior" by reason of its clearly evident effect. He speaks adversatively: *alla basileuō* (yet it reigns) because he opposes the reason to the next section. Sin, you say, was not imputed without the law: "yet death reigned."

The summary is: where there is death, there is sin and it is imputed (apart from God the protector, of course). For death is the perpetual effect and payment for sin. But from Adam to Moses, death not only existed, but even reigned. That is, it ran riot and it raged horribly in the world, the picture of an inconceivably vast tyrant. The word *basileuō* (reigned) has this emphasis, for it refers not merely to the death of the fathers, who were as *makrobia* (long-lived) as you like, yet in the end are said to be dead, but it especially refers to the horrible judgments of God imposed on the world for sins: the flood, the destruction of Sodom, the plagues and drowning of the Egyptians in the Red Sea, and so on, by which the dreadful kingdom or tyranny of death asserts itself. Who, then, would deny that the charge of the first sin was in the world before the law?

Observe the skill of the apostle. Before, he was demonstrating the effect from the cause: death passed to all men and women because all sinned. Now he infers the cause from the effect: all sinned. Because death passed to all, all died. The demonstration (*apodeixis*) is valid, in which the cause (*synechon*[†]) switches back and forth with its effect. Aristotle demonstrates this. Just as it is valid: there is an interposition of the earth, therefore there is no moon; there is no moon, therefore there is an interposition of the earth.[‡] . . . Just as these two evils, sin and death, were indivisibly bound together by Adam, so one could not be taken away by Christ without the other. Those whom Christ liberates from sin are also liberated from the charge of death, and vice versa. And he demonstrates that the penalty of death immutably remains on all sinners, however long they may be allowed to go

---

[20]Hemmingsen, *Commentarius in Epistolam*, 192.
[21]Valdés, *Commentary upon St. Paul's Epistle*, 70-71*.

unpunished—a consideration which should deter us from sinning. Finally, he refutes the lie of the Pelagians and Socinians that death is the lot of human nature per se. For death cannot reign where there is no sin. COMMENTARY ON ROMANS (1608).[22]

THE CONTRAST OF THE TWO ADAMS. JACQUES LEFÈVRE D'ÉTAPLES: There were two Adams: the first, a prevaricator with respect to the commands of God, was cast out of paradise; the second, a constant observer of the commandments of God, was assumed into paradise. The first was the author of sin and of death for human beings; the second was the giver of justification and of life. The first was old, the second new; the first earthly, the second heavenly, and the earthly one was a type of the heavenly, that is representing a kind of figure and shadowy likeness to him, in some respects being directed by the law of proportion and analogy.

In many respects, however, it was the other way around. For since the old Adam was taken up from the virgin earth, and the second from virgin flesh; since God breathed the breath of life on the man formed of mud, and the Holy Spirit, the power of the Most High overshadowed the Virgin; since, while the old Adam slept in the garden, Eve was formed from his side, and while the Lord "slept" on the cross, the church was formed from his opened side. These analogies correspond directly, and the first Adam is a form of the one to come, that is of the Christ and Word of God Incarnate.

But since Adam was a transgressor, and Christ was innocent; since the former was disobedient and the latter obedient; since the former was the author of death, and Christ the author of life; since the former was earthly and the latter heavenly; the former a figure and type, and the latter the real thing, and innumerable similar contrasts of this kind, they show that the first Adam and the second relate to one another as opposites. And Paul's thought follows this format. For transgression

belongs to the first Adam; grace and gift belong to the second, and these are opposites and relate to one another as opposites. For transgression—as it is privation and nonbeing—is weak and ineffective, while a habit of grace—affirmation and being—is strong and effective.

Who, therefore, will not see when the argument is so obvious: if the weak, sick sin of the first Adam could cast many down to death, much more the grace and gift of Christ the Lord, the second and true Adam who is the image of the true and living God—the grace and gift of Christ I say—indeed strong and effective, is able to supply life for many more. Therefore, let us fly together to the grace of Christ, most mighty to save, and infinitely more powerful to save than the sin of Adam (and our own) can be to damn. For the power of grace excels that of sin as that which is something excels that which is nothing. May this hope animate us, convert us, burning with love for him who wills and is so mighty to save. Sin and the gift (for understand that grace and gift are one and the same) do not have equal powers. For sin is through one who sinned; the gift through the One who did not sin. From one sin judgment came unto condemnation, but the gift is unto justification from many sins. The gift of grace is so powerful unto salvation and justification, that it is impossible for even countless sins to resist it. The gift and sin are therefore not equals. Therefore let us aspire to the grace of Christ, which resists countless sins. And the one who has it is able to contend against infinite sins in the manner in which light is able to drive away infinite darkness. For one who does not sense this efficacy of the grace of Christ is blind, denying the power of light in the darkness and believing the power of darkness of nothingness to be stronger than light. Therefore, if by the offense of one, death reigned in many through one, how much more strongly will life rightly reign for many having abundance of grace, gift and justification through one, Jesus Christ. Accordingly *this* one is most powerful, *that* one indeed (namely the one who fell) weak and infirm. Grace, gift, and justification are strong; sin and death weak and ineffective.

---

[22]Pareus, *In Divinam ad Romanos*, 495-96. †Self-sufficient cause of an effect. ‡In a lunar eclipse. See Aristotle, *Posterior Analytics*.

And although man of himself and with regard to himself cannot overcome sin and death, since darkness cannot drive away the dark, nevertheless, when he looks at the grace of Christ he does not see himself but the grace of Christ, and so, as rays from the sun drive away darkness from the dark, he is able to drive off both offense and death.

And so, you will easily understand all Paul's reasoning if you know that the analogy follows from a series of opposites. You need to attribute the stronger parts (as is suitable) to Christ, toward salvation, and the weaker parts—and certainly they are so much the weaker inasmuch as a human being is able to do less than God—to Adam, toward damnation; and the stronger parts to grace, toward justification, but the weaker ones to sin, toward mortification. The apostle deduces all this by most certain reasoning, which no one who is not entirely unformed in good dialectic will be ignorant is most sound. COMMENTARY ON ROMANS (1517).[23]

TWO ADAMS, TWO SPRINGS. WALTER CRADOCK: Now both these Adams are as two springs in a hill, conveying their streams to two rivers. They are springs from which arise all our thoughts, and imaginations, and actions, and proceedings, all the wisdom and righteousness. Whatsoever is in us, it springs either from the second Adam, the Lord Jesus planted in the soul, or else it flows from old Adam, from natural Adam that is in us. Therefore, they are called the roots; the Lord Jesus is the root of Jesse. Why so? Because all the new creation, all the work for grace, all the principles, and thoughts, and actions of a saint, so far as they are of grace, they rise from the new Adam, the Lord Jesus Christ. Therefore, I say, to understand this a little in general before I go further: a man that walks according to the flesh, who is he? He is a man that walks according to anything of old Adam, whether it is good or evil. And usually in the New Testament, it is taken for the good. There, flesh is taken for the good of old Adam, when a man walks according to

the wisdom of Adam, according to natural wisdom and according to the righteousness of old Adam that is done by us; or when we walk according to the sins, and lusts, and corruptions of Adam; for both are put together, and all makes but flesh, and whole flesh strives against whole spirit. Now I say take it in a general sense, to walk after the flesh is not only to walk sinfully and carnally, but when a person walks, though devoutly and righteously in the eye of the world, yet if it is according to the principles of old Adam, if they do not walk by a principle planted in them from the new Adam, the Lord Jesus Christ, all this is just flesh.

Now then, for men and women to walk according to the spirit. What is that? All their principles spring from the root of Jesse, from the spirit of the Lord Jesus; all their actions are on another ground. Now, I say, all the principles and actions of every man and woman in the world spring from one of these. Therefore it is convenient and necessary that you consider how the two Adams are the two springs of all humanity, the two pillars (as it were) on which God has laid all humanity, and all that is done in the world, and those that are after the other walk after the spirit. SERMON ON ROMANS 8:4 (1649).[24]

5:15 Grace Is Greater Than Sin

THE "ONE" AND THE ONE. JACQUES LEFÈVRE D'ÉTAPLES: Behold the sin of the one, to which the stronger grace of the One is opposed. That one, Adam, is mortal and earthly; this One, Christ, is immortal and divine. Death followed sin; on the other side, life followed to a far greater extent. Sin brought the condemnation of all humanity unto death; grace brought forgiveness and the justification of all humanity unto life. Behold the disobedience of one, to which a stronger obedience is opposed. That one's disobedience was split into the sins of many. This One's obedience brought righteousness that will reach a much larger multitude. And if it should not reach us, this is not

---

[23]Lefèvre, *Epistole divi Pauli*, 63r-63v.

[24]Cradock, *Gospel-Holiness*, 254-55*; citing 1 Cor 1.

on account of the insufficiency of his grace, righteousness, and obedience, but on account of our perversity, by which we are refusing to be partakers of as great a grace, righteousness and obedience as possible. . . . He, by himself, holds our redemption, not only for us, but for countless people—indeed, it is sufficient to redeem the world. COMMENTARY ON ROMANS (1517).[25]

THE GIFTS OF GOD'S BENEVOLENCE. MARTIN BUCER: "The gift of God through Jesus Christ." Let us also always keep in mind that all the benefits that Christ bestows on us are given so that we might flourish through the gift of righteousness, living upright and orderly lives, adorned with every virtue, that is, restored to the image of God. In this is eternal life: namely that we live rightly and that we live so forever, furnished with a true and full liberty in all things. And let us by no means pass over the fact that everything has been received and flows out of overabounding grace, and nothing at all is to be attributed to us. All these things are the gifts of divine and freely given benevolence. COMMENTARY ON ROMANS (1536).[26]

WHAT GRACE IS. JOHN CALVIN: Grace is properly set in opposition to offense, the gift that proceeds from grace to death. Hence "grace" therefore means the free goodness of God or gratuitous love, of which he has given us a proof in Christ, that he might relieve our misery. "Gift" is the fruit of this mercy, and has comes to us, even the reconciliation by which we have obtained life and salvation, righteousness, newness of life, and every other blessing. We hence see how absurdly the schoolmen have defined grace who have taught that it is nothing else but a quality infused into the human heart. Grace, properly speaking, is in God, and what is in us is the effect of grace. And he says that it is by one man, for the Father has made him the fountain out of whose fullness all must draw. And thus he teaches us that not even the last drop

of life can be found out of Christ, that there is no other remedy for our poverty and want than what he conveys to us from his own abundance. COMMENTARY ON ROMANS 5:15.[27]

GRACE AND GIFT BY GRACE. CASPAR CRUCIGER: There are two terms found in Paul in Romans 5: "grace" (*gratia*) and "gift by grace." There, "grace" means the freely bestowed remission of sins and acceptance on account of the Mediator. "Gift by grace" means the granting of the Holy Spirit and of eternal life. There is no doubt that this is the simple and natural meaning of the words. For Paul is speaking of all of the benefits that come through the Mediator: life, wisdom, and an everlasting righteousness that has already begun in this life. This is why he chose to say, "How much more will the grace of God and the gift by grace, by which one Man, Jesus Christ" makes peace with God "has abounded to many." Likewise does John speak in chapter 1: "Grace and truth have come by Jesus Christ"—"grace" is the remission of sins or his free acceptance of us on account of his Son, while "truth" means that through the Son of God they are not merely the shadow of good things that are given, nor goods that perish like the Aaronic priesthood or the Mosaic civil society and all those other material benefits that were things that pass away, but rather eternal goods: life, wisdom, and everlasting righteousness. Here also, then, the whole package of benefits is to be understood. COMMENTARY ON ROMANS (1567).[28]

JESUS IS THE GIFT OF GOD. HEINRICH BULLINGER: This *anthypophora*[†] qualifies the immediately preceding sentence. He says, in effect, "Nevertheless, nobody should understand this as meaning that the gift spread in quite the same way that we hear that sin had spread since Adam; the typology consists only in the fact that justification comes from Christ alone." For if by his transgression this one Adam gave over a multitude as a whole to

---

[25]Lefèvre, *Epistole divi Pauli*, 63v.
[26]Bucer, *Metaphrases et Enarrationes*, 263.
[27]CTS 38:207-8* (CO 49:98-99).
[28]Cruciger, *In Epistolam Pauli*, 13-14, citing Jn 1:17.

death, likewise the grace of the one Jesus Christ managed to restore to life a whole multitude of those who were dead. For the grace of God is greater and more efficacious than our sins. Further, "just as all died through Adam, so also all will be made alive through Christ." In a beautiful antithesis, he correlates grace with sin and "the gift" with death. For grace is the undeserved favor and benevolence of God toward us, freely and divinely bestowed. But the generous gift of forgiveness of sins, which arises out of divine grace, is conferred through Jesus Christ, who also is himself sometimes called the "grace of God" and sometimes "the gift of God." COMMENTARY ON ROMANS (1533).[29]

5:16 The Free Gift Is Greater Than Many Sins

GRACE OVERCOMES SIN. ERASMUS SARCERIUS: The conscience must be led away, with greatest care, from this impious and dangerous judgment, so that those who think sin is greater than grace do not charge headlong into a despair from which they are not able to defend themselves. You see an example of this care in 1 John 3, when he says: "By this we know that we are of the truth, and in his sight we will reassure our hearts. Because when our hearts condemn us, God is greater than our hearts." John speaks about the accusation of the conscience when it accuses us sinners that our sins are so great that they will not be able to attain forgiveness.

And when such an accusation of the conscience regards despair as its end goal, it is from the devil, the tempter, who works to drive the conscience to despair. In this temptation there is no greater truth than that the end goal is not always desperation. Undoubtedly, when God tests with this temptation, he is not one who tempts to evil. Thus Christ tested the Canaanite woman in Matthew 15: "I was not sent but to the lost sheep of the house of Israel." Likewise, "it is not honest to take the bread of the sons and give it to the dogs."

It is not easy to stand fast in the face of temptation of this kind, for the devil presses in from one direction to make us think that our sins are stronger than grace, and from another direction, passages of Scripture that judge sinners as unworthy of grace are applied against us, such as: "God does not listen to sinners." . . . [and] "All things are defiled for those already defiled."

But concerning these and similar sayings, we must employ suitable and true interpretations. In this way, the truth is that God does not listen to "sinners," that is to those who are destroyers, stubborn, and not seeking grace, but rashly disdaining it. Thus, with the holy, God is holy; with the destructive, he is destructive. That is, whoever one judges God to be, such he is for that person. So, the one who judges that God is merciful toward him, to that one he is merciful. The one who judges that God is an unjust ruler toward himself, to that one he is a tyrant. Finally, the apostle wants us, in this present passage, to judge that grace is greater than sin, that forgiveness is greater than guilt. NOTES ON ROMANS (1541).[30]

NOTHING CAN RESIST THE POWER OF GRACE. JOHN COLET: Now if there was such force in sin for destruction—and that too the sin of one man—then there ought to be a much greater force and power in grace, for bringing men and women to life and restoring them to an entire and sure salvation. And that this is so, one may discern from this: namely, that whatever grew from one sin for destruction (and sin did grow manifold and infinite), when the tale thereof was all made up, and the virulence of the disease, as it were, at fever height, then at the same time all-powerful grace, by its prevailing and marvelous force, dispelled it, and destroyed all the sin. For grace was mightier to take away the evil when completed, than the evil was to begin. Thus it happens that men and women, being laid hold of by the love and grace of God and drawn to God will, if they have hope, be more

---

[29]Bullinger, *In Sanctissimam Pauli*, 78r-v; citing Rom 5:14; 1 Cor 15:22. †An *anthypophora* is a rhetorical device in which one raises a question and immediately answers it.

[30]Sarcerius, *In Apostolam ad Romanos*, T2v; citing 1 Jn 3:19; 1 Jn 3:20; Jas 1:13; Mt 15:24; Mt 15:26; Jn 9:31; Tit 1:15.

strongly and firmly sustained and preserved unto life by that same prevailing grace, than they had been thrust down and kept under by sin unto death. Sin is indeed a violent and aggressive thing. But the glorious power of sweet and pleasant grace that works softly and marvelously, and with a secret and wonderful effect, nothing can resist. Wherefore we must believe that grace, which reconciles to God, has far more power in the world than sin, which estranges from God. And hence, that the righteousness and obedience of Christ has far more power to recall to God men and women who are to be recalled, than the sin and disobedience of Adam had to call them away from God. For without doubt, virtue is a much more life-giving thing than sin is deadening, and the Author of virtue far more powerful than the cause of sin. EXPOSITION ON ROMANS (1497).[31]

ADAM'S ONE SIN VERSUS CHRIST'S DEFEAT OF MANY SINS. HULDRYCH ZWINGLI: Adam condemns us all with one sin. Christ has freed us not merely from one sin, namely, by that inborn disease (i.e., original sin), but from many disgraces and crimes. For as in Adam, just as in a root, we have all become infected and diseased. This disease has burst into the wicked fruits and evil works that are contrary to the law and will of God, and those sins are likewise taken away through Christ. This Paul shows here. All those things, nevertheless, are able to be said by *anthypophora*[†] to those who claim that they are justified by works of the law rather than by the death of Christ. They are being said so that they won't despair of consolation for their sins, or regard their sins as greater and weightier than they are able to obtain pardon for. NOTES ON ROMANS (1539).[32]

THE FREE GIFT COVERS ALL OUR SIN. JUAN DE VALDÉS: "God's free gift" extends itself to both the original sin and the particular sins of every person. And here it goes beyond the opinion of those who

restrict the benefit of Christ to original sin only, and even that of those who will have it that Christ has made satisfaction for the *offense* only, and that every one has to give satisfaction individually for the *penalty*. And it likewise goes beyond what a godly person might have doubted, saying, "I confess that just as God contemplating me not in myself but in Adam has condemned me to death, so likewise contemplating me not in myself but in Christ, he accepts me as just and entitles me to resurrection. But as to the times that I myself have sinned, why will he not contemplate me in myself?" And I say that it goes beyond that, for St. Paul states that "the free gift" is of *many* offenses unto justification. So that God contemplates those who believe—even in the offenses they themselves commit—only through Christ and in Christ, with whose righteousness he covers and enfolds them. COMMENTARY ON ROMANS (1556).[33]

5:17 Adam's Sin, Christ's Redemption

WHAT ADAMS FORFEITS, CHRIST KEEPS. GEORGE HERBERT:

> I threaten'd to observe the strict decree
> Of my dear God with all my power and might:
> But I was told by one, it could not be;
> Yet I might trust in God to be my light.
>
> Then will I trust, said I, in him alone.
> Nay, e'en to trust in him, was also his:
> We must confess, that nothing is our own.
> Then I confess that he my succor is:
>
> But to have nought is ours, not to confess
> That we have nought. I stood amazed at this,
> Much troubled, till I heard a friend express,
> That all things were more ours by being his.
> What Adam had, and forfeited for all,
> Christ keepeth now, who cannot fail or fall.
>
> THE HOLDFAST.[34]

---

[31]Colet, *Exposition of Romans*, 10*.
[32]Zwingli, *In Evangelicam Historiam*, 420. [†]An *anthypophora* is a rhetorical device in which one raises a question and immediately answers it.
[33]Valdés, *Commentary upon Romans*, 73*.
[34]Herbert, *Works*, 2:161-62*.

ADAM IS A TYPE OF CHRIST. JOHANNES BRENZ:
Adam, Paul says, bears the form of the future One,
who is the Christ. Therefore, let us carefully
consider in which things Adam is a type of Christ
in order that we may not only comprehend them,
but so that our hope may be truly strengthened,
and so that we will not be ashamed. But although
it is rightly asserted that Adam bears the form of
Christ, it nevertheless must be explained, so that
no one will think that Adam bears the form from
every side and in every way. Therefore a correction
should be added. But by no means does he say that
the gift is just like the one who sinned, for indeed
Adam is in many, but not in all things, a type of
Christ. Adam and Christ are presented in a similar
way, but so that Christ is far superior to Adam. For
in the first place, Adam is a type of Christ by
means of leadership because, to the extent that
Adam was the first, or the patriarch of his offspring
who descended from him, so also is Christ the first
and the patriarch of his who descended from him,
of his family. Next, Adam is a type of Christ by
means of propagation, because just as Adam
propagated any in his posterity, so Christ propagated many in his posterity. And at this point the
likeness ceases, for in the case of their propagation,
there is the greatest difference in regard to virtue.
For Adam propagated sin, suffering, death, and hell
into his posterity. But Christ propagates righteousness, peace, life, and heaven into his posterity. What
is dissimilar in this one and that One? In like
manner, Adam is of such efficacy that however
many are born from him are liable to sin and death.
But Christ, the Son of God, is much more
efficacious, because one may clearly see that those
who are born again by him through faith, are
considered righteous, and are made perpetually
blessed. COMMENTARY ON ROMANS (1564).[35]

DEFINING ORIGINAL SIN. MARTIN BUCER:
David said that he had been conceived in sins [sic].
Everything that pertains to our renovation and
rebirth has reference to this original sin.

Accordingly, from these passages of Scripture that
affirm that we have been corrupted from our first
origin and sold to sin and hence are held under the
reign of Satan and under the wrath of God, it is
quite clear, to all who insist on having a simple
faith in the Word of God, that original sin is a
corruption and depravation of the whole man or
woman by which neither God nor the things
pleasing to God, that is, things that are truly good,
can either be known or pursued with any mind but
by a perverse judgment of things. Nothing at all is
possessed or even sought after in its proper place
and measure, but all things are abused and
perverted. COMMENTARY ON ROMANS (1536).[36]

5:18 One Sin, One Act of Righteousness

SIN IS SERIOUS. JOHANNES BRENZ: If you regard
only the external appearance of sin, it often seems
most trivial and undeserving of censure. But if you
examine and judge carefully, you will discover, on
the other hand, a Lerna[†] of most serious sins
against God. Let us place Adam's disobedience
before our eyes, about which we are now discussing.
Indeed, what is more pitiful, what is more childish,
than to secretly enjoy an apple? But when God
prohibited it and added threats that on whatever
day you shall eat you shall surely die, Satan taught
differently, namely, that Adam would not die but
would become as God, but Adam, forsaking the
Word of God, agreed with Satan and ate. Reflect
with me, I ask, how great a sin was perpetrated?
For first, Adam declared Satan farseeing—one who
understood what would profit the welfare of
humanity and what would not profit—but God a
fool who is ignorant of this. How great is this
profanity? Next, he declared God deceitful, but
Satan truthful. What is more monstrous than this
offense? Certainly this would be: if you have
decided to deny that God is God. In addition, each
one thought themselves to be wiser than his
Creator, and more able to judge what is proper for
themselves than God. And also, perhaps Adam did

---

[35]Brenz, *In Epistolam*, 139.

[36]Bucer, *Metaphrases et Enarrationes*, 267-68; citing Ps 51:5.

not consider the things in his heart to be perceivable by God. In any case, after he perpetrated that sin, he and Eve hid these things in the recesses of their hearts. But they were most plainly visible to God. COMMENTARY ON ROMANS (1564).[37]

THE NECESSITY OF CHRIST'S HUMANITY. JOHN CALVIN: In Hebrews 9:26, it is said, in speaking of Christ, "But now, once in the end of the world, he has appeared, to put away sin by the sacrifice of himself." And why so? St. Paul shows us the reason in Romans 5:18, "As by the offense of one, judgment came on all people to condemnation; even so by the righteousness of one, the free gift came on all people to justification of life." If we do not know this, that the sin that was committed in our human nature was repaired in the same nature, where are we? On what foundation can we stay ourselves? Therefore, the death of our Lord Jesus Christ could not have profited us at all if he had not been made human, like us. SERMON ON 1 TIMOTHY 3:16.[38]

DISTINGUISHING *DIKAIŌSIN* FROM *DIKAIŌMA*. THEODORE BEZA: "Unto justification of life," *eis dikaiōsin zōēs*. Paul has a peculiar way of speaking that folks cannot easily change, nor by any means should they, since it is far more fitting that we become familiar with his personal mode of speech, for nobody has ever touched on the divine mysteries more truly, more weightily or more clearly than he did. And I would here have willingly complained of our inability to speak as clearly as the Greeks, if someone did not permit me here to use the word *iustificamen* (just conduct) or *iustificamentum*[†] (righteous act) according to the Theologians'[‡] technical sense of "justification."

I will, therefore, never admit what some say, that in this passage *dikaiōma* (act of righteousness) and *dikaiōsin* (justification) mean the same thing, not only lest a certain kind of cunning sleight of hand be attributed to the apostle, or rather to the Holy Spirit, but much more so because the term *dikaiōma* here refers to the material cause of our justification (if I might speak in this way), named after its effect, namely, that obedience of Christ, the imputation of which makes us righteous in him, just as a bit earlier he had called it a *charisma* (gift), because God bestows it upon us freely. Whereas *dikaiōsis* is the opposite of *katakrima* (that is, the sentence of condemnation). Therefore, just as condemnation is the result of the charged offense, so the righteousness of Christ that is imputed to us by faith—taking the place of the offense that his blood washed away—causes us to be declared just by God, and therefore we obtain eternal life.

Now I thought this worth being clearly explained, not only to show the distinction between *dikaiōsin* and *dikaiōma* in this passage, but also that the reader might understand that in this chapter *dikaiōsin* means something more than it did in the previous chapter. For we are said to be justified not only by the remission (that is, by the imputed satisfaction of Christ) of our sins, or set free by him from our punishment and absolved as if we were innocent, but also in that the obedience of Christ is also imputed, we are likewise declared "just" so that we too might seek eternal life from that same legal condition, since Christ, whom we possess by faith, has fulfilled all righteousness for us. MAJOR ANNOTATIONS (1594).[39]

INFANTS ARE SAVED. DIRK PHILIPS: Since then infants are saved and included in the hand and grace of God, and the kingdom of heaven belongs to them, therefore, it is a great lack of understanding that one should baptize children so that through this they might be kept and saved, and besides this condemn children who die without baptism. This is an open diminishing and denial of the grace of God and merit of Jesus

---

[37]Brenz, *In Epistolam*, 142-43. [†]"A Lerna of evils" was a common phrase (see Erasmus, *Adages* 4.1.1). *Lerna* is the term for the body of water, sometimes referred to as a swamp, in which Heracles killed the Hydra. It was considered by some to be the mouth of hell.
[38]Calvin, *Selection of Celebrated Sermons*, 28*.

[39]Beza, *Annotationes Majores*, 68. [†]It appears that at least one of these terms has been coined by Beza. [‡]Referring to the scholastic theologians.

Christ. For since the sin of Adam, yes, of the whole world, is paid for and taken away through Jesus Christ, and sin may not be ascribed to children except what comes from Adam, how then may children be condemned on account of Adam's sin? Yes, who may condemn the children for whom Christ shed his precious blood? Who will damn the children to whom the Lord in his boundless grace has promised the kingdom of heaven? Or who can forsake holy Scripture, which so expressly testifies that the sins of Adam and the whole world are taken away, the handwriting that was against us is wiped away and nailed to the cross, that grace has taken the upper hand over sin, and that life has overcome death through Jesus Christ, our Lord and Savior? THE BAPTISM OF OUR LORD JESUS CHRIST.[40]

ADAM'S SIN IS INHERITED. JOHN CALVIN: We thus see that the impurity of parents is transmitted to their children, so that all, without exception, are originally depraved. The commencement of this depravity will not be found until we ascend to the first parent of all as the fountainhead. We must, therefore, hold it for certain that, in regard to human nature, Adam was not merely a progenitor, but as it were a root, and that accordingly, by his corruption, the whole human race was deservedly vitiated. This is plain from the contrast which the apostle draws between Adam and Christ, "Wherefore, as by one man sin entered into the world, and death by sin; and so death passed on all men, for that all have sinned; even so might grace reign through righteousness unto eternal life by Jesus Christ our Lord." To what quibble will the Pelagians here recur? That the sin of Adam was propagated by imitation? Is the righteousness of Christ then available to us only insofar as it is an example held forth for our imitation? Can any man tolerate such blasphemy? But if, out of all controversy, the righteousness of Christ, and thereby life, is ours by communication, it follows that both of these were lost in Adam that they

might be recovered in Christ, whereas sin and death were brought in by Adam, that they might be abolished in Christ. There is no obscurity in the words, "As by one man's disobedience many were made sinners, so by the obedience of one shall many be made righteous." Accordingly, the relation subsisting between the two is this, as Adam, by his ruin, involved and ruined us, so Christ, by his grace, restored us to salvation. In this clear light of truth I cannot see any need of a longer or more laborious proof. INSTITUTES OF THE CHRISTIAN RELIGION 2.1.6 (1559).[41]

RESTORED BY THE RIGHTEOUSNESS OF THE SON OF GOD. DIRK PHILIPS: Since the person was created by God the Father after his image and likeness, that is, after the image and likeness of Christ, and after his fall was by grace again restored through the obedience and righteousness of the Son of God, therefore also every person must (as he comes to maturity and is able to distinguish good from evil) be born again through the enlightenment, activity, and illumination of the Holy Spirit to a new divine being. Yes, be born again to the fellowship and likeness of Jesus Christ, and be glorified in this same image from one glory to another (nevertheless all from the Spirit of the Lord), and thus again be created anew after the image of God and to his likeness through Jesus Christ in the Holy Spirit. THE NEW BIRTH AND THE NEW CREATURE.[42]

5:19 Adam's Disobedience, Christ's Obedience

ADAM'S SIN SEEMS SMALL AT FIRST. JOHANNES BRENZ: "Through disobedience of the one man." The disobedience of Adam is that sin which is the source of so much evil. For the law was given to him: "Do not eat from the fruit of the tree of wisdom." Therefore, when Adam did not obey this law, his disobedience introduced an ocean of evil

---

[40]CRR 6:92*; citing Mt 19:14; Jn 1:29; Rom 5:18; Col 2:14.

[41]Calvin, *Institutes*, 1:215*; citing Rom 5:19-21.
[42]CRR 6:295*; citing 2 Cor 3:18.

into the world. Is it, you will say, so great a crime to enjoy fruit that because of it, not only Adam, but indeed all of his descendants should be condemned? Or is it not a childish sin to steal apples and pears from parents? And it seems a great cruelty for a parent to disinherit his own son on account of the surreptitious taking of one or two apples. Rather, it seems more shameful that such a sin would be magnified and exaggerated. But here we must be trained not to judge sin according to our human opinion, but according to the opinion of our Lord God, and not according to the thing's appearance, but according to the truth. To eat an apple is not a big thing by itself, but to scorn and transgress the Word of God, which forbade the eating of the fruit, that is a big thing. It does not take long to eat an apple, but in the end, revolting against eternal Good and calling forth an eternal anger upon oneself endures a long time. Thus, with regard to the doctrine of repentance, it is required from us that we recognize our sin and understand that we deserve eternal condemnation on account of it. COMMENTARY ON ROMANS (1564).[43]

CHRIST'S OBEDIENCE SEEMS SMALL AT FIRST.
JOHANNES BRENZ: Let us now also consider the righteousness of Christ. What then is that righteousness of Christ that is not only on his own account, but also for all his descendants who are believers in him, for their obtaining of salvation? First, Paul says it is through obedience. That is, Christ's obedience. But just as the disobedience of Adam is not seen at first as being particularly significant, so also the obedience of Christ at first appears neither great nor admirable. Christ led an honest and devout life, but many of the patriarchs also led that kind of life. Christ suffered death innocently, but many of the prophets also suffered death innocently and obediently. What then does Christ's obedience have that is more excellent than others'? If it were possible to explain it by his dignity itself, no virtues would be more admirable and distinguished. For after the only-begotten and

eternal Son of God assumed the Son of Man in the unity of his person, he was adorned with all fullness of the divine nature bodily (as Paul says) in order that immediately from the beginning of his incarnation or of his conception, he would be in the form of God and would have all of the divine majesty. But he was not able to display this immediately in public or to openly seize upon it in front of the whole world, for God the heavenly Father willed that by his suffering and death he would atone for the sins of the human race and regain men and women from eternal ruin. Hence Christ obeyed the will of God his Father in order that he might first restore all human weaknesses to heavenly happiness, and while he could have enjoyed continual happiness, he preferred to be afflicted rather than to oppose the calling of God his Father. Next, when he could have escaped the hands of all his enemies, he preferred to be hostilely captured than not to sufficiently do the will of God. In addition, when he had to die, he could have chosen a calm sort of death, but he preferred to undergo the most disgraceful, bitter death of the cross that he might obey God the Father. Finally, when his enemies cursed him on the cross with the most virulent taunts, he had the ability to cause the earth to split open, not only—I will now say—by a single word, but even by a mere nod. But he preferred to bear it patiently— indeed to actually intercede for their salvation— rather than to fight with the will of God the Father and to do nothing about the salvation of the human race.

What is greater than this work? Christ, by his own obedience, fulfilled the entire law of God so absolutely and to such a degree—in accordance with loving God with his entire heart, and loving his neighbor as himself—that no fault was found in him. Nothing more perfect, nothing more complete can be imagined than this obedience. Hence this obedience was achieved while he by no means exalted himself to the highest height. But also all his descendants—whether they were before or after his advent in the flesh—would acquire eternal righteousness and happiness through him.

---

[43]Brenz, *In Epistolam*, 141.

Consider the antitheses of Adam and Christ, from which it is clear that although Adam's disobedience was greatly effective, nevertheless, Christ's obedience was much greater and more effective. While one brought sin and death into the world, the Other brought in righteousness and life. COMMENTARY ON ROMANS (1564).[44]

THE NEW MAN AND A NEW PEOPLE. CONSTANTINO PONCE DE LA FUENTE: You have descended to become man, and a new man, of the same lineage as Adam, but without Adam's sin, for thus it comported with our justification. You have taken on humanity and have been born of a Virgin Mother, in order that you might favor us in everything, and you might, in everything, be the kind of man that reason required that you should be, who being man was God. You have called us to be new people, in order that by the privilege and favor that your association gave us, we should eradicate our father's original sin, and should take a new origin with a new inheritance in you; that as we had borne the image of the old man, and of the guilty one, we should afterward bear and represent that of the new and innocent one. I, sympathizing with my old nature, and satisfied with my old sins, as though they had made me happy, was content that you should be innocent, and that I should continue to be guilty, without considering that I not only lost myself and became thereby the sufferer, but that I greatly dishonored your goodness, in having come to seek me, by rejecting it and neglecting it.

The whole earth has been filled by your Spirit, and by the new nature that you have brought into the world. Very many have left slavery and the old garb to clothe themselves with the new righteousness that you have given to us. CONFESSION OF A SINNER.[45]

DIFFERENTIATING CAUSES OF GUILT AND RIGHTEOUSNESS. NIELS HEMMINGSEN: I carefully note the difference between the cause of guilt and the cause of righteousness. The cause of guilt exists in Adam and in us, but the cause of justification exists in Christ alone, by whom we are also being sanctified, in order that in us new obedience might begin. Finally, here we see this solid refutation of the error of Osiander who contends that men and women are justified through the essential righteousness of God. Therefore, as above, the apostle distinguishes between the righteousness of God and that of men and women. But Paul here most freely defines that righteousness of God as the obedience of Christ, by which many men and women will be decreed righteous. Therefore, it is said that Christ's obedience is the righteousness of God, and this is because God is its Author, and he commends it as the greatest. COMMENTARY ON ROMANS (1562).[46]

THE IMPORTANCE OF OBEDIENCE. MARTIN BUCER: Now the first of all of God's commandments is that we have faith in him who promises that he will be our God, that is, our Savior (in Christ, of course). Our first parent did not persevere in applying his faith to this dictate; but he acquired the persuasive counsel of Satan and at the same time ruined his entire posterity. Christ, wishing to put this to rights, rendered himself obedient to the Father in undoing "death, even the death of the cross," and even to "set joy before him." For he willed to submit to the Father's command, to look for life in the midst of death from the One commanding him. And as it was with him, so it is with all those who believe in him. That's why he would say to his disciples, "As the Father has commanded me, even so I do." He did not hesitate in yielding himself to an attendant of the prince of this world, even though he had no authority over him. In the same way, Christ's justification will be obtained among us if we obey the divine voice of the One commanding us to expect all our happiness from Christ the Lord, to be conformed to him, enduring adversities until we escape them. We will be obeying the divine voice only when—all the interrogations of our reason being set aside—it

---

[44]Brenz, *In Epistolam*, 143-44*.
[45]Fuente, *Confession* 92-93*.

[46]Hemmingsen, *Commentarius in Epistolam*, 199-200.

becomes enough for us that "the Lord has said so." The Lord himself testifies that he requires of his people that they carefully attend to his voice. Therefore, let us above all pray to the Lord, that he would cause us to recognize his voice; for it is this to which, once we have recognized it, we must render our obedience without any delay. Therefore, whenever Satan manages to persuade our flesh, as he did to our first parents, something serious takes place that is gravely contrary to the Lord's righteousness. God is to be obeyed, whose will ought to suffice in the place of our reason. The world perished by disobedience; it will be restored only by obedience. Therefore "Christ became obedient even to death." COMMENTARY ON ROMANS (1562).[47]

CHILDREN NOT DAMNED ON ACCOUNT OF ADAM. DIRK PHILIPS: No one may either accuse or damn young children on account of original sin except they deny the death, blood, and merit of Jesus Christ. For if children may be damned through Adam and on account of his transgression, then Jesus Christ has died in vain for them, and the guilt of Adam that has come on us . . . has not been paid for through Jesus Christ. Then grace has not become mightier than sin, and life has not overcome death through Jesus Christ. This be far hence! But the Scripture, which so expressly testifies about the great and saving grace of God, which he has so richly and abundantly shown humanity through Jesus Christ, stands steadfast and immovable and may not be broken. THE BAPTISM OF OUR LORD JESUS CHRIST.[48]

5:20 Grace Abounds Where Sin Abounds

THE LAW IS LIKE A DOCTOR. JACQUES LEFÈVRE D'ÉTAPLES: "The law" certainly "entered, so that"—not from intention, but from opportunity—"sin might abound." The one giving the law is like a doctor. The law itself includes commands, all of which are poisonous and unhealthy, but also all of which help spread health. Those who accept the law are like healthy specimens who, if they are exposed to worldly desires and advised of many poisonous and unhealthy things of which they were ignorant and did not desire, now desire them and make use of them, and become even sicker from them. Again, from opportunity, and not from intention. So it is with those who transgress the law. In this way the first parent sinned. God had wished to safeguard and save him through the commandment, for he knew the future, that the enemy would entice him into eating the fruit, which was poisonous to him; otherwise Adam could have eaten the fruit through ignorance. . . . But Adam did not obey his "doctor" and his God, and given the opportunity, he offended more gravely. For the tree was good and fulfilled its universal category—as a fire is good, as hemlock is good, when fulfilling their types—but fire is bad for you if you touch it, and hemlock is bad if you eat it. COMMENTARY ON ROMANS (1517).[49]

THE LAW. JOHANNES BUGENHAGEN: When the law came, sin was found in the world, for it had reigned in unawakened humans since Adam, and because we were not concerned about it, the law (as is its nature) immediately revealed that reality to our consciences. For that reason, it became much more burdensome and difficult for humans than it had formerly been, because the law had not been perceived. Now, when it is perceived and understood by their consciences, it produces an extraordinary kind of terror about death and despair. They might wish that the law, which stands against our passionate desires, did not exist altogether. Indeed, they grumble against God, who condemns us by the law. This is the innermost state of our hearts, which few realize. That the law might justify, Paul therefore says, is very far from the truth; on that account, one must not be mindful of the law's works, but of Christ.

[47]Bucer, *Metaphrasis et Enarrationes*, 304 (this is a reprint of the 1536 edition); citing Phil 2:8; Heb 12:2; Jn 14:31.
[48]CRR 6:92-93*; citing Rom 5:18; Tit 2:11; 1 Tim 2:6.
[49]Lèfevre, *Epistole divi Pauli*, 63v.

The law was given in the first place so that it might reveal sin. Second, so that it might increase sin. But what do you say? Is the law, therefore, an evil thing? Paul responds that the law is holy (as you shall see in the seventh chapter). Yet God deals thus with us by means of the law, just as a physician deals with a person who is sick through medicine, which on its own is good and salutary, but nevertheless often supplies the conditions for wrongdoing. For example, if someone who is sick should be ordered not to eat the flesh of a pig, immediately some kind of appetite is stirred up in that person for eating pork, since nature strives after that which is forbidden. In the same way, there is opportunity for much sinning when, in spite of this, God wills us to be burdened through the law so that, by seeing our sin and condemnation, we may press forward in order to seek his grace. After all, the more burdensome and unbearable a transgression is, the more quickly do we seek Christ. And so that the more someone is forgiven, the more they love, as Christ says in Luke, in the story about the sinful woman. INTERPRETATION OF ROMANS (1531).[50]

USES OF THE LAW. PHILIPP MELANCHTHON: To begin with, the reader must be reminded that Paul is not speaking about the political use of the law, or about the pedagogical, but about the use of the law in a conscience which is dealing with God and seeking justification. The first is the pedagogical or political use, namely, to coerce the flesh and to furnish outward works commanded by the law.... With respect to this political or pedagogical use one must also know that the law is needed because it is the highest gift for bodily life, which God also gives and preserves.... The second and chief use of the law is to accuse and terrify consciences when it judges and condemns sin.... Paul speaks of this use in the entire letter to the Romans.... Paul teaches that this is the foremost task of the law—that it accuses, terrifies, and condemns. It does not justify; it does not announce forgiveness

of sins; it does not liberate from sin and from death. Thus Paul distinguishes the law from the gospel. COMMENTARY ON ROMANS (1540).[51]

ADD THE MISSING OPPOSITE TO GET THE FULL MEANING. JACQUES LEFÈVRE D'ÉTAPLES: When the most blessed Paul, arguing from opposites, adds more in one small point of opposition than another, if you assume there is as much on the other side, you will not go astray. For example, when it says, "so that just as sin reigned in death, so also grace will reign through justice unto eternal life through Jesus Christ our Lord," he adds in the second phrase, "through justice, through Jesus Christ our Lord," for which, opposing terms are not placed in the first phrase. Therefore, if you understand the whole thus, supplying the opposing terms: "so that just as sin reigned" through injustice unto eternal death through Adam, "so also grace reigns through justice unto life eternal through Jesus Christ our Lord," you will not go astray. And you will see each particular opposed more visibly to its opposing term: reign (tyrannical) to reign, sin to grace, injustice to justice, eternal death to eternal life, Adam to Christ. (And the one who does this in other passages as well will be greatly helped to understand. For Paul, usually by expressing a few things, intends for many things to be understood.) And so, grace, justice, life, eternity, and even more magnificent things than these, which Adam had lost for himself and us, Christ restored. To whom be honor and glory forever and ever. COMMENTARY ON ROMANS (1517).[52]

THE GOSPEL IS MORE POWERFUL THAN THE LAW. JUAN DE VALDÉS: What he says, that is, that the grace of God is more abundant where there is greater knowledge of sin, and that there is greater vehemence of the affections and lusts, is to be understood when this knowledge and this vehemence take occasion through the law. For I understand it to be St. Paul's design to say that precisely there where the law is most powerful,

---

[50]Bugenhagen, *In D. Pauli ad Romanos*, 55r -56r*.

[51]Melanchthon, *Commentary on Romans*, 140-42*.
[52]Lèfevre, *Epistole divi Pauli*, 63v.

there the gospel is most powerful. The law is powerful to condemn, but the gospel is more powerful to justify. The law is more powerful to give men and women self-knowledge, the gospel is much more powerful to give them the knowledge of God and of Jesus Christ. COMMENTARY ON ROMANS (1556).[53]

GRACE ABOUNDS IN A DOUBLE MANNER. GEORG MAJOR: Which has the greater strength, sin or grace? Indeed when sin abounds, can grace? Paul replies, "Through the law, sin abounded in condemnation unto death in order that we, terrified by the law, would experience the anguish of death and hell. But a far greater strength is the grace abounding and reigning through righteousness unto eternal life through Jesus Christ, who is triumphant over sin, death, and hell. For those who lay hold of this grace and mercy by faith, are freed from these terrors and the anguish of the law and hell, and they have peace and life and happiness in God. For grace abounds in a double manner.

First, it abounds by imputation, because sin is not imputed to those who believe in the Son of God, but rather, their faith is imputed to them as righteousness, and they are received by God on account of the Son. Although the remainder of evil from original sin may continue, yet they resist it, according to that Word: "There is no condemnation for those who are in Christ Jesus."

Second, grace abounds also by the effect it accomplishes when the Son of God pours out the Holy Spirit into the hearts of believers, and through him hearts are freed from an experience of death and hell, and he brings them back to life and sanctifies them, and even though the body of sin is destroyed through physical death, the Son of God, nevertheless, from his abounding grace and mercy, will raise them up into eternal life and happiness. Therefore, the strength of grace abounding—which is the conqueror of sin, the law, death, the devil and hell—is much more powerful and fruitful and efficacious than the abounding of sin.

This doctrine must be transferred into use when sin abounds in us, when "the sting of death is sin," when we perceive that "the power of sin is the law" accusing and condemning us. And by this temptation, we are pushed into believing we could be saved if we did not have so many and such great sins. To these temptations is opposed this most sweet expression and encouragement: "Grace abounds over sin." The Son of God is stronger than the entire reign of sin. And let us consider examples of those who were converted and saved when they had the most extensive sins: David, Mannaseh, Nebuchadnezzar, Peter, Paul. The eternal Father desires the Son to be believed; he desires us to think the Son to be true. The witness to the Father's will is that "all who look to the Son and believe in him have eternal life." Similarly, "I do not desire the death of the sinner but that they be converted and live." For grace abounds over sin. According to the saying of Psalm 103:11-13: "As high is the heaven above the earth, so he causes his mercy to prevail over those who fear him. As far as the east is from the west he has made us from our iniquities. As a father views his sons with compassion, the Lord himself has shown compassion to you." Likewise Micah 7:19: "He will throw all our sins into the depths of the sea." By this we are buttressed by comfort, and we believe in the Son of the abounding God, and in him we give thanks. Oh, the immeasurable goodness of God, because where our sin abounded, there the grace and mercy of God abounded even more. EXPOSITION OF THE EPISTLES OF PAUL (1569).[54]

THE TENDENCY TO MISUSE GRACE. MARTIN LUTHER: In this letter, St. Paul teaches Christians *to live a Christian life here on earth*, and connects with it the *hope of another, future, eternal life*, for which they are baptized and become Christians. For he makes out of the life here on earth, a dying, yes, a grave; with the view, however, that from now on, the essence of the resurrection and new life

---

[53]Valdés, *Commentary upon Romans*, 77*.

[54]Major, *Enarrationes Epistolarum S. Pauli*, 116-17; citing Rom 8:1; 1 Cor 15:56; Ezek 33:11; Jn 6:40; Ps 103:11-13; Mic 7:19.

must be found in us. And he introduces this doctrine, because it always happens in the world that when we preach concerning grace and the forgiveness of sins bestowed on us independent of any of our own merits, that people wish to be free and to perform no works, except those that suit them. This was the course pursued in regard to St. Paul also, when he extolled the grace of Christ in a manner that was both elevated and consoling, as he says a little before: "But where sin abounded, grace did much more abound." So that, where great and numerous sins exist, there also exists a great, abundant, and rich grace. "O! If this is true," said the illiterate multitude, "that abundant grace will be given and will follow great sins, we will freely heap up sins, and easily remedy the matter, so that we, too, may have the more and greater grace!" POSTILS ON EPISTLES.[55]

5:21 Where Sin Reigned, Grace Will Reign

THE CONTRAST BETWEEN CHRIST AND US. HEINRICH BULLINGER: Truly we hold this, dear reader, concerning the first part of the gospel, which is about justification, or the forgiveness of sins, which is not conferred except by believing in Jesus Christ, by that most powerful name, because that one alone is righteous and holy. We, conversely, are all corrupted sinners by nature, and for that reason are dead and condemned. We are all, therefore, justified freely without our merit or works, but only through faith that is in the Lord Jesus, to whom always belongs praise and acts of gratitude. COMMENTARY ON ROMANS (1533).[56]

THE KING OF BOTH GRACE AND RIGHTEOUS-NESS. WOLFGANG MUSCULUS: Whoever one heeds, he is in that one's power. There are two kingdoms: one of sin unto death, the other of grace unto life. The one who fights under the reign of sin knows he will be a soldier until death, and

the wages for his military service will be the receiving of eternal death. However, those who desire to be under the reign of grace know that the grace of God will reign until death is annihilated—indeed, until sin is also annihilated and the kingdom is administered through righteousness. For the apostle does not simply say "and thus grace reigned unto eternal life through Jesus Christ" but that it is combined with righteousness. Therefore, Christ is indeed the King of grace and at the same time also King of righteousness: therefore let us juxtapose the grace of righteousness and the righteousness of grace. Truly, as long as we believe that the reign of grace is contrary to the pursuit of righteousness, we surrender a place to unholiness and unrighteousness, and again, truly, as long as we believe that the reign of righteousness is without grace, we either open the door to desperation or to dependence on our merit. COMMENTARY ON ROMANS (1555).[57]

THE POWER OF SIN, THE POWER OF GRACE. NIELS HEMMINGSEN: The sweetest end of victorious grace is emphasized by means of contrasting the power of sin and the power of grace. The reign of sin passes away in death and condemnation; the reign of grace has eternal life through our Lord Jesus Christ, the Victor over death. This should be noted in the first place, for it shows the division between these two most different kingdoms, of which one is of sin, the other of grace. The kingdom of sin is governed by disobedience, unto death; the other one, through righteousness, unto eternal life. But wherever there is no faith in the Mediator, there sin reigns unto death. On the other hand, where faith is, there is the reign of grace unto life. For by believing, sins are forgiven and the righteousness of Christ is imputed, by which we have peace with God. So then we are here reminded that while we hold fast to faith, we do not allow sin to reign in us, so that we may stir up the spirit of true repentance through fruit, prayer, reading of and meditation on the Word,

---

[55]Luther, *Church-Postil: Sermons on the Epistles*, 74*.
[56]Bullinger, *In Sanctissimam Pauli*, 81r-81v.
[57]Musculus, *In Epistolam Apostoli Pauli*, 132.

patience, and other virtues, by which at last we will arrive at the desired goal, through our Lord, Jesus Christ. COMMENTARY ON ROMANS (1562).[58]

THE DIFFERENT KINDS OF GRACE. ANDREW WILLET: The [scholastic theologians] have certain distinctions of grace that either are not to be admitted at all, or else must be qualified first before they can be received.

1. Of the first kind is that distinction of grace between *gratia gratis data* and *gratia gratum faciens*, grace freely given, and grace that makes us acceptable to God. Two exceptions may be made to this. (1) There is no grace that is not freely given; otherwise it would not be of grace, that is, from favor. But they, in making only one kind of grace be freely given insinuate that there are other graces that are not freely given. (2) They hold the grace that makes us acceptable to God to be an infused grace or habit by which we are accepted. In this they err, ascribing to a created or infused grace that which is the work only of the free grace and favor of God toward us. This word (grace) is either taken actively for the love, grace, and favor of God, or passively for those gifts and graces that are effects. The first is outside of us, the other within us. The first is the original grace in God, the other are created graces. Now, we hold that we are made acceptable to God only by the first grace of God toward us, which is grounded in Christ;

the [Catholics] ascribe our acceptance with God to the other. . . .

2. Of the other sort is the distinction of grace, *operans* and *cooperans*, "working" and "working together." While the "working" grace is that that alone changes the will and makes it willing, the "working together" grace is that by which the will of man or woman works for the effecting of that which it wills. This distinction must be qualified, for to make the will of man or woman a joint worker with grace is against the apostle, who says that it is God who works "in us both the will and the deed." But thus it may be admitted that one's will being once moved and regenerated by grace is not idle but then works with grace, not by its own strength, but as it is still moved and stirred by grace. . . .

3. Of this sort is that distinction of grace between *praeveniens* and *subsequens*, grace "preventing and going before," and "following" grace, which are not indeed two different graces but diverse effects of one and the same grace. God's grace prevents one's will and changes it from unwilling to making it willing and then it follows to make the will of man fruitful and effectual; and this we acknowledge. But the "subsequent or following" grace is not merited or procured by well using the first, preventing grace, in which sense this distinction is to be rejected. A SIX-FOLD COMMENTARY ON THE EPISTLE TO THE ROMANS (1611).[59]

---

[58]Hemmingsen, *Commentarius in Epistolam*, 205-206.

[59]Willet, *Hexapla*, 283*; citing Phil 2:13.

6:1-7 BURIED AND RAISED IN CHRIST TO A NEW LIFE

What shall we say then? Are we to continue in sin that grace may abound? ²By no means! How can we who died to sin still live in it? ³Do you not know that all of us who have been baptized into Christ Jesus were baptized into his death? ⁴We were buried therefore with him by baptism into death, in order that, just as Christ was raised from the dead by the glory of the Father, we too might walk in newness of life.

⁵For if we have been united with him in a death like his, we shall certainly be united with him in a resurrection like his. ⁶We know that our old self[a] was crucified with him in order that the body of sin might be brought to nothing, so that we would no longer be enslaved to sin. ⁷For one who has died has been set free[b] from sin.

a Greek *man* b Greek *has been justified*

OVERVIEW: Paul answers the logical question of whether believers should keep sinning so that grace has more opportunity to grow by stating that we have been buried in baptism into the death of Christ so that, as a result of his resurrection, we might live a new life. The interpreters explore the implications of this death and new life.

The topic of baptism raises one of the key issues that divides the magisterial reformers from the Anabaptists, that of infant versus adult baptism. The Anabaptists argue against infant baptism; the magisterial reformers defend it and are concerned about the rebaptism that they believe the Anabaptists—who were baptized as infants—are engaging in when they are then baptized as adults. The reformers, both magisterial and radical, then explore the connection of regeneration and baptism and the role of symbolism in the sacrament. What they all agree about is that baptism should lead to a new life.

The commentators elaborate on various aspects of this new life. Christ has rescued us from death and, like a king, sets us free from prison. But the resulting freedom does not grant a license to sin. Rather Christ intends for us to strive for righteousness. The same power that raised him from the dead is at work in us to turn our impiety into holy living. Calvin, with his characteristic emphasis on

union with Christ, points out that the dying in baptism linkage goes beyond mere imitation to participation. The Anabaptists' emphasis on transformation emerges here as well. We have a new nature, and so we should exhibit new fruits, new acts, new habits. Using Erasmus's translation of *symphytoi* as "engrafted," a number of the reformers use the metaphor of a plant or tree to illustrate the progress of the new life. Our old will fought against God, but the new self should be in concert with the Holy Spirit's will. In the same way that a physically dead body cannot engage in its previous activities, so we, having died to our old lives, should not engage in sinful activities.

6:1 Should We Continue in Sin?

ANSWERING OBJECTIONS. HULDRYCH ZWINGLI: In this chapter Paul answers those who were objecting, "If everyone's sins are taken away through Christ, and grace is more abundant and clearer by the multiplication of sins, then what else should be done but to keep on sinning so that the grace of God may all the more abound?" Paul anticipates these arguments, showing that a faithful person not only does not speak in this way, but that one should never sin in this way. Let the faithful ones beware of every eagerness for sin, and let them take care that they daily die to sin, and having both cast off and rejected the "old self," let them rise again as a new one.... When we have not yet been regenerated, still do not rightly recognize God nor place our faith in the one God, when we still live by our passions and live without God, this is the sin which we have as transmitted from Adam, and this is the "old self." The "new self," on the other hand, is the one who truly recognizes the true God, places their faith in him alone, hopes in him, loves him above all things, who knows that God is everything, and who lives guided by the Spirit, joined with the will of God. Notes on Romans (1539).[1]

Our Freedom Is Not a Wild Fleshy Freedom. Martin Luther: In chapter 6, St. Paul takes up the special work of faith, the struggle that the spirit wages against the flesh to kill off those sins and desires that remain after a person has been made just. He teaches us that faith doesn't so free us from sin that we can be idle, lazy, and self-assured, as though there were no more sin in us. Sin *is* there, but, because of faith that struggles against it, God does not reckon sin as deserving damnation. Therefore we have in our own selves a lifetime of work cut out for us; we have to tame our body, kill its lusts, force its members to obey the spirit and not the lusts. We must do this so that we may conform to the death and resurrection of Christ and complete our baptism, which signifies a death to sin and a new life of grace. Our aim is to be completely clean from sin and then to rise bodily with Christ and live forever.

St. Paul says that we can accomplish all this because we are in grace and not in the law. He explains that to be "outside the law" is not the same as having no law and being able to do what you please. No, being "under the law" means living without grace, surrounded by the works of the law. Then surely sin reigns by means of the law, since no one is naturally well-disposed toward the law. That very condition, however, is the greatest sin. But

grace makes the law lovable to us, so there is then no sin anymore, and the law is no longer against us but one with us.

This is true freedom from sin and from the law; St. Paul writes about this for the rest of the chapter. He says it is a freedom only to do good with eagerness and to live a good life without the coercion of the law. This freedom is, therefore, a spiritual freedom which does not suspend the law but which supplies what the law demands, namely, eagerness and love. These silence the law so that it has no further cause to drive people on and make demands of them. It's as though you owed something to a moneylender and couldn't pay him. You could be rid of him in one of two ways: either he would take nothing from you and would tear up his account book, or a pious man would pay for you and give you what you needed to satisfy your debt. That's exactly how Christ freed us from the law. Therefore our freedom is not a wild, fleshy freedom that has no obligation to do anything. On the contrary, it is a freedom that does a great deal, indeed everything, yet is free of the law's demands and debts. Preface to the Letter of St. Paul to the Romans (1545).[2]

Sin Is Not the Cause of Salvation. Johannes Bugenhagen: Look at the manifest folly of the flesh: it desires sin to be the cause of grace! What could be a more insulting claim against God than that my sin is the cause of salvation? "I am saved, so I sin." This interpretation that thinks such things must be brought to what Paul talks about in chapter 5. The gospel does not teach us to sin, but rather it teaches that if you have sinned, you are not damned. It promises you forgiveness of your sins from the good will of God, and his grace, not so you can sin, but so you can *stop* sinning! Here you must look back to this grace alone, not to your own sin and wickedness, which earns not salvation, but damnation. Indeed, the magnitude of grace is apportioned out of our sin, but the sin is not the cause of salvation. Not to mention, it is grace itself

---

[1] Zwingli, *In Evangelicam Historiam*, 420.

[2] Luther, *Preface to the Letter**.

that sends away sin. For if salvation were attributed to sin, many—even all—impious ones would be saved! Interpretation of Romans (1531).[3]

Two Parts of Being a Christian. Martin Luther: We have heard above what the two parts are to being together in a Christian and emphasized in Christian teaching. The first part is faith, that we are redeemed from sin through the blood of Christ and have forgiveness. The second part, after we have [faith], is that afterward we should become different people and live a new life. In baptism, or when we begin to believe, we receive not only the forgiveness of sins (which is the grace that makes us God's children) but also the gift that must do away with the remaining sins and kill them. Our sins are not forgiven so that we would continue in them (as St. Paul says in Rom 6), as the insolent spirits and despisers of grace allege. Rather, even though sins have been blotted out through Christ's blood, so that we do not need to pay or make amends for them, and we now are children of grace and have forgiveness, yet that does not mean sin has been entirely done away with and killed in us. Summer Postil (April 27, 1539).[4]

A Digression on a Weighty Matter. Viktorin Strigel: This chapter is a digression set forth on a weighty matter, from which he will later come back to the comparison of sin, law, and grace. Since it has already been said that sins are not taken away through the law, nor are people become righteous by the law, a great tumult of questions arise. If good works do not merit forgiveness of sins, to what end is it beneficial to take great care to do what is right? Indeed, if we are not justified by the law, what need is there to curb our desires? He answers these questions in a most learned and weighty manner, affirming that a new obedience should follow. Notes on Romans (1565).[5]

We Have Two Births. Jacques Lefèvre d'Étaples: A little earlier the blessed Paul said, "Where transgression abounded, there grace also superabounded." Those who failed to understand him were capable of saying, "Then let transgression abound in us so that grace might superabound in us; let us persist in sin so that we might receive an abundance of grace!" Paul slams the door on such insane impiety when he says, "What then shall we say? Shall we remain in sin so that grace might abound? By no means!" He gives the reason why not and also sheds light on the sacrament when he goes on to say, "We who have died to sin, how will we still live in it? Or do you not know that each and every one of us who have been baptized into Christ Jesus have been baptized into his death? We were therefore buried with him through baptism into death, so that just as Christ arose from the dead through the glory of the Father, so we also are to walk in newness of life."

We have two births in this world: one from Adam, and one from Christ. By the former we are born sons of the flesh, of wrath, of sin, of debt, and of death. But from the latter we are born sons of the Spirit, of glory, of grace, of redemption and of eternal life. From the former, we are sons and daughters of men and women, and are slaves. From the latter, sons and daughters of God, and freeborn. Adam and all his sons and daughters are united in one body of sin with Adam as its head. Christ and all his sons and daughters are united in one body of righteousness, with Christ as head. Over the former reigns a death that is a bondage and death of the worst kind, as has been written: "the worst kind of death for sinners." Over the latter a death reigns by means of imitation and of the best sort, concerning which it is said, "Precious in the sight of the Lord is the death of his saints."

This precious death happens to us first by sacred shadows[†] in holy baptism, whereby we transition from the body of sin to the body of righteousness, from the body of Adam to the body of Christ, which can never happen unless we die to sin and live to righteousness. But this death

---

[3]Bugenhagen, *In D. Pauli ad Romanos*, 57v.
[4]LW 77:194-95*.
[5]Strigel, *Hypomnemata in Omnes Epistolas*, 39.

happens in us through the washing of the baptismal laver; we are then signed with crosses† that represent the cross of Christ, as if to say that we have sacramentally (*in mysterio*) died together with Christ and have been crucified with him. We are immersed three times, pointing to the burial of Christ that lasted three days; we are sacramentally buried with him. Finally, we completely rise up out of the water. This rising up is a sign of the resurrection of Christ and also of our final resurrection. Just as we have risen up following Christ's example, so also we will rise in the last day in the true resurrection.

This is our second birth. The first was carnal; the second is spiritual. The first was old, the second is new, and the life that we live after this rising up from the water and this new birth ought to be a following in his footsteps and an imitation of his life, which life we expect to receive as a gift from God after our final resurrection. But what is that life except the everlasting beatific vision of God, and the ceaseless, ineffable praise of his goodness? Therefore, our manner of life after baptism ought to be wholly occupied in the contemplation and praise of God, albeit dimly and in a mirror, whereas then it will be in truth. COMMENTARY ON ROMANS (1517).[6]

TRUE REPENTANCE. DIRK PHILIPS: Could Miriam come to the camp of Israel and be admitted except she was first cleansed of her leprosy? And if one would then present to us that the transgressor is cleansed through repentance, through his sorrowful lament and confession of his guilt, we answer to it that no one can repent and still live in sin. The reason for this is: true repentance always has these following points or characteristics (which one calls properties), and which cannot be separated from it, namely: a proper sadness and sorrowful state about the preceding sin; after that a true confession of the

sin before God; praying and sighing before the throne of grace with a genuine faith for the forgiveness of sin and with a firm trust in God's bottomless mercy. But above all there must be a good and firm resolve to sin no more and to refrain from the sin. That is then true repentance which is valid before God, that one refrains from sin, yes, that is the true worship which pleases the Lord. And that one ceases from unrighteousness, that is a true atonement for sin. ABOUT THE MARRIAGE OF CHRISTIANS.[7]

6:2 How Can the Dead Live to Sin?

CHRISTIANS HAVE TRANSFORMED NATURES. HEINRICH BULLINGER: Christians through faith have transformed natures, having put to death the customs of their former and inherited lives. They live a new life—which, unless one has come to such a life, one is not a Christian. Therefore, the apostle presently returns to the inquiry with an emphatic oration, and he says, "Can it be true that someone is so foolish that he would rely on impiety as much as piety? The least of the Gentiles obtains by faith what you oppose. For it is as impossible for the faithful to remain in their sins as it is for one who has died to either eat or argue. Certainly, we sin as Christians, but we do not remain in our sins. For the Christian's life is a continual repentance, mourning, and guarding of one's life. For in regard to this, we certainly succumb to sin; however, we soon overcome again." COMMENTARY ON ROMANS (1533).[8]

EAGER FOR A NEW AND HOLY LIFE. NIELS HEMMINGSEN: This prayer of aversion (i.e., "God forbid!") is due to the wickedness of his opponents. And Paul then incorporates his opponents' way of thinking, as if he were to say, "From here on, absolutely no one may seek permission to sin because by abounding in sin grace much more

---

[6]Lefèvre, *Epistole divi Pauli*, 64v; citing Rom 5:20; Ps 34:21; 116:15; 1 Cor 13:12. †*Velamina* are coverings; the sacramental signs that conceal sacred mysteries are contained in them. ‡On the forehead; part of the medieval baptismal rite.

[7]CRR 6:565*; citing Num 12:1-2; Ezek 18:21-22; Mt 3:1-2; Ps 32:1-2; Rom 3:21-25; Heb 5:7-8; Sir 35:1-2.
[8]Bullinger, *In Sanctissimam Pauli*, 82r.

abounds! But instead, we must consider the goodness of God and practice a pious and holy life so that we do not provoke the wrath of God against us. On the contrary, let us escape by grace." Therefore, from this answer we ought to deduce this proposition: having been justified by faith, you ought to be eager for a new and holy life. So then, let us observe in this place the catholic doctrine that one may clearly see, that the companion of justification ought to be sanctification, which is the beauty of regeneration, whose external and internal fruit comes by obedience toward God. This is confirmed in 1 Corinthians 1:30. "He was made for us wisdom, justification, sanctification, and redemption." COMMENTARY ON ROMANS (1562).[9]

SIN WAS SLAIN IN CHRIST'S HOLY BODY.
MARTIN LUTHER: It would not be right for us to explain the salutary doctrine of the grace of Christ and the forgiveness of sins to mean that we now should live as we lived before and do whatever we want. It does not follow, says St. Paul, that we should be under grace and have the forgiveness of sins so that we could live in sin. How should we who have died to sin live in it? We died to it just so that it would no longer live and rule in us. It was slain and killed in Christ's holy body so that it would also be killed in us. SUMMER POSTIL (APRIL 15, 1537).[10]

DEAD OR ALIVE TO SIN. THE ENGLISH ANNOTATIONS: Those who are made partakers of the virtue of Christ are said by Paul to be dead to sin. Natural corruption is dead in them, that is, the force of it is taken away so that it does not bring forth its bitter fruits. On the other side, those who are in the flesh, that is, whom the Spirit of God has not delivered from the slavery of this corruption of nature, are said to live in sin. ANNOTATIONS ON ROMANS 6:2.[11]

6:3 *We Are Baptized into Christ's Death*

BAPTISM AND THE ARK OF CHRIST. DIRK PHILIPS: Again, just as the flood drowned all flesh that was outside of the ark, and the ark was preserved through the same water, so also in baptism all fleshly lusts must drown and be killed, but the soul is preserved to eternal salvation in the ark of Christ, through the power of his Word, Spirit, and blood. Again, just as few persons, namely, eight souls, were preserved and kept alive in the ark, so also there are few who with Noah find grace before God's eyes because they rightly believe in God, enter into the Christian congregation, and are baptized in the name of the Lord. [Through this] they have and guard the power, meaning, and mysteries of true faith and the baptism of Christ for the mortification of the flesh and the resurrection to eternal life. The Lord himself testified that there are few who find the true and narrow way, few are chosen, few believe and are saved. THE BAPTISM OF OUR LORD JESUS CHRIST.[12]

BAPTISM IS A SECRET, SEVERE WATER. PILGRAM MARPECK: However, almost everyone babbles and boasts deceitfully about the height and divinity of Christ and uses reason and scriptural subtleties to find a false sufficiency of joy in themselves. Yet, no one is prepared to go down with Christ into death and be buried with him. They begin with the height [of Christ], in order to deceive themselves and others. Thus they must go down to destruction and suffer eternal exclusion from the height of Christ.

Baptism is a secret, severe water that drives all reason down into the depth to die with Christ and be buried in his death. Only then can the soul rise with Christ and become a partaker of his gifts and the treasures of his kingdom, which he distributes to all his chosen ones and gives to his own. Thus the Son makes the Father known, and the Father

---

[9]Hemmingsen, *Commentarius in Epistolam*, 208-9; citing 1 Cor 1:30.
[10]LW 77:168*.
[11]Downame, ed., *Annotations*, AAA4v*.

[12]CRR 6:81-82*; citing Gen 6:21; Col 2:12; 1 Pet 3:20; Mt 7:13; 2 Esdr 7:7; Mt 20:16.

makes known and reveals the Son. The elect are glorified in them, just as the Father and Son are glorified in and with themselves. CONCERNING THE LOWLINESS OF CHRIST.[13]

CHILDREN ARE UNABLE TO DIE WITH CHRIST. BALTHASAR HUBMAIER: Further, you write concerning the word: *In mortem Christi* that the secret of baptism is that we are baptized into the death of Christ and learn how Christ Jesus died and thus did enough for our sin so that we also die to sins. Again, such learning and dying to sins cannot be said of a child one day old. ON INFANT BAPTISM.[14]

BAPTISM'S BENEFIT OF MORTIFICATION AND NEW LIFE. JOHN CALVIN: Another benefit of baptism is that it shows us our mortification in Christ and our new life in him. "Do you not know," says the apostle, "that as many of us as were baptized into Jesus Christ, were baptized into his death? Therefore we are buried with him by baptism into death," that we "should walk in newness of life." By these words, he not only exhorts us to imitation of Christ, as if he had said that we are admonished by baptism in like manner as Christ died, to die to our lusts, and as he rose, to rise to righteousness, but he traces the matter much higher, that Christ by baptism has made us partakers of his death, engrafting us into it. And as the twig derives substance and nourishment from the root to which it is attached, so those who receive baptism with true faith only feel the efficacy of Christ's death in the mortification of their flesh, and the efficacy of his resurrection in the quickening of the spirit. On this he founds his exhortation, that if we are Christians we should be dead unto sin and alive unto righteousness. He elsewhere uses the same argument—that is, that we are circumcised and put off the old man after we are buried in Christ by baptism. And in this sense, in the passage that we formerly quoted, calls it "the

washing of regeneration, and renewing of the Holy Ghost." We are promised, first, the free pardon of sins and imputation of righteousness; and, second, the grace of the Holy Spirit, to form us again to newness of life. INSTITUTES OF THE CHRISTIAN RELIGION 4.15.5 (1559)[15]

BAPTISM AS CONSECRATION INTO A HEAVENLY KINGDOM. JOHANNES BRENZ: For this is "his glory": that we might be stirred up out of our dead works to walk in newness of life. Here the role of baptism can be learned, namely, that it is an engrafting into the death, burial and resurrection of Christ so that he who is baptized might be sanctified by that baptism unto a participation in every good thing that Christ obtained by his death, burial, and resurrection. We must, therefore, make much of baptism and consider it nothing other than the King's public consecration of members into his kingdom, or, as a great many people suppose, that whereas the kings of this world are consecrated only unto an earthly kingdom, by baptism we are consecrated into a heavenly kingdom. COMMENTARY ON ROMANS (1564).[16]

BAPTISM SHOULD NOT BE REPEATED. MARTIN BUCER: The reason why the baptism that the church observes today is not to be repeated appears to be that it is the symbol of that fully revealed knowledge of Christ by which we embrace him, a knowledge that has been given indiscriminately to all the saints before the coming of the gospel. This is done so that Christ himself, rather than anything of our own, might live within us in every facet of our lives. We are made full sharers in his death and resurrection so that we might never relapse such that sin reigns again within us. Those enduring symbols that exhibit and commend the most important things are done only once. Kings are anointed only once. Bishops are consecrated only once. Only once is a wedding ring given. The remission of sins, which is the chief thing of all,

---

[13]CRR 2:434-35*.
[14]CRR 5:294*.

[15]Calvin, *Institutes*, 2:515*; citing Col 2:11-12; Tit 3:5.
[16]Brenz, *In Epistolam*, 174.

remains perpetually exhibited in those baptized among the saints. Further, baptism was intended to avail among the baptized so that they would not easily relapse. While true regeneration had always been conferred upon the baptized to whom the Lord's first covenant was given, it was not conferred so fully or with such great revelation as it is now that Christ has been glorified. The death of sins and the life of God are now revealed so absolutely that we are said to be buried in the death of Christ, to be incorporated into Christ, and to be clothed with Christ. Therefore, we should not look for a more perfect exhibition of Christ than happens in these symbols and that can be apprehended by faith. And, therefore, it is not at all appropriate to repeat our baptisms. For not even the baptisms of old, by which the Lord's first covenant was conferred, were repeated. But because we have no practice of observing those washings that were repeated, it therefore falls to us to possess such a living and active communion with Christ that the daily handling of the holy gospel, the practice of prayer, and the sacred Supper should suffice to keep it renewed. In all other respects it is intended that the Spirit of Christ give us aid, an internal force within us to stir us up and move us to contemplate the goodness of God, so that all the many symbols that the saints of old possessed have no further use among us. COMMENTARY ON ROMANS (1536).[17]

GOOD WORKS ARE OUR DUTY, NOT OUR MERIT. JOHANNES BRENZ: We can also learn from this passage what the role is of those who are baptized, namely, that since they have been absolved from sin and consecrated unto righteousness and life, they must no longer walk in sinful works. For this would be to profane one's consecration and return to death. For this reason, even though good works are not merits that earn righteousness, they are nevertheless the fruits of righteousness and are to be done *ex officio*.[†] For just

like a king who is consecrated unto a kingdom does not "earn" the kingdom by issuing judgments in civil controversies, but rather obtains the kingdom either by succession, or by adoption, or by election, and yet to pronounce justice is the duty of a king, so also a Christian who is consecrated unto the heavenly kingdom does not earn that kingdom by good works, but has obtained it freely solely because of Christ through faith. And yet, to do good works is the duty of a Christian, to which role a Christian is assigned. It has not been ordained that we should merely eat and drink, but that we should do good works. Therefore they are not merits, but they *are* our duty. COMMENTARY ON ROMANS (1564).[18]

THERE IS NO BETTER BAPTISM. MARTIN BUCER: Baptisms are symbols that declare the remission of sins by the divine benevolence through the gospel, and exhibit the renewal of the Holy Spirit. Therefore those baptisms that were practiced by our first fathers, as well as those among the Gentile Godfearers, were symbols of a more generic "gospel" and a less developed experience of the Spirit. Jewish baptisms signified the proclamation of grace more openly, since they contained in themselves the promise of Christ more clearly depicted, and they conferred the renewing Spirit more fully. Both the baptism of John and that of the apostles conveyed the same two realities. But the baptism of the church so excels that of John's with respect to Christ having already been glorified, the brightness of the gospel, the extent of the redemption which Christ conferred on us, and the power of the Spirit which he gives, that there remains no more excellent baptism to take its place. But what we do further await is that Christ, when he returns in his glorious body, will abolish sin entirely and fully complete our renewal. This is why, as we've said, our baptism cannot be repeated. COMMENTARY ON ROMANS (1536).[19]

---

[17]Bucer, *Metaphrases et Enarrationes*, 290.

[18]Brenz, *In Epistolam*, 174. [†]I.e., by virtue of one's status.
[19]Bucer, *Metaphrases et Enarrationes*, 292-93.

BATH OF REGENERATION EXTENDED TO INFANTS. MARTIN BUCER: There is also in these verses the opportunity for an excursus. Just because all in whom an obvious communion with Christ is evident are to be baptized, it does not therefore follow that all who are to be baptized are already furnished with an obvious and manifest communion with Christ. Likewise, just because all in whom an obvious communion with Christ is evident are to be baptized, it does not follow that those in whom a communion with Christ is *not* apparent are therefore *not* to be baptized. Rather, it does mean that in those who are not to be baptized there is no communion with Christ. In order that Christ's salvation might be made available more extensively than either the confession of faith or a living of communion with Christ in one's habits of life, it cannot be inferred that one in whom is lacking a confession or an evident exhibition of Christ in his actions of life should not be baptized. Christ's salvation is communicated to infants. And Christ himself placed his hands on infants to convey that he grants them his communion, even though they are not yet able to confess or display a life. And so, seeing that baptism is a bath of regeneration, it is presented to all. COMMENTARY ON ROMANS (1536).[20]

BAPTIZED IN HIS NAME. DIRK PHILIPS: That is what the apostle also meant when he wrote thus to the Romans: And do you not know that you who are baptized in Jesus Christ are baptized in his name? The meaning of the apostle is that the believers and penitents are baptized into the fellowship of the death of Jesus Christ, first therein, that they share in his suffering and dying and everything that he has therewith fulfilled in God and extended to our salvation, and that we participate in these, and second, that they die with him, have become conformed to his suffering, and walk in a new spiritual and Christlike being. THREE ADMONITIONS.[21]

BAPTISM AND COMMUNION WITH CHRIST. MARTIN BUCER: Our baptism is, therefore, an immersion[†] in the name of the Father, of the Son, and of the Holy Spirit, by which both the remission of sins and communion with Christ is exhibited, and this is so openly and fully displayed that we draw as near as possible to this fellowship of heavenly life. Now, because the remission of sins and communion with Christ our sole Mediator is exhibited by baptism, it is customary for us to say of all baptisms observed according to divine institution that it belongs to it to display such a full communion with Christ that nothing remains for us except that he, when he comes back in his glorious body, might conform our lowly bodies to his glorious body, and that we might attain to his stature then fully developed within us and perfected according to the heavenly image. COMMENTARY ON ROMANS (1536).[22]

REFLECT ON CHRIST'S DEATH. DIRK PHILIPS: Let now your faith in Christ Jesus be revealed, that you are truly baptized into his death, in order to live and die with him. Reflect now on your pioneer and king of our faith, Jesus Christ, what he has done and has suffered on our behalf, how he has come out of heaven, yes, out of the bosom of his Father into this world, and after much pain and scorn which was done to him by the godless, at last came to the cross, and there was offered for us as our Passover Lamb; there he was through his fiery love on the wood of the cross, roasted as a spiritually sacrificed Lamb, becoming food to all believing souls who eat him spiritually, through faith holding Passover with the unleavened bread of purity and truth. TWO ADDITIONAL LETTERS.[23]

THE DEATH OF DEATH. MARTIN LUTHER: Hence we must note that death is of two kinds: natural, or better, temporal death and eternal death. Temporal death is the separation of the body and

---

[20]Bucer, *Metaphrases et Enarrationes*, 293.
[21]CRR 6:420*.

[22]Bucer, *Metaphrases et Enarrationes*, 296-97. [†]*Tinctio* means "dipping," as one would dip something in a dye.
[23]CRR 6:629*; citing Heb 12:2; Jn 16:30; Mt 27:34; Jn 6:1-14, 50.

the soul. But this death is only a figure, a symbol, and like death painted on a wall when compared with eternal death, which is also spiritual. Hence in the Scripture it is very often called a sleep, a rest, a slumber. Eternal death is also twofold. The one kind is good, very good. It is the death of sin and the death of death, by which the soul is released and separated from sin and the body is separated from corruption and through grace and glory is joined to the living God. This is death in the most proper sense of the word, for in all other forms of death something remains that is mixed with life, but not in this kind of death, where there is the purest life alone, because it is eternal life. For to this kind of death alone belong in an absolute and perfect way the conditions of death, and in this death alone whatever dies perishes totally and into eternal nothingness, and nothing will ever return from this death, because it truly dies an eternal death. This is the way sin dies; and likewise the sinner, when he is justified, because sin will not return again for all eternity, as the apostle says here, "Christ will never die again." This is the principal theme in Scripture. For God has arranged to remove through Christ whatever the devil brought in through Adam. And it was the devil who brought in sin and death. Therefore God brought about the death of death and the sin of sin, the poison of poison, the captivity of captivity. LECTURE ON ROMANS (1516).[24]

THE SINFUL BODY DIES WITH CHRIST'S DEATH. DIRK PHILIPS:

We are also buried with him by baptism into death, that as Christ was awakened from the dead by the glory of his father, so we too shall walk in a newness of life. For if we have now been planted with him in a death like his, we shall also be partakers of the resurrection. Thereby we know that our old self was crucified with him, so that the sinful body might cease and we now no longer serve sin. THE BAPTISM OF OUR LORD JESUS CHRIST.[25]

CHRIST IS STRONGER THAN DEATH.

JOHANNES BUGENHAGEN: Christ has died for us so that all of us who have died might be with him. We were all liable to death on account of sin; we were destined to die, but Christ paid this debt for us. We were too weak to conquer death, but he swallowed it up and did away with it for us. Truly Christ is stronger than death. He absorbed it not for himself but for us. While we were not paying back our debt, he dissolved it so effectively that even if *we* did not satisfy it, death is now satisfied. Therefore, we have died in his death—just as he paid what was owed for me. Even though I have not paid that greatest price, yet I am now free from debt, because he satisfied it on my behalf. INTERPRETATION OF ROMANS (1531).[26]

6:4 We Are Raised with Christ to a New Life

BURIED WITH CHRIST IN BAPTISM. MARTIN BUCER:

"Therefore we have been buried together with him in baptism." From these passages from which we can easily learn the nature of the sacraments, it is to be observed to *whom* fellowship with Christ is held out. Since the chief aspect of our salvation comes about when the power of sin is extinguished within us, which could not be accomplished apart from the death of Christ, the apostle writes that we are buried with Christ through baptism. Consequently, Christ's power and fellowship are present in the sacraments, and that fellowship is such that we are engrafted into him fully, and we contemplate him by faith and embrace him with all reverence. COMMENTARY ON ROMANS (1536).[27]

BAPTISM BURIES THE OLD BEING. PILGRAM MARPECK:

Listen to what Paul says here. We are, he says, buried with Christ in baptism. How so? Is it because we were thrust into the water and because the words, "I baptize you in the name of

---

[24]LW 25:310*; citing Rom 6:9.
[25]CRR 6:75*.

[26]Bugenhagen, *In D. Pauli ad Romanos*, 58r.
[27]Bucer, *Metaphrases et Enarrationes*, 297.

the Father, the Son, [and the Holy Spirit]," were spoken over us? No, my dear friend, more is involved here. When we allow ourselves to be baptized with our whole hearts, we deny the devil, lay aside our fleshly lust, and, henceforth, desire to live a new life, with good conscience toward God. But only the power of faith, and not the act of baptism, will accomplish this rebirth. When such things happen in our baptism, we bury the old being and commit ourselves to live in a new way of life. Without commitment, baptism is *useless* and incorrect. Only the flesh is washed and thus, baptism is without power and becomes vain child's play. God is mocked; God's eyes look *only* and primarily on the heart, and not on the external work, to see with what kind of faith his will is sought. The Admonition of 1542.[28]

Baptism Does Not Apply to Children.

Felix Manz: From these words we clearly see what baptism is and when it shall be practiced, namely, on one who having been converted through God's Word and having changed his heart now henceforth desires to live in newness of life, as Paul clearly shows in the letter to the Romans, the sixth [chapter], dead to the old life, circumcised in his heart, having died to sin with Christ, having been buried with him in baptism and arisen with him again in newness of life. To apply such things as have just been related to children is without any and against all Scriptures. Petition of Defense (1524).[29]

Baptism and Participation in Grace. John

Calvin: Let us know that the apostle does not simply exhort us to imitate Christ, as though he said that the death of Christ is a pattern that all Christians are to follow, for no doubt he ascends higher as he announces a doctrine, with which he connects, as it is evident, an exhortation. His doctrine is this, that the death of Christ is efficacious to destroy and demolish the depravity of our

flesh, and his resurrection to effect the renovation of a better nature, and that by baptism we are admitted into a participation of this grace. This foundation being laid, Christians may very suitably be exhorted to strive to respond to their calling. Further, it is not to the point to say that this power is not apparent in all the baptized, for Paul according to his usual manner, where he speaks of the faithful, connects the reality and the effect with the outward sign, for we know that whatever the Lord offers by the visible symbol is confirmed and ratified by their faith. In short, he teaches what is the real character of baptism when rightly received. So he testifies to the Galatians, that all who have been baptized into Christ have put on Christ. This indeed we must speak as long as the institution of the Lord and the faith of the godly unite together, for we never have naked and empty symbols, except when our ingratitude and wickedness hinder the working of divine beneficence. Commentary on Romans 6:4.[30]

The Significance of Baptism. John Frith:

Now will I proceed with the second point of this sacrament, which is its signification. The signification of baptism is described of Paul in the sixth chapter of Romans: that, as we are plunged bodily into the water, even so we are dead and buried with Christ from sin. And as we are lifted again out of the water, even so we are risen with Christ from our sins, that we might thereafter walk in a new conversation of life. So that these two things, that is, to be plunged in the water and lifted up again, signify and represent the whole pith and effect of baptism, that is, the modification of our old Adam, and the rising up of our new self. What is the old Adam? Truly, it is what, by natural inheritance, was planted in us through Adam's fall, making us unfaithful, angry, envious, covetous, slothful, proud, and ungodly. These and other such uses, wherewith our nature is poisoned, we ought to cut off and modify with all diligence, so that we might daily be more patient, generous, and merciful, according to

---

[28]CRR 2:191-92*.
[29]CRR 4:313*; citing Acts 22:14-16.

[30]CTS 38:221* (CO 49:105-6); citing Gal 3:27.

what our baptism signifies. Insomuch that a Christian person's life is nothing else save a continual baptism, which is begun when we are dipped in the water, and is put in continual use and exercise as long as the infection of sin remains in our bodies, which is never utterly vanquished until the hour of death. And there the great Goliath is slain with his own sword, that is, death, which is the power of sin, and the gate of everlasting life is opened to us. And thus is Paul to be understood where he says, "All you that are baptized into Christ, have put Christ on you"; that is, you have promised to die with Christ as touching your sins and worldly desires past, and to become new men and women, or creatures, or members of Christ. This have we all promised unto the congregation, and it is represented in our baptism. But alas! There are but few who indeed fulfill what they promise, or rather that the sacrament promises for them. And for this cause Paul calls it the fountain of the new birth and regeneration because it signifies that we will indeed renounce and utterly forsake our old life, and purge our members from the works of iniquity through the virtue of the Holy Spirit, which, as the water or fire cleanses the body, even so it purifies the heart from all uncleanness. Yes, it is a common phrase in Scripture to call the Holy Spirit water and fire, because these two elements express so lively his purging operation. A Mirror, or Looking Glass wherein You May Behold the Sacrament of Baptism Described (1533).[31]

Living as Buried by Baptism. Hans Hotz: As said before, we do not deny that you of the preachers made a beginning and were the origin. But by God's providence it happened that the books were put into German. To the extent that you contributed to it, God thank you, although much was pointed out to us by the books of Luther, Zwingli, and others, so that we soon understood regarding the Mass and other [Catholic] ceremonies that they are of no benefit. Nevertheless, I saw

great lack in that they do not lead to Christian living, repentance, or conduct, on which I for my part set my mind and directed my thought and spirit toward a Christian life. So I put it off a year or two and waited, while there was preaching everywhere. The priest said much about reform, sharing, loving one another, desisting from evil, and forming community. I always felt that there was a lack in that we did not follow or establish what we were taught and what the Word of God can accomplish. There was no initiation of godly conduct, for not all were so minded. And although the Mass and images were abolished, there was still no penitence or mercy, and everything remained in evil living, gluttony, drunkenness, envy, hatred, and so on, that should not have been in all the people. Because of this I found a reason for inquiring further in this matter. Then God sent his messengers, Conrad Grebel and others, with whom I conferred on the basis of the apostles as to how one should live and also with whom. I started and established a church as those who had yielded themselves in true repentance according to the teaching of Christ concerning hearts, who by abstaining from wrongdoing, prove that they are in Christ, buried in baptism, and risen in newness of life. Bern Disputation of 1538.[32]

The Characteristics of Buried and Risen Lives. Menno Simons: I admonish all our beloved brothers and sisters in the Lord never to let it go out of your mind how precious Christ Jesus is to you, but to remember always for what purpose you are called, taught, and baptized. Remember the covenant of the Most High God, that into which you voluntarily entered, which you have voluntarily desired and accepted, being taught by the Word of God and operated on by the Holy Spirit. And remember that according to the doctrine of Paul, you have voluntarily buried in baptism all your avarice, uncleanness, pride, hatred, envy, abuse of the sacramental signs, idolatry, gluttony, drunkenness, sensuality, falsehood, deceit,

---

[31]Frith, *Works of the English Reformers*, 289-90*; citing Gal 3; Tit 3.

[32]CRR 4:521*.

and so on, and that you have risen with Christ Jesus into newness of life if you are rightly risen with him. And this new life is nothing else than righteousness, blamelessness, love, mercy, humility, long-suffering, peace, truth—yes, the whole, gentle life that is taught by the gospel and was found in Christ Jesus. A KIND ADMONITION.[33]

EXCLUDING ABSURDITIES. WOLFGANG MUSCULUS: This argument has two parts, related to the imagery of Christ's death and resurrection, both intended to exclude absurdities:

First, it is said that "our old self has been buried with Christ through baptism." But Paul makes use of the word "buried" to suggest the completion and reliability of the event of his death, which happened by his being made completely dead. Therefore since the body of sin, the old self, is buried with Christ into death through baptism, how will we be able to live in sin?

Second, it is said that "we are raised to new life with Christ being raised." This is the new creature, the new self, being born again, a renewal. This is symbolically represented in baptism, a genuine event during the life of each Christian, from the Spirit of Christ. And so accordingly, when we are renewed and raised to new life with Christ—which is entirely incompatible with the old—how can we then remain in sin? COMMENTARY ON ROMANS (1600).[34]

THE KING RELEASED US FROM PRISON. JOHANNES BUGENHAGEN: The Father raising his Son Christ out of a disgraceful death and established him in glory—as it says in John 17, "Father, glorify your Son"—and he gave him new life. He did this likewise to us, thus raising us also out of death and establishing us in a new life. Let us continue in that new life, not returning to death. Once Christ was dead, but now he lives forever. Death will not rule over him. Also, therefore, we who were brought back to life in him should not be eager to die a second time. Christ already reigns in the kingdom of life, not of death. Therefore, he is today declared in his glory throughout every region. We will cause him the highest disgrace if, disregarding the new life, we prefer to sink toward death, which they do who say, "Therefore we will sin, preferring death to life." Consider how absurd that is. Sin is forgiven not so that you can sin, but because God hates sin. Therefore, sin does not extend into Christ's kingdom and the new life. By the kindness of a particular King, I was released from prison. I am a fool if I now think his kindness was for captivity, not for liberty. For that reason I was not released in order to remain in prison, but rather, to be free. INTERPRETATION OF ROMANS (1531).[35]

WALKING IN THE NEWNESS OF LIFE. WOLFGANG MUSCULUS: "Let us walk in newness of life." He does not say, "In new life" but "In newness of life." This means being alive in a new form, in acts, and by fruits. For the apostle considers not a new aspect of regeneration, which they already have through the renewal of their minds by the Spirit of Christ, but rather, a greater effectiveness and devotion. And here also pertains the word "walking,"—that is, working, doing, moving—which Paul seizes upon in order that he might portray zeal, deeds of righteousness, and the new life. Moreover, he thus allows it to be inferred that the new nature has new movements, new affections, new acts. We are in a new nature, having been begotten according to the likeness of Christ through baptism, just as if through a bath of renewal. Therefore, it is necessary that we should devote ourselves well to new acts of righteousness and to bearing fruit. How, then, can we remain in sin? COMMENTARY ON ROMANS (1600).[36]

GRATITUDE FOR DEATH AND REBIRTH. ELIZABETH I: Great Framer and Preserver of things, God, before whom here at the feet of your Majesty I humbly lie prostrate, I consider seriously

---

[33]Simons, *Complete Works*, 444*.
[34]Musculus, *In Epistolam Apostoli*, 134.
[35]Bugenhagen, *In D. Pauli ad Romanos*, 57v; citing Jn 17:1.
[36]Musculus, *In Epistolam Apostoli*, 134.

with myself how unworthy I am, to whom you kindly offer your ear. Suffused all over with shame, I scarcely dare to lift up mine eyes to you. For formerly when I was in my mother's womb, a fall into sin stained me, on account of which, like the rest of the descendants of Adam, I was most worthy of miscarriage; yet your fatherly hand led me out from thence and allowed me to be born into light—born to die with Christ and, dead, be reborn to enjoy eternal life. PRAYER FOR THE ADMINISTRATION OF THE KINGDOM.[37]

BY THE GLORY OF THE FATHER. WOLFGANG MUSCULUS: Observe that Paul inserts the idea that Christ was raised to new life from the dead by the glory of the Father, that he might reveal and restore the glory of the Father. And this is also in us, if, according to the likeness of Christ in our life, having been made righteous from wickedness, having been raised, we henceforward strive for righteousness. Otherwise we would remain in sin. And here also he beautifully depreciates the glory of human strength, distinguishing not the raising of ours, but of our Father's strength and glory. For so great is the work of the Father and the glory of the Father, that we are raised up to new life because Christ has been raised from the dead. And certainly the power required to turn impiety to righteousness is no less than that to bring a dead body back to life. COMMENTARY ON ROMANS (1600).[38]

WASHING AND THE NEWNESS OF LIFE. HEINRICH BULLINGER: For nobody is buried with him physically, but only mentally, as is seen clearly when one renounces the world. This glory is not owing to human powers, but to that heavenly virtue that is breathed into us. For Christ himself was "raised by the glory of the Father," that is, by the divine nature. Hence, from the obligation of the sacrament of baptism, Paul has summoned proof that all who are baptized are obligated to newness or innocence of life; believers are, therefore, not to

remain in their sin. From this text it will be easy to see what the ordinance or mystery [sacrament] of baptism is. First of all, it binds us under the worship and religion of the one God: Father, Son and Holy Spirit. Second, it obliges us to live in holiness and piety while in this world. But above all, there is a correspondence in this ordinance between the element of water, by which we wash off and purge filth, and sprinkling or immersion by which we make the sign. COMMENTARY ON ROMANS (1533).[39]

PRAYER FOR A NEW LIFE. KATHARINA SCHÜTZ ZELL: May we be granted to sin no more, but henceforth to lead a new life according to Your will, so that we may willingly come to You out of this world, comforted and happy, as a pilgrim out of exile and a foreign place comes home to the fatherland, as children whose accounts have been settled come to their Father who wills them good. And so may we come to a blessed resurrection: not to the severe judgment of those on the left side, but that we may arise with the righteous to everlasting life and nothing may hinder us from that. THE MISERERE PSALM MEDITATED, PRAYED, AND PARAPHRASED.[40]

6:5 Planted Together with Him

A FRUITFUL COMPARISON. THEODORE BEZA: By an elegant comparison, the apostle likens the Christ who died, was buried, and rose, with a seedling that being planted in the ground, sprouted forth in its own time.[†] Then, however, he said that we who died together with Christ and were buried to sin, are to rise again to righteousness, and he declared that these things happened to us as if by that "sap" that we expelled from Christ. He says we are nourished together with him as in a single plant, as by *symphytos* (growing together), when trees so closely join together that they live by a common sap. So, then,

---

[37]Elizabeth I, *Collected Works*, 158-59*.
[38]Musculus, *In Epistolam Apostoli*, 134.

[39]Bullinger, *In Sanctissimam Pauli*, 83r.
[40]Zell, *Church Mother*, 168*; citing Rom 6:4; Heb 11:13-14; Mt 25:41, 46.

the apostle, with the most suitable comparison—the closest is that of our having been joined spiritually to Christ himself through faith—that is, by our acquiring a union, and at the same time Christ pressed out that life-giving power that flowed into us. Furthermore, by this reckoning, Christ himself is the vine, but we compare to the branches. And we rise in accordance with him, and in turn it is said that we will grow up. Thus Christ is compared to brushwood by Isaiah, the Word is compared to a seed, we are called fruitful trees, ministers are said to plant and water, and the faithful in Christ to take root. Truly, that is a fruitful comparison! MAJOR ANNOTATIONS (1594).[41]

TREES AND GARDENS TEACH US PIETY.

JOHANNES BRENZ: For what occurs in the planting of a tree, or in grafting, this is the same as happens in baptism, in which we have been incorporated into the death of Christ. In the planting of a tree, a wild and unfruitful tree is transplanted from barren soil to a garden and is grafted into the fruit bearing shoot. Then what happens? The fruit bearing shoot is not changed into the nature of the wild tree, but on the contrary, the wild tree is changed into the nature of the fruit bearing shoot. Therefore, the entire tree is made fruitful by means of grafting into the fertile shoot. In such a way we humans also are born a fruitless and wild tree. But we are transplanted through baptism into the garden of God's church, and we are planted into the death of Christ just as a fruitful shoot. Then what happens? It is necessary to mention the kind of fruit the shoot of Christ's death bore corresponds to his own character, and furthermore is such in us who have been grafted into the death of Christ and who are his members. But the death of Christ in itself bore that fruit because Christ having atoned for sin, he returned to true and everlasting life. Therefore, we also ought to bear that fruit to destroy sin in us, indeed let us in the first place walk in newness of life, then also let us rise again from death with Christ into eternal life. Therefore it is necessary that Christ is not changed into our nature, but we be changed into the nature of Christ. You see, the garden as well as the tree teach us piety if, after being taught by the Word of God, we observe them with proper eyes. By this and other ways Christ teaches us to learn piety from the vineyard. Saying, "I am the true vine and you are the branches. . . ." Likewise he proposed another similarity about the barren fig tree, by which we are exhorted toward repentance, and indeed when man was created in the beginning, God placed him in the Garden of Eden so that he would cultivate it. And even the Son of God, while praying, withdrew frequently into a garden. Therefore, trees and gardens are not only to be contemplated according to the human nature of this age, which inquires only to the external pleasure and advantage of it, but they are also to be considered according to the nature of the Holy Spirit in order that they would be for our instruction in true piety. COMMENTARY ON ROMANS (1564).[42]

THREE KINDS OF DYING.
MARTIN LUTHER: There are . . . three kinds of people in this order. First there are those who are impatient with a crisis and a dying of this kind, and they are unwilling to die. These people are like the robber on the left, for they blaspheme Christ, at least in their heart and also in their work. The second class, however, are those who endure it, but with great feeling, difficulty, and groaning; yet they finally overcome, so that at least they die with patience. It is very hard for them that they are despised and detested by all. They are like the robber on the right. Indeed, a grieving and sympathetic Christ carried them in his body. But the third class are those who, as I have said, enter upon this death with joy, whom Christ himself prefigured when he died with a loud shout like the most courageous giant. LECTURES ON ROMANS (1516).[43]

---

[41]Beza, *Annotationes Majores*, 71; citing Jn 15:5; Mt 13:22-23; Is 64:2; Mk 4:1-20. †A number of translations, including the Vulgate, used the phrase "planted together with him." Erasmus translated *symphytoi* as "engrafted."

[42]Brenz, *In Epistolam*, 148v; citing Jn 15:5.
[43]LW 25:312*.

6:6 *Crucified to Be Set Free*

ALL PARTS OF A CRUCIFIED PERSON DIE.
WOLFGANG MUSCULUS: "We know" this, he says.
What? "Our old self"—that is, that corrupt
nature—"has been crucified with Christ." Where?
"In baptism." For what purpose? "In order that the
sinful body may be destroyed." Why did this
happen? "So that after this, we might not be
enslaved to sin." How, therefore, shall we remain in
sin? The apostle compares the power of sin to a
human who has a body and lives for his or her own
nature as long as life endures. If this person's body
is crucified and dies, then certainly all their limbs,
and whatever belonged to the person's substance
and action, have at the same time been crucified
and have died. COMMENTARY ON ROMANS (1555).[44]

THE DIVIDED SELF. JOHANNES BUGENHAGEN:
Paul describes a divided self, the old and the new.
The old is the one "born of the flesh," as Christ says.
What is born from flesh, is flesh. That is, everything which pertains to the self and its capacities,
the entirety of what was born—the soul and the
body, including reason and the senses—is flesh and
sin. Hence Christ says, "It is necessary that you be
born again." Indeed, nothing in that first birth of
yours is good; everything is found guilty, and you
are not able to will and to think the things of God.
And because the law of God displeases you, you
murmur against it and would prefer it did not exist.
By no means is your will able to be in harmony
with the will of God. Therefore, whatever you will,
whatever you reason or desire, is contrary to God.

But the new self is the one in whom there is
nothing of nature, nothing of human capacities,
but only of the Spirit of God who moves and
impels it, who, whatever he does, he certainly
knows he does God's good will. He knows
everything that pleases him, and that there is
nothing in him that he hates or condemns.
INTERPRETATION OF ROMANS (1531).[45]

OLD SELF, NEW LIFE. ELISABETH CRUCIGER:

Lord Christ, God's only Son
Sprung from the Father's heart
From all eternity.
Just as it is written,
He is the Morning Star
Who shines from afar
Brighter than all other stars.

For us a Man was born
In the ripeness of time,
To the blessed Mother,
The chaste Virgin.
Death was destroyed for us,
The heavens were unlocked,
And life restored.

Let us in your love
Find wisdom
So that we stay in the faith
And serve in the Spirit.
And savoring the taste
Of your sweetness in our hearts,
May we always thirst for You.

Creator of all things
Fatherly in power
Rule the Earth's four corners,
Strong in Your might.
Turn our hearts to you
And [guide] our senses
So that we do not stray from you.

Kill us with your goodness
Awaken us by your grace
Shrink in us the old self
Increase in us the new life
That here on this earth
All our senses, desires,
And thoughts may be for you.

"HERR CHRIST, DER EINIG GOTTS SOHN" IN
ERFURT ENCHIRIDION (1524)[46]

---

[44]Musculus, *In Epistolam Apostoli Pauli*, 135.
[45]Bugenhagen, *In D. Pauli ad Romanos*, 79v; citing Jn 3:6.
[46]Cruciger, *Ein Enchiridion*, 66.

6:7 *The Dead Are Emancipated from Sin*

FREED FROM SIN. LUCAS OSIANDER: For the ones (mentioned earlier) who have died with Christ in a spiritual manner through baptism, have been justified from sin. So sin is no longer imputed to them, whether original sin or sins committed. Therefore, having been freed from sin, let us have no more relations with it; and although sin remains within this life as a result of our inability to tear out the flesh, nevertheless let us not yield to its lusts. EXPLICATION OF PAUL'S EPISTLES (1583).[47]

THE DEAD DON'T BITE. PETER MARTYR VERMIGLI: "For he who is dead, is justified from sin." The reason why one should not serve cupidity,[†] of course, is that we have been absolved from it through death. For this means to be justified from sin, to be liberated from it, so that it no longer has power in us. And Paul appears to speak here not of natural death, but of mortification, of which we have spoken many times. And justification can be accepted properly, so that mortification is the effect of it. For we cannot proceed to that effect unless we have been justified beforehand.

Certain others, not unfittingly, understand this passage as referring to everyday things and natural death, for the dead cease from the depraved actions in which they used to live. So we speak of a thief who has been hanged: he has now ceased to steal. And it is a proverb that "the dead don't bite." For which reason, if we follow this sense, it serves as a metaphor for the way that those who are naturally dead leave and finish with the sins that they carried on while living. In this way we—when we have died with Christ and have professed that we wish to be dead to sin—must entirely desist from sin. These words of Paul are not to be taken otherwise, as well as those of John, "the one who is born of God does not sin"; that is, so far as whoever it is lives and acts out of the beginning of his heavenly birth, for that beginning is the Spirit and the Word of God. Therefore, he who is dead to sin—and one with Christ, affixed to the cross—is said to be absolved from sin. To the extent that he is dead and affixed to the cross, he does not to do anything from the impulse of sin. And Peter does not teach otherwise in the fourth chapter of the earlier letter: "Christ having suffered for us in the flesh, arm yourself also with the same thought. For he that has died has ceased from sin and lives not according to human desires, but according to the will of the Lord God." COMMENTARY ON ROMANS (1559).[48]

MORTIFY THE REMNANTS OF SIN. THE ENGLISH ANNOTATIONS: This is not said as if evil lusts were in the body alone—or as if they had the original [sin] only from it and not from the soul, for Christ teaches the contrary—but because these evil lusts do most of all show and manifest themselves in and through the body. Or the words may bear this interpretation: Do not let sin reign in your mortal body, that is, while you live this bodily life here, which, being subject unto death, it appears thereby that there are some remnants of sin yet behind, to be striven against that we may mortify and destroy them more and more. ANNOTATIONS ON ROMANS 6:12.[49]

---

[47]Osiander, *Epistolae S. Pauli*, 65.

[48]Vermigli, *In Epistolam S. Pauli*, 347-48; citing 1 Jn 3:9; 1 Pet 4:1.
   [†]Cupidity is excessive desire.
[49]Downame, ed., *Annotations*, AAA4v*; citing Mt 15:19, 20; Gal 5:19.

6:8-14 DEAD TO SIN, ALIVE TO GOD

[8]*Now if we have died with Christ, we believe that we will also live with him. [9]We know that Christ, being raised from the dead, will never die again; death no longer has dominion over him. [10]For the death he died he died to sin, once for all, but the life he lives he lives to God. [11]So you also must consider yourselves dead to sin and alive to God in Christ Jesus.*

[12]*Let not sin therefore reign in your mortal body, to make you obey its passions. [13]Do not present your members to sin as instruments for unrighteousness, but present yourselves to God as those who have been brought from death to life, and your members to God as instruments for righteousness. [14]For sin will have no dominion over you, since you are not under law but under grace.*

OVERVIEW: Paul—and, therefore, the commentators as well—continues to explore the results of the impact that our being buried and raised to life with Christ should have on our lives as Christians. Eternal life starts now. It is, admittedly, imperfect at the moment, contrasting with the perfection of the life to come. But it is meant, nevertheless, to be lived, guided, and empowered by the Holy Spirit.

The reformers agree that the regenerate person will still struggle with sin. However, they express a variety of views on "reigning sin," about whether it can occur in the regenerate, and if so, whether it can lead to the loss of salvation. We will sin, but we must not do so willfully out of contempt toward God or with determination to do evil. And when we sin, we must repent and fight against our flesh. We must use the "weapons of righteousness," for God, with no need on his part, invites us to fight alongside him against Satan and sin, exhibiting his grace in our lives. These weapons include such disciplines as fasting, prayer, and the sacraments. The reformers are concerned that some Protestants have overreacted to some medieval spiritual practices and have eliminated them because of their association with Catholic piety.

Paul teaches that Christ died once for all, and a number of commentators contrast this to a popular—albeit not universally held—medieval view that the Mass involved resacrificing Christ, and that each Mass was itself a propitiatory sacrifice.

In addition, the theme of law versus grace continues in these comments. We have been given freedom in Christ, but we must not abuse this liberty. We have not been freed from sin in order to sin. Instead, we have been freed from the law in order to live by love, which means that we should obey the law, but out of grace rather than under constraint. The commentators urge us to seek to obey God's commandments, engage in good works, exhibit integrity of morals, and live with spiritual joy.

6:8 We Died with Christ, We Live with Christ

ETERNAL LIFE STARTS NOW. PETER MARTYR VERMIGLI: So that we will not be afraid at the name of death, which he mentioned so often before, here Paul adds a consolation, declaring that to this death that he has spoken of, the life of Christ is added. So that if we die together with Christ, we shall also live together with him. And this life is not only that which we look for in the world to come, but also it is the life that we lead even now. The life here is the same as the life to come, but this one has just begun and is imperfect, whereas the other is perfect and absolute. For we who believe in Christ and are justified, also lead the life of God even now. For we are driven and moved not by ourselves, but by the Spirit of God. LEARNED AND FRUITFUL COMMENTARY ON ROMANS (1558).[1]

---

[1]Vermigli, *Learned and Fruitfull Commentaries*, 149*.

A SHIFT IN THE TERM *JUSTIFICATION*.

AEGIDIUS HUNNIUS: It is as if you had said, those who crossed over from slavery into freedom are vindicated. They did not originally submit their necks easily to the yoke. In fact, rather, they strove to retain the freedom they gained. But having been justified because they have died to sin, they have been freed from its dominion and rule. Therefore, they do not serve it any longer. For just as previously they were slaves for a long time, they were liable to their masters for such a long time, but by the intervention of death they are freed from the power of the owner. And just as previously through physical death the saints were fully freed from sin, so through spiritual death those who are dead to sin have been freed or justified from sin by reason of the Lord. For the word "justification" does not mean the same thing in this passage as it did in the above chapter, as indicating the free forgiveness of sins that does not happen through our spiritual death but through and because of the death of Christ alone. Therefore, in this passage, "to be justified" does not signify to be freely absolved from sin, or that it is not imputed, but it indicates to be free from the law and dominion of sin, so that it does not reign through the work of the flesh. EXPOSITION ON ROMANS (1592).[2]

CHRIST AS THE HEAD ABOVE WATER. JUAN DE VALDÉS: And seeking to give us assurance as to this resurrection, he says that we may base it on Christ's having risen again, not to revert to die like other people that have been resuscitated, but to live for ever, Christ having passed beyond the dominion and jurisdiction of death. By this St. Paul means that just as when a person about to be drowned in a river gets their head out of water so that the water cannot again get above it, all the other members of the body hold themselves to be safe and free from danger, not because they are out of the water, but because the head is out. So too we who are members of Christ, since we see that he, our Head, is now raised again, and that he has

passed beyond the dominion and jurisdiction of death, we esteem ourselves to be risen too, and to have passed beyond the dominion and jurisdiction of death; not that we do not have to die, but because we have to follow our Head in being resurrected. COMMENTARY ON ROMANS (1556).[3]

6:9 Christ Will Never Die Again

CHRIST'S DEATH WAS OF ONE SORT, OURS OF ANOTHER. PETER MARTYR VERMIGLI: Just as the life of Christ is never extinguished by death, so the lives of the children of God and brothers and sisters of Christ ought not to be quenched by sins. The reason why Christ dies no more is that he has overcome death and has taken away sin, which was the only means by which death was upheld and held dominion. For to the Corinthians it is written, "The sting of death is sin," and in this letter, "death reigned by sin." Therefore, those that are partakers of Christ's death neither ought nor can any longer be subject to either sin or death. But our death is one kind and Christ's is another. "For his death"—as Augustine says in *De Trinitate*—"was simple and of only one sort, but ours is double, or of two sorts."[†] For in Christ only the body died, for his soul was never without the eternal and true life, for sin never had a place in him. But in us both body and soul were dead because of sin. Therefore, just as Christ does not die again physically, so we should not die again either physically or in our souls. Otherwise only one death of Christ should not (as he says) bring remedy unto our double death. The apostle emphasizes this when he doubles this in the same sentence, saying: "He dies no more," also, "death has no more dominion over him." For he wants us to understand fully that death is completely and forever removed from Christ. Neither should we infer by these words that death at any time had such dominion over Christ, that he was compelled to die. For Christ says that no one could

---

[2]Hunnius, *Epistolae Divi Pauli*, 214-15; citing 1 Cor 15:56; Rom 5:21.

[3]Valdés, *Commentary upon St. Paul's Epistle*, 84*. [†]Augustine, *De Trinitate* 4.2.

take away his life from him but that he himself had power both to lay down his life, and also to take it up again. Christ freely and willingly became subject to death. Therefore, since we are members of his mystical body, we ought to freely and of our own accord die together with Christ. And in such a way that we will die no more, that is we will no longer be subject to the guilt, death, and damnation of our sins. A LEARNED AND FRUITFUL COMMENTARY (1558).[4]

THE MASS IS NOT A PROPITIATORY SACRIFICE.

WILLIAM GUILD: The Mass is not a propitiatory sacrifice. . . . Seeing then from this verse that Christ died only once and dies no more, and that his death was the sole propitiatory sacrifice, offered on the cross once for all time, never to be reiterated, as we are clearly taught in Hebrews. Therefore, it follows that there is no propitiatory sacrifice offered up in the Mass, but only a commemoration in the sacrament of Christ's death and Passion. THE OLD ROMAN CATHOLIC (1649).[5]

OUR DEATH AND FULL SANCTIFICATION.

NIELS HEMMINGSEN: Having to this point drawn his arguments from the power of our communion with Christ, whereby he proved that we are dead to sin and ought to live to righteousness, he now reasons by way of example. There is here a twofold enthymeme,[†] the first drawn from the example of his death:

(P2) Christ died once for all.

(C) Therefore we, having died to sin, ought not to go back to living in sin.

The second is drawn from the example of his resurrection:

(P2) Rising again, Christ lives an everlasting life.

(C) Therefore we also should apply ourselves to perpetual newness of life.

We can summarize the main idea this way: just as by the example of Christ's death we should die to sin so that we no longer obey it, so by the same example we ought to live to God so that we do the things that are pleasing to him. Of course here we may observe a dissimilarity: Christ died to his natural body and died while expiating sin. We, however, who are justified by faith, die to the body of sin, and die to sin not by expiating it, but by mortifying sins in our flesh, since he cannot abolish sin fully until we die in this mortal body. For our sanctification, which flows out of the power of Christ, is never completed in us as long as the consummation of our sanctification hinges upon death itself. COMMENTARY ON ROMANS (1562).[6]

PREACHING RESURRECTION AT HER HUSBAND'S GRAVE.

KATHARINA SCHÜTZ ZELL: I stand here today by the holy body of my husband and confess with him and all believers the forgiveness of our sins only through the blood of our Lord Jesus Christ the spotless Lamb, who was with the Father from eternity and was killed in the flesh for us. Likewise I confess the only righteousness that counts before God: our inheritance of eternal life through the resurrection of our Lord Jesus Christ from the dead. And so I say today, with and in the place of my dear husband, with Mary Magdalene, "The Lord is truly risen and lives for us all!" And on the contrary the devil and eternal death have died and are dead to us all and have no further power over all those who are in Christ Jesus. LAMENT AND EXHORTATION OF KATHARINA ZELL TO THE PEOPLE AT THE GRAVE OF MASTER MATTHEW ZELL, MINISTER AT THE CATHEDRAL IN STRASBOURG, HER UPRIGHT HUSBAND, OVER HIS DEAD BODY, THE 11TH OF JANUARY 1548.[7]

---

[6]Hemmingsen, *Commentarius in Epistolam*, 219-20. [†]An enthymeme is a syllogism in which one of the premises is implied rather than stated.

[7]Zell, *Church Mother*, 114-15*; citing 1 Pt 1:19-20; 3:18; 1 Cor 1:30; Mt 19:29; Rom 6:4; Jn 20:18.

---

[4]Vermigli, *Learned and Fruitfull Commentaries*, 149; citing 1 Cor 15:56.
[5]Guild, *The Old Roman Catholik*, 71-72*; citing Heb 9:25; 10:14.

CHRIST HAS CONQUERED DEATH.

GEORGE WITHER:

1.

This is the day the Lord has made,
And therein joyful we will be;
For, from the black infernal shade
In triumph back returned is he.
The snares of Satan, and of Death,
He has victoriously undone,
And fast in chains he bound them hath,
His triumph to attend upon.

2.

The grave, which all men did detest,
And held a dungeon full of fear,
Is now become a bed of rest,
And no such terrors find we there.
For Jesus Christ has taken away
The horror of that loathed pit;
Even ever since that glorious day,
In which he himself came out of it.

3.

His mockings, and his bitter smarts,
He to our praise and case does turn,
And all things to our joy converts,
Which he with heavy heart has borne:
His broken flesh is now our food,
His blood he shed, is ever since
That drink, which does our souls most good,
And that which will our foulness cleanse.

4.

Those wounds so deep, and torn so wide,
As in a rock our shelters are;
And that they pierced through his side,
Is made a dovecote[†] for his dear;
Yea, now we know, as was foretold,
His flesh did no corruption see;
And that hell wanted strength to hold
So strong, and one so blest as he.

5.

Oh let us praise his name therefore
(Who thus the upper hand has won)
For we had else, for evermore,

Been lost, and utterly undone.
Whereas this favor does allow
That we with boldness thus may sing,
Oh Hell, where is your conquest now?
And you, oh Death, where, is your sting.

HYMNS AND SONGS OF THE CHURCH (1625).[8]

6:10 *Christ Died to Sin and Lives to God*

THE IMPLICATIONS OF CHRIST'S DYING ONCE.

THOMAS WILSON: Timotheus: What is contained in the tenth verse?

Silas: The telos of Christ's death, which was to abolish and wholly take away sin, touching on both the punishment and the power of it. Therefore it is said, he died once to sin, that is, to take away sin from his members by that one death that he once suffered. Also, it contains the telos of his life, which he now lives in heaven: to wit, the glory of his Father. Therefore, it is written that he lives to God, that is to the praise of God, and in his glorious presence, or most gloriously.

Timotheus: What are we to learn from this, that Christ is said to die once to sin?

Silas: First, that our sin was the cause of his death. Second, that sin in the elect shall be destroyed and taken away by the merit and virtue of his death. The time will come (to wit, after this life) that the children of God shall be as free from sin as Christ himself is. Third, that for the destruction of sin, it was sufficient for Christ once to die, and therefore the sacrifice or offering of Christ in the Mass to take away sin is absurd and abominable. It is absurd because it implies a taking away of sin without death and a sacrifice for sin without blood, or else an iteration of his death, or often shedding of his blood, all which is most absurd. It is abominable [first] because it is directly against the Scripture, which speaks of Christ as of one once dead, and once offered. Second, because it derogates from the all sufficiency and perfection of Christ's only sacrifice in his death. For if his

---

[8]Wither, *Hymns and Songs*, 206-7*. †A dovecote was a shelter with holes for doves to enter and find safety.

sacrifice is sufficient for this purpose to take away sin, their sacrifice of the Mass is superfluous; if it is necessary, then Christ's is weak. COMMENTARY ON ROMANS (1614).[9]

BAPTISM AND DEATH TO SIN. GEORG MAJOR: That is, just as Christ died once to sin, meaning on account of *our* sin, and he is now forever immortal, and lives to God, so we have been reborn once through baptism and are dead to sin. So let us not slide back into sin, and let us live not for the flesh and the old self, but for God, and let us obey the Director, the Holy Spirit, just as chapter 8 says below: "If you live according to the flesh, you will die. But if you put to death the deeds of the body, you will live." EXPOSITION ON THE EPISTLES OF PAUL (1569).[10]

BE A NEW PERSON. HULDRYCH ZWINGLI: Christ was dead to sin, that is, on account of sin. Christ died so that sin would be destroyed and taken away. Truly, we ought to be dead to sin, that is, to the flesh, so that we may live no longer for the flesh, but for God through Christ, and so that we may be a new creature in Christ. So it is not enough to have been baptized, but to have been baptized *in him*, so that we may be new people. ANNOTATIONS ON ROMANS (1539).[11]

6:11 We Are Dead to Sin, Alive to God

SANCTIFICATION. AEGIDIUS HUNNIUS: Regarding sanctification and the new obedience, which follows justification as fruit: sanctification consists in this, that whoever dies to sin, crucifies and kills the old self along with his or her own carnal desires. In other words, let them despise the world and that which is in the world, and abstain from sins which battle against his soul, and let them reject impiety and the desires of the world. Let them, conversely, walk in newness of life, live in

righteousness, be eager for a new obedience, run after the way of the commandments of the Lord, and let them be found in a state of good works. Indeed, if these things are not in this person, or they have not yet begun to be, it is sure that he has not yet been justified. . . . But those who are Christ's have crucified the flesh along with their affections and desires. And on the other side, one can gather that those who indulge in sins against their conscience are not Christ's. EXPOSITION ON ROMANS (1592).[12]

LEAD A HEAVENLY LIFE. LUCAS OSIANDER: You should lead a heavenly life in the spiritual joy that comes from a quietness of conscience and in integrity of morals, so that now, having abandoned your former ungodly manner of life, you are entirely dedicated to God so that you might desire his will because—as it has already been said often—you have been grafted into Jesus Christ, the Son of God, with whom you died to sin and are alive to God. You see, the gospel's doctrine concerning the forgiveness of sins, which we have because of Christ's merit, does not teach impiety, but a pious life. Therefore, whoever is willing under the pretext of the gospel's doctrine to live according to the desires of his own corrupt flesh, these should know that they have not yet grasped the gospel itself, which is about true faith in Christ. It follows as a corollary of the preceding discussion that sin must be avoided. EXPLICATION OF ST. PAUL'S EPISTLES (1583).[13]

THE SWEET FRUITS OF RIGHTEOUSNESS BLOSSOM. DIRK PHILIPS: Here it now proceeds spiritually in full power so that the Bridegroom says to the bride: my beautiful friend, come and see; the winter is past, the rain is gone and has passed by; the flowers have come forth in the land; spring has come forth; the turtledoves let themselves be heard in our land; the fig tree has received buds; the vines have blossomed and given forth a lovely

[9]Wilson, *Commentarie*, 359-60*.
[10]Major, *Enarrationes Epistolarum S. Pauli*, 118-19; citing Rom 8:13.
[11]Zwingli, *In Evangelicam Historiam*, 421.

[12]Hunnius, *Epistolae Divi Pauli*, 117.
[13]Osiander, *Epistolae S. Pauli*, 66.

fragrance. That is, the time of the law has run its course, the wrath of God is stilled, the punishment of the Lord is taken away, the joyful time of grace has come. The comforting gospel has been heard, the sweet fruits of righteousness blossom. CONCERNING SPIRITUAL RESTITUTION.[14]

HOW TO PRESERVE THE SPIRITUAL LIFE.
THOMAS WILSON: Timotheus: What is meant here by living unto God?

Silas: When not sin, but the Spirit and the Word of God are the grounds of all our thoughts, words, and deeds.

Timotheus: How is this spiritual life by which we live to God to be preserved and maintained?

Silas: First, by the means of spiritual nourishment, the flesh and blood of Christ, spiritually eaten and drunk by faith. Second, by recreation, that is, the singing of psalms with joyfulness. Third, by exercise of prayer, repentance, and good works. Fourth, by sleep, even by meditation of the Word, law, and gospel. Fifth, by the physic [medicine] and good use of affliction, both on ourselves and others. Sixth, the avoiding of hindrances, namely, of sin, evil company, evil example, and evil counsel. COMMENTARY ON ROMANS (1614).[15]

6:12 Do Not Let Sin Reign

CAN SIN REIGN IN THE REGENERATE? DAVID
PAREUS: Doubt 7: whether reigning sin remains in the regenerate? This doubt arises from the same passage: whether reigning sin remains in the regenerate. About this there are disagreeing opinions among orthodox theologians. Ursinus in volume one affirms: "that even the regenerate can fall into reigning sin is sufficiently shown by the tragic falling away of men even from among the saints, such as when Aaron made the golden calf, for which cause in his wrath God purposed to destroy him; and also David when he committed adultery and murder, to whom Nathan said, 'you

are the man worthy of death.'" But against this Zanchius in his *Miscellanies* seems to deny that reigning sin and a ravaged conscience can have a place in the elect who are regenerate.[†]

Response: The resolution to this question lies in discerning between different definitions. For we call "reigning sin" that which a man embraces out of contempt for God with all his heart and against his conscience, without any struggle or feeling of penitence—which is the sense that Zanchius holds it—then clearly it must be denied that sin of this kind can exist in the sons and daughters of God. But those who occasionally fall mortally to their ruin against the dictates of their conscience, such as Aaron, David, and Peter did, and yet who sin not out of contempt for God or a fixed resolution toward wickedness, nor with all their heart, but rather by being won over by the weakness of their flesh—these by an earnest struggle between the flesh and the Spirit, by whose grace through true penitence, are such who are able to raise themselves back up again and turn back to God. Those who sin in this manner do devastate their conscience, grieve the Holy Spirit, lose all inner joy, and incur the wrath of God, but they do not completely shut out all fear of God, nor faith, but the seed that God planted remains in them, by which they are called to repentance and so arise from their fall. The apostle John openly teaches this in 1 John 3:9: "Whoever is born of God does not sin, nor can sin, for the seed of God remains in him," and the psalmist in Psalm 37:24, "If the righteous fall he will not be in ruins, for the Lord holds him by the hand." Peter denied Christ out of fear of death, but he soon afterward was weeping bitterly, for as Augustine said, although the confession of Christ had failed in his mouth, faith in him had not failed in his heart.

Further, even if "reigning sin" refers to mortal sin, which sometimes by one act trips up God's children who are self-secure and not watchful, even then it cannot be denied that such sin occurs in the regenerate, since this is all too often witnessed by the examples of the saints in sacred history and by common experience. For sin is said to be "reigning"

---

[14]CRR 6:340*; citing Song 2:10-13; Rom 11:25-27.
[15]Wilson, *Commentarie*, 361*; citing Ps 1:1; 26:1-12; 119:1-176.

only in an improper sense when by its forcefulness it seizes power over someone in the spur of the moment. Thus it is improperly termed "reigning sin" when it sometimes, for a short while, catches in its snare those of God's children who are not being watchful, but is then soon afterward again brought into subjection and driven away, as is seen in the case of David and Peter. Even Zanchius explains and allows this resolution to the problem in his *Miscellanies*. As for the difference in how the regenerate and the unregenerate customarily sin, let the reader consult Ursinus in the same volume and in the catechism on "a threefold difference." COMMENTARY ON ROMANS (1608).[16]

SALVATION MAY BE LOST. FRIEDRICH BALDUIN: Q: The apostle exhorts Romans who were born again that they must not permit sin to reign in their mortal bodies, from which it follows that reigning sin can hold sway even over the regenerate, driving away faith and the Holy Spirit. Why, therefore, did the apostle John write that "he who is born of God does not sin, nor can sin, because the seed of God remains in him"?

A: I answer, it is rightly inferred from this passage of our Paul that even the regenerate can fall back into reigning sin, which not only leaves their conscience in ruins but also drives away faith and the Holy Spirit; and, further, that those who do this are excluded from the inheritance of eternal life, since otherwise this exhortation would be pointless. A prime example of this is David, who defiled himself with adultery against the dictates of his conscience, a crime of such a nature and such dimensions that the Scriptures judge it worthy of exclusion from eternal life. Another example is Saul, who had certainly been born again but who drove away the Spirit of God. Also Aaron who made the golden calf, for which crime of idolatry St. Paul assigns eternal condemnation.

There are even some among the Calvinists who assign reigning sin even to the regenerate, but they say that this is only improperly speaking, "since it seizes dominion over the regenerate only by force, trapping the careless in its snare but for only a little while, and soon afterward it is conquered again and driven out from them."[†] Other Calvinists say that the regenerate are unable to sin out of contempt for God or hopelessness, but only out of ignorance or weakness, which they refer to as human temptation.[‡] But the most common opinion of the Calvinists is that the children of God never wholly lose their faith on account of their sins, nor do they lose the Holy Spirit, since the seed of God remains in them, which will recall them to repentance and lift them up from their fall (which is found in the passages from Pareus and Zanchius already cited, and also in Ursinus, *Catechism*, p. 71). But this doctrine is repugnant to the Scriptures and above all to this apostolic text of ours before us. St. Paul exhorts the regenerate that they beware of sin reigning in them, but in such a way that to those who strenuously wage war, a sure victory is promised. He also does not distinguish between reigning sin properly speaking versus improperly speaking. For a dominion lasting only a short while is still a dominion, properly speaking. Neither can sin be said to take dominion only by force over those who willingly and consciously violate their consciences, which David confessed that he had done. "To a willing person no violence or injury is done," as the common saying goes. Therefore our Paul does not attribute a tyranny to sin, but simply a reign; for a tyranny is exercised over unwilling subjects, but a reign over those who are willing to be ruled over, a point made by Theodoret when discussing this text. Therefore Pareus errs when he calls the sin of the regenerate, even that which is done against the conscience, only improperly speaking a "reigning" sin. Zanchius also errs when he suggests that the children of God cannot fall into contempt of God or unbelief, but can sin only out of weakness. For it is quite clear that Saul and Judas were at one time children of God, since they had been engrafted into the covenant of God by

---

[16]Pareus, *In Divinam ad Romanos*, 600-601; citing 2 Sam 12:7; 1 Jn 3:9; Ps 37:24. [†]Zacharias Ursinus, *Explicationum Catecheticarum D. Zachariae Ursini Silesii: Absolutum Opus, Totiusque Theologiae Purioris Quasi Novum Corpus* (Neostadii Palatinorum, 1593), 1:63; Jerome Zanchi, *Miscellanea Theologica* (1566), 293.

the sacrament of initiation, but both of them nevertheless fell into a horrible contempt for God and unbelief.

Therefore if the question is one of possibility, whether the children of God can fall into a contempt for God, the Scriptures everywhere affirms that it is so, frequently exhorting that "those who stand must watch lest they fall," "nor permit sin to reign in their mortal bodies," but that they should "work out their own salvation with fear and trembling." But in other respects we freely concede that contempt of God, or rather any other sin, cannot exist together with our adoption and gift of rebirth, but that when the regenerate fall into sins of this kind they immediately cease to be regenerate and the children of God, until by means of conversion, the gift of rebirth is restored in them. It was with this meaning that John wrote the passage mentioned above, saying that "those who are born of God cannot sin," namely, as long as they are regenerate. But it can so happen that they come to lose both the name and the essence of being the "born again." The fact that it is said that the seed of God remains in them does not mean that they cannot fall from the grace of God or lose their faith and the Holy Spirit, which the Scriptures testify in a loud voice in many passages. For this "seed of God" is not the residue of some faith that remains hidden in the souls of the lapsed, as if it were fire latent under ashes, but is that very faith itself and the adoption to which they are "born again by the incorruptible seed of the Word of God," all of which remains in them as long as they remain reborn; but they can totally lose this seed of God and with it, God himself, which is why St. John also wrote concerning the same people that if they sin, they do not have God, "nor does eternal life remain in them." COMMENTARY ON ROMANS (1620).[17]

AN EXHORTATION IN PASSING. WOLFGANG MUSCULUS: There are certain related reasons in that exhortation, some of which are hidden and ought to be carefully observed. For they seem as though they were inserted quickly, in passing, so that if you don't pay close attention, you will not notice them. Indeed, such a statement is added here, inasmuch as he says, "For you are not under the law, but under grace." This admonition has two parts. One is exhorting *from* the slavery of sin, and the other exhorting *toward* the slavery of righteousness. For a person who lives under the reign of sin cannot serve righteousness. For this also is the truth: Christ said that no one is able to serve two masters. Again, it is not enough to be free from the tyranny of sin, unless one also agrees to be a slave of righteousness. COMMENTARY ON ROMANS (1555).[18]

VENIAL VERSUS MORTAL SINS. FRIEDRICH BALDUIN: The distinction between "venial" and "mortal" sin has its foundation in this apostolic text, where he expressly distinguishes between the lust or desire for sin and a voluntary submission rendered to it. No man or woman can avoid evil desires, on account of original sin, which is never idle. But as long as a godly person fights against them and does not render assent, it is only venial sin, so called not because it is worthy of pardon on account of its own nature or in any way deserving pardon, but because it is not imputed to believers, on account of Christ. But submission to sin makes it mortal sin, which does violence to the conscience and drives away both faith and the Holy Spirit. COMMENTARY ON ROMANS (1620).[19]

DO NOT LET SIN REIGN. HULDRYCH ZWINGLI: It was already revealed, Paul says, what any of us who are of Christ ought to be: truly, to be a new person, a new creation in Christ, living a new life. This is what I want: that sin may not reign in your mortal body. It is as if he were to say,

---

[17]Balduin, *Catechesis Apostolica*, 417-19; citing Jn 3:9; 1 Cor 6:9; Gal 5:19; Eph 5:5; 1 Sam 16:14; Deut 9:20; 1 Cor 6:9; 10:12; Phil 2:12; Ezek 18:26; Rom 8:8; 1 Cor 11:29; Heb 6:6; 10:1; 1 Jn 3:15; 2 Pet 2:3; 1 Jn 3:6, 15. †Pareus, *Romans*, chap. 6, q. 7. †See Zanchius, *Miscellanies*, 133.

[18]Musculus, *In Epistolam Apostoli Pauli*, 136; citing Mt 6:24; Rom 6:15. [19]Balduin, *Catechesis Apostolica*, 427.

"Indeed I know the nature of the flesh; I know that it never rests while we reside here; I know that it always devours bad fruit. But most carefully watch out! Do not let it rule over you! Do not let yourself be dominated! Do not let it gain authority! This is what happens as long as you are living close to the passions of the flesh." "Let a person deny himself," says Christ. And Paul says, "Do not let sin reign." So Christ teaches us to pray, "Lead us not into temptation." Annotations on Romans (1539).[20]

Sin Reigns When We Yield to Its Passion.

Johannes Brenz: Now it is required from us that sin, which was active in us until now, no longer reign in us or be our king or lord. During the time, however, when we excelled in its service with enthusiasm and passion, sin was our king or lord. For example, if someone is caused injury by a neighbor, the injured neighbor is provoked and boils over into anger or hatred, like heat being stirred up when water is poured into a jar, for the sin lies hidden within the flesh. The sin commands the one injured to repay the one doing the injury and to administer vengeance. This is the lust, the passion of sin. If we yield to this lust or command, then sin is king and we are its servant. But if we do not yield to it but rather repress it by faith, then we are kings with regard to sin. Another example: if anyone is afflicted by poverty or hunger, then in that place the sin lurking within us is aroused. The first things to be aroused are unbelief and despair; then they command the person to either steal or participate in fraud, or also to hang himself from a tree. This is the passion of sin. Therefore it is required of us not to let sin reign; nor should we be subject to its passion. As for the one who is said to be typically very angry, anger has conquered him entirely. Therefore, we are conquered by sin when we yield to its passion. Commentary on Romans (1564).[21]

Sin Remains but Should Not Reign.

Georg Major: This is the conclusion of Paul's response, wherein he countered the previously cited objection: "A person who is dead to sin does not permit sin to reign within themselves, but rather they resist it. By baptism, you are buried with Christ in death (that is, in putting to death and laying to rest your old self); therefore 'let not sin reign' in you." He did not say, "Let not sin exist within you," since original sin—that depravity of nature, the *anomia* (lawlessness) that struggles against the law of God—remains in all the saints, for which it is to be prayed by all the saints that this might be forgiven. But because he said, "Let not sin reign within you" some immorality, therefore, remains in the saints: concupiscence,[†] manifold immoral affections, doubt concerning God, a failure to burn with both the fear and love of God, lack of trust, sluggishness in prayer or in thanksgiving, impatience, and the flames of lust, wrath, hate, the desire for revenge, pride, and avarice—all of which the saints resist, as well as a multitude of sins of omission and ignorance. Such diseases as these in the saints, even if they are in their nature "mortal" sins, that is, sins worthy of eternal death, are forgiven for those who believe in Christ, who both turn away in horror from these diseases and by faith lay hold of Christ as Mediator. Accordingly, they become "venial" sins, that is, forgiven and remitted,[‡] covered over and not imputed, and these believers retain the Holy Spirit and their faith and remain in grace. On the other hand, they are truly mortal sins for those who, having already been sanctified, indulge in and become obedient to these sinful affections, who neither turn away from them nor repent [*poenitentiam agunt*], such as King Saul. Such people lose their faith and the Holy Spirit and are condemned to eternal death if they do not return to repentance. "Those who practice these things will not inherit the kingdom of God." Exposition of the Epistles of Paul (1569).[22]

---

[20]Zwingli, *In Evangelicam Historiam*, 421; citing Lk 9:23; Mt 6:13.
[21]Brenz, *In Epistolam*, 152.

[22]Major, *Ennarationes Epistolarum S. Pauli*, 119; citing Ps 32; Gal 5:21. [†]Sinful desires. [‡]A variation on the Catholic idea of venial sins as forgivable and remissible.

6:13 *Present Yourself to God, Not to Sin*

WE DIE AND LIVE AT THE SAME TIME. JO-
HANNES BUGENHAGEN: And now I will go over
this again rather briefly: that external sign has two
features: immersing and drawing out. And there
are two parts of Scripture, or two duties of
preaching, that is the law and the gospel. By the law
we are immersed, not only in body, but in our soul,
that is, our whole self. And it should be shown that
our whole body, great as it is, must die. And it does
not only mean this, but we truly die with Christ
through baptism. And in baptism, we are also
drawn out—that is, we rise again with Christ—
with a new spirit growing in us. Therefore it
happens that we die and live at the same time: we
die through the law, but we live through the gospel.
INTERPRETATION OF ROMANS (1531).[23]

**WARFARE AND THE WEAPONS OF RIGHTEOUS-
NESS.** WOLFGANG MUSCULUS: "Unto sin as
weapons of unrighteousness." In the Greek the
word is *hopla* (shield), not *skeue* (equipment).
With this word, the apostle is implying that sin is
engaged in warfare and battle. We see this also in
1 Peter 2, where a warring against the soul is caused
by fleshly lusts. Now the material for this war is
unrighteousness. But since it's through our sin that
unrighteousness stirs up war against us, which it
could not do without our help, what kind of
blindness is it, or rather by what deranged insanity
do we join an enemy that's violently attacking us
with our own weapons turned against ourselves?
Who is so out of his mind that, knowing that there
is a war against him waged by his enemy, if he had
some weapons, would offer them to his enemy?
Would he not effectively be using them against
himself, by his own orders, especially since he
knows that his enemy can do nothing unless he
himself contributes to the effort?

"And your members as weapons of righteousness
to God." The war that God wages against Satan
and against sin has for its material this righteousness. Our warfare is to be waged by this means. He
rightly includes in this the presentation of our
bodily members, for it is through them that it is
plainly seen how a person makes himself useful to
God. But why is this? Can't God carry out this war
without our weapons? Of course he can. But both
our salvation and the exhibition of his grace—not
any need on his part—requires that we not fail to
contribute our own small part in this war. COM-
MENTARY ON ROMANS (1555).[24]

EITHER WAY, THERE'S A FIGHT. MARTIN
BUCER: "Weapons of unrighteousness." We observe
in the use of the word "weapons" that there is a
fight either in sinning or in living well. There is a
fight when you sin, since your mind, being guided
by your conscience, protests in such a way that you
have to struggle against righteousness. And there is
also a fight when you pursue righteousness, since
the flesh is carried along in a different direction, or
rather has to be struggled with, contrary to
unrighteousness. It is therefore necessary that we
take great care for ourselves and be cautious about
all things; in particular, a strengthening of the soul
is required, by means of devout prayers, by holy
admonitions, and especially by the divine mysteries,[†] so that when struggling against our natural
inclinations, with unrighteousness being conquered,
we might enlist in the service of righteousness.
COMMENTARY ON ROMANS (1536).[25]

6:14 *You Are Under Grace, Not Law*

RESIST THE TYRANT WHO HAS NO POWER.
WOLFGANG MUSCULUS: For sin will not have
dominion among you. For you are not under the
law, but under grace. This reasoning has clearly
been put forth by the apostle. It is an argument
that proceeds from the effectiveness of the grace of
Christ, and the weakness of sin. For the grace of
Christ made us free from the power and force of
sin, so much so that unless we should voluntarily

---

[23]Bugenhagen, *In D. Pauli ad Romanos*, 61v.

[24]Musculus, *In Epistolam Apostoli Pauli*, 138-39; citing 1 Pet 2:11.
[25]Bucer, *Metaphrases et Enarrationes*, 300. [†]I.e., sacraments.

submit ourselves to sin, it has no stranglehold on us, nor any rightful power. Since this is so, I ask you: How easy is it to resist a tyrant whom you know to have been stripped of all power, and is not able to do anything against you, unless you should arm him and voluntarily submit yourself to him? And moreover, this is the strongest possible argument for stirring up zeal for piety and rebellion against sin, especially since sin by itself is not able to rule over those who are Christ's. COMMENTARY ON ROMANS (1555).[26]

HOPE DOES NOT MAKE US ASHAMED.

JOHANNES BRENZ: Although Paul makes use of that saying, "You are not under the law, but under grace" in order to demonstrate the ease of doing good, just as it was stated, nevertheless it is also the argument that proves the truth of the chief proposition in this second part of the letter, which proposition is, "Hope does not make us ashamed." For since those born again in Christ are no longer under the law and wrath, but under the gospel and grace, hope immediately follows, which they have concerning the future eternal happiness on account of Christ, who by no means deceives and causes shame. Nothing could be more true than the gospel of Christ, nothing more certain than grace on account of Christ. COMMENTARY ON ROMANS (1564).[27]

COMFORT FOR BELIEVERS.

JOHN CALVIN: It seems to me that there is here especially a consolation offered, by which the faithful are to be strengthened, lest they should faint in their efforts after holiness through a consciousness of their own weakness. He had exhorted them to devote all their faculties to the service of righteousness, but as they carry about them the relics of the flesh, they cannot do otherwise than walk somewhat lamely. Hence, lest being broken down by a consciousness of their infirmity they should lead them to despondence, he seasonably comes to their aid by interposing a consolation, derived from this circumstance, that their words are not now tested by the strict rule of the law, but that God, remitting their impurity, does kindly and mercifully accept them. The yoke of the law cannot do otherwise than tear and bruise those who carry it. It hence follows that the faithful must flee to Christ, and implore him to be the defender of their freedom. As such he exhibits himself, for he underwent the bondage of the law, to which he himself was no debtor, for this end, that he might, as the apostle says, redeem those who were under the law. COMMENTARY ON ROMANS 6:14.[28]

ABUSING CHRISTIAN LIBERTY.

JOHANNES BUGENHAGEN: To "be under the law" means to be condemned in one's conscience by its sentence, for we have sinned. To "be under grace" is a conscience fully confident that one belongs to God, that he is one's Father, and that every sin is forgiven by his kindness. Therefore, where will sin be, when it is forgiven? Who will condemn, when the law itself cannot condemn? But there's something else that must be said about this: there are many today who abuse Christian liberty, who say, "since the law has been abrogated, therefore nothing is commanded of Christians," or "the fasting that papists practice is worthless; therefore we will not fast," or "prayers decreed by the pope are unprofitable, therefore we ought not to pray." This is how they think, and such people abuse Christian liberty. INTERPRETATION OF ROMANS (1531).[29]

THE SPIRIT SETS US FREE FROM BONDAGE.

RICHARD SIBBES: Are we troubled with any corruptions? Go to the Spirit of liberty in Christ, and desire him to set us at liberty from the bondage and slavery of our corruptions. And remember what Christ has done for us, and where he is now: in heaven. Let us raise our thoughts so that we may see ourselves in heaven already; that we may be ashamed to defile our bodies and souls

---

[26]Musculus, *In Epistolam Apostoli Pauli*, 139.
[27]Brenz, *In Epistolam*, 155.

[28]CTS 38:232-33* (CO 49:112-13).
[29]Bugenhagen, *In D. Pauli ad Romanos*, 62v.

with the base drudgery of sin and Satan, for our bodies and souls are sanctified in part in this world, and shall be glorified in heaven. Certainly faith would raise our souls so. We betray ourselves, when, being once in the state of grace, we are enslaved immorally to any sin. "For sin shall not have dominion over you, because you are under grace," says the apostle. Being under grace, if we just use our reasoning, and use faith, and exercise the grace we have been given, we cannot be enslaved to corruptions. We shall have remainders to trouble us, but not to rule, and reign, and domineer. For sin never takes control except when we betray ourselves and either do not believe what Christ has done for us, or else do not exercise our faith. Christians are never overtaken morally, except when they neglect their privileges and prerogatives and do not stir up the grace of God within. SERMON ON THE SPIRITUAL JUBILEE.[30]

ONLY A FOOL GOES BACK TO JAIL AFTER BEING FREED. JOHANNES BUGENHAGEN: Paul is saying here: "You are not under the law, that is, the law has no right to condemn you, even if it is true that when you look at yourselves, you see that you still have sin. For insofar as you are under grace, in that respect you have no sin, for all sins have been forgiven, and you only do those things that are in accordance with the divine will." Therefore we "owe nobody anything, except love to our neighbor." Those who are Christians cannot fail to have love for God, and so that commandment isn't given, but only that which concerns our neighbor. From all of these considerations you can see the folly of those who reason: "According to this, we will continue to sin. Where then is that liberation from the law, if we are still held captive by it?" No—we have been liberated from death, from the law, and from sin, and therefore we must not at all continue to sin; anyone who says "I have been freed from jail, therefore I will go back to jail" is a fool. INTERPRETATION OF ROMANS (1531).[31]

SERVING THROUGH LOVE RATHER THAN UNDER CONSTRAINT. JUAN DE VALDÉS: Here it appears to be St. Paul's meaning that Christians are not under the law, because they keep no account with it. They indeed abstain from things prohibited by the law, not because the law prohibits them, but because they are unsuitable to the man or woman who is dead to sin and alive to God. . . .

To be under this law is, as I understand, to be under grace, like the master's servants who serve through love rather than under either constraint or force. COMMENTARY ON ROMANS (1556).[32]

GRACE AND MERCY. PHILIPP MELANCHTHON: Here the meaning of the word *grace* should be prudently observed. For the entire meaning is corrupted and ruined by those who explain: "You are under grace, that is, under the moral law," since the moral law condemns very sternly. But grace is to be understood of imputation, by which believers are righteous, that is, accepted because of Christ. This imputation is proclaimed in the gospel. Although effects and renewal accompany imputation, the conscience must nevertheless look to the promised imputation and to Christ the Mediator, and not to its own qualities or condition. This statement sets before us a very rich teaching and comfort: "You are not under the law, but under grace"; that is, the law has no right to condemn believers. Therefore, although obedience is imperfect in believers, it is nevertheless pleasing because the persons are accounted righteous or accepted on account of Christ, the High Priest.

Here mercy must be greatly exalted in order that it may arouse us to doing good. The goodness of God is very great and inexpressible, that God approves of this obedience in believers, even though it has strange weakness and dissimilarity and is contaminated with much filth and offenses. Doubt should not weaken or scare off minds. The very greatness of the mercy which approves of all kinds of weak persons, provided only that they believe in Christ, invites us to do good. It is

---

[30]Sibbes, *Complete Works* 5:244*.
[31]Bugenhagen, *In D. Pauli ad Romanos*, 64; citing Rom 13:8.
[32]Valdés, *Commentary upon St. Paul's Epistle*, 87*.

necessary that this teaching and comfort should be found in the church, in order that we may know to what extent and where good works are to be rejected, and to what extent required, and how they may please God. COMMENTARY ON ROMANS (1540).[33]

LIVING UNDER GRACE. HEINRICH BULLINGER: Since we are often frightened by the thought of the difficulty of things that are simultaneously most useful and most virtuous, the apostle anticipates this and says that there is no danger that sin will overthrow those who do not wish it to, nor that it will be so strong that we will not be able to resist it when it rushes on us and fights against us. No, instead we will prevail decisively against it, since we are "no longer under the law, but under grace." In other words, having laid hold of faith in the Lord Jesus, after this we are no longer what we were when we were still under the law, that is, when we conducted ourselves as we did in our earlier life.

For we, made to be new men and women, are now "able to do all things through him who strengthens us" by his Spirit and who called us into this grace. For to be "under the law" is nothing other than to live that life that the trembling and terrified live who are still under the law, trusting in their own powers and yet accomplishing nothing. Or rather, to be "under the law" is to be under the dominion of sin, if "the law" is taken to mean "the sin that is recognized by the law pointing it out." Whereas, to be "under grace" is to be made a new self set free from sin, to experience divine assistance and to be led by the Holy Spirit. Which, if certain worthless persons were to carefully consider this, they would not say, "I am unable to resist this sin." By this very statement they reveal that they have no faith. For as many of us are faithful believers living under grace, we can do all things, certainly not by our own power, but by the Holy Spirit, who works all good things in those who believe. COMMENTARY ON ROMANS (1533).[34]

---

[33]Melanchthon, *Commentary on Romans*, 149-50*.

[34]Bullinger, *In Sanctissimam Pauli*, 87v-88r; citing Phil 4:13.

6:15-23 FROM SLAVES OF SIN TO SLAVES TO RIGHTEOUSNESS

15What then? Are we to sin because we are not under law but under grace? By no means! 16Do you not know that if you present yourselves to anyone as obedient slaves, you are slaves of the one whom you obey, either of sin, which leads to death, or of obedience, which leads to righteousness? 17But thanks be to God, that you who were once slaves of sin have become obedient from the heart to the standard of teaching to which you were committed, 18and, having been set free from sin, have become slaves of righteousness. 19I am speaking in human terms, because of your natural limitations. For just as you once presented your members as slaves to impurity and to lawlessness leading to more lawlessness, so now present your members as slaves to righteousness leading to sanctification.

20For when you were slaves of sin, you were free in regard to righteousness. 21But what fruit were you getting at that time from the things of which you are now ashamed? For the end of those things is death. 22But now that you have been set free from sin and have become slaves of God, the fruit you get leads to sanctification and its end, eternal life. 23For the wages of sin is death, but the free gift of God is eternal life in Christ Jesus our Lord.

OVERVIEW: With their strong emphasis on justification by faith alone, the reformers were sometimes accused of not affirming the importance of good works. However, as their comments on this passage make evident, they were careful to argue that we are still called to live holy lives. We are free from the law, but that does not mean that we are therefore permitted to sin. Being free from the law means no longer being under its curse, but we still need to obey it. Now we do so under the reign of grace, not under the law itself. Although we do not fulfill it perfectly, we are no longer condemned, for we are under Christ's protection. Yes, the gospel teaches imputation, but it also teaches repentance. The reformers speak against antinomianism, and they affirm that while God no longer punishes us, he still disciplines us. We are slaves to something, either to sin or to righteousness. If we are regenerate believers, then we should pursue righteousness.

The reformers further clarify that the good works that matter follow justification rather than precede it. They argue that we need to approach these works with a desire for our hearts to be formed by Christ and for our selves to be conformed to his image. We are weak, but that does not give us an excuse to not pursue holiness. Moreover, we have God's power working on our behalf. The Holy Spirit stirs us up, sets us on fire, and establishes holiness in our hearts. While we are slaves to righteousness, we are heirs to God, and he treats us as sons and daughters. The ends of the two ways of living are radically different. As slaves of sin, we would reap impurity in this life and eternal death in the next; as slaves of righteousness, we reap the fruit of sanctification in this life and eternal life in the next. We have moved from being slaves to our emotions and lusts and doing things that brought us shame, to serving God and being saints. The reformers remind us that although, as believers, we are to pursue a life of holiness, that holiness will not save us. Our salvation is still a free gift from Christ, and what awaits us is the unimaginable beauty of the happiness of heaven.

6:15 Shall We Go On Sinning?

THE ONE TRULY SACRED ANCHOR. PHILIPP
MELANCHTHON: Is everything then permissible?
To kill the innocent? To lie? The same question is
posited by Paul in Romans 6, when he says, "Since
we are not under the law, shall we therefore sin?"
But our freedom consists in this, that every right of
accusing and condemning us has been removed
from the law. The law curses those who fail to keep
it entirely and constantly. But the entire law
demands perfect love of God and exacts the most
vehement fear of God, does it not? And since our
entire nature is thoroughly inimical to these
commands, although we present the greatest and
most attractive Pharisaism, we are nevertheless
guilty and deserving of the curse. Christ has taken
away this curse and right of the law, so that
although you have sinned and although you have
sin even now—for we should use the terminology
of Scripture—you are nevertheless saved. Our
Samson has crushed the power of death, the power
of sin, and the gates of hell. This is what Paul
writes to the Galatians, "Christ has redeemed us
from the curse of the law, having become a curse
for us." And again, "When the fullness of time had
come, God sent his Son, born of a woman, born
under the law, to redeem those who were under the
law." And in Romans 6, he writes, "Sin will not have
dominion over you, for you are not under the law,
but under grace." This is the security that the
prophets loudly and constantly celebrate, that
those who are in Christ are above all the power of
the law. That is, even though you have sinned, even
though you have sin, you cannot be condemned, as
Scripture decrees, "Death has been swallowed up
in victory. Where, O death is your victory?" These
passages should always be impressed on Christians,
but especially when they are about to die, since to
them this one truly sacred anchor alone is left, as
the proverb says. LOCI COMMUNES (1521).[1]

WHY IS LAW THE OPPOSITE OF GRACE?

WOLFGANG MUSCULUS: "For you are not under
that law," he says, "but under grace." What does
this mean—"You are not under the law"? Why
does he not say, "You are not under sin"? What is
it that he is thinking of concerning the law? Why
does he set the law as the opposite of grace? He
does not simply use "the law" in place of sin, but as
the opposite of grace. The law is holy and just and
full of divine benefit. Yet, being "under the law" is
what he sets up as the opposite of the grace of
Christ. So, what does it mean to be under the law?
And what does it mean to be under grace? To the
apostle, to be under the law is the same as being
under the duty and condemnation of the law, to
be destitute of the spirit and grace of Christ, and
for that reason to even be subject to the tyranny of
sin. For where sin reigns, there the law condemns.
Where the law has a place, there sin must surely
be. To truly be under grace is to be under the
power and dominion of grace—to be led and
ruled by the grace of Christ. COMMENTARY ON
ROMANS (1600).[2]

FREED FROM THE CURSE, NOT FROM OBEDI-

ENCE. GEORG MAJOR: The second objection is
taken from the next sentence. If we are free from
the law, will we then be permitted to sin? Paul
answers in two similes, of which the first is taken
from the condition and station of slaves, in this
way: To whom has one sold oneself and obeyed,
whether for sin unto death, or for righteousness
unto eternal life? You all are holy slaves of Christ
and righteousness and are justified by faith.
Therefore, you ought to obey Christ and righteousness, not the devil and unrighteousness. For to be
free from the law is not to be freed from obedience
to the law. Rather, you are freed from its curse, so
that even though the saints do not fulfill the whole
law, nevertheless because they are under grace—
even a gracious mercy, and under Christ who gives
protection—the law in no way has anything more

---

[1]Melanchthon, *Loci Communes*, 153*; citing Gal 3:13; 4:4-5; 1 Cor
15:55.

[2]Musculus, *In Epistolam Apostoli*, 139.

against them, for there is no condemnation for those who are in Christ. EXPOSITION OF THE EPISTLES OF PAUL (1569).[3]

LAW ABROGATED FOR JUSTIFICATION BUT NOT FOR OBEDIENCE. PHILIPP MELANCH-THON: The gospel does not grant license to sin, since it preaches not only about imputation, but also about repentance, and it brings in the new obedience, and shows in which way it is pleasing. Meanwhile the law remains, as far as discipline and external life are concerned. Likewise, as far as rebuking and mortifying the old nature is concerned, but in such a way that when faith is victorious the law has no power to condemn. Therefore, I answer simply: The law has been abrogated as far as justification is concerned, but not as far as obedience is concerned. Obedience must be rendered, and indeed is begun. Nevertheless we must know that we are righteous because of Christ, in order that the benefit may remain sure. COMMENTARY ON ROMANS (1540).[4]

AGAINST THE ANTINOMIAN LIBERTARIANS.
JOHN TRAPP: Some antinomian libertines want to persuade men and women that God is never displeased with his people, even if they fall into adultery or similar sin, no not even with a fatherly displeasure. That God never chastises his people for any sin, no not even with a fatherly chastisement. That God sees no sin in his elect, that the very being of their sin is abolished out of God's sight, that they cannot sin, or if they do, it is not they but sin that dwells in them. What is this but to turn the grace of God into wantonness, which then becomes the savor of death to them. Like Moses' rod cast on the ground turned into a serpent, or as dead men's bodies bring forth serpents when the marrow melts? COMMENTARY ON ROMANS (1656).[5]

6:16 If You're a Slave

PAUL PRESSES THE CONSCIENCE. MARTIN BUCER: "Or do you not know?" It should be noted that Paul is always pressing the conscience, for we ourselves are driven by our wills, nor are we able to not pursue with devotion those things that we have judged will be profitable to us. Those who possess faith in Christ do possess the knowledge of what is true and good, but they do not always act according to this knowledge, since the judgment of the senses, perverted by innate desires, often overturns the judgment of faith about what is to be done. Paul, therefore, is always trying to stir up their minds so that they might pay attention to the saving truths they already know and might judge all matters according to these truths. This is why it is his custom to frequently pray for his hearers, that they might be perfected in knowledge and spiritual understanding, by which they might prove all that is fitting, that is, that they might dispose themselves toward them. We find this prayer prefixed to the beginning of the letters to the Ephesians, Philippians, and Colossians. COMMENTARY ON ROMANS (1536).[6]

OBEDIENCE IS A SIGN OF SLAVERY. ERASMUS SARCERIUS: Obedience testifies about slavery. The apostle sets obedience as a sign of slavery, no matter what the category. Thus, the one who obeys sin is a slave of sin. The one who obeys righteousness is a slave of righteousness. The one who obeys the flesh is a slave of the flesh. And so on.

Therefore, the apostle wants both ends to be known: that of obedience, and that of the things that we obey. And both of them in relation to Christian liberty, justification, and so on, and in relation to truth and falsehood. Hence, the one who obeys sin testifies by himself that he has set sin itself as the goal of Christian liberty, justification, and so on. And the one who obeys righteousness, testifies that he has set the new life itself as the goal of Christian liberty, justification, and so on. NOTES ON ROMANS (1541).[7]

---

[3]Major, *Enarrationes Epistolarum S. Pauli*, 119.
[4]Melanchthon, *Commentary on Romans*, 150*.
[5]Trapp, *A Commentary or Exposition upon the Epistle of St. Paul*, 631*.

[6]Bucer, *Metaphrases et Enarrationes*, 302.
[7]Sarcerius, *In Apostolam ad Romanos*, A4r-A4v.

A SERVANT OF OBEDIENCE. NIELS HEMMING-SEN: This argument is taken from the civil law: to whomever a slave belongs, to that person he presents himself to obey. This proposition is the premise from which he infers these two conclusions: (1) Those who present themselves to sin in order to obey it are the slaves of sin. And, (2) those who present themselves to God to obey him are *his* servants. An exact corollary would require that in the second conclusion it be added: "a servant of righteousness (or of God) leading to life." But rather than "of righteousness" or "of God" he says "of obedience," so as to expound what is meant by "righteousness," namely, obedience to God, which is the goal of justification. Next, in the place of what he was going to say, "leading to life," he says "leading to righteousness" because righteousness is the close attendant of life, or rather of vivification and that which demonstrates it. COMMENTARY ON ROMANS (1562).[8]

TWO KINDS OF RIGHTEOUSNESS. ERASMUS SARCERIUS: The apostle places obedience to righteousness as the entirety of the new life, in accordance with all good and righteous works. Next, just as sin is something that enslaves, so righteousness is something that enslaves. Here is obedience and life, both external and holy at the same time. Here "righteousness" means all righteous works that are signs or evidence of true righteousness being received through faith. This righteousness, concerning which Paul presently makes mention, is a testimony of the true righteousness that is apprehended by faith for the forgiveness of sins.

One ought to distinguish between the righteousness that we seek after, by faith, for the forgiveness of sins, and the righteousness that follows the preceding. One is the cause, the other the effect. Augustine is here most correct: "Good works do not precede justification, but follow justification."[†] NOTES ON ROMANS (1541).[9]

6:17-19 *Slaves of Righteousness*

THE AUTONOMOUS AND DIVINELY ASSISTED WILL. JOHANNES LONICER: It is as if he had said that their will is autonomously self-moved, and at the same time, he adds immediately after, enabled by divine assistance. "You," he says, "obeyed voluntarily. But it was God who delivered you to this form of teaching." What kind of teaching? "That you should will and desire to live rightly, as well as being sound and vigorous concerning the doctrine of Christ's religion." He calls it a "form of teaching" in that it is a definition and rule thereof. EXEGESIS OF ROMANS (1537).[10]

FORMED BY THE EVANGELICAL DOCTRINE. WOLFGANG MUSCULUS: "Unto that form of doctrine into which you have been delivered." Here we see what that "obedience unto righteousness" is of which he speaks. Naturally, it is that by which one submits to the teaching of the gospel.

"The form of doctrine." It is not as though the doctrine itself is formed according to the desire of the teacher. Rather, it is that those who submit themselves to him for formation are formed by the doctrine of the truth. For the doctrine of the gospel forms the minds of believers to Christ the archetype, who has been placed before all as the express exemplar of all righteousness and piety.

"From the heart" and "you have been delivered." These two come together in the dispute over free will. When we consecrate our hearts to the pattern of the teaching of the gospel, we are formed by it. And nevertheless, this will not come about unless we are delivered over to that pattern by divine favor. Therefore, both the grace of God and our desire to be formed come together in the work of this formation.

Note also in this passage that those who think they are profound and learned philosophers are unable to be hearers of the teachings of the gospel; they do not put up with the shaping hand of doctrine. For it is concerned entirely

---

[8]Hemmingsen, *Commentarius in Epistolam*, 225.
[9]Sarcerius, *In Apostolam ad Romanos*, A5r-A5v. [†]Augustine, *Enarratio in Psalmum* 110.3.

[10]Lonicer, *Veteris Cuiuspiam Theologi*, 45.

with the modest and compliant mind, not the proud and inflexible.

Therefore, those who use the doctrine of the faith and sacred Scripture in such a way that they make it a matter for exercising their wits—and what they judge themselves to have from their own particular effort—certainly cannot be formed to zeal for piety and Christian righteousness by this, because they come to this pattern not as one to be shaped, but as a sculptor and artisan comes to the material of his art. Thus, the simple ones who modestly and humbly allow themselves to be shaped by this doctrine, disputing nothing, but simply accepting what is true in faith, are formed to true piety, while meanwhile learned people are rendered more wicked. And I anxiously fear that there are many today who approach this holy doctrine with an attitude far different from that by it and through it they may be formed to the image of Christ, but rather that they may form others to their own opinion, or that they may show the sharpness of their wits. COMMENTARY ON ROMANS (1555).[11]

MOLDED INTO THE GOSPEL. THE ENGLISH ANNOTATIONS: The word in the original signifies most properly a pattern or mold, and the apostle would thereby have us understand that the doctrine of the gospel is such a pattern or mold that we are cast into, that we may be formed and fashioned into its likeness. ANNOTATIONS ON ROMANS 6:17.[12]

NOT LIKE HORSES LET LOOSE IN THE FIELDS. JOHN CALVIN: Paul compares here the hidden power of the Spirit with the external letter of the law, as though he had said, "Christ inwardly forms our souls in a better way than when the law constrains them by threatening and terrifying us." Thus is dissipated the following calumny, "If Christ frees us from the subjection to the law, he brings liberty to sin." He does not indeed allow his people

unbridled freedom, that they might frisk about without any restraint, like horses let loose in the fields, but he brings them into a regular course of life. COMMENTARY ON ROMANS 6:17.[13]

THE PRIVILEGE OF BECOMING A SLAVE OF RIGHTEOUSNESS. NIELS HEMMINGSEN: Simply, it is as if he said, "But you all are slaves of righteousness, or of God. Truly, it is a great privilege to become a slave of God, from being a slave of sin." He begins this consideration by an act of thanks, by which he gives thanks to God, so that he shows him to be the author of such kindness, and arouses the righteous to gratitude. Then he calls to mind their condition before their justification had been secured, for they were in the most unhappy slavery of sin. He means to arouse their obedience to God, whose slaves they have now become. Third, he indicates the cause of their change in status when he says that they have obeyed the form of teaching that has been handed down to them by the preaching of the gospel. Let it be first observed here from the antithesis, that all who do not obey the gospel are slaves of sin unto death. With respect to which, the gospel is a sort of type—that is, a form by which new people are molded and formed—so that they may be restored to the form of the doctrine. In addition, just as the Word (with which the Holy Spirit is united) is one necessary part, thus our will (by which we obey the Word), is the part required from us, so that we may be able to be slaves of righteousness. Therefore, those who have converted do not view themselves as stones that have been violently dragged against their wills to be a slave to righteousness. COMMENTARY ON ROMANS (1562).[14]

A TRANSITION BETWEEN TWO PARTS OF CHRISTIAN FREEDOM. DAVID PAREUS: This verse is clear: it now joins together the whole argument. It connects both parts of Christian freedom: freedom from sin and slavery to righteousness.

---

[11]Musculus, *In Epistolam Apostoli Pauli*, 141.
[12]Downame, ed., *Annotations*, BBB1r*.
[13]CTS 38:236* (CO 49:115).
[14]Hemmingsen, *Commentarius in Epistolam*, 226.

Therefore, it relates to the teaching above. COM-
MENTARY ON ROMANS (1608).[15]

BEING MADE FREE FROM SIN. BENEDICT
ARETIUS: We here find a third argument that
derives its force from its contraries and draws a
conclusion in two ways: (1) First, since you are set
free from sin, therefore sin is no longer to be
obeyed. (2) Second, you have changed over to a
service, not of the Lord, but of righteousness, that
is, to the innocence of that life which we profess in
Christ. Therefore it is manifestly clear that we are
no longer to live in sin. COMMENTARY ON RO-
MANS (1579).[16]

**THE LOVING BOND-SERVICE OF RIGHTEOUS-
NESS.** JUAN DE VALDÉS: The bond-service of
righteousness obliges the man or woman to believe,
to love, to hope, and to do everything else that is
associated with these and especially to the obligation of Christian regeneration. But this obligation
does not work wrath as does that of the law, for the
affections and lusts are not irritated with it, for it is
loving and not rigorous. It entreats and does not
threaten, and, better still, because the Holy Spirit
is the one that is at work. COMMENTARY ON
ROMANS (1556).[17]

SET FREE TO BE ENTHRALLED. JOHN DONNE:

Batter my heart, three-person'd God; for you
As yet but knock; breathe, shine, and seek to mend;
That I may rise, and stand, o'erthrow me, and bend
Your force, to break, blow, burn, and make me new.
I, like an usurp'd town, to another due,
Labor to admit you, but O, to no end.
Reason, your viceroy in me, me should defend,
But is captive, and proves weak or untrue.
Yet dearly I love you, and would be loved fain,
But am betroth'd unto your enemy;
Divorce me, untie, or break that knot again,
Take me to you, imprison me, for I,

Except you enthrall me, never shall be free,
Nor ever chaste, except you ravish me.

DIVINE POEMS.[18]

THREE REASONS NOT TO LIVE IN SIN. THOMAS
WILSON: Timotheus: What does this text contain?
  Silas: Three new reasons to dissuade men and
women from living in the service of sin.
  Timotheus: What is the first reason?
  Silas: Because Christ having set them free from
the bondage of sin, they are now not bound to
obey the lusts of it. As bondmen and servants give
obedience to their lords while they are their
servants, but once being free, they do not serve
them any more. No, now they overrule sinful lusts,
or else in vain they profess Christianity: it is to no
purpose to put on the purple kingly robe if there is
no one to command. So, in vain do you profess
yourself a Christian if you have no command over
your passions and lusts.
  Timotheus: What is the second reason?
  Silas: They are made the servants of righteousness; therefore, they must not serve nor obey sin,
but God. This reason may be declared two ways.
First, by comparison of bodily servants who are
careful to please their masters, so ought Christians
to be, being God's servants. Second, by consideration of his goodness and bounty, whom we serve,
declared both in the many good things—both spiritual and corporeal—that we have from him; and in
those that we further hope for, to wit, the preservation and sustaining of our lives in this world, and
eternal life in heaven with God and his angels.
  Timotheus: What is the third reason?
  Silas: The third reason is taken from things
that are similar or equal, such as this: The elect
before their conversion diligently served sin in
performing its lusts. Therefore, being converted,
they must with like diligence serve God in doing
his will as revealed in his Word. COMMENTARY ON
ROMANS (1614).[19]

---

[15]Pareus, *In Divinam ad Romanos*, 586.
[16]Aretius, *Commentarii in Epistolam*, 196.
[17]Valdés, *Commentary upon St. Paul's Epistle*, 90*.

[18]Donne, *Poems*, 1:165*.
[19]Wilson, *Commentarie*, 381*; citing Rom 14:4.

SIN LEADS TO MORE SIN. MARTIN BUCER: Let us observe here that for the apostle, among the strongest arguments by which he can deter us from all sin is the fact that whatever particular sin we give permission to, it ends up promoting every kind of iniquity and depravity of life, just as each particular deed we do that is right and pious and serves to advance the whole of our sanctification. For a Christian man or woman, nothing ought to be more dreaded than that he should degenerate into perversity, that is, to a manner of life at odds with the expressed will and life of Christ our Savior. For those reborn in the Lord, no other life is fitting but that life that is holy and lived in accordance with the commandment of Christ. Just as those who love this life fear any sickness that might impede or subvert the functions of this life, so also should Christians fear sins, by which the functions of their new and blessed life are removed or impeded. COMMENTARY ON ROMANS (1536).[20]

RIGHTEOUSNESS AND HOLINESS. NIELS HEMMINGSEN: Here a double antithesis should be noticed. The first is that in which righteousness is set in opposition to both filthiness and lawlessness. The second is that in which sanctification or holiness is set in opposition to lawlessness. The first antithesis teaches us what the apostle means by "righteousness": it is the cleanness of heart that comes about by means of faith (for such cleanness is the opposite of filthiness of heart), and it is obedience to the law, the opposite of *anomia* (which means whatever is contrary to the law of God). Therefore inchoate righteousness in those who are justified refers to the cleanness of heart that comes about by faith, and obedience to God insofar as one is able to render it in this state of weakness.

The second antithesis teaches what the word "holiness" means: it is the pursuit of innocence and obedience toward God (which is the opposite of the pursuit of lawlessness) that we might be holy. From this it, therefore, follows that the duty of the justified is to continually pursue holiness, which is rooted in that same righteousness that is comprised of cleanness of heart and inchoate obedience toward God. COMMENTARY ON ROMANS (1562).[21]

THE REASONABLE PURSUIT OF SANCTIFICATION. MARTIN BUCER: Here it should be said that for a teacher of the gospel, there is cause for taking human weakness into account, but only in order to lift it up to divine strength. The apostle here is being careful lest he appear to demand things that are too lofty and thus make room for those Romans who were indulging their sinful desires to find an excuse for their spiritual laziness. He therefore draws them away from their weakness, showing that nothing that he is demanding is too much for them, but at the same time points them to divine power when he urges them to devote themselves to the pursuit of righteousness with as much effort as they previously, when left to themselves, had pursued the desires of the flesh. It is assuredly within this pursuit that all our sanctification and eternal life itself is found. Therefore, let us study to persuade ourselves as much as others that what God requires of us is entirely humane and reasonable, so that it must put us to shame if we do not respond to everything he has commanded us as dutifully as we should. But let us at the same time be diligent to explain that in this pursuit lies everything that pertains to our full restoration. To this end we will be urged on both by shame arising from the fairness and reasonableness of the One commanding, and by hope rooted in the dignity and excellence of the value of the works commanded. COMMENTARY ON ROMANS (1536).[22]

6:20-21 *When You Were Slaves to Sin*

A MISERABLE FREEDOM. RICHARD BAXTER: And that the world is an enemy to your happiness may appear in two ways. First, in its deceitfully pretending to be your happiness, when it is not;

---

[20]Bucer, *Metaphrases et Enarrationes*, 305.

[21]Hemmingsen, *Commentarius in Epistolam*, 227-28.
[22]Bucer, *Metaphrases et Enarrationes*, 305.

and so turning away your hearts from that which is. Second, in that by either allurements or discouragements, it is always hindering you in the way to life, and is continually a snare to you in all that you do. And isn't it necessary to your salvation for you to be delivered from the enemies of your salvation? And to be freed from such perilous snares? Can you conquer while you are conquered? And if the world is not crucified to you, it conquers you, for its victory is on your will and affections. And if it conquers you, it will condemn you. To be servants to the world is to be servants to sin. And the servants of sin are free from righteousness, and free from Christ, and free from salvation. A miserable freedom! THE CRUCIFYING OF THE WORLD (1658).[23]

PREPARATORY WORKS THROWN OUT. PETER MARTYR VERMIGLI: Paul explains the reason why he admonished them to give their members as servants unto righteousness. It is, he says, that before, when you were servants of sin, you were utterly free in relation to righteousness; that is, you were utterly strangers from it. . . . And such a liberty is pernicious, and far worse than all servitude; it is most like the liberty that the prodigal son so much desired. Again, this passage throws out preparatory works, for Paul says, "when you were servants of sin"—that is, not yet regenerate, and still strangers from Christ—"you were free unto righteousness." That is, you were wholly out of agreement with it. And if such men and women have no fellowship with righteousness, how can they work good works, which should "of congruity" merit grace? LEARNED AND FRUITFUL COMMENTARIES (1558).[24]

THE SON, NOT THE SLAVE, REMAINS IN THE HOUSE ETERNALLY. JOHANNES BRENZ: But if he had wanted to speak accurately and clearly, he would have said this: "You, while you were

formerly a slave to sin, now you have been made free, or in the liberty of righteousness on account of Christ." For it is done between God and the Christian, as between a father and a son, for a son is not the father's slave, nor does he yield to the father as a slave, but freely, voluntarily, cheerfully, and as they say, with a filial affection. "The slave," Christ says, "does not remain in the house eternally." Therefore, whatever he would have done is tainted by sadness, bitterness, in short, is done in an ignoble and servile spirit. With this nature, all are hypocrites. But the son remains in the house as an heir. Therefore he yields to his parent eagerly and with free affection. COMMENTARY ON ROMANS (1564).[25]

SIN'S FRUIT AND DISGRACE. NIELS HEMMINGSEN: This question contains two arguments. One is taken from sin's fruit, the other from its disgrace. The fruit of sin is most wicked, and sin itself is repulsive. Therefore, those who have been justified by faith and have renounced sin do not owe any more service to it. The adverbs, "then and now,'" denote a double-status relationship—indeed, the first, before justification, and the latter, after justification has been received. Observe that those who have been justified ought to be ashamed of their prior status, in which they placed themselves as slaves to the vilest master, namely, sin. The worst fruit of sin is death, and that is eternal. COMMENTARY ON ROMANS (1562).[26]

WE OUGHT TO FEEL SHAME. HULDRYCH ZWINGLI: Here he answers the previous question more extensively: "Therefore, shall we sin?" It is as if he says, "You faithful, far from wanting to sin, ought to be greatly ashamed of your previous sins." Just as we see among drunks and those who commit other crimes that when they come to their senses and return to their minds, they are greatly ashamed. But the wicked, when they sink to the depths, think little of it. God's grace has

---

[23]Baxter, *Crucifying of the World*, 65*.
[24]Vermigli, *Learned and Fruitfull Commentaries*, 156v*. See the introduction for discussion of *de congruo* merit.

[25]Brenz, *In Epistolam*, 157.
[26]Hemmingsen, *Commentarius in Epistolam*, 229.

been imparted to us, and it should, therefore, not make us arrogant and shameless, but thankful, modest, and circumspect. ANNOTATIONS ON ROMANS (1539).[27]

SIN'S MEMORY SHOULD CAUSE SHAME.
MARTIN BUCER: "Of which things you are now ashamed." Let us take care that, if we truly live in Christ, we should always be ashamed of those sins we wrongfully committed in the past, even though we ought not to doubt that they have been forgiven. Such is the disposition of Christ that governs true believers, that it necessarily follows that in those in whom the memory of their sins causes no shame, nor in the least troubles them in their soul, Christ's disposition must be lacking. Therefore, let those for whom it is an unhappy thing to frequently bring to mind the impure deeds formerly committed, know that it is because they are led by the Spirit. Assuredly, those who know and love Christ cannot fail to greatly execrate anything that is detested by him, so that the memory of their sins will never come to their minds without bringing with it not merely shame but even horror and a full-throttled sense of disgust. COMMENTARY ON ROMANS (1536).[28]

THE RESULTS OF VICES AND VIRTUES. HEINRICH BULLINGER: He now turns us away from the profitability or unprofitability and vileness of carnal things to consider innocence of life, and he compares and contrasts the ends and rewards of both in a rather remarkable way, as much that of sin as of righteousness, extolling everything belonging to the latter while demeaning everything associated with the former, in very few words: "Tell me, if you will, what return did you get from your earlier way of life? Do not these very sins confer their own punishment when they so pollute a person that now, after you have come to your senses out of the drunkenness, as it were, and the insanity of your vices, you yourselves are ashamed in your hearts and shrink from even thinking about the things in which you once delighted?" We might here refer to the case of that famous Greek orator Demosthenes, how that when he had asked the noble courtesan Lais for the price of her body—a woman who valued herself so highly that she demanded ten thousand denarii—he answered, "I am not going to buy remorse for such a high price!"[†] Further, that the end, or the fully earned wages, of wicked deeds is death and condemnation is made clear by the tragic story of the rich man and the beggar that the Lord set forth in the gospel as a startling illustration for us to reflect on. But as for virtues that are inherently beautiful and desirable, not only do they bring great happiness and satisfaction in this life, but they will also be rewarded with everlasting joys in the age to come. Or rather, those who live in moderation and maintain a principle of sobriety and reasonable well-being even in this life, live with much greater satisfaction and pleasantness than those who have a taste for luxury, drunkenness, and every other manner of intemperance. Diseases of both body and soul arise from these vices, as do many other evils that are listed by Pliny [the Elder] in *Natural History*, book 14, chapter 22.[‡] If someone should collect the statements of Scripture on this subject, as well as those of Seneca and other writers, it would wonderfully illustrate the truthfulness of this passage. COMMENTARY ON ROMANS (1533).[29]

6:22 *The Results of Following God*

ON SANCTIFICATION. JOHANN GRYNAEUS: Concerning sanctification, the following should be believed:

First, regeneration is elsewhere called a gift of Christ, because it consists of mortification of the flesh and vivification in the Spirit, or rather death to sin and life unto righteousness, which in turn results in justification.

---

[27]Zwingli, *In Evangelicam Historiam*, 422.
[28]Bucer, *Metaphrases et Enarrationes*, 305.

[29]Bullinger, *In Sanctissimam Pauli*, 90v-91r; citing Lk 16:19-31.
[†]Aulus Gellius, *Attic Nights* 1.8. [‡]Pliny the Elder, *Natural History* 26. Bullinger refers to 4.22, but book 26 is the one in which diseases and their remedies are cataloged.

Second, the strongest inducements to it are (1) because being engrafted into him, we participate in the death, burial, and resurrection of Christ, so we must therefore walk in newness of life; (2) because we have been signed by its sacrament, namely, baptism; (3) because we are not under law but under grace; (4) because it is fitting that our life be different after regeneration than it was before it; (5) since although the flesh wages a pitched battle against the Spirit, "there is no condemnation to those who are in Christ Jesus"; (6) because not being able to fulfill the law, but it being fulfilled on our behalf by Christ, it should no longer have any reason to complain against us; (7) because the Holy Spirit leads us, enlightens us, and exhorts us to prayers; (8) and because those things that gratify the flesh, which needs to be mortified, should give way in us to good. A BRIEF CHRONOLOGY OF THE HISTORY OF THE GOSPEL (1580).[30]

THE FRUIT OF SLAVERY TO SANCTIFICATION. NIELS HEMMINGSEN: Its antithesis is what he said a little earlier: "When you were slaves to sin." Here the argument is concluded in this way: That slavery is deservedly to be preferred whose fruit is sanctification, and whose end is eternal life. The fruit of slavery to righteousness in this life is sanctification, and the end is eternal life. Therefore, slavery to righteousness should be preferred to slavery to sin (which is slavery to sin in this life). It has a fruit that is impurity, and its end is eternal death. Eternal life is said to be the end of slavery to righteousness, not because we earn it by our righteousness, but because it is the central path in justification. COMMENTARY ON ROMANS (1562).[31]

SET ON FIRE BY THE SPIRIT. GEORG MAJOR: When the Son of God sent forth the Holy Spirit— who is holiness himself—into your hearts, he also established holiness in you. You might describe being stirred up by the Holy Spirit as being set on

fire. What is the goal of the Holy Spirit's actions and rewards? It is the free gift of eternal life, on account of Christ, not on account of our merit. EXPOSITION OF THE EPISTLES OF PAUL (1569).[32]

FOUR ADVANTAGES FOR CHRISTIANS. JUAN DE VALDÉS: St. Paul here adduces four advantages that those Christians had that respond to four other disadvantages that they had had before they became Christians. It is as though he said, "Previously you were the servants of sin, subject to your affections and lusts, but now you are free from this servitude and from this subjection, because Christ, when he slew his flesh, slew yours. Previously you served the world, that most cruel tyrant, while now you serve God. Previously you practiced things that you are ashamed of now, while now the fruit of your having become servants of God is your sanctification, that you are saints. Previously the wages paid to you were death, while those you now receive are eternal life." All who feel the benefit of Christ and assume that all this is especially spoken to them may arrogate these four things to themselves. COMMENTARY ON ROMANS (1556).[33]

BENEFITS THAT LEAD TO HOLINESS. BENEDETTO DA MANTOVA AND MARCANTONIO FLAMINIO: We say that those who become righteous through faith, since they know themselves to be righteous through God's righteousness, purchased by Christ, do not bargain with God for their works, as though they would buy their manner of justification, as it is with those who hold the other view. But, being inflamed with the love of God, and desirous to glorify Jesus Christ who has made them righteous by giving them his merits and riches, they bestow their whole study and labor to do God's will, fighting valiantly against the love of themselves, and against the world and the devil. And when they fall through frailty of the flesh, they recover themselves by and by, and are that much more desirous to do good. And they are so much

---

[30]Grynaeus, *Chronologia Brevis Evangelicae Historiae*, 63-65; citing Rom 8:1.
[31]Hemmingsen, *Commentarius in Epistolam*, 229-30.
[32]Major, *Enarrationes Epistolarum S. Pauli*, 120.
[33]Valdés, *Commentary upon St. Paul's Epistle*, 92-93*.

more in love with their God, considering that he does not lay their sins to their charge, because they are engrafted into Jesus Christ, who has made full amends for all his members on the tree of his cross, and makes continual intercession for them to the eternal Father. He, for the love of his only-begotten Son, beholds them always with a gentle countenance, governing and defending them as his most dear children, and in the end giving them the heritage of the world, fashioning them to the likeness of the glorious image of Christ. THE BENEFIT OF THE CROSS.[34]

6:23 The Wages of Sin, the Free Gift of God

ALL SINS ARE DEADLY SINS. WILLIAM GUILD: All sins are mortal by nature, and no sin is venial. . . . From this verse we reason thus: Anything that deserves death as its wages is, therefore, mortal. Any sin—if it is sin by its nature—deserves death as its wages, no matter the degree of sin, as the apostle affirms. Therefore, each sin is mortal. Of this Jerome says, "Even the sins that we consider to be the smallest exclude us from the kingdom of God."[†] THE OLD ROMAN CATHOLIC (1649).[35]

PROVISIONS FROM A VIOLENT TYRANT. NIELS HEMMINGSEN: He demonstrates from the contrary position, that the end of slavery to righteousness is eternal life. The end of sin is eternal death. Therefore, the end of righteousness is eternal life. However, lest anyone conclude that this life depends on one's merits, the apostle anticipates this, and declares that it is a gift of God through Jesus Christ. Let it be observed in the expression, *obsonia* (provisions), meanwhile signifying royal provisions and supplies, and gifts that are given, by law, to those who are worthy. Therefore, since sin is a violent tyrant, it gives its own soldiers the provisions they deserve: death, hell, and perpetual torture. COMMENTARY ON ROMANS (1562).[36]

DEATH IS THE WAGES DUE TO SIN. GEORGE WITHER:

> Remember death! For now my tongue
> To sing of death shall tuned be:
> Remember Death! Which else ere long,
> Will to your pain remember you.
> > Remember Death! Whose voice does say,
> > This night a man, tomorrow clay.
> If lucre shall your heart entice,
> Your needy neighbor to oppress;
> If pride shall tempt you to despise,
> Or slight your brother in distress.
> > Remember death! And then, I know,
> > More just, more humble you wilt grow.
> When lust shall woo you to commit
> What soul and body may defile,
> When sloth shall make you lazy sit,
> And let your talent rust the while,
> > Remember, death of old hath been,
> > And is the wages due to sin.
> When envy shall your heart possess,
> When you shall cheat, curse, swear, or lie,
> When you shalt wallow in excess,
> Your faith abuse, or God deny.
> > Remember death, and what attends
> > On willful sinners' latter ends.
> Remember, Death no truce has made,
> A year, a month, or week to stay;
> Remember how your flesh doth fade,
> And how your time does steal away.
> > Remember, death will neither spare
> > Wit, wealth, nor those that lovely are.
> Remember, death foregoes the dooms
> Which due to your deservings be;
> Remember this before it comes,
> And that despair oppress not you.
> > Remember death! Remember him,
> > Who does from death and hell redeem.

A HYMN PUTTING US IN REMEMBRANCE OF DEATH.[37]

---

[34]Benedetto and Flaminio, *Benefit of the Cross*, 68-69*.
[35]Guild, *The Old Roman Catholik*, 51-52*. [†]Jerome, *Commentary on Galatians* 5:19-21, in book 3.
[36]Hemmingsen, *Commentarius in Epistolam*, 230.

[37]Wither, *Hallelujah*, 80-81*.

IT's ABOUT THE LEADER, NOT THE FIGHT.

GEORG MAJOR: For all who are soldiers of righteousness and God, to these God gives eternal life—but not as something earned, to be sure, but as a free gift, only because of the merit and obedience of Christ. Therefore, he calls it a "gift in Christ Jesus" so that it excludes our merit. For although we are required to fight the good fight, yet the crown of righteousness and eternal life are not given on account of our fight, but freely on account of the leader and completer of faith, Jesus. Hebrews 12:2 considers soldiers who run, and in that passage those soldiers depend only on their leader. It is not about running, or fighting, or laboring, but about the God who shows mercy. EXPOSITION OF THE EPISTLES OF PAUL (1569).[38]

THE WAGES OF OUR SIN PIERCED CHRIST.

JOHN COTTON: "Pierced by us." This implies . . . that we look at all our sins as piercing Christ. A person that is led by a spirit of grace to a penitential and godly sorrow is brought on to consider this much: That all the sins he has committed have been a piercing and crucifying of Christ; the sin of his nature, the vanity of his childhood, the rebellions of his youth, and sins of riper times, whatever they are, whether against nature or the moral law of God. This is one work that the Spirit of grace effects in the hearts of all God's people. It opens their eyes to see that all their sins in the end have reflected on Christ. The burden and sting of them have fallen on him, for "the wages of sin is death." Either we must die for every one of our sins, or else the Lord Jesus Christ must die for every one of us. Every sin must either pierce us or him to the death. And, therefore, when we see that there is life and hope of life in us, it makes us see that "by his stripes we are healed." THE WAY OF LIFE (1641).[39]

THE TREE OF DEATH AND THE TREE OF LIFE.

JOHN BOWLE: This Scripture is of the sort that craves your attention while it is interpreted and craves your affection when it is applied. And it

justly craves both, the Holy Spirit joining together the highest and lowest things, as Leo says. The first proposition being of death, the second of life. Death, of all things the most terrible. Life, of all things the most comfortable.

To leave an impression in you, I will compare them to the two remarkable trees in Paradise. The first is as the tree of the knowledge of good and evil. The second, as the tree of immortality. The first the experimental tree of death. The second as the sacramental tree of life.

Both of these have a double consideration. In the tree of death, you may consider first the bitter root, which is sin; and the evil fruit, which is death, the wages of sin. In the tree of life, you may consider the sacred root, which is God's gift, and the happy fruit, which is eternal life by Jesus Christ our Lord. . . .

I will conclude this point with another passionate meditation. It's about a sorrowful soul apprehending the wrath of God and the infinite punishment due to sin. Such a sinner goes to heaven by the very gates of hell; his sighs as pillars of smoke perfumed with myrrh ascend up into the presence of God to implore mercy, being fully assured in the midst of all his fears that however "Eternal death is the wages of sin," yet that the "Gift of God is eternal life through Jesus Christ our Lord."

This is the tree of life, the foot of which is the grace and gift of God by Jesus Christ: the fruit eternal life and happiness. . . .

When your eyes shall see God and enjoy heaven, you will confess that not half the glory was reported on earth that you will find in heaven, when the queen, that is the church, shall stand on the right hand of the Lamb, glorious in diverse colors, in the infinite, incomprehensible variety of happiness.

To this kingdom, this crown, this eternal weight of glory, good Lord bring us, for the infinite mercies, for Jesus Christ's infinite merits. Amen. SERMON ON ROMANS 6:23 (1616).[40]

---

[38]Major, *Enarrationes Epistolarum S. Pauli*, 121; citing Heb 12:2; Rom 9:16; Mt 20:9-15.
[39]Cotton, *Way of Life*, 31-32*; citing Is 53:15.

[40]Bowle, *A Sermon Preached at Mapple-Durham*, 2-3, 21, 28*.

7:1-6 DYING TO THE LAW,
LIVING IN THE SPIRIT

Or do you not know, brothers[a]*—for I am speaking to those who know the law—that the law is binding on a person only as long as he lives?* [2]*For a married woman is bound by law to her husband while he lives, but if her husband dies she is released from the law of marriage.*[b] [3]*Accordingly, she will be called an adulteress if she lives with another man while her husband is alive. But if her husband dies, she is free from that law, and if she marries another man she is not an adulteress.*

[4]*Likewise, my brothers, you also have died to the law through the body of Christ, so that you may belong to another, to him who has been raised from the dead, in order that we may bear fruit for God.* [5]*For while we were living in the flesh, our sinful passions, aroused by the law, were at work in our members to bear fruit for death.* [6]*But now we are released from the law, having died to that which held us captive, so that we serve in the new way of the Spirit and not in the old way of the written code.*[c]

a Or brothers and sisters; also verse 4   b Greek law concerning the husband   c Greek of the letter

OVERVIEW: These Reformation-era interpreters see Paul's addressing his readers as "brethren" as modeling the kind of affection that there should be between a preacher of the Word and the people. They then exegete Paul's analogy of a remarried widow to illustrate the implications of Christians no longer being under the law. The story has three items that are key: the woman, her new husband, and the law. The law was an abusive, controlling husband, but it is now dead, or, in theological terms, we are dead to it. Sin and death are also dead to us, and we have a new "husband" in Christ. Where the law was tyrannical, Christ is a loving husband. He gives his name to us and shares in our sufferings, and we should live our lives for him. In addition to interpreting the theological symbolism of the various pieces of the parable, several commentators take the opportunity to give advice about marriage and how to avoid adultery. Their comments are made against the backdrop of having rejected the mandatory clerical celibacy of the medieval Catholic Church. Many of the reformers got married as pastors, thus elevating the status of marriage in general.

The reformers then parse the ways in which the law applies or no longer applies to the believer. The Ten Commandments still function as the rule of good living. What no longer remain are the curse and the rigorous demands of the law. When attempting to obey Christ, however, we run into the weakness of our sinful flesh, and the commentators suggest ways to overcome it, including leaning on Christ, studying his Word, and avoiding situations that stir up the desire to sin. Having emphasized the negative aspects of the law, Paul turns to defend it. The interpreters use various analogies (e.g., caustic powder, a medical doctor, a mirror) to show the necessity of the law in pointing to the disease of sin so that it can be dealt with. According to the reformers, the law should spur us to seek Christ as our safe harbor.

7:1 Addressing the Reader

UNDER GRACE. JOHANN GRYNAEUS: Here is instruction in which he teaches what it means to be not under the law, but under grace. Like a woman whose husband is dead is freed from the law binding her to him and is free to marry another, so also we have "become dead to the law through the body of Christ that we might be joined to another, namely, to him who rose again from the dead that we might bear fruit to God." He then last goes on to amplify his point by arguing its effects: "when we were in the flesh."

Then there is an apology in favor of the law against that slander: "Is the law therefore sin?" He commends the law by these descriptions of it: (1) It points out sin. (2) The generation of lusts on its own finds occasion in the law on account of something extrinsic to it (*kat' allo*)—sinning because of sin. (3) It is "holy, righteous, and good," such that it clearly shows itself to have become the cause of death in men and women only accidentally.[†] (4) It is "spiritual, while" we ourselves are "carnal and sold under sin."

Then comes a lament over the struggle between the flesh and the Spirit. "The inner person delights in the law of God, but sees another law in their members fighting against the law of their mind." HISTORY OF THE GOSPEL (1580).[1]

RESPONDING TO ACCUSATIONS OF DEBASING THE LAW. EDWARD ELTON: In this seventh chapter, the apostle applies his strength against slander and false accusations that some wicked or weak people did (or might) cast on him, namely this: That when he said that the law increased, he vilified and debased the law of God too much, and more than was appropriate. In that he said that the law increased sin, that when the law entered, sin abounded. When the apostle stated that, some perhaps thought—and it may be that some did not hesitate to utter it—that the apostle wronged the law and debased it too much. And therefore, in this chapter, he clears himself from doing any wrong at all to the law, and shows how his speech may be understood, and how it may receive an accurate and good inter-

pretation, and not be in any sort prejudicial to the law. And in this chapter, the general argument and matter is this: the apostle shows how true believers are freed and delivered from the law, and upon occasion of that, he meets with some cavils and calumnies that might be brought against the law. He commends the law, showing the true use of it, and sets forward in his own example the combat and fight that is between the flesh and the Spirit in those that are truly regenerate. In these things stands the sum and substance of this seventh chapter.

Now, these are the three parts of the chapter:

The first is a declaration how true believers are freed from the law, from the beginning of the chapter to the seventh verse.

The second is a clearing of the law from some foul blots that some might happen to seek to blemish it with, and a commendation of the law, with a manifestation of the true use of it, from verses 7 to 14.

The third and last is a troubled complaint of the apostle: that though he were regenerate and had received a great measure of grace and sanctification, yet through the relics of sin still abiding in him, he was far from the spirituality (as I may say) of the law, and that he was even carnal in respect to the spiritual nature of the law. And so, he set forth in his own particular life an example of the combat between the flesh and the Spirit in those that are truly regenerate, from verse 14 to the end of the chapter. THE COMPLAINT OF A SANCTIFIED SINNER (1618).[2]

PARABLE OF THE WIDOW WHO REMARRIES. JOHANNES BUGENHAGEN: Paul regards the parable in this way: Since we are dead, even the law and sin are dead to us through the death of Christ. It is just like when a husband is dead, that man's wife is also "dead." She does not bear any more liability toward the law, since the law itself has said that she is no longer under the rule

---

[1]Grynaeus, *Chronologia Brevis Evangelicae Historiae*, 72-73; citing Rom 7:12, 14, 22-23. [†]*Per accidens*: as opposed to by its very nature.

[2]Elton, *The Complaint of a Sanctified Sinner*, 1-2*; citing Rom 5:20.

of her former husband, nor is she able to bear him children. Now that she is married to another, the law is transferred to her new husband, having forgotten the former. Therefore, she does those things desired of her by her living husband who is not dead, paying attention to bearing children, giving birth not for the former, but for her new husband. The Christian life can be considered in a similar way. Sin and the law are dead to us, and we to them through Christ. Therefore freed from the law—and just as if we were previously married, and because we are not able to be without a husband—we choose for ourselves Jesus Christ. He is far more blessed than the previous husband, and it is to his law that we have subjected ourselves, with whom we are made one, and because of whom we are inspired by one Spirit. In a similar way, therefore, we should bear offspring for Christ, namely, righteousness and the fruit of the Spirit, not looking back at the obsolete husband, that is, the law. Interpretation of Romans (1531).[3]

Brethren as a Term of Affection. Edward Elton: The apostle stills them to whom he wrote, by the name "brethren," thereby signifying . . . his own kind and loving affection toward them, that he tenderly and dearly has affection for them in the Lord and respects them as those that are conjoined with him by the bond of one truth, one faith, and one hope of salvation. By this, he also implies a similar loving affection in them toward him again. The point hence is this:

There ought to be a special and mutual love and good affection between the teachers of the Word and God's people. The teachers of the Word are to love and care for God's people with a brother-like affection, and to care for their good, and to demonstrate that they care for it by all good means with all their power. And the people of God are to take notice of that love, and to acknowledge it and to answer it with similar love and good affection in return. The Complaint of a Sanctified Sinner (1618).[4]

Dying to the Law and to Sin. Martin Luther: It is evident that the apostle is not speaking of the law in a metaphysical or moral sense, but in a spiritual and theological sense, as is sufficiently discussed above in chapter 4. That is, he is dealing with the law as it applies to the inner self and the will and not with respect to the works of the outer self. Once we have understood his customary propositions and his bases and principles, all the rest is easy. The first of these principles is:

Sin and the wrath of God come through the law. Therefore no persons die to the law unless they die also to sin, and those who die to sin die also to the law. And as soon as persons are free from sin, they are also free from the law. And when people become servants of sin, they also become slaves of the law, and while sin rules over them and dominates them, the law also rules over and dominates them. Lectures on Romans.[5]

The Law Sends Us to Christ. Peter Martyr Vermigli: The test of what he has said, that we are free from the law, comes from nothing other than that we are dead, for those who are dead are not bound by the law. And he shows that we are dead through the body of Christ, in which, he said, we have become dead to the law. And by this argument, therefore, the apostle diligently teaches what to the Jews—of whom the church was mostly constituted in those early times—seemed disgraceful and wicked: to suddenly die to the law that they had received both from their ancestors and by divine revelation. And now, therefore, the apostle says that after we have been exempted from the law, we must not turn to vice, nor should we withdraw from it unwillingly. For that very law sends

---

[3]Bugenhagen, *In D. Pauli ad Romanos*, 67r-67v.

[4]Elton, *The Complaint of a Sanctified Sinner*, 11*.
[5]LW 25:322*.

us from itself to Christ. COMMENTARY ON ROMANS (1560).[6]

WEDDED TO THE HORRID MONSTER OF SIN. HEINRICH BULLINGER: The gist of the matter is captured in this metaphor: we are wedded to sin as if to an abusive and foul husband, and as long as this remains we are not free from the law. But "those who have crucified their flesh along with its passions" are dead to sin, and accordingly are now free from the law so that they can be wed to Christ, who made an end to this horrid monster of sin so that mortals, being freed from its companionship and the sway of its tyranny, might be joined to Christ himself, a kind and most noble husband. COMMENTARY ON ROMANS (1533).[7]

THE LAW DOES NOT DAMN THOSE WHO ARE DEAD. PETER MARTYR VERMIGLI: But although a double death is proposed, ours and the law's, Paul only pursues ours explicitly, from which the death of the law also follows. For the law does not sting, does not force, does not accuse, and does not condemn those who are dead. Nor is any covenant troublesome or hateful to them. And those who are dead and conjoined with Christ by no means expect that they will be justified by the law, partly because the law cannot perform that, and partly because they have already obtained true righteousness through the grace of Christ. We are said to be mortified, either through Christ's body, or because, once made members of the Lord, we follow our Head, so that just as he was crucified and died in relation to this mortal and corruptible life, so we also die to sin. COMMENTARY ON ROMANS (1560).[8]

BETROTHED BY FAITH. GEORG MAJOR: A previous similitude, which led to the objection answered above, was of the person purchased from slavery. What follows is a similitude that obtains to

the law of marriage. It is just as when a woman whose first husband has died is released from him by law and marries another; she is bound to submit to that second husband. So when we were annulled by the law or by a handwritten document, through the body being destroyed—that is through the sacrifice of Christ—being freed from the curse and condemnation of the law, and now being betrothed by faith to a second husband, to Christ the Son of God, we owe obedience to him, to serve him through newness of the Spirit. EXPOSITION OF THE EPISTLES OF PAUL (1569).[9]

7:2 When a Married Woman's Husband Is Alive

A CHANGE IN THE ANALOGY. WOLFGANG MUSCULUS: Here the apostle introduces a major change in analogy in order to more strongly demonstrate this. The law of the husband in relation to a wife is what is contained in Genesis 3: "You will be under the rule of your husband and he will rule over you." Under the vigor of this law, a married woman is liable to her husband, and thus she cannot be given to another. But for how long? Certainly not beyond the time of his life. Because if death should intervene, the wife is free from this law. The apostle applies this to the universal dominion of the law. But this paradigm has two aspects: first, after the intervention of death the law is void, because it does not rule over the dead, but the living. Thus he indicates this part by means of an analogy in order to teach—stealthily!—that those who believe in Christ are also free from the law on account of him, because in him the law itself is dead. Second, because already freed from the law, one is able to be joined to another, to the Lord himself. Paul uses the analogy not in order to teach that Christians should bring about a marriage contract contrary to the law, but because through Christ himself, they judge the dominion of the law as inconsequential, it now being invalid and devoid of vigor. In the analogy, it does not square up to say that

[6]Vermigli, *In Epistolam S. Pauli*, 504.
[7]Bullinger, *In Sanctissimam Pauli*, 92.
[8]Vermigli, *In Epistolam S. Pauli*, 506.

[9]Major, *Enarrationes Epistolarum S. Pauli*, 121.

the wife is liable to the husband as long as *she* lives. But where there is a death, she is already free from the law of her husband so that she may marry another. For a wife who has died is free from the law of her husband, yet she is not able to marry another, since *she* is dead! But the apostle was not delivering this analogy in order to indicate only that we are free from the law of sin, but that thus being free, we are married to another, that is, to Christ. So then, in this way the analogy has been used in order to demonstrate that when death intervenes, the dominion of the law is loosened. However, in the application of the analogy he does not say that the law is dead, but that we are dead to the law. COMMENTARY ON ROMANS (1555).[10]

THE LAW IS A TYRANNICAL HUSBAND.

JOHANNES BRENZ: During the government of Moses, wives were dominated by their husbands—especially the harsh and tyrannical ones—practically being in the position of maid servants. They were treated unmercifully and scorned, being given the writ of divorce for any reason. In the same way, as long as the law ruled over men and women, it managed them inhumanely. For although the law was holy and just, it nevertheless became a tyrant over men and women because of their sin. Therefore, just as the tyrannical husband manages his wife most cruelly and demands servility in everything, even in the most difficult of things, so that the wife does not even dare to murmur dissent, so also the law requires from men and women the most thorough righteousness, not excusing even an iota. Likewise, the husband becomes such a tyrant by his inconsiderateness that the wife, even while she is his own flesh, becomes morose, and her subservience to her husband in everything is most spiritless, and indeed she fears his blows and attends him in hatred. COMMENTARY ON ROMANS (1564).[11]

CHRIST IS THE MOST BENEVOLENT HUSBAND.

JOHANNES BRENZ: In the comparison, the discord between the tyrant and his wife, and thus between the law and men and women, is everlasting, until either they are separated or divorced. Therefore, Christ, the Son of God, came into this world in order to reconcile this discord and first the most suitable method of reconciling this discord appeared that the tyrant be slaughtered through his body or death, that is, that he would abolish the law by his death in order to free man and woman from the law. But how? Did he then liberate men and women from the law, so that it would be permissible to do evil against the law? Certainly not, but he expiated our sin, by means of which the law was confounded, and he gives us his most perfect righteousness, so that the law is not able to administer its great tyranny in us.

Then he joined the pious man to a wife, so that between them is true and legitimate marriage. But Christ is not a tyrant, but the most benevolent husband. But the example of being brought together in marriage in the situation of Christ and the church is useful to us in the first place, that we may be stirred up and inflamed toward faith. For there isn't any example in the whole world that more clearly pronounces, by itself, in what way the relationship between Christ and men and women who have been born again in Christ is managed than the example of the human body, between its head and members, or the example of marriage between a husband and wife. For the wife is a partaker of every good dignity of her husband. . . . The wife has both name and position from the husband. If her husband should be the king, the wife will be the queen. And to the contrary, if some disgrace should fall on the wife, it also overflows onto the husband. And in such a way the church is a partaker in the majesty of Christ, and in turn Christ assigns to himself the sufferings that the wicked inflict on his church. Therefore, let us

---

[10]Musculus, *In Epistolam Apostoli Pauli*, 249; citing Gen 3:16.
[11]Brenz, *In Epistolam*, 162.

confirm our faith by the example of marriage, so that in our afflictions we may endure. Then, being stirred up by this example, to obey. Indeed, if those born in Christ are the wife of Christ, certainly they owe Christ, their husband, obedience. They have, therefore, the peace of marriage, who he himself gives to them by his righteousness, and he gives the Holy Spirit, so that they are able to obey him, even though they cannot fulfill the law. Further, if anyone sins from weakness, he forgives and remits it, and similarly, for anyone who is unable to fulfill the law because of its strictness. Therefore, for those who are born again, in no way is it permitted to serve the flesh or sin. For this is what spiritual adultery is. COMMENTARY ON ROMANS (1564).[12]

A WIDOW IS FREE TO REMARRY. DIRK PHILIPS: We refer to the word of Paul to the Romans, namely, that the woman is bound to the law of the husband as long as he lives. But if the husband dies, she is free from the law of the husband, in order to wed, and to give herself in marriage with whomever she wills, only that it must happen in the Lord. We put this apostolic word there as a foundation from our earlier explanation. Yes, we put it as an irrefutable testimony to the truth that we believe as an unconquerable argument against all our opposition. The reason is this: the apostle presents the free, unbound person with the freedom to change, but with the condition that it happen in the Lord. What now happens in the Lord cannot be done against his Word and will. Here Paul's words to the Corinthians serve well, noted and taken to heart, namely, that one shall not pull together on a strange yoke with unbelievers. Read the text and understand it well. ABOUT THE MARRIAGE OF CHRISTIANS.[13]

7:3 If a Married Woman's Husband Dies

THE ADULTERESS. ERASMUS SARCERIUS: Now, through the adulteress, Paul allegorically designates the conscience of the one who feigns peace, tranquility, delight, and gladness. She is not content with the law and does not exert herself in its duty and performance. She disparages the law, rules, obedience, and so on. She pretends to love the law, does not believe or trust the law, and promises nothing good for herself concerning the law. She does not cling only to the law, nor submit only to the law, nor fear nor honor it only. And she is even pleased when the law is dishonored. The woman who has said and done these and similar things is called an adulteress.

These actions of the adulteress are not only evil, but also shameful and dangerous. In a similar way, the actions of the one whose conscience feigns peace under the law are evil, shameful, and dangerous. In addition, just as the adulteress is not commended because of these actions, so is the conscience on account of its actions. And, just as the adulteress injures herself by her actions and works, so also does the conscience that desires to heal itself before liberation from the law. The adulteress gazes in vain on honesty and chastity, and the conscience attempts in vain to heal itself before it is freed from the law.

On the other hand, the honest and reputable wife who, expecting the death of her husband, does not marry another while he is still alive, upholds the family name. Just so, the conscience that waits for the liberation from the law is declared honest and good.

Note carefully that the conscience is to be compared to the adulteress who lays claim to peace prior to being set free from the law. For her love is unprofitable and unfruitful, not to mention dangerous. From this we learn that we need to wait until the time that liberation is revealed, if we desire to be "married" honorably and with the enjoyment of favor. NOTES ON ROMANS (1541).[14]

---

[12]Brenz, *In Epistolam*, 162-63.
[13]CRR 6:562*; citing 1 Cor 7; 2 Cor 6:14-18.

[14]Sarcerius, *In Apostolam ad Romanos*, C5r-C6r.

DIAGRAM OF OUR FIRST AND SECOND MARRIAGES. THEODORE BEZA:

Diagram of Our First Marriage		
The domineering husband	**The wife (*hypandros*)**	**The offspring of this marriage**
This is sin leading to more sin, that is, the debased passions toward sinning that exist in the unregenerate. When its opportunity for sin is hindered by the law, it gets stirred up; otherwise it would be dead, as explained in verses 11, 13, and 14. For this reason it happens that to be "under the law" and to be "under the dominion of sin" are logically corollaries.	This is the carnal self, which is the condition in which one is born, in whom sin takes the lead just as a husband leads his wife.	These are all the thoughts, words, and deeds of a wife (*hypandros*), that is, one bound to sin as to a husband. These are the works, conceived from sin as by a husband, that we formerly gave birth to, leading to death.
True Description of Our Latter Nuptials		
The husband	**The wife freed from her first husband and wedded to another**	**The offspring**
This is the Spirit, or that power of Christ communicated to us. When the first husband is removed, the Spirit takes its place and stirs up holy impulses within us. Consequently "to be dead to the law" and "to be dead to sin" are corollaries, as are "to not be under the law" and "to be under grace."	This is the spiritual self, which is the condition of a man or woman reborn in Christ, in whom the Spirit takes the lead as a husband leads his wife.	These are the fruits of the Spirit, as listed by the apostle in Galatians 5:22, that we conceive by our second husband, the Spirit, and that we give birth to.

MAJOR ANNOTATIONS (1594).[15]

7:4 We Have Died to the Law

FOUR WAYS WE ARE FREED FROM THE LAW.
FRIEDRICH BALDUIN: Our apostle does not say that the *law* is dead, as if it had been entirely abrogated, but rather that we are dead to the law. Therefore the law is abrogated and we are freed from the law only (1) insofar as it pertains to justification, for no law was given that could justify; (2) insofar as it pertains to the curse, for "Christ redeemed us from the curse of the law, having been made a curse for us" and conferring on us the right of adoption; (3) with respect to the rigor of what was demanded, for since Christ perfectly fulfilled the law for us, for believers God now relaxes something of the rigor of the law. For according to this rigor, the only obedience he accepts is that which is pure and perfect; he promises nobody life and salvation unless under the condition of perfect fulfillment of the law. Every-

thing to which some vice adheres without mercy (*epieikeia*) is subject to condemnation. But now even the novice obedience of those who are regenerate is pleasing to God, to whom he promises life and salvation—not as merit for their imperfect obedience, but for the most perfect obedience of Christ. And therefore, the defects that still adhere to even the regenerate, although in and of themselves they incur the sentence of eternal damnation he does not impute on account of his Son, but rather covers them with the mantle of Christ's righteousness so that they cannot be seen and thus condemned. (4) We are also loosed from the law with respect to that servile coercion that you find in the unregenerate, who observe the precepts of the law out of fear of punishment and not without tediousness. Believers are freed from this tedium, for because they are led by the Spirit, the law now gives them delight according to the inner self so that they observe its precepts willingly insofar as they are able,

---

[15]Beza, *Annotations Majores*, 79.

"not in the oldness of the letter, but in the newness of the Spirit," for which reason they are called "God's willing people." COMMENTARY ON ROMANS (1620).[16]

SNATCHED FROM THE CONDEMNATION OF THE LAW. HULDRYCH ZWINGLI: "Therefore, brethren." He explains that on account of the body of Christ being put to death for our sakes we are now dead to the law. That is, by reason of the death to which Christ was condemned, which death was required by the law, we are therefore dead in that the law cannot condemn us anymore. Understand, therefore, that the term "the law" refers to that which domineers over us, condemns us, and executes justice against us. For it says, "cursed is he who will not continue in all of the things that the law commands." Also, by "the woman" is meant a person whom the law condemns. But we have been snatched out of law's condemnation by the death of Christ. Paul does not, however, teach that we are so liberated from the law that we need not do the things which the law commands and prescribes, for the law of God is nothing other than the will of God, which remains the same forever. ANNOTATIONS ON ROMANS (1539).[17]

FREEDOM FROM THE LAW. EDWARD ELTON: Now, this freedom from the law (understanding by "the law" the moral law) is not to be conceived as a freedom from all obedience to the law or as an exemption from the law where it is the rule of good life. Adam before his fall was not so freed from the law, and the angels and saints in heaven are not now freed from it in that respect; none yield more obedience to the law than they. But we are to conceive this freedom from the law to be in three other respects: namely, in respect of the rigor of the law, of the curse of the law, and of the power of it to stir us up to sin through the corruption of our nature. THE COMPLAINT OF A SANCTIFIED SINNER (1618).[18]

NUANCING THE ABROGATION OF THE LAW. JOHN CALVIN: We must remember that Paul refers here only to that office of the law which was peculiar to the dispensation of Moses. As far as God has in the Ten Commandments taught what is just and right and given directions for guiding our life, no abrogation of the law is to be dreamed of, for the will of God must stand the same forever. We ought carefully to remember that this is not a release from the righteousness that is taught in the law, but from its rigid requirements and from the curse that then follows. The law, then, as a rule of life, is not abrogated, but what belongs to it as opposed to the liberty obtained through Christ, that is, as it requires absolute perfection, for as we fail to render this perfection, it binds us under the sentence of eternal death. COMMENTARY ON ROMANS 7:3.[19]

TWO VIEWS ON FAITH AND WORKS. BENEDETTO DA MANTOVA AND MARCANTONIO FLAMINIO: In the current discussion, one can clearly see the difference between us and those who defend justification by both faith and works. Here we agree with them: that we establish works, affirming that the faith that justifies cannot be without good works, and that those that become righteous are those that do the good works that may rightly be called good works. But we differ from them in this: that we say that faith makes us righteous without the help of works. And the reason is ready, namely, that it is by faith that we "put on Christ" and make his holiness and righteousness ours. And, seeing the case so stands that Christ's righteousness is given to us by faith, we cannot be so thankless, blind, and unhappy, as to not believe that he is of sufficient ability to make us acceptable and right before God. . . .

Good and devout Christian, I ask you to seriously consider which of these two opinions is the truest, holiest, and worthiest to be preached: ours, which advances the benefit of Jesus Christ and tears down the pride of those who would exalt

---

[16]Balduin, *Catechesis Apostolica*, 444-45; citing Gal 3:21; Gal 3-4 Ps 110:3.
[17]Zwingli, *In Evangelicam Historiam*, 422; citing Deut 27:26; Gal 3:10.
[18]Elton, *The Complaint of a Sanctified Sinner*, 44*.

[19]CTS 38:236-37* (CO 49:120-21).

their own works against Christ's glory. Or the other, which, by affirming that faith by itself doesn't justify, defaces the glory and benefit of Jesus Christ, and puffs up the pride of those who cannot abide to be justified freely by our Lord Jesus Christ without some merit of their own. But, they say, it provides a great motivation for good works to say that people make themselves righteous before God by means of them. I answer that we also confess that good works are acceptable to God, and that he, out of his mere grace and free liberality, rewards them in paradise. But going further, we say that no works are good except for those that (St. Augustine says) are done by those that have become righteous through faith; because if the tree is not good, it cannot yield good fruit. THE BENEFIT OF THE CROSS.[20]

DEATH OF SIN AND LAW CAME THROUGH CHRIST'S DEATH. NIELS HEMMINGSEN: Here the matter is pressed. The parable just adduced serves the matter that must be explained and proved about the woman. In this matter there are three things: a person, sin, and the law, just as there are three in the proposed parable: the woman, the husband, and the law. And so the woman, while her husband is alive, is under his law, and when her husband dies, she is free from his law. It happens like this: While a person lives with sin in himself, he is under the law. This is the power of sin. But when sin is dead, the person is no longer under the law's condemnation. Besides, as a woman is free from the law of her first husband, when she remarries she ought to obey her new one. In this way a person is justified by faith, free from the accusing and damning power of the law. He ought to obey Christ as a new husband, and bear him children, which are the fruits of the Spirit. Thus far have we explained the apostle's opinion. Now we will further weigh his words. So, first he says, "You have died to the law." The following statement is put in place of the antecedent, which is, "And you

all are dead to sin, that is, to you sin is dead." Indeed, this is a *hypallage*.[†] From here it follows that you are not under the law. This being the case, the law is the power of sin, and it condemns. Then, since it is the power of sin, the cause of the death of sin, or of the law, is given. It is by the body of Christ, that is, through the sacrifice of Christ. And through communion, which the justified have with the body of Christ. For, as was said above, our old self has been crucified with Christ. Now the end of the death of sin is added, so that you who have been raised from the dead may belong to one another, that is, new "brides" of Christ, so that we may bear fruit for Christ. Here the apostle passes over from the second to the first person; this is a Hebrew idiom. And then he returns to a summary of the comparison: Namely, that since sin has died in us, that we may not be under the condemning power of the law, but be new "brides" of Christ under grace, to whom we should bear children, that is, the fruits of the Spirit, as it is said. COMMENTARY ON ROMANS (1562).[21]

THAT YOU MIGHT BE JOINED TO ANOTHER. MARTIN BUCER: Let us stir ourselves up by this passage to be ever diligent in all circumstances to be mindful that we are not our own but belong to Christ. Let us bear fruit to him; that is, let us be as instruments for Christ the Lord through whom he can dispense his work, which is the salvation of humankind. Let this thought light a flame within us: that he regards us as worthy of occupying the role not only of servants, but also of his wife and the members of his body! COMMENTARY ON ROMANS (1536).[22]

THE COMFORT OF CHRIST IN TIMES OF LOSS. EDWARD ELTON: We know it is a comfort to a wife in the time of some great loss that her husband is still alive. Even though her goods may be taken away and lost by fire, by water, or the like; though

---

[20]Benedetto and Flaminio, *Benefit of the Cross*, 66-67*; 1 Pet 2:12; Gal 3:26-27.

[21]Hemmingsen, *Commentarius in Epistolam*, 235-37. [†]A *hypallage* is a literary device in which two elements of a phrase or sentence or exchanged unexpectedly.
[22]Bucer, *Metaphrases et Enarrationes*, 313-14.

she may have lost her children, and her dearest and nearest friends have been taken away from her, yet this is a stay to her fainting heart, and this cheers her up, that her kind and loving husband is yet alive, and she has him still with her. For she is sure that he will bear part of it with her in her distress and trouble, and that he will be a guide, comfort, and help to her in any thing for her good as far as he is able. This she is sure of, and this comforts her. Oh, how much more may true believers comfort themselves and cheer up their hearts in their greatest troubles, crosses, and losses, whatever they are. I say, much more may they comfort themselves with this; that their head and husband Christ Jesus is yet alive, for he is an all-sufficient husband, able to provide help and comfort them. . . . They may assure themselves of this, there is not any affliction they suffer, but Jesus Christ their head and husband bears part of it with them and suffers with them. THE COMPLAINT OF A SANCTIFIED SINNER (1618).[23]

ALL BEARING FRUIT IN CHRIST. PETER MARTYR VERMIGLI: And the Lord said in John's writing, "When I have been raised from the earth, I will draw all people to myself." This is what Paul said, "That we may bear fruit to God." But this is only done when we not only present our good works to him, but also truly lead others to Christ. These two goals are not disunited. For neither are we able to win others to Christ—if we consider the matter as it mostly happens—except that the pattern of an honest life should follow sound doctrine in us. Nor did the apostle randomly change the "person."[†] For he used the second person when he previously wrote, "You have died to the law through the body of Christ in order that you might exist for another." But immediately he adds, "In order that we may bear fruit to God," when the natural sequence would have been "in order that *you* may bear fruit to God." But he changed the person to declare that this is a general statement. So that no persons would think

themselves so holy that they do not need these fruits, the apostle places himself among them as well. COMMENTARY ON ROMANS (1560).[24]

LOVE CHRIST AS YOUR HUSBAND. EDWARD ELTON: There is that relation and that near union between Christ and the church that there is between a husband and wife. True believers must learn their duty: They must learn to love Christ as their husband, they must give to him the chief affection of their hearts, their love, their joy, and their delight, and they must yield their bodies and souls wholly to him.

Do you persuade yourself that Christ is your husband? Oh, let him have the chief love of your heart. In this, many in the world are exceedingly faulty. They think they have Christ as their head and husband, and yet the chief love of their hearts is not given to him. No, they set their love and delight chiefly on the world and the things of it, on the profits, pleasures and vanities of the world, and they will not be driven from the love and liking of those things. . . .

Now this is how it is with you in respect to Christ, if he has the chief love of your heart; if Christ is the one that your soul chiefly loves, then you make more account of him than of all riches and treasures in the world. Yes, you hold all things loss and dung in comparison to him; you delight in his presence and company. It is the joy of your heart and the rejoicing of your soul to be where you may see the face and glorious beauty of your Beloved, Jesus Christ, even to come to the house of God, to the Word and sacraments, where Christ is set before you in lively manner. THE COMPLAINT OF A SANCTIFIED SINNER (1618).[25]

7:5 When We Were Under the Law

THE SHEEP DOES NOT MAKE THE WOLF DEVOUR HIM. JOHANNES BRENZ: What happens

---

[23]Elton, *The Complaint of a Sanctified Sinner*, 67-68*.

[24]Vermigli, *In Epistolam S. Pauli*, 508; collated with *Learned and Fruitfull Commentaries*, 161; citing Jn 12:32. [†]Used as a grammatical term.

[25]Elton, *The Complaint of a Sanctified Sinner*, 61-63*.

when we are yet in the flesh, or under the law, or under sin and Satan? Paul says that the passions of sinners that are aroused through the law are thriving in our members. Here we must pay attention to how it begins, which is what he says, "The passions of sinners exist or are awakened through the law." For we are in the habit of regularly complaining that it is others' persistent lack of consideration, and their annoying us that causes us to be evil and angry. And we think ourselves as having a quiet and good nature, and that it is the faults of others that make us bad. But we err greatly. For the passions of sinners—that is, the will and delight of those who sin—dwell in us by nature. Paul says, "I find another law in my flesh rebelling against the law of my mind." And the senses as well as the thinking of men and women are evil from adolescence. Therefore no one causes the evil of another person, but the one only awakens the other's evil, which was already adhering to and hiding in him. A sheep does not make a wolf passionate to devour, but by being seen, the sheep only awakens in the wolf the passion to devour. Money does not make the thief, but by being seen it only awakens in him the desire for stealing. Thus one man or woman does not make another evil, but usually, given the opportunity, the evil that was already dwelling in the other is dragged out of its hiding place. And the sin in us is dragged out and brought into the light partly by the purity of the law, partly by example, or by the provocation of other people. COMMENTARY ON ROMANS (1564).[26]

THE FLESH IS POWERLESS. BALTHASAR HUB-MAIER: Here one sees truly how the flesh after the fall can do wholly and completely nothing; and how, as far as good is concerned, it is completely unprofitable and dead, in all its powers incapable of doing good, and is impotent, an enemy of the law, to whom it does not want to be subservient even unto the grave. FREEDOM OF THE WILL.[27]

THE MEANS OF COUNTERING STIRRINGS TO SIN. EDWARD ELTON: Let no persons then fancy to themselves that they can at their own time and pleasure vanquish and subdue the evil motions that are stirring in their hearts and so neglect the timely use of the means that serve to subdue them, but let every one of us learn to use the means that serve to that purpose, namely, a diligent hearing, reading, and meditating in the Word of God. And let us apply the threats in it that are directly against our evil motions. And let us labor to get faith into our hearts, by which we may draw virtue from the death of Christ, to mortify, kill, and crucify the flesh, with the evil affections and lusts of it. And let us be careful to avoid all occasions that may stir up evil motions in our hearts, and be earnest and frequent in calling on God, that he would give us the strength of grace against all our evil motions and stirrings to sin. THE COMPLAINT OF A SANCTIFIED SINNER (1618).[28]

LEAN ON CHRIST RATHER THAN SLIPPERY FLESH. PETER MARTYR VERMIGLI: Thus, because sins and desires are increased in us, this comes about from it, since we are in the flesh. People are accustomed, as much as they are able, to avoid unwholesome and toxic air. And so we also, if we want to be saved, ought to shrink from and flee this contagion of the flesh, and fly upward into the sky toward Christ. However, it is not possible to be separated from the flesh, except by death. And so Paul urges us to die to sin through the body of Christ. Indeed, the flesh is a slippery part of us. And so, as long as we cling to the flesh, we will slip often. And so we need to lean on Christ, who reigns over and sustains us in this way, so that we may not collapse from this slipperiness of the flesh, leading to eternal destruction. COMMENTARY ON ROMANS (1560).[29]

---

[26]Brenz, *In Epistolam*, 164.
[27]CRR 5:438*; citing Jn 12:40; Gal 5:17; Gen 6:3; Rom 8:1-8; 1 Jn 2:16-17.

[28]Elton, *The Complaint of a Sanctified Sinner*, 102-3*.
[29]Vermigli, *In Epistolam S. Pauli*, 510.

7:6 Now That We Have Died to the Law

SERVITUDE TO AND FREEDOM FROM THE LAW.
PHILIPP MELANCHTHON: He has described the
servitude under the law in a few words in the latest
conclusion, namely, that the law holds hearts
captive and increases mistrust and doubting, which
lead to despair and blasphemy, and turn the hearts
away from God, and rush them into various sins.

Then he adds a description of freedom and says
first that we are dead to the law, that is, freed from
that captivity, because the gospel brings forgiveness
of sins. One cannot call on God or obey God
unless one has first received remission of sins. As
long as we are prisoners of the law and have not yet
heard about the remission of sins, and the goodness of God is not yet known to us and hearts do
not feel that we are heard, we flee from the wrath
of God and are turned away from God. But after
the remission of sins has been received through the
gospel and the knowledge of Christ, then obedience begins because now we know the will of
God—that he wants to hear us, wants to take pity
on us; then we call on him. COMMENTARY ON
ROMANS (1540).[30]

LETTER CAN BE LAW OR CORRUPTION. THE
ENGLISH ANNOTATIONS: Either by "the letter" he
means the law in respect to our old condition, for
before our will is framed by the Holy Spirit, the
law speaks to us only as to deaf men, and therefore
it is dumb and dead to us as touching the fulfilling
thereof. And in the word "oldness" he insinuates
also the abolishing thereof in regard to the
insufficiency thereof. Or, by the oldness of the
letter he understands the old corruption, which by
the outward letter of the law is more and more
stirred and provoked in us, inasmuch as the law,
though it condemned the sinner, yet affords no
power at all to abolish or destroy sin, in which
regard it is called a killing letter and the administration of death. ANNOTATIONS ON ROMANS 7:6.[31]

RECONCILING WITH 2 TIMOTHY 3:16. MARTIN
BUCER: "We were freed from the law; we have died
to the law" and "when the law came, sin revived,
and so the law turned out for me to result in death."

How is it that this harsh testimony agrees with
what the apostle wrote in 2 Timothy 3:16 ("All Scripture is divinely inspired and profitable for doctrine"),
or with any of the Scriptures that are again and
again proclaiming the excellency of the law?

The things the apostle wrote about the law—
that when it is undertaken in our natural strength
and separated from the grace of Christ it increases
sin and brings condemnation—do not in any way
contradict those things that Scripture attributes to
the law simply and by itself, that is, as it was
handed down to the elect and to those given to
Christ: namely, that it is wisdom for life, that it
instructs unto salvation and builds us up in every
good work.

By way of analogy, if someone should claim that
some powder or cauterizing agent when applied to
a bandage is effective for healing rotten flesh being
eaten away by an ulcer, a person would not be
contradicting themselves if they should reply that
caustic powder used in this way can do nothing but
increase the pain and make the ulcer even more
harmful, whereas if they were asked about the *same*
caustic powder considered in and of itself, if rightly
applied, that is, if after the cleansing of the wound
is complete [it is removed and] the appropriate
medications are applied, and they should affirm
that this kind of caustic powder is not just useful
but even necessary for healing the wound, it would
in fact be true if he were to simultaneously say,
"This caustic powder will increase the pain and be
harmful," and "This caustic powder will take the
pain away and do some good." He might as well say,
"If the wound is to be healed, this caustic powder
should be applied," and at the same time, "The
wound cannot be healed unless this powder is
washed off and the wounded member is freed from
the action of the cauterizing agent." For if the
caustic powder is the only thing applied, it can
accomplish nothing but increase the pain and make
the wound even worse. But if it has been applied in

---

[30]Melanchthon, *Commentary on Romans*, 154*.
[31]Downame, ed., *Annotations*, BBB1r*; citing Heb 8:13; 2 Cor 3:7.

the proper manner and the appropriate medications have also been added, such corrosive agents will have served in some degree to promote health and remove the pain. Once again: unless the wound is cleansed, the other medicines will not do any good; therefore, if this caustic powder is not applied, the wound cannot be healed. But at the same time, because in the case of rotten flesh that has been eaten away the wound must be healed by other poultices so that healthy flesh might grow in its place, the wound, therefore, cannot be healed unless the corrosive action of any powders of this kind or cauterizing agents first be removed.

In like fashion, if Christ does not breathe his Spirit on us, the law—which is meant to suppress sin in us, impel us to righteousness, and above all lift us to faith in the goodness of God through Christ—by itself will be able to do nothing but increase sin and kill us. But when it is set before those who believe in Christ, in whom the faith and life of Christ is present, it has a cleansing effect so that the grace and righteousness of Christ are perceived more perfectly.

By these analogies I think I have made it abundantly clear how the harsher things that Paul seems to say about the law in this present chapter and in other places beautifully agree with all those other utterances in which the law is preached throughout the Scriptures. COMMENTARY ON ROMANS (1536).[32]

THE LAW IS LIKE A DOCTOR EMPHASIZING THE SEVERITY OF OUR DISEASE. JOHANNES BRENZ: Here the end of these things must be considered by us. For just as a doctor at the first meeting does not heal the patient, but indicates to him the magnitude of the disease, that is, he makes himself greater than the patient not in order to cause him to remain in his sickness, but in order to stir him up that he might accept the medicine and so regain his health. . . . So when we think that we are properly healthy—especially if we consider the

prosperous success of our businesses—the law, and whatever pertains to its thinking, stirs up sin in us and it exhibits its magnitude not that it should destroy us, but in order to temper us so that we might search for and accept the true medicine against sin. COMMENTARY ON ROMANS (1588).[33]

WE STILL NEED THE LAW. PETER MARTYR VERMIGLI: So because of the death of our flesh and of sin, the law also has died and ceased. It is a truth to be noted that meanwhile, as long as we live here, we are not perfectly dead. And, therefore, the law is not useless for the present. For we are not provided with such a well supplied spirit that we may act on every impulse. So there are many things in us for which the law may accuse and blame us, for which reason the saints, while they live here may not cease to consider the law by which, the more they flee from its damnation, the more they are converted to Christ. For if we are incorporated into Christ by faith, that conjoining can be made greater over time. For the life of the pious is said to be a perpetual mortification and penance. Neither does our admitting that much of the old Adam remains in us get in the way of our regeneration. Therefore, when we consider the law and see what in us still needs to be mortified, we are more and more impelled toward Christ. And this is why Paul writes to the Galatians that he was "dead to the law through God." This is the reason why Christians must settle for themselves that as long as they see anything remaining in their consciences related to blame, or some incitement to sin, or some hatred and loathing for the divine law, or some unwillingness to be drawn toward doing good, sin is not dead in them, and they can be reproved by the law. COMMENTARY ON ROMANS (1560).[34]

IMMODERATE AFFECTIONS AS SPURS TO VIRTUE. CATHERINE PARR: He has also vanquished sin, because he has taken away the force of the same. That is, he has canceled the law, which

---

[32]Bucer, *Metaphrases et Enarrationes*, 309, 312; citing Rom 7:9; 2 Tim 3:16.

[33]Brenz, *In Epistolam*, 603.
[34]Vermigli, *In Epistolam S. Pauli*, 511-12; citing Gal 2:19.

was the occasion of sin in sinful men and women. Therefore, sin has no power against them that are, by the Holy Spirit, united to Christ; there is nothing worthy of damnation in them. And although the dregs of Adam do remain—that is, our concupiscences,[†] which indeed are sins—nevertheless they are not imputed as sins if we are truly planted in Christ. It is true that Christ could have taken away all our immoderate affections, but he has left them for the great glory of his Father, and for his own greater triumph. It is similar to when a prince fights with his enemies who for a while had sovereignty over his people, and after subduing them, he could kill them if he wished to, yet he allows them to live; and whereas they used to be lords over his people, from then on, he makes them serve those whom they before had ruled. Now, in such a case, the prince shows himself a greater conqueror—in that he made those who had been rulers to obey, and the subjects to be lords over those whom they had served—than if he had utterly destroyed them upon the conquest. For now he leaves continual victory to those whom he redeemed, whereas otherwise the occasion of victory would have been taken away if none had been left to be the subjects. Even so, in like case, Christ hath left in us these concupiscences, for the intent that they should serve us to exercise our virtues, where first they reigned over us to exercise our sin. And it may be plainly seen that whereas first they were such impediments to us that we could not move ourselves toward God, now, by Christ, we have so much strength, that in spite of their force, we will assuredly walk to heaven. And although the children of God sometimes fall by frailty into some sin, yet, that falling makes them to humble themselves, and to acknowledge the goodness of God, and to come to him for refuge and help. THE LAMENTATION OF A SINNER.[35]

LAW AS MIRROR, CHRIST AS HARBOR. PETER MARTYR VERMIGLI: Certain people are inspired by the law only to engage in certain external ceremonies and lifeless works that can pertain only to some particular discipline: and they do not at all arrive at a just and solid observation of the divine will. There are others who, when they more carefully study the law, consider the horror of sin and uncleanness and the weakness of their powers, and, at their wits' end, completely despair, and begin to hate and detest God and to blaspheme him and his law, and to rush headlong into every iniquity and crime, until they plunge themselves into their eternal destruction. But for pious persons, considering the law is useful and healthful. For when they behold their infirmity in it, as in a mirror, they are compelled to bring themselves to Christ as if to a harbor, from whom they may each day obtain both pardon for their sins and the restoration of their greater powers. COMMENTARY ON ROMANS (1560).[36]

TRUE SPIRITUAL SERVICE. EDWARD ELTON: First, the ground of true spiritual service of God is a true knowledge of God as he has revealed himself in his Word, to know God to be infinite in power, wisdom, justice, mercy, holiness, goodness, and so on and that he is a beholder and a judge of all secrets and will render to all men and women according to their works. This is the very root and ground of all sound, hearty, and sincere affection in the service of God. . . .

Now we should conceive of the true spiritual service of God as follows: It is a true acknowledgment of God's power, justice, mercy, and goodness, with an inward and sincere affection in some proportion agreeable to that acknowledgment. For as we know by the light of the Word that God is just, good, and omnipotent, so must we that are in his service acknowledge in our hearts that he is so, and be affected toward him accordingly in all duties of God's service. With the outward work must go inward and good affections, and then we serve God with spiritual service. And this is what the Lord in all times has called for: throughout the book of God we are taught to serve God in

---

[35]*Writings of Edward VI*, 44*. [†]I.e., sinful desires.

[36]Vermigli, *In Epistolam S. Pauli*, 514.

pureness of Spirit, in simplicity and soundness of heart; and that is spiritual service of God.

Now in the third place, this service has two kinds. Either it is such as is immediately performed to God, as in all action of religious worship, in hearing, in speaking the Word of God, in prayer, in receiving the sacraments, and the like. Or such as is mediately offered up to God, as in the duties of love, mercy, equity, and justice to men and women, for we serve God in those as well. THE COMPLAINT OF A SANCTIFIED SINNER (1618).[37]

HERMENEUTICS OF THE SPIRIT. DIRK PHILIPS: Again, that Moses allowed circumcision to lapse in the wilderness does not prove that Christian baptism may be discontinued in the same manner. For, in principle, we are not to be guided by the figures, images, and incompleteness of the Old Testament, but by the true and perfect being and spirit of the New Testament. We are not under the law but under the gospel. We are not to serve according to the old nature of the letter but according to the new nature of the Spirit. Finally, we are not disciples of Moses but of Christ. Therefore, we have also received a command from the heavenly Father that we shall hear Jesus Christ, his dear Son, and be obedient to his words and follow his example. Nevertheless, we do not wish herewith to despise Moses with his law, figures, and schemes, but to look on them with spiritual eyes, yes, to have them judged and understood according to the true spirit and being of the New Testament. THE BAPTISM OF OUR LORD JESUS CHRIST.[38]

---

[37]Elton, *The Complaint of a Sanctified Sinner*, 127-28*.

[38]CRR 6:108-109*; citing Heb 7:11; Rom 6:14; Mt 3:17; 17:5.

7:7-13 THE LAW, SIN, AND DEATH

7What then shall we say? That the law is sin? By no means! Yet if it had not been for the law, I would not have known sin. For I would not have known what it is to covet if the law had not said, "You shall not covet." 8But sin, seizing an opportunity through the commandment, produced in me all kinds of covetousness. For apart from the law, sin lies dead. 9I was once alive apart from the law, but when the commandment came, sin came alive and I died. 10The very commandment that promised life proved to be

death to me. 11For sin, seizing an opportunity through the commandment, deceived me and through it killed me. 12So the law is holy, and the commandment is holy and righteous and good.

13Did that which is good, then, bring death to me? By no means! It was sin, producing death in me through what is good, in order that sin might be shown to be sin, and through the commandment might become sinful beyond measure.

OVERVIEW: As in the earlier part of the chapter, this passage continues to explore the topic of the law and sin in the life of the believer. The commentators interpret the fact that Paul is using an example (the prohibition of covetousness) from the Ten Commandments as illustrating that it is not only the ceremonial law that is abrogated by Christ's death but *all* of the law. Medieval theologians had divided the law into civil/judicial, ceremonial, and moral categories, and the reformers continued with that threefold categorization. But where they differed from their predecessors was in arguing that, in relation to salvation, the death of Christ dealt with all three of these facets of the law, and they discuss various ways of dividing the functions of the law or of defining the law. While the law plays a role in relation to our sin—identifying and highlighting it—it is not the actual cause of it. The cause is our sinful hearts, our fleshly desires. The law is not merely about external actions. Rather, it commands us *fully*. It either requires that we do something with our whole heart, soul, and mind (as with the greatest commandment), or it prohibits that we do something at all, even in our hearts and minds (as with the command not to covet).

The interpreters point out that at first it seems that Paul is accusing the law of killing him. But

then he makes it clear that it is the sin, not the law that kills him. The law is good, and its work of pointing out our sin is crucial. All of Scripture either points out our sin (law) or points us to Christ (gospel), the one who can free us from sin, thus revealing both our depravity and his mercy.

7:7 *The Law Is Not Sin*

IS THE LAW SIN? HULDRYCH ZWINGLI: Is the law, therefore, sin? In these things that follow, Paul describes sin, that is, the old self, which he already discussed above in chapters 5 and 6. He shows, however, that sin is a disease and scourge. Likewise, he depicts the power, nature, and efficacy of the law. Then he describes the fight between flesh and spirit. Since he said above that he who is Christ's is dead to the law and to sin, someone might object, "Paul, you said that we were dead with respect to the law and sin through the death of Christ, and so sin and the law are the same thing." "God forbid!" says Paul, "but through the law sin abounds, that is, through the law one comes to know how weighty sin really is." A person does not know what sin is and what it is not, unless God shows him this by his (own) Word, that is, what he ought to have done and not done. For the law being portrayed is the doctrine regarding the will of God, what he wants, what he doesn't want, what he requires, and what he forbids. ANNOTATIONS ON ROMANS (1539).[1]

CORRECTING TWO OPINIONS ABOUT THE LAW. PHILIPP MELANCHTHON: Having completed his digression, he returns to the comparison that he began above between the law and grace. And most of all he speaks here about the use of the law, in order that he may correct two opinions that persist not only in Jews, but universally in the minds of all. For all imagine that the righteousness of the law which a person is able to offer satisfies the law and is righteousness in the sight of God. People do not see sin and the corruption of nature, nor do they see that the discipline which they offer as best they can[†] through the law, does not satisfy the law, nor is it righteousness in the sight of God. Although it was the Jews who most of all defended these opinions about the law, they are nevertheless common to all. But they are refuted by the gospel, which teaches that the law is not only an external discipline, and that people are not righteous by means of the law. Therefore it is necessary that the apostles speak about this matter. Neither is Paul here quarreling only about ceremonies, but he is speaking about the whole law, and chiefly about the Decalogue, since he cites an example from the Decalogue and argues that no one satisfies the law, and that all are accused by the law, and that for this reason the law is a ministry of wrath and of death.

It is necessary that this be taught in the church in order that the benefit of Christ may become clear, and that the need of the gospel, and the need of grace and righteousness other than the righteousness of the law, may be understood. Because we are not justified by the law, God gave his Son for us. God reveals the gospel—that he wants to forgive us gratis on account of his Son, pronounce us righteous, and renew us. COMMENTARY ON ROMANS (1540).[2]

FIVE OFFICES OF THE LAW. BENEDETTO DA MANTOVA AND MARCANTONIO FLAMINIO: Our God, therefore, mindful of his infinite goodness and mercy, sent his only Son to set free the wretched children of Adam. Knowing that first of all it was important for him to make them understand their own misery, he chose Abraham (in whose seed he promised to bless all nations), and accepted his offspring as his particular people, to whom (after their departure out of Egypt and deliverance from the bondage of Pharaoh) he, by means of Moses, gave the law. The law forbids all lust, and commands us to love God with all our heart, with all our soul, and with all our strength, in such a way that our whole trust is reposed in him, and we are ready to leave our life for his sake, to suffer all torments, and to be bereft of all our goods, dignities, and honors, for the love of our God, choosing to die rather than to do anything that may displease him, no matter how little, and doing all things for him with a merry heart, and with all boldness and cheerfulness. Moreover, the law commands us to love our neighbor as ourselves, meaning by the neighbor all types of people, both friends and foes. And it wills us to do to every person as we would want them to do to us, and to care about other people's situations as much as our own. And so, by looking in this holy law, as in a clear mirror, we see our own great imperfection and inability to obey God's commandments, and to render him the honor and love that we ought to yield to our Maker. The first office of the law, then, is to make sin known, as St. Paul affirms. And in another place he says, "I did not know what sin was except by the law."

The second office of the law is to make sin increase. Being quite gone from obeying God, and having become bond slaves to the devil, being full of sinful works and inordinate affections, we cannot tolerate God forbidding us to lust, which increases the more it is prohibited. For this reason, St. Paul says that sin was dead but the law came and raised it up again, and so it became immeasurably great.

The third office of the law is to show the wrath and judgment of God, who threatens death and

---

[1]Zwingli, *In Evangelicam Historiam*, 423.
[2]Melanchthon, *Commentary on Romans*, 155-56*. [†]*Facere quod se est.* See introduction for discussion of this medieval doctrine.

everlasting punishment to those who do not keep the law throughout in all points. . . . St. Paul says that the law is a ministry and that it brings forth wrath. The law, then—having discovered sin and increased it and shown forth the wrath and indignation of God, who threatens death—executes his fourth office, that is, to put a person in fear; who then falls into sorrow and fails to satisfy the law. But, when he sees clearly that he is not able to, he becomes angry against God, and wishes with all his heart that there were no God, because he fears he will be chastised and punished by him, as St. Paul says that "the wisdom of the flesh is the enemy of God; because it neither is, nor can be subject to the law of God."

The fifth office of the law (which is the principal end, and the most excellent and necessary office of it) is to constrain us to go to Jesus Christ. It is similar to the Hebrews, who being dismayed, were constrained to appeal to Moses, saying, "Don't let the Lord speak to us or we may die; but you speak to us, and we will obey you in all things." And the Lord answered, "Truly, they have spoken exceedingly well." Yes, they were not praised for any thing other than for their desiring of a mediator between God and them, which was Moses, who represented Jesus Christ, who would be the Advocate and Mediator between God and us. With respect to this, God said to Moses, "I will raise up a prophet among their brothers, like you, and I will put my word in his mouth. And he will speak to them all the things that I shall command him, and I will punish all those that will not obey my word, which he will speak in my name." THE BENEFIT OF CHRIST'S DEATH.[3]

PAUL INCLUDES BOTH THE CEREMONIAL AND MORAL LAW. PETER MARTYR VERMIGLI: This passage manifestly teaches that Paul is not only speaking of ceremonies, but also includes the very Decalogue itself. For he appeals to it as a confirmation of his opinion: "You shall not covet." And it is

this very law that he is referring to when he proclaims that we have been liberated from the law. COMMENTARY ON ROMANS (1560).[4]

THE LAWGIVER IS A PHYSICIAN. JACQUES LEFÈVRE D'ÉTAPLES: The One giving the law was like a physician, and the one receiving it like a sick person. The law itself was the medicine prescribed by the Physician, the One giving instruction about things that are healthy and things that are unhealthy, who forbids this and prescribes that. Sin is the disease. Therefore the law itself is, in and of itself, a good thing—in fact a very good thing. This is confessed by the one who said, "I regard the law of your mouth as a good thing, better than thousands of gold and silver coins." But the Lord implies through Ezekiel that it is sometimes an evil, when he says: "I gave you precepts that were not good, and judgments in which they could not live." Accordingly, the law was given to them for their salvation, but because it was the law of flesh given to heal the infirmities of the flesh, and because it itself was weak because of the flesh, therefore at times the desires of the flesh's infirmity actually increase by means of the law. Just like if a physician should command a person with dropsy not to drink, his appetite for drinking will increase all the more due to the command. It seems that because of the command, he will not at all avoid it, because he now feels a desire for it. Just so, the desires that sinners feel appear to be in them as a result of the law, and this does sometimes happen, although it is especially and causally a result of sin and the flesh's infirmity. COMMENTARY ON ROMANS (1517).[5]

PAUL'S EXPLANATION OF THE LAW'S POWER. PHILIPP MELANCHTHON: Paul explains the power of the law most thoroughly in Romans 7 when he writes, "I did not know sin except through the law; for I did not know concupiscence except the law said: 'You shall not covet.'" Paul says the same thing

---

[3]Benedetto and Flaminio, *The Benefit of Christ's Death*, 11-14*; Rom 3:20; 2 Cor 3:7; Rom 4:15; 8:7; Ex 20:19; Deut 18:17-19.

[4]Vermigli, *In Epistolam S. Pauli*, 516; for a concise summary of Aristotle's *Ten Categories*, see Augustine, *Confessions* 4.16.
[5]Lefèvre, *Epistole divi Pauli*, 67r; citing Ps 119:72; Ezek 20:25.

in Romans 3, "through the law is the knowledge of sin." It is as if he were saying that hypocrites are falsely convinced that righteousness is obtained by the law, since the law only reveals sin to the heart. Then "taking occasion through the commandment, sin worked all manner of concupiscence[†] in me," that is when I began to feel the weight of the law, still less did anything come from the law, so that instead concupiscence was aroused all the more and began to rage against the judgment and will of God. For "without the law sin was dead," that, unless the law had shown me the sin in my heart, unless the recognition of my sin had terrified me, sin would have been dead and would not have burst forth. "For once I was alive without the law." There was once a time when I thought I was righteous, when I did not understand the law and so did not recognize my sin. And at that point sin was quiet, nor did it show open hostility to God. "But when the commandment came, sin came back to life, but I died." That is, after God had shown me my sin through the law, I was confounded, terrified and trembling. In short, I died. And then, finally the power of the law became clear. The law was given so that we would live, but since we cannot do it, it is the instrument of death. Why, then, does the law kill? "The law is spiritual"; that is, it demands spiritual things—truth, faith that glorifies God, love of God. "But I am carnal," unbelieving, ignorant of God, foolish, full of self-love.

Nowhere does the apostle Paul so thoroughly treat the power and nature of the law than in the passage just cited. I do not see that there is anything lacking in it. There is no obscurity, no impediment. Everything in it is clear and evident, so that its meaning cannot be doubted. LOCI COMMUNES (1521).[6]

LIVING BY THE LAW IS LIKE A SEED. JACQUES LEFÈVRE D'ÉTAPLES: The law by its very nature leads toward salvation, but it is incapable of granting a perfect salvation, for perfect salvation happens through grace, not through the law and the works of the law. But those who performed the works of the law, as it is written, lived by them: "Keep," he says, "my law and my judgments, which if a man does, he will live by them." This "living by the law" or "living by them" is not a perfect life, but only a kind of beginning aimed at a more perfect life, just as the life of a seed is the beginning that leads toward the life of the plant. But so that this might happen, it is necessary that it cease to be what it is and die: "Unless," the Truth says, "a grain of wheat that falls on the earth dies, it remains alone; but if it dies," it is certain that a plant will arise "and produce much fruit." Just so, he who lives by the law, who performs the works of the law and lives by them, must die to the law so that he might live by grace, which is the consummate life that only God gives. The law does not give it, nor do its works. Therefore "to live by them" is a kind of disposition preparing them for the consummate life, like the life of the grain, for the consummate life that is in the plant. And as the life of the grain is shadowy and buried in the dirt, so also the life that is by the law and its works is shadowy, and those who lived that life and in those works descended to hell. But they were alive with this shadowy life as it were under the dirt, feeling no punishment among the infernal spirits but were awaiting that better and illuminated life which Christ the eternal King and Lord brought to them. COMMENTARY ON ROMANS (1517).[7]

THE LAW AND SIN DO NOT AGREE. WILLIAM AMES: The apostle, so that he might stir up the faithful to a new obedience, had proposed to them the difference of the condition of those who are under the law and of those that are under grace; to wit, that those that are under the law of the flesh and sin bring forth fruits unto death; but those that are under the grace of the Spirit bring forth fruits in a new obedience unto eternal life. But because of this opposition between the law and

---

[6]Melanchthon, *Loci Communes*, 102*; citing Rom 7:14. [†]Sinful desire.

[7]Lefèvre, *Epistole divi Pauli*, 67r; citing Lev 18:5; Jn 12:24.

grace, some might gather that then there was a very great agreement between the law and sin. Therefore in this seventh verse, the apostle (1) proposes an objection: "What shall we say? Is the law sin?" (2) It is rejected with a certain kind of detestation: "God forbid!" (3) The case is set down plainly and resolved in these words: "I had not known sin, etc." Thus, the singular effect and use of the law is declared; to wit, that by forbidding and reproving, the law begets in us a sense and acknowledgment of sin, as of that which is contrary to itself; and therefore the law cannot be the cause of sin.

The Explication: By the term *law* we commonly understand a way and rule of walking. Now this way and rule is imposed on reasonable creatures by divine authority and the greatest obligations that can be. And this is the law of God, which the apostle here understands, especially the moral law. "Sin" here means not only the transgression of God's will, but also all those things that follow after such a transgression, which in this chapter is defined by the term "death," and is sometimes called misery. Sin is either known confusedly and speculatively only, or more exactly and practically. Now the accurate and practical knowledge of sin is here understood—and therefore effectively concluded by our consciences—that sin is a detestable thing, and by all means to be avoided. THE SUBSTANCE OF CHRISTIAN RELIGION.[8]

LAW NOT NECESSARY FOR CHILDREN. JACQUES LEFÈVRE D'ÉTAPLES: But some who are already living that illuminated life that is by grace and in a bright place still desire to live the life that is by law. How can they live a life that is shadowy and illuminated at the same time? But you may be asking, "When is the physician's prescription not necessary, since there is no infirmity?" When there is no sin, the law isn't needed, just as the law is not necessary for a little child since it does not yet have any sin, not having yet become ill by the flesh. But like Adam, they first begin to become ill by the flesh when they come to possess an understanding

of good and evil; it is then that the lusts of their infirmity arise. The law is necessary then that prohibits evil things and commands good ones, that if it is obeyed they will live by the law, being prepared to receive afterward by grace the best life. But if they do not follow it, the law which was good, will at times lead them to the death of the law and afterward the death of outer darkness, which is the opposite of the best life. Therefore, before the time of the law, they were *dead to sin* and sin in them was dead. But when the time came in which the law became necessary, sin arose. This is what Paul implies when he says, "apart from the law sin is dead; I was alive once apart from the law." COMMENTARY ON ROMANS (1517).[9]

THE VARIOUS USES OF THE LAW. JOHANNES BRENZ: Paul's discourse about the true use of the law must diligently be observed. But meanwhile it should also be known that in this passage Paul is not treating the political or civil use of the law, which the law has in the external state. . . . Indeed, a magistrate necessarily must assert the laws, so that he may keep people safe, in peaceful and respectable society. . . . This is the outward use of the law. Paul, however, treats in this passage the spiritual use of the law, in the conscience, and before the judgment seat of God. This is necessary, as much for those who are *going* to be justified—so that they may recognize the greatness and severity of sin, by which they are aroused to seek out forgiveness of sin in Christ—as for those who *have* been justified, so that on account of the recognized magnitude of their sin, and having received his forgiveness, they might come to know of the immense grace and mercy of God through Christ, and they might be pleasing to God. COMMENTARY ON ROMANS (1564).[10]

GUILT EXISTED BEFORE THE LAW. PETER MARTYR VERMIGLI: The apostle prudently said he would not have recognized sin and would have been

---

[8]Ames, *The Substance of Christian Religion*, 13-14*.

[9]Lefèvre, *Epistole divi Pauli*, 67r.
[10]Brenz, *In Epistolam*, 166-67.

ignorant about his covetousness if the law had not said, "You shall not covet." But he did not say that he was not guilty of sin before the law came, for he was even then guilty of that sin, only he did not recognize it. COMMENTARY ON ROMANS (1560).[11]

THE LAW IS A RULE THAT DEFINES SIN.

HEINRICH BULLINGER: Marcus Tullius Cicero, in whose possession were Plato's twelve books of *On the Laws*, being a most careful reader, regarding the origin of the laws says in his dialogue *For Sestius*:[†] "There used to be a time when, neither natural or civil law having yet been articulated, men and women wandered around, spread out and scattered in the countryside. They possessed only that which they were able to seize with their own hands and strength, by shedding blood. But those who excelled in wisdom and virtue . . . congregated together in one place and brought those who were scattered out of their former savagery to a state of justice and civility." He says that this is how the laws of society and of households began. Accordingly, they speak rightly who say, "Good laws arose because of evil customs." Undoubtedly, the written law of God, which we call the "Mosaic law," was also laid down under the same circumstances. For the Israelites were degenerate and depraved through their living together with the Egyptians to such an extent that they no longer recognized what was righteousness and what was sin, and the Lord, being moved to anger by their wickedness, wanted to drive out the darkness of their errors by laying down the law. So he brought the law and inscribed it on tablets of stone, since the inertia and blindness of the human mind had neglected or was unwilling to pay attention to the law of nature written in the heart. For by means of the law being written, like visible testimonies brought forth to be looked at, he wished to reaffirm and renew that law written within. For just as human laws, which at one time were just, flowed out of the natural law as from a fountain, so also the divine laws were laid down in order to repair the natural law and to purge from it the stains of human corruption. However, one cannot deny that in the case of some of these laws, they were constituted on account of the times and character of the people, most especially in the case of the ceremonial laws, and to a great degree also in the civil laws, or as others would have it, the "judicial" part of the law. For when the occasion demanded it, they were either altered or entirely abolished. But that which belongs to the heart of the law, namely, piety, faith, innocence, and charity, has never at any time been repealed, as not a single part of this can ever be altered.

Now, Paul in this passage is principally speaking of the "moral law" (as they call it), proclaiming the very thing that we said a little earlier, that it was set forth in order to disclose the way of truth and goodness, and that by pointing this out it might clarify what true righteousness is before God and from whence it springs, namely, not from humanity but from God. The law, therefore, shows what sin is, and also that inside man and woman, there is nothing but sin. This is what the apostle narrates in very few words when he says, "I did not know sin except through the law." From which words it is now clear that the law itself was not given in order to justify, but rather to cast out, dig up and bring into the light of day the sin that is shut up and hidden by hypocrisy and impudence in the secret lurking places of the human breast. From this it follows that the law is nothing other than a rule that defines sin, like the rules of a judicial investigation that define what is to be investigated and how it is to be evaluated. A determination of this kind (provided that it deserves this label) is drawn from judicial cases and is adapted to the law by synecdoche. There are also other effects of the law, but the effect that pertains to our subject is the most important. COMMENTARY ON ROMANS (1533).[12]

COOL WELLS UNDER A GLARING SUN. PETER

MARTYR VERMIGLI: So that the things which

---

[11]Vermigli, *In Epistolam S. Pauli*, 519.

[12]Bullinger, *In Sanctissimam Pauli*, 93-95. [†]Cicero, *Pro Sestio* 1.42.91.

follow might be understood more easily and clearly, you must observe that Paul does not attribute the efficient cause of sin to law. For sin follows from the law only in an accidental fashion. The true and proper cause of sin is located within ourselves. For when they are opposed by the divine law, the fleshly desires that are rooted and fixed within us break out afresh and are inflamed with greater vehemence. It is not because the law offers occasions for disease, for its role is only to point out evils, proposing to us what should be done and what should be avoided. But when the corruption of nature senses that the things set forth by the law are contrary to it, it gathers courage, fortifies itself, and exerts its greatest powers to put up as much resistance as it can. It is like what we sometimes see in the summertime: when there are cool clouds overhead, in the lowest parts of these regions one finds the greatest heat, and likewise when everything is inflamed by the glaring sun and is steaming hot, by way of *antiperistasis*,[†] wells and subterranean places become even colder. For these are of a contrary nature, so that they seek more vehemently to push away the presence of things contrary to themselves. COMMENTARY ON ROMANS (1560).[13]

SPEAKING TRUTH AGAINST THE SUGGESTIONS OF DESPAIR. GEORGE WITHER:

What hellish doubt, what cursed fear,
    Is that which now begins
Unto my conscience to appear,
    And threatens me for my sins?
In myself I think I somewhat feel
    My heart oppressing so,
That faith and hope begin to reel,
    And faint my spirits grow.
Assist me, Lord! For I perceive
    My ghostly foe intends,
Of that assurance to bereave
    Whereon my soul depends.
He whispers to my troubled mind
    Suggestions of despair,

And says I shall no mercy find,
    Though I to you repair.
But all untruth in him is found,
    And truth itself does say,
That you in mercy do abound,
    And hear all those that pray.
Oh! Hear me, Lord! Oh, hear me now!
    And since my God you are,
Against despair enable you
    My much oppressed heart.
Say to my soul you are her friend,
    Her comfort and her aid;
From those distresses me defend
    Which make me now afraid.
For weak, and sick, and faint, alas!
    My faith begins to be;
And, Lord! Without your saving grace,
    There is no hope for me.
My sins before my face appear
    In their most loathsome dress;
My conscience tells me when and where,
    And how I did transgress.
Your law declares what for my sins
    Your justice did foredoom,
And Satan lays a thousand gins,
    That snared I may become.
That hell which in my soul I find,
    Is to my friends unknown;
The world her own affairs does mind,
    And leaves me oft alone.
And but that I to you as yet
    Remember to repair,
My passions would in me beget
    A merciless despair.
Preserve, O Lord! preserve in me,
    And all men thus oppressed.
A hopeful heart to seek from you
    Our much desired rest.
And still when Satan snares does lay,
    To work our overthrow,
Still frustrate what he does assay,
    And stronger make us grow.

HYMN AGAINST DESPAIR.[14]

---

[13]Vermigli, *In Epistolam S. Pauli*, 515. [†]An *antiperistasis* is a process in which one thing heightens the force of its opposite.

[14]Wither, *Hallelujah*, 142-43*.

THE SOUL OF THE LAW. PETER MARTYR
VERMIGLI: Paul aims at the very root of all sins,
and he explains that that which is lurking and
hidden is brought out by the law of God and
dragged into the light. In order for us to explain
this more clearly, we must observe that every one
of God's commandments either command
something or forbid it. But when they command,
it is not so that something should be done in a
merely trivial way, but that it should be done with
the whole soul, the whole heart, with all of one's
powers and in the most exact way, in such a
fashion that there is nothing whatsoever within
us that does not comply with the divine will. And
when they forbid something, it does not merely
forbid that it should occur among us, but also
that not even the desire or inclination for it
should remain within us. Therefore God decreed
"you shall not covet" so that we might shrink from
the things God prohibited with our mind, will,
and every last part of our soul and body. It's in
this way that these two commandments, "You
shall love the Lord your God with all your soul,
with all your heart" and so on (which is something that must be repeated after all of the
precepts that are commanded), and the last of the
Ten Commandments, "You shall not covet"
(which is to be understood in turn to apply to all
things that are forbidden). Hence in these two
commandments the force and, if I might say so,
the "soul" of the law is to be found, without which
the remainder of God's commandments would
not be full and complete. But all mortals, however
holy they may be, are by both of these precepts
accused, convicted, and condemned. Indeed, if
the grace of God through his Christ had not
come, we would have nothing to look forward to
but certain destruction. COMMENTARY ON
ROMANS (1560).[15]

DO NOT PLACE FAIR NAMES ON FOUL SINS.
EDWARD ELTON: Again, is it so that men and

women come to a sound and thorough knowledge of sin only by the law of God? Surely then,
if we would soundly and thoroughly know sin, if
we would know what things are sin, and how
foul, ugly, and monstrous a thing sin is, we must
look into the book of God, and not rest in our
own sense and understanding; we must not
judge of sin by the crooked rule of our own
reason, for this is that which deceives many, they
judge of sin by their own corrupt sense and
reason. For example, they think it is nothing to
take the name of God into their mouths at every
turn, and to say, Oh God! O Lord! O Jesus!
God's sonty![†] and the like. They think their
words are but wind, and that it is nothing to
open their mouths against those that fear God
and to revile and to reproach them, and they
think it nothing to lie for advantage, and to
swear by faith or "troth." . . . And hence it is that
men and women put fair names on foul sins and
call covetousness good husbandry; pride, comeli-
ness; and drunkenness, good fellowship; and
such like. THE COMPLAINT OF A SANCTIFIED
SINNER (1618).[16]

**ARISTOTLE'S TEN CATEGORIES AND THE TEN
COMMANDMENTS.** PETER MARTYR VERMIGLI:
If I might say so, it sometimes comes to my mind
that the Ten Commandments of the Decalogue,
in all its parts, broadly correspond, in my opinion,
to the discussion of nobility and dishonor, virtue
and vice, and to Aristotle's *Ten Categories*. For just
as nothing can be found in nature that does not
pertain to those Aristotelian categories, so there is
no virtue, no vice, nothing noble, and nothing
dishonorable that cannot also be referred to one
of the Ten Commandments. Just as all genera and
species are reducible to the category of "substance,"
so all external sins can be reduced to disordered
desire.[†] Hence each precept has the same material
substance and form as this first and highest
principle, such that every consent to sin within

---

[15]Vermigli, *In Epistolam S. Pauli*, 518.

[16]Elton, *The Complaint of a Sanctified Sinner*, 143*. [†]Shortened
form of "sanctity"; used as an oath.

our soul is reducible to the depravity of our nature. Commentary on Romans (1560).[17]

The Law Rather Than Reason Shows Us What Is Sin. Edward Elton: Thus men and women deceive themselves in judging sin by their own sense and reason. We must learn not to rest in our own sense and reason in relation to sin. Rather, we are to look into the book of God and to examine our hearts and lives by the law of God published in his Word, the sum of which we have in the Ten Commandments. And we shall there find thousands of things to be sins that we never thought to be so. The Complaint of a Sanctified Sinner (1618).[18]

7:8 The Law Awoke Sin

The Spirit and Death Are Contraries. Jacques Lefèvre d'Étaples: A disease reveals itself as disease most of all when it yearns for things forbidden and flees from things commended, and hence takes occasion from the prescriptions of the physician, which themselves were good and health-giving, to kill more quickly and cause the disease (if I may say so) to become even graver. This is how sin is. When the disease burns within us like a fever, what will the law given by the Physician command for the fever? No doubt, that it be cooled down. But if instead, sin chills us like a paralysis, is it not necessary to be warmed? And since sin is an infirmity of the flesh, what kind of law will be given for sin by One who recognizes the nature of the transgression? Will it not be a spiritual one? For the Spirit and the flesh are contraries, just as to heat and to cool are. And thus the Spirit heals the infirmity of the flesh, as a source of warmth cures a frigid paralysis. And just as warmth is friendly to life

and the cold is friendly to death, so the Spirit is always friendly to life whereas the flesh is friendly to death. And just as for cold to live in the body without any heat is death, so in those who have arrived at the time of the Spirit, the flesh without the Spirit is death. Sin dwells in the flesh; the Spirit dwells in the mind. I say that sin dwells in the flesh, but only in that flesh that is the ground of and feels the weight of Adam's curse. But the flesh that does not feel that curse does not germinate thorns and thistles and noxious lusts. Therefore, just as sin is the infirmity of the flesh, so the Spirit is the health of the mind. The latter was implanted in every mind by God, whereas the former, except where prevented by divine blessing, is inseminated in all flesh from Adam. For Christ received flesh, but without Adam's infirmity. . . . And just as the flesh that is obedient to the Spirit and to the mind is healed from Adam's infirmity, so the spirit perishes when due to the infirmity of the flesh it is not cherished, and the mind grows ill from contagion by the flesh. The flesh that yields to the Spirit is assimilated to the flesh of Christ, which did not feel the sting of illicit desires, but experienced only harmless passions such as thirst, hunger, cold, heat, tiredness, pain from bad sensations, and enjoyment of good ones and other passions of this kind which even in our case do not proceed from the infirmity of the flesh but from our imitation of Christ. And along the same lines, if the flesh bears a similarity with Christ's flesh, then much more does our spirit—which is alive by grace and the Spirit of Christ—bear a similarity with his Spirit. Commentary on Romans (1517).[19]

Restraining Sin Through Faith and the Holy Spirit. Martin Luther: It is unusual language to say "dead and risen with Christ." This means that they are truly holy, and yet they are to kill their earthly vices in their own bodies and

---

[17]Vermigli, *In Epistolam S. Pauli*, 522-23; conflated with *Learned and Fruitfull Commentaries*, 166*. †Augustine's concept, expressed in *Confessions* 2 as *cupiditas*, and its opposite, *ordo amoris*, in *City of God*.
[18]Elton, *The Complaint of a Sanctified Sinner*, 144*.

[19]Lefèvre, *Epistole divi Pauli*, 67r.

members. The apostle often points out (in Rom 7 and elsewhere) that there will remain in the saints all kinds of sinful desires from original sin, which are always active and want to break out into coarse external vices, unless they are opposed. It is so strong and powerful that it wants to take the person completely captive and make him subject to sin (as St. Paul himself laments). It does this if he does not restrain and overcome it through faith and the help of the Holy Spirit. SUMMER POSTIL (APRIL 7, 1534).[20]

HEALTHY FLESH IMITATES CHRIST'S. JACQUES LEFÈVRE D'ÉTAPLES: Why is there so much warring between us—to whom Christ's flesh[†] is given for our healing—and the law of the flesh in which there is nothing at all spiritual? Where does this come from? It's because we are carnal, sold, conceived, brought forth, and, if I may speak of it, obtained by our parents under sin,[†] that is, in lusts that have their source in sin and the infirmity of the flesh. For the flesh does not understand what is good, nor does it desire it (for such belong to the mind and the spirit; not that the mind understands what is good or desires it by its own nature and will), and we perform our acts in this flesh. But the flesh is ill, so it is this infirmity rather than the flesh itself that appears to be acting in us. Healthy flesh imitates Christ's own flesh and never acts in such fashion, as a healthy woman never acts in a manner similar to a woman who is weak from childbearing or one in whom perhaps tumors or growths or hemorrhages are eating the flesh. COMMENTARY ON ROMANS (1517).[21]

ORDERING SIN AND LUST. THE ENGLISH ANNOTATIONS: These words seem to be contrary to the words of St. James, for St. James says "lust brings forth sin," but St. Paul here says that "sin brought forth, or wrought in him concupiscence."[†] But these may be easily reconciled, for they do not take the words in the same sense. For St. Paul, by "sin," as before has been shown, understands the corruption of our nature and proneness to sin, which produces in us actual lusts, called by him all kinds of concupiscence. But St. James by "lust" understands the depravity of our appetite, and by "sin," actual outward sins, in which sense we construe their words. The apostles are so far from contradicting each other that they both affirm the self-same thing, though differently expressed. ANNOTATIONS ON ROMANS 7:8.[22]

THE WHOLE LAW IS ABROGATED. JOHANNES BUGENHAGEN: "All kinds of coveting." That is, "I then began to have a conscience about the sinfulness of covetousness, for prior to that I did not know that it was sin; I thought that only external acts were prohibited by the law. But when I saw that even sinful affections are condemned, I began to hate the law." Hence those "great" interpreters of Scripture are to be laughed at who say that only the ceremonial law was abrogated by Christ. What benefit then would Christ bring us? Would his coming not then have been pointless? By Christ the *whole* law is abrogated, and unless it is also abrogated in us today by faith, we will be detained under its perpetual condemnation. The law says: "you shall not covet." Unless you see this law as being dead to you and abrogated by Christ—which, when it happens, you have an honest and transparent heart toward your neighbor, to whom if it were possible you would choose to pour yourself out entirely with all readiness and sense of duty—you will always hate God and will say that he gave a bad law. INTERPRETATION OF ROMANS (1531).[23]

---

[20]LW 77:112*; citing Rom 7:23.
[21]Lefèvre, *Epistole divi Pauli*, 67r-v. [†]That is, in the Eucharist. [†]A patristic concept according to which original sin is conveyed through the sinful desires of parents engaged in the act of conceiving.

[22]Downame, ed., *Annotations*, BBB1r*; citing Jas 1:15. [†]Sinful desire.
[23]Bugenhagen, *In D. Pauli ad Romanos*, 72v-73r.

THE ROMANS 7 MAN AND THE MAN WITH THE SPIRIT. FAUSTO SOZZINI:

The man of whom the apostle Paul speaks in Romans chapter 7:	The man endowed with the Spirit of Christ according to the apostle Paul's words, described:
1. In him sin produces all manner of lust (7:8).	1. He has crucified the flesh together with its stirrings and lusts (Gal 5:24).
2. In him sin so continues to live that it sells him into the bondage of death and kills him (7:9-11).	2. In him the body of sin (that is, sin itself) is so destroyed that he is dead to sin and sin no longer reigns in him, nor has dominion over him (6:2, 6, 11-12, 14).
3. This man is carnal (7:14)	3. This man is no longer in the flesh (7:5; 8:8-9)
4. This man is sold under sin (7:14).	4. This man is freed from sin (6:18, 22).
5. This man does not do the good that he wishes to do, but the evil he does not wish, that he does (7:19).	5. This man walks not according to the flesh, but according to the Spirit (8:1, 4), and by the Spirit he puts to death the deeds of the body (8:18).
6. This man is a captive of the law of sin (7:23)	6. This man is set free from the law of sin (8:2).
7. This man is hindered by this body of death (that is, by death itself) from which he miserably longs to be freed (7:24)	7. This man has been freed from the law of death (8:2).

DISPUTATIONS ON ROMANS 7 (1583).[24]

A JADE HORSE AND A STUBBORN CHILD.

EDWARD ELTON: We hold a horse to be a very jade[†] when the more he is spurred, the more he goes backward. And we hold a child to be a stubborn and desperate child if because his father wills him to do a thing he therefore sets himself against it, and the more earnest his father is to have him do it, the more backward he shows himself to the doing of it. Now this is the case of every one of us by nature. So sinful and so perverse is our nature that the more the Lord requires good duties at our hands, the more untoward we are to the doing of them; and the more any evil is forbidden, the more eagerly we desire it, and seek to do it, if we are left to ourselves. Therefore, do not think it does not matter if you are in your natural state and condition. As long as you are in that state, you are in a miserable state. And, therefore, finding yourself in that state and condition, hasten out of it and never rest until you have been renewed by grace and worked upon by the Spirit of grace and sanctification. THE COMPLAINT OF A SANCTIFIED SINNER (1618).[25]

7:9 I Died When Sin Came Alive

CHRIST KILLS SIN. PETER MARTYR VERMIGLI: "Sin," he says, "is alive again, and I am dead." Thus does he strongly consider the matter. When sin is dead, then we seem to ourselves to live. But when that thing has come alive once again, we immediately die, for we perceive God's wrath and damnation in us. And when the elect have died in this way, Christ wakes them up and kills the sin in them. Whatever the crime is, he pardons, and whatever remains of depraved desire, he shatters and destroys. Therefore, sin's death is twofold. One is not real, but an illusion, insofar as when the law is absent, sin is not recognized without the law, nor does it stir us up. The other death is the true death of sin, since it is killed by Christ, and since it is fastened to the very cross. COMMENTARY ON ROMANS (1560).[26]

THE LAW AND TRUE CONTRITION. MARTIN

LUTHER: This is true contrition. It suddenly attacks the heart and makes it afraid and

---

[24]Sozzini, *De Loco Pauli*, 16; citing Rom 6:2, 6, 11-12, 14, 18, 22; 7:5, 8, 9-11, 14, 19, 23, 24; 8:1, 2, 4, 8-9, 18; Gal 5:2.
[25]Elton, *The Complaint of a Sanctified Sinner*, 171-72*. [†]A worn-out horse.

[26]Vermigli, *In Epistolam S. Pauli*, 528-29.

alarmed, so that it feels God's wrath and condemnation lying on it and beings to know the real, strong, hidden sins, of which it previously did not know. Such a heart must now say: "Alas! What shall I do? There is nothing but sin and wrath here, which—sadly!—I did not know or think about before." St. Paul also speaks of the strength of the Word, which confronts us with God's wrath: "I was once alive apart from the law"; that is, I was arrogant and secure and knew neither sin nor God's wrath. But when the law came and struck my heart, then sin became alive, so that only then did I begin to sense God's wrath, and so I died, that is, experienced trembling, anguish, and trepidation, which I could not endure. I would have had to perish in eternal death, if I had not again been delivered. SUMMER POSTIL (APRIL 11, 1531).[27]

THE LAW WORKS TERROR; THE GOSPEL WORKS JOY.

EDWARD ELTON: It serves first, for the use of it, for us to discover the manifest differences between the law and the gospel in regard to the effects and workings of them: the law works terror, fear, and dread; and the gospel works comfort, joy, and peace. The law discovers sin and what sin deserves, wounds the soul, and works legal repentance, properly called penitence or contrition. This differs from evangelical repentance, that repentance that is wrought by the gospel, which is a turning from sin to God, or a thorough change of the purpose of heart, and the course of life, from evil to good. This is how the law differs from the gospel. And this is what deceives some; they cannot distinguish between these two. They cannot put a difference between penitence or contrition, which is the effect of the law, and repentance or turning from sin to God, or a thorough change of the purpose of heart, and course of life, from evil to good, which is the proper effect of the gospel. THE COMPLAINT OF A SANCTIFIED SINNER (1618).[28]

I WILL MAKE AN EXAMPLE OF MYSELF.

HEINRICH BULLINGER: But why are we anxious about this passage, when the apostle uses himself as his own example just so that we might more accurately and easily follow him as he enters into a difficult disputation? "I will make," he says, "an example of myself.' 'I once was alive apart from the law,' either because I was ignorant of the law's claims, or because while I led a Pharisee's life and was unaware that all men and women are accused by the law, I was quite pleased with myself and regarded myself as both righteous and holy. 'But when the commandment came'—that is, when the force of the law became known—'sin revived,' that is, as soon as the covetousness, hypocrisy and spiritual plague lurking in the dark recesses within my breast were detected, it became apparent what its true nature was in God's sight, and I came to truly know myself when I saw myself being exposed as a son of wrath and death. For what I perceived within myself was the lust of the flesh, of the eyes, of the hands, of the stomach, and an immense pride of life, from which nothing except despair of life could be born in me." COMMENTARY ON ROMANS (1533).[29]

THE TASTE OF HELL PRECEDES THE DESIRE OF HEAVEN.

JOHANNES BRENZ: Because they live without the law, that is, without the recognition of sin, they are hitherto distant from salvation. Indeed, there are so many generations that are as children, who are weak by nature; such are the men and women whom we call simple, who even by a simple recognition of sin, by faith in Christ—for apart from faith in Christ, there is no salvation—seek after salvation on account of Christ. But that is the customary and ordinary way of seeking salvation, that the one who desires heaven should first taste hell, and the one who reaches for the forgiveness of sins should first recognize their magnitude. Nor should he recognize only with a slight meditation of the heart or by words of the mouth, but with a perpetual sense of damnation. . . .

---

[27]LW 77:95*.
[28]Elton, *The Complaint of a Sanctified Sinner*, 206-7*.

[29]Bullinger, *In Sanctissimam Pauli*, 95v-96r.

Therefore, that we might cast out our fleshly carelessness, and that we might restrain what is in us, and in recognition of our sins, that we might walk in that way and regulation which arrives at true salvation, it is necessary that we have before us an eye set on the Decalogue, and that we diligently reflect on it, not that we might cling to it, but that by acknowledging sin, we might be stirred up in order to seek for the forgiveness of sin and the true salvation which is in Christ Jesus our Savior. COMMENTARY ON ROMANS (1588).[30]

THE LAW AND REASON AS THE OLD SERPENT.

PILGRAM MARPECK: The letter to the Romans testifies to this fact everywhere, namely, that the law and the commandments only work death in us, which otherwise is life in Christ Jesus. As soon as our devastated reason hears the proclamation of the law and the good commandments of God, she finds herself condemned under it, and would gladly keep the law in order to be saved, of which, however, our own fallen reason is not capable. Because reason herself presumed to be a god and lord, and to have the power that belongs to God alone, the ability to keep the law has been taken away. She imagines that she can be saved or condemned by her own power, and not by God's, who alone has all power. That is why God has likened our reason to the head of the serpent. This old serpent constantly resists God and now presumes to be saved through its own ability. Oh, how the poison of the serpent works its destruction in all humanity through presumptuousness! CONCERNING HASTY JUDGMENTS AND VERDICTS.[31]

7:10-11 The Law Was Death to Me

I AM UNABLE TO LOVE WITH ALL MY HEART.

JOHANNES BUGENHAGEN: "And I died." That is, "By means of the law I came to know sin and condemnation. Before then, I appeared to live holily, when I was 'living apart from the law.' But now that the law is revealed, I am no longer alive, for 'I died.'" That is, "I see that I am in contempt of the Word of God." For when the law said, "Love with all your heart," I am unable to do this. Therefore, it resulted in me being dead, that is, in not having any righteousness and being clearly condemned. INTERPRETATION OF ROMANS (1531).[32]

WHAT WAS LIFE, TO ME WAS DEATH. WOLF-

GANG MUSCULUS: "And the law was found." It is the justification and cleansing of the law, and the accusation of sin, as if to say: this is the perversity of sin, that the commandment that is for life, to me was for death. The emphasis in this place is on the pronoun, *to me*. For he is not saying simply that a commandment for death had been issued, but that it had come to him in practice. COMMENTARY ON ROMANS (1555).[33]

THE LAW IS THE POWER OF SIN. DAVID

PAREUS: "But sin, taking occasion": that he may even more vindicate the law from guilt, all the while repeating its lethal effects, from verse 8, Paul shows its cause in itself, and how through the ministry of the law it was, as it were, abused for its [sin's] products. Sin, he says, is the architect of evil. Taking the occasion given by the law, it (*exapataō me*) deceived me: that is, it urged me on to not observe the law, by persuading me that it would be easier to indulge my desires than to follow the commands of the law. And so "through the law, sin killed me," as if he were saying, therefore the sin, uncovered by the law, then on that occasion, excited by my depravity, won me over to death—not the law itself. Many times he emphasizes that it is sin that is properly and per se the cause of death, yet by occasion of the law. For the law is the standard of universal justice, and also the norm of particular distributive justice. But it requires these sinners to be punished. Apart from this, sin would go unpunished. Therefore, the law is called the power of sin. COMMENTARY ON ROMANS (1608).[34]

[30]Brenz, *In Epistolam*, 606-7.
[31]CRR 12:145-46*; citing Gen 3:5.

[32]Bugenhagen, *In D. Pauli ad Romanos*, 73v; citing Deut 6:5.
[33]Musculus, *In Epistolam Apostoli Pauli*, 151.
[34]Pareus, *In Divinam ad Romanos*, 632-33.

THE LAW KILLS. ERASMUS SARCERIUS: The law kills. That means that the law terrorizes, passes judgment on, and condemns the conscience on account of sin and the wrath of God concerning sin. And it disquiets and disturbs the conscience on account of sin and the wrath of God concerning sin. Truly, here the effect of the law does not begin quickly, unless sin has been already recognized by the law. Until the law reveals sins, judges, terrifies, condemns, and kills, it is not truly the law, it does not truly administer its own obligations. And from this effect of the law, one may gather the definition of the law. Therefore, the law is a killing doctrine, or one that kills. NOTES ON ROMANS (1541).[35]

ADAM AS A NOBLEMAN LOSING HIS FIEF. BALTHASAR HUBMAIER: After our first father Adam transgressed the commandment of God by his disobedience, he lost this freedom for himself and all his descendants. Likewise, if a nobleman receives a fief from a king and if he acts against the king, the king will take this fief from the nobleman and all his heirs, for they must all carry the guilt of their forefather. Thus the flesh has irretrievably lost its goodness and freedom through the fall of Adam and has become entirely and wholly worthless and hopeless unto death. It is not able or capable of anything other than sin, striving against God and being the enemy of his commandments. FREEDOM OF THE WILL.[36]

HOW TO ARM YOURSELF AGAINST THE SUBTLETIES OF YOUR DECEIVING HEART. EDWARD ELTON: Work to spy out the sleights and subtleties of your own deceiving heart, how your own heart is ready to join hands with the devil, to deceive you, and to draw you to the practice of sin by blinding your judgment, by the pleasure of sin, by the profits of the world, by turning away your mind from thinking of the punishment of sin seriously, and many other ways, and arm yourself against their subtleties and sleights, and endeavor to prevent them.

Perhaps you will ask me, How?

I answer, By these means:

First, get your judgment cleared in respect of yourself. Never rest until you are able to judge rightly of sin in yourself, by the Word of God.

Second, often meditate on and think of the fearful consequence and fruits of sin, such as the horror of a guilty conscience, anguish, fear, dread, trembling, amazement, a fearful expectation of God's wrath and vengeance, a standing subject to all the plagues and judgments of God in this world, and everlasting perdition in the life to come.

Third, remember that God's eye looks on you, and you are ever in his presence; and he sees you, wherever you are. Yes, he sees the very secrets of your heart.

Fourth, carry in you a godly jealousy and suspicion of yourself, lest your own deceitful heart should draw you to sin before you are aware. For "blessed is the one who always fears, but the one who hardens their heart shall fall into evil." And add to these frequent, earnest, and hearty prayer. Often and earnestly call on the Lord, that he would give you wisdom and strength against the strength and subtlety of your own deceiving heart.

And if you carefully use these means, you will find yourself in some good measure armed against the subtleties and sleights of your own deceiving heart and be able to prevent them. And therefore be careful in the use of these means, and know, whoever you are, that it is a work of your whole life to spy out the subtleties of your own deceiving heart and to arm yourself against them. And if you slack in this duty, sin will deceive you. Remember the example of David and Solomon; they were men of great wisdom and grace and yet slacking this duty. They were surprised by their own deceiving hearts and brought to the practice of sin. THE COMPLAINT OF A SANCTIFIED SINNER (1618).[37]

---

[35]Sarcerius, *In Apostolam ad Romanos*, C7r.
[36]CRR 5:433*.

[37]Elton, *The Complaint of a Sanctified Sinner*, 236-37*; citing Prov 28:14.

7:12 *The Law Is Holy, Righteous, and Good*

ALL SCRIPTURE TEACHES OUR DEPRAVITY OR GOD'S MERCY. PETER MARTYR VERMIGLI: If anyone asks what usefulness comes from the law—insofar as our cupidity is aroused by it, and it points out more serious sins and bears us on to death—he replies that it is that we might be openly acquainted with the wickedness of inborn depravity, which is very greatly entrenched in us, so that the best of God's laws is perniciously abused, so that that which was established for good now gives birth to destruction in us. Nor is it fitting to cling and remain fixed to this knowledge of our misery. For the more we know ourselves to be lost, the more we must fly with greater zeal to Christ, from whom alone we hope for our salvation, and the single remedy for our great calamity. And here is the scope of the whole of the holy Scripture, for everywhere either our depravity is shown, or the mercy of God through Christ is preached. COMMENTARY ON ROMANS (1560).[38]

THE EPITOME OF THE LAW. JOHANNES BRENZ: For there are two tablets of the law. The epitome of the first is: "You shall love the Lord your God with all your heart, with all your soul, and with all your strength." Nothing can be commanded in God's worship that is more perfect or more complete than this. In this are demanded all works of service to God that are perfectly pure, righteous, and holy. "With all," it says, "your heart, with all your soul, with all your strength." The epitome of the second table is: "You shall love your neighbor as yourself." Once again, in this there is nothing omitted that pertains to perfect justice being rendered to one's neighbor. COMMENTARY ON ROMANS (1564).[39]

PAUL'S CLEAR CONSCIENCE DID NOT SAVE HIM. PETER MARTYR VERMIGLI: Lest you say that Paul was removed or rescued from these sins when he began to zealously attack the teachings of the law—in which he was so proficient that he could neither be accused nor killed by it—he himself asserts in the letter to Titus that he had been justified by Christ alone and absolved by the blessing of the Holy Spirit. He says this because before he had come to Christ, knowledge of the law could only have killed him. He says so because the kindness and humanity of God our Protector began to shine not from the works of righteousness which we performed, but because he saved us because of his mercy, through the washing of regeneration, and by the renewal of the Holy Spirit, whom he most abundantly poured out on us through Jesus Christ our Protector, so that having been justified by his grace, we might be made heirs according to the hope of eternal life. And on this subject he wrote to Timothy that he had "served God from his forefathers with a clear conscience," so that one could answer: although he did not have a protesting conscience, nevertheless this did not free him from sin. COMMENTARY ON ROMANS (1560).[40]

THE SCRIPTURES ARE ABOVE THE CHURCH. EDWARD ELTON: This property of the Word of God, the purity and holiness of it, is one infallible note and mark by which we may know and be persuaded that it is the very Word of God. This one note, even if we had no other, carries with it and contains in it sufficient evidence against all contradiction, that it is from God, and has a sacred authority in itself, and depends not on the church or the pope as the Catholics teach. The Scripture is holy and pure, like God himself. And therefore certainly it is of God and from God. It is not the testimony and tradition of the church that is able to resolve and settle the conscience which is Scripture and which is not, as the Catholics teach. No, no: the testimony of the church is inferior to the evidence of the Scripture. For the Scripture points out the church and contains in it the true notes of the church. Yes, the Scripture—as an instrument and means—sanctifies the church and

---

[38]Vermigli, *In Epistolam S. Pauli*, 531-32.
[39]Brenz, *In Epistolam*, 171-72; citing Deut 6:5; Lev 19:18.
[40]Vermigli, *In Epistolam S. Pauli*, 534; citing Tit 3:4-7; 2 Tim 1:3.

members of it. THE COMPLAINT OF A SANCTIFIED SINNER (1618).[41]

7:13 It Was Sin That Brought Death

THE LAW MAKES SIN APPEAR EVEN MORE SEVERE. WOLFGANG MUSCULUS: Paul relates the reasoning of the divine plan, why God desired to give the law, by which occasion sin was not taken away but rather grew more abundant and long-living. Therefore, he says, "that it might appear," that is that it should become evident and plain how strong and wicked sin is. That is, that we are so corrupted and crooked that even that which is good is unable to cure us of our evil, but it rather drives us toward death. Therefore, it was necessary that sin be represented as exceedingly sinful through the law; that is, it was necessary that the preeminence of sin's evil become clear by the opportunity of the law. For in fact, the depravity of a sickness must be great if the medicine not only does nothing to cure it, but

also causes it to return even more severely. COMMENTARY ON ROMANS (1555).[42]

SUNLIGHT BOTH ILLUMINATES AND BLINDS. JOHANNES BRENZ: The sun is an immensely brilliant part of creation and sheds light on the whole world. However, it blinds the eyes that are fixed directly on its brilliance. How, I ask, does it happen that it has this effect on eyes gazing on it, when blindness is so completely contrary to its nature? Certainly it doesn't happen due to some defect of the sun, but rather due to the defect of feeble eyes. Similarly, Christ is the very light of the world, "illuminating every one coming into the world." And he says, "I have come into this world for judgment, that those who do not see might see, and those who do see might become blind." Consider this: from Christ who is Light itself comes blindness! How so? It is not because of a defect in Christ, but because of the defect of the unbelief of men and women. COMMENTARY ON ROMANS (1564).[43]

---

[41]Elton, *The Complaint of a Sanctified Sinner*, 253-54*.

[42]Musculus, *In Epistolam Apostoli Pauli*, 252.
[43]Brenz, *In Epistolam*, 172; citing Jn 1:9; 9:39.

7:14-25 THE LAW AND THE WAR WITHIN

¹⁴*For we know that the law is spiritual, but I am of the flesh, sold under sin.* ¹⁵*For I do not understand my own actions. For I do not do what I want, but I do the very thing I hate.* ¹⁶*Now if I do what I do not want, I agree with the law, that it is good.* ¹⁷*So now it is no longer I who do it, but sin that dwells within me.* ¹⁸*For I know that nothing good dwells in me, that is, in my flesh. For I have the desire to do what is right, but not the ability to carry it out.* ¹⁹*For I do not do the good I want, but the evil I do not want is what I keep on doing.* ²⁰*Now if I do what I do not want, it is no longer I who do it, but sin that dwells within me.*

²¹*So I find it to be a law that when I want to do right, evil lies close at hand.* ²²*For I delight in the law of God, in my inner being,* ²³*but I see in my members another law waging war against the law of my mind and making me captive to the law of sin that dwells in my members.* ²⁴*Wretched man that I am! Who will deliver me from this body of death?* ²⁵*Thanks be to God through Jesus Christ our Lord! So then, I myself serve the law of God with my mind, but with my flesh I serve the law of sin.*

OVERVIEW: Most of the reformers believe that when referring here to his struggles with sin, Paul is speaking of himself as a regenerate person. There are a few dissenting voices, such as Sozzini (Socinus) and Arminius, who argue that he is referring to himself as he was while still under the law.

The commentators then explore what it means to be carnal/flesh/fleshly, both before and after regeneration. They then examine the battle between flesh and spirit/Spirit/the spiritual. True believers may fall into sin, as David did with Bathsheba, but they will not dwell in it, and they repent and turn from it. The interpreters differentiate the Christian, flesh/spirit model from the Aristotelian, philosophical model that sees the higher part of a human mind being good and the coarser parts inferior. Philosophy elevates reason, whereas the Pauline model sees all parts of the person, including reason, as being in conflict with the Spirit.

The reformers encourage the believer to seek after Christ, to cry out to him, to take encouragement from the fact that even Paul struggled with sin, and to keep persevering in overcoming sin. We have the will to do good, but our sinful natures fight against that. Thankfully, we have the Holy Spirit in us, who can help us overcome our sinful natures and help our new self triumph over our old self. Our deliverance comes from one Mediator, Christ—in contrast to medieval piety's involvement of Mary and other saints—and it is to him that we must give thanks. The knowledge that the God who is the crucified Christ's Father is our Father too propels us into the battle against sin and fills us with joy.

7:14 The Law Is Spiritual; We Are of the Flesh

RECONCILING ROMANS 7:14 WITH JOHN 3:6.
FRIEDRICH BALDUIN: Q: How can Paul write of himself, being regenerate, "I am carnal," since Christ says in John 3:6 that "whatever is born of the flesh is flesh"? But Paul, since he is regenerate, is born not of flesh but of God.

A: I answer that that saying of Christ is true with respect to nature that is not yet regenerate—it is entirely and wholly carnal, corrupt, and therefore an enemy of God, no matter how wise one might be in the things of this world and no matter how many moral deeds they might perform. Paul, however, is born of God according to that aspect of him that is regenerate, and to that degree he is called "not carnal." But because the regeneration of a man or woman is imperfect and many blemishes still adhere to the regenerate that they will at last put off only when they quit this mortal life, therefore according to this aspect by which they still struggle against the law of the Lord, they are called "carnal." Accordingly, the Corinthians were "saints," but when they indulged in contentions and immoderate zeal, they are called "carnal": and said to walk after the manner of humans. In short, a man or woman is called "carnal" in two senses: (1) insofar as they serve, consent to and delight in sin; and it is in this sense that those yet unregenerate are carnal; (2) insofar as one still experiences the illicit desires of the flesh, against which the spirit of the mind struggles, and in this sense even the regenerate are "carnal." The former are so completely, whereas the latter are so only in part; the former are called "flesh," while the latter are called merely "fleshly." The entire self will be spiritual only when the body itself becomes spiritual, that is, in the age to come. COMMENTARY ON ROMANS (1620).[1]

THE LAW REQUIRES THE HOLY SPIRIT. JOHANNES BRENZ: Right up front, Paul says that the law is "spiritual," since in order to bring about perfect righteousness, it requires the Holy Spirit within a person. It also requires not only external works of piety, but also every internal affection that is of the Spirit and entirely holy. "You shall love," it says, "God with all your heart," and "You shall not covet." This is what the law really requires. COMMENTARY ON ROMANS (1564).[2]

WILLS AND AFFECTIONS LIKE BLOOD-WARM WATER. ANTHONY CADE: These words bring to a close the discourse of that troublesome combat (which Saint Paul describes from the thirteenth verse) between the flesh and the Spirit. That is, between our natural corruption lusting one way, and God's Holy Spirit moving us another way. For in this life our understanding is enlightened only in part ("now we see but as through a glass darkly").

So our wills and affections are only partly reformed, following very weakly that little which we see ("We cannot do the things that we would"). Our corruptions, though abated, are not yet extinguished by regeneration. Rather, our mind and will continue still partly flesh and partly spirit, that is, partly grace and partly corruption. A reformation begun, but not finished, like the air in the dawning of the day, neither wholly yet enlightened, nor wholly remaining dark; or blood-warm water, neither perfectly hot nor perfectly cold. But the light and darkness of the mind, the heat and cold of the will, so mixed and intermeddled together throughout, that there is a continual strife between them, which shall overcome the other, and overrun the soul. This combat the apostle describes most movingly and feelingly in his own person, finding his own soul (as it were) distracted into two contrary factions, and subject to two contrary rulers, and guided by two contrary laws (as a ship tossed by two contrary winds or tides). The inner person (or regenerate part) ever eyeing the law of God and striving for perfection, but hindered by another law in his members (the unregenerate part) rebelling against the law of his mind, and striving both against his will, and against his knowledge to carry him away to sin, so hindering the good which he would do and drawing him to the evil which he would not do. He repeats this again in the following verse, as a thing never observed enough. At last, as one amazed and much astonished to find so much imperfection in himself, he breaks out into this passionate exclamation, "O wretched man that I am, who shall deliver me from the body of this death?" SAINT PAUL'S AGONY (1618).[3]

SLAVES OF SIN. JOHANNES BRENZ: We must consider the customs observed by the ancients in the sale of lands, or even of slaves. Power over that which is sold to another is totally transferred to that other to whom it is sold, nor is it any longer the care of the seller. Just so, humanity was sold to sin as a

---

[1]Balduin, *Catechesis Apostolica*, 484-85; citing Jn 3:6; 1 Cor 3:3.
[2]Brenz, *In Epistolam*, 173; citing Deut 6:5; Ex 20:17.
[3]Cade, *Saint Paul's Agony*, 1-3*; citing 1 Cor 13:12.

result of Adam's sin. For after Adam sinned, he was deprived of the Holy Spirit and handed over to captivity and enslavement to sin. But with our first parent being sold into foreign servitude, all his posterity that were present in the body of that parent are likewise sold into servitude of sin, so that they not only have sin in them, they are also the very slaves of sin. COMMENTARY ON ROMANS (1564).[4]

WE REMAIN PARTIALLY CARNAL. JOHANNES BRENZ: But whoever is a slave of sin, because he is slave to a foreign power, holds the Holy Spirit to be of little account, nor does he bother himself further concerning him. Nevertheless, the Holy Spirit does not abandon *his* care in converting ungodly men and women to true godliness. We obtain the firstfruits of the Holy Spirit by the grace of God through the gospel on account of Christ— and yet we remain by nature the slaves of sin as long as we live this bodily life. For nature is not abolished even if we receive the firstfruits of the Spirit through the gospel. For this reason, because those born again in Christ remain in their nature slaves to sin, they are still rightly said to be in a certain manner "carnal." COMMENTARY ON ROMANS (1564).[5]

THE FLESH AND THE SPIRIT.
ANNE BRADSTREET:

In secret place where once I stood
Close by the banks of Lacrim flood
I heard two sisters reason on
Things that are past and things to come.
One Flesh was call'd, who had her eye
On worldly wealth and vanity;
The other Spirit, who did rear
Her thoughts unto a higher sphere.
"Sister," quotes Flesh, "what live you on
Nothing but Meditation?
Doth Contemplation feed you so
Regardlessly to let earth go?
Can Speculation satisfy

Notion without Reality?
Do you dream of things beyond the Moon
And do you hope to dwell there soon?
Have treasures there laid up in store
That all in th' world you count but poor?
Art fancy-sick or turn'd a Sot
To catch at shadows which are not?
Come, come. I'll show unto your sense,
Industry has its recompense.
What can you desire, but you may see
True substance in variety?
Do you honor like? Acquire the same,
As some to their immortal fame;
And trophies to your name erect
Which wearing time shall ne'er deject.
For riches do you long full sore?
Behold enough of precious store.
Earth has more silver, pearls, and gold
Than eyes can see or hands can hold.
Affects your pleasure? Take your fill.
Earth has enough of what you will.
Then let not go what you may find
For things unknown only in mind."
Spirit: Be still, you unregenerate part,
Disturb no more my settled heart,
For I have vow'd (and so will do)
You as a foe still to pursue.
And combat with you will and must,
Until I see you laid in th' dust.
Sisters we are, yea twins we be,
Yet deadly feud 'twixt you and me;
For from one father are we not,
You by old Adam wast begot,
But my arise is from above,
Whence my dear father I do love.
You speaks me fair, but hat'st me fore,
Your flatt'ring shows I'll trust no more.
How oft your slave have you me made,
When I believed what you have said,
And never had more cause of woe
Than when I did what you bad'st do.
I'll stop mine ears at these your charms,
And count them for my deadly harms.
Your sinful pleasures I do hate,
Your riches are to me no bait,

---

[4]Brenz, *In Epistolam*, 174.
[5]Brenz, *In Epistolam*, 174.

Your honors do, nor will I love;
For my ambition lies above.
My greatest honor it shall be
When I am victor over you,
And triumph shall, with laurel head,
When you my captive shall be led,
How I do live, you need'st not scoff,
For I have meat you know not of;
The hidden Manna I do eat,
The word of life it is my meat.
My thoughts do yield me more content
Than can your hours in pleasure spent.
Nor are they shadows which I catch,
Nor fancies vain at which I snatch.
But reach at things that are so high
Beyond your dull capacity;
Eternal substance I do see,
With which enriched I would be:
Mine eye does pierce the heavens, and see
What is invisible to you.
My garments are not silk nor gold,
Nor such like trash which Earth does hold.
But royal robes I shall have on,
More glorious than the glistering Sun;
My crown not diamonds, pearls, and gold.
But such as angels heads infold.
The city where I hope to dwell,
There's none on earth can parallel;
The stately walls both high and strong,
Are made of precious jasper stone;
The gates of pearl, both rich and clear,
And angels are for porters there;
The streets therof transparent gold,
Such as no eye did e're behold,
A crystal river there does run,
Which does proceed from the Lamb's Throne.
Of Life, there are the water sure,
Which shall remain for ever pure,
Nor Sun, nor Moon, they have no need,
For glory does from God proceed:
No candle there, nor yet torch light,
For there shall be no darksome night.
From sickness and infirmity,
For evermore they shall be free,
Nor withering age shall e're come there,

But beauty shall be bright and clear;
This city pure is not for you,
For things unclean there shall not be:
If I of Heaven may have my fill,
Take you the world, and all that will.

THE FLESH AND THE SPIRIT (BEFORE 1650).[6]

PAUL IS SPEAKING OF THE REGENERATE.
JOHANNES BRENZ: He explains in what way he is "carnal." But it must again be observed that Paul here speaks not of the ungodly, but of himself, in the condition in which he was *after* his conversion to Christ, and in which all the saints are who still live their life in this world. For they who are not yet born again to Christ by faith do not have within themselves any such fight between the Spirit and flesh such as Paul depicts, since they lack the Spirit and are therefore so dominated by the flesh that they live entirely according to the flesh. Therefore, in this passage Paul is speaking of the saints, or those who believe in Christ. COMMENTARY ON ROMANS (1564).[7]

THE LAW IS SPIRITUAL. HULDRYCH ZWINGLI: "The law is spiritual." He now begins to describe the war between the flesh and the spirit that is waged within believers. The law is not to blame for my failure. The reason why it is "spiritual" is that if we could keep the law in its entirety and carry it out fully according to the divine will, we would live. But this is impossible for the flesh. "The law is spiritual but I am carnal"; that is, I am nothing but flesh. Using himself, he sketches a picture of all men and women. "And I am sold under sin"—that is, he is wholly sold into slavery to and given over to sin, that is, to the old self, to death, and to the corrupt Adamic nature, entirely inclining toward doing evil. Note that "to be sold under sin" is to be completely given over to sin. "The law is spiritual," which I cannot attain to since I am carnal." If Adam had kept the first law, he would not have

---

[6]Bradstreet, *Works of Anne Bradstreet*, 381-85*; citing Rev 21:10-27; 22:1-5.
[7]Brenz, *In Epistolam*, 174.

been cast out of Paradise. If we could keep the law, we would be righteous. But we do not keep it, because we are sold under sin. Therefore, we cannot be righteous by our own strength, but we do obtain righteousness by Christ. Notes on Romans (1539).[8]

Paul Is Referring to One Under the Law, Not Grace. Jacobus Arminius: Having, in the preceding manner, considered the disposition and economy of the whole chapter, let us now somewhat more strictly investigate the question proposed by us, which is this: "Are those things that are recorded, from the fourteenth verse to the end of the seventh chapter, to be understood concerning a man who is under the law, or concerning one who is under grace?"

First of all, let some attention be bestowed on the connection of the fourteenth verse with those that preceded it; for the rational particle *gar*, "for," indicates its connection with the preceding. This connection shows that the same subject is discussed in this verse, as in those before it; and the pronoun *ego*, "I," must be understood as relating to the same man, as had been signified in the previous verses by the same pronoun. But the investigation in the former part of the chapter was respecting "a man who is under the law," and the pronoun "I" had previously denoted the man who was under the law: Therefore, in this fourteenth verse also, in which a cause is given of that which had been before explained, a man under the law is still the subject. If it were otherwise, the whole of it is nothing less than loose reasoning; nor, in this case, have we ever been able to perceive even any probable connection, according to which these consequences that follow can be in coherence with the matters preceding, and which has been adduced by those who suppose that, in the first thirteen verses of this seventh chapter, the discourse refers to a man under the law, but that in the fourteenth verse and those that follow, the subject of the discourse is a

man under grace. If any one denies this, let him attempt to make out the connection between the two portions of the chapter that have just been specified. Some of those who have entertained that opinion, perceiving the difficulty of such an undertaking, interpret this fourteenth verse as well as those that preceded it, as relating to a man under the law, but the fifteenth and following verses as applicable to a man under grace. This, also, we shall hereafter perceive.

Second, in the same fourteenth verse, that man about whom the apostle treats under his own person is said to be carnal; but a man who is regenerate and placed under grace is not carnal, but spiritual. Therefore, it is a matter of the greatest certainty that the subject of the apostle in this verse is not a man placed under grace. But a man who is under the law is carnal; therefore, it is plain that the subject of discourse in this verse is a man under the law. I prove that a regenerate man, one who is placed under grace, is neither carnal, nor designated so in the Scriptures. In Romans 8:9, it is said "but you are not in the flesh, but in the Spirit." And in the verse preceding, it is said, "so then they that are in the flesh cannot please God." But a regenerate man, one who is placed under grace, pleases God. In Romans 8:5 it is said, "They that are after the flesh do mind the things of the flesh," but as it is expressed in the same verse, a man under grace "minds the things of the Spirit." In Galatians 5:24, it is said, "They that are Christ's have crucified the flesh, with the affections and lusts"; and they that "have crucified the flesh" are not carnal. But men and women who are regenerate and placed under grace "are Christ's and have crucified the flesh." Therefore, such men as answer this description are not carnal. In Romans 8:14 it is said, "As many as are led by the Spirit of God, they are the sons of God." Therefore, they are "led by the Spirit of God"; but such persons are spiritual. Dissertation on Romans 7 (c. 1599).[9]

[8]Zwingli, *In Evangelicam Historiam*, 424; citing Is 52:3; 2 Kings 21:1-26.

[9]Arminius, *Works*, 2:245-47*; citing Rom 8:9, 5; Gal 5:24; Rom 8:14.

PAUL IS NOT REFERRING TO A REGENERATE

MAN. JACOBUS ARMINIUS'S NINE CHILDREN: In this number of abused passages is included the seventh chapter of the letter of Paul to the Romans, from the fourteenth verse to the end of the chapter, that is, if the apostle be understood in that chapter to be speaking about a man who is regenerated. For then it will follow that a renewed man or woman is still "carnal and sold under sin," that is, the slave of sin; that "he wills to do good, but does it not." . . . If this view of that chapter is correct, then all attention to piety, the whole of new obedience, and thus the entire new creation will be reduced to such narrow limits as to consist not in effects, but only in affections or feelings. Every man and woman, at first sight, perceives how languid, cold, and remiss such a belief would render all of us, both in our abstaining from evil, and in the performance of that which is good. DEDICATION TO THEIR FATHER'S DISSERTATION ON ROMANS 7 (1612).[10]

PAUL IS REFERRING TO A REGENERATE

PERSON. JOHN CALVIN: He now comes to a more particular case, that of a person already regenerated, in whom both the things that he had in view appear more clearly. These show the great discord there is between the law of God and the natural person, and how the law does not of itself produce death. For since carnal people rush into sin with the whole propensity of their mind, they seem to sin with such a free choice, as though it were in their power to govern themselves. Thus a most pernicious opinion has prevailed almost among all people, that persons, by their own natural strength, without the aid of divine grace, can choose what they please. But though the wills of faithful people are led to good by the Spirit of God, yet in them the corruption of nature appears conspicuously, for it obstinately resists and leads to what is contrary. Hence the case of a regenerated person is most suitable, for by this you may know how much is the contrariety between our nature and the

righteousness of the law. COMMENTARY ON ROMANS 7:15.[11]

SOLD INTO SLAVERY BY ORIGINAL SIN. PETER

MARTYR VERMIGLI: When he calls himself carnal, he means that he was infected with original sin and corruption. For that evil is derived from Adam through the flesh, yet it is itself not confined to the flesh, but it overtakes the entire self and all of its strength. And in order to demonstrate more clearly what the term "carnal" means, he prefers to add "sold under sin." For as slaves are often drawn or are impelled by a master to that which they were unwilling, thus we are carried off by original sin toward many things that we do not sanction. COMMENTARY ON ROMANS (1560).[12]

DON'T JUDGE SOMEONE FOR SLIPPING. ED-

WARD ELTON: The dearest saints and servants of God that live in the world still have inbred corruption in part abiding in them. And though they are freed by the power of grace that is in them from the full force and strength of it, and from a willing subjection to it, yet they are still in part in thralldom, and in bondage under it. And sometimes it overwhelms them by its strength and makes them yield at times to its evil motions and lusts. Sometimes it strikes them and wounds them and gives them such a blow of such a sort that its points and strokes are seen and appear openly even to the view of the world. And therefore we are not to judge them harshly because of some slip and some failing or because sometimes they are overtaken by some sin. No, take this for a general and certain rule: we are not to judge any person to be good or bad by any one or few acts, but by their walking, and by the course of their life. If the course of their life is carnal, earthly, and sensual, certainly then they are a carnal person, and we may so judge them. If the course of their life is holy and such as it ought to be, then doubtless they are holy, and their state is good, and we may so judge of

---

[11]CTS 38:261-62* (CO 49:129).

[12]Vermigli, *In Epistolam S. Pauli*, 536.

[10]Arminius' *Works*, 2:209-10*.

them, though sometimes they fail, and be sometimes overtaken by some sin. THE COMPLAINT OF A SANCTIFIED SINNER (1618).[13]

THE NECESSITY OF CHRIST NOT BEING A SLAVE TO SIN. PETER MARTYR VERMIGLI: Suppose there were someone who was willing to redeem us, would it not be necessary for him to be free from the common master whom we serve, that is, free from sin? I believe it would be. For otherwise, whatever he might obtain would be bound by sin, to which the redeemer would still be a slave. But no one can be found free from sin, except only our Lord Jesus Christ. Therefore, whoever desires to be free from sin must go to him. COMMENTARY ON ROMANS (1560).[14]

THE LAW IS SPIRITUAL IN TWO WAYS. PETER MARTYR VERMIGLI: It is called the spiritual law for two reasons: the first is that it was not devised by human counsel as civil laws, but it was written when at Mount Sinai God himself was speaking through his Spirit to Moses. Therefore, it is called spiritual because it proceeds from the Spirit as its author. It is also called spiritual because it is not satisfied with external actions but extends to the will, the mind, the senses, and the inmost movements of men and women. And it orders us to obey it with our entire soul and spirit. For which reason they are disgracefully mistaken who distinguish the old law from the new, thinking the old is confined only to the hand, while the new extends also to the affection of the mind. For those who only observe an outward righteousness must not be considered to be satisfying the old law. COMMENTARY ON ROMANS (1560).[15]

THE SPIRIT OF THE LAW ACCORDS WITH THE GOSPEL. DIRK PHILIPS: Therefore the gospel and the law are divided so far as the figures, shadows, and letter of the law are concerned or involved, which are all removed through the

gospel. But it is because of this that one observes the spirit of the law (for the law is also spiritual, as Paul says). So we discover that the meaning, content, and actual understanding of the law accords with the gospel in every way and corresponds with it, yes, is one truth. For just as there is not more than one God, so also there is not more than one truth: for God himself is the truth. But the letter (in which the truth is hidden) will indeed come to an end. Thus that literal command of the Lord about the circumcision of the flesh has come to an end. Nevertheless, that command of the spiritual circumcision of the heart thus remains. Yes, thus have all the figures of the law (which are too long to relate here) come to an end so far as the letter is concerned. Nevertheless, the genuine and essential significance of these same figures remains and harmonizes with the gospel. THE TABERNACLE OF MOSES.[16]

7:15 I Do What I Do Not Want to Do

DAVID'S STRUGGLE OVER BATHSHEBA. MARTIN BUCER: When David saw Bathsheba, his flesh recognized a pleasurable prospect and was inflamed with depraved lust. An awareness of the law in his mind was protesting against this lust, reminding him that it was wicked adultery and destruction for the one committing it. But the judgment of his physical senses was telling him the contrary, that this woman was elegant, and that it would be a delightful thing to enjoy her. This reasoning of the senses was striving to convince him that that which gives delight is to be sought after. But the reasoning of the mind illuminated by the law is this: that which is an abomination to God and fraud against one's neighbor is destructive and to be fled from. But whereas the proposition that even to ask for this wife of your neighbor is an abomination to God and fraud against your neighbor should have been taken to heart, the power of lust prevailed and was taken in under the other proposition: that it would be delightful to

---

[13]Elton, *The Complaint of a Sanctified Sinner*, 309-10*.
[14]Vermigli, *In Epistolam S. Pauli*, 539-40.
[15]Vermigli, *In Epistolam S. Pauli*, 536.

[16]CRR 6:268*; citing Rom 2:29; Col 2:11.

enjoy such an elegant woman. Some consideration of this kind—that it would be a pleasure to enjoy such a woman, by the power of lust that had already inflamed his entire body—prevailed to such a point that the consideration that Bathsheba was the wife of another man and therefore must not even be desired was weakened and gave place to the passion of lust until that passion had passed and the law was restored in his soul by Nathan. At that time the consideration was restored to David that there was nothing so destructive and to be so zealously avoided than what he had done, and that he had done something that God opposed and that was fraud against his neighbor. He then came to have a sense of nothing but God's displeasure—that is, of eternal death, the very fire of hell. David's soul then came under a loathing not only of that which he had done, but also of himself, since all the while that he was indeed taking it on himself to seek after illicit embraces, he was also being impelled by the power of that lust that burned within him.

Therefore, David committed that evil that he detested, while with his mind he agreed with the law. And since he did not do it by the free judgment of his mind but rather by being assaulted by violent lust, it was not he himself as a man, nor as a man taught in the law of God that he did it, but it was the sin present in his flesh that did it. That depraved and profligate nature that is against God and all that is pleasing to God was carried away by sin. Hence it came to pass that he did that which he at the same time both willed and did not will. It was something he did *not* will—not, of course, at the time that he was doing it, but—while the consideration of the divine law remained intact, and again when it was restored in him. And it was something he *did* will, when he resolved and decided to put into action his desire for the woman set before him. COMMENTARY ON ROMANS (1536).[17]

A REMINDER THAT WE CANNOT RELY ON OUR RIGHTEOUSNESS. JOHANNES BRENZ: These are mutually opposed to each other, so that whatever you should not desire, this is the same thing that you do. That is, contrary to the Spirit, you do not perfectly and actually obey the law of God to the extent that you desire. These things must be diligently learned in order that we might know how imperfect human righteousness is and, indeed, what things must be like in order to move forward in the calling and obedience of God. But here our righteousness must not be relied on. You see, therefore, how necessary Christ is to us, on account of whom we have the forgiveness of sin, which is our chief righteousness, not by works, but by an unwavering faith. COMMENTARY ON ROMANS (1564).[18]

SIN ADHERES TO US. MARTIN BUCER: It is sin, which even now still adheres to us, that does these things. For those of us who have already now begun to live the life of Christ, not we, but sin, will eventually be destroyed and abolished by the Spirit of Christ. But because it is true that evil is never committed by us without us in the end giving our consent, and that we invite it in (which the Scriptures everywhere testify), he threatens us with the punishment it deserves. But this judgment will ultimately be abolished through Jesus Christ and the new self will prevail, clothed in him. Paul rightly pronounces over us the judgment that is according to this grace, which will prevail and prove more eternal than that judgment that is according to this present death and slavery to sin, which, even though it still adheres to us, will nevertheless shortly after be completely removed and vanish from us.

From these considerations I think that it is clear how a man, Paul, wills to do what he does not do, and does what he detests, and how also it is and is not he who does what is evil, and also in which men and women such things happen in the same way. COMMENTARY ON ROMANS (1536).[19]

---

[17]Bucer, *Metaphrases et Enarrationes*, 325.

[18]Brenz, *In Epistolam*, 175-76.
[19]Bucer, *Metaphrases et Enarrationes*, 326-27.

Paul Is Referring to a Regenerate Person.

John Calvin: He now comes to a more particular case, that of a man already regenerated, in whom both the things which he had in view appear more clearly. These were the great discord there is between the law of God and the natural man, and how the law does not of itself produce death. For since the carnal man rushes into sin with the whole propensity of his mind, he seems to sin with such a free choice, as though it were in his power to govern himself. Thus a most pernicious opinion has prevailed almost among all men, that man, by his own natural strength, without the aid of divine grace, can choose what he pleases. But though the will of a faithful man is led to good by the Spirit of God, yet in him the corruption of nature appears conspicuously, for it obstinately resists and leads to what is contrary. Hence the case of a regenerated man is most suitable, for by this you may know how much is the contrariety between our nature and the righteousness of the law. Commentary on Romans.[20]

True Believers May Fall Into Sin but Do Not Persevere in It.

Edward Elton: I briefly answer the propounded question this way: That children of God, and ones that are truly regenerate, may give in so much to the lusts of their own hearts that they may delight in them. Yes, they may consent to them, though not ordinarily, nor wholly, but at some times, and then only in part. And they may sometimes—not ordinarily, but sometimes—proceed to the act and execution of lust. Yet so—as they may truly say—they hate the evil they do. Yes, sometimes being suddenly surprised by the violence of temptation and the strength of their own corruptions, they may fall into some particular, foul, and gross evil and sin. But to persevere in the act of evil and to hold on a course in doing evil with pleasure, that is never found in any child of God and one that is truly regenerate. And thus we see

this truth confirmed and cleared, that true believers and those that are truly regenerate are sometimes drawn by the strength of their own corruption, still in part abiding in them, to do that evil that is hateful to them. They are sometimes over-carried to the doing of even that evil they in part loathe and abhor. The Complaint of a Sanctified Sinner (1618).[21]

Paul Is Referring to an Unregenerate Person.

Jacobus Arminius: He who does not approve of what he does, and does not do what he wishes, is the slave of another, that is, of sin. But the man about whom the apostle is writing does not approve of that which he does, nor does what he wishes, but he does that which he hates. Therefore, the man who is the subject of discussion in this passage is the slave of another, that is, of sin. And therefore, the same man is unregenerate, and not placed under grace. Dissertation on Romans 7 (c. 1599).[22]

The Comfort That Paul Also Did the Evil That He Hated.

Edward Elton: This being a truth, the use of it is for comfort; it serves as a ground of comfort to God's children in relation to their falling sometimes into some sin. Do you find—you that are a child of God—that you are sometimes drawn by the strength of your own corruption still in part abiding in you, to do that evil that is hateful to you? Are you sometimes carried too far to do that evil you in part loathe and abhor? It is no different with you than it was with the holy apostle Paul; he did the evil he hated. And it is no different with you than with others of the dearest saints and servants of God. Thus it has been with them, and thus it is with true believers and such as are truly regenerate. They are sometimes drawn by the strength of their own corruption to do that evil that is hateful to them. The Complaint of a Sanctified Sinner (1618).[23]

---

[20]CTS 38:261-62* (CO 49:129).

[21]Elton, *The Complaint of a Sanctified Sinner*, 314*.
[22]Arminius, *Works*, 2:253*.
[23]Elton, *The Complaint of a Sanctified Sinner*, 314*.

7:16 The Law Is Good

THE DIVINE LAW IS GOOD. NIELS HEMMING-SEN: He sums up the defense of the law from what has been said. Divine law requires that which the will reformed by the Spirit of God approves. Therefore the divine law is good. For it is evident that those commands are best that most closely agree with the Spirit of God and with the will of the man or woman who has been renewed and reformed by the Spirit of God. COMMENTARY ON ROMANS (1562).[24]

THE TESTIMONY OF ONE WHO HAS TRANS-GRESSED THE LAW. WOLFGANG MUSCULUS: He now draws conclusions from the preceding premises. He first infers that the innocence of the law of God is as pure as that of his law that is internal to man and woman, dismissing all accusation of evil from either of these laws. It is as if he were saying, "By the very fact that contrary to the law I repeatedly yield, unwillingly, to the very evil that I detest, it is clear that I bear witness to the sanctity, goodness, and righteousness of the law of God, as a good thing that admonishes my conscience. How then could I bring an accusation of evil against it?"

But the most powerful testimony that is given concerning the law—the affirmation that it is good, holy, and righteous—is the one that comes from one who has trespassed against it. For by this it is shown that the goodness of the law is so incontrovertible and obvious that not only those who do not sin against it, but even sinners are forced to acknowledge its goodness, even when they sin against it, whatever manner of offense against it they may be guilty of. Notice how effectively Paul rids himself of the suspicion that he was being hounded by: that he allegedly despised and condemned the law of God. COMMENTARY ON ROMANS (1555).[25]

7:17 The Sin Within Me Does It

THE TWOFOLD SELF. JOHANNES BRENZ: For each saint is a twofold self, namely, outer and inner, carnal and spiritual, earthly and heavenly, old Adam and new Adam. For in this way Paul also speaks of the righteous self in this letter and others. "The law of God," he says, "delights me as to the inner self." And Ephesians 4: "take off the old self and put on the new." And 1 Corinthians 15, on the earthly and the heavenly self. COMMENTARY ON ROMANS (1564).[26]

THE WHOLE PERSON AFFECTED BY ORIGINAL SIN. PETER MARTYR VERMIGLI: Aristotle says that in each sin, some kind of ignorance is involved. Nevertheless, there is a difference between the Philosophers and Paul's sense. For they judged a power to be innate in the nature of mind, reason, and will—that it always desires and approves the good—so confusion arises only in the coarser parts of the mind. The apostle, on the other hand, asserts that all parts of the man or woman, both inferior and superior, because of original sin, are opposed to the Spirit of God. COMMENTARY ON ROMANS (1560).[27]

THE NEW SELF'S DOMINION OVER THE OLD. JOHANNES BRENZ: So also these two selves coexist in the man or woman reborn by faith. One from the first nativity, the other from the second. And each lives, but with this difference, that in the saints, because they trust in Christ, the new or spiritual self dominates the old, neither does it permit it to perform sins according to its lust, but controls its desires. Certainly, it sometimes happens that the old self overtakes the new and masters it—after the manner you see took place in David, in Peter, in Paul, and in innumerable others—but as a result of coming to its senses, the new self recovers dominion over the old. COMMENTARY ON ROMANS (1564).[28]

[24]Hemmingsen, *Commentarius in Epistolam*, 257.
[25]Musculus, *In Epistolam Apostoli Pauli*, 155.

[26]Brenz, *In Epistolam*, 177; citing Eph 4:22-24; 1 Cor 15:40.
[27]Vermigli, *In Epistolam S. Pauli*, 543.
[28]Brenz, *In Epistolam*, 177.

ALIVE TO SIN, DEAD TO MYSELF. MICHELANGELO:

> Alive to Sin, dead to myself I live;
> My life is not my own—Sin masters it,
> Around me an obscuring cloud it spreads,
> So that I wander blind, to reason lost.
> My liberty, of which I boasted once,
> Is now enslaved; oh, miserable fate!
> To what excess of woe and grief I'm born,
> If Lord, through you, I be not born again!
> When I look back, retracing the sad course
> Of my past years, with error thickly strewn,
> Sole I accuse my insane hardihood.
> 'Twas thus I loosed the curb to my desires,
> Quitting the radiant path which to your Love
> Conducts. Oh! Still stretch out your arm to save.

SONNET 52.[29]

MANICHEES ON EVIL NATURE AS A SUBSTANCE. PETER MARTYR VERMIGLI: Truly we must beware here of the error of the Manichees, who stated that human beings were composed of a double nature, one good, the other evil, and that both were comingled, but that through Christ it came about that the evil was separated from the good and thrust out to a race of darkness. For to them it did not seem that evil was a corruption of nature that happened to the one who had been otherwise good. Rather, they said that it existed per se, and had a certain substance, and was separated from good people by means of ejection and flight, rather than that it ceased to be. Truth, however, teaches that Christ heals sin and defect, and heals it in such a way that it remains nowhere. COMMENTARY ON ROMANS (1560).[30]

DWELLING. WOLFGANG MUSCULUS: When he openly expresses this tyranny and violence of sin, he does not say: "sin *existing* in me" but "sin *dwelling* within me." By the word *dwelling* he shows that sin had obtained a complete dominion over him, as if sin had firmly established its throne inside him. Evil nowhere reigns so powerfully as where it sets up its throne, as can be seen in the case of tyrants. In an altogether contrary fashion, God is said to have dwelt in the midst of Israel, since to no other people did he thereby grant so great a display of his goodness, according to this verse: "He has not dealt thus with any other nation." The word *dwelling* is used frequently in this sense in the Scriptures. When, therefore, the apostle wished to declare the power and tyranny of sin with himself, he said that it "dwelt" within him, as a man does in his own home, and so sin exercised a total reign within him. COMMENTARY ON ROMANS (1555).[31]

PAUL REFERS TO HIS REGENERATE SELF. ROBERT ROLLOCK: "Now therefore." From here to the end of the chapter Paul draws three conclusions from what precedes. The first follows upon his last argument, wherein he agreed with the law of God, that it is holy. But it provides something of an excuse for him, for if he "agrees with the law that it is holy, it follows that it is no longer he who acts, but rather the sin that dwells within" him. Take note that the apostle refers to his whole self, using a pronoun belonging to his stronger part, that is, that part that is regenerate, just as earlier he had referred to his whole will with the same pronoun, referring to himself as born again. COMMENTARY ON ROMANS (1595).[32]

WATCH YOUR HEART IN TIMES OF ABUNDANCE. EDWARD ELTON: Thus it ought to be with all God's children: they are to make covenants with their eyes, ears, and all the parts and members of their bodies, and to watch carefully over their hearts. They have a secret foe that dwells in them, ready to betray them into the hands of Satan, who seeks their destruction. And therefore they cannot be too heedful and watchful over their own hearts in regard to indwelling

---

[29]Michelangelo, *Life of Michael Angelo*, 165*.
[30]Vermigli, *In Epistolam S. Pauli*, 545-46.
[31]Musculus, *In Epistolam Apostoli Pauli*, 136; citing Ps 147:20.
[32]Rollock, *In Epistolam S. Pauli*, 136-37; citing Rom 7:12.

corruption. And they should especially watch over themselves in time of prosperity and when they have an abundance of outward things, for then they are in the greatest danger to be surprised and overtaken with pride, deadness of heart, self-love, and the like. THE COMPLAINT OF A SANCTIFIED SINNER (1618).[33]

PAUL ADMITS TO INDWELLING SIN. ROBERT ROLLOCK: "For I know." He says this in order to head off an inference from his saying that sin dwells in him, for someone might say to him: "Then isn't sin still dwelling in you even when you are born again? For you say that sin indwells in you and that it perpetrates evil within." The apostle answers by way of concession that there is indeed something of sin dwelling within him, and when he says "I know" he admits that he knows this fact all too well—or perhaps it refers to what his conscience is saying. COMMENTARY ON ROMANS (1595).[34]

SIN AFTER SALVATION. THE ENGLISH ANNOTATIONS: That natural corruption that cleaves fast even to those who are regenerated and is not quite conquered. He speaks this for the comfort of himself and others who groan under the servitude of their natural corruption, and what he would infer is this, that he stands not in fear to be rejected by God for these remains of sin in him, because God judges his children who are thus divided between flesh and spirit according to the better and sounder part, which is that of the spirit as most prevailing in them, and unto which they do most heartily and willingly adhere, which has likewise a subsistence and root of permanent life, and not according to the flesh, which they renounce and resist, and which little by little decays in them, and in the end is reduced to nothing. ANNOTATIONS ON ROMANS 7:17.[35]

7:18 I Have the Desire but Not the Ability to Do Good

SORROW FOR NOT DOING ACCEPTED AS DOING. SAMUEL RUTHERFORD: Light remains, you say, but you cannot attain to perfection. See if this complaint is not written in the New Testament, like this, "To will is present with me, but I do not know how to perform that which is good." But not all of us have the same spirit as Paul's when we complain, for often, in us, complaining is simply backbiting and denigrating Christ's new work in our souls. But about the matter of the complaint: I would say that the light of glory is perfectly obeyed in loving, and praising, and rejoicing, and resting in a seen and known Lord. But that light is not here in any clay body. For while we are here, light is, for the most part, broader and longer than our narrow and inept obedience. But if there is light [accompanied by] armies of challenging thoughts, and sorrow for coming short of performance in what we know and see ought to be performed—then that sorrow for *not* doing is accepted by our Lord for *doing*. Our honest sorrow and sincere aims—together with Christ's intercession pleading that God would welcome that which we have and forgive what we have not—must be our life, till we cross over the boundary road into the other country, where the law will get a perfect soul. LETTER CCLXXXVI TO PARISHIONERS OF KILMALCOLM.[36]

THE BESTIAL NATURE OF FALLEN MAN. JOHN COLET: Now all the evil that man has springs up from him out of that lower part of his nature, which may be called the animal and bestial part of man. This was committed to the inner person and soul to be ruled by it. But after humanity loosed itself from God through ungodliness and want of faith and sank to the corporeal, our bestial nature—now that humanity's state was so changed

---

[33]Elton, *The Complaint of a Sanctified Sinner*, 355*; Prov 1:32.
[34]Rollock, *In Epistolam S. Pauli*, 137.
[35]Downame, ed., *Annotations*, BBB1v*.

[36]Rutherford, *Letters*, 561-62*. The letter was written to the parishioners of Kilmalcolm on August 5, 1639, in response to their complaints of "dead ministry in their bounds" [561].

and overturned—broke forth at once in riot and madness and seized on the reins of government in humanity. It placed our soul in miserable subjection to folly and lust and dealt with everything according to the judgment of the senses. Then, in humanity, a republic grew strong, as it were, wholly of the people and the commonalty,† administered by the decision and decrees of sense, with no interposition of the authority of understanding and reason. It was a republic held in blind subjection, forced in a measure to be the slave—the voluntary slave, I might almost say—of the dominant senses. This miserable and forlorn condition of humanity, and the lamentable bondage of the soul is here bewailed by St. Paul; and he complains bitterly of the injustice and tyranny of the sensual body. Under that bondage, he says, he does not know what he does in his actions; that he wills but cannot perform what is good; that he agrees that the law is an admonisher of righteousness but cannot obey it. Our bestial nature so goads, presses, and orders us with such blandishments and inveigles the soul and binds it to itself with such false enticements that our soul cannot see how it can release itself, unless aided by divine grace. . . .

Thus it was marvelously brought about in merciful justice and just mercy, that men's and women's sins were taken away out of the world, not by their own death for endless destruction afterward, but by the saving of their lives. That, if willing, they may live in this world so as to possess eternal life with God. And that they may do this, he who, of his singular love toward them, even when they were aliens, was willing to die for all, will give them the needful strength, and will preserve them; especially those whom he has recalled to himself and reconciled to himself and God. This St. Paul implies by saying, "Much more, being now justified by his blood, we shall be saved," and a little after, "Much more, being reconciled, we shall be saved by his life." Exposition on Romans (1497).[37]

Sin Still Dwells in the Regenerate Person. Robert Rollock: "That is, in my flesh." . . . He injects this clarification in order to correct a misunderstanding: for sin dwells in his other self, the part that is not regenerate. This is inserted in passing, lest someone should think that he is speaking of himself as a regenerate man and according to his *to einai* (being), for his essential being as a regenerate man comes from the Spirit of sanctification.

"For to will. . . ." He argues that sin dwells within him by showing the effect of sin, namely, that by it he is impeded from carrying out noble works. This effect is discovered and amplified by the contrary will and choice to do good. "For I will what is good, but how to carry it out I do not find." But this is nothing other than "sin that dwells in me." You can see, therefore, that his argument is drawn from the fact that being impeded, he is unable to carry out good works, which is the effect of indwelling sin.

"For it is not I who does it." He plainly shows this effect of indwelling sin, namely, a good work that is impeded, or the impediment to the good work, from the opposite effect of inhabiting sin, namely, the doing of an evil work. It is as if he said, "It is so far from me to be able to carry out the good work that I wish, that to the contrary, I do that evil thing which I do not wish."

"But if. . . ." Having digressed until now in explaining the indwelling sin within him, he now returns to his self-defense, and wraps it up by taking for his argument what he had just said, that he does the evil that he does not wish to do. Commentary on Romans (1595).[38]

The Regenerate Life Does Not Imply Perfection. Edward Elton: I answer that it is indeed true that God works both the will and the deed in the regenerate. Whenever they both will good and perform good, it is God that works both. But hence it follows not that regenerate persons do always and in every particular act, both will good

---

[37]Colet, *Exposition of St. Paul's Epistle*, 22-24*. †The common people.

[38]Rollock, *In Epistolam S. Pauli*, 137-38.

and do good. No, sometimes they will and desire to do good and either they do not do it, or at the least they do not do it as it ought to be done. But when they will good and do good, it is God that works both in them. That is the meaning of the apostle. And so notwithstanding this, it remains a truth that the apostle was truly regenerate when he spoke in this way of himself, "To will is present with me, but I find no means to perform that which is good." THE COMPLAINT OF A SANCTIFIED SINNER (1618).[39]

THERE IS GOOD IN HUMANS. BALTHASAR HUBMAIER: From this you will note: If one says there is nothing good in us, that is saying too much. As Paul also said too much when he said, I know that nothing good dwells within me. But he hastens to explain this by adding to this concept: I know that nothing good dwells within me, that is, in my flesh. Likewise all the other Scriptures must be understood that indicate that there is nothing good in us, that is, in our flesh, for God's image has never yet been completely obliterated in us. How can it be evil, for (like the law) it shows and teaches us the good. Far be it from us then to call it evil. For we know that it is holy, makes us righteous, and is wholly good. A CHRISTIAN CATECHISM.[40]

CHRISTIANS HAVE BOTH CARNAL AND SPIRITUAL NATURES. DIRK PHILIPS: Since, then, both of these births now occur in all Christians, namely, while they are in part born out of the flesh and in part out of the Spirit. Therefore they must have both a carnal and a spiritual nature. According to the outward person, they are thus carnally minded, but according to the inner person, they are spiritually minded. Through the carnal nature they fall and sin, but through the divine nature they have a desire toward righteousness and wish to fulfill the will of God. The carnal nature must be overcome by the Spirit of God; nevertheless, flesh and blood retains its nature as long as it lives.

Therefore, although someone has become participant of the spiritual and divine nature, he nevertheless remains frail and sinful, for he remains a human being; he is flesh and blood, and therein dwells nothing good, just as Paul says. For it has become corrupted, sinful, and desirous of evil through the disobedience of the first human being, so that no person who lives is entirely innocent before the Lord, and that is on account of his evil nature and the carnal lusts that tempt and cling to him. Because of these reasons the justified person is still accused by the Scripture. THE TABERNACLE OF MOSES.[41]

CHRISTIANS STILL STRUGGLE WITH THEIR FLESH. BALTHASAR HUBMAIER: It is not sufficient that sin be recognized through the law, nor that we know what is good or evil. We must bind the commandments on our hand, grasp them, and fulfill them in deeds. To do this is easy and a small thing to the believer, but to those who walk according to the flesh, all things are impossible. Yet the believing and newly born person under the gospel is still also [a person] under the law. They have just as many trials as before, or even more. They find (however holy they may be) nothing good in their own flesh, just as St. Paul laments the same with great seriousness regarding the conflict and the resistance of the flesh. A FORM FOR CHRIST'S SUPPER.[42]

PRAYER FOR OVERCOMING SIN. KATHARINA SCHÜTZ ZELL: O righteous Father, also help us to be strengthened and made sure by you, to break through the afflictions of this flesh and be able to enter through the narrow gate. Grant us your Spirit of knowledge and strength, that we may not deny you [in this temptation of the enemy] because of the sin that sticks in our flesh with evil desires and unceasingly stirs it up. Therefore the flesh struggles against the spirit and the spirit against the flesh and its evil fruits. So there is a

---

[39]Elton, *The Complaint of a Sanctified Sinner*, 369*.
[40]CRR 5:360-61*.

[41]CRR 6:284-85*.
[42]CRR 5:400*; citing Deut 6:8; Mt 11:30; Jn 3:1-36.

great conflict and struggle in us: we have the will but we do not have the ability to fulfill it, yet both of these are yours. O holy Father, grant us help that in this affliction we may not be servants of sin but may overcome sin and be free children of your grace through Jesus Christ—Who, being without sin, became sin for us that he might make us free. However, so long as there is this great struggle in us and we are weak and fleshly, strengthen us, dear Father. Grant us weapons to fight against such affliction and sins so that we may put on your yoke against the cunning assault of the devil and, with our loins girded with truth and the breastplate of righteousness and the shield of faith, we can extinguish all the arrows of the devil and our flesh. By that, dear Father, through your help we may not deny you in the afflictions and temptations of this world, even though poverty, sickness, insult, exile, prison, torment, and death come on us. O God, we could not pass through these dangers if we were abandoned and if you did not bring us out of them; therefore help us and grant that we may from the heart entrust ourselves to you and set ourselves willingly to obey you through the crucified Jesus. THE MISERERE PSALM MEDITATED, PRAYED, AND PARAPHRASED.[43]

7:19 I Do the Wrong, Not the Right That I Desire

NO ONE'S PIETY IS PERFECT, EVEN ABRAHAM'S. JOHANNES BRENZ: Those who are pious, who have been born again in Christ, and who lead an honest life, though they relapse a number of times because of weakness in relation to external sins, nevertheless, in the greatest part of their life, they do good and honest works. For piety in God and faith in Christ brings this about. But it must be understood that when the pious and holy obey the law of God and do good work, nevertheless they do not bring this work about. That is, they themselves do not do it perfectly without any fault.

For all work—even when one has done one's best—yet has sin in it to some degree, so it is not perfect, and it does not satisfy God's law. Let us take, for example, the patriarch Abraham. He did a good work excellently when he forsook his own country and obeyed God's calling, which is what God wanted. But nevertheless, this work was not perfectly good, because love for God from his whole heart, soul, and strength was not in Abraham. For Abraham had preferred his own flesh rather than the calling of God, wanting to stay in his own country and to delight in his father's goods rather than to give them up and pursue the uncertain. Likewise, Abraham had offered, according to the command of God, his only-begotten son Isaac. That work was so excellent that even God himself was pleased with it. And yet it was not perfect righteousness, for Abraham had the flesh that fought against the spirit, and that meant that this work of his would have fault. Indeed, Abraham wished he could be free from this fight and rebellion, and to yield perfectly to the will of God, not only in the external work, but truly with his whole heart and his whole spirit, but he did not find this perfection in his own flesh. COMMENTARY ON ROMANS (1564).[44]

THE REGENERATE HAVE BEEN GIVEN A WILL TO OBEY GOD. NIELS HEMMINGSEN: The reason for this sentence is taken from the experience of the apostle. Those who do not do the good that they desire but do evil that they do not desire, have the faculty of will, but are without the power of accomplishing it. The apostle—regenerated or converted—does not do the good that he desires, but he does the evil that he does not desire. So indeed the apostle has the faculty of will, along with not having the ability to accomplish it. From this may be taken up a general doctrine about those who are reborn, namely, that indeed grace brings forth a will to obey God. However, having made the attempt, that grace is thrown into confusion by the weakness of the flesh and

---

[43]Zell, *Church Mother*, 170*; citing Mt 7:13-14; Gal 5:17; Rom 6:17; Heb 4:15; 2 Cor 5:21; Eph 6:11, 14, 16.

[44]Brenz, *In Epistolam*, 179-80.

depravity of their nature. Moreover, those who deduce from this passage that free will exists in a corrupt nature are greatly mistaken. For Paul speaks here about himself being justified, and about the will that he has from the grace of renewal by the Holy Spirit. COMMENTARY ON ROMANS (1562).[45]

THE SOUL CAN CHOOSE NOTHING GOOD ON ITS OWN. BALTHASAR HUBMAIER: The soul, the third part of the human being, has through this disobedience of Adam been wounded in the will in such a way and become sick unto death so that it can on its own choose nothing good. Nor can it refuse evil since it has lost the knowledge of good and evil. There is nothing left to it but to sin and to die. Yes, as far as doing good goes, the soul has become entirely powerless and ineffective. Only the flesh can act, without which the soul is outwardly able to do nothing, for the flesh is its instrument. Since, however, the instrument is incapable of doing anything, how can anything good be done with it, even if the soul gladly wanted to and made every effort. FREEDOM OF THE WILL.[46]

ONLY GOD'S MERCY CAN DELIVER ME. MARGUERITE DE NAVARRE: Now as far as I can see, I have no hope of aid except through the grace of God, which I cannot deserve, but which may raise everyone from death. By his brightness he gives light to my darkness, and by his power examining my faults he breaks the whole veil of ignorance and gives me clear understanding, not only of what comes from me, but also what things abide in me. . . . For I never had the power to observe even one of the commandments of God. I feel the strength of sin within me. Therefore my sin cannot be hidden; the more it dissembles outwardly, the more it increases within the heart. What God wills, I cannot will. And what he does not will, I often times desire to have. These things constrain me with unbearable sorrow to wish for

the end of this miserable life, through desiring death because of my weary and ragged life. Who can deliver and recover such good for me? Alas, it cannot be a mortal person, for his power and strength are not such. But it shall be only by the good grace of almighty God, which is never slack in protecting us with his mercy. THE MIRROR OF THE SINFUL SOUL (1544).[47]

7:20 It Is No Longer I Who Do It

LIKE A HORSEMAN AND HIS HORSE. MARTIN LUTHER: It is not he who sins, because his flesh lusts without his consent, indeed he himself does not lust because he dissents from the lusts of the flesh. And yet he says: "I do not do the good I want." Because the same person is both spirit and flesh, therefore what he does in the flesh the whole self is said to do. And yet because he resists, it is rightly said that the whole self is not doing it, but only a part of him. Therefore both expressions are true, that he himself does it and he himself does not do it.

He is like a horseman. When his horses do not trot the way he wants them to, it is he himself and yet not he himself who makes the horse run in such and such a way. For the horse is not without him, and he is not without the horse. But because a carnal person certainly consents to the law of his members, he certainly himself does what sin does. For now it is the mind and flesh not only of one person but also of one will. LECTURES ON ROMANS.[48]

CLASH OF WILL AND DEEDS FOUND ONLY IN THOSE BORN AGAIN. NIELS HEMMINGSEN: Here we find a redirection of guilt to inherited sin. This argument concludes as much:

(P1) If I do that which I do not will, it is no longer I who do it.

(P2) But I do that which I do not will.

(C) Therefore, it is no longer I who do it.

---

[45]Hemmingsen, *Commentarius in Epistolam*, 260.
[46]CRR 5:435*; citing Gen 2, 3; Rom 7.

[47]De Navarre, *Mirror of the Sinful Soul*, 64-65*; citing Rom 5. Translated into English by Elizabeth I when she was eleven years old.
[48]LW 25:331*; citing Rom 7:19.

But if it is not I who do it, then it must be someone else who is doing it. But no other can be found except for our hereditary disease. In this we observe the conflict between the flesh and the spirit,[†] and the distinction between the old and new self. The new is the one who wills, whereas the old is the one who opposes, all in one and the same person. The new self is whatever a person possesses from the grace of regeneration, whereas the old self is the entire condition of an unregenerate person, which puts up resistance to God. Therefore this clash of will versus deeds is not to be found in any person whatever, but only in those born again by the Spirit and by grace. COMMENTARY ON ROMANS (1562).[49]

SIN IS AN "ACCIDENT." DIETRICH SCHNEPFF: From this statement of Paul and from other passages of Scripture it has been shown that human powers can contribute nothing to regeneration, and therefore should not be adorned with false praises.

But on the other hand, from the same Pauline passage we show those are out of their minds who say that after that mortal wound[†] not only was our beauty [ornament] lost that in the beginning glittered on man and woman—namely, the image of God—but also our very substance was lost and transformed into sin.

Against this pernicious error, the mere word indwelling that Paul uses three times in this seventh chapter is enough to silence them.

For just as a house and he who inhabits it are two different things, so likewise sin and the substance in which it inheres are necessarily two different things.

Whereas "substance" is the thing in and of itself, and whereas "accidents"[‡] inhere in substances, it is certain that sin is an "accident" and Paul is witnessing several times in this chapter that sin adheres to man and woman in this way.

"Good does not dwell within me." Also, "I see another law in my members." Again: "making me

captive to the law of sin which is in my members." And writing to the Romans he exhorts them, "let not sin reign in your mortal bodies." He even said that evil was present with him. From these testimonies it is clear that sin inheres within man and woman, and it therefore ought not to be called a substance but rather an accident. DISPUTATIONS ON ROMANS 7:20 (1585).[50]

7:21 Evil Is Nearby When I Desire to Do Good

OUR WEAKNESS. HEINRICH BULLINGER: This is a complete reversal of what is expected. Then what, you might ask, is the use of the law? What power does it have? What is its role? From his preceding arguments, it follows (he says) that the law, whether you will it or not, convicts us that we are sinners and that human powers contribute nothing to being good. For the righteous, just, holy, and good law of God commands that we love God before all else, that we devote ourselves to innocence, that we not lust, that we not harm our neighbor but rather that we ought to love them as ourselves. By reason of which things, what I ask can be more noble, more valuable, or better than the law? But quite to the contrary: men and women, attracted by the nobility of these things, initially strain themselves to pay heed to the Lawgiver, but when they have mentally weighed this holy undertaking even a little, they see how miserably base human powers are, how the human mind is slow to turn itself to heavenly things, and how it automatically inclines toward the most detestable vices of the flesh; or rather, it is so drawn by such vices that it altogether shrinks from heavenly things. COMMENTARY ON ROMANS (1533).[51]

---

[49]Hemmingsen, *Commentarius in Epistolam*, 260-61. [†]Possibly, "Spirit."

[50]Schnepff, *Disputatio de Sententia*, C4; citing Rom 6:12. [†]Caused by the fall. [‡]Substance and accidents are Aristotelian categories of analysis (see his *Ten Categories*) in which the essence (stable) of something is differentiated from its characteristics (changeable).
[51]Bullinger, *In Sanctissimam Pauli*, 99r-99v.

THE HOLY SPIRIT WORKS WITHIN US.
JOHANNES BUGENHAGEN: "I find two things," he says, "within me: the flesh willing evil, and the Spirit opposing the flesh." Therefore those commentaries are vain that imagine that here "free will" is attributed to us, by which we are able to will what is good, since Paul wished it to be understood that this is not by any powers within us but by the very Spirit of God himself who wills what is good, who works within us "both to will and to do according to his good pleasure in us." Also senseless are those who pretend that Paul is speaking here only of sensuality, that wills evil. But is this not to spit in Jesus' face and to punch him in the jaw? He said that the whole of man, insofar as he is according to nature, cannot do or will anything good; or you might say of "free will" or natural reasoning and anything that is in man, that all are under the curse—everything you contemplate, purpose to do, or struggle to do out of your own nature or by the wisdom of the flesh. For Paul said "I find," that is, I perceive, "then by the law" of God that was intended to do me good (for it only reveals sin in me that I might learn not to trust my own powers but to call on the mercy of God) "that when I will to do good" (which is not done by me, but by the Spirit of God), "there is something else present within me," that is, innate to and implanted in every part of my flesh, *evil*, or sin. In other words, I see myself willing according to my own powers only that which is contrary to God. If I may summarize: I am partly spiritual, partly carnal, and there is no agreement at all between what the Spirit wills and what the flesh wills. INTERPRETATION OF ROMANS (1531).[52]

WHEN YOU PURPOSE TO DO GOOD, TEMPTATIONS WILL ARISE. EDWARD ELTON: Is it so that no sooner do the best of God's children purpose and desire to do any good thing, or set on the doing of it, but some evil motion or lust starts up, looks them in the face, countermands them, and either hinders them from doing it or intermingles

in the doing of it? Surely then it concerns us, when any good thought is put into our hearts and when we have a purpose or desire of doing any good thing, to look to it, to watch over our own hearts, and to make much of that good thought, purpose, and desire, and to cherish it, and to labor by all good means to bring it forth into act. If we do not do so, certainly some evil motion or lust starting up in our hearts will outface it and will bear it down. Perhaps in the time of hearing the Word you have a good motion put into your heart, and on the hearing of your own sin reproved you then have a purpose to leave it—as to lay aside your pride, your garishness in apparel, your drunkenness, your swearing, and such things. Oh, if you make much of that good purpose, there will be some evil motion or lust ready to countermand it, and when you come abroad in the air of the world, a thousand to one it will be quenched and gone, and it will vanish and come to nothing. Your own heart will then furnish you with a thousand excuses to the contrary. THE COMPLAINT OF A SANCTIFIED SINNER (1618).[53]

7:22 Deep Within, I Delight in the Law

MEANING OF THE LAW OF GOD. JUAN DE VALDÉS: Here by "the law of God," St. Paul means the Decalogue, the Ten Commandments, because he neither rejoiced in nor delighted himself in the remainder of the law, since he preached against it, because it was not conformable to the obligations of Christian regeneration. To men and women the law of God is the will of God, in whatever aspect they may envisage it. It does not operate on those who have died with Christ, exerting the functions of the law, but of the gospel. For they do not take it as a law to justify themselves by, but as instruction on how to live conformably with it. It does not irritate them, nor does it make them enemies to God, but it attaches them—and makes them friends—to God. Some understand that St. Paul in all this does not speak of his own experience nor

---

[52]Bugenhagen, *In D. Pauli ad Romanos*, 76v-77r; citing Phil 2:13.

[53]Elton, *The Complaint of a Sanctified Sinner*, 400-401*.

of what transpired in himself, but of the experience of those who have not yet attained justification through Christ, and of what transpired in them. I think that St. Paul speaks of himself, and that which really had passed and was passing through him. And I am moved to believe this to be so, both because this is not alien to a person already justified through Christ—nay, it is peculiar to him, and is, as it were, consequent on justification—and because all that has been spoken of is alien to a person who is not justified through Christ. To such persons it is most alien to rejoice in the law of God and to keep it in their minds. COMMENTARY ON ROMANS (1556).[54]

THE LAW OF GOD VERSUS THE LAW OF SIN. JUAN DE VALDÉS: Here I understand St. Paul to lay it down that there are two laws that he says are hostilely arrayed against each other. The one is the law of God, the other the law of sin. Of the law of God, he states that he rejoices and inwardly delights in it; and of the law of sin, he states that it was against the law of God, even subduing and enslaving the man or woman. So that when he says, "the law of my mind," he means the law of God that I have in my mind, loving it, rejoicing, and delighting myself in it. And when he speaks of that "which is in my members," he means the law of sin, and the law of the members, which is all one. COMMENTARY ON ROMANS (1556).[55]

THE FOURFOLD LAW. NIELS HEMMINGSEN: We should observe in this passage what Ambrose[†] also urges, namely, the fourfold law proposed here by Paul, for he regards that there is all the more clearly a conflict of flesh and spirit among those who have been born again, and he shows the difference between the old and new self. First is the law of God, which is justice's proper norm, according to which the inner self aspires to live. Second is the law of the mind, namely, the new self who was begotten of the Spirit through grace. Third, the law of the

members—which is assembled according to a framework—is the impetus toward sinning. Fourth is the law of sin, that is, original sin itself and the natural brutality of humankind; this differs from the third as a cause does from its effect. For as this fourth law is itself the depravity of nature, so the third has in view corrupt desires from which they spring forth. These four laws are in the regenerate, but the law of the mind—which is a good will, a holy resolution, an inclination, propensity, and impetus toward good—is awoken first in the heart through the grace of regeneration, unto obedience to God, which those not regenerated are incapable of fulfilling. Hence they do not perceive the battle of the spirit and the flesh. So then, it should here be observed that the doctrine concerning original sin and the evil in its desires is most evident. For first, it is a foe ferociously matched as against a soldier, and in this it attacks in order to seize him. It exhausts and overwhelms him. Next, victory being obtained, the conqueror himself attempts to bind and take captive his adversary in order that he might sell him into perpetual servitude. But how true this is may be shown by the lapsing of the greatest saints—as with David and others. However, the spirit, in turn, rouses itself by grasping faith and beats down the enemy with spiritual weapons. COMMENTARY ON ROMANS (1562).[56]

DEFINING THE "INWARD PERSON" AND "MEMBERS." JOHN CALVIN: We ought to notice carefully the meaning of the "inner person" and "members," which many have not rightly understood and therefore have stumbled at this stone. The inner person then is not simply the soul, but that spiritual part that has been regenerated by God. The members signify the other remaining part, for as the soul is the superior and the body the inferior part of the person, so the spirit is superior to the flesh. Then as the spirit takes the place of the soul in a person, which is the corrupt and polluted soul, that of the body, the former has the name of the

---

[54]Valdés, *Commentary upon St. Paul's Epistle*, 111-12*.
[55]Valdés, *Commentary upon St. Paul's Epistle*, 111*.

[56]Hemmingsen, *Commentarius in Epistolam*, 262-63. [†]Hemmingsen elaborates on Ambrosiaster, *Ad Romanos* 7.22.

inner person, and the latter has the name of members. The inner person has indeed a different meaning in 2 Corinthians 4:16, but the circumstances of this passage require the interpretation that I have given. It is called the inner person by way of excellency, for it possesses the heart and the secret feelings, while the desires of the flesh are vagrant and are, as it were, on the outside of a person. Doubtless it is the same thing as though one compared heaven and earth, for Paul by way of contempt designates whatever to be in a person by the term "members," that he might clearly show that the hidden renovation is concealed from and escapes our observation, except it be apprehended by faith. COMMENTARY ON ROMANS 7:22.[57]

INWARD AND OUTWARD, NEW AND OLD SELVES. THEODORE BEZA: The new inner self (which is also called spirit) is undoubtedly the same that is indicated by Paul—which everyone will acknowledge—here and at Ephesians 3:16 when compared with Colossians 2:9-10. But to this is opposed the outward or old self, which is also understood by the terms "flesh" and "members." But it must be carefully observed that most of the ancients (and especially the Greeks from the time of Pelagius) . . . had not sufficiently considered that, truly, the distinction between the internal and external self, between spirit and flesh, cannot rest on a distinction in the faculties of the person, as if the spirit and the inner self were the mind and reason, while the flesh and outward self (who also is understood by the name "members") being summed up merely by the remaining inferior parts, what the philosophers call *alogos* (without reason). For this is a philosophical—and not a Christian—division of the parts of the self. Therefore the Spirit of God calls flesh members, or the outward self whatever is in a person either inside or outside, from head to heel, indeed to whatever extent a person is not regenerated by the grace of God. And indeed, for this reason, it is proved that the apostle numbers reason among the most corrupt parts of

the self. He desires to extend the renewing according to the Spirit to every part of the mind. In the end, it is plain that it is nonsense to struggle against the Spirit, and moreover, human wisdom and reasoning are darkness. But from this, in turn, that Word is understood that states that the Spirit opposes the flesh, or that he makes known the inner and new self. MAJOR ANNOTATIONS (1594).[58]

THE LAW AND THE INNER SELF. ROBERT ROLLOCK: "I find therefore a law." This is another conclusion inferred from the points he has made, for he discovers imposed in himself a law, as it were, that induces to sinning, which he explains and amplifies by contrasting it with the contrary will and choice to do good works. He therefore begins by setting forth this imposed "law."

"For I delight in the law of God." Here is the reason why that law of which he spoke, and the necessity of sinning as its effect, "wars against the law of his mind" and takes him "captive to the law of sin." He explains and amplifies this warfare by asserting the contrary delight, which he generally feels toward the law of God according to the inner self. In this passage as a whole, you see in the apostle's experiences that which they refer to as the struggle between the Spirit and the flesh.

"According to the inner self." The "inner self" is, most properly speaking, the person in his or her interior part, that is, the renewed mind. For renewal or regeneration is usually attributed, in a particular way, to the mind and the purer part of the self: "Be renewed in the spirit of your mind." But this is not to say that the body and the other parts of the self are not renewed, but only that regeneration is more easily seen in the higher part than it is in the coarser parts, and it is from the former that it spreads to the rest of the self. Here, however, the "inner self" refers to that holy condition not only of the mind but of the whole person. COMMENTARY ON ROMANS (1595).[59]

---

[57]CTS 38:271-78 (CO 49:133-34).

[58]Beza, *Annotationes Majores*, 86-87; citing Eph 3:16; Col 2:9-10; Rom 1:28; 1 Tim 6:5; 2 Tim 3:8; Tit 1:15; Eph 4:23.
[59]Rollock, *In Epistolam S. Pauli*, 138-39; citing Eph 4:23.

PAINTERS AND PEACOCKS. PETER MARTYR VERMIGLI: The saints are not, however, greatly overjoyed by true knowledge of solid and perfect righteousness, because they do not know it perfectly. Indeed, they, on the contrary, are always casting their eyes to the law of God. And when they see outlined in it the figure of the righteous man or woman, and the perfect image of God to which we were built, they cannot but be wonderfully overjoyed. But afterward, when they turn their gaze to their own works, they are greatly afflicted that they see them fall so far short of the proposed example. So painters, when they see some figure admirably expressed, seize on it with great pleasure. But when, having tried to produce the same, they see themselves unable to equal its grace and elegance, they begin to be afflicted and indignant. The same nature of inclination is also noted in peacocks, for when they have erected their plumes, they may be seen to exult, seized by their delightful variety. But again, when they perceive their malformed, black feet, immediately their hearts are cast down and they let down their feathers. In this way the pious are delighted by the law of God, and are captivated by a powerful love for its commands. Conversely they are grieved and afflicted by the baseness that they discover in all their works. COMMENTARY ON ROMANS (1560).[60]

7:23 The War Within

MIND AND FLESH AS STATES WITHIN THE SELF. FRIEDRICH BALDUIN: By the term "flesh" the Scriptures mean the man or woman who is not yet regenerate, which elsewhere is referred to as the "old self" or the "outer self," since however much it might be wise in fleshly affairs, even if it ranks with the very best in wisdom, it does not receive the things that are of the Spirit of God. But by the term "mind," the Scriptures mean a man or woman who is regenerate, one who is ready and eager for spiritual things, the obtaining of which is however frequently hindered by the flesh. Therefore "mind"

and "flesh" are opposites, not as different parts or powers, but as different *states* in a person. The "mind" denotes the self as regenerate; the "flesh" denotes the lingering remains of sin still adhering to the regenerate nature, by which through its corruption the best actions of the mind are impeded. COMMENTARY ON ROMANS (1620).[61]

THE POWER IN THE FLESH. JOHANNES BUGENHAGEN: But I see another law. It is another power in my flesh, which fights back against the law of the mind, that is, against the Holy Spirit in my heart. It is a power that holds me captive under the law of sin. That is, I see that the sin in me is not yet entirely dead. It lives, and my flesh gives in to its allurement. The flesh has its own desires, which Paul here calls a law. And the Spirit thinks that between the two, there is never agreement. The Spirit says, "Don't covet." The flesh says, "I will covet." Since in this way these things are embedded in us, should we not be crying out with Paul? INTERPRETATION OF ROMANS (1531).[62]

HOW TO STRENGTHEN YOUR DELIGHT IN THE GOOD. EDWARD ELTON: Thus it is that no sooner do God's children find delight in good things but their own corruption makes resistance and opposition against that delight of theirs and seeks to hinder it and to shake it out of their hearts. And therefore know this, whoever you are, that you cannot expect to always find the same measure of delight in good things. Your delight in good things will sometimes be greater and sometimes less. For why? Your own corruption makes resistance and stands in opposition against that delight of yours, and you will find it will sometimes hinder it, weaken it, and lessen it in measure. And therefore, when you find in yourself any measure of delight in good things, make much of it, cherish it, and labor to keep it in your heart, and to that purpose do these two things:

First, esteem good things according to the worth and excellency of them, as Job did: "I have

---

[60]Vermigli, *In Epistolam S. Pauli*, 552-53.

[61]Balduin, *Catechesis Apostolica*, 489.
[62]Bugenhagen, *In D. Pauli ad Romanos*, 77r-77v.

esteemed the words of his mouth more than my appointed food."

Second, establish your delight by counsel, as it says in Proverbs 20:18. I mean, by taking counsel with God. Go to the Lord by prayer, be earnest and instant with him to help and assist you by his grace, that you may continue delighting in good things.

And if you do these two things, doubtless you shall be able to keep your heart in some good measure delighting in good things. Yes, you shall find your delight in those things much increased. THE COMPLAINT OF A SANCTIFIED SINNER (1618).[63]

THE LAW OF MEMBERS. PETER MARTYR VERMIGLI: This law that he is describing is the power for sin and innate depravity. He calls it "the law of members," because above he referred to the whole as, "this wicked body of sin," and the body holds the members. Then "the members" in this place, as I indicated above, signify all the powers of the mind and all the parts of the body yet contaminated by sin. The apostle wished to indicate that this sickness, contracted from birth itself, remains not only in some one of our parts, but throughout the whole self, and has pervaded all its parts. COMMENTARY ON ROMANS (1560).[64]

FIGHT LIKE A KING AGAINST THE REBELS IN YOUR HEART. EDWARD ELTON: Grace and corruption are mingled together throughout, in every power and faculty of the soul of the person that is truly regenerate, as light and darkness are mingled together in the dawning of the day, and as heat and cold are mingled together in lukewarm water. We know that lukewarm water is not in one part hot and in another part of it cold, but it is partly hot and partly cold throughout. And there is a similar mixture of grace and corruption in those that are truly regenerate. And with all there is a flat contrariety between grace and corruption, and they are as contrary one to the other as light

and darkness, and as fire and water; and therefore it must be that the corruption of nature that still in part abides in God's children, and like a rebel violently and strongly opposes and intrigues against the power of grace that is in them, and it makes not a weak and feeble resistance but a mighty, strong, and violent opposition against it, and the lusts that arise from this mightily war and rebel against the working and the fruits of grace, as unbelief against faith, ignorance against knowledge, despair against hope, hypocrisy against singleness of heart, pride against humility, and so in other particulars.

Now this being a truth, for use it serves as a ground of admonition to all God's children: for here they are to be warned and to be stirred up to set themselves against the rebellion of their hearts. . . . Will a king be secure and careless, having many strong rebels up in arms against him in his own kingdom seeking to pull the crown from his head? Surely not! If he cares for his own safety he will not; rather, he will seek, with all possible speed, to subdue them, and to bring them down, yes to take away their heads. THE COMPLAINT OF A SANCTIFIED SINNER (1618).[65]

7:24 Repenting of Wretchedness

AN EXAMPLE OF TRUE REPENTANCE. PETER MARTYR VERMIGLI: When he feels himself in a manner oppressed in the conflict of these two laws, he cries out and confesses himself to be miserable, something he would not have done unless he had felt himself oppressed with some great and grievous evil. But there can be nothing more grievous than misery and death. Paul joins these two together and complains that he is drawn to them against his will. . . . And this exclamation comes neither from an ungodly man nor from one living in security, but from one converted to Christ, and striving against sin and detesting it, which he feels to be very strong in him. Here an example of true repentance is set forth for us, which the life of a Christian ought

---

[63]Elton, *The Complaint of a Sanctified Sinner*, 419-20*; citing Job 23:12; Prov 20:18.
[64]Vermigli, *In Epistolam S. Pauli*, 553.

[65]Elton, *The Complaint of a Sanctified Sinner*, 432-33*.

never to lack. Paul in this place wishes not for death, but to be delivered from depravity and corruption. And he uses an interrogation to signify that he cannot be delivered either by the law, or by a good conscience, or by the show of good works. Delivery is to be hoped for at Christ's hands only. COMMENTARY ON ROMANS (1558).[66]

STUNNING CHRIST WITH OUR CRIES. SAMUEL RUTHERFORD: To the Parishioners of Kilmalcolm, 1639: In Christ's absence, there is—as you write—a willingness to use means, but a sense of heaviness after using them, because performing them feels formal and shallow. In Christ's absence, I confess, it feels like work. But if you mean absence of comfort, and absence of a sense of his sweet presence, I think *that* absence is Christ's testing us, not simply our sin against him. Therefore, although our obedience is not sugared and sweetened with joy (which is the sweetmeat little children desire), yet the less sense, and the more willingness we have in obeying, the less formality there is in our obedience. However, we tend not to think so. For I believe that many think obedience is formal and lifeless unless the wind is fair in the west, and the sails are filled with joy and emotion, until souls, like a ship fair before the wind, can spread no more sail. But I am not of the same mind as those who think so.

But if, by the absence of Christ, you mean the withdrawal of his working grace, I do not see how willingness to use means could exist at all under that kind of absence. Therefore, be humbled that you feel a sense of heaviness in your obedience, and thankful that you have willingness. For the Bridegroom is preparing his spouse, often while she is half sleeping; and your Lord is working and helping more than you see. Also, I recommend to you that sense of heaviness, in place of formality and lifeless deadness in obedience. Be cast down, as much as you will or can, instead of being dead; and in your spiritual obedience, challenge that dull and slow carcass of sin rather than letting it lead or drive you. Oh, how sweet to lovely Jesus are bills

and grievances that we bring against corruption and the body of sin! I would have Christ, in such a case, bothered (if I may speak so) and stunned by our cries, as you see the apostle does, "Oh, wretched man that I am, who shall deliver me from the body of this death?" Protestations against the law of sin in you are law-grounds why sin can have no law against you. Seek to have your protestation discussed and judged, and then you will find Christ on your side of it. LETTER CCLXXXVI TO PARISHIONERS OF KILMALCOLM.[67]

TOO MUCH TO HOPE? MICHELANGELO:

Much it afflicts, and yet it soothes my mind
To dwell upon each thought of time gone by
Which memory recalls; though reason mourns
The irreparable ill of wasted hours.
It soothes me, when the thought of death suggests,
How brief, how transient is each human joy;
It grieves me, since I scarcely dare to hope
Pardon and grace thus late for all my sins.
Despite thy promises, O Lord, it would seem
Too much to hope that even love like thine
Can overlook my countless wanderings:
And yet your blood helps us to comprehend
That if your pangs for us were measureless
No less beyond all measure is your grace.

SONNET 50.[68]

SAINTS CARRY FORGIVEN SIN. JOHANNES BRENZ: The saints, in recognition of this wickedness, are therefore so troubled and crushed that they groan by night and by day. They sigh and they cry out for God's presence, where they are freed from this blight that is more horrible and grievous than death itself. But they are freed through Christ. Thus it follows: "I thank God through Jesus Christ our Lord." That is, although this blight is most burdensome, nevertheless, the pious must not give up hope. Rather, they are to give thanks to God who has given us his Son, our Lord

---

[66]Vermigli, *Learned and Fruitfull Commentaries*, 176*.

[67]Rutherford, *Letters*, 562-63*.
[68]Michelangelo, *Life of Michael Angelo*, 166-67*.

Jesus Christ. For he took up our sin in himself in order to make atonement, and he reconciled us to God so that although we still carry sin in our flesh, nevertheless, its guilt has been forgiven, and perfect and absolute righteousness has been given to us in Christ our Lord, through faith. COMMENTARY ON ROMANS (1564).[69]

THE MORE HOLY, THE MORE ONE GRIEVES SIN. HEINRICH BULLINGER: He emphasizes the distress by an exclamation. In truth, all the saints of God cry out together with Paul, bewailing this unhappy captivity. In fact, the more holy a person is, the more frequently and ardently they cry out, grieving over the incurable misery of the human heart, by which we are so often drawn away from better things to worse. For he calls a body subject to the impulses of sin "this body of death." COMMENTARY ON ROMANS (1533).[70]

HOLY DISCONTENTMENT. EDWARD ELTON: Let us be restless and discontented in this respect: It is a holy discontentment when we find ourselves clogged with unbelief, with doubting, with distrust, and the like, and we try to shake them off but cannot. And then to be in a sort of discontent, and even restless in our desire to be rid of them, and in our care to use the means to that purpose, that is a holy discontentment. And know it—whoever you are, that are thus restless and thus discontented—know it, I say, to your comfort, that though you cannot be freed completely from that spiritual evil that lies heavy on your soul, and you desire to shake off, and you use all good means to that purpose, yet that evil will never be imputed to you. Though the Lord is pleased to keep you in exercise under it, yet he will never charge it to your soul but will accept your will and desire to be freed from it, as if you were indeed freed from it. Think on that to your comfort. THE COMPLAINT OF A SANCTIFIED SINNER (1618).[71]

SIN IS BRED IN THE BONE. JOHN TRAPP: We must discontentedly be contented to be exercised with sin while we are here. It is so bred in the bone that until our bones—like Joseph's—are carried out of the Egypt of this world, it will not out. The Romans so conquered Chosroes the Persian that he made a law that no king of Persia should ever again move war against the Romans. But whatever we do to subdue sin, it will be a Jebusite, a false borderer, yes, a rank traitor rebelling against the Spirit. But we may take for a comforting sign of future victory only this: that we are discontented with our present ill estate. Grace will get the upper hand as nature does when the humors are disturbed, and after many fits. And as until then there is no rest to the body, so neither is there to the soul. The conflict between flesh and spirit is like when two opposite things meet together—like cold saltpeter and hot brimstone—and make a great noise. So does Paul here: Miserable me, and so on. He is fitly compared to a man thrown off his horse and dragged after him, crying out for help. Or he is like one that is troubled with a disease called the *Mare* or *Ephialtes*, which (in his slumber) makes him think that he feels a thing as big as a mountain lying on his breast, which he can no way remove, but desires to be rid of. COMMENTARY ON ROMANS (1656).[72]

LIKE A NEWBORN STRUGGLING FOR LIFE. JOHN COTTON: The spirit of grace is a spirit of supplication. . . . [The first reason is that the spirit reveals our lack of grace and leads us to humbly pray.] It becomes even clearer if you add this second reason; and it is taken from the estate of the spirit of grace in those in whom it is received. And what is that? It is a spirit of life in Christ Jesus, the same spirit of which he speaks in verse 15. Yet it is a spirit of life that is an imperfect life, a weak life, like that of a newborn child. True life, but very weak, being pained and bruised in the birth, it cries out bitterly. So a newborn babe in Christ, as soon as it has received the spirit of grace,

[69]Brenz, *In Epistolam*, 183.
[70]Bullinger, *In Sanctissimam Pauli*, 99v-100r.
[71]Elton, *The Complaint of a Sanctified Sinner*, 475-76*.

[72]Trapp, *A Commentary or Exposition upon the Epistle of St. Paul*, 634*.

feels itself in a cold and naked condition, and then feels its own weakness and hunger. An imperfect life strongly desires relief, and if it is afflicted with any sense of death, it will struggle exceedingly, and strive, and grasp every way, if it is possible, to preserve its life. So we no sooner receive a spirit of grace than we find ourselves encompassed about with a body of death. Now all life, when it is encompassed about by death, will so strive to preserve itself that you would think the dying man to be the most lively. So there is no Christian soul that receives a spirit of grace but then finds itself encompassed about with enemies, the flesh lusting against the spirit, so that there is a great strife in him. His heart being changed, faith strives against doubting; his heat and zeal against coldness; humility and meekness against pride and wrath. And thus he strives earnestly for the preservation of his life. Now, then you will no longer need to make up prayers. For if a man becomes aware of his own weakness, he then has enough matters to complain of to God and himself. He sees what he stands in need of: he wants faith, and a soft heart, a humble spirit, and zeal for God's glory. Now he wants everything; so as (if I may speak so) he can tell God stories of his misery, and that with some earnestness and heartiness. As a man struggling for his life, he can now plead for anything that might make him live in God's sight. And the Spirit teaches us all this. THE WAY OF LIFE (1641).[73]

CHRIST ALONE IS INNOCENT. BALTHASAR HUBMAIER: Now these brethren see the truth and must confess that our kingdom is of this world, about which we are sincerely sorry. However, Christ alone can say in truth, "My kingdom is not of this world," because he was conceived and born without sin, an innocent little lamb, in whom there is no deception, without sin or blemish. He alone could say in truth, "The prince of this world has come, but in

me he found nothing," which we here on earth could never truthfully say. For as often as that prince, the devil, comes, he finds in us evil lusts, evil desires, evil inclinations. Therefore also St. Paul, while filled with the Holy Spirit, calls himself wretched. Likewise the most righteous and pious Christians must also confess their wretchedness until death, no matter what we make of ourselves. ON THE SWORD.[74]

7:25 The Complexity of Human Nature

THE LIFELONG FEUD OF SPIRIT AND FLESH. MARTIN LUTHER: Then St. Paul shows how spirit and flesh struggle with each other in one person. He gives himself as an example, so that we may learn how to kill sin in ourselves. He gives both spirit and flesh the name "law," so that, just as it is in the nature of divine law to drive a person on and make demands of them, so too the flesh drives and demands and rages against the spirit and wants to have its own way. Likewise the spirit drives and demands against the flesh and wants to have its own way. This feud lasts in us for as long as we live, in one person more, in another less, depending on whether spirit or flesh is stronger. Yet the whole human being is both: spirit and flesh. The human being fights with himself until he becomes completely spiritual. PREFACE TO THE LETTER OF ST. PAUL TO THE ROMANS (1545).[75]

THANKS TO THE ONE MEDIATOR. PETER MARTYR VERMIGLI: Another is the truth that when one has heard, been helped by, and experienced freedom, he gives thanks. And he does this through Jesus Christ our Lord, not through Mary, or through John the Baptist, or through their works, or through any other thing of this kind, but only through that One who alone is the one Mediator between God and humankind. COMMENTARY ON ROMANS (1560).[76]

---

[73]Cotton, Way of Life, 3-7*; citing Heb 10:29; Rom 8:2; Gal 5:17; Rom 8:26.

[74]CRR 5:497*; citing Jn 14:30.
[75]Luther, Preface to the Letter*.
[76]Vermigli, In Epistolam S. Pauli, 556.

UNDER THE INFLUENCE OF BOTH GOD'S AND SIN'S LAWS. HEINRICH BULLINGER: Let it never be said that justification begins from us, that is, from our merits and righteous deeds. Nor are we speaking of the ungodly here, but of saints. For with their mind and spirit they serve the law of God, but they have not stopped being men and women, and therefore they are under the influence of the flesh; or rather, they are subservient to the law of sin as well. Therefore, the law of God brings it about that, having been convicted by our own misery and experience, we are compelled to confess that justification is solely of grace. What will those who attribute justification to the works produced by grace[†] answer to this? They doubtless say that Paul spoke not in his own person but in the assumed persona of someone else. But this opinion is refuted by Paul's own words. COMMENTARY ON ROMANS (1533).[77]

FOUR STATES OF HUMANITY. PETER MARTYR VERMIGLI: Whether there is a faculty of this kind in human beings, or in what manner it is in them, cannot be defined by a single answer. It is first necessary to define the state and condition of humanity. For there are at least four categories in humankind. For the status of Adam, when he was created at the beginning, was far different from after he had fallen, and the status of his whole posterity is still of this kind. Furthermore, those who have been regenerated in Christ are in a far better state than those who live apart from Christ. And we are to have a most happy and free state when we have gone forth from this mortal body. COMMENTARY ON ROMANS (1560).[78]

EVEN THE RIGHTEOUS DO GOOD WORKS IMPERFECTLY. JOHANNES BRENZ: The thought is "I myself love the law of God, I delight in the law of God, and I am eager to perfectly satisfy it, because it indeed pertains to the renewing of my will. But

because it pertains to my old nature, which clings to me until death, I am much more lured by that which is in me, the flesh, and a passion for sin, than that which is of the Spirit and is subjugated to the law of God." Here it is now possible to understand what that common saying means: "The righteous person sins in every good work."[†] It seems that the expression is nonsensical, for if one sins in doing good works, it is not certain that works are good, or that they are not sin. And when they see somebody inexperienced praying or distributing alms, they ridicule them and shout, "What are you doing? Do you not know that you are doing evil, since those new preachers teach and say that we sin in whatever good work we do?" But this is refuted in this place by Paul, who explains what is the meaning of that saying. For the truth is that although the righteous person sins in every good work, this does not mean that the work itself that was commanded by God is sin, or that it is not beneficial. For God commands good works, and the Spirit of faith demands that we walk in the commands of God. But it must be understood in the way that Paul explains it: "I myself serve the law of God in my mind, but in my flesh I serve the law of sin." That is, "In every good work, I do two things. The first is that I desire—as one who was born again from faith by the Spirit—to perfectly satisfy the law of God. The other is that the flesh, or the old Adam, because it opposes and resists the Spirit, does not permit my obedience to be perfect and my work to be complete in every aspect. Therefore, I sin in every good work, not because the things that are commanded by God are sins, but because I do the good work imperfectly." COMMENTARY ON ROMANS (1564).[79]

WE USED TO BE WILD OLIVE TREES. PETER MARTYR VERMIGLI: And in this letter to the Romans, he calls people not yet grafted into Christ "wild olive trees." However, we know that wild olive trees are sterile and are not able to bear fruit. And

---

[77]Bullinger, *In Sanctissimam Pauli*, 100r-100v. [†]*Operibus gratiae:* term in Catholic theology referring to works (deserving of merit) that are enabled by God's grace.
[78]Vermigli, *In Epistolam S. Pauli*, 558-59; citing Ps 8:5; Heb 2:7.

[79]Brenz, *In Epistolam*, 183-84. [†]Luther, *Assertio*, article 31 (WA 7:136.21).

yet it is not possible for works to be good unless they either satisfy the law, or if they veer to some degree from the law, by means of Christ they may not be imputed. But people who are not born again are not able to satisfy the law: for they have not been regenerated. Truly, a benefit of Christ is that our failings are mended. At the same time, if they are not joined to Christ by faith, they are not able to be restored. And the one who teaches that a person, apart from the grace of God, is able to do works that are pleasing to him is the sort of one who teaches, essentially, that Christ is not the Redeemer of all people. The one who teaches that we are able to do good works, and to live rightly, apart from the grace of Christ assigns to our nature too much credit for salvation apart from Christ. Indeed, Paul says in this passage that although we were slaves of sin, we are now children of righteousness. COMMENTARY ON ROMANS (1560).[80]

It Is Not the Tree Itself That Is Bad.

WOLFGANG MUSCULUS: Here's how I understand the "law of sin": first, I understand "sin" here not as referring to some external act, nor to some affection of the soul such as anger, hatred, love, joy, fear, or lust, but instead to that original corruption of all of these things that is passed down to us from our heritage in Adam. Just as we do not say the badness and sin of a bad tree is its fruit, or its leaves, or its bark, or its twigs, or the sap itself or the arteries through which the sap flows, but that it is the *corruption* and *infection* of the sap that arises from its roots that produces bad fruit, just so, in this passage sin is that infection and original corruption by which all of our affections are riddled with vices. Insofar as they are natural, however, they are not evil. It is not even an evil to "lust," since even the Spirit "lusts," nor is it evil to become angry, since even God becomes angry (humanly speaking), nor is hatred an evil, since David says: "I pursue the enemies of God with a perfect hatred." But rather, it is the *perversion* of

this or that affection or desire that is sin. This is the evil that the apostle said was present in himself. COMMENTARY ON ROMANS (1555).[81]

When Sin Lies Heavy on Your Soul, Look to Christ.

EDWARD ELTON: Let us learn that when sin lies heavy on our souls and we feel the weight and the burden of it—yes, we being God's children and feeling sinful infirmities lying heavy on our souls that we are weary of and would willingly shake off and cannot—let us learn, I say, where we are to seek and to look for ease, comfort, and refreshing. Surely not in ourselves, nor in anything in ourselves, nor elsewhere in the world, but only in Jesus Christ the storehouse of all true comfort. THE COMPLAINT OF A SANCTIFIED SINNER (1618).[82]

The Importance of Personal Experience.

JUAN DE VALDÉS: To be perfectly understood, this whole chapter requires personal experience. Indeed, people will understand as much of it as they have experienced, having themselves passed through the things that are here written. These things give great satisfaction and greatly console Christians in their weaknesses, considering that since so great an apostle experienced them and passed through them, it is no great thing that they should experience them and pass through them. COMMENTARY ON ROMANS (1556).[83]

Gratitude Propels Us into the Battle.

JOHANNES BUGENHAGEN: "I give thanks to God." Earlier when he said, "What a miserable man I am!" Paul was looking at his sin. Here, his attention is turned to the grace of God: "Every day, whenever condemnation, death and sin rage against me, I nevertheless know that I am in God's grace and am accepted through Christ. When I see that I am unable to overcome sin, I am driven to despair; but when I see that God is the Father of Christ

---

[80]Vermigli, *In Epistolam S. Pauli*, 569.

[81]Musculus, *In Epistolam Apostoli Pauli*, 160-61; citing Gal 5:17; Ps 139:22.

[82]Elton, *The Complaint of a Sanctified Sinner*, 488-89*.

[83]Valdés, *Commentary upon St. Paul's Epistle*, 114*.

crucified, and that insofar as he is Christ's Father, he is for this very reason my Father as well—how can I not be transported with joy? How can I not rejoice and exult, seeing that I now behold all that sin to be abolished and not imputed? Therefore, because God wishes it so, I will gladly restrain and push back against the sin that is in me. By the power of God, may I not allow it to rule over me!"

All these things are intended to make you understand what he has just said: that the sin in us is plainly not dead yet, but there is a perpetual battle for us to wage with remaining sin, like the Israelites who perpetually waged war against the Canaanites. INTERPRETATION OF ROMANS (1531).[84]

---

[84]Bugenhagen, *In D. Pauli ad Romanos*, 78v-79r.

8:1-11 LIVING IN THE SPIRIT

There is therefore now no condemnation for those who are in Christ Jesus.[a] [2]*For the law of the Spirit of life has set you*[b] *free in Christ Jesus from the law of sin and death.* [3]*For God has done what the law, weakened by the flesh, could not do. By sending his own Son in the likeness of sinful flesh and for sin,*[c] *he condemned sin in the flesh,* [4]*in order that the righteous requirement of the law might be fulfilled in us, who walk not according to the flesh but according to the Spirit.* [5]*For those who live according to the flesh set their minds on the things of the flesh, but those who live according to the Spirit set their minds on the things of the Spirit.* [6]*For to set the mind on the flesh is death, but to set the mind on the Spirit is life and peace.* [7]*For the mind that is set on the flesh is hostile to God, for it does not submit to God's law; indeed, it cannot.* [8]*Those who are in the flesh cannot please God.*

[9]*You, however, are not in the flesh but in the Spirit, if in fact the Spirit of God dwells in you. Anyone who does not have the Spirit of Christ does not belong to him.* [10]*But if Christ is in you, although the body is dead because of sin, the Spirit is life because of righteousness.* [11]*If the Spirit of him who raised Jesus from the dead dwells in you, he who raised Christ Jesus*[d] *from the dead will also give life to your mortal bodies through his Spirit who dwells in you.*

a Some manuscripts add *who walk not according to the flesh (but according to the Spirit)* **b** Some manuscripts *me* **c** Or *and as a sin offering* **d** Some manuscripts lack *Jesus*

OVERVIEW: In the previous pericope, the reformers emphasized the struggle that goes on within the regenerate person between their flesh and their spirit. Now they shift to contrasting those who live according to the flesh (the unregenerate) with those who live according to the Spirit (the regenerate).

The reformers take the opportunity to present the gospel and explore how justification works, including examining the role of the Trinity in it. We do not need to be afraid, for in Christ we are no longer under condemnation. The "in Christ" state matters, for it is an engrafting, a sharing, a becoming like him. We gain more in the second Adam than we lost with the first, and Christ was able to do what the law had not been able to do due to our sinful nature. The reformers also argue against a medieval pope who used Romans 8:8 as a justification for requiring clerical celibacy, and against the medieval doctrine of transubstantiation in the Eucharist (Rom 8:10).

The interpreters explore the contrast of walking according to the flesh and walking according to the Spirit. Although there is still within the believer a struggle between the flesh and the Spirit, there is a contrast between believers and those who are living entirely according to the flesh. Those who are still under law, who live and breathe the life of the flesh, and who tend toward sin are under condemnation and headed toward eternal death. Those who live under grace think, feel, and desire the things of the Spirit. Although they have to fight against the flesh that remains, their sin is covered by Christ's grace, and they have peace with God and are headed for eternal life. The reformers emphasize that we are not beyond condemnation because of some inherent change that has been worked in us, but because of grace alone, because we are in Christ. But that doesn't mean that our actions are inconsequential. Obedience to the Spirit is key, and we should ask ourselves how much we have grown in it. The Holy Spirit will do the same thing in us that he did in Christ: raise us from the dead. Thus, we no longer need to be afraid of death, for it is no longer a punishment, for God does not punish his children, but rather only chastises them or allows afflictions for their training.

8:1 *No Condemnation for Those in Christ*

THERE IS NO LONGER ANYONE TO CONDEMN US. JUAN DE VALDÉS: It is as though St. Paul had said, "I say there is no condemnation to those who are members of Christ; meaning that there is in them all an inward experience, concurrent with my own, as to the mode in which the faith is obtained, by which the Spirit of life has made me free (exempted) from the law, which discovers sin and aggravates it, and which by such discovery and aggravation works death. By this I come to understand that there is no condemnation either to me or those who are members of Christ. For neither they nor I have any accuser, since we have been freed from the law. And having no accuser, there is no one to condemn us." COMMENTARY ON ROMANS (1556).[1]

NO NEED TO FEAR. JOHN COLET: Being assured and certain of this, I say, there is, beyond question, nothing further for them to fear, depending as they do in steadfast hope on God. Nor, while they retain God as their helper, do they have reason to think anything able to withstand and be dangerous to them. But, embracing God, or rather embraced by God, they may feel confident that they are altogether shielded and safe in God. These are they, as St. Paul records, whom the divine purpose has marked out to be called to him by his grace for justification, whom by his free inspiration he has moved and formed anew after the likeness of his Son, and drawn from their human and customary affections, and translated to a new and divine state of life, in such wise that they should from now on appear in no degree the men and women that they were before. But as being begotten again and entirely born anew, they should in all their life and actions image forth God himself within them, so far as human dimness allows. EXPOSITION ON ROMANS (1497).[2]

IMPERFECTION, MERCY, AND REGENERATION INTERTWINED. JOHN CALVIN: After having described the contest that the godly have perpetually with their own flesh, he returns to the consolation, which was very needful for them and which he had before mentioned. It was this, that though they were still beset by sin, they were yet exempt from the power of death, and from every curse, provided they lived not in the flesh but in the Spirit. He joins together these three things: the imperfection under which the faithful always labor, the mercy of God in pardoning and forgiving, and the regeneration of the Spirit. COMMENTARY ON ROMANS 8:1.[3]

CAIN, ABEL, AND CONDEMNATION. JOHANNES BRENZ: Therefore, there is no condemnation—and that only on account of Jesus Christ our Lord, who is the propitiation for our sin. But the wicked not only have the flesh and sin; they also live according to the flesh, and they submit to their passion for sin, so they bear its fruit. Cain, when he saw that Abel was preferred over himself, feared that dominion of the earth would be snatched away from him, and he was indignant with Abel. This sin incited him so that he envied his brother and killed him. And indeed, up till this point, Cain and Abel were not dissimilar. For if Abel had been the elder, and he had seen that Cain the younger was preferred, certainly as the one abandoned by himself he would have been afraid of his own flesh, lest the rank of authority being snatched away from him he be stirred up toward hatred and murder. But in that event is the greatest distinction, because Cain did not believe in the seed of the woman, who is Christ, but rather, he thought himself to be this seed. Thereafter he yielded to the love of sin, he virulently envied his brother, and when given the opportunity, he killed him. But Abel believed in the seed of the woman; he did not pursue Cain with virulent hatred, nor did he kill him. . . . Therefore, that is the distinction between the faithful and the wicked, because even if both

---

[1] Valdés, *Commentary upon St. Paul's Epistle*, 116*.
[2] Colet, *Exposition of St. Paul's Epistle*, 25*.

[3] CTS 38:275-76* (CO 49:136).

have sin in the flesh, nevertheless the faithful believe in Christ and do not submit to the love of sin, but the wicked do not actually believe in Christ and they do not oppose the love of sin, but instead relax the harness on it, and therefore, they have both sin and condemnation. But there is no condemnation for the faithful. COMMENTARY ON ROMANS (1588).[4]

DISCHARGED FROM THE FEAR OF DAMNATION. ANTONIO DEL CORRO: Romans:[†] You have so plainly and enlighteningly, in your own person, shown how great the worthiness and holiness of God's law is, and how it is meant to execute a variety of offices toward men and women, until they are truly and perfectly born anew in Christ. So now, by this talk of yours, I understand one of the hardest points of this letter, which point consists in knowing of the offices that God's law uses toward a person. Now, if it pleases you, let us discuss the third state of men and women, that is, to wit, when they are justified and made holy. But first of all, I pray you show me more plainly what kind of state this state of the regenerated sort is: and afterward by what marks the person that is godly minded may be certified (reassured) of their regeneration or new birth.

Paul: Just as in considering the first and second state of man or woman, namely, "unregenerated" and "regenerated," I used my own life as an example: so in laying forth this third member of our partition, I will allege my own experiences as a pattern to represent the image of a regenerated man or woman. As touching the first part of your demand, surely the state and dignity of those that are justified and regenerated is most excellent. They, being dead to the old Adam and grafted into the new Adam, Christ, are no longer in danger of any damnation. For how is it possible that Christ our head would give up his own members to destruction? Here may also be gathered an answer to the other part of our demand. For Christ's work is so great in the minds of those who are

truly regenerated, that their life is consecrated to holiness. By which they are, in a way, certified that the presence of Christ dwells in them. But we will speak more about these things hereafter. Now, to use my own experience as an argument, the reason why these most excellent effects are worked in my mind, is this: that the law of the life-giving Spirit in Jesus Christ, has set me free from the law of sin and death, insomuch that by the gift of faith, and the record of God's Spirit, I feel my self discharged from the fear of damnation. And I think the same thing has befallen all the true members of Christ. A THEOLOGICAL DIALOGUE EXPOUNDING ROMANS.[5]

THE NECESSITY OF SANCTIFICATION. ANDREW WILLET: Sanctification must not be severed from justification. "There is no condemnation for those who do not walk after the flesh." The apostle here evidently shows that those who walk according to the flesh are not in Christ Jesus, nor justified by him and freed from condemnation; although our sanctification is not a meritorious or efficient cause of salvation, yet it is such a cause as sine qua non, without the which there is no salvation: (1) Because regeneration is inseparably joined with justification. (2) Sanctification is a testimony and evidence of our faith, without which it is dead. (3) It is a fruit of the Spirit. (4) And it necessarily follows true repentance. A SIX-FOLD COMMENTARY ON THE EPISTLE TO THE ROMANS (1620).[6]

8:2 *The Spirit of Life*

THE LAW OF THE SPIRIT OF LIFE. HEINRICH BULLINGER: Here is the reason why the faithful are freed from the fear of condemnation: The law of the Spirit of life, through Christ, has freed us from sin and death. Significantly, he has connected death to sin. For no one is freed from sin so that they may not be—or be perceived as—sinful. But

---

[4]Brenz, *In Epistolam*, 618.

[5]Del Corro, *A Theological Dialogue*, 69v-70v*. [†]Del Corro sets up an imaginary dialogue between the Romans and Paul.
[6]Willet, *Hexapla*, 402*.

rather so that he may not be imputed as sinful, nor be able to die. He calls the life-giving Spirit the law of the Spirit of life, according to antithesis. Moreover, that life-giving power of faith is indeed the very Spirit of God, by whom life, redemption, and sanctification were given; we know that these things were given to us through Christ. COMMENTARY ON ROMANS (1533).[7]

BEING "IN CHRIST." PETER MARTYR VERMIGLI: It seems necessary to understand what it means to be "in Christ." In the first place there is something common to all mortals that answers to this, for in that the Son of God received human nature, he is thereby conjoined to all men and women. For since they have commerce with flesh and blood, he also was made a sharer in flesh and blood, as the letter to the Hebrews testifies. But this is only a general conjunction, and a weak one at that, one that is, if I can so speak, only according to physical matter. For the nature of men and women is far removed from that nature that Christ took unto himself. For the human nature existing in Christ is both immortal and exempt from sin, and adorned with all purity; whereas ours is impure, corruptible, and wretchedly contaminated by sin. But if our nature is gifted with the Spirit of Christ, it is so renewed that it becomes not that much different from Christ's human nature. Or rather, there is such an increased likeness to him that Paul says in the letter to the Ephesians that we are flesh "of his flesh" and bone "of his bones," a manner of speaking that seems to have been taken from the wording of the Old Testament, where brothers and relatives customarily say to each other, "my bone and my flesh." They seem to be acknowledging a single substance common between them, derived from the same paternal seed and the same maternal womb. To this point, it even happens that children do not derive from the parents merely their fleshly and bodily substance, but also their natural character, impulses, and disposition. This same manner of speaking comes to be applied to us when we are

given the Spirit of Christ. For we possess a common mind with him that surpasses the common nature we have with him, as Paul instructs us in his first letter to the Corinthians and, with the same meaning, as he demands of the Philippians when he says "let this same mind be in you which was also in Christ Jesus." Paul expresses this conjunction we have with Christ in this same letter with the concept of engrafting, wherein the two aspects that we've already mentioned are best grasped. For since the shoot that is grafted in and the plant in which it is grafted are made one, in a certain sense, not only are two substances that were formerly different conjoined together, but they are invigorated by the same sap, spirit, and life. The apostle bore witness that this same thing takes place in us when he said that we are engrafted into Christ. Even Christ teaches the same thing in the gospel according to John when he calls himself the "vine" and us the "branches." COMMENTARY ON ROMANS (1560).[8]

DELIVERED FROM THE DOMINION OF THE LAW. BENEDETTO DA MANTOVA AND MARCANTONIO FLAMINIO: He has delivered us from the dominion of the law, in that he has given us his Holy Spirit who teaches us all truth, and he has satisfied the law to the full and given the same satisfaction to all his members (that is, to all true Christians), so that they may safely appear at God's throne, because they are clothed with the righteousness of Christ, and delivered by him from the curse of the law. Then the law cannot accuse us or condemn us any more, nor move our affections or appetites, nor increase sin in us. And, therefore, St. Paul says that the obligation that was against us is canceled by Jesus Christ and discharged on the tree of the cross, as he has set us free from the subjection of the law, and consequently from the tyranny of sin and death, which can no more hold us oppressed because it is overcome by Jesus Christ in

[8]Vermigli, *In Epistolam S. Pauli*, 611-12; citing Eph 5:30; Gen 2:23; 29:14; Judg 9:2; 2 Sam 5:1; 19:12-13; 1 Chron 11:1; Phil 2:5; Rom 11:16-24; Jn 15:5.

[7]Bullinger, *In Sanctissimam Pauli*, 101v.

his resurrection, and so consequently by us, which are his members, in such a way that we may say with St. Paul, and with the prophet Hosea, "Death is quite vanquished and destroyed." THE BENEFIT OF CHRIST'S DEATH (1543).[9]

UNDER THE LEADING OF THE HOLY SPIRIT. JOHANNES COCCEIUS: Because they are sanctified through the Spirit of Christ, they are not under the law as they once were under the law, as miserable sinners, but by the "law of the spirit of life in Christ they are set free from the law of sin and death"—that is, from the dominion of sin and the curse that leads to death. So they are, therefore, not under the covenant of works, which prescribes the condition of righteousness and life, and that requires either that [condition] or the punishment for disobedience. Rather, they are under the leading of the Holy Spirit, who inscribes the law on the heart and renews them according to the image of God. SUMMARY OF THE DOCTRINE OF THE COVENANT AND TESTAMENT OF GOD.[10]

8:3 God Sent His Son to Do What the Law Couldn't

THE LAW IS LIKE WINE THAT CANNOT HEAL. MARTIN LUTHER: The apostle argues against their empty faith in the law and their knowledge of it when he says that it was impossible for the law to accomplish that which they presumptuously thought, namely, the abolition of sin and the acquisition of righteousness. In this the law is not at fault, but their opinion of and confidence in the law is vain and stupid. To be sure, the law in itself is very good. It is as with a sick man who wants to drink some wine because he foolishly thinks that his health will return if he does so. Now if the doctor, without any criticism of the wine, should say to him: "It is impossible for the wine to cure you, it will only make you sicker," the doctor is not

condemning the wine but only the foolish trust of the sick man in it. For he needs other medicine to get well, so that he then can drink his wine. Thus also our corrupt nature needs another kind of medicine than the law, by which it can arrive at good health so that it can fulfill the law. LECTURES ON ROMANS.[11]

JUSTICE AND MERCY KNIT TOGETHER. THOMAS CRANMER: Although this justification is free for us, it was not free without any ransom being paid at all. Here we may be astonished, reasoning after this fashion: If a ransom was paid for our redemption, then it was not given to us freely. For prisoners who pay their ransom are not let go freely; for if they go freely, then they go without ransom. For what does it mean to go freely, other than to be set at liberty without the payment of ransom? This reason is satisfied by the great wisdom of God in the mystery of our redemption, who so tempered his justice and mercy together that he would neither by his justice condemn us to the perpetual captivity of the devil and his prison of hell, remediless for ever, without mercy; nor by his mercy deliver us without justice or payment of a just ransom. Rather, he joined his most upright and equal justice to his endless mercy. He showed his great mercy to us in delivering us from our former captivity without requiring any ransom to be paid or amends to be made on our part, which would have been impossible for us to do. And since it did not lie within us to do that, he provided a ransom for us; that was the most precious body and blood of his dearest and most beloved Son Jesus Christ, who, besides his being a ransom, fulfilled the law for us perfectly. And so the justice of God and his mercy embraced together and fulfilled the mystery of our redemption. HOMILY ON SALVATION.[12]

WE GAIN MORE IN THE SECOND ADAM THAN WE LOST IN THE FIRST ADAM. THEODORE

---

[9]Benedetto and Flaminio, *Benefit of Christ's Death*, 26-27*; citing Gal 3:13, Hos 13:14.
[10]Cocceius, *Foedere*, 459-60.

[11]LW 25:350*.
[12]Cranmer, *Miscellaneous Writings*, 129*.

BEZA: We find here a strengthening of the conclusion drawn in the previous verse. For Paul would not have been able to argue successfully that our sins have been forgiven in Christ unless he also taught that Christ had been promised and revealed to us for this very purpose, and that our guilt was covered by his obedience. He also needed to demonstrate by a rather lengthy comparison between Christ and Adam that in Christ being made man so that he might be, as it were, another Adam, we receive much more and better things in him than we had lost in the first Adam. Thus he would have tried to argue in vain that our corruption is covered over in the sight of God by that most perfect sanctification of our nature in Christ, freely imputed to us, unless he added that the Father willed that our nature be assumed by his Son so that he might restore it to wholeness. In this nature which through faith we possess in common with Christ, we are found in God's sight, if not in ourselves yet, so in Christ, to be completely everything that the written ordinance of the law requires of us.

He now adds the reason why this was necessary: because the law—whose general function and role was to lead us to that perfect goal of righteousness—was utterly unable to carry this out. By no means was this its own fault (as he explained in the previous two chapters) but rather due to our flesh, that is, that nature corrupted and made repugnant to God by our guilt, which therefore had to be restored whole in Christ unless God wished us to be utterly lost. This is the true explanation of this passage, insofar as I'm able to judge. MAJOR ANNOTATIONS (1594).[13]

How Justification Happens. JOHANNES BRENZ: From where are we justified? What follows it? God has brought this about. The law was not able to justify us on account of the flesh. Much less is the flesh itself—that is, all human capacities—able to justify us. Therefore, God's mercy was such that he destroyed sin, and he also considers us all

as perfectly righteous. But how is this possible? It is not simply because God is himself merciful, for he is not merciful and tenderhearted except to this one: the one who satisfies his commands. For thus says the Decalogue. "The one bringing about mercy on thousands, to those who love me and keep my commandments." Therefore, God, who is All, is so righteous that he has a hatred for sin, and therefore also he has a hatred for sinners, which all men and women are. But because he is merciful and tenderhearted toward those who are unworthy and sinners, he forgave them their sins, which he did on account of Christ his Son. For God supplied what was lacking in the law, that is, he forgives sin, he frees us from sin, and he perceives us as righteous according to this mode, as may be clearly seen:

First, he sent his Son into the world. And he did not send him as an angel, appearing only by an external image, but he sent him assuming human flesh into his very person. And so exactly did he assume flesh—which, in his case, was not sinful, but nevertheless was similar to our flesh, which is liable to sin. For although the flesh of Christ is not liable to sin, nevertheless he was liable to every suffering of sin, which includes corporeal as well as spiritual sufferings, among which the foremost is the horror of death and of hell. And therefore, Christ had truly human flesh, which indeed pertains to nature, but not to sin. But which was subject to the sufferings of sin, which are poverty, sadness, and every other sort of curse that was enumerated in Leviticus and Deuteronomy. "We do not have," he says in the letter to the Hebrews 4, "a High Priest who is not able to be affected with the experience of our weaknesses, but one who was tempted in all respects according to the likeness, yet without sin."

Second, with regard to sin, Christ—having been sent by God the Father, in the flesh—condemned sin by means of the flesh, as a sacrifice for sin. That is, Christ offered the flesh—or his body—as a sacrifice for sin, by which sacrifice he atoned for sin and by it he bore his own law, and thus he condemned sin by his own sacrifice, that although there is a remainder of sin until now in the saints, it is yet

---

[13]Beza, *Annotationes Majores*, 91; citing Rom 3:23-26; 5:1-21.

not able to condemn them. Nor was he only condemned, but he also brought about the truth that he would fulfill the righteousness of the law for us. Again, the righteousness of the law is a perfect righteousness, which remains valid in the presence of the tribunal of God. The law does not itself bring forth this righteousness. Moreover, no man or woman has fulfilled this righteousness. Only Christ fulfilled the law perfectly. Therefore, when Christ assumed human flesh, he presented his entire self to us—however great that is—that if we believe in him and take hold of him through faith, then we would also take hold of in him what he himself held and took hold of. He had a perfect righteousness, or the "justification of the law." Therefore, we also have in Christ a perfect righteousness, indeed not on account of our worth, but on account of Christ through faith. And God, when he finds in us Christ his Son, also imputes to us his perfect righteousness. Just as in a body, the members enjoy the dignity of the head, so when Christ is the head of believers, believers are his members, and therefore they enjoy his righteousness.

Finally, we should not suppose that this faith in Christ and the righteousness of Christ are idle within us. Paul adds, "Who move about not according to the flesh, but according to the Spirit." Many people thought that when the righteousness of Christ was given to us, it might be permitted for us to lead life according to our desire, and meanwhile to boast about the righteousness of Christ. Therefore Paul adds, "Who not according to the flesh," that he might make clear that faith and the righteousness of Christ are effective in believers. Although until now, there is a remainder of sin in the flesh, nevertheless, the righteousness of Christ, which we have through faith, does not permit us to walk according to the flesh and to follow the desire of sin, but to put the harness onto sin, and to continually follow the affection of the Spirit and the command of God. Therefore, where do all of these things point? Without doubt, in order to prove the truth of the chief proposition, that hope does not make us ashamed. If there is no condemnation for the saints, even if they still have sin, if

Christ has atoned for sin by his sacrifice and has given to those who trust in him the entirety of his own righteousness, how is it possible for those who hope in him, who await the heavenly blessedness, to be defrauded and put to shame? Commentary on Romans (1588).[14]

The Death of Christ Is Both Virtue and Sin. Peter Martyr Vermigli: "But what was impossible for the law, insofar as it was weak through the flesh, God did by sending his own Son." Here the reason is given whereby it is shown that the liberating Spirit of God was given to us, so that we might be made more confident that it is so. For when people hear that the Spirit of Christ is to be possessed, they customarily think that on account of impure affections and depraved habits of life they are unworthy to receive him. Paul removes this doubt and says that this benefit is conferred on us by virtue of the death of Christ. For this was the end for which Christ was willing to die: that by his Spirit the "justification of the law† might be fulfilled in" the elect. Nor did he take on himself flesh for any other reason than that he might give aid to the weakness of our flesh. The apostle here touches on this purpose and counsel of God. From this passage it becomes quite clear how that one and the same act—the death of Christ—depending on whether it is considered as being advanced by God or by men and women, is either a virtue or a sin. Commentary on Romans (1560).[15]

Christ's Sacrifice Fulfills the Righteousness of the Law in Us. Christoph Corner: This is the goal, that the *dikaiōma tou nomou*, the "'righteousness of the law' might be fulfilled in us." That is, that that righteousness which the law requires might be imputed to us on account of Christ's satisfaction and obedience which he rendered in our flesh to God for us, that we might be accounted righteous through him, and

---

[14]Brenz, *In Epistolam*, 619-20; citing Heb 4.
[15]Vermigli, *In Epistolam S. Pauli*, 613. †*Iustificatio legis*, following the Vulgate of Rom 8:4, whereas the Greek has *dikaiōma*, "righteous requirements" or "precepts."

that we might thus "do" the righteousness of the law. The righteousness of the law is fulfilled in us through the offering of Christ's sacrifice, so that we are said to have "done" it, first by imputation, and then afterward after we've been justified also by those things beginning to be fulfilled by us through the Spirit which will be perfected in the next life. COMMENTARY ON ROMANS (1583).[16]

CHRIST IS OUR SANCTIFICATION. THE ENGLISH ANNOTATIONS: He uses no argument here but instead expounds the mystery of sanctification, which is wrought in us, because, he says, the virtue of the law was not such—by reason of the corruption of our nature—that it could make us pure, perfect, and free. For it kindled the fiery malady of sin, rather than putting it out and extinguishing it. Therefore God clothed his Son with flesh like our sinful flesh, wherein he utterly abolished our corruption, that being accounted thoroughly pure and without fault in him, apprehended and laid hold of by faith, we might be found to have fully that singular perfection which the law requires, and therefore that there might be no condemnation in or to us. ANNOTATIONS ON ROMANS 8:3.[17]

THE TRINITY IMPLIED. PETER MARTYR VERMIGLI: "He sent his own Son in the likeness of sinful flesh and on account of sin condemned sin in the flesh." Both the number and distinctions of divine persons in the holy Triad are clear from these words. For if the Son is sent by the Father, it is necessary that one be distinct from the other, contrary to Photinus, Sabellius, the patripassians, and other pests of their ilk, who taught that the Son and Holy Spirit were distinguished from the Father and from each other in name only. But we can easily see what order Paul placed among the persons: he first says that the Spirit liberates us; then that this same Spirit is given through Christ; and finally, that the Son was sent by the Father. In

this way the ultimate effect of our salvation resolves back to the First Cause.[†] COMMENTARY ON ROMANS (1560).[18]

8:4 So That the Law May Be Fulfilled in Us

CAN A REGENERATE PERSON FULFILL THE LAW? FRIEDRICH BALDUIN: Q: Can it not be inferred from this passage that a regenerate man or woman is able to fulfill the law, since the apostle writes in verse 4 that "Christ died so that the justification of the law might be fulfilled in us"?

A: I answer, it is in this sense that Pererius distorts this passage, in disputation 5 on this chapter. He says, "The apostle manifestly teaches that through his bodily passion and death, Christ condemned the sin that was preventing the law from being fulfilled by man and woman, so that with sin being taken away, the justification of the law might be fulfilled in us." So says he. But this commentary is refuted by the passage itself, which attributes expiation and fulfillment of the law to Christ alone; nor can any saint attain to so much perfection in this life, which is proved by those perpetual complaints we experience and especially by Paul in the preceding chapter. Nor is this the fruit or effect of Christ's passion, for how it was that he took away sins has been most ably stated and proved—not that they no longer exist, but that they are not imputed. Therefore, he alone is the fulfillment of the law, and is called such. But when it says here that "Christ condemned sin so that the justification of the law might be fulfilled in" the saints, it is not what the saints are capable of doing or experiencing that is being taught, but what he does in the saints, or what Christ has already done for the saints' benefit, namely, that he suffered and died for this purpose, that a fulfillment of the law might be accomplished, which required two things: (1) the expiation of sins and (2) the observing of the

---

[16]Corner, *In Epistolam Pauli ad Romanos*, 100v.
[17]Downame, ed., *Annotations*, BBB2r*.

[18]Vermigli, *In Epistolam S. Pauli*, 616. [†]It was common in trinitarian theology to use the Aristotelian term *primam causam* (first cause) for God the Father to identify him as the ultimate, uncaused cause.

law's precepts. Christ accomplished both, not we. And thus the fulfillment was accomplished by him; but it is said to occur "in us" because it was done on our behalf[†] and has been imputed to us through faith. Therefore, the apostle here points his finger at imputation, and thus the law is fulfilled by the saints, not by their working, but by their believing. COMMENTARY ON ROMANS (1620).[19]

THE GROUNDS OF FULFILLING THE LAW. WALTER CRADOCK: I say first, the law requires a righteousness from every person to fulfill it. Or, every person is bound to fulfill the law of God. That is the first thing. The grounds of that are these; I will just touch on them.

First, because God made humanity, humans were his creatures, and the Lord was their sovereign. And when God made all creatures, he made laws for them; he made a law for the sun, and moon, and stars, and so on. And everything goes according to the law that God determined for it. Now when God made humans (who were merely his creatures, though more excellent creatures) he made a law for them, this blessed law of God that is in his book here, the covenant of works, as it was sometimes called. Therefore, as all the other creatures were required to go in their course, and keep their peculiar laws that God laid on them, so humans also were bound to keep the law of God that God had made for them.

Second, there is another thing—besides the sovereignty of God—that might impose a law on humanity. That was that there was a compact between God and humanity, and so there was a kind of bargain. For God laid that law on humanity, and Adam as a public[†] person undertook to keep that law by contract or bargain. If God (as it were) previously had no right to lay it on him, yet now man undertook it—by way of a bargain—to keep the law of God. First, Adam did it. . . . And afterward the people of Israel professed to do it: "All these works we will do. We will keep them."

That is another reason it appears that every man and woman in the world is bound to fulfill the law of God.

Third, another thing is this: If you consider what might free people from keeping a law that is laid on them, you will see that none of those things can help them in this.

For first of all, our human laws are often repealed. And a law that people were bound to keep a few years ago they are now bound to protect against. For example, in relation to the service book, the Book of Common Prayer, and so on, there is now a penalty for using it, whereas a few years ago there was a penalty for not using it. But it is not so with the law of God. Heaven and earth will pass away, but not one jot or tittle of the law will pass. That law is an eternal law; there is no repealing of it.

Then second, you know that human judges and lawgivers may be corrupted and bribed, and may be brought to dispense with their own laws, even sometimes to go against their own laws. But God is a just God. And when his own Son, the Son of his love, took on himself to be born under the law, and to be a surety for us, he endured the smart of the law, and was treated just as if he had been any other person. SERMON ON ROMANS 8:4 (1649).[20]

THE RIGHTEOUSNESS OF GOD FULFILLED IN US. PETER MARTYR VERMIGLI: "So that the righteousness of God may be fulfilled in us, who walk not according to the flesh, but according to the Spirit." What we translate "righteousness," and others "justification," is *dikaiōma* in Greek. And it means uprightness, rectitude, that which is commanded in the law, by which, however much it is called such, we are yet not justified, for execution of it is had in no one's case, except for the one who is justified. It is certainly true that we are to be judged according to works by their sort. For God renders to individuals according to their works, as the form of the sentence is to be expected according to the state of the works. Nevertheless, good

---

[19]Balduin, *Catechesis Apostolica*, 519-20*; citing Rom 10. [†]The key theological terms here are *in nobis* versus *propter nos*.

[20]Cradock, *Gospel-Holiness*, 208-9*. [†]Representing a constituency.

works are not the causes of the happiness that we hope for from him. For if they were the causes, either they would equal the reward, or they would be greater than it. For it is in the nature of causes to be either greater than their effects or at least equal to them; which cannot be ascribed to good works. Paul says enough when he says that "the present afflictions are not worthy of being compared with the coming glory which will be revealed" *in us*. Rather, the manner in which the precepts of the law may be fulfilled in us through communion with Christ, who died for us, may be thus declared: that the Spirit is conceded to those who believe in him, by whom their powers are restored, so that they may fulfill obedience to the law, yet not perfectly and absolutely; for this obedience is not to be had while they live here. Therefore the complement of the law is situated in this: that confessed sins are pardoned in Christ, and the righteousness which is fulfilled by him is imputed to us: because he is our head and we, in turn, are his members. Finally, it is to be expected that when we have come to the hoped-for end of final happiness, then nothing will come about in us that is contrary to the law of God. By this compact Christ is called the end of the law: as the one who did not dissolve it but fulfilled it—not only that he wrested it from the depraved interpretations of the scribes and Pharisees with his doctrine, but also that by those means which we have already discussed, he perfected it both in himself and in us. COMMENTARY ON ROMANS (1560).[21]

THREE BENEFITS FROM CHRIST. ANDREW WILLET: The apostle in this place sets forth three benefits purchased for us by Christ: (1) Remission of our sins, in that Christ bore in himself the punishment due for our sins. (2) Then the imputation of Christ's obedience and his performing of the law. (3) Our sanctification, that we by the spirit of Christ die to sin and rise into newness of life. Our sanctification is necessarily joined with our justification, but is not a part of it: (1) because

it is imperfect in this life; it is perfect after a sort of *perfectione partium*, by the perfection of the parts, because regeneration is both in the body and soul, but not *perfectione graduum*, by the perfection of degree; for so it is only begun here, and will be perfected in the next life: (2) and sanctification follows after justification, and so is not a part of it; for first we are justified, then sanctified. A SIXFOLD COMMENTARY ON THE EPISTLE TO THE ROMANS (1620).[22]

THE HOLY SPIRIT IS ESSENTIAL TO FULFILLING THE LAW. JOHANNES BUGENHAGEN: "Who not according to the flesh." Lest any should here act boldly by his reason or the temerity of his flesh, he says that the "justification of the law" is fulfilled in us, who are constant in watching by the Spirit against the ambushes of the flesh, or who relinquish nothing to the flesh. Truly, everything is done through that Spirit who has been given to us through Christ. Therefore, no one who is devoid of this Spirit fulfills the law. You are unable to fulfill—by your own strength—the commandment to love your neighbor as yourself. But you are able to when you have the Spirit. INTERPRETATION OF ROMANS (1531).[23]

ACCORDING TO THE FLESH, ACCORDING TO THE SPIRIT. NIELS HEMMINGSEN: Now a fair confirmation is made clear as to why the above proposition was added—"Those who do not walk according to the flesh but according to the Spirit"—and then the same was impressed again in the next explanation. The foundation of this reasoning is this: there are two ways of life, one is of the flesh, the other of the Spirit. One is of the old self, the other of the new. One is of those who live under the law, the other of those who live under grace. Both of these are known by their own nature and are discovered from their own fruit. Therefore, those who live according to the flesh (that is, those in whom the corrupt nature is master, by which

---

[21]Vermigli, *In Epistolam S. Pauli*, 620-21.

[22]Willet, *Hexapla*, 392.
[23]Bugenhagen, *In D. Pauli ad Romanos*, 81r.

they are of the flesh), understand (that is, they judge, they think, they meditate, they feel, they desire, and so on) the things that are of the flesh. That is, the entirety is brought under the rule of the flesh. And that is the life of those who have not yet been renewed by the grace of regeneration. Therefore, it is not remarkable that those who are of such a kind remain under the damnation of the law until now. But on the contrary, those who are "according to the Spirit"—that is, those in whom the new self is in control and who are led by the Spirit of Christ—these are those who are "of the Spirit." They understand (that is, they judge, they think, they meditate, they desire, they feel) the things that are of the Spirit. That is, they permit the Spirit himself to reign supreme, and by him they oppose every attack of the flesh, groaning under the bitterest grief between the Spirit and the flesh. Therefore, this sort of person is no longer under the law of damnation but under grace, which covers the remnants of sin by the shadow of Christ. COMMENTARY ON ROMANS (1562).[24]

WALKING ACCORDING TO THE SPIRIT AND THE FLESH. WOLFGANG MUSCULUS: It is not because of some new quality worked in us by the grace of the Holy Spirit that we are beyond condemnation, but on account of the grace of God alone, which we lay hold of by faith in Christ. We are saved because we are in Christ. The death of Christ is what saves us. Nevertheless, it is still true that those who are in Christ "do not walk according to the flesh, but according to the Spirit." But they are not saved *by* so doing; rather, they are led by the Spirit of God *because* they are saved by the grace of Christ.

But what does it mean to walk according to the flesh or to walk according to the Spirit? By the term "flesh," the apostle here means man or woman as an animal, a totally corrupt nature, not only because it tends to wantonness and carnal pleasures, but also because it refers to the human's animal nature insofar as he or she is outside of

Christ and destitute of the Spirit of God. By "to walk according to the flesh" he means to live according to the leading and rule of this corrupt nature, of its corrupt affections, and of its corrupt judgment. The flesh is not being condemned here, because it is a good creature of God, nor is our life in the flesh condemned insofar as it pertains to meeting our necessities. Rather, what is condemned is its corruption, by which it comes about that, vitiated by its affections, we make our choices and live contrary to the mind of God and his glory. For this same reason we also abuse those things that are given for the sustenance of nature, using them contrary to their intended mode or purpose, and perverting everything.

The "Spirit" here is to be understood not as a person's spirit, but as the Spirit of God. We should here beware the philosophical distinction of those who understand the word "flesh" to mean bestial wantonness and pleasures as opposed to reason, and who understand the word "spirit" to mean reason as the more important faculty of a person which, they say, always inclines toward what is best and that is present in every person because it is something we are born with. But by the very context itself the apostle declares that he is speaking of the Spirit of God. It is the Spirit's law that is life, not the law of reason.

Therefore to "walk according to the Spirit" means to live by the leading and governance of the Spirit, which Spirit is given to those who believe in Christ. COMMENTARY ON ROMANS (1555).[25]

THE MYSTERY OF BEING JUST AND SINFUL AT THE SAME TIME. WALTER CRADOCK: I have seen people quarrel with themselves and complain, "Oh, I have a hard heart and I desire the preachers to pray for me." And when you have fallen into weakness, you go and confess your sins and strive to break your heart and mourn for your worldliness and your pride and disobedience. But it does not work, for your hearts grow harder than they were before. When you have committed a sin today,

---

[24]Hemmingsen, *Commentarius in Epistolam*, 247.

[25]Musculus, *In Epistolam Apostoli Pauli*, 163-64; citing Jn 7:39.

you think you can go and reform tomorrow and turn over a new leaf. But tomorrow you will be worse than today. Because you think you can make amends to God, he leaves you to yourselves and you grow worse. The reason is this: because in some sort, even to this day, you mix sanctification with justification. Now, I know it; I speak what I know. If only you would leave your justification alone in the hands of Jesus Christ and look on it (as I said) as cash in the cupboard, not to be touched, and as long as Christ is righteous say, "I am righteous." See yourselves always as just men and women that in Jesus Christ have fulfilled the law of God, and then you will find your hearts inclined toward goodness. Then your hearts would break and shatter to pieces when you have done the least evil against God. Then you will know what true sorrow and what true repentance are, and not before. Then you will know those things that you do not know now, nor cannot know. Therefore strive to learn that lesson; it is one of the greatest mysteries in the world. And that is the reason that worldly people complain about these things. What greater mystery is there than that I am a just and righteous person through Christ, and yet I am so sinful? That I can say there is no one who is more sinful than I am, and yet I am as righteous as Abraham or Paul? In respect to the righteousness of Christ I have as large a share as Abraham or Paul, and yet I am full of sin? A Christian knows this, and knows why it is so. Well, that is one lesson. Ponder it, so that you will know where to plant your justification: that is, on the death and resurrection of Jesus Christ. May the Lord teach it to you, and me. SERMON ON ROMANS 8:4 (1649).[26]

CHRIST WAS SACRIFICED FOR US. ERASMUS SARCERIUS: Now follows the goal of Christ's being sent in the likeness of sinful flesh and also of Christ's being made a sacrifice on our behalf: that the justification of the law might be fulfilled in us. Christ was made a sacrifice and made satisfaction

to the law not because of his own sins, but on account of our sins. Christ did not need a sacrifice for sins; we did.

This goal is connected to the preceding words to head off the possibility that, since the apostle said that Christ was made a sacrifice for sin, the Romans might think that it was for Christ's own sin and not that of another, and also lest they should object that by offering himself, Christ merited righteousness only for himself, but not for us. The apostle meets these objections here when he makes us participants in Christ's offering in which he offered himself.

The passages of Scripture that indicate the same intention, that of making Christ and all his benefits ours: Isaiah 9: "For us a child is born, for us a son is given." Isaiah 7: "His name will be called 'Immanuel.'" Isaiah 53: "My righteous servant will justify many by his knowledge. . . . He took away the sins of many." Also later in this very chapter: "He who did not spare his own Son, but delivered him up for us all, how will he not also with him give us all things?" NOTES ON ROMANS (1541).[27]

SNOW CANNOT BE HOT. PETER MARTYR VERMIGLI: Augustine[†] has a sound interpretation of this passage. The same soul, he says, can be subject to both the dispositions[†] of the flesh and the dispositions of the Spirit, just as the same water is capable both of heating up and of freezing in the cold and making snow. If you should then say that snow does not heat up, you speak truly, and if you should add also that snow is incapable of heating up, this would still be true, since snow cannot heat up as long as it remains snow. But it is possible for it to come under the influence of heat and the snow to melt and become hot. But it cannot happen that snow both retains its proper nature and at the same time heats up. In this same way, the dispositions of the flesh can be taken away or at least subdued so that the dispositions of the Spirit might take their place. But the dispositions

---

[26]Cradock, *Gospel-Holiness*, 234-35*.

[27]Sarcerius, *In Apostolam ad Romanos*, h8r-v; citing Heb 10:12; Is 9:6; 7:14; 53: 11, 12; Rom 8:32.

of the flesh themselves can in no way become spiritual. But if you should ask, "Aren't spiritual observances of God's commandments impossible?" I would answer that they are in fact impossible in the oldness of the flesh, but if the Spirit and regeneration are added, they are not *entirely* impossible, however true it is that God's law cannot be perfectly obeyed in this life even by the most holy people. For the Spirit of Christ is with us to subdue the depravity of our flesh and, when we die, to fully extinguish it. COMMENTARY ON ROMANS (1560).[28]

8:5 Setting Our Minds on the Spirit

THE DISPOSITIONS OF THE FLESH AND OF THE SPIRIT. WOLFGANG MUSCULUS: This must not be read as indicating that the flesh aspires to or loves death, for no one "of the flesh" loves death. However, because of the fleshly dispositions in them—which are nothing other than the dispositions toward sin, disorder, and opposition to the divine will—men and women deserve death and, as guilty people, are delivered over to death.

The dispositions of the Spirit are contrary to this. Those who have been purified and regenerated by the Spirit of Christ are pleasing to God, and they enjoy life and peace with God. COMMENTARY ON ROMANS (1555).[29]

SCRIPTURAL TRUTH AND THE STRUGGLE BETWEEN SPIRIT AND FLESH. JÖRG HAUG: I must test the witness of the Scriptures to see if it is true in me. But if I am of a different mind and have a wrong understanding, it will hinder me and hold me back from a true, divine understanding. I must then examine what it is that I love more than God. This is where the struggle between spirit and flesh begins. If the flesh is victorious and the person falls under the sway of the creaturely, the person will be worse off than before; but if the

spirit is victorious, then one truth after another will emerge from such a person. When the spiritually illuminated person reads and considers the Scriptures, they witness to him of an unchanging God, while he recognizes himself as the opposite—a changeable human being. A CHRISTIAN ORDER OF A TRUE CHRISTIAN.[30]

THREE WAYS OF RELATING TO GRACE. JOHANNES OECOLAMPADIUS: Paul distinguishes in three ways between those who are in need of grace and those who are affected by grace. (1) The fleshly are devoid of grace. He sums this up: those who are "of the flesh" have an appetite for it. That is, they follow after their own interests. You should understand this concerning not only the externals, but also concerning the internals. (2) But on the other hand, there are those who satisfy themselves with the *gifts* of the Spirit. While they may have understanding, endurance, and similar things, they are actually still fleshly. (3) But those who pursue spiritual things and grace, these are those who are striving for the things of the Spirit *himself*, which is to say, the things that are of God. For although you strive for that which makes the internal self beautiful, that is, to meditate or to pray, if you do not freely render praise to God, you are by no means spiritual. But if the Spirit of God is working in you, then let him work so that in everything, even the internal, you might proclaim his praise. ANNOTATIONS ON ROMANS (1525).[31]

GOD DEALS MARVELOUSLY WITH HIS CHILDREN. KATHARINA SCHÜTZ ZELL: May you also receive these sufferings with great patience and thankfulness, as special fatherly gifts sent from God, which he does not give to any but his best beloved children. For indeed to an unbeliever it would look strange that God should give such gifts to his children whom he loves! Such an unbeliever would much rather not be God's child but a child of the world, which does not treat its children that

---

[28]Vermigli, *In Epistolam S. Pauli*, 626. †Vermigli paraphrases Augustine, *On Romans* 49.5. ‡*Affectus* may be translated variously as affections, dispositions, motions, or impulses.
[29]Musculus, *In Epistolam Apostoli Pauli*, 128.

[30]CRR 10:18*.
[31]Oecolampadius, *In Epistolam Pauli*, 66.

way: the world disciplines its children softly and tenderly. It is true, as Paul says, that faith is not everyone's thing, and the worldly, that is, the carnal person cannot understand what is godly. But the spiritual, that is, the believing person, understands that God deals marvelously, surprisingly, with his own, completely contrary to the world and its children. As also he says in the prophet Isaiah, chapter 55: "My thoughts (that is, his will) are not like your thoughts, and my way (that is, his ways of acting) are not like your ways." Therefore he says in another place in the prophet, "The one whom I want to make alive, that one I cause to die, the one whom I want to make well, that one I strike." In sum, he wills that those whom he has eternally chosen and whom he has written as his children in the book of his heirs should also be won away from this world, and he wants to teach us to depend on him in one strong faith and not expect or take anything from anyone else but only from him. LETTER TO THE SUFFERING WOMEN OF KENTZINGEN (1524).[32]

8:6 There Is Life and Peace in the Spirit

WHAT HUMAN REASON IS GOOD FOR. JO-HANNES BUGENHAGEN: "For the disposition of the flesh is death." That is to say, the discretion that is in us, the human reasoning, all of our human resources, are death. That is, you are not able to be saved by the help of even those things in you that are healthy and from God. Therefore, is human reasoning (phronema) useful for anything? Yes, for governing the republic, or forming civil customs, or tending fields, or for building, as long as everything is done without placing your confidence or rest in them. For it is not permitted—for those that are Christ's—for their old self to place its hope in created things. Moreover, if anyone desires to use them as if they were means of eternal life and salvation, this work brings about the death of any not living in the presence of God, for nothing other

than death comes by means of human effort. INTERPRETATION OF ROMANS (1531).[33]

THE DISPOSITION OF THE SPIRIT. JOHANNES BRENZ: But let us also explain another part of the antithesis. When Paul spoke of the disposition of the flesh, he also brought in the disposition of the Spirit, saying, "The disposition of the Spirit is life and peace." The Spirit in this place is accepted as the gift of the Holy Spirit, which men and women are divinely given through the proclamation of the gospel in order that they might also believe in the Son of God and be born again through faith. Therefore, this gift of the Spirit chiefly brings life and peace with himself, because he vivifies men and women, so that they may be heirs of heaven in an eternal life of good things. And he restores a peaceful or tranquil mind to men and women, because they recognize themselves as those who have been reconciled to God through Christ, just as it says above, "Having been justified by faith, we have peace with God through Jesus Christ." Next, this gift of the Spirit stirs up the self so that it might not desire, nor long for, nor endeavor after anything other than the things which are of heavenly life and tranquility. Nor ought this to be seen as strange. For to the one who has been born again through the Spirit, Christ himself is given, together with all of his good things. For what else is Christ than life and peace, than salvation and blessedness? COMMENTARY ON ROMANS (1588).[34]

THE DISPOSITION OF THE SPIRIT IS LIFE. JOHANNES BUGENHAGEN: "But the disposition of the Spirit is life." In other words, the prudence and wisdom that is from God alone, through grace, makes us understand spiritually. That is, so far as these things are of God, they are not of our flesh. That, I say, is nothing other than life and peace, for it is through it that we who were dead through sin are reborn, and we have peace and tranquility in our conscience now that it does not hurt. And the

---

[32]Zell, Church Mother, 50-51*; citing Eph 2:8; Is 55:8l; Rev 20:15; Eph 1:4; Rev 20:15; Eph 1:4.

[33]Bugenhagen, In D. Pauli ad Romanos, 81v.
[34]Brenz, In Epistolam, 623; citing Rom 5:1.

sting of death (which is sin) is overthrown. INTERPRETATION OF ROMANS (1531).[35]

HOLINESS AND THE HOPE OF FUTURE SWEETNESS. WALTER CRADOCK: Beloved, I say there is more ease, and sweetness, and contentedness—by a hundredfold—in going on in the ways of God spiritually. For the other will be rough, and that is how God has designed it. God has put a curse on all old Adam; he cursed it with death, and therefore whoever walks according to the flesh must die, and that is the reason that all your natural thoughts and actions are so bitter. God has cursed them; they must die. At the same time, the ways of holiness offer enough to induce you to choose them. As someone has said, the gleanings of the saints are better than the harvest of the wicked. Even if there were no hell or heaven in the hereafter, but all there was was the here and now, with the wicked having the pleasures of sin here, and the saints having the consolations of the Spirit dwelling in them, the difference would be more than a hundredfold. The one is nothing but crackling of thorns under a pot, and its end is smoke and stink, while the other is sweet here, and in the end brings eternal blessing. But even if it were not, you should still choose holiness, for even if the way to heaven is bitter here, yet it will be sweet in the end; and even if the way of the world is sweet here, it will be bitter in the end. As a philosopher asked, "If you had to take both a bitter and a sweet thing, which would be best to take first?" He says to take the sour or the evil first and then the sweet, for the hope of the good to come will sweeten the present evil. But if you take the good first, the fear of the evil to come will mar everything. Therefore, seeing that there is a reward in holiness both along the way as well as in the end, it should move us to strive after holiness. SERMON ON ROMANS 8:4 (1649).[36]

8:7 *The Mind of the Flesh Is Hostile to God*

CONTRITION FOR HOSTILITY AGAINST GOD. MARTIN LUTHER: First, in Scripture true contrition is not our own self-made thoughts, which the monks call contrition and attrition, whole or half contrition. Rather, true contrition is when your conscience begins to sting and alarm you, and your heart is seriously frightened of God's wrath and judgment, not only because of obvious, coarse sins but also because of the truly strong, knotty doubts that you see and sense, which put in your flesh and blood nothing but unbelief, contempt, and disobedience for God and (as St. Paul says) "hostility against God." This makes itself felt with all kinds of evil lust and desires, by which you have brought God's wrath on yourself and have deserved to be rejected eternally from his sight and to burn in hellfire.

Thus contrition does not apply piecemeal to some works that you have committed publicly against the Ten Commandments—that is where the dream and delusion of the hypocritical monkish repentance stays; they invent for themselves this distinction in their works and nevertheless find something good in themselves. Rather, contrition applies to the whole person with all their life and being, even to your whole nature, and shows that you are under God's wrath and condemned to hell. Otherwise the word *contrition* still sounds too juristic the way people speak about sin and contrition in worldly matters as about something someone did and then thinks differently and wishes that he had not done it. SUMMER POSTIL (APRIL 11, 1531).[37]

THE INABILITY TO SATISFY THE LAW OF GOD. JOHANNES BRENZ: The disposition of the flesh is hostile toward God because it is not subject to the law of God, and indeed it cannot be. Whoever has not been born again, although they be the most just and the most honest, yet they do not perfectly satisfy the law of God. And so great is their

---

[35]Bugenhagen, *In D. Pauli ad Romanos*, 81v-82r; citing 1 Cor 15:55.
[36]Cradock, *Gospel-Holiness*, 413-14*.

[37]LW 77:90-91*.

corruption that they are not able to satisfy it in the least. For the law of God demands a perfect knowledge of God, but men and women are not perfectly acquainted with God by their natural strength. The law of God demands a perfect faith and love of God. But men and women, when they are either ignorant of God, or inconsistently know him, do not have either a perfect faith or love of God. The law of God demands a perfect love of neighbor. But men and women, however, love themselves more than their neighbors. COMMENTARY ON ROMANS (1588).[38]

FRIENDSHIP AND ENMITY WITH GOD. WOLFGANG MUSCULUS: We plainly see in this passage what it means to be a friend of God and what it is to be his enemy. The friends of God are those who submit to his will. Christ said, "You are my friends if you do the things that I command you." Let us ponder whether we are friends of God, and try to perceive whether we deceive ourselves with an empty hope and opinion. It is true that by Christ we have been reconciled and made to be God's friends. But it is necessary that that friendship express itself as authentic by our submitting to God's will. Those who have been already reconciled and received into friendship do not have the same disposition or life as those who are still in a state of enmity. By grace, Christians have been reconciled by the blood of Christ interceding on their behalf, but they have been reconciled in truth, not only in outward appearance as it happens with the sons and daughters of this age. If they have truly been made friends, they altogether will the same thing that God wills, and they will not the same things that God wills not. The carnal do not do this and, therefore, are God's enemies; they are still under the power of death and therefore not in Christ. COMMENTARY ON ROMANS (1600).[39]

OUR WISDOM IS A SLAVE TO OUR LUSTS. RICHARD SIBBES: This is the nature of this tyrant,

sin. It takes such possession of people that until they have got out of it and are in Christ; it takes away their perception of itself. It hinders the knowledge of itself; it puts out a person's eyes. For that by which a person should judge corruption is corrupt itself. "The wisdom of a person is death; it is enmity to God." The wit that we have that should be able to discern our degrading courses instead tangles us more and more in our own lusts; so that wit and wisdom, the highest part of the soul, are imprisoned by base affections; and that power that should discern corruption is instead set to work on satisfying corruption. What is the wit of a person—that is not in Christ—occupied about all his or her lifetime? It is nothing but a drudge and a slave, devising means to satisfy one's degrading lusts. Take worldly people: they are exceedingly witty in contriving worldly plots and business, even though they are dunces and drunkards in spiritual matters. In their own tracts and courses, they have a shrewd wit. Why? Because their worldly lusts whet their wit. So we see the best thing in a person—his or her wisdom—is now enthralled to sin; therefore, it is enmity to God. SPIRITUAL JUBILEE SERMON.[40]

8:8 *We Cannot Please God in the Flesh*

NOT AGAINST MARRIAGE. WOLFGANG MUSCULUS: Pope Siricius uses—indeed, misuses—this passage in his decretals against clerical marriage† to imply that for the apostle, to be married is the same as to be "in the flesh." Hence Satan appears to have defamed the marriage bed in those times as an unclean thing, from which, and openly in that time, he introduced the apostle's text, where it said, "For the unclean, nothing is pure, but for the pure, all things are."

Certainly, elsewhere the Holy Spirit says that the marriage bed is honorable and holy. And the apostle, in Galatians 5, does not number marriage among the works of the flesh, but adultery, fornication, and so on. What then, I ask, are Christians

[38]Brenz, *In Epistolam*, 622.
[39]Musculus, *In Epistolam Apostoli*, 171; citing Jn 15:14.
[40]Sibbes, *Complete Works*, 5:232-33*.

who are married to think, if this passage is to be cited against matrimony? Evidently those who are married cannot please God. Therefore, away with divinely instituted marriage from the midst of Christians! This is exactly what the apostle foresaw in 1 Timothy 4. Otherwise, there they could have inferred that the apostle was writing only to priests and celibates when he concluded, "but you are not in the flesh." COMMENTARY ON ROMANS.[41]

A WOLF, A SERPENT, AND FORGIVENESS IN SPITE OF THE OLD NATURE. JOHANNES BRENZ: For just as a wolf by its natural disposition prowls about against the sheep—nor can it be that either the wolf should become a sheep, or that he may pursue the sheep with a pure and spotless mind—thus the natural man or woman is an enemy to God, nor can it be that according to this nature that the one corrupted by sin can become a friend of God. And just as there is a natural enmity between the serpent and man, therefore, the man was led astray by the craft of the serpent and being made its captive by nature, he is not able to *not* hate God. Therefore, what shall we say? If the nature of the self is not able to not hate God, nor is it able to yield to the law of God—which is God's justice—should that person be condemned? Can it be that all sin is voluntary? Can it be that God is angry against his own creation, which cannot change itself? It was said above concerning the saints, although they still have sin and have enmity toward God in their flesh or their old nature, nevertheless they have no damnation, because they have Christ through faith, and they fight with the flesh through the Holy Spirit, and the enmity that they have after their rebirth against God is left in their nature. But the wicked are justly condemned, because not only are they captives of their own flesh, but also, though God influences them by his great kindness and his grace, which he clearly offers through the gospel of his Son, they oppose

him with an obstinate zeal. COMMENTARY ON ROMANS (1564).[42]

LED BY THE FLESH. THE ENGLISH ANNOTATIONS: The apostle here by this phrase means not those that are married, as Siricius the pope absurdly interpreted this Scripture and wrested it to the disparagement of holy wedlock in the clergy, nor does he thereby understand all that are clothed with flesh, for then no one upon earth should please God. Rather, to be "in the flesh," and to be "after the flesh," and to "war," and "walk after the flesh," signify one and the same thing, to remain still in our carnal estate, and to be led by the motions and lusts of the flesh. Those that are so led, until God gives them a better guide and delivers them out of their corrupt estate by nature, cannot please God. ANNOTATIONS ON ROMANS 8:8.[43]

8:9 The Spirit Is in You If You Belong to Him

GIFTS OF THE HOLY SPIRIT. JOHANNES BRENZ: For if you profess yourself to be a Christian, by this you also profess to have the Spirit of Christ who is the Holy Spirit. With respect to this, it must be explained more fully in order that we should be rightly understood a little more deeply. We know, therefore, that there is certainly only one Holy Spirit in essence, but many and various are the gifts of the Holy Spirit. For some are personal and heroic, which are certainly admirable and deserving of great praise, but they are not necessary for the salvation of those who possess them, nor were they bestowed for the sake of individual believers in Christ. Such a gift is prophecy concerning things about to occur on this earth. COMMENTARY ON ROMANS (1564).[44]

THE SPIRIT OF SANCTIFICATION. RICHARD SIBBES: Again, there is a freedom in sanctification;

---

[41]Musculus, *In Epistolam Apostoli Pauli*, 129; citing Tit 1:15; Heb 13:4; Gal 5:19; 1 Tim 4:1-16. †The *Directa Decretal*, issued by Pope Siricius in 385, seemed to imply that sexual relations with one's wife was "of the flesh."

[42]Brenz, *In Epistolam*, 191.
[43]Downame, ed., *Annotations*, BBB2r*.
[44]Brenz, *In Epistolam*, 194.

that is, when I believe that Christ is mine, and that his sufferings are mine, then the same Spirit that reveals this to be mine, it works a change and alteration in my nature, and frees me from the dominion of sin. The obedience of Christ frees me from the condemnation of sin, and the Spirit of sanctification frees me from the dominion of sin. This is the freedom of sanctification, which faith lays hold on. "Whoever does not have the Spirit of Christ is not his." Christ as a head communicates to me the Holy Spirit to sanctify my nature; and "of his fullness we receive grace for grace." So the Spirit of sanctification in Christ frees me from the dominion of sin and death. SPIRITUAL JUBILEE SERMON.[45]

PERSONAL AND GENERAL GIFTS OF CHRIST'S SPIRIT. JOHANNES BRENZ: The gift of healing, or of raising the dead, must also be counted among the heroic gifts of the Spirit, of which sort the apostles had following the day of Pentecost. And this gift is indeed illustrious and most useful in confirming the truth of the gospel of Christ: but it is not necessary for salvation that anyone should be furnished with this gift. To this list, the singular gift of industry in the workman's trade also extends, which was declared in Exodus 31. Concerning Bezalel, the Lord said, "I filled him with the Spirit of God, with wisdom and understanding and knowledge in all the work." But neither is such a gift necessary for the personal salvation of a man or woman. And indeed, the discussion here does not concern these personal and heroic gifts of the Holy Spirit. Rather, it concerns the general gifts of Christ's Spirit, which are necessary in everyone for true and eternal salvation. For first, the Spirit of Christ produces faith. This faith, by which it is believed that we have a propitious God on account of Christ, the Son of God, is a gift of the Holy Spirit necessary for salvation. The one who does not have this gift is not in Christ. Next, the Spirit of Christ produces an obedience in the believer, by which the sinful disposition is restrained and the

disposition of the Spirit advanced. And this gift is necessary, because naturally it should be necessary that the flesh be mortified and the Spirit reign in the person. Finally, the Spirit of Christ works not only in order that we should acquire good, mortified flesh, but also that we might patiently bear with evil or adversity. Therefore, patience and steadfastness in the faith and hope in adversity are gifts of the Spirit necessary for salvation. These are the general gifts of the Spirit—which are not only for those who are ordinary persons, but for even those that were adorned with the personal and heroic gifts—which are necessary if they desire to attain the true, eternal salvation. COMMENTARY ON ROMANS (1564).[46]

ADVANCING IN OBEDIENCE TO THE SPIRIT. PETER MARTYR VERMIGLI: There are some who are so inept that they think that this passage opposes the church's ministry of matrimony. If this were the case, then it would have to be concluded universally that all Christians ought to live without wives. Christians, after they believe in Christ, are no longer "in the flesh." We indeed have a body, flesh, and bodily parts, bread and drink and marriage, all of which seem to pertain to the flesh, but we have these things in God that we might employ them in accordance with the Spirit, not according to the flesh. Nor does it seem that Paul intended in this passage anything other than what the Lord said to his disciples in the gospel: "You are not of this world." Similarly, Ambrose said that our nature is defined by the beliefs we hold, and he adds that the wise of this world are "in the flesh" because they resist the faith and are willing to believe only those things that agree with reason. This passage also teaches us that Ambrose understood the term "carnal reason" to apply also to the highest parts of the soul. Therefore, we say that to be "in the flesh" according to the apostle is nothing other than to be ruled and governed in all our actions by beliefs and natural affections that have not yet been reborn in Christ. It is, therefore, clear

---

[45]Sibbes, *Complete Works*, 5:242-43*; citing Jn 1:16.

[46]Brenz, *In Epistolam*, 194-95; citing Ex 31:3.

from this that it belongs to a Christian man or woman to pursue those things that are of the Spirit and to avoid those things that are of the flesh. Also, this property of the Christian life in part serves to admonish us that we not fall away from it, and in part is a mark by which we can be made more certain about our justification and liberation from our sins. But since it belongs to man or woman to act out of the soul and by human reason; and to philosophers to be directed by the instruction and discipline of wisdom; and to soldiers to regulate themselves according to the whole art of soldiery, so it is proper to a Christian man or woman to be moved by the Spirit and motions of Christ. And however it may be that all persons have their own proper vocations and ought to pursue the duties that are appropriate for them, nevertheless as many of us as belong to Christ ought to measure ourselves by this proper and certain rule: that we perpetually consider how much we have advanced in obedience to the Spirit. COMMENTARY ON ROMANS (1560).[47]

FAITH AND THE HOLY SPIRIT CANNOT BE SEPARATED.

BENEDETTO DA MANTOVA AND MARCANTONIO FLAMINIO: There are some who say that no one ought to presume to boast that he has the Spirit of God. They speak this way, as if Christians should boast of having it because of their own deserving, and not by the mere mercy of God. And as though it were presumptuous to profess themselves to be Christians. Or as though someone could be a Christian without having Christ's Spirit; or as though we could say without straight out hypocrisy that Jesus Christ is our Lord, or call God our Father, if the Holy Spirit didn't move our hearts and tongues to say such sweet words. And yet, in spite of that, even those who consider us presumptuous for saying that God has given us his Holy Spirit with faith, command us to say the "Our Father" every day. But I would ask them, how is it possible to separate faith and the Holy Spirit, seeing that faith is the

unique work of the Holy Spirit? THE BENEFIT OF CHRIST'S DEATH (1543).[48]

INSTRUMENTS OF THE SPIRIT.

JOHANNES BRENZ: What, therefore, must be done? We do not have this Spirit naturally, but he is given to us from heaven through Christ. And he is given through his own instruments. For Christ established the preaching of his gospel and the use of his own sacraments, which are instruments through which the Spirit of Christ is conferred to us. For faith, obedience in doing good, and patience in suffering evil, all come from the gospel of Christ, and are conceived by the authority of the Holy Spirit. These are the gifts of the Spirit. "Faith comes from hearing, and hearing from the Word of God." But faith is secured and preserved by the use of the sacraments. Therefore, the greatest part of our zeal should be that we might take hold of the instruments of the Spirit, by which we obtain the gifts of the Spirit themselves. COMMENTARY ON ROMANS (1564).[49]

NO ONE WITHOUT THE SPIRIT OF GOD CAN TEACH GOD'S WORD.

DIRK PHILIPS: Since then a godless person cannot teach correctly, and the one who is actually godless transgresses and does not abide in the doctrine of Christ as John says, it follows therefrom without contradiction that no one can teach God's Word correctly unless they themselves remain in Christ and his doctrine. But no one can understand Christ's doctrine, much less abide in it, except through the Holy Spirit. And no one has the Holy Spirit except one who is no longer carnally but spiritually minded, as Paul says, "But you are not in the flesh, you are in the Spirit, if the Spirit of God really dwells in you. Any one who does not have the Spirit of Christ does not belong to him. But if Christ is in you, although your bodies are dead because of sin, your spirits are alive because of righteousness." Therefore, those who have not died to sin and do not live in

---

[47]Vermigli, *In Epistolam S. Pauli*, 628-29; citing Jn 15:19.

[48]Benedetto and Flaminio, *Benefit of Christ's Death*, 106-7*.
[49]Brenz, *In Epistolam*, 195; citing Rom 10:17.

righteousness do not have the Spirit of God. But those who do not have the Spirit of the Lord do not understand the Word of the Lord and do not experience what is spiritual. How should they then be able to teach God's Word correctly or correctly distribute the gifts of the Spirit? Therefore everyone may well see to it that they do not accept the office of teacher before they themselves have been taught by God and enlightened with the Holy Spirit through whom he may speak God's Word correctly. THE SENDING OF PREACHERS.[50]

8:10 The Spirit Is Life

LIVE BY THE SPIRIT. HULDRYCH ZWINGLI: This is the justification that is accomplished by Christ. Thus the Christian that is concerned only with the body is always dead, whereas one who pays attention to the mind and spirit adheres always to God and always lives by the Spirit. From which it should be observed that man or woman can live by nothing external, but only by the Spirit.[†] NOTES ON ROMANS (1539).[51]

"SPIRIT" REFERS TO THE HOLY SPIRIT. JOHN CALVIN: Readers have already been reminded that by the word "Spirit" they are not to understand the soul but the Spirit of regeneration. Paul calls the Spirit life, not only because he lives and reigns in us, but also because he quickens us by his power, until at length, having destroyed the mortal flesh, he perfectly renews us. COMMENTARY ON ROMANS 8:10.[52]

SICK OF MANNA AND GRACE. JOHANNES BUGENHAGEN: For you have been justified by him. This is a proclamation of that grace of God on account of which sin is not imputed. These days when we hear of grace, we have no taste for it and begin to tire of it; our soul is sick of this bread, just like the sons of Israel were of the manna. For the power of faith is not easily understood, and while we neglect this, it necessarily comes to pass that we seek after something new. We enter into various and overly inquisitive disputes, here about the sacrament, there about the resurrection, then about Christian liberty and an endless number of relics. We do this not to believe, but only to dispute, that we might be somebody. INTERPRETATION OF ROMANS (1531).[53]

THE TRINITY. PETER MARTYR VERMIGLI: The apostle said, "If, however, Christ is in you." When he uses the phrase "Christ is in you," he shows that he regards it as the same thing for the Spirit of God or the Spirit of Christ to indwell us and for Christ himself to be in us. He does not mean, however, that the Holy Spirit and Christ are the same, that the Son of God is the same *hypostasis* or person. As Chrysostom observed, it is the nature of the three persons that wherever one may be, the others are also present at the same time. Therefore, since the Holy Spirit is in us, it necessarily follows that the Son of God, who is Christ, together with the Father, is in us as well. This is what Paul clearly declared in Ephesians when he said "that Christ may dwell in our hearts by faith." It does not, however, follow that wherever Christ may be according to his divine nature he is also there according to his human nature. For that nature—whether we're thinking of his soul or his body—is finite and cannot be diffused everywhere without bounds so that it occupies and fills every place as his divine nature does. In this way it is conceded that the Son and the Father are everywhere that the Holy Spirit is, and wherever we confess that the Son of God is, we also confess that Christ is, just not always according to his human nature. For that cannot be done. COMMENTARY ON ROMANS (1560).[54]

THE CONSOLATION THAT CHRIST IS IN US. JOHANNES BUGENHAGEN: "If, however, Christ is

---

[50]CRR 6:206*; citing 2 Jn 1:9; 1 Cor 2:14.
[51]Zwingli, *In Evangelicam Historiam*, 427. [†]Or "spirit."
[52]CTS 38:291* (CO 49:145).
[53]Bugenhagen, *In D. Pauli ad Romanos*, 85r-85v.
[54]Vermigli, *In Epistolam S. Pauli*, 632; citing Eph 3:17.

in you." This is the greatest consolation there is to the saints still living in the flesh, who on their own account are condemned but on Christ's account are justified. It is for this reason that sin cannot agitate or afflict them, and although it on occasion burns within them, it does not accomplish its purpose; they do not deny that they have sin, but they rejoice that it is put out of the way by Christ. For they say from their hearts, "This is our righteousness; this is the death of sin and victory over it. All the gates of hell will be unable to prevail against it," as long as, he says, Christ—that is, the Spirit of Christ—is in us. INTERPRETATION OF ROMANS (1531).[55]

OF CHRIST IN THE LORD'S SUPPER. PETER MARTYR VERMIGLI: But that what Paul said, "if Christ is in you," is not to be understood of his human nature or his body, is sufficiently shown by those things that are said concerning the Spirit. From this passage of Paul we are sufficiently taught how it is that we lay hold of Christ in the Eucharist and how we're conjoined to him. For we hear that by the death of Christ we have come to possess his Spirit. But in the Lord's Supper, a commemoration of Christ's death, both of his body nailed to the cross and his blood poured out on our behalf, is celebrated. What is more, it is celebrated not only in words, but with symbols of bread and wine that point to the body and blood of Christ. Accordingly, if we embrace by faith those things that are being commemorated, we come to possess the Spirit of Christ and Christ himself is in us, as Paul testifies in this passage. But it is unfitting to invoke the very body and flesh of Christ according to its own proper nature and real presence,[†] although we fully have their presence in a spiritual manner when we lay hold of them by faith. COMMENTARY ON ROMANS (1560).[56]

8:11 *The Spirit Will Bring You Life*

RESURRECTION IS BOTH PHYSICAL AND SPIRITUAL. MARTIN LUTHER: It is also in itself certain that if we are to rise to blessedness bodily with this flesh and blood on the last day, then we also must previously have risen spiritually on earth, as St. Paul says. . . . That is, because he has already made you inwardly alive, righteous, and in bliss, he also will not leave behind your body, which is the tent and house of the living spirit. Rather, because the spirit has already here risen from sin and death, the tent and the corruptible garment, which is the flesh and blood, must again come forth from the dust of the earth, since it is the inn and dwelling of that risen spirit, so that both should come together again and live eternally. SUMMER POSTIL (APRIL 6, 1534).[57]

THE SAME SPIRIT. JOHANNES BUGENHAGEN: "But if his Spirit. . . ." See with how much diligence and love he emphasizes this chief aspect of our salvation! Paul is so concerned to preach about this grace that he feared lest he might be unable to describe it with sufficiently clear words and statements. He therefore repeats what he had already said, saying again and again: "the Spirit reigns in you," "the Spirit stirs you up and makes you alive," "the Spirit mortifies your flesh," "the Spirit works all things." "And if he does all things while dwelling within you, he will therefore raise you up, infuse new life, and will cause that which was mortal to be abolished and then brought back to life. For the Father who raised Jesus from the dead will also raise you by the very same Spirit."

Therefore the end, consummation, and the principle of our baptism is this same Spirit. The water with which we are outwardly baptized immediately passes away, but the Spirit cleanses through our entire life all the way until the end, when this animal self will fall away and the spiritual self will rise up in its place. Hence this passage overthrows those heretics who deny that

---

[55]Bugenhagen, *In D. Pauli ad Romanos*, 84v-85r.
[56]Vermigli, *In Epistolam S. Pauli*, 634. [†]Speaking against the medieval Catholic doctrine of real presence according to transubstantiation.

[57]LW 77:104-5*; citing Jude 23.

the Spirit of Christ and of God the Father are one and the same. He proceeds from both; he is One and the one life of both God and Christ, for he had previously said "if the Spirit of Christ dwells in you" and then later, "if the Spirit of him," that is, of God the Father, "dwells in you." Clearly Paul is saying these things about one and the same Spirit. We wished to point this out in passing, not because I think it is doubtful to anybody now, but because we know that there will not be lacking those who will turn this into a doubt, whose mouths should be shut by plain passages of this kind.

Further, just as the Spirit of the Father and of Christ is the same, so also the Spirit is both the Father's and ours. He who is the life and bond between the Father and Christ is also that between the Father and us, so that you can perceive what our adoption really is and how it comes about, namely, by means of the same Spirit by which Christ is united to the Father, uniting us also with the Father. And, just as he is the natural Son through this Spirit, so also we are adoptive sons and daughters by that same Spirit, by whom we are one with the Father and with Christ. Oh that we understood this with greater light! We would not then fall into foolish disputations. INTERPRETATION OF ROMANS (1531).[58]

AFFLICTIONS OF THE RECONCILED ARE CHASTISEMENTS, NOT PUNISHMENTS. PETER MARTYR VERMIGLI: Though with regard to the elect, who have already been reconciled to God, death and such afflictions have not been inflicted as punishments, but rather as a cross sanctified by God, and in order that we might understand by paternal reproof to what degree sin displeases God, and that we might be called back to repentance more and more, and that death might be for

us the way through which whatever survives of sin in us might be destroyed. Therefore, although death is said to possess a place in us on account of sin—because it is entirely impossible that it would not—nevertheless, it is not inflicted on the pious and the elect as a punishment. And although the body is called dead on account of sin, we ought not to think that it is because of it that God retains hatred or anger toward his own, whose sins have been forgiven. For death and the enemy are those who harass the pious; they ought not be reckoned among penalties or punishments. Indeed, God is in the habit of training the faithful with adverse things, as we read concerning David, who, after he heard his sins were forgiven, nevertheless both lost his son and experienced in his family the most cruel calamities. COMMENTARY ON ROMANS (1560).[59]

THE SPIRIT IS STRONGER THAN THE FLESH. DAVID JORIS: The sincere Israelites will be known from the struggle and victory in which they must persevere and not lose, or they are not Israelites in deed. And the final struggle is against death, which is concealed in the flesh and which wounds the living. Indeed, its defeat must be completed by the Spirit, through the power of the Spirit. You will not die in this, but instead be victorious, for the Spirit is stronger and greater in power than the flesh. Therefore, blessed are those who are united in this, yes, those who have lusted after and desired this. These ones will not be ashamed but are able to remain standing against the death in the flesh. Observe this well. Now death is, I say, the last enemy. Therefore, arm yourselves! It comes on you. Do not be defeated by it, else it will remain your lord and eternally gnaw at you. Pay attention. HEAR, HEAR . . . (1536).[60]

---

[58]Bugenhagen, *In D. Pauli ad Romanos*, 83v-84r; citing Jn 17:22.

[59]Vermigli, *In Epistolam S. Pauli*, 638.
[60]CRR 7:135*; citing 1 Cor 15:26.

8:12-17 THE CHILDREN OF GOD

12So then, brothers,ᵃ we are debtors, not to the flesh, to live according to the flesh. 13For if you live according to the flesh you will die, but if by the Spirit you put to death the deeds of the body, you will live. 14For all who are led by the Spirit of God are sons of God. 15For you did not receive the spirit of slavery to fall back into fear, but you have received the Spirit of adoption as sons, by whom we cry, "Abba! Father!" 16The Spirit himself bears witness with our spirit that we are children of God, 17and if children, then heirs—heirs of God and fellow heirs with Christ, provided we suffer with him in order that we may also be glorified with him.

a Or *brothers and sisters*; also verse 29

OVERVIEW: Paul and the reformers focus here on the role of the Holy Spirit in leading us to live holy lives and in confirming that we are God's children. Living according to the flesh is not merely about outward acts but also about inner thoughts. Thus, everyone—even monks who claim to have never done sinful acts—has sinned.

Paul is exhorting believers to live holy lives. He appeals to their sonship through referring to the "Spirit of adoption" and their being coheirs with Christ.

The commentators remind readers that before the gospel, we had fear of God that made us flee from him. But as a result of the gospel, because we know we are loved, we do not need to fear, for as God's sons and daughters we can draw near to him in joy. Where the preaching of the law had produced fear, the preaching of the gospel brings "filial confidence." We serve God now out of affection and love rather than out of fear of punishment.

The interpreters present various views about whether one can be certain of one's election by sensing the actions of the Holy Spirit in one's heart. Paul has exhorted believers to mortify their flesh and live a new life of holiness. Now he starts transitioning to strengthening us to be able to endure suffering for Christ's sake. Knowing that we are coheirs with Christ gives us the impetus to suffer with him, for we know that we will share with him in his glory. But, the reformers point out, we do not earn salvation by our suffering. That comes to us as a free gift from God through his Son's death. We are headed toward certain glory. What would we not be willing to endure for the sake of that?

8:12-13 *Live by the Spirit, Not the Flesh*

FAITH HELPS US FACE TEMPTATION. ERASMUS SARCERIUS: *Objection.* We must not live according to the flesh; therefore the flesh will not tempt us? We must not live according to sins of the flesh; therefore the sins of the flesh will not tempt us?

Response. The flesh does not cease to tempt us with sin, but where it tempts us, there is also faith to fight against it. When we do fight against it by faith, those sins become venial because they obtain pardon, nor will they be imputed to us on account of our faith in Christ, as the passage in the beginning of this chapter states: "There is therefore now no condemnation for those who are in Christ Jesus." And in John 6, "He who believes in me has eternal life." NOTES ON ROMANS (1541).[1]

THE STRUGGLE. MARTIN LUTHER: Here it is necessary that the saints engage in a strong, eternal controversy and struggle, if they do not want to lose God's grace and their faith again, as St. Paul

---

[1]Sarcerius, *In Apostolam ad Romanos*, k7r; citing Rom 8:1; Jn 6:47.

also says, "If you live according to the flesh, then you must die, but if by the Spirit you put to death the deeds of the body, you will live." Christians have to struggle and contend with themselves so that they retain the Spirit and the beginning, new, divine life.

This is not done with monkish begging by which they think they can restrain sin. This filth does not adhere to the clothing or outwardly to the skin, so that we can wash and scrape it off or fast and castigate it out. Rather, it is stuck inwardly in the blood and flesh and is active throughout a human being; it must simply be killed, or it will kill you. It will be killed if you acknowledge it through repentance, are earnestly displeased with it, and seek and receive forgiveness through faith in Christ. Thus you will oppose the sinful desires so that they do not become deeds and rule over you. SUMMER POSTIL (APRIL 7, 1534).[2]

THINKING ACCORDING TO WISDOM OF THE FLESH. JOHANNES BUGENHAGEN: "You will die." That is, if you follow the wisdom of the flesh, you will be liable to damnation. He here alludes to the law that was given to Adam, where it was said: "In the day that you eat of it, you will die." Observe also—I point this out for the sake of those who are dim-witted—what Paul says is to live according to the flesh. It is not merely the things that those who have written precepts concerning civil ethics impose on you, for they think that those who do not fornicate, or live as gluttons, or squander everything they have, do not live according to the flesh. But this is human wisdom, not the wisdom of the Word, which calls the impulses and wisdom of the flesh a "carnal life," not merely fornication and drunkenness. You can see this in the case of Eve, who was deceived not by a deed, but by the very wisdom of the flesh. For she, having heard the divine commandment, thought to herself, "This tree is so beautiful and pleasing, how can it be that its fruit could be evil or harmful? It has no poison that God should strictly forbid it to be eaten; it is a

creature of God like I am—how can it not be good? I will surely taste it—a mere taste will do no harm." In these thoughts Eve sinned, even when she had not yet actually touched the apple, for she had accused God and his Spirit of being liars. What outward act was there in this to which we ascribe sin? Therefore, the sin of the flesh is to live, think, and act according to the wisdom of the flesh. From this not even monks and petty saints can escape, who pretend that they have never done any sinful work, and that they are therefore blameless and worthy to set their seats next to the throne of the Most High. INTERPRETATION OF ROMANS (1531).[3]

THE DIVINE SPARK REMAINS. BALTHASAR HUBMAIER: If before the fall God's likeness was free and unbound in us, since the fall it is held captive and the sin of the fall is damning. After the restoration of the fall through Christ, this likeness is made free again, although captive in the sinful and poisoned body; but the curse has been removed from the sin of the fall insofar as we do not by our own wickedness make it damning again by rebelliously walking in it. Thus Paul teaches us in Romans 8:13. Here you see clearly that the image or inbreathing of God is still in us all, although captive and as a live spark covered with cold ashes is still alive and will steam if heavenly water is poured on it. It also lights up and burns if one blows on it. That is the source of the conscience in the Jews, pagans, and Christians, as Paul writes about it. But Christ restored the quenched spark of flame on Easter Day when he breathed on his disciples and said, "Receive the Holy Spirit." Now Christ has ordered his servants to inbreathe and blow by the proclaiming of his holy Word, that the wounded soul may be reawakened from sleep. A CHRISTIAN CATECHISM.[4]

LIVE ACCORDING TO THE SPIRIT. WOLFGANG MUSCULUS: If it pleases anyone, this sentence can be formed into an exhortatory argument, so that

---

[2]LW 77:112*.

[3]Bugenhagen, *In D. Pauli ad Romanos*, 85r-85v; citing Gen 2:17.
[4]CRR 5:360*; citing Rom 2:15; Jn 20:22.

we might be persuaded, if we are Christians, to live not according to the flesh, but according to the Spirit—that is, to meditate on the life, not of sin and the flesh, but of righteousness and the Spirit. As such, it is an argument drawn from the nature and efficacy of the Spirit of Christ and what is proper for Christians:

(P1) It belongs to Christians to be led by the Spirit of God.

(P2) It belongs to the Spirit of Christ to extinguish sin and death, and to bring to life and justify.

(C) Therefore Christians are unable to live in sins and the flesh; rather, it is necessary that they live in righteousness and in the Spirit.

COMMENTARY ON ROMANS (1600).[5]

KEEPING THE HEART WELL. JOHN COTTON: Given the mixture of graces and corruption in every person's heart, and the strong power corruption has to deaden grace, it will deaden our liveliest performances if the heart is not well kept and corruption kept under control so that grace may be kept lively. This is what it means to keep the heart well: To keep under control those corruptions that abound in our hearts, to keep them subdued, and as much as it lies in us, mortified; and then the strength of them will be broken; and throughout it all to exercise the graces of the Spirit. If we do not keep the heart well, then in regard to the body of the corruptions of our hearts—which are older than the graces of God in us, and therefore more subtle and strong than grace is—it will come to pass that the weight of corruption will press down on the life of grace in us. I do not say it will kill it, but it will dull and deaden it. For although grace is eternal, it may still be cast into such loathing and fainting that you may truly say your heart is dead within you: "If you walk after the flesh, you will die." You to whom there is no condemnation, yet if you walk after the flesh, you will die. That is, your best graces and works will be dead. But if, by the Spirit,

you mortify your corruptions, you will live in grace and in every duty you perform to God and others. Therefore, from a heart well kept flow the springs of life, because it keeps corruption under control, for unsubdued corruption will choke grace greatly. Worldly cares, sensual lusts, proud affections, these either not being espied, or being winked at, will dull the sweetest graces in any spirit; but if we, by the Spirit, mortify these, then all our performances will be fruitful, our buying and selling lovely, not relishing oppression and deceit. Let us keep the beds of graces well and clean, and our whole life and conversation will be sweet and savory. But if we suffer a spirit of pride, or worldliness, or emulation in us, or if we don't bring them lower and take care to weed and root them out, our walks will be unsavory and our best duties yield us little or no comfort. WAY OF LIFE (1641).[6]

MORTAL VERSUS VENIAL SINS. PETER MARTYR VERMIGLI: The apostle also seems here to touch on the distinction between mortal and venial sin. It is not that only some sins are deadly in their nature, but that when the death and Spirit of Christ come to bear on it, some sins are forgiven and therefore called "venial." But those are deemed "mortal" that are not mortified in us when we indulge our lusts, live without repentance, sin against our conscience, put up no resistance against our lusts, hold on to our intention of living perversely, and set against our sin neither Christ's Spirit nor his death. COMMENTARY ON ROMANS (1560).[7]

WE MUST COOPERATE WITH GOD. BALTHASAR HUBMAIER: On this basis, true health and freedom must be in humanity after the restoration, or these Scriptures must fall to the ground, which God forbid. Therefore Christ and Paul ascribe this freedom to humanity and say, "If you will enter into life, then keep the commandments. If you live after the flesh, then you will die. If you will walk according to the Spirit, then you will live." Here is

---

[5]Musculus, *In Epistolam Apostoli Pauli*, 130.

[6]Cotton, *Way of Life*, 218-19*; alluding to Prov 4:23; citing Rom 8:1.
[7]Vermigli, *In Epistolam S. Pauli*, 644.

confirmed that ancient proverb: "Man, help yourself; then I also will help you." Yes, God speaks first and gives power through his Word. Now the human being can also help himself through the power of the Word or he can willfully neglect; that is up to him. Therefore one says: God has created you without your help, but without your help he will not save you. Since God first created the light, whoever wants to accept it will do so on the basis of the commandment of God; whoever despises it falls into darkness because of the just judgment of God. And the talent that he has and does not want to use, but hides in the handkerchief, will therefore be simply taken from him. FREEDOM OF THE WILL.[8]

8:14 Everyone the Spirit Leads Is a Child of God

CERTAINTY NOT FOUND IN MOTIONS OF THE HOLY SPIRIT. FRIEDRICH BALDUIN: Q: Aren't the motions of the Holy Spirit that a man or woman feels but once, sufficient to be certain of our election, since it here says that those who are led by the Spirit of God are sons and daughters of God?

A: I answer, this is the teaching of the Calvinists, but it is false and in error. It is certainly true that even those motions of the Holy Spirit are not entirely excluded from functioning as a certification of our election. For we hear that the Holy Spirit "gives testimony to our spirit that we are the sons of God"; therefore we are commanded to test ourselves, whether we are in the faith. But we can test our faith by its effects, by those motions of the Holy Spirit in us, such as a desire for God, patience in adversities, a hope for a better world, and so on. But this does not yet suffice: for the Holy Spirit can be grieved within us by our sins against conscience, which sins extinguish those motions in our heart, as demonstrated by the examples of Saul, Judas, and similar reprobates who certainly had received the Holy Spirit

through the ministry of regeneration and even at times felt his movements and guidance, but who nonetheless, being given over to reprobation, were in the end deprived of God's grace. Therefore, certainty of our election is not something to be sought for in the motions of the Holy Spirit alone. COMMENTARY ON ROMANS (1620).[9]

THE SPIRIT DRAWS US GENTLY. JOHANNES OECOLAMPADIUS: "Those who are led by the Spirit of God are the sons and daughters of God." The Spirit brings it about that our weakness does not prevail. But he does not drag us against our wills, but with a kind of interior gentleness. He draws us to imitating the example of Christ, who obeyed his Father even until death, that his glory might become known throughout all the world. For this reason, the sons and daughters of God are said to be drawn in this way, because they are regenerated by the Spirit of Christ. And just as he is the Son of God by nature, so they are by adoption. ANNOTATIONS ON ROMANS (1525).[10]

THE SPIRIT GATHERS GOD'S CHILDREN. PAUL GLOCK: Whoever has heard from us the word of preaching and of repentance (the judgment also, on those who will not repent) and allows the preaching of repentance to drive, frighten, and force them, such people will begin to recognize their sin, vice, burden of wrong, labor, and weariness. They will come to Christ and to his church. They will permit their sins to be removed and prayer for them to be made to God. Those who thus allow themselves to be compelled, urged, and driven through God's Word become God's children and true wedding guests of Christ. Matthew the publican as well as Mary Magdalene did this. They all were compelled when they heard the preaching of Christ, to recognize their sins and repent. Therefore, those whom the Spirit of God drives, says Paul, they are God's children, and are brought and led to the Lord's house, that it might be filled. But those who

---

[8]CRR 5:440*; citing Jn 1:5-9; 3:19.

[9]Balduin, *Catechesis Apostolica*, 524-25; citing 2 Cor 13:5.
[10]Oecolampadius, *In Epistolam Pauli*, 68v-69r.

will not accept the Word of the Lord from us and will not be compelled by it, will bear their own judgment. FIRST DEFENSE.[11]

YOU ARE THE HEIRS OF GOD'S GOOD THINGS.
JOHANNES PISCATOR: With these four verses he strengthens the argument by which he has exhorted us to a life of holiness. Those who live holily will be victorious; that is, as he says here, they will be the heirs of God. He proves this assertion, I would say, from the efficient cause, the right of sons.

(P1) Sons are the heirs of their fathers' goods.

(P2)You are the sons of God.

(C) Therefore you are the heirs of God's good things, or, what is the same thing, you will live.

He proves the assumed premise of this syllogism, namely, that the Roman believers are the sons and daughters of God, first by appealing to what is adjoined to them,† namely, the indwelling Holy Spirit whom he calls the "Spirit of adoption," since the Holy Spirit witnesses to believers that they have been adopted, as is clear from verse 16. But he proves this indwelling of the Holy Spirit in believers by appeal to its effects, namely, the invocation in which believers in filial confidence call on God as their Father. For it is the indwelling Holy Spirit who produces in them this confidence and invocation.

He then proves the assumed premise of the proposed syllogism by means of a twofold testimony, that of the Holy Spirit and that of the conscience. He further expands on the argument by means of an antithesis in which he sets against each other the contrary effects of the Holy Spirit that he produces in the elect through the preaching of the law, and through the preaching of the gospel. For he produces, by the law, a servile fear, but by the gospel, a filial confidence.

Last, he establishes his conclusion from both propositions in verse 17 where he says, "you are coheirs of Christ." As if to say, "Christ is the heir of God; therefore believers also are heirs of God," since just as Christ is the Son of God by nature, so believers are the sons and daughters of God by grace in that by grace they have been adopted by the Father in Christ his only-begotten Son and received into the number of his sons. Therefore, Christ is the principal heir, or rather the "firstborn among many brethren," but believers are coheirs with Christ and heirs because of Christ since it is because of him that they have been adopted. LOGICAL ANALYSIS OF ROMANS (1589).[12]

NO ONE CAN ORDER THE CHILDREN OF GOD.
PILGRAM MARPECK: Of what value would it be to escape the verdicts, bonds, cords—yes, the imprisonment—of conscience and human rules, only to run into the devil's hands because you falsely boast of new insight and indulge in the self-will of carnal liberty? For it is surely true and certain that neither flesh nor blood nor any creature in heaven or on earth has such power over a free conscience that it can command or forbid those of the true nature and character of God. Those who do possess the true Spirit of God are one nature, born again as they are by the Word and Holy Spirit.

Those who are driven by God's Spirit are children of God. One can no more order or forbid the children of God than one can order or forbid the Holy Spirit of God. Only the Holy Spirit is the commander and prohibitor in those to whom he has given birth. CONCERNING THE LIBERTARIANS.[13]

TRUE CHRISTIANS ARE LED BY THE SPIRIT OF GOD.
MENNO SIMONS: Water, bread, wine, and name do not make anyone a Christian, but

---

[11]CRR 10:320*; citing Mt 9:9; Lk 7:36.

[12]Piscator, *Analysis Logica*, 140-41; citing Rom 8:29. †*Ex/ab adjuncto*. A technical term in logic, in which, if a subject is changed by an adjunct, the adjunct must have the qualities in and of itself that adhere to the subject. For example, the rain that changes the parched ground from dry to wet must be wet itself. Thus, in this case, believers' ability to call on God must mean that they have the Holy Spirit in them, who gives them this ability.
[13]CRR 12:93*.

those are Christians who are born of God; are of a divine nature, are of the same mind as Christ Jesus; led by the Spirit of God, who daily crucify their evil and corrupt flesh; do not walk after the flesh, but after the Spirit; love nothing above God's Word; love their neighbors as themselves; lead a blameless, humble, pious life; who meekly walk in the footsteps of Christ and who have become new, changed, and converted men and women and creatures in Christ. These the Word of God calls Christians. A HUMBLE AND CHRISTIAN DEFENSE.[14]

THE TRUE LIBERTY OF CHRIST. PILGRAM MARPECK: In short, the true liberty of Christ, and the love that belongs to it, is a free surrender, denial, and forgetting of self. The true liberty of Christ fervently desires to serve everyone in that which is good, to the praise of God and the salvation of humankind. Yes, even though something is legitimate for them, they surrender it all for the sake of love and growth. CONCERNING THE LIBERTARIANS.[15]

8:15 The Spirit of Adoption

NO LONGER A SPIRIT OF BONDAGE. WALTER CRADOCK: That is one fruit of it, that as soon as someone comes to walk according to the Spirit, they no longer have a spirit of bondage. What is a spirit of bondage? It is nothing but this: a temper of soul like a slave. It is just as you might imagine of a man who has been taken prisoner in [in a faraway country], what his temper might be: he is grateful for a crust of bread, and he fears being whipped, and beaten, and even killed. Such is the temper of a person's soul who is in a spirit of bondage. When one is in such a temper, they are always in fear of being whipped and scourged, and they have hard thoughts about God, and they fear that they will prove to be a hypocrite, and the like.

Now, the apostle says we do not have the spirit of fear but we have the spirit of adoption, by whom we cry, "Abba Father." That is, there is a sweet temper, such as a loving child has toward his dear Father; there is a boldness, a love, delight, and rejoicing and sweetness. This is one fruit of it, therefore. As long as you are under horror, and moping, and howling, and crying, you come short of walking according to the Spirit. For if you have a spirit of adoption, your soul will always be full of sweetness during great affliction; and under the worst sins you commit, though there may be sorrow, yet you will be full of sweetness and joy. SERMON ON ROMANS 8:4 (1649).[16]

LINKING COMFORT AND CALLING ON GOD. PHILIPP MELANCHTHON: As long as the conscience is without faith and about to despair in fears, it flees from God, doubts whether he hears, whether he has regard for them, and so on. It does not call on God. Therefore Paul links together comfort and calling on God, and ascribes this only to those who have already been raised up by faith through the gospel. For when he says: "We cry 'Abba, Father,'" this signifies: Now we acknowledge that God is a Father, that he truly hears us, and by means of this faith we receive comfort and call on God.

This faith and acknowledgment of the mercy of God really makes a distinction between the Christian and the ungodly, because doubt and anger against God remain in the wicked. But in believers, faith is a new recognition of the mercy of God. It fights against doubting and declares that we are truly heard on account of Christ. This same faith is the comfort and vivification, and the testimony of the Holy Spirit in hearts about which he says here: "The Spirit bears witness to our spirit." The Holy Spirit works comfort in the midst of true terrors through the word of the gospel. COMMENTARY ON ROMANS (1540).[17]

[14]Simons, *Complete Works*, 444*; citing 2 Pet 1:4; Phil 2:5; Gal 5:24; Rom 8:2; Mt 10:37; 7:12; 16:24.
[15]CRR 12:404*.
[16]Cradock, *Gospel-Holiness*, 280*.
[17]Melanchthon, *Commentary on Romans*, 175*.

Children, Servants, and Fear. Johannes Bugenhagen: "For you have not received a spirit of servitude." There is one kind of spirit in slaves, another in sons. . . . Sons know that they are free and do not fear being ejected from the home of their father. They are secure in their certain inheritance and know that their father is theirs and that everything that belongs to their father belongs to them as well. They also know that they have not merited their inheritance by any duty they have rendered to their father, since they already possess it in common with him from the sole fact that they are his sons. But no fleshly person can lay claim to the right to such an inheritance and liberty, unless he knows that he himself is a son of God. Contrariwise, a slave possesses no liberty and does not know when he might be cast out of the home. For they are not sons, nor does anything in the home belong to them. They do all things by coercion and fear and are pressed by the grievous tyranny of the law that always says, "Do! Do! Love! Love!" But they are unable to. While sons and daughters do not hear this, for they do all things and love God of their own accord—for how can they not love the Father?

Take note of how elegantly Paul expresses himself in very brief arguments that intertwine among themselves:

1. You must not sin, for you are not debtors to the flesh.

2. If you are followers of the flesh, you will die.

3. If you walk according to the Spirit, you will live.

4. By this Spirit you are sons and daughters of God, not slaves.

But we should see clearly in the text this point: When you were once enslaved and under the law it was impossible for you not to be afraid of God, whom you knew not as a father, but as a judge, for this is what your bad conscience that was guilty was teaching you. You did not then wish to approach him with trust, but rather were fleeing from him with great terror and fear; you were feeling the weight of sin and the wrath of the law,

and when you believed that we would be absolved through external works and hypocrisy, you fell into an even greater fear, or rather, into desperation, and this is what we have experienced. Are we not driven by papal decrees [and so on] to "good works" because of our sins? We have done many things, in fasting, praying, singing, building the temples of the saints, now for St. James, now for Veronica, or in making pilgrimage to some other extravagant marvel—but what has it done for us? We were not able to be absolved from our sins. For it was only the spirit of bondage; we never felt our consciences being set at ease, even though wherever the Spirit of God and of sons is found, the conscience is rendered completely at peace. Is it not true of us what the apostle says in the ninth chapter, about the Jews: "In pursuing the law of righteousness, we have not attained to the law of righteousness." We see that that same fear was in Adam, who after he had sinned, hid, fleeing from God's sight, for . . . he now began to possess a spirit of bondage. John speaks of this fear in his letter: "Perfect love casts out fear." Love does not cause you to fear God, for when you know that you are his son or daughter, you draw near to him with a joyful heart, acknowledging him as your Father. But he does not say this about that fear that the Scriptures greatly commend, which is nothing other than the worship of and reverence for God, concerning which it is written: "The fear of the Lord drives away sin" and "the fear of the Lord is the beginning of wisdom." There, fear draws near to God, while the other servile kind of fear flees from God's sight, which was the kind operative in us before the gospel of Christ was preached. But now, because we have the fear appropriate for sons and daughters, we draw near with great joyfulness of conscience. Interpretation of Romans (1531).[18]

Father, Father! Heinrich Bullinger: This "Father, Father!"—by being repeated—points to the ardor in the breast of a Christian. For one who

---

[18]Bugenhagen, *In D. Pauli ad Romanos*, 86r-87r; citing Rom 9:31; 1 Jn 4:18; Sir 1:27; Ps 111:10; Prov 9:10.

believes in the gospel of God does not cry out "St. Martin, pray for us! For we are sinners and do not dare draw near to God's throne!" But rather they cry out along with the prodigal son, "Father, I have sinned against heaven and against you; I am no longer worthy to be called your son." Think of me through your Son Jesus Christ, who taught us to pray thus: "our Father who is in heaven," and so on. COMMENTARY ON ROMANS (1533).[19]

ABBA, PADRE. JUAN DE VALDÉS: In saying, "whereby we cry Abba, Father," he means that the filial spirit that dwells in us who are Christians, is that which gives us boldness to call on God loudly and plainly when we seek something from him, and to call him Father. For St. Paul, writing in Greek, used the Hebrew word "Abba," which signifies Father. And by way of expounding it, he employed the Greek word. I likewise have left "Abba," and have employed the Spanish word *padre*. COMMENTARY ON ROMANS (1556).[20]

THE PRAYER COMES ONLY FROM THE SPIRIT OF GOD. WOLFGANG MUSCULUS: "For you have not again received the spirit of servitude unto fear." This is the minor premise.[†] It is the same as if he had simply said, "but you are the sons of God." For he said that they had have received the Spirit of adoption, that is, of divine sonship. He proves this by that solemn prayer of Christians in which we call God "our Father," which form of address cannot be made unless it comes from the Spirit of God, which is why he says that it is by him that we cry out, "Abba, Father!" COMMENTARY ON ROMANS (1555).[21]

SERVING OUT OF LOVE, NOT FEAR. HULDRYCH ZWINGLI: "A spirit of servitude." You who have been made sons and daughters of God through Christ and by his Spirit ought not to henceforth serve God out of the fear of punishment or the terrors of the law like servants who serve only for

wages, but willingly, freely, and voluntarily out of love as sons and daughters who do all things of their own will. For they know that they will be heirs of their father's goods. We have the Spirit, not of servants, but of adopted sons and daughters. The believer therefore does good works not by force, nor compelled by fear of the law or of punishment, but out of love and affection for the Father. ANNOTATIONS ON ROMANS (1539).[22]

GOD IS OUR FATHER AND GRANDFATHER. KATHARINA SCHÜTZ ZELL: It is like the way a grandfather loves the child of his child and also the father and the child are his heirs because the child is born (*geboren*) of his child. So also God is our Father, yes, our grandfather, and we are his heirs through Jesus Christ his Son, through whom we are given birth (*geboren*) again by God as new people. And so we dare confidently to cry out and say, "Abba, dear Father," through the adopting Spirit whom we have received from Christ, the Spirit who assures us that we are God's children and fellow heirs of God with Christ, as the apostle has clearly taught in his letter to the Romans and all his letters. As also all the other apostles have taught. And John in all his writing always calls God our Father and us his beloved little children. THE MISERERE PSALM MEDITATED, PRAYED, AND PARAPHRASED.[23]

8:16 The Spirit Witnesses to Our Adoption

THE HOLY SPIRIT BEARS WITNESS TO OUR SPIRIT. JOHN DONNE: So then our spirit bears witness sometimes when the Spirit does not. That is, nature testifies some things without the addition of particular grace. And then the Spirit—the Holy Spirit—testifies often when ours does not. How often does he stand at the door and knock? How often does he spread his wings to gather us as a hen does her chickens? How often does he present

---

[19]Bullinger, *In Sanctissimam Pauli*, 106; citing Lk 15:18-19.
[20]Valdés, *Commentary upon St. Paul's Epistle*, 127*.
[21]Musculus, *In Epistolam Apostoli Pauli*, 177. [†]For the major premise see the previous verse.

[22]Zwingli, *In Evangelicam Historian*, 427.
[23]Zell, *Church Mother*, 154*; citing Jn 3:3; 2 Cor 5:17; Rom 8:15-17; Gal 4:6, 3:26; Eph 1:11; Phil 2:15; Col 1:12; Jas 2:5; Jn 1:12; 1 Jn 3:1, 2, 9; 5:1-2.

us the power of God in the mouth of the preacher, and we then bear witness to one another of the wit and of the eloquence of the preacher, and no more? How often does he bear witness that a certain action is odious in the sight of God, and then our spirit bears witness that it is acceptable, profitable, honorable in the sight of men and women? How often does he bear witness for God's judgments and our spirit deposes for mercy, by presumption, and how often does he testify for mercy, and our spirit swears for judgment, in desperation? But when the Spirit and our spirit agree in their testimony that he has spoken comfortably to my soul, and my soul has taken comfort in his speech, that—to use Christ's similitude—"He has piped, and we have danced," he has shown me my Savior, and my spirit has rejoiced in God my Savior, then he deposes for the decree of my election, and I depose for the seals and marks of that decree, these two witnesses, the Spirit, and "my spirit," and they induce a third witness, the world itself, to testify that which is the testimony of this text, "That I am the child of God." SERMON ON ROMANS 8:16.[24]

Two Witnesses to Our Adoption. NIELS HEMMINGSEN: The apostle produces two witnesses of our adoption in Christ, which are (1) the Spirit of God, and (2) our spirit made more certain by him. "Our spirit" is that burning affection stirred up by the Holy Spirit in the hearts of believers. Of this Paul writes in 2 Corinthians in the first chapter: "He who establishes us with you and anointed us is God, who also sealed us and gave his Spirit in our hearts as a guarantee." By this guarantee, by which a surety is made firm, the spirit of believers being confirmed persuades itself with certainty that it has been adopted by God and is now truly a son in Christ. Therefore, when these two testimonies agree, a believer ought not be in any further doubt about the grace of adoption, but through patience should look for the promised inheritance. COMMENTARY ON ROMANS (1562).[25]

Because the Holy Spirit First Touched Our Heart. PETER MARTYR VERMIGLI: "The Spirit himself testifies with our spirit that we are the children of God." He shows that by these prayers in which we call on God we are made more certain of that adoption of which he had just previously made mention. For since we are stirred up by the Holy Spirit praying within us we ought to be wholly persuaded that when we call God "Father" it is truly so, inasmuch as we know that the Spirit of God cannot lie. . . . He said here that nobody can pray in such a way that he calls God his "Father" unless this had been prompted by the Holy Spirit. We see from this that those things that have been handed down to us to be believed and those things that the Lord himself taught cannot be received by us unless the Holy Spirit first touches our heart. COMMENTARY ON ROMANS (1560).[26]

The Holy Spirit, Assurance, and Prayer. JOHN CALVIN: Paul means that the Spirit of God gives us such a testimony that when he is our guide and teacher, our spirit is made assured of the adoption of God, for our mind, of its own self, without the preceding testimony of the Spirit, could not convey to us this assurance. There is also here an explanation of the former verse, for when the Spirit testifies to us that we are the children of God, he at the same time pours into our hearts such confidence that we venture to call God our Father. Doubtless, since the confidence of the heart alone opens our mouth, except the Spirit testifies to our heart respecting the paternal love of God, our tongues would be dumb, so that they could utter no prayers. For we must ever hold fast to this principle, that we do not rightly pray to God unless we are surely persuaded in our hearts that he is our Father, when we so call him with our lips. To this there is a corresponding part, that our faith has no true evidence, except we call on God. It is not then without reason that Paul, bringing us to this test,

---

[24]Donne, *Works*, 2:54-55*.
[25]Hemmingsen, *Commentarius in Epistolam*, 292; citing 2 Cor 1:21-22.

[26]Vermigli, *In Epistolam S. Pauli*, 662.

shows that it then only appears how truly anyone believes, when they who have embraced the promise of grace exercise themselves in prayers. COMMENTARY ON ROMANS 8:16.[27]

8:17 We Are Heirs and Cosufferers with Christ

SINCE WE ARE COHEIRS, WE CAN SUFFER WITH PATIENCE. MARTIN BUCER: "If indeed we suffer with him." *Eiper sympaschomen*. This saying can be taken in two respects, both causally and conditionally. If we take it in the first sense, it has this meaning: we are coheirs with Christ. Since we draw near to this inheritance together with him—that is, since we will be glorified together with Christ—we can therefore suffer so many things together with him, which we would by no means be able to patiently endure unless we were certain that we are sharers with him in his glory and that we will more fully see this glory, on account of which we will tolerate many adverse things for the Lord's sake and together with the Lord. Therefore, when we suffer so many things together with Christ, we testify about ourselves that we are persuaded beyond all doubt that we are coheirs with Christ and sharers in his own glory. Let us therefore prepare ourselves for this glory with all of our strength by repressing the desires of the flesh that draw us away from this glory and by zealously making advances in that newness of life that is a kind of foretaste of his glory. COMMENTARY ON ROMANS (1536).[28]

COHEIRS MUST BE COMARTYRS. MARTIN LUTHER: He intentionally makes the connection that whoever wants to be Christ's brother and coheir should reflect that he is also a comartyr and cosufferer. It is as if he means to say: There are many Christians who would gladly be coheirs and occupy the whole fief with the Lord Christ, but they do not want to suffer with him; rather, they separate from him on this point: they do not want to participate in his suffering. "But this will not do" (he says). "The inheritance will not follow unless the suffering precedes." The reason is that Christ, our dear Lord and Savior, himself had to suffer first before he attained to glory. So also we must be comartyrs and together with the Lord Christ be mocked, despised, spit on, crowned with thorns, and killed by the whole world, before we attain to the inheritance. Otherwise it will not happen.

This faith and teaching brings with it that there is to be an equality there in every respect, namely, whoever wants to be a brother and coheir of Christ must also suffer with him. Whoever wants to live with him must first die with him. Similarly, in one house many brothers must tolerate not only the good but also the bad. As people say, "Whoever wants to share in the meal must also contribute to the work." SUMMER POSTIL.[29]

WE SHARE WITH HIM IN HIS SUFFERING SO THAT WE MAY SHARE IN HIS GLORY. MARTIN BUCER: If . . . we accept this saying in a conditional sense, Paul is providing a rhetorical transition in order to fortify the tolerance with which we bear afflictions for Christ's sake. That we are coheirs with Christ and of his glory will be clearly beyond all doubt if, as we are approaching this glory and are to be glorified together with him, there is nothing that we will refuse to suffer patiently for Christ's sake, but rather, we undergo all things with a lively spirit. I affirm that we are, indeed, coheirs with Christ and sharers of his glory, but only according to this law: if we are afflicted together so that we might be glorified together. It is on this path that Christ entered into his glory, so that he suffered many things beforehand; therefore it is by this same path that this glory will be entered by us as well. COMMENTARY ON ROMANS (1536).[30]

---

[27]CTS 38:299-300* (CO 49:150).
[28]Bucer, *Metaphrases et Enarrationes*, 338.
[29]LW 78:153-54*; citing 2 Thess 3:10.
[30]Bucer, *Metaphrases et Enarrationes*, 338.

CLOTHED WITH THE IMAGE OF CHRIST CRUCIFIED AND GLORIFIED. BENEDETTO DA MANTOVA AND MARCANTONIO FLAMINIO: So then, by patience we find that our Lord gives us the help that he has promised us in our need, by which our hope is confirmed. And it would be exceedingly ungrateful not to trust to such aid and favor in the future when we have found it, by experience, to be so certain and steadfast up until now. But what do we need with so many words? It ought to suffice us to know that true Christians, while going through tribulation, are clothed with the image of our Lord Jesus Christ crucified. And if we bear tribulation willingly and with a good heart, we shall in the end be clothed with the image of Jesus Christ glorified. THE BENEFIT OF CHRIST'S DEATH.[31]

FROM NEW LIFE, TO SUFFERING, TO GLORY. MARTIN BUCER: It is abundantly clear that the apostle in this passage is transitioning from his exhortation to mortify the flesh and meditate on our new life, to an exhortation of tolerance in adversities and persecutions that must be born patiently for Christ's sake. But it is no less clear that the apostle wrote everything in the section that follows that he might be seen to have especially set out to enlarge on the glory of the sons and daughters of God, unto which glory we have been adopted and sealed by the Spirit of Christ. And certainly it is needful that this glory be of the highest degree, with which nothing that we suffer here can be compared, and which the prayers of all creatures and especially of the holiest men and women so anxiously aspire to and look forward to.

Also, this amplification of the heavenly inheritance in which we have been enrolled is most effective in both inflaming the pursuit of a new life and in strengthening our tolerance of adversities. If there is so much glory that God made us to be sharers in—not by any merits of our own but only by his grace—who of us will not prepare ourselves for it with the greatest effort, disowning whatever is contrary to it in our lives,

such as all the lusts of the flesh, and giving our assent to those things that are agreeable with that glory, such as all the duties of piety and moral purity? Again, when we consider how immense that glory is that has been ascribed to us, and that it will certainly come when we suffer for Christ's sake, what will we not endure with a noble spirit? COMMENTARY ON ROMANS (1536).[32]

WE MUST SUFFER WITH CHRIST RATHER THAN TAKE UP ARMS. BALTHASAR HUBMAIER: Here anyone who has ears can hear that on the authority of these Scriptures we are to be completely docile, submissive, and obedient to the authorities and ready to prevent and repudiate all disturbances, rebellions, and disunity. For this reason I am greatly displeased with Hans Hut and his followers for stirring up and misleading the populace secretly in corners, provoking conspiracy and sedition under the pretense of baptism and the Supper of Christ as if one had to take up the sword and the like. No, No! That is not the way. A Christian does not fight, strike, or kill unless in a seat of authority and is ordered to do it or is called to do it by the properly instituted government. Otherwise, before Christians draw swords, they will give up their cloak and coat. They also offer the other cheek, yea even their body and life. Christian conduct is so peaceable because this is the Christian's victory, our faith, which overcomes the world. Accordingly, Christians' lives are set toward suffering in order that they may in some measure become like Christ in suffering, fulfill Christ's suffering in their bodies and with their crosses follow in the path that he has prepared for us and on which he himself has gone before us with his cross and suffering. Then we shall also inherit eternal life with him. This is what I told Hut and others to their face, and reproved them severally for their seductive and seditious doctrines, as one finds in my theses that I publicly presented against him and his followers. APOLOGIA.[33]

---

[31]Benedetto and Flaminio, *Benefit of Christ's Death*, 80-81*.

[32]Bucer, *Metaphrases et Enarrationes*, 338.
[33]CRR 5:560*; citing 1 Jn 5:4; Col 1:24; Lk 24; Acts 14:22.

WE DO NOT EARN GLORY BY OUR SUFFERING.
MARTIN BUCER: I do not accept the saying before us in a conditional sense, since while this glory is certainly more revealed in us when we suffer for Christ's sake, and is in some sense attained when we bravely suffer death for the name of Christ, nevertheless we do not acquire it for ourselves by any of our afflictions. It is God's inheritance, on the basis of his mercy alone, to which God adopted us as a result of his Son's death, and to which he draws us through his Son. COMMENTARY ON ROMANS (1536).[34]

CHRISTIAN FREEDOM IS TO SERVE. DIRK PHILIPS: This is now the freedom of God's children in which they have been placed by God through Jesus Christ, and this freedom is nowhere except where the kinship of God and the spirit of the Lord is. Therefore this freedom does not exist in order to sin, or not to walk according to the flesh, or not to become like the world, but to serve God and the neighbors. For Christian freedom (of which it is now spoken) is actually serving God and the neighbor, as the apostle Peter said: That is God's will that you with right doing will shut up the ignorance of foolish persons, as the free ones, not as if you had freedom as a cover for wickedness but as God's servants. THREE ADMONITIONS.[35]

THE BRIDE HEADS TOWARD HER INHERI-TANCE. DAVID JORIS: The blessed Lord God will at once give might and power to his children. Namely, to the bride who has come to maturity in order to stand against the devil and death. For the devil has been allowed an ordained time, in order to torment and to rule, or so that he may be led to the scene of the last battle. This does not mean that the thorns will do damage to the flowers of life. Let them grow up unhindered and as abominable as they will. Pay attention and understand it well, beloved. There exists a time for conversion and restoration. Hasten therefore to the time of renewal. In this time the Leviathan, the wily devil, will be captured between the teeth and his head will be split open. Furthermore, he will be bound and placed under our knees or feet. Nevertheless, the bride is chased by him to old age. But when the morning star rises and draws near in her heart, she will be strengthened against the deceiver so that she can stand against the strong devil. She can then turn freely to him, asking him what he wants and freely and unconcernedly examining him in his light. For in her the love of her Lord is perfected. She will shame him in his vile, evil lusts or look in his face, to see that he is still proud and that he has not ceased from his path. See, she becomes inflamed with wrath from the earnest love of her God. She therefore grasps him by the head and devours or defeats the power or the force of death. She brings it all under her through the power of God in the name of Jesus her Lord whom she loves alone with a full heart. She hates what he hates. The struggle is a witness of this. In this way will he be captured by his own eyes. He will be repudiated and his might will be robbed. Then the brilliant banner of righteousness will be raised up or it will appear. And she will appropriate the crown of life which belongs to her by the right of inheritance. Observe this well. HEAR, HEAR . . . (1536).[36]

---

[34]Bucer, *Metaphrases et Enarrationes*, 338-39.
[35]CRR 6:393*; citing 2 Cor 3:18; 1 Pet 2:15.

[36]CRR 7:141*; citing Rev 20:7-10; Mt 13:39-43; Ps 74:14; Rev 20:2; 1 Pet 5:8-9.

8:18-25 SUFFERING AND THE HOPE OF GLORY

[18]*For I consider that the sufferings of this present time are not worth comparing with the glory that is to be revealed to us.* [19]*For the creation waits with eager longing for the revealing of the sons of God.* [20]*For the creation was subjected to futility, not willingly, but because of him who subjected it, in hope* [21]*that the creation itself will be set free from its bondage to corruption and obtain the freedom of the glory of the children of God.* [22]*For we know that the whole creation has been groaning together in the pains of childbirth until now.* [23]*And not only the creation, but we ourselves, who have the firstfruits of the Spirit, groan inwardly as we wait eagerly for adoption as sons, the redemption of our bodies.* [24]*For in this hope we were saved. Now hope that is seen is not hope. For who hopes for what he sees?* [25]*But if we hope for what we do not see, we wait for it with patience.*

OVERVIEW: The Reformation was a time of suffering. Just as Paul faced suffering and persecution, many of the reformers faced the threat of exile, imprisonment, or death. Many even lost their lives as martyrs. Both Paul and the reformers reflect on the theme of suffering and the awaiting glory that will make it all worthwhile. Almost every time that the Scriptures mention our suffering, they also allude to the good that is awaiting us. It helps us to know that the tribulations are temporary and that they will turn into everlasting joy. Not only will our sufferings eventually be replaced by the eternal blessings we look toward, but God promises to work them to our good now as well. Moreover, they argue that suffering is simply part of the Christian life. The commentators point to numerous entities that are groaning as they wait: the creation, the church, the ungodly and the godly, the apostles, and the Holy Spirit.

The interpreters suggest different meanings for the "firstfruits of the Spirit." It is perhaps what the apostles were given after the resurrection; or it may be the gifts given to all believers; or perhaps it was the apostles themselves; or it is a metaphor taken from the ceremonial law, involving giving one's best to God, something we need to do as well.

The commentators explore the roles of faith, hope, and love. In the midst of our suffering, faith and hope are closely linked and help us to survive as we learn to endure all sorts of unhappiness here in the promise of great happiness in the world to come. Faith grabs ahold of the forgiveness of sins and the imputation of Christ's righteousness in the present. Hope is future oriented, keeping our eyes focused on the glory that awaits us. Hope is also linked to patience, which is essential to it. Faith, hope, and love are also connected: They start with faith, which points to the God we trust; then hope helps us to wait for what faith taught us; and love is the pinnacle and extends to God and others.

8:18 The Glory Will Be Greater Than Our Suffering

SUFFERING CAN'T COMPARE TO THE JOY AND GLORY AWAITING US. MARTIN LUTHER: Only look at how he turns his back on the world and his face to the future revelation, as if he saw no misfortune or misery anywhere on earth, but only joy! "In truth," he says, "even if things go badly for us, what is our suffering compared to the inexpressible joy and glory which is to be revealed in us? It is not worth comparing with that or even with being called 'suffering.'" However, what is lacking is that we do not see with our bodily eyes the great and excellent glory for which we are to wait. We do not grasp with our hands that we will never die, and besides will obtain a body that need not suffer or be sick. Whoever could take that to heart would have to say that even if he were burned or drowned ten times, if that were possible, it would still be nothing at all compared to the future life of glory. What is temporal suffering, no matter how long it is, compared with eternal life? It is not worth boasting that it is suffering or calling it meritorious.

"Thus I hold," says St. Paul, "and you Christians should also learn to hold this." Then they would find that the infinite is not at all to be compared with the finite. What is a single halfpenny compared to a world full of gold coins? Yet even such a parable does not fit here, because both are perishable. Therefore, even all the world's suffering is to be counted as nothing at all compared to the glorious, eternal reality that we shall see and possess eternally. "Therefore, I ask you, dear brothers and sisters, to be afraid of no suffering, even if you should be slaughtered. If you are genuine coheirs, then a part of your inheritance will be that you also suffer at the same time. However, what does this suffering amount to, if it is compared with the eternal glory that has been prepared for you and already earned by your Savior, Jesus Christ? It is not worth comparing." Thus St. Paul makes all suffering on earth into a droplet and tiny spark, but he makes the glory we are to hope for into an infinite ocean and a great fire. SUMMER POSTIL (JUNE 20, 1535).[1]

SUFFERING IS A LESSON. NIELS HEMMINGSEN: The first argument is taken from a comparison of the present toil with future glory.

(P1) Evils that will be shortly brought to an end and followed by glory that will have no end are to be born with a steady soul.

(P2) The sufferings of this life are of this kind.

(C) Therefore, they are to be patiently born with.

The apostle calls *pathēmata* those things that we suffer in this life, such as every kind of calamity of which it is said *ta pathēmata mathēmata esti* (suffer-

ings are lessons). The "glory that will be revealed in us" is that eternal blessedness and enjoying of God through all eternity. Let us, therefore, keep our eyes fixed on this glory as often as we are pressed by some cross, and let us hold onto both faith and a good conscience lest we fall short of this hope of glory. COMMENTARY ON ROMANS (1562).[2]

TEMPORARY SUFFERING FOLLOWED BY ENORMOUS REWARDS. ANTONINUS CORVINUS: It gives no little amount of strength to the souls of us on whose shoulders the cross is laid to know that those things we endure are temporary and will not last forever. This is the foremost consolation by which the apostle wished to console those living under the cross. Not only are our tribulations in this age temporary, but also after this life they will be transformed into everlasting joy that will never end. If that famous proverb about the change that overtook Glaucus and Diomedes[†] applies anywhere it applies here most of all. Who, therefore, would let himself be driven to impatience or escape in some way from the Lord's rod and discipline when it is to be compensated with so many and so great goods in Christ's coming kingdom? Note that the Scriptures nearly everywhere, when they announce the coming cross to be born by Christians, also hold out this consolation as a kind of recompense. This can, for example, be seen in that sentence that is found in the book of Acts: "It is necessary that through many tribulations we enter the kingdom of heaven." Is there not mention first of tribulation, and then of the kingdom of heaven? Christ also spoke of himself in the same manner, that he could not return to glory except through death and suffering. Given that this is common to both Christ and the apostles, by what means could we think to escape the same? Or are we better than they? Or should the condition of a servant be better than that of the Master? Nobody would say anything of the sort! But this will be the lot of all, as many of those who believe. Hence St. James wrote likewise: "Esteem it all joy, my brethren, if you fall into

---

[1]LW 78:155-56*.

[2]Hemmingsen, *Commentarius in Epistolam*, 294-95.

various trials." He was not ignorant of the fact that the afflictions suffered by Christians are not only temporary but also after this life will be compensated for and transformed into enormous rewards.

So much for this first consolation by which Paul wished to ease the suffering of those souls sweating under a cross. COMMENTARY ON EPISTLES AND GOSPELS (1540).[3]

THIS WORLD'S TROUBLES AND HEAVEN'S JOYS.

THOMAS WILCOX: When the apostle says, "I count," he means that he comes with an upright judgment, in an even pair of balance and scales, as it were, having rightly and religiously examined reasons on both sides and gathering all into a just sum, to weigh the troubles of this world, and the joys of heaven together. He does not deal with it as worldly persons do, who regard nothing but their miseries and afflictions, by means of which they become not only impatient and wayward, but past all hope of being able to receive comfort and consolation. Nor do they play the part of the profane and unfeeling Stoics, who again on the other side, by reason of their beastly blockishness that they bring to themselves, having both their souls and bodies benumbed as it were, are no whit at all touched with the sense of the same. Nor yet being so rapt and ravished with these eternal joys that they utterly forget, or feel not at all the miseries and afflictions of this life, a matter that the contemplative persons, in their trances, dreams, and revelations, make the height and top of all perfection in this world. But as wise physicians, yes as good Christians, intermingling sweet things and sour things together, and comparing one of them so with another, that as they see in their afflictions an evident pattern of the misery and mortality of their own lives, and a plain proof of the justice and judgment of God against sin, so they make the same a profitable mean to themselves, not only in a Christian and comfortable death, but in a holy life

also, so long as God will have them to live on the face of the earth, to meet with the Lord and to glorify his most blessed name. A CHRISTIAN AND LEARNED EXPOSITION (1587).[4]

PAUL SPEAKS FROM PERSONAL EXPERIENCE.

WILLIAM COWPER: The apostle St. Paul, that chosen vessel of God, was his ambassador sent forth into the world to bring the house of Japheth into the tents of Shem. In his peregrination—undertaken for preaching from "Jerusalem to Illyricum"—he had seen the most pleasant parts of the world. In an ecstasy, transported from earth into the third heaven, he had also seen the pleasures of paradise. Thus, as one who knew both—not by naked speculation, but by experience—he presents his judgment of both: that the most excellent things of this world are but dung in relation to the Lord Jesus, and that whatever pleasures on earth might delight our eyes or ears are infinitely inferior to those that God has prepared for his children. And therefore, ignoring both the pleasures of life and the terrors of death, he fixed his eyes steadfastly on that "prize of the high calling of God." Forgetting all other things, he came to care about only one thing: to run in such a way—and to fulfill his course with joy—that he might obtain the crown. This he had learned like a good disciple in the school of Christ. So, like a faithful doctor, he delivers it to others, letting us see that the only comfort of a Christian on earth consists in this: to know that his name is written in heaven in the book of life, which, as in this treatise he confirms to us by the inseparable mixture of the links of the golden chain of salvation, especially of our calling, election, and glorification. In this way, he endeavors to draw the hearts of all the children of God toward it as that main and only point in which true peace and joy can be found, and without which all other comforts in the world . . . shall be found in the end but miserable comforters. HEAVEN OPENED (1632).[5]

---

[3]Corvinus, *Postilla in Epistolas*; 204v-205r; citing Acts 14:22; Jas 1:2.
†In Homer's *Iliad*, Glaucus and Diomedes meet as enemies on the battlefield, discover that their grandfathers had been friends, and agree to continue the friendship rather than fight.

[4]Wilcox, *A Christian and Learned Exposition*, 31-32*.
[5]Cowper, *Heaven Opened*, A3r-A4v*; citing Rom 15:19; Phil 3:14.

The Afflictions Are Only in This Present Time. Thomas Wilcox: The word *afflictions* imports all the troubles and calamities that God's children suffer in this life, whether they are outward in the body, such as sickness, poverty, nakedness, banishment, persecution, and such, or whether they are inward in the mind, such as temptations from our corrupted nature, assaults from Satan's malice, grief of heart for sin, fear of judgment in this life or in that that is to come, and so on. And yet he restrains, as it were, that general term by the following words, when he called them "the afflictions of this present time," meaning that they do not last longer than this life nor indeed can last in the children of God, because by our death God not only wipes all tears from our eyes, ends our miseries, and utterly kills the strength and body of sin, but not leaving things there, he begins and perfects our blessedness, where there are "unspeakable joys, and crowns of incomprehensible glory laid up for us, and for all those that do unashamedly love him and look for his coming." A Christian and Learned Exposition (1587).[6]

Troubles as Airy Bubbles. George Wither:

By your grace the passions, troubles,
And what most my heart expressed,
Have appeared as airy bubbles,
Dreams or suff'rings but in jest;
And with profit that has ended,
Which my foes for harm intended

Those afflictions and those terrors
Which did plagues at first appear,
Did but show me what my errors
And my imperfections were;
But they wretched could not make me,
Nor from your affection shake me.

Therefore as your blessed psalmist,
When his warfare had an end,
And his days were at the calmest,
Psalms and hymns of praises penned;

So my rest by you enjoyed,
To your praise I have employed.

The Author's Hymn for Himself.[7]

It Is Harder to Suffer for What We Cannot See. Martin Luther: With these words, in which he speaks of a glory which is to be revealed, he points out what people lack, so that they are so reluctant to suffer, namely: faith is still weak and does not perceive the hidden glory that is still to be revealed in us. If it were a glory that we could see with our eyes, what excellent, patient martyrs we would be! If someone stood on the other side of the Elbe with a chest full of gulden and said, "The chest with the gulden will belong to whoever dares to swim across," everyone would begin swimming for the sake of the gulden that they could see!

What does a daring mercenary do? For four gulden a month, he sets himself against spears and rifles, into certain death. Thus a merchant runs and races throughout the world and back again for the sake of money and goods, risks his body and life, no matter if he suffers harm or not. What must a person suffer at court before they arrive where they intend—unless it turns out differently? Thus in the world one can do and suffer everything for the sake of honor, goods, and power, for they are obvious to the eyes. Summer Postil (June 20, 1535).[8]

Glorification Includes Deliverance. Miles Coverdale: Glorification includes deliverance, that is, the laying away and clear discharge of all these miseries and sorrows. So that now glorification is called (and also is in very deed) purity, perfect strength, immortality, and joy; yes, a sure, quiet, and everlasting life. For Paul says, "We who are in this tabernacle sigh and grieve; because we do not want to be unclothed, but rather to be clothed, so that mortality might be swallowed up by life." And to the Romans he says, "I suppose that the afflictions of this life are not worthy of the

---

[6]Wilcox, *A Christian and Learned Exposition*, 34*; citing 2 Tim 4:8; Acts 14:22; Ps 125:3.

[7]Wither, *Hallelujah*, xvii-xviii.
[8]LW 78:157*.

glory that will be shown on us. For the fervent desire of the creature abides, waiting for the appearing of the children of God."

All these words sufficiently declare what glorification means and what is understood by it: namely, a freedom or discharge from this frail servitude and bondage, and a deliverance into the glorious and comfortable liberty of God's children. By which freedom we are delivered from all sickness and frailty, and from all the imprisonment of weakness, that is, from all that brings sickness, heaviness, and frailty. We are freed, discharged, and delivered from all of that, having now the perfect fruition of God, and being made into a similar shape to his Son Jesus Christ. . . . Paul serves this well when he says: "When the corruptible has put on incorruption, and the mortal has put on immortality, then the saying that is written, 'Death is swallowed up in the victory' will be brought to pass." HOPE OF THE FAITHFUL.[9]

THE CONSOLATION OF THE BREVITY OF LIFE. JOHANNES OECOLAMPADIUS: If someone should object, "It seems ridiculous that one should be a son or daughter of God who is afflicted by those who take pleasure in the evils of this age," it is answered that it is not to be regarded by those things which we experience in this age. For the glory of the sons and daughters of God is now hidden, but in the future age it will be revealed. Hence he sets forth in order many consolations and benefits by which they who are the sons and daughters of God now receive consolation. First, they are consoled by the brevity of this life. For that which is eternal is not to be compared with that which is but momentary, nor can the purest joy be compared with that which is interspersed with sadness. I call "interspersed with sadness" that which has some admixture of consolation. For there is nothing so sad for believers that it might not in some measure be tempered by consolation. But neither can this light suffering that is brought

to us by the creation be compared with that highest joy that is received from the Creator himself. ANNOTATIONS ON ROMANS (1525).[10]

FREE SERVANTS OF ONE ANOTHER. PILGRAM MARPECK: O dearest friends of God, if we really reflect on it, let us not become lazy, dull, or careless. It will cheer up our hearts, regardless of all the offense, frustration, and affliction of the enemy and our own flesh and blood and what we must endure and suffer because of it. None of this compares to the inexpressible glory which we have through the knowledge of Christ. What therefore should prevent, vex, and hinder us in our godly life, conduct, and service in the love which is in Christ? May the Lord Jesus Christ give us the gifts and aid of his Holy Spirit. Indeed, may the Holy Spirit himself as the mind, will, and pleasure of the Father and the Son be in us the Giver and Doer, Ruler and Accomplisher, Teacher and Leader, Reminder and Urger, that we may be found to be free servants of one another in Christ until our end. Amen. THE SERVANTS AND SERVICE OF THE CHURCH.[11]

8:19 The Creation Waits Expectantly

CREATION AWAITS LIBERATION. NIELS HEMMINGSEN: The second argument is taken from the entire creation. The entire realm of nature has been subjected to misuse by the wicked and is corrupted as by the contagion of wicked men and women, yet it is awaiting liberation when the Son of God will free it. Therefore, let us also bravely bear the present calamities by the hope of the future liberation. The word *apokaradokia*, which Paul uses, signifies a certain eager carrying on of an expectation, as if intently extending one's head and eye toward something, looking out for its coming from some distance. COMMENTARY ON ROMANS (1562).[12]

[9]Coverdale, *Remains*, 180*; citing 1 Cor 15:54.

[10]Oecolampadius, *In Apostolam Pauli*, 69v-70r.
[11]CRR 2:553-54*.
[12]Hemmingsen, *Commentarius in Epistolam*, 295.

CREATION SUFFERS WITH CHRIST. MARTIN LUTHER: Nowhere else in holy Scripture do we find similar words, in which St. Paul speaks about "the final expectation and waiting of creation for the revelation of the children of God." He describes it not only as much yearning, longing, and sighing for their redemption but also as a woman in childbirth. Then he always says afterward that creation is afraid and cries out like a woman in childbirth. Sun and moon, stars, heaven and earth, the grain that we eat, the water or wine that we drink, oxen, cows, sheep—in summary, everything we use raises an outcry about the world because they are subjected to vanity and must suffer together with Christ and all his brothers. It is impossible for a person to express that outcry, for who can count up all of creation? This is why it formerly was said correctly from the pulpit that on the last day all creation will raise an outcry against the godless because they abused it here on earth and will accuse them of being tyrants to whom they had to be subjected against all justice and fairness. SUMMER POSTIL (1544).[13]

THE SUFFERING OF CREATION. PETER MARTYR VERMIGLI: This passage is indeed difficult. Nevertheless, I consider the sense to be sufficiently clear. The entire creation is reeling in labor pains until our full redemption; it is fatigued by toilsome labors. For the earth is subjected to the curse and thorns because of us, and it produces briers, and after nourishing us with the fallen fruit . . . it is forced to endure devastation and destruction on account of our sins. The air becomes pestilential; now it is stiff with cold, now it burns with heat, now it is covered with clouds, now in rain. All kinds of living things are propagated and die in order that we might be sustained. The heavenly orbs are constantly enraged; they fall, they rise, they suffer eclipse; the moon grows weak and is restored; in the death of Christ the light of the sun is darkened, and when Christ will come forth to the judgment as the Gospels tell, the hosts of heaven will be troubled. COMMENTARY ON ROMANS (1560).[14]

CREATION AS CONSOLATION. JOHANNES OECOLAMPADIUS: "For the eager expectation of the creation." This is another consolation. He is in effect saying, "Look at how all creatures were made for men and women's sake, that they might serve them. It is for man and woman that the sun shines, the earth bears its fruit, and fire gives warmth. And there is no creature that does not acknowledge humankind as its lord just as he himself acknowledges God as his Lord. Since they all groan, are in pain, are in travail and labor for men and women's sake so that they might be conducted toward their proper end, how can they themselves not be diligent and labor and with patience bear affliction? For the creatures are said to eagerly await, to not want, to sigh, to be in travail—not that they have feelings, but by a certain figure of speech, just as they are said to praise the Lord insofar as they bear a face full of pain, opposition, and travail."

For each and every thing wishes to endure in an incorruptible condition, just as we say that all things seek to be, and seek life. But God ordained otherwise, that they would be consumed and altered for humanity's utility. For what need does a tree have for so many fruit, or a hen have for so many eggs? And so on with the rest of the creatures. Do not all these exist for man and woman's sake? But even where humanity did not have need of their service, God will still endow the remainder of the creatures with nobility, and will liberate them from the bondage of corruption so that they themselves become incorruptible. It is in this sense that heaven and earth are said "to pass away." ANNOTATIONS ON ROMANS (1525).[15]

IF CREATION CAN ENDURE, SO CAN WE. ANTONINUS CORVINUS: "For the eager expectation of the creation awaits the revelation of the sons and daughters of God." The meaning of these

---

[13]LW 78:160*.

[14]Vermigli, *In Epistolam S. Pauli*, 674-75.
[15]Oecolampadius, *In Apostolum Pauli*, 70r-70v; citing Lk 21:33.

words of Paul is this: if the condition of the creatures is such that they are forced to await their liberation from the enslavement of corruption with firm composure, why should we hesitate to the same? Do we not have more hope than they? But the apostle is not amiss in attributing affection and sense to the creatures. Whenever something like this is done, he does it for our benefit, so that the thought is this: there is no creature in the whole world that does not know the purpose for which it was made, namely, for good and not for evil. But because they also see and experience the ungodly wretchedly abusing all things, they are vehemently tortured so that it hurts them not a little that they are forced to see themselves subjected for such a long time to this abuse and vanity. As things stand now, they long to restrain the wickedness of the ungodly within limits, if that were possible by some means. Nevertheless, no thanks to humanity because of whom they have been subjected to vanity of this kind, they patiently endure and bear all these things, not doubting that they will at last by liberated by God and see the end of this vanity. Now, seeing that the creation suffers so and in hope is compelled to await its liberation, why should we not do the same also with equal patience and composure? Or do you think it too little a consolation that not only the Holy Spirit but also the whole creation is said to suffer with us in our sufferings? Observe that in the Scriptures we find sense, reason and speech attributed to the elements in this way, such as the text in Isaiah that says, "Listen, O heavens, and lend your ears, O earth, for the Lord has spoken." It is not that they are actually capable of listening or understanding the speech of the one speaking, but so that when those who hear the Word of God reject it, their guilt might become that much heavier. COMMENTARY ON EPISTLES AND GOSPELS (1540).[16]

THE HOLY SPIRIT USES PERSONIFICATION.
THOMAS WILCOX: Now when Paul attributes "fervent desire" to the animals—and that may seem strange to us, who know by common sense and daily experience that animals have no such reasonable affections—we are to understand that the apostle does it by that figure of speech that rhetoricians term *prosopopoeia*,[†] which is when an author ascribes—to dumb, unreasonable, or senseless things—such a person, speech, or action as indeed and properly belong to human beings. . . . All writers, both profane and sacred, use this technique, including Virgil and Homer, who personify fame . . . and the same technique is used in this passage, wherein reasonable affections, for example, desire, waiting, groaning, travailing in pain, and so on are attributed to unreasonable creatures. . . .

In this we are to note that the Holy Spirit does not use this manner of speech as a vain affection or imitation of human eloquence. . . . Rather, he uses it to cause his truth to sink more deeply into their souls and hearts. . . . Rather than allowing us to lack learning, as you would say, the Lord will give us all means whereby we may attain sound knowledge, steadfast belief, and holy obedience of his blessed will. A CHRISTIAN AND LEARNED EXPOSITION (1587).[17]

8:20 *The Creation Was Subjugated*

CREATION IS SUBJECTED, BUT UNDER HOPE.
MARTIN BUCER: "But by reason of him who subjected it." Because, in general, all things shrink from the corruption of nature, they could not serve us in it to this degree, unless God had condemned them to corruption for some special reason. For what things are there in earth, air, and water that we have not destroyed, that we have not corrupted? As there are no birds that fly in the heights, no fish that swim in the depths, so there are no beasts inhabiting the remote wastes that we do not reduce, that we do not kill, when it is in our power. No strength, no agility, much less any cunning or trickery can render them safe from our corrupting power. No rock is so hard, no mountains so high

---

[16]Corvinus, *Postilla in Epistolas*, 205r-v; citing Is 1:2.

[17]Wilcox, *A Christian and Learned Exposition*, 89-91*. [†]The personification of an abstract thing or a nonhuman entity.

or vast, no trees so great, that we do not smash it all to pieces. Since we have been subjected to corruption, and hence spare nothing from corruption, all things are forced to serve.

How did this come about? By that singular virtue of the Creator by which he subjected all things to this vanity. But it is under hope, because he established . . . that they be restored. Indeed, because all things are designed so that some take care of others, and so that these lower things are ruled and driven by higher ones, this corruption of corporal things in its own way pertains to angels and heavenly bodies, so that they also feel its repugnance when things die and are destroyed, and hence also the hope of restoration, by which they put up with serving our corruption.

Further, among those things that were enslaved more closely to our customs, it is discerned more clearly that they may both oppose the corruption of nature and yet subject themselves to it. Indeed you very obviously see divine power subjecting it, but with the hope of restitution. Thus we see that cows, horses, camels, and elephants dread dying and fight against death. But how do they, with no trouble, still suffer themselves to be led and driven to death by a stupid little man? Therefore, that they resist indicates that there is in them a desire to endure, which, because God placed it in them, cannot be in vain: and so they serve corruption, in hope. Indeed, if you consider that they so easily suffer themselves to be led and driven to death by a human gifted with no such physical powers as they have, that subjection appears divine. For these carry and perform for God, who subjected them to this vanity. All things together have still been so made that they hold some kinship and consent one with another, and once all served humankind. Therefore what we discern so clearly in the animals that are more enslaved to our customs, we ought not doubt to be applicable in its own way to the rest of the animals, even if it is not so clearly evident. COM-MENTARY ON ROMANS (1536).[18]

THE PROPER USE OF CREATION. ERASMUS SARCERIUS: "The creatures are subject to vanity," that is, to abuse, and the ungodly world abuses them when it does not use them for their right and true purpose, which is the necessary sustenance of the body. Thus, wine is a creature intended to assuage thirst, but we abuse wine when we use it for drunkenness. In sum, we abuse all of God's creatures when we do not use them according to the true use for which they were created by God.

This vanity is the reason for the eager expectation of the creation for the revelation of the sons and daughters of God, for whose use they were ultimately created. NOTES ON ROMANS (1541).[19]

8:21 *The Creation Will Be Set Free*

ELECTION UPON ENTRANCE. DAVID JORIS: Break forth. Come to the day, you children of light, truth, and Spirit. Appear now with new power, you kingdom of God. Now the world will perish and her glory will be extinguished; this is certain and it will appear in this way. My mouth will have spoken lies and not spoken through the Lord if it does not happen this way. Pay attention. When the time has come that the children of God are fit to enter or receive their glorious divine freedom, then they are the elect, beloved flower of Jacob. Take heed. HEAR, HEAR . . . (1536).[20]

PAUL'S SOLILOQUY. MARTIN BUCER: It seems that Paul needs to respond to these questions from the Christian person: "The whole creation groans and is in birth pains until now," eagerly waiting and looking for my restoration, for "it was unwillingly subjected to corruption" on my account. "It will all be set free" through my Christ "from its bondage to corruption" when he restores us, the members of his body. I will contemplate and carefully weigh this in my mind, so that I might fully recognize in myself the enormity of sin that dwells within me and in all things, and that I might surrender myself

[18]Bucer, *Metaphrases et Enarrationes*, 343.

[19]Sarcerius, *In Apostolam ad Romanos*, Miv.
[20]CRR 7:128*.

entirely to Christ my Lord and Savior, and consecrate and entrust myself to him in whatever way he wills to make in me an end of sin by his cross, and by whatever path and calling he wills to lead me to newness of life, to which end I will devote myself to him with all my heart by my efforts in mortifying the flesh and striving to apply myself to the Spirit, to the life of God. So that I might eagerly pursue this life and hasten on without interruption in this pursuit and effort, I will fix my mind on what the Lord himself will give me, in the contemplation of this great happiness that will be mine, to which I will be restored in the resurrection, which he will assuredly adorn me with when the whole fabric of the world is liberated from corruption. I will contemplate these things; I will immerse my soul in these truths, unconcerned with what parts of the world Christ the Lord is going to restore together with me, or how he will do so, or what condition he is going to give to them. It is more than enough for me that I and the whole creation around me will be in a happier state than my mind is now capable of imagining. Hence I will preach and glorify my Lord, and by his own gift I will pursue him with all my heart, all my soul, all my powers, singing to him that he has both done and will do all things well, to him be glory forever, Amen. COMMENTARY ON ROMANS (1536).[21]

TOWARD THE GLORIOUS DIVINE FREEDOM.

DAVID JORIS: I maintain that the true restitution is the first, which has thus occurred in Christ. Put briefly, everything we have lost in the first Adam, by disobedience through the devil, is restored by and through the obedience of Jesus Christ. Also, that those who now believe in the name of Jesus, that he is Christ, and call on him as his head and Lord and prove to be obedient, in these people all things will be restored and renewed; changed from flesh into spirit, from death into life, from the earthly into the heavenly beings, until they have become once again the likeness and true image of

God through Christ Jesus, by grace. They will be just as God made Adam in the beginning as an image of God: immortal, pure, without spot or sin, simple and innocent, just like God. We must again put on these clean, unspotted, white garments of simplicity and innocence, else we cannot enter into Eden, that is, into the life and kingdom of God. Pay attention.

These are the pure wedding garments that few people on the earth have known. Yes, these are the garments of faith, in which exist the union and incorporation. These were given first to Adam from the rising of the sun, and now have been entrusted to me through grace, from the rising of the sun. Yes, to me, unworthy, in order to admonish and proclaim to all those who desire to be saved how to come to victory. See, all of it must be completed in us. The beloved or the saved of the Father will be seen publicly, and all things will be restored in their first condition, as God has promised from the beginning through his holy prophets. To say this briefly, it is the abandonment of evil. To this we ought to pray, that we might receive the glorious divine freedom of the children of God, for which we long and seek. Pay attention. OF THE WONDERFUL WORKING OF GOD (1535).[22]

HOPE AND THE DIN OF FALLING LEAVES.

JOHANNES BUGENHAGEN: "The liberty of the glory of the sons and daughters of God." That is, when the sons and daughters of God are glorified, the creatures themselves will also be freed from their bondage, nor will we then have need for their service, when we see all things made new.... We can have a presentiment now within us of a kind of early experience of this mystery. In a trial in which all creatures appear to be contrary to us and even the sun that is the brightest of all becomes dark to us according to that which we read in the Prophets: All that was formerly pleasant and delightful we feel has been turned to bitterness for us, or rather we tremble at the din of leaves falling from a tree. But where we harbor some hope in

---

[21]Bucer, *Metaphrases et Enarrationes*, 343; citing Mk 7:37.

[22]CRR 7:122-23*.

God in the midst of that trial, there is nothing that does not stand by us, there is nothing that terrifies us. All creatures seem to smile at us and rejoice with us because God the Father smiles at us. This is a taste of the firstfruits of this glory, and we experience here that which Paul said, "All things work together for the good for those who love God"; that is, all creatures and whatever other things there are, including adverse things, promote our salvation. We will see this in the resurrection when all ungodliness will be wiped out. INTERPRETATION OF ROMANS (1531).[23]

COMING INTO THE GLORIOUS FREEDOM OF THE CHILDREN OF GOD. DAVID JORIS: At the last day there will be a holy mountain and a beloved city of the Lord, which shall be very blessed and be made fruitful by the beautiful bridegroom of righteousness. For the citizens inside it will bloom as the grass on the meadow. Yes, they will increase, grow, and become great. They will then fill the whole earth and possess it, bringing it under them. This the mountain of the Lord will do, and the city of the Lord will have authority over everything, as it is written. Blessed are they who first receive the benediction and blessing in the Spirit, for they will observe and produce fruit in the Lord. These ones are circumcised in their hearts from all the lusts of the flesh. . . . For they die and are mortified to all things of the world and in peace they leave behind the goods of this life for the faith of Jesus Christ. In particular, they forsake and abandon the evil will, and stand against the lusts of the flesh, the covetousness of the eyes, the haughtiness of life. They are brought low, to absolute nothing: poor, humble, meek, needy, simple, innocent, foolish in the flesh. They suffer violence and injustice on account of the faith of Jesus, on account of the gospel, on account of righteousness, or on account of the kingdom of our Lord, without quarreling or murmuring. See, they will receive again here a hundredfold, and will come into the glorious freedom of the children of

God. They will forever possess eternal life and find rest from all the work of the Spirit; that is, those (I say) who rest now from the work and evil labor of the sinful flesh, which is eternally damned with its seed. Pay attention. Yes, pay attention indeed, and always and eternally praise the Lord, the Lord Sabbaoth. Amen. Alleluias will be sung by the victorious. OF THE WONDERFUL WORKING OF GOD (1535).[24]

8:22 Creation Has Been Groaning

THE GROANING OF CREATION AND THE CHURCH. NIELS HEMMINGSEN: This is a repetition of the same assertion, unless he is expounding with a most elegant similitude the magnitude of the affliction suffered by the creatures and its longing to emerge from its present evils, and at the same time pointing to what will happen in the future. For just as when a woman gives birth she has the severest pains, but once the infant is brought forth into the light she rejoices and forgets the pains that she had suffered, so also the creation being oppressed by abuses groans as if it were giving birth. In a similar fashion, the church groans as if giving birth, being exposed to the various hardships of this life until she is liberated by the coming of the Son of God, and then because of the magnitude of the glory that will be revealed will forget all her afflictions which she suffered in this life. COMMENTARY ON ROMANS (1562).[25]

WAITING FOR FREEDOM. DAVID JORIS: We must work and desire greatly this glorious divine freedom and rest of the true children of God. Yes, for the creation itself cries out and wishes for the revelation of the children of God, so that it will be subjected without its vain will on account of the will of the one who has subjected it, and it must remain bowed down in all submissiveness. So it waits for this; hoping for, expecting, and desiring

---

[23]Bugenhagen, *In D. Pauli ad Romanos*, 92v-93r; citing Rom 8:28.

[24]CRR 7:124-25*; citing Rev 21:1–22:21; Ps 72:16; Gen 1:28; Phil 2:14; Mk 10:29-30.

[25]Hemmingsen, *Commentarius in Epistolam*, 296-97.

the childhood and revelation of the children of God, so that it will be subjected without its vain will. For this reason it will yet be freed from the service of the perishable nature, to the glorious, divine freedom of the elect children of God. For this reason we must proceed roughly in pain and suffering, like the burdened. But we have great longing for the time of the restitution and the deliverance from evil and service to the perishable nature, and to see the transfiguration; so that we might experience the rest in the garden, the eternal life. Therefore, fight and pray that you might be delivered. Pay attention, you seed of Jacob and David. HEAR, HEAR, HEAR, GREAT WONDER, GREAT WONDER, GREAT WONDER (1536).[26]

THE CONSOLATION THAT THE APOSTLES ALSO GROANED. WOLFGANG MUSCULUS: This is a magnificent consolation. The apostles themselves were constituted in bodies that were weighed down by corruption, and they groaned in hope of the adoption and liberation of their bodies, looking for their full redemption. If, therefore, we also are groaning, and we also are looking for our future redemption and glory, and we also are weighed down in this mortal body of ours, then we have this experience in common not only with every creature universally but also with the very apostles themselves. There was something for those who had received the firstfruits of the Spirit to groan for and look forward to—how can that not be true of us as well? For what else does he mean by "groaning" and "expectation of redemption" other than what the apostles themselves were afflicted by? COMMENTARY ON ROMANS (1600).[27]

AWAITING THE HAPPY CATASTROPHE. DAVID PAREUS: "The whole creation groans." The metaphor of groaning under a weight; to "groan together" is to groan with one who is groaning. We, he says, groan with cause; that is, we lament our own vanity. Nevertheless, the creation groans

together, as if furthering our groans, and in part demanding God's vengeance against the impious, and in part desiring liberation for the sons and daughters of God. Together it brings forth in labor; that is, it suffers and groans in the manner of a woman giving birth. Therefore God will heed these groans. There is comfort in the latter metaphor. The suffering of the one giving birth ends when the child is born, and joy replaces the pain. Thus will the suffering of the present vanity be ended by the happy catastrophe. COMMENTARY ON ROMANS (1608).[28]

8:23 Firstfruits of the Spirit in the Midst of Suffering

THE FIRSTFRUITS OF THE SPIRIT AID US. ANTONINUS CORVINUS: "But these things are not all—we also having the firstfruits of the Spirit." It has already been shown how the creation itself both suffers and eagerly awaits the liberation of the sons and daughters of God. Now he wishes by his own example as much as by that of all the other apostles both to strengthen us and to call us to the endurance of suffering. It is just as if he had said, "If we who have received the firstfruits of the Spirit cannot escape the world's hatred and its afflictions—good God!—what privilege could there be that would make you immune to persecutions? Or do you think that your condition will be better than ours?" Did not St. Peter say that they shared in the same afflictions as all the brethren throughout the world? It's certain that the storms of adversities pose no hindrance whatsoever to the adoption of the sons and daughters of God—since this can by no means be easily lost if we have a determined faith and a firmly held hope. For even though this liberation of ours may be delayed for a long time, we must not let our hope falter and become discouraged; it is certain that in its proper time it will come, and we will at last be set free. We can know beforehand neither the season nor the hour of this liberation, but it is certain that it will

---

[26]CRR 7:135*.
[27]Musculus, *In Epistolam Apostoli Pauli*, 139.

[28]Pareus, *In Divinam ad Romanos*, 738.

come, at a time of his choosing, not ours. Therefore make yourselves ready for enduring suffering, and keep far from the vice of impatience. The "firstfruits of the Spirit" in my judgment refers to those abundant gifts of the Holy Spirit with which all the apostles were first endowed after the resurrection. His meaning is therefore this: If such excellent and magnificent gifts through Christ came to us before others, enabling us to await with calm self-composure that day in which the Lord will free us from this body tainted by sin, why can't you await that same event with equal self-composure? Will you give up in despair when faced with a few light afflictions? For they are most certainly light if compared to the blessedness to come.

Even if you think the firstfruits of the Spirit are those common gifts given to all Christians equally, but not so abundantly as they were given to the apostles, I will not argue with you very much, as long as you hold the essential meaning of this passage rightly and learn from it how you ought to console and strengthen your soul when the tempest of persecutions rolls in. COMMENTARY ON EPISTLES AND GOSPELS (1540).[29]

THE APOSTLES ARE THE FIRSTBORN CHILDREN OF GOD. DIRK PHILIPS: The children of God now grow and they become stronger and more mature in the faith and more perfect in the knowledge of God and his Son, Jesus Christ, but they are not born out of God more than once. Beyond this young and weak Christians may not be called firstborn children of God. For if it is so that we regard and observe the letter of the law, then the firstborn in the family in the Old Testament was the greatest. But if we observe the Spirit of the New Testament, then the apostles were the firstborn children of God, in part because they were first chosen of Christ to the faith and called to the office of preaching and came to the fellowship of the gospel. And also in part because they were the first, that is, they have had the most glorious and greatest gifts of the Holy Spirit, as

Paul says, "We who have the first fruits of the Spirit." And James says, God who is the Father of lights, "he has borne us by the word of truth that we should be the first fruits of his creatures." THE TABERNACLE OF MOSES.[30]

WE SHOULD GIVE GOD THE BEST WE POSSESS AND ENJOY. THOMAS WILCOX: Now, when Paul adds "the first fruits of the Spirit," we need to know that it is a metaphor borrowed from the ceremonial law. The Lord appointed that the first fruits of all their increase should be dedicated as a holy thing to his majesty and serve especially for these two ends: the one was the maintenance of the priests, and the other to be a pledge, that the remainder that was left in the hands of the owners for the lawful use was now sanctified unto them since God, the author of holiness, had graciously agreed to receive a portion of it for his own service and other holy uses. All of this is plainly put down in many places of the books of the law, and namely in Leviticus and Deuteronomy. From which we may learn many good and profitable instructions, such as that the firstfruits of every thing were consecrated to the Lord. That therefore, in the service of our God we should employ not only the meanest things that we have—a fault, as in the past, so also now, too common in this unthankful world, either in contempt will yield God nothing, or in carelessness offer him the worst of all the flock— but even the best we possess and enjoy, if we have anything better than another, either within us or without. Neither was this obscurely only figured in the law by this ceremony, but plainly and expressly put down in these terms: "You shall love the Lord your God with all your heart, with all your soul, and with all your mind," we knowing and confessing that we have nothing more excellent than our inward parts, since therein consists all our affection, reason, yes, and natural life itself. A CHRISTIAN AND LEARNED EXPOSITION (1587).[31]

---

[29]Corvinus, *Postilla in Epistolas*, 205v-206r; citing 1 Pet 5:9.

[30]CRR 6:282*; citing Jas 1:18.
[31]Wilcox, *A Christian and Learned Exposition*, 134-35*; citing Mal 1:8-9-10; Deut 6:5.

THE GROANS OF THE UNGODLY AND GODLY.

JOHANNES OECOLAMPADIUS: "We groan within ourselves." The groans of the ungodly belong to those who wish to be liberated from the cross of this life but who do not long for God as the living fount. For this is to fight against the divine will like a person fights who dies unwillingly. But the groans of the godly are of those who do not shirk the difficulties of this age, but who "desire to be dissolved and be with Christ." ANNOTATIONS ON ROMANS (1525).[32]

WILL ALL SPECIES BE RESURRECTED? PETER

MARTYR VERMIGLI: When Paul says that the creation is to be "liberated from the bondage of corruption," it can in general terms be understood to refer to the world, since it will no longer be compelled to renew the creation by always generating anew, but it does not follow from this that all creatures, as it respects each individual species, will be preserved. It's my judgment that it belongs to the pious soul to affirm neither position stubbornly. For we do not have a full or certain clarity either way. But I do dare to assert that from among those creatures that will have been buried, only men and women are to be awakened from the dead. But of other creatures of heaven and earth that survive the Day of Judgment, about which the Scriptures make some mention, I judge that nothing should be said. For when we are left without answers by the Scriptures, nothing should be investigated by us in an overly speculative manner. It is sufficient that we understand that it was on our account that the corruption of things was introduced, and conversely, when we will be restored all things that are to continue in existence will be better than they were before. COMMENTARY ON ROMANS (1560).[33]

THE CONSOLATION THAT THE APOSTLES CARRIED HEAVY CROSSES. ERASMUS

SARCERIUS: The apostles and the other saints who outshone others in gifts did not despair in their cross, nor do those who are still around despair. Therefore, neither are we to despair in our cross.

This is a consolatory argument in the face of a particularly substantial cross, since equal burdens are carried more lightly, and inequity in bearing one's cross can easily produce impatience. For it often happens that an ordinary person bears their cross in a wicked fashion when they see their superiors neglecting that cross, and when they see the ministers of the Word and those who possess many gifts not having to cross the straits of this life in the same boat of cross-bearing as he does. NOTES ON ROMANS (1541).[34]

STRETCHING THE SINEWS OF THE MIND ON THE ESSENTIALS. PETER MARTYR VERMIGLI:

The sinews of our mind should be stretched so that those things that are necessary for our salvation do not escape our understanding. These would include such things as dogmas concerning God, justification, divine worship, good works, the observance of the sacraments, and so on, which will never be clean and pure unless their nature is well perceived and understood. For if we attribute either more or less to them than we ought, we will always be erring. The Scriptures often touch on these chief points especially, "that the man or woman of God might be perfect and equipped for every good work." But those things that the Scriptures do not touch on, we should reckon as things that are not necessary for our salvation. For the Holy Spirit is good, so that if those things were necessary he would have handed them down to us in the Scriptures. COMMENTARY ON ROMANS (1560).[35]

8:24 Hope Is in the Unseen

ASSURANCE OF SALVATION. JUAN DE VALDÉS:

And that expression, "for we are saved" is worthy of consideration, as leading us to see how certain St. Paul held his salvation and that of Christians to be, so that he spoke of it as though already attained,

---

[32]Oecolampadius, *In Apostolum Pauli*, 71r; citing Phil 1:23.
[33]Vermigli, *In Epistolam S. Pauli Apostoli*, 698.
[34]Sarcerius, *In Apostolam ad Romanos*, M3v.
[35]Vermigli, *In Epistolam S. Pauli Apostoli*, 698; citing 2 Tim 3:7.

understanding that since God had called them to the grace of the gospel, they might already hold themselves to be saved, assured of their firmness in faith, and assured of their constancy and perseverance in hope, and assured also of their warmth of love, whereby faith is upheld to justification and hope is upheld to salvation. COMMENTARY ON ROMANS (1556).[36]

SALVATION BY FAITH AND HOPE. JOHANNES BRENZ: What need is there to say more? The Scriptures everywhere teach that it is the one who hopes in the Lord who will obtain salvation. Therefore, it remains that when salvation is promised to hope, by this it implies that true and heavenly happiness, in its fullest sense, is not to be received in this age but rather, afflictions are to be endured now so that there might be place for hope, by which we await our certain future redemption. What then will we say? Was it not said earlier that we obtain salvation only by faith? Why is it now said that we obtain it by hope? While it is true that the distinction between faith and hope can be examined in some contexts, because they both look to the same Christ (whose name alone has been given to us "by which we must be saved") and at the same salvific blessings that are provided to us through Christ, it is therefore rightly said that we are as much saved by faith as we are by hope. For faith believes that Christ is the expiator of our sins and our Savior from death unto an eternal inheritance. But that which faith believes, hope lays hold of and in the midst of all adversities—"Even if the broken world should fall to pieces"[†]—awaits, without doubting, what Christ has merited for us by his death. Faith and hope are so conjoined in the matter of obtaining true and eternal salvation that they cannot nor ought not be separated, since that which we accept by faith in the midst of various trials, afflictions, and miseries we preserve by hope. Therefore may it never be said that we should not endure all manner of unhappiness in this age, since we await a certain happiness in Christ. Or rather, because we hope and are looking for this, therefore the unhappiness of this world is to be endured with a strong soul. COMMENTARY ON ROMANS (1564).[37]

FAITH AND HOPE DEFINED. JOHN CALVIN: Wherever this living faith exists, it must have the hope of eternal life as its inseparable companion, or rather it must of itself beget and manifest it. Where it is wanting, however clearly and elegantly we may discourse about faith, it is certain we do not have it. For if faith is (as has been said) a firm persuasion of the truth of God—a persuasion that it can never be false, never deceive, never be in vain—those who have received this assurance must at the same time expect that God will perform his promises, which in their conviction are absolutely true; so that in one word hope is nothing more than the expectation of those things that faith previously believes to have been truly promised by God. Thus faith believes that God is true; hope expects that in due season he will manifest his truth. Faith believes that he is our Father; hope expects that he will always act the part of a Father toward us. Faith believes that eternal life has been given to us; hope expects that it will one day be revealed. Faith is the foundation on which hope rests; hope nourishes and sustains faith. For as no one can expect anything from God without previously believing his promises, so, on the other hand, the weakness of our faith, which might grow weary and fall away, must be supported and cherished by patient hope and expectation. For this reason Paul justly says, "We are saved by hope." For while hope silently waits for the Lord, it restrains faith from hastening on with too much precipitation, confirms it when it might waver in regard to the promises of God or begin to doubt of their truth, refreshes it when it might be fatigued, extends its view to the final goal, so as not to allow it to give up in the middle of the course or at the very outset. In short, by constantly renovating and reviving, it is always furnishing more vigor for

---

[36]Valdés, *Commentary upon St. Paul's Epistle*, 134*.

[37]Brenz, *In Epistolam*, 216; citing Acts 4:12. [†]Horace's *Odes* 3.3: *si fractus illabatur orbis*, a reference to standing firm on principles no matter what may be happening around one.

perseverance. INSTITUTES OF THE CHRISTIAN RELIGION 3.2.42 (1559).[38]

HOPE IN THE UNSEEN. WOLFGANG MUSCULUS Paul develops in more detail what he has already said, but in such a way that from this very declaration of what has preceded, he might by yet another argument make the consolation of those who are afflicted more solid, in order to fortify their patience. For he said that even the apostles groan within themselves and are still in expectation of their adoption and redemption, which could be thought to not agree very well with the things he has already said, in which he had asserted that we are the sons and daughters of God and have received the Spirit of adoption. An ignorant reader might immediately think to themselves, "What is this? I thought we were already saved and redeemed. But now he says that the apostles themselves still await their redemption and groan within themselves? If they have already been redeemed, what redemption are they waiting for? If they have already been saved, what are they groaning for?" He sweeps away such thoughts by what he subjoins to explain what he means, an argument drawn from the logic of our salvation that he regards as something we have not yet laid hold of in its essence, but only by means of hope. And because this is beyond all doubt, instead of a proposition, he speaks by way of a simple assertion: "for we have been saved by hope," which is the same thing as saying "we have laid hold of our salvation in hope and not yet in its essence." He does not support this statement with any proof. For Christians who cannot deny that they have been saved by Christ and yet are clearly not yet blessed in the fullness thereof but remain exposed to miseries and corruption, it is self-evident, certain and beyond all doubt, that they have received this salvation not in its essence but only by way of hope. He now explains by this certain and manifest proposition what he had earlier said, that the apostles themselves are still waiting for the redemption of their bodies and their full adoption.

But he employs an argument drawn from the very nature of hope when he says, "for hope which is seen is not hope. For who hopes for what he sees?" By these words he is merely saying that the nature of hope is such that it is unable to look to present realities, but is necessarily meant to be applied to things yet absent and future. He here gathers and infers that if we hope for what we do not see, it follows that we wait for it with patience. This passage, therefore, follows this pattern:

(P1) Whatever is hoped for is not possessed presently but is looked forward to as something future. (To this major premise pertain those words: "If hope is seen, it is not hope—for why does one hope for that which he sees?")

(P2) Our salvation and our full redemption are hoped for. (To this is to be referred what he said: "For we have been saved by hope.")

(C) Therefore our salvation is not presently possessed but is looked forward to as something future. (This is what he said: "But if we hope in what we do not see, we eagerly wait for it through patience.")

COMMENTARY ON ROMANS (1555).[39]

HOPE IS THE GUARDIAN OF SALVATION. JOHN CALVIN: Paul strengthens his exhortation by another argument, for our salvation cannot be separated from some kind of death, and this he proves by the nature of hope. Since hope extends to things not yet obtained, and represents to our minds the form of things hidden and far remote, whatever is either openly seen or really possessed is not an object of hope. But Paul takes it as granted, and what cannot be denied, that as long as we are in the world, salvation is what is hoped for. It hence follows that it is laid up with God far beyond what we can see. By saying that hope is not what is seen, he uses a concise expression, but the meaning is not obscure, for he means simply to teach us that since hope regards some future and not present good, it can never be connected with what we have in possession. If then it be grievous

---

[38]Calvin, *Institutes*, 1:506*.

[39]Musculus, *In Epistolam Apostoli Pauli*, 185.

to any to groan, they necessarily subvert the order laid down by God, who does not call his people to victory before he exercises them in the warfare of patience. But since it pleased God to lay up our salvation, as it were, in his closed bosom, it is expedient for us to toil on earth, to be oppressed, to mourn, to be afflicted, yea, to lie down as half dead and to be like the dead, for they who seek a visible salvation reject it, as they renounce hope which has been appointed by God as its guardian. COMMENTARY ON ROMANS 8:24.[40]

HOPE, ABSENCE, AND EXPECTATION. PETER MARTYR VERMIGLI: Here we see how it is that hope and faith are to be distinguished with respect to the goods that they pertain to, goods to which hope and faith direct us. Faith already lays hold of the remission of sins and the imputation of righteousness through Christ. But hope continues to look forward to our complete restitution and full liberation from all evils. We have this hope now. Neither groaning nor sighing are inconsistent with this hope, but rather are most well fitted to it. For hope holds before itself two things, namely, the absence of the thing that is desired, and the firm expectation of it. Because that good which we desire is deferred and yet absent, we are anguished in our soul and cannot fail to feel pain. But since we have a certain expectation that what God has promised will come to pass, we are cheered up and rejoice. This is why the Scriptures everywhere proclaim the gladness and joy of the saints. Paul demonstrates from the nature of hope the absence of the thing expected. For he says that "hope that is seen is not hope." These words are to be understood as a metonymy[†] where "hope" is substituted for the thing hoped for. But Paul wishes to say nothing else than that hope is not concerned with those things that are seen. He calls those things "seen" which belong to the present, things we can now enjoy and take delight in. COMMENTARY ON ROMANS (1559).[41]

8:25 We Wait Patiently in Hope

RHETORICAL ANALYSIS AND ADAGES OF HOPE. HEINRICH BULLINGER: This is an *epanaphora*, or repetition. For he has just said that God had subjected believers to hope, and now he encourages those engaged in the contest by pointing to the nature of hope. He says, "Hope concerns those things that are not seen. You have been saved by hope, so, therefore, salvation is to be waited for with long-suffering and patience, nor must we lose hope if things other than what we had expected take place before our eyes."

Meanwhile, let the reader take clear note of how he wrote all these things in such an excellent manner and with such effectual words. First, so that he might depict the certainty of salvation, a *heterōsis*[†] is fittingly employed in its proper place. For nobody is saved while he still lives here, but still he said, "We have been saved by hope." For faith makes the future to be present, and makes what is at other times uncertain to be most certain. Next, in the second place he used the term "hope" in place of the thing hoped for by way of a metonymy or *metalepsis*.[†] Likewise by the word "seen" he means "experienced." For I call "visible" both those things that are perceived by the senses as well as those that are already possessed now in present circumstances. Then the most elegant sentence follows, being composed of opposites and in the shape of a question: "For why does one hope for that which he sees?" For hope pertains to things that are absent. Therefore he rightly concludes that "if we hope for what we do not see" as we hope in salvation and redemption, these are not to be expected without patience. Hence there never ceases to be adversities to be borne with on all sides and dangers to be endured. COMMENTARY ON ROMANS (1533).[42]

---

[40]CTS 38:309-10* (CO 49:155).

[41]Vermigli, *In Epistolam S. Pauli*, 519. [†]Metonymy is a rhetorical device that substitutes an associated item for the original term.

[42]Bullinger, *In Sanctissimam Pauli*, 108v-110r. [†]Latin transliteration of the Greek, indicating the process or phenomenon of variation or alteration. [†]Metonymy is a rhetorical device that substitutes an associated item for the original term. Metalepsis is a figure of speech in which another figure of speech is alluded to. It adds layers of symbolism and poetic expression.

EXPECTATION, HOPE, AND TRUST. JUAN DE
VALDÉS: For "expectation" some read "hope," not
understanding that hope consists in expectation, it
being, as they say, not merely being on the alert, but
having assured certainty. I read "expectation" as
meaning to be on the alert; the good men and
women of whom the gospel speaks were so, who
expected their Lord's return. This does not
contradict the other reading. And it is certain that
those who expect, hope and trust, while those who
hope and trust, expect. COMMENTARY ON RO-
MANS (1556).[43]

NO HOPE WITHOUT PATIENCE. HEINRICH
BULLINGER: But there is no hope without patience.
So says Hebrews 10. "Patience is necessary for us,"
says the apostle, "that having fulfilled the will of
God we might receive the promise." For that which
faith clearly beholds and understands, hope waits
for with long-suffering. Hence hope is sometimes
put in the place of faith, just as faith is in place of
hope. Hebrews 11 defines "faith as the assurance of
things hoped for," and in Ephesians, "by grace you
have been saved," he says, "and that by faith." But in
our text he says, "by hope you have been saved."
Therefore, if we wish to confess the truth about
faith and hope, or even about love, they are
altogether the same thing, except that they are
given one or the other names as increments of one
and the same reality. Hence in 2 Corinthians,
"Now," he says, "remain faith, hope and love, these
three, but the greatest of these is love." For these
three constitute a single piety and true religion, nor
are they anything other than a heart full of zeal for
the Lord. Faith is naturally first, by which we
recognize the One in whom we trust. Then comes
hope, by which we presently endure for the thing
we've come to recognize, and by which we await
that which we learned from faith was to be waited
for. But charity, that is, love for God, is the summit
and extends itself also to one's neighbor, whereupon it extends in the widest possible way to all
people. Therefore, you see that these things that

obtain various names by way of effect and incre-
ment are really one and the same thing. For it is
called "faith," then "hope," then finally, "love," even
though it is one and the same piety. Or if you will,
consider our subject after the figure of the *Charites*,
or "Graces." Pagan poets have handed it down that
there are three Graces, but who are so conjoined
that they are understood to be one reality, each
bringing with them the others. Perhaps also
pertaining to this is that phrase of Sophocles:
charis charin gar estin hē tiktous' aei[†] (Grace is
forever giving birth to grace). There is also that
very popular proverb among the Latins that says
"Grace begets grace." We have belabored this point
a bit more because of those who being ignorant of
divine things cry aloud that "we are saved by hope,
therefore not by faith!" And again, "righteousness is
merited by love and not by faith alone!" They act
as if Paul were contradicting himself when he
wrote that "love is the fulfillment of the law." And
elsewhere, "Christ is the fulfillment of the law for
justification to all who believe."

But let's return to our text. By these words, Paul
wanted to encourage all believers, as if to say, "The
Lord prompts us to hope; he did not will to confer
absolute happiness on those living on the earth and
in the flesh, but he injected the hope that someday in
the future those who will have lawfully struggled
in this life and subdued the impulses of the flesh
might then fully enjoy eternal blessedness." COM-
MENTARY ON ROMANS (1533).[44]

WAITING PATIENTLY. JOHANNES BUGENHAGEN:
The patience, that is, of the cross. For in the present,
long-suffering is needful. Consider carnal examples
of this same thing, as when you are waiting to
marry a beautiful and good woman you put up
with everything, enduring cares on every side or
even consigning yourself to servitude on her
account, as Jacob did. It is hope that preserves you
and helps you to bear all things with long-suffering.
Also, if some great thing should be promised to you,

---

[43]Valdés, *Commentary upon St. Paul's Epistle*, 1-2*.

[44]Bullinger, *In Sanctissimam Pauli*, 108v-110r; citing Heb 10:36; 11:1;
Eph 2:8; Rom 13:10; 10:4. [†]Sophocles, *Ajax* l.522.

you wait for it with the greatest desire, but before it comes many things intervene that must be put up with in the meantime. It's similar to when a father hands over his child to a pedagogue to be instructed. The child is at times compelled to endure tyranny and stripes until he knows himself to have matured in character and in teaching. Only then is such a thing fully agreeable, even though it seemed earlier to be a most bitter experience that he had to overcome through long-suffering. In like manner, the Christian is not meant to persevere in his cross-bearing except through the virtue of long-suffering or patience, until he who is coming finally comes. INTERPRETATION OF ROMANS (1531).[45]

---

[45]Bugenhagen, *In D. Pauli ad Romanos*, 95r; citing Hab 2:3-5.

8:26-30 GOD WORKS IN ALL
THINGS FOR OUR GOOD

26Likewise the Spirit helps us in our weakness. For we do not know what to pray for as we ought, but the Spirit himself intercedes for us with groanings too deep for words. 27And he who searches hearts knows what is the mind of the Spirit, becausea the Spirit intercedes for the saints according to the will of God. 28And we know that for those who love God all things work together for good,b for those who are called

according to his purpose. 29For those whom he foreknew he also predestined to be conformed to the image of his Son, in order that he might be the firstborn among many brothers. 30And those whom he predestined he also called, and those whom he called he also justified, and those whom he justified he also glorified.

a Or that   b Some manuscripts God works all things together for good, or God works in all things for the good

---

OVERVIEW: In this passage, Paul explores God's work in the lives of believers. First, he discusses the role of the Holy Spirit in the Christian's prayer life. The commentators compare the Holy Spirit to an artist, speak of his coming on both men and women, and explore the implications of the term "groaning." They then console and exhort their readers with the promise in Romans 8:28 that God will redeem their suffering, for our crosses lead to glory.

Paul then lists the stages in a believer's life with God. The reformers outline in various ways what will eventually come to be known as the *ordo salutis* (order of salvation). In light of Romans 8:28-30, the idea of temporal gradations or degrees of salvation became common in Reformation and Puritan writings, with Calvin referring to it as a climax (a rhetorical term for concepts listed in ascending order) and the Puritans calling it the "golden chain."[1]

In particular, the commentators discuss the role of predestination in that graduated life, from election to calling. They argue against election being done on the basis of foreseeing our good works, and they differentiate between foreknowl-

edge and predestination. We are predestined solely through God's mercy. In this regard, they are careful to specify that God does not cause evil. We are also predestined to suffer, to be siblings to Christ, and to be conformed to his image. The commentators have various answers as to whether all those who are called remain believers until the end. They also suggest various lists of the order of salvation, including elements such as foreknowledge, predestination, election, calling, faith, justification, suffering, sanctification, hope, love, and glorification. At the end of this many-stepped journey, happiness awaits.

8:26 The Spirit Helps Us

WHAT IS THE FEELING OF THE SPIRIT?
DESIDERIUS ERASMUS: *Quid desideret spiritus,* "what the Spirit desires"; *to phronēma,* that is, "the feeling" [of the Spirit] or "what the Spirit feels," that is, the "disposition" [*affectus*] of the Spirit—which Terence terms *sensus* [feeling]: "I well understand his feeling." This is the same Greek word that he has so many times already translated as *prudentia* [prudence]. I do not know what that man is thinking of who imagines that *feeling* and *disposition* are words appropriate to the flesh, not to the divine Spirit. Do we suppose the man was sober

---

[1]For discussion of the development of the "golden chain," see Richard Muller, *Calvin and the Reformed Tradition: On the Work of Christ and the Order of Salvation* (Grand Rapids: Baker Academic, 2012), 161-201.

when he wrote that? Was it not said of God: "Who has known the mind of the Lord?" Is pity not a disposition of mind [*affectus*] attributed especially to God? And if the Spirit of God is rightly said to long for, to desire, to groan, and to appeal, is it absurd to attribute states of feeling to it? But in God, the "affections" are not as they are in us; but neither are understanding and living and taking pity and loving the same in him as they are in us. And yet, frequently in speaking of him Scripture uses words of this sort appropriate to our human condition. ANNOTATIONS ON THE EPISTLE TO THE ROMANS (1516, 1519, 1522, 1527, 1535).[2]

THE HOLY SPIRIT IS LIKE AN ARTIST. MARTIN LUTHER: It is always the case that we understand our own work before it is done, but we do not understand the work of God until it has been done: "In the latter days you will understand his counsel," which is to say that in the beginning or at first we understand our own counsel, but in the end we understand God's. "So that when it does take place, you may believe." Because, as I have said, just as in the case of an artist who comes on some material that is suitable and apt for making into a work of art, the suitableness of the material is in a certain sense an unfelt prayer for the form, which the artist understands and heeds, as he gets ready to make what this material calls for through its suitability, so God comes on our feeling and thinking, seeing what it is praying for, what it is suitable for, and what it desires; then heeding the request he begins to mold the form which suits his art and his counsel. Then of necessity the form and the model of our thinking is destroyed. Thus we read in Genesis 1:2: "The spirit of the Lord was moving over the waters, and darkness was on the face of the deep." Notice that it says, "on the face of the deep," and not just "on the deep," for according to appearances it seems to be opposed to us, when the Spirit comes over us and is about to do what we pray. LECTURES ON ROMANS.[3]

THE HOLY SPIRIT HELPS US PRAY. JOHN CALVIN: As our faculties are far from being able to attain to such high perfection, we must pursue some means to assist them. As our mind's eye should be intent on God, so our heart's affection ought to follow in the same course. But both fall far beneath this, or rather, they faint and fail, and are carried in a contrary direction. To assist this weakness, God gives us the guidance of the Spirit in our prayer to dictate what is right, and regulate our affections. For seeing "we know not what we should pray for as we ought . . . the Spirit itself makes intercession for us with groanings that cannot be uttered"; not that he actually prays or groans, but he excites in us sighs, and wishes, and confidence, which our natural powers are not able to conceive at all. Nor is it without cause that Paul gives the name of "groanings that cannot be uttered" to the prayers that believers send forth under the guidance of the Spirit. For those who are truly exercised in prayer are aware that blind anxieties so restrain and perplex them that they can barely find what is appropriate for them to say; no, in attempting to lisp, they halt and hesitate. Thus it appears that to pray aright is a special gift. We do not speak this way in indulgence to our laziness (sloth), as if we were to leave the office of prayer to the Holy Spirit and give way to that carelessness to which we are too prone. Thus we sometimes hear the impious expression that we are to wait in suspense until he takes possession of our minds while we are otherwise occupied. Rather, our meaning is that, weary of our own heartlessness and laziness, we are to long for the aid of the Spirit. INSTITUTES OF THE CHRISTIAN RELIGION 3.20.5.[4]

THE SPIRIT OF GRACE IS A PROFOUND SPIRIT. JOHN COTTON: The Spirit of Grace in the heart is greater than the world; nothing can do what the Spirit of Grace can do. It teaches us to cry with sighs and unutterable groans. A soul cannot tell God how much it grieves in such a case as this, because the principle of it is the Spirit of grace. We

---

[2]CWE 56:222-23*.
[3]LW 25:367*; citing Jer 23:20; Jn 14:29; Gen 1:2.

[4]Calvin, *Institutes*, 2:150*.

are shallow and can soon run our eyes and hearts dry for any grief we take up ourselves. But where the Spirit of grace works, the grief that it puts forth cannot be expressed. As it comes from a deeper fountain, the eternal love of Christ, so it has a deeper work. It searches the deep things of God. It is a profound spirit, and so it works a profound work. WAY OF LIFE (1641).[5]

THE IMPORTANCE OF PRAYER TO ABBA. JOHN CALVIN: The apostle, to show that a faith unaccompanied with prayer to God cannot be genuine, states this to be the order: as faith springs from the gospel, so by faith our hearts are framed to call on the name of God. And this is the very thing that he had expressed some time before—that is, that the "Spirit of adoption," which seals the testimony of the gospel on our hearts, gives us courage to make our requests known to God, calls forth groaning that cannot be uttered, and enables us to cry, Abba Father. This last point, as we have so far only touched on it slightly in passing, must now be treated more fully.

To *prayer*, then, we are indebted for penetrating to those riches that are treasured up for us with our heavenly Father. For there is a kind of intercourse between God and us, by which, having entered the upper sanctuary, we appear before him and appeal to his promises, that when necessity requires, we may learn by experience, that what we believed merely on the authority of his Word was not in vain. Accordingly, we see that nothing is set before us as an object of expectation from the Lord which we are not enjoined to ask of him in prayer, so true it is that prayer digs up those treasures which the gospel of our Lord reveals to the eye of faith. No words can sufficiently express the necessity and utility of this exercise of prayer. Assuredly it is not without cause our heavenly Father declares that our only safety is in calling on his name, since by it we invoke the presence of his providence to watch over our interests, of his power to sustain us when weak and almost fainting,

of his goodness to receive us into favor, though miserably loaded with sin; in short, call on him to manifest himself to us in all his perfections. Hence, admirable peace and tranquility are given to our consciences; for the straits by which we were pressed being laid before the Lord, we rest fully satisfied with the assurance that none of our evils are unknown to him, and that he is both able and willing to make the best provision for us. INSTITUTES OF THE CHRISTIAN RELIGION 3.20.1-2.[6]

THE GROANINGS OF THE HOLY SPIRIT. WOLFGANG MUSCULUS: In this way our weaknesses lead us to not despise or detest the Holy Spirit, so that he might more help us, lest what is already weak should be snuffed out entirely and perish. I ask by what spirit are they led who with unbelievable and Pharisaic fastidiousness reject and despise weak sinners, as we see it being done by Anabaptists? The Holy Spirit is not a despiser of the weak, but a helper. Those who do not demonstrate the same soul cannot be furnished with the same Spirit. See Galatians 6, "you who are spiritual."

"But if this is what we are to pray for." These words are an explanation and evidence for his statement that the Spirit helps our weaknesses. He teaches how it is that he does this when he says, "The Spirit importunes for us with unutterable groanings." He is speaking of groanings of our hearts so hidden that they simply cannot be articulated, and he assigns them to the Holy Spirit, since it is by his motion within us that he generates and produces them. I say this in agreement with older writings lest anyone should question how it is that groaning and importunity can be fittingly ascribed to the Holy Spirit, since he is God in whom neither groaning nor importuning can have any place. Just like when we cry out "Abba, Father!" in the Holy Spirit, so also do we groan in him when we are moved by him to these hidden groanings.

It, therefore, would appear that the apostle in a marvelous fashion has taken a closer and more

---

[5]Cotton, *Way of Life*, 8-9, 50-51*.

[6]Calvin, *Institutes*, 2:146-47*; citing Rom 10:14.

careful look at the groaning of the saints for the sake of those for whom it seems a miserable and lamentable thing that he would have used this as an argument of greatest consolation, since he understands as evidence the fact that the Spirit of God inhabits us, groans within us and importunes on our behalf. Human reason would interpret these groanings as marks of impatience and of a soul fighting against the divine will. But the apostle understands these groanings to be elicited by the motion of the Holy Spirit, and as being precisely the very importunings of the Holy Spirit on our behalf, which beyond all doubt are a real help for our weaknesses. COMMENTARY ON ROMANS (1555).[7]

No Set Form of Prayer and Praise. JOHN COTTON: If having one set form of spiritual worship in prayer and praises had been necessary, Christ would have left one. But the prophets, Christ, and the apostles never prayed nor praised God by any set form of worship invented by human beings, but by the powerful work of the Holy Spirit. CONFERENCE (1646).[8]

Holy Spirit Given to Both Men and Women. ARGULA VON GRUMBACH:

That this is promised to us all
Is seen in chapter two of Joel:
Neither man, nor womankind
Is excluded there, you'll find.
For God would let his Spirit flow
Upon all flesh—and will not store
His Spirit in some narrow stall
Which only a tonsured monk can call
His own; and understand alone.
No, God strikes up a different tone:
Your sons and daughters, servants, maids
Will prophesy; read Scripture straight,
And learn from God what this could mean:
That old folk dream new dreams,
Heaven and earth tell wonders abroad

Before the dread day of the Lord.
Look up and read the Gospel of John
In chapter seven the lesson's drawn:
Loudly Christ, our Lord, cries out:
"Come to me now, whoever thirsts!
From those who follow my decrees,
Living waters will flow free."
Tidings of the Spirit he did preach
Who each of us will truly teach.
Explain all this, please, if you may,
God's Word stands here, as plain as day.
Are peasants or women excluded here?
Show me where that's said, good sir!
Who were the apostles—after all
What higher learning could they recall?
Though John was but a fisherman
So profound yet clear is no other man;
And Peter was of identical breed,
A fisherman, as we can read.
And furthermore, as Paul makes known,
God sent the Holy Spirit down
To help us in our poor, weak state
It's there in Romans, chapter eight:
We do not know how we should pray
Unless the Spirit shows the way.
So listen, as all Christians should,
The Spirit leads us to the truth.

POEM TO "JOHANNES OF LANZHUT."[9]

The Consolation of Paul's Admitting to His Own Weakness. WOLFGANG MUSCULUS: As it pertains to our weaknesses, it brings no little consolation that the apostle himself acknowledges that same human and common weakness and applies it to himself. For he did not say, "The Spirit helps you in your weaknesses," as if the apostles did not themselves have any human weakness so that they had no need of this help of the Spirit. Rather, he includes himself among the feeble as one who is himself weak uplifting and administering strength to the weak. God so willed that those whose efforts

---

[7]Musculus, *In Epistolam Apostoli Pauli*, 187*; citing Gal 6:1.
[8]Cotton, *Conference*, 56-57*; citing Gal 4:6.

[9]Matheson, *Argula von Grumbach*, 175-77*. Grumbach is responding to the anonymous accusations made against her for reading and interpreting the Scriptures as a woman.

he decreed would be used to teach and strengthen others, would themselves be weak and furnished with that common fragility and imperfection. Lest by weaker folk being weighed down with faint-heartedness there be any cause for being despondent in their soul or that they should despise themselves because they are weak. Those who in the church have preached only of sublime and strong things concerning the saints have obscured this consolation of the weak. COMMENTARY ON ROMANS (1555).[10]

PRAYER FOR POWER TO PRAY. MICHELANGELO

What sweetness will attend my acts of prayer,
If you, to pray to you, will give me power!
Within my heart's bleak soil, no means
    are found
Fruits to produce of innate excellence.
You are the seed of just and holy works;
Wherever your power is felt they germinate:
None have the heroic will to follow you,
Unless you teach them first your
    beauteous ways;
Pour into my mind prolific thoughts
Of vital energy, that so my feet
May in the track of your blessed footsteps tread;
And that my tongue with pure impressive words,
All ardent for your glory, your great name;
May ever magnify, exalt, adore.

SONNET 53.[11]

THE IMPRESSIVE VOICE. VITTORIA COLONNA:

Would that a voice impressive might repeat,
In holiest accents to my inmost soul,
The name of Jesus; and my words and works
Attest true faith in him, and ardent hope;
The soul elect, which feels within itself
The seeds divine of this celestial love,
Hears, sees, attends on Jesus; grace from him
Illumines, expands, fires, purifies the mind;
The habit bright of thus invoking him,

Exalts our nature so that it appeals
Daily to him for its immortal food.
In the last conflict with our ancient foe,
So dire to nature, armed with faith alone,
The heart, from usage long, on him will call.

SONNET 29.[12]

8:27 *The Spirit Intercedes for Us*

GOD LISTENS TO PRAYERS ACCORDING TO THE HOLY SPIRIT. JOHANNES BUGENHAGEN:

God, who knows the depths of our hearts and who hears the praying Holy Spirit, immediately inclines himself to our prayers, for when he sees the Spirit interceding not according to the will of our flesh, he sees that his will and that of the Spirit are one and the same. Therefore, God listens to nobody unless that person prays according to his Spirit, who cannot go astray in prayer. INTERPRETATION OF ROMANS (1531).[13]

THE HOLY SPIRIT'S DESIRE, PRAYER, AND WORK. JUAN DE VALDÉS:

In saying "according to God," he means, according to that which is the will of God. In this the intense love that God bears to those whom he has chosen for himself is to be considered. Since it is his will that they should desire and ask glorification and eternal life, and knowing that they will never of themselves do either one or the other, as is meet, he gives them his Holy Spirit, that he may do both the one and the other in them. And it comes to pass frequently that these persons desire and ask with the Holy Spirit, without knowing that it is the Holy Spirit in them that desires and asks, as I believe to have happened to Cornelius, of whom St. Luke speaks in the Acts of the Apostles 10, who desired, prayed, and worked with the Holy Spirit, without knowing that it was the Holy Spirit. And that it was the Holy Spirit appears from what he obtained by his desire, prayer, and work. And I understand that that which occurred to Cornelius occurs to all who

---

[10]Musculus, *In Epistolam Apostoli Pauli*, 187.
[11]Michelangelo, *Life of Michael Angelo*, 2:167-68*.
[12]Michelangelo, *Life of Michael Angelo*, 2:66*.
[13]Bugenhagen, *In D. Pauli ad Romanos*, 97r-v.

are admitted to the grace of the gospel. They desire, they labor, and they pray with the Holy Spirit, without knowing that the Holy Spirit within them is he that desires, prays, and labors, until having believed, they feel the Holy Spirit within them. COMMENTARY ON ROMANS (1556).[14]

STANDING AS SAINTS. THE ENGLISH ANNOTATIONS: Though the remains of sin cleave so fast to the best of God's children, they cannot utterly shake them off. Yet they are here termed saints, partly in regard to their sincere and unstained desire for sanctity and earnest striving for it, partly in regard to God's gracious acceptance, who takes the will for the deed and out of his infinite mercy in Christ accounts them for saints by not imputing their sins to them. ANNOTATIONS ON ROMANS 8:27.[15]

8:28 All Things Work Together for the Good of Those in Christ

POISON, RIGHTLY USED, DRAWS OUT POISON. PETER MARTYR VERMIGLI: Since the apostle had begun to speak a word about the adversities that would perhaps have to be endured, he wished to follow the subject a little longer, mostly due to the fact that such adversities foster that which is contrary to our salvation. For since, treating each separately, he had explained how we are helped by both hope and the Spirit's intercession and had just taught above that all the creation groans together with us, he now declares in a universal sense that all things cooperate for our good. He did not say that God would make sure that we are not vexed by adverse things, but rather teaches that God overturns their adverse nature so that those things that considered in themselves are only capable of bringing about our destruction now, quite to the contrary, furnish what is useful to us and bring us salvation. They do this not by their own virtue, but due to God's election and predestination. Nor

should it be shocking if we attribute so much power to God, for we sometimes see physicians doing the same thing. They frequently draw out poisons from human bodies by employing poisonous drugs, and hemlock, however much it might otherwise be a quick-acting poison, yet when tamed by the pharmaceutical art, is so far from causing harm that it even drives out poison. In a similar fashion, afflictions for godly men and women do not fight against them but against the lingering remains of sin. COMMENTARY ON ROMANS (1559).[16]

OUR CROSSES LEAD TO GLORY. ERASMUS SARCERIUS: "To them that are called according to his purpose." He explains that for those afflicted by some cross that cross leads to glory; but not so for all, but only for those "who are called according to his purpose." The apostle here distinguishes between a cross that is saving and one that is not saving, between a cross that is a path to glory and one that is not a path to glory, between those who by their cross suffer unto glory and those who by their cross do not suffer unto glory.

That cross is glorious that belongs to those "who are called according to purpose." Therefore, the glory of a cross is not the effect of our merit or of our afflictions *ex opere operato*.[†]

This calling according to purpose can also be here understood simply as the cause of our cross, so that it has this sense: that we are not to fear our cross, but that it has come about by God's call. NOTES ON ROMANS (1541).[17]

TRIBULATION TEACHES THE BELIEVER. HANS HAS VON HALLSTATT: Now I acknowledge first and foremost, dear brothers, that either you,

---

[14]Valdés, *Commentary upon St. Paul's Epistle*, 137-38*; citing Acts 10.
[15]Downame, ed., *Annotations*, BBB2v*; citing Rev 8:3; Ps 32:1; Rom 1:7.

[16]Vermigli, *In Epistolam S. Pauli*, 529.
[17]Sarcerius, *In Apostolam ad Romanos*, N2r-v. [†]The Latin phrase *ex opere operato*, "by the work performed," affirmed the medieval Catholic view that the correct and priestly performance of the sacrament conveyed grace to the recipient unless the recipient placed an obstacle to grace. By comparison, *ex opere operantis*, "by the work of the worker," affirmed that the moral condition of the priest or the proper attitude of the recipient in the celebration of the sacrament would determine its efficacy.

together with those who are now imprisoned and hunted, are true Christians, or that the overwhelming riches of fatherly mercy see fit to make you true Christians through his most beloved Son Christ, our Redeemer. For persecution and oppression make genuine Christians and strengthen them, so that they become truly experienced and well practiced in true faith and strong reliance on God. Indeed, they become truly educated and experienced, more bold and unwavering, since one learns and studies more of the gospel through a little tribulation than in any other way in one's entire life. Thus the elect must undergo all misfortunes as best they can. For no persecution or tribulation will come on them that is not entirely profitable for their salvation. They will become even stronger and more fruitful in their faith in God, and boldly trust him. For one sees, notices, and acknowledges how all of this together rests solely on God's power, might, and strength. Indeed, not a hair will fall from the heads of the truly faithful against his will (according to the words of Christ). CONCERNING THE COMFORT OF CHRISTIANS UNDER PERSECUTION.[18]

UNCRUCIFIED CHRISTIANS. LEONHARD SCHIEMER: An even greater form of unbelief that tortures us is the godless thoughts that invade us, such as "Yes, but God will forget me. He will not keep his true faithfulness toward me. He is a respecter of persons and won't help me as he helps others." Could there be a greater form of unbelief! Take note of how it thinks, "If I commit myself to God, I will never be secure. I will perish! If I depend on the world, I am safer and won't perish so miserably." In the same vein, I think, "If I become or remain a Christian, maybe God won't sustain me. However, if I become a heathen, I can easily sustain myself. Or, if I become a Christian, my children will die of hunger, but if I don't, they will survive."

In that case, of course, you are not yet a Christian but a bad heathen, and you will suffer pain until unbelief is separated from faith. What you need is a good smelting house, a strong ordeal, some sharp nitric acid, for an uncrucified Christian is like untested ore or like a house whose boards are still uncut trees. Nothing keeps us from the love of God, except that we do not know him. For since he is the greatest good, it would be impossible not to love God alone and above all things, if only one knew him. Indeed, whoever truly knows God begins so to love him that from now on it is no longer possible to love anything else besides, even if ordered to do so by threat of eternal damnation. Yes, and if I knew God truly, my spirit and soul would be so jubilant that the inward joy would surge into my body, so that even my body would be completely insensible, impassable, immortal, and glorified. CONCERNING THE GRACE OF GOD.[19]

HOW TO RESPOND TO PERSECUTORS. HANS HAS VON HALLSTATT: One should have a heartfelt pity for them, and pray to God regarding their ignorance, whether he might have a Saul among them whom he would transform into a Paul. For goodness' sake, do not oppose them with your fist, or wish something horrible on them or curse them. For they will all be richly rewarded by the stern judge who will not suffer any injustice.

My dear brothers and sisters, have you understood (I hope) how all of this comes together from God alone, be it persecution or any other misfortune? God brings us this out of pure grace and love. All these things assist us greatly to eternal salvation; they provoke and motivate us, that we may learn to recognize God more and more—he who is wonderful in our eyes through the deeds he does for his elect. Even the evil that is present in the world has to serve the good of the pious, and the glory and honor of God. To us, however, who remain steadfast in the Word of God, it brings eternal life. Amen.

May all of this be a farewell and last word to you, written before my end. May God give grace through his Jesus Christ, that it may be fruitful for

---

[18]CRR 12:441-42*; citing Mt 10:30; Lk 21:18.

[19]CRR 12:218-19*; citing Mt 10:30; Lk 21:18; 23:34; Jn 17:3; 1 Cor 13:3.

many and bring healing to many to God's praise. Amen. CONCERNING THE COMFORT OF CHRISTIANS UNDER PERSECUTION.[20]

PREDESTINATION AND GOOD WORKS. PETER MARTYR VERMIGLI: God predestines even those means by which it will eventually lead to its ultimate end. In a similar way we also, after we have resolved to employ some piece of wood for some household use, customarily adorn it and smooth it into that form that is most suitable for the service it will perform. But here we must diligently take note of four things:

First, the will to believe and the purpose and determination to live a godly life will come about at some point in those who are elected and does not have its source in them nor does it naturally inhere in them. For these are God's gifts, not the endowments of nature, nor is anybody able on their own to furnish themselves with them. "For what do you have," Paul says, "that you did not receive?" But if they are given by God, as they most certainly are, it necessarily follows that they come about not by chance, nor rashly, but by God's counsel and predestination. Therefore, these fall under the category of predestination. For just as God predestines his elect unto eternal life, so also he predestines them to good counsel, holy works, and right use of God's gifts.

Here follows that which is to be noted in the second place: that neither our good intention, nor our faith, nor our good works that God foresees can be the causes of our predestination. For if they were, this would result in an infinite chain of cause and effect. For since these things, as we've said, result from predestination and not from ourselves, it can again be asked why God willed to give them to some people rather than others. If you were to answer like many do, that God foresaw that they would make good use of them but that others wouldn't, there would be another no less serious question concerning this good use itself, since it also is God's gift: why do these people rather than

others come to have it as a result of God's predestination? And in this manner there will be no end to inquiry, unless at least we wish to pretend that there is something good found in us that we do not have from God, to say which is not only absurd but also impious.

Third, it is needful to determine that just as foreseen good works cannot be the cause of predestination, so likewise they are not furnished to men and women on the basis of predestination in order that they might then be the cause of that highest good, that is, eternal blessedness, to which we are predestined. They are indeed means by which God leads us to eternal life. But they are not for this reason causes, since blessedness is given freely and we are predestined to it by the sheer mercy of God.

Last, we must establish that these works are not always foreseen in God's predestination. For many in the age of childhood that are swept away while yet immature still attain to eternal life on the basis of God's predestination, even though they were not seen as ever going to have any good works. For God foresaw that they would die as infants. This sufficiently proves that foreknowledge of good works is not to be posited as the cause of predestination, for a genuine effect cannot lack a real cause. COMMENTARY ON ROMANS (1559).[21]

ELECTION SAVES. HULDRYCH ZWINGLI: "To them who according to purpose. . . ." Namely, those who have been called from eternity. For I understand this to refer to inner calling, that is, of election, not of the external calling by hearing of the Word. He is basically saying, "I have already said that all things happen for good to the saints or the called-out ones, which I can demonstrate since all children of God are made so by election." The God who knows all things before they exist also predestined us that we should be coheirs of his Son, so that just as Christ is the firstborn—that is, the natural and essential Son of God—we are the sons of adoption. Those whom he predestined and

[20]CRR 12:454*; citing Lk 23:34; Jn 17:3.

[21]Vermigli, *In Epistolam S. Pauli*, 533-34; citing 1 Cor 4:7.

foreordained, he then calls by an inner calling; that is, he draws us inwardly, which is to say he renders us believers by so drawing us that our mind adheres to him and trusts in him. Those whom he thus renders believers he also justifies on account of their firm faith in his Son, and finally at length he glorifies them. Although Paul touches somewhat here on the topic of predestination, it will be in the ninth chapter that he fully works it out. Therefore, if we wish to speak properly, it is *election* that saves, not faith, but since faith is a sure sign that one is elect, that which properly belongs to election is commonly attributed to faith. ANNOTATIONS ON ROMANS (1539).[22]

8:29 Predestined to Be Conformed to His Image

THE ETIOLOGY OF SALVATION AND GLORY. ERASMUS SARCERIUS: This etiology is drawn from the manner and order in which by means of the cross one reaches glory. Herein the apostle declares how it is that glory comes about through the cross, or rather he furnishes the reason why those who are called according to purpose are afflicted so much: it is so that they might be glorified.

The means, shape and order of our salvation as well as that of glory is described by this etiology.[†]

The order is this: we are first foreknown, then we are predestined that we might suffer according to the example of Christ, and third we are called, then justified, and last we are glorified. NOTES ON ROMANS (1541).[23]

ELECTION. ANDREW WILLET: Concerning election these points are hence concluded: (1) That God has decreed some to be elected unto salvation before the beginning of the world. (2) That the decree of election is the purpose of God to show mercy on some in bringing them unto glory. (3) That the free and gracious purpose of God is

the only cause of election, without the foresight of faith or works. (4) That it is certain and immutable. (5) The effects of which are vocation, justification, sanctification: "Those whom he predestined, he called," and so on. (6) The ends are two: the happiness of the elect, and the glory and praise of God in the setting forth of his mercy. A SIX-FOLD COMMENTARY ON THE EPISTLE TO THE ROMANS (1620).[24]

ELECTION AND AFFLICTION. JOHN CALVIN: Paul then shows, by the very order of election, that the afflictions of the faithful are nothing else than the manner by which they are conformed to the image of Christ, and he had declared that this was necessary. There is, therefore, no reason for us to be grieved, or to think it hard and grievous, that we are afflicted, unless we disprove the Lord's election, by which we have been foreordained to life, and unless we are unwilling to bear the image of the Son of God, by which we are to be prepared for celestial glory. COMMENTARY ON ROMANS 8:29.[25]

FOREKNOWLEDGE AND PREDESTINATION. JOHANNES OECOLAMPADIUS: "Moreover those whom he foreknew." Persons are neither truly trained nor truly justified if they do not persevere, for it is by the perseverance and long-suffering of the cross that we are most glorified and will be made sharers in the image of his Son. Some ask at this juncture, "Doesn't predestination impose a necessity on things?" Those who are believers live in obedience to the Word, nor do they desire to understand more than what has been entrusted to them in their weakness. Nonetheless, we know that both the knowledge and will of God are immutable, but by this very fact God ineffably comforts his people, since by the Spirit and their faith in his Word they know that he wills rightly, and because they have the Spirit they do not seek their own desires, but rather those of God. Therefore, both God's will and his knowledge are pleasing to them,

---

[22]Zwingli, *In Evangelicam Historiam*, 428; citing Jn 6:1-71; 1 Cor 7:12-14; 2 Cor 4:1-18.
[23]Sarcerius, *In Apostolam ad Romanos*, N3r. [†]"Etiology" refers to the cause of a given condition.

[24]Willet, *Hexapla*, 433*.
[25]CTS 38:316-17* (CO 49:159-60).

no matter how they may be disposed or what they may decree, even if there is some impossibility standing in their way. But observe in this text that "to foreknow (*prescire*)" is not the same as "to foreknow (*praecognoscere*)."† For *praescientia* is to have *praecognitio* of something in such a way as to also determine it, since it is certain that he has a mere *praecognitio* of many who are to be damned.

Foreknowledge (*praescientia*) and predestination (*praedestinatione*) are, however, distinguished by some. According to them, God foreknows even the wicked with *praescientia*, but they are not, however, regarded as wicked on account of his action. But those whom God predestined, he foreknew in his *praecognitio* in such a way that he is the author of everything that they do. And so you must acknowledge that God is not properly the author of evil deeds, but he is properly the author of good deeds. Hence Hosea says, "Your destruction, O Israel, is your own, but your help is found only in me." Therefore, all good deeds are to be referred to God who furnishes them and cooperates with us in them, whereas evil deeds are to be referred to the willful wickedness of the rational creature. Nor should you interpret the term *predestination* as a forceful decree, which is a groundless opinion. For it is not lawful to ascribe to God the blame for the evil things that we do. ANNOTATIONS ON ROMANS (1525).[26]

GOD'S FOREKNOWLEDGE DOESN'T CAUSE EVIL TO BE EVIL. ERASMUS SARCERIUS: On the basis of his foreknowledge, God knows future events, both good and bad, and which people would be both good and bad. But it does not follow from this that God is therefore the author of evil or of evil deeds. For one is able to foreknow an evil even if he is not the cause of that evil. God foreknows those who are good and at the same time brings it about that they are good. But he merely foreknows those who are evil. NOTES ON ROMANS (1541).[27]

CHRIST SET BEFORE US IN AFFLICTION.
PHILIPP MELANCHTHON: God is glorified in no other way except through afflictions. Therefore endure them, since they are the road to glorification. He proves the antecedent by setting forth the picture of Christ. We need to become similar to the image of the Son of God; he was glorified through suffering. Therefore it is necessary that we also be afflicted. This is the chief comfort of the godly, to gaze on this picture of the Son of God. No philosophy and no human wisdom can see why this infirm human nature should be burdened with such extraordinary calamities. Reason wonders whether they happen by chance. The law of God proclaims that they are punishments of sin and signs of the wrath of God that testify that we have been rejected.

But the gospel chides both errors and sets before us the Son of God. It testifies that we are subjected to afflictions not by chance, but according to the sure counsel of God, not in order that we may be lost, but that we may be exercised. When God comforts us, faith and the knowledge of God increase in us. This wisdom about the cause and purpose of human calamities is wholly above and beyond the grasp of reason. It is revealed only in the gospel, and is seen chiefly in this picture of the Son of God. COMMENTARY ON ROMANS (1540).[28]

BECOMING LIKE CHRIST IN WORKS AND HAPPINESS. PETER MARTYR VERMIGLI: Since Christ is the perfect image of the Father, when we are conformed to him we approach a likeness to God. What this conformation to Christ rests on is to be understood in this way: Christ is now in glory and is seated at the right hand of the Father, happy, blessed, and immortal, and it is for this same happiness that we also have been destined. God so ordained that that which will be perfected in the next life should in some sense be begun in us now in this life. We are accordingly rendered as those conformed to Christ by good works, holy

---

[26]Oecolampadius, *In Epistolam Paulus*, 72v-73a; citing Hos 13:9.
†*Praecognoscere* is simply to foreknow; *praescire* is to foreknow and predestine.
[27]Sarcerius, *In Apostolam ad Romanos*, N3r-v.

[28]Melanchthon, *Commentary on Romans*, 181*.

manners, and a blameless life. Just as it was for this purpose that he was continually harassed by crosses and tribulations while he walked in this world, so we also must undergo crosses and torments for the same reason. Just as these trials worked together in Christ for his happiness and glory, so they will work together in us for a similar purpose. COMMENTARY ON ROMANS (1560).[29]

TWOFOLD IMAGE OF CHRIST. JOHANNES BRENZ: "Those whom he had foreknown" or purposed that they should be called to lay hold of the heavenly inheritance on account of Christ, "these he also preordained, or predestined, that they should be conformed to the image of the Son" of God. Now there is a twofold image (at least that applies to this text) of the Son of God: one is that of the cross, the other is that of resurrection. One is that of humiliation, the other of glorification. Therefore those whom God purposed to call to the gospel of the kingdom of heaven, these he also ordained so that, just as Christ, his only-begotten Son, did not enter into the glory of the kingdom of heaven except by the cross and by affliction, so also those who believe in Christ would not enter into the heavenly kingdom except through various hardships. "For a servant is not greater than his master." COMMENTARY ON ROMANS (1564).[30]

CHRIST THE FIRSTBORN. MARTIN BUCER: "That he might be the firstborn." We ought to often ponder with admiration that we are regarded by God as Christ's brothers, and that he is to us what a firstborn is to his brothers, that is, their prince and father who looks out for us in everything. Let us, therefore, surrender ourselves to our firstborn brother and Savior with all our heart, and let us be devoted with all our strength. COMMENTARY ON ROMANS (1536).[31]

PREDESTINED TO BE CHRIST'S SIBLINGS. JACOPO SADOLETO: The sole reason that he said,

"All things work together for good to those that love God," and the reason for the other promises that he will make immediately afterward in this same sentence, is founded on the mere fact that God established and decreed that it would be so. For insofar as it pertains to our own roles, we have nothing stable, nothing lasting in ourselves, and we are constantly tossed about by fluctuating pursuits and desires. But it is the gift of God himself and his own resolved purpose that we remain fixed and steadfast in this good so that we might never be separated from the grace of God. He therefore decreed eternally from the beginning those who were to be called to his righteousness and glory, and these he predestined that they might be the brothers and companions of Christ Jesus, insofar as Christ is man. For it was as a man that he was adopted, and yet that adoption was the image of his natural generation; he who is Son by nature was adopted by the common accord of laws, and thus portrayed in a certain fashion a similitude of his generation. Therefore God "predestined those whom he foreknew that they might be conformed to the image of his Son," who as God is the Son of God by nature, and as man, the Son by way of adoption. Hence they were predestined to be his brethren by way of adoption, and Christ, who is the *only*-begotten of God by nature was predestined to be the *first*-begotten by adoption. For there were many brethren that were to be brought to God through him, and he would see to it that they also were adopted as sons of God. For it was for no other reason than this that he came into this world, and that while he already possessed this relationship with God the Father, he received its like by means of adoption, something which he certainly was not lacking: that those many brethren whom he could not have by natural generation he might obtain by the law of adoption. COMMENTARY ON ROMANS (1536).[32]

SHARING IN THE SUFFERINGS OF THE FIRST-BORN. JOHN CALVIN: The pious mind must

[29]Vermigli, *In Epistolam S. Pauli Apostoli*, 724.
[30]Brenz, *In Epistolam*, 226; citing Jn 15:20.
[31]Bucer, *Metaphrases et Enarrationes*, 362.

[32]Sadoleto, *In Pauli Epistolam*, 129.

ascend still higher—namely, to where Christ calls his disciples when he says, that every one of them must "take up his cross." Those whom the Lord has chosen and honored with relationship must prepare for a hard, laborious, troubled life, a life full of many and various kinds of evils, it being the will of our heavenly Father to exercise his people in this way while putting them to the test. Having begun this course with Christ the firstborn, he continues it toward all his children. For though that Son was dear to him above others, the Son in whom he was "well pleased," yet we see that far from being treated gently and indulgently, we may say that not only was he subjected to a perpetual cross while he dwelt on earth, but his whole life was nothing else than a kind of perpetual cross. The apostle assigns the reason: "Though he was a Son, yet he learned obedience by the things that he suffered." Why then should we exempt ourselves from that condition to which Christ our Head was willing to submit, especially since he submitted on our account so that he might, in his own person, exhibit a model of patience? Because of this, the apostle declares, that all the children of God are destined to be conformed to him. Hence it affords us great consolation in hard and difficult circumstances, which people deem evil and adverse, to think that we are holding fellowship with the sufferings of Christ; that as he passed to celestial glory through a labyrinth of many woes, so we too are conducted there through various tribulations. For, in another passage, Paul himself says, "We must through much tribulation enter the kingdom of God"; and again, "that I may know him, and the power of his resurrection, and the fellowship of his sufferings, being conformed to his death." How powerfully should it soften the bitterness of the cross, to think that the more we are afflicted with adversity, the surer we are made of our fellowship with Christ. By communion with him our sufferings are not only blessed to us, but tend greatly to the furtherance of our salvation. Institutes of the Christian Religion 3.8.1 (1559).[33]

---

[33]Calvin, *Institutes*, 2:16-17*; citing Mt 16:24; Heb 5:8; Acts 14:22.

Conforming to the Image of Christ Through Suffering. Olympia Morata: The bishops and their adherents, having besieged Schweinfurt, threw fire into it night and day, from every quarter. Such was the constant fury of their cannonade, that the garrison declared they had not witnessed the like of it in any former siege. . . . The besiegers treacherously and unexpectedly entered and, having plundered every thing the town contained, set it on fire.

But God delivered us from the flames also, and that by the counsel of one of the enemy. My husband was twice made prisoner, and you may believe that if ever I knew sorrow, or if ever I prayed heartily in my life, it was then! From the bottom of my anguished heart, I cried with unutterable groans, "Help, Lord! Help me, for the sake of Christ!" Nor did I cease until it pleased God to hear me and to deliver my husband. Oh, if you had seen me disheveled and covered with rags—for they took our clothes from us—and in the haste of the flight I had lost my shoes along the way, so that only God can tell how I got over the sharp stones and flints! Often I said, "I can't proceed any further; I must lie down and die." Often I cried to God in my despair, "Lord, if you would have me live, bid your angels carry me, for I can do no more myself." It is still a matter of astonishment to me how I made it ten miles in one day, weak as I was, emaciated and exhausted, having even been ill before, and now, from fatigue, I was attacked with intermittent fever, which hung on to me during all my wanderings.

But God did not forsake us, though everything, even our very clothing, was taken from us. He sent us, by the hands of an unknown nobleman, fifteen gold crowns; and he conducted us to other princes, who clothed us honorably and entertained us. Now, thanks be to him, we are settled at Heidelberg (where my husband is a public lecturer on medicine) and we are almost as well supplied with household furniture as before our misfortune.

These things I have written to you so that you may thank God with us, and observe that he never abandons in their miseries those that are his; and thus, be confirmed in your faith that he will never forsake you, should you be called on to suffer for the truth. For we must all be (as Paul says) "conformed to the image of Christ"—we must suffer with him, if we would reign with him, and only those who overcome can have the crown.

If you feel yourself weak, my dearest lady, as indeed I am myself (but the Lord makes me strong when I call on and pray to him), go to Christ. LETTER TO MADONNA CHERUBINA ORSINI FROM HEIDELBERG, AUGUST 8, 1554.[34]

8:30 Predestined, Called, Justified, and Glorified

THE MOST DIVINE VERSE. ANTHONY MAXEY: The blessed apostle says that every Scripture is given by inspiration, is profitable to instruct the man and woman of God, and to make them perfect toward good works. Yet notwithstanding, if someone should seek on purpose to trace through the whole body of the Scripture, line by line, they will find that of all others, this one short verse is the most divine, most excellent. . . .

In the holy Scripture, every speech and sentence, every verse, every point and syllable is rich in sense and full of divine and holy mysteries. So it is here: As to its relation to points of doctrine, it contains the whole sum of our religion. As to manner, it consists of a sweet gradation. As to matter, it is full of comforting instruction. And as to depth of understanding, it has in it such sweet, profound, and heavenly mysteries that it is like the saying, "The head of the River Nile can never be found." So the height, depth, and spiritual knowledge that lies couched in this whole verse, in every point, in every word, is unsearchable; it cannot be found. THE GOLDEN CHAIN OF MAN'S SALVATION (1606).[35]

PREDESTINATION, JUSTIFICATION, AND GLORIFICATION. JOHANN VON STAUPITZ: Since

justification is due to grace and not to nature since acceptation of works performed in grace is grace, and since it is again grace that the merits of Christ are made ours, it is appropriate to attribute the whole Christian life to grace. And thus the claim for humans, namely, that they are master over their works from beginning to end, is destroyed. So, therefore, the origin of the works of Christian life is predestination, its means is justification, and its aim is glorification or thanksgiving—all these are the achievements not of nature but of grace. ETERNAL PREDESTINATION AND ITS EXECUTION IN TIME (1517).[36]

THE ORDER AND ASSURANCE. JUAN DE VALDÉS: All this depends on what he has stated. That is, that those who love God are called of God by divine ordinance. Here St. Paul means that God first knew his people, and that after he had known them, he predestined them, and that after having predestined them, he has gone on calling them from time to time as they have been born into the world, and that after having called them, he justifies them. And they have responded to his call by accepting as their own the justice of God executed on Christ. And after having justified them, God glorifies them.

So that two things precede vocation or calling: knowledge and predestination. And two other things follow: justification and glorification. Now it is perfectly understood that when a person feels himself inwardly invited or called of God to be Christ's, without his having made it his aim to seek Christ or to go to Christ—as in the instance of a person who goes to hear a sermon or something else through curiosity or any other whim of his, and there hears some word which penetrates his soul and makes him seek Christ, and then he desires Christ (even without knowing why he desires him or how he seeks him), until having sought him, he has found him and then knows that he sought him because he is Christ's and that as such God accepts him as just—he then properly

---

[34]Smyth, *Olympia Morata*, 221-23*. She died the following year of the illness contracted then.
[35]Maxey, *Golden Chain*, A2r-v*.

[36]Oberman, *Forerunners of the Reformation*, 186*.

feels his vocation and rests assured as to the two things that precede vocation. That is, that God has known him and has predestinated him. And he is assured of the two things that follow on vocation: justification and glorification. And being assured of all these things is the highest and most excellent thing to which a man or woman can attain in the present life. COMMENTARY ON ROMANS (1556).[37]

ORDER OF SALVATION. ANDREW WILLET: "Whom he justified, he glorified." Glorification does not follow immediately on predestination, but vocation, faith, justification, and sanctification must come between. Those who without these presume on election pervert the revealed counsel of God to his destruction. A SIX-FOLD COMMENTARY ON THE EPISTLE TO THE ROMANS (1620).[38]

WHY IT IS CALLED THE GOLDEN CHAIN. ANTHONY MAXEY: The ancient Fathers, in the course of their writings, call it the golden chain of our salvation because each one of these: predestination, calling, justification, and glorifying, are so coupled and knit together that if you hold fast to one link, you draw to yourself the whole chain. And if you let one go, you lose all. THE GOLDEN CHAIN OF MAN'S SALVATION (1606).[39]

THE PERMANENCE OF THE GOLDEN CHAIN. WILLIAM PERKINS: Once someone is in the state of grace, they will be in that state forever. This appears in Romans 8:30, where Paul sets down the golden chain of the causes of salvation that can never be broken, so that those who are predestined will be called, justified, and glorified. And a little after that, he says, "Who shall lay any thing to the charge of God's elect?" And, "Who shall sever us from the love of Christ?" And, "I am persuaded that no creature shall be able to sever us from the love of Christ," which he would not have said if a person who was in the state of grace could fall from grace. And how could those who are justified

have peace with God if they were not certain to persevere as righteous before God to the end? And how can it be said, "that hope makes not ashamed, because the love of God (by which God loves his elect) is shed abroad in their hearts by the Holy Spirit who is given to them," if any can utterly fall from that love? How could the testimony of the Spirit, which testifies to the elect that they are the children of God, be true and certain if it can be quite extinguished? Last, how shall what John says be true, "They went out of us, because they were not of us; if they had been of us, they would have remained with us" if a person can wholly fall from Christ when they have once been made a true member of him? Our Savior Christ says, "My sheep hear my voice, and I know them, and they follow me; and I give eternal life to them, and no one shall take them out of my hand or out of my Father's hand, and whoever my Father gives me shall come to me, and whoever comes to me, I will not cast out." And if any of the elect being effectually called could fall wholly from grace, then there would have to be a second insertion or engrafting into the mystical body of Christ, and therefore a second baptism. For every fall, a new engrafting and a new baptism would be needed; but there is no way that could be granted. Therefore, those that are predestined to be in the state of grace are also predestined to persevere in that same state to the end. A GOLDEN CHAIN.[40]

THE PEACE THE GOLDEN CHAIN BRINGS. ANTHONY MAXEY: For the comfort of their soul and the assurance of their salvation forever may every true Christian thus conclude:

I am truly justified by a lively and working faith; therefore I am called. I am effectively called by his Word; therefore, I am predestined. I am predestined and chosen by his free love from eternity, and therefore I shall be glorified to all eternity.

O settled comfort! O sweetly conceived hope of joy! That joy that the strength of hell's ten thousand can never take away. Why, therefore, should

---

[37]Valdés, *Commentary upon St. Paul's Epistle*, 140-41*.
[38]Willet, *Hexapla*, 402*.
[39]Maxey, *Golden Chain*, A2v-A3r*.
[40]Perkins, *A Golden Chaine*, 678*; citing Jn 10:27-28; 6:37.

we fear? Of what should we be afraid? The
Golden Chain of Man's Salvation (1606).[41]

God Knows More Than You Do. Johannes
Bugenhagen: Then, "those whom he had
predestined." As you can see, he asserts that the fact
that these are to be saved is "not of him who wills
nor of him who runs but of him who shows mercy."
This, however, is deeply offensive to the flesh, for
which reason you must settle it firmly that God
knows more than you do. This commendation that
freely belongs to all Christians is of grace, not of
merit. For Erasmus here says that they were
enemies of God for a time, but now have been
made sons of God by grace. Interpretation of
Romans (1531).[42]

Called and Chosen. Friedrich Balduin: Q:
How does what the apostle Paul says agree with
Christ, since Christ said, "Many are called, but few
are chosen." But the apostle says, "Those whom he
predestined these he also called." Are we to
conclude that as many as are called are also
predestined or elect?

A: I answer that "they are called" can be
understood chiefly in five different ways.

First, there are those who are called but who do
not obey that call, and these are called the
keklēmenoi. They are those whom God does in truth
sincerely call and desires that they should come, as a
sign not only of his will but also of his good
pleasure: "he stretches out his hands all day long to a
rebellious people" and threatens punishment to
those refusing him. Therefore, the fact that they do
not come happens para prothesin (contrary to God's
purpose), whence we conclude that even they are
"called kata prothesin (according to his purpose)."

Second, those are also "called" people who show
up in the meetings of the church and these are
called not only keklēmenoi but also klētoi.

Third, among those who come, there are some
who show up not with seriousness but in dissimulation and hypocrisy of soul, without a wedding

garment, among whom of their own fault, para
prothesin (contrary to the purpose) of God, his
calling does not attain to its intended outcome.

Fourth, there are yet others who are made
sharers in the divine calling; that is, they are reborn
through the Word, they receive the Holy Spirit,
and for awhile they obey the divine calling, but
then they fall back and do not retain the beginning
of their faith until the end. These also, by their
own fault, fall away from the freely given calling of
God, contrary to his purpose and will.

Last, there are those who are not only called
but who also obey the Holy Spirit and make their
calling sure until the end of their life. The calling
of which Paul here conjoins to predestination is
to be understood as referring to these last kind.
For they are these who truly are called kata
prothesin (according to purpose) and who
ultimately obtain the end of their protheseōs
(calling), namely, glory and eternal salvation.
Christ speaks of all the other kinds of people for
whom the calling of God does not attain its goal,
of whom there are a great many distinguished
into four categories as we have seen. In light of all
these, the number of those who fall into the
category of both called and chosen is extremely
small. Commentary on Romans (1620).[43]

Seeding on Sterile and Fertile Soils.
Wolfgang Musculus: When a farmer is sowing
seed he does not intend to sow on sterile ground
such as on a path, or a thorn thicket, or soil that is
full of rocks, but rather on good and fertile soil.
But it nevertheless sometimes happens that while
he is sowing, some seed falls not only on good
ground but also on sterile ground, such as on the
path. What prevents us from calling the path
"seeded" even if the farmer did not purpose to sow
seed there? Accordingly, you can rightly say that
while much ground is "seeded" only some of it is
fertile. And yet nothing prohibits you from
applying a series of steps here, in this way: "That
ground that the farmer elected, this he also

[41]Maxey, Golden Chain, C1r-C2v*.
[42]Bugenhagen, In D. Pauli ad Romanos, 99r; citing Rom 9:16.

[43]Balduin, Catechesis Apostolica, 569-70; citing Mt 22:1-46; 20:1-34;
Lk 14:1-35; Is 65:2; Prov 1:24-33; Heb 9:15; Mt 20:16; 22:14.

destined for planting; that which he destined, this he also sowed; that which he sowed, this he made fertile, and that which he made fertile this he also harvested." Nothing about this stands in the way of what I said above, that "much ground is 'seeded' but only a little is fertile."

For according to this sentence, the seeded ground is not said to be seeded for any other reason than insofar as it received some seed beyond the intention of the farmer while he was sowing, not because it was seeded according to his purpose. So also in this passage. The "called" are properly those who are called "according to God's purpose." These are the elect. For God purposed to call nobody else than them. And in Christ's statement the "many" who are called are those who, when the elect and sons and daughters of God are called to life, even though they themselves are not elect, will also run to him, and having been externally called, are joined to him. I wished to point these things out so that we might determine with certainty and simplicity who are the called of God and who are not, according to the logic of this chain of steps. Who they are is not to be looked for here at this step of calling, but rather only in the next step, that of justification. COMMENTARY ON ROMANS (1555).[44]

WE ARE CONFORMED TO THE SON BY THE CROSS. THEODORE BEZA: "These he glorified," *edoxasen*. Paul uses the perfect tense in place of the present tense, not only after the manner of a common Hebrew speech, but also so that he might declare a continuous act. He is, in effect, saying that when the Lord instructs his people under the rod of the cross, he is still presently calling, justifying, and in a certain sense already glorifying them. For we are conformed to the Son of God by means of the cross. Hence it happens that by this very cross believers have something of which to glory in, since to them "it was granted to suffer for Christ's sake." MAJOR ANNOTATIONS (1594).[45]

GOD WILL GLORIFY THOSE HE HAS SANCTIFIED. JOHN CALVIN: The Lord thus keeps them all their lifetime under the discipline of the cross, lest they should allow their hearts to long for or confide in present good. In short, his treatment is usually such that wherever they turn their eyes, as far as this world extends, they see nothing before them but despair. And hence, Paul says, "If in this life only we have hope in Christ, we are of all men most miserable." So that they may not fail in these great straits, the Lord is present, reminding them to lift their head higher and extend their view farther, that in him they may find a happiness that they do not see in the world. To this happiness he gives the name of reward, hire, or recompense—not as estimating the merit of works, but intimating that it is a compensation for their straits, sufferings, and affronts, and so on. Therefore, there is nothing to prevent us from calling eternal life a recompense, after the example of Scripture, because in it the Lord brings his people from labor to quiet, from affliction to a prosperous and desirable condition, from sorrow to joy, from poverty to affluence, from ignominy to glory. In short, all the evils that they endured, he exchanges for blessings. Thus there will be no impropriety in considering holiness of life as the way, not indeed the way which gives access to the glory of the heavenly kingdom, but a way by which God conducts his elect to the manifestation of that kingdom, since his good pleasure is to glorify those whom he has sanctified. Only let us not imagine that merit and reward are correlative terms, a point on which the scholastic theologians absurdly insist, from their not having attended to the end we advert. How preposterous is it when the Lord calls us to one end, to look to another? Nothing is clearer than that a reward is promised to good works in order to support the weakness of our flesh by some degree of comfort, but not to inflate our minds with vainglory. He, therefore, who infers merit from reward, or weighs works and reward in the same balance, errs very widely from the end that God has in view. INSTITUTES OF THE CHRISTIAN RELIGION 3.18.4 (1559).[46]

---

[44]Musculus, *In Epistolam Apostoli Pauli*, 193-94.
[45]Beza, *Annotationes Majores*, 100; citing Phil 1:29.

[46]Calvin, *Institutes*, 2:123*; citing 1 Cor 15:19.

**Thirsting After the Graces of Sanctifi-
cation.** Richard Rogers: This doctrine is a
double link of that golden chain, mentioned by the
apostle in these words in Romans 8 (whom he
predestined, those he called, justified, and glorified).
There is no other way to seek out the certainty of our
election, but by the means that serve our calling. And
our calling never goes without the gift of faith, and
the Spirit of God sanctifying, which is the beginning
of our glorifying in heaven. So that as predestination
itself is manifested in time by the enlightening and
opening of the heart to receive the glad tidings of the
gospel, so when Christ is embraced by faith, the
Holy Spirit is given to the believer, who quickens the
heart with spiritual grace, and fits such a party to the
work of God. He does this both by inwardly
renewing and changing our nature, and by outwardly
framing the life to his will. And thus he works in all
that are his. Though he gives greater measure to
some who are deputed and appointed by him to
greater employment and service. I mean he gives
them more zeal, courage, love, diligence, constancy,
experience, judgment, and the like. And yet (lest any
should err about this point) we know that he works
none of these without means. Those therefore whom
he will thus sanctify he will also prepare, by stirring
up in them an earnest coveting after these graces, a
special hunger and thirst after them, a high opinion
and account of them, and a singular affection of love
to them, with a fervent desire of honoring the giver
of them, and a studious endeavor by all means both
of prayer and labor to attain them. Yes, look what
affections he works in those he will bring to the
certainty and assurance of salvation. And he
preserves and nourishes these in believers, for the
increasing of grace, and the enabling of them to his
service in better manner. He does not allow them to
just sit still or take their ease until these gifts drop
into their mouths. Nor does he allow them to be
indifferent as to whether they will attain and come
by them or not. But rather, he causes them to give
themselves no rest until they are satisfied, from time
to time, with the good things that they desire.
Commentary on Judges.[47]

**The Inner Calling to a Renovation of
the Heart.** Wolfgang Musculus: I said above
that I would leave this distinction alone and
untouched. And yet I have been moved contrary to
that opinion of mine by the present passage, since
that inner calling which is the renovation of our
hearts here is shown to be nothing different from
what justification itself is, unless we wish to
distinguish between inner calling and justification
insofar as that inner calling is not the same
illumination of the heart and transformation or
purgation that properly belongs to justification and
faith, but rather an earlier and initial movement of
the heart in this direction, so that the preaching of
the gospel might be listened to and received, which
we might call the "opening of the heart" as in the
example of Lydia the seller of purple in Acts 16.
There is as a result a certain eagerness to hear the
Word, and this certainly must come about divinely
and inwardly. This is similar to how the opening of
the stomach produces an eagerness of taking food
that precedes eating itself and prepares the
stomach so that it is ready to receive the food. In
this sense, that inner calling can be rescued from
being thought to coincide exactly with justification
itself. And so it can easily be answered how those
who were unworthy can be said to be called and yet
not elect unto life, since the apostle here says, "and
those whom he called, these he also justified." For
the unworthy are called only by an external calling,
not by an internal calling. Commentary on
Romans (1555).[48]

**Affliction and the Glory of the Kingdom
of Heaven.** John Calvin: That he might now by
a clearer proof show how true it is that a conformity
with the humiliating state of Christ is for our good,
he adopts a climax, by which he teaches us that a
participation of the cross is so connected with our
vocation, justification, and, in short, with our future
glory, that they can by no means be separated. . . .
What Paul then means by this climax is that the
afflictions of the faithful, having obtained the glory

---

[47]Rogers, *Commentary upon the Whole Book*, 656*.

[48]Musculus, *In Epistolam Apostoli Pauli*, 195; citing Acts 16:14.

of the celestial kingdom, may reach the glory of Christ's resurrection, with whom they are now crucified. Commentary on Romans 8:30.[49]

Crosses Have a Happy Ending. Erasmus Sarcerius: "These he also glorified." Glorification is the effect of justification. Therefore, glorification does not come to any but to the justified. Hence, glorification will not come to those who are not first justified, even if they are afflicted and pressed by some cross.

It is here important to know that justification is both an occasion for facing a cross, as well as the subject matter for a legitimate cross.

Justification is certain. Therefore a cross together with glorification is also certain.

Even here a question arises about the goal of crosses, which is glorification. It is needful to keep one's eye on this goal, so that no cross might be irksome to us nor overly difficult.

Glorification is the goal of any cross arranged or ordained by God. Glorification applies not so much to the present life as it does to the one yet to come. This glorification means that crosses have a happy ending and a salvific outcome. Notes on Romans (1541).[50]

For All These Gracious Favors. George Wither:

O Lord! I long to sing your praise,
But know not where I should begin;
So often and in so many ways
Your favors have conferred been. . . .

But most of all I praise you, Lord!
For pardoning what is done amiss;
And for the means you do afford
To bring me to eternal bliss.

For choosing me before time was made,
For your creating me in time,
For my redemption when I had
Well being lost by Adam's crime.

For me enlightening by those rays,
By which the paths of truth I see;
For bringing me from error's ways,
For these things, Lord! I honor thee.

I bless your name that by your grace
I freely justified am,
And that when I polluted was,
I thereby sanctified became.

I praise you too that I abide
Preserved in the state of bliss,
And that of being glorified
My woeful soul kept hopeful is.

O Lord! To sum up all in One,
In One which every bliss contains;
I give You thanks for Christ your Son,
Who all these gracious favors deigns.

To him for whatsoever he
Has suffered, said, or done, be praise;
And to that Spirit who to me
The means of all this grace conveys.

Hymn of General Thanksgiving.[51]

---

[49]CTS 38:319-20 (CO 49:160-61).
[50]Sarcerius, *In Apostolam ad Romanos*, N5r.
[51]Wither, *Hallelujah*, 25-27*.

8:31-39 NOTHING CAN SEPARATE
US FROM HIS LOVE

³¹*What then shall we say to these things? If God is for us, who can be*ᵃ *against us?* ³²*He who did not spare his own Son but gave him up for us all, how will he not also with him graciously give us all things?* ³³*Who shall bring any charge against God's elect? It is God who justifies.* ³⁴*Who is to condemn? Christ Jesus is the one who died—more than that, who was raised—who is at the right hand of God, who indeed is interceding for us.*ᵇ ³⁵*Who shall separate us from the love of Christ? Shall tribulation, or distress, or persecution, or famine, or nakedness, or danger, or sword?* ³⁶*As it is written,*

"For your sake we are being killed all the day long; we are regarded as sheep to be slaughtered."

³⁷*No, in all these things we are more than conquerors through him who loved us.* ³⁸*For I am sure that neither death nor life, nor angels nor rulers, nor things present nor things to come, nor powers,* ³⁹*nor height nor depth, nor anything else in all creation, will be able to separate us from the love of God in Christ Jesus our Lord.*

a Or *who is* b Or *Is it Christ Jesus who died… for us?*

OVERVIEW: As Paul's argument moves toward a crescendo by the end of this chapter, the reformers exhort their readers to stand strong against the suffering and opposition that might come at them. God is for us, and he has proved this by giving over his Son to die for us rather than allowing us to be destroyed. He is a very unusual father in that instead of handing over a ransom to redeem his Son, he handed over his Son to redeem others. This Son, Christ, is the treasury of all good things, and he will give us righteousness, freedom from sin, and eternal life. We should look to him, rather than Mary or the saints, as our intercessor.

The commentators explore many aspects of persevering in the face of allegations. There are two primary accusers of the elect: the law (esp. the Ten Commandments) and our consciences. If we were making a claim for our own good works or sinlessness as the justification for right standing with God, then perhaps someone could successfully accuse us before God, but since our salvation depends on God's free acceptance of us in Christ, any charges against us are irrelevant to our security in our future glorification.

Commentators speak against a medieval viewpoint that the love referred to in the phrase "nothing can separate us from the love of God" refers to our love for God rather than his love for us. God's love for us is extraordinary and unbreakable. It is also surprising, given the immensity of the gap between us and him. When we are aware of God's benevolence toward us, we can stand strong against any afflictions that come against us.

The reformers—especially the Anabaptists and the later Puritans—lived under the threat of persecution, even to the point of death, and so the "sheep for slaughter" phrase is not merely theoretical for them. They compose prayers for endurance in persecution. They exhort readers, when facing tribulation, to keep their eyes on Christ (and the church), for the strength for our victory comes from him who loves us, and his cross enables us to have victory in our own cross-bearing experiences.

In the end, in all our trials, God reveals his faithfulness to us as our Father and shows us "something lovely and wonderful" that deepens our love for him as we wait for the joy of eternity in the midst of this dark world. After all the theological and exegetical explications of the reformers on everything from predestination to glorification, it comes down to this: the "chief voice of the gospel" is that God loves us.

8:31 Who Can Be Against Us If God Is for Us?

PULLING THE THREADS TOGETHER. WILLIAM COWPER: Now follows the conclusion of the whole chapter, in which the apostle breaking off the course of his former speech gathers up all that he has spoken, into a short summary. He began at the first and lowest benefit that God in Christ has bestowed on us: deliverance from condemnation. This is indeed the least of his mercies, yet it is so great that if we had received no more we would never be able to yield to the Lord the praise that is due for it. Yet, as I said, it is but little in respect to that which God has done to us. And, therefore, the apostle beginning at it, ascends continually, until he comes to the last and highest, which is our estate of glorification. And so, having run so high in the enumeration of God's mercies toward us that he can't go any higher, he bursts out into an exclamation, as if he said, "More cannot be spoken. Further comfort cannot be given." So he contents himself with making a brief recapitulation of all that he has said, in which he first triumphs generally and afterward, particularly. And he does so first against sin: "Who shall accuse? Who shall condemn?" And second, against affliction: "Who shall separate us from the love of God?" Outward and visible enemies cannot do it, not by any sort of trouble. Nor are inward and invisible enemies able to do it. Thus, like a valiant man established on Christ, in his own name and in the name of the rest of God's children, Paul proclaims defiance to all his enemies, both visible and invisible. HEAVEN OPENED: TREATISE ON ROMANS 8 (1632).[1]

LIKE A VICTOR, PAUL SCOFFS AT HIS SUFFERINGS. JOHANNES BRENZ: To this point Paul has cited many and clear arguments by which he has proved that the hope that by faith we have received from our Lord Jesus Christ concerning eternal salvation will not put us to shame, even when the greatest and most weighty afflictions seem to be warring against us. So much is it not the case that those afflictions that overwhelm us nullify in any way our hope and are harmful to us or are hindrances to our heavenly salvation, that they are rather helps for us to attain to eternal happiness, especially since the whole creation groans together with us under a cross, and the Holy Spirit himself intercedes for us. And briefly, afflictions have the same outcome in us who believe in Christ that they had in Christ himself: namely, the highest glory and majesty in heaven. Therefore by these arguments and reasoning Paul is so animated and kindled against all afflictions and hardships that we can only regard him as a victor and conqueror over them who with great ardor of soul cries out at them and scoffs at them and regards them as unworthy to be compared with those things on account of which we are shaken and perturbed in our soul actually only a little. COMMENTARY ON ROMANS (1588).[2]

SEEKING THE DEEPER PRINCIPLE IN SUFFERING. JOHN CALVIN: The subject discussed having been sufficiently proved, Paul now breaks out into exclamations by which he sets forth the magnanimity with which the faithful ought to be furnished when adversities urge them to despond. And he teaches us in these words that with the paternal favor of God is connected that invincible courage that overcomes all temptations. We indeed know that judgment is usually formed of the love or of the hatred of God, in no other way than by a view of our present state, hence, when things fall out untowardly, sorrow takes possession of our minds and drives away all confidence and consolation. But Paul loudly exclaims that a deeper principle ought to be inquired after, and that those who confine themselves to the sad spectacle of our present warfare reason absurdly. I indeed allow that the scourges of God are in themselves justly deemed to be tokens of God's wrath, but as they are consecrated in Christ, Paul bids the saints to lay hold, above all things, on the paternal love of

---

[1]Cowper, *Heaven Opened*, 399-400*.

[2]Brenz, *In Epistolam*, 227.

God, that relying on this shield they may boldly triumph over all evils. This is a brazen wall to us, so that while God is propitious to us, we shall be safe against all dangers. He does not, however, mean that nothing shall oppose us, but he promises a victory over all kinds of enemies. COMMENTARY ON ROMANS 8:31.[3]

THE MOST CAPABLE INTERCESSOR. CATHARINA REGINA VON GREIFFENBERG: With his drops of blood, the eternal Word divided himself up into pure pomegranate seeds, and from each seed a word came to speak the Word to us. In each ruby of blood resides heavenly eloquence, and [it] wins over the heart of the omnipotent Father so that he grants the wish. Why then do we want, for God's sake, to run after a handful of water when the divine primal spring gushes forth in superabundance? How should a little wax candle light [the way] for us in the bright midday sunshine? If God (Jesus) is for us, who can be against us? How should the words of this Word that in eternity emerged from God not enter into God's heart to be granted a favorable hearing, especially after he has done penance for our sins and so superabundantly atoned them. But whom can one have eternally more capable as an intercessor with God than him with whom God himself conversed about our creation and redemption? TWELVE DEVOUT MEDITATIONS ON THE SUPREMELY HOLY AND SUPREMELY SALVIFIC SUFFERING AND DYING OF JESUS CHRIST (1683).[4]

GOD-WITH-US IS A SEA. CATHARINA REGINA VON GREIFFENBERG: One can just as little leave off contemplating and admiring as leave off praising itself; for the fact that God-with-us is a sea [composed of] individual droplets merits the contemplation of all the grains of sand of time running through an eternally running hourglass. How can he whom we oppose with our sins be with us? For is it not written: These sins separate

us and our God from one another? But for precisely this reason God, who is good through and through, means to be with us in order to separate this separation from us, for he is and loves unity. In order, however, that what he cut in two may become one with him again, the one from the one also becomes one with what has been cut in two and will nevertheless remain one in the one so that in him both flow together and become one, because he is both in one. MEDITATIONS ON THE INCARNATION OF JESUS CHRIST (1678).[5]

THE WAYS GOD IS PRESENT IN SUFFERING. WILLIAM COWPER: To make this clear, let us know that God is present with his children in many ways. First, he is with them by preventing a danger, not allowing the intended evil of the enemy to come near them. For example, he brought Sennacherib to see Jerusalem from the outside, but he did not allow him to shoot so much as a dart against it inside. Second, the Lord sometimes enters his children into trouble, as with Daniel into the den, Joseph into prison, and the three men into the fire. But he delivers them in such a way that both his glory and their comfort is greater than if they had not been in trouble at all. Third, sometimes he allows his children to end their mortal lives in trouble, and yet he is with them, strengthening them by his glorious might, giving them all patience and long-suffering, filling them with such a sense of his love that in death they rest under the assurance of life. HEAVEN OPENED: TREATISE ON ROMANS 8 (1632).[6]

8:32 If He Gave Up His Own Son, Won't He Give Us All Things?

THE FATHER DID NOT SPARE HIS SON. PILGRAM MARPECK: The Father did not spare the Son, but gave him up so that all who believe in him may have eternal life. The Father sealed the guilt of sin in death and in the prison of hell forever. In his human

---

[3]CTS 38:321* (CO 49:162).
[4]Greiffenberg, *Meditations on the Incarnation*, 144*.

[5]Greiffenberg, *Meditations on the Incarnation*, 270-71*.
[6]Cowper, *Heaven Opened*, 405*.

poverty, the payer of the debt, the true warrantor, went himself into the depths of hell with our sins, and yet without any sin of his own, through his torment on earth in order to make payment. Moreover, he took the power away from death and from him who has the dominion over pain and death. The whale could not hold Jonah, nor could the pit hold him there. Life broke through in its power, which the Lord had had in himself against all the power of hell. By means of the glory, dominion, and power of life he took life back again out of the midst of death, together with all who have hoped for the Lord and his salvation. Their hope, and also the hope of the apostles on earth, was gone. For their very sakes, the joy, splendor, and glory of Christ has ascended to the heights, not only with all the imprisoned, but with the prison itself. Paul's question is appropriate here: "Death, hell, devil, and sin, where is your power and dominion?" CONCERNING THE LOWLINESS OF CHRIST.[7]

PRAYER OF PRAISE FOR GOD'S GIVING US HIS SON. BALTHASAR HUBMAIER: The bishop takes the bread and with the church lifts his eyes to heaven, praises God and says: "We praise and thank you, Lord God, Creator of the heavens and earth, for all your goodness toward us. You especially so sincerely loved us that you gave your most beloved Son for us unto death so that each one who believes in him may not be lost but have eternal life. May you be honored, praised, and magnified now, forever, always and eternally. Amen." A FORM FOR CHRIST'S SUPPER.[8]

CHRIST'S DEATH PROVES GOD IS FOR US. JOHANNES BRENZ: It was most truly said, "If God is for us who is against us?" But how do we know that God is for us and stands on our side? Paul explains this quite clearly for us when he says: "who did not spare his own Son, but delivered him up for us all; how therefore could it happen that he would not with his Son also give us all things?"

Here you have a very clear argument proving the favor and clemency of God toward us, since he did not spare even his very own Son but chose to hand him over to the most shameful death rather than to pay no heed to our destruction. COMMENTARY ON ROMANS (1588).[9]

CHRIST IS GIVEN FOR US AND TO US. THEODORE BEZA: "Together with him" (*syn auto*). It was not enough that Christ was given over to death for our sakes, unless the Crucified One is also given to us now, that is, unless it is applied to us by faith. Just as it is not enough to be nourished by food that is seen, unless we are actually fed by it, so also he who surrendered himself freely for our sakes is also bestowed on us, when he grants us that faith by which we lay hold of him unto eternal life. Further, two things are mentioned here that are given freely: Christ himself and those things that we obtain in him. It follows from this that we do not receive Christ apart from his gifts, nor his gifts (that is, the spiritual gifts belonging to the elect that we obtain in him) apart from Christ. That teaching is therefore most false and absurd which says that among those who come to the Lord's Supper, he himself is partaken of, but by some unto salvation and by others unto judgment. No, Christ will judge those who come to the table unworthily, not because he himself was partaken of unworthily (which cannot happen), but because he was disregarded in the sacrament by its being received in an unworthy manner, just as he also is when the Word is heard in an unworthy manner. MAJOR ANNOTATIONS (1594).[10]

CHRIST IS THE TREASURY OF ALL GOOD THINGS. JOHANNES BRENZ: What more? From such an immense love of God toward us it necessarily follows that together with Christ whom he gave to us, he will also give us all good things that Christ possesses. What, therefore, are those good things that Christ as the Son of God

---

[7]CRR 2:432-33*.
[8]CRR 5:404*; citing Jn 3:16; 1 Jn 4:9.

[9]Brenz, *In Epistolam*, 650.
[10]Beza, *Annotationes Majores*, 100.

possesses? First, Christ possesses righteousness: "He committed no sin, nor was deceit found in his mouth." Second, he possesses victory over all afflictions, over death and hell. He also has the highest and eternal happiness. In short, the good things that Christ possesses are innumerable, since he is the treasury of all good things. Therefore, since God gave us his own Son, it cannot be denied that he will along with him also give us righteousness, liberation from all evils, and the enjoyment of eternal beatitude. COMMENTARY ON ROMANS (1588).[11]

HIS MERITS MAKE US MERRY. BENEDETTO DA MANTOVA AND MARCANTONIO FLAMINIO: To be clothed with Jesus Christ is nothing else than believing for a certainty that Christ is wholly ours; and so he is, in very deed, if we believe so, and hold ourselves assured that by the same heavenly garment we are received into favor before God. For it is most certain that he, as a most dear Father, has given us his Son, meaning that all his righteousness and all that he always is, can, or has done, can be in our power and jurisdiction, in such a way that it should be lawful for us to make our boast of them, as if we had done, purchased, and deserved them by our own strength. And whoever believes this shall find that his belief is good and true, as we have shown. Then the Christian must have a steadfast faith and belief that all the goods, all the graces, and all the riches of Jesus Christ are his; for, since God has given us Jesus Christ himself, how could it be possible that he has not given us all things along with him? Now if this is true, as true it is indeed, the Christian may rightly say, "I am the child of God; and Jesus Christ is my brother. I am lord of heaven and earth, and of hell and of death, and of the law; insofar as the law cannot accuse me, nor lay any curse on me, because the righteousness of God is become mine." And it is this faith alone that causes us to be called Christians and that clothes us with Jesus Christ; as we have said before. ... This belief and trust that we have in the merits

of Jesus Christ makes us true Christians, stout, cheerful, merry, lovers of God, ready to do good works, possessors of God's kingdom and of God himself, and his right dear beloved children, in whom the Holy Ghost truly dwells. THE BENEFIT OF CHRIST.[12]

THE JOYFUL GIFT OF FORGIVEN SIN. WILLIAM COWPER: First we have to consider who he is that triumphs in this way. Isn't it Paul, who before his conversion was a persecutor, a blasphemer, and an oppressor, who now confesses himself to be the chief of all sinners, and the least of all saints? Yes, indeed, he is the same one. But note, he indeed *was* such a one, but now he has received mercy. And, therefore, like a man now relieved of a heavy burden that oppressed him before, he rejoices and triumphs. Certainly, no greater comfort can come to man than to feel that his sins have been forgiven; this alone causes true rejoicing. You can see this in David. As long as the burden of sin lay on his conscience, it pressed out the very natural moisture of his body. He had no rest night or day, but once Nathan proclaimed remission to him, and he, in his own conscience, felt his sin had been forgiven, he then cried out, "O blessed is the one whose wickedness is forgiven, whose sin is covered, and to whom the Lord does not impute his iniquity." Similarly, the man that lay sick for thirty-six years with paralysis arose with great joy when Jesus healed him. And the man that was a cripple, when he found that his feet that had failed him so long now served him, leaped for joy and followed the apostles into the temple to praise God. In the same way, the soul that finds itself freed from the guilt and servitude of sin—the heaviest to bear of all burdens that ever lie on a person—will exult and triumph with much more abundant joy in that mercy of God that has made it free. HEAVEN OPENED: TREATISE ON ROMANS 8 (1632).[13]

---

[11]Brenz, *In Epistolam*, 650; citing 1 Pet 2:22.

[12]Benedetto and Flaminio, *The Benefit of Christ*, 72-74*.
[13]Cowper, *Heaven Opened*, 413-14*; citing Ps 32:2; Jn 5:1-47; Acts 3:1-26.

Does God Stand by Sinners? Johannes Brenz: Why does God embrace us with so much benevolence that he is still for us and stands on our side when we sin and follow wicked deeds and despise his calling? To which I answer that if God were to cast away even his elect and wholly abandon them when they sin, who then would be saved? Nevertheless, because God does have a hatred for sin and detests iniquity, it must never be thought that he is in favor of sin or stands with those who abandon his calling and perpetrate wicked crimes. He altogether—and with severity—demands that all must follow their calling and flee from sin: "Depart from evil and do the good." "If you choose not to listen to the voice of the Lord your God . . . you will be cursed in the city, cursed in the field."

There are also examples that bear witness to the same thing. When Pharaoh was chasing the Israelites down to the Red Sea, he was not walking according to God's calling but rather fighting against God. He was therefore deservedly abandoned by God and drowned in the waters: "Let us flee from Israel, for God fights for them!" When Absalom held the reigns of the kingdom of Israel while his father was ejected, he was not walking according to God's calling. God, therefore, did not stand on his side, and consequently he was suspended in the air by his own deserts.

It was different with the Israelites, who when they set forth in the desert were walking in God's calling. God was, therefore, for them and protected them against their enemies. David, when he approached Goliath, was walking in God's calling, and therefore, God stood with him against Goliath. Hence, if you want God to stand with you, it is necessary that you remain in God's calling and walk by faith. And it sometimes happens that God even saves and protects those who act wickedly. This doesn't happen by the promised and ordinary divine benevolence, nor does it happen out of any kind of favor shown toward the crime, but by an extraordinary grace by which he invites the sinner to repentance. Hence if someone should take

advantage of this grace as an excuse for even greater ungodliness, "he will store up for himself even greater wrath in the day of wrath in which the righteous judgment of God will be revealed," as Paul explained above in chapter 2. Commentary on Romans (1588).[14]

The Unusual Father. Peter Martyr Vermigli: He says that God gave up his Son for us. Therefore, what things for our sake will he hold back, who did not spare his own Son? Fathers customarily spend everything they have to ransom their sons back, but God did the opposite: in order to redeem us, he handed his Son over. When Abraham had brought his son to the altar and was going to offer him as a sacrifice at God's command, God himself testified that he would one day be seen to do that very thing that was going to be done by Abraham. If that testimony of Abraham's was to God proof of his great love and sincere charity toward him, what ought we to think of God himself who handed over his own Son for our sake? "For God so loved the world that he gave his only-begotten Son." This is the banner that Paul continually waves and extolls. Commentary on Romans (1560).[15]

Who Can Sit at Supper Table with a Good Conscience? Balthasar Hubmaier: Since now these ceremonies and signs have to do completely and exclusively with fraternal love, and since one who loves their neighbor like themselves is a rare bird, yea even a . . . phoenix on earth, who can sit at the supper table with a good conscience? Answer: One who has thus taken to heart and has thus shaped themselves in mind and heart and senses inwardly that they truly and sincerely can say, "The love of God that he has shown to me through the sacrifice of his only-begotten and most beloved Son for the payment of my sins, of which I have heard and been certainly assured through his

---

[14]Brenz, *In Epistolam*, 650; citing Ps 34:14; 37:27; Deut 28:15-16; Ex 14:25; 2 Sam 18:9-15; Rom 2:5.

[15]Vermigli, *In Epistolam S. Pauli*, 729; citing John 3:16.

holy Word, has so moved, softened, and penetrated my spirit and soul that I am so minded and ready to offer my flesh and blood, furthermore so to rule over and so to master it, that it must obey me against its own will, and henceforth not take advantage of, deceive, injure, or harm my neighbor in any way in body, soul, honor, goods, wife, or child, but rather go into the fire for them and die as Paul also desired to be accursed for his brethren and Moses to be stricken out of the book of life for the sake of his people." Such a person may with good conscience and worthiness sit at the Supper of Christ. A FORM FOR CHRIST'S SUPPER.[16]

8:33 Who Can Accuse God's Elect?

GOD HIMSELF STANDS BESIDE US WHEN WE ARE ACCUSED. JOHANNES BRENZ: There are two principal accusers of God's elect, those who are believers in Christ. One is the law or the Decalogue. This shuts up all men and women under sin. The other is our own conscience, which recognizes sins by means of the law and makes us aware of our sins. It is not our only accuser—there are a thousand witnesses against us. And Satan, assisted by these accusers or witnesses, threatens and demands that we be condemned on account of our sins. But if we have believed in Christ, we have God himself standing by our side, who when he gave us Christ his own Son, also together with him gave us his righteousness and on that account absolved us of all unrighteousness. COMMENTARY ON ROMANS (1564).[17]

PAUL ESTABLISHES THE CERTAINTY OF GOD'S FATHERLY KINDNESS. JOHN CALVIN: The first and chief consolation of the godly in adversities is to be fully persuaded of the paternal kindness of God, for hence arises the certainty of their salvation and that calm quietness of the soul through which it comes that adversities are sweetened, or at least the bitterness of sorrow

mitigated. Hardly then a more suitable encouragement to patience could be adduced than this, a conviction that God is propitious to us. Hence Paul makes this confidence the main ground of that consolation, by which it behooves the faithful to be strengthened against all evils. And as the salvation of people is first assailed by accusation, and then subverted by condemnation, he in the first place averts the danger of accusation. There is indeed but one God, at whose tribunal we must stand, then there is no room for accusation when he justifies us. The antithetic clauses seem not indeed to be exactly arranged, for the two parts that ought rather to have been arranged are these: "Who shall accuse? Christ is he who intercedes," and then these two might have been connected: "Who shall I condemn? God is he who justifies," for God's absolution answers to condemnation, and Christ's intercession to accusation. But Paul has not without reason made another arrangement, as he was anxious to arm the children of God, as they say, from head to foot, with that confidence which banishes all anxieties and fears. He then more emphatically concludes that the children of God are not subject to an accusation, because God justifies, than if he had said that Christ is our advocate, for he more fully expresses that the way to a trial is more completely closed up when the judge himself pronounces him wholly exempt from guilt, whom the accuser would bring in as deserving punishment. COMMENTARY ON ROMANS 8:33.[18]

THE SECURITY OF KNOWING NO ONE CAN ACCUSE THOSE ELECTED BY GOD. JUAN DE VALDÉS: St. Paul, desiring to make us feel still more sure of our glorification, asks himself the question if there will ever be any creature so bold as to dare to make a charge at the day of judgment against us whom God has elected and taken for himself? And the question is to be understood as involving the negative, and he means that there will be no creature who will have this audacity.

---

[16]CRR 5:399-400*; citing Jn 3:16; 1 Jn 4:9; Rom 9:3; Ex 32:32. [17]Brenz, In Epistolam, 230. [18]CTS 38:323* (CO 49:163).

The expression "God's elect" is significant, as it implies that had they at their own caprice applied to God, there might well have been one to accuse them who might have had ground for accusing them. But since they have been elected by God himself, there will never be anyone who will think of accusing them, even though there might be ground for accusation.

Afterward he says, "Since God is he who justifies those whom he elects, who is he that shall condemn them?" meaning nobody. Had they justified themselves, alleging that they had satisfied the law by good works, then when they failed, there might well have been those who might condemn them. But since God is the one who has freely accepted them as just, who shall be able to condemn them as unjust?

And to heighten more the security that Christians can have in relation to their glorification, by which they can be without any mental anxiety whatsoever in relation to the day of judgment, he adds, "It is Christ that dies," meaning, "Shall Christ, peradventure, accuse us or condemn us?—he who died to justify us, who rose again to glorify us, and who is exalted in the highest degree proximate to God, who wills what God wills, and who continuously intercedes for us?!" This is like a mother saying to her child, "Are you afraid that your mother will accuse you? She who carried you for nine months in her womb, who labored for you in birth, and who has suffered and endured innumerable labors and cares in rearing you?!"

By the words "has died," I understand justification; and by the words "is risen again," I understand glorification. And by being "at the right hand of God," I understand both the highest favor and the entire conformity to the will of God. And by "making intercession for us," I understand the great love Christ has for us. He, while representing to God what he has suffered, asks of him to confirm his predestination, his vocation, and his justification in us until he brings us to the glory of the resurrection and glorification. COMMENTARY ON ROMANS (1556).[19]

OUR REDEEMER-JUDGE WILL RATIFY HIS PROMISE. JOHN CALVIN: It is highly consoling to think that our judgment is vested in the one who has already destined us to share with him in the honor of judgment; so it is far from being true that he will ascend to the judgment seat to condemn us. How could a most merciful prince destroy his own people? How could the head destroy his own members? How could the advocate condemn his clients? For if the apostle, when contemplating the interposition of Christ, is bold to exclaim, "Who is he that condemns?" it is much more certain that Christ, the intercessor, will not condemn those whom he has admitted to his protection. It certainly gives us no small security that we shall be assisted at no other tribunal than that of our Redeemer, from whom salvation is to be expected; and that he who in the gospel now promises eternal blessedness, will then as judge ratify his promise. INSTITUTES OF THE CHRISTIAN RELIGION 1.16.18 (1559).[20]

MEMORY OF SIN LIKE THORNS IN A PROTECTIVE HEDGE. WILLIAM COWPER: Sometimes our consciences present sins to us that we have done many years ago, and of which we have repented. For we need to know that although the Lord, after we repent, forgives the guilt of our sin, yet he will allow the memory of our sin to remain in the conserving faculty of conscience . . . that it may both serve to humble us for the evil we have done, and also preserve us from sin in the time to come. And sin retained this way in the memory, I compare to thorns and briars that in the middle of a garden are hurtful and hinder the growth of good fruit, but when placed in the hedge are profitable to preserve the garden. So sin, as long as it is in the affections, is very pernicious. For then it chokes the seed of the Word of God in them. But being taken out of the affection and set in the memory, it is a hedge to the soul, to preserve it from wild and raging beasts that would otherwise come in and devour it. Thus, for our humiliation, the Lord keeps in us a remembrance

---

[19]Valdés, Commentary upon St. Paul's Epistle, 143-44*.

[20]Calvin, Institutes, 1:451*; citing Mt 19:28.

even of those sins that he has pardoned. But he does so in such a way that with the remembrance of the evil that we have done, our conscience also excuses and comforts us with the remembrance of our sincere repentance toward God. HEAVEN OPENED: TREATISE ON ROMANS 8 (1632).[21]

BOLD DEMANDS AND DECLARATIONS. RICHARD SIBBES: Now, since the Spirit of life in Christ Jesus has quickened his body, the soul may make a bold demand to God, as in 1 Peter 3:16. It may make that demand, "Who shall lay anything to the charge of God's elect? It is Christ that died, no, rather, that is risen again, and ascended into heaven, and makes intercession for us. Who shall lay anything to the charge of God's people? It is God that justifies; who shall condemn?" Our sins? Christ has taken our sins on him, and satisfied divine justice for them. And by the Spirit of life has quickened that dead body of his that was surety for us himself. We may well say, "Who shall lay anything to our charge?" He that is our surety is dead. Dead? No, risen again; no, ascended, and sitting at the right hand of God. Therefore now the conscience of any Christian may make that interrogation and bold demand. It may stand against any that dare to oppose the peace of his conscience, now that he may say, "Who is it?" It is the God-man that died. It is Christ that died in our nature, and has raised that nature of ours again, and is at the right hand of God. Who shall lay anything to our charge? The Spirit of life in Christ that brought him back to life has brought us to life together with him. So now we may state boldly, we are freed from our sins, because our Surety is freed from all. SERMON ON THE SPIRITUAL JUBILEE.[22]

8:34 Christ Intercedes for Us at the Right Hand of God

DEATH, RESURRECTION, KINGDOM, AND PRIESTHOOD. PHILIPP MELANCHTHON: He amplifies this statement by mentioning Christ, the Mediator, and he mentions first death, then the resurrection, third, the kingdom, and fourth, the priesthood. He mentions these things briefly, but they are not to be looked at only in passing.

First, he speaks about death and about the sacrifice in order to remind us that it is the height of disgrace [to] make any sin greater than this sacrifice.

Second, by his resurrection Christ overcame all the power of the devil. We should know that this victory is efficacious and that it will profit us also.

In the third place, his reign is not idle: He sits at the right hand of the Father and saves the believers with divine power, sustains and vivifies them, if only we do not fall away from him.

Fourth, he adds the priesthood and intercession of Christ. Neither is there any sweeter comfort than knowing that Christ is the priest and intercessor for us. However, it would be a disgrace against the priesthood of Christ if we were to think that his intercession was ineffective, or if we were not to join our calling on God to his intercession. COMMENTARY ON ROMANS (1540).[23]

THE TRINITY WORKS ON OUR BEHALF. WOLFGANG MUSCULUS: We see in this passage what confidence a Christian man or woman should have in God in the face of sin, death, and Satan. The Father elected, justified and gave up his Son. The Son died, rose again, and is at the right hand of God interceding for us. The Holy Spirit, as we heard earlier, also intercedes for us with groanings that cannot be expressed. With this divine majesty operating unilaterally on our behalf, who is it that will be able to condemn us? COMMENTARY ON ROMANS (1555).[24]

CHRIST STANDS GUARD OVER US. JOHANNES BRENZ: What can we be troubled by? Christ has been given to us, and in him we have liberation. For in the first place, he died so that he might free us from death and condemnation. Second, he

---

[21]Cowper, *Heaven Opened*, 420-21*.
[22]Sibbes, *Complete Works*, 5:239*.

[23]Melanchthon, *Commentary on Romans*, 182-83*.
[24]Musculus, *In Epistolam Apostoli Pauli*, 300.

didn't just die; he also rose again, and rose again not only for himself but for us also, so that he might call us back from death to life together with himself. Further, he not only rose again, but also is seated at the right hand of God his omnipotent Father and is there arrayed in majesty and omnipotence equally with God the Father so that that which he obtained by means of his death and resurrection he might also preserve by means of his omnipotence. Last, he does not sit at God's right hand idly doing nothing; he is interceding for us. But this should not be understood as meaning that Christ in his majesty intercedes for us in a human fashion and with the gestures that are customary in this world, in the way a friend might petition a worldly judge on behalf of a friend. No, it rather means that although he is now reigning, Christ is nevertheless still moved even today (though in a heavenly and divine manner) by our weaknesses and afflictions, and that he stands guard over us before the judgment seat of God. Commentary on Romans (1564).[25]

Christ, Not the Saints, Is Our Intercessor. Balthasar Hubmaier: Because our Head, Christ Jesus, intercedes for us with the Father, I hold that also the dear saints who are in heaven and are of one will with their Head, Christ, and with members of his body, intercede along with him, for their will is subject to the will of Christ. But I know of no Scripture at all that says we are to call on them for help and salvation in our needs, for all the Scriptures point us to Christ as our advocate and Mediator, as I have also noted in my catechism. Apologia.[26]

We Are Not Alone in the Battle. Thomas Wilcox: First he tells us that we are not alone in that case and conflict, but that we have Christ our head and captain not only as a common companion—as you would say—with us in those afflictions, but one that has gone before us in that path

and straight way, as having broken—as you would say—the ice for us and before us, so that we might go forward with less danger and more boldness.

In worldly warfare it doubtless adds no small courage to the common soldier that he has others with him to sustain the hard assaults of the enemy. Yet if he has a valiant and courageous captain he is much more cheered and heartened, for soldiers do not look as much at each other as they do at their ringleader. And if they are persuaded that he is someone that can, as it were, with a word or expression confound their adversaries, how valiantly they not only mount the first attack but mightily hold on to the end of the field. So that every one of them may at the end of the skirmish or pitched battle carry away with them some notable ensign or token of the victory. Oh, how much more ought this to comfort us in spiritual combats and conflicts, that we do not come alone to the field but have with us—besides the rest of God's saints and infinite number of holy angels—God and all his graces to be, as it were, a brazen wall for us. Yes, Christ Jesus himself, the head of men and women and angels, who has not only all creatures at his command to use for our good and the hurt of his and our enemies, but with the least breath of his mouth, is able to overthrow them, as "he did those that came to take him," and with the meanest spark of his majesty, to confound and abolish them, as he shall do to the "Antichrist with the brightness of his coming." A Christian and Learned Exposition (1587).[27]

Rightly Learn to Know the Ascended Christ. Menno Simons: O my faithful reader, rightly learn to know Christ Jesus. He is not like the fabled Proteus, but he is now the everlasting, almighty Son of the eternal, omnipotent God, and not a perishable creature, bread and wine. Oh no! he is unchangeable through all eternity. Neither can he be confined in any house, church, or chamber, in silver or golden vessels; for, according

---

[25]Brenz, *In Epistolam*, 230-31.
[26]CRR 5:556*; citing Mt 11; 1 Tim 2:5; 1 Jn 2:1.

[27]Wilcox, *A Christian and Learned Exposition*, 14-15*; citing Jn 18:4-6; 2 Thess 2:8.

to his eternal, divine being, heaven is his throne and the earth his footstool, and according to his holy humanity, he ascended into heaven and sits at the right hand of his Father. He is the eternal and almighty power, brightness, Word, truth, wisdom, and image of God. He has all power in heaven above and on earth below; all things are under him. Every knee has to bow, and every tongue to confess to him, that he is Lord, to the honor and glory of his Father, and he will not again appear in the flesh, but he will come in the clouds of heaven, to judge the goats and sheep. OF THE CORRUPTIONS OF THE HOLY SUPPER (1565).[28]

THE SIGNIFICANCE OF CHRIST'S ENTRY INTO GLORY. VAVASOR POWELL: The first reason is this: that otherwise Christ would never have entered into glory. Note that the apostle places emphasis on this, "that God raised him up from the dead and gave him glory."

Once Jesus Christ had come down from heaven and had undertaken this work, there were doubtless no admissions into heaven until he had finished it. If you should see a judge take a malefactor that had been arraigned before him at the bar and lead him by the hand and exalt him to sit at his own right hand, would you not conclude and say, "Surely this man is not only acquitted from all that was laid to his charge, but he is in great favor also with the judge"? Now, God the Father judged and condemned his Son, for—if I may say so—humankind had not as great a hand in the crucifying of Christ as God had. Mark that it is said, "Thus he was put to death by the determinate counsel of God." Now, after his death, God led him out of his grave into his glory, and this was a sign that there was nothing that could be further laid to the charge of Christ, nor to the charge of those that Christ then undertook for. This is the argument of the apostle, "Who shall lay anything (he says) to the charge of God's elect? It is Christ that died, yes,

rather, who is risen, who also sits at the right hand of God." And he puts a "rather" on it. "Yes, *rather*, who is risen, and sits on the right hand of God."

The second reason is this, that the gospel is now published to men and women. We would never have had the gospel had not Jesus Christ finished the work. You know, until Christ was taken up into glory there were *two* great things that were kept back in heaven from men and women. First, there was the Spirit of God, and second, the counsel of God. Both these are wrapped up in the gospel. These two (I say) were kept back from men and women until Christ went up, the Spirit immediately came down, and the counsel of the Lord began to be revealed in a marvelous way unto men and women. This is an absolute and clear sign the work was done; for Christ said, "Except I go away, the Comforter cannot come." I say it is a sign Jesus Christ had finished the work, for do you think that the Lord would have sent his gospel to men and women to tell others, or his Spirit to assure men and women that it was done, if it had not been done. GOD THE FATHER GLORIFIED (1650).[29]

CERTAINTY ABOUT THE PROMISES OF GOD. BENEDETTO DA MANTOVA AND MARCANTONIO FLAMINIO: When I look to the promises of God, who promises me forgiveness of my sins by the blood of Jesus Christ, I am as sure that I have obtained it, and that I have his favor, as I am sure that he who has made the promises and covenants cannot lie or deceive. And through this steadfast faith I become righteous by Christ's righteousness, through which I am saved, and my conscience quieted. Has he not given his most innocent body into the hands of sinners for our sins? Has he not shed his blood to wash away my iniquities? Why then do you vex yourself, O my soul? Put your trust in the Lord, who bears you so great love that to deliver you from eternal death it pleased him that his only Son should suffer death and passion.

[28]Simons, *A Foundation and Plain Instruction*, 77-78*; citing Is 66; Acts 7; 17; Mk 16; Acts 1; Rom 8; Heb 1; Mt 28; Eph 1; Phil 2; Mt 26; Rev 1; Mt 25.

[29]Powell, *God the Father Glorified*, 27-28*; citing 1 Pet 1:21; Acts 4:28; Jn 16:7.

He took upon himself our poverty to give us his riches; laid our weakness upon himself to establish us in his strength; became mortal to make us immortal; came down to earth to bring us up to heaven; and became the Son of Man with us to make us the children of God with himself. "Who then is he that shall accuse us?" . . . Is there not now to be seen grace, remission of sins, righteousness, consolation, joy, peace, life, heaven, Christ, and God? Trouble me no more then, O my soul. For what is the law? What is sin? What is death and the devil in comparison of these things? Therefore, trust in God, who has not spared his own dear Son, but given him to the death of the cross for your sins and has given you victory through him. THE BENEFIT OF CHRIST'S DEATH.[30]

CHRIST IS OUR MODEL FOR TRUSTING GOD.

THOMAS GOODWIN: This challenge we first hear published by Jesus Christ himself, our only Champion. "He is near that justifies me. Who will contend with me?" They were Christ's words there and spoken of God's justifying him; and these are every believer's words here intended of God's justifying them. Christ is brought in there uttering them as standing at the high priest's tribunal, when they spat on him and buffeted him, as in verses 4 and 5 when he was condemned by Pilate. Then he exercised this faith on God his Father, saying, "He is near that justifies me." And as in the time of his condemnation he stood in our stead, so in this his hope of his justification, he speaks in our stead also and as representing us in both. And on this the apostle here pronounces, in similar words, about all the elect, "It is God that justifies. Who shall accuse? Christ was condemned, yea, has died. Who, therefore, shall condemn?" See here the commu-nion we have with Christ in his death and condem-nation, yes, in his very faith: if he trusted in God, so may we, and we shall as certainly be delivered. SERMON ON ROMANS 8:34.[31]

8:35 What Can Separate Us from the Love of God?

WHAT DOES IT MEAN TO BE VICTORIOUS?

JOHANNES BRENZ: "What then?" you ask, "Is it really to overcome, if someone should be cruelly slaughtered by an enemy? Stephen was stoned; James and Paul were killed with a sword—who would say that they carried away the victory?"

Think with me now what it really means to "carry away the victory" from the enemy. It is not to deprive an enemy of his faculties or even of his life, just as being "overcome" by an enemy is not the same as being slain by an enemy. Rather, to be victorious is to retain and preserve inviolate those things that the enemy attacks in order to take from you. Through his instruments, Satan attacks the saints by stealing their faculties, by exile, torture, and death so that he might take from them their heavenly goods, their eternal homeland, their true happiness, and their eternal righteousness and life. Consequently, the saints "carry away the victory from Satan" when they retain their true and eternal goods, even if they should lose their worldly faculties and bodily life. Christ speaks of this kind of victory when he says, "Whoever should love his life for my sake will find it." COMMENTARY ON ROMANS (1564).[32]

THE LOVE OF CHRIST.

THEODORE BEZA: "From the love of Christ?" *Apo tēs agapēs tou Christou?* This is the love with which Christ loved us, or rather God in Christ, as verse 39 will soon explain. Therefore not a few interpret this wrongly in an active sense as the love with which we love Christ in return. For they are deceived by the notion that the apostle is speaking of our own constancy and not that of Christ himself. They ought, however, to have perceived that Paul has set the love with which God in Christ pursued us as the basis for this constancy of ours, from which we would be separated only if in some way we were able to fall away from his freely given kindness. But this love

---

[30]Benedetto and Flaminio, *Benefit of Christ's Death*, 89-90*; citing Rom 4:5, 24.

[31]Goodwin, *Christ Set Forth*, 1-2*; citing Is 50:8.

[32]Brenz, *In Epistolam*, 233; citing Mt 10:39; 16:25.

of God rests, says the apostle, on his purpose, which is unchangeable, and Christ himself is the guarantee of God's kindness toward us. Therefore, what calamity can there be that would persuade us that God is estranged from us? So beginning from the lesser, he proceeds to the greater: from "affliction" he passes over to "anguish," and from there to "persecution," from which follow those things he mentions last. Major Annotations (1594).[33]

The Saints Overcome by the Strength of the Son. Johannes Brenz: Hilary wrote: "When it is slaughtered, the church prevails."[†] And Tertullian: "The blood of the martyrs is the seed of the church."[‡] Even if the saints are handed over to death, they still carry away the victory—that is, the one that is heavenly. This is the highest and everlasting victory. By whose strength, then, or by whose power do the saints overcome? Is it by their own strength? Absolutely not! But it is by him who loved us, namely, he who so loved us that he chose to see his own Son cruelly lacerated on a cross rather than to pay no heed to our destruction. Commentary on Romans (1564).[34]

Stirring Up the Constancy of Believers. Wolfgang Musculus: Indeed, the verb "separate" implies this very thing. Love unites the lover and the beloved. If a separation occurs so that one party is shut out of the communion of love by the other, it's the one who ceases to be loved that is said to be "excluded," not the one who stops loving. Now the apostle does not say, "who will separate God from our love," but rather "who will separate us (that is, exclude us) from the love of God?"

It is also clearly intelligible what he means, for it can be expounded in this way: "Who can cause us to stop being loved by God? Who would be able to make God angry at us so that he ceases to love us?" It's also along these lines that the constancy of God's love is proclaimed, a love so firm that it can

in no way change or collapse or be hindered, so that those whom he began to love before they even existed he continues to love until the end. And if the words that followed did not hinder this meaning, it would be a most beautiful reading and wholly comforting. . . .

But it can also be explained in another way: "Who will separate us from the love of God?" That is, "What thing can be of such great weight or so efficacious that it could snatch us away from this love of God so that we do not endure in his grace or we wholly despise his grace so that we let it become nullified within us? What thing can go so far as to compel us to render ourselves destitute of this love that is so ineffable and amazing, that we should forsake it and deprive ourselves of it, which is what we would do if we failed to continue in our faith in Christ?" According to this sense, it is more the constancy of believers in their faith that is commended or stirred up rather than God in his love.

It's this latter explanation that pleases me most, on account of the things that Paul adds afterward, which are the kind of things that by the cunning of Satan are more aimed at dislodging us from our constancy in faith rather than pushing God out of his love for us. For if he had added instead, "or weakness of faith? or impatience?" or other things of this kind it would seem more fitting that we should understand the verse in the first sense. But because he makes mention of adversity and tribulation, I think it is clear that the apostle was setting forth the latter sense. Commentary on Romans (1555).[35]

Disposition of the True Christian's Heart Toward God. Benedetto da Mantova and Marcantonio Flaminio: This holy predestination maintains true Christians in a continual spiritual joy, increases in them the endeavor of good works, inflames them with the love of God, and makes them an enemy to the world and to sin. Who is so fierce and hard-hearted,

---

[33]Beza, *Annotationes Majores*, 101.
[34]Brenz, *In Epistolam*, 234. [†]Hilary, *On the Trinity* 4. [‡]Tertullian, *Apologeticum* 50.

[35]Musculus, *In Epistolam Apostoli Pauli*, 203.

who, knowing that God of his mercy has made him his child from everlasting, will not by and by be inflamed to love God? Who are of so vile and base courage that they will not esteem all the pleasures, all the honors, and all the riches of the world as filthy mire, when they know that God has made them a citizen of heaven? Yes, these are the ones that worship God rightly in spirit and truth, receiving all things (as well in prosperity as in adversity) at the hand of God their Father, and always praising and thanking him for all, as their good Father who is righteous and holy in all his works. These, being inflamed with the love of God and armed with the knowledge of their predestination, fear neither death, nor sin, nor the devil, nor hell. Neither do they know what the wrath of God is, for they see nothing in God except love and fatherly kindness toward them. And if they fall into any troubles, they accept them as tokens of God's favor, crying out with St. Paul, "Who is it that shall separate us from God's love? . . . In all these things we get the upper hand through him that has loved us." THE BENEFIT OF CHRIST'S DEATH.[36]

NOT "NOTHING CAN SEPARATE US FROM HIS RIGHTEOUSNESS." WOLFGANG MUSCULUS: Otherwise what point is there in separating what is not united? Or rather, who would be able to separate what is not united? A separation cannot occur except among those who are united. Therefore, he declares that we are united to God in God's love when he says "from the love of God." Seeing that there is so great a discontinuity between humanity and God, it is an amazing thing that humanity is united with God, and so united that humanity is completely unable to be separated from him. Therefore, I admonish not in vain that we must observe where the apostle locates this unity. He doesn't locate it in the truth. For among our ranks there is only the lie. He doesn't locate it in righteousness, for in this we fail most of all. Nor does it place it in ability, for we are weak. If he had said,

"'Who will separate us from' the truth, or from righteousness, or from ability, or from the holiness 'of God?'" we would not have near as much consolation as we do by his saying "Who will separate us from the love of God?" It is God's love that preserves us in unity with God. Why? Because it altogether absorbs all our uncleanness, weakness, imperfection, and injustices, and makes saints and righteous men and women out of sinners, perfect men and women out of the imperfect, clean men and women out of the unclean. There is nothing that it does not pardon, for it is attributed to love that it "covers a multitude of sins." Therefore, it is this same love that both unites us with God and that preserves us so united. COMMENTARY ON ROMANS (1555).[37]

BORNE UP BY THE WINGS OF THE PROMISES OF GOD. JOHN CALVIN: Those who are persuaded of God's kindness toward them are able to stand firm in the heaviest afflictions. These usually harass people in no small degree, and for various reasons; because they interpret them as tokens of God's wrath, or think themselves to be forsaken by God, or see no end to them, or neglect to meditate on a better life, or for other similar reasons. But when the mind is purged from such mistakes, it becomes calm and quietly rests. The import of the words is this, that whatever happens, we ought to stand firm in this faith, that God, who once in his love embraced us, never ceases to care for us. For he does not simply say that there is nothing which can tear God away from his love to us, but he means that the knowledge and lively sense of the love that he testifies to us is so vigorous in our hearts that it always shines in the darkest afflictions. As clouds, though they obscure the clear brightness of the sun, do not yet wholly deprive us of its light, so God, in adversities, sends forth through the darkness the rays of his favor, lest temptations should overwhelm us with despair. Nay, our faith, supported by God's promises as by wings, makes its way upward to heaven through all

---

[36]Benedetto and Flaminio, *Benefit of Christ's Death*, 99-100*.

[37]Musculus, *In Epistolam Apostoli Pauli*, 204; citing 1 Pet 4:8.

intervening obstacles. It is indeed true that adversities are tokens of God's wrath when viewed in themselves, but when pardon and reconciliation precede, we ought to be assured that God, though he chastises us, yet never forgets his mercy. He indeed thus reminds us of what we have deserved, but he no less testifies that our salvation is an object of his care, while he leads us to repentance. COMMENTARY ON ROMANS 8:35.[38]

WHATEVER COMES, FAITH RESIDES IN THE BELIEVER'S HEART. LEUPOLD SCHARN-SCHLAGER: Any believer who should fall into this blindness and presumptuousness, claiming to become holy or a Christian before God through good works, falls from faith and from all aforementioned gifts that come through faith. But whoever has the faith stated above has a comfort that works can never achieve. Indeed, those in the Old Testament did not achieve it through the external keeping of God's laws and commandments, not to mention other works of human invention. For what can harm, horrify, or damn a believer, as Paul proclaims? If sin and death come on believers, faith resides in their heart—faith that Christ died for their sins, that Christ has become theirs, and that their unrighteousness and sins are no longer theirs but Christ's. CONCERNING TRUE FAITH AND COMMON SALVATION IN CHRIST.[39]

THE SECURITY OF HIS LOVE. JUAN DE VALDÉS: It appears that St. Paul by these words satisfies the doubt that might lie repressed in the mind of one weak in the faith, who might say, "But the thing is, how can I maintain the love of God in myself, so that all these privileges may attach to me?" I understand Paul to satisfy this person by saying, "Since it is a fact that when we love God all things work together for our good, that the creatures desire our welfare, that the Holy Spirit himself desires it, and asks it, that God himself is on our side, and Christ intercedes for us, rest assured

there is nothing in the personal life that can separate us from the love of God, through which we enjoy so many privileges." COMMENTARY ON ROMANS (1556).[40]

THE GRAND MANNER OF THE RHETORIC EMPHASIZES IMPORTANCE. DESIDERIUS ERASMUS: Now the whole passage abounds with inquiries and questions. If one distinguishes sharpness or intensity in speech from sublimity (which among the rhetoricians is the third style of speaking), a question, which is more forceful than even an emphatic assertion, contributes to sharpness. It is more forceful to say: "How will he not give us all things along with him?" than to say: "Beyond a doubt, he will give us all things along with him." For the listener is thus hard-pressed by this confidence in the manifest truth—as though he would have nothing to say in reply. Likewise there is more intensity [in the questions]: whether tribulation? or distress? or persecution? or famine? than in statements of denial. Contributing to the intensity are phrases that begin with the same expression, such as I have just now quoted; also, for example, "neither death, nor life, nor angels." At the same time, it is these phrases in particular that make the speech elevated, because Paul, breathed on, as it were by the divine power, says nothing in the low style. For loftily does he declare: "We know that to those who love God all things," and so on. Furthermore the whole passage consists of both things and persons that are great and eminent: death, life, might, height, God, Christ, at the right hand of God, angels, principalities, powers. This too no doubt has a grand air: "In all these things *hypernikōmen* [we are more than conquerors]," and "for I am certain." What did Cicero ever say that effected more fully the grand manner? ANNOTATIONS ON THE EPISTLE TO THE ROMANS (1516, 1519, 1522, 1527, 1535).[41]

---

[38]CTS 38:326-27* (CO 49:165-66).
[39]CRR 12:537*.

[40]Valdés, *Commentary upon St. Paul's Epistle*, 145*.
[41]CWE 56:233-34*.

THE CHURCH IS INSEPARABLE FROM GOD AND HIS LOVE. LEUPOLD SCHARNSCHLAGER: The church of Christ is preserved in God's grace and favor through the great treasure of faith we have mentioned. This grace and favor are the church's constant help. However dark the times may appear, faith persists all the way, with its attendant love and accompanying Holy Spirit as comforter. The church of Christ remains inseparable from God and his love; fellow travelers and mercenaries damage only themselves—and the gates of hell will not overcome the rightly built church of Christ. May God help us to that end, through Jesus Christ. Amen. CONCERNING TRUE FAITH AND COMMON SALVATION IN CHRIST.[42]

8:36 Regarded as Sheep for Slaughter

SHEEP FROM THE FLOCK OF THE ONLY GOOD SHEPHERD. DIRK PHILIPS: You also [are] a sheep from the flock of the only Good Shepherd, Jesus Christ; [you have been] led for a long time on his precious pasture and were given to drink the clear water out of the fountain of his grace and truth. Through that your soul is fattened well according to my undoubted hope, through such spiritual food and drink. [Therefore], be still, patient, and courageous in your suffering, so that you conquer for the sake of righteousness; and if you will be led to the slaughter bench at any time, reflect on your only good, trustworthy Shepherd Jesus Christ, who has gone before you [and] left you an example that you should follow in his footsteps. For it happens with the Christians just as the prophet said, Oh Lord, we are killed daily for your sake and counted as sheep for the slaughter, but in all this we conquer, says the apostle, through the one who has loved us. TWO ADDITIONAL LETTERS.[43]

LIKE SHEEP DESTINED FOR THE KITCHEN. PETER MARTYR VERMIGLI: Since it is difficult to persuade our reason and our flesh that we are loved by God when we are suffering affliction, Paul adds a proof from the Scriptures to confirm this paradox. And here we need faith, which depends on the Word of God. This testimony was taken from Psalm 44 in which those people—we are not to doubt that they were most dear to God—are shown complaining about their tribulations. "We are," they say, "like sheep set aside for slaughter." That is, there is nothing more certain than that they are destined to be killed. For there are certain sheep that are raised for their wool or for breeding. For those sheep, life is permitted for a certain time. Others are destined for the kitchen. They are killed on particular days, just as they were meant to be. And so the saints complain in the same psalm that they are the same as the sheep intended for food. They complain that they are dealt with differently than their elders had been, to whom God had shown great favor. God had enriched them, fought on their behalf, permitted them the victory, and made them well-known, with excellent names and titles. But we were dealt with differently, they say. For we have been given over to the enemy, just like sheep for slaughter, so that they can do with us whatever they please. Indeed the truth is that God desired this, and when he declared his love for the saints and confirmed the truth of his doctrine, he adorned them with good things and abilities of this kind, so that even idolaters would understand that God, whom the patriarchs worshiped, was the Creator of the world and giver of all good things, and that everything that people desire is in his pleasure. So when he had declared it sufficiently, he also made them so valiant by adversity that their stout courage and invincible steadfastness testified that the doctrine of God is true. God has likewise declared in this matter that he is the giver of all the good things of the mind and of heroic virtues, and that his power is so great that he is able to draw out the same result from contrary events. COMMENTARY ON ROMANS (1560).[44]

---

[42]CRR 12:544*.
[43]CRR 6:622*; citing Ezek 34:18; Mal 4:3; Rom 12:12; Mt 5:10; 1 Pet 2:21; Ps 44:22.

[44]Vermigli, *In Epistolam S. Pauli*, 740-41; collated with *Learned and Fruitfull Commentaries*, 232v*; citing Ps 44:11, 22.

Prayer for the Persecuted. Hans Schla⁻fer and Leonhard Frick:

> O compassionate God,
> we pray to you for all our brothers and sisters
> wherever they might be around the world—
> persecuted, hunted, scattered, imprisoned, anc
>   killed daily.
> Look down on them and us from your holy
>   place,
> your heavenly dwelling!
> Look down with the eyes
> of your fatherly compassion and goodness!
> Do not let us be swallowed and destroyed, body
>   and soul,
> by lions, wolves, and a seven-headed dragon
> with its huge, gaping jaws.

A Simple Prayer, Confession of Sin, and Open Confession of Faith.[45]

Fix Your Eyes on Christ and the Endur⁻ing Church. Niels Hemmingsen: He lists those things by which the souls of believers are greatly shaken for a while, and so that believers might know that it is not unusual for the sons and daughters of God to be afflicted in this life, he adds a testimony from Psalm 43 in which the church complains that she is exposed to so many various misfortunes because of her confession of Christ. But because God is always present to his Christ, he promises that we will overcome through Christ who loved us. Therefore, this statement of Paul's also contrasts the image of the enduring church with carnal judgment and human reason. Reason concludes that God is angry with us and that's why we are under a perpetual cross. But the spirit of believers fixes its eyes on the enduring image of the church, and on Christ himself, whence the godly conclude that God cares for them and someday in the future all the trials of this life will have a happy end. Commentary on Romans (1562).[46]

Prayer for Endurance in Persecution. Hans Schlaffer and Leonhard Frick:

> O heavenly Father, we appeal to you
> most diligently, most reverently
> concerning the hour you alone know,
> when you will fully justify us, each of us.
> "For your sake we are killed every day
> and considered as sheep for the slaughter"—
> daily they take us to the butcher.
> When the tyrants, your servants,
> come to interrogate, torture, and kill us,
> let us not be so terrified that we fall into dismay
> but wait patiently with a willing and joyful spirit
> and so overcome the weakness of the flesh.

A Simple Prayer, Confession of Sin, and Open Confession of Faith.[47]

8:37 In Him We Are More Than Conquerors

The Unusual Victors. Wolfgang Musculus: "The nature of this victory." Consider how wonderful this victory is, how admirable are the victors, and how different it is from the ways and nature of the world. In the world, those who heap affliction on others are considered the victors, but here they are those who suffer. There the victors are those who oppress others, but here it is those who are oppressed; there it is those who persecute others, but here it is those who endure persecution; there it is those who revel in pleasures and abound with wealth, but here it is those who are beset by hunger and nakedness; there it is those who bring dangers with them, but here it is those who are endangered; there it is those who slay others, but here it is those who are slain. Who, I ask, recognizes the afflicted, oppressed, agitated, famished, naked, endangered, and those everywhere subject to death as *victors*? How are they victors? This victory is not located in preserving bodily goods and this bodily life, but in preserving that which Satan desires to wrest away from us. He wants to

---

[45]CRR 12:274-75*; citing Rev 12:13-17; 13:1-10.
[46]Hemmingsen, *Commentarius in Epistolam*, 307.

[47]CRR 12:276*.

wrest away faith in Christ since he knows that it is believers that are saved; he wants any of them who will, to be under his power and be lost. But because he is unable in any way to achieve this, he is rightly said to be overcome so that his attendants, such as troublemakers, oppressors, persecutors, plunderers, robbers . . . and murderers, who are regarded in this world as having the greatest power and reigning over others, are in reality the defeated ones, overcome by the long-suffering of the saints. An example of this is Job and Satan: which one was the victor? Which one was defeated? Satan struck him with calamity and harassed him, but Job endured all of it and so emerged as the victor by his long-suffering, so that he not only did not lose his faith in God, but also received back twofold what he had lost and in the end had seven more sons and three daughters. So it is with us also, if we are long-suffering we will not only preserve our faith but also "receive a hundredfold and life eternal" when we inherit much more glorious and better things than our present bodily goods. Is this not *hypernikaō*, "being more than conquerors"? COMMENTARY ON ROMANS (1555).[48]

THE TWO PARTS OF A CROSS. ERASMUS SARCERIUS:

We overcome by a cross. Therefore, one ought not be downcast under one's cross; one ought not grieve because of a cross. Please understand what a cross is, and what are its parts. A cross is: to be mortified all the day on account of righteousness or the truth, and it is to overcome in all these trials, by the cross, through the power of God who loves and watches over us.

There are two parts to a cross: to suffer and to overcome, to die and to live, to be oppressed, and to be set free. Here many notable doctrines are involved. The first is, that the first part of a cross, which is to suffer, will most certainly be followed by the second part, which is victory and liberation. Second, that God the Father and Christ are stronger than our cross. Third, that we overcome the cross, and overcome every danger in that cross,

not by our own powers, but by the protection and presence of God the Father loving us together with his Son. The fourth concerns the lack of power that crosses and dangers have over us, and the superior power of God and of Christ. NOTES ON ROMANS (1541).[49]

THE STRENGTH FOR THE VICTORY COMES FROM THE ONE WHO LOVED US. WOLFGANG MUSCULUS:

In the end, this constancy and strength for emerging victorious does not come from us. It is, he says, "through him who loved us." It is something to recognize one's own weakness. But so far from making any progress, this will only cause despair unless it is also known from whom our help is to be sought. Further, he does not say "we are unable to do this by ourselves, but we can do it with the help of others." Instead he points to him from whom this constancy and this power of overcoming is furnished. It is "through him who loved us." Who is that? There are many who preach about the love of the saints. Why, therefore, did he mention only one, and not many? Why didn't he say "through *them* who loved us, angels and saints?" Instead he said, "through him who loved us." Is there, therefore, only one who has loved us? Have not the saints loved us and still love us? Certainly they do—who denies that? But why is it that only one is set forth here? It's because in order to sustain those who are loved it isn't enough to love them if one lacks the power to sustain them. Only One has this power, and therefore mention of this One alone is made. It is by him that we overcome all things. Who is he? It is enough for the apostle to simply say, "through him who loved us," for he judged that this description would be clear from what he had said earlier, so that there was no need for him to specify whom he was speaking of expressly by name. Do you want to know who it is? Who was it that "did not spare his own Son, but delivered him up for us all"? Who else do you think has shown a love for us equivalent to this? The phrase "through him who loved

---

[48]Musculus, *In Epistolam Apostoli Pauli*, 207; citing Mt 19:29.   [49]Sarcerius, *In Apostolam ad Romanos*, O4r-v.

us" is therefore a most sweet and brilliant periphrasis.[†] For in it is everything that is necessary for the purpose at hand, which is rooted in these two things: first, there must be power, and second there must be a will. The first is clear from the one being described, that is, God. He is omnipotent. This is not expressly stated since it is beyond doubt in the consciences of even the feeble-minded. The other is expressed in the description itself, since it is possible for this to be doubted. That's why he did not say "through him who is omnipotent, to whom nothing is impossible," but rather "through him who loved us." Which lover abandons the weak person whom he loves? The powerful easily desert the weak, but not lovers, as long as they have the ability. COMMENTARY ON ROMANS (1555).[50]

CHRIST'S VICTORY IS THE CAUSE OF OUR VICTORY IN THE FACE OF A CROSS. ERASMUS SARCERIUS: See here the reasons for our victory by the cross, which are not our powers, but by the power and protection of God the Father and of Christ. Therefore, our victory or liberation through a cross is the effect of God's power, not the work of our own powers. Christ hinted in this direction in the book of John, in which text Christ makes his own victory the cause of our victory in the face of a cross. NOTES ON ROMANS (1541).[51]

8:38-39 Nothing Can Separate Us from His Love

GOD'S LOVE FOR US FOUNDED ON THE SURE, FIXED, AND STABLE. JOHANNES BRENZ: What is the reason that no adverse matter, no afflictions, no labors are able to turn God away from that very love by which he embraces the believers in Christ? There is one—put forth a little earlier—namely, that the love of God, which pursues us, has not been established on something that is changeable and unsteady, that is, on our righteousness, wisdom,

or other human qualities, virtues, or merits, but on Christ the Son of God, who is perpetually righteous, who has atoned for our sins, sits at the right hand of God, and intercedes for us. All these things are sure, fixed, and stable. COMMENTARY ON ROMANS (1588).[52]

NOR THE ANGELS. PETER MARTYR VERMIGLI: The angels, as it is in the letter to the Hebrews, are ministering spirits who are sent out to do their work on behalf of those who will be heirs of salvation. This applies only to the good angels. Indeed, evil ones are often sent out to punish the impious and tempt humans, although their temptation among the predestined may not be harmful. Therefore, it stands that the evil angels contend in all ways to snatch us from God. However, they will not be able to bring this thing about, because of God's love toward us. About the good angels, however, we are able to suppose no such thing. Indeed, they go abroad as much as they are able, calling people back to God. And they rejoice wonderfully at the repentance of sins. Although even they are sometimes sent for the purpose of punishment. COMMENTARY ON ROMANS (1560).[53]

TERTULLIAN ON CHRIST'S LOVE. JOHANNES BRENZ: Before we undertake the explanation of the ninth chapter, we see added in this place, Tertullian's notable passage about the certainty of God's love toward us, so that we may learn from it why we ought to be persuaded that nothing in creation is able to separate us from the love by which God embraces us who believe in Christ. Therefore, Tertullian writes in his book *Of the Resurrection of the Flesh*, "We know," he says, "that God is good, and we further learn from Christ that he alone is the greatest. After commanding that we love our neighbor like ourselves, he will himself bring about that which he has instructed. He will love, in so many ways, the flesh that is close to him.

---

[50]Musculus, *In Epistolam Apostoli Pauli*, 207. [†]Indirect speech.
[51]Sarcerius, *In Apostolam ad Romanos*, O4v.
[52]Brenz, *In Epistolam*, 655.
[53]Vermigli, *In Epistolam S. Pauli Apostoli*, 748.

Though it is weak: but virtue is perfected by
    weakness.
Though feeble: but they do not desire a doctor
    unless they are sick.
Though shameful: but we surround with greater
    honor those who are more honorable.
Though ruined: But I, he says, have come to save
    that which has perished.
Though sinful: But for myself, he says, I prefer
    the salvation of a sinner, more than their
    death.
Though damned: But I, he says, will heal the
    flesh that is pierced."[†]
Thus says Tertullian.

COMMENTARY ON ROMANS (1564).[54]

PERSECUTION IS THE CHRISTIANS' BADGE.

JOHANNES BUGENHAGEN: "From the love of God."
This is that love that we laid hold of through Jesus
Christ our Lord. Notice how the words that have
been written to this point contain fire; they ought
to move our hearts so that we do not shrink back
from dangers, since one ought to persevere in them
according to the Lord's will. And unless we do this,
he will not acknowledge us as his. For persecution,
or "the cross," is the Christians' badge by which we
know that we are his children. INTERPRETATION
OF ROMANS (1531).[55]

A MARTYR'S SONG OF PRAYER.

URSULA HELLRIGEL:

Everlasting Father in heaven,
I call on you so ardently,
Do not let me turn from you.
Keep me in your truth
Until my final end.

O God, guard my heart and mouth,
Lord watch over me at all times,
Let nothing separate me from you,
Be it affliction, anxiety, or need,
Keep me pure in joy.

My everlasting Lord and Father,
Show and teach me,
Poor unworthy child that I am,
That I heed your path and way.
In this lies my desire.

To walk through your power into death,
Through sorrow, torture, fear, and want.
Sustain me in this,
O God, so that I may nevermore
Be separated from your love.

HYMN 36 IN *AUSBUND*.[56]

I AM PERSUADED.

MARTIN BUCER: Apart from
this exultation of the mind now proudly disdain-
ful of any evil whatsoever, there is also an issue
that Paul explains and enumerates by name and
with much repetition, because it is counted by
human beings among the special evils. "Who," he
says, "shall separate us from the love of God?" It
looks back on this: "Who shall accuse the elect of
God? Who is he that condemns?" For these also
pertain to the proof of the proposition made at
the beginning of the section: that "all things work
for the good of those who love God." Therefore,
the first argument is led here from the property of
love. For those who truly love can only act for the
benefit of those they love. God loves us lavishly
and constantly to such a degree that no one could
turn his love from us. And he works all in all.
Therefore, all things ought to benefit us. When
adverse things appear to be sent from an angry
God, far from his hating or not loving us, it shows
that there is nothing so adverse that can come
about that it excludes the love of God. That is, it
is for us an argument that we are still loved no
less by God. . . . So he says in the first place that
there is absolutely nothing that could exclude us
from the love of God, and by questioning, he
urges the confession of which he speaks in a very

---

[54]Brenz, *In Epistolam*, 657. [†]Tertullian, *De Resurrectione Carnis* 9.
[55]Bugenhagen, *In D. Pauli ad Romanos*, 103.

[56]Snyder and Huebert Hecht, *Profiles of Anabaptist Women*,
199-200*. Hymn printed in *Ausbund*, a Swiss Brethren hymnal.
Written most likely by Ursula Hellrigel, an Anabaptist
imprisoned for five years and then exiled. Sometimes attributed
to Annelein of Freiburg, an Anabaptist martyred in 1529.

bold manner, and even in a mocking tone: there is nothing whatever that is able to turn the love of God away from us. But he says *who*, not *what*, "shall separate us," that he may show himself to be secure from anything whatsoever that contends— even with the greatest strength—to pull us way from the love of God. And therefore, the proposition is this: of all things, nothing whatever shall be able to separate us from love. He does not prove this, but only states it and professes it to be true of him in these matters, not only with certainty, but also with security. And from then on, when a reason had to be offered for this holy confidence, he offers nothing other than, "I am persuaded" that there is nothing anywhere that can turn us away from love. COMMENTARY ON ROMANS (1536).[57]

No One Can Pluck Us from His Love.

ANTONIO DEL CORRO: A Roman Christian: These proofs of true faith so move my mind, that from now on I will not set a straw by the threats and intimidations of our emperor, or (to speak more rightly) of our tyrants, for their power may show cruelty to the body, but it can not pluck the mind away from faith and the love of God.

Paul: Now, to make an end of this treatise of justification, I am fully persuaded that we that are born anew and grafted into Christ are never overcome, neither by death, nor by life, nor by any other thing that can happen to us alive or dead. Yes, I am fully persuaded that neither angels, nor principalities, nor powers, nor things present, nor things to come, nor height, nor depth, nor any other thing that is in nature, is able to pluck us from the love of God which is in Christ Jesus our Lord, and much less that any torments of tyrants, no matter how cruel, can drive us away from Christ's declaration of friendship.† A THEOLOGICAL DIALOGUE (1575).[58]

Through Jesus Christ Our Lord. JUAN DE

VALDÉS: It is well to consider that to strengthen the love that we Christians have to God, Paul says that it is "through Jesus Christ our Lord," meaning that we love God because Christ has reconciled us with him. And our love increases by considering the love that God has shown in Jesus Christ our Lord, in executing the rigor of his justice upon his most precious flesh for that which had to be executed upon all who, through believing, come to be his members. For he is the Head that gives existence and life to those who are his members, and in this consists the benefit that the human race has received from God, through Jesus Christ our Lord. COMMENTARY ON ROMANS (1556).[59]

The Fountain of Love Flows from Christ.

JOHN CALVIN: He is the beloved son, in whom the Father is well pleased. If, then, we are through him united to God, we may be assured of the immutable and unfailing kindness of God toward us. He now speaks here more distinctly than before, as he declares that the fountain of love is in the Father and affirms that it flows to us from Christ. COMMENTARY ON ROMANS 8:39.[60]

The Infinite Benefits of God. THOMAS

CRANMER: To conclude, let us consider the infinite benefits of God mercifully shown and exhibited to us without our deserving them. He has not only created us from nothing, but as touching our soul, out of his infinite goodness he has exalted us from a piece of vile clay to his own similitude and likeness. And where we were condemned to hell and eternal death, he has given his own natural Son, being God eternal, immortal, and equal to himself in power and glory, to be incarnated and to take our mortal nature on him, with the infirmities of the same, and in the same nature to suffer the most shameful and painful death for our offenses, with the intent to justify us and to restore us to life everlasting. And doing so, he also made us his dear,

---

[57]Bucer, *Metaphrases et Enarrationes*, 363.
[58]Del Corro, *A Theological Dialogue*, 80v-81r*. †Lit. "the professing of Christ," which might refer to his acknowledgment of us or ours of him.

[59]Valdés, *Commentary upon St. Paul's Epistle*, 148*.
[60]CTS 38:332* (CO 49:168).

beloved children, brothers and sisters to his only Son our Savior Christ, and inheritors forever with him of his eternal kingdom of heaven. These great and merciful benefits of God, if they are considered, neither minister to us occasion to be idle and to live without doing any good works, nor stir us by any means to do evil things. But to the contrary, if we are not desperate persons with our hearts harder than stones, his benefits move us to render ourselves wholly to God and with all our will, hearts, might, and power, to serve him in all good deeds, obeying his commandments during our lives, and seeking in all things his glory and honor, not our sensual pleasures and vainglory. They move us evermore to dread willingly offending such a merciful God and loving Redeemer, whether in word, thought, or deed. And the benefits of God, deeply considered, move us for his sake also to be always ready to give ourselves to our neighbors, and, as much as we are able, to study with all our endeavor to do good to everyone. These are the fruits of the true faith: to do good to everyone as much as we are able, and, above all things, and in all things, to advance the glory of God, from whom alone we have our sanctification, justification, salvation, and redemption. To whom be ever glory, praise, and honor, world without end. Amen. HOMILY ON SALVATION (1547 AND 1560).[61]

ROMANS 8 AS HER DYING WORDS. EDWARD RAINBOW: A little before her death, patience, meekness, and low thoughts about herself, which had been her practice, now became her argument. Discoursing frequently with one of her nearest attendants, and seeing her and others passionately concerned and busily taking care of her, she willed them not to take so many pains for her who deserved less. Expostulating why any, especially herself, should at any time be angry; why any of these outward things should trouble her who deserved so little and had been blessed with so much? By which it might appear that she had brought into subjection all great thoughts; she had

cast down imaginations and every high thing, bringing into captivity every high thought, and submitting the world and her soul to the obedience of Christ, her passions were mortified and dead before her. So that for three or four days of her last sickness (for she endured no more) she lay as if she endured nothing; she called for her Psalms, which she could not now, as she had usually done, read herself (the greatest symptom of her extremity), and she caused them to be read to her. But that cordial of which I have spoken (kept in Romans 8, and in her heart), this her memory held to the last. This she soon repeated. No doubt to secure her soul against all fear of condemnation, being now wholly Christ's, having served him in the spirit of her mind and not loved to walk after the flesh, having (as often as she affectionately pronounced the words of this chapter) called in the testimony of the Spirit to bear her witness that she desired to be delivered from this bondage of corruption into the glorious liberty of the children of God; and so to strengthen her faith and hope by other comfortable arguments, contained in the rest of that chapter, being the last coherent words which this dying lady spoke.

The rest of the time—as if it had been spent in ruminating, digesting, and speaking inwardly to her soul what she had uttered with broken words—she lay quiet, and without any sign of distress. After a while, in a gentle, scarcely perceptible breath, she breathed out the soul that God had breathed into her, rendering it to the God who had given it to her. So she breathed her last and slept quietly, not to be awakened again except by the archangel's trumpet, which will call her to the resurrection of the just.

Thus at last, this goodly building fell; thus died this great wise woman, who while she lived was the honor of her sex and age, fitter for a history than a sermon.

. . . Let us all endeavor to follow her to the blessed mansions, by treading in the steps of her faith, virtue, and patience. That having fought the good fight, finished our course, and kept the faith, we may receive the crown of righteousness that the Lord, the righteous Judge shall give at that day to

---

[61]Cranmer, *Miscellaneous Writings*, 134*.

all that love his appearing. SERMON AT THE FUNERAL OF ANNE, COUNTESS OF PEMBROKE, DORSET, AND MONTGOMERY (1676).[62]

SOMETHING LOVELY AND WONDERFUL. HANS HAS VON HALLSTATT: One takes note of and recognizes this most clearly, however, when one is in fear, need, and tribulation; there he learns best what the eternal providence of God is, what good it is, how comforting it is. Otherwise one cannot lay hold of and experience it without danger, regardless of how attractively or beautifully one may debate the issue. All this can obviously be received and acknowledged only through the living Spirit. Here one learns with the heart that all our deeds and salvation arise from no other power than God's might. However much and often one rants against the elect, however much one wishes to push them into hell and afflict them with all plagues, nonetheless they are certain that no one may harm them and rip them from the hand of God, though all the world were against them—indeed, all the might of the devil.

Behold, this is why God sends his elect so many trials: so that his fatherly faithfulness might be recognized. For no misfortune comes to God's elect in which they do not experience something wonderful of the depths of God. For in all cases he reveals to them something lovely and wonderful, through which they love him more and become bolder in the face of all misfortune. CONCERNING THE COMFORT OF CHRISTIANS UNDER PERSECUTION.[63]

THE CHIEF VOICE OF THE GOSPEL: GOD LOVES US. PHILIPP MELANCHTHON: The conclusion of the last argument is as follows: Since God loves us so much he certainly will not cast us away, even though we are weak and are troubled by every kind of affliction. He calls the love of God that love with which God loves us, as Paul himself later interprets: "Because of him who loved us." At the end of the consolation Paul repeats this proper and chief voice of the gospel—that God loves us—because that is the most effective comfort in all afflictions, yes, in every act of calling on God. It far surpasses the understanding of the human heart, which is filled with doubting and fear and does not dare to declare that we are loved by God. Paul makes this comfort great with many words, as though he said: "Do not let the greatness of the afflictions break you, but in all terrors look upon this comfort, that God certainly loves you." COMMENTARY ON ROMANS (1540).[64]

---

[62]Rainbow, *Sermon*, 62-64*; citing Rom 8:1, 5, 4, 16, 21; 2 Tim 4:7-8.

[63]CRR 12:452*; citing Is 26:16; Jn 10:28; 17:12; 18:9.
[64]Melanchthon, *Commentary on Romans*, 183*.

Map of Europe at the Time of the Reformation

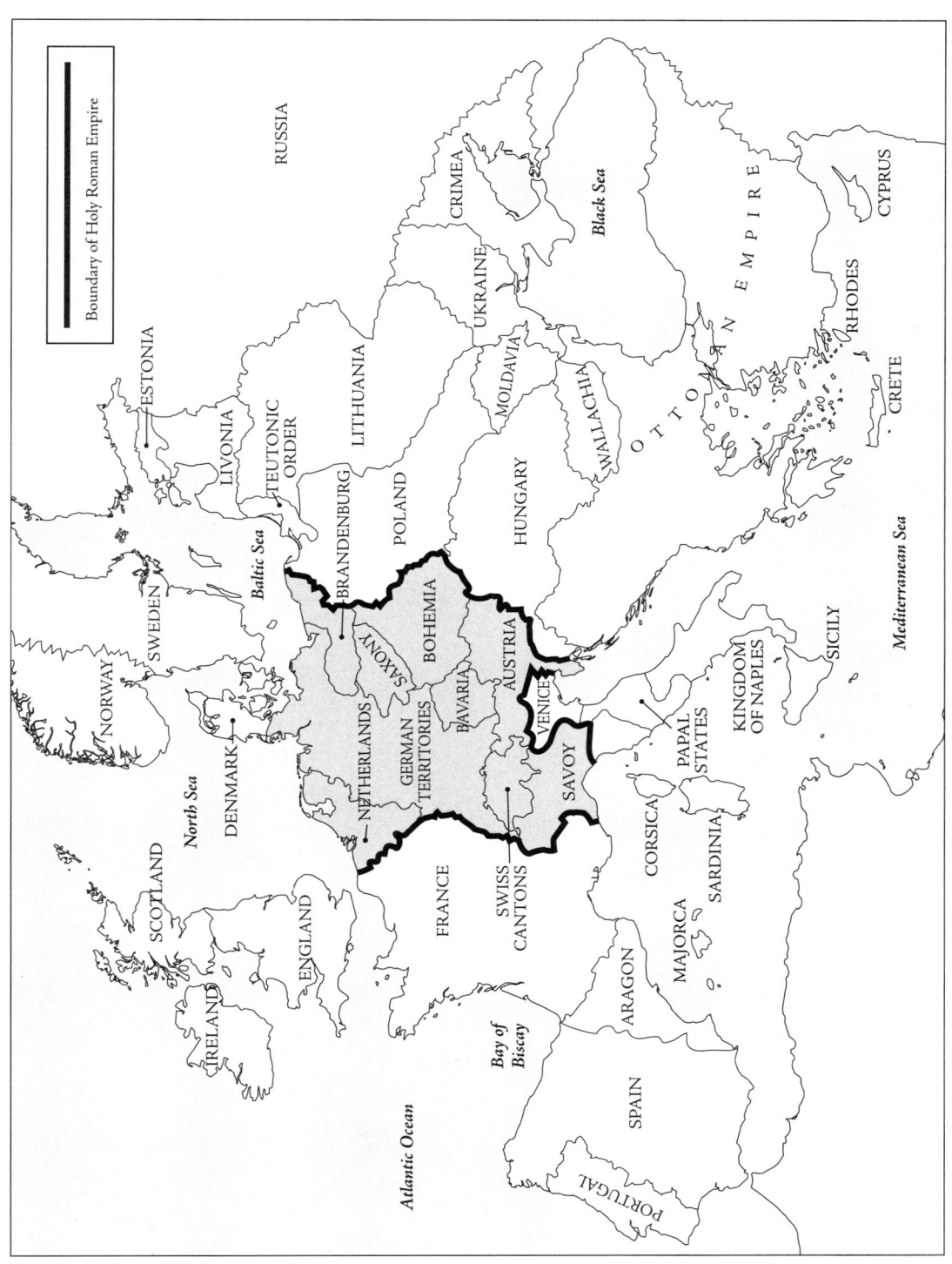

Timeline of the Reformation

	German Territories	France	Spain	Italy	Switzerland	Netherlands	British Isles
1309–1377		Babylonian Captivity of the Papacy					
1337–1453		d. Nicholas of Lyra Hundred Years' War	b. Paul of Burgos (Solomon ha-Levi)(d. 1435) Alonso Tostado (1400–1455)				Hundred Years' War
1378–1415		Western Schism (Avignon Papacy)		Western Schism			
1384							d. John Wycliffe
1414–1418					Council of Basel (1431–1437)		
1415				Council of Constance; d. Jan Hus; Martin V (r. 1417–1431); Council of Florence (1438–1445)			
1450	Invention of printing press						
1452				b. Leonardo da Vinci (d. 1519)			
1453				Fall of Constantinople			
1455–1485	b. Johannes Reuchlin (d. 1522)						War of Roses; rise of House of Tudor
1456	Gutenberg Bible						
1460				Pope Pius II issued *Execrabilis*			
1466		b. Jacques Lefèvre d'Étaples (d. 1536)					
1467						b. Desiderius Erasmus (d. 1536)	b. John Colet (d. 1519)
1469	b. Antoius Broickwy von Königstein (d. 541)						
1470				b. Santes Pagninus (d. 1541)			b. John (Mair) Major (d. 1550)
1475				b. Michelangelo (d. 1564)			
1478	b. Wolfgang Capito (d. 1541)		Ferdinand and Isabella	b. Jacopo Sadoleto (d. 1547)			b. Thomas More (d. 1535)

	German Territories	France	Spain	Italy	Switzerland	Netherlands	British Isles
1480	b. Balthasar Hubmaier (d. 1528); b. Andreas Bodenstein von Karlstadt (d. 1541)						
1481–1530			Spanish Inquisition				
1482					b. Johannes Oecolampadius (d. 1531)		
1483	b. Martin Luther (d. 1546)						
1484	b. Johann Spangenberg (d. 1550)				b. Huldrych Zwingli (d. 1531)		
1485	b. Johannes Bugenhagen (d. 1554)						b. Hugh Latimer (d. 1555)
1486	r. Frederick the Wise, Elector (d. 1525); b. Johann Eck (d. 1543)						
1488	b. Otto Brunfels (d. 1534)						b. Miles Coverdale (d. 1568)
1489	b. Thomas Müntzer (d. 1525); b. Kaspar von Schwenckfeld (d. 1561)						b. Thomas Cranmer (d. 1556)
1491	b. Martin Bucer (d. 1551)		b. Ignatius Loyola (d. 1556)				
1492			Defeat of Moors in Grenada; Columbus discovers America; expulsion of Jews from Spain	Alexander VI (r. 1492–1503)			
1493	b. Justus Jonas (d. 1555)						
1494							b. William Tyndale (d. 1536)
1496	b. Andreas Osiander (d. 1552)					b. Menno Simons (d. 1561)	
1497	b. Philipp Melanchthon (d. 1560); b. Wolfgang Musculus (d. 1563) b. Johannes (Ferus) Wild (d. 1554)						

	German Territories	France	Spain	Italy	Switzerland	Netherlands	British Isles
1498				d. Girolamo Savonarola	b. Conrad Grebel (d. 1526)		
1499	b. Johannes Brenz (d. 1570) b. Justus Menius (d. 1558)			b. Peter Martyr Vermigli (d. 1562)			
1500			b. Charles V (−1558)				
1501	b. Erasmus Sarcerius (d. 1559)						
1502	Founding of University of Wittenberg			Julius II (r. 1503–1513)		b. Frans Titelmans (d. 1537)	
1504					b. Heinrich Bullinger (d. 1575)		
1505	Luther joins Augustinian Order			b. Benedict Aretius (d. 1574)			
1506		b. Augustin Marlorat (d. 1562)		Restoration of St. Peter's begins			
1507				Sale of indulgences approved to fund building			
1508	b. Lucas Lossius (d. 1582)						
1509		b. John Calvin (d. 1564)					r. Henry VIII (−1547)
1510	Luther moves to Rome			b. Immanuel Tremellius (d. 1580)			b. Nicholas Ridley (d. 1555)
1511	Luther moves to Wittenberg						
1512				Sistine Chapel completed			
1512–1517				Fifth Lateran Council; rejection of conciliarism			
1513	Luther lectures on Psalms			r. Pope Leo X (−1521)			b. John Knox (d. 1572)
1515	Luther lectures on Romans	r. Francis I (−1547); b. Peter Ramus (d. 1572)					
1516		Est. French National Church (via Concordat of Bologna)		Concordat of Bologna		Publication of Erasmus's Greek New Testament	
1517	Tetzel sells indulgences in Saxony; Luther's Ninety-five Theses						

	German Territories	France	Spain	Italy	Switzerland	Netherlands	British Isles
1518	Heidelberg Disputation; Luther examined by Cajetan at Diet of Augsburg			Diet of Augsburg			
1519	Leipzig Disputation	b. Theodore Beza (d. 1605)	Cortés conquers Aztecs; Portuguese sailor Magellan circumnavigates the globe		Zwingli appointed pastor of Grossmünster in Zurich; b. Rudolf Gwalther (d. 1586)		
1520	Publication of Luther's "Three Treatises"; burning of papal bull in Wittenberg		Coronation of Charles V	Papal Bull v. Luther: *Exsurge Domine*			
1521	Luther excommunicated; Diet/Edict of Worms—Luther condemned; Luther in hiding; Melanchthon's *Loci communes*	French-Spanish War (–1526)	French-Spanish War; Loyola converts	Papal excommunication of Luther			Henry VIII publishes *Affirmation of the Seven Sacraments* against Luther; awarded title "Defender of the Faith" by Pope
1521–1522	Disorder in Wittenberg; Luther translates New Testament						
1521–1525		First and Second Habsburg–Valois War					
1522	Luther returns to Wittenberg; Luther's NT published; criticizes Zwickau prophets; b. Martin Chemnitz (d. 1586)		Publication of Complutensian Polyglot Bible under Cisneros		Sausage Affair and reform begins in Zurich under Zwingli		b. John Jewel (d. 1571)
1523	Knight's Revolt	Bucer begins ministry in Strasbourg	Loyola writes Spiritual Exercises	r. Pope Clement VII (–1534)	Iconoclasm in Zurich		
1524	Luther criticizes peasants; d. Johann von Staupitz					Erasmus's disputation on free will	
1524–1526	Peasants' War						
1525	Luther marries; execution of Thomas Müntzer; publication of Luther's *Bondage of the Will*				Abolition of mass in Zurich; disputation on baptism; first believers' baptism performed in Zurich		

	German Territories	France	Spain	Italy	Switzerland	Netherlands	British Isles
1526					Zurich council mandates capital punishment of Anabaptists	Publication of Tyndale's English translation of NT	
1527	d. Hans Denck (b. c. 1500) d. Hans Hut (b. 1490) b. Tilemann Hesshus (d. 1588)			Sack of Rome by mutinous troops of Charles V	First Anabaptist executed in Zurich; drafting of Schleitheim Confession		
1528	Execution of Hubmaier						
1529	Second Diet of Speyer; evangelical "protest"; publication of Luther's catechisms; Marburg Colloquy; siege of Vienna by Turkish forces	Abolition of mass in Strasbourg			d. Georg Blaurock (b. 1492)		Thomas More appointed chancellor to Henry VIII
1530	Diet of Augsburg; Confession of Augsburg	d. Francois Lambert (Lambert of Avignon) (b. 1487)	Charles V crowned Holy Roman Emperor				
1531	Formation of Schmalkaldic League				d. H. Zwingli; succeeded by H. Bullinger		
1532		Publication of Calvin's commentary on Seneca; conversion of Calvin	b. Francisco de Toledo (d. 1596)				
1533	b. Valentein Weigel (d. 1588)	Nicholas Cop addresses University of Paris; Cop and Calvin implicated as "Lutheran" sympathizers	b. Juan de Maldonado (d. 1583)				Thomas Cranmer appointed as Archbishop of Canterbury; Henry VIII divorces
1534	First edition of Luther's Bible published	Affair of the Placards; Calvin flees d. Guillame Briçonnet (b. 1470)		Jesuits founded; d. Cardinal Cajetan (Thomas de Vio) (b. 1469)			Act of Supremacy; English church breaks with Rome
1535	Bohemian Confession of 1535; Anabaptist theocracy at Münster collapses after eighteen months				b. Lambert Daneau (d. 1595)		d. Thomas More; d. John Fisher

	German Territories	France	Spain	Italy	Switzerland	Netherlands	British Isles
1536	Wittenberg Concord; b. Kaspar Olevianus (d. 1587)				First edition of Calvin's *Institutes* published; Calvin arrives in Geneva (–1538); First Helvetic Confession	Publication of Tyndale's translation of NT; d. W. Tyndale	d. A. Boleyn; Henry VIII dissolves monasteries (–1541)
1537					Calvin presents ecclesiastical ordinances to Genevan Council		
1538					Calvin exiled from Geneva; arrives in Strasbourg (–1541)		
1539		Calvin publishes second edition of *Institutes* in Strasbourg		d. Felix Pratensis			Statute of Six Articles; publication of Coverdale's Great Bible
1540				Papal approval of Jesuit order			d. Thomas Cromwell
1541	Colloquy of Regensburg	French translation of Calvin's *Institutes* published	d. Juan de Valdés (b. 1500/1510)		d. A. Karlstadt; Calvin returns to Geneva (–1564)		
1542	d. Sebastian Franck (b. 1499)			Institution of Roman Inquisition			War between England and Scotland; James V of Scotland defeated; Ireland declared sovereign kingdom
1543	Copernicus publishes *On the Revolutions of the Heavenly Spheres*; d. Johann Eck (Johann Maier of Eck) (b. 1486)						
1545–1547	Schmalkaldic Wars; d. Martin Luther			First session of Council of Trent			b. Richard Bancroft (d. 1610)
1546	b. Johannes Piscator (d. 1625)						
1547	Defeat of Protestants at Mühlberg	d. Francis I; r. Henri II (–1559)					d. Henry VIII; r. Edward VI (–1553)
1548	Augsburg Interim (–1552) d. Caspar Cruciger (b. 1504) b. David Pareus (d. 1622)						

	German Territories	France	Spain	Italy	Switzerland	Netherlands	British Isles
1549	d. Paul Fagius (b. 1504)	d. Marguerite d'Angoulême (b. 1492)			Consensus Tigurinus between Calvin and Bullinger		First Book of Common Prayer published
1550	b. Aegidius Hunnius (d. 1603)						
1551–1552				Second session of Council of Trent			
1552	d. Sebastian Münster (b. 1488) d. Friedrich Nausea (b. c. 1496)						Book of Common Prayer revised
1553	d. Johannes Aepinus (b. 1449)				Michael Servetus executed in Geneva		Cranmer's Forty-Two Articles; d. Edward VI; r. Mary I (d. 1558)
1554							Richard Hooker (d. 1600)
1555	Diet of Augsburg; Peace of Augsburg establishes legal territorial existence of Lutheranism and Catholicism b. Johann Arndt (d. 1621)	First mission of French pastors trained in Geneva				b. Sibbrandus Lubbertus (d. 1625)	b. Lancelot Andrewes (d. 1626) b. Robert Rollock (d. 1599); d. Hugh Latimer; d. Nicholas Ridley d. John Hooper
1556	d. Pilgram Marpeck (b. 1495) d. Konrad Pellikan (b. 1478) d. Peter Riedemann (b. 1506)		Charles V resigns			d. David Joris (b. c. 1501)	d. Thomas Cranmer
1557							Alliance with Spain in war against France
1558			d. Charles V				b. William Perkins (d. 1602); d. Mary I; r. Elizabeth I (–1603)
1559		d. Henry II; r. Francis II (–1560); first national synod of French reformed churches (1559) in Paris; Gallic Confession		First index of prohibited books issued	Final edition of Calvin's Institutes; founding of Genevan Academy	b. Jacobus Arminius (d. 1609)	Elizabethan Settlement

	German Territories	France	Spain	Italy	Switzerland	Netherlands	British Isles
1560	d. P. Melanchthon	d. Francis II; r. Charles IX (1574); Edict of Toleration created peace with Huguenots	d. Domingo de Soto (b. 1494)		Geneva Bible		Kirk of Scotland established; Scottish Confession
1561-1563				Third session of Council of Trent			
1561						Belgic Confession	
1562	d. Katharina Schütz Zell (b. 1497/98)	Massacre of Huguenots begins French Wars of Religion (–1598)					The Articles of Religion—in Elizabethan "final" form (1562/71); publication of Latin edition of Jewel's *Apology*
1563	Heidelberg Catechism						
1564				b. Galileo (d. 1642)	d. J. Calvin		b. William Shakespeare (d. 1616); publication of Lady Ann Bacon's English translation of Jewel's *Apology*
1566	d. Johann Agricola (b. 1494)			Roman Catechism	Second Helvetic Confession		
1567						Spanish occupation	Abdication of Scottish throne by Mary Stuart; r. James VI (1603–1625)
1568						d. Dirk Phillips (b. 1504) Dutch movement for liberation (–1645)	*Bishops' Bible*
1570		d. Johannes Mercerus (Jean Mercier)		Papal Bull *Regnans in Excelsis* excommunicates Elizabeth I			Elizabeth I excommunicated
1571	b. Johannes Kepler (d. 1630)		Spain defeats Ottoman navy at Battle of Lepanto				b. John Downame (d. 1652)
1572		Massacre of Huguenots on St. Bartholomew's Day		r. Pope Gregory XIII (1583–1585)		William of Orange invades	b. John Donne (d. 1631)
1574		d. Charles IX; r. Henri III (d. 1589)					

	German Territories	France	Spain	Italy	Switzerland	Netherlands	British Isles
1575	d. Georg Major (b. 1502); Bohemian Confession of 1575						
1576		Declaration of Toleration; formation of Catholic League		b. Giovanni Diodati (d. 1649)		Sack of Antwerp; Pacification of Ghent	
1577	Lutheran Formula of Concord						England allies with Netherlands against Spain
1578	Swiss Brethren Confession of Hesse d. Peter Walpot		Truce with Ottomans				Sir Francis Drake circumnavigates the globe
1579			Expeditions to Ireland			Division of Dutch provinces	
1580	Lutheran Book of Concord						
1581			d. Teresa of Avila				Anti-Catholic statutes passed
1582				Gregorian Reform of calendar			
1583							b. David Dickson (d. 1663)
1584		Treaty of Joinville with Spain	Treaty of Joinville; Spain inducted into Catholic League; defeats Dutch at Antwerp			Fall of Antwerp; d. William of Orange	
1585	d. Josua Opitz (b. c. 1542)	Henri of Navarre excommunicated		r. Pope Sixtus V (−1590)			
1586							Sir Francis Drake's expedition to West Indies; Sir Walter Raleigh in Roanoke
1587	d. Johann Wigand (b. 1523)	Henri of Navarre defeats royal army					d. Mary Stuart of Scotland
1588		Henri of Navarre drives Henri III from Paris; assassination of Catholic League Leaders	Armada destroyed				English Navy defeats Spanish Armada
1589		d. Henri III; r. Henri (of Navarre) IV (−1610)	Victory over England at Lisbon				Defeated by Spain in Lisbon
1590		Henri IV's siege of Paris		d. Girolamo Zanchi (b. 1516)			Alliance with Henri IV

	German Territories	France	Spain	Italy	Switzerland	Netherlands	British Isles
1592	d. Nikolaus Selnecker (b. 1530)						
1593		Henri IV converts to Catholicism					Books I-IV of Hooker's *Laws of Ecclesiastical Polity* published
1594		Henri grants toleration to Huguenots					
1595		Henri IV declares war on Spain; received into Catholic Church		Pope Sixtus accepts Henri IV into Church			Alliance with France
1596		b. René Descartes (d. 1650) b. Moïse Amyraut (d. 1664)					
1597							Book V of Hooker's *Laws of Ecclesiastical Polity* published
1598		Edict of Nantes; toleration of Huguenots; peace with Spain	Treaty of Vervins; peace with France				
1600	d. David Chytraeus (b. 1531)						
1601							b. John Trapp (d. 1669)
1602					d. Daniel Toussain (b. 1541)		
1603							d. Elizabeth I; r. James I (James VI of Scotland) (–1625)
1604	d. Cyriacus Spangenberg (b. 1528)						d. John Whitgift (b. 1530)
1605						b. Rembrandt (d. 1669)	Guy Fawkes and gunpowder plot
1606							Jamestown Settlement
1607							b. John Milton (d. 1674)
1608							
1610		d. Henri IV; r. Louis XIII (–1643)	d. Benedict Pererius (b. 1535)			The Remonstrance; Short Confession	

	German Territories	France	Spain	Italy	Switzerland	Netherlands	British Isles
1611							Publication of Authorized English Translation of Bible (AV/KJV); George Abbot becomes Archbishop of Canterbury (–1633)
1612							b. Richard Crashaw (d. 1649)
1616							b. John Owen (d. 1683)
1617							b. Ralph Cudworth (d. 1689)
1618–1619						Synod of Dordrecht	
1618–1648	Thirty Years' War						
1620							English Sepratists land in Plymouth, Massachusetts
1621							d. Andrew Willet (b. 1562)
1628							Puritans establish Massachusetts Bay colony
1633	d. Christoph Pelargus (b. 1565)						Laud becomes Archbishop of Canterbury
1637	d. Johann Gerhard (b. 1582)					*Statenvertaling*	
1638							d. Joseph Mede (b. 1638)
1640				Diodati's Italian translation of Bible published			
1642–1649							English civil wars; d. Charles I; r. Oliver Cromwell (1660)
1643		d. Louis XIII; r. Louis XIV (–1715)					
1643–1649							Westminster Assembly
1645							d. William Laud (b. 1573)

	German Territories	France	Spain	Italy	Switzerland	Netherlands	British Isles
1648		Treaty of Westphalia ends Thirty Years' War					Books VI and VIII of Hooker's *Laws of Ecclesiastical Polity* posthumously published
1656	d. Georg Calixtus (b. 1586)						
1658							d. Oliver Cromwell
1659							Richard Cromwell resigns
1660							English Restoration; r. Charles II (–1685)
1662							Act of Uniformity; Book VII of Hooker's *Laws of Ecclesiastical Polity* posthumously published
1664						d. Thieleman Jans van Braght (b. 1625)	d. John Mayer (b. 1583)
1671							d. William Greenhill (b. 1591)
1677							d. Thomas Manton (b. 1620)
1678						d. Anna Maria von Schurman (b. 1607)	
1688							Glorious Revolution; r. William and Mary (-1702); d. John Bunyan (b. 1628)
1691							d. Richard Baxter (b. 1615)

BIOGRAPHICAL SKETCHES OF
REFORMATION-ERA FIGURES AND WORKS

This list is cumulative, including all the authors cited in the Reformation Commentary on Scripture to date as well as other people relevant to the Reformation and Reformation-era exegesis. For works consulted, see "Sources for Biographical Sketches," p. 587.

Cornelius À Lapide (1567–1637). Flemish biblical exegete. A Jesuit, Lapide served as professor of Holy Scripture and Hebrew at Louvain for twenty years before taking a similar role in Rome, where he taught until his death. He is best known for his extensive commentaries on the Scriptures. Encompassing all books of the Bible except Job and the Psalms, his work employs a fourfold hermeneutic and draws heavily on the work of patristic and medieval exegetes.

Thomas Adams (1583–1653). Anglican minister and author. He attended the University of Cambridge where he received his BA in 1601 and his MA in 1606. Following his ordination in 1604, Adams served as curate at Northill in Bedfordshire. In 1611, he became vicar of Willmington. Three years later he served the parish of Wingrave, Buckinghamshire, where he remained until 1618. From 1618 to 1623 Adams was preacher at St. Gregory by St. Paul's. He also served as chaplain to Henry Montague, First Earl of Manchester, and Lord Chief Justice of England. Among his most important works are the *Happiness of the Church* (1618) and an extensive commentary on 2 Peter (1638).

Johannes Aepinus (1499–1553). German Lutheran preacher and theologian. Aepinus studied under Martin Luther,* Philipp Melanchthon* and Johannes Bugenhagen* in Wittenberg. Because of his Lutheran beliefs, Aepinus lost his first teaching position in Brandenburg. He fled north to Stralsund and became a preacher and superintendent at Saint Peter's Church in Hamburg. In 1534, he made a diplomatic visit to England but could not convince Henry VIII* to embrace the Augsburg Confession.* His works include sermons and theological writings. Aepinus became best known as leader of the Infernalists, who believed that Christ underwent torment in hell after his crucifixion.

Johann Agricola (c. 1494–1566). German Lutheran pastor and theologian. An early student of Martin Luther,* Agricola eventually began a controversy over the role of the law, first with Melanchthon* and then with Luther himself. Agricola claimed to defend Luther's true position, asserting that only the gospel of the crucified Christ calls Christians to truly good works, not the fear of the law. After this first controversy, Agricola seems to have radicalized his views to the point that he eliminated Luther's *simul iustus et peccator* ("at the same time righteous and sinful") paradox of the Christian life, emphasizing instead that believers have no need for the law once they are united with Christ through faith. Luther responded by writing anonymous pamphlets against antinomianism. Agricola later published a recantation of his views, hoping to assuage relations with Luther, although they were never personally reconciled. He published a commentary on Luke, a series of sermons on Colossians, and a massive collection of German proverbs.

Henry Ainsworth (1571–1622/1623). English Puritan Hebraist. In 1593, under threat of persecution, Ainsworth relocated to Amsterdam, where he served as a teacher in an English congregation. He composed a confession of faith for the community and a number of polemical and exegetical works, including annotations on the Pentateuch, the Psalms and Song of Songs.

Henry Airay (c. 1560–1616). English Puritan professor and pastor. He was especially noted for his preaching, a blend of hostility toward Catholicism and articulate exposition of English Calvinism. He was promoted to provost of Queen's College Oxford (1598) and then to vice chancellor of the university in 1606. He disputed with William Laud* concerning Laud's putative Catholicization of the Church of England, particularly over the practice of genuflection, which Airay vehemently opposed. He also opposed fellow Puritans who wished to separate from the Church of England. His lectures on Philippians were his only work published during his lifetime.

Albert the Great (1201–1280). German theologian, philosopher, scientist, and ecclesiastic. Albert was born in Lauingen, located in the Bavarian-Swabian region. After completing his studies at Padua, Albert joined the Dominicans in 1220s. Upon finishing further theological studies at Cologne, Albert became a conventual lecturer during the 1230s at Hildesheim, Freiberg (Saxony), Regensburg, and Strasbourg. In the early 1240s, Albert was sent to Paris where he became a master of theology, and regent of the university in 1245. He served as regent until 1248. While at Paris, Albert commenced his paraphrases of Aristotle's works. Furthermore, Albert authored a systematic theology, and lectured on the four Gospels and nine books of the Old Testament. Albert is best known for having taught Thomas Aquinas,* who, as his assistant, transcribed his course on the works of Dionysius and Aristotle's *Nicomachean Ethics*.

Alexander (Ales) Alesius (1500–1565). Scottish Lutheran theologian. Following the martyrdom of his theological adversary Patrick Hamilton (c. 1504–1528), Alesius converted to the Reformation and fled to Germany. In 1535 Martin Luther* and Philipp Melanchthon* sent him as an emissary to Henry VIII* and Thomas Cranmer.* He taught briefly at Cambridge, but after the Act of Six Articles reasserted Catholic sacramental theology he returned to Germany, where he lectured at Frankfurt an der Oder and Leipzig. Alesius composed many exegetical, theological and polemical works, including commentaries on John, Romans, 1–2 Timothy, Titus and the Psalms.

Andreas Althamer (c. 1500–1539). German Lutheran humanist and pastor. Forced from the chaplaincy at Schwäbisch-Gmünd for teaching evangelical ideas, Althamer studied theology at Wittenberg before serving as a pastor in Eltersdorf, Nuremberg, and Ansbach. A staunch Lutheran, he contended against Reformed theologians at the 1528 disputation at Bern and delivered numerous polemics against Anabaptism. He also composed an early Lutheran catechism, published at Nuremberg in 1528.

William Ames (1576–1633). English Puritan theologian. Heavily influenced by William Perkins* while at Cambridge, Ames was unable to find employment in the English church due to his Puritan commitments. Most of his life was spent in exile in the Netherlands, where he served as chaplain to English forces at The Hague and was the pastor of a small congregation. Best known as a controversialist during his early career, Ames was the theological advisor to the president of the Synod of Dort (1618–1619) and was later installed as chair of theology at the University of Franeker in Friesland. *The Marrow of Theology* (1627) is viewed as a model of seventeenth-century Puritan theology.

Moïse Amyraut (1596–1664). French Reformed pastor and professor. Originally intending to be a lawyer, Amyraut turned to theology after an encounter with several Huguenot pastors and having read Calvin's* *Institutes*. After a brief stint as a parish pastor, Amyraut spent the majority of his career at the Saumur Academy. He was well known for his irenicism and ecumenicism (for example, in advocating intercommunion with Lutherans). Certain aspects of his writings on justification, faith, the covenants and especially predestination proved controversial among the Reformed. His doctrine of election is often called hypothetical universalism or Amyraldianism, stating that Christ's atoning work was intended by God for all human beings indiscriminately, although its effectiveness for salvation depends on faith, which is a free gift of God given only to those whom God has chosen from eternity. Amyraut was charged with grave doctrinal error three times before the National Synod but was acquitted each time. Aside from his theological treatises, Amyraut published paraphrases of almost the entire New Testament and the Psalms, as well as many sermons.

Anabaptists of Trieste (1539). Following a meeting between Swiss Brethren and the Hutterites at Steinabrunn on December 6, 1536, around 140 radicals were arrested and imprisoned in Falkenstein Castle. After six weeks in captivity, the ninety men of the group were forced to march to Trieste to be sold as galley slaves. Twelve days after arrival, all but twelve prisoners managed to escape and return to Moravia, where they published a confession of their beliefs.

Jakob Andreae (1528–1590). German Lutheran theologian. Andreae studied at the University of Tübingen before being called to the diaconate in Stuttgart in 1546. He was appointed ecclesiastical superintendent of Göppingen in 1553 and supported Johannes Brenz's* proposal to place the church under civil administrative control. An ecclesial diplomat for the duke of Württemberg, Andreae debated eucharistic theology, the use of images and predestination with Theodore Beza* at the Colloquy of Montbéliard (1586) to determine whether French Reformed exiles would be required to submit to the Formula of Concord.* Andreae coauthored the Formula of Concord. He and his wife had eighteen children.

Lancelot Andrewes (1555–1626). Anglican bishop. A scholar, pastor and preacher, Andrews

prominently shaped a distinctly Anglican identity between the poles of Puritanism and Catholicism. He oversaw the translation of Genesis to 2 Kings for the Authorized Version.* His eight-volume collected works—primarily devotional tracts and sermons—are marked by his fluency in Scripture, the Christian tradition and classical literature.

Thomas Aquinas (1225–1274). Dominican medieval theologian. Thomas Aquinas was born into a noble family in Rocasecca, Italy. In 1230 Thomas's father sent him to the abbey at Monte Casino as a child oblate. When, at age fourteen, Thomas was given the choice between taking his final vows and leaving, he chose to go to Naples to study at the school recently founded by the Holy Roman Emperor. While studying at Naples, Thomas came into contact with the Dominicans, and joined this order in 1244. Although his family objected to his decision at first, to the point of actually imprisoning Thomas, they came to accept his decision the following year. Afterwards, Aquinas traveled to Paris where he began his formal studies under Albert the Great (1200–1280). Aquinas followed his teacher to Cologne in 1248 where he was ordained a priest, and completed his course in theology. Four years later, he was appointed a bachelor in the Dominican convent in Paris where he lectured on Peter Lombard's (1096–1160)* Sentences. In 1256, Thomas was incepted as a master of the sacred page, and he taught in Paris until 1259. In 1261, he was appointed lecturer at a school in Orvieto. Four years later, Aquinas was transferred to Rome, and in 1268 returned to Paris. In 1272, the Dominican order appointed Aquinas to start a new school in Naples. A mystical experience reportedly caused Aquinas to abruptly cease his writing. Aquinas died at a monastery in Fossanova. In addition to his major works, *Summa Theologia* and *Summa Contra Gentiles*, Aquinas's voluminous corpus includes extensive commentaries on Jeremiah, Lamentations, Isaiah, Job, and an incomplete one on the Psalms. Aquinas also wrote commentaries on the Gospels of Matthew and John as well as the Pauline Epistles. Furthermore, at the request of the pope, Aquinas produced the *Catena Aurea*, a commentary on the four Gospels consisting of exegetical statements by the Latin and Greek fathers. One of the most significant features of Aquinas's biblical commentaries is his emphasis on the literal meaning of a Scriptural text. As a representation of medieval Catholic theology, Aquinas's theology was regularly challenged by the Protestant reformers.

Benedict Aretius (d. 1574). Swiss Reformed professor. Trained at the universities of Bern, Strasbourg and Marburg, Aretius taught logic and philosophy as well as the biblical languages and theology. He advocated for stronger unity and peace between the Lutheran and Reformed churches. Aretius joined others in denouncing the antitrinitarian Giovanni Valentino Gentile (d. 1566). He published commentaries on the New Testament, as well as various works on astronomy, botany and medicine.

Aristotle (388–322 BC). Ancient Greek philosopher and scientist. Aristotle was born in Stagira, Chalkdice, northern Greece. He is considered the "Father of Western Philosophy" along with his teacher, Plato, because his teaching produced the bases for almost every discipline studied in the Western world. After his father's death while he was still a child, Aristotle was raised by his guardian, Proxenus of Atarneus. At the age of about eighteen, Aristotle joined Plato's Academy in Athens, where he remained until his was thirty-seven. Aristotle's writings cover a wide range of subjects: physics, biology, zoology, metaphysics, logic, ethics, aesthetics, poetry, theater, music, rhetoric, psychology, linguistics, and politics. Shortly after Plato's death, King Philip II of Macedonia requested his services as a tutor to his son, Alexander the Great. Aristotle began tutoring the young prince in 343 BC. While teaching Alexander, Aristotle was able to acquire hundreds of books for the library of what would become his Lyceum. Aristotle's work profoundly shaped scholarship during the Middle Ages and early modern period as his logic was employed in the exegesis of Scripture and forma-

tion of theology. Among the major theologians who incorporated Aristotle's methods into their theological systems was Thomas Aquinas.* Aristotle's methods and categories would also be utilized by many Protestant theologians throughout the sixteenth and seventeenth centuries.

Jacobus Arminius (1559–1609). Dutch Remonstrant pastor and theologian. Arminius was a vocal critic of high Calvinist scholasticism, whose views were repudiated by the Synod of Dordrecht. Arminius was a student of Theodore Beza* at the academy of Geneva. He served as a pastor in Amsterdam and later joined the faculty of theology at the university in Leiden, where his lectures on predestination were popular and controversial. Predestination, as Arminius understood it, was the decree of God determined on the basis of divine foreknowledge of faith or rejection by humans who are the recipients of prevenient, but resistible, grace.

Johann Arndt (1555–1621). German Lutheran pastor and theologian. After a brief time teaching, Arndt pastored in Badeborn (Anhalt) until 1590, when Prince Johann Georg von Anhalt (1567–1618) began introducing Reformed ecclesial policies. Arndt ministered in Quedlinberg, Brunswick, Eisleben and Celle. Heavily influenced by medieval mysticism, Arndt centered his theology on Christ's mystical union with the believer, out of which flows love of God and neighbor. He is best known for his *True Christianity* (1605–1609), which greatly influenced Philipp Jakob Spener (1635–1705) and later Pietists.

John Arrowsmith (1602–1659). English Puritan theologian. Arrowsmith participated in the Westminster Assembly, and later taught at Cambridge. His works, all published posthumously, include three sermons preached to Parliament and an unfinished catechism.

Articles of Religion (1562; revised 1571). The Articles underwent a long editorial process that drew from the influence of Continental confessions in England, resulting in a uniquely Anglican blend of Protestantism and Catholicism. In their final form, they were reduced from Thomas Cranmer's*

Forty-two Articles (1539) to the Elizabethan Thirty-Nine Articles (1571), excising polemical articles against the Anabaptists and Millenarians as well as adding articles on the Holy Spirit, good works and Communion. Originating in a 1535 meeting with Lutherans, the Articles retained a minor influence from the Augsburg Confession* and Württemberg Confession (1552), but showed significant revision in accordance with Genevan theology, as well as the Second Helvetic Confession.*

Anne Askew (1521–1546). English Protestant martyr. Askew was forced to marry her deceased sister's intended husband, who later expelled Askew from his house—after the birth of two children—on account of her religious views. After unsuccessfully seeking a divorce in Lincoln, Askew moved to London, where she met other Protestants and began to preach. In 1546, she was arrested, imprisoned and convicted of heresy for denying the doctrine of transubstantiation. Under torture in the Tower of London she refused to name any other Protestants. On July 16, 1546, she was burned at the stake. Askew is best known through her accounts of her arrests and examinations. John Bale (1495–1563), a bishop, historian and playwright, published these manuscripts. Later John Foxe (1516–1587) included them in his *Acts and Monuments*, presenting her as a role model for other pious Protestant women.

Augsburg Confession (1530). In the wake of Luther's* stand against ecclesial authorities at the Diet of Worms (1521), the Holy Roman Empire splintered along theological lines. Emperor Charles V sought to ameliorate this—while also hoping to secure a united European front against Turkish invasion—by calling together another imperial diet in Augsburg in 1530. The Evangelical party was cast in a strongly heretical light at the diet by Johann Eck.* For this reason, Philipp Melanchthon* and Justus Jonas* thought it best to strike a conciliatory tone (Luther, as an official outlaw, did not attend), submitting a confession rather than a defense. The resulting Augsburg Confession was approved by many of the rulers of the northeastern Empire; however, due to differences in eucharistic

theology, Martin Bucer* and the representatives of Strasbourg, Constance, Lindau and Memmingen drafted a separate confession (the Tetrapolitan Confession). Charles V accepted neither confession, demanding that the Evangelicals accept the Catholic rebuttal instead. In 1531, along with the publication of the Augsburg Confession itself, Melanchthon released a defense of the confession that responded to the Catholic confutation and expanded on the original articles. Most subsequent Protestant confessions followed the general structure of the Augsburg Confession.

Augustine of Hippo (354–430 AD). North African bishop and theologian. Augustine was born in Thagaste (Ahras, Algeria), a small town in the Roman province to Numidia, the son of a Christian mother, Monica, and a non-Christian father, Patricius, a local official of modest means. Enabled by local patronage, Augustine received a classical education, which afforded him the opportunity to pursue advanced training in rhetoric at Carthage. Upon completing his education at Carthage, Augustine taught rhetoric there as well as in Rome and Milan, where he was appointed official rhetorician of that city. Inspired by his reading of Cicero's *Hortensius*, Augustine embarked upon a quest for wisdom. While in Carthage, Augustine was repulsed by the seemingly simplistic Christianity he encountered, and therefore joined the Manicheans. Having become disillusioned by the Manichaeans' failure to lead him to the wisdom they promised, Augustine was eventually drawn to orthodox Christianity by the preaching of Ambrose (340–397) and his reading of the Neo-Platonist philosopher Plotinus (204–270). As a result of his conversion in 386, Augustine abandoned his secular ambitions in favor of a celibate life fully committed to intellectual and spiritual devotion to God. Towards this end, Augustine returned to north Africa to establish a semi–monastic community. However, in 391, while visiting Hippo Regius, he was forcibly ordained into the priesthood, and made bishop of that church in 396. In addition to his many duties as a bishop, Augustine engaged in controversies against the Manicheans, Donatists, and Pelagians, which took up the remainder of his life and career. He died in 430 while the Vandals besieged Hippo. Among his many works, Augustine devoted several to exegesis. He outlines exegetical principles in his *De Doctrina Christiana* ("On Christian Doctrine"), and he authored extensive series of homilies on most of the books of the New Testament as well as the Old Testament books of Psalms and Genesis (incomplete). During the Reformation era, both Catholic and Protestant theologians appealed to and engaged with Augustine's theology, especially his emphases upon original sin and humanity's need for God's grace.

Authorized Version (1611). In 1604 King James I* commissioned this new translation—popularly remembered as the King James Version—for uniform use in the public worship of the Church of England. The Bible and the Apocrypha was divided into six portions and assigned to six companies of nine scholars—both Anglicans and Puritans—centered at Cambridge, Oxford and Westminster. Richard Bancroft, the general editor of the Authorized Version, composed fifteen rules to guide the translators and to guard against overly partisan decisions. Rather than offer an entirely fresh English translation, the companies were to follow the Bishops' Bible* as closely as possible. "Truly (good Christian Reader)," the preface states, "we neuer thought from the beginning that we should need to make a new Translation, nor yet to make of a bad one a good one . . . but make a good one better, or out of many good ones, one principall good one, not iustly to be excepted against: that hath bene our endeauour, that our mark." Other rules standardized spelling, dictated traditional ecclesial terms (e.g., *church*, *baptize* and *bishop*), and allowed only for linguistic marginal notes and cross-references. Each book of the Bible went through a rigorous revision process: first, each person in a company made an initial draft, then the company put together a composite draft, then a supercommittee composed of representatives from each company reviewed these drafts, and finally two bishops and Bancroft scrutinized the final edits. The text and

translation process of the Authorized Version have widely influenced biblical translations ever since.

Robert Bagnall (b. 1559 or 1560). English Protestant minister. Bagnall authored *The Steward's Last Account* (1622), a collection of five sermons on Luke 16.

Friedrich Balduin (1575–1627). German Lutheran theologian. After spending time in the pastorate at Freiberg and Oelsnitz, Balduin was appointed professor of theology at Wittenberg in 1604, where he remained until the end of his life. He also served as head of the theology faculty, superintendent of churches, and assessor of the consistory. Known for his commitment to Lutheran orthodoxy, Balduin's major works include a commentary on the Pauline letters and writings on exegesis, homiletics, and casuistry.

John Ball (1585–1640). English Puritan theologian. Ball was a respected educator. He briefly held a church office until he was removed on account of his Puritanism. He composed popular catechisms and tracts on faith, the church and the covenant of grace.

Thomas Bastard (c. 1565–1618). English Protestant minister and poet. Educated at Winchester and New College, Oxford, Bastard published numerous works, including collections of poems and sermons; his most famous title is *Chrestoleros* (1598), a collection of epigrams. Bastard was alleged to be the author of an anonymous work, *An Admonition to the City of Oxford*, which revealed the carnal vices of many clergy and scholars in Oxford; despite denying authorship, he was dismissed from Oxford in 1591. Bastard was recognized as a skilled classical scholar and preacher. He died impoverished in a debtor's prison in Dorchester.

Jeremias Bastingius (1551–1595). Dutch Reformed theologian. Educated in Heidelberg and Geneva, Bastingius pastored the Reformed church in Antwerp for nearly a decade until the Spanish overran the city in 1585; he later settled in Dordrecht. He spent the last few years of his life in Leiden on the university's board of regents. He wrote an influential commentary on the Heidelberg Catechism that was translated into English, Dutch, German and Flemish.

Johann (Pomarius) Baumgart (1514–1578). Lutheran pastor and amateur playwright. Baumgart studied under Georg Major,* Martin Luther* and Philipp Melanchthon* at the University of Wittenberg. Before becoming pastor of the Church of the Holy Spirit in 1540, Baumgart taught secondary school. He authored catechetical and polemical works, a postil for the Gospel readings throughout the church year, numerous hymns and a didactic play (*Juditium Salomonis*).

Richard Baxter (1615–1691). English Puritan minister. Baxter was a leading Puritan pastor, evangelist and theologian, known throughout England for his landmark ministry in Kidderminster and a prodigious literary output, producing 135 books in just over forty years. Baxter came to faith through reading William Perkins,* Richard Sibbes* and other early Puritan writers and was the first cleric to decline the terms of ministry in the national English church imposed by the 1662 Act of Uniformity; Baxter wrote on behalf of the more than 1700 who shared ejection from the national church. He hoped for restoration to national church ministry, or toleration, that would allow lawful preaching and pastoring. Baxter sought unity in theological, ecclesiastical, sociopolitical and personal terms and is regarded as a forerunner of Noncomformist ecumenicity, though he was defeated in his efforts at the 1661 Savoy Conference to take seriously Puritan objections to the revision of the 1604 Prayer Book. Baxter's views on church ministry were considerably hybrid: he was a paedo-baptist, Nonconformist minister who approved of synodical Episcopal government and fixed liturgy. He is most known for his classic writings on the Christian life, such as *The Saints' Everlasting Rest* and *A Christian Directory*, and pastoral ministry, such as *The Reformed Pastor*. He also produced *Catholick Theology*, a large volume squaring current Reformed, Lutheran, Arminian and Roman Catholic systems with each other.

Thomas Becon (1511/1512–1567). English Puritan preacher. Becon was a friend of Hugh Latimer,* and for several years chaplain to Archbishop Thomas Cranmer.* Becon was sent to the Tower of London by Mary I and then exiled for his controversial preaching at the English royal court. He returned to England upon Elizabeth I's* accession. Becon was one of the most widely read popular preachers in England during the Reformation. He published many of his sermons, including a postil, or collection of sermon helps for undertrained or inexperienced preachers.

Belgic Confession (1561). Written by Guy de Brès (1523–1567), this statement of Dutch Reformed faith was heavily reliant on the Gallic Confession,* although more detailed, especially in how strongly it distances the Reformed from Roman Catholics and Anabaptists. The Confession first appeared in French in 1561 and was translated to Dutch in 1562. It was presented to Philip II (1527–1598) in the hope that he would grant toleration to the Reformed, to no avail. At the Synod of Dordrecht* the Confession was revised, clarifying and strengthening the article on election as well as sharpening the distinctives of Reformed theology against the Anabaptists, thus situating the Dutch Reformed more closely to the international Calvinist movement. The Belgic Confession in conjunction with the Heidelberg Catechism* and the Canons of Dordrecht were granted official status as the confessional standards (the Three Forms of Unity) of the Dutch Reformed Church.

Robert Bellarmine (1542–1621). Italian Catholic cardinal. A Jesuit, Bellarmine first taught at Louvain before being appointed chair of polemical theology at the Roman College. Much of Bellarmine's career was devoted to the refutation of Protestant teachings, and his three volume work, the *Controversies* (1586–93), was widely disseminated in the post-Tridentine era as the foremost refutation of the evangelical message. He was influential in the official revision of the Vulgate* text during the reign of Pope Clement VIII (1536–1605), with the resulting version, the Sixto-Clementine Vulgate, providing the basic biblical text for Catholics until Vatican II. Bellarmine is also a controversial figure in the history of science. Appointed to the Holy Office, also known as the Inquisition, by Pope Paul V

(1550–1621), it was he who examined Galileo Galilei (1564–1642) and ordered him to treat heliocentrism as a hypothesis rather than a reality, believing the evidentiary threshold had not yet been met. Later in his career, Bellarmine's attention turned to works on devotion and piety. and include his extensive commentary on the Psalms (1611).

Bernard of Clairvaux (1090–1153). French abbot and theologian. Born the son of a Bugundian knight, Bernard became interested in the new reforming movement at Citeaux, and thus abandoned his preparation for a secular career in favor of monastic life there. Towards this end, Bernard persuaded thirty-one of his friends and relatives to follow him to Citeaux, and join the Cistercian order. Among this group were four of Bernard's brothers. In 1115, Bernard went with others of his order to found a Cistercian monastery at Claivaux. Bernard's austere approach to the monastic life attracted many followers to the point that by the time of his death there were sixty-eight Cistercian houses. Throughout his career, Bernard preached, mediated theological disputes, and advised. Bernard is best known for having preached the Second Crusade (1147–1150) as well as advising his former student, Pope Eugenius III (r. 1145–1153), and engaging in theological controversies with Peter Abelard (1079–1142) and Gilbert of Poitiers (1085–1154). One of the distinguishing characteristics of Bernard's theology is his Christocentric mysticism. Among Bernard's most important works are his treatises *On Consideration* and *On Loving God* along with his *Sermons on the Song of Songs* as well as many other sermons on the liturgical year and other subject. Many of the reformers in the sixteenth century cited Bernard extensively, especially Martin Luther* and John Calvin*.

Theodore Beza (1519–1605). French pastor and professor. Beza was compatriot and successor to John Calvin* as moderator of the Company of Pastors in Geneva during the second half of the sixteenth century. He was a noteworthy New Testament scholar whose *Codex Bezae* formed the basis of the New Testament section of later English translations. A leader in the academy and the church, Beza served as professor of Greek at the Lausanne Academy until 1558, at which time he moved to Geneva to become the rector of the newly founded Genevan Academy. He enjoyed an international reputation through his correspondence with key European leaders. Beza developed and extended Calvin's doctrinal thought on several important themes such as the nature of predestination and the real spiritual presence of Christ in the Eucharist.

Theodor Bibliander (1504?–1564). Swiss Reformed Hebraist and theologian. Professor of Old Testament at the Zurich Academy from 1531, Bibliander published two Hebrew grammars, a collection of letters by Zwingli* and Oecolampadius*, commentaries on Isaiah, Ezekiel, and Nahum, a Latin translation of the Qur'an, and a tract warning Christians against the threat of Islam. He taught a universalist view of predestination, arguing that God saved all people unless they rejected divine grace. Following a dispute with double-predestinarian Peter Martyr Vermigli*, he was forced into retirement in 1560.

Hugh Binning (1627–1653). Scottish Presbyterian theologian. At the age of eighteen, Binning became a professor of philosophy at the University of Glasgow. In his early twenties he left this post for parish ministry, and died of consumption a few years later. His commentary on the Westminster Confession and a selection of his sermons were published after his death.

Samuel Bird (d. 1604). Anglican minister and author. A native of Essex, Bird matriculated at Queen's College, Cambridge, where he received his BA in 1570 and his MA in 1573, at which time he was also elected a fellow of Corpus Christi College, Cambridge. For reasons unknown, Bird resigned his fellowship sometime in 1576. He spent nearly the entirety of his post-university career as rector of St. Peter's in Ipswich until his death in 1604. Among Bird's major works are *A Friendlie Communication or Dialogue Betweene Paule and Demas, wherein is Disputed How We are to Use the*

Pleasures of This Life (1580), *Lectures upon the 11. Chapter of Hebrews and upon the 38. Psalme* (1598), and *Lectures upon the 8 and 9 Chapters of the Second Epistle to the Corinthians* (1598).

Bishops' Bible (1568). Anglicans were polarized by the two most recent English translations of the Bible: the Great Bible (1539) relied too heavily on the Vulgate* and was thus perceived as too Catholic, while the Geneva Bible's* marginal notes were too Calvinist for many Anglicans. So Archbishop Matthew Parker (1504–1575) commissioned a new translation of Scripture from the original languages with marginal annotations (many of which, ironically, were from the Geneva Bible). Published under royal warrant, the Bishops' Bible became the official translation for the Church of England. The 1602 edition provided the basis for the King James Bible (1611).

Georg Blaurock (1492–1529). Swiss Anabaptist. Blaurock (a nickname meaning "blue coat," because of his preference for this garment) was one of the first leaders of Switzerland's radical reform movement. In the first public disputations on baptism in Zurich, he argued for believer's baptism and was the first person to receive adult believers' baptism there, having been baptized by Conrad Grebel* in 1525. Blaurock was arrested several times for performing mass adult baptisms and engaging in social disobedience by disrupting worship services. He was eventually expelled from Zurich but continued preaching and baptizing in various Swiss cantons until his execution.

Bohemian Confession (1535). Bohemian Christianity was subdivided between traditional Catholics, Utraquists (who demanded Communion in both kinds) and the *Unitas Fratrum*, who were not Protestants but whose theology bore strong affinities to the Waldensians and the Reformed. The 1535 Latin edition of this confession—an earlier Czech edition had already been drafted—was an attempt to clarify and redefine the beliefs of the *Unitas Fratrum*. This confession purged all earlier openness to rebaptism and inched toward Luther's* eucharistic theology. Jan Augusta (c. 1500–1572) and Jan Roh (also Johannes Horn; c.

1490–1547) presented the confession to King Ferdinand I (1503–1564) in Vienna, but the king would not print it. The *Unitas Fratrum* sought, and with slight amendments eventually obtained, Luther's advocacy of the confession. It generally follows the structure of the Augsburg Confession.*

Bohemian Confession (1575). This confession was an attempt to shield Bohemian Christian minorities—the Utraquists and the *Unitas Fratrum*—from the Counter-Reformation and Habsburg insistence on uniformity. The hope was that this umbrella consensus would ensure peace in the midst of Christian diversity; anyone who affirmed the 1575 Confession, passed by the Bohemian legislature, would be tolerated. This confession was, like the Bohemian Confession of 1535, patterned after the Augsburg Confession.* It emphasizes both justification by faith alone and good works as the fruit of salvation. Baptism and the Eucharist are the focus of the sacramental section, although the five traditional Catholic sacraments are also listed for the Utraquists. Though it was eventually accepted in 1609 by Rudolf II (1552–1612), the Thirty Years' War (1618–1648) rendered the confession moot.

Book of Common Prayer (1549; 1552). After the Church of England's break with Rome, it needed a liturgical manual to distinguish its theology and practice from that of Catholicism. Thomas Cranmer* drafted the Book of Common Prayer based on the medieval Roman Missal, under the dual influence of the revised Lutheran Mass and the reforms of the Spanish Cardinal Quiñones. This manual details the eucharistic service, as well as services for rites such as baptism, confirmation, marriage and funerals. It includes a matrix of the epistle and Gospel readings and the appropriate collect for each Sunday and feast day of the church year. The 1548 Act of Uniformity established the Book of Common Prayer as *the* authoritative liturgical manual for the Church of England, to be implemented everywhere by Pentecost 1549. After its 1552 revision, Queen Mary I banned it; Elizabeth I* reestablished it in 1559, although it was rejected by Puritans and Catholics alike.

The Book of Homilies (1547; 1563; 1570). This collection of approved sermons, published in three parts during the reigns of Edward VI and Elizabeth I,* was intended to inculcate Anglican theological distinctives and mitigate the problems raised by the lack of educated preachers. Addressing doctrinal and practical topics, Thomas Cranmer* likely wrote the majority of the first twelve sermons, published in 1547; John Jewel* added another twenty sermons in 1563. A final sermon, *A Homily Against Disobedience*, was appended to the canon in 1570. Reprinted regularly, the *Book of Homilies* was an important resource in Anglican preaching until at least the end of the seventeenth century.

Martin (Cellarius) Borrhaus (1499–1564). German Reformed theologian. After a dispute with his mentor Johann Eck,* Borrhaus settled in Wittenberg, where he was influenced by the radical Zwickau Prophets. He travelled extensively, and finally settled in Basel to teach philosophy and Old Testament. Despite his objections, many accused Borrhaus of Anabaptism; he argued that baptism was a matter of conscience. On account of his association with Sebastian Castellio (1515–1563) and Michael Servetus (1511–1553), some scholars posit that Borrhaus was an antitrinitarian. His writings include a treatise on the Trinity and commentaries on the Torah, historical books, Ecclesiastes and Isaiah.

John Bowle (d. 1637). Anglican pastor. After matriculating from Cambridge, Bowle was household pastor to Sir Robert Cecil (1563–1612) and held a pastorate at Tilehurst in Berkshire. He was appointed dean of Salisbury in 1620 and bishop of Rochester in 1629.

John Boys (1571–1625). Anglican priest and theologian. Before doctoral work at Cambridge, Boys pastored several parishes in Kent; after completing his studies he was appointed to more prominent positions, culminating in his 1619 appointment as the Dean of Canterbury by James I.* Boys published a popular four-volume postil of the Gospel and epistle readings for the church year, as well as a companion volume for the Psalms.

John Bradford (1510-1555). English Reformer, prebendary of St. Paul's, and martyr. Bradford was born in Blackley, Manchester, to an affluent family. After grammar school, Bradford at first began legal studies at the Inner Temple in London. However, while there, he heard the preaching of a fellow student, and thus converted to an evangelical faith. This conversion caused Bradford to abandon his study of law and enroll at St. Catherine's Hall, Cambridge, to study theology. He completed his MA in 1549, and in the same year, received an appointment of fellow at Pembroke Hall, Cambridge. In August, 1550, Bishop Nicholas Ridley ordained Bradford a deacon, and appointed him his personal chaplain. Bradford's exceptional preaching moved King Edward VI to select him as his chaplain and prebendary at St. Paul's Cathedral. After Mary Tudor succeeded her half-brother to throne, Bradford was tried and convicted of heresy on January 31, 1555. He was executed at the stake on July 1 of the same year.

Anne Bradstreet (1612–1672). English-American Puritan poet. Born in Northampton, Bradstreet married at sixteen and emigrated to the Massachusetts Bay Colony, of which both her father and husband would serve as governors. Mother to eight children, Bradstreet also wrote poetry. Much of her verse reflects on marriage, children, and her Puritan faith. While her writing received a mixed reception from contemporaries, many of whom viewed poetry as outside a woman's purview, she is today celebrated as the most significant early English poet in North America.

Thieleman Jans van Braght (1625–1664). Dutch Radical preacher. After demonstrating great ability with languages, this cloth merchant was made preacher in his hometown of Dordrecht in 1648. He served in this office for the next sixteen years, until his death. This celebrated preacher had a reputation for engaging in debate wherever an opportunity presented itself, particularly concerning infant baptism. The publication of his book of martyrs, *Het Bloedigh Tooneel of Martelaersspiegel* (1660; *Martyrs' Mirror*), proved to be his lasting contribution to the Mennonite tradition. *Martyrs' Mirror* is heavily indebted to the earlier martyr book

Offer des Heeren (1562), to which Braght added many early church martyrs who rejected infant baptism, as well as over 800 contemporary martyrs.

Johannes Brenz (1499–1570). German Lutheran theologian and pastor. Brenz was converted to the reformation cause after hearing Martin Luther* speak; later, Brenz became a student of Johannes Oecolampadius.* His central achievement lay in his talent for organization. As city preacher in Schwäbisch-Hall and afterward in Württemberg and Tübingen, he oversaw the introduction of reform measures and doctrines and new governing structures for ecclesial and educational communities. Brenz also helped establish Lutheran orthodoxy through treatises, commentaries and catechisms. He defended Luther's position on eucharistic presence against Huldrych Zwingli* and opposed the death penalty for religious dissenters.

Guillaume Briçonnet (1470–1534). French Catholic abbot and bishop. Briçonnet created a short-lived circle of reformist-minded humanists in his diocese under the sponsorship of Marguerite d'Angoulême. His desire for ecclesial reform developed throughout his prestigious career (including positions as royal chaplain to the queen, abbot at Saint-Germain-des-Prés and bishop of Meaux), influenced by Jacques Lefèvre d'Étaples.* Briçonnet encouraged reform through ministerial visitation, Scripture and preaching in the vernacular and active study of the Bible. When this triggered the ire of the theology faculty at the Sorbonne in Paris, Briçonnet quelled the activity and departed, envisioning an ecclesial reform that proceeded hierarchically.

Thomas Brightman (1562–1607). English Puritan pastor and exegete. Under alleged divine inspiration, Brightman wrote a well known commentary on Revelation, influenced by Joachim of Fiore (d. 1202). In contrast to the putatively true churches of Geneva and Scotland, he depicted the Church of England as a type of the lukewarm Laodicean church. He believed that the Reformation would result in the defeat of the Vatican and the Ottoman Empire and that all humanity would be regenerated through the spread of the gospel before Christ's final return and judgment.

Otto Brunfels (c. 1488–1534). German Lutheran botanist, teacher and physician. Brunfels joined the Carthusian order, where he developed interests in the natural sciences and became involved with a humanist circle associated with Ulrich von Hutten and Wolfgang Capito.* In 1521, after coming into contact with Luther's* teaching, Brunfels abandoned the monastic life, traveling and spending time in botanical research and pastoral care. He received a medical degree in Basel and was appointed city physician of Bern in 1534. Brunfels penned defenses of Luther and Hutten, devotional biographies of biblical figures, a prayer book, and annotations on the Gospels and the Acts of the Apostles. His most influential contribution, however, is as a Renaissance botanist.

Martin Bucer (1491–1551). German Reformed theologian and pastor. A Dominican friar, Bucer was influenced by Desiderius Erasmus* during his doctoral studies at the University of Heidelberg, where he began corresponding with Martin Luther.* After advocating reform in Alsace, Bucer was excommunicated and fled to Strasbourg, where he became a leader in the city's Reformed ecclesial and educational communities. Bucer sought concord between Lutherans and Zwinglians and Protestants and Catholics. He emigrated to England, becoming a professor at Cambridge. Bucer's greatest theological concern was the centrality of Christ's sacrificial death, which achieved justification and sanctification and orients Christian community.

Johannes Bugenhagen (1485–1558). German Lutheran pastor and professor. Bugenhagen, a priest and lecturer at a Premonstratensian monastery, became a city preacher in Wittenberg during the reform efforts of Martin Luther* and Philipp Melanchthon.* Initially influenced by his reading of Desiderius Erasmus,* Bugenhagen grew in evangelical orientation through Luther's works; later, he studied under Melanchthon at the University of Wittenberg, eventually serving as rector and faculty member there. Bugenhagen was a versatile commentator, exegete and lecturer on Scripture. Through these roles and his development of lectionary and devotional material,

Bugenhagen facilitated rapid establishment of church order throughout many German provinces.

Heinrich Bullinger (1504–1575). Swiss Reformed pastor and theologian. Bullinger succeeded Huldrych Zwingli* as minister and leader in Zurich. The primary author of the First and Second Helvetic Confessions,* Bullinger was drawn toward reform through the works of Martin Luther* and Philipp Melanchthon.* After Zwingli died, Bullinger was vital in maintaining adherence to the cause of reform; he oversaw the expansion of the Zurich synodal system while preaching, teaching and writing extensively. One of Bullinger's lasting legacies was the development of a federal view of the divine covenant with humanity, making baptism and the Eucharist covenantal signs.

John Bunyan (1628–1688). English Puritan preacher and writer. His *Pilgrim's Progress* is one of the best-selling English-language titles in history. Born to a working-class family, Bunyan was largely unschooled, gaining literacy (and entering the faith) through reading the Bible and such early Puritan devotional works as *The Plain Man's Pathway to Heaven* and *The Practice of Piety*. Following a short stint in Oliver Cromwell's parliamentary army, in which Bunyan narrowly escaped death in combat, he turned to a preaching ministry, succeeding John Gifford as pastor at the Congregational church in Bedford. A noted preacher, Bunyan drew large crowds in itinerant appearances and it was in the sermonic form that Bunyan developed his theological outlook, which was an Augustinian-inflected Calvinism. Bunyan's opposition to the Book of Common Prayer and refusal of official ecclesiastical licensure led to multiple imprisonments, where he wrote many of his famous allegorical works, including *Pilgrim's Progress, The Holy City, Prison Meditations* and *Holy War*.

Michelangelo Buonarroti (1475–1564). Italian Catholic artist and poet. Michelangelo was born in Florence but spent the majority of his career in Rome, completing artworks commissioned by the popes of the early sixteenth century. One of the most recognized artists of all time, his artworks include the *Pietà* (1499), *David* (1501–1504), the

ceiling of the Sistine Chapel (1508–1512), *Moses* (1515), and the *Last Judgment* (1536–1541), which remain famous and have done much to shape Western aesthetics. Toward the end of his life, his interests shifted toward architecture, culminating with his contributions to the designs of St. Peter's Basilica in Rome. Michelangelo is thought to have been devoutly Catholic throughout his life, but recent scholarship has considered the complexity of his relationship with the Catholic Reformation and the Protestant movement.

Jeremiah Burroughs (c. 1600–1646). English Puritan pastor and delegate to the Westminster Assembly. Burroughs left Cambridge, as well as a rectorate in Norfolk, because of his nonconformity. After returning to England from pastoring an English congregation in Rotterdam for several years (1637–1641), he became one of only a few dissenters from the official presbyterianism of the Assembly in favor of a congregationalist polity. Nevertheless, he was well known and respected by presbyterian colleagues such as Richard Baxter* for his irenic tone and conciliatory manner. The vast majority of Burroughs's corpus was published posthumously, although during his lifetime he published annotations on Hosea and several polemical works.

Anthony Cade (d. 1641). Anglican pastor. Cade served as tutor and chaplain to George Villiers, First Duke of Buckingham (1592–1628), a close confidante of King James I* before holding a number of pastoral positions in Leicestershire and Northamptonshire.

Cardinal Cajetan (Thomas de Vio) (1469–1534). Italian Catholic cardinal, professor, theologian and biblical exegete. This Dominican monk was the leading Thomist theologian and one of the most important Catholic exegetes of the sixteenth century. Cajetan is best-known for his interview with Martin Luther* at the Diet of Augsburg (1518). Among his many works are polemical treatises, extensive biblical commentaries and most importantly a four-volume commentary (1508–1523) on the *Summa Theologiae* of Thomas Aquinas.*

Georg Calixtus (1586–1656). German Lutheran theologian. Calixtus studied at the University of

Helmstedt where he developed regard for Philipp Melanchthon.* Between his time as a student and later as a professor at Helmstedt, Calixtus traveled through Europe seeking a way to unite and reconcile Lutherans, Calvinists and Catholics. He attempted to fuse these denominations through use of the Scriptures, the Apostles' Creed, and the first five centuries, interpreted by the Vincentian canon. Calixtus's position was stamped as syncretist and yielded further debate even after his death.

John Calvin (1509–1564). French Reformed pastor and theologian. John Calvin was born in Noyon, France. After receiving his primary education in the aristocratic family of Charles de Hangest, he attended the University of Paris to prepare for further study of theology. However, after completing his BA degree, as per his father's instructions, Calvin proceeded to the study of the law at Orleans of Bourges. While at Orleans, Calvin's interests in Greek and Latin literature were reawakened. Upon his father's death, Calvin resumed his study of classical literature at the newly founded College of Royal Readers in Paris under the direction of Guillaume Bude. The product of these studies was his commentary on Seneca's *De Clementia* (1532). Sometime between 1533 and 1534 Calvin experienced a "sudden conversion" due largely to the influence to Martin Luther's 1520 treatises. Calvin's embracing of an evangelical faith forced him to flee France. From there he went to Basel, where he wrote the first edition of his *Institutes of the Christian Religion* in 1536. The *Institutes* became a theological dogmatics for the Reformed churches. Calvin spent most of his career in Geneva (excepting a three-year ministry in Strasbourg with Martin Bucer*). In Geneva, Calvin reorganized the structure and governance of the church and established an academy that became an international center for theological education. He was a tireless writer, revising his *Institutes* several times, and authoring theological treatises as well as biblical commentaries. Calvin is also known for his debates with his contemporaries, including Michael Servetus, whose anti-Trinitarian views led to his execution in Geneva in 1553. Calvin also maintained friendly correspon-

dence with many reformers, including Melanchthon* and Bullinger*, the latter of whom he was able to come to an agreement with regarding the presence of Christ in the Lord's Supper with the signing of the *Consensus Tigurinus* in 1551, which brought a degree of unity between Geneva and Zurich and to the Reformed tradition. One of the foremost figures during the Reformation period, Calvin has an extensive exegetical and theological legacy.

Wolfgang Capito (1478?–1541). German Reformed humanist and theologian. Capito, a Hebrew scholar, produced a Hebrew grammar and published several Latin commentaries on books of the Hebrew Scriptures. He corresponded with Desiderius Erasmus* and fellow humanists. Capito translated Martin Luther's* early works into Latin for the printer Johann Froben. On meeting Luther, Capito was converted to Luther's vision, left Mainz and settled in Strasbourg, where he lectured on Luther's theology to the city clergy. With Martin Bucer,* Capito reformed liturgy, ecclesial life and teachings, education, welfare and government. Capito worked for the theological unification of the Swiss cantons with Strasbourg.

Pietro Carnesecchi (1508–1567). Italian humanist. Carnesecchi rose in the papal bureaucracy under Medici patronage, but after the death of Clement VII* he began to deviate from Catholic orthodoxy, aligning himself with Juan de Valdés.* While he retained relations with the established church, he also read Protestant works by theologians such as Luther,* Calvin,* and Bucer,* and his only extant doctrinal writing defends Bucer's view of the Eucharist over that of Zwingli.* Carnesecchi was able to avoid arrest by the Inquisition for a time, and his condemnation to death in absentia was pardoned under Pope Pius IV (1499–1565). However, Pius V (1504–1572) was a longtime opponent of Carnesecchi, and upon his election to the papal office, reopened the case and those of a number of others suspected of Protestant leanings. While seeking refuge in Florence, Carnesecchi was betrayed to the Inquisition by Cosimo I de' Medici, and following trial he was beheaded.

Thomas Cartwright (1535–1606). English Puritan preacher and professor. Cartwright was educated at St. John's College, Cambridge, although as an influential leader of the Presbyterian party in the Church of England he was continually at odds with the Anglican party, especially John Whitgift.* Cartwright spent some time as an exile in Geneva and Heidelberg as well as in Antwerp, where he pastored an English church. In 1585, Cartwright was arrested and eventually jailed for trying to return to England despite Elizabeth I's* refusal of his request. Many acknowledged him to be learned but also quite cantankerous. His publications include commentaries on Colossians, Ecclesiastes, Proverbs and the Gospels, as well as a dispute against Whitgift on church discipline.

Mathew Caylie (unknown). English Protestant minister. Caylie authored *The Cleansing of the Ten Lepers* (1623), an exposition of Luke 17:14-18.

John Chardon (d. 1601). Irish Anglican bishop. Chardon was educated at Oxford. He advocated Reformed doctrine in his preaching, yet opposed those Puritans who rejected Anglican church order. He published several sermons.

Martin Chemnitz (1522–1586). German Lutheran theologian. A leading figure in establishing Lutheran orthodoxy, Chemnitz studied theology and patristics at the University of Wittenburg, later becoming a defender of Philipp Melanchthon's* interpretation of the doctrine of justification. Chemnitz drafted a compendium of doctrine and reorganized the structure of the church in Wolfenbüttel; later, he led efforts to reconcile divisions within Lutheranism, culminating in the Formula of Concord*. One of his chief theological accomplishments was a modification of the christological doctrine of the *communicatio idiomatium*, which provided a Lutheran platform for understanding the sacramental presence of Christ's humanity in the Eucharist.

David Chytraeus (1531–1600). German Lutheran professor, theologian and biblical exegete. At the age of eight Chytraeus was admitted to the University of Tübingen. There he studied law, philology, philosophy, and theology, finally receiving his master's degree in 1546. Chytraeus befriended Philipp Melanchthon* while sojourning in Wittenberg, where he taught the *Loci communes*. While teaching exegesis at the University of Rostock Chytraeus became acquainted with Tilemann Heshusius,* who strongly influenced Chytraeus away from Philippist theology. As a defender of Gnesio-Lutheran theology Chytraeus helped organize churches throughout Austria in accordance with the Augsburg Confession.* Chytraeus coauthored the Formula of Concord* with Martin Chemnitz,* Andreas Musculus (1514–1581), Nikolaus Selnecker* and Jakob Andreae.* He wrote commentaries on most of the Bible, as well as a devotional work titled *Regula vitae* (1555) that described the Christian virtues.

David Clarkson (1622–1686). English Puritan theologian. After his dismissal from the pastorate on account of the Act of Uniformity (1662), little is known about Clarkson. At the end of his life he ministered with John Owen* in London.

Robert Cleaver (1571–1613). English Puritan pastor. Cleaver served as rector at Drayton in Oxfordshire until silenced by Archbishop Richard Bancroft for advocating Nonconformity. Despite opposition from ecclesiastical authorities, Cleaver enjoyed a reputation as an excellent preacher. His published works include sermons on Hebrews 4 and Song of Songs 2 as well as one on the last chapter of Proverbs. Cleaver also authored *The Parsimony of Christian Children*, which contained a defense of infant baptism against Baptist criticisms.

Michael Cobabus (d. 1686). German Lutheran theologian and mathematician. Trained in philosophy, mathematics, and theology at the University of Rostock, Cobabus remained in the city, serving as rector of the city school until appointed professor of mathematics at the university. He later received a doctorate in theology from the University of Griefswald and exchanged his position in the Rostock mathematics faculty for a professorship in theology.

Johannes Cocceius (1603–1669). German Reformed theologian. Cocceius first served as professor of biblical philology in his hometown of Bremen before moving to Franeker, where he taught Hebrew and theology, and finally to Leiden, where he spent the majority of his career as professor of theology. Cocceius is perhaps best remembered for his exposition of Reformed federal theology, defining the relationship between humanity and God in terms of progressive covenants. His critics, chief among them Gisbertus Voetius (1589–1676), argued that Cocceius's view of salvation history ignored the unity of the Scriptures and spiritualized the Old Testament. His other writings are extensive, including commentaries on all the books of the Bible, an influential Hebrew and Aramaic lexicon, and numerous works on theology, ethics, and philology.

John Colet (1467–1519). English Catholic priest, preacher and educator. Colet, appointed dean of Saint Paul's Cathedral by Henry VII, was a friend of Desiderius Erasmus,* on whose classical ideals Colet reconstructed the curriculum of Saint Paul's school. Colet was convinced that the foundation of moral reform lay in the education of children. Though an ardent advocate of reform, Colet, like Erasmus, remained loyal to the Catholic Church throughout his life. Colet's agenda of reform was oriented around spiritual and ethical themes, demonstrated in his commentaries on select books of the New Testament and the writings of Pseudo-Dionysius the Areopagite.

Vittoria Colonna (1490–1547). Italian Renaissance poet. Born into a noble family, Colonna was betrothed at three years of age to Fernando d'Ávalos (1489–1525), and they married in 1509. D'Ávalos was largely absent on military campaigns during their marriage, while she exercised his governorship of Benvenuto and became involved in the literary circles of Rome and Naples. One of the most important writers of her age, her friends included Pietro Bembo (1470–1547), Marguerite de Navarre,* and Michelangelo Buonarroti.* Writing primarily in the Petrarchan style, Colonna's reputation as a poet grew after the death of her husband, and much of her poetry was dedicated to his memory. Spiritual concerns form a major element of Colonna's writings, promoting contemplation and the ascetic life. While denied her

desire to take holy orders in widowhood, Colonna spent much of her life residing in religious communities, and she was actively involved in movements seeking their improvement, collaborating with reformers such as Reginald Pole,* Juan de Valdés,* and Bernardo Ochino.*

Gasparo Contarini (1483–1542). Italian statesman, theologian and reform-minded cardinal. Contarini was an able negotiator and graceful compromiser. Charles V requested Contarini as the papal legate for the Colloquy of Regensburg (1541), where Contarini reached agreement with Melanchthon* on the doctrine of justification (although neither the pope nor Luther* ratified the agreement). He had come to a similar belief in the priority of faith in the work of Christ rather than works as the basis for Christian life in 1511, though unlike Luther, he never left the papal church over the issue; instead he remainied within it to try to seek gentle reform, and he adhered to papal sacramental teaching. Contarini was an important voice for reform within the Catholic Church, always seeking reconciliation rather than confrontation with Protestant reformers. He wrote many works, including a treatise detailing the ideal bishop, a manual for lay church leaders, a political text on right governance and brief commentaries on the Pauline letters.

Christoph Corner (1518–1594). German Lutheran theologian. Professor of philosophy, rhetoric, and theology at the University of Frankfurt, Corner participated in the drafting of the Formula of Concord.* He also served as superintendent of churches in Mark Brandenberg.

Antonio del Corro (1527–1591). Spanish Reformed pastor and theologian. After encountering the ideas of Martin Luther* and other reformers, Corro abandoned the Hieronymite order. Leaving Spain to avoid charges of heresy, he traveled through Europe, spending time in Geneva and Lausanne before pastoring churches in France and the Low Countries. The arrival of Spanish armies in the Netherlands saw Corro and his family relocate to England, where he pastored a church of Spanish exiles in London and taught at Temple

Church and Oxford. Corro courted controversy throughout his career, entering into debates with a wide array of Protestant theologians. In England he was suspended from his pastorate for slander and examined a number of times for heresy, with some finding suggestions of Arianism in his Christology. Although these charges were never upheld, they clouded his later career and legacy.

Antonius Corvinus (1501–1553). German Lutheran theologian, pastor, and church administrator. Influenced by evangelical ideas, Corvinus left the Cistercian order to study at Wittenberg. He held a number of pastoral and administrative positions and published numerous works, including exegetical postils on Genesis, the Psalms, the Gospels, and Letters. Perhaps his greatest influence was his role in the composition of numerous church orders, including Northeim, Calenberg, Wolfenbüttel, and Hildesheim, giving the organizational foundation for the Lutheran church in Northern Germany and establishing its autonomy from regional rulers.

John Cosin (1594–1672). Anglican preacher and bishop. Early in his career Cosin was the vice chancellor of Cambridge and canon at the Durham cathedral. But as a friend of William Laud* and an advocate for "Laudian" changes, he was suspected of being a crypto-Catholic. In 1640 during the Long Parliament a Puritan lodged a complaint with the House of Commons concerning Cosin's "popish innovations." Cosin was promptly removed from office. During the turmoil of the English Civil Wars, Cosin sojourned in Paris among English nobility but struggled financially. Cosin returned to England after the Restoration in 1660 to be consecrated as the bishop of Durham. He published annotations on the Book of Common Prayer* and a history of the canon.

John Cotton (1584–1652). New England Puritan minister. Cotton was born to Puritan parents in Derby, England. He entered Trinity College, Cambridge, graduating with his bachelor's degree in 1603. Afterward, Cotton became a fellow at Emmanuel College, Cambridge, which at the time was heavily influenced by Puritanism. There, Cotton finished his master's degree in 1606.

Cotton then served as head lecturer, dean, and catechist for the college. It was in this period that he heard the preaching of Richard Sibbes,* which proved instrumental in Cotton's personal conversion. Cotton received a bachelor of divinity in 1610 from Cambridge and was shortly thereafter ordained into the priesthood of the Church of England. However, Cotton's increasing nonconformity brought him into conflict with episcopal authorities, which prompted him to move to the colony of Massachusetts in July 1633. Upon his arrival, he immediately assumed a position of leadership as the teacher of the First Church of Boston. Throughout his tenure, Cotton exerted significant influence in the civic and ecclesiastical affairs of the colony. He continued in his ministry at First Church until his death on December 23, 1652. Over the course of his ministry, Cotton wrote nearly forty works. Among these were the *Keys of the Kingdom of Heaven, and the Power Thereof* (1644) and *Exposition upon the Thirteenth Chapter of Revelation* (1655).

Council of Constance (1414–1418). Convened to resolve the Western Schism, root out heresy and reform the church in head and members, the council asserted in *Sacrosancta* (1415) the immediate authority of ecumenical councils assembled in the Holy Spirit under Christ—even over the pope. Martin V was elected pope in 1417 after the three papal claimants were deposed; thus, the council ended the schism. The council condemned Jan Hus,* Jerome of Prague (c. 1365–1416) and, posthumously, John Wycliffe. Hus and Jerome, despite letters of safe conduct, were burned at the stake. Their deaths ignited the Hussite Wars, which ended as a result of the Council of Basel's concessions to the Bohemian church. The council fathers sought to reform the church through the regular convocation of councils (*Frequens*; 1417). Martin V begrudgingly complied by calling the required councils, then immediately disbanding them. Pius II (r. 1458–1464) reasserted papal dominance through *Execrabilis* (1460), which condemned any appeal to a future council apart from the pope's authority.

Council of Trent (1545–1563) Convoked by Pope Paul III (r. 1534–1549) with the support of Charles V*, the nineteenth ecumenical council was convened in the northern Italian city of Trent. Attended primarily by Italian clerics, it met in three distinct phases. Beginning in December 1545, during its first eight sessions, the council issued doctrinal decrees, asserting the authority of tradition alongside Scripture, the authenticity of the Vulgate, the prerogative of the church in interpretation, and the necessity of human cooperation in the work of salvation. Ecclesial abuses were also addressed, as attempts were made to eliminate absenteeism and pluralism and devolve power from Rome to bishoprics and parishes. The council was suspended following the outbreak of the plague in Trent in March 1547. A number of Protestant delegates were present during the second phase of the council, which met between May 1551 and April 1552 under the supervision of Pope Julius III (r. 1550–1555). The primary achievement of this period of the council was the clarification of teachings on the seven sacraments, with transubstantiation, the objective efficacy of the Eucharist, and the necessity of auricular confession confirmed as dogma. Reconvened by Pope Pius IV (r. 1559–1565) in 1561, the third phase of the council addressed the relationship between bishops and Rome, resulting in affirmations of the divine appointment of the church hierarchy and the obligation of bishops to reside in their dioceses. Clerical education, the regulation of marriage, and teachings on purgatory, indulgences, the use of images, and the saints were also addressed.

Miles Coverdale (1488–1568). Anglican bishop. Coverdale is known for his translations of the Bible into English, completing William Tyndale's* efforts and later producing the Great Bible commissioned by Henry VIII* (1539). A former friar, Coverdale was among the Cambridge scholars who met at the White Horse Tavern to discuss Martin Luther's* ideas. During Coverdale's three terms of exile in Europe, he undertook various translations, including the Geneva Bible*.

He was appointed bishop of Exeter by Thomas Cranmer* and served as chaplain to Edward VI. Coverdale contributed to Cranmer's first edition of the Book of Common Prayer.*

William Cowper (Couper) (1568–1619). Scottish Puritan bishop. After graduating from the University of St. Andrews, Cowper worked in parish ministry for twenty-five years before becoming bishop. As a zealous Puritan and advocate of regular preaching and rigorous discipline, Cowper championed Presbyterian polity and lay participation in church government. Cowper published devotional works, sermon collections and a commentary on Revelation.

Walter Cradock (1606–1659). Welsh Anglican minister. Cradock was born in Llangwm, Monmouthshire, Wales. After completing his education at the University of Oxford, Cradock assumed his first position as curate at Peterson-super-Ely, Glamorgan. In 1633, Cradock, along with some other Welsh ministers, was reported to Archbishop William Laud* and the Court of High Commission for preaching nonconformity and for refusing the *Book of Sports*. In 1634 Cradock traveled throughout Wexham and Herefordshire encouraging the establishment of Welsh Nonconformist congregations. Cradock later became pastor of an Independent congregation at Llanfair Waterdine in 1639. When the English Civil War began, Cradock and his conventicle moved to Bristol, but when Royalist forces came to occupy the city, he and some of his group departed for All-Hallows-the-Great, where he preached regularly with Henry Jessey (1603–1663). In 1641, Cradock was among the group of preachers for Wales commissioned by the Long Parliament. Later, he served as regular preacher for the Barebones Parliament. Throughout this period, Cradock was an ardent supporter of Oliver Cromwell. Cradock lived the remainder of his life quietly while ministering to a congregation at Llangwm. Throughout his career, Cradock authored a number of devotional works, among which were *Gospel Liberty* (1648) and *Gospel Holiness* (1655).

Thomas Cranmer (1489–1556). Anglican archbishop and theologian. Cranmer supervised church reform and produced the first two editions of the Book of Common Prayer.* As a doctoral student at Cambridge, he was involved in the discussions at the White Horse Tavern. Cranmer contributed to a religious defense of Henry VIII's* divorce; Henry then appointed him Archbishop of Canterbury. Cranmer cautiously steered the course of reform, accelerating under Edward VI. After supporting the attempted coup to prevent Mary's assuming the throne, Cranmer was convicted of treason and burned at the stake. Cranmer's legacy is the splendid English of his liturgy and prayer books.

Richard Crashaw (1612–1649). English Catholic poet. Educated at Cambridge, Crashaw was fluent in Hebrew, Greek and Latin. His first volume of poetry was *Epigrammatum sacrorum liber* (1634). Despite being born into a Puritan family, Crashaw was attracted to Catholicism, finally converting in 1644 after he was forced to resign his fellowship for not signing the Solemn League and Covenant (1643). In 1649, he was made a subcanon of Our Lady of Loretto by Cardinal Palotta.

Herbert Croft (1603–1691). Anglican bishop. As a boy Croft converted to Catholicism; he returned to the Church of England during his studies at Oxford. Before the English Civil Wars, he served as chaplain to Charles I. After the Restoration, Charles II appointed him as bishop. Croft ardently opposed Catholicism in his later years.

John Crompe (d. 1661). Anglican priest. Educated at Cambridge, Crompe published a commentary on the Apostles' Creed, a sermon on Psalm 21:3 and an exposition of Christ's passion.

Oliver Cromwell (1599–1658). Commander of the Parliamentary forces during the English Civil War. Lord Protector of the Commonwealth of England, Scotland, and Ireland. Cromwell was born in Huntingdon, East Anglia, the only surviving son of Robert Cromwell. In 1616, he enrolled at the University of Cambridge as a fellow commoner. However, he withdrew from the university the following year due to his father's death. He represented Huntingdon in Parliament in 1628, and later Cambridge in the Short and Long Parliaments. During the Civil War, he commanded the Parliamentary forces, which he led to victory at the Battles of Marston Moor (1644) and Naseby (1645). After the execution of King Charles I in 1649, he became a member of the Council of State. It was at this time that the monarchy was abolished. In 1653, he was elevated to the position of Lord Protector of the Commonwealth. He declined the crown, though it was offered him in 1657. As Lord Protector, he endeavored to lead the postwar recovery, suppress military resistance, and advance British influence throughout Europe and the world. Moreover, he promoted a limited religious toleration in the kingdoms of England, Scotland, and Ireland. After his death in 1658, his son Richard (1626–1712) succeeded him as Lord Protector. However, due to incompetence, Richard was forced to resign, which paved the way for the Restoration of the monarchy in 1660 with the ascension of Charles II (1630–1685) to the throne. One year after the Restoration, Oliver Cromwell's body was disinterred from Westminster Abbey, hung on the gallows at Tyburn, and cast into an unmarked grave.

Caspar Cruciger (1504–1548). German Lutheran theologian. Recognized for his alignment with the theological views of Philipp Melanchthon,* Cruciger was a scholar respected among both Protestants and Catholics. In 1521, Cruciger came Wittenberg to study Hebrew and remained there most of his life. He became a valuable partner for Martin Luther* in translating the Old Testament and served as teacher, delegate to major theological colloquies and rector. Cruciger was an agent of reform in his birthplace of Leipzig, where at the age of fifteen he had observed the disputation between Luther and Johann Eck.*

Elisabeth Cruciger (c. 1500–1535). German Lutheran hymnist. Following her conversion to Lutheranism, Cruciger left the Praemonstratensian order and relocated to Wittenberg, where she married Caspar Cruciger.* While her authorship has been contested, recent scholarship has assigned Cruciger the place of the first female

Lutheran hymnist for her composition of "Lord Christ is the Only Son of God" (Herr Christ der einig Gotts Sohn) (1524).

Ralph Cudworth (d. 1624) English Protestant minister. Father of noted Cambridge Platonist Ralph Cudworth (1617–1688), the elder Cudworth was a fellow of Emanuel College, Cambridge and rector of Aller in Somersetshire.

Marguerite d'Angoulême (1492–1549). French Catholic noblewoman. The elder sister of King Francis I of France, Marguerite was the Queen of Navarre and Duchess of Alençon and Berry. She was a poet and author of the French Renaissance. She composed *The Mirror of a Sinful Soul* (1531)—condemned by the theologians of the Sorbonne for containing Lutheran ideas—and an unfinished collection of short stories, the *Heptaméron* (1558). A leading figure in the French Reformation, Marguerite was at the center of a network of reform-minded individuals that included Guillame Briçonnet,* Jacques Lefèvre d'Etaples,* Gérard Roussel (1500–1550) and Guillaume Farel (1489–1565).

Jakob Dachser (1486–1567). German Anabaptist theologian and hymnist. Dachser served as a Catholic priest in Vienna until he was imprisoned and then exiled for defending the Lutheran understanding of the Mass and fasting. Hans Hut* rebaptized him in Augsburg, where Dachser was appointed as a leader of the Anabaptist congregation. Lutheran authorities imprisoned him for nearly four years. In 1531 he recanted his Radical beliefs and began to catechize children with the permission of the city council. Dachser was expelled from Augsburg as a possible insurrectionist in 1552 and relocated to Pfalz-Neuberg. He published a number of poems, hymns and mystical works, and he versified several psalms.

Jean Daillé (1594–1670). French Reformed pastor. Born into a devout Reformed family, Daillé studied theology and philosophy at Saumur under the most influential contemporary lay leader in French Protestantism, Philippe Duplessis-Mornay (1549–1623). Daillé held to Amyraldianism—the belief that Christ died for all humanity inclusively, not particularly for the elect who would inherit salvation (though only the elect are in fact saved). He wrote a controversial treatise on the church fathers that aggravated many Catholic and Anglican scholars because of Daillé's apparent demotion of patristic authority in matters of faith.

Lambert Daneau (1535–1595). French Reformed pastor and theologian. After a decade of pastoring in France, following the St. Bartholomew's Day Massacre, Daneau fled to Geneva to teach theology at the Academy. He later taught in the Low Countries, finishing his career in southern France. Daneau's diverse works include tracts on science, ethics and morality as well as numerous theological and exegetical works.

John Davenant (1576–1641). Anglican bishop and professor. Davenant attended Queen's College, Cambridge, where he received his doctorate and was appointed professor of divinity. During the Remonstrant controversy, James I* sent Davenant as one of the four representatives for the Church of England to the Synod of Dordrecht.* Following James's instructions, Davenant advocated a *via media* between the Calvinists and the Remonstrants, although in later years he defended against the rise of Arminianism in England. In 1621, Davenant was promoted to the bishopric of Salisbury, where he was generally receptive to Laudian reforms. Davenant's lectures on Colossians are his best-known work.

William Day (1605–1684). Anglican theologian. Born and raised in Windsor, Berkshire, Day received his early education from Eton College. Afterward, he matriculated at King's College, Cambridge, where he was elected a fellow in 1624. Day received his BA in 1629, and MA in 1632. In 1635, Day was incorporated MA at Oxford and in 1637 became vicar of Mapledurham, Oxfordshire. Throughout his long career, Day conformed to all the ecclesiastical changes dictated by the government through the Restoration, during which he retained his vicarage. Finally, Day was made divinity reader at the King's Chapel, Windsor Chapel. He published two commentaries, *An Exposition of the Book of the Prophet Isaiah* (1654) and *A Paraphrase and Commentary upon the*

Epistle of St. Paul to the Romans (1666).

Defense of the Augsburg Confession (1531). See *Augsburg Confession.*

Hans Denck (c. 1500–1527). German Radical theologian. Denck, a crucial early figure of the German Anabaptist movement, combined medieval German mysticism with the radical sacramental theology of Andreas Bodenstein von Karlstadt* and Thomas Müntzer.* Denck argued that the exterior forms of Scripture and sacrament are symbolic witnesses secondary to the internally revealed truth of the Sprit in the human soul. This view led to his expulsion from Nuremberg in 1525; he spent the next two years in various centers of reform in the German territories. At the time of his death, violent persecution against Anabaptists was on the rise throughout northern Europe.

Stephen Denison (unknown). English Puritan pastor. Denison received the post of curate at St. Katherine Cree in London sometime in the 1610s, where he ministered until his ejection from office in 1635. During his career at St. Katherine Cree, Denison waded into controversy with both Puritans (over the doctrine of predestination) and Anglicans (over concerns about liturgical ceremonies). He approached both altercations with rancor and rigidity, although he seems to have been quite popular and beloved by most of his congregation. In 1631, William Laud* consecrated the newly renovated St. Katherine Cree, and as part of the festivities Denison offered a sermon on Luke 19:27 in which he publicly rebuked Laud for fashioning the Lord's house into a "den of robbers." Aside from the record of his quarrels, very little is known about Denison. In addition to *The White Wolf* (a 1627 sermon against another opponent), he published a catechism for children (1621), a treatise on the sacraments (1621) and a commentary on 2 Peter 1 (1622).

Marie Dentière (1495–1561). Belgian Reformed theologian. Dentière relinquished her monastic vows and married Simon Robert (d.1533), a former priest, in Strasbourg. After Robert died, she married Antoine Froment (1508–1581), a reformer in Geneva, and became involved in the reform of that city. Her best-known writings are a tract

addressed to Marguerite d'Angoulême,* the *Very Useful Epistle* (1539), in which she espoused the evangelical faith and the right of women to interpret and teach scripture, and a preface to Calvin's sermon on 1 Timothy 2:8-12. Dentière is the only woman to have her name inscribed on the International Monument to the Reformation in Geneva.

Edward Dering (c.1540–1576). English Puritan preacher. An early Puritan, Dering's prospects of advancement in the Elizabethan church were effectively ended after a sermon in front of the Queen in which he described her as an "untamed and unruly heifer" while criticizing the state of the church and clergy. While continuing with intemperate and critical attacks throughout his career, Dering established himself as a preacher at St. Paul's Cathedral in London, where he became known for his pastoral concern and desire to teach the assurance of salvation.

David Dickson (1583?–1663). Scottish Reformed pastor, preacher, professor and theologian. Dickson defended the Presbyterian form of ecclesial reformation in Scotland and was recognized for his iteration of Calvinist federal theology and expository biblical commentaries. Dickson served for over twenty years as professor of philosophy at the University of Glasgow before being appointed professor of divinity. He opposed the imposition of Episcopalian measures on the church in Scotland and was active in political and ecclesial venues to protest and prohibit such influences. Dickson was removed from his academic post following his refusal of the oath of supremacy during the Restoration era.

Veit Dietrich (1506–1549). German Lutheran preacher and theologian. Dietrich intended to study medicine at the University of Wittenberg, but Martin Luther* and Philipp Melanchthon* convinced him to study theology instead. Dietrich developed a strong relationship with Luther, accompanying him to the Marburg Colloquy (1529) and to Coburg Castle during the Diet of Augsburg (1530). After graduating, Dietrich taught on the arts faculty, eventually becoming dean. In 1535 he returned to his hometown, Nuremberg, to pastor.

Later in life, Dietrich worked with Melanchthon to reform the church in Regensburg. In 1547, when Charles V arrived in Nuremberg, Dietrich was suspended from the pastorate; he resisted the imposition of the Augsburg Interim to no avail. In addition to transcribing some of Luther's lectures, portions of the Table Talk and the very popular *Hauspostille* (1544), Dietrich published his own sermons for children, a manual for pastors and a summary of the Bible.

Louis de Dieu (1590–1642). Dutch Reformed pastor and linguist. Committed to his pastoral and teaching ministry in Leiden, Dieu turned down the opportunity to teach theology and Old Testament at the University of Utrecht. He published grammars of Hebrew (1626) and Persian (1639); a comparative grammar of Hebrew, Aramaic, and Syriac (1628); and a collection of writings on the New Testament text.

Giovanni Diodati (1576–1649). Italian Reformed theologian. Diodati was from an Italian banking family who fled for religious reasons to Geneva. There he trained under Theodore Beza;* on completion of his doctoral degree, Diodati became professor of Hebrew at the academy. He was an ecclesiastical representative of the church in Geneva (for whom he was a delegate at the Synod of Dordrecht*) and an advocate for reform in Venice. Diodati's chief contribution to the Italian reform movement was a translation of the Bible into Italian (1640–1641), which remains the standard translation in Italian Protestantism.

John Dod (c. 1549–1645). English Puritan pastor. Over the course of his lengthy pastoral career (spanning roughly sixty years), Dod was twice suspended for nonconformity and twice reinstated. A popular preacher, he published many sermons as well as commentaries on the Ten Commandments and the Lord's Prayer; collections of his sayings and anecdotes were compiled after his death.

John Donne (1572–1631). Anglican poet and preacher. Donne was born into a strong Catholic family. However, sometime between his brother's death from the plague while in prison in 1593 and the publication of his *Pseudo-Martyr* in 1610,

Donne joined the Church of England. Ordained to the Anglican priesthood in 1615 and already widely recognized for his verse, Donne quickly rose to prominence as a preacher—some have deemed him the best of his era. His textual corpus is an amalgam of erotic *and* divine poetry (e.g., "Batter My Heart"), as well as a great number of sermons.

Dordrecht Confession (1632). Dutch Mennonite confession. Adriaan Cornelisz (1581–1632) wrote the Dordrecht Confession to unify Dutch Mennonites. This basic statement of Mennonite belief and practice affirms distinctive doctrines such as nonresistance, shunning, footwashing and the refusal to swear oaths. Most continental Mennonites subscribed to this confession during the second half of the seventeenth century.

John Downame (c. 1571–1652). English Puritan pastor and theologian. See *English Annotations.*

Charles Drelincourt (1595–1669). French Reformed pastor, theologian and controversialist. After studying at Saumur Academy, Drelincourt pastored the Reformed Church in Paris for nearly fifty years. He was well known for his ministry to the sick. In addition to polemical works against Catholicism, he published numerous pastoral resources: catechisms, three volumes of sermons and a five-volume series on consolation for the suffering.

The Dutch Annotations (1657). See *Statenvertaling.*

Daniel Dyke (d. 1614). English Puritan preacher. Born of nonconformist stock, Dyke championed a more thorough reformation of church practice in England. After the promulgation of John Whitgift's* articles in 1583, Dyke refused to accept what he saw as remnants of Catholicism, bringing him into conflict with the bishop of London. Despite the petitions of his congregation and some politicians, the bishop of London suspended Dyke from his ministry for refusing priestly ordination and conformity to the Book of Common Prayer.* All of his work was published posthumously; it is mostly focused on biblical interpretation.

Johann Eck (Johann Maier of Eck) (1486–1543). German Catholic theologian. Though Eck was not an antagonist of Martin Luther* until the dispute over indulgences, Luther's Ninety-five Theses (1517) sealed the two as adversaries. After their debate at the Leipzig Disputation (1519), Eck participated in the writing of the papal bull that led to Luther's excommunication. Much of Eck's work was written to oppose Protestantism or to defend Catholic doctrine and the papacy; his *Enchiridion* was a manual written to counter-Protestant doctrine. However, Eck was also deeply invested in the status of parish preaching, publishing a five-volume set of postils. He participated in the assemblies at Regensburg and Augsburg and led the Catholics in their rejection of the Augsburg Confession.

Edward VI of England (1537–1553). English monarch. Son of Henry VIII* and Jane Seymour (1508–1537), Edward ascended to the throne as a minor, leaving the practical power of the monarchy in the hands of those appointed by the Regency council as Lord Protector of the Realm, first, his uncle, Edward Seymour, duke of Somerset (1500–1552), and afterwards, John Dudley, duke of Northumberland (1504–1553). Under Somerset and Northumberland, and with Thomas Cranmer* installed as Archbishop of Canterbury, the eclectic reforms made during the reign of Henry VIII were drawn into the service of a thoroughly Protestant transformation. During the reign of Edward, communion in two kinds was instituted, all services were held in the vernacular, and a series of ecclesiastical visitations oversaw the suppression of Catholic religion. Alongside the flood of Protestant refugees from the continent that sheltered in the kingdom, the publication of the revised Book of Common Prayer*, the Book of Homilies* and the Forty–Two Articles (1553) helped establish the future direction of Anglicanism.

Elizabeth I of England (1533–1603) English monarch. The daughter of Henry VIII* (r. 1509–1547) and Anne Boleyn (c. 1501–1536), Elizabeth outwardly conformed to Catholicism during the reign of her sister Mary I (r. 1553–1558), but her Protestant upbringing encouraged the hopes of many reformers upon her accession in 1558. With the 1559 Elizabethan Settlement, Elizabeth redefined England as a Protestant country, with the Act of Supremacy asserting the monarch as the head of the English church, and the Act of Uniformity establishing the 1559 *Book of Common Prayer** as the valid order of service within the realm. However, Elizabeth resisted the aggressive persecution of Catholics for political reasons, while also allowing some traditional vestments, furniture and ceremonies to be retained. Her moderate and pragmatic reforms frustrated many who wished for more thorough change and led to the emergence of the Puritan movement. Elizabeth faced numerous threats during her reign, including the machinations of Scottish Catholics and claims to the throne of Mary Stuart (1542–1547), leading to her rival's imprisonment and execution in 1587; the attempted invasion of England by Spain, which culminated in the celebrated defeat of the Spanish Armada in 1588; and a Catholic rebellion in Ireland that was suppressed during the Nine Years War (1594–1603). Elizabeth never married, and was succeeded on the throne by James I* following her death in 1603.

Edward Elton (1569–1624). Puritan minister. Elton served as pastor of St. Mary Magdalen's Church in Bermondsey, Surrey. Richard Baxter* praised him for his exegetical works, among which were *Three Excellent Pious Treatises in Sundry Sermons upon the Whole Seventh, Eighth, and Ninth Chapters of the Epistle to the Romans* and *An Exposition of the Epistle of St. Paul to the Colossians*.

English Annotations (1645; 1651; 1657). Under a commission from the Westminster Assembly, the editors of the English Annotations—John Downame* along with unnamed colleagues—translated, collated and digested in a compact and accessible format several significant Continental biblical resources, including Calvin's* commentaries, Beza's* *Annotationes majores* and Diodati's* *Annotations*.

Desiderius Erasmus (1466–1536). Dutch Catholic humanist and pedagogue. Erasmus, a celebrated humanist scholar, was recognized for translations of ancient texts, reform of education according to classical studies, moral and spiritual writings and the first printed edition of the Greek New Testament. A former Augustinian who never left the Catholic Church, Erasmus addressed deficiencies he saw in the church and society, challenging numerous prevailing doctrines but advocating reform. He envisioned a simple, spiritual Christian life shaped by the teachings of Jesus and ancient wisdom. He was often accused of collusion with Martin Luther* on account of some resonance of their ideas but hotly debated Luther on human will.

Paul Fagius (1504–1549). German Reformed Hebraist and pastor. After studying at the University of Heidelberg, Fagius went to Strasbourg where he perfected his Hebrew under Wolfgang Capito.* In Isny im Allgäu (Baden-Württemberg) he met the great Jewish grammarian Elias Levita (1469–1549), with whom he established a Hebrew printing press. In 1544 Fagius returned to Strasbourg, succeeding Capito as preacher and Old Testament lecturer. During the Augsburg Interim, Fagius (with Martin Bucer*) accepted Thomas Cranmer's* invitation to translate and interpret the Bible at Cambridge. However, Fagius died before he could begin any of the work. Fagius wrote commentaries on the first four chapters of Genesis and the deuterocanonical books of Sirach and Tobit.

Guillaume Farel (1489–1565) French Reformed preacher and theologian. At the vanguard of the French Reformation, Farel was a student of Jacques Lefèvre d'Étaples* and member of Archbishop Briçonnet's* circle in Meaux until his desire for more rapid change saw him depart in 1523 to preach the Protestant message in Basel, Montbéliard, Strasbourg, Bern, and Aigle. During this period of his ministry, he composed the first French Protestant book, an evangelical commentary on the Lord's Prayer and the Apostle's Creed, as well as the first French Confession of Faith. A catalyst in Geneva's acceptance of the Reformation in 1536, it was Farel who persuaded Calvin* to settle in the city. After he and Calvin were banished from Geneva in 1538, Farel accepted the pastorate in Neuchâtel, a position he held until his death while continuing to travel and support the Reformation in the French-speaking lands.

John Fary (unknown). English Puritan pastor. Fary authored *God's Severity on Man's Sterility* (1645), a sermon on the fruitless fig tree in Luke 13:6-9.

William Fenner (1600–1640). English Puritan pastor. After studying at Cambridge and Oxford, Fenner ministered at Sedgley and Rochford. Fenner's extant writings, which primarily deal with practical and devotional topics, demonstrate a zealous Puritan piety and a keen interest in Scripture and theology.

Charles Ferme (1566–1617). Scottish Reformed pastor and educator. After studying and teaching at the University of Edinburgh, Ferme pastored in Philorth, where he later served as the principal of a newly chartered university. The reconstitution of the episcopacy brought challenges for Ferme, and his resistance saw him imprisoned a number of times, including a three-year incarceration on the Isle of Bute. His only extant writing is a logical analysis of Romans.

First Helvetic Confession (1536). Anticipating the planned church council at Mantua (1537, but delayed until 1545 at Trent), Reformed theologians of the Swiss cantons drafted a confession to distinguish themselves from both Catholics and the churches of the Augsburg Confession.* Heinrich Bullinger* led the discussion and wrote the confession itself; Leo Jud, Oswald Myconius, Simon Grynaeus and others were part of the assembly. Martin Bucer* and Wolfgang Capito* had desired to draw the Lutheran and Reformed communions closer together through this document, but Luther* proved unwilling after Bullinger refused to accept the Wittenberg Concord (1536). This confession was largely eclipsed by Bullinger's Second Helvetic Confession.*

John Fisher (1469–1535). English Catholic bishop and theologian. This reputed preacher defended Catholic orthodoxy and strove to reform abuses in the church. In 1521 Henry VIII* honored Fisher with the title *Fidei Defensor* ("defender of the faith"). Nevertheless, Fisher opposed the king's divorce of Catherine of Aragon (1485–1536) and the independent establishment of the Church of England; he was convicted for treason and executed. Most of Fisher's works are polemical and occasional (e.g., on transubstantiation, against Martin Luther*); however, he also published a series of sermons on the seven penitential psalms. In addition to his episcopal duties, Fisher was the chancellor of Cambridge from 1504 until his death.

Matthias Flacius (1520–1575). Lutheran theologian. A native of Croatia, Matthias Flacius commenced his studies at the University of Tubingen, and completed them at Wittenberg, where through Luther's influence, he embraced the university's evangelical theology. Flacius began his career as instructor of Hebrew at the University of Wittenberg in 1544, and remained in this post until 1549. As a devoted follower of Luther's teachings, Flacius sought to defend them in their purity which drove him and Nikolaus von Amsdorf as leaders of the Gnesio-Lutherans to oppose the more moderate positions of Philipp Melanchthon and his sympathizers, the Philippists, in several controversies concerning the role of free will and good works in justification as well as relations with Calvinism. After serving as a professor at the University of Jena (1557–1561), Flacius spent the remainder of his life as an independent scholar, frequently moving from one city to another to escape persecution. Flacius died in Frankfurt am Main in 1575. His important exegetical works are *De vocabula Dei* (1549), *Clavis Scripturae Sacrae* (1567), and *Glossa Novi Testamenti* (1570). Flacius also published two historical works, *Catalogus Testium Veritatis* (1556) and the *Magdeburg Centuries*.

Marcantonio Flaminio (1498–1550). Italian humanist and poet. Flaminio was dependent on patronage, and he spent much of his life in the houses of noble benefactors in Bologna, Genoa, and Verona. While he never left the Roman church, he was drawn to intellectual currents that sought reform. In Naples, he participated in an intellectual circle that included Juan de Valdés* and Pietro Carnesecchi* before joining the house of Cardinal Pole* in Viterbo. Alongside his poetry and humanistic writings, Flaminio also edited one of the most significant Italian texts of the Reformation, Benedetto de Mantova's* *The Benefit of Christ* (1543).

John Flavel (c. 1630–1691). English Puritan pastor. Trained at Oxford, Flavel ministered in southwest England from 1650 until the Act of Uniformity in 1662, which reaffirmed the compulsory use of the Book of Common Prayer. Flavel preached unofficially for many years, until his congregation was eventually allowed to build a meeting place in 1687. His works were numerous, varied and popular.

Giovanni Battista Folengo (1490–1559). Italian Catholic exegete. In 1528 Folengo left the Benedictine order, questioning the validity of monastic vows; he returned to the monastic life in 1534. During this hiatus Folengo came into contact with the Neapolitan reform-minded circle founded by Juan de Valdés.* Folengo published commentaries on the Psalms, John, 1–2 Peter and James. Augustin Marlorat* included Folengo's comment in his anthology of exegesis on the Psalms. In 1580 Folengo's Psalms commentary was added to the Index of Prohibited Books.

Formula of Concord (1577). After Luther's* death, intra-Lutheran controversies between the Gnesio-Lutherans (partisans of Luther) and the Philippists (partisans of Melanchthon*) threatened to cause a split among those who had subscribed to the Augsburg Confession.* In 1576, Jakob Andreae,* Martin Chemnitz,* Nikolaus Selnecker,* David Chytraeus* and Andreas Musculus (1514–1581) met with the intent of resolving the controversies, which mainly regarded the relationship between good works and salvation, the third use of the law, and the role of the human will in accepting God's grace. In 1580, celebrating the fiftieth anniversary of the presentation of the Augsburg Confession to Charles V (1500–1558), the *Book of Concord* was printed as the authoritative interpretation of the Augsburg Confession; it included the three ancient creeds, the Augsburg Confession, its Apology (1531), the Schmalkald Articles,* Luther's *Treatise on the Power and Primacy of the Pope* (1537) and both his Small and Large Catechisms (1529).

John Foxe (1516–1587). English Protestant martryrologist, historian. John Foxe was born in Boston, Lincolnshire. After completing his early education, Foxe became a fellow at Magdalen College, Oxford, where he completed his BA degree in 1537, and MA in 1543. Also he was lecturer in logic from 1539 to 1540. However, in 1545, Foxe was forced to resign from Magdalen because he had adopted Protestant beliefs. After leaving Oxford, Foxe became tutor to the children of the Earl of Surrey. During this time Foxe made the acquaintance of John Bale (1495–1562) who fostered his interest in history. When Mary Tudor ascended the throne of England in 1553, Foxe fled to the continent. While there, Foxe traveled to Frankfurt, where in 1555 he met Edmund Grindal (1519–1583), who had been composing accounts of Protestant martyrs. Foxe later joined Grindal in Basel, where he translated his narratives into Latin. Foxe published the book resulting from his labors in Basel in 1559. After Elizabeth I* succeeded to the throne in the same year, Foxe returned to England. Upon his return he began working with the printer, John Day, who published the first English edition of Foxe's work. This voluminous work, *The Acts and Monuments*, underwent four editions during the remainder of the author's lifetime. *The Acts and Monuments* contributed significantly to the development of the national identity and piety of Elizabethan England. Shorter versions of this work are known simply as *Foxe's Book of Martyrs*.

Francis I of France (1494–1547). French monarch. Francis ascended to the French throne following the death of Louis XII (1462–1515), who was both his cousin and father-in-law. Much of Francis's reign was dominated by warfare. In Italy, victory over the Swiss allowed him to assert his dynastic claim to the Duchy of Milan, and extract liberties for the French church from Pope Leo X* through the Concordat of Bologna. His campaign against Charles V* was less successful, however, as Milan was lost and following defeat at the Battle of Pavia, Francis was taken prisoner. His release was negotiated by his sister, Marguerite d'Angouleme*, though he reneged in its terms once reaching safety, ensuring continued conflict with the Holy Roman Emperor throughout his reign. Francis fostered humanistic learning within his kingdom, and while he resisted Lutheran and other evangelical thought, he gave some space for its expression, giving protection to scholars such as those gathered around his sister and Bishop Guillaume Briçonnet* at Meaux. His desire for social order saw him take increasingly strident steps against the Reformation, however, particularly after his bedchamber was pamphleted during the Affair of the Placards, and the final years of his reign saw a significant increase in attempts to reassert Catholic doctrine and stamp out Protestantism with persecution.

Sebastian Franck (1499–1542). German Radical theologian. Franck became a Lutheran in 1525, but by 1529 he began to develop ideas that distanced him from Protestants and Catholics. Expelled from Strasbourg and later Ulm due to his controversial writings, Franck spent the end of his life in Basel. Franck emphasized God's word as a divine internal spark that cannot be adequately expressed in outward forms. Thus he criticized religious institutions and dogmas. His work consists mostly of commentaries, compilations and translations. In his sweeping historical *Chronica* (1531), Franck supported numerous heretics condemned by the Catholic Church and criticized political and church authorities.

Leonhard Frick (d. 1528). Austrian Radical martyr. See *Kunstbuch*.

John Frith (1503–1533). English reformer, author, and martyr. Frith was born in Westerham, Kent. He was the son of Richard Frith, the innkeeper of the White Horse Inn. After receiving his earlier education at Sevenoaks Grammar School and Eton College, Frith matriculated at Queen's College, Cambridge, where Stephen Gardiner (1497–1555), future bishop of Winchester, and opponent of the English Reformation, was his tutor. Frith graduated with his BA degree in 1525, having obtained proficiency in Latin and mathematics. While still a student, Frith met Thomas

Bilney (1495–1531), who most likely introduced him to evangelical faith. After graduating, Frith became a junior canon at Christ Church, Oxford. However, while at Oxford, Frith along with nine others was imprisoned in a fish cellar for possessing what ecclesiastical authorities considered "heretical books." Upon his release, Frith traveled to the Continent, where he assisted William Tyndale* with his translation work. Also while on the Continent, Frith translated some antipapal polemical works, and authored *A Disputation of Purgatory*. Upon Frith's return to England in 1532, he was arrested and imprisoned several times for publicly preaching against transubstantiation and purgatory. Eventually, Frith was imprisoned in the Tower of London, and later transferred to Newgate Prison. He was burned at the stake on July 4, 1533.

Gallic Confession (1559). This confession was accepted at the first National Synod of the Reformed Churches of France (1559). It was intended to be a touchstone of Reformed faith but also to show to the people of France that the Huguenots—who faced persecution—were not seditious. The French Reformed Church presented this confession to Francis II (1544–1560) in 1560, and to his successor, Charles IX (1550–1574), in 1561. The later Genevan draft, likely written by Calvin,* Beza* and Pierre Viret (1511–1571), was received as the true Reformed confession at the seventh National Synod in La Rochelle (1571).

Geneva Bible (originally printed 1560). During Mary I's reign many English Protestants sought safety abroad in Reformed territories of the Empire and the Swiss Cantons, especially in Calvin's* Geneva. A team of English exiles in Geneva led by William Whittingham (c. 1524–1579) brought this complete translation to press in the course of two years. Notable for several innovations—Roman type, verse numbers, italics indicating English idiom and not literal phrasing of the original languages, even variant readings in the Gospels and Acts—this translation is most well known for its marginal notes, which reflect a strongly Calvinist theology. The notes explained Scripture in an accessible way for the laity,

also giving unlearned clergy a new sermon resource. Although controversial because of its implicit critique of royal power, this translation was wildly popular; even after the publication of the Authorized Version (1611) and James I's* 1616 ban on its printing, the Geneva Bible continued to be the most popular English translation until after the English Civil Wars.

Johann Gerhard (1582–1637). German Lutheran theologian, professor and superintendent. Gerhard is considered one of the most eminent Lutheran theologians, after Martin Luther* and Martin Chemnitz.* After studying patristics and Hebrew at Wittenberg, Jena and Marburg, Gerhard was appointed superintendent at the age of twenty-four. In 1616 he was appointed to a post at the University of Jena, where he reintroduced Aristotelian metaphysics to theology and gained widespread fame. His most important work was the nine-volume *Loci Theologici* (1610–1625). He also expanded Chemnitz's harmony of the Gospels (*Harmonia Evangelicae*), which was finally published by Polykarp Leyser (1552–1610) in 1593. Gerhard was well-known for an irenic spirit and an ability to communicate clearly.

George Gifford (c. 1548–1600). English Puritan pastor. Gifford was suspended for nonconformity in 1584. With private support, however, he was able to continue his ministry. Through his published works he wanted to help develop lay piety and biblical literacy.

Anthony Gilby (c. 1510–1585). English Puritan translator. During Mary I's reign, Gilby fled to Geneva, where he assisted William Whittingham (c. 1524–1579) with the Geneva Bible.* He returned to England to pastor after Elizabeth I's* accession. In addition to translating numerous continental Reformed works into English—especially those of John Calvin* and Theodore Beza*—Gilby also wrote commentaries on Micah and Malachi.

Bernard Gilpin (1517–1583). Anglican theologian and priest. In public disputations, Gilpin defended Roman Catholic theology against John Hooper (c. 1495-1555) and Peter Martyr Vermigli.* These debates caused Gilpin to reexamine his faith. Upon Mary I's accession, Gilpin resigned his benefice. He sojourned in Belgium and France, returning to pastoral ministry in England in 1556. Gilpin dedicated himself to a preaching circuit in northern England, thus earning the moniker "the Apostle to the North." His zealous preaching and almsgiving roused royal opposition and a warrant for his arrest. On his way to the queen's commission, Gilpin fractured his leg, delaying his arrival in London until after Mary's death and thus likely saving his life. His only extant writing is a sermon on Luke 2 confronting clerical abuses.

Paul Glock (c. 1530–1585). German Radical preacher. A teenage convert to Hutterite Anabaptism, Glock spent nineteen years imprisoned at Hohenwittlingen, unwilling to recant. While incarcerated, he wrote hymns, a confession and defense of his beliefs, and numerous letters that proved influential in the development of Anabaptist thought. After helping extinguish a fire at the prison in 1576, Glock was freed and settled with the Brethren in Moravia.

Thomas Goodwin (1600–1679). Puritan minister. Goodwin was born October 5, 1600, in Norfolk. After receiving his early education from local schools, Goodwin matriculated at Christ College, Cambridge, which was a prime center of Puritan influence. He graduated with the BA degree in 1616 and MA in 1620. Upon receiving his MA, Goodwin became a fellow and lecturer at the university. In October 1620, Goodwin experienced a profound conversion on his twentieth birthday. After his conversion, Goodwin joined the Puritan party at Cambridge. He was licensed to preach in the Church of England in 1625. Three years later, Goodwin became lecturer at Trinity Church. He served as vicar of this church from 1632 to 1634. Unwilling to comply with Archbishop William Laud's* directives for conformity, Goodwin was forced to resign all of his ecclesiastical and academic positions, and leave Cambridge. During the remainder of the 1630s, due to John Cotton's* influence, Goodwin came to adopt the principles of Independency. In 1639, in order to escape the increasing restrictions of

unauthorized preachers, Goodwin fled to the Netherlands, where he worked with other English Independent exiles. In 1641, Goodwin returned to England per Parliament's request, and preached before it on April 27, 1642. Goodwin was later appointed a delegate to the Westminster Assembly. In the Assembly, Goodwin proved himself to be one of the foremost advocates of Independency. After the Westminster Assembly adjourned, Goodwin was appointed a lecturer at Oxford, and a year later became president of Magdalen College. Furthermore, Goodwin served as an advisor to Oliver Cromwell (1599–1658) and as the Lord Protector's Oxford commissioner. Goodwin also tended to Cromwell on his deathbed. In addition to his university and advisory duties, Goodwin pastored an Independent church at Oxford. Notably, Goodwin was one of the primary authors of the Savoy Declaration of Faith (1658), which served as the confession of faith for the Independent/Congregational churches. When Charles II ascended to the throne of England in 1660, Goodwin withdrew from Oxford to London, where he pastored an Independent congregation until his death at the age of eighty. Throughout his career, Goodwin produced an enormous literary corpus, which includes many exegetical works. Best known among these are his expositions of Ephesians and Revelation.

Glossa ordinaria. This standard collection of biblical commentaries consists of interlinear and marginal notes drawn from patristic and Carolingian exegesis appended to the Vulgate*; later editions also include Nicholas of Lyra's* Postilla. The Glossa ordinaria and the Sentences of Peter Lombard (c. 1100–1160) were essential resources for all late medieval and early modern commentators.

Simon Goulart (1543–1628) French Reformed pastor, translator, and theologian. Goulart spent most of his career as a pastor in Geneva and its surrounds, particularly at the city parish of St. Gervais, and was the leader of the Company of Pastors during the last decades of his life. A prolific translator, he published numerous French editions of classical, patristic, and contemporary works from diverse authors including Plutarch, Seneca, Chrysostom, Cyprian, Tertullian, Beza*, Perkins* and Vermigli*. He also composed numerous devotional writings, important histories of early French Protestantism, and polemical treatises supporting the Huguenot cause.

Conrad Grebel (c. 1498–1526). Swiss Radical theologian. Grebel, considered the father of the Anabaptist movement, was one of the first defenders and performers of believers' baptism, for which he was eventually imprisoned in Zurich. One of Huldrych Zwingli's* early compatriots, Grebel advocated rapid, radical reform, clashing publicly with the civil authorities and Zwingli. Grebel's views, particularly on baptism, were influenced by Andreas Bodenstein von Karlstadt* and Thomas Müntzer.* Grebel advocated elimination of magisterial involvement in governing the church; instead, he envisioned the church as lay Christians determining their own affairs with strict adherence to the biblical text, and unified in volitional baptism.

William Greenhill (1591–1671). English Puritan pastor. Greenhill attended and worked at Magdalen College. He ministered in the diocese of Norwich but soon left for London, where he preached at Stepney. Greenhill was a member of the Westminster Assembly of Divines and was appointed the parliament chaplain by the children of Charles I. Oliver Cromwell included him among the preachers who helped draw up the Savoy Declaration. Greenhill was evicted from his post following the Restoration, after which he pastored independently. Among Greenhill's most significant contributions to church history was his *Exposition of the Prophet of Ezekiel*.

Catharina Regina von Greiffenberg (1633–1694). Austrian Lutheran poet. Upon her adulthood her guardian (and half uncle) sought to marry her; despite her protests of their consanguinity and her desire to remain celibate she relented in 1664. After the deaths of her mother and husband, Greiffenberg abandoned her home to debtors and joined her friends Susanne Popp (d. 1683) and Sigmund von Birken (1626–1681) in Nuremberg. During her final

years she dedicated herself to studying the biblical languages and to writing meditations on Jesus' death and resurrection, which she never completed. One of the most important and learned Austrian poets of the Baroque period, Greiffenberg published a collection of sonnets, songs and poems (1662) as well as three sets of mystical meditations on Jesus' life, suffering and death (1672; 1683; 1693). She participated in a society of poets called the Ister Gesellschaft.

Lady Jane Grey (1537–1554). English Protestant monarch, sometimes known as "the Nine Days Queen." The eldest daughter of Henry Grey and Frances Brandon, the daughter of Henry VIII's* younger sister Mary, Jane received an extensive Protestant and humanist education. She married Lord Guildford Dudley (c. 1535–1554), son of Edward VI's* chief minister John Dudley, Duke of Northumberland (1504–1553). Seeking to avoid succession by Edward's Catholic half-sister Mary I, Edward and Northumberland conspired to alter the order of succession, naming Jane as heir in the king's will. Following Edward's death, Jane reluctantly took the crown on July 9, 1553, but Northumberland and other Protestants were unable to raise adequate support for her claim and the Privy Council proclaimed Mary queen on July 19. Upon Mary's accession, Jane was imprisoned in the Tower of London and after trial was executed alongside her husband for treason. A handful of her writings exist demonstrating her religious affections, while the story of her martyrdom is prominent in John Foxe's Acts and Monuments.

Argula von Grumbach (c. 1490–c. 1564) German Lutheran noblewoman. Grumbach, an attendant of Queen Kunigunde of Austria (1465–1520), was one of the first women to publish in support of the Reformation. She is best known for letters from 1523 and 1524 written in defense of Arsacius Seehofer (1503–1545), a lecturer at the university of Ingolstadt accused of Lutheranism. For unknown reasons, Grumberg ceased to publish after 1524, although her private correspondence after this time demonstrates a continued effort to support evangelical reform.

Johann Jacob Grynaeus (1540–1617). Swiss Reformed theologian. Raised Lutheran, Grynaeus replaced his father as pastor at Rotelen. After becoming professor of Old Testament at Basel, however, Grynaeus caused conflict by embracing Reformed theology. He avoided controversy by spending two years at the University of Heidelberg. Upon his return to Basel, his opponents had largely died, and he was made superintendent of the church in the city and professor of New Testament. Grynaeus aligned the Basel church with his Reformed convictions and reorganized the city's educational system while preaching regularly and composing numerous theological, exegetical, and practical works.

William Guild (1586–1657). Scottish Reformed minister and theologian. Guild was born in Aberdeen and educated at Marischal College. He was licensed to preach in 1605 and ordained to serve as minister of the parish of King Edward in 1608. In 1617, Guild joined the protest for the liberties of the Scottish national church. While in Edinburgh, Guild met the acquaintance of Bishop Lancelot Andrewes,* who was accompanying King James VI/I* on his royal visit to the city. Moreover, Guild dedicated his best-known work, *Moses Unveiled* (1620), to both Andrewes and the king. He was later appointed chaplain to Charles I, and shortly thereafter received the degree of doctor of divinity. In 1631, Guild was given his second charge in Aberdeen. When he assumed this charge, Guild expressed his support for episcopacy. He signed the National Covenant in 1638 with some conditions. However, when in 1640 an army came to Aberdeen to enforce full subscription to the Covenant, Guild fled to the Netherlands. After returning to Scotland later that year, he was appointed Guild Principal for King's College Aberdeen, but was deprived of this post by Oliver Cromwell's (1599–1658) military commissioners in 1651. Following his deprivation, Guild lived in retirement until his death in Aberdeen.

Rudolf Gwalther (1519–1586). Swiss Reformed preacher. Gwalther was a consummate servant of the Reformed church in Zurich, its chief religious officer and preacher, a responsibility fulfilled previously by Huldrych Zwingli* and Heinrich Bullinger.* Gwalther provided sermons and commentaries and translated the works of Zwingli into Latin. He worked for many years alongside Bullinger in structuring and governing the church in Zurich. Gwalther also strove to strengthen the connections to the Reformed churches on the Continent and England: he was a participant in the Colloquy of Regensburg (1541) and an opponent of the Formula of Concord.*

Matthias Hafenreffer (1561–1619). German Lutheran theologian. After holding pastoral positions in Herenberg, Ehingen, and Stuttgart, Hafenreffer was appointed professor of theology at Tübingen, a position he held for more than twenty-five years. He composed exegetical works on Nahum, Habakkuk, and Ezekiel, a number of polemical works, and a theological *loci communes* that served as a common textbook within the Lutheran churches for much of the seventeenth century.

Hans Has von Hallstatt (d. 1527). Austrian Reformed pastor. See *Kunstbuch.*

Henry Hammond (1605–1660). Anglican priest. After completing his studies at Oxford, Hammond was ordained in 1629. A Royalist, Hammond helped recruit soldiers for the king; he was chaplain to Charles I. During the king's captivity, Hammond was imprisoned for not submitting to Parliament. Later he was allowed to pastor again, until his death. Hammond published a catechism, numerous polemical sermons and treatises as well as his *Paraphrase and Annotations on the New Testament* (1653).

Jörg Haug (Unknown) German Anabaptist leader. Haug was a radical preacher during the 1525 Peasant's Revolt and composed a tract entitled *A Christian Order of a True Christian* (1524) enumerating seven degrees of faith reached by Christians.

Peter Hausted (d. 1645). Anglican priest and playwright. Educated at Cambridge and Oxford, Hausted ministered in a number of parishes and preached adamantly and vehemently against Puritanism. He is best known for his play *The*

Rival Friends, which is filled with invective against the Puritans; during a performance before the king and queen, a riot nearly broke out. Haustead died during the siege of Banbury Castle.

Erhart Hegenwald (Unknown). Swiss Protestant teacher and doctor. A teacher at the Pfäffen Monastery in St. Gallen and at the Schola Carolina in Zurich, Hegenwald recorded the minutes of Zwingli's* First Zurich Disputation in 1523. Correspondence demonstrates he remained in contact with the Zurich reformers while he studied medicine at Wittenberg, and after graduating in 1526, he may have practiced as a physician in Frankfurt.

Heidelberg Catechism (1563). This German Reformed catechism was commissioned by the elector of the Palatinate, Frederick III (1515–1576) for pastors and teachers in his territories to use in instructing children and new believers in the faith. It was written by theologian Zacharias Ursinus (1534–1583) in consultation with Frederick's court preacher Kaspar Olevianus* and the entire theology faculty at the University of Heidelberg. The Heidelberg Catechism was accepted as one of the Dutch Reformed Church's Three Forms of Unity—along with the Belgic Confession* and the Canons of Dordrecht—at the Synod of Dordrecht,* and became widely popular among other Reformed confessional traditions throughout Europe.

Ursula Hellrigel (b. c. 1521). Austrian Anabaptist. Imprisoned for her heterodox beliefs at 17, authorities sought Hellrigel's recantation, but she refused to acquiesce. After five years she was released from prison and exiled from the Tyrol. The thirty-sixth hymn in the first known Anabaptist hymnal, the *Ausbund* (1654), is commonly attributed to her.

Niels Hemmingsen (1513–1600). Danish Lutheran theologian. Hemmingsen studied at the University of Wittenberg, where he befriended Philipp Melanchthon.* In 1542, Hemmingsen returned to Denmark to pastor and to teach Greek, dialectics and theology at the University of Copenhagen. Foremost of the Danish theologians, Hemmingsen oversaw the preparation and publication of the first Danish Bible (1550). Later in his career he became embroiled in controversies because of his Philippist theology, especially regarding the Eucharist. Due to rising tensions with Lutheran nobles outside of Denmark, King Frederick II (1534–1588) dismissed Hemmingsen from his university post in 1579, transferring him to a prominent but less internationally visible Cathedral outside of Copenhagen. Hemmingsen was a prolific author, writing commentaries on the New Testament and Psalms, sermon collections and several methodological, theological and pastoral handbooks.

Henry IV of France (1553–1610). French monarch. Son of Jeanne of Navarre* and Antoine de Bourbon (1518–1562), Henry's religious loyalties wavered throughout his life. Raised Protestant at the behest of his mother, he practiced Catholicism while attending the Valois court. After his mother's death in 1572, Henry succeeded her as King of Navarre and soon afterwards married Margaret of Valois (1553–1615), the daughter of Henry II of France (1519–1559) and Catherine de' Medici (1519–1589). Their wedding provided the occasion for the St. Bartholomew's Day Massacre, when Catholic forces seized the opportunity to decimate the Huguenot leadership gathered to celebrate the nuptials in Paris, leading to an outbreak of mob violence that devastated the Huguenot movement. A great proportion of the Protestants in France were killed in the weeks that followed the wedding, while many others, including Henry, reconverted to Catholicism. In 1576, Henry escaped the influence of the Valois court, returned his allegiance to Protestantism and took a leadership role amongst the Huguenots. Following the assassination of Henry III of France (1551–1589), Henry was the presumptive heir, but French Catholics were unwilling to accept his rule and Henry was unable to assert his prerogative outside Huguenot strongholds. In 1593, therefore, Henry converted again to Catholicism, with legend claiming he justified his decision with the phrase "Paris is worth a mass." Over the following years, Henry established his authority throughout his kingdom, and while remaining Catholic, provided some relief to Protestants, particularly through the Edict of Nantes (1598), essentially ending the Religious Wars. Henry's pragmatic reign ended with his assassination by a Radical Catholic in 1610.

King Henry VIII of England (1491–1547). English monarch. The second son of Henry VII (r. 1485–1509) and Elizabeth of York (1466–1503), Henry VIII succeeded his father to the English throne, his elder brother Edward having died in 1502. Soon after accession, he married his brother's widow, Catherine of Aragon (1485–1536). Following several stillbirths and the birth of a daughter, Mary, Henry, who was desperate for a male heir to head off dynastic challenges, wished separation from Catherine in order to marry Anne Boleyn (c. 1501–1536). Believing his marriage cursed as it transgressed the commands in Leviticus against marrying a brother's widow, Henry sought dispensation from the church for his annulment and remarriage. While the case was first heard by a papal legate in England, it was transferred to Rome upon the order of Pope Clement VII*, who wished to placate Charles V, Catherine's nephew, whose troops had recently sacked Rome and held the pope under house arrest. Henry asserted praemunire, arguing that as king, he was supreme in his own kingdom. With the formation of the Reformation Parliament in 1529, the legislative process to disentangle the English Church from the Roman was begun. The issue of Henry's divorce was finalized in 1533, after Thomas Cranmer* became Archbishop of Canterbury and declared his marriage to Catherine invalid. While Henry's divorce, assertion of royal supremacy, and subversion of Catholic institutions gave impetus to English Protestantism, Henry's beliefs remained essentially Catholic, and these continued to be enforced by law. He ultimately married six times, and was succeeded by Edward VI*, his son by his third wife, Jane Seymour (1508–1537). Elizabeth I*, Henry's daughter by Anne Boleyn, later became Queen and with the Elizabethan Settlement in 1559, redefined England as a Protestant country.

George Herbert (1593–1633). Anglican minister, theologian, and poet. Herbert was born in Montgomery Powys, Wales, on April 3, 1593, to a noble family. After completing his early education at Westminster School, Herbert matriculated at Trinity College, Cambridge, in 1609. He graduated with both his bachelor's and master's degrees. Shortly thereafter Herbert was elected a fellow of the college, and then became Reader of Rhetoric. From 1620 to 1627, Herbert was Public Orator for the University of Cambridge. In 1624, Herbert was elected to Parliament. However, after the death of King James I,* and of his other major patrons, Herbert withdrew from politics to pursue a career in the church. Toward this end, Herbert was ordained to the priesthood of the Church of England in 1630, and appointed rector of Fugglestone St. Peter and later Bemerton St. Andrews in Wiltshire near Salisbury. While at St. Andrews, Herbert composed his collection of poems titled *The Temple* and his guide for rural ministers, *A Priest to the Temple, or The Country Parson: His Character and Rule of Holy Life.* Twice a week Herbert traveled to Salisbury, where he attended services at Salisbury Cathedral. Following the services, Herbert would compose music with the cathedral musicians. Herbert died of consumption in 1633.

Tilemann Hesshus (1527–1588). German Lutheran theologian and pastor. Hesshus studied under Philipp Melanchthon* but was a staunch Gnesio-Lutheran. With great hesitation—and later regret—he affirmed the Formula of Concord.* Heshuss ardently advocated for church discipline, considering obedience a mark of the church. Unwilling to compromise his strong convictions, especially regarding matters of discipline, Hesshus was regularly embroiled in controversy. He was expelled or pressed to leave Goslar, Rostock, Heidelberg, Bremen, Magdeburg, Wesel, Königsberg and Samland before settling in Helmstedt, where he remained until his death. He wrote numerous polemical tracts concerning ecclesiology, justification, the sacraments and original sin, as well as commentaries on Psalms, Romans,

1–2 Corinthians, Galatians, Colossians and 1–2 Timothy, and a postil collection.

Cornelis Hoen (c. 1460–1524). Dutch humanist, jurist, and theologian. A lawyer at the Court of Holland at the Hague, Hoen was prosecuted in 1523 over his sympathy for the evangelical message. He proposed a symbolic interpretation of Christ's presence in the Eucharist justified with reference to Matthew 24:23 in an influential, posthumously-published treatise.

Melchior Hoffman (1495?–1543). German Anabaptist preacher. First appearing as a Lutheran lay preacher in Livonia in 1523, Hoffman's claim to direct revelation, his perfectionist teachings and his announcements that the end of the world would occur in 1533 saw him alienated from both Lutheran and Reformed circles. After converting to Anabaptism in Strasbourg in 1530, a city he claimed would rise as the spiritual Jerusalem, Hoffman escaped brief arrest and fled to the Netherlands, where his preaching made him the first to bring the radical faith to the Low Countries. Believing himself to be Elijah, Hoffman gathered numerous followers, including future Anabaptist leaders Obbe Philips* and Jan Mathijs (d. 1534), until his arrest in Strasbourg in 1533, whereupon he was imprisoned for the final decade of his life. A tendency toward mystical allegory and apocalyptic exegesis supported by direct revelation is found in his writings, which include commentaries on Romans, Revelation, and Daniel 12 alongside numerous tracts, pamphlets, and letters.

Nathaniel Holmes (1599–1678). English Puritan theologian. Educated at Oxford, Holmes was a preacher in the Anglican Church until his millenarian views led him to establish an independent congregation. His publications include defenses of infant baptism and exclusive psalmody; treatises against witchcraft, usury, and astrology; and a commentary on the Song of Solomon.

Christopher Hooke (unknown). English Puritan physician and pastor. Hooke published a treatise promoting the joys and blessings of childbirth (1590) and a sermon on Hebrews

12:11-12. To support the poor, Hooke proposed a bank funded by voluntary investment of wealthy households.

Richard Hooker (c. 1553–1600). Anglican priest. Shortly after graduating from Corpus Christi College Oxford, Hooker took holy orders as a priest in 1581. After his marriage, he struggled to find work and temporarily tended sheep until Archbishop John Whitgift* appointed him to the Temple Church in London. Hooker's primary work is *The Laws of Ecclesiastical Polity* (1593), in which he sought to establish a philosophical and logical foundation for the highly controversial Elizabethan Religious Settlement (1559). The Elizabethan Settlement, through the Act of Supremacy, reasserted the Church of England's independence from the Church of Rome, and, through the Act of Uniformity, constructed a common church structure based on the reinstitution of the Book of Common Prayer.* Hooker's argumentation strongly emphasizes natural law and anticipates the social contract theory of John Locke (1632–1704).

Thomas Hooker (1586–1647) English-American Puritan Preacher. Hooker ministered at churches in Surrey and Essex and established a school to teach pastors until threatened with arrest as Archbishop Laud* worked to suppress Puritanism. Fleeing to Holland and then New England, he pastored a church in New Town (later Cambridge), Massachusetts before playing an important role in the foundation of Hartford, Connecticut and assisting with the composition of the state constitution.

John Hooper (d. 1555). English Protestant bishop and martyr. Impressed by the works of Huldrych Zwingli* and Heinrich Bullinger,* Hooper joined the Protestant movement in England. However, after the Act of Six Articles was passed, he fled to Zurich, where he spent ten years. He returned to England in 1549 and was appointed as a bishop. He stoutly advocated a Zwinglian reform agenda, arguing against the use of vestments and for a less "popish" Book of Common Prayer.* Condemned as a heretic for denying transubstantiation, Hooper was burned at the stake during Mary I's reign.

Rudolf Hospinian (Wirth) (1547–1626). Swiss Reformed theologian and minister. After studying theology at Marburg and Heidelberg, Hospinian pastored in rural parishes around Zurich and taught secondary school. In 1588, he transferred to Zurich, ministering at Grossmünster and Fraumünster. A keen student of church history, Hospinian wanted to show the differences between early church doctrine and contemporary Catholic teaching, particularly with regard to sacramental theology. He also criticized Lutheran dogma and the Formula of Concord*. Most of Hospinian's corpus consists of polemical treatises; he also published a series of sermons on the Magnificat.

Hans Hotz (dates unknown). Swiss Anabaptist leader. Born in Grüningen, near Zurich, Hotz was an associate of Georg Blaurock.* He defended Anabaptism as spokesman for the Swiss Brethren at disputations in Zofingen (1532) and Bern (1538).

Caspar Huberinus (1500–1553). German Lutheran theologian and pastor. After studying theology at Wittenberg, Huberinus moved to Augsburg to serve as Urbanus Rhegius's* assistant. Huberinus represented Augsburg at the Bern Disputation (1528) on the Eucharist and images. In 1551, along with the nobility, Huberinus supported the Augsburg Interim, so long as communion of both kinds and regular preaching were allowed. Nevertheless the people viewed him as a traitor because of his official participation in the Interim, nicknaming him "Buberinus" (i.e., scoundrel). He wrote a number of popular devotional works as well as tracts defending Lutheran eucharistic theology against Zwinglian and Anabaptist detractions.

Balthasar Hubmaier (1480/5–1528). German Radical theologian. Hubmaier, a former priest who studied under Johann Eck,* is identified with his leadership in the peasants' uprising at Waldshut. Hubmaier served as the cathedral preacher in Regensberg, where he became involved in a series of anti-Semitic attacks. He

was drawn to reform through the early works of Martin Luther*; his contact with Huldrych Zwingli* made Hubmaier a defender of more radical reform, including believers' baptism and a memorialist account of the Eucharist. His involvement in the Peasants' War led to his extradition and execution by the Austrians.

Aegidius Hunnius (1550–1603). German Lutheran theologian and preacher. Educated at Tübingen by Jakob Andreae (1528–1590) and Johannes Brenz,* Hunnius bolstered and advanced early Lutheran orthodoxy. After his crusade to root out all "crypto-Calvinism" divided Hesse into Lutheran and Reformed regions, Hunnius joined the Wittenberg theological faculty, where with Polykarp Leyser (1552–1610) he helped shape the university into an orthodox stronghold. Passionately confessional, Hunnius developed and nuanced the orthodox doctrines of predestination, Scripture, the church and Christology (more explicitly Chalcedonian), reflecting their codification in the Formula of Concord.* He was unafraid to engage in confessional polemics from the pulpit. In addition to his many treatises (most notably *De persona Christi*, in which he defended Christ's ubiquity), Hunnius published commentaries on Matthew, John, Ephesians and Colossians; his notes on Galatians, Philemon and 1 Corinthians were published posthumously.

Jan Hus (d. 1415). Bohemian reformer and martyr. This popular preacher strove for reform in the church, moral improvement in society, and an end to clerical abuses and popular religious superstition. He was branded a heretic for his alleged affinity for John Wycliffe's writings; however, while he agreed that a priest in mortal sin rendered the sacraments inefficacious, he affirmed the doctrine of transubstantiation. The Council of Constance* convicted Hus of heresy, banned his books and teaching, and, despite a letter of safe conduct, burned him at the stake.

Hans Hut (1490–1527). German Radical leader. Hut was an early leader of a mystical, apocalyptic strand of Anabaptist radical reform. His theological views were shaped by Andreas Bodenstein von Karlstadt,* Thomas Müntzer* and Hans Denck,* by whom Hut had been baptized. Hut rejected society and the established church and heralded the imminent end of days, which he perceived in the Peasants' War. Eventually arrested for practicing believers' baptism and participating in the Peasants' War, Hut was tortured and died accidentally in a fire in the Augsburg prison. The next day, the authorities sentenced his corpse to death and burned him.

George Hutcheson (1615–1674). Scottish Puritan pastor. Hutcheson, a pastor in Edinburgh, published commentaries on Job, John and the Minor Prophets, as well as sermons on Psalm 130.

Roger Hutchinson (d. 1555). English reformer. Little is known about Hutchinson except for his controversies. He disputed against the Mass while at Cambridge and debated with Joan Bocher (d. 1550), who affirmed the doctrine of the celestial flesh. During the Marian Restoration he was deprived of his fellowship at Eton because he was married.

Andreas Hyperius (1511–1564). Dutch Protestant theologian. After a peripatetic humanist education that encompassed studies in theology, canon law, and medicine, Hyperius became professor of theology at Marburg in 1541 and held this position until his death. Often viewed as mediating between Lutheran and Reformed thought, Hyperius was particularly concerned with the practical application of theology, demonstrated in his composition of the first Protestant text on homiletic method.

Abraham Ibn Ezra (1089–c. 1167). Spanish Jewish rabbi, exegete and poet. In 1140 Ibn Ezra fled his native Spain to escape persecution by the Almohad Caliphate. He spent the rest of his life as an exile, traveling through Europe, North Africa and the Middle East. His corpus consists of works on poetry, exegesis, grammar, philosophy, mathematics and astrology. In his commentaries on the Old Testament, Ibn Ezra restricts himself to *peshat* (see *quadriga*).

Valentin Ickelshamer (c. 1500–1547). German Radical teacher. After time at Erfurt, he studied under Luther,* Melanchthon,* Bugenhagen* and

Karlstadt* in Wittenberg. He sided with Karlstadt against Luther, writing a treatise in Karlstadt's defense. Ickelshamer also represented the Wittenberg guilds in opposition to the city council. This guild committee allied with the peasants in 1525, leading to Ickelshamer's eventual exile. His poem in the Marpeck Circle's *Kunstbuch** is an expansion of a similar poem by Sebastian Franck.*

Thomas Jackson (1579–1640). Anglican theologian and priest. Before serving as the president of Corpus Christi College at Oxford for the final decade of his life, Jackson was a parish priest and chaplain to the king. His best known work is a twelve-volume commentary on the Apostles' Creed.

King James I of England (VI of Scotland) (1566–1625). English monarch. The son of Mary, Queen of Scots, James ascended to the Scottish throne in 1567 following his mother's abdication. In the Union of the Crowns (1603), he took the English and Irish thrones after the death of his cousin, Elizabeth I.* James's reign was tumultuous and tense: Parliament and the nobility often opposed him, church factions squabbled over worship forms and ecclesiology, climaxing in the Gunpowder Plot. James wrote treatises on the divine right of kings, law, the evils of smoking tobacco and demonology. His religious writings include a versification of the Psalms, a paraphrase of Revelation and meditations on the Lord's Prayer and passages from Chronicles, Matthew and Revelation. He also sponsored the translation of the Authorized Version*—popularly remembered as the King James Version.

Jeanne of Navarre (1528–1572) French Reformed noblewoman. Daughter of Henry II, King of Navarre (1503–1555) and Marguerite d'Angoulême*, Jeanne was forced into a strategic marriage at age 12 by her uncle, Francis I* to William, Duke of Cleves (1516–1592). Shifting political alignments allowed her an annulment after four years and in 1548 she wed the first Prince of the Blood, Antoine de Bourbon (1518–1562). Jeanne took the throne of her father, and after making a public announcement of her conversion to the evangelical faith, established a

Reformed community at Béarn. A regular correspondent of reformers such as Calvin* and Beza* and an advocate for the reformation of her lands, Jeanne nevertheless remained largely neutral and advocated tolerance during the first years of religious war. At the outbreak of the Third War of Religion (1569–1570), however, she recognized her moderate position was untenable, and from the Protestant stronghold of La Rochelle served as political head for the Huguenot cause alongside Gaspard de Coligny (1519–1572), commander of the Huguenot armed forces.

John Jewel (1522–1571). Anglican theologian and bishop. Jewel studied at Oxford where he met Peter Martyr Vermigli.* After graduating in 1552, Jewel was appointed to his first vicarage and became the orator for the university. Upon Mary I's accession, Jewel lost his post as orator because of his Protestant views. After the trials of Thomas Cranmer* and Nicholas Ridley,* Jewel affirmed Catholic teaching to avoid their fate. Still he had to flee to the continent. Confronted by John Knox,* Jewel publicly repented of his cowardice before the English congregation in Frankfurt, then reunited with Vermigli in Strasbourg. After Mary I's death, Jewel returned to England and was consecrated bishop in 1560. He advocated low-church ecclesiology, but supported the Elizabethan Settlement against Catholics and Puritans. In response to the Council of Trent, he published the *Apoligia ecclesiae Anglicanae* (1562), which established him as the apostle for Anglicanism and incited numerous controversies.

St. John of the Cross (Juan de Yepes y Álvarez) (1542–1591). Spanish Catholic mystic. Born into poverty, Álvarez entered the Carmelite order in Medina del Campo, where, after studying theology at Salamanca, he met the famed mystic Teresa of Ávila (1515–1582). Drawn to her vision of the contemplative life, with two others, he established the first house of Discalced (barefoot) Carmelite Friars and became a leader in the Catholic reform movement. An exceptional administrator and spiritual leader, for more than twenty years, John of the Cross sought to return his order to its original vision of asceticism and

prayer while establishing many new reformed Carmelite houses. He encountered significant resistance in his work for renewal, however, and spent nine months imprisoned and tortured by his Carmelite superiors. Considered among the foremost poets in Spanish literary history, his poems, including *The Spiritual Canticle, Ascent of Mount Carmel*, and *The Dark Night of the Soul* demonstrate his overriding desire for spiritual growth and closeness to God.

Justus Jonas (1493–1555). German Lutheran theologian, pastor and administrator. Jonas studied law at Erfurt, where he befriended the poet Eobanus Hessus (1488–1540), whom Luther* dubbed "king of the poets"; later, under the influence of the humanist Konrad Muth, Jonas focused on theology. In 1516 he was ordained as a priest, and in 1518 he became a doctor of theology and law. After witnessing the Leipzig Disputation, Jonas was converted to Luther's* cause. While traveling with Luther to the Diet of Worms, Jonas was appointed professor of canon law at Wittenberg. Later he became its dean of theology, lecturing on Romans, Acts and the Psalms. Jonas was also instrumental for reform in Halle. He preached Luther's funeral sermon but had a falling-out with Melanchthon* over the Leipzig Interim. Jonas's most influential contribution was translating Luther's *The Bondage of the Will* and Melanchthon's *Loci communes* into German.

William Jones (1561–1636). Anglican minister and theologian. After teaching at Cambridge, Jones ministered at East Bergholt in Suffolk for forty-four years, publishing a commentary on Philemon and Hebrews and tracts on suffering, the nativity, and arrangements to be made before one's death.

David Joris (c. 1501–1556). Dutch Radical pastor and hymnist. This former glass painter was one of the leading Dutch Anabaptist leaders after the fall of Münster (1535), although due to his increasingly radical ideas his influence waned in the early 1540s. Joris came to see himself as a "third David," a Spirit-anointed prophet ordained to proclaim the coming third kingdom of God, which would be established in the Netherlands with Dutch as its *lingua franca*. Joris's interpretation of Scripture, with his heavy emphasis on personal mystical experience, led to a very public dispute with Menno Simons* whom Joris considered a teacher of the "dead letter." In 1544 Joris and about one hundred followers moved to Basel, conforming outwardly to the teaching of the Reformed church there. Today 240 of Joris's books are extant, the most important of which is his *Twonder Boek* (1542/43).

Jörg Haugk von Jüchsen (unknown). German Radical preacher. Nothing is known of Haugk's life except that during the 1524–1525 Peasants' War in Thuringia, he was elected as a preacher by the insurrectionists in his district. He composed one extant tract, titled *A Christian Order of a True Christian: Giving an Account of the Origin of His Faith*, published in 1526 but likely written before the Peasants' War. While lacking reference to most distinctive Anabaptist doctrines, this pamphlet became popular among radicals as it set out the stages of Christian growth toward perfection.

Andreas Bodenstein von Karlstadt (Carlstadt) (1486–1541). German Radical theologian. Karlstadt, an early associate of Martin Luther* and Philipp Melanchthon* at the University of Wittenberg, participated alongside Luther in the dispute at Leipzig with Johann Eck.* He also influenced the configuration of the Old Testament canon in Protestantism. During Luther's captivity in Wartburg Castle in Eisenach, Karlstadt oversaw reform in Wittenberg. His acceleration of the pace of reform brought conflict with Luther, so Karlstadt left Wittenberg, eventually settling at the University of Basel as professor of Old Testament (after a sojourn in Zurich with Huldrych Zwingli*). During his time in Switzerland, Karlstadt opposed infant baptism and repudiated Luther's doctrine of Christ's real presence in the Eucharist.

Edward Kellett (d. 1641). Anglican theologian and priest. Kellett published a sermon concerning the reconversion of an Englishman from Islam, a tract on the soul and a discourse on the Lord's Supper in connection with Passover.

David Kimchi (**Radak**) (1160–1235). French Jewish rabbi, exegete and philosopher. Kimchi wrote an important Hebrew grammar and dictionary, as well as commentaries on Genesis, 1–2 Chronicles, the Psalms and the Prophets. He focused on *peshat* (see *quadriga*). In his Psalms commentary he attacks Christian interpretation as forced, irrational and inadmissible. While Sebastian Münster* censors and condemns these arguments in his *Miqdaš YHWH* (1534–1535), he and many other Christian commentators valued Kimchi's work as a grammatical resource.

Moses Kimchi (**Remak**) (1127–1190). French Jewish rabbi and exegete. He was David Kimchi's* brother. He wrote commentaries on Proverbs and Ezra-Nehemiah. Sebastian Münster* translated Kimchi's concise Hebrew grammar into Latin; many sixteenth-century Christian exegetes used this resource.

Andreas Knöpken (c. 1468–1539). German Lutheran pastor. Knöpken worked in Pomerania as assistant to Johannes Bugenhagen* before relocating to Riga. Here he served as pastor of St. Peter's, and after a brief setback that saw him return to his previous position, he returned and won a disputation before the authorities, which allowed him to undertake the evangelical reform of the city. Knöpken oversaw the reorganization of the churches and schools, composed the church order, wrote a commentary on Romans, and arranged a number of hymns based on the Psalms.

John Knox (1513–1572). Scottish Reformed preacher. Knox, a fiery preacher to monarchs and zealous defender of high Calvinism, was a leading figure of reform in Scotland. Following imprisonment in the French galleys, Knox went to England, where he became a royal chaplain to Edward VI. At the accession of Mary, Knox fled to Geneva, studying under John Calvin* and serving as a pastor. Knox returned to Scotland after Mary's death and became a chief architect of the reform of the Scottish church (Presbyterian), serving as one of the authors of the Book of Discipline and writing many pamphlets and sermons.

Antonius Broickwy von Königstein (1470–1541). German Catholic preacher. Very little is known about this important cathedral preacher in Cologne. Strongly opposed to evangelicals, he sought to develop robust resources for Catholic homilies. His postils were bestsellers, and his biblical concordance helped Catholic preachers to construct doctrinal loci from Scripture itself.

Kunstbuch. In 1956, two German students rediscovered this unique collection of Anabaptist works. Four hundred years earlier, a friend of the recently deceased Pilgram Marpeck*—the painter Jörg Probst—had entrusted this collection of letters, tracts and poetry to a Zurich bindery; today only half of it remains. Probst's redaction arranges various compositions from the Marpeck Circle into a devotional anthology focused on the theme of the church as Christ incarnate (cf. Gal 2:20).

Osmund Lake (c. 1543–1621). English Pastor who ministered at Ringwood in Hampshire.

François Lambert (Lambert of Avignon) (1487–1530). French Reformed theologian. In 1522, after becoming drawn to the writings of Martin Luther* and meeting Huldrych Zwingli,* Lambert left the Franciscan order. He spent time in Wittenberg, Strasbourg, and Hesse, where Lambert took a leading role at the Homberg Synod (1526) and in creating a biblically based plan for church reform. He served as professor of theology at Marburg University from 1527 to his death. After the Marburg Colloquy (1529), Lambert accepted Zwingli's symbolic view of the Eucharist. Lambert produced nineteen books, mostly biblical commentaries that favored spiritual interpretations; his unfinished work of comprehensive theology was published posthumously.

Eitelhans Langenmantel (d. 1528). German Radical writer. The son of the mayor of Augsburg, Langenmantel was converted to Anabaptism and was rebaptized by Hans Hut* in 1527. Arrested for his heterodox views later that year, he was freed after accepting the validity of infant baptism during a debate, but after renouncing his recantation in 1528, he was rearrested and beheaded. Seven tracts he composed during 1526 and 1527 survive, focusing on the Lord's Supper and the moral life.

Hugh Latimer (c. 1485–1555). Anglican bishop and preacher. Latimer was celebrated for his sermons critiquing the idolatrous nature of Catholic practices and the social injustices visited on the underclass by the aristocracy and the individualism of Protestant government. After his support for Henry's petition of divorce he served as a court preacher under Henry VIII* and Edward VI. Latimer became a proponent of reform following his education at Cambridge University and received license as a preacher. Following Edward's death, Latimer was tried for heresy, perishing at the stake with Nicholas Ridley* and Thomas Cranmer.*

William Laud (1573–1645). Anglican archbishop, one of the most pivotal and controversial figures in Anglican church history. Early in his career, Laud offended many with his highly traditional, anti-Puritan approach to ecclesial policies. After his election as Archbishop of Canterbury in 1633, Laud continued to strive against the Puritans, demanding the eastward placement of the Communion altar (affirming the religious centrality of the Eucharist), the use of clerical garments, the reintroduction of stained-glass windows, and the uniform use of the Book of Common Prayer.* Laud was accused of being a crypto-Catholic—an ominous accusation during the protracted threat of invasion by the Spanish Armada. In 1640 the Long Parliament met, quickly impeached Laud on charges of treason, and placed him in jail for several years before his execution.

Ludwig Lavater (1527–1586). Swiss Reformed pastor and theologian. Under his father-in-law Heinrich Bullinger,* Lavater became an archdeacon in Zurich. In 1585 he succeeded Rudolf Gwalther* as the city's Antistes. He authored a widely disseminated book on demonology, commentaries on Chronicles, Proverbs, Ecclesiastes, Nehemiah and Ezekiel, theological works, and biographies of Bullinger and Konrad Pellikan.*

Laws and Liberties of the Inhabitants of Massachusetts (1647). North American colonial constitution. The first printed set of laws in the American colonies, the 1647 *Laws and Liberties of the Inhabitants of Massachusetts* was a revision of the *Massachusetts Body of Liberties* (1641), a legal code collected by Puritan minister Nathaniel Ward (1578–1652). The *Laws and Liberties* codified Puritan expectations of doctrine and morality, and included provision for the punishment for heresy, stipulating banishment for Anabaptism. The majority of the document consists of practical clauses addressing general and specific aspects of communal and commercial life.

John Lawson (unknown). Seventeenth-century English Puritan. Lawson wrote *Gleanings and Expositions of Some of Scripture* (1646) and a treatise on the sabbath in the New Testament.

Jacques Lefèvre d'Étaples (Faber Stapulensis) (1460?–1536). French Catholic humanist, publisher and translator. Lefèvre d'Étaples studied classical literature and philosophy, as well as patristic and medieval mysticism. He advocated the principle of *ad fontes*, issuing a full-scale annotation on the corpus of Aristotle, publishing the writings of key Christian mystics, and contributing to efforts at biblical translation and commentary. Although he never broke with the Catholic Church, his views prefigured those of Martin Luther,* for which he was condemned by the University of Sorbonne in Paris. He then found refuge in the court of Marguerite d'Angoulême, where he met John Calvin* and Martin Bucer.*

Edward Leigh (1602–1671). English Puritan biblical critic, historian and politician. Educated at Oxford, Leigh's public career included appointments as a Justice of the Peace, an officer in the parliamentary army during the English Civil Wars and a member of Parliament. Although never ordained, Leigh devoted himself to the study of theology and Scripture; he participated in the Westminster Assembly. Leigh published a diverse corpus, including lexicons of Greek, Hebrew and juristic terms, and histories of Roman, Greek and English rulers. His most important theological work is *A Systeme or Body of Divinity* (1662).

John Lightfoot (1602–1675). Anglican priest and biblical scholar. After graduating from Cambridge, Lightfoot was ordained and pastored at several small parishes. He continued to study classics under the support of the politician Rowland Cotton (1581–1634). Siding with the Parliamentarians during the English Civil Wars, Lightfoot relocated to London in 1643. He was one of the original members of the Westminster Assembly, where he defended a moderate Presbyterianism. His best-known work is the six-volume *Horae Hebraicae et Talmudicae* (1658–1677), a verse-by-verse commentary illumined by Hebrew customs, language and the Jewish interpretive tradition.

Wenceslaus Linck (1482–1547). German Lutheran theologian and preacher. As dean of the theology faculty at the University of Wittenberg and successor to Johannes von Staupitz* as the prior of the Augustinian Monastery, Linck worked closely with Martin Luther* and attended the Heidelberg Disputation with him. He replaced Staupitz as vicar-general of the Augustinian order in 1520 in Germany, a capacity in which he pronounced all members free from their vows before renouncing the order himself. After periods of ministry in Munich and Altenburg, Linck settled in Nuremberg, where he became known as an exemplary preacher and an advisor to cities undertaking Protestant reform. He published a significant number of sermons and practical tracts as well as a paraphrase and annotations on the Old Testament.

Peter Lombard (1095–1160). Scholastic theologian, bishop of Paris. Though little is known about his life, some records indicate that Lombard came from the region of Novara in Lombardy. Bernard of Clairvaux* patronized his studies at Reims, and later recommended him for further study at St. Victor in Paris. In 1144, Lombard participated in an examination of the writings of Gilbert of Poitiers for heresy. Lombard became a canon at Notre Dame in 1145, and an archdeacon there in 1156. Meanwhile he spent a year and a half in Rome as an assistant to Theobald, bishop of Paris. Lombard was elected bishop of Paris in 1159. He died less than a year later. Lombard's most important work was the *Four Books of the Sentences*, which served as the standard textbook for theology throughout the remainder of the Middle Ages, and at the beginning of the early modern period. Additionally, Lombard produced commentaries on the Psalms and Pauline epistles.

Johannes Lonicer (1499–1569). German Lutheran theologian and linguist. After studying in Erfurt and Wittenberg, Lonicer renounced his Augustinian vows. He briefly taught Hebrew at the University of Freiburg, but controversy saw him flee to Strasburg, where he worked with a printer, translating some early Lutheran vernacular works into Latin. At the opening of the University of Marburg, Lonicer was appointed to teach Greek and Hebrew, and he later also served as professor of theology.

Lucas Lossius (1508–1582). German Lutheran teacher and musician. While a student at Leipzig and Wittenberg, Lossius was deeply influenced by Melanchthon* and Luther,* who found work for him as Urbanus Rhegius's* secretary. Soon after going to work for Rhegius, Lossius began teaching at a local gymnasium (or secondary school), *Das Johanneum*, eventually becoming its headmaster. Lossius remained at *Das Johanneum* until his death, even turning down appointments to university professorships. A man of varied interests, he wrote on dialectics, music and church history, as well as publishing a postil and a five-volume set of annotations on the New Testament.

Sibrandus Lubbertus (c. 1555–1625). Dutch Reformed theologian. Lubbertis, a key figure in the establishment of orthodox Calvinism in Frisia, studied theology at Wittenburg and Geneva (under Theodore Beza*) before his appointment as professor of theology at the University of Franeker. Throughout his career, Lubbertis advocated for high Calvinist theology, defending it in disputes with representatives of Socinianism, Arminianism and Roman Catholicism. Lubbertis criticized the Catholic theologian Robert Bellarmine and fellow Dutch reformer Jacobus Arminius*; the views of the latter he opposed as a prominent participant in the Synod of Dordrecht.*

Martin Luther (1483–1546). German Lutheran priest, professor, and theologian. Martin Luther was born in Eisleben, Saxony, to an entrepreneurial minor. Upon completing his earlier education at Eisenach, Luther matriculated at the University of Erfurt where he completed his BA in 1502, and MA in 1505. While at Erfurt, Luther studied the philosophy of William of Ockham (1285–1347), and his disciple, Gabriel Biel (1420–1495). After receiving his MA, Luther proceeded to the study of law. However, a number of events culminating in his promise to St. Anne (the patron saint of minors) to become a monk compelled Luther to withdraw from law school and join the Augustinian monastery at Erfurt in 1505. At this monastery, Luther was ordained a priest. Later, the Augustinians sent Luther to the University of Wittenberg to study theology. In 1512, Luther received his doctorate, and took up the post of lecturer in Bible at Wittenberg, a position he would hold the rest of his life. While a professor at this university, Luther reinterpreted the doctrine of justification. Convinced that righteousness comes only from God's grace, he disputed the sale of indulgences with his *Ninety–Five Theses*, which he reportedly posted to the door of All Saints' Church in Wittenberg on October 31, 1517. Luther's positions brought conflict with Rome. He challenged the Mass, transubstantiation, and communion in one kind, and his denial of papal authority led to excommunication. Though Luther was condemned by the Diet of Worms, Frederick III, the Elector of Saxony, provided him safe haven. Luther later returned to Wittenberg with public order collapsing under Andreas Bodenstein von Karlstadt* and steered a more cautious path of reform. Among his most influential works are three treatises published in 1520: *To the Christian Nobility of the German Nation, On the Babylonian Captivity of the Church*, and *On the Freedom of a Christian*. His rendering of the Bible and liturgy in the vernacular, as well as his hymns and sermons, proved extensively influential.

Georg Major (1502–1574). German Lutheran theologian. Major was on the theological faculty of the University of Wittenberg, succeeding as dean Johannes Bugenhagen* and Philipp Melanchthon.* One of the chief editors on the Wittenberg edition of Luther's works, Major is most identified with the controversy bearing his name, in which he stated that good works are necessary to salvation. Major qualified his statement, which was in reference to the totality of the Christian life. The Formula of Concord* rejected the statement, ending the controversy. As a theologian, Major further refined Lutheran views of the inspiration of Scripture and the doctrine of the Trinity.

John (Mair) Major (1467–1550). Scottish Catholic philosopher. Major taught logic and theology at the universities of Paris (his alma mater), Glasgow and St Andrews. His broad interests and impressive work drew students from all over Europe. While disapproving of evangelicals (though he did teach John Knox*), Major advocated reform programs for Rome. He supported collegial episcopacy and even challenged the curia's teaching on sexuality. Still he was a nominalist who was critical of humanist approaches to biblical exegesis. His best-known publication is *A History of Greater Britain, Both England and Scotland* (1521), which promoted the union of the kingdoms. He also published a commentary on Peter Lombard's *Sentences* and the Gospel of John.

Juan de Maldonado (1533–1583). Spanish Catholic biblical scholar. A student of Francisco de Toledo,* Maldonado taught philosophy and theology at the universities of Paris and Salamanca. Ordained to the priesthood in Rome, he revised the Septuagint under papal appointment. While Maldonado vehemently criticized Protestants, he asserted that Reformed baptism was valid and that mixed confessional marriages were acceptable. His views on Mary's immaculate conception proved controversial among many Catholics who conflated his statement that it was not an article of faith with its denial. He was intrigued by demonology (blaming demonic influence for the Reformation). All his work was

published posthumously; his Gospel commentaries were highly valued and important.

Thomas Manton (1620–1677). English Puritan minister. Manton, educated at Oxford, served for a time as lecturer at Westminster Abbey and rector of St. Paul's, Covent Garden, and was a strong advocate of Presbyterianism. He was known as a rigorous evangelical Calvinist who preached long expository sermons. At different times in his ecclesial career he worked side-by-side with Richard Baxter* and John Owen.* In his later life, Manton's Nonconformist position led to his ejection as a clergyman from the Church of England (1662) and eventual imprisonment (1670). Although a voluminous writer, Manton was best known for his preaching. At his funeral in 1677, he was dubbed "the king of preachers."

Benedetto da Mantova (c. 1495–c. 1556). Italian Catholic monk. Benedetto entered the Benedictine order in Mantua and served as dean at San Giorgio Maggiore in Venice. At San Nicolò l'Arena on Mt. Etna, he became acquainted with Waldensian and Protestant thought, which influenced his composition of *The Benefit of Christ*, one of the most significant Italian writings of the Reformation. Marcantonio Flaminio* was asked to rewrite the text in more elegant prose before its anonymous publication in 1543, and although the work drew the ire of the Inquisition, Benedetto's authorship was not uncovered during his lifetime. His increasingly radical spiritualism saw him arrested in Padua, though nothing of his later life is known.

Felix Mantz (d. 1527). Swiss Anabaptist Leader. An early supporter of Zwingli* in Zurich, Mantz's frustration with the pace of the magisterial Reformation led him to found an independent congregation, the Swiss Brethren, with Conrad Grebel,* Georg Blaurock,* and others. Mantz and Grebel represented the Brethren in two disputations with Zwingli over infant baptism in 1525. Defeated, the Brethren refused to cease meeting and rebaptizing adults, which they considered a first baptism, leading to suppression by the Zurich authorities. Mantz was able to spread his message for a time, traveling through a number of Swiss regions despite several arrests. Imprisoned by the Zurich authorities in March 1526 with Grebel and Blaurock, he briefly escaped, but having broken his commitment not to rebaptize adults, he was executed by drowning, the stipulated punishment for Anabaptism, in January 1527.

Augustin Marlorat (c. 1506–1562). French Reformed pastor. Committed by his family to a monastery at the age of eight, Marlorat was also ordained into the priesthood at an early age in 1524. He fled to Geneva in 1535, where he pastored until the Genevan Company of Pastors sent him to France to shepherd the nascent evangelical congregations. His petition to the young Charles IX (1550–1574) for the right to public evangelical worship was denied. In response to a massacre of evangelicals in Vassy (over sixty dead, many more wounded), Marlorat's congregation planned to overtake Rouen. After the crown captured Rouen, Marlorat was arrested and executed three days later for treason. His principle published work was an anthology of New Testament comment modeled after Thomas Aquinas's* *Catena aurea in quatuor Evangelia*. Marlorat harmonized Reformed and Lutheran comment with the church fathers, interspersed with his own brief comments. He also wrote such anthologies for Genesis, Job, the Psalms, Song of Songs and Isaiah.

Pilgram Marpeck (c. 1495–1556). Austrian Radical elder and theologian. During a brief sojourn in Strasbourg, Marpeck debated with Martin Bucer* before the city council; Bucer was declared the winner, and Marpeck was asked to leave Strasbourg for his views concerning paedobaptism (which he compared to a sacrifice to Moloch). After his time in Strasbourg, Marpeck traveled throughout southern Germany and western Austria, planting Anabaptist congregations. Marpeck criticized the strict use of the ban, however, particularly among the Swiss brethren. He also engaged in a christological controversy with Kaspar von Schwenckfeld.*

Mary I of England (1516–1558). English monarch. Daughter of Henry VIII* and his first wife Catherine of Aragon (1509–1553), Mary was raised in the strict Catholicism of her mother. Her succession of Edward VI, her half-brother, was briefly contested by Lady Jane Grey*, daughter of Henry VIII's younger sister, in whom Protestants placed their hopes, but unable to raise adequate support, this challenge was quickly dismissed. Upon her ascent, Mary set about the task of restoring the Catholic religion, a reversal of royal policy that was positively received by much of the populace. While able to reestablish relations with the Pope and reassert the mass and other aspects of Catholicism, the impoverishment of the church following the dissolution of the monasteries and the closure of the chantries was difficult to overcome. Other aspects of popular piety, including the cult of the saints, pilgrimages, and the doctrine of purgatory, were not restored during her reign. Mary looms large in the Protestant imagination, and her persecution of evangelicals led to the moniker "Bloody Mary." The accounts of martyrs such as Thomas Cranmer*, Hugh Latimer*, and Nicholas Ridley* were immortalized in John Foxe's (1516–1587) *Acts and Monuments** and became a mainstay of Protestant propaganda.

Johannes Mathesius (1504–1565). German Lutheran theologian and pastor. After reading Martin Luther's* *On Good Works*, Mathesius left his teaching post in Ingolstadt and traveled to Wittenberg to study theology. Mathesius was an important agent of reform in the Bohemian town of Jáchymov, where he pastored, preached and taught. Over one thousand of Mathesius's sermons are extant, including numerous wedding and funeral sermons as well as a series on Luther's life. Mathesius also transcribed portions of Luther's Table Talk.

Anthony Maxey (d. 1618). Anglican minister. Maxey was born in Essex and educated at Westminster School. After completing his early education at Westminster, Maxey matriculated at Trinity College, Cambridge, in 1578. Maxey graduated Cambridge with the BA (1581), MA (1585), BD (1594), and DD (1608) degrees. However, he was unable to obtain a fellowship at Trinity. King James I* appointed Maxey as his chaplain and dean of Windsor on June 21, 1612. Maxey was also inducted into the Order of the Garter. He died on May 3, 1618. Maxey's published works consist of three sermons: *The Churches Sleep*; *The Golden Chain of Man's Salvation*; and *The Fearful Point of Hardening*.

John Mayer (1583–1664). Anglican priest and biblical exegete. Mayer dedicated much of his life to biblical exegesis, writing a seven-volume commentary on the entire Bible (1627–1653). Styled after Philipp Melanchthon's* *locus* method, Mayer's work avoided running commentary, focusing instead on textual and theological problems. He was a parish priest for fifty-five years. In the office of priest Mayer also wrote a popular catechism, *The English Catechisme, or a Commentarie on the Short Catechisme* (1621), which went through twelve editions in his lifetime.

Joseph Mede (1586–1638). Anglican biblical scholar, Hebraist and Greek lecturer. A man of encyclopedic knowledge, Mede was interested in numerous fields, varying from philology and history to mathematics and physics, although millennial thought and apocalyptic prophesy were clearly his chief interests. Mede's most important work was his *Clavis Apocalyptica* (1627, later translated into English as *The Key of the Revelation*). This work examined the structure of Revelation as the key to its interpretation. Mede saw the visions as a connected and chronological sequence hinging around Revelation 17:18. He is remembered as an important figure in the history of millenarian theology. He was respected as a mild-mannered and generous scholar who avoided controversy and debate, but who had many original thoughts.

Philipp Melanchthon (1497–1560). German Lutheran educator, reformer, and theologian. Philipp Melanchthon was born in the Palatinate, the son of an armorer. He attended the Latin school in Pforzheim, where he lived with the sister of Johannes Reuchlin* to whom he was related by marriage. Having completed his early education, Melanchthon went on to attend the University of Heidelberg, where he received his BA in 1511. Afterwards, he earned his MA from the University

of Tubingen in 1514. In 1518, Reuchlin recommended Melanchthon for the new professorship of Greek at the University of Wittenberg, where he remained for the rest of his life. There, Melanchthon taught Greek, rhetoric, and logic. Melanchthon is known as the partner and successor to Martin Luther* in reform in Germany and for his pioneering *Loci Communes*, which served as a theological textbook. Melanchthon participated with Luther in the Leipzig disputation, helped implement reform in Wittenberg, and was a chief architect of the Augsburg Confession.* Later, Melanchthon and Martin Bucer* worked for union between reformed and Catholic churches. On account of Melanchthon's ecumenical disposition and his modification of several of Luther's doctrines, he was held in suspicion by some.

Andrew Melville (1545–1622). Scottish Reformed theologian. Melville was born at Baldovie on August 1, 1545, to an evangelical family. After finishing his early education at Montrose Grammar School, he matriculated at St. Mary's College, St. Andrews, in 1559. Melville graduated St. Andrews in 1564, after which he traveled to Paris, where he studied Greek, Hebrew, mathematics, and other languages. While in Paris, Melville came under the influence of Petrus Ramus,* whose pedagogical methods he would later utilize in Scotland. From there, he proceeded to Poitiers to study law. There, he became regent of the College of St. Marceon. However, when Poitiers came under siege, Melville departed the city for Geneva, where Theodore Beza* warmly received him. Shortly after Melville's arrival in Geneva, he assumed the chair of humanities at the academy. Melville remained in this position at the academy until 1573, when he returned to Scotland. In 1574, Melville was appointed principal of the College of Glasgow. While in this post, Melville led in the reform of the college's curriculum, and engaged in ecclesiastical controversy. He served on the committee that drafted the Second Book of Discipline, and was elected moderator of the General Assembly in 1578. In 1580, Melville became principal of St. Mary's College, St.

Andrews, where he initiated the same types of reform as he did at Glasgow. Throughout his career, Melville denounced royal ecclesiastical supremacy, arguing strongly for the autonomy of the national church. For this he was summoned to the Privy Council in Edinburgh in 1584 on the possible charge of treason for his resistance to royal ecclesiastical authority. Though they could not charge Melville with sedition, the Privy Council still determined to consign him to trial, but Melville managed to escape to England. While in England, he visited Puritan leaders at Oxford and Cambridge. He also lectured on Genesis in London. Melville returned to Scotland in 1585, and became rector of the University of St. Andrews in 1590. He was eventually deprived of this rectorship in 1587 for his opposition to episcopacy. In 1606, along with several ministers, he was summoned to appear before Hampton Court, where he gave some uncompromising speeches. These speeches resulted in Melville's imprisonment in several places, including the Tower of London. Melville was released from the Tower on April 19, 1611, and from there traveled to France. Having arrived in France, Melville proceeded through Paris and Rouen to Sedan, where he assumed the chair of theology. He remained in Sedan until his death in 1622. Melville authored an extensive literary corpus, which includes a commentary on Romans.

Justus Menius (1499–1558). German Lutheran pastor and theologian. Menius was a prominent reformer in Thuringia. He participated in the Marburg Colloquy and, with others, helped Martin Luther* compose the Schmalkald Articles.* Throughout his career Menius entered into numerous controversies with Anabaptists and even fellow Lutherans. He rejected Andreas Osiander's (d. 1552) doctrine of justification—that the indwelling of Christ's divine nature justifies, rather than the imputed alien righteousness of Christ's person, declared through God's mercy. Against Nikolaus von Amsdorf (1483–1565) and Matthias Flacius (1520–1575), Menius agreed with Georg Major* that good works are necessary

to salvation. Osiander's view of justification was censored in Article 3 of the Formula of Concord*; Menius's understanding of the relationship between good works and salvation was rejected in Article 4. Menius translated many of Luther's Latin works into German. He also composed a handbook for Christian households and an influential commentary on 1 Samuel.

Johannes Mercerus (Jean Mercier) (d. 1570). French Hebraist. Mercerus studied under the first Hebrew chair at the Collège Royal de Paris, François Vatable (d. 1547), whom he succeeded in 1546. John Calvin* tried to recruit Mercerus to the Genevan Academy as professor of Hebrew, once in 1558 and again in 1563; he refused both times. During his lifetime Mercerus published grammatical helps for Hebrew and Chaldean, an aid to the Masoretic symbols in the Hebrew text, and translated the commentaries and grammars of several medieval rabbis. He himself wrote commentaries on Genesis, the wisdom books, and most of the Minor Prophets. These commentaries—most of them only published after his death—were philologically focused and interacted with the work of Jerome, Nicholas of Lyra,* notable rabbis and Johannes Oecolampadius.*

Ambrose Moibanus (1494–1554). German Lutheran bishop and theologian. Moibanus helped reform the church of Breslau (modern Wrocław, Poland). He revised the Mass, bolstered pastoral care and welfare for the poor, and wrote a new evangelical catechism.

Olympia Morata (1526/27–1555). Italian Protestant humanist and theologian. Daughter of a humanist scholar, her father taught in the court of Ferrara, and she was raised alongside Anna d'Este (1531–1607), daughter of Protestant Renée of France (1510–1574) and later wife of Francis, Duke of Guise (1519–1563), a central antagonist in the St. Bartholomew's Day Massacre. A precocious scholar, Morata's classical, humanist, and biblical studies drew her toward the evangelical currents of the court, but these Protestant leanings also raised the constant suspicion of the Inquisition. In 1550, Morata married Andreas

Grundler (unknown), a German Protestant doctor, and moved to his native Schweinfurt, where, facing limited opportunities due to her gender, she continued her studies and privately tutored in Greek and the classics. She developed an extensive correspondence with friends, especially noblewomen she had met at court, and Protestant leaders including Luther*, Melanchthon* and Matthias Flacius (1520–1575), whom she asked to translate some of Luther's work into Italian. Most of Morata's writings were destroyed during the siege of Schweinfurt in 1553–1554, and while she was able to resettle in Frankfurt, she died of tuberculosis soon afterwards. In her writings that survived the siege, her scholarly erudition is clear, and her letters demonstrate a ministerial care for her correspondents and desire for the spread of the Reformation message.

Thomas More (1478–1535). English Catholic lawyer, politician, humanist and martyr. More briefly studied at Oxford, but completed his legal studies in London. After contemplating the priesthood for four years, he opted for politics and was elected a member of Parliament in 1504. A devout Catholic, More worked with church leaders in England to root out heresy while he also confronted Lutheran teachings in writing. After four years as Lord Chancellor, More resigned due to heightened tensions with Henry VIII* over papal supremacy (which More supported and Henry did not). Tensions did not abate. More's steadfast refusal to accept the Act of Supremacy (1534)—which declared the King of England to be the supreme ecclesial primate not the pope—resulted in his arrest and trial for high treason. He was found guilty and beheaded with John Fisher (1469–1535). Friends with John Colet* and Desiderius Erasmus.* More was a widely respected humanist in England as well as on the continent. Well-known for his novel *Utopia* (1516), More also penned several religious treatises on Christ's passion and suffering during his imprisonment in the Tower of London, which were published posthumously.

Sebastian Münster (1488–1552). German Reformed Hebraist, exegete, printer, and geographer. After converting to the Reformation in 1524, Münster taught Hebrew at the universities of Heidelberg and Basel. During his lengthy tenure in Basel he published more than seventy books, including Hebrew dictionaries and rabbinic commentaries. He also produced an evangelistic work for Jews titled *Vikuach* (1539). Münster's *Torat ha-Maschiach* (1537), the Gospel of Matthew, was the first published Hebrew translation of any portion of the New Testament. Despite his massive contribution to contemporary understanding of the Hebrew language, Münster was criticized by many of the reformers as a Judaizer.

Thomas Müntzer (c. 1489–1525). German Radical preacher. As a preacher in the town of Zwickau, Müntzer was influenced by German mysticism and, growing convinced that Martin Luther* had not carried through reform properly, sought to restore the pure apostolic church of the New Testament. Müntzer's radical ideas led to expulsions from various cities; he developed a highly apocalyptic theology, in which he heralded the last days that would establish the pure community out of suffering, prompting Müntzer's proactive role in the Peasants' War, which he perceived as a crucial apocalyptic event. Six thousand of Müntzer's followers were annihilated by magisterial troops; Müntzer was executed.

John Murcot (1625–1654). English Puritan pastor. After completing his bachelor's at Oxford in 1647, Murcot was ordained as a pastor, transferring to several parishes until in 1651 he moved to Dublin. All his works were published posthumously.

Simon Musaeus (1521–1582). German Lutheran theologian. After studying at the universities of Frankfurt an der Oder and Wittenberg, Musaeus began teaching Greek at the Cathedral school in Nuremberg and was ordained. Having returned to Wittenberg to complete a doctoral degree, Musaeus spent the rest of his career in numerous ecclesial and academic administrative posts. He opposed Matthias Flacius's (1505–1575) view of original sin—that the formal essence of human beings is marred by original sin—even calling the pro-Flacian faculty at Wittenberg "the devil's latrine." Musaeus published a disputation on original sin and a postil.

Wolfgang Musculus (1497–1563). German Reformed pastor and theologian. Musculus produced translations, biblical commentaries and an influential theological text, *Loci communes Sacrae Theologiae* (*Commonplaces of Sacred Theology*), outlining a Zwinglian theology. Musculus began to study theology while at a Benedictine monastery; he departed in 1527 and became secretary to Martin Bucer* in Strasbourg. He was later installed as a pastor in Augsburg, eventually performing the first evangelical liturgy in the city's cathedral. Displaced by the Augsburg Interim, Musculus ended his career as professor of theology at Bern. Though Musculus was active in the pursuit of the reform agenda, he was also concerned for ecumenism, participating in the Wittenberg Concord (1536) and discussions between Lutherans and Catholics.

Georg Mylius (1548–1607). German Lutheran pastor and theologian. Mylius began his career as a preacher in Augsburg, rising to superintendent of the churches in the city after receiving his doctorate in theology. He was arrested and ejected from the city by the Catholic-dominated council for his opposition to the Gregorian calendar, returning briefly to learn of the death of his pregnant wife and child. After grieving in Ulm, Mylius spend the remainder of his career as a preacher and professor of theology at Wittenberg, with a brief hiatus teaching at Jena.

Hans Nadler (unknown). German Radical layperson. An uneducated and illiterate needle salesman, after receiving baptism from Hans Hut* in 1527, Nadler sought to share the faith with those he met during his extensive travels. He is remembered through the records of his arrest and examination, recorded by a court reporter, which give insight into his beliefs and activities as a committed Anabaptist layperson, whereby he affirmed believer's baptism, the spiritual reception of the Eucharist, and nonresistance.

Friedrich Nausea (c. 1496–1552). German Catholic bishop and preacher. After completing his studies at Leipzig, this famed preacher was appointed priest in Frankfurt but was run out of town by his congregants during his first sermon. He transferred to Mainz as cathedral preacher. Nausea was well connected through the German papal hierarchy and traveled widely to preach to influential ecclesial and secular courts. Court preacher for Ferdinand I (1503–1564), his reform tendencies fit well with royal Austrian theological leanings, and he was enthroned as the bishop of Vienna. Nausea thought that rather than endless colloquies only a council could settle reform. Unfortunately he could not participate in the first session of Trent due to insufficient funding, but he arrived for the second session. Nausea defended the laity's reception of the cup and stressed the importance of promulgating official Catholic teaching in the vernacular.

Melchior Neukirch (1540–1597). German Lutheran pastor and playwright. Neukirch's pastoral career spanned more than thirty years in several northern German parishes. Neukirch published a history of the Braunschweig church since the Reformation and a dramatization of Acts 4–7. He died of the plague.

Nicholas of Lyra (1270–1349). French Catholic biblical exegete. Very little is known about this influential medieval theologian of the Sorbonne aside from the works he published, particularly the *Postilla litteralis super totam Bibliam* (1322–1333). With the advent of the printing press this work was regularly published alongside the Latin Vulgate and the *Glossa ordinaria*. In this running commentary on the Bible Nicholas promoted literal interpretation as the basis for theology. Despite his preference for literal interpretation, Nicholas also published a companion volume, the *Postilla moralis super totam Bibliam* (1339), a commentary on the spiritual meaning of the biblical text. Nicholas was a major conversation partner for many reformers though many of them rejected his exegesis as too literal and too "Jewish" (not concerned enough with the Bible's fulfillment in Jesus Christ).

John Norden (1547–1625). English devotional writer. Norden was born at Somerset, and in 1564 entered Hart Hall, Oxford where he graduated with his BA in 1568, and MA in 1573. Norden spent most of his life Middlesex, moving later to St. Giles in the Fields in 1619, where he remained until his death in 1625. Throughout his life, Norden distinguished himself also as a cartographer, chorographer, and antiquarian. His best known devotional work was his Progress of Piety (1596).

Alexander Nowell (1517–1602). Anglican theologian. Born in Lancashire, Nowell was educated at Brasenose College, Oxford where he shared a room with the future martyrologist John Foxe. Nowell was elected a fellow at the same college, where he spent thirteen years. In 1543, he was appointed master of Westminster School, and in December, 1551, a prebendary of Westminster Abbey. Though elected to the House of Commons in 1553, Nowell was permitted to assume his seat because as a prebendary, he had a seat in Convocation. Because of his evangelical convictions, Nowell lost prebendary in 1554, after which he fled to the Continent, traveling first to Strasbourg, and then to Frankfurt. When Elizabeth I ascended the throne, Nowell returned to England where he afterwards served as chaplain to Edmund Grindal. In 1561 Nowell became Dean of St. Paul's Cathedral, a post which he held until his death. Nowell's best known work was his Catechism originally written in Latin (1563), and translated into English by Thomas Norton in 1570.

Bernardino Ochino (1487–1564). Italian Reformed theologian. After serving as vicar general of the Franciscan order, Ochino left the foundation of the Capuchins, where he assisted in the composition of their constitution and served as vicar general. A famed preacher, his teaching came to the attention of the Inquisition as it began to reflect the thought of Juan de Valdés. Summoned to Rome in 1542, he fled to Geneva with Peter Martyr Vermigli* where his Reformed orthodoxy, tinged with Franciscan mysticism, was brought into the open. Following his flight, Ochino led an unstable life, with brief stays in Basel, Strasbourg, and Augsburg before moving to England with Vermigli in 1548 where he was able to compose a significant treatise against the Roman church. His doctrinal orthodoxy was questioned by the pastor of the Italian congregation in London, but his case left unresolved when he departed for Geneva, then Basel and Zurich, at the accession of Mary*. As pastor of a congregation of Italian refugees in Zurich, Ochino courted considerable controversy. He refused to have his works approved by the city magistrates before publication, and his opponents alleged that his *Dialogi XXX* (1563) included questionable teachings on the Trinity and divorce while seeming to advocate polygamy. Expelled from Zurich in 1563, he died in Moravia the following year.

Johannes Oecolampadius (Johannes Huszgen) (1482–1531). Swiss-German Reformed humanist, reformer and theologian. Oecolampadius (an assumed name meaning "house light") assisted with Desiderius Erasmus's* Greek New Testament, lectured on biblical languages and exegesis and completed an influential Greek grammar. After joining the evangelical cause through studying patristics and the work of Martin Luther,* Oecolampadius went to Basel, where he lectured on biblical exegesis and participated in ecclesial reform. On account of Oecolampadius's effort, the city council passed legislation restricting preaching to the gospel and releasing the city from compulsory Mass. Oecolampadius was a chief ally of Huldrych Zwingli,* whom he supported at the Marburg Colloquy (1529).

Kaspar Olevianus (1536–1587). German Reformed theologian. Olevianus is celebrated for composing the Heidelberg Catechism and producing a critical edition of Calvin's *Institutes* in German. Olevianus studied theology with many, including John Calvin,* Theodore Beza,* Heinrich Bullinger* and Peter Martyr Vermigli.* As an advocate of Reformed doctrine, Olevianus oversaw the shift from Lutheranism to Calvinism throughout Heidelberg, organizing the city's churches after Calvin's Geneva. The Calvinist ecclesial vision of Olevianus entangled him in a dispute with another Heidelberg reformer over the rights of ecclesiastical discipline, which Olevianus felt belonged to the council of clergy and elders rather than civil magistrates.

Josua Opitz (c. 1542–1585). German Lutheran pastor. After a brief stint as superintendent in Regensburg, Opitz, a longtime preacher, was dismissed for his support of Matthias Flacius's (1520–1575) view of original sin. (Using Aristotelian categories, Flacius argued that the formal essence of human beings is marred by original sin, forming sinners into the image of Satan; his views were officially rejected in Article 1 of the Formula of Concord.*) Hans Wilhelm Roggendorf (1533–1591) invited Opitz to lower Austria as part of his Lutheranizing program. Unfortunately Roggendorf and Opitz never succeed in getting Lutheranism legal recognition, perhaps in large part due to Opitz's staunch criticism of Catholics, which resulted in his exile. He died of plague.

Lucas Osiander (1534–1604). German Lutheran pastor. For three decades, Osiander— son of the controversial Nuremberg reformer Andreas Osiander (d. 1552)—served as pastor and court preacher in Stuttgart, until he fell out of favor with the duke in 1598. Osiander produced numerous theological and exegetical works, as well as an influential hymnal.

John Owen (1616–1683). English Puritan theologian. Owen trained at Oxford University, where he was later appointed dean of Christ Church and vice chancellor of the university, following his service as chaplain to Oliver Cromwell. Although Owen began his career as a Presbyterian minister, he eventually departed to the party of Independents. Owen composed many sermons, biblical commentaries (including seven volumes on the book of Hebrews), theological treatises and controversial monographs (including disputations with Arminians, Anglicans, Catholics and Socinians).

Santes Pagninus (c. 1470–1541). Italian Catholic biblical scholar. Pagninus studied under Girolamo Savonarola* and later taught in Rome, Avignon and Lyons. He translated the Old Testament into Latin according to a tight, almost wooden, adherence to the Hebrew. This translation and his Hebrew lexicon *Thesaurus linguae sanctae* (1529) were important resources for translators and commentators.

Johann Pappus (1549–1610). German Lutheran theologian. After a decade as a teacher of Hebrew and professor of theology at the Strasbourg academy, Pappus was appointed president of the city's company of pastors. Despite resistance from the Reformed theologian Johann Sturm (1507–1589), he led the city away from its Swiss Reformed alliances and toward subscription to the Lutheran Formula of Concord. A talented humanist, Pappus published more than thirty works on controversial, theological, historical, and exegetical subjects.

David (Wängler) Pareus (1548–1622). German Reformed pastor and theologian. Born at Frankenstein in Lower Silesia, Pareus studied theology at Heidelberg under Zacharias Ursinus (1534–1583), the principal author of the Heidelberg Catechism.* After reforming several churches, Pareus returned to Heidelberg to teach at the Reformed seminary. He then joined the theological faculty at the University of Heidelberg, first as a professor of Old Testament and later as a professor of New Testament. Pareus edited the *Neustadter Bibel* (1587), a publication of Martin Luther's* German translation with Reformed annotations—which was strongly denounced by Lutherans, especially Jakob Andreae* and Johann Georg Sigwart (1554–1618). In an extended debate, Pareus defended the orthodoxy of Calvin's exegesis against Aegidius Hunnius,* who accused Calvin of "judaizing" by rejecting many traditional Christological interpretations of Old Testament passages. Towards the end of his career, Pareus wrote commentaries on Genesis, Hosea, Matthew, Romans, 1 Corinthians, Galatians, Hebrews and Revelation.

Catherine Parr (1512–1548). The last of King Henry VIII's* six wives, Catherine Parr was Queen Consort to Henry from 1543 until his death in 1547. She enjoyed a close relationship with two of her step children, Elizabeth and

Edward (the future Queen Elizabeth I* and King Edward VI), involving herself extensively in their education. Having married three more times after the death of Henry VIII, Catherine died in 1548. Her published works are *Psalms or Prayers* (1543) and a *Lamentation of a Sinner* (1548).

Paul of Burgos (Solomon ha-Levi) (c. 1351–1435). Spanish Catholic archbishop. In 1391 Solomon ha-Levi, a rabbi and Talmudic scholar, converted to Christianity, receiving baptism with his entire family (except for his wife). He changed his name to Paul de Santa Maria. Some have suggested that he converted to avoid persecution; he himself stated that Thomas Aquinas's* work persuaded him of the truth of Christian faith. After studying theology in Paris, he was ordained bishop in 1403. He actively and ardently persecuted Jews, trying to compel them to convert. In order to convince Jews that Christians correctly interpret the Hebrew Scriptures, Paul wrote *Dialogus Pauli et Sauli contra Judaeos, sive Scrutinium Scripturarum* (1434), a book filled with vile language toward the Jews. He also wrote a series of controversial marginal notes and comments on Nicholas of Lyra's* *Postilla*, many of which criticized Nicholas's use of Jewish scholarship.

Christoph Pelargus (1565–1633). German Lutheran pastor, theologian, professor and superintendent. Pelargus studied philosophy and theology at the University of Frankfurt an der Oder, in Brandenburg. This irenic Philippist was appointed as the superintendent of Brandenburg and later became a pastor in Frankfurt, although the local authorities first required him to condemn Calvinist theology, because several years earlier he had been called before the consistory in Berlin under suspicion of being a crypto-Calvinist. Among his most important works were a four-volume commentary on *De orthodoxa fide* by John of Damascus (d. 749), a treatise defending the breaking of the bread during communion, and a volume of funeral sermons. He also published commentaries on the Pentateuch, the Psalms, Matthew, John and Acts.

Konrad Pellikan (1478–1556). German Reformed Hebraist and theologian. Pellikan attended the University of Heidelberg, where he mastered

Hebrew under Johannes Reuchlin. In 1504 Pellikan published one of the first Hebrew grammars that was not merely a translation of the work of medieval rabbis. While living in Basel, Pellikan assisted the printer Johannes Amerbach, with whom he published some of Luther's* early writings. He also worked with Sebastian Münster* and Wolfgang Capito* on a Hebrew Psalter (1516). In 1526, after teaching theology for three years at the University of Basel, Huldrych Zwingli* brought Pellikan to Zurich to chair the faculty of Old Testament. Pellikan's magnum opus is a seven-volume commentary on the entire Bible (except Revelation) and the Apocrypha; it is often heavily dependent upon the work of others (esp. Desiderius Erasmus* and Johannes Oecolampadius*).

William Pemble (1591–1623). Puritan theologian and author. Pemble was born in Egerton, Kent. He was educated at Magdalen College, Oxford, where he graduated with his BA degree in 1614. Afterward he moved to Magdalen Hall, where he became a reader and tutor in divinity. He received his MA in 1618. Primarily a Hebrew scholar, Pemble authored commentaries on Ecclesiastes (1629), the first nine chapters of Zechariah (1629), and portions of Ezra, Nehemiah, and Daniel. Pemble also wrote *An Introduction to the Worthy Receiving the Sacrament* (1628), as well as treatises on predestination and justification. He died of a fever on April 14, 1623.

Benedict Pererius (1535–1610). Spanish Catholic theologian, philosopher and exegete. Pererius entered the Society of Jesus in 1552. He taught philosophy, theology, and exegesis at the Roman College of the Jesuits. Early in his career he warned against neo-Platonism and astrology in his *De principiis* (1576). Pererius wrote a lengthy commentary on Daniel, and five volumes of exegetical theses on Exodus, Romans, Revelation and part of the Gospel of John (chs. 1–14). His four-volume commentary on Genesis (1591–1599) was lauded by Protestants and Catholics alike.

William Perkins (1558–1602). English Puritan preacher and theologian. Perkins was a highly regarded Puritan Presbyterian preacher and biblical commentator in the Elizabethan era. He studied at Cambridge University and later became a fellow of Christ's Church college as a preacher and professor, receiving acclaim for his sermons and lectures. Even more, Perkins gained an esteemed reputation for his ardent exposition of Calvinist reformed doctrine in the style of Petrus Ramus,* becoming one of the first English reformed theologians to achieve international recognition. Perkins influenced the federal Calvinist shape of Puritan theology and the vision of logical, practical expository preaching.

François Perrault (1577–1657). French Reformed pastor for over fifty years. His book on demonology was prominent, perhaps because of the intrigue at his home in 1612. According to his account, a poltergeist made a commotion and argued points of theology; a few months later Perrault's parishioners slew a large snake slithering out of his house.

Dirk Philips (1504–1568). Dutch Radical elder and theologian. This former Franciscan monk, known for being severe and obstinate, was a leading theologian of the sixteenth-century Anabaptist movement. Despite the fame of Menno Simons* and his own older brother Obbe, Philips wielded great influence over Anabaptists in the Netherlands and northern Germany where he ministered. As a result of Philips's understanding of the apostolic church as radically separated from the children of the world, he advocated a very strict interpretation of the ban, including formal shunning. His writings were collected and published near the end of his life as *Enchiridion oft Hantboecxken van de Christelijcke Leere* (1564).

Obbe Philips (1500–1568) Dutch radical leader. Trained as a physician, Philips was drawn to mystical Anabaptism, as taught by Melchior Hoffman (1495–1543) in his hometown of Leewarden. After adult rebaptism and ordination, he preached in Amsterdam, Delft, Appingedam, and Grongen, and he ordained other leaders including his brother Dirk Philips*, David Joris*, and Menno Simmons*. Disillusioned with the growth of revolutionary, enthusiastic, and

apocalyptic elements within Anabaptism and unable to reconcile any visible church with the church of God, Philips withdrew from the radical movement in 1540, after which nothing is known of his life. His only extant writing, entitled *The Confession of Obbe Philips*, was published after his death and recounts elements of the history of the Anabaptist movement and defends his departure from the movement.

James Pilkington (1520-1576). Protestant bishop of Durham and Elizabethan author. Born in Lancashire, Pilkington received his early education at Manchester Grammar School. Afterwards, he entered Pembroke College, Cambridge, and later transferred to St. John's College, Cambridge, from where he graduated with his BA degree in 1539, and MA in 1542. Pilkington was appointed vicar of Kendal in 1545, but resigned this position shortly thereafter in order to return to Cambridge. While there, Pilkington was granted a license to preach, and was awarded the degree of Bachelor of Theology in 1551. In this same year, Pilkington became president of the college. When Mary Tudor succeeded her half-brother, Edward VI, in 1553, Pilkington fled to the Continent where he traveled to Zurich, Geneva, Frankfurt, and Strasbourg. He returned to England in 1559 when Elizabeth I ascended the throne of England. After returning to England, Pilkington became Regius Professor of Divinity at Cambridge and after, bishop of Durham in 1560. Pilkington's major work was his voluminous commentary on the Prophet Haggai.

Hector Pinto (c. 1528–1584). Portuguese Catholic theologian and exegete. A member of the order of Saint Jerome, Pinto taught theology and Scripture at the Universities of Sigüenza and Coimbra. A respected theologian and exegete, he published commentaries on Daniel, Nahum, Jeremiah, and Isaiah and an influential devotional work, *The Image of the Christian Life*.

Johannes Piscator (1546–1625). German Reformed theologian. Educated at Tübingen (though he wanted to study at Wittenberg), Piscator taught at the universities of Strasbourg and Heidelberg, as well as academies in Neustadt and Herborn. His commentaries on both the Old and New Testaments involve a tripartite analysis of a given passage's argument, of scholia on the text and of doctrinal loci. Some consider Piscator's method to be a full flowering of Beza's* "logical" scriptural analysis, focused on the text's meaning and its relationship to the pericopes around it.

Constantino Ponce de la Fuente (1502–1559). Spanish Protestant theologian and preacher. A priest in Seville, Ponce de la Fuente was a critic of the established church and associated with the evangelical circle in the city. A popular preacher, he authored a catechism and a number of books on doctrine and the Christian life that focused on the work of Christ. Charged with heresy by the Inquisition, he admitted to the authorship of a number of heretical writings and died in prison awaiting trial while his works were added to the Index of Prohibited Books.

Gabriel Powell (1575–1611). Puritan minister. Powell was born at Ruabon in Denbigshire in 1575. Having completed his studies at Jesus College, Oxford, Powell became master of the free-school in Ruthen. During his tenure at Ruthen, Powell closely studied the writings of the church fathers as well as philosophy, and afterward endeavored to publish several works based on this research. Finding his present location to be a hinderance to his literary objectives, Powell relocated to Oxford, entering St. Mary's Hall, where he finished his anticipated projects. Powell is chiefly known for his literary debate with Thomas Bilson (1547–1619) concerning Christ's descent into hell. Later, Richard Vaughan (1550–1607), bishop of London, appointed Powell his domestic chaplain. Powell died on December 31, 1611. In addition to many controversial and polemical works, Powell wrote a commentary on Romans 1.

Vavasor Powell (1617–1670). Welsh Puritan minister and author. Powell was born at Knucklas, Radnorshire, Wales. After completing his education at Jesus College, Oxford, Powell returned to Wales to assume the position of a local schoolmaster. During this time, Powell came under the influence of Walter Cradock's* preach-

ing as well as the writings of Richard Sibbes* and William Perkins,* resulting in his conversion to Puritanism. Soon thereafter he became an itinerant preacher, traveling throughout Wales. He was arrested twice for nonconformity. During the Civil War, Powell first preached in London, and shortly thereafter pastored an Independent congregation in Wales. On December 26, 1641, Royalist forces arrested and imprisoned Powell. In 1646, as victory for the Puritans appeared inevitable, Powell was released, and allowed to return to Wales, having received a letter of endorsement from the Westminster Assembly. Back in Wales, Powell played a prominent role in the Westminster Assembly's 1650 commission for the better propagation of the gospel throughout Wales. In 1653, Powell returned to London, where he preached at St. Ann Blackfriars. It was at this time that Powell denounced Oliver Cromwell (1599–1658) for assuming the position of Lord Protector. For this reason, he was arrested and imprisoned. At the Restoration in 1660, Powell was again arrested and imprisoned for unauthorized preaching for seven years. Though released in 1667, Powell was once more arrested and incarcerated. He remained in custody until his death on October 27, 1660. Powell authored many poems and a concordance to the Bible.

Felix Pratensis (d. 1539). Italian Catholic Hebraist. Pratensis, the son of a rabbi, converted to Christianity and entered the Augustinian Hermits around the turn of the sixteenth century. In 1515, with papal permission, Pratensis published a new translation of the Psalms based on the Hebrew text. His *Biblia Rabbinica* (1517–1518), printed in Jewish and Christian editions, included text-critical notes in the margins as well as the Targum and rabbinic commentaries on each book (e.g., Rashi* on the Pentateuch and David Kimchi* on the Prophets). Many of the reformers consulted this valuable resource as they labored on their own translations and expositions of the Old Testament.

John Preston (1587–1628). Puritan minister and author. Preston was born at Upper Heyford,

Northamptonshire, on October 27, 1587. He studied philosophy at King's College and Queen's College, Cambridge, earning his bachelor's degree in 1607. He became a fellow at Queen's in 1609, and a prebendary at Lincoln Cathedral a year later. During this period, Preston studied medicine and astronomy. In 1611, he received the MA degree. Sometime afterward, he experienced a conversion under the preaching of John Cotton.* After his conversion, Preston went on to study theology, concentrating mainly on Thomas Aquinas,* Duns Scotus, and William of Ockham. From there, he proceeded to the reformers, especially John Calvin.* Preston was appointed court chaplain in 1615. In this position he was influential in the promotion of Puritans to high civil office. Preston later assumed the positions of dean and catechist at Queen's College, Cambridge, where he distinguished himself by preaching a series of sermons that formed the basis of his body of divinity. In 1622, he received the degree of bachelor of divinity, becoming thereafter master of Emmanuel College, Cambridge. While at Emmanuel, Preston participated in the conflict between Calvinism and Arminianism. Moreover, in the same year, Preston succeeded John Donne* as preacher at Lincoln's Inn. Two years later, Preston accepted the lectureship at Trinity Church. He died at the age of forty in 1628. Throughout his prodigious career, Preston authored a sizable corpus, which includes published sermons on Romans.

Quadriga. The *quadriga*, or four senses of Scripture, grew out of the exegetical legacy of Paul's dichotomy of letter and spirit (2 Cor 3:6), as well as church fathers like Origen (c. 185–254), Jerome (c. 347–420) and Augustine* (354–430). Advocates for this method—the primary framework for biblical exegesis during the medieval era—assumed the necessity of the gift of faith under the guidance of the Holy Spirit. The literal-historical meaning of the text served as the foundation for the fuller perception of Scripture's meaning in the three spiritual senses, accessible only through faith: the allegorical sense taught what should be believed, the tropological or moral sense taught what should be done, and the anagogical or eschatological sense taught what should be hoped for. Medieval Jewish exegesis also had a fourfold interpretive method—not necessarily related to the *quadriga*—called *pardes* ("grove"): *peshat*, the simple, literal sense of the text according to grammar; *remez*, the allegorical sense; *derash*, the moral sense; and *sod*, the mystic sense related to Kabbalah. Scholars hotly dispute the precise use and meaning of these terms.

Edward Rainbow[e] (1608–1684). Anglican minister, scholar, and bishop. Rainbow was born at Lincolnshire on April 20, 1608. After completing his education, Rainbow matriculated at Corpus Christi College, and later transferred to Magdalene College, Cambridge, where he graduated with the BA (1627), MA (1630), BD (1637), and DD (1643). He was elected a fellow at Magdalene in 1633 and a master there in 1642. In 1630, Rainbow accepted the mastership of the Kirton-in-Lindsey but shortly afterward moved to London. In 1632, Rainbow took holy orders and preached his first sermon in April of that year. His first appointment was that of curate of Savoy Hospital. Rainbow was recalled to Cambridge in 1633 and elected a fellow. Four years later he became dean of Magdalene and master of the same college in 1642. Though dismissed from his mastership by Parliament in 1650, Rainbow was restored to it in the year of the Restoration (1660). At the same time, he was appointed chaplain to the king. In 1661, Rainbow became dean of Peterborough, and appointed vice chancellor of Cambridge a year later. Rainbow was elected bishop of Carlisle in 1664. As bishop, Rainbow led in the systemic reform of his diocese. Rainbow died March 26, 1684. His published works consist of three published sermons and an incomplete treatise, *Verba Christi*.

Petrus Ramus (1515–1572). French Reformed humanist philosopher. Ramus was an influential professor of philosophy and logic at the French royal college in Paris; he converted to Protestantism and left France for Germany, where he came under the influence of Calvinist thought.

Ramus was a trenchant critic of Aristotle and noted for his method of classification based on a deductive movement from universals to particulars, the latter becoming branching divisions that provided a visual chart of the parts to the whole. His system profoundly influenced Puritan theology and preaching. After returning to Paris, Ramus died in the Saint Bartholomew's Day Massacre.

Rashi (Shlomo Yitzchaki) (1040–1105). French Jewish rabbi and exegete. After completing his studies, Rashi founded a yeshiva in Troyes. He composed the first comprehensive commentary on the Talmud, as well as commentaries on the entire Old Testament except for 1–2 Chronicles. These works remain influential within orthodox Judaism. Late medieval and early modern Christian scholars valued his exegesis, characterized by his preference for peshat (see quadriga).

Remonstrance (1610). See *Synod of Dordrecht*.

Johannes Reuchlin (1455–1522). German Catholic lawyer, humanist and Hebraist. Reuchlin held judicial appointments for the dukes of Württemberg, the Supreme Court in Speyer and the imperial court of the Swabian League. He pioneered the study of Hebrew among Christians in Germany, standing against those who, like Johannes Pfefferkorn (1469–1523), wanted to destroy Jewish literature. Among his many works he published a Latin dictionary, an introductory Greek grammar, the most important early modern Hebrew grammar and dictionary (*De rudimentis hebraicis*; 1506), and a commentary on the penitential psalms.

Edward Reynolds (1599–1676). Anglican bishop. Reynolds succeeded John Donne* as the preacher at Lincoln's Inn before entering parish ministry in Northamptonshire. During the English Civil Wars, he supported the Puritans because of his sympathy toward their simplicity and piety—despite believing that Scripture demanded no particular form of government; later he refused to support the abolition of the monarchy. Until the Restoration he ministered in London; afterward he became the bishop of Norwich. He wrote the general thanksgiving prayer which is part of the morning office in the *Book of Common Prayer*.*

Urbanus Rhegius (1489–1541). German Lutheran pastor. Rhegius, who was likely the son of a priest, studied under the humanists at Freiburg and Ingolstadt. After a brief stint as a foot soldier, he received ordination in 1519 and was made cathedral preacher in Augsburg. During his time in Augsburg he closely read Luther's* works, becoming an enthusiastic follower. Despite his close friendship with Zwingli* and Oecolampadius,* Rhegius supported Luther in the eucharistic debates, later playing a major role in the Wittenberg Concord (1536). He advocated for peace during the Peasants' War and had extended interactions with the Anabaptists in Augsburg. Later in his career he concerned himself with the training of pastors, writing a pastoral guide and two catechisms. About one hundred of his writings were published posthumously.

Lancelot Ridley (d. 1576). Anglican preacher. Ridley was the first cousin of Nicholas Ridley,* the bishop of London who was martyred during the Marian persecutions. By Cranmer's* recommendation, Ridley became one of the six Canterbury Cathedral preachers. Upon Mary I's accession in 1553, Ridley was defrocked (as a married priest). Ridley returned to Canterbury Cathedral after Mary's death. He wrote commentaries on Jude, Ephesians, Philippians and Colossians.

Nicholas Ridley (c. 1502–1555). Anglican bishop. Ridley was a student and fellow at Cambridge University who was appointed chaplain to Archbishop Thomas Cranmer* and is thought to be partially responsible for Cranmer's shift to a symbolic view of the Eucharist. Cranmer promoted Ridley twice: as bishop of Rochester, where he openly advocated Reformed theological views, and, later, as bishop of London. Ridley assisted Cranmer in the revisions of the Book of Common Prayer.* Ridley's support of Lady Jane Grey against the claims of Mary to the throne led to his arrest; he was tried for heresy and burned at the stake with Hugh Latimer.*

Peter Riedemann (1506–1556). German Radical elder, theologian and hymnist. While traveling as a Silesian cobbler, Riedemann came into contact with Anabaptist teachings and joined a congregation in Linz. In 1529 he was called to be a minister, only to be imprisoned soon after as part of Archduke Ferdinand's efforts to suppress heterodoxy in his realm. Once he was released, he moved to Moravia in 1532 where he was elected as a minister and missionary of the Hutterite community there. His *Account of Our Religion, Doctrine and Faith* (1542), with its more than two thousand biblical references, is Riedemann's most important work and is still used by Hutterites today.

John Robinson (1576–1625). English Puritan pastor. After his suspension for nonconformity, Robinson fled to the Netherlands with his congregation, eventually settling in Leiden in 1609. Robinson entered into controversies over Arminianism, separation and congregationalism. Most of his healthy congregants immigrated to Plymouth in 1620; Robinson remained in Leiden with those unable to travel.

John Rogers (1505–1555). English Protestant Bible translator. Rogers was born in Deritend, Birmingham. After receiving his early education at the Guild School of St. John the Baptist, Rogers matriculated at Pembroke Hall, Cambridge, where he graduated with the BA degree in 1526. He served as rector of Holy Trinity the Less in London from 1532 to 1534, when he left for the Continent to serve as chaplain to the English merchants of the Company of the Merchant Adventurers. It was at this time that he met William Tyndale,* under whose influence he came to embrace an evangelical faith. After Tyndale's death, Rogers completed his late colleague's translation of the Old Testament, which had ended with 2 Chronicles, by adding Miles Coverdale's translation of the remainder, including the Apocrypha. The resulting work, known as the "Matthew Bible" (Rogers published it under the pseudonym "Thomas Matthew") was published in 1537. It has the distinction of being the first complete English Bible translated essentially from the original languages to be printed. "Matthew's Bible" served as the basis for the Great Bible (1540), which in turn was used by those who prepared the Bishops' Bible (1568), on which later the King James Version (1611) was produced. In 1540, Rogers enrolled at the University of Wittenberg, where he became close friends with Philipp Melanchthon.* During his three years at Wittenberg, Rogers was a superintendent of the Lutheran Church in northern Germany. When Rogers returned to England in 1548, he published a translation of Melanchthon's *Considerations of the Augsburg Interim*, and later served in a variety of ecclesiastical roles. Rogers was burned at the stake for heresy during the reign of Mary Tudor on February 4, 1555.

Nehemiah Rogers (1593–1660). Anglican priest. After studying at Cambridge, Rogers ministered at numerous parishes during his more than forty-year career. In 1643, he seems to have been forced out of a parish on account of being a Royalist and friend of William Laud.* Rogers published a number of sermons and tracts, including a series of expositions on Jesus' parables in the Gospels.

Thomas Rogers (d. 1616). Anglican theologian and translator. Rogers attended Christ Church, Oxford, where he completed his BA degree in 1573 and MA in 1576. Later he served as rector of Horrigner in Suffolk, and chaplain to Archbishop of Canterbury, Richard Bancroft. He died at Horringer and was buried in his church. Among his many works were an exposition of the Thirty-Nine Articles as well as a paraphrase of the Psalms and a translation of Niels Hemmingsen's commentary on Psalm 84.

Robert Rollock (c. 1555–1599). Scottish Reformed pastor, educator and theologian. Rollock was deeply influenced by Petrus Ramus's* system of logic, which he implemented as a tutor and (later) principal of Edinburgh University and in his expositions of the Bible. Rollock, as a divinity professor and theologian, was instrumental in diffusing a federalist Calvinism in the Scottish church; he lectured on theology using the texts of Theodore Beza* and articulated a highly covenantal interpretation of the biblical narratives. He was a prolific writer of sermons, expositions, commentaries, lectures and occasional treatises.

David Runge (1564–1604). German Lutheran theologian. First appointed professor of Hebrew at the University of Greifswald, Runge supported and later replaced his father in teaching philosophy and theology. After receiving his doctorate, he was named to the theological faculty at Wittenberg, where he also served as dean and rector of the university.

Johann Rurer (1480–1542) German Lutheran pastor. Rurer was court chaplain to Margrave Casimir of Brandenberg–Kulmbach (1481–1527), and the first Protestant pastor in Ansbach. Conflict over church order and his desire for reform led to his expulsion, but he was recalled after Casimir's death by his successor, George (1484–1543), who sought a throughgoing Lutheran reformation of the town and appointed Rurer preacher at the collegiate church.

Samuel Rutherford (1600–1661). Scottish Reformed theologian. Rutherford was born in Nisbet, Roxburghshire. After completing his early education at Jedborough, Rutherford enrolled at the University of Edinburgh, where he received his MA degree in 1621. In 1623, Rutherford was appointed professor of humanities at Edinburgh. Two years later, he was dismissed from his position on account of misbehavior with the woman who would later be his wife. Sometime after this incident, he underwent a spiritual conversion. In 1625, Rutherford commenced the study of theology at Edinburgh. Upon finishing his studies, Rutherford was called to pastor a church in Antwoth by Solway in Kirkcudbrightshire. Throughout his ministry, Rutherford proved to be an ardent opponent to episcopacy. For this, he was summoned to appear before the Court of High Commission in 1630. Despite the court's warnings to cease and desist, Rutherford continued his nonconformity. Rutherford also participated extensively in the Arminian controversy, writing treatises against Arminius as well as the Jesuits. Since Rutherford's virulent opposition to Arminianism placed him in direct opposition with the English episcopacy, he was once again summoned by the Court of High Commission in 1636. After a three-day trial, Rutherford was deprived of his ministerial office and ordered not to preach anywhere in Scotland. Meanwhile he was confined to Aberdeen. In 1638, when the National Covenant was signed and Presbyterianism restored in Scotland, Rutherford left Aberdeen and assumed the post of professor of theology at St. Mary's College, St. Andrews. Later, Rutherford served as a commissioner to the Westminster Assembly, where he contributed to the discussions related to the Shorter Catechism. In 1647, Rutherford returned to Scotland, where he was appointed principal of St. Mary's College, and rector of the university in 1651. After the monarchy was restored, Rutherford was charged with treason, and deprived of all his ecclesiastical and university positions. He died on March 30, 1661. Throughout his career, Rutherford published many sermons and theological works, most famous of which is *Lex Rex* (The law is king), a treatise arguing against the divine right of kings.

Jacopo Sadoleto (1477–1547). Italian Catholic Cardinal. Sadoleto, attaché to Leo X's court, was appointed bishop in 1517, cardinal in 1536. He participated in the reform commission led by Gasparo Contarini.* However, he tried to reconcile with Protestants apart from the commission, sending several letters to Protestant leaders in addition to his famous letter to the city of Geneva, which John Calvin* pointedly answered. Sadoleto published a commentary on Romans that was censored as semi-Pelagian. His insufficient treatment of prevenient grace left him vulnerable to this charge. Sadoleto emphasized grammar as the rule and norm of exegesis.

Heinrich Salmuth (1522–1576). German Lutheran theologian. After earning his doctorate from the University of Leipzig, Salmuth served in several coterminous pastoral and academic positions. He was integral to the reorganization of the University of Jena. Except for a few disputations, all of Salmuth's works—mostly sermons—

were published posthumously by his son.

Robert Sanderson (1587–1663). Anglican bishop and philosopher. Before his appointment as professor of divinity at Oxford in 1642, Sanderson pastored in several parishes. Because of his loyalty to the Crown during the English Civil Wars, the Parliamentarians stripped Sanderson of his post at Oxford. After the Restoration he was reinstated at Oxford and consecrated bishop. He wrote an influential textbook on logic.

Edwin Sandys (1519–1588). Anglican bishop. During his doctoral studies at Cambridge, Sandys befriended Martin Bucer.* Having supported the Protestant Lady Jane Grey's claim to the throne, Sandys resigned his post at Cambridge upon Mary I's accession. He was then arrested and imprisoned in the Tower of London. Released in 1554, he sojourned on the continent until Mary's death. On his return to England he was appointed to revise the liturgy and was consecrated bishop. Many of his sermons were published, but his most significant literary legacy is his work as a translator of the Bishop's Bible (1568), which served as the foundational English text for the translators of the King James Bible (1611).

Erasmus Sarcerius (1501–1559). German Lutheran superintendent, educator and pastor. Sarcerius served as educational superintendent, court preacher and pastor in Nassau and, later, in Leipzig. The hallmark of Sarcerius's reputation was his ethical emphasis as exercised through ecclesial oversight and family structure; he also drafted disciplinary codes for regional churches in Germany. Sarcerius served with Philipp Melanchthon* as Protestant delegates at the Council of Trent, though both withdrew prior to the dismissal of the session; he eventually became an opponent of Melanchthon, contesting the latter's understanding of the Eucharist at a colloquy in Worms in 1557.

Michael Sattler (c. 1490–1527). Swiss Radical leader. Sattler was a Benedictine monk who abandoned the monastic life during the upheavals of the Peasants' War. He took up the trade of weaving under the guidance of an outspoken Anabaptist. It seems that Sattler did not openly join the Anabaptist movement until after the suppression of the Peasants' War in 1526. Sattler interceded with Martin Bucer* and Wolfgang Capito* for imprisoned Anabaptists in Strasbourg. Shortly before he was convicted of heresy and executed, he wrote the definitive expression of Anabaptist theology, the Schleitheim Articles.*

Girolamo Savonarola (1452–1498). Italian Catholic preacher and martyr. Outraged by clerical corruption and the neglect of the poor, Savonarola traveled to preach against these abuses and to prophesy impending judgment—a mighty king would scourge and reform the church. Savonarola thought that the French invasion of Italy in 1494 confirmed his apocalyptic visions. Thus he pressed to purge Florence of vice and institute public welfare, in order to usher in a new age of Christianity. Florence's refusal to join papal resistance against the French enraged Alexander VI (r. 1492–1503). He blamed Savonarola, promptly excommunicating him and threatening Florence with an interdict. After an ordeal by fire turned into a riot, Savonarola was arrested. Under torture he admitted to charges of conspiracy and false prophecy; he was hanged and burned. In addition to numerous sermons and letters, he wrote meditations on Psalms 31 and 51 as well as *The Triumph of the Cross* (1497).

Leupold Scharnschlager (d. 1563). Austrian Radical elder. See *Kunstbuch.*

Leonhard Schiemer (d. 1528) Austrian radical martyr. Troubled by the hypocrisies he experienced, Scheimer left the Franciscan order and spent a period of time wandering. Attracted to the teachings of Hans Hut* after hearing him debate Balthasar Hubmaier* in Moravia, he was rebaptized and traveled widely throughout Austria and Southern Germany, spreading the Anabaptist message until he was arrested in Rattenberg, where he was condemned to death and beheaded. A number of his essays and hymns survive, dispersed among the *Kunstbuch** and other collections of radical writings.

Hans Schlaffer (c. 1490–1528). Austrian Radical martyr. Drawn by Luther's theology, Schlaffer resigned his priesthood in 1526 only to turn to Anabaptism soon afterward. While contemporaries recognized his ability as a preacher, he never settled in a ministry position. He spent time among Radical congregations in Freistadt, Nicholsburg, Augsburg, Nuremberg, and Regensburg before his arrest in Schatz, where he was executed. Nine writings by Schlaffer remain, most of which were composed during his imprisonment. They include confessions of his beliefs and devotional works, which have been preserved among Hutterite churches.

Schleitheim Articles (1527). After the death of Conrad Grebel* in 1526 and the execution of Felix Manz (born c. 1498) in early 1527, the young Swiss Anabaptist movement was in need of unity and direction. A synod convened at Schleitheim under the chairmanship of Michael Sattler,* which passed seven articles of Anabaptist distinctives—likely defined against both magisterial reformers and other Anabaptists with less orthodox and more militant views (e.g., Balthasar Hubmaier*). Unlike most confessions, these articles do not explicitly address traditional creedal interests; they explicate instead the Anabaptist view of the sacraments, church discipline, separatism, the role of ministers, pacifism and oaths. Throughout the document there is a resolute focus on Christ's example. Also referred to as the Schleitheim Confession and the Schleitheim Brotherly Union, the Schleitheim Articles are considered the definitive statement of Anabaptist theology, particularly regarding separatism.

Schmalkald Articles (1537). In response to Pope Paul III's (1468–1549) 1536 decree ordering a general church council to solve the Protestant crisis, Elector John Frederick (1503–1554) commissioned Martin Luther* to draft the sum of his teaching. Intended by Luther as a last will and testament—and composed with advice from well-known colleagues Justus Jonas,* Johann Bugenhagen,* Caspar Cruciger,* Nikolaus von Amsdorf (1483–1565), Georg Spalatin (1484–1545), Philipp Melanchthon* and Johann Agricola*—these articles provide perhaps the briefest and most systematic summary of Luther's

teaching. The document was not adopted formally by the Lutheran Schmalkald League, as was hoped, and the general church council was postponed for several years (until convening at Trent in 1545). Only in 1580 were the articles officially received, by being incorporated into the *Book of Concord* defining orthodox Lutheranism.

Dietrich Schnepff (1525–1586). German Lutheran pastor and theologian. Schnepff taught briefly at the city school in Tübingen while working toward his theological doctorate before taking pastorates in Derendingen and Nürtingen. Returning to Tübingen as professor of theology, Schnepff also took on additional roles as rector of the university and pastor of the Collegiate Church.

Anna Maria van Schurman (1607–1678). Dutch Reformed polymath. Van Schurman cultivated talents in art, poetry, botany, linguistics and theology. She mastered most contemporary European languages, in addition to Latin, Greek, Hebrew, Arabic, Farsi and Ethiopian. With the encouragement of leading Reformed theologian Gisbertus Voetius (1589–1676), van Schurman attended lectures at the University of Utrecht—although she was required to sit behind a wooden screen so that the male students could not see her. In 1638 van Schurman published her famous treatise advocating female scholarship, *Amica dissertatio . . . de capacitate ingenii muliebris ad scientias*. In addition to these more polemical works, van Schurman also wrote hymns and poems, including a paraphrase of Genesis 1–3. Later in life she became a devotee of Jean de Labadie (1610–1674), a former Jesuit who was also expelled from the Reformed church for his separatist leanings. Her *Eucleria* (1673) is the most well known defense of Labadie's theology.

Kaspar von Schwenckfeld (1489–1561). German Radical reformer. Schwenckfeld was a Silesian nobleman who encountered Luther's* works in 1521. He traveled to Wittenberg twice: first to meet Luther and Karlstadt,* and a second time to convince Luther of his doctrine of the "internal word"—emphasizing inner revelation so strongly that he did not see church meetings or the sacraments as necessary—after which Luther considered him heterodox. Schwenckfeld won his native territory to the Reformation in 1524 and later lived in Strasbourg for five years until Bucer* sought to purify the city of less traditional theologies. Schwenckfeld wrote numerous polemical and exegetical tracts.

Scots Confession (1560). In 1560, the Scottish Parliament undertook to reform the Church of Scotland and to commission a Reformed confession of faith. In the course of four days, a committee—which included John Knox*—wrote this confession, largely based on Calvin's* work, the Confession of the English Congregation in Geneva (1556) and the Gallic Confession.* The articles were not ratified until 1567 and were displaced by the Westminster Confession (1646), adopted by the Scottish in 1647.

Second Helvetic Confession (1566). Believing he would soon die, Heinrich Bullinger* penned a personal statement of his Reformed faith in 1561 as a theological will. In 1563, Bullinger sent a copy of this confession, which blended Zwingli's and Calvin's theology, to the elector of the Palatinate, Frederick III (1515–1576), who had asked for a complete explication of the Reformed faith in order to defend himself against aggressive Lutheran attacks after printing the Heidelberg Confession.* Although not published until 1566, the Second Helvetic Confession became the definitive sixteenth-century Reformed statement of faith. Theodore Beza* used it as the organizing confession for his *Harmonia Confessionum* (1581), which sought to emphasize the unity of the Reformed churches. Bullinger's personal confession was adopted by the Reformed churches of Scotland (1566), Hungary (1567), France (1571) and Poland (1571).

Obadiah Sedgwick (c. 1600–1658). English Puritan minister. Educated at Oxford, Sedgwick pastored in London and participated in the Westminster Assembly. An ardent Puritan, Sedgwick was appointed by Oliver Cromwell (1599–1658) to examine clerical candidates. Sedgwick published a catechism, several sermons and a treatise on how to deal with doubt.

Nikolaus Selnecker (1530–1592). German Lutheran theologian, preacher, pastor and hymnist. Selnecker taught in Wittenberg, Jena and Leipzig, preached in Dresden and Wolfenbüttel, and pastored in Leipzig. He was forced out of his post at Jena because of suspicions that he was a crypto-Calvinist. He sought refuge in Wolfenbüttel, where he met Martin Chemnitz* and Jakob Andreae.* Under their influence Selnecker was drawn away from Philippist theology. Selnecker's shift in theology can be seen in his *Institutio religionis christianae* (1573). Selnecker coauthored the Formula of Concord* with Chemnitz, Andreae, Andreas Musculus (1514–1581), and David Chytraeus.* Selnecker also published lectures on Genesis, the Psalms, and the New Testament epistles, as well as composing over a hundred hymn tunes and texts.

Short Confession (1610). In response to some of William Laud's* reforms in the Church of England—particularly a law stating that ministers who refused to comply with the Book of Common Prayer* would lose their ordination—a group of English Puritans immigrated to the Netherlands in protest, where they eventually embraced the practice of believer's baptism. The resulting Short Confession was an attempt at union between these Puritans and local Dutch Anabaptists ("Waterlanders"). The document highlights the importance of love in the church and reflects optimism regarding the freedom of the will while explicitly rejecting double predestination.

Richard Sibbes (1577–1635). English Puritan preacher. Sibbes was educated at St. John's College, Cambridge, where he was converted to reforming views and became a popular preacher. As a moderate Puritan emphasizing interior piety and brotherly love, Sibbes always remained within the established Church of England, though opposed to some of its liturgical ceremonies. His collected sermons constitute his main literary legacy.

Menno Simons (c. 1496–1561). Dutch Radical leader. Simons led a separatist Anabaptist group in the Netherlands that would later be called Mennonites, known for nonviolence and renunciation of the world. A former priest, Simons rejected Catholicism through the influence of Anabaptist disciples of Melchior Hoffmann and based on his study of Scripture, in which he found no support for transubstantiation or infant baptism. Following the sack of Anabaptists at Münster, Simons committed to a nonviolent way of life. Simons proclaimed a message of radical discipleship of obedience and inner purity, marked by voluntary adult baptism and communal discipline.

Henry Smith (c. 1550–1591). English Puritan minister. Smith stridently opposed the Book of Common Prayer* and refused to subscribe to the Articles of Religion,* thus limiting his pastoral opportunities. Nevertheless he gained a reputation as an eloquent preacher in London. He published sermon collections as well as several treatises.

Domingo de Soto (1494–1560). Spanish Catholic theologian. Soto taught philosophy for four years at the University in Alcalá before entering the Dominican order. In 1532 he became chair of theology at the University of Salamanca; Soto sought to reintroduce Aristotle in the curriculum. He served as confessor and spiritual advisor to Charles V, who enlisted Soto as imperial theologian for the Council of Trent. Alongside commentaries on the works of Aristotle and Peter Lombard (c. 1100–1160), Soto commented on Romans and wrote an influential treatise on nature and grace.

Fausto Sozzini (1539–1604). Italian theologian. Without a formal education, Sozzini used his inherited wealth to travel widely throughout Europe after his family came under the suspicion of the Inquisition for Lutheranism. Spending time in Lyons, Zurich, and Geneva, he published his first work, an explanation of the prologue to John's Gospel, claiming Christ was not divine, but a human worthy of respect due his divinely appointed office. Returning to Italy, Sozzini served at the Florentine court of Isabella de Medici (1542–1576) for more than a decade, departing for Basel, then Transylvania and Poland after her death. His thoroughgoing rationalism saw him elevate human reason over divine revelation and

traditional doctrine. He rejected the doctrine of the Trinity and Nicene orthodoxy, instead arguing that Christ was not divine and did not make atonement for humanity, but rather served as a model of victory over death for all people.

Cyriacus Spangenberg (1528–1604). German Lutheran pastor, preacher and theologian. Spangenberg was a staunch, often acerbic, Gnesio-Lutheran. He rejected the Formula of Concord* because of concerns about the princely control of the church, as well as its rejection of Flacian language of original sin (as constituting the "substance" of human nature after the fall). He published many commentaries and sermons, most famously seventy wedding sermons (*Ehespiegel* [1561]), his sermons on Luther* (*Theander Luther* [1562–1571]) and Luther's hymns (*Cithara Lutheri* [1569–1570]). He also published an analysis of the Old Testament (though he only got as far as Job), based on a methodology that anticipated the logical bifurcations of Peter Ramus.*

Johann Spangenberg (1484–1550). German Lutheran pastor and catechist. Spangenberg studied at the University of Erfurt, where he was welcomed into a group of humanists associated with Konrad Muth (1470–1526). There he met the reformer Justus Jonas,* and Eobanus Hessius (1488–1540), whom Luther* dubbed "king of the poets." Spangenberg served at parishes in Stolberg (1520–1524), Nordhausen (1524–1546) and, by Luther's recommendation, Eisleben (1546–1550). Spangenberg published one of the best-selling postils of the sixteenth century, the *Postilla Teütsch*, a six-volume work meant to prepare children to understand the lectionary readings. It borrowed the question-answer form of Luther's *Small Catechism* and was so popular that a monk, Johannes Craendonch, purged overt anti-Catholic statements from it and republished it under his own name. Among Spangenberg's other pastoral works are *ars moriendi* ("the art of dying") booklets, a postil for the Acts of the Apostles and a question-answer version of Luther's *Large Catechism*. In addition to preaching and pastoring, Spangenberg wrote pamphlets on controversial topics such as purgatory, as well as textbooks on music, mathematics and grammar.

Georg Spindler (1525–1605). German Reformed theologian and pastor. After studying theology under Caspar Cruciger* and Philipp Melanchthon,* Spindler accepted a pastorate in Bohemia. A well-respected preacher, Spindler published postils in 1576 which some of his peers viewed as crypto-Calvinist. To investigate this allegation Spindler read John Calvin's* *Institutes*, and subsequently converted to the Reformed faith. After years of travel, he settled in the Palatinate and pastored there until his death. In addition to his Lutheran postils, Spindler also published Reformed postils in 1594 as well as several treatises on the Lord's Supper and predestination.

Statenvertaling (1637). The Synod of Dordrecht* commissioned this new Dutch translation of the Bible ("State's Translation"). The six theologians who undertook this translation also wrote prefaces for each biblical book, annotated obscure words and difficult passages, and provided cross-references; they even explained certain significant translation decisions. At the request of the Westminster Assembly, Theodore Haak (1605–1690) translated the *Statenvertaling* into English as *The Dutch Annotations Upon the Whole Bible* (1657).

Johann von Staupitz (d. 1524). German Catholic theologian, professor and preacher. Frederick the Wise summoned this Augustinian monk to serve as professor of Bible and first dean of the theology faculty at the University of Wittenberg. As Vicar-General of the Reformed Augustinian Hermits in Germany, Staupitz sought to reform the order and attempted unsuccessfully to reunite with the conventional Augustinians. While in Wittenberg, Staupitz was Martin Luther's* teacher, confessor and spiritual father. He supported Luther in the early controversies over indulgences, but after releasing Luther from his monastic vows (to protect him), he distanced himself from the conflict. He relocated to Salzburg, where he was court preacher to Cardinal Matthäus Lang von Wellenburg (d. 1540) and abbot of the Benedictine monastery. Staupitz wrote treatises on predestination, faith

and the love of God. Many of his sermons were collected and published during his lifetime.

Michael Stifel (1486–1567). German Lutheran mathematician, theologian and pastor. An Augustinian monk, Stifel's interest in mysticism, apocalypticism and numerology led him to identify Pope Leo X as the antichrist. Stifel soon joined the reform movement, writing a 1522 pamphlet in support of Martin Luther's* theology. After Luther quelled the fallout of Stifel's failed prediction of the Apocalypse—October 19, 1533 at 8 a.m.—Stifel focused more on mathematics and his pastoral duties. He was the first professor of mathematics at the University of Jena. He published several numerological interpretations of texts from the Gospels, Daniel and Revelation. However, Stifel's most important work is his *Arithmetica Integra* (1544), in which he standardized the approach to quadratic equations. He also developed notations for exponents and radicals.

Viktorin Strigel (1524–1569). German Lutheran theologian. Strigel taught at Wittenberg, Erfurt, Jena, Leipzig and Heidelberg. During his time in Jena he disputed with Matthias Flacius (1520–1575) over the human will's autonomy. Following Philipp Melanchthon,* Strigel asserted that in conversion the human will obediently cooperates with the divine will through the Holy Spirit and the Word of God. In the Weimar Disputation (1560), Strigel elicited Flacius's opinion that sin is a substance that mars the formal essence of human beings. Flacius's views were officially rejected in Article 1 of the Formula of Concord*; Strigel's, in Article 2. In 1567 the University of Leipzig suspended Strigel from teaching on account of suspicions that he affirmed Reformed Eucharistic theology; he acknowledged that he did and joined the Reformed confession on the faculty of the University of Heidelberg. In addition to controversial tracts, Strigel published commentaries on the entire Bible (except Lamentations) and the Apocrypha.

Johann Sutell (1504–1575). German Lutheran pastor. After studying at the University of Wittenberg, Sutell received a call to a pastorate in Göttingen, where he eventually became superintendent. He wrote new church orders for Göttingen (1531) and Schweinfurt (1543), and expanded two sermons for publication, *The Dreadful Destruction of Jerusalem* (1539) and *History of Lazarus* (1543).

Swiss Brethren Confession of Hesse (1578). Anabaptist leader Hans Pauly Kuchenbecker penned this confession after a 1577 interrogation by Lutheran authorities. This confession was unusually amenable to Lutheran views—there is no mention of pacifism or rejection of oath taking.

Synod of Dordrecht (1618–1619). This large Dutch Reformed Church council—also attended by English, German and Swiss delegates—met to settle the theological issues raised by the followers of Jacobus Arminius.* Arminius's theological disagreements with mainstream Reformed teaching erupted into open conflict with the publication of the *Remonstrance* (1610). This "protest" was based on five points: that election is based on foreseen faith or unbelief; that Christ died indiscriminately for all people (although only believers receive salvation); that people are thoroughly sinful by nature apart from the prevenient grace of God that enables their free will to embrace or reject the gospel; that humans are able to resist the working of God's grace; and that it is possible for true believers to fall away from faith completely. The Synod ruled in favor of the Contra-Remonstrants, its Canons often remembered with a TULIP acrostic—total depravity, unconditional election, limited atonement, irresistible grace, perseverance of the saints—each letter countering one of the five Remonstrant articles. The Synod also officially accepted the Belgic Confession,* Heidelberg Catechism* and the Canons of Dordrecht as standards of the Dutch Reformed Church.

Arcangela Tarabotti (1604–1652). Italian Catholic nun. At the age of eleven, Tarabotti entered a Benedictine convent as a student-boarder; three years later her father forced her to take monastic vows. The dignity of women and their treatment in the male-controlled institutions of early modern Venice concerned Tarabotti deeply. She protested forced cloistering, the denial of education to women, the exclusion of women from public life and the double standards by which men and women were judged. Tarbotti authored numerous polemical works and an extensive correspondence.

Johannes Tauler (c. 1300–1361) German mystical theologian. A Dominican friar and disciple of Meister Eckhart (c. 1260–c. 1328), Tauler spent most of his career as a mendicant preacher in Strasburg and Basel. Known through a collection of about eighty German sermons, Tauler taught a practical spirituality, accessible to those outside the cloister and intended to draw his audience to deeper contemplation of the divine nature.

Richard Taverner (1505–1575). English Puritan humanist and translator. After graduating from Oxford, Taverner briefly studied abroad. When he returned to England, he joined Thomas Cromwell's (1485–1540) circle. After Cromwell's beheading, Taverner escaped severe punishment and retired from public life during Mary I's reign. Under Elizabeth I,* Taverner served as justice of the peace, sheriff and a licensed lay preacher. Taverner translated many important continental Reformation works into English, most notably the Augsburg Confession* and several of Desiderius Erasmus's* works. Some of these translations—John Calvin's* 1536 catechism, Wolfgang Capito's* work on the Psalms and probably Erasmus Sarcerius's* postils—he presented as his own work. Underwritten by Cromwell, Taverner also published an edited version of the Matthew Bible (1537).

Jeremy Taylor (1613–1667) Anglican theologian, preacher, and author. Son of a barber, Taylor studied at Cambridge before the patronage of Archbishop Laud* drew him into the work of the English church. After serving as chaplain to Laud and King Charles I (1600–1649), he entered parish ministry. Following the outbreak of the Civil War (1642–51), his commitment to the Royalist cause saw him imprisoned at least three times. Withdrawing to Wales, he ran a school preparing students for university while serving as chaplain to the earl of Carbery. Known for his skill as a writer, it was here that Taylor composed many of his best known works, including his popular devotional manuals, *The Rules and Exercises of Holy Living* (1650), and *The Rules and Exercises of Holy Dying* (1651). After the Restoration, Taylor was made Bishop of Down and Connor in Ireland and served as vice-chancellor of the University of Dublin.

Thomas Taylor (1576–1632). Puritan minister and commentator. Taylor was born in Richmond, Yorkshire. He was educated at Christ's College, Cambridge, where he earned the degrees of Bachelor of Arts (1595) and Master of Arts (1598). Prior to entering pastoral ministry, Taylor served as a fellow and lecturer in Hebrew at the university. Throughout his academic career, Taylor was significantly influenced by the writings of William Perkins.* At the age of twenty-five, Taylor preached a virulent sermon against the papacy before Queen Elizabeth I.* As a Puritan, Taylor denounced the ecclesiastical policies of Archbishop Richard Bancroft.* In 1612, Taylor became minister of a church in Watford, Hertfordshire. While serving this charge, Taylor preached regularly in Berkshire and Reading. Moreover, Taylor formed and led a Puritan seminary, where he personally trained Nonconformist preachers. In the early 1620s, Taylor served as a chaplain to Edward Conway (1564–1631), secretary of state under James VI/I* (1566–1625). In 1625, Taylor was called to be curate and lecturer at St. Aldermanbury, London. While there, he organized and ran another Puritan seminary. Two years later, Taylor joined several other Puritans' efforts to send relief to oppressed Reformed ministers on the Continent. Taylor retired from his labors in 1630 due to ill health. He died of pleurisy in 1632. His main works include *Christ Revealed; or The Old Testament Explained* and *An Exposition of Titus.*

Thomas Thorowgood (1595–1669). English Puritan pastor. Thorowgood was a Puritan minister in Norfolk and the chief financier of John Eliot (1604–1690), a Puritan missionary among the Native American tribes in Massachusetts. In 1650, under the title *Jews in America, or, Probabilities that Americans be of that Race*, Thorowgood became one of the first to put forward the thesis that Native Americans were actually the ten lost tribes of Israel.

Frans Titelmans (1502–1537). Belgian Catholic philosopher. Titelmans studied at the University of Leuven, where he was influenced by Petrus Ramus.* After first joining a Franciscan monastery, Titelmans realigned with the stricter Capuchins and moved to Italy. He is best known for his advocacy for the Vulgate and his debates with Desiderius Erasmus* over Pauline theology (1527–1530)—he was deeply suspicious of the fruits of humanism, especially regarding biblical studies. His work was published posthumously by his brother, Pieter Titelmans (1501–1572).

Francisco de Toledo (1532–1596). Spanish Catholic theologian. This important Jesuit taught philosophy at the universities of Salamanca and Rome. He published works on Aristotelian philosophy and a commentary on Thomas Aquinas's* work, as well as biblical commentaries on John, Romans and the first half of Luke. He was also the general editor for the Clementine Vulgate (1598).

Laurence Tomson (1539–1608). English Reformed politician and translator. Tomson was born in Northhamptonshire and educated at Magdalen College, Oxford. He graduated with his BA degree (1559) and MA degree (1564). Tomson was a fellow at Magdalen until he resigned in 1569. Prior to this resignation, Tomson was part of a diplomatic delegation to France. From 1575 to 1587, Tomson served in the House of Commons and attended the royal court at Windsor in 1582. He went on further embassies throughout Europe, where he occasionally lectured on Hebrew. Tomson died on March 29, 1608. Tomson's chief exegetical contribution was his revised text and annotations of the New Testament of the Geneva Bible.

Alonso Tostado (1400–1455). Spanish Catholic bishop and exegete. Tostado lectured on theology, law and philosophy at the University of Salamanca, in addition to ministering in a local parish. Tostado entered into disputes over papal supremacy and the date of Christ's birth. Tostado's thirteen-volume collected works include commentaries on the historical books of the Old Testament and the Gospel of Matthew.

Daniel Toussain (1541–1602). Swiss Reformed pastor and professor. Toussain became pastor at Orléans after attending college in Basel. After the third War of Religion, Toussain was exiled, eventually returning to Montbéliard, his birthplace. In 1571, he faced opposition there from the strict Lutheran rulers and was eventually exiled due to his influence over the clergy. He returned to Orléans but fled following the Saint Bartholomew's Day Massacre (1572), eventually becoming pastor in Basel. He relocated to Heidelberg in 1583 as pastor to the new regent, becoming professor of theology at the university, and he remained there until his death.

John Trapp (1601–1669). Anglican biblical exegete. After studying at Oxford, Trapp entered the pastorate in 1636. During the English Civil Wars he sided with Parliament, which later made it difficult for him to collect tithes from a congregation whose royalist pastor had been evicted. Trapp published commentaries on all the books of the Bible from 1646 to 1656.

Immanuel Tremellius (1510–1580). Italian Reformed Hebraist. Around 1540, Tremellius received baptism by Cardinal Reginald Pole (1500–1558) and converted from Judaism to Christianity; he affiliated with evangelicals the next year. On account of the political and religious upheaval, Tremellius relocated often, teaching Hebrew in Lucca; Strasbourg, fleeing the Inquisition; Cambridge, displaced by the Schmalkaldic War; Heidelberg, escaping Mary I's persecutions; and Sedan, expelled by the new Lutheran Elector of the Palatine. Many considered Tremellius's translation of the Old Testament as the most accurate available. He also published a Hebrew grammar and translated John Calvin's* catechism into Hebrew.

Richard Turnbull (d. 1593). English minister. A preacher in London, Richard Turnbull published sermons on James, Jude, and Psalm 15.

William Tyndale (Hychyns) (1494–1536). English reformer, theologian and translator.

Tyndale was educated at Oxford University, where he was influenced by the writings of humanist thinkers. Believing that piety is fostered through personal encounter with the Bible, he asked to translate the Bible into English; denied permission, Tyndale left for the Continent to complete the task. His New Testament was the equivalent of a modern-day bestseller in England but was banned and ordered burned. Tyndale's theology was oriented around justification, the authority of Scripture and Christian obedience; Tyndale emphasized the ethical as a concomitant reality of justification. He was martyred in Brussels before completing his English translation of the Old Testament, which Miles Coverdale* finished.

Guillaume du Vair (1556–1621). French Catholic priest, lawyer, and writer. While du Vair took holy orders in his youth, much of his life was spent serving the state as a counselor of the parliament of Paris, a representative of King Henry IV both in France and abroad, and as Keeper of the Seals, the highest legal office in the country. The last four years of his life were spent as the bishop of Lisieux. His studies on Epictetus and the Stoics, and attempts to relate Stoicism to the Christian faith, were influential in the dissemination of this philosophy during the seventeenth and eighteenth centuries. He also wrote significant works on politics, the moral life, prayer, and the use and abuse of the French language.

Juan de Valdés (1500/10–1541). Spanish Catholic theologian and writer. Although Valdés adopted an evangelical doctrine, had Erasmian affiliations and published works that were listed on the Index of Prohibited Books, Valdés rebuked the reformers for creating disunity and never left the Catholic Church. His writings included translations of the Hebrew Psalter and various biblical books, a work on the Spanish language and several commentaries. Valdés fled to Rome in 1531 to escape the Spanish Inquisition and worked in the court of Clement VII in Bologna until the pope's death in 1534. Valdés subsequently returned to Naples, where he led the reform- and revival-minded Valdesian circle.

Peter Martyr Vermigli (1499–1562). Italian Reformed humanist and theologian. Vermigli was one of the most influential theologians of the era, held in common regard with such figures as Martin Luther* and John Calvin.* In Italy, Vermigli was a distinguished theologian, preacher and advocate for moral reform; however, during the reinstitution of the Roman Inquisition Vermigli fled to Protestant regions in northern Europe. He was eventually appointed professor of divinity at Oxford University, where Vermigli delivered acclaimed disputations on the Eucharist. Vermigli was widely noted for his deeply integrated biblical commentaries and theological treatises.

Vulgate. In 382 Pope Damasus I (c. 300–384) commissioned Jerome (c. 347–420) to translate the four Gospels into Latin based on Old Latin and Greek manuscripts. Jerome completed the translation of the Gospels and the Old Testament around 405. It is widely debated how much of the rest of the New Testament was translated by Jerome. During the Middle Ages, the Vulgate became the Catholic Church's standard Latin translation. The Council of Trent recognized it as the official text of Scripture.

George Walker (1581–1651). Puritan minister. Walker was born at Hawkshead, Lancashire, and educated at St. John's College, Cambridge. After graduating Cambridge, Walker moved to London, where he became rector of St. John the Evangelist on Watling Street in 1614. He served this parish for nearly forty years. Throughout his ministry, Walker showed himself to be an ardent opponent of the papacy and practices within the Church of England that he deemed not sufficiently reformed. Toward this end, Walker engaged numerous disputations and literary debates with both conformists and Catholics. For his sermons that were critical of the Church of England, he was summoned to appear before Archbishop Laud in 1635 and the Star Chamber in 1638, which fined and imprisoned him for twelve weeks. On another occasion, Walker was incarcerated for as long as two years for his nonconformity until released by the Long Parliament. In 1643, Walker was selected to serve in the Westminster Assembly and to participate in the trial of Laud. Walker died in London. Among his many published sermons and polemical works is a treatise on justification.

Thomas Walkington (d. 1621). Anglican minister and author. Born in Lincoln, he was educated at Cambridge, graduating with his BA in 1597 and his MA in 1600. Walkington was elected a fellow at St. John's College, Cambridge, in 1602. Later, he received a BD from Oxford and a DD from Cambridge. He served as rector of parishes in Northamptonshire, Lincolnshire, and Middlesex. A prolific author, Walkington published works on diverse subjects. Among his biblical works are *An Exposition of the First Two Verses of the Sixth Chapter to the Hebrews in form of a Dialogue* (1609) and *Theologicall Rules to Guide Us in the Understanding and Practice of Holy Scripture* (1615).

Peter Walpot (d. 1578). Moravian Radical pastor and bishop. Walpot was a bishop of the Hutterite community after Jakob Hutter, Peter Riedemann* and Leonhard Lanzenstiel. Riedemann's *Confession of Faith* (1545; 1565) became a vital authority for Hutterite exegesis, theology and morals. Walpot added his own *Great Article Book* (1577), which collates primary biblical passages on baptism, communion, the community of goods, the sword and divorce. In keeping with Hutterite theology, Walpot defended the community of goods as a mark of the true church.

Valentin Weigel (1533–1588). German Lutheran pastor. Weigel studied at Leipzig and Wittenberg, entering the pastorate in 1567. Despite a strong anti-institutional bias, he was recognized by the church hierarchy as a talented preacher and compassionate minister of mercy to the poor. Although he signed the Formula of Concord,* Weigel's orthodoxy was questioned so openly that he had to publish a defense. He appears to have tried to synthesize several medieval mystics with the ideas of Sebastian Franck,* Thomas Müntzer* and others. His posthumously published works have led some recent scholars to suggest that Weigel's works may have deeply influenced later Pietism.

Hieronymus Weller von Molsdorf (1499–1572). German Lutheran theologian. Originally intending to study law, Weller devoted himself to theology after hearing one of Martin Luther's* sermons on the catechism. He boarded with Luther and tutored Luther's son. In 1539 he moved to Freiburg, where he lectured on the Bible and held theological disputations at the Latin school. In addition to hymns, works of practical theology and a postil set, Weller published commentaries on Genesis, 1–2 Samuel, 1–2 Kings, Job, the Psalms, Christ's passion, Ephesians, Philippians, 1–2 Thessalonians and 1–2 Peter.

John Whitgift (1530–1604). Anglican archbishop. Though Whitgift shared much theological common ground with Puritans, after his election as Archbishop of Canterbury (1583) he moved decisively to squelch the political and ecclesiastical threat they posed during Elizabeth I's* reign. Whitgift enforced strict compliance to the Book of Common Prayer,* the Act of Uniformity (1559) and the Articles of Religion.* Whitgift's policies led to a large migration of Puritans to Holland. The bulk of Whitgift's published corpus is the fruit of a lengthy public disputation with Thomas Cartwright,* in which Whitgift defines Anglican doctrine against Cartwright's staunch Puritanism.

Johann Wigand (1523–1587). German Lutheran theologian. Wigand is most noted as one of the compilers of the *Magdeburg Centuries*, a German ecclesiastical history of the first thirteen centuries of the church. He was a student of Philipp Melanchthon* at the University of Wittenburg and became a significant figure in the controversies dividing Lutheranism. Strongly opposed to Roman Catholicism, Wigand lobbied against innovations in Lutheran theology that appeared sympathetic to Catholic thought. In the later debates, Wigand's support for Gnesio-Lutheranism established his role in the development of confessional Lutheranism. Wigand was appointed bishop of Pomerania after serving academic posts at the universities in Jena and Königsburg.

Thomas Wilcox (c. 1549–1608). English Puritan theologian. In 1572, Wilcox objected to Parliament against the episcopacy and the Book of Common Prayer,* advocating for presbyterian church governance. He was imprisoned for sedition. After his release, he preached itinerantly. He was brought before the courts twice more for his continued protest against the Church of England's episcopal structure. He translated some of Theodore Beza* and John Calvin's* sermons into English, and he wrote polemical and occasional works as well as commentaries on the Psalms and Song of Songs.

Johann (Ferus) Wild (1495–1554). German Catholic pastor. After studying at Heidelberg and teaching at Tübingen, this Franciscan was appointed as lector in the Mainz cathedral, eventually being promoted to cathedral preacher—a post for which he became widely popular but also controversial. Wild strongly identified as Catholic but was not unwilling to criticize the curia. Known for an irenic spirit—criticized in fact as *too* kind—he was troubled by the polemics between all parties of the Reformation. He preached with great lucidity, integrating the liturgy, Scripture and doctrine to exposit Catholic worship and teaching for common people. His sermons on John were pirated for publication without his knowledge; the Sorbonne banned them as heretical. Despite his popularity among clergy, the majority of his works were on the Roman Index until 1900.

Andrew Willet (1562–1621). Anglican priest, professor, and biblical expositor. Willet was a gifted biblical expositor and powerful preacher. He walked away from a promising university career in 1588 when he was ordained a priest in the Church of England. For the next thirty-three years he served as a parish priest. Willet's commentaries summarized the present state of discussion while also offering practical applications for preachers. They have been cited as some of the most technical commentaries of the early seventeenth century. His most important publication was *Synopsis Papismi, or a General View of Papistrie* (1594), in which he responded to many of

Robert Bellarmine's critiques. After years of royal favor, Willet was imprisoned in 1618 for a month after presenting to King James I* his opposition to the "Spanish Match" of Prince Charles to the Infanta Maria. While serving as a parish priest, he wrote forty-two works, most of which were either commentaries on books of the Bible or controversial works against Catholics.

Thomas Wilson (d. 1586). English Anglican priest. A fellow of St John's, Cambridge, Wilson fled to Frankfurt to escape the Marian Persecution. After his return to England, he served as a canon and Dean of Worcester.

George Wither (1588–1667). English poet, satirist, and hymn writer. Wither was born in Bentworth, Hampshire. After finishing his early education under the tutelage of a local minister, Wither continued his studies at Magdalen College, Oxford. Afterward, he studied law at the Inns of Chancery. Wither commenced his literary career with the publication of an elegy on the occasion of the death of Henry Frederick, Prince of Wales (1594–1612). Most of Wither's literary works consist of satirical pamphlets for which he was regularly arrested, imprisoned, and released. He fought in the Parliamentary Army during the Civil War. A conforming Anglican, Wither composed numerous hymns as well as translations of the Psalms. Two of Wither's major works are *Preparation to the Psalter* (1619), in which he explores various literary aspects of the Bible, and *Hymns and Songs of the Church* (1622/1623). He died in London.

John Woolton (c. 1535–1594). Anglican bishop. After graduating from Oxford, Woolton lived in Germany until the accession of Elizabeth I.* He was ordained as a priest in 1560 and as a bishop in 1578. Woolton published many theological, devotional and practical works, including a treatise on the immortality of the soul, a discourse on conscience and a manual for Christian living.

Girolamo Zanchi (1516–1590). Italian Reformed theologian and pastor. Zanchi joined an Augustinian monastery at the age of fifteen, where he studied Greek and Latin, the church

fathers and the works of Aristotle and Thomas Aquinas.* Under the influence of his prior, Peter Martyr Vermigli,* Zanchi also imbibed the writings of the Swiss and German reformers. To avoid the Inquisition, Zanchi fled to Geneva where he was strongly attracted to the preaching and teaching of John Calvin.* Zanchi taught biblical theology and the *locus* method at academies in Strasbourg, Heidelberg, and Neustadt. He also served as pastor of an Italian refugee congregation. Zanchi's theological works, *De tribus Elohim* (1572) and *De natura Dei* (1577), have received more attention than his commentaries. His commentaries comprise about a quarter of his literary output, however, and display a strong typological and christological interpretation in conversation with the church fathers, medieval exegetes, and other reformers.

Katharina Schütz Zell (1497/98–1562). German Reformed writer. Zell became infamous in Strasbourg and the Empire when in 1523 she married the priest Matthias Zell, and then published an apology defending her husband against charges of impiety and libertinism. Longing for a united church, she called for toleration of Catholics and Anabaptists, famously writing to Martin Luther* after the failed Marburg Colloquy of 1529 to exhort him to check his hostility and to be ruled instead by Christian charity. Much to the chagrin of her contemporaries, Zell published diverse works, ranging from polemical treatises on marriage to letters of consolation, as well as editing a hymnal and penning an exposition of Psalm 51.

Ulrich Zwingli (1484–1531). Swiss Reformed humanist, preacher and theologian. Zwingli studied at the University of Vienna, and afterwards the University of Basel, where he received his BA and MA in 1504 and 1506. Ordained in September 1506, Zwingli became priest of the church in Glarus where he taught himself Greek, and read deeply in the church fathers. During this period, Zwingli was also greatly impacted by the writings of Desiderius Erasmus*. In 1516, Zwingli accepted the position of priest at the Benedictine Abbey at Einsiedeln in Schwyz, where he intently studied the Greek New Testament, and learned Hebrew. When he became a preacher in the city cathedral at Zurich, Zwingli enacted reform through sermons, public disputations, and conciliation with the town council, abolishing the Mass and images in the church. Zwingli broke with the lectionary preaching tradition, instead preaching serial expository biblical sermons. He later was embroiled in controversy with Anabaptists over infant baptism and with Martin Luther* at the Marburg Colloquy (1529) over their differing views of the Eucharist. Zwingli, serving as chaplain to Zurich's military, was killed in the Second Battle of Kappel.

SOURCES FOR
BIOGRAPHICAL SKETCHES

General Reference Works

Allgemeine Deutsche Biographie. 56 vols. Leipzig: Duncker & Humblot, 1875–1912; reprint, 1967–1971. Accessible online via deutsche -biographie.de/index.html.

Baskin, Judith R., ed. *The Cambridge Dictionary of Judaism and Jewish Culture.* New York: Cambridge University Press, 2011.

Benedetto, Robert, ed. *The New Westminster Dictionary of Church History.* Vol. 1. Louisville: Westminster John Knox Press, 2008.

Bettenson, Henry and Chris Maunder, eds. *Documents of the Christian Church.* 3rd ed. Oxford: Oxford University Press, 1999.

Betz, Hans Dieter, Don Browning, Bernd Janowski and Eberhard Jüngel, eds. *Religion Past & Present: Encyclopedia of Theology and Relgion.* 13 vols. Leiden: Brill, 2007–2013.

Bremer, Francis J. and Tom Webster, eds. *Puritans and Puritanism in Europe and America: A Comprehensive Encyclopedia.* 2 vols. Santa Barbara, CA: ABC-CLIO, 2006.

Gritsch, Eric W. *A History of Lutheranism.* Minneapolis: Fortress Press, 2002.

Haag, Eugene and Émile Haag. *La France protestante ou vies des protestants français.* 2nd ed. 6 vols. Paris: Sandoz & Fischbacher, 1877–1888.

Hillerbrand, Hans J., ed. *Oxford Encyclopedia of the Reformation.* 4 vols. New York: Oxford University Press, 1996.

Kolb, Robert, and Timothy J. Wengert, eds. *The Book of Concord: The Confessions of the Evangelical Lutheran Church.* Translated by Charles Arand et al. Minneapolis: Fortress, 2000.

McKim, Donald K., ed. *Dictionary of Major Biblical Interpreters.* Downers Grove, IL: InterVarsity Press, 2007.

Müller, Gerhard, et al., ed. *Theologische Realenzyklopädie.* Berlin: Walter de Gruyter, 1994.

Neue Deutsche Biographie. 28 vols. projected. Berlin: Duncker & Humblot, 1953–. Accessible online via deutsche-biographie.de/index.html.

New Catholic Encyclopedia. 15 vols. New York: McGraw-Hill, 1967; 2nd ed., Detroit: Thomson-Gale, 2002.

Oxford Dictionary of National Biography. 60 vols. Oxford: Oxford University Press, 2004.

Pelikan, Jaroslav. *The Christian Tradition.* 5 vols. Chicago: University of Chicago Press, 1971–1989.

Stephen, Leslie, and Sidney Lee, eds. *Dictionary of National Biography.* 63 vols. London: Smith, Elder and Co., 1885–1900.

Terry, Michael, ed. *Reader's Guide to Judaism.* New York: Routledge, 2000.

Wordsworth, Christopher, ed. *Lives of Eminent Men connected with the History of Religion in England.* 4 vols. London: J. G. & F. Rivington, 1839.

Additional Works for Individual Sketches

Akin, Daniel L. "An Expositional Analysis of the Schleitheim Confession." *Criswell Theological Review* 2 (1988): 345-70.

Bald, R. C. *John Donne: A Life.* Oxford: Oxford University Press, 1970.

Beeke, Joel, and Randall J. Pederson. *Meet the Puritans.* Grand Rapids: Reformation Heritage Books, 2006.

Bireley, Robert, *The Refashioning of Catholicism, 1450–1700,* Washington, DC: Catholic University of America Press, 1999.

Blok, P. J., and P. C. Molhuysen, eds. *Nieuw Nederlandsch Biografisch Woordenboek.* 10 vols.

Brackney, William H. *A Genetic History of Baptist Thought: With Special Reference to Baptists in Britain and North America.* Atlanta: Mercer University Press, 2004.

Brook, Benjamin. *The Lives of the Puritans.* 3 vols. London: James Black, 1813. Reprint, Pittsburgh, PA: Soli Deo Gloria, 1994.

Brown, Peter. *Augustine of Hippo: A Biography.* Berkeley & Los Angeles, CA: University of California Press, 1967.

Burke, David G. "The Enduring Significance of the KJV." *Word and World* 31, no. 3 (2011): 229-44.

Campbell, Gordon. *Bible: The Story of the King James Version, 1611–2011*. Oxford: Oxford University Press, 2010.

Charles, Amy. *A Life of George Herbert*. Ithaca, NY: Cornell University Press, 1977.

Coffey, John. *Politics, Religion, and the British Revolutions: The Thought of Samuel Rutherford*. Cambridge: Cambridge University Press, 1997.

Colish, Marcia. *Peter Lombard*, 2 vols. Leiden, Netherlands: Brill, 1993.

Doornkaat Koolman, J ten. "The First Edition of Peter Riedemann's 'Rechenschaft.'" *Mennonite Quarterly Review* 36, no. 2 (1962): 169-70.

Emerson, Everett H. *John Cotton*. New York: Twayne, 1990.

Fischlin, Daniel and Mark Fortier, eds. *Royal Subjects: Essays on the Writings of James VI and I*. Detroit: Wayne State University Press, 2002.

Fishbane, Michael A. "Teacher and the Hermeneutical Task: A Reinterpretation of Medieval Exegesis." *Journal of the American Academy of Religion* 43, no. 4 (1975): 709-21.

Friedmann, Robert. "Second Generation Anabaptism as Illustrated by the Walpot Era of the Hutterites." *Mennonite Quarterly* 44, no. 4 (1970): 390-93.

Frymire, John M. *The Primacy of the Postils: Catholics, Protestants, and the Dissemination of Ideas in Early Modern Germany*. Leiden: Brill, 2010.

Furcha, Edward J. "Key Concepts in Caspar von Schwenckfeld's Thought, Regeneration and the New Life." *Church History* 37, no. 2 (1968): 160-73.

Gordon, Bruce, *The Swiss Reformation*. Manchester: Manchester University Press, 2002.

Greaves, Richard L. *Society and Religion in Elizabethan England*. Minneapolis: University of Minnesota, 1981.

Greiffenberg, Catharina Regina von. *Meditations on the Incarnation, Passion and Death of Jesus Christ*. Edited and translated by Lynne Tatlock. The Other Voice in Early Modern Europe. Chicago: University of Chicago Press, 2009.

Grendler, Paul. "Italian biblical humanism and the papacy, 1515-1535." In *Biblical Humanism and Scholasticism in the Age of Erasmus*. Edited by Erika Rummel, 225-76. Leiden: Brill, 2008.

Haemig, Mary Jane. "Elisabeth Cruciger (1500?–1535): The Case of the Disappearing Hymn Writer."

Sixteenth Century Journal 32, no. 1 (2001): 21-44.

Heiden, Albert van der. "Pardes: Methodological Reflections on the Theory of the Four Senses." *Journal of Jewish Studies* 34, no. 2 (1983): 147-59.

Hendrix, Scott H., ed. and trans. *Early Protestant Spirituality*. New York: Paulist Press, 2009.

Hvolbek, Russell H. "Being and Knowing: Spiritualist Epistelmology and Anthropology from Schwenckfeld to Böhme." *Sixteenth Century Journal* 22, no. 1 (1991): 97-110.

Kahle, Paul. "Felix Pratensis—a Prato, Felix. Der Herausgeber der Ersten Rabbinerbibel, Venedig 1516/7." *Die Welt des Orients* 1, no. 1 (1947): 32-36.

Kelly, Joseph Francis. *The Ecumenical Councils of the Catholic Church: A History*. Collegeville, MN: Liturgical Press, 2009.

Lake, Peter. *The Boxmaker's Revenge: "Orthodoxy", "Heterodox" and the Politics of the Parish in Early Stuart London*. Stanford, CA: Stanford University Press, 2001.

Lane, Anthony N. S. *Calvin and Bernard of Clairvaux*. Princeton, NJ: Princeton Theological Seminary, 1996.

Lane, Belden C. *Ravished by Beauty: The Surprising Legacy of Reformed Spirituality*. Oxford: Oxford University Press, 2011.

Lockhart, Paul Douglas. *Frederick II and the Protestant Cause: Denmark's Role in the Wars of Religion, 1559–1596*. Leiden: Brill, 2004.

Lubac, Henri de. *Medieval Exegesis: The Four Senses of Scripture*. 3 vols. Translated by Mark Sebanc and E. M. Macierowski. Grand Rapids: Eerdmans, 1998–2009.

Manetsch, Scott, *Calvin's Company of Pastors: Pastoral Care and the Emerging Reformed Church, 1536–1609*. Oxford: Oxford University Press, 2013.

Manschereck, Clyde Leonard. *Melanchthon, the Quiet Reformer*. New York: Abingdon, 1958.

Matheson, Peter, *Argula von Grumbach: A Woman's Voice in the Reformation*. Edinburgh: T&T Clark, 1995.

McGuire, Daniel Patrick. *The Difficult Saint: Bernard of Clairvaux and his Tradition*. Collegeville, MN: Cistercian Publication, 1991.

McKinley, Mary B. "Volume Editor's Introduction." In *Epistle to Marguerite of Navarre and Preface to a Sermon by John Calvin*, edited and translated by Mary B. McKiney. Chicago: University of Chicago Press, 2004.

M'Crie, Thomas. *The Life of Andrew Melville*. 2 vols. Edinburgh: William Blackwood, 1819.

Norton, David. *A Textual History of the King James Bible.* New York: Cambridge University Press, 2005

Nuttall, Geoffrey. *The Welsh Saints, 1640–1660: Walter Cradock, Vavasor Powell, Morgan Llwyd.* Cardiff: University of Wales Press, 1957.

Oberman, Heiko A. *Luther: Man Between God and the Devil.* New York, NY: Doubleday, 1989.

O'Meara, Thomas F. *Albert the Great: Theologian and Scientist.* Chicago: New Priory Press, 2013.

Packull, Werner O. "The Origins of Peter Riedemann's Account of Our Faith." *Sixteenth Century Journal* 30, no. 1 (1999): 61-69.

Papazian, Mary Arshagouni, ed. *John Donne and the Protestant Reformation: New Perspectives.* Detroit: Wayne State University Press, 2003.

Paulicelli, Eugenia. "Sister Arcangela Tarabotti: Hair, Wigs and Other Vices." In *Writing Fashion in Early Modern Italy: From Sprezzatura to Satire,* by idem, 177-204. Farnham, Surrey, UK: Ashgate, 2014.

Pragman, James H. "The Augsburg Confession in the English Reformation: Richard Taverner's Contribution." *Sixteenth Century Journal* 11, no. 3 (1980): 75-85.

Rashi. *Rashi's Commentary on Psalms.* Translated by Mayer I. Gruber. Atlanta: Scholars Press, 1998.

Raynor, Brian. *John Frith: Scholar and Martyr.* Kent, UK: Pond View Books, 2000.

Reid, Jonathan A. *King's Sister—Queen of Dissent: Marguerite of Navarre (1492–1549) and her Evangelical Network.* Leiden: Brill, 2009.

Schmidt, Josef, "Introduction" in Johannes Tauler, *Sermons.* New York: Paulist Press, 1985, 1-34.

Spinka, Matthew. *John Hus: A Biography.* Princeton, NJ: Princeton University Press, 1968.

———. *John Hus at the Council of Constance.* New York: Columbia University Press, 1968.

———. *John Hus and the Czech Reform.* Hamden, CT: Archon Books, 1966.

Steinmetz, David C. *Reformers in the Wings: From Geiler von Kayserberg to Theodore Beza.* Oxford: Oxford University Press, 2000.

———. "The Superiority of Pre-Critical Exegesis." *Theology Today* 37, no. 1 (1980): 27-38.

Stjerna, Kirsi. *Women of the Reformation.* Malden, MA: Blackwell Publishing, 2009.

Synder, C. Arnold. "The Confession of the Swiss Brethren in Hesse, 1578." In *Anabaptism Revisited: Essays on Anabaptist/Mennonite Studies in Honor of C. J. Dyck.* Edited by Walter Klaassen, 29-49. Waterloo, ON; Scottdale, PA: Herald Press, 1992.

———. "The Schleitheim Articles in Light of the Revolution of the Common Man: Continuation or Departure?" *Sixteenth Century Journal* 16, no. 4 (1985): 419-30.

Todd, Margo. "Bishops in the Kirk: William Cowper of Galloway and the Puritan Episcopacy of Scotland." *Scottish Journal of Theology,* 57 (2004): 300-312.

Thornton, Wallace. *John Foxe and His Monument: A Theological-Historical Perspective.* Birmingham, AL: Aldersgate Heritage Press, 2013.

Van Liere, Frans. *An Introduction to the Medieval Bible.* New York: Cambridge University Press, 2014.

Voogt, Gerrit. "Remonstrant-Counter-Remonstrant Debates: Crafting a Principled Defense of Toleration after the Synod of Dordrecht (1619–1650)." *Church History and Religious Culture* 89, no. 4 (2009): 489-524.

Wallace, Dewey D. Jr. "George Gifford, Puritan Propaganda and Popular Religion in Elizabethan England." *Sixteenth Century Journal* 9, no. 1 (1978): 27-49.

Wawrykow, Joseph P. *The Westminster Handbook to Thomas Aquinas.* Louisville, KY: Westminster John Knox, 2005.

Wendel, Francois. *Calvin: The Origins and Development of His Religious Thought.* New York: Harper & Row, 1963.

Wengert, Timothy J. "'Fear and Love' in the Ten Commandments." *Concordia Journal* 21, no. 1 (1995): 14-27.

———. "Philip Melanchthon and John Calvin against Andreas Osiander: Coming to Terms with Forensic Justification." In *Calvin and Luther: The Continuing Relationship,* edited by R. Ward Holder, 63-87. Göttingen: Vandenhoeck & Ruprecht, 2013.

Wilkinson, Robert J. *Tetragrammaton: Western Christians and the Hebrew Name of God.* Leiden: Brill, 2015.

BIBLIOGRAPHY

Primary Sources Cited in This Volume

Alesius, Alexander. *Omnes disputationes d. Alexandri Alesii de tota Epistola ad Romanos diversis temporibus propositae ab ipso.* Leipzig, 1553. Digital copy online at www.bsb-muenchen.de.

Ames, William. *The Svbstance of the Christian Religion or a Plain and Easie Draught of the Christian Catechisme in XII. Lectures.* London: T. Mabb, 1659. Digital copies online at EEBO-TCP and books.google.com.

Aretius, Benedict. *Commentarii in Epistolam d. Pauli ad Romanos.* Lausanne: D. Berensium, 1579. Digital copy online at www.e-rara.ch.

Arminius, Jacobus. *The Works of James Arminius.* 3 vols. Translated by James Nichols. Auburn, NY: Derby, Miller and Orton, 1853. Digital copy online at archive.org.

Balduin, Friedrich. *Catechesis Apostolica: hoc est, S. Apostoli Pauli: Epistola ad Romanos, commentario perspicuo illustrata.* Wittenberg: Augusti Boreck, Samuelis Selfisch & Pauli Helwichij, 1620. Digital copy online at archive.org.

Baxter, Richard. *Aphorismes of Justification, with Their Explication Annexed.* Hague: Abraham Brown, 1655. Digital copy online at EEBO.

———. *The Crucifying of the World by the Cross of Christ.* London, R. W., 1658. Digital copy online at EEBO-TCP.

Beza, Theodore. *Annotationes Majores in Novum Dn. Nostri Jesu Christi Testamentum. In duas distinctae partes, quarum prior explicationem in quatuor Evangelistas et Acta Apostolorum. Posterior vero in Epistolas.* Geneva, 1594. Digital copy online at www.e-rara.ch.

———. *Cours Sur Les Épîtres aux Romains et aux Hébreux: 1564–1566 d'après les notes de Marcus Widler. Thèses disputées à l'Académie de Genève: 1564–1567.* Edited by Pierre Fraenkel and Luc Perrotet. Travaux d'Humanisme et Renaissance. Genève: Librarie Droz, 1988.

The book of the general lauues and libertyes concerning the inhabitants of the Massachusets collected out of the records of the General Court for the several years wherin they were made and established, and now revised by the same Court and disposed into an alphabetical order and published by the same authoritie in the General Court held at Boston the fourteenth of the first month anno 1647. Cambridge, MA: Matthew Day, 1648. Digital copy online at University of Oxford Text Archive.

Bowle, John. *A Sermon Preached at Mapple-Durham.* London: T. S. for John Hodges, 1616. Digital copy online at EEBO.

Bradstreet, Anne. *The Works of Anne Bradstreet in Poetry and Prose.* Edited by John Harvard Ellis. Charleston: A. E. Cutter, 1867 (based on 2nd ed. of 1678). Digital copy online at archive.org.

Brenz, Johannes. *In Epistolam, quam Apostolus Paulus ad Romanos scripsit, commentariorum libri tres.* Frankfurt: Petri Brubacchii, 1564. Digital copy online at books.google.com.

———. *In epistolam, quam Apostolus Paulus ad Romanos scripsit, commentariorum libri tres.* Tübingen: Georgius Gruppenbachius, 1588. Digital copy online at DLCPT.

Bucer, Martin. *Metaphrases et enarrationes perpetuae Epistolarum D. Pauli Apostoli, quibus singulatim Apostoli omnia, cum argumenta. . . .* Strasbourg, 1536. Digital copy online at books.google.com.

———. *Metaphrasis et enarratio in Epist. d. Pauli Apostoli ad Romanos, in quibus singulatim apostoli omnia, cum argumenta, tum sententiae & verba, ad autoritatem divinae scripturae, fidem[que] Ecclesiae Catholicae tam priscae quàm praesentis, religiosè ac paulò fusius excutiuntur.* Basel: Peter Pernam, 1562. Digital copy online at digitale.bibliothek.uni-halle.de.

Bugenhagen, Johannes. *In D. Pauli ad Romanos Epistolam interpretatio.* Haguenau: Iohan Secer, 1531. Digital copy online at www.bsb-muenchen.de.

Bullinger, Heinrich. *Commentarii in omnes Pauli Apostoli Epistolas, atque etiam in Epistolam ad Hebraeos.* Zurich: Christophorum Froschoverum, 1582. Digital copy online at DLCPT.

———. *In Sanctissimam Pauli ad Romanos epistolam Heinrychi Bullingeri Commentarius.* Zurich: Christophorum Froschoverum, 1533. Digital copy online at www.e-rara.ch.

Bunyan, John. *A Defence of the Doctrine of Iustification by Faith in Jesus Christ: Shewing True Gospel-Holiness Flows from Thence.* London: Francis Smith, 1672. Digital copy online at EEBO.

Cade, Anthony. *Saint Paul's Agonie: A Sermon Preached at Leicester.* London: Bernard Alsop, 1618. Digital copy online at EEBO.

Cajetan, Cardinal (Thomas de Vio). *Epistolae Pauli et Aliorum Apostolorum ad Graecam veritatem castigatae.* Paris, 1550. Digital copy online at books.google.com.

———. *In omnes D. Pauli et aliorum Apostolorum Epistolas commentarii.* Lyon: Sumptibus Iacobi and Petri Prost, 1639. Digital copy online at books.google.com.

Calixtus, Georg. *In Epistolam Sancti Apostoli Pauli ad Romanos expositio litteralis.* Helmstedt: Henningus Mullerus, 1665. Digital copy online at diglib.hab.de.

Calvin, John. *Commentaries on the Epistle of Paul the Apostle to the Romans.* Translated and edited by John Owen. Edinburgh: Calvin Translation Society, 1899.

———. *Commentarii in omnes Epistolas S. Pauli Apostoli.* Amsterdam: Ioannis Iacobi Schipperi, 1667. Digital copy online at DLCPT.

———. *The Epistles of Paul the Apostle to the Romans and to the Thessalonians.* Translated by Ross Mackenzie. Calvin's New Testament Commentaries 8. Grand Rapids: Eerdmans, 1960.

———. *In omnes Pauli Apostoli Epistolas, atque etiam in Epistolam ad Hebraeos, item in canonicas Petri, Johannis, Jacobi, et Judae, quae etiam catholicae vocantur, Joh. Calvini Commentarii.* Geneva: Oliva Roberti Stephani, 1556. Digital copy online at www.e-rara.ch.

———. *Institutes of the Christian Religion.* Translated by Henry Beveridge. Edinburgh: T&T Clark, 1863. Digital copy online at books.google.com.

———. *Iohannis Calvini Commentarius in Epistolam Pauli ad Romanos.* Edited by T. H. L. Parker. Leiden: Brill, 1981.

———. *A Selection of the Most Celebrated Sermons of John Calvin, Minister of the Gospel, and One of the Principal Leaders of the Protestant Reformation . . . to Which is Prefixed a Biographical History of His Life.* Philadelphia: S. & D. A. Forbes, 1830. Digital copy online at books.google.com.

———. *Sermons de Jean Calvin sur L'Epistre S. Paul Apostre aux Galates.* Geneva: Francois Perrin, 1563. Digital copy online at books.google.com.

———. *Sermons of M. Iohn Calvine upon the Epistle of Saincte Paule to the Galathians.* London: Lucas Harison and George Bishop, 1574. Digital copy online at books.google.com.

Carnesecchi, Pietro. *Report of the Trial and Martyrdom of Pietro Carnesecchi, Sometime Secretary to Pope Clement VII.* Edited and translated by Richard Gibbings. Dublin: University Press, 1856. Digital copy online at books.google.com.

Clendon, Thomas. *Justification Justified.* London: Robert Ibbitson, 1653. Digital copy online at EEBO.

Cobabus, Michael, and Johanne Quistorp. *Disputationum in Epistolam ad Romanos Prima Philologico-Theologica*. Rostock: Johannes Richelius, 1644. Digital copy online at www.dilibri.de.

Cocceius, Johannes. *Summa Doctrinae de Foedere et Testamento Dei*. London: Elseviriorum, 1654. Digital copy online at books.google.com.

Colet, John. *An Exposition of St. Paul's Epistle to the Romans: Delivered as Lectures in the University of Oxford about the Year 1497*. Translated by J. H. Lupton. London: Bell and Daldy, 1873. Digital copy online at books.google.com.

Contarini, Gasparo. *Gasparis Contareni Cardinalis Opera*. Paris: Sebastianum Nivellium, 1571. Digital copy online at books.google.com.

Corner, Christoph. *In Epistolam D. Pauli Ad Romanos Scriptam Commentarius*. Heidelberg: Ioannes Spies, 1583. Digital copy online at DLCPT.

Corro, Antonio del. *A Theological Dialogue. Wherin the Epistle of S. Paul the Apostle to the Romanes is Expounded. Gathered and Set Together out of the Readings of Antonie Corranus of Siville, Professor of Divinitie*. London: Thomas Purfoote, 1575. Digital copy online at EEBO.

Cotton, John. *A conference Mr. John Cotton held at Boston with the elders of New-England 1. concerning gracious conditions in the soule before faith, 2. evidencing justification by sanctification, 3. touching the active power of faith: twelve reasons against stinted forms of prayer and praise: together with the difference between the Christian and antichristian church*. London: J. Dawson, 1646. Digital copy online at EEBO-TCP.

———. *The Way of Life, or, God's Way and Course in Bringing the Soul into, Keeping it in, and Carrying it on in the Ways of Life and Peace*. London: M. F. at Brazen Serpent, 1641. Digital copy online at books.google.com.

Corvinus, Antonius. *Postilla in Epistolas et Evangelia*. Strasbourg: Wolfgang Köpfel, 1540. Digital copy online at books.google.com.

Coverdale, Miles, trans. *Biblia: the Byble, that is the Holy Scrypture of the Olde and New Testament*. Antwerp and Southwark: Jacob van Meteren and J. Nycolson, 1535. Digital copy online at EEBO.

———. *Remains of Myles Coverdale, Bishop of Exeter*. Edited by George Pearson. Cambridge: University of Cambridge Press for Parker Society, 1846.

Cowper, William. *Heaven Opened*. London: William Stansby, 1632. Digital copy online at books.google.com.

Cradock, Walter. *Gospel-Holiness or the Saving Sight of God Laid open from Isa. 6.5 Together with the Glorious Priviledge of the Saints. From Rom. 8.4,5*. London: M. Simmons, 1651. Digital copy online at EEBO.

Cranmer, Thomas. *Miscellaneous Writings and Letters of Thomas Cranmer, Archbishop of Canterbury, Martyr, 1556*. Parker Society. Cambridge: Cambridge University Press, 1846. Digital copy online at books.google.com.

Cruciger, Caspar. *In Epistolam Pauli ad Romanos Scriptam Commentarius*. Wittenberg: Iohannes Crato, 1567. Digital copy online at books.google.com.

Cruciger, Elisabeth. *Ein Enchiridion oder Handbüchlein geistelicher Gesänge und Psalmen* (Erfurt, 1524). Edited by Christiane and Kai Brodersen. Speyer: Kartoffeldruck-Verlag, 2011.

Da Mantova, Benedetto, and Marcantonio Flaminio (incorrectly attributed to Aonio Paleario). *The Benefit of Christ's Death or, the Glorious Riches of God's Free Grace, which Every True Believer Receives by Jesus Christ, and Him Crucified*. Introduction by John Ayre. London: Religious Tract Society, 1847. Digital copy online at books.google.com.

Day, William. *A Paraphrase and Commentary upon the Epistle of Saint Paul to the Romans.* London: S. Griffin for Joshua Kirton, 1666. Digital copy online at EEBO.

De Dieu, Louis. *Animadversiones in D. Pauli Apostoli Epistolam ad Romanos.* Leiden, 1646. Digital copy online books.google.com.

Dentiére, Marie. *Epistle to Marguerite de Navarre and Preface to a Sermon by John Calvin.* Edited and translated by Mary B. McKinley. The Other Voice in Early Modern Europe. Chicago: University of Chicago Press, 2004.

D'Étaples, Jacques Lèfevre. *Contenta Epistola ad Rhomanos.* Paris: Henrici Stephani, 1512. Digital copy online at books.google.com.

———. *Epistole divi Pauli Apostoli: cum commentariis preclarissimi viri Jacobi Fabri Stapulensis.* Paris: Francisci Regnault et Joannis de la Porte, 1517. Digital copy online at books.google.com.

Dickson, David. *An Exposition of All St. Pauls Epistles, Together with an Explanation of those other Epistles of the Apostles, St. James, Peter, John & Jude.* London: R. I. for Francis Eglesfield, 1659. Digital copy online at EEBO-TCP.

Diodati, Giovanni. *Pious and Learned Annotations upon the Holy Bible.* London: Nicolas Fussell, 1651. Digital copy online at DLCPT.

Donne, John. *Poems of John Donne.* 2 vols. Edited by E. K. Chambers. London: Lawrence and Bullen, 1896. Digital copy online at books.google.com.

———. *The Works of John Donne.* 6 vols. Edited by Henry Alford. London: John Parker, 1839. Digital copy online at archive.org.

Downame, John. *Annotations upon all of the Old and New Testament.* London: John Legate, 1645. Digital copy online at EEBO.

Elizabeth I. *Collected Works.* Edited by Leah S. Marcus, Janel Mueller, and Mary Beth Rose. Chicago: University of Chicago Press, 2000.

Elton, Edward. *The Complaint of a Sanctified Sinner Answered: Or an Explanation of the Seventh Chapter of the Epistle of Saint Paul to the Romans.* London: W. Stansby for Robert Mylbourne, 1618. Digital copy online at EEBO.

Erasmus, Desiderius. *Annotations on Romans.* Edited by Robert T. Sider. Translated by John B. Payne. CWE 56. Toronto: University of Toronto Press, 1994.

———. *Des Erasmi Roterodami in Novum Testamentum Annotationes* Basel: Inclytam Ravracorum, 1527. Digital copy online at books.google.com.

———. *Paraphrases on Romans and Galatians.* Edited by Robert D. Sider. Translated by John B. Payne. CWE 42. Toronto: University of Toronto Press, 1984.

———. *The Seconde Tome or Volume of the Paraphrase of Erasmus upon the Newe Testament: Conteynyng the Epistles of S. Paul, and Other the Apostles. Whereunto is added a Paraphrase upon the Revelacion of S. John.* London: Edwarde Whitchurche, 1549. Digital copy online at EEBO.

Ferme, Charles, and Andrew Melville. *A Logical Analysis of the Epistle of Paul to the Romans by Charles Ferme . . . and a Commentary on the Same Epistle by Andrew Melville.* Edited by William Lindsay Alexander. Edinburgh: Wodrow Society, 1850. Digital copy online at books.google.com.

Frith, John. *Works of the English Reformers: William Tyndale and John Frith.* Vol. 3. Edited by Thomas Russell. London: Printed for Ebenezer Palmer, 1831. Digital copy online at books.google.com.

Fuente, Constantino Ponce De La. *The Confession of a Sinner.* Edited by John T. Betts. London: Bell and Daldy, 1869. Digital copy online at archive.org.

Gardiner, Stephen. *A Declaration of such true articles as George Ioye hath gone about to confute as false.* London: Johannes Herford for Robert Toye, 1546.

Gerhard, Johann. *Adnotationes ad Priora Capita Epistolae D. Pauli ad Romanos.* Jena: Christianus Saher; Ern. Steinmann, 1645. Digital copy online at books.google.com.

———. *Summae Evangelii Aphorismi Apostolici Rom. 4. v. 25. qui traditus est propter delicta nostra, et resurrexit propter justificationem nostram.* Wittenberg: Casp. Freyschmid, 1635. Digital copy online books.google.com.

Goodwin, Thomas. *Christ Set Forth in His Death, Resurrection, Ascension, Sitting at God's Right Hand, and Intercession as the Cause of Justification and Object of Justifying Faith.* London: W. E. and F. G. for Robert Dawlman, 1642. Digital copy online at EEBO.

Greiffenberg, Catharina Regina von. *Meditations on the Incarnation, Passion, and Death of Jesus Christ.* Edited and translated by Lynne Tatlock. The Other Voice in Early Modern Europe. Chicago: University of Chicago Press, 2009.

Grey, Jane. *Here in this booke ye haue a godly epistle made by a faithful Christian. A comunication betwene Feckna and the Lady Iane Dudley. A letter that she wrote to her syster Lady Katherin. The ende of the Ladye Iane vpon the scaffolde. Ye shal haue also herein a godly prayer made by maister Iohn Knokes.* London, c. 1554. Digital copy online at EEBO.

Grey, Lady Jane, and Anonymous. *The life, death and actions of the most chast, learned, and religious lady, the Lady Iane Gray, daughter to the Duke of Suffolke Containing foure principall discourses written with her owne hands. The first an admonition to such as are weake in faith: the second a catechisme: the third an exhortation to her sister: and the last her words at her death.* London: Printed by G. Eld for John Wright, 1615. Digital copy online at EEBO.

Grynaeus, Johann. *Chronologia brevis Evangelicae Historiae: logicique artificii in Epistola Apostoli Pauli ad Romanos.* Basel, 1580. Digital copy online books.google.com.

Guild, William. *The old Roman Catholik, as at first he was taught by Paul, in opposition to the new Roman Catholik, as of latter he is taught by the Pope. The one being Apostolicall, the other apostaticall. Descrived and proven only out of the Epistle of Paul, to the Romanes.* Aberdeen: E. Raban, 1649. Digital copy online at EEBO.

———. *Argumenta omnium, tam Veteris quam Novi Testamenti, capitum elegiaco carmine conscripta.* Zurich, 1543. Digital copy online at www.e-rara.ch.

Gwalther, Rudolf. *In D. Pauli Apostoli Epistolam ad Romanos homiliae XCVI.* Zurich: Froschoviana, 1590. Digital copy online at DLCPT.

Hafenreffer, Matthias. *Disputatio de iustificatione hominis coram Deo gratuita ex Epistola D. Pauli ad Romanos.* Tübingen: Philippum Gruppenbachium, 1606. Digital copy online at www.bsb-muenchen.de.

Harder, Leland, trans. and ed. *Sources of Swiss Anabaptism.* CRR 4. Scottdale, PA: Herald Press, 1985.

Hemmingsen, Niels. *Commentarius in Epistolam Pauli ad Romanos.* Leipzig: Voegeliana, 1562. Digital copy online at books.google.com.

Herbert, George. *The Temple: Sacred Poems and Private Ejaculations.* Edited by Christopher Harvey. London: William Pickering, 1838. Digital copy online at books.google.com.

———. *The Works of George Herbert, in Prose and Verse.* 2 vols. London: William Pickering, 1853.

Herlin, Johann. *Isagoge ad lectionem librorum Novi Testamenti omnium.* Bern: D. D. Bernensium, 1605. Digital copy online at books.google.com.

Hesshus, Tilemann. *Commentarius in Omnes D. Pauli Epistolas, et Eam quae Scripta est as Hebraeos.* Zurich, 1605. Digital copy online at www.slub-dresden.de.

———. *Explicatio Epistolae Pauli ad Romanos Tradita. piae iuventuti in Academia Ienensi.* Jena: Guntherus Huttichius, 1571. Digital copy online at www.bsb-muenchen.de.

Holmes, Nathaniel. *Gospel Musick, or the Singing of Davids Psalms, etc. in the Publick Congregations, or Private Families Asserted, and Vindicated.* London, 1644. Digital copy online at archive.org.

Hooker, Thomas. *Three Godly Sermons.* London, 1639. Digital copy online at EEBO.

Hubmaier, Balthasar. *Balthasar Hubmaier: Theologian of Anabaptism.* Translated and edited by H. Wayne Pipkin and John H. Yoder. CRR 5. Scottdale, PA: Herald Press, 1989.

Hunnius, Aegidius. *Epistolae Divi Pauli Apostoli ad Romanos expositio plana et perspicua.* Frankfurt: Ioannes Spies, 1592. Digital copy online at books.google.com.

Hyperius, Andreas. *Commentarii d. Andreae Hyperii, doctissimi ac clarissimi theologi, in Epistolam D. Pauli Ad Romanos, et utramque ad Corinthios.* Zurich: Christophorum Froschoverum, 1583. Digital copy online at www.bsb-muenchen.de.

Joris, David. *The Anabaptist Writings of David Joris.* Translated and edited by Gary K. Waite. CRR 7. Waterloo, ON: Herald Press, 1994.

Karlstadt, Andreas Bodenstein von. *The Essential Carlstadt.* Translated and edited by E. J. Furcha. CRR 8. Waterloo, ON: Herald Press, 1995.

Knopken, Andreas. *In Epistolam ad Romanos Andreae Knopken Costerinen.* Nuremberg, 1524. Digital copy online at books.google.com.

Lonicer, Ioanne. *Veteris cuiuspiam Theologi Graeci succincta in D. Pavli ad Romanos Epistolam exegesis, ex Graecis Sacrae Scripturae interpretibus desuripta.* Basel: Roberti Winter, 1537. Digital copy online at books.google.com.

Luther, Martin. *Church-Postil: Sermons on the Epistles for the Different Sundays and Festivals in the Year.* New Market, VA: New Market Evangelical Lutheran Publishing Company, 1869. Digital copy online at books.google.com.

———. *Lectures on Romans.* Edited and translated by Wilhelm Pauck. LCC 15. Philadelphia: Westminster, 1961.

———. *Luther's Works.* American ed. 82 vols. planned. St. Louis: Concordia; Philadelphia: Fortress, 1955–1986; 2009–.

———. *Preface to the Complete Edition of Luther's Latin Works* (1545). Translated by Andrew Thornton, OSB. Manchester, NH: Saint Anselm College Humanities Program, 1983. Translation online at iclnet.org.

———. *Preface to the Letter of St. Paul to the Romans.* Translated by Andrew Thornton, OSB. Manchester, NH: Saint Anselm College Humanities Program, 1983. Translation online at www.ccel.org.

———. *Sermons of Martin Luther.* 3 vols. Edited by John Nicholas Lenker. Reprint, Grand Rapids: Baker, 1988. Digital copy online at books.google.com.

Major, Georg. *Primus tomus operum reverendi viri D. Georgii Maioris: continens enarrationes Epistolarum S. Pauli, electi organi Dei.* Wittenberg: Johanne d. Ä. Krafftt, 1569. Digital copy online at digitale.bibliothek.uni-halle.de.

———. *Vita S. Pauli Apostoli.* Wittenberg: Hans Lufft, 1555. Digital copy online at gateway-bayern.de.

Maler, Jörg. *Jörg Maler's Kunstbuch: Writings of the Pilgram Marpeck Circle.* Translated and edited by John D. Rempel. CRR 12. Kitchener, ON: Pandora, 2010.

Matheson, Peter, ed. *Argula von Grumbach: A Woman's Voice in the Reformation.* Edinburgh: T&T Clark, 1995.

Mayer, John. *A Commentarie Upon all the Epistles of the Apostle Saint Paul, Being Fourteene.* London: John Haviland for John Grismond, 1631. Digital copy online at EEBO.

Maxey, Anthony. *The Golden Chaine of Man's Saluation and the Fearefull Point of Hardening, Opened and Set Downe in Two Severall Sermons Preached Before the King.* London: G. Eld for Clement Knight, 1606. Digital copy online at EEBO.

Melanchthon, Philipp. *Commentarii in epistolam Pauli ad Romanos hoc anno M.D.XL. recogniti et locupletati*. Strasbourg: Cratonem Mylium, 1540. Digital copy online at DLCPT.

———. *Commentary on Romans*. Translated by Fred Kramer. St. Louis: Concordia, 1992.

———. *Commonplaces: Loci Communes, 1521*. Translated by Christian Preus. St. Louis: Concordia, 2014.

———. *Operum Philippi Melanchtonis tomi quinque*. Basel: Ioan. Hervagium, 1541. Digital copy online at www.e-rara.ch.

Michelangelo. *The Life of Michael Angelo Buonarroti with Translations of Many of His Poems and Letters; Also Memoirs of Savonarola, Raphael, and Vittoria Colonna*. Edited by John Scandrett Harford. 2 vols. London: Longman, Brown, Green, Longmans, and Roberts, 1858. Digital copy online at books.google.com.

Müntzer, Thomas. *The Collected Works of Thomas Müntzer*. Translated by Peter Matheson. Edinburgh: T&T Clark, 1988.

Musculus, Wolfgang. *In Epistolam Apostoli Pauli ad Romanos: Commentarii, per Wolfganum Musculum*. Basel: Hervagios, 1555. Digital copy online at books.google.com.

———. *In Epistolam D. Apostoli Pauli ad Romanos, commentarii, per Wolfgangum Musculum Dusanum*. Basel: Sebastianum Henricpetri, 1600. Digital copy online at DLCPT.

Mylius, Georg. *Disputatio ex capite primo Epistolae ad Romanos: ad cuius conclusiones, iuvante aspiranteque Deo optimo maximo*. Jena: Tobiae Steinmanni, 1590. Digital copy online at www.bsb-muenchen.de.

Navarre, Marguerite de. *The Mirror of the Sinful Soul*. Translated by Elizabeth I. Edited by Percy Ames. London: Asher, 1897. Digital copy online at books.google.com.

Oberman, Heiko A. *Forerunners of the Reformation: The Shape of Late Medieval Thought*. Cambridge: James Clarke, 1967.

Ochino, Bernardino. *Expositio Epistolae divi Pauli ad Romanos*. Augsburg: Philippus Ulhardus, 1545. Digital copy online at books.google.com.

Oecolampadius, Johannes. *In Epistolam B. Pauli Apost. ad Rhomanos adnotationes à Ioanne Oecolampadio Basilae praelectae*. Basel: Andream Cratandrum, 1525. Digital copy online at DLCPT.

———. *In Epistolam Pauli ad Rhomanos adnotationes*. Basel: Andream Cratandrum, 1525. Digital copy online at www.bsb-muenchen.de.

Olevianus, Kaspar. *In Epistolam D. Pauli Apostoli ad Romanos notae*. Geneva: Eustathium Vignon, 1579. Digital copy online at www.e-rara.ch.

Osiander, Lukas. *Epistolae S. Pauli Apostoli omnes quotquot extant. Iuxta Veterem, seu vulgatam translationem, as graecum textum emendata, et brevi ac perspicua explicatione illustrata: insertis etiam praecipuis Locis communibus, in lectione sacra observandis*. Tübingen: Georgius Gruppenbachius, 1583. Digital copy online at books.google.com.

Owen, John. *Works of John Owen*. 24 vols. Edited by William Goold. Edinburgh: T&T Clark, 1862. Digital copy online at books.google.com.

Pareus, David. *In Divinam ad Romanos S. Pauli Apostoli Epistolam commentarius*. Frankfurt: Iohannis Lancelloti, 1608. Digital copy online at books.google.com.

Pellikan, Konrad. *In omnes Apostolicas Epistolas, Pauli, Petri, Iacobi, Ioannis et Iudae D. Chuonradi Pellicani tigurinae ecclesiae ministri commentarii*. Zurich: Froschouiana Mense Augusto, 1539. Digital copy online at www.e-rara.ch.

Pemble, William. *Vindiciae Fidei, or a Treatise of Iustification by Faith, wherein that point is fully cleared and vindicated from cauils of its aduersaries*. Oxford: John Lichfield and William Turner, 1625. Digital copy online at EEBO-TCP.

Perkins, William. *A Golden Chaine: or the Description of Theologie containing the Order of the Salvation and Damnation, According to God's Word*. Cambridge: John Legate for the University of Cambridge, 1600. Digital copy online at EEBO-TCP.

Philips, Dirk. *The Writings of Dirk Philips, 1504–1568*. Translated and edited by Cornelius J. Dyck, William E. Keeney, and Alvin J. Beachy. CRR 6. Scottdale, PA: Herald Press, 1992.

Piscator, Johannes. *Analysis logica Epistolae Pauli ad Romanos*. Herborn: Christophori Corvini, 1589. Digital copy online at digitale.bibliothek.uni-halle.de.

Pole, Reginald (Cardinal). *A Treatie of Iustification*. Leuven: John Foulerum, 1569. Digital copy online at books.google.com.

Powel, Gabriel. *Prodromus: A Logical Resolutior of the First Chapter of the Epistle of the Apostle Paul unto the Romanes*. Oxford: Joseph Barnes, 1602. Digital copy online at EEBO.

Powell, Vavasor. *God the father glorified: and the worke of mens redemption, and salvation, finished by Jesus Christ on earth. Opened in a sermon before the Right Honourable the Lord Maior, and the Right Worshipfull the sheriffes, aldermen, and recorder of the city of London, the second day of the tenth moneth (called December) 1649*. London: Charles Sumptner, 1650. Digital copy online at EEBO.

Preston, John. *The Breast-plate of Faith and Love*. London: George Purflow, 1651. Digital copy online at EEBO.

Rainbow, Edward. *A Sermon Preached at Appleby, April 14, 1676, at the Funeral of the Right Honourable Anne Clifford, Countess of Pembroke, Dorset and Montgomery*. Carlisle, UK: Samuel Jefferson, 1839. Digital copy online at books.google.com.

Riedemann, Peter. *Love Is Like Fire: The Confession of an Anabaptist Prisoner*. Edited by Emmy Barth Maendel. 1993. Reprint, Walden, NY: Plough, 2016.

———. *Peter Riedemann's Hutterite Confession of Faith*. Translated and edited by John J. Friesen. CRR 9. Waterloo, ON: Herald Press, 1999.

Rollock, Robert. *In Epistolam S. Pauli Apostoli ad Romanos . . . commentarius, analytica methodo conscriptus*. Geneva: Franc Le Preux, 1595. Digital copy online at www.e-rara.ch.

Rogers, Richard. *A Commentary Upon the Whole Booke of Iudges*. London: Felix Kyngston for Thomas Man, 1615. Digital copy online at EEBO-TCP.

Runge, David. *Disputatio Prima ex Epistola Pauli Apostoli ad Romanos, complectens quaedam Prolegomena*. Wittenberg: M. Bartholomaeus Battus, 1595. Digital copy online at digitale.bibliothek.uni-halle.de.

Rutherford, Samuel. *Letters of Samuel Rutherford*. Edited by Andrew A. Bonar. Edinburgh & London, 1891. Digital copy online at books.google.com.

Sadoleto, Jacopo (Cardinal). *Iacobi Sadoleti Episcopi Carpentoractis in Pauli Epistolam ad Romanos commentariorum libri tres*. Lyon: Sebastianum Gryphium, 1535. Digital copy online at books.google.com.

Sarcerius, Erasmus. *In Epistolam ad Romanos. pia et erudita scholia, pro rhetorica dispositione, ad perpetuum coherentiae filum, conscripta*. Frankfurt: Chr. Egenolphum, 1541. Digital copy online at books.google.com.

Schnepff, Dietrich. *Disputatio de Sententia D. Pauli ad Romanos septimo: Novi quod non habitet in me, hoc est, in carne mea bonum. . . .* Tübingen: Alexandrum Hoggium, 1585. Digital copy online at www.bsb-muenchen.de.

Sibbes, Richard. *The Complete Works of Richard Sibbes*. Edited by Alexander B. Grosart. 7 vols. Edinburgh: James Nichol, 1863. Digital copy online at books.google.com.

Simons, Menno. *The Complete Works of Menno Simon*. Elkhart, IN: John F. Funk and Brother, 1871.

———. *A Foundation and Plain Instruction.* Lancaster, PA: Boswell & M'Cleery for John Herr, 1835.

Snyder, C. Arnold, and Linda A. Huebert Hecht, eds. *Profiles of Anabaptist Women: Sixteenth-Century Reforming Pioneers.* Waterloo, ON: Wilfred Laurier University Press, 1996.

Snyder, C. Arnold, ed., Walter Klaassen, Werner O. Packull, C. and F. Friesen, trans. *Sources of South German/Austrian Anabaptism.* CRR 10. Kitchener, ON: Pandora Press, 2001.

Sozzini, Fausto. *De loco Pauli Apostoli in Epistola ad Rom. cap. septimo. Disputatio.* Krakow: Alexius Rodecius, 1583. Digital copy online at books.google.com.

Strigel, Viktorin. *Hypomnēmata in omnes epistolas Pauli et aliorum apostolorum et in Apocalypsin.* Leipzig: Ernesti Voegelini Constantiensis, 1565. Digital copy online at www.bsb-muenchen.de.

Tomson, Laurence, trans. *The Bible, that is, the Holy Scriptures conteined in the Olde and New Testament, translated according to the Ebrew and Greeke, and conferred with the best translations in diuers languages. With most profitable annotations vpon all the hard places, and other things of great importance.* [= Geneva Bible] London: Deputies of Christopher Barker, 1595. Digital copy online at archive.org.

Toussain, Daniel. *Synopsis Doctrinae Apostoli Pauli de Iustificatione ex Primis Capitibus Epistolae ad Romanos Desumta, et certis Thesibus comprehensa.* Heidelberg, 1588. Digital copy online at www.bsb-muenchen.de.

Trapp, John. *A Commentary or Exposition Upon the Epistle of St. Paul to the Romanes* in *A Commentary or Exposition upon All the Books of the New Testament.* London: R. W., 1656. Digital copy online at books.google.com.

Tyndale, William. *Doctrinal Treatises and Introductions to Different Portions of the Holy Scriptures by William Tyndale, Martyr, 1536.* Edited by Henry Walter. Cambridge: The Parker Society, 1848. Digital copy online at books.google.com.

Valdés, Juan de. *Alfabeto Christiano: A Faithful Reprint of the Italian of 1546 with Two Modern Translations, in Spanish and in English.* London, 1861. Digital copy online at books.google.com.

———. *Commentary Upon St. Paul's Epistle to the Romans.* Translated by John T. Betts. London: Trübner, 1883. Digital copy online at books.google.com.

———. *In Epistolam S. Pauli Apostoli ad Romanos . . . commentarii doctissimi, cum tractatione per utili rerum et locorum, qui ad eam epistolam pertinent.* Zurich, 1559. Digital copy online at books.google .com (= *In Epistolam S. Pauli*).

———. *In Epistolam S. Pauli Apostoli ad Rom. D. Petri Martyris Vermilii Florentini . . . commentarii doctissimi, cum tractatione perutili rerum et locorum, qui ad eam epistolam pertinent.* Basel: Petrum Pernam, 1560. Digital copy on DLCPT (= *In Epistolam S. Pauli Apostoli*).

Vermigli, Peter Martyr. *Most Learned and Fruitfull Commentaries of D. Peter Martir Vermilius Florentine . . . upon the Epistle of S. Paul to the Romanes.* Translated by H. B. London: Iohn Daye, 1558. Digital copy online at EEBO.

Wigand, Johann. *In Epistolam S. Pauli ad Romanos Annotationes.* Frankfurt am Main: Georgium Corvinum, 1580. Digital copy online at books.google.com.

Wilcox, Thomas (T. W.). *A Christian and learned exposition upon certaine verses of that eight chapter of the Epistle of that blessed Apostle Paule to the Romanes, and namely, upon verse, 18.19.20.21.22.23. Written long agoe, by T. W. for a most deare friend of his in Christ, and now lately published in print, for the benefite and good of Gods people wheresoever.* London: Robert Walde-grave, 1587. Digital copy online at EEBO.

Wild, Johann. *Exegesis in Epistolam Pauli ad Romanos.* Mainz: Francisus Behem, 1558. Digital copy online at www.bsb-muenchen.de.

Willet, Andrew. *Hexapla: That is, a Six-fold Commentarie vpon the Most Diuine Epistle of the Holy Apostle S. Paul to the Romanes*. Cambridge: Leonard Greene, 1611. Digital copy online at EEBO.

———. *Hexapla: That is, a six-fold commentarie upon the most Divine Epistle of the holy Apostle S. Paul to the Romanes: wherein according to the authors former method sixe things are observed in every chapter. 1. The text with the divers readings. 2. Argument and method. 3. The questions discussed. 4. Doctrines noted. 5. Controversies handled. 6. Morall uses observed*. Cambridge: Leonard Greene, 1620. Digital copy online at DLCPT.

Williams, George Huntston, ed. *Spiritual and Anabaptist Writers*. LCC 25. Philadelphia: Westminster, 1957.

Wilson, Thomas. *A Commentarie upon the most Divine Epistle of S. Paul to the Romanes*. London: W. Iaggard, 1614. Digital copy online at EEBO.

Wither, George. *Hallelujah, or Britain's Second Remembrancer; Bringing to Remembrance, (In Praiseful and Penitential Hymns, Spiritual Sons, and Moral Odes,) Meditations, Advancing the Glory of God, in the Practice of Piety and Virtue*. London: John Russell Smith, 1857. Digital copy online at books.google.com.

———. *Hymns and Songs of the Church*. London: T. Bensley, 1815. Digital copy online at books.google.com.

Writings of Edward VI, William Hugh, Queen Catherine Parr, Anne Askew, Lady Jane Grey, Hamilton, and Balnaves. London: The Religious Tract Society, 1831. Digital copy online at archive.org.

Zell, Katharina Schütz. *Church Mother: The Writings of a Protestant Reformer in Sixteenth-Century Germany*. Translated by Elsie McKee. The Other Voice in Early Modern Europe. Chicago: University of Chicago Press, 2006.

Zwingli, Huldrych. *In Evangelicam Historiam de Domino Nostro Iesu Christo, per Matthaeum, Marcum, Lucam et Ioannem conscriptam, epistolasque aliquot Pauli annotationes D. Huldrychi Zvinglii*. Zurich, 1539. Digital copy online at www.e-rara.ch.

Secondary Sources Cited in This Volume

Adams, Gwenfair Walters. "Shock and Awe: The Reformers and the Stunning Joy of Romans 1–8." *Journal of the Evangelical Theological Society* 61, no. 2 (2018): 231-44.

Bietenholz, Peter G., and Thomas B. Deutscher, eds. *Contemporaries of Erasmus: A Biographical Register of the Renaissance and Reformation*. 3 vols in 1. Toronto: University of Toronto Press, 2003.

Bizer, E., ed. *Texte aus der Anfangszeit Melanchthons*. Neukirchen-Vluyn: Neukirchener, 1966.

Bray, Gerald L., ed. *Galatians, Ephesians*. RCS NT 10. Downers Grove, IL: IVP Academic, 2011.

———, ed. *Romans*. ACCS NT 6 Downers Grove, IL: IVP Academic, 1998.

Brundin, Abigail. *Vittoria Colonna and the Spiritual Poetics of the Italian Reformation*. New York: Routledge, 2008.

———, ed. *Vittoria Colonna: Sonnets for Michelangelo: A Bilingual Edition*. Chicago: University of Chicago Press, 2005.

Cummings, Brian. *The Literary Culture of the Reformation: Grammar and Grace*. Oxford: Oxford University Press, 2002.

Demson, David. "John Calvin." In *Reading Romans Through the Centuries: From the Early Church to Karl Barth*, edited by Jeffrey P. Greenman and Timothy Larsen, 137-48. Grand Rapids: Brazos, 2005.

Duffy, Eamon. *The Stripping of the Altars: Traditional Religion in England, 1500–1580*. 2nd ed. New Haven CT: Yale University Press, 2005.

Edwards, John. *Archbishop Pole*. Burlington, VT: Ashgate, 2013.

Ehrensperger, Kathy, and R. Ward Holder, eds. *Reformation Readings of Romans*. Romans Through History and Cultures. New York: T&T Clark, 2008.

Fenlon, Dermot. *Heresy and Obedience in Tridentine Italy: Cardinal Pole and the Counter Reformation.* Cambridge: Cambridge University Press, 1972.

George, Timothy. "Martin Luther." In *Reading Romans Through the Centuries: From the Early Church to Karl Barth*, edited by Jeffrey P. Greenman and Timothy Larsen, 101-20. Grand Rapids: Brazos, 2005.

———. *Reading Scripture with the Reformers.* Downers Grove, IL: IVP Academic, 2011.

———. *Theology of the Reformers.* Rev. ed. Nashville: B&H Academic, 2013.

Gleason, John B. *John Colet.* Berkeley: University of California Press, 1989.

Greenman, Jeffrey P. "William Tyndale." In *Reading Romans Through the Centuries: From the Early Church to Karl Barth*, edited by Jeffrey P. Greenman and Timothy Larsen, 121-36. Grand Rapids: Brazos, 2005.

Holder, R. Ward. "Calvin as Commentator on the Pauline Epistles." In *Calvin and the Bible*, edited by Donald K. McKim, 224-56. Cambridge: Cambridge University Press, 2006.

Jensen, Robin M. *The Cross: History, Art, and Controversy.* Cambridge, MA: Harvard University Press, 2017.

Kolb, Robert. "Philipp Melanchthon's Reading of Romans." In *Reformation Readings of Paul: Explorations in History and Exegesis*, edited by Michael Allen and Jonathan A. Linebaugh, 73-96. Downers Grove, IL: IVP Academic, 2015.

Kreitzer, Beth, ed. *Luke.* RCS NT 3. Downers Grove, IL: IVP Academic, 2015.

Kroeker, Greta Grace. *Erasmus in the Footsteps of Paul: A Pauline Theologian.* Toronto: University of Toronto Press, 2011.

Le Goff, Jacques. *The Birth of Purgatory.* Translated by Arthur Goldhammer. Chicago: University of Chicago Press, 1984.

Lugioyo, Brian. *Martin Bucer's Doctrine of Justification: Reformation Theology and Early Modern Irenicism.* Oxford Studies in Historical Theology. Oxford: Oxford University Press, 2010.

Luther, Martin. *The Bondage of the Will.* Translated by J. I. Packer and O. R. Johnston. 1957. Reprint, Grand Rapids: Baker Academic, 2012.

Manetsch, Scott M., ed. *1 Corinthians.* RCS NT 9A. Downers Grove, IL: IVP Academic, 2017.

Martin, John Jeffries. *Venice's Hidden Enemies: Italian Heretics in a Renaissance City.* Baltimore: Johns Hopkins University Press, 2003.

McGrath, Alister E. *Iustitia Dei: A History of the Christian Doctrine of Justification.* 3rd ed. Cambridge: Cambridge University, 2005.

McLaughlin, R. Emmet. "Paul in Early Anabaptism." In *A Companion to Paul in the Reformation*, edited by R. Ward Holder, 215-42. Brill's Companions to the Christian Tradition. Leiden: Brill, 2009.

Morison, James. *A Critical Exposition of the Third Chapter of St. Paul's Epistle to the Romans.* London: Hamilton, Adams, 1866.

Muller, Richard. *Calvin and the Reformed Tradition: On the Work of Christ and the Order of Salvation.* Grand Rapids: Baker Academic, 2012.

———. *Christ and the Decree: Christology and Predestination in Reformed Theology from Calvin to Perkins.* Grand Rapids: Baker, 1986.

———. *Dictionary of Latin and Greek Theological Terms: Drawn Principally from Protestant Scholastic Theology.* Grand Rapids: Baker, 1985.

Null, Ashley. "Thomas Cranmer's Reading of Paul's Letters." In *Reformation Readings of Paul: Explorations in History and Exegesis*, edited by Michael Allen and Jonathan A. Linebaugh, 211-34. Downers Grove, IL: IVP Academic, 2015.

Oberman, Heiko A. "*Facientibus Quod in se est Deus non Denegat Gratiam*: Robert Holcot, O.P. and the Beginnings of Luther's Theology." *Harvard Theological Review* 55 (1962): 317-42.

O'Connor, Michael. "Cajetan on Paul." In *A Companion to Paul in the Reformation*, edited by R. Ward Holder, 337-62. Brill's Companions to the Christian Tradition. Leiden: Brill, 2009

Parker, T. H. L. *Calvin's New Testament Commentaries*. 1971. Reprint, Edinburgh: T&T Clark, 1993.

———. *Commentaries on the Epistle to the Romans, 1532–1542*. Edinburgh: T&T Clark, 1986.

Pitkin, Barbara. *What Pure Eyes Could See: Calvin's Doctrine of Faith in Its Exegetical Context*. Oxford: Oxford University Press, 1999.

Raith, Charles, II. *Aquinas and Calvin on Romans: God's Justification and Our Participation*. Oxford: Oxford University Press, 2014.

Rittgers, Ronald, ed. *Hebrews, James*. RCS NT 13. Downers Grove, IL: IVP Academic, 2015.

Schnabel, Eckhard. *Der Brief des Paulus an die Römer*. Vol. 1, *Kapitel 1–5*. Historisch-Theologische Auslegung. Witten: SCM R-Brockhaus, 2015.

Seifrid, Mark. "The Text of Romans and the Theology of Melanchthon." In *Reformation Readings of Paul: Explorations in History and Exegesis*, edited by Michael Allen and Jonathan A. Linebaugh, 97-122. Downers Grove, IL: IVP Academic, 2015.

Shell, Marc. *Elizabeth's Glass*. Lincoln: University of Nebraska Press, 1993.

Smyth, Amelia Gillespie, ed. *Olympia Morata: Her Times, Life, and Writings*. London: Smith, Elder, 1834.

Steinmetz, David C. *The Bible in the Sixteenth Century*. Durham, NC: Duke University Press, 1990.

———. "Calvin and Abraham: The Interpretation of Romans 4 in the Sixteenth Century." *Church History* 57 (1988): 12-35.

———. "Calvin and the Divided Self of Romans 7." In *Augustine, the Harvest, and Theology: Essays Dedicated to Heiko Augustinus Oberman in Honor of His Sixtieth Birthday*, edited by Kenneth Hagen, 300-313. Leiden: Brill, 1990.

———. *Calvin in Context*. 2nd ed. Oxford: Oxford University Press, 2010.

———. *Reformers in the Wings: From Geiler von Eysersberg to Theodore Beza*. 2nd ed. Oxford: Oxford University Press, 2001.

Viladesau, Richard. *The Beauty of the Cross: The Passion of Christ in Theology and the Arts from the Catacombs to the Eve of the Renaissance*. Oxford: Oxford University Press, 2005.

Wengert, Timothy. "Biblical Interpretation in the Works of Philip Melanchthon." In *A History of Biblical Interpretation*. Vol. 2, *The Medieval Through Reformation Periods*, edited by Alan J. Hauser and Duane F. Watson, 319-40. Grand Rapids: Eerdmans, 2009.

———. "Philip Melanchthon's 1522 Annotations on Romans and the Lutheran Origins of Rhetorical Criticism." In *Biblical Interpretation in the Reformation*, edited by Richard A. Muller and John L. Thompson, 118-40. Grand Rapids: Eerdmans, 1996.

Wengert, Timothy, and M. Patrick Graham, eds. *Philip Melanchthon (1497–1560) and the Commentary*. Sheffield: Sheffield Academic, 1997.

Westerholm, Stephen. *Perspectives Old and New on Paul: The "Lutheran" Paul and His Critics*. Grand Rapids: Eerdmans, 2004.

Wright, Shawn. *Theodore Beza: The Man and the Myth*. Tain, Scotland: Christian Focus, 2015.

Author and Writings Index

Subject Index

Scripture Index